Research Design and Statistical Analysis

Third Edition

Research Design and Statistical Analysis

Third Edition

Jerome L. Myers
University of Massachusetts at Amherst

Arnold D. Well
University of Massachusetts at Amherst

Robert F. Lorch, Jr.
University of Kentucky

Routledge
Taylor & Francis Group

NEW YORK AND LONDON

Published in 2010
by Routledge
270 Madison Avenue
New York, NY 10016
www.psypress.com
www.researchmethodsarena.com

Published in Great Britain
by Routledge
27 Church Road
Hove, East Sussex BN3 2FA

Routledge is an imprint of the Taylor & Francis Group, an Informa business

Typeset in Times by RefineCatch Limited, Bungay, Suffolk, UK
Printed and bound by Sheridan Books, Inc. in the USA on acid-free paper
Cover design by Design Deluxe

10 9 8 7 6 5 4 3 2 1

Library of Congress Cataloging-in-Publication Data
Myers, Jerome L.
   Research design and statistical analysis / Jerome L. Myers, Arnold D. Well. –3rd ed. / Robert F. Lorch, Jr.
      p. cm.
   Includes bibliographical references.
   1. Experimental design.   2. Mathematical statistics.   I. Well, A. (Arnold).   II. Lorch, Robert Frederick, 1952– .   III. Title.
   QA279.M933 2010
   519.5—dc22   2009032606

ISBN: 978–0–8058–6431–1 (hbk)

To Nancy, Susan, and Betty

Contents

Preface

Like the previous editions, this third edition of *Research Design and Statistical Analysis* is intended as a resource for researchers and a textbook for graduate and advanced undergraduate students. The guiding philosophy of the book is to provide a strong conceptual foundation so that readers are able to generalize concepts to new situations they will encounter in their research, including new developments in data analysis and more advanced methods that are beyond the scope of this book. Toward this end, we continue to emphasize basic concepts such as sampling distributions, design efficiency, and expected mean squares, and we relate the research designs and data analyses to the statistical models that underlie the analyses. We discuss the advantages and disadvantages of various designs and analyses. We pay particular attention to the assumptions involved, the consequences of violating the assumptions, and alternative analyses in the event that assumptions are seriously violated.

As in previous editions, an important goal is to provide coverage that is broad and deep enough so that the book can serve as a textbook for a two-semester sequence. Such sequences are common; typically, one semester focuses on experimental design and the analysis of data from such experiments, and the other semester focuses on observational studies and regression analyses of the data. Incorporating the analyses of both experimental and observational data within a single textbook provides continuity of concepts and notation in the typical two-semester sequence and facilitates developing relationships between analysis of variance and regression analysis. At the same time, it provides a resource that should be helpful to researchers in many different areas, whether analyzing experimental or observational data.

CONTENT OVERVIEW

Also like the previous editions, this edition can be viewed as consisting of four parts:

1. Data exploration and basic concepts such as sampling distributions, elementary probability, principles of hypothesis testing, measures of effect size, properties of estimators,

and confidence intervals on both differences among means and on standardized effect sizes.

2. Between-subject designs; these are designs with one or more factors in which each subject provides a single score. Key elements in the coverage are the statistical models underlying the analysis of variance for these designs, the role of expected mean squares in justifying hypothesis tests and in estimating effects of variables, the interpretation of interactions, procedures for testing contrasts and for controlling Type 1 error rates for such tests, and trend analysis—the analysis and comparison of functions of quantitative variables.

3. Extension of these analyses to repeated-measures designs; these are designs in which subjects contribute several scores. We discuss nesting and counterbalancing of variables in research designs, present quasi-F ratios that provide approximate tests of hypotheses, and consider the advantages and disadvantages of different repeated-measures and mixed designs.

4. The fourth section provides a comprehensive introduction to correlation and regression, with the goal of developing a general framework for analysis that incorporates both categorical and quantitative variables. The basic ideas of regression are developed first for one predictor, and then extended to multiple regression. The expanded section on multiple regression discusses both its usefulness as a tool for prediction and its role in developing explanatory models. Throughout, there is an emphasis on interpretation and on identifying common errors in interpretation and usage.

NEW TO THIS EDITION

Although the third edition shares the overall goals of the previous editions, there are many modifications and additions. These include: (1) revisions of all of the chapters from the second edition; (2) seven new chapters; (3) more examples of the use of SPSS to conduct statistical analyses; (4) added emphasis on power analyses to determine sample size, with examples of the use of G*Power (Faul, Erdfelder, Lang, & Buchner, 2007) to do this; and (5) new exercises. In addition to the modifications of the text, there is a substantial amount of additional material at the website, www.psypress.com/research-design. The website contains the following: (1) SPSS syntax files to perform analyses from a wide range of designs and a hotlink to the G*Power program; (2) all of the data files used in the text and in the exercises in SPSS and Excel formats; (3) technical notes containing derivations of some formulas presented in the book; (4) extra material on multiple and on logistic regression; and (5) a solutions manual and the text's figures and tables for instructors only.

Additional chapters

There are seven new chapters in the book. Chapters 1, 13, and 27 were added to provide more emphasis on the connections between design decisions, statistical analyses, and the interpretation of results from a study. In addition, a chapter has been added at the end of each of the four sections noted above to provide integrated examples of applications of the principles and procedures covered in the sections.

Planning the Research.   The first chapter provides a schema for thinking about the major steps involved in planning a study, executing it, and analyzing and interpreting the results. The emphasis is on the implications of decisions made in the planning study for subsequent analyses and interpretation of results. The chapter establishes a critical theme for the rest of the book; namely, that design and statistical analyses go hand-in-hand.

Comparing Experimental Designs.   Chapter 13, the first chapter in the third section on repeated-measures, provides a bridge between the second and third sections. It introduces blocking in research designs, the analysis of covariance, and repeated-measures and Latin square designs. Advantages and disadvantages of these designs and analyses are discussed. In addition, the important concept of the relative efficiency of designs is introduced, and illustrated with data and the results of computer sampling studies. This chapter reinforces the theme of the intimate connection between design and statistical analysis.

Review of Important Points and Cautions About Common Errors.   Chapter 27 is intended to remind readers of points discussed in the book—points we believe to be important but sometimes overlooked—and to warn against common errors in analyzing and interpreting results. For example, the chapter reminds readers of the importance of carefully choosing a research design and the need for *a priori* power calculations. As another example, the chapter again emphasizes the distinction between statistical and practical, or theoretical, significance.

Integrated Analysis Chapters.   Each chapter in the book covers a lot of conceptual and procedural territory, so the integrated analysis chapters provide opportunities to see how the concepts and analyses come together in the context of a research problem. In these chapters, we consider the design of a study and the analysis of the resulting data. The presentation includes discussion of the pros and cons of possible alternative designs, and takes the analysis through exploration of the data to inferential procedures such as hypothesis tests, including, where applicable, tests of contrasts, estimates of effect size, and alternatives to the standard analyses in consideration of possible violations of assumptions. These chapters also serve as a review of the preceding chapters in the section and, in some cases, are used to introduce additional methods.

Use of Statistical Software

We assume that most readers will have access to some statistical software package. Although we have used SPSS for most of our examples, the analyses we illustrate are available in most packages. At several points, we have indicated the relevant SPSS menu options and dialog box choices needed to carry out an analysis. In cases where certain analyses are not readily available in the menus of current versions of SPSS (and possibly other statistical packages), we have provided references to Internet sites that permit free, or inexpensive, downloads of relevant software; for example, programs for obtaining confidence intervals for various effect size measures. Also, although their use is not required in the book, we have provided a number of SPSS syntax files available at the book's website (see below) that can be used to perform analyses for a wide range of designs. We note that the syntax files were written using SPSS 17 and that the analyses reported in the book are also based on that version. Future versions may provide slightly different output, other options for analysis, or somewhat different syntax.

We have used G*Power 3 for power analyses in many of the chapters and in some exercises. This very versatile software provides both *a priori* and post hoc analyses for many designs and analyses, as well as figures showing the central and noncentral distributions for the test and parameters under consideration. The software and its use are described by Faul, Erdfelder, Lang, and Buchner (2007). G*Power 3 can be freely downloaded from the website (http://www.psycho. uni-duesseldorf.de/abteilungen/aap/gpower3/). Readers should register there in order to download the software and to be notified of any further updates. Description of the use of G*Power 3 and illustrations in the current book are based on Version 3.0.9. An excellent discussion of the use of that program has been written by Faul, Erdfelder, Lang, and Buchner (2007).

Exercises

As in previous editions, each chapter ends with a set of exercises. Answers to odd-numbered exercises are provided at the back of the book; all answers are available in the password-protected Instructor's Solution Manual available at the book's website. There are more than 40 exercises in the four new integrated-analysis chapters to serve as a further review of the material in the preceding chapters.

The Book Website

For the third edition, a variety of materials are available on the website, www.psypress.com/ research-design. These include the following.

Data Files

A number of data sets can be accessed from the book's website. These include data sets used in analyses presented in the chapters, so that these analyses can be re-created. Also, there are additional data sets used in the exercises. All data files are available both in SPSS and Excel format, in order to make them easily accessible. Some of these data sets have been included in order to provide instructors with an additional source of classroom illustrations and exercises. For example, we may have used one of the tables in the book to illustrate analysis of variance, but the file can also be used to illustrate tests of contrasts that could follow the omnibus analysis. A listing of the data files and descriptions of them are available on the website.

SPSS Syntax Files

As mentioned above, a number of optional syntax files are provided on the website that can be used to perform analyses for a wide range of designs. These include analyses involving nesting of variables having random effects; tests involving a variety of contrasts, including comparisons of contrasts and of trend components; and a varied set of regression analyses. These files, together with a Readme Syntax file that describes their use, are available at the website.

Technical Notes

For the sake of completeness, we wanted to present derivations for some of the expressions used in the book—for example, standard errors of regression coefficients. Because these derivations are not necessary to understand the chapters, and may be intimidating to some readers, we have made them available as optional technical notes on the website.

Additional Chapters

Here we present two supplementary chapters in pdf format that go beyond the scope of the book. One is a brief introduction to regression analysis using matrix algebra. The other is an introduction to logistic regression that is more comprehensive than the brief section that we included in Chapter 23. Other material will be added at various times.

Teaching Tools

There is information on the website for instructors only. Specifically, there is a solutions manual for all the exercises in the book and electronic files of the figures in the book.

Errata

Despite our best intentions, some errors may have crept into the book. We will maintain an up-to-date listing of corrections.

ACKNOWLEDGMENTS

We wish to express our gratitude to Axel Buchner for helpful discussions about G*Power 3; to J. Michael Royer for permission to use the data from his 1999 study; to Jennifer Wiley and James F. Voss for permission to use the Wiley-Voss data; to Melinda Novak and Corrine Lutz for permission to use the self-injurious behavior data set; and to Ira Ockene for permission to use the Seasons data. The *Seasons* research was supported by National Institutes of Health, National Heart, Lung, and Blood Institute Grant HL52745 awarded to University of Massachusetts Medical School, Worcester, Massachusetts.

Special thanks go to those individuals who reviewed early chapters of the book and made many useful suggestions that improved the final product: Jay Parkes, University of New Mexico; John Colombo University Kansas; William Levine, University of Arkansas; Lawrence E. Melamed, Kent State University; and one anonymous reviewer. We also wish to thank our colleagues, Alexander Pollatsek and Caren Rotello, and the many graduate assistants who, over the years, have contributed to our thinking about the teaching of statistics.

We also wish to express our gratitude to several individuals at Routledge. We have been greatly helped in the development and publication of this book by Debra Riegert, Senior Editor, and her Editorial Assistant, Erin Flaherty, as well as by Nicola Ravenscroft, the Project Editor for this book, and Joseph Garver, who was responsible for the final technical editing. We also wish to thank the American Statistical Association, the Biometric Society, and the Biometrika Trustees for their permission to reproduce statistical tables.

Finally, as always, we are indebted to our wives, Nancy A. Myers, Susan Well, and Elizabeth Lorch, for their encouragement and patience during this long process.

PART 1
Foundations of Research Design and Data Analysis

Chapter 1
Planning the Research

1.1 OVERVIEW

There are three essential stages in carrying out an effective research project. In the first stage, the research is planned: objectives are stated; decisions are made about the treatments to be included, the measures to be obtained, and the type and number of subjects; the research design is determined; and possible patterns of results and their implications are contemplated. This stage is reflected primarily in the Method section of the final research report. In the second stage, the data are collected and analyzed: descriptive statistics are calculated; population parameters are estimated; and inferential tests are performed to determine whether any obtained effects are larger than those we would expect to occur due to chance. The outcomes of the analyses are presented in words, tables, and graphs in the Results section of the final report. The final stage is the interpretation of the results, which typically is presented in the Discussion section of the research report: What do the results tell us about the answers to the questions we initially asked? Answering the questions that motivated the research is, of course, our ultimate goal; however, correct conclusions about what our results mean are totally dependent upon the first two stages. If the study is designed in such a way that factors other than the independent variable may have influenced the results, we may be led to incorrect conclusions. Even if the design of the study is sound, our statistical tests may fail to reveal effects that are present in the population from which we have sampled if our measures are very variable, or if we collect too few data. Finally, despite a sound design and adequate procedures, data analyses that violate assumptions underlying the statistical procedures may lead us to incorrect inferences. We may think of the planning and analysis stages as providing input to the inferential stage and, as an old adage states, "garbage in, garbage out."

In this chapter, we focus on the initial stage of planning the research. We will present an overview of the decisions that confront the researcher at the onset of a new project, and of the factors that should influence those decisions. In subsequent chapters, we will return to many of the issues raised in this chapter, explicitly linking the decisions made in the planning stage to aspects of the data analysis. Indeed, the decisions made in planning the research are the major factors influencing the results of statistical analyses, and subsequently influencing the conclusions that are drawn.

Chapter 1 is organized by the major decisions that must be made in planning a study:

- *The independent variable.* What is the question being asked in the research study? The question must be translated into an independent variable to be manipulated in an experiment or a predictor variable to be measured in an observational study.
- *The dependent variable.* What measure or measures should we use? In any study, there is a choice of measures. Different measures will provide different information and have different psychometric properties. Some measures may be better windows than others on the phenomenon we are studying. Some measures may be more sensitive than others to variation in the behaviors that are of interest. Some measures may be more reliable than others as indicators of some aspect of ability or performance. How should we balance these considerations in deciding among alternative measures?
- *The subject population.* Who is the target of the research question? Are we interested in healthy, elderly adults? Do we wish to study brain development in rats? And how should observations be sampled from the relevant population? Shall we sample from a diverse population, perhaps varying widely in attributes such as age, intelligence, and ethnicity? Or should our sampling process be more tightly constrained? What are the implications of our decisions about sampling for conclusions that we hope to be able to make?
- *Nuisance variables.* In addition to decisions about the independent and dependent variables, the researcher must carefully consider the possible influences of other variables in the research study. What other variables may plausibly influence the dependent variable? These other variables are potentially a nuisance in two very important respects. First, if they are not taken into account, they may confound the independent variable. In that case, it may be impossible to determine whether a difference in the mean scores across various conditions is due to an effect of the independent variable, or to effects of the nuisance variables that are correlated with the independent variable. Second, even if steps are taken to make certain that the independent variable is not confounded with other variables, nuisance variables contribute random variability to the data. This "error variance" is a concern because it can result in our failing to detect effects of the independent variable.
- *The research design.* In some circumstances, the research question demands an observational study; in other circumstances, the research question can be addressed by an experiment; in all circumstances, there are many options in designing the final study. The choice among the options must be informed by all of the questions considered to this point: What is the independent variable? What is the population to be studied? What measure has been chosen? What are the potential nuisance variables, and how—and how much—are they expected to influence the dependent variable?
- *The statistical analyses.* The statistical analyses should be planned before collecting the data for two reasons. First, planning the analyses has the healthy effect of forcing the researcher to specify the questions to be addressed by the data. Second, it enables the researcher to be sure that, given the planned research design, the targeted questions can be answered by a statistical analysis.

The decisions made in the planning stage are interrelated; therefore, any sequencing of those decisions is a bit arbitrary and may be somewhat misleading. Nevertheless, for expository purposes, we will sequence the six categories of considerations by the order in which the decisions are typically first confronted by the researcher.

1.2 THE INDEPENDENT VARIABLE

Research begins with a question. What is the best way to teach the logic of a simple experiment to fourth-graders? Do people's attitudes toward gay marriage affect the likelihood that they will vote in a presidential election? Which dosage schedule minimizes side effects of a drug? The answer to the question begins with the identification of a variable to be manipulated in an experiment or observed in a natural setting. In an experiment, we call that variable an "independent variable"; in an observational setting, we often refer to the variable as a "predictor variable"; for the present, we will use the term "independent variable" to apply to both situations. The translation of a research question into a relevant independent variable is guided, in part, by the researcher's assumptions about plausible answers to the question. In the question about science teaching, for example, the choice of teaching interventions might be based on current theory about science teaching. In the drug example, the selection of different dosages for comparison will likely be based on existing knowledge of the drug.

Beyond the general process of translating a question into a relevant independent variable, it is useful to distinguish between quantitative and qualitative variables. *Quantitative variables* are defined by the *amount* of a variable. The research question about drug dosage provides an example of a quantitative variable. The conditions of an experiment to relate drug dosage to the occurrence of side effects will compare conditions that differ solely in the amount of drug administered to subjects. *Qualitative variables* involve the *type* of treatment. The research question about science teaching provides an example of a qualitative variable. The relevant experiment will compare two or more teaching interventions to determine which is the most effective. In this example, the different teaching methods would constitute the levels of the independent variable.

1.2.1 Quantitative Independent Variables

In the case of a quantitative independent variable, the experimenter is generally interested in questions relating to the form of the function relating the independent variable, X, to the dependent variable, Y. What is the rate of change in the incidence of side effects as drug dosage is increased? At what point on the dose effect function are side effects at a minimum? Does the function that relates side effects to drug dosage differ for two alternative drug treatments? Given the focus on the form of the function, the levels of the independent variable should be chosen to cover a wide enough range to detect any behavioral change within that range. Further, the number and spacing of levels across that range should be sufficient to clearly define the shape of the function, including its maximum or minimum (e.g., the drug dosage that minimizes side effects).

Theoretical considerations may also dictate the choice of levels of a quantitative independent variable. Suppose the investigator is trying to decide between two theories, one of which predicts a stepwise function and one of which predicts a gradual change in Y as a function of X. In this case, examination of a broad range of levels may be sacrificed in order to concentrate on more levels with a narrow range, presumably permitting a clearer view of the shape of the function within that range.

1.2.2 Qualitative Independent Variables

In studies investigating a quantitative independent variable, the specific numerical levels are of less interest in themselves than in the information they provide about a function relating the independent and dependent variables. In our drug dosage example, it is probably not critical whether the levels of drug dosage are 10, 20 and 40 mg, or 15, 25 and 50 mg. In contrast, a qualitative independent variable is one whose levels have typically been chosen specifically because they are of direct interest to the researcher. In our science teaching example, the teaching interventions to be compared in such an experiment will be specifically chosen. The choice may be based on theory, or on previous research findings, or on observations of behavior in naturally occurring circumstances. For example, two teaching interventions might be constructed to represent opposing teaching philosophies. Alternatively, an educational researcher may observe that a novel method of teaching science has produced impressive scores relative to national norms, so it is decided to compare the novel method with a more conventional method in a controlled experiment.

1.3 THE DEPENDENT VARIABLE

In addition to the independent variable, a researcher must also select a dependent variable, or measure of performance. The choice of the dependent variable should be based on several considerations. First, the dependent variable should be a *valid* measure of the behavior of interest. By valid, we mean that the measure should reflect the behavior of interest in the research. It is often a straightforward matter to select a valid measure. For example, if a researcher wishes to study how the organization of information in a text influences recall of the text, the dependent variable will be recall. If the incidence of side effects of a drug is of interest, the researcher will probably have a list of side effects to check and will simply count the number of instances of side effects for each subject in each condition. However, there are many situations where the selection of a valid measure is less straightforward. If a researcher wants to study how the organization of information in a text influences comprehension of the text, the use of recall as a measure of comprehension is less convincing because recall is influenced by factors other than comprehension. A researcher wishing to assess teaching effectiveness might use student ratings of the overall quality of instruction. However, if by "effectiveness" we mean how well students learned in a course, student ratings may not be a good measure of their learning.

The choice of a valid measure should be guided by the goals of the research and what the researcher knows about the domain. This includes both theory and the empirical literature. For example, if a clinical researcher hypothesizes specific factors that underlie depressive behavior, scales designed to measure those factors may be included in a study of depression. Similarly, if an experimenter has a theory that predicts effects on response time as well as accuracy in studies of memory, then both types of measures should be recorded. Further, as a measure is used by many researchers over time, a knowledge base develops that should inform future use of the measure. For example, recall measures were common in early studies of text comprehension, but have fallen into disfavor as it was discovered that recall performance is influenced by memory factors that have little to do with what most would define as comprehension.

Practical constraints are frequently an important influence on choice of measures. A personality researcher may feel that the ideal way to measure some clinical state is in an intensive interview, but if the research goal requires a large number of subjects, a paper-and-pencil scale may be used because it is easily administered to many individuals, and can also be scored by machine.

Within the constraints imposed by the researcher's goals and by practical limits of time in administration and scoring, statistical considerations are relevant to selection of the dependent variable. All other factors being equal, the most *reliable* measure—the one that is least variable within conditions—should be chosen. In some instances, high reliability is easily attained. For example, response times may be consistently accurately recorded. However, in other cases, reliability is less easily assured. For example, reliability is a major consideration in research in which the dependent variable is an attitude scale or other measurement instrument. Many articles and books have been written on the topic of measurement, and we cannot do justice to the issues here. Interested readers should consult some of the many sources available (e.g., Downing & Haladnya, 2006; Martin & Bateson, 2007; Nunnally & Berstein, 1994).

The *sensitivity* of the measure is also an important concern when selecting a dependent variable. All else being equal, a measure that is capable of detecting small differences in performance is preferable to a measure that can detect only gross differences. In our example of a study of drug side effects, the ultimate side effect would be death of a subject; however, if that was the only category measured, the resulting failure to record less drastic side effects would seriously compromise our ability to identify an optimal dosage to minimize side effects. Perhaps less obviously, measures that are relatively sensitive across many ranges of behavior will not be able to reveal differences among experimental conditions if performance is close to some maximum or minimum value. This would be the case, for example, if two methods of teaching are evaluated by scores on a test so easy that the scores are high regardless of the instructional method. In this example, simply increasing the difficulty of the test should improve its sensitivity.

Another factor that may affect the outcome of the statistical analysis is the *distribution of the dependent variable*. Many common statistical procedures rest on the assumption that the data are normally distributed; that is, that the distribution curve has, at least approximately, a bell shape. This is but one of several assumptions that underlie various methods for estimating and testing effects. We will have much to say throughout this book about the assumptions that underlie the methods we discuss—what these assumptions are, the consequences when they are violated, and the alternative methods appropriate when the consequences may invalidate our conclusions.

Finally, we do not want to leave the impression that there is a single "best" dependent variable in a given experiment. Different measures provide different information, so it is often advisable to use multiple measures of behavior in the same experiment. The result will be a richer understanding of behavior.

1.4 THE SUBJECT POPULATION

With the independent variable identified and the dependent variable(s) selected, who will participate in the study? The answer to this question has immediate implications for our ability to generalize our research conclusions. Several considerations shape the choice of subjects in most research.

Practical considerations often play a major role in defining the subject population. In clinical research, for example, financial and time limitations may force a researcher to draw a sample of subjects from the local Veterans Administration hospital. In social and cognitive research, the easy accessibility of students in introductory psychology courses makes them a nearly irresistible source of study subjects. These practical considerations are understandable, but it is important to recognize that the constraints on sampling that they represent serve to define the subject population. The sampling process, in turn, has implications for how our research conclusions may be generalized. In some situations, practical constraints on sampling may not seriously constrain conclusions. If the study involves basic sensory or perceptual processes, the results from a sample of college students can probably be generalized to individuals of a similar age who do not attend college. On the other hand, if a study of problem-solving strategies is conducted on students from a highly selective college, the conclusions may not be applicable to individuals who do not attend college or, for that matter, to students at less selective colleges.

Beyond the reality of practical limitations, the purpose of the research should be an important factor in the sampling of subjects. If the investigator wants to investigate the cognitive abilities of older adults, then that is the population to be represented in the study. This seems obvious but matters usually are more complicated. For example, what range of older ages will be included in the study? The actual sample of subjects may be a function of several considerations beyond the very general goal.

Theoretical considerations may influence the choice of subjects. Suppose the investigator who is studying cognitive functioning of older adults hypothesizes that speed and accuracy in memory and problem-solving tasks are a direct function of the degree to which people continue to engage in intellectual pursuits. Of course, this depends on the definition of intellectual activities, but the researcher might administer a questionnaire to ensure that he had a range of individuals with respect to whether they participated in activities such as doing puzzles, reading and discussing those readings, or learning new things such as a foreign language.

The subjects' previous histories will be an important constraint on the sample. If the investigator wants older individuals with no obvious cognitive impairments, individuals who may be suffering from such impairments should be excluded from the study. If part of the research goal is to generalize to a population of older individuals representing a broad spectrum of experience, some attempt should be made to include people from various social and economic classes, ethnic backgrounds, and work experiences.

Although perhaps less obvious than the preceding considerations, the control of error variance is an issue in selecting research subjects. The investigator may want to include a wide range of attributes in the study so that there is a firm statistical basis for generalizing to a broad population. However, the more diversified the sample, the more variable the data will be and, therefore, the less clear will be the effects of independent variables on the behavior of interest. For example, if we want to evaluate some method of improving memory in a sample of older adults, we are likely to have a better estimate of the effect of the method in a sample whose members are similar in attributes such as age, experience, and intelligence than in one with wide variation in these attributes.

The tradeoff in sampling from a more narrowly defined population is that, although the data are less variable, inferences about individuals outside the range studied are more speculative. For example, we may assume that if a method of improving memory is less effective for the older members of our sample, it will be even less effective with individuals older than those in our sample. However, that is a hypothesis that is only indirectly supported by our data. Ideally, investigators should think about the population to which they wish to generalize, consider the implications for the possible variability of the data, and then come to a decision about the attributes to be controlled in recruiting subjects. Often, we can compensate for a heterogeneous sample by having a larger sample (see Section 1.6), by the choice of the research design (Chapter 13), and by statistical means (Chapters 13 and 25).

1.5 NUISANCE VARIABLES

Many of the decisions facing the researcher reflect the fact that scores are influenced by variables other than the independent variables of interest. Such variables have been labeled "irrelevant" (to the researcher's interest; Myers, 1979) or "nuisance" variables (Kirk, 1995). Subjects in research differ in ability, prior experience, attitudes, age, gender, and many other attributes that may influence their responses in a study. Even a single individual may make different responses to the same stimulus at different points in time because of factors such as fatigue or practice, a change in calibration of equipment, a change in room temperature, or variation in items on a test or rating instrument.

The presence of nuisance variables is a threat to the success of a study in two potential ways. First, care must be taken to ensure that nuisance variables are not confounded with the independent variable; otherwise, differences among experimental conditions may not be unambiguously attributed to the independent variable. Second, the presence of nuisance variables may make it more difficult to decide whether the independent variable has had an effect, or whether the effect is due to chance.

1.5.1 Confounding

Suppose we observe that students taught science by a lab-based curriculum show higher achievement than students taught science by a text-based curriculum. Can we be sure that the difference in achievement is due to the difference in the curricula? Are the students taught by the lab-based approach more likely to come from an environment that provides more parental support or more resources (e.g., lab equipment)? Are the teachers using the lab-based curriculum better trained in science or more experienced? These are just some of the potential *confounds* that may compromise our hypothetical comparison of curricula. This is but one illustration of how differences between the means of various conditions may be attributed to the effects of the independent variable when those differences are in part, or entirely, due to effects of one or more nuisance variables. Such incorrect attribution of effects may occur whenever variables that are not of primary interest are related to the independent variable.

Issues of public policy provide an important example because they often involve separating the contributions of many variables from those of the variable of interest. For example, a relevant policy issue is whether giving vouchers to poor children to enable them to attend private schools results in more effective education of those children. However, differences in academic performance between students who obtain vouchers and those who remain in public schools, cannot simply be attributed to differences in the schools. Children who obtain vouchers and transfer to private schools may be more able, or have more motivated parents, than those public school students who do not opt out of the public school system.

Many other examples of possible confounds due to nuisance variables could be presented. Relations among variables cause problems of interpretation for true experiments, for observational studies, and for correlational studies. Campbell and Stanley (1963, 1966) present an excellent discussion of several classes of nuisance variables, together with consideration of the advantages and disadvantages of relevant research designs. Although primarily concerned with educational research, their discussion is relevant to any area.

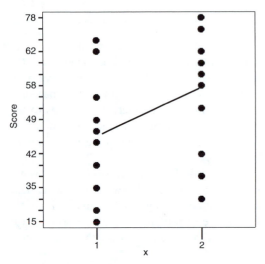

Fig. 1.1 Two data sets with a line connecting mean scores.

1.5.2 Error Variance

Error variance consists of those chance fluctuations in scores that are attributable to the effects of nuisance variables. Consider Fig. 1.1. The two points on the x-axis represent two levels of an independent variable, perhaps two methods of teaching science. In that example, the individual points on the graph represent the scores of individual students on a science achievement test, and the points connected by the line would represent the average scores of individuals in the two groups. The average score at Method 2 is higher than that at Method 1, suggesting that the second method is superior. However, error variance weakens that conclusion. Note that several scores at Method 2 are lower than some of the scores at Method 1, even lower than the mean score at Method 1. Can we be sure that Method 2 represents the better method? Or might the difference in mean performance be due to chance differences between the groups in average ability or motivation, or some other factor? Note that if there were no variability within a condition, all the points would fall at the means, and the advantage of Method 2 would be clear. Unfortunately, error variance is always present, albeit to varying degrees, in behavioral research.

1.6 RESEARCH DESIGN

In an ideal world, a well-articulated research question would be rewarded by definitive empirical results. But an ideal world would not include nuisance variables, so even well-articulated research questions are sometimes answered in a misleading way or not at all. The study of research design and inferential statistics deals to a large extent with the problems posed by nuisance variables. We have already encountered the two main problems: nuisance variables can introduce confounds that make it difficult or impossible to know the true effect of our independent variables; and nuisance variables produce error variance that hinders a researcher's ability to discern the effects of independent variables. In this section, we elaborate these two problems and discuss some strategies for coping with them.

1.6.1 Observation Versus Experimentation

Not all research questions may be approached in the same way. The nature of the approach taken by a researcher has important implications for the researcher's ability to cope with potential confounds and with error variance.

Some questions readily lend themselves to experimentation. Our example of determining the relationship between drug dosage and the incidence of side effects is a good case in point. Typically, an animal model would be used to investigate this question in a laboratory setting. The experimenter has precise control over the administration of drug dosages and extensive control over the conditions under which the drug is administered (e.g., animal weight, feeding and watering, time of day). As we will see, the control associated with experiments makes experimentation eminently suited to dealing with the threats of confounds and error variance.

However, many important questions necessitate a loss of experimental control. For example, if we want to know the effects of a traumatic event on depression, a true experiment is not possible because manipulating the independent variable would be unethical. Instead, a researcher might collect relevant information through interviews or questionnaires administered to individuals who have undergone some trauma. In such circumstances, a researcher cannot prevent nuisance variables from confounding variables of interest. For example, if the researcher is specifically interested in the effects of a traumatic combat experience on depression, a comparison of individuals who have experienced combat trauma with individuals who have not experienced combat trauma could easily be compromised by other differences between the groups. Some of the potential confounds might be avoided by careful selection of a comparison group (e.g., a comparison group comprised of soldiers not involved in combat would be preferable to a comparison group comprised of college students). Still, it is often impossible to identify comparison groups that are matched in all respects to the group of interest. Similarly, the loss of control inherent to observational studies is frequently associated with increased error variance.

Finally, there are many examples of questions that may be approached through either experimentation or observation. Our example of comparing science curricula is relevant. Many educational researchers would approach this question with observational methods, comparing the achievement levels of schools that use a lab-based curriculum with those of schools using a text-based curriculum. One argument for adopting this approach is that an experimental approach disrupts the natural educational environment, with the consequence that the findings of an experiment will ultimately not generalize to the classroom. Another argument is that the barriers to a true experimental approach are so great as to render an experiment impractical. However, many educational researchers counter that an experimental approach can be situated in the classroom without seriously compromising the natural educational environment. Although conceding that the barriers to such an approach are significant, they argue that the effort to surmount the barriers is rewarded by a clearer understanding of what instructional methods are effective and why. There are valid points on both sides of the argument, and there is a place for both observational and experimental research. Thus, it is important to have tools to address the effects of nuisance variables in both types of research.

1.6.2 Dealing with Threats to Valid Inferences

In order to draw a valid conclusion about the effect of an independent variable, a researcher must be able to rule out the possibility that nuisance variables could explain the apparent effect of the independent variable.

Control of Nuisance Variables by Random Assignment.   The most effective means for ruling out nuisance variables as an alternative explanation of an observed effect is to guarantee that the independent variable is not confounded with any relevant nuisance variables. This is possible only in a true experiment. When the independent variable is manipulated, we have control over which individuals are assigned to which treatments. In such cases, the potential effects of many nuisance variables can be countered by *random assignment* of individuals to conditions. For example, in a study comparing effects of several instructional methods on problem solving, we would not want to select subjects in such a way as to increase the likelihood that more motivated individuals would be assigned to a particular method. However, that might happen if the first volunteers, possibly the more motivated individuals, were assigned to one method. One solution is to randomly assign subjects to conditions, using a method that ensures that each subject has an equal chance of being assigned to each instructional method. Randomization does not ensure that the various instructional groups are perfectly matched on those nuisance variables that might influence learning. However, randomization does ensure that over many replications of the experiment, no treatment will have an advantage. In any one experiment, one condition might have an advantage (e.g., include more motivated, or more intelligent, subjects) but statistical analyses that are based on the assumption of randomization take these chance differences into account.

Randomization does not apply only to the assignment of subjects to conditions. In many studies, the subject is tested on several different items in each condition. For example, a researcher might be interested in whether there is a difference in ease of understanding sentences as a function of whether they are in the active or passive voice. Accordingly, the researcher might create an active and a passive version of each member of a set of sentences. The time each subject needed to read each sentence would be recorded; half of the sentences would be randomly selected for presentation in the active voice, and the other half of the sentences would be in the passive voice. A different random assignment could be used for each subject. In addition, the order of presentation of the sentences could be randomly sequenced for each subject. Random assignment of sentences to the active and passive voices addresses the possibility that some sentences are inherently more difficult to read by providing an equal chance of their being presented in either condition to each subject. Similarly, random sequencing of the presentation of the sentences addresses concerns about the influences on reading time of fatigue, boredom, practice, or other time-related effects that influence reading time.

Randomization guards against attributing effects to an independent variable when other variables are responsible for the effects. However, it is not a cure-all. For example, we might wish to study the effects on depression of a newly developed pill. We could have interviewers rate the state of depression before and after treatment. However, just the knowledge of being treated might influence the subjects' responses. One solution would be to have a control condition, a second group of depressed patients who are given a placebo (e.g., a sugar pill). Subjects would be randomly assigned to either the experimental or the control condition. However, if the interviewer is aware of the condition of each individual being interviewed, this could (presumably unintentionally) bias the results. The response to this concern is to run what is termed a double-blind experiment, in which neither interviewer nor subject is aware of the condition. Kirk (1995, pp. 22–24) discusses several other methods that supplement randomization.

Measurement of Nuisance Variables.   In the absence of experimental control, a researcher can never be completely certain that a nuisance variable might not be responsible, at least in part, for an apparent effect of an independent variable. The researcher's best strategy is to identify and measure relevant nuisance variables, and then hope to demonstrate that those variables cannot account for the observed results. For example, consider a study that attempts to determine the effect of combat trauma on depression. A comparison of soldiers who have with those who have not experienced trauma might be compromised by, say, differences in the gender or average education levels of the two groups. Men may be more likely to encounter traumatic combat experiences than women because of different assignments. Similarly, better educated soldiers may be more likely to receive assignments that make them less likely to experience combat. If gender and education level are recorded and included in the analyses of the data, it may be possible to demonstrate that neither variable is related to depression and therefore cannot explain an observed relation between combat trauma and depression. Or gender and/or education level might be related to depression, but not in a way that can explain an observed relation between trauma and depression. Of course, it is possible that the nature of the relations between gender, education, and trauma make it impossible to clearly discern the nature of the relation between trauma and depression. Measurement is the best a researcher can do in this situation, but it does not substitute for the ability to exert control over variables.

1.6.3 Dealing with Error Variance

If there is an effect of our independent variable in the population, we hope that the effect will be clearly evident in our sample. Unfortunately, that doesn't always happen. The reason is error variance. An analogy is useful here. Think of error variance as noise and the effect of the independent variable as a signal embedded in that noise. If the signal is sufficiently strong relative to the noise, it will be detected; however, if the signal is too weak, it will be missed. A well-designed and conducted study will establish circumstances in which the signal-to-noise ratio is high and thus the probability of detecting an effect of the independent variable is high. This detection probability is the concept of statistical power: *Power* is the probability of detecting an effect of an independent variable in an experiment when an effect exists in the population. We seek to conduct studies with high power; our primary means to accomplish this goal is to minimize error variance. Several strategies are available.

Control by Uniform Conditions. Random assignment of subjects or items to treatments provides protection against wrongly attributing effects to the independent variable. However, randomization does not reduce error variance. One way to reduce error variance is to hold the conditions of the study constant except for variation in the levels of the independent variables. For example, all subjects should receive the same instructions in the same environment, and all animal subjects should receive the same handling, feeding, and housing. To the extent that sources of variance other than the independent variable are held constant, error variance will be reduced and effects of independent variables will be more easily detected.

It is possible and desirable to seek uniformity of conditions in observational studies, as well as experiments. A good example is found in a study by Räkkönen et al. (1999). They studied the relation between ambulatory blood pressure (BP) and personality characteristics, taking BP measurements from all subjects in the same time period on the same three days of the week, two work days and one nonwork day. In this way, they reduced possible effects of the time at which measurements were taken. Similarly, researchers have the option of selecting the subjects of observational studies in such a way as to match subjects on attributes (e.g., age and intelligence) that may influence the behavior of interest (e.g., learning in a study comparing teaching interventions), but which are not of interest to the researcher.

Control by Design.   The design of the research is a plan for data collection. We can minimize the effects of error variance by choosing a design that permits us to calculate the contribution of one or more nuisance variables. In the data analysis, that error variance is subtracted from the total variability in the data set. Many of the design variations also enable the researcher to equate treatment conditions for one or more nuisance variables, thus ensuring that those variables are not responsible for any differences that are found between conditions.

One procedure that is often used in experiments is *blocking,* sometimes also referred to as *stratification*, or *matching*. Typically, we divide the pool of subjects into blocks on the basis of some variable whose effects are not of primary interest to us, such as gender or ability level. Then we randomly assign subjects within each block to the different levels of the independent variable. As an example of the blocking design, suppose we wish to carry out a study of memory in which subjects are taught to use one of three possible mnemonic strategies. We might measure the memory span of subjects before the start of the research. We could then randomly distribute the three subjects with the highest memory span score among the three conditions, then do the same with the three next highest scoring subjects, and so on, until all three conditions are filled. In this design, the groups are roughly matched on initial memory ability, a variable that might influence their memory of materials in the experiment. Thus, any possible differences between means of the strategy groups cannot be attributed to initial memory span. As an added result of the matching, a statistical analysis that treats the level of initial memory span as a second independent variable can now remove the variability due to that variable. The blocking design is said to be more *efficient* than a simpler design that randomly assigns subjects to conditions without regard to memory span. (Chapter 9 presents the analysis of data when a blocking design has been used.)

Blocking can also be used in some studies that are not true experiments. If we wish to study attitudes in different ethnic groups about some issue, we can attempt to recruit subjects of different ethnicities who are matched on variables which might influence responses, such as age, income, and education.

For some independent variables, even greater efficiency can be achieved if we test the same subject at each level of the independent variable. This variant of blocking is known as a *repeated-measures design*. A common example occurs in studies of forgetting in which measures are obtained at various times after the material was studied. The advantage of repeated-measures designs is that subjects can be treated as another independent variable in the statistical analysis, thus removing from the data variability due to differences among subjects. Ideally, the remaining error variance will be due to errors of measurement caused by random fluctuations over time in factors such as the subject's attentiveness, the difficulty of the stimuli, and the temperature in the room. Thus, the repeated-measures design is a particularly effective way to minimize error variance, although it is not without its drawbacks. The major drawbacks of the design are the possibility of systematic biases due to time-related effects (e.g., practice and fatigue) and the possibility of *carry-over effects* (i.e., influences of participation in earlier conditions on performance in subsequent conditions). (A full treatment of this design is presented in Chapters 14–17.)

Control by Measurement.   Often, blocking is not practical. Morrow and Young (1997) studied the effects of exposure to literature on the reading scores of third-graders. Although reading scores were obtained before the start of the school year (pretest scores), the composition of the third-grade classes was established by school administrators prior to the study. Therefore, the blocking design was not a possibility. However, the pretest score could still be used to reduce error variance by removing that portion of the variability in the dependent variable (i.e., the posttest score) that was predictable from the pretest score. This adjustment, called *analysis of covariance*, is thus a statistical means to reduce error variance, as opposed to the design approach of blocking. (Analysis of covariance is discussed in Chapters 13 and 25.)

Usually, the greater efficiency that comes with more complicated designs and analyses has a cost. For example, additional information is required for both blocking and the analysis of covariance. Furthermore, the appropriate statistical analysis associated with more efficient approaches is usually based on more assumptions about the nature of the data. In view of this, a major theme of this book is that there are many possible designs and analyses, and many considerations in choosing among them. We would like to select our design and method of data analysis with the goals of minimizing potential confounds and reducing error variance as much as possible. However, our decisions in these matters may be constrained by the resources that are available and by the assumptions that must be made about the data. Ideally, the researcher should be aware of the pros and cons of the different designs and analyses, and the tradeoffs that must be considered in making the best choice.

Control by Sample Size. The final strategy for dealing with error variance is through the choice of sample size. The size of the sample does not actually affect the individual error variance in the design; however, it does influence the amount of error in estimates of the effects of the independent variables. As sample size increases, estimates of effects become more precise; as a consequence, the power to detect the effects improves. Thus, in general, increasing sample size increases statistical power in any design. The relationship between sample size and power is well defined for a given design, so we can—and should—use that relationship in planning how many observations to make in a given experiment or observational study. Sometimes, we may find that the sample size required to achieve a certain level of power is impractical. However, it is better to know that before we begin a study so that we can modify our plans by revising our research design, or choosing other, less variable, measures.

1.7 STATISTICAL ANALYSES

Statistical analyses are performed after the data are collected, of course. However, the analyses should be planned *before* the data are collected, as part of the process of evaluating the adequacy of the research design. The analysis of data broadly consists of two phases: (1) an *exploratory phase*, in which measures of central tendency (e.g., means, medians), variability, and shape of distributions should be calculated and graphed; and (2) an *inferential phase*, in which population parameters are estimated and hypotheses about them are tested.

Too often, researchers neglect the first, exploratory phase. However, the descriptive statistics *are* the results of an experiment and they therefore deserve particular attention. That attention begins during the planning phase. The research plans should include decisions about what descriptive statistics will be calculated and what plots of the data will be useful to view. The researcher should imagine, for example, possible patterns of means across conditions, and what different patterns would reveal about the behavior being studied. We will present the reasons for, and examples of, exploratory analyses in the next chapter. For now, we note that such analyses may suggest additional hypotheses and also inform us about potential problems for the statistical analyses to be carried out in the next phase.

The goals of the research will often dictate very specific hypotheses or questions. For example, if there are several levels of the independent variable, are there comparisons between certain levels that are of particular interest? Or, if the independent variable is quantitative, is it of interest to examine certain features of the function relating the dependent and independent variables, such as whether it is best represented by a straight line or a curve? These rather specific sorts of questions should be considered before the data are collected for two reasons. First, considering specific questions before the data are collected ensures that the design allows us to answer those questions. Second, inferences based on tests of hypotheses formulated before the results are viewed have less likelihood of yielding erroneous conclusions than tests of hypotheses suggested by the observed results.

The power of the statistical test should be an important consideration in planning the research. Estimates of error variance obtained from related research or pilot studies, together with a desired level of power to detect effects of a certain size, should determine the amount of data collected. Just how this is done is considered in several chapters in this book and computer software is provided on the website for the book to carry out the calculations.

Finally, it is useful to specify the planned inferential tests in detail to make certain that the experimental design has been thoroughly evaluated and all potential sources of variability have been identified. This practice will help guard against oversights in planning the design. For example, an educational researcher planning an experiment to compare two methods of teaching science might assign two classes of students at random to a lab-based teaching method and two other classes to a text-based method. However, this plan is flawed because it neglects an important potential influence on performance; namely, individual classes may differ in performance regardless of their assignment to different teaching methods. An implication of this observation is that the research plan should include many more than four classes so that variability due to classes may be adequately evaluated.

1.8 GENERALIZING CONCLUSIONS

A final planning consideration is to identify issues concerning the generalizability of any findings to emerge from the research. Campbell and Stanley (1963) distinguished between internal and external validity of inferences. *Internal validity* refers to the question of whether observed effects can validly be attributed to the independent variable. *External validity* refers to the extent to which the inferences that are drawn can be generalized to other conditions or populations. In much of this chapter, we have been concerned with internal validity; in particular, we have discussed the role of randomization and research design in protecting against potential confounds. We touched briefly on the subject of external validity when we cautioned that researchers should consider the population to which their inferences apply. For example, if a treatment of depression is successful in a study with all female subjects, or in one with individuals in a certain age range, we should not conclude that the treatment would also reduce depression in males, or in older subjects, without some firm basis in theory or data. Perhaps the most common setting in which we need to be careful about generalizing beyond the population sampled is the academic, in which the subjects are usually college students within a limited range of age and intelligence, or the children of faculty and students.

Similar issues arise with respect to generalizing conclusions based on a particular method or measure. For example, recall and recognition scores have been shown to reflect very different memory processes. And different results have been obtained in studies of reading in which reading times are calculated as differences between button presses that bring on successive words in a text and studies in which reading times are recorded by tracking eye movements.

Studies in which the independent variable is quantitative confront the researcher with other problems of generalization. There are practical limits to the levels that can be included. Conclusions about the shape of the function relating dependent and independent variables require interpolation between, and extrapolation beyond, the levels observed.

Still another common problem for external validity involves generalization to a population of items. When emotional states or attitudes are inferred from responses to a set of pictures, we have to consider whether the results are specific to those particular pictures or have more general implications. Similar inferential issues confront researchers in the area of language comprehension, whose stimuli are sentences, or words that are usually constrained as to length or familiarity.

One approach to the issue of external validity is to systematically vary the populations sampled or the measures obtained. This can be done within a study or over a series of studies. For example, a study of the effects of some treatment might include gender of the subjects as a second variable. Or, as has often been done, both recall and recognition measures might be recorded in studies of memory. The inclusion of variables that enable tests of the generalizability of results should be a consideration in planning the research. Nevertheless, it is important to understand that results can never be generalized on every dimension. As Campbell and Stanley (1963) have pointed out, the very act of conducting an experiment raises the question of whether the results would apply in a less controlled, real-world setting. Whereas we can provide a logical basis for arguing that certain methods, such as randomization, increase internal validity, we can only argue for external validity by extrapolating beyond the methods and results of the current study. We should take great care before making such extrapolations.

1.9 SUMMARY

Careful planning of a study may save much wasted effort. Such plans should have several goals:

- The research plan should include steps to ensure that results attributed to the independent variable are not due to other uncontrolled variables. In experiments, random assignment is the key procedure for guarding against systematic biases due to nuisance variables. In less controlled research environments, the researcher must identify nuisance variables of interest and measure them so that their influences may be assessed.
- Error variance should be controlled as much as possible to ensure maximal power to detect effects of the independent variable. Several strategies address control of error variance, including ensuring uniformity of conditions, selecting reliable dependent variables, choice of research design, and measurement of nuisance variables for purposes of statistical adjustment.
- Decisions about the number of observations to collect in a study should be informed by power considerations.
- Statistical analyses, including descriptive statistics, should be planned as part of the process of planning the research design.
- Issues pertaining to the bases for generalizing conclusions should be considered during the planning phase.

EXERCISES

1.1 A researcher requested volunteers for a study comparing several methods to reduce weight. Subjects were told that if they were willing to be in the study, they would be assigned randomly to one of three methods. Thirty individuals agreed to this condition and participated in the study.

(a) Is this an experiment or an observational study?

(b) Is the sample random? If so, characterize the likely population.

(c) Describe and discuss an alternative research design.

1.2 A study of computer-assisted learning of arithmetic in third-grade students was carried out in a private school in a wealthy suburb of a major city.

(a) Characterize the population that this sample represents. In particular, consider whether the results permit generalizations about computer-assisted instruction (CAI) for the broad population of third-grade students. Present your reasoning.

(b) This study was done by assigning one class to CAI and one to a traditional method. Discuss some potential sources of error variance in this design.

1.3 Investigators who conducted an observational study reported that children who spent considerable time in day care were more likely than other children to exhibit aggressive behavior in kindergarten (Stolberg, 2001). Although this suggests that placement in day care may cause aggressive behavior—either because of the day-care environment or because of the time away from parents—other factors may be involved.

(a) What factors other than time spent in day care might affect aggressive behavior in the study cited by Stolberg?

(b) If you were carrying out such an observational study, what might be done to attempt to understand the effects upon aggression of factors other than day care?

(c) An alternative approach to the effects of day care upon aggressive behavior would be to conduct an experiment. How would you do this and what are the pros and cons of this approach?

1.4 It is well known that the incidence of lung cancer in individuals who smoke cigarettes is higher than in the general population.

(a) Is this evidence that smoking causes lung cancer?

(b) If you were a researcher investigating this question, what further lines of evidence would you seek?

1.5 In the *Seasons* study (the data are in the *Seasons* file in the *Seasons* folder on the CD accompanying this book), we found that the average depression score was higher for males with only a high-school education than for those with at least some college education. Discuss the implications of this finding. In particular, consider whether the data demonstrate that providing a college education will reduce depression.

1.6 In a 20-year study of cigarette smoking and lung cancer, researchers recorded the incidence of lung cancer in a random sample of smokers and nonsmokers, none of whom had cancer at the start of the study.

(a) What are the independent and dependent variables?

(b) For each, state whether the variable is discrete or continuous.

(c) What variables other than these might be recorded in such a study? Which of these are discrete or continuous?

Chapter 2
Exploring the Data

2.1 OVERVIEW

Too often, students—and even established researchers—begin data analysis by calculating a few statistics, usually means or correlations, and then immediately perform statistical tests. This common approach to data analysis puts the cart before the horse by emphasizing inferential statistics over descriptive statistics. In fact, a thorough description of the data is critical to both a complete understanding of the data and appropriate application of inferential tests. Data analyses should begin with graphing of the distribution of observations and calculation of several descriptive statistics. Such exploration of the data serves several purposes.

First, a data set is a researcher's window on the population under study. Inferential tests perform the important function of helping researchers to determine which trends in the data reflect corresponding characteristics of the population, but inferential tests will only be applied to those aspects of the data that are considered by the researcher in the first place. For example, consider a clinical researcher studying depression who observes that the pattern of means on the Beck Depression Inventory appears to vary as a function of marital status. If information is not also gathered about the distribution of scores for each marital category, the researcher is likely to overlook the possibility that a few extreme scores are responsible for the pattern of means. As Hoaglin, Mosteller, and Tukey (1983, p. 2) have said: "Exploratory data analysis emphasizes flexible searching for clues and evidence, whereas confirmatory data analysis stresses evaluating the available evidence." We must look for the evidence before we can evaluate it.

Second, in many instances, description is an end in itself. Consider the example of a school district superintendent who wishes to evaluate the scores on a standardized reading test. The superintendent has several questions she would like to answer. How should the overall level of performance of students in the district be characterized relative to national norms? Are most students performing near the average? Or is there considerable variability in reading level? If there is variability, are there students whose scores clearly indicate the need for remediation? Are there factors that seem related to variation in performance, such as gender or school?

Yet a third reason for a thorough descriptive analysis is that careful examination of the data may serve to generate hypotheses that the investigator had not had in mind when the study was designed. For example, our hypothetical district superintendent may find an unexpected difference between the means of male and female students. She may then ask whether this is a difference that would hold for similarly instructed students with the same prior experiences, or whether it is due to a chance fluctuation in performance of the two groups. Or the superintendent may note that the average score in her district is below that for the state as a whole. She may ask whether this is a chance result or one that will repeat itself with future generations of students.

Finally, description of the data is important to ensure that assumptions underlying subsequent, inferential statistics will be valid for the data being analyzed. Questions about group differences (e.g., boys and girls), or the difference in performance between a group (e.g., the school district) and some standard (e.g., scores for the state as a whole), are questions of statistical inference. Such questions require further analyses and those analyses rest on certain assumptions about the shape and variability of the distribution of data. Therefore, we first must explore our data to assess whether assumptions underlying planned inferential analyses are being met. If not, we may consider modifications of our planned analyses. Among many possibilities, such modifications may include deleting extreme scores, transforming data, or using statistical procedures other than those originally planned.

In this chapter, we present the tools for the necessary exploration of data. The major objectives of this chapter are to:

- *Present several ways of graphing the data that provide different views of the distribution of scores.* We graph the data in different ways because different graphs provide different sorts of information. Some data plots provide only a general sense of the distribution, whereas others provide a more detailed look, and enable us more readily to address questions such as whether there are scores that are markedly different from most of the others.
- *Present several summary statistics to reflect key properties of distributions.* Specifically, we will present measures of the average, variability, and shape of the distribution of scores. In the case of measures of average and variability, alternative statistics will be presented because they provide somewhat different information about a distribution. In addition, different indices of the same general characteristic have different properties that make them more or less desirable, depending upon the situation. Thus, in addition to the mean and standard deviation, we will consider the median and interquartile range.
- *Introduce ways of characterizing relationships between two variables.* We will present examples of scatter diagrams, which graphically present such relationships. We will also present and illustrate the application of the correlation coefficient, which is a numerical measure of the direction and strength of a relationship.

Good statistical practice should begin with the exploration of the data, using graphs and statistics such as those presented in this chapter.

2.2 PLOTS OF DATA DISTRIBUTIONS

The first step in describing a data set is to get an overall view of the data by graphing the distribution of observations. An understanding of the distribution of scores provides fundamental information, as well as a context for interpreting specific properties of the distribution, such as its mean and standard deviation.

Table 2.1 The *Royer* second-grade addition scores

47	50	50	69	72	74	76	82	82	83
84	85	88	89	89	90	93	94	94	94
94	95	95	100	100	100	100	100		

In a study of basic arithmetic skills, Royer et al. (1999) collected both accuracy and response time scores from male and female students in grades 1 to 8 for addition, subtraction, and multiplication.[1] Table 2.1 presents the percent correct addition score for 28 male students in the second grade. The mean is 84.607 and the middle score, the median, is 89.[2] This indicates that, on the average, the students did quite well. What it does not reveal is whether everyone scored close to the average or whether there was considerable variability. Nor does the average reveal anything about the shape of the distribution. If most students have scored near the median but a few students have much lower scores, we should know this because it alerts us to the fact that there are children having problems with simple addition. We also may want to determine whether the distribution is at least approximately bell-shaped because the assumption that scores have been drawn from a normally distributed population underlies many inferential procedures. Considerations such as these suggest that we look at the distribution of scores.

The answers to the concerns just raised seem evident from an examination of the table. However, they would not be so evident in larger data sets, or even in this one if we had not sorted the data from lowest to highest score before entering them into the table. In most cases, graphic aids will be needed to tell us about the characteristics of the distribution of scores. In this section, we consider several graphs available from the Explore module of SPSS. Most can also be generated from other SPSS menus (e.g., "Graphs") or by any of several other statistical programs (e.g., SAS, Systat, Minitab), as well as by graphics programs (e.g., Sigma Plot, StatGraphics, PsiPlot) and spreadsheets (e.g., Excel, Quattro Pro).

2.2.1 Histograms

Histograms are graphs of the frequency of groups of scores. They provide one way to quickly view the data. Fig. 2.1 presents a histogram for the data set of Table 2.1. In this graph, the label on the left hand y-axis (the ordinate) is the frequency, the number of scores represented by each bar; the label on the right side is the proportion of the 28 scores represented by each bar. The x-axis (the abscissa) presents the addition scores, which have been divided into eight intervals, called bins, of five points each. Actually, the default histogram plotted in SPSS would have had six bins of 10 points each, so we used an option to decrease the width of the bins and thus increase the number of bins. This raises an important point. The goal in constructing a graph of a distribution is to summarize the important characteristics of the distribution. A summary involves data reduction and a corresponding loss of information; however, an accurate summary must retain any important information. Thus, researchers must exercise judgment in deciding on an appropriate degree of resolution (i.e., bin size) for a graph.

---

[1] The complete data set can be downloaded by following the link from the home page of the book's website to *Data Files*, and then to *Royer*; also see the *Royer Readme* file there.

[2] Table 2.1 contains values that have been rounded to the nearest integer, and the statistics and graphs we present for the second-grade addition accuracy are based on these integer values.

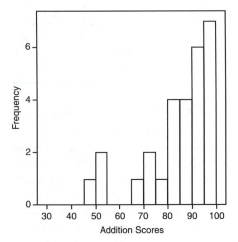

Fig. 2.1 Histogram of the data in Table 2.1.

Once the histogram is constructed, important characteristics of the distribution should now be more evident than they would be from a listing of the scores. It is clear in Fig. 2.1, as the mean and median cited earlier indicated, that most students performed very well. Indeed, the most frequent score is 100%. However, it is also evident that a few students performed very poorly, and there is a gap between the three lowest scores and the lowest of the remaining 25 scores. This gap is typical of many real data sets, as is the obvious asymmetry in the distribution. Micceri (1989) examined 440 distributions of achievement scores and other psychometric data and noted the prevalence of such departures from the classic bell shape as asymmetry (skew) and "lumpiness" (more than one mode, the most frequently observed value). Similarly, after analyzing many data distributions based on standard chemical analyses of blood samples, Hill and Dixon (1982) concluded that their real-life data distributions were "asymmetric, lumpy, and have relatively few unique values" (p. 393). We raise this point because the inferential procedures most commonly encountered in journal reports rest on strong assumptions about the shape of the distribution of data in the population. These assumptions are often not met, and it is therefore important to understand the consequences of the mismatch between assumptions and the distribution of data. We will consider those consequences and possible alternative analyses later in this book. For now, we again emphasize that exploring the data is a first step in evaluating the validity of assumptions that play a role in the next, inferential, stage of analysis.

2.2.2 Box Plots

Histograms provide only one way to look at our data. A very different view is provided by box plots, which emphasize important characteristics of the data while sacrificing much of the detail available in a histogram. Fig. 2.2 presents an SPSS box plot of the same data depicted in the histogram in Fig. 2.1. The box plot quickly provides information about the main characteristics of the distribution of scores: (1) the median, the value at the center of the distribution; (2) the variability, or spread, of the scores; (3) the degree of skewness, or asymmetry, in the distribution; and (4) extreme scores, or outliers. We will consider each of these aspects of the box plot but we first provide an overview of its elements.

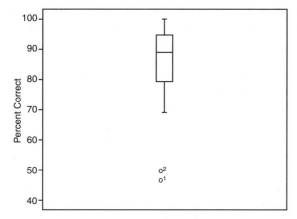

Fig. 2.2 Box plot of the data in Table 2.1.

Creating the Box. The construction of a box plot begins by placing the scores of the data set in order by rank, from lowest to highest. Once this is done, we can draw the box depicted in Fig. 2.2. The high end corresponds to the score that exceeds 75% of the scores; this is the third quartile. The lower end corresponds to the score that exceeds 25% of the scores; this is the first quartile. Thus, 50% of the data lies between the limits indicated by the top and bottom of the box.

There are several ways to calculate the quartiles. The definition usually found in introductory statistics texts is often awkward, requiring linear interpolation. Somewhat simpler to calculate are the *hinges* (Tukey, 1977). SPSS bases its calculation of the top and bottom of the box plot on this statistic. As an example of their calculation, consider the *Royer* data of Table 2.1. Then take the following steps.

1. Find the location, or *depth*, of the median; $d_M = (n + 1)/2$. With 28 scores, $d_M = 29/2 = 14.5$. When d_M has a fractional value—that is, when n is an even number—drop the fraction. We use brackets to represent the integer; that is, $[d_M] = 14$.

2. Find the depth of the lower and upper hinges, d_{LH} and d_{UH}. These are simply the medians of the lower and of the upper 14 scores. The depth of the lower hinge is

$$d_{LH} = ([d_M] + 1)/2 \tag{2.1a}$$
$$= (14 + 1)/2 = 7.5$$

and the depth of the upper hinge is

$$d_{UH} = (n + 1) - d_{LH} \tag{2.1b}$$
$$= (28 + 1) - 7.5 = 21.5$$

The depth of 7.5 for the lower hinge means that the lower hinge is the score midway between the seventh score (76) and the eighth score (82), or 79. The depth of the upper hinge is 21.5, which is midway between the seventh and eighth scores from the top; the corresponding score is 94.5 in the *Royer* data. The length of the box in Fig. 2.2 is therefore 94.5 − 79, or 15.5. This distance between the hinges is one measure of variability, and is usually referred to as the *H-spread*, to signify the spread of scores between the hinges. An option available in SPSS's Explore module is to request that box-plot statistics be expressed in percentiles. If that option is selected, quartiles are computed by linear interpolation and the values of the first and third quartiles are 77.5 and 94.75.

The Median.   The horizontal line between the top and bottom of the box represents the median. The median is the middle score in an ordered set of scores. In the data of Table 2.1, in which the number of scores, n, is an even number, the median falls halfway between the middle two scores. Those scores are in the 14th and 15th positions when the scores are ordered from lowest to highest. Both of the scores are 89, and so the median has that value. If the two scores had differed, the median would have been computed as the mean of the two values.

The median is useful in an initial exploration of data because it is not affected by extreme scores. Unlike the mean, whose value changes if any individual score is changed, the median is considered a *resistant statistic* because it is unaffected by changes in the value of any single score. For example, if we replaced the 47 in the data set of Table 2.1 with a score of 67, the median would be unchanged but the mean would be increased. Because of this property of the median, there are circumstances in which it provides a more representative index of the location of a distribution than does the mean. For example, if the salaries of corporate officers are included in reporting mean salaries at a company we may have a distorted sense of how well everyone is paid because the officers' salaries will greatly increase the mean.

The Whiskers.   The lines extending vertically from the box are often called whiskers, and they extend to the lowest and highest scores that are not outliers. Note that the median is closer to the top of the box than to the bottom and also that the top whisker is shorter than the bottom one. This reflects the same straggling left tail that we saw reflected in the histogram of Fig. 2.1. In other words, both figures illustrate that half of the data fall in a relatively narrow range between 89 and 100, whereas the remaining half are spread over a wider range of scores; the distribution is asymmetric, or *skewed*.

Outliers.   The circles in the box plot represent outliers, the two scores of 50 and the score of 47 in Table 2.1. The numbers next to the outliers are case numbers; because we sorted the data file, cases 1 and 2 have the lowest scores, and are outliers in this data set. The steps to define an outlier are as follows:

1. Calculate the H-spread. This is $94.5 - 79$, or 15.5, in the present example.
2. Find 1.5 times the H-spread; this is $(1.5)(15.5) = 23.25$.
3. Subtract the preceding result (23.25) from the bottom limit of the box and add it to the top limit. In the current example, these values are $79 - 23.25 = 55.75$ and $94.5 + 23.25 = 117.75$.
4. An outlier is any score beyond those limits. Therefore, the scores of 47 and 50 are outliers. It might also be noted that SPSS distinguishes outliers from extreme outliers, which are scores that are more than three times the H-spread above or below the hinges. Extreme outliers are denoted by an asterisk rather than a circle.

Outliers are important to detect because they often correspond to cases that merit special attention. In the current example, they draw attention to three students who are performing much worse than any other student in the group of second-grade males. These students may require remedial aid, or there may be other causes of their poor performance that require investigation.

Outliers are also important to detect in studies where the goal is to draw inferences about the population from which the sample has been drawn. Many statistical tests involve calculating the sample mean, which, as we have already noted, is quite sensitive to extreme scores. Thus, it is important to be aware of outliers when interpreting patterns of means. In addition, many statistical tests assume a normal distribution of scores. Inferences based on such tests can be suspect when the distribution is asymmetric and asymmetry is often associated with extreme scores. In the current example, our estimate of the population mean is the sample mean, 84.61. If we eliminate the three outlying scores, the mean is now estimated to be 88.88, close to the sample median. Furthermore, the distribution is far more symmetric in shape when the outliers are eliminated. Thus, our interest in both the individuals who had the outlying scores and the effects of outliers on inferences drawn from the sample dictates a need to identify outliers.

Integrating the Components.   Our box plot provides a sense of several important aspects of the data. The median of 89 tells us that at least half of the second-grade students have a good grasp of addition. We also can see from the position of the lower hinge that approximately 75% of the students have scored in the high 70s or above. We can also see the straggling lower tail, usually referred to as *negative skew*; the top 25% of the students have scores between 95 and 100 whereas the lowest 25% fall between 47 and 79, reminding us that there are several students who have had problems with the test.

2.2.3 Stem-and-Leaf Displays

The histogram and box plot provide an overview of shape, variability, and location, but often we prefer a more detailed view of the data. In that event, a good option is the stem-and-leaf graph. Fig. 2.3 presents a stem-and-leaf display of the *Royer* data. We might think of this as a histogram laid on its side. The length of each row gives a sense of the frequency of a particular range of scores, just as in the histogram. However, this plot provides more information because it allows us to reconstruct the numerical values of Table 2.1 The left-most column is the frequency associated with each row. The middle column of values is called the "stem." For the *Royer* data, to obtain a score we multiply the stem by 10 and add the "leaf," the value to the right of the stem. We know that the multiplier of the stem is 10 because the SPSS output states that the stem width is 10. In this data set, SPSS has indicated that there are three extreme scores; they are scores of 50 or less, and they correspond to the outliers noted in the preceding section. The second row of the plot represents a score of 69. The next row contains the scores 72 and 74.

ADD_ACC Stem-and-Leaf Plot

Frequency Stem & Leaf

```
 3.00 Extremes (=<50)
 1.00 6 . 9
 2.00 7 . 24
 1.00 7 . 6
 4.00 8 . 2234
 4.00 8 . 5899
 6.00 9 . 034444
 2.00 9 . 55
 5.00 10 . 00000
```

Stem width: 10
Each leaf: 1 case(s)

Fig. 2.3 Stem-and-leaf plot of the data of Table 2.1.

X Stem-and-Leaf Plot

Frequency Stem & Leaf

```
    2.00 Extremes (=<182)
    4.00 2 . 7788
    5.00 3 . 22244
   15.00 3 . 667777777789999
    8.00 4 . 00234444
    9.00 4 . 667778899
    3.00 5 . 112
    2.00 5 . 89
    1.00 6 . 2
    1.00 Extremes (>=749)
```

Stem width: 100
Each leaf: 1 case(s)

Fig. 2.4 Stem-and-leaf plot of a data set (X).

Histograms and stem-and-leaf plots display much the same information. However, histograms usually provide a more immediate sense of the overall shape, whereas stem-and-leaf plots provide more detail about the numerical values. In addition, they indicate outliers.

The values by which the stem and leaf should be multiplied depend on the numerical scale. Consider a set of 50 scores, the first 10 of which are 168, 182, 273, 273, 280, 287, 322, 322, 329, and 343. Fig. 2.4 presents the SPSS stem-and-leaf display for the entire data set. Because the scores are in the hundreds, we have to multiply the stem by 100 and the leaf by 10. Unlike the example of Fig. 2.3, this doesn't give us the exact value for each score, but we have an approximation. The first row tells us that there are two low outliers, scores at or below 182. If we multiply the stem in the second row by 100 and each of the four leaves by 10, we know that there are two scores between 270 and 279, and two scores between 280 and 289. Although we can't tell the exact score from this plot, we have approximate values and know that there are three outliers, two extremely low scores and one extremely high score. Thus, we still have more information than the histogram would have provided, and we still have a sense of the shape of the distribution.

2.2.4 A Graphic Check on Normality

Because many commonly used statistical procedures are based on the assumption that the data were sampled from a normally distributed population, it is helpful to have ways of looking at possible violations of this assumption. Specific characteristics of a distribution imply nonnormality. For example, because the normal distribution is symmetric, *skewness* (asymmetry) in a data plot indicates a distribution that is not normal. Another indication is a nonzero value of *kurtosis* (roughly, more or fewer scores in the tails than we would expect in a normal distribution). However, a more direct indication is available in many computing packages. These programs rank order the scores and then plot the standardized scores (z scores; see Section 2.4 for further discussion) against the actual scores. Fig. 2.5 presents two such plots. Using SPSS's Q–Q plot option (in the Graphs or Explore menus), we first plotted multiplication response times for students in the fifth through eighth grades. If data are normally distributed, the points will fall on a straight line. This is clearly not the case for the multiplication response times (RT). However, if we transform the multiplication times into response speeds by taking the reciprocals of the response times, we obtain the second plot

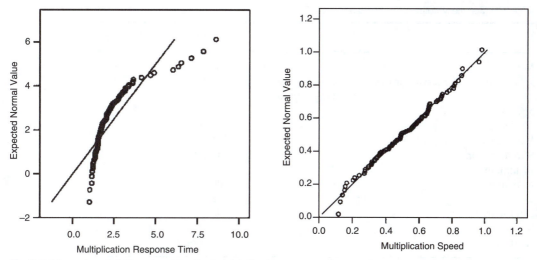

Fig. 2.5 Normal probability plots (Q–Q) of multiplication response times and speeds.

shown in Fig. 2.5. The multiplication speeds, except for a few scores at each extreme, do fall quite close to the line, indicating that the response speeds are more nearly normally distributed than the response times. Implicit in this illustration is a possible strategy for dealing with situations where we desire normally distributed observations, but the data do not conform to the distribution; namely, we can sometimes transform the data. We will have more to say about transformations in later chapters.

We might ask whether departures from the straight line that we observe are large enough to affect subsequent inferential analyses. Although we have not included the information in Fig. 2.5, SPSS's Explore module does include the results of two different tests of the assumption of normality with the Q–Q plot. We will provide examples of this output and its implication for data analysis in Chapter 6, in which we discuss the t test and its assumptions. Similar tests may be found in other software packages.

2.3 MEASURES OF LOCATION AND SPREAD

A graph provides an immediate picture of the overall shape of a distribution, the variability in the observations, and whether there are outliers in the data. Additionally, stem-and-leaf plots and box plots provide specific information about the location of the distribution (i.e., the median); box plots provide a specific measure of variability, too (i.e., the H-spread). Numerical estimates of specific characteristics of a distribution are very useful in helping us to understand a data set. Further, some measures are prominent in inferential procedures, most notably the mean and standard deviation. Thus, in this section, we focus on the mean and measures of variability that complement the mean; specifically, the standard deviation, variance, and standard error of the mean.

Most statistical packages readily provide several useful descriptive statistics for a data set. The data of Table 2.1 were submitted to the Explore module in SPSS to generate the statistics presented in Table 2.2. Let us consider some selected statistics in the table.

Table 2.2 Summary statistics for the data of Table 2.1

		Statistic	Std. error
Mean		84.61	2.89
95% Confidence interval for mean	Lower bound	78.68	
	Upper bound	90.54	
5% Trimmed mean		85.79	
Median		89.00	
Variance		234.025	
Std. deviation		15.298	
Minimum		47	
Maximum		100	
Range		53	
Interquartile range		17.25	
Skewness		−1.326	.441
Kurtosis		1.124	.858

2.3.1 The Arithmetic Mean

The familiar arithmetic mean, symbolized by $\bar{Y}$ (Y bar), is just the sum of all scores divided by the number of scores. Expressing this as an equation, we have

$$\bar{Y} = \sum_{i=1}^{n} Y_i / n \tag{2.2}$$

where Σ represents the mathematical operation of summation,[3] Y_i represents an individual score, and n represents the number of scores in a sample. For example, the mean of $Y = [1, 2, 3, 5, 9, 10, 12]$ is $42/7 = 6$.

The widespread use of the mean reflects two advantages it has over other measures of location. First, it has certain properties that are desirable when estimating the mean of the population from which the sample was drawn. Discussion of the role of the sample mean as an estimator of the population mean will be reserved for Chapter 5. Second, unlike the median or mode, the mean can be manipulated algebraically. The algebraic properties of the mean can be proven by the rules of summation in Appendix A. They can be demonstrated by using the preceding set of numbers, or any other numbers you choose.

1. Adding a constant, k, to every score in the sample results in the mean being increased by the amount k; that is, $\Sigma(Y + k)/n = \bar{Y} + k$. For example, if we add 10 to each of the values in the preceding set of 12 numbers, the mean increases from 6 to 16.
2. Multiplying every score in the sample by a constant, k, results in the mean being multiplied by k; that is, $\Sigma(kY)/n = k\bar{Y}$. For example, multiplying each of the scores in the example by 2 increases the mean from 6 to 12.

---

[3] The presentation of formulas for some of these statistics involves the use of a summation sign, a capital Greek sigma, Σ. Although our use of notation is intended to be easily understood, readers may find it helpful to refer to Appendix A, which reviews the algebra of summation, and derives several properties of statistics that we state in this chapter.

3. Perhaps most importantly, means can be combined. For example, given the means of depression scores and the sample sizes from several clinics, we are able to calculate the mean based on the combined data sets. Note that you cannot meaningfully combine other measures of location, such as medians or modes.

The means and sample sizes (n) for each of four clinics are presented in Table 2.3. It is tempting to add the four means and divide by 4 to get the mean of the combined data sets. However, because the four ns vary, this won't do. The mean for Clinic C should carry more weight and that for Clinic B less weight in combining the means because of their relative sample sizes. The correct approach requires us to obtain the sum of all the scores in all four data sets and then divide by N, the sum of the ns. We obtain the sum of scores for each clinic by multiplying the clinic mean by the number of scores for that clinic. Summing these four sums, and dividing the grand total by N, the total number of scores, we have the grand mean of all the scores:

$$\bar{Y} = [(26 \times 17.5) + (17 \times 18.3) + (31 \times 19.2) + (24 \times 22.6)]/98 = 19.426$$

We might have slightly rewritten this:

$$\bar{Y} = \left(\frac{26}{98}\right)(17.5) + \left(\frac{17}{98}\right)(18.3) + \left(\frac{31}{98}\right)(19.2)\left(\frac{24}{98}\right)(22.6)$$

This equation suggests that the mean can be represented as a sum of weighted values, where the weights are proportions or probabilities. The weight for Clinic A is 26/98 because 26 of the 98 depression scores come from Clinic A. To take a somewhat different example, consider a student who has spent two semesters in College A and compiles a 3.2 average. She then transfers to College B, where she earns a 3.8 average for the next three semesters. The student's overall grade point average (GPA) for the five semesters is calculated as in the preceding example of the clinic means. The overall GPA is a weighted mean where the weights are 2/5 and 3/5:

$$\bar{Y} = (2/5)(3.2) + (3/5)(3.8) = 3.56$$

In general, the preceding calculations may be represented by

$$\bar{Y} = \Sigma \, p(y) \cdot y \tag{2.3}$$

Equation 2.3 is the formula for a *weighted mean*. It indicates that each distinct value of Y is to be multiplied by its weight, $p(y)$, the proportion of all scores with that value. All of these products are then added together. Note that the usual expression for the arithmetic mean, $\bar{Y} = \Sigma \, Y/n$, is a special case of the preceding formula for the weighted mean; here each of the n scores in the sample is given a weight of $1/n$.

Table 2.3 Example of means based on different sample sizes

	Clinics			
	A	B	C	D
Mean	17.5	18.3	19.2	22.6
n	26	17	31	24

Two other properties of the mean, proven in Appendix A, may help convey the sense in which it reflects the central tendency of a data set:

1. The mean is the balance point of the data in the sense that the sum of the deviations about the mean is zero; that is, $\Sigma(Y - \bar{Y}) = 0$.
2. The sum of squared deviations of scores from the mean is smaller than the sum of squared differences taken from any point other than the mean; that is, $\Sigma[Y - (\bar{Y} + k)]^2$ has its smallest value when $k = 0$.

Many of the advantages of the mean as a descriptive statistic are attributable to the fact that every value in a set of scores is incorporated into the calculation of the mean. However, the mean has a potential weakness that derives from this same fact. Namely, a few extreme scores can bias the value of the mean, and may result in the mean taking on a value that does not typify the distribution of scores. We gave an example earlier in this chapter where a single outlier had a substantial effect on the value of the mean. In such a situation, the median is the better description of location because its value is affected only by score ranks, not by their individual values. Because the median changes little when values of individual scores are changed, we say that the median is a *resistant statistic*. Resistance is a desirable property in a statistic, but it is not a property of the mean. We will find that this fact has several implications for our analyses of means when we study inferential tests.

2.3.2 The Variance and the Standard Deviation

One common way to measure the spread of scores in a distribution is to compute the variance of the scores. The sample variance, S^2, is computed as: $S^2 = \Sigma(Y - \bar{Y})^2/n$. Consider the information summarized by this formula. First, note that the calculation is based on a measure of the discrepancy of individual scores with respect to the average score in the distribution, $(Y - \bar{Y})$. This makes the variance a nice complement to the mean. Also, like the mean, the variance incorporates the value of each individual score and, thus, the variance possesses some of the same statistical properties we observed in the mean. Second, the squaring of the deviation scores is necessitated by the fact that $\Sigma(Y - \bar{Y}) = 0$, as we discovered earlier. Finally, the squared deviations are summed and divided by n, so the final value represents *the average squared deviation of scores about the mean*.

Although the formula defining the sample variance involves division by n, we will divide by $n - 1$, as most statistical packages do. The divisor $n - 1$, is used instead of n because it results in a better estimate of the population variance, a fact that will be explained in Chapter 5. We denote this revised definition by s^2, rather than S^2, to indicate that we are dividing by $n - 1$. Thus, our formula for s^2 is:

$$s^2 = \Sigma(Y - \bar{Y})^2/(n - 1) \qquad (2.4)$$

Generally, s^2 will be computed with the aid of a calculator or statistical package; however, we illustrate its calculation here with a simple data set to make sure that the formula is understood. For the following set of seven scores, $Y = [1, 2, 3, 5, 9, 10,$ and $12]$, the sum of the scores is 42, and, therefore, $\bar{Y} = 42/7 = 6$. The deviations from the mean are $(Y - \bar{Y}) = -5, -4, -3, -1, 3, 4,$ and 6. Squaring these deviations, $(Y - \bar{Y})^2 = 25, 16, 9, 1, 9, 16,$ and 36. Summing the squared deviations, we have $\Sigma(Y - \bar{Y})^2 = 112$. Then, $s^2 = 112/6 = 18.667$. In words, the variance of the scores is 18.667 squared units.

As a descriptive measure, the variance is rather awkward because it expresses the variance on a different scale (i.e., squared units) than the distribution being described. Because of this, the preferred measure of spread for descriptive purposes is the standard deviation, which is simply the square root of the variance. In the preceding example, $s = \sqrt{18.667} = 4.320$.

Two properties of the standard deviation should be noted:

1. *If $Y' = Y + k$, $s_{Y'} = s_Y$.* When a constant is added to all scores in a distribution, the standard deviation is unchanged. Each score is increased (or decreased) by the same amount so the spread of scores is unchanged. The range and the H-spread are also unchanged when a constant is added, and it is a desirable property of any measure of variability.
2. *If $Y' = kY$, $s_{Y'} = |k| s_Y$,* where $|k|$ indicates the absolute value of k. When each score is multiplied by a constant, k, the standard deviation of the new scores is the absolute value of k times the old standard deviation. Thus, the standard deviation of the transformed distribution is changed by multiplication.

These properties are proven in Appendix A.

Although the standard deviation is less intuitive than other measures of variability (e.g., H-spread), it has two important advantages. First, the standard deviation is important in drawing inferences about populations from samples. It is a component of formulas for many significance tests, for procedures for estimating population parameters and the bounds on them, and for measures of relations among variables. Second, the standard deviation (and the variance) can be manipulated arithmetically in ways that other measures cannot. For example, if we know the standard deviations, means, and sample sizes of two sets of scores, we can calculate the standard deviation of the combined data set without access to the individual scores. This relation between the variability within groups of scores and the variability of the total set plays an important role in data analysis. Both of the properties just noted will prove important throughout this book.

The main drawback of the standard deviation is that, like the mean, it can be greatly influenced by a single outlying score. Recall that for $Y = [1, 2, 3, 5, 9, 10,$ and $12]$, $\bar{Y} = 6$ and $s = 4.320$. Suppose we add one more score. If that score is 8, a value within the range of the scores, the new mean and standard deviation are 6.25 and 4.062, a fairly small change. However, if the added score is 20, we now have $\bar{Y} = 7.75$ and $s = 6.364$. The standard deviation has increased by almost 50% with the addition of one extreme score. In contrast, the H-spread is resistant to extreme scores and is often a more useful measure for describing the variability in a data set. We again emphasize that there is no single best measure of variability (or of location or shape), but that there is a choice, and that different measures may prove useful for different purposes, or may sometimes supplement each other.

2.3.3 The Standard Error of the Mean (*SEM*)

Ordinarily, we view the data set as a sample from some population. If we are studying the arithmetic scores of second-grade boys, we may wish to draw conclusions about the performance of second-grade boys who were not in our study but who share many of the attributes of our sample that might affect performance, such as the range of arithmetic ability, similar learning experiences, and similar family background. The standard error of a statistic provides some sense of how much the statistic might vary if other samples were taken from the same population. A familiar example is the *SEM*. This statistic tells us how much error there is in the sample mean as an estimate of the mean of the population from which the sample was drawn. The *SEM* can be best understood if we assume that many random samples of size n are drawn from the same population, and the mean is calculated each time. If we record all of the values of the sample mean we observe and tabulate the proportion of times each value occurs, we have constructed the *sampling distribution of the mean* for samples of size n. The *SEM* that is calculated from a single sample is an estimate of the standard deviation of the sampling distribution of the mean. If the *SEM* is small, the one sample mean we have is likely to be a good estimate of the population mean because the small *SEM* suggests that the mean will not vary greatly across samples, and therefore any one sample mean will be close to the population mean. We will have considerably more to say about the *SEM* and its role in drawing inferences in later chapters. At this point, we introduced it because of its close relation to the standard deviation, and because it provides an index of the variability of the sample mean.

The *SEM* (in the column labeled "Std. error" in the SPSS output of Table 2.2) is a simple function of the standard deviation:

$$SEM = s/\sqrt{n} \tag{2.5}$$

For example, in Table 2.2 the standard deviation is 15.298. Dividing by the square root of 28 (the n based on Table 2.1), we have 15.298/5.292, or 2.89, the value given in the Std. error column of Table 2.2. Note an immediate and important implication of Equation 2.5: The error in the sample mean as an estimate of the population mean depends on both the variability in the sample and the size of the sample. Specifically, as the variability in the sample increases, the variability in the sample mean also increases. However, as the size of the sample increases, the variability in the sample mean decreases.

2.3.4 The Confidence Interval (*CI*) for the Mean

If we wish to use the sample mean as an estimate of the value of the population mean, we should recognize the error associated with the sample mean. We can do this by calculating a "margin of error" and including it in our statement of our estimate. A quick procedure for doing this is to take the sample mean as our best single or *point estimate* of the population mean, and then compute an upper and lower boundary on that estimate to create an *interval estimate*. The upper bound (*UB*) can be computed as the sample mean plus 2 times the *SEM*; the lower bound (*LB*) is the sample mean minus approximately 2 times the *SEM*:

$$UB = \bar{Y} + 2 \times SEM \tag{2.6a}$$

$$LB = \bar{Y} - 2 \times SEM \tag{2.6b}$$

Applying Equation 2.6, we estimate that the population mean falls between 79.43 and 89.79. This differs slightly from the boundaries listed for the "95% Confidence interval for mean" in Table 2.2. The discrepancy is because we multiplied the *SEM* by 2, rather than the precise value used by SPSS, a number that changes slightly depending on sample size. As can be seen, the results are not much affected by using this approximation.

For the moment, it is sufficient for our purposes to introduce the notion of taking sampling error into account when estimating a population mean, and to have a rough, easy procedure for doing so. In fact, confidence intervals are a very important tool, so we will have considerably more to say about them throughout the book. The explicit formulas for computing the bounds in Table 2.2 will be presented in Chapter 5. At that time, we will also develop a more precise interpretation of the meaning of a confidence interval.

2.3.5 The 5% Trimmed Mean

The sample mean, as calculated by Equation 2.2, is the best estimator of the population mean under rather constrained assumptions; for example, that the population distribution is normal. Unfortunately, we have already noted that distributions often depart from normality in a variety of ways; for example, asymmetry, lumpiness, and long or heavy tails. In particular, when the population distribution is symmetric but has longer tails than the normal, the sample mean may not be the optimal way to estimate the population mean. The reason is that the *SEM* will be large; consequently, the confidence interval will be quite wide. In such circumstances, a more precise estimate of the population mean may be generated by trimming a percentage of the scores from each tail of the sample distribution. This has the effect of reducing sample variability and, hence, *SEM*; thus, the confidence interval on the mean will be narrower.

The SPSS output of Table 2.2 includes the value of the 5% trimmed mean. This is calculated by rank ordering the scores, dropping the highest and lowest 5%, and recalculating the mean. Although the trimmed mean may provide a better estimate of the population mean than the untrimmed mean, decisions about when to trim and how much to trim are not simple. Chapter 6 discusses trimming further, as well as statistical tests based on trimming.

2.3.6 Displaying Means and Standard Errors

A graph of the means for various conditions often provides a quick comparison of those conditions. The graph is more useful still when accompanied by a visual representation of variability, such as *s*, the *SEM*, or the confidence interval bounds. The selection of a procedure for graphing the data should depend upon the nature of the independent variable. Although graphics programs will provide a choice, the American Psychological Association's *Publication Manual* (2001) recommends that "*Bar graphs* are used when the independent variable is categorical" and "*Line graphs* are used to show the relation between two quantitative variables" (p. 178). We believe this is good advice.

When the independent variable consists of categories that differ in type rather than in amount, we should make it clear that the shape of a function relating the independent and dependent variables is not a meaningful concept; thus, the choice of a bar graph. Fig. 2.6 presents mean depression scores[4] from the *Seasons* data set (found on the *Data Files* page on the book's website) as a function of marital status and sex; the numbers on the *x*-axis are the researchers' codes: 1 = single; 2 = married; 3 = living with partner; 4 = separated; 5 = divorced; 6 = widowed. At least in this sample, depression means are highest for single males and females, and for divorced females, and the means are low for those living with a partner. Without a more careful statistical analysis, and without considering the size of these samples, we hesitate to recommend "living in sin," but merely note that the bar graph presents a starting point for comparing the groups. The vertical lines at the top of each bar represent the *SEM*s. Note that the *SEM* bars indicate that the male data are more variable than the female data, particularly in categories 3 and 6.

When the independent variable consists of categories that do differ in amount, it is meaningful to illustrate the shape of a function relating the independent and dependent variables; thus, a line graph is a good choice. Fig. 2.7 presents mean times in seconds to do subtraction problems (*subrt*)

---

[4] The means are averages of the four seasonal depression scores and were calculated only for those subjects who had been tested in all four sessions. The absence of a bar for females in category 4 indicates not that there were no females in that category but only that there were no females for whom all four seasonal scores were available.

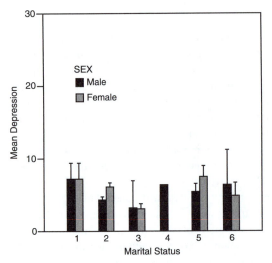

Fig. 2.6 Bar graph of mean depression scores as a function of sex and marital status.

from the *Royer* data set as a function of grade and gender. Because grade level is quantitative, it is useful to plot the data as line curves, providing a sense of the shape of the functional relation. Although it is often useful to plot multiple functions on a single graph for ease of comparison, we plotted these data in two panels because the two curves are close together and the error bars are difficult to disentangle if presented within a single panel. From Fig. 2.7, it appears that response times for both genders decrease as a function of grade and seem to level off in around the sixth grade. It also appears that variability decreases with grade as indicated by the general decrease in the length of the *SEM* bars. Comparing across panels, the main difference between boys' and girls' times appears to be in the early grades.

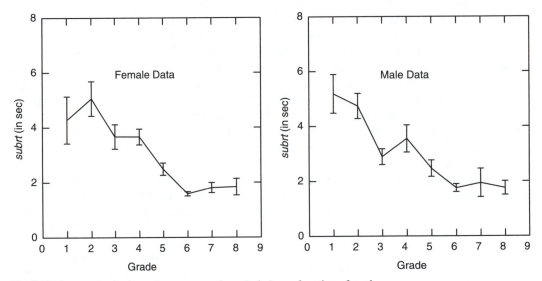

Fig. 2.7 Line graph of subtraction response times (*subrt*) as a function of grade.

Software capable of bar and line plots usually offers several options such as the choice of placing different plots in one panel (as in Fig. 2.6) or in separate panels (as in Fig. 2.7), or choosing the error bars to represent standard deviations, standard errors, or confidence intervals. The best advice is to become thoroughly familiar with the software being used, and then to think carefully about which options will enable you to best communicate the points you believe are important.

2.3.7 The Interquartile Range (*IQR*)

Table 2.2 presents one other measure of spread that deserves mention here. The value of the *IQR*, like the closely related *H*-spread of the box plot, provides a measure of spread that is more resistant to extreme scores than is the standard deviation. Like the *H*-spread measure, *IQR* is a resistant statistic because it ignores scores in the tails of a distribution. The value of the *IQR* is the difference between the 75th and 25th percentiles. Percentiles can be obtained from statistical software such as the Explore module of SPSS. However, to illustrate their computation, consider the data in Table 2.2. First, to obtain the location of the score at the 25th percentile, find .25 times $n + 1$. For the 28 scores in Table 2.1, the location is 7.25. When the 28 scores are rank ordered, the seventh score is 76 and the eighth score is 82. One-fourth of the distance between them yields a value of 77.5 for the 25th percentile. Similarly, the value of the 75th percentile is the score 3/4 of the way between the 21st and 22nd scores; this is 94.75. Therefore, the *IQR* is 94.75 − 77.50 = 17.25, the value reported in Table 2.2.

2.4 STANDARDIZED (z) SCORES

An individual's score, by itself, is not very informative. If a student earns a score of 70 on a math test, is that good or bad? If told that a score of 70 was at the 90th percentile—that it had been exceeded by only 10% of all scores—we would probably feel that the performance was quite good. On the other hand, we would be considerably less impressed if the same raw score fell at the 40th percentile. Although information about percentile values tells us where a score ranks relative to other scores, it provides no information about distances among scores. For example, a score at the 90th percentile could be many points higher than the average or only a little higher; it depends on how variable the scores are. Standardized, or *z*, scores tell us more about where the score is located within the distribution—specifically, how many standard deviation units the score is above or below the mean. Given a distribution of scores with mean, $\overline{Y}$, and standard deviation, s, the z score corresponding to a score Y is calculated as

$$z_Y = (Y - \overline{Y}) / s \tag{2.7}$$

For example, if the mean is 75 and the standard deviation is 15, for a score of 90, we would have $z_{90} = (90 - 75)/15 = 1.0$; thus, this score is one standard deviation above the mean. Statistical packages generally include an option such as SPSS's Descriptive Statistics (in the "Analyze" menu) for calculating z scores.

Standardizing a group of scores changes the scale to one of standard deviation units, permiting comparisons with scores that were originally on a different scale. Nevertheless, there are aspects of the original distribution that remain unchanged. The following are two things that remain constant:

1. *An individual's z score has the same percentile rank as did that individual's original score.* This is because subtracting a constant, $\overline{Y}$, from every score does not change the rank order of the scores, nor is the order changed by dividing all scores by a constant, s.
2. *The shape of the distribution of z scores is the same as that of the original data.* Subtraction of $\overline{Y}$ shifts the original distribution and division by s squeezes the points closer together, but shape information is preserved. If the original distribution was symmetric, the distribution of z scores will also be symmetric. However, if the original distribution was skewed, this also will be true of the distribution of z scores.

As we shall see in Chapter 5, z scores are used in drawing inferences when scores can reasonably be assumed to be normally distributed. However, the preceding point should make clear that *z scores are not necessarily (or even usually) normally distributed*. Their distribution depends on the distribution of the scores prior to the z transformation.

Two other characteristics of z scores should be noted:

1. *The mean (and therefore also the sum) of a set of z scores is zero.* We stated earlier that when a constant is subtracted from every score, the mean is also changed by that constant. In the case of z score, $\overline{Y}$ is subtracted from each of the Y values. Therefore, the mean of the z scores is $\overline{Y} - \overline{Y}$, or 0.
2. *The variance of a group of z scores is 1.0 and, therefore, so is the standard deviation.* Because the average z score is zero, we need only square each member of the group of z scores, sum the squared values, and divide by $n - 1$ to obtain the variance, s_z^2. Doing so,

$$s_z^2 = \sum \frac{(Y - \overline{Y})^2}{s^2} \Big/ (n - 1)$$

$$= \sum \frac{(Y - \overline{Y})^2}{n - 1} \Big/ s^2$$

$$= s^2 / s^2 = 1$$

Standardized scores can be useful in our understanding of a data set because they provide a way of comparing performances on different scales. For example, the mean and standard deviation of the subtraction accuracy scores in the *Royer* data set were 88.840 and 11.457, respectively; the corresponding values for multiplication accuracy scores were 87.437 and 13.996. Even though a subtraction score of 70 is higher than a multiplication score of 65, it is actually slightly worse, relative to the other scores in the distribution. For subtraction, $z_{70} = -1.64$ (that is, the score of 70 is 1.64 standard deviations below the mean of the subtraction scores), whereas for multiplication, $z_{65} = -1.60$.

Standardized scores play other roles as well. In Chapter 5, we will discuss how z scores provide percentile information when the population distribution has an approximate bell shape. Also, in Chapter 18, we will consider the correlation coefficient as an average product of z scores.

2.5 MEASURES OF THE SHAPE OF A DISTRIBUTION

We have considered several measures of location (the mean, the trimmed mean, the median) and variability (the variance, standard deviation, *IQR*, and *H*-spread) that summarize important properties of a distribution. In addition to these measures, it is often also useful to obtain measures of the shape of a distribution. Measures of shape permit a more precise description of a data set than measures of location and variability alone. They also provide another way to assess the validity of the assumption of normality. This is important because when a data distribution departs markedly from normality, reliance on the mean and standard deviation may lead to incorrect inferences. For example, although the mean and median of a symmetric population distribution are identical, the sample mean is usually considered the better estimate of the location of the population distribution. However, if the population distribution has long straggling tails, the sample median, or a trimmed mean, is more likely to have a value close to that of the center of the population distribution (Rosenberger & Gasko, 1983), and therefore would be a better estimate of the location of the population. If the distribution is skewed, a transformation may be helpful, or a test based on ranks (see Chapter 6 for a discussion of these alternatives). The data plots in Section 2.2 provide a first step in assessing the shape of the distribution, but the measures in this section will provide summary numbers, aiding in the evaluation of shape.

There is yet a third reason for our interest in measures of shape. An important stage in understanding the processes that underlie behavior is the construction of mathematical or computer models, models precise enough to predict the behavior in question. Comparing predicted and observed measures of the shape of the data distribution provides additional tests of such models.

Two aspects of shape have received the most attention from statisticians: (1) the degree of *skewness*, or departure from symmetry; and (2) *tail weight*, or the proportion of data in the extreme tails of the distribution. Indices of these two attributes of shape can be obtained from various computer packages; those in Table 2.2 were generated by SPSS, but most packages will yield the same results.

2.5.1 Skewness

Skewness statistics are designed to reflect departures from symmetry. The standard definition of skewness is the average cubed deviation of scores from the mean divided by the cubed standard deviation. However, several other measures of skewness can be found in the statistical literature (e.g., Hillebrand, 1986, pp. 43–45). The value reported in Table 2.2 is labeled $g1$.

There are two points to consider about the $g1$ value in the table. First, it is negative, indicating that the distribution is skewed to the left. This reflects the fact that the left tail in Fig. 2.1 is considerably longer than the right tail of its distribution. It is also consistent with the fact that the median has a higher value than the mean; the long left tail reduces the value of the mean. If the distribution had been perfectly symmetric, $g1$ would have been zero. A positive skewness value would have indicated skew to the right, a longer right tail; this often is seen in response-time data.

Second, note how much larger the absolute skewness value is than its standard error, the *SE skewness* value. The *SE* of $g1$, like the *SE* of the mean encountered earlier, is based on the idea of drawing many random samples of size n from the same population, and then calculating the skewness value for each sample. The *SE* is an estimate of the standard deviation of those values. A ratio of skewness (ignoring the sign) to its *SE* greater than 2 suggests that asymmetry is present in the population from which we sampled; that is, it did not occur in the sample just by chance. Given the skewness value and its *SE* in Table 2.2, we have strong evidence that the population of male second-grade addition scores is negatively skewed. Our description of the sample data, based on Figs. 2.1–2.3, indicated that there were students whose scores trailed those of the majority of the class; the numerical values in Table 2.1 lead us to believe that this may be true of the population represented by these 28 students.

2.5.2 Kurtosis

Kurtosis values also reflect departures from the normal distribution, and are generally sensitive to the height of the peak and to the tail weight of a distribution. The value reported in Table 2.2 is often labeled $g2$. It has a value of zero for the normal distribution. Distributions with high peaks and heavy tails (relative to the normal distribution) will have positive $g2$ values whereas the $g2$ values will be negative for flatter, shorter-tailed distributions. Heavy-tailed distributions are of particular interest because inferences based on the assumption of normality have often been shown to be affected by this departure from normality. With such data, increasing the sample size or removing extreme scores ("trimming") may improve the accuracy of our inferences. However, kurtosis is sensitive to more than just the tails of the distribution and therefore interpretation is often difficult. Good discussions of kurtosis, together with figures illustrating various shapes and the accompanying effect on $g2$, are provided in several sources (e.g., Balanda & MacGillivray, 1988; DeCarlo, 1997). These and other articles and chapters (e.g., Hogg, 1974; Rosenberger & Gasko, 1983) also suggest alternative measures of tail weight that are often more resistant to outlying points.

2.6 COMPARING TWO DATA SETS

Our focus up until now has been on examining the characteristics of single data sets. However, a comparison of graphs and statistics for two or more data sets can often be even more useful, suggesting hypotheses about the effects of variables and providing an initial assessment of assumptions underlying subsequent statistical tests. In this section, we review what we have done previously, but now in the context of comparisons of data sets. We look at two examples.

2.6.1 Example: The *Royer* Data Revisited

A particularly clear example of how just comparing measures of location and variability can obscure potentially important differences between conditions is provided by comparing the distribution of the data in Table 2.4 with that in Table 2.1. The data in Table 2.4 are artificial and we have used the letter Y to label the dependent variable. Table 2.5 presents statistics that provide a comparison of the two data sets. In most respects the statistics based on Tables 2.1 and 2.4 are either identical or very similar. The means are both 84.61 and the medians are both 89. The trimmed means, confidence interval bounds, variances, and standard errors are very similar for the two data sets. These statistics would lead us to believe that the two distributions also are very similar. However, the Y data have much larger skewness and kurtosis values, indicating some difference in shape of the distributions. Replotting the *Royer* data, together with plots of the Y data, provides more information about the difference between the two distributions.

Fig. 2.8 presents box plots of the two data sets. A comparison of the plots reveals that despite being equal in both means and medians, the Y distribution contains two scores much lower than

Table 2.4 Data (Y) to be compared with the data of Table 2.1

	31	32	79	83	83	85	85	85	87	87
Y	87	89	89	89	89	89	89	90	90	91
	91	91	91	92	92	93	95	95		

Table 2.5 Comparison of statistics for the *Royer* data of Table 2.1 with those for the *Y* data of Table 2.4

		Royer		Y	
		Statistic	Std. error	Statistic	Std. error
Mean		84.61	2.89	84.61	2.92
95% Confidence interval for mean	Lower bound	78.68		78.62	
	Upper bound	90.54		90.59	
5% Trimmed mean		85.79		86.99	
Median		89.00		89.00	
Variance		234.025		238.099	
Std. deviation		15.298		15.530	
Minimum		47		31	
Maximum		100		95	
Range		53		64	
Interquartile range		17		6	
Skewness		−1.326	.441	−3.195	.441
Kurtosis		1.124	.858	9.664	.858

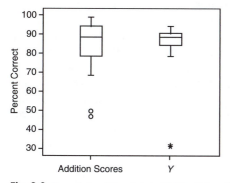

Fig. 2.8 Box plots of the data in Tables 2.1 and 2.4.

any in the *Royer* data. Furthermore, despite the near equality of the variances in Table 2.5, the *Y* data are actually less variable when the outliers are excluded from the two data sets. If the two data sets represented two methods of teaching arithmetic, we might prefer that associated with the *Y* data; if outliers are excluded from both sets of data, the mean is higher for the *Y* data, and scores fall within a narrower range.

2.6.2 Example: Age Differences in Depression Scores

In the preceding section, we contrived a comparison between a real data set, the *Royer* addition scores, and one we created to make the point that the summary statistics usually examined (e.g., mean, variance) can be misleading, or at least fail to provide a complete understanding of the data. Real data can make the same point. In examining Beck Depression scores for the winter season for males of various ages, we found a difference between the mean of the youngest group (< 40 years, mean = 6.599) and that of a group between 50 and 59 years old (mean = 4.613). However, the medians were identical, 4.500.

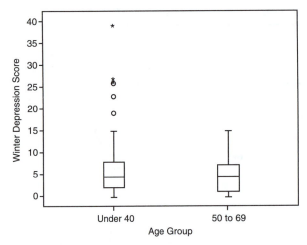

Fig. 2.9 Box plots of winter depression scores for two age groups of men.

Plotting the Beck Depression data for the two groups is a first step in clarifying why the means are further apart than the medians. Fig. 2.9 presents box plots for the two groups. As in all plots of Beck Depression scores, most of the scores are at the low (normal) end of the scale for both age groups. We say that the distributions are skewed to the right because of the straggling right-hand (upper) tails. The explanation for the difference in means is readily apparent. The younger group has several individuals with scores above 18; these are depicted as outliers in the box plot for that group, some of which are extreme. In contrast, no score is an outlier in the older group. Although the medians are identical, the greater number of extremely high scores in the younger group has moved that mean higher than the mean of the older group. Just why there are more extremely depressed males in the under-40 group is not clear. However, the point for the present is that only by comparing the distributions of the two age groups do we achieve a full understanding of the nature of the difference between the two groups. Consideration of just the means and/or medians is misleading.

2.7 RELATIONSHIPS AMONG QUANTITATIVE VARIABLES

Thus far, we have considered how to graph and summarize distributions of single variables. However, we are often interested in how two or more variables are *related* to one another. For example, we may wish to know how cholesterol level changes with age, or whether mathematics skills are related to verbal skills in children. Because variability is always present, when variables are related, they are usually not perfectly related. Tall fathers tend to have tall sons, but because of a host of factors, the tallest fathers do not always have the tallest sons.

Variables may be related in ways that vary in type and degree, so we need ways to graphically represent these relationships and statistics to characterize them. In this section, we very briefly introduce:

- *Scatterplots* as a way of graphically exploring the relationship between two variables.
- The *correlation coefficient* as an index of the extent to which the relationship is linear.
- *Regression* as a way of generating the linear equation that best predicts one variable from another.

2.7.1 Scatterplots

Consider how subtraction and multiplication performance might be related in elementary school children. We might expect that children who are better at subtraction will also be better at multiplication. Perhaps the best way of determining whether there is a relationship between the two variables is to use a *scatterplot*, a plot in which each data point has coordinates that represent the scores for one of the students. The scatterplot for the 28 third-graders for whom we have both multiplication accuracy (percent correct) and subtraction accuracy scores in the *Royer* data set is presented in Fig. 2.10. The scatterplot in Fig. 2.11 shows the mean time to answer multiplication problems plotted against accuracy.

In both scatterplots, we see some organization to the distribution of data points, although it is imperfect. In Fig. 2.10, there is a tendency for higher multiplication scores to go together with higher subtraction scores; when this happens we say there is a *positive relationship* between the two variables. In Fig. 2.11, there is a tendency for children who are more accurate to take less time to answer; this is an example of a *negative* relationship. In both scatterplots, there is a good deal of variability in the distribution of scores. Although we might imagine a line being drawn through

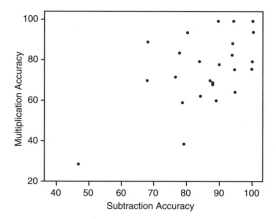

Fig. 2.10 Scatterplot of multiplication and subtraction accuracy for 28 third-grade children.

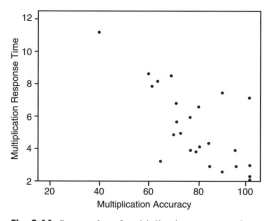

Fig. 2.11 Scatterplot of multiplication response time and accuracy for 28 third-grade children.

the scatterplot to summarize the general tendency in the distribution, there is a lot of "scatter" of points about that line. Next, we would like to discuss some statistics that characterize the relationship.

2.7.2 Correlation

Correlation is an index of strength of linear relationship between two variables. The equation for a straight line is given by

$$Y = b_0 + b_1 X \tag{2.8}$$

All data points (X, Y) that satisfy this equation fall on a straight line. The constant b_1 is the *slope* of the line—the amount by which Y changes when X is increased by one unit. The slope is *positive* if Y increases as X increases; it is *negative* if Y decreases as X increases. The constant b_0 is the value of Y when $X = 0$.

The *correlation coefficient, r,* is a number between 1 and −1 that provides a measure of the extent to which the relationship between Y and X is "captured" by a straight line, and whether the straight line has a positive or negative slope. If r is +1, all the data points fall exactly on a straight line with a positive slope; if r is −1, all data points fall on a straight line with a negative slope; if r is 0, there is no overall tendency for there to be a linear relationship. Intermediate values of r are used as measures of the strength of the linear relationship. All other things being equal, scatterplots with higher rs will display tighter clustering of data points around a straight line.

A useful formula for the correlation coefficient is given by

$$r_{XY} = \frac{1}{N-1} \sum_{i=1}^{N} z_{X_i} z_{Y_i} \tag{2.9}$$

Although there are many expressions for the correlation coefficient, they are all equivalent to Equation 2.9 and will give the same result within rounding error. Values of r are readily obtained from any statistical package. When the correlation is computed for the multiplication and subtraction accuracy data for third-graders in the *Royer* data set, $r = .59$. For accuracy and response time on multiplication tests, $r = -.49$. Both values indicate strong linear relationships. Because the correlation coefficient is inherently a z score measure, it should be interpreted with caution. We discuss interpretation of correlation in great detail in Chapter 18.

2.7.3 Linear Regression

Although the correlation coefficient is an index of how well a bivariate distribution is fit by a straight line, it does not describe the line. In Chapter 18, we show that the straight that best predicts Y from X has its slope and intercept given by

$$b_1 = r\frac{s_Y}{s_X} \tag{2.10a}$$

and $$b_0 = \bar{Y} - b_1 \bar{X} \tag{2.10b}$$

For example, the regression equation that predicts multiplication accuracy from subtraction accuracy for third-graders in the *Royer* data set is

predicted multiplication accuracy = 1.631 + 0.883 × *subtraction accuracy*

Therefore, we would predict that a student with subtraction accuracy of 90 would have a multiplication accuracy of 81, rounding to the nearest integer. The regression equation is useful for predicting and also provides a useful description of the relationship between multiplication and subtraction accuracy. There are also other regression statistics that quantify the degree of scatter around the regression line.

There is much more to be said about correlation and regression, and more generally about measures relating two or more variables. Chapters 18–20 expand upon this very brief introduction to bivariate relationships, and Chapters 21–25 continue our discussion by considering more than two variables and nonlinear relationships.

2.8 SUMMARY

In this chapter, we presented various ways of looking at data. The process of understanding our results begins with exploration of the data. Exploration should go beyond computing means and standard deviations and correlation coefficients. Therefore, we considered ways of graphing the distribution of observations (histograms, box plots, stem-and-leaf plots, and scatterplots), of calculating resistant measures of location (median and trimmed mean) and variability (IQR and H-spread), and of calculating measures of shape (skewness, kurtosis). Data exploration serves several important purposes:

- Exploration is necessary to achieve a thorough description of the data. And a thorough description is essential to understanding the data.
- Exploration can be a source of hypotheses. A thorough description of a data set often leads to discovery: Unexpected differences between conditions may be noticed and pursued. Or details of a distribution of scores may produce a deeper understanding of the nature of the effect of a manipulation.
- Exploration provides a check on assumptions underlying subsequent statistical tests, such as the assumption of a normal distribution of scores.

More extensive discussions of ways of plotting data and of resistant statistics may be found in many sources. In particular, we recommend the three volumes edited by Hoaglin, Mosteller, and Tukey (1983, 1985, 1991). They provide a clear presentation of many topics beyond the scope of this book, as well as further discussion and examples of topics we have introduced. Other suggestions of possible ways of plotting data, and references to useful sources, may be found in the report of the American Psychological Association's Task Force on Statistical Inference (Wilkinson & Task Force, 1999).

EXERCISES

2.1 We have scores for 16 individuals on a measure of problem-solving ability: $Y = 21, 40, 34, 34, 16, 37, 21, 38, 32, 11, 34, 38, 26, 27, 33, 47$. Without using statistical software, find (a) the mean, (b) the median, (c) $(\Sigma_i Y_i)^2$, (d) $\Sigma_i Y_i^2$, (e) the standard deviation, and (f) the upper and lower hinges for these data.

2.2 **(a)** Transform the scores in Exercise 2.1 to a new scale so that they have a mean of 100 and a standard deviation of 15.
   (b) What will the new values of the median and hinges be?

2.3   Given the five scores 37, 53, 77, 30, and 28,

   (a) What sixth score must be added so that all six scores together have a mean of 47?

   (b) What sixth score should be added so that the set of six scores has the smallest possible variance?

2.4   Following are several sets of scores in ranked order. For each data set is there any indication that it does not come from a normal distribution? Explain, citing graphic evidence to support your conclusion.

   (a) $X = 10\ 16\ 50\ 50\ 50\ 55\ 55\ 55\ 57\ 61\ 61\ 62\ 63\ 72\ 73\ 75\ 83\ 85\ 107\ 114$

   (b) $Y = 15\ 25\ 26\ 37\ 37\ 39\ 45\ 45\ 48\ 49\ 49\ 52\ 53\ 61\ 61\ 63\ 68\ 70\ 72\ 76$

   (c) $Z = 9\ 9\ 10\ 12\ 14\ 14\ 15\ 16\ 16\ 16\ 17\ 18\ 24\ 28\ 31\ 32\ 32\ 35\ 47\ 59$

   (d) Find the mean, median, and 10% trimmed mean of data set (c). How do the results relate to your conclusion based on the graphic evidence?

2.5   We have the following data set:

$$X = 6 \quad 5 \quad 7 \quad 1 \quad 11$$
$$Y = 7 \quad 11 \quad 14 \quad 21 \quad 9$$

Find (a) $\sum_{i=1}^{5} (X_i + Y_i)$;   (b) $\sum_{i=1}^{5} X_i^2$;   (c) $\left(\sum_{i=1}^{5} X_i\right)^2$;   (d) $\sum_{i=1}^{5} X_i Y_i$;   (e) $\sum_{i=1}^{5} (X_i + 5Y_i^2 + 27)$.

2.6   We have five subjects tested in conditions C_1–C_3:

Subject	C_1	C_2	C_3
1	7	11	3
2	31	15	12
3	16	40	5
4	21	42	19
5	35	45	4

Given that Y_{ij} is the ith score in the jth column, find (a) $\bar{Y}_{.1}$; (b) $\bar{Y}_{.2}$; (c) $\bar{Y}_{..}$; (d) $\sum_{i=1}^{5} \sum_{j=1}^{3} Y_{ij}^2$;

(e) $\sum_{j=1}^{3} \bar{Y}_{.j}^2$.

2.7   In Exercise 2.6, find (a) $\sum_{i=1}^{5} (\bar{Y}_{i.} - \bar{Y}_{..})^2$;   (b) $\sum_{j=1}^{3} (\bar{Y}_{.j} - \bar{Y}_{..})^2$;   (c) $\sum_{j=1}^{3} \sum_{i=1}^{5} (Y_{ij} - \bar{Y}_{..})^2$.

2.8   This problem uses the *EX2_8* data set at the website. Using any software that you have, explore the distributions and compare them by graphing one or more of the following: histograms, box plots, or stem-and-leaf plots. In addition, base your discussion on descriptive statistics (include the median, as well as measures of skewness and kurtosis) and probability (Q–Q) plots. Summarize what you have learned about the distributions of X, Y, and Z. Be sure to refer to such concepts as the location, spread, and shapes of the distributions, in particular, whether or not they seem to be normally distributed, and how they compare in spread and shape.

2.9   Suppose we standardize *X, Y, Z* (that is, convert to standard or *z* scores) in the *EX2_8* data set. How would this affect the characteristics of the distributions? Do the standardization to check your answer.

2.10   Find the *Royer* multiplication accuracy and response time data (*Royer Mult Data* file) on the *Royer* page of the book's website. Using whichever descriptive statistics and graphs you find useful, describe any differences in location, variability, and shape of male and female distributions in the third and fourth grades. In particular, comment on whether gender differences change from third to fourth grade. Also, comment on whether the patterns you note are the same or different for accuracy and for *RT*. Finally, consider whether outlying scores may have an influence on any of these comparisons.

2.11   The *Sayhlth* data set on the *Seasons* page of the book's website includes self-ratings from 1 (excellent health) to 4 (fair); only three participants rated themselves in poor health, and they were excluded from this file. The file also includes *Beck_D* (depression) scores for each season. It is reasonable to suspect that individuals who feel less healthy will be more depressed.

(a)   Selecting any statistics and graphs you believe may help, evaluate this hypothesis.

(b)   Discuss any trends over seasons. Are there differences in trends as a function of self-ratings of health?

2.12   The *Seasons* study was carried out to see whether there was variation in the physical or psychological characteristics of the sampled population over seasons.

(a)   Using the data in the *Seasons* file on the book's website, plot *Beck_A* (anxiety; *BeckA1 . . . BeckA4*) means as a function of seasons for each age group (*Agegrp*). Use either a bar or line graph. Which do you think is preferable? Why?

(b)   Discuss the graph in part (a), noting any effects of age, seasons, or both.

(c)   Box or stem-and-leaf plots reveal a skewed distribution with many outliers. Do you think the pattern of outliers contributed to your conclusions in part (b)?

2.13   Scores for 50 students on two tests may be found in the *EX2_13* file. One student received a score of 41 on Test 1 and a 51 on Test 2. She was delighted with the improvement.

(a)   Should she have been? Explain.

(b)   What is the minimum score on Test 2 that would be an improvement for this student?

(c)   Graph the data for each test and describe the distributions.

(d)   Plot the data to show the relationship between scores on the two tests and provide a statistic summarizing that relationship.

(e)   If a student had a score of 40 on Test 1, what score would you predict for Test 2?

2.14   The file *mlb salaries 86_07* at the website contains major league baseball player average salaries by team and league for the years 1986 and 2007.

(a)   Describe the distribution of the team payrolls in 2007. Support any conclusions by citing statistics and graphs.

(b)   Do this again but separately for each league. What differences or similarities do you see between the leagues?

(c)   We might ask about the relationship between salaries in 1986 and 2007. (Ignore any team that is not present in both years—e.g., Tampa Bay and Florida in 2007; the Montreal Expos became the Washington Nationals in 2005 and can be considered present in both years.) Include comparisons of measures of location, shape, and spread, as well as graphs showing the relation, and a measure of the relation, between the two sets of payrolls. Does the relationship between relative payroll sizes in the two years depend on which league we look at?

2.15 The file *mlb86 summary stats* contains offensive and defensive statistics, as well as other information, for major league baseball players for the year 1986. Salaries are reported in hundreds of thousands; for example, 575 is (approximately) $575,000.

(a) One hypothesis is that players who hit more home runs (*HR*s) also draw more bases on balls (*BB*s). Based on the data, what do you think of that hypothesis?

(b) Two of the variables are *OBP* (on-base percentage) and *DP* (defensive percentage). $OBP = (Hs + BBs)/(ABs + BBs)$ where *Hs* = no. of hits, *BB*s = no. of bases on balls, and *AB*s = no. of official at-bats; $DP = (\text{Assists} + \text{Putouts})/(\text{Assists} + \text{Putouts} + \text{Errors})$. Then plot the relationship between *OBP* and *DP* and calculate the correlation. What is your assessment of the relationship between offensive and defensive performances as reflected in these statistics?

(c) In the 1986 World Series, the New York Mets represented the National League (NL) and the Boston Red Sox represented the American League. The individual batting averages (*BA*s) are listed for all position (non-pitchers) players; they were calculated as *Hs/AB*s (hits divided by number of official at-bats). Find the mean *team* batting averages for the Red Sox and the Mets.

(d) Find the correlation between *BA*s and *AB*s for the Red Sox.

Chapter 3
Basic Concepts in Probability

3.1 OVERVIEW

In Chapter 2, we discussed various descriptive statistics and their uses. These statistics summarize important aspects of a sample of data and form the basis for making inferences about the population from which the sample was obtained. However, because statistics vary from sample to sample, our inferences may be incorrect. A sample is not a miniature version of the population, so the mean or variance of a sample is not likely to be the same as the mean or variance of the population from which the sample was selected. This is true for any other statistic we might calculate. How then can we justify using statistics from a single sample to draw inferences about the population?

Let's begin by considering an example. Imagine that we want to test whether extrasensory perception (ESP) exists. We decide to conduct an experiment to test the ability of Rachel, who claims to have ESP. An experimenter is seated in a room with a pack consisting of four different cards. On each of 20 trials, the experimenter shuffles the cards well, then randomly picks one, looks at it, and tries to transmit its contents mentally. Rachel sits in a room in a different building, is familiar with the pack of cards, and knows when each trial of the experiment is to occur. For each trial, she tries to "perceive" and then record the card chosen by the experimenter.

How well must Rachel perform before we decide that the evidence is sufficiently strong to support her claim to have ESP? We first note that if Rachel is guessing randomly, the most likely outcome is that she will be correct on 25% of the trials. However, we must recognize that Rachel may do better than 25% correct even if she guesses. Before we can conclude that Rachel is not simply guessing, we want convincing evidence that her performance cannot easily be attributed to guessing alone. How much better than 25% correct must Rachel do before we are convinced? Twenty correct responses (i.e., 100% correct) would be impressive support for Rachel's claim of ESP because such a high level of performance is extremely unlikely to result if she was just guessing. But what about 19 correct in 20 trials? Or 12? Or 8? Those outcomes still seem very unlikely given guessing, but how much evidence against guessing do they provide? To answer this question, we must be able to calculate the probability of any possible outcome under the assumption that Rachel is guessing. We should also note that we are concerned with the entire population of potential responses that characterizes Rachel's ESP ability, not just the 20 responses we happen to collect in the experiment. If we ran the experiment several times, it would almost certainly turn out somewhat differently each time.

This example makes the important point that in order to draw inferences in an objective manner, we must be able to find the probabilities of different possible outcomes. Suppose that Rachel makes eight correct responses. Is this strong enough evidence to reject the hypothesis that Rachel is randomly guessing on each trial? Later, we will show that there is a better than 10% chance that Rachel would make eight or more correct responses even if she randomly guessed on each trial. This is very useful information on which to base a decision. We might decide that a 10% chance of being wrong is too high, and therefore conclude that obtaining eight correct responses is not sufficiently strong evidence to reject the guessing hypothesis.

The subsequent chapters of this book are concerned with procedures for drawing inferences about characteristics of populations from samples of observations. The ability to assign probabilities to possible outcomes is central to statistical inference. Therefore, some background in probability will be useful in order to understand the logic and assumptions underlying statistical tests, as well as how to interpret the tests. In this chapter, we provide a basic introduction to probability. The organization of topics is as follows:

- *Basic concepts for analyzing structure.* The ability to compute probabilities of events depends, in part, on being able to analyze how simple events (e.g., specific sequences of correct and incorrect guesses) comprise more complex events (e.g., total number of correct guesses in a 20-trial experiment). The starting point for our study of probability is therefore to introduce concepts that form the basis for such analyses.
- *Computing probabilities.* Once we have the tools for analyzing the structure of events, we will introduce a definition of the probability of an event and some basic rules of probability. We will use the rules and our analysis of the structure of events to develop two important laws—the additive and multiplicative laws—that will be very useful in computing probabilities of complex events. We will also discuss concepts such as independence and conditional probability that are important for understanding many statistical tests.
- *Probability distributions.* The first two sections of the chapter provide the foundation for the concept of a distribution of a random variable, or probability distribution.
- *Connecting probability theory to real-world experiments.* The final section will provide a transition from the theoretical constructs of probability theory to the real world of experiments and data. In this section, probability distributions will be presented as hypothetical distributions that may be used to evaluate empirical results.

3.2 BASIC CONCEPTS FOR ANALYZING THE STRUCTURE OF EVENTS

3.2.1 Simple Experiments and Elementary Events

Suppose we have a class of 100 students, 60 men and 40 women. The instructor, a kindly statistician, gives no grades lower than C. The number of male and female students receiving each grade is presented in Table 3.1.

Suppose further that the sex of each student, along with his or her grade, is written on a separate slip of paper and the 100 slips are placed in a box. We can determine the probability that

Table 3.1   Distribution of grades for men and women

Sex	Grade			Total
	A	B	C	
Female	12	24	4	40
Male	15	36	9	60
Total	27	60	13	100

a slip of paper randomly selected from the box has a particular sex and/or grade written on it. We can use this *simple experiment* to introduce some basic ideas about probability.

A simple experiment is a well-defined process that leads to a single outcome (Hays, 1981). All probabilities are defined with respect to an experiment. Randomly drawing a slip of paper from the box and observing the grade and sex listed on the slip is an example of a simple experiment. Another example is recording whether each of Rachel's 20 responses is correct or wrong.

The possible outcomes of a simple experiment are called *elementary events*, and the complete set of elementary events is called the *sample space* for the experiment. In the statistics class example, the sample space consists of the 100 combinations of sex and grade across all of the students in the class. In the ESP example, the sample space consists of every possible sequence of correct and incorrect guesses across 20 trials.

3.2.2 Combining Elementary Events into Event Classes

We are often not so much interested in the probability of a particular elementary event as we are in the probability of meaningful collections of elementary events that are called *event classes* or, simply, *events*. For example, a student in the statistics class might be interested in the probability of getting a grade of A or B. In the ESP experiment, we would likely be interested in a summary of performance (e.g., proportion of correct responses) across all of the trials in the experiment.

Events can be combined in important ways. Events may be "joined" such that an elementary event may be simultaneously classified into two (or more) event classes. In our statistics class example, a person may be both female *and* have earned an A in the class. In our ESP experiment, Rachel might pick the correct card on every trial of the experiment; that is, she may be correct on the first and second and third and . . . and twentieth trial. Thus, we can talk about *joint events* that are comprised of the *intersections* of two or more events. We will use the conjunction "and" to refer to the joining of two or more events, but we will understand the term to refer to the logical operation of intersection.

Events may also "unite" to form *compound events*. In contrast to joint events such as "*F and A*," we can have compound events (or unions of events) such as "*F or A*." The *union* of two events occurs if an elementary event may be classified as either or both of the two events. In our statistics class experiment, the union of *female* with *A* occurs if we observe "*female*" or "*A*" or "*female and A*" (i.e., a female student who earned a grade of A). In a simplified version of our ESP example, the outcome of at least one correct guess in *two* trials is comprised of the events: "correct on the first trial only" *or* "correct on the second trial only" *or* "correct on both trials" (i.e., correct on trial 1 and on trial 2). We will use the disjunction "or" to refer to the union of two or more events, but understand the term to refer to the logical operation of union (i.e., either or both).

3.2.3 Characterizations of Sets of Events

Event classes may be related to one another in different ways. One important kind of relationship is *complementarity*. The complement of event A is the collection of elementary events that do not qualify as instances of event A. The complement of A is expressed as "*not-A*" or $\bar{A}$. In our statistics example, the complement of *male* is *female*; the complement of the C is "A or B." One useful application of the concept of complementarity is that it is sometimes easier to approach the analysis of a problem by redefining it in terms of the complement of the event specified in the problem. For example, if asked to compute the probability that Rachel will make at least one correct guess in five trials of our ESP experiment by guessing, we could approach the calculation by computing the probability of one correct, the probability of two correct, the probability of three correct, etc. But a simpler approach would be to realize that getting at least one correct is equivalent to *not* making errors on all five trials; this realization would suggest an approach based on computing the probability of zero correct in five trials.

Another kind of relationship that characterizes some sets of events is *mutual exclusion*. Two events are mutually exclusive if they cannot jointly occur. The events A, B, and C are mutually exclusive, as are *male* and *female*, and *correct* and *incorrect*. If you get an A on an exam, you do not get a B. In contrast, A and *male* are not mutually exclusive; it is possible that a male student will get a grade of A. We will find that it is easier to compute probabilities of mutually exclusive events than those involving events that are not mutually exclusive.

In part because of the tractability of probability calculations involving mutually exclusive events, it is generally desirable to define the outcomes for an experiment in terms of event classes that are *mutually exclusive* and *exhaustive* (i.e., account for all possible elementary events in a sample space). A set of mutually exclusive and exhaustive events partitions the sample space. That is, it accounts for every possible event, and it does so such that each possible outcome is unambiguously classified into a single event class. For example, the set of events "A, B, and C" partitions the sample space for the statistics class; so does the set "*male* and *female*." Similarly, the six cells of Table 3.1, corresponding to the six combinations of sex and grade, also partition the sample space. As a final example, any event and its complement partition a sample space.

Another important possible relationship between events is that of *independence*. A formal definition of independence must be deferred until probability calculations are introduced. An informal definition is that two events are independent if the occurrence of one event provides no information about the likelihood of occurrence of the other event. That is, independent events are unrelated events. In our ESP example, it is probably reasonable to assume that the trial-to-trial outcomes are independent of one another. If Rachel is randomly guessing, knowing that she made a correct response on the first trial does not help us to predict her performance on any other trial. Because the way in which the terms "independence" and "mutual exclusion" are commonly used in everyday language, some students confuse the two concepts. However, the two terms have very different meanings when we talk about probability: If two events, E_1 and E_2, are mutually exclusive (e.g., male, female), then knowing that E_1 occurs tells us that E_2 does not occur (i.e., their joint probability is zero). However, if E_1 and E_2 are independent, then the probability of their joint occurrence is greater than zero, except in the trivial case where the probability of one of the events is zero. Thus, mutually exclusive events are not independent. As we will see, the concept of independence is often a major assumption of statistical tests.

3.2.4 Combining Events in the ESP Experiment

To illustrate the potential usefulness of some of the concepts introduced to this point, suppose that Rachel does not have ESP and randomly guesses on every trial. If so, we would expect her to be correct 25% of the time in the long run because there are four equally likely choices on each trial. In evaluating the strength of the evidence against guessing, we want to be able to translate our hypothesis that she is guessing on each trial into the probability that she makes a specific number of correct responses in a given number of trials. In order to do this, we need to consider all of the possible sequences of correct and incorrect guesses that might occur. A useful conceptual tool for this purpose is a tree diagram like the one in Fig. 3.1. Each branch of the diagram in Fig. 3.1 represents a distinct combination of possible outcomes for a four-trial experiment.

Suppose that we want to compute the probability that Rachel makes exactly one correct guess in a four-trial experiment (i.e., 25% correct). To do this, we must analyze the various ways in which individual trial outcomes may produce one correct result in four trials. Looking at Fig. 3.1, we can distinguish four distinct sequences of trial outcomes that correspond to one correct guess: Rachel can be correct on the first trial, but wrong on trials 2 through 4 (call this "sequence 1"), or she can be correct on only the second trial (sequence 2), or only on the third trial (sequence 3), or only on the fourth trial (sequence 4). Each of these sequences represents a joint event; e.g., (correct on trial 1) and (error on trial 2) and (error on trial 3) and (error on trial 4). We do not care on which trial the

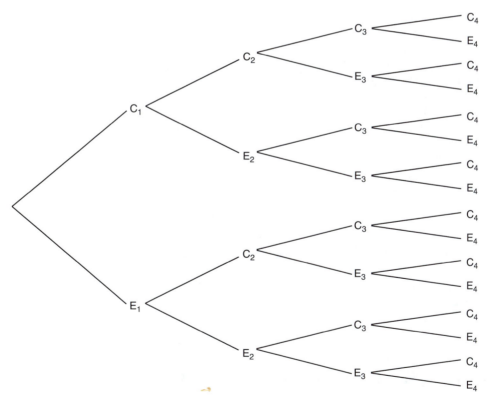

Fig. 3.1 Tree diagram for four trials with two possible responses on each trial (C = correct, E = error). The numerical subscripts represent trial number.

correct response occurs—the outcome of one correct response occurs if sequence 1 or sequence 2 or sequence 3 or sequence 4 is observed. Further, the four sequences are mutually exclusive events. Thus, the response of one correct in four trials can be represented as the union of four, mutually exclusive joint events (i.e., the four sequences of trial outcomes). This precise specification of the relationship between individual trial outcomes and one possible experimental outcome is necessary if we are to translate a hypothesis about the probability of a correct response on any trial into a calculation of the probability (p) of a given experimental outcome.

3.3 COMPUTING PROBABILITIES

In probability theory, probabilities are numbers assigned to the events in a sample space. We will denote the probability of an event, A, by $p(A)$. The assignment of probabilities to events follows some simple rules.

3.3.1 Some Basic Rules of Probability

The sample space, S, consists of all of the elementary events, and the probabilities of the elementary events must sum to 1. This must be the case because the elementary events are by definition mutually exclusive and exhaustive. In the simplified ESP experiment example, the set of events (0, 1, 2, 3, and 4 correct responses) are mutually exclusive and exhaustive, so their probabilities must also sum to 1. In general,

$$p(S) = 1 \tag{3.1}$$

It should be evident from the definition of probability in Equation 3.1 that a probability must have a value within the range from 0 to 1. More precisely,

$$0 \le p(A) \le 1 \tag{3.2}$$

It is meaningless to speak of an event as having less than no chance, or more than a 100% chance of occurring.

The sample space can always be partitioned into two mutually exclusive and exhaustive sets of elementary events; call these A and $\tilde{A}$ ("not-A," which is called the "complement of A"). Given that $p(S) = 1$, it follows that $p(A \text{ or } \tilde{A}) = p(A) + p(\tilde{A}) = 1$, and therefore that

$$p(\tilde{A}) = 1 - p(A) \tag{3.3}$$

For example, if event A is "zero correct responses" in the four-trial ESP experiment, then $\tilde{A}$ is "one or more correct responses." Given that $p(S) = 1$, $p(\text{one or more correct})$ must equal $1 - p(\text{zero correct})$.

Finally, it follows from the preceding rules that if we define a set of events that are mutually exclusive and exhaust the possible events in a sample space, then the sum of their probabilities will equal 1. That is, if the set of events $A, B, C, \ldots$ constitute a partition of S, then

$$p(A \text{ or } B \text{ or } C \text{ or } \ldots) = p(A) + p(B) + p(C) + \ldots = 1 \tag{3.4}$$

3.3.2 Assigning Probabilities to Marginal Events

We have some simple rules that define properties of probabilities, but how do we assign probabilities to actual events in a meaningful way? In the case where all of the elementary events in a sample space are equally likely, the probability of event A is simply the ratio of the number of elementary events in A to the total number of events, $n(A)$, in the sample space, $n(S)$. That is, the probability of an event A is its relative frequency in the sample space:

$$p(A) = \frac{n(A)}{n(S)} \tag{3.5}$$

To be concrete, let's return to Table 3.1 and the example of grades in a statistics class. Suppose we want to find the probability that a slip of paper randomly selected from the box will correspond to a person who got a B; $p(B)$ is simply the number of slips of paper with a B divided by the total number of slips of paper:

$$p(B) = \frac{60}{100} = .60$$

In the preceding example, we computed the probability of a particular grade without regard to the sex of the student. In Table 3.1, the numbers of students with As, Bs, and Cs and the numbers of men and women are presented in the margins of Table 3.1. Because of this, the probability of observing a particular value of some variable (e.g., grade) without respect to any other variable (e.g., sex) is sometimes referred to as a *marginal probability*.

3.3.3 Joint Probabilities

The probability of obtaining a particular *combination* of events is referred to as a *joint probability*. For example, $p(A \text{ and } M)$, which is read as "the probability of A and M," is the probability of the joint event $<A, M>$; that is, the probability of selecting a slip of paper with both "A" and "male" written on it. If the probabilities of the elementary events are equal, $p(A \text{ and } M)$ can be obtained by computing the relative frequency of the joint event in the sample space:

$$p(A \text{ and } M) = \frac{n(A \text{ and } M)}{n(S)} \tag{3.6}$$

where $n(A \text{ and } M)$ is the number of elementary events that belong to *both* the events A and M. For the data of Table 3.1, $p(A \text{ and } M) = .15$, because 15 of the 100 slips of paper correspond to grades of A obtained by male students. Similarly, if the events B and F correspond to "getting a grade of B" and "being female," respectively, $p(B \text{ and } F) = 24/100 = .24$. Note that $p(A)$ must always be at least as large as $p(A \text{ and } M)$ because the event A will always contain at least as many elementary events as the joint event $<A, M>$. These ideas may be clarified by reconsidering Table 3.1. Each column represents the event of a letter grade and has two nonoverlapping parts. For example, the column representing the event $<A>$ consists of the joint events $<A, M>$ and $<A, F>$. Note that $n(A) = n(A \text{ and } M) + n(A \text{ and } F)$, and it follows from Equations 3.5 and 3.6 that $p(A) = p(A \text{ and } M) + p(A \text{ and } F)$. Also note that $p(A \text{ and } M) = p(M \text{ and } A)$.

3.3.4 Probabilities of Unions of Events

The *union* of two events consists of all the elementary events belonging to either or both of them. The elementary events forming the union of events A and M are the following cells of Table 3.1: $<A, F>$, $<A, M>$, $<B, M>$, and $<C, M>$. The expression $p(A \text{ or } M)$ refers to the probability of obtaining an elementary event belonging to either A or M; that is, falling into any of the four cells just noted. Therefore,

$$p(A \text{ or } M) = \frac{n(A \text{ or } M)}{n(S)} \qquad (3.7)$$

$$= \frac{12 + 15 + 36 + 9}{100} = .72$$

because 72 of the 100 elementary events belong either to A or to M or to both. Note that $n(A \text{ or } M)$ does not generally equal $n(A) + n(M)$. As should be clear from Table 3.1, this sum counts twice the 15 elementary events that belong to both A and M. Verify for yourself that $p(A \text{ or } M) = p(A) + p(M) - p(A \text{ and } M)$. Also verify that $p(A \text{ or } F) = 55/100 = .55$. In general, if E_1 and E_2 are two events of interest,

$$p(E_1 \text{ or } E_2) = p(E_1) + p(E_2) - p(E_1 \text{ and } E_2) \qquad (3.8)$$

We subtract $p(E_1 \text{ and } E_2)$ because E_1 and E_2 are not mutually exclusive. If they were, the probability of their intersection would be zero.

3.3.5 Conditional Probabilities

We are often interested in computing the probabilities of events when considering only a subset of events in a sample space. For example, we may be interested in the probability of obtaining a grade of A if only the male students are considered. This probability is called a *conditional probability* because it is the probability of *A given the condition that M occurs*. It is represented by $p(A|M)$, and is read as "the probability of A given M." There are 60 slips of paper labeled "male" and 15 of them correspond to grades of A. Therefore, $p(A|M) = 15/60 = .25$. More generally, $p(A|M)$ is the proportion of all elementary events in M that also belong to A; that is,

$$p(A|M) = \frac{n(A \text{ and } M)}{n(M)} = \frac{p(A \text{ and } M)}{p(M)} \qquad (3.9)$$

Verify that for the current example, $p(B|M) = 36/60 = .60$; $p(M|A) = 15/27 = .56$; and $p(A|B) = 0/60 = 0$.

Two important things about conditional probabilities should be noted. First, people have a tendency to confuse conditional probabilities with joint probabilities. Look carefully at Equations 3.6 and 3.9. The conditional probability $p(A|M)$ is the probability of selecting a slip of paper that is labeled "A" if the selection is made from only the 60 slips labeled "male." The joint probability $p(A \text{ and } M)$ is the probability of selecting a slip labeled both "A" and "male" if selection is randomly made from *all* 100 slips of paper. A conditional probability has to be at least as large as— and is generally larger than—the corresponding joint probability because the set from which we sample is a subset of the entire sample. For example, when we calculate $p(A|M)$, we divide by only the number of male students, a number less than the size of the total sample. Bear in mind, however, that although joint and conditional probabilities are not the same, they are related, as can be seen in Equation 3.9.

The second thing to note about conditional probabilities is that for any two events, A and M, there are two *opposite* conditional probabilities, $p(A|M)$ and $p(M|A)$. These two conditional probabilities will generally not have the same values; in our current example, $p(A|M) = 15/60 = .25$ and $p(M|A) = 15/27 = .56$. As this example illustrates, the denominators are based on different subsets of the entire sample, and these often will have different numbers of elementary events. As we will see, conditional probabilities are very useful in characterizing relationships between events.

3.3.6 Mutually Exclusive and Independent Events

Two events E_1 and E_2 are *mutually exclusive* if they are incompatible; that is, if an elementary event belongs to E_1, it cannot belong to E_2. It follows that if E_1 and E_2 are mutually exclusive, $p(E_1$ and $E_2) = 0$, $p(E_1|E_2) = 0$, and $p(E_2|E_1) = 0$. In our current example (Table 3.1), $p(A$ and $B) = 0$, because a student who receives a grade of A in the course did not receive a B. Earlier, we encountered the partitioning rule (Equation 3.4), in which we summed the probabilities of the elementary events in a sample space. It is because any partitioning is based on mutually exclusive events that we summed the probabilities of events in Equation 3.4; it is because the set of events in any partitioning is also *exhaustive* that the sum equals 1.

We introduced the concept of independence in discussing concepts for analyzing the structure of events. At that time, we said that two events are independent if the occurrence of one event provides no information about the likelihood of occurrence of the other event. Now that we have introduced the concept of conditional probabilities, we can state the concept of independence more precisely: Two events E_1 and E_2 are *independent* if $p(E_1|E_2) = p(E_1)$; that is, if the probability of event E_1 is the same whether or not event E_2 occurs.

We may wish to ask questions such as "Is getting a grade of A independent of the sex of the student?" This is another way of asking whether the probability of getting an A is the same for male and female students. If there is independence, $p(A|M) = p(A|F) = p(A)$. Returning to Table 3.1, $p(A|M) = 15/60 = .25$, $p(A|F) = 12/40 = .30$, and $p(A) = .27$. Clearly, for this data set, getting an A is not independent of being a male or female student because $p(A|M)$ is not equal to $p(A|F)$; therefore, $<A, M>$ and $<A, F>$ are pairs of events that are not independent. On the other hand, $p(B|M) = p(B|F) = p(B)$, so that, for this data set, getting a grade of B is independent of the student's sex. For both male and female students, the probability of getting a B is .60.

We may also wish to ask more general questions such as "Are the variables of grade and sex independent of each other?" In order for the answer to be "yes," each of the six pairs of events formed by combining levels of sex and grade (specifically, $<A, M>$, $<A, F>$, $<B, M>$, $<B, F>$, $<C, M>$, and $<C, F>$) would have to be independent. The variables sex and grade are not independent of each other in this example because, as we have already shown, $<A, M>$ and $<A, F>$ are pairs of events that are not independent.

Two important points about independence should be noted. First, if E_1 and E_2 are two independent events, $p(E_1$ and $E_2) = p(E_1) \times p(E_2)$. To see why this is so, consider the definition of conditional probability given by Equation 3.9:

$$p(E_1|E_2) = p(E_1 \text{ and } E_2) / p(E_2)$$

Multiplying both sides of this equation by $p(E_2)$ yields

$$p(E_1|E_2) \times p(E_2) = p(E_1 \text{ and } E_2)$$

But we know that if E_1 and E_2 are independent, $p(E_1|E_2) = p(E_1)$. Replacing $p(E_1|E_2)$ by $p(E_1)$ in the last equation, we have, *if E_1 and E_2 are independent events*,

$$p(E_1 \text{ and } E_2) = p(E_1) \times p(E_2)$$

The second important point is that if events E_1 and E_2 are mutually exclusive, they cannot be independent. By definition, if E_1 occurs, then E_2 cannot occur if the two events are mutually exclusive. Therefore, if E_1 and E_2 are mutually exclusive, their joint probability and both conditional probabilities must be zero; that is

$$p(E_1 \text{ and } E_2) = 0, \ p(E_1|E_2) = 0, \text{ and } p(E_2|E_1) = 0$$

In contrast, if E_1 and E_2 are independent and their probabilities are both greater than zero, then their joint probability is greater than zero.

3.3.7 The Additive Law for Compound Events

We are now ready to integrate much of what we have developed to this point into two very useful probability laws. The first law is the *additive law for compound events*. We will often apply this law in the special case in which we have two or more mutually exclusive events, so we begin with that situation:

If E_1 and E_2 are mutually exclusive events,

$$p(E_1 \text{ or } E_2) = p(E_1) + p(E_2) \tag{3.10}$$

This can be extended to any number of mutually exclusive events:

$$p(E_1 \text{ or } E_2 \text{ or } \ldots \text{ or } E_n) = p(E_1) + p(E_2) + \ldots + p(E_n) \tag{3.11}$$

In English, the probability of the union of two or more mutually exclusive events is the sum of their individual probabilities.

Of course, events are not always mutually exclusive. As we explained in Section 3.2.4, if events E_1 and E_2 are not mutually exclusive, then the probability of their joint occurrence is (usually) greater than zero and must be taken into account, so that

$$p(E_1 \text{ or } E_2) = p(E_1) + p(E_2) - p(E_1 \text{ and } E_2) \tag{3.12}$$

For example, in Table 3.1, $p(A \text{ or } M) = p(A) + p(M) - p(A \text{ and } M) = .27 + .60 - .15 = .72$.

3.3.8 The Multiplication Law for Joint Events

As we did for the additive law, we start with a special case. If E_1 and E_2 are two independent events,

$$p(E_1 \text{ and } E_2) = p(E_1) \times p(E_2) \tag{3.13}$$

The law can be extended to any number of independent events, $E_1, E_2, \ldots E_n$:

$$p(E_1 \text{ and } E_2 \text{ and } \ldots \text{ and } E_n) = p(E_1) \times p(E_2) \times \ldots \times p(E_n) \tag{3.14}$$

In English, if two or more events are independent, then the probability of their joint occurrence is equal to the product of their individual probabilities.

Note that Equations 3.13 and 3.14 do not hold if the events are not independent. For example, A and M are not independent and $p(A \text{ and } M) = .15$, but $p(A)p(M) = (.27)(.60) = .162$. However, the multiplication rule can be extended to events that are not independent. In this case,

$$p(E_1 \text{ and } E_2) = p(E_1) \times p(E_2 | E_1) = p(E_2) \times p(E_1 | E_2) \tag{3.15}$$

Equation 3.15 follows directly from the definition of conditional probability, $p(E_1 | E_2) = p(E_1 \text{ and } E_2)/p(E_2)$. Multiplying both sides of this last equation by $p(E_2)$ yields $p(E_2) \times p(E_1 | E_2) = p(E_1 \text{ and } E_2)$. For example, applying Equation 3.15 to the data of Table 3.1, we can see that $p(A \text{ and } M) = p(M)p(A | M) = (.60)(15/60) = .15$.

Table 3.2 summarizes much of what has been presented in Section 3.3. It includes important definitions and the rules embodied in Equations 3.10–3.15.

Although the multiplication and addition rules are quite simple, people often mix them up, possibly because the statement of the multiplication rule uses the word "and" and the statement of

Table 3.2 Some probability definitions and rules

Some probability definitions	
Probability of event A	$p(A) = n(A)/n(S)$
Probability of the joint events A and B	$p(A \text{ and } B) = n(A \text{ and } B)/n(S)$
Probability of the union of events A and B	$p(A \text{ or } B) = n(A \text{ or } B)/n(S)$
Conditional probability of A given B	$p(A\,|\,B) = p(A \text{ and } B)/p(B)$
	$= n(A \text{ and } B)/n(B)$
Some probability rules	
The addition rule for unions of events	$p(A \text{ or } B) = p(A) + p(B) - p(A \text{ and } B)$
Special case of the addition rule if the events are mutually exclusive	$p(A \text{ or } B) = p(A) + p(B)$
The multiplication rule for joint events	$p(A \text{ and } B \text{ and } C)$
	$= p(A)\,p(B|A)\,p(C|A \text{ and } B)$
Special case of the multiplication rule for independent events	$p(A \text{ and } B \text{ and } C) = p(A)\,p(B)\,p(C)$

the addition rule does not. It should be emphasized that the multiplication rule tells us how to calculate $p(E_1 \text{ and } E_2)$, the probability of the joint occurrence of E_1 *and* E_2. The addition rule tells us how to calculate $p(E_1 \text{ or } E_2)$, the probability that E_1 *or* E_2 occurs. This union of E_1 and E_2 (E_1 or E_2) includes the joint event $<E_1 \text{ and } E_2>$ but it also includes occurrences of E_1 without E_2 and of E_2 without E_1.

3.3.9 Computing Probabilities of Events in the ESP Experiment

Let's apply what we have learned about probability to calculate the probability of one correct guess in a four-trial ESP experiment. In Section 3.2.4, we established that there were four sequences of trial outcomes corresponding to the experimental outcome of exactly one correct guess in four trials. If C and E are used to denote guesses that are "correct" and in "error," and we use subscripts to denote trials, then the four sequences of interest are: $<C_1\,E_2\,E_3\,E_4>$, $<E_1\,C_2\,E_3\,E_4>$, $<E_1\,E_2\,C_3\,E_4>$, and $<E_1\,E_2\,E_3\,C_4>$. Each of these sequences represents a joint event, and it is reasonable to assume that trial outcomes are independent. If we hypothesize that Rachel guesses on every trial, then $p(C) = .25$ and $p(E) = 1 - p(C) = .75$. Applying the multiplicative law, the probability of each sequence is $(.25)(.75)(.75)(.75) = .1055$. However, we are interested not in the probability of a specific sequence, but in the probability of any one of the sequences occurring. That is, we wish to compute:

$$p[<C_1\,E_2\,E_3\,E_4> \text{ or } <E_1\,C_2\,E_3\,E_4> \text{ or } <E_1\,E_2\,C_3\,E_4> \text{ or } <E_1\,E_2\,E_3\,C_4>]$$

The sequences are mutually exclusive and we want the probability of their union, so we may apply the additive law and sum their probabilities. Thus, the probability of exactly one correct guess in four trials if Rachel is guessing is $(.1055 + .1055 + .1055 + .1055) = .422$. In English, if Rachel is guessing from among four equally likely alternatives, then the probability is .422 that she will be correct exactly once in the four-trial experiment.

3.4 PROBABILITY DISTRIBUTIONS

We are not interested in just one possible outcome of an experiment. It is possible that Rachel will get 0, 1, 2, 3, or 4 items correct in our four-trial ESP experiment. The probabilities of each of these possible outcomes based on a *statistical model* – a set of assumptions about how the responses are generated that can be used to calculate the probabilities – is referred to as a probability distribution.

3.4.1 Random Sampling, Random Variables, and Distributions of Random Variables

In any experiment, we consider our observations to be a sample from a much larger, possibly infinite, population of observations. We attempt to obtain a sample that is representative of the population from which the observations are drawn. In calculating probabilities, we often assume *random sampling*. In our ESP example, the set of trials in the experiment is considered to be a sample from an infinite number of trials that characterizes Rachel's ability to generate correct responses. Random sampling means that each of these potential trials with its accompanying response has an equal opportunity of being sampled.

Although the goal of random sampling is to obtain a representative set of observations from a population, samples will differ from one another and thus are not perfect miniatures of the population from which they are drawn. Put another way, sample statistics are *variables* because they can take on different values for different samples. When the numerical value of a variable is determined by a chance event, that variable is called a *random variable*. Therefore, sample statistics as well as the outcomes of chance events, such as throwing a pair of dice or guessing the identity of a card (scored 1 if correct and 0 if wrong), are random variables.

3.4.2 Discrete Random Variables

In many situations, a random variable may take only a limited number of values within its range. In our ESP experiment, if the random variable of interest is the number of correct responses in 20 trials, the possible values are the 21 integers from 0 to 20. Alternatively, we might characterize the results of the ESP experiment in terms of the *proportion* of correct responses, in which case the possible values of our random variable would be each of the integers divided by 20. In either case, there is a relatively small number of possible values so that the variable is discrete. This is in contrast to other variables such as the amount of time taken to make a response. Time to respond is a continuous variable that can take on an infinite number of possible values if measured precisely enough.

We will encounter many situations involving discrete variables that are of interest. We have already given a great deal of attention to one—the number (or proportion) of correct guesses in an ESP experiment. Probability calculations for discrete random variables are often simple. With just a basic knowledge of probability, we were able to compute the probability that Rachel makes exactly one correct guess in a four-trial ESP experiment by randomly guessing. We could similarly calculate the probability of each other potential outcome of the four-trial experiment, and will do so in Chapter 4. The graph of the resulting probability distribution is given in Fig. 4.1. In general, a probability distribution associates a probability with every possible value of a random variable.

3.4.3 Continuous Random Variables

Imagine that we are interested in the distribution of times it takes healthy adults in the 20–40-year age range to complete a mile run. The range of times will be finite (i.e., presumably between 3.75 and, say, 25 minutes). However, if we could measure time to any degree of precision, then any value between the extremes might be observed. Unlike our example of correct guesses in an ESP experiment, the random variable of time to complete a mile run is a *continuous random variable*.

Arguably, we deal only with discrete random variables in practice because there are always limits to the precision of our measurements. However, continuous functions often provide excellent approximations to distributions of discrete random variables, so they will turn out to be very useful to us in many inferential applications. Therefore, it is important to develop a basic understanding of the properties of distributions of continuous random variables.

In general, the probability of occurrence of any *exact* value of a continuous random variable is essentially zero. For this reason, we do not talk about the probability of a value of a continuous random variable. Instead, we refer to the *probability density* at a particular value of a continuous random variable. We will symbolize the probability density of a variable Y at value a by

$$f(a) = \text{probability density of } Y \text{ at } a$$

Graphically, the probability density at a particular value of a continuous random variable is the height of the probability distribution at that value.

Although an exact value of a continuous random variable has a probability of zero, it is meaningful to talk about the probability of observing a value within an *interval*. Graphically, the probability of observing a value within some interval is the area under the curve for the distribution of that random variable. This is how we will typically work with probability computations when dealing with distributions of continuous random variables. For example, if we know that IQ scores in a population are normally distributed with a certain mean and standard deviation, we can find the probability that a person randomly selected from the population has an IQ of, say, 130 or greater, by using the characteristics of the normal distribution.

3.5 CONNECTING PROBABILITY THEORY TO DATA

Probability distributions are theoretical entities, but they have very useful applications. We have already hinted frequently at some of those applications. At least three closely related applications of probability distributions to data interpretation can be identified. First, we have already seen that we can, in some circumstances, use probability to calculate the probabilities of various experimental outcomes given an explicit model of performance. In our ESP example, we calculated the probability that Rachel would make exactly one correct guess in a four-trial experiment given the assumption that she was guessing randomly among four, equally likely alternatives on each trial. We indicated that we could also compute the probability of any other possible outcome of the ESP experiment. Thus, a basic knowledge of probability allows a precise statement of the predictions of a specific hypothesis for the possible outcomes of an experiment.

A second application of a probability distribution is related to the first. Namely, a probability distribution like the one that we generated for our four-trial ESP experiment provides us with two clear expectations regarding the experimental outcome. One is that the probability distribution identifies the most likely outcome of an experiment. In our ESP example, that outcome is one correct in four trials, or 25% correct, if Rachel is guessing. The other expectation is that there will be *sampling error* in any experiment. Although the most likely outcome of the experiment is one correct response, that outcome has only a .422 probability of occurring; there is a .578 probability of observing a different outcome. The very fact that there is a *distribution* of possible outcomes embodies the reality of sampling error in an experiment.

Finally, the ability to generate a probability distribution representing the potential outcomes of an experiment and their corresponding probabilities provides us with critical information for evaluating the actual outcome of an experiment. In our ESP example, if Rachel makes only one correct guess in four trials, we will doubt that she has ESP because that outcome is quite likely under the hypothesis that she is simply guessing. On the other hand, if she is correct on all four trials, we will doubt that her performance is due to guessing because the probability of being correct on all four trials is very low (i.e., .004).

Although we can see the relevance of probability theory and probability distributions to interpreting empirical observations in scientific studies, we must make an additional link between probability theory and the process of interpreting data. We have defined probability as the relative frequency of an event in a sample space. If we select a piece of paper with a grade and sex written on it from the distribution given in Table 3.1, all the elementary events are specified, so computing the probability of an event is simple. However, in most real experiments, we do not have such comprehensive knowledge of the characteristics of the sample space, so we are unable to compute the precise probability of each possible event. Indeed, the reason for conducting studies is to learn about the characteristics of populations of interest. We sample observations from populations and use characteristics of samples to estimate corresponding characteristics of populations. We define the probability of an event in these circumstances as its relative frequency of occurrence in the long run.

The definition of probability as the long-run relative frequency of an event is obviously related to our initial definition of probability as the relative frequency of an event in a sample space. However, defining probability in terms of long-run relative frequency has the advantage of suggesting a way to empirically estimate the probability of an event; namely, by computing the proportion of times the event occurs in some large number of observations. For example, we can compute the proportion of times that Rachel responds correctly in our ESP experiment and use that as our best indication of the level of Rachel's ESP ability. By "long run," we mean the relative frequency of occurrence of an event in an infinite number of observations. Because we can never make an infinite number of observations, we must assume that any calculation we base on a finite sample of observations is an imperfect estimate. However, *if we make N independent observations under the exact same conditions, then the observed relative frequency of occurrence of an event, Y, approaches the probability of the event, p(Y), as N approaches infinity.* This statement is usually referred to as Bernoulli's theorem. It tells us that the relative frequency of some event Y in a sample of observations may be used to estimate the probability of Y, and that the accuracy of the estimate will increase with the number of observations. This provides the connection we need to relate the probability to the application of analyzing and interpreting empirical observations.

3.6 SUMMARY

Our goal in this chapter was to present the rudiments of probability theory in preparation for developing basic concepts in statistical inference in Chapters 4 and 5. Our major points were:

- Observations in behavioral experiments are probabilistic, so we must be able to compute the probabilities of events under different assumptions about the population if we are to have a basis for interpreting experimental outcomes.
- The starting point for computing probabilities is the ability to analyze the structure of events; that is, to determine how elementary events are combined to form the event classes. Such an analysis involves both determining how events may be combined (i.e., joint events and compound events) and how events are related (i.e., mutual exclusion, independence).
- The structure of events has implications for computing the probabilities of those events from a knowledge of the probabilities of the elementary events comprising them. We will have particular use for two probability laws. The *additive law* states that the probability of a compound event is the sum of the probabilities of its component events if the component events are mutually exclusive. The *multiplicative law* states that the probability of a joint event is the product of its component events if the component events are independent.
- An important application of probability theory is the derivation of probability distributions that provide fundamental information to guide processes of statistical inference.
- Finally, defining the probability of an event in terms of its long-run relative frequency provides a connection between probability theory and empirical observations that provides the basis for data analysis. We develop that connection further in Chapter 4.

EXERCISES

3.1 Suppose an experiment similar to the one described in the chapter is designed to test for the existence of ESP. The major difference is that now there are five cards in the pack instead of four. Suppose that the subject, S, has no ESP and randomly picks one of the five cards on each trial. Assuming independence, what is the probability that S is (a) correct on the first trial? (b) correct on each of the first three trials? (c) correct on the second trial but wrong on the first and third? (d) correct on exactly one of the first three trials? (e) correct on at least one of the first three trials? (f) correct on exactly two of the first three trials? (g) correct for the first time on the fifth trial?

3.2 Suppose a certain trait is associated with eye color. Three hundred randomly selected individuals are studied with the following results:

	Eye color		
Trait	Blue	Brown	Other
Yes	70	30	20
No	20	110	50

Suppose a person is chosen at random from the 300 in the study.

(a) For each of the following pairs of events, indicate whether or not they are exhaustive, whether or not they are mutually exclusive, and whether or not they are independent: (i) "Yes" and "No"; (ii) "Blue" and "Brown"; (iii) "Yes" and "Brown".

(b) Find: (i) $p(\text{Blue}|\text{Yes})$; (ii) $p(\text{Yes}|\text{Blue})$; (iii) $p(\text{Yes or Blue})$; (iv) $p(\text{Yes and Blue})$.

Suppose two people are chosen at random from the 300.

(c) What is the probability that the first person has the trait and has brown eyes?

(d) What is the probability that both people have the trait and have brown eyes if they are selected *with replacement* (that is, after the first person is selected, he or she is returned to the pool and may be selected again)?

(e) What is the probability that both people have the trait and have brown eyes if they are selected *without replacement* (that is, once the person has been selected on the first choice, he or she is no longer available to be chosen)?

3.3 Two individuals, A and B, shoot at a target. The probability of hitting the target on a given trial is .7 for A and .6 for B—i.e., $p(A) = .7$ and $p(B) = .6$. Assuming that the results of these shots are *independent* of one another, answer the following: If A and B each take a single shot at the target, what is the probability that

(a) both A and B hit the target?

(b) neither A nor B hit the target?

(c) A hits the target and B misses it?

(d) A misses the target and B hits it?

(e) the target is hit at least once?

If A and B each shoot at the target twice, what is the probability that

(f) the target is hit at least once?

(g) the target is missed at least once?

3.4 Consider the following table to indicate the number of degrees awarded by a university in a particular year, classified by the type of degree and the sex of the recipient. Assume that nobody received more than one degree during the year.

Sex	Type of degree				Total
	Bachelor's	Master's	Professional	Doctorate	
Female	645	227	32	18	922
Male	505	161	40	26	732
Total	1,150	388	72	44	1,654

Suppose a person is chosen at random from the 1,654 degree recipients in the study.

(a) For each of the three following pairs of events, indicate whether or not they are exhaustive, whether or not they are disjoint (i.e., mutually exclusive), and whether or not they are independent: (i) "Professional" and "Doctorate"; (ii) "Professional" and "Male"; (iii) "Professional" and "Female".

(b) Find: (i) p(Bachelor's|Female); (ii) p(Female|Bachelor's); (iii) p(Female or Bachelor's); (iv) p(Female and Bachelor's).

3.5 The following demonstrates why it is hard to screen populations for the presence of low-incidence diseases: enzyme-linked immunosorbent assays (ELISA) are used to screen donated blood for the presence of the HIV virus. The test actually detects antibodies, substances that the body produces when the virus is present. But the test is not completely accurate. It can be wrong in two ways: (1) by giving a positive result when there are no antibodies (false positive) or (2) by giving a negative result when there actually are antibodies (false negative). When antibodies are present, ELISA gives a positive result with probability about .997 and a negative result (false negative) with probability about .003. When antibodies are not present,

ELISA gives a positive result (false positive) with a probability of about .015 and a negative result with probability .985. That is, $p(\text{correct positive}) = p(\text{positive}|\text{HIV}) = .997$; $p(\text{false negative}) = p(\text{negative}|\text{HIV}) = .003$; $p(\text{false positive}) = p(\text{positive}|\text{no HIV}) = .015$; $p(\text{correct negative}) = p(\text{negative}|\text{no HIV}) = .985$. Suppose 100,000 blood samples are obtained from a population for which the incidence of HIV infection is 1.0%; that is, $p(\text{HIV}) = .01$.

(a) Using the information given above, fill in the cells in the following 2×2 table.

Test results	HIV	No HIV	Total
Positive			
Negative			
Total			

(b) Given that a randomly chosen sample tests positive, what is the probability that the donor is infected?

(c) Given that a randomly chosen sample tests negative, what is the probability that the donor is not infected?

3.6 We are often able to use key words such as "and", "or", and "given" to decide among probability rules. In the following problem, we use more everyday language. So read carefully and for each part think about whether the wording dictates marginal, joint, or conditional probability.

Suppose that a survey of 200 people in a college town has yielded the following data on attitudes toward liberalizing rules on the sale of liquor. Suppose a person is selected at random.

Attitude	Men Student	Men Non-student	Women Student	Women Non-student	Row total
For	70	10	40	0	120
Against	5	30	10	20	65
No opinion	5	0	10	0	15
Col. total	80	40	60	20	200

(a) What is the probability that someone is *for* if that person is a man?

(b) What is the probability that a randomly selected individual is a woman who has no opinion?

(c) What is the probability that a female student has no opinion?

(d) What is the probability that a student has no opinion?

(e) What is the probability that someone with no opinion is a man?

3.7 Order the following three quantities from largest to smallest on the basis of your knowledge of the world, assuming a person is chosen at random from American adults: Explain your ordering. $p(\text{woman}|\text{schoolteacher})$; $p(\text{schoolteacher}|\text{woman})$; $p(\text{woman and schoolteacher})$.

3.8   A study reported in the local newspapers indicated that a psychological test has been developed with the goal of predicting whether elderly people are at high risk of developing dementia in the near future. For healthy people at age 79, the probability of developing dementia within the next 4 years is approximately .20. In the study, a group of healthy 79-year-olds was given the test. For those who went on to develop dementia within the next 4 years, the probability of a positive test at age 79 was found to be .17; that is, p(positive|dementia) = .17. For those who did not develop dementia within the next 4 years, the probability of a positive test was .008; that is, p(positive|no dementia) = .008.

(a) What is p(negative|dementia)?

(b) What is p(negative|no dementia)?

From the data given above, find the predictive accuracy of the test. That is, find the probability that a 79-year-old who takes the test will develop dementia within the next 4 years (c) if the test result is positive? (d) if the test result is negative?

3.9   Many states have, as part of their lottery offerings, a game in which you can choose to bet by choosing any four digits. The winning number is a four-digit number chosen at random with replacement (i.e., the same digit can be chosen more than once).

(a) What is the probability that your chosen number will exactly match the winning number?

(b) What is the probability that the digits in your chosen number will match those in the winning number without regard to order?

3.10   Given a pair of fair dice (i.e., for each die, the probability of getting any of the outcomes 1, 2, 3, 4, 5, or 6 is 1/6), if you roll the dice after shaking them well,

(a) What is the probability of getting a 12?

(b) What is the probability of getting a 7?

3.11   Generate the probability distribution for the outcome of a roll of a pair of dice. What is the probability of getting an outcome of 8 or greater?

Chapter 4

Developing the Fundamentals of Hypothesis Testing Using the Binomial Distribution

4.1 OVERVIEW

Our goal in conducting research is to use our data as a window on the population from which they are sampled. To make this generalization, we must have a way to distinguish trends in the data that reflect corresponding patterns in the population from trends in the data that may be specific to the sample. The procedures for making this critical distinction are collectively known as *inferential statistics*. Most of the subsequent chapters of this book are concerned with two very general inferential procedures: testing specific hypotheses about population parameters and estimating the values of population parameters. The focus of the current chapter is on developing the logic of *hypothesis testing*. Parameter estimation will be discussed in Chapter 5.

In Chapter 3, we established that probability theory is central to the decision-making process of inferential statistics. To elaborate that role and to facilitate presentation of some of the rather abstract concepts underlying hypothesis testing, we will continue to use our ESP experiment as an example. We again have Rachel choosing among four different cards in a 20-trial experiment. Because we are skeptics, we are unwilling to concede that Rachel has ESP unless guessing can be ruled out as a reasonable explanation of her performance in our experiment. If Rachel simply randomly guesses on each trial, the probability of a correct response is 1/4 or .25. Therefore, a finding of five correct responses on the 20 trials is consistent with chance performance, and would provide no evidence whatsoever for ESP. But suppose that 7/20 or .35 of Rachel's responses were correct. Is this result different enough from five correct to convince us that she performed better than what could reasonably be expected by guessing? If not, how many correct responses would it take to convince us? 10/20? 15/20? 20/20? How are we to select a criterion level of performance to decide that Rachel is not simply guessing?

We must develop a conceptual framework in order to answer this question. Suppose that Rachel achieved a .35 success rate in the sample of 20 trials (i.e., seven correct choices). In addressing the issue of ESP, we are concerned with the entire population of potential responses that characterizes Rachel's ESP ability, not just the 20 responses we happened to collect in the experiment. If we ran the experiment again, it would almost certainly turn out somewhat differently. This is the fundamental obstacle to making correct inferences from a sample to a population: Because our observations are subject to *sampling error*, any conclusion we make about the population may be wrong. Therefore, we must be able to assess the likelihood of making an error if we decide on the basis of our experimental results to reject the hypothesis that Rachel is simply guessing.

The major topics of this chapter are organized as follows:

- *What are the requirements for a test of a hypothesis?* Before developing the machinery of hypothesis testing, we will consider what we need to specify to have a testable hypothesis. This discussion will provide us with a framework for the topics that follow.
- *The binomial distribution as a sampling distribution.* We will apply our knowledge of probability to derive a specific theoretical probability distribution called the *binomial distribution*. Our interest in the binomial is that it serves as the *sampling distribution* for the ESP experiment and similar types of experiments. We will see that the concept of a sampling distribution is fundamental to the process of making statistical inferences.
- *Hypothesis testing.* Hypothesis testing uses the concept of a sampling distribution, along with a decision rule, to decide whether the sample of data we collected provides sufficient evidence to reject some hypothesis about the population. For example, if we determined that the data we actually obtained in our experiment were very improbable assuming that Rachel was guessing throughout the experiment (i.e., $p = .25$), this would be strong evidence that she was doing something other than guessing.
- *Power.* In testing hypotheses, we run the risk of two kinds of errors. Namely, we may conclude that Rachel has ESP when she is actually guessing or we may conclude that she is guessing when she really does have some degree of ESP. The researcher's decision rule controls the probability of the first kind of error, but the design of the experiment affects the probability of the second kind of error. We would like to minimize the chance of committing the second error of failing to detect actual effects. This requires us to design experiments with adequate *statistical power*.
- *Assumptions.* Finally, statistical procedures are always based on assumptions that may not be valid in some applications. When assumptions fail, the probability of inferential errors may increase. Therefore, we must consider the implications of violating assumptions.

4.2 WHAT DO WE NEED TO KNOW TO TEST A HYPOTHESIS?

Not all hypotheses that a researcher might generate are amenable to the procedures of hypothesis testing. We need two things in order to directly test a hypothesis. First, we must be able to specify a "point hypothesis." A *point hypothesis* is an exact statement about the state of the world. For example, the hypothesis that Rachel is guessing is a point hypothesis because it can be expressed by a precise probability statement. In our four-choice procedure, the guessing hypothesis can be stated as $p(\text{correct on any trial}) = .25$.

Second, we must be able to use the point hypothesis to derive the "sampling distribution" for the outcomes of interest in an experiment. A *sampling distribution* is a probability distribution that assigns a probability to every possible outcome that might be observed (i.e., is "sampled") in an experiment. A sampling distribution may be thought of as the predictions of a hypothesis. As such, a sampling distribution provides the objective information needed to evaluate the tenability of a hypothesis. For example, the guessing hypothesis predicts that a result of four correct guesses in a four-trial ESP experiment has a probability of only $(1/4)^4$ or .0039. This probability information provides an objective basis for deciding that if Rachel is correct on all four trials, she almost surely is not guessing in the experiment.

Let's develop these ideas with our ESP example. To keep things manageable, we will start by considering a four-trial experiment. We will measure performance in the experiment by counting the number of correct responses across the four trials; we will call this measure Y. Given that each response is either correct (C) or in error (E), Y can now take on only five possible values (0–4 correct).

We want to determine the probability of each possible experimental outcome under the hypothesis that Rachel does not have ESP and is randomly guessing on each trial. Under this hypothesis, $p(C) = .25$ because she is guessing among four equally likely alternatives. This hypothesis refers to performance on individual trials, but our interest is using the summary measure of performance in the experiment, Y, to evaluate the hypothesis. Therefore, we must translate our hypothesis about trial performance into corresponding probabilities for the different values of Y.

The first step in deriving the probability distribution for Y is to identify all of the ways in which trial outcomes may combine to form the five possible experimental outcomes. With four trials that can each have two outcomes, there are 2^4 or 16 possible distinct patterns of correct and error responses, each associated with a possible value of Y. In Chapter 3, we found that a *tree diagram* is a useful way to enumerate all possible sequences of trial outcomes. Fig. 3.1 diagramed the sequences for our four-trial experiment and Table 4.1 summarizes those patterns. The 16 possible sequences of trial outcomes may be considered elementary events that partition the sample space for the experiment.

Table 4.1 Possible patterns of correct (C) and error (E) responses for four trials; the subscripts denote the trial numbers

Pattern	Number correct (Y)
$<E_1\,E_2\,E_3\,E_4>$	0
$<E_1\,E_2\,E_3\,C_4>$	1
$<E_1\,E_2\,C_3\,E_4>$	1
$<E_1\,C_2\,E_3\,E_4>$	1
$<C_1\,E_2\,E_3\,E_4>$	1
$<E_1\,E_2\,C_3\,C_4>$	2
$<E_1\,C_2\,E_3\,C_4>$	2
$<E_1\,C_2\,C_3\,E_4>$	2
$<C_1\,E_2\,E_3\,C_4>$	2
$<C_1\,E_2\,C_3\,E_4>$	2
$<C_1\,C_2\,E_3\,E_4>$	2
$<C_1\,C_2\,C_3\,E_4>$	3
$<C_1\,C_2\,E_3\,C_4>$	3
$<C_1\,E_2\,C_3\,C_4>$	3
$<E_1\,C_2\,C_3\,C_4>$	3
$<C_1\,C_2\,C_3\,C_4>$	4

Having specified the structure of the sample space for the experiment, we want to use our analysis to compute the probability of each possible value of Y. The probability distribution for Y is obtained by using a *statistical model*, which is a set of assumptions about how the responses are generated that can be used to calculate the probabilities. In the current example, a desirable model would be one that captures the essential features of what we mean by random guessing and allows us to calculate the probability of each possible value of Y. We employ the following model for the simplified ESP experiment:

1.   The probability of a correct response, π, is .25 on each trial.[1]
2.   The responses are *independent* of one another; that is, the probability of a correct response on any trial does not depend on the outcomes of any other trials.

The first assumption is based on the fact that Rachel chooses from among four equally likely card values. The independence assumption seems reasonable because each card is replaced in the pack after each trial, the cards are well shuffled, and the selection of each card is done at random. The result on each trial should not be influenced by the outcome of any previous trial.

Given these assumptions, we can apply the multiplicative law to compute the probability of each sequence of trial outcomes because each sequence corresponds to a joint event. We assume trial outcomes are independent, so the probability of any sequence may be found by multiplying probabilities. The probability of the sequence $<C_1\ C_2\ C_3\ C_4> = (.25)(.25)(.25)(.25) = .0039$. The probability of the sequence $<E_1\ E_2\ E_3\ E_4> = (.75)(.75)(.75)(.75) = .3164$. The probability of each single sequence corresponding to one correct and three errors is $(.25)(.75)(.75)(.75) = .1055$. However, there are four distinct sequences corresponding to the outcome of one correct in four trials, so the probability of observing one correct is greater than .1055. The four sequences are mutually exclusive and we are interested in any one of them occurring, so the additive law may be used to compute the probability of the compound event. Summing up the probabilities of the four possible sequences gives us a value of .4220 for the probability of one correct in four trials. By the same approach, we can compute that the probability of two correct in four trials is .2109, and the probability of three correct in four trials is .0469.

We have now translated our hypothesis that Rachel is guessing into a distribution that represents the probability of each possible outcome of our four-trial experiment if Rachel does, indeed, guess on each trial. That probability distribution is summarized graphically in Fig. 4.1.

Keep in mind why the probability distribution presented in Fig. 4.1 is useful: In order to decide whether the responses were produced by guessing, we have to get some idea of what to expect if they were, in fact, produced by guessing. The probability distribution we generated is a *theoretical* probability distribution because it was generated on the basis of a statistical model. Here, our statistical model is a theory about the patterns of responses that would be produced by guessing. If the assumptions we made are valid and if we performed many random replications of the ESP experiment, then in .3164 of the experiments there would be zero correct responses; in .4220 of the experiments there would be one correct response; and so on. In short, the proportions of experiments yielding various values of Y would match the theoretical probability values in Fig. 4.1.

---

[1] We will use π (the Greek letter *pi*) to represent the proportion of correct responses in the population from which the sample was selected and p to represent the proportion of correct responses in the sample. We often use Greek letters to represent population parameters and Latin letters to represent sample statistics in order to lessen confusion between them.

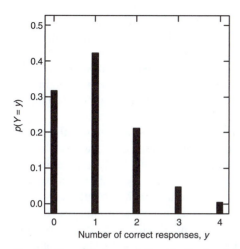

Fig. 4.1 Theoretical probability distribution for the number of correct responses, Y, with $n = 4$ and $p(C) = .25$.

The idea of repeating an experiment many times and obtaining the value of some statistic from each experiment is basic to the inferential procedures described throughout this book. The idea is important enough to summarize the general steps:

1. A model is formulated.
2. On the basis of this model, we obtain the theoretical distribution of a statistic of interest given many repetitions of the experiment. This is the *sampling distribution* of the statistic.
3. The sampling distribution is then used together with the collected data to draw inferences about the population.

How can we use the theoretical sampling distribution (Fig. 4.1) to evaluate the hypothesis that Rachel is guessing on each trial (i.e., $\pi = .25$)? We are interested in knowing whether Rachel actually has ESP, which would mean that the true probability of her making a correct response is really greater than .25. Therefore, a finding that Rachel is correct more than 25% of the time would be evidence supporting the ESP hypothesis over the guessing hypothesis. But how much better than 25% correct must Rachel be before we conclude that she is not just guessing? One possible decision rule is to conclude that the population probability is greater than .25 if two or more responses in the sample (i.e., at least 50%) are correct. However, this is not a very good rule because from Fig. 4.1 we see that it would not be surprising to get at least two correct responses simply by guessing. The probability of two or three or four correct responses if $\pi = .25$ is $(.2109 + .0469 + .0039) = .2617$. That is, even if Rachel is just guessing, there is greater than one chance in four of getting at least two correct responses in the four trials. A better rule would be to require that all four responses be correct before concluding that something besides random guessing was going on. Four correct responses could also occur just by random guessing, but this is much less likely. According to our guessing model, the probability of correct responses on all four trials is only .0039. Therefore, if all four responses are correct, either the subject is guessing and an unlikely event has occurred, or the value of π in the population of responses is really greater than .25.

We can now summarize the rationale underlying hypothesis testing. If in the context of a particular experiment we wish to examine the hypothesis that only chance is involved, a model of chance performance is used to generate a sampling distribution. There are certain outcomes, consistent with an alternative hypothesis (e.g., that the probability of a correct response is above the chance level), that will be very unlikely if the model is valid. If one of these outcomes is obtained in the experiment, we will conclude that the model is not valid and that something other than chance is involved.

We have developed a simple example of an experiment for the purposes of sketching the role of a sampling distribution in the process of evaluating a specific hypothesis. The example that we used—a four-trial experiment in which Rachel guessed among four equally likely alternatives—is one specific example from a much more general class of experiments. If we had chosen to do a 20-trial experiment and changed the experimental procedure to require Rachel to guess among 10 alternatives, it should be obvious that we would need to specify a new sampling distribution to describe the possible outcomes for this more ambitious experiment. However, the approach to deriving the appropriate sampling distribution would be the same as that illustrated for our simpler experiment. We turn now to the task of generalizing our approach.

4.3 THE BINOMIAL DISTRIBUTION

Fig. 4.1 presents the probability distribution for the number of correct responses when there are four trials ($n = 4$) and the probability of a correct response on each trial is .25 ($\pi = .25$). For different values of n and π we could always find the desired probabilities by drawing the appropriate tree diagram and applying the multiplicative and additive laws. A tree diagram is very helpful for understanding the probability calculation; however, using a tree diagram quickly becomes very tedious as the sample size, n, increases.[2] It is useful to have a general formula for the probability distribution given any combination of n and π. This general formula is developed in the next two sections.

4.3.1 Basic Assumptions

We are interested in developing a formula that will give us a way to derive the sampling distribution for any experiment with the same general characteristics. The following assumptions about a series of n trials constitute a statistical model that will produce a binomial distribution:

1. On each trial there are exactly *two* possible outcomes; examples might be correct/error, success/failure, head/tail, or live/die. The two outcomes possible on each trial might be referred to as A and $\tilde{A}$ with probabilities π and $1 - \pi$, respectively.
2. The value of π stays the same over trials.
3. Trials are independent. The probability of an outcome of any trial does not depend on the outcome of any other trial.

---

[2] With four trials each with two possible outcomes, the tree diagram consists of $2^4 = 16$ branches. With 20 trials, there would be $2^{20} = 1,048,576$ branches.

4.3.2 The Binomial Function

Here, we develop a formula for calculating the probability of y responses as a function of n and π. We denote the binomial probability function by $p(y; n, \pi)$ to indicate that it is the probability of obtaining y responses of type A when there are n trials with $p(A) = \pi$ on each trial.

Table 4.1 presents the 16 possible sequences for a four-trial experiment.[3] Suppose we wish to find the probability of obtaining exactly three A responses in four trials. Assuming that the responses A and $\tilde{A}$ are independently distributed over trials, the multiplication rule developed earlier can be used to calculate the probability for each combination of A and $\tilde{A}$ responses. For example, the probability of the combination $<A, A, A, \tilde{A}>$ would be $(\pi)(\pi)(\pi)(1 - \pi)$ or $\pi^3(1 - \pi)$.

But there are four combinations with three As and one $\tilde{A}$, so that $p(3, 4, \pi)$, the probability of exactly three A responses in four trials, is equal to $p(<\tilde{A}, A, A, A>$ or $<A, \tilde{A}, A, A>$ or $<A, A, \tilde{A}, A>$ or $<A, A, A, \tilde{A}>)$. These four combinations are mutually exclusive (i.e., only one of them will occur in a single, four-trial experiment in which there are three A responses and one $\tilde{A}$ response). Therefore, the probability of three A responses and one $\tilde{A}$ response in any order is the sum of the probabilities of these four combinations, or $4\pi^3(1 - \pi)$. In general, to find the probability of having y A responses, we calculate the probability of a combination having y A responses and then multiply by the number of such combinations.

The approach can be generalized to any value of n. If we can assume independence, the probability of any one specific combination of y A responses and $n - y$ $\tilde{A}$ responses is $\pi^y(1 - \pi)^{n-y}$. The probability of exactly y A responses and $n - y$ $\tilde{A}$ responses is

$$p(y; n, \pi) = k\pi^y (1 - \pi)^{n-y} \tag{4.1}$$

where k is the number of combinations consisting of y A and $n - y$ $\tilde{A}$ responses.

We just about have our binomial function; all we still need is a formula for k, the number of ways in which y A and $(n - y)$ $\tilde{A}$ responses can be combined. This number of combinations can be shown to be (see Appendix 4.1):

$$k = \binom{n}{y} = \frac{n!}{y!(n-y)!} \tag{4.2}$$

where $n! = (n)(n - 1)(n - 2) \ldots (3)(2)(1)$ and $0! = 1$. Note that

$$\binom{n}{y} \text{ and } \binom{n}{n-y}$$

have the same value. Substituting $y = 0, 1, 2, 3,$ and 4 in turn into Equation 4.2, verify that k takes on the values 1, 4, 6, 4, and 1, respectively; these are the numbers of combinations that appear in Table 4.1. Replacing k in Equation 4.1 with the expression on the right side of Equation 4.2 yields the binomial probability function:

$$p(y; n, \pi) = \binom{n}{y}\pi^y(1 - \pi)^{n-y} = \frac{n!}{y!(n-y)!}\pi^y(1 - \pi)^{n-y} \tag{4.3}$$

---

[3] Note that the trial outcomes need not come from the same individual as they do in our ESP example. For example, each A or $\tilde{A}$ could represent a single success or failure by n different participants on a single trial. Then each pattern would represent a possible set of outcomes for the n subjects and π would be the proportion of correct responses in the population from which the sample of subjects was selected. From now on, we will use the more general term *combination* to refer to a pattern of A and $\tilde{A}$ responses.

Equation 4.3 describes a family of distributions, with a different probability distribution for each distinct combination of values of π and n. Table C.1 in Appendix C presents specific binomial distributions for selected values of π and n. We will restrict our examples to situations that are described by the distributions in Table C.1 to save ourselves the trouble of computing binomial distributions from scratch.

Now we can calculate the probabilities of various outcomes in the ESP experiment if Rachel was generating responses by random guessing. If $n = 20$ and $\pi = .25$, we can find the probability of, say, seven or more correct responses. In Table C.1, we first find the part of the table that corresponds to $n = 20$, and then we use the column corresponding to $p = .25$. Reading from the table, we see that $p(Y = 0) = .0032$, $p(Y = 1) = .0211$, $p(Y = 2) = .0669$, and so on. These are the same values that would be obtained using Equation 4.3. We can find the probability of seven or more responses in several ways. One way is to find the probabilities for 7, 8, 9, …, 20 correct and add these 14 numbers together. The other is to find the probabilities of 0, 1, 2, …, 6 correct, add these seven numbers together, and then subtract the sum from 1. The probability of getting 0–6 correct responses is $.0032 + .0211 + .0669 + .1339 + .1897 + .2023 + .1686 = .7852$. So the probability of seven or more correct responses must be $1 - .7852 = .2143$. We see that a result of seven correct responses in 20 tries is not very convincing evidence that Rachel was doing anything other than randomly guessing on each trial because there would be better than 2 chances in 10 of getting at least seven correct just by guessing. However, if Rachel got, say, 13 correct responses in 20 trials, we could pretty much rule out the random guessing model, because we can see from Table C.1 that there is only a probability of about .0002 (two chances in 10,000) of getting 13 or more correct responses by random guessing.

4.3.3 What Happens When n and π Change?

Fig. 4.2 presents several binomial distributions for various values of n and π. For easier comparisons across different values of n, the outcome probability is plotted as a function of the proportion of A responses in the sample, $P = Y/n$. For example, when $n = 10$ and $\pi = .5$, we expect to observe 40% correct responding (four A responses in 10 trials) with probability .2051. In the long run (i.e., if the experiment were repeated many times), the proportion of experiments with four A and six $\tilde{A}$ responses should equal .2051, if the binomial model is correct. Several points should be noted about these distributions. First, when $\pi = .5$, the distributions are more symmetric than for values closer to 0 or to 1. Second, when $\pi = .25$ and skewness (asymmetry) is present, as n increases, the distribution becomes more symmetric about the value of $P = Y/n$ that corresponds to π. Third, the distributions appear more continuous in form as n increases. These observations are important because if n is sufficiently large, particularly when π is close to .5, the binomial distribution looks much like the normal distribution, which then can be used to get binomial probabilities with considerably easier calculations.

A fourth point to note about Fig. 4.2 is that the probability of getting a value of Y/n close to π increases as n increases. This illustrates Bernoulli's theorem in action. For example, consider the probability that Y/n lies in the range from .4 to .6; that is, $p(.4 \geq Y/n \geq .6)$ when π is actually .5. When n is 10, $p(.4 \geq Y/n \geq .6)$ is the probability that $Y = 4$, 5, or 6, which is $.2051 + .2461 + .2051$, or .6563. When n is 20, $p(.4 \geq Y/n \geq .6)$ is the probability that $Y = 8$, 9, 10, 11, or 12, which is $.1201 + .1602 + .1762 + .1602 + .1201$, or .7368. When n is 40, the probability is .8461. This point is very important; it means that as n grows larger, the proportion of A responses observed in a single experiment is more likely to be close to the proportion of A responses in the population. We prefer larger data sets to smaller ones not because of some deeply ingrained work ethic; we do so because larger data sets

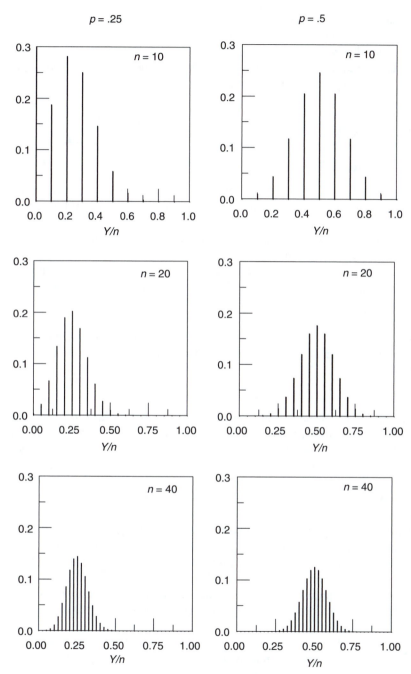

Fig. 4.2 Binomial distributions as a function of sample size and probability.

are more likely to produce sample statistics that are closer to the corresponding population parameters. Statistics that have a higher probability of being within any fixed range of the population parameter as *n* increases are called *consistent* estimators of the parameter. We will have more to say about this desirable property of sample statistics, and about other properties important to estimating population parameters, in Chapter 5.

4.4 HYPOTHESIS TESTING

4.4.1 What Is a Hypothesis Test?

Having derived the binomial distribution as a family of sampling distributions that characterizes a general domain of experiments, we move on to formally develop a general procedure for testing hypotheses.

A hypothesis test consists of a set of procedures to determine whether a sample of collected data provides sufficient evidence to reject some hypothesis of no effect in the population, often called the *null hypothesis* (H_0). In the ESP example, the null hypothesis is that Rachel is guessing or, more formally, that the true probability of a correct guess is .25. We represent this hypothesis as

$$H_0: \pi = .25$$

In contrast to the null hypothesis is the *alternative hypothesis* (H_1), which is motivated by the claim that Rachel has ESP and therefore the probability of a correct response is higher than chance. We represent this hypothesis as

$$H_1: \pi > .25$$

In our 20-trial experiment, the experimenter randomly chooses among four cards on each trial and Rachel attempts to identify each card without seeing it. We consider the sample of 20 responses to be a random sample selected from the hypothetical population of responses that characterizes Rachel's ESP ability. Our estimate of the probability of a correct response in the population is the proportion of correct responses in the sample, $P = Y/n$. We can use our estimate as evidence to evaluate the null hypothesis because we can generate the probabilities of possible outcomes assuming that the null hypothesis is true. If we assume that the null hypothesis is true and that trials are independent, Y should have a binomial distribution. Letting $n = 20$ and $\pi = .25$ (the value if H_0 is true) in Equation 4.3, we can generate the values of $p(Y = y)$ found in the $\pi = .25$ column of Table 4.2.

Next, we determine whether our sample of data provides sufficient evidence to reject H_0 in favor of H_1. There are two closely related but slightly different procedures for doing this, the "*p*-value" and the "rejection region" approach. Box 4.1 summarizes the steps following the *p*-value approach; Box 4.2 summarizes the steps following the rejection region approach. We illustrate each approach for our 20-trial ESP experiment.

We have already done much of the work required for a hypothesis test; namely, we have completed the first three steps in the process. To summarize:

1. Our hypotheses are: $H_0: \pi = .25$, $H_1: \pi > .25$.
2. Our test statistic is the number of correct guesses, Y.
3. Assuming that the probability of a correct response remains constant over the 20 trials and that the trial outcomes are independent, our test statistic, Y, will follow a binomial distribution with $n = 20$ and $\pi = .25$, as presented in Table 4.2.

Table 4.2 The binomial distribution for $n = 20$, and $\pi = .25$, .35, and .50

Number correct y	$p(Y = y)$		
	$\pi = .25$	$\pi = .35$	$\pi = .50$
0	.0032	.0002	.0000
1	.0211	.0020	.0000
2	.0669	.0100	.0002
3	.1339	.0323	.0011
4	.1897	.0738	.0046
5	.2023	.1272	.0148
6	.1686	.1712	.0370
7	.1124	.1844	.0739
8	.0609	.1614	.1201
9	.0271	.1158	.1602
10	.0099	.0686	.1762
11	.0030	.0336	.1602
12	.0008	.0136	.1201
13	.0002	.0045	.0739
14	.0000	.0012	.0370
15	.0000	.0003	.0148
16	.0000	.0000	.0046
17	.0000	.0000	.0011
18	.0000	.0000	.0002
19	.0000	.0000	.0000
20	.0000	.0000	.0000

Box 4.1 Steps for Testing Hypotheses Using the *p*-Value Approach

1. State the null and alternative hypotheses, H_0 and H_1.
2. Decide on the *test statistic* that will be used to assess the evidence against H_0.
3. Decide, making reasonable assumptions, what *sampling distribution* the test statistic should have if H_0 is true.
4. Decide on the *significance level* that will be used as the criterion for deciding whether or not to reject the null hypothesis. We will reject H_0 only if our result is very unlikely under the assumption that H_0 is true. The significance level (denoted by α, the Greek letter alpha) specifies exactly how unlikely the result must be.
5. Use the sampling distribution that assumes H_0 is true to find the probability of getting a value for the statistic that is at least as "extreme" as what was actually obtained in our sample of data— call this probability the *p-value*. In finding the *p*-value, use only the part or parts of the sampling distribution that are consistent with H_1.
6. Reject H_0 in favor of H_1 if $p \leq \alpha$. If we reject H_0, we say that our result is "statistically significant at level α." If $p > \alpha$, we say that we have failed to reject H_0 or that we have insufficient evidence to reject H_0.

Box 4.2 Steps for Testing Hypotheses Using the Rejection Region (or Critical Region) Approach

Steps 1–4 are the same as for the *p*-value approach of Box 4.1.

5. Identify values of the test statistic that would constitute the most convincing support for the *alternative* hypothesis. Using the sampling distribution that assumes H_0 is true, determine the set of those values whose cumulative probability equals α. Call the part of the distribution that is beyond the critical value the *rejection region* or *critical region*. Call the value of the test statistic that demarcates the boundary of the rejection region from the rest of the sampling distribution the *critical value* of the test statistic.
6. Reject the H_0 in favor of H_1 if the value of the test statistic falls in the rejection region.

Next, according to both approaches, we must decide on an appropriate significance level, the criterion for how unlikely a result must be if the null hypothesis is true, before we are willing to reject the null hypothesis. In theory, the significance level, α, may be set at different values, and the value chosen for a particular situation may depend on a variety of considerations. For example, in a pilot experiment, a researcher may select a relatively lenient criterion, perhaps $\alpha = .10$. In contrast, if the efficacy of some new drug treatment is being tested against an established drug that has already been proven effective, a researcher might decide on a stringent criterion before rejecting the old treatment in favor of the new, perhaps $\alpha = .001$. In practice, only relatively small values of α are considered; generally, $\alpha = .05$ or less.

The remaining steps are as follows:

4. We will select a significance level of $\alpha = .05$.
   It is at this point that the two hypothesis-testing approaches diverge. According to the *p*-value approach in Box 4.1, we next conduct our experiment and convert our observed result into its corresponding *p*-value. For example, suppose that our experimental result is seven correct responses in 20 trials. The *p*-value is the probability of observing a result at least as extreme as seven assuming that the null hypothesis is true. This corresponds to the conditional probability $p(Y \geq 7 | \pi = .25)$.
5. Using the $\pi = .25$ column of Table 4.2, we see $p(Y \geq 7 | \pi = .25)$ equals $.1124 + .0609 + 0271 + .0099 + .0030 + .0008 + .0002 + 0 = .2143$.
6. Comparing the *p*-value to α, we fail to reject H_0 because the *p*-value of .2143 is not less than or equal to $\alpha = .05$.

Because statistical packages display *p*-values in their outputs, it is probably most natural to think about hypothesis testing in terms of *p*-values. However, the alternative approach of framing hypothesis tests in terms of rejection regions makes it easier to think about important concepts such as statistical power (see Section 4.5). Thus, we illustrate the approach summarized in Box 4.2 for the same example.

In determining the rejection region for a hypothesis test, we must first identify the types of outcomes that would favor the alternative hypothesis because we never reject the null unless the alternative provides a better account of the data. In our example, the alternative hypothesis claims that $\pi > .25$, so it predicts that Rachel will make more correct choices than expected by chance. The outcome that would be the most convincing support for the alternative would be 20 correct guesses in the 20-trial experiment, 19 correct would be pretty convincing, and 18 correct would be a little less so; in short, we will consider rejecting the null hypothesis only if Rachel makes lots of correct responses. Our goal is to specify the range of number of correct responses that (a) would be consistent with the alternative hypothesis, but (b) very unlikely under the null hypothesis. Our significance level guides our determination of the appropriate rejection region. Using the sampling distribution specified by the null hypothesis (i.e., the $\pi = .25$ column of Table 4.2), we sum the probabilities beginning at the bottom of the column (i.e., 20 correct, 19 correct, etc.). We cumulate the probabilities at the upper tail of the distribution until the cumulative probability is as close to α as possible, without exceeding it. In our example, if H_0 is true, the probability that Y has a value of 9 or greater is $p(Y \geq 9) = .0271 + .0099 + .0030 + .0008 + .0002 + 0 = .0410$. We call the part of the distribution for which $Y \geq 9$ the "rejection region" because we will reject H_0 if the test statistic, Y, falls in this region. Therefore, our decision rule for this experiment is to reject H_0 if nine or more responses are correct. Given the value $Y = 7$ in our sample, we fail to reject H_0 because this value of Y does not fall in the rejection region. In this example, the rejection region actually consists of the uppermost .041 of the distribution, so, in effect, we have specified that $\alpha = .041$. Because Y is a discrete variable, we cannot find a value of Y that cuts off exactly .05 of the distribution.

Several important points should be noted about the logic of hypothesis testing. First, a statistically significant result means that a value of the test statistic has occurred that is very unlikely if H_0 is true. However, "unlikely" is not the same as "impossible," and we may sometimes reject a null hypothesis even when it is true. Such incorrect rejections of the null hypothesis are called *Type 1 errors*. The significance level α is the probability of such errors; that is, $\alpha = p(\text{reject } H_0 | H_0 \text{ true})$, the conditional probability of rejecting H_0 given that H_0 is true. A useful way to conceptualize this is that if the responses were generated by random guessing (H_0 true), and if we were to replicate the experiment many times, we can expect to obtain $Y \geq 9$ in .041 of these experiments. If we obtain Y greater than or equal to 9 when H_0 is true, we will incorrectly reject H_0. By setting α at a particular level, we specify the level of risk of a Type 1 error that we are willing to tolerate.

Two types of errors are often made in interpreting p-values. First, the p-value is the probability of the observed data given that the null hypothesis is true, or $p(\text{observed data} | H_0 \text{ true})$. However, it is common to confuse this conditional probability with its opposite, $p(H_0 \text{ true} | \text{observed data})$, the probability that the null hypothesis is true given the results of the experiment. This is not correct. It would be nice if a significance test gave us the probability that H_0 was true, but it does not.

The second error that researchers often make is to interpret p-values as measures of effect size. For instance, if a test of an effect produces a smaller p-value in Experiment A than in Experiment B, it is sometimes asserted that the effect is larger or more important in Experiment A. This is also not correct: p-values convey useful information, but they depend on sample size and variability as well as effect size, so direct comparisons of p-values are rarely useful. This is one reason why we will present ways to find confidence intervals and estimate effect sizes in the following chapters.

4.4.2 One- and Two-Tailed Tests

The test we just discussed is an example of a *one-tailed* or *directional* test. Because we were interested in whether performance was *better* than chance, the rejection region consisted of only the largest possible values of Y (the upper tail of the binomial distribution). Not all hypothesis tests are directional. There are many situations in which a departure from the null hypothesis in either direction would be of interest. For example, in the case of Royer's data on arithmetic skills (see Chapter 2), we might wish to know whether there is a significant difference in performance for arithmetic and subtraction; if there was, it might influence the way in which these skills were taught.

To test for a difference, we could assign a plus to each student who had a higher addition than subtraction score and a minus to each student who had a higher subtraction score. Then we could ask whether the probability of a plus (or a minus) was significantly *different from* .5. A result in either direction (i.e., addition better than subtraction or subtraction better than addition) would be of interest. As another example, University of Massachusetts medical school researchers collected data on seasonal variation in clinical states such as depression and anxiety. Comparing depression scores in winter and summer, we might assign a plus if the winter score was higher, and a minus if it was lower. In both of these examples, H_0 would be

$$H_0: \pi = .5$$

The alternative hypothesis would be

$$H_1: \pi \neq .5$$

In this case, H_1 is nondirectional; that is, we will reject H_0 if we find strong evidence that π is greater than *or* is less than .5. We may want α to be .05, but now the rejection region is split in two—half in the upper tail and half in the lower tail of the distribution. Suppose n is again 20. Turning to the column labeled $\pi = .50$ in Table 4.2, assuming equal weight is given to both directions, and that α is to be close to .05, H_0 would be rejected if $Y \leq 5$ *or* $Y \geq 15$. This is usually referred to as a *two-tailed* or *nondirectional* test. Note that if we use these rejection regions, the actual probability of a Type 1 error is $.021 + .021 = .042$. If we found $Y = 16$, we would reject H_0 because the statistic falls in the rejection region. What is the p-value? Using Table 4.2, we find $p(Y \geq 16 | \pi = .50) = .0046 + .0011 + .0002 + 0 = .0059$. But because H_1 is nondirectional, we must also consider equally extreme results in the lower tail of the distribution, so that the p-value is equal to $p(Y \geq 16 | \pi = .50) + p(Y \leq 4 | \pi = .50) = 2 \times .0059 = .0118$. The procedure we have just outlined (using the binomial distribution to test the hypothesis $H_0: \pi = .50$) is called the *sign test*.

4.5 THE POWER OF A STATISTICAL TEST

4.5.1 Errors in Decision Making

In deciding to reject or not to reject a null hypothesis, we can make two types of errors. If the null hypothesis is true, rejecting it is called a *Type 1 error*. As we have just discussed, the probability of a Type 1 error is α, the significance level. If the null hypothesis is false, we can make a different kind of error by failing to reject it. Failure to reject a null hypothesis when it is false is called a *Type 2 error*, and its probability, p(fail to reject $H_0 | H_0$ is false), is referred to as β (Greek letter beta). The complementary conditional probability, that is, p(reject $H_0 | H_0$ is false), is called the *power* of the test. When H_0 is false, only two decisions are possible: fail to reject it (with probability β) or reject it (with probability $1 - \beta$). Therefore, power $= 1 - \beta$.

The following table may help to clarify the meanings of α, β, and power:

	Decision	
H_0	Reject	Fail to reject
H_0 True	α	$1 - \alpha$
H_0 False	power $= 1 - \beta$	β

The rows represent two mutually exclusive events: H_0 is either true or false. Given either of these events, the researcher may make one of two mutually exclusive decisions: reject or fail to reject H_0. The cell probabilities are conditional probabilities representing the probability of the decision given the event. Because one of the two decisions must be made, the probabilities in each row sum to 1.

4.5.2 Computing Power

Power is a conditional probability: it is the probability of rejecting the null hypothesis when the null hypothesis is wrong. Thus, the first step in computing power is to determine the conditions under which the null hypothesis will be rejected (see Box 4.2). Once the rejection region for H_0 is found, we must compute the probability of observing a result in the rejection region assuming that H_0 is wrong and that some alternative hypothesis, H_A, is correct. It is important to be clear about the distinction between H_1 and H_A. H_1 is the class of alternative hypotheses which determines where the rejection region is placed (right or left tail, or in both tails). In contrast, H_A is a *specific alternative hypothesis*; power is calculated for the test of H_0 assuming H_A to be true. Of course, the true value of the population parameter is never known. However, if some value of the parameter is assumed, the power of the test against that alternative can be calculated.

Let's illustrate the calculation of power for our ESP experiment. Suppose we wish to test H_0: $\pi = .25$ against the alternative hypothesis H_1: $\pi > .25$. Further, let's assume that Rachel has rather weak ESP abilities; more specifically, we will assume that her abilities will permit her to correctly choose the identity of a card 35% of the time. In this example, this is our *specific alternative hypothesis*,

$$H_A: \pi = .35$$

The H_0 and H_A specify different sampling distributions for our experiment, as illustrated in Fig. 4.3. Our example assumes that H_A correctly describes the probabilities of different possible

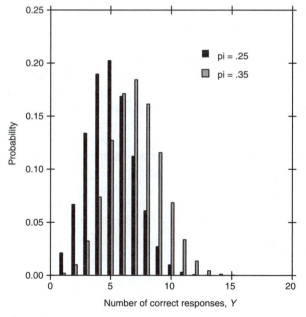

Fig. 4.3 Binomial distributions for Y for $\pi = .25$ and $\pi = .35$ with $n = 20$.

Box 4.3 Steps in Computing the Power of a Test

1. Determine the theoretical sampling distribution of Y assuming H_0 to be true.
2. Determine the rejection region.
3. Assume that the null hypothesis is incorrect and that some specific alternative hypothesis, H_A, is correct.
4. Compute the probability of a result in the rejection region using the sampling distribution specified by the alternative hypothesis. The resulting value is the conditional probability of observing an outcome in the rejection region given that H_A is true. This is the *power* of the test.

---

outcomes for the experiment, but the extensive overlap between the two distributions means that the two hypotheses will not be easy to discriminate empirically. Thus, we can expect that power will be low.

The general steps in computing power are the same for all statistical tests. These steps are summarized in Box 4.3. Applying this procedure to our example:

1. Calculate the theoretical sampling distribution of Y assuming H_0 to be true. In this example, the distribution is presented in the .25 column of Table 4.2.
2. Determine the rejection region. In this example ($n = 20$, $\alpha = .05$, H_1: $\pi > .25$), the rejection region is $Y \geq 9$.
3. Calculate the probability distribution of Y assuming H_A is true. In this example, π in Equation 4.3 is replaced by .35. The results are presented in the $\pi = .35$ column of Table 4.2.
4. Sum the probabilities for $Y \geq 9$ (the rejection region) in the .35 column. This sum is the conditional probability $p(Y \geq 9 \mid H_A = .35)$ and is the power of the test of H_0 against H_A. In this case, power $= .1158 + .0686 + .0336 + .0136 + .0045 + .0012 + .0003 = .2376$.

These calculations mean that a test of H_0: $\pi = .25$ has .238 probability of yielding a significant result if π is actually .35. Stated in terms of the probability that the experimental results will lead to a wrong conclusion, the probability of a Type 2 error, β, is $1 - .238$, or .762. As anticipated, our experiment does not have a very good chance of discriminating H_0 from the assumed true state of the world, H_A.

Power is one of the most difficult concepts for students to grasp—probably because so many different things have to be kept in mind. It is necessary to consider two sampling distributions (those specified by H_0 and H_A), as well as the information provided by H_1 and α. To find the rejection region for the test, we start with the sampling distribution that assumes H_0 is true. We then need α to tell us how big the rejection region is, and we need H_1 to tell us where it is. Power is just the proportion of the sampling distribution specified by H_A that falls in the rejection region.

4.5.3 Factors Affecting Power

Fig. 4.4 presents the power of the binomial test of H_0: $\pi = .50$ against several alternatives. The power functions have been plotted for three conditions: (1) $n = 20$, $\alpha = .15$; (2) $n = 20$, $\alpha = .06$; and (3) $n = 15$, $\alpha = .06$; Π_A represents specific alternative values of π. The top panel presents power when the alternative is one-tailed, and the bottom panel presents power when the alternative is two-tailed. Four points should be noted that are typical of power functions for all statistical tests:

1. *Power increases as the effect size increases.* If H_0: $\pi = .25$ and H_1: $\pi > .25$, Y is more likely to fall in the rejection region the larger the true value of π. This is illustrated in Fig. 4.4 by the fact that the curves rise as the value of Π_A increases and becomes increasingly different from the null-hypothesis value of π.
2. *Power increases as α increases.* This is because an increase in α means the size of the rejection region becomes larger. For example, when $n = 20$ and the alternative is one-tailed, the rejection region increases from $Y \geq 14$ to $Y \geq 13$ as α increases from .06 to .15. Because power is also calculated for this larger set of Y values, it too becomes larger.
3. *Power is affected by whether or not H_1 is directional.* Compare the curves in the top panel of Fig. 4.4 to the right-hand side of the corresponding curves in the bottom panel. Notice that the curves in the top panel begin to rise sooner, and rise faster, than the curves in the

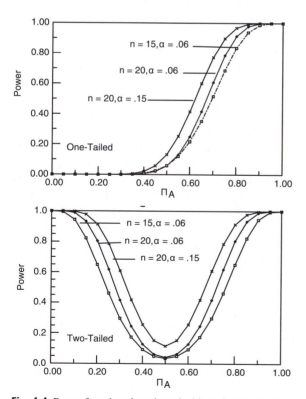

Fig. 4.4 Power functions based on the binomial distribution.

bottom panel. This illustrates that a one-tailed test has more power than the corresponding two-tailed test whenever π is greater than .5. This is because the rejection region is concentrated in that tail of the distribution in the case of the one-tailed test, whereas it is divided in half and distributed over the two tails in the case of the two-tailed test. On the other hand, the one-tailed test has virtually no power against specific alternatives of the form $\pi < .5$, whereas the two-tailed test does have power to reject H_0 against these alternatives. In short, a one-tailed test has more power than a two-tailed test if—and only if—the directional hypothesis is correct.

4.   *Power increases as n increases.* Compare the two curves for $\alpha = .06$ in either panel and note that the $n = 20$ curve rises more rapidly than the $n = 15$. This demonstrates the effect of n on power and it follows from our discussion of the fact that Y/n is a consistent estimator of π. Recall that the property of consistency (see Section 4.3.3) means that as n increases, Y/n is more likely to be close to the true value of the parameter. Therefore, if H_0 is false, it is more likely that the data will demonstrate that as n increases.

4.5.4 The Usefulness of Power Calculations

For several reasons, it is important for researchers to understand and be able to calculate power. First, there may be different statistical tests of the same H_0. Assuming that the choice among tests is not dictated by some other factor (such as validity of assumptions, ease of calculations, or availability of tables or software), the test with the greater power should be chosen. Second, the effects of violations of assumptions on power functions can be assessed. Finally, and most important, the relationship between power and sample size can be used to decide how much data should be collected. For example, suppose we want power of at least .90 to reject H_0 if π is at least .35. We can derive power functions for various values of n similar to those depicted in Fig. 4.4. The n we want for our study is the one that gives rise to a power function such that there is an ordinate value (power) of at least .90 when the abscissa value (π) is .35.

The last point deserves further comment. The null hypothesis is almost always false. If we collect enough data, we are likely to obtain statistically significant results. Whether the results will be of practical importance or theoretical significance is another matter. The effect may be trivially small, or in a direction that makes no sense in terms of any theory, or practical concern. Therefore, it makes good sense before we collect data to ask the following questions: What is the smallest size effect that would be of interest and what power do we want to detect (i.e., find significance for) such an effect? The answer to these two questions will be major factors in determining the sample size for our research. Sometimes the required n will be impractically large and we will have to compromise, have less power, and/or target a larger effect; or we may be able to redesign the research so that a smaller sample will achieve the desired power against the specific alternative hypothesis we had in mind.

Suppose we wish to test H_0: $\pi = .25$ against H_1: $\pi > .25$, with $\alpha = .05$. If we have reason to believe that $\pi = .35$ or if we are only interested in the effect of π if it is at least .35, how large a sample do we need to have, say, a power of .8? Some statistical packages will do these power calculations for many statistical tests. A very convenient and flexible power program is G*Power 3 (Faul, Erdfelder, Lang, & Buchner, 2007).[4] To perform the power computation, open G*Power 3 and select *Exact* as the *Test family*, then select *Proportions: Difference from Constant (one sample*

---

[4] Versions of G*Power 3 are available on the Internet at http://www.psycho.uni-duesseldorf.de/abteilungen/aap/gpower3/download-and-register

case) as the *Statistical test*. Then, for *Type of power analysis*, select *A priori: Compute required sample size—given α, power, and effect size*. Here, the constant proportion is .25; the effect size, *g*, is .35 − .25 = .10; and α = .05. We want the power to be .80, and we have a one-tailed test. Insert these values, and then click the *Calculate* button in the lower right of the dialog box. The results are displayed in Fig. 4.5. We see that we need a sample size of 129 (i.e., 129 trials) to get the desired power.

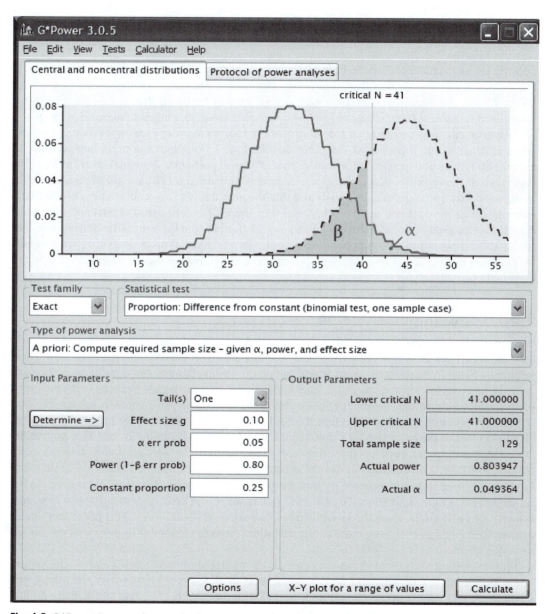

Fig. 4.5 G*Power 3 output for sample size necessary to have power = .80 given H_0: π = .25, H_1: π > .25, and H_A: π = .35.

The figure at the top of the results box deserves some explanation: The distribution on the left is the binomial for $n = 129$ and $\pi = .25$ and has a mean of $n\pi = (129)(.25) = 32.25$. The distribution on the right is for $\pi = .35$ and has a mean of $(129)(.35) = 45.15$. The critical N of 41 informs us that if we get 41 or more correct in 129 trials, we can reject the null hypothesis at $\alpha = .05$. We can also use G*Power 3 to show that if we had only 20 trials, the power to reject $\pi = .25$ is only .2376 if π is really .35 (Select *Post hoc: Compute achieved power given α, sample size, and effect size* for *Type of power analysis*).

4.6 WHEN ASSUMPTIONS FAIL

Suppose the significance test on the ESP data allows us to reject the null hypothesis that H_0: $\pi = .25$ at $\alpha = .05$. Do we conclude that Rachel has ESP? Not necessarily. For one thing, we may have made a Type 1 error. For a controversial effect such as ESP, we may well want stronger evidence than that determined by the $\alpha = .05$ significance level, and therefore insist on a much smaller value for α.

We must also keep in mind that the validity of our calculations depends on the assumptions we made in order to use a particular sampling distribution. Throughout the preceding sections on hypothesis testing and power, we assumed that Y has a particular binomial distribution. The derivation of the equation that provides the binomial probabilities (Equation 4.3) rests upon the assumption that π is constant across trials and that the probability of an outcome on any one trial is independent of the outcome on any other trial. For the ESP experiment, the particular binomial distribution we used is the one with $n = 20$ and $\pi = .25$ (for random guessing with 20 trials and four cards). If these assumptions do not hold, we cannot take our calculations at face value. We generally try to design our studies so that the assumptions are satisfied, but we must consider ways in which they might be violated.

4.6.1 Nonrandom Sampling

Suppose in the ESP experiment the four cards are blue, black, red, and white. We would normally have the experimenter shuffle the pack before selecting a card so that on any trial each card would be equally likely to be selected. What would happen if we just handed the experimenter the pack and told him to select any sequence of 20 cards he desired? Suppose he just happens to have a strong preference for blue, so that the proportions of blue, black, red, and white cards he selects are .7, .1, .1, and .1, respectively. Suppose also that Rachel has no ESP but that she also has a preference for blue (or knows of the experimenter's preference). Say she responds randomly, but with probability .4 for blue and .2 for each of the other colors (as though she was randomly selecting with replacement from a box containing two blue cards and one black, one red, and one white card). Under these conditions, the probability that she would be correct by chance would not be .25 but rather $p(C) = p(\text{Blue}_R \text{ and Blue}_E) + p(\text{Black}_R \text{ and Black}_E) + p(\text{Red}_R \text{ and Red}_E) + p(\text{White}_R \text{ and White}_E) = (.4)(.7) + (.2)(.1) + (.2)(.1) + (.2)(.1) = .28 + .02 + .02 + .02 = .34$. This may seem like an extreme example; however, even more subtle deviations from the binomial assumptions can undermine our calculations.

It is important to distinguish between general knowledge about preferences and psychic ability. For example, given k options and no obvious reason to choose one option over the others, you might think that people would choose each option with probability $1/k$—but they usually do not. Conduct your own "experiment": If you tell a group of people that you are thinking of a number between 1 and 10 and that you want them to guess that number and write it down, the integers 1–10 will not be chosen equally often. Usually, the extremes 1 and 10 will be avoided and more people will guess "7" than any other number. People do have preferences, and the design of ESP research has to take this into account. If the cards were well shuffled before each selection, there would be no preference for Rachel to capitalize on. We should also point out that although here we have been talking about the ESP example, response preferences must be considered in other kinds of research as well.

4.6.2 Violation of the Independence Assumption

The assumption of independence can also be problematical for many kinds of social science research. Several measures taken from the same subject will usually be correlated. Also, whenever responses are obtained from members of the same discussion group, school class, or litter of animals, the responses obtained are likely to be correlated. Social, environmental, and biological factors will tend to affect the members of such units in a similar way. Violations of the independence assumption will frequently result in a Type 1 error rate very different from the error rate assumed by the experimenter. Some assumptions can be violated with minor consequences, but the independence assumption is often quite critical. Moreover, this assumption plays some role in all statistical test procedures. Here, the binomial test will be used to illustrate the consequences of violating the independence assumption, but the implications are much more general.

Consider a study in which 10 pairs of subjects discuss a topic. After the discussion, each of the 20 subjects casts a "yes" or "no" vote on the issue under consideration. Suppose that previous research has established that votes are evenly divided between the two positions when there is no discussion. However, theoretical principles lead the researcher to believe that "yes" votes will be more frequent than "no" votes following discussion. Thus, the null hypothesis is H_0: $\pi(\text{yes}) = .5$ and the alternative hypothesis is H_1: $\pi(\text{yes}) > .5$. If the significance level α is set equal to .06, the binomial table indicates that H_0 should be rejected if the observed number of "yes" responses is 14 or more.

There is a problem with this procedure: the two individuals in each discussion pair may have influenced each other and their responses may not be independent. In order to make clear the consequences for the binomial test of this dependency, let's consider an extreme example. Suppose the joint probabilities of votes were:

		M_1		
		Yes	No	
M_2	Yes	.50	0	.50
	No	0	.50	.50
		.50	.50	

In this case, the dependence within pairs is complete: The conditional probability of a "yes" vote is 1 when the partner votes "yes" and 0 when the partner votes "no." Note, however, that the null hypothesis is true; $\pi(\text{yes}) = .5$.

Recall that the researcher had sampled 10 pairs from this population and, on the basis of the binomial distribution table, had decided to reject H_0 if there were 14 or more "yes" votes from the 20 individuals. Unknown to the researcher, the two members of each pair vote the same way. Therefore, the probability of 14 or more "yes" votes is really the probability that 7, 8, 9, or 10 pairs vote "yes." There are only 10 independent events; they are the pair (not the individual) votes. If this violation of the independence assumption occurs, the probability of a Type 1 error is not the .058 computed by the researcher; rather it is the probability that $Y = 7$, 8, 9, or 10 when $n = 10$ and $p(\text{yes}) = .5$. Using Table C.1, that probability can be shown to be .172. This means that the actual Type 1 error rate is actually about three times the size of the rate expected by the researcher. Most researchers would feel that a Type 1 error rate of .172 was unacceptably high.

Although complete dependence between the members of the pair is improbable in a real experiment, some dependence is often likely. Consequently, the distortion in Type 1 error rate will be less than in our example, but there will be distortion. Frequently, the true error rate will be intolerably high. The opposite result occurs when responses are negatively related. For example, suppose that the null hypothesis is false, but in a high proportion of pairs, the partners agree to split their votes. In cases such as this, power will be greatly reduced. Thus, depending on the nature of the dependency, either Type 1 or Type 2 error rates will be increased. Positive dependencies are far more likely and, therefore, the greatest danger is an increased rate of rejection of true null hypotheses.

Independence is only one assumption that plays a role in many statistical tests. In general, the consequences of failures of assumptions are not simple and have to be thought through in each research situation. Many factors affect error rates. We have already discussed the effects of both the magnitude and direction of failures of the independence assumption. A third factor is the particular assumption that is violated. Some assumptions, despite being used in the derivation of the test statistic, are less critical, so their violation has little effect on error rates. A fourth factor is sample size; certain (but not all) assumptions are less critical when there are many observations. Appendix 4.2 provides an example of the interaction of assumptions and sample size.

In summary, every inferential procedure involves a statistical distribution and the derivation of that distribution rests on certain assumptions. The consequences of violating these assumptions will vary depending on the factors noted above. Throughout this book, we will emphasize the statistical model underlying each inferential procedure, detailing the conditions that cause assumptions to be violated, the results of such violations, and alternative analyses that remedy the situation when the violations are severe enough to make the proposed analysis untrustworthy.

4.7 SUMMARY

Our goal in Chapter 4 was to introduce the basic concepts of statistical inference in the context of a relatively simple probability distribution, the binomial.

- The conceptual framework for statistical inference is based on the idea of taking a *sample* from a *population* and using the information in the sample to make certain claims about the population. The process of inferring population characteristics from sample characteristics involves sampling error and is, therefore, probabilistic in nature.
- We applied our knowledge of probability to derive the probability of each possible outcome of an ESP experiment according to the hypothesis that the subject was guessing on each trial. The resulting hypothetical probability distribution, a *sampling distribution*, is

fundamental to the process of statistical inference because it provides the probabilities upon which we base our statistical decision making.

- The nature of the sampling distribution that is relevant to a given experiment depends on certain assumptions we make about the population. For our ESP experiment and related types of experiments, the *binomial distribution* is the appropriate sampling distribution. We therefore used the binomial distribution to illustrate the role of sampling distributions for an important procedure in inferential statistics, *hypothesis testing*.

- We developed the logic of hypothesis testing and identified the two types of errors we may commit when we conduct a significance test: We may reject H_0 when it is true (*Type 1 error*) or fail to reject H_0 when it is false (*Type 2 error*).

- We also developed an important topic in hypothesis testing, *power*. Statistical power is the probability of rejecting H_0 when it is false. Given H_0, H_1, and α, we can find the power to test H_0 against a specific alternative hypothesis, H_A. Power is a particularly important consideration during the planning stage of research. Power considerations inform the choice of experimental design and power calculations should be used in making decisions about sample size.

- Finally, we discussed the fact that any statistical procedure is based on certain assumptions associated with the derivation of the sampling distribution on which the procedure is based. If these assumptions are not valid, any decisions based on our calculations may also not be valid.

Appendix 4.1

Understanding the Combinatorial Formula (Equation 4.2)

Consider five individuals who are running for positions on the city council; the two top vote getters will be elected. First consider all the possible assignments of individuals to ranks where the ranks are the position in the final vote. There are five possibilities for the first position in the vote count, four possibilities for the second position (e.g., A could be followed by B, C, D, or E). The total number of sequences is (5)(4)(3)(2)(1) or 5!. In general there are $n!$ sequences of n objects.

Suppose the question is: How many outcomes can this election have? Here, by "outcome" we mean patterns of election and non-election. For example, A and B might be elected and C, D, and E fail to be elected. Notice that the order of finish within each of the two classes (elected and non-elected) is irrelevant. The following sequences are all equivalent in that they constitute the same outcome: A and B elected, and C, D, and E not elected:

$$A,B/C,D,E \quad B,A/C,D,E$$

$$A,B/C,E,D \quad B,A/C,E,D$$

$$A,B/D,C,E \quad B,A/D,C,E$$

$$A,B/D,E,C \quad B,A/D,E,C$$

$$A,B/E,C,D \quad B,A/E,C,D$$

$$A,B/E,D,C \quad B,A/E,D,C$$

Note that the two (2!) possible sequences of A and B, paired with the six (3!) possible combinations of C, D, and E correspond to one *combination* (A and B elected; C, D, and E not elected). In general, $r!(n - r)!$ sequences will correspond to a single combination when n items are split into one class with r items and one with $n - r$ items. Therefore, the number of combinations is $n!/r!(n - r)!$. In our example, the number of ways the election can turn out is

$$\binom{5}{3} = \binom{5}{2} = \frac{5!}{2!3!} = \frac{120}{(2)(6)} = 10$$

In general, the number of different ways of selecting r items from n items is

$$\binom{n}{r} = \frac{n!}{r!(n - r)!}$$

Appendix 4.2

Sample Size and Violations of the Independence Assumption

Although violations of assumptions can often lead to erroneous inferences, the consequences can sometimes (though not always) be minimized by using large samples. The violation of the independence assumption in calculating probabilities provides a nice illustration of this point. Consider an urn containing five red and five black balls. We draw a marble three times from the urn. If we assume that the marble is replaced and the urn is thoroughly shaken after each draw, so that we have independence, according to the multiplication rule, the probability of drawing three red marbles is $p(R_1 \text{ and } R_2 \text{ and } R_3) = p(R)p(R)p(R) = (5/10)^3 = .125$. However, suppose that the drawn marble has not been replaced each time. This violates our assumption of independence. We can see this by the following analysis: If a red ball is drawn on trial 1, the probability of drawing a second red ball is now 4/9, whereas if a black ball is drawn on the first draw, the probability of a red on the second draw is 5/9. In fact, the probability of drawing a red (or black) ball on any trial depends on the sequence of preceding draws. So, although our assumption of independence leads us to conclude that $p(R_1 \text{ and } R_2 \text{ and } R_3) = .125$, the true probability is $p(R_1 \text{ and } R_2 \text{ and } R_3) = p(R_1) \, p(R_2|R_1) \, p(R_3|R_1 \text{ and } R_2) = (5/10)(4/9)(3/8) = .063$, roughly half the inferred probability.

Suppose the urn consists of 50 red and 50 black balls. Our assumption of independence leads us to the same probability, .125. This time, however, the true probability if we select without replacement is $p(R_1 \text{ and } R_2 \text{ and } R_3) = (50/100)(49/99)(48/98) = .121$, and the true and inferred probabilities are quite close; that is, the violation of the independence assumption did not lead to a very large error.

There are two implications of our examples that extend beyond simple probability calculations and violations of the independence assumption. First, violations may lead to very wrong conclusions, as the urn with 10 marbles attests. Second, the consequences of violations of assumptions may be less damaging when sample size is large. Neither of these statements will be true for every inferential procedure, but they are often true and therefore worth bearing in mind.

EXERCISES

4.1 Assume that in a particular research area .30 of the null hypotheses tested are true. Suppose a very large number of experiments are conducted, each with $\alpha = .05$ and power $= .80$.
  (a) What proportion of true null hypotheses will be rejected?
  (b) What proportion of false null hypotheses will not be rejected?
  (c) What proportion of nonrejected null hypotheses will actually be true?
  (d) What proportion of all null hypotheses will be rejected?

4.2 For each of the following, state the null and alternative hypotheses:
  (a) The recovery rate for a disease is known to be .25. A new drug is tried with a sample of people who have the disease in order to determine whether the probability of recovering is increased.
  (b) An experiment such as that described in Exercise 3.1 is conducted to provide evidence for the existence of ESP.
  (c) In the ESP experiment of Exercise 3.1, a proponent of ESP (Claire Voyant?) claims that she will be successful on greater than 60% of the trials.

4.3 Use the binomial table (Appendix Table C.1) to find the rejection region in each of the following cases (π is the population probability):

Case	H_0	H_1	n	α
(a)	$\pi = .25$	$\pi > .25$	20	.01
(b)	$\pi = .25$	$\pi > .25$	5	.01
(c)	$\pi = .25$	$\pi < .25$	20	.05
(d)	$\pi = .5$	$\pi \neq .5$	20	.01

4.4 In an experiment, data are collected such that when a hypothesis test is conducted, the null hypothesis is rejected with $p = .003$.
  (a) Can you conclude that H_0 is true with probability .003? Why or why not?
  (b) Can you conclude that H_1 is true with probability .997? Why or why not?

4.5 In each of the following, (i) state the null and alternative hypotheses, (ii) state n, and (iii) state the appropriate rejection region, assuming $\alpha = .05$.
  (a) An important quality in clinical psychologists is empathy, the ability to perceive others as they perceive themselves. In a simplified version of one investigation of empathy, five first-year graduate students were asked to rate a target individual on a particular trait, as they believed the individual would rate herself. A four-point scale was used. The question of interest was whether the raters would do better than chance.
  (b) In a study of group problem solving, the investigator uses the solution rate for individuals in a previous study to predict that 40% of three-person groups will reach the correct solution. Fifteen groups are run in the study. The question of interest is whether the theory is correct.

4.6 Suppose a sign test is to be done with H_0: $\pi = .50$, H_1: $\pi < .50$, $n = 20$, $\alpha = .05$. Suppose further that the number of successes, y, is 7.
  (a) What is the rejection region?
  (b) What do we conclude?
  (c) What is the power of the test if π is actually .35?

(d) If π is actually .35, how many cases do we need to have power = .90?

(e) If π is actually .35, how many cases do we need to have power = .90 for a two-tailed test?

4.7 The data set *EX4_7* contains data for 20 cases on two variables, *Y*1 and *Y*2. Each variable is dichotomous; *Y*1 has seven values of 1 and thirteen of 0 whereas *Y*2 has five values of 1 and fifteen of 0. Use a statistical package to perform a binomial test. Test the hypothesis H_0: $\pi = .5$ at $\alpha = .05$ for both *Y*1 and *Y*2. In SPSS, you would start by selecting *Nonparametric Tests* from the *Analyze* menu. In the *Binomial Test* dialog box, add both *Y*1 and *Y*2 to the *Test Variable List*, and insert .50 for the *Test Proportion*, and then click on *OK*.

4.8 Ten students take a course to improve reasoning skills. Before the course, they took a pretest designed to measure reasoning ability and after the course they took a posttest of equal difficulty. The results for the 10 students are as follows:

Student	1	2	3	4	5	6	7	8	9	10
Pretest Score	25	27	28	31	29	30	32	21	25	20
Posttest Score	28	29	33	36	32	34	31	18	32	25

The instructors of the course want to decide whether performance on the posttest is significantly better than performance on the pretest by looking at the signs of the difference scores, on the reasoning that if the course had no effect whatsoever, each student would be equally likely to get a + or −.

(a) State H_0 and H_1.

(b) Perform a sign test on these data (here, use $\alpha = .06$) and report your conclusion.

4.9 A researcher studying memory performs an experiment that compares two strategies for remembering pairs of words. Twelve students are each given a number of sets of word pairs to learn. They learn half the sets by rote memorization and the other half by using imagery. The order of conditions is counterbalanced appropriately. It is found that nine students do better with the imagery strategy and three do better with rote memorization.

(a) Using the binomial distribution, test the null hypothesis that both strategies are equally effective using $\alpha = .05$. Write down the appropriate null and alternative hypotheses and describe the steps you take in testing the null hypothesis. What is the result of the significance test?

(b) What is the power of this test if the probability of doing better using the imagery strategy is actually .9 in the population (so that the probability of doing better using the rote strategy would be .1)?

4.10 Reconsider the study of empathy described in Exercise 4.5, part (a).

(a) If the true probability of an empathetic response is .5, what is the power of the significance test in your answer to the earlier question.

(b) How many subjects would be required to get power = .80 for the test of the null hypothesis at $\alpha = .05$?

(c) What is meant by "true probability" here?

Chapter 5

Further Development of the Foundations of Statistical Inference

5.1 OVERVIEW

In Chapter 2, we explored a subset of data in the study in which Royer and his colleagues collected accuracy scores and response times on simple arithmetic skills from students in first to eighth grades. Usually, this is a preliminary step in addressing questions about the data of a population of students represented by our sample. Among the many questions we might ask of the data we collect are:

- What is the average addition score of the population of first-grade boys?
- What are reasonable bounds on our estimate of the population average.

The answers to questions such as the first one involve *point estimates*; we use sample data to estimate a point, a single value, in the population of scores. The answer to questions such as the second one involves *interval estimates*; we use sample data to estimate an interval within which we believe the population parameter falls.

There are many other questions we could ask of these data. For example,

- Does the average score of the sampled population differ from some standard set by the government?
- Does the average score differ from that of some other population of first-graders, perhaps first-grade students taught by a different method?

These last two questions imply tests of the null hypothesis, tests that are based on the logic presented in Chapter 4. Most researchers are primarily concerned with these questions. However, point and interval estimates of population parameters should take precedence. For example, rather than immediately ask whether there is a statistically significant difference between two means, we should first ask what the size of the difference is, and place some bounds on our estimate. Testing for significance is equivalent to asking whether there is an effect, but our understanding of the behavior in question will proceed more rapidly if we ask what the magnitude of the effect is, a question that encompasses the possibility that there is no, or little, effect.

Both estimates and significance tests are influenced by the variability in our data. The variability in the population distribution is reflected in the variability of the distribution of the sample data and in the distribution of sample statistics. The greater the population variability, the more a sample statistic, such as the sample mean or variance, will vary from sample to sample; that is, the greater will be the variance of the *sampling distribution* of the statistic. As a result of sampling variability, no statistic from a single sample will exactly match the parameter it estimates, and inferences about the parameter may be in error. In this chapter, we consider the relation between the sampling distribution of a statistic and both estimation and hypothesis testing.

The major topics of this chapter are organized as follows:

- *The use of sample statistics to estimate population parameters.* Familiar statistics such as the sample mean and standard deviation are useful estimators because they provide important information about the "typical" score and variability of scores in a population. However, other sample statistics can be used to estimate the average score or the variability in a population. We will see that the choice among the estimators of a parameter rests on comparisons of characteristics of the sampling distributions of the sample statistics.
- *The sampling distribution of the sample mean* plays a critical role in many inferential procedures. This is because the central limit theorem assures us that the sampling distribution of the mean is approximately normal in shape under a wide range of circumstances. For this reason, we are able to use the normal distribution as a basis for probability computations underlying inferential procedures concerning means of populations.
- *The normal distribution may be used to construct interval estimates and hypothesis tests concerning population means.* The construction and interpretation of interval estimates is introduced in this chapter. In addition, we present the use of the normal distribution to test hypotheses about means and to do power calculations. The discussion of hypothesis testing and power calculations serves, in part, to emphasize that the logic of those procedures is the same regardless of the particular application. Relations among interval estimates, hypothesis tests, and power calculations are also discussed.
- *The validity of the assumptions* underlying our inferential procedures affects the validity of the inferences we draw from our data. Using confidence intervals and hypothesis tests based on the normal distribution, we discuss these assumptions and the consequences of violating them.
- *Relations between the normal distribution and other theoretical distributions* are discussed in the final sections of the chapter.

In summary, in this chapter we will discuss sampling distributions and their role in estimating population parameters and in testing hypotheses about those parameters. We introduce the normal distribution to exemplify these concepts and procedures, in part because the normal distribution plays several important roles in inferential procedures that we will study in subsequent chapters of this text.

5.2 USING SAMPLE STATISTICS TO ESTIMATE POPULATION PARAMETERS

5.2.1 Populations, Samples, and Sampling Distributions

Usually, a researcher has a sample and wants to draw inferences about a population. As we discussed in Chapter 4, there is a basic problem in drawing inferences from the sample to the population: The values of the sample statistics are not identical to those of the population parameters in which we are interested. For example, the sample mean will vary over independent replications of a study, as will all other statistics we can compute from a sample. Two important questions this raises are:

- How is a particular statistic distributed over repeated samples?
- Can more than one statistic be used to estimate a particular population parameter? If so, how do we decide between these possible estimates of the parameter?

These are some of the questions we will consider in Section 5.2. The answers require an understanding of sampling distributions, the topic we turn to next.

5.2.2 What is a Sampling Distribution?

The concept of a sampling distribution was introduced in Chapter 4, where we developed the binomial as a sampling distribution for frequency (or proportions). However, the concept of a sampling distribution is much more general than the context in which it was introduced in Chapter 4. It is implicit in statistical inference. For example, consider the following marketing study. Fifty individuals are sampled from some well-defined population and asked to rate a new brand of breakfast cereal. The ratings range from 1 ("strongly dislike") to 11 ("strongly like") with 6 as the neutral point. We might wish to test whether the mean of the sampled population is different from the midpoint of the scale, 6. The mean of the sampled ratings is 8.6. If the sample mean changed little from one sample to another, this value would provide strong evidence against the hypothesis that the population mean equaled 6, and thus would suggest that the new cereal is worth marketing further. On the other hand, if the sample mean was quite variable over samples, then a sample value of 8.6 could well have occurred even when the population mean was 6. It is useful to picture many random replications of the 50-subject sampling experiment, with each replication giving rise to a value of the mean, $\bar{Y}$. If we tabulate all of the possible values of $\bar{Y}$ and their associated relative frequencies of occurrence, the result is called the *sampling distribution of the mean* for samples of size 50. Knowing the properties of this sampling distribution will help us evaluate inferences made on the basis of a single sampled value of $\bar{Y}$. If we know that the sampling distribution has little variability, we have considerable confidence that our one estimate is close to the population parameter; conversely, we are less satisfied with an estimate when the variability of the sampling distribution is high. Furthermore, as we shall see, if we have knowledge of the shape of the sampling distribution—e.g., that the population of scores is normally distributed—we can draw various inferences about the parameter. This application of sampling distributions to statistical inference was introduced in Chapter 4, and we return to it soon to develop procedures for drawing inferences about population means. However, before doing so, we will consider another important use of sampling distributions of statistics; namely, to study properties of statistics as estimators of population parameters.

5.2.3 Criteria for Estimators

We have established that researchers usually want to draw inferences about population parameters from their sample data. For example, they want to know the mean of the population, or estimate some measure of variability (e.g., the standard deviation). In fact, there are often multiple ways to estimate the value of a given population parameter. For example in a distribution that is unimodal and symmetric, the sample mean, median, and mode all estimate the population mean. Given this, what criteria should be used in selecting the statistics to provide a point estimate of such population parameters?

In our marketing example, we focused on the sampling distribution of the mean. However, it should be understood that every statistic has a sampling distribution, because each time a new sample is drawn from a population, the sample statistic is based on a new set of values. Just as we can imagine a distribution of sample means, there are sampling distributions of medians, modes, variances, standard deviations, etc. And like any distribution of a random variable, any sampling distribution has a characteristic shape, a mean, a variance, and other properties. The criteria we will require for good point estimates relate to several properties of the estimator's sampling distribution: the mean and variance of that distribution, and how rapidly the mean of the sampling distribution approaches the parameter value as sample size increases. Before discussing these properties, it will prove useful to briefly consider the concept of an expected value.

5.2.4 Expected Values

The *expected value of a random variable* is the mean of the variable's theoretical distribution. In the case of an individual score, Y, its expected value is the population mean; that is, $E(Y) = \mu$. The theoretical variance of Y is $\sigma^2 = E(Y - \mu)^2$; that is, the population variance is the average squared deviation of scores about the population mean. With respect to the issue of criteria for selecting estimators, we are interested in the mean and variance of the sampling distribution of potential estimators of population parameters. (For more information about expected values, and important proofs involving them, see Appendix B.) In general, we may think in terms of a population parameter that we will represent by the Greek letter θ (theta); this could be the population mean, variance, a measure of skewness, or any other measure that in theory might be a function of the random variable of interest. There are many possible estimators of θ; we will use the symbol $\hat{\theta}$ (theta-hat) to represent an estimator. We will consider three criteria:

1. *Unbiasedness*—does $E(\hat{\theta}) = \theta$?
2. *Consistency*—does the probability increase that $\hat{\theta}$ is within some small distance of θ as sample size increases?
3. *Relative efficiency*—what are the relative variances of the sampling distributions of two estimators of θ, $\hat{\theta}_1$ and $\hat{\theta}_2$?

5.2.5 Unbiasedness

Suppose we wish to estimate some population parameter, θ. A statistic, $\hat{\theta}$, is calculated from a sampled set of n scores. One desirable quantity for a good estimator is that the mean of its sampling distribution should equal the parameter being estimated; that is, a statistic $\hat{\theta}$ is an *unbiased estimator* of θ if

$$E(\hat{\theta}) = \theta \tag{5.1}$$

If Equation 5.1 holds for an estimator, the mean of its sampling distribution will equal the population parameter. In Appendix B, we show that the sample mean, $\overline{Y}$, is an unbiased estimate of the population mean, μ. That seems intuitively reasonable. However, just because a statistic and a parameter share the same name does not guarantee that the statistic is an unbiased estimator of the parameter. An example of biased estimation is the use of the largest score in a sample (g) to estimate the largest score in a population (G). It is unlikely that the largest score in the population would be contained in the sample, Therefore, $E(g) < G$. A second example is S^2 as an estimator of σ^2 where $S^2 = \Sigma(Y_i - \overline{Y})^2/n$. In Appendix B, we show that

$$E(s^2) = \sigma^2 \tag{5.2}$$

where $s^2 = \Sigma(Y - \overline{Y})^2/(n-1)$. Therefore, because $S^2 = [(n-1)/n]s^2$,

$$E(S^2) = \left(\frac{n-1}{n}\right)\sigma^2 \tag{5.3}$$

so $E(S^2) < \sigma^2$. Thus, S^2 is a biased estimator of the population variance (although the bias grows smaller as n increases), but s^2 is an unbiased estimate. Equations 5.2 and 5.3 together convey this message: if we were to take many samples, and compute S^2 and s^2 each time, the average value of S^2 would be smaller than the population variance, σ^2, whereas the average value of s^2 would equal σ^2. Because S^2 tends to underestimate σ^2, we will follow the usual practice of calculating s^2 rather than S^2 for the sample variance.

Bias, or the lack of it, cannot be the sole, or even the most important, property of an estimator. Suppose we took the first score drawn from a sample, Y_1, as an estimate of μ. If we drew many samples, discarded all but the first score drawn each time, and then calculated the mean of the sampling distribution of Y_1, that mean would equal μ. Thus, the first score (or, for that matter, any single score) drawn from a sample is an unbiased estimate of μ. Nevertheless, this estimator does not feel right. For one thing, it violates our work ethic; collecting more data in the sample does not improve our estimate because we are discarding all but one score. This line of reasoning suggests the next criterion for an estimator.

5.2.6 Consistency

Again, let $\hat{\theta}$ be some estimator of θ. $\hat{\theta}$ is a *consistent estimator* of θ if its value is more likely to be close to θ as n increases.[1] A familiar example of a consistent estimator is the sample mean of n independently distributed scores. From Appendix 5.1, $\sigma_{\overline{Y}}^2 = \sigma_Y^2/n$; therefore, the sampling variability of $\overline{Y}$ about μ must decrease as n increases. Because inferences based on consistent estimators are more likely to be correct as sample size increases, consistency is an important property of an estimator. Nevertheless, even consistency combined with unbiasedness is not a sufficient basis for choosing between possible estimators of a parameter. A very important consideration in selecting an estimator of a parameter is its variance about the parameter being estimated. The less variable the sampling distribution is, the more likely it is that any single estimate will have a value close to that of the population parameter. We consider this criterion next.

---

[1] Technically, $\hat{\theta}$ is a consistent estimate of θ if the probability approaches 1 as n increases that the absolute distance between $\hat{\theta}$ and θ is less than any arbitrarily chosen small value.

5.2.7 Relative Efficiency

Assume that a sample of size n has been drawn from a symmetric population. In that case, the sample mean and median are both unbiased estimators of the population mean because the population mean and median have the same value in any symmetric distribution. Furthermore, both the sample mean and median are consistent estimates of μ. However, they do differ in one respect: For any sample of size n, the sampling distributions of the median and mean will differ in their variances. Assume that many samples are drawn from a normally distributed population and the average squared deviations of the sample means and medians about μ are then calculated. For very large samples, the variance of the sample means will be approximately 65% of the variance of the sample medians *if the population is normally distributed*. This smaller variance of the mean relative to that of the median is expressed by saying that the *relative efficiency* of the median to the mean as estimator of the mean of a normally distributed population is .65. Conversely, the relative efficiency of the mean to the median is 1/.65 or 154%. Because of its greater efficiency, the mean is preferred to the median as an estimator of the mean of a normally distributed population.

In general, assume a population parameter, θ, which can be estimated by either of two statistics, $\hat{\theta}_1$ or $\hat{\theta}_2$. The relative efficiency (RE) of $\hat{\theta}_1$ to $\hat{\theta}_2$ is:

$$RE_{1\,to\,2} = \frac{E(\hat{\theta}_2 - \theta)^2}{E(\hat{\theta}_1 - \theta)^2} \tag{5.4}$$

Thus, relative efficiency is the ratio of two averages of squared deviations of estimates about the same population parameter. Note that this is a measure of the efficiency of the estimator in the denominator relative to that in the numerator.

5.2.8 Which Estimator?

Most of the estimation and hypothesis-testing procedures presented in statistics texts, and in published journal articles, make use of the sample mean, and the unbiased variance estimate, s^2. If the population from which the data are drawn has a normal distribution, these statistics will be efficient relative to their competitors. Consequently, estimates based upon them are more likely to be close to the true value of the parameter being estimated, and hypothesis tests are more likely to lead to correct inferences. But what if the population distribution is not normal? We will address this question by considering the relative efficiencies of several estimators of μ for different population distributions.

Rosenberger and Gasko (1983) derived the variances of various estimators for several population distributions and sample sizes. Table 5.1 presents their results for $n = 20$ for the mean ($\bar{Y}$), the

Table 5.1   Variances and relative efficiencies (RE) of three estimators of the population mean for $n = 20$

Statistic	Normal distribution		Mixed-normal distribution	
	Variance	RE	Variance	RE
$\bar{Y}$	.050	1.000	.298	1.000
$\tilde{Y}$	.073	.685	.079	3.772
$\bar{Y}_{.10}$	.053	.943	.061	4.885

Note: For the mixed-normal, one observation comes from a normal distribution with $\sigma = 10$.

median ($\tilde{Y}$), and the 10% trimmed mean ($\overline{Y}_{.10}$); this last statistic is obtained by rank ordering the scores in the sample, discarding the highest and lowest 10% (the top and bottom two scores for $n = 20$), and then calculating the arithmetic mean of the remaining scores. The theoretical variances of these three statistics when the distribution of the random variable is normal are presented in the second column of Table 5.1. The third column contains the efficiencies (RE) of $\tilde{Y}$ and $\overline{Y}_{.10}$ relative to $\overline{Y}$; these are obtained by taking ratios of the variances, as in Equation 5.4. When the population of scores is normal, the mean is the most efficient statistic and therefore the best estimator of the population mean. However, the situation is quite different if we make one change in our sampling procedure. Suppose 19 of the 20 scores in each sample are drawn from the population having $\mu = 0$ and $\sigma = 1$; however, one score is drawn at random from a population for which $\mu = 0$ and $\sigma = 10$. This second population looks much like the first except that extreme scores are more likely. Think of the extreme scores as coming from those rare individuals who come to the experiment hung over from the previous night's party. Such scores might contribute to the variance, increasing the proportion of very small and very large scores. Variances of the three statistics, and efficiencies relative to the mean are presented in the fourth and fifth columns of Table 5.1. The interesting result here is that the variances of the sampling distributions of both the trimmed mean and the median are markedly less than that of the mean, and their relative efficiencies, accordingly, are greater. In fact, Rosenberger and Gasko found that, for the seven distributions they studied, the mean was the most efficient estimator only when samples were drawn from a normally distributed population. In the other six distributions they investigated, some other estimator (not necessarily the two alternatives reported in Table 5.1) was at least slightly more efficient, and sometimes much more so.

Contrary to intuition and popular usage, the sample mean is not always the best estimator of the population mean. Other estimators may be more efficient when the population is skewed, or is symmetric but with long tails (i.e., high variability), or when there are a few outlying scores, as in the example of Table 5.1. This happens because the sampling variance of the mean is increased much more than that of a trimmed mean or median by the inclusion of even a few extreme scores. Micceri's (1989) review of many real data sets suggests that normality is the exception. In many cases, inferential procedures that do not rest upon the sample mean may provide more powerful tests of hypotheses. Several procedures based on assigning ranks to scores, and analyzing those ranks, are presented in this book; these *nonparametric procedures* will be useful in fairly simple designs, but less so in more complex designs involving several independent variables. Another possible approach is implicit in the results presented in Table 5.1. This involves *trimming data* from the tails of the data set, thus reducing the effect of extreme scores. Inferences based on trimming require the adjustment of estimates of population variances. Hogg, Fisher, and Randles (1975) described a test based on trimming, and compared it with several other tests for distributions exhibiting various degrees of tail weight and skew. The article also suggests ways of estimating tail weight and skew, and of using these estimates to select the best hypothesis-testing procedure.

5.2.9 Summary

To sum up the developments of this section, unbiasedness, consistency, and efficiency are desirable properties in the statistics we use in drawing inferences. However, in some situations, there may be a tradeoff between bias and efficiency; a biased estimator may have less sampling variability than an available unbiased one. Unless the bias is very extreme, and no correction for bias can be found, the more efficient estimator is to be preferred. It is more important to have an estimate that is more likely to be close to the parameter being estimated, than to have one that, if many such estimates were obtained, would be correct on the average. The prevalent use of inferential procedures based on $\overline{Y}$ and $\sigma_{\overline{Y}}$ reflects the fact that these statistics are known to be both unbiased and efficient when the data are normally distributed. However, there will be situations in which we will encounter distributions for which other statistics will be more efficient. Exploring data using the sorts of graphs and tabular outputs illustrated in Chapter 2 will help the researcher in determining when alternative estimators and approaches to inference should be considered.

5.3 THE SAMPLING DISTRIBUTION OF THE SAMPLE MEAN

Despite the observation that the sample mean is not always the best choice of estimator, it is conventionally the estimator of choice in procedures designed for making inferences about population means. The reason for this is that we are able to specify the sampling distribution of the mean for a wide range of circumstances. The theoretical key to this fact is the central limit theorem.

5.3.1 The Central Limit Theorem

The central limit theorem states that:

If a sample is large enough, the sampling distribution of its mean will be approximately normal, regardless of the shape of the underlying population.

This theorem about the large-sample shape of the sampling distribution is important because it establishes that the normal distribution may be used to compute probabilities of values of sample means under a wide range of circumstances. This will be true even when samples are drawn from a population that is not normally distributed. Probability statements, such as "the Type 1 error rate is .05" will be at least approximately correct. As one example, we will demonstrate in Section 5.8.2 that the normal distribution may be used to perform significance tests when dealing with a population that is binomially distributed. This is because the proportion of successes, y/n, is actually a mean. If we assign a score of 1 to a success and 0 to a failure, y (the number of successes) is a sum of these zeros and ones, and a sum divided by the number of observations is a mean.

How rapidly the sampling distribution approaches normality as the sample size, n, increases will depend on the shape of the population. A sample size of 30 is usually "large enough" to ensure that the normal closely approximates the shape of the sampling distribution; however, a larger sample size may be necessary if the population is skewed, or is lumpy (i.e., has few values and several modes). We saw an example of the influence of population shape on the sampling distribution in Fig. 4.2 of the preceding chapter: When the population is symmetrically distributed ($p = .5$), the sampling distribution is approximately normal for samples of size 20, whereas there is still some slight asymmetry in the sampling distribution for $n = 40$ when the population parameter, p, is .25.

One other point about the central limit theorem should be noted. It applies not only to means, but to all linear combinations. A *linear combination* is a sum of scores, each multiplied by some number, or weight, w. That is,

$$linear\ combination = w_1 Y_1 + w_2 Y_2 + \ldots + w_j Y_j + \ldots + w_n Y_n \tag{5.5}$$

We saw an example of a linear combination in Chapter 2, in which the means of four different clinics of different sizes were combined to obtain an overall, or grand, mean. The weights in that example were the n_j/N, the proportion of scores in the jth clinic divided by the total number of scores.

Finally, we note that there is a tendency to overgeneralize in applying the central limit theorem.

Although it holds for all linear combinations, it does not hold for nonlinear combinations of variables such as sums or averages of scores raised to a power. For example, the sampling distribution of the variance is not normal because it involves sums of squared deviations. A second exception is the correlation coefficient, which was defined in Chapter 2 and is discussed further in Chapter 18.

5.3.2 The Mean and Variance of the Sampling Distribution of the Mean

Knowing that the sampling distribution of the mean is normal in shape is just part of the information needed to completely specify the sampling distribution. The normal distribution has two parameters, its mean and variance; therefore, we must know the values of the mean and variance of the relevant sampling distribution. Fortunately, even though we never observe the sampling distribution of a statistic, we can derive its properties without actually drawing even one sample. This point may be clearer if we consider an example.

Assume that we toss a single die. As usual, the die has six sides, each with a different one of the values from 1 to 6. If this experiment is carried out many times, and the resulting number is recorded each time, we have the distribution displayed in Fig. 5.1(a); in the long run, each possible integer from 1 to 6 will occur on 1/6 of the trials, assuming the trial outcomes are independent and that each value has probability 1/6 of occurring. This is the population distribution.

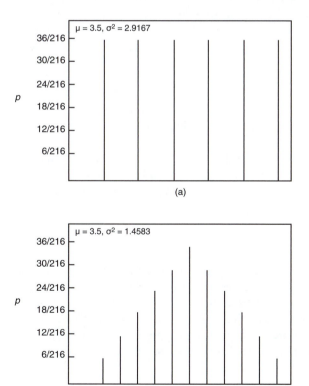

Fig. 5.1 (a) A discrete population distribution and (b) the sampling distribution of the mean for $n = 2$.

Now let us change the experiment slightly so that a trial consists of tossing two dice. If we record the mean of the two numbers that come up on each of many trials and—still assuming independence and equal probability of the six values for each die—the sampling distribution of the trial mean will be that depicted in Fig. 5.1(b). The distribution now has a definite peak. For example, the sample mean is more likely to equal 3.5 than 1 or 6. The reason for this follows from the multiplication rule for independent events. The mean will equal 1 only if both dice on a trial result in a 1, an event that occurs with probability $p = 1/6 \times 1/6$. On the other hand, the mean will equal 3.5 if one die shows a 1 and the other shows a 6, or if either die has a 2 while the other shows a 5, or if the result is a 3 and a 4. Therefore, there are six outcomes which can yield a sum of 7, or a mean of 3.5. Each outcome has a probability of 1/36, so the probability of a mean of 3.5 is $6 \times 1/36$. If we were to further increase the number of dice tossed in each replication of the experiment, the resulting sampling distribution of the mean would be more closely approximated by the normal distribution, as expected under the central limit theorem.

Fig. 5.1(a) includes values of the population mean and variance, and Fig. 5.1(b) includes the mean and variance of the sampling distribution when two dice are thrown; that is, when $n = 2$. Note that the mean of the sampling distribution of the mean, $\mu_{\bar{y}}$, is identical to the mean of the population, μ_Y; both are 3.5. Also note that when there are two scores in the sample, the variance of the sample means, $\sigma_{\bar{Y}}^2$, is ½ the population variance; in Fig. 5.1, the population variance, σ^2, is 2.917 and the variance of the sampling distribution, $\sigma_{\bar{Y}}^2$, is 2.917/2, or 1.458. In general, if the scores are independently distributed, $\sigma_{\bar{Y}}^2 = \sigma_Y^2/n$, where n is the sample size. If we constructed the sampling distribution of means for samples of size 10, its variance would be .2917. This relation between the variance of the sampling distribution and that of the population holds regardless of the shape of the population, *provided the scores are independently distributed*. Appendix 5.1 contains a proof that $\sigma_{\bar{Y}}^2 = \sigma_Y^2/n$, as well as more general results for linear combinations, including cases in which scores are not independently distributed.

In summary,

- The average of many sample means will be the same as the population mean.
- The sample-to-sample variability of the sample mean will be less when n is large.

Therefore, the value of a sample mean is more likely to be close to the value of the population mean it estimates as sample size increases. This makes sense; the larger the sample, the more likely it is to resemble other samples from the same population and the closer its mean will be to those of other samples and to the population mean.

5.3.3 Summary

We have determined that sample means are unbiased and consistent estimators of population means. Under some conditions—but not all—sample means are also relatively efficient estimators. Most importantly, the central limit theorem tells us that the sampling distribution of the sample mean is approximately normally distributed, with $E(\bar{Y}) = \mu$ and $\sigma_{\bar{Y}}^2 = \sigma_Y^2/n$ if the sample size is sufficiently large. Thus, we are able to use the normal distribution as a basis for making inferences about population means. To do this, we need to know something about the normal distribution.

5.4 THE NORMAL DISTRIBUTION

5.4.1 Why Is the Normal Distribution Important?

The justification we have presented for using the normal distribution as the basis for making inferences about means is sufficient to establish the importance of the normal distribution in statistics. However, there are other important roles played by the normal distribution that are worth considering before we take up the task of examining the properties of the normal distribution.

A second reason for the importance of the normal distribution is that the derivations of several important theoretical distributions rest upon that assumption. Specifically, the derivations of the chi-square, t, and F distributions all assume that scores are sampled from a normally distributed population. In fact, many random variables do have at least an approximately normal distribution. Consideration of an individual's score on a test such as the Scholastic Aptitude Test (SAT) may clarify why this is so. The score might be represented as

$$Y = \mu + \varepsilon \tag{5.6}$$

where Y is the obtained score, μ is the mean of the population of test scores, and ε (epsilon) is a sum of "errors," positive and negative deviations from the population mean due to many random factors that affect the score being considered. Such factors would include test-taking skills, amount of knowledge relevant to the test, amount and type of preparation, motivation, and the current state of alertness. The central limit theorem states that the sum of many such effects will be normally distributed. Therefore, if ε can be viewed as a sum of many independent random effects like the ones we have indicated, it (and therefore Y) will tend to be normally distributed.

Finally, just as the central limit theorem provides the basis for assuming that the sampling distribution of the mean is normal, it also underlies the fact that the normal distribution provides a reasonable approximation to the distribution of many discrete random variables (e.g., the binomial). Thus, when sample sizes are sufficiently large, we can approximate results of tests based on discrete distributions with procedures based on the normal distribution. The advantage is that normal probabilities are more accessible than probability calculations based on discrete distributions such as the binomial.

We do not want to leave the reader with the impression that the normality assumption applies in all circumstances. Although the normal distribution is a reasonable approximation to the distribution of many variables, many others are not normally distributed. We cited published reviews of data sets in Chapter 2 and presented examples from the *Royer* and *Seasons* data sets that make this point. With this in mind, in later chapters, we will consider the consequences of nonnormality and alternatives to those classical statistical procedures that rest on the assumption of normality. Nevertheless, because of its central role in statistical inference, we will devote the remainder of this chapter to considering the normal distribution. The normal distribution also merits our consideration because it provides a relatively simple context within which to continue our development of inferential procedures such as interval estimation and hypothesis testing.

5.4.2 The Normal Distribution's Probability Density Function and z Scores

The normal distribution is characterized by its density function:

$$f(y) = \frac{1}{\sigma\sqrt{2\pi}} e^{-(y-\mu)^2/2\sigma^2} \tag{5.7}$$

where μ and σ are the mean and standard deviation of the population and π and e are mathematical constants. The random variable Y can take on any value between $-\infty$ and $+\infty$, and the curve is symmetric about its mean, μ.

Infinitely many normal distributions are possible, one for each combination of mean and variance. However, inferences based on these normal distributions are made possible by the fact that all of the possible normal distributions are related to a single distribution. This *standardized normal distribution* is obtained by subtracting the distribution mean from each score and dividing the difference by the distribution standard deviation; specifically, it is the distribution of the z score

$$z = (Y - \mu)/\sigma \qquad (5.8)$$

As we showed in Chapter 2, the mean of the distribution of z scores is zero and its standard deviation is one. This is true of any complete set of z scores. In addition, if the variable Y is normally distributed, the corresponding distribution of z scores also will be normal. In this case, the variable z is often referred to as a *standardized normal deviate*.

Standardization provides information about the relative position of an individual score. For example, assume a normally distributed population of scores with μ = 500 and σ = 15. A value Y of 525 would correspond to a z score of 1.67; $z = (525 - 500)/15 = 1.67$, meaning that a raw score of 525 is 1.67 standard deviation units above the population mean of 500. Turning to Appendix Table C.2, we find that $F(z) = .9525$ when z is 1.67. $F(z)$ is the proportion of standardized scores less than z in a normally distributed population of such scores. In this example, we may conclude that the score of 525 exceeds .9525 of the population. Of course, this conclusion may not be valid if our values of μ and σ are incorrect or if Y is not normally distributed.

Equation 5.8 defined a z score as $(Y - \mu)/\sigma$. In fact, this is just a special case of a general formula for a z score. Instead of Y, we could have any observed quantity; examples would be the sample mean, the difference between two sample means, or some other statistic. Call this V for *observed variable*. To transform V into a z score, subtract the expected value of V, and then divide the difference by the standard deviation of the sampling distribution of V. Thus, a general formula for z is

$$z_V = [V - E(V)]/\sigma_V \qquad (5.9)$$

The variable z_V will be normally distributed if—*and only if*—V is normally distributed. In that case, we can assess the probability that V exceeds some specified value by referring to Appendix Table C.2, which tables probabilities under the normal distribution.

5.5 INFERENCES ABOUT POPULATION MEANS

In this section, we apply concepts developed in Chapter 4 to inferences based on the normal distribution. The application of normal probabilities assumes knowledge of the population variance. Using the data we have collected, we can only estimate that variance, a fact that introduces some error into our calculations. Although more accurate results would be obtained by basing our inferences on the t distribution, we will wait until the next chapter to develop this topic. For now, we will continue to focus on the normal distribution to further illustrate and extend ideas introduced in Chapter 4.

One of the measures available to us in the *Seasons* data set is the seasonal total cholesterol score ($TC1, ..., TC4$). We calculated the average over the four seasons for those subjects who had been measured in all four seasons (some subjects missed at least one of the four sessions); the data are in the file, *TC_Data*; the link is on the *Seasons* page on the website. We used the sample data to estimate the mean *TC* of a subpopulation—namely males 50 and older (Agegrps 3 and 4 in the file). These data are in the file *TC_Data over 50*. Keeping in mind that doctors frequently recommend that *TC* should be at 200 or less, we wanted to know whether the subpopulation mean differed from this recommended maximum level. In what follows, we analyze the *TC* data of the 117 males in *Agegrps* 3 and 4 to estimate the mean of a population of such individuals, and to test the null hypothesis that the population mean equals 200.

5.5.1 A First Look at the Data

As we emphasized in Chapter 2, we should explore our data before conducting any inferential procedures. We begin our exploration of the *TC* data with Fig. 5.2, which presents a box plot (using SPSS's Graphs module) of the data. Several aspects of the plot are of interest. First, because the median approximately bisects the box and the whiskers are of about equal length, it appears that the distribution is symmetric. Second, the median is clearly above the recommended maximum *TC* level of 200. Furthermore, the lower hinge is above the y-axis tick that represents this level, meaning that at least 75% of the participants have *TC* scores above the recommended maximum. There is some good news, however. None of the participants have a *TC* level as high as 300, a value that would clearly signal a high-risk patient. Nevertheless, the box plot warns us that cholesterol level may be a problem for many of the patients. One other point should be noted about the box plot. There is one extreme outlier, a *TC* score close to 100 that was obtained from Case 214. This is such an unusual score that it might be wise to recheck this patient's cholesterol level. One possibility that should be considered is that the score represents a clerical error.

The *Q–Q* plot in Fig. 5.3 shows the expected scores (on the y-axis) under the assumption that *TC* is normally distributed. The great majority of scores fall on or very near the straight line; the one clear exception is the outlier noted previously. Confirmation that the data are approximately normally distributed is provided by the nonsignificant results of two tests (Kolmogorov–Smirnov and Shapiro–Wilk) included in SPSS's output. Although these test results provide confirmation, we should be aware that there are occasions where they will be misleading. In particular, when samples are large, even small departures from normality may yield significant results. Small, but statistically significant deviations from the expected normal distribution may have little effect on subsequent hypothesis tests that are based on the assumption of normality. In view of this, we are concerned

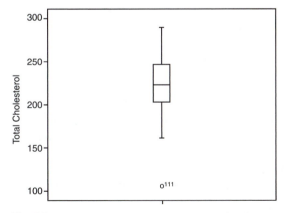

Fig. 5.2 Box plot of total cholesterol scores of males age 50 and older.

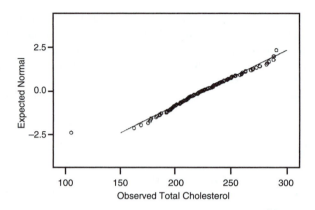

Tests of normality

	Kolmogorov–Smirnov[a]			Shapiro–Wilk		
	Statistic	df	Sig.	Statistic	df	Sig.
TC_mean	.043	117	.200 *	.979	117	.060

* This is a lower bound of the true significance.

a Lilliefors significance correction.

Fig. 5.3 *Q–Q* plot of the total cholesterol scores of men age 50 and older and tests of normality.

only when the *Q–Q* plot signals marked departures from normality or the presence of outliers that require our attention.

Given the findings of our data exploration, it seems reasonable to assume that the population from which the *TC* scores were sampled has a normal distribution. Therefore, our subsequent analyses will be based on the normal probability table in Appendix C.2. We were troubled by the one outlier, so we performed the analyses to be described with and without Case 214. We found little difference in our two sets of results and therefore will report the analyses based on the entire sample of 117 scores. The values we need for this example are $n = 117$, $\bar{Y} = 224.684$, and $s = 31.302$. We are now ready to estimate an interval containing the population mean, and test whether that mean differs significantly from the theoretical value of 200.

5.5.2 A Confidence Interval for μ

In Chapter 4, we introduced the inferential procedure of hypothesis testing. In this section, we introduce a new inferential procedure called *interval estimation*. Interval estimation answers the question, "What is the plausible range of values of θ?", where θ is a population parameter. Thus, interval estimation is a very general and useful procedure.

Although various population parameters may be estimated, at the moment we are interested in estimating the mean of a population, μ. Let's begin by illustrating the procedure for our current example. The sample mean, $\bar{Y} = 224.684$, provides a point estimate of μ, the population mean *TC* score for males older than 50 years. However, the sample mean might be close to the parameter, or it might be considerably in error. In order to have a sense of the accuracy of such estimates, we calculate an interval estimate or *confidence interval*, a pair of numbers which provide bounds for the parameter being estimated.

The procedure for constructing a confidence interval for μ is based on what we have learned about the sampling distribution of the sample mean; namely, that the distribution of the sample mean is normal with an expected value equal to μ and variance equal to the population variance divided by the sample size, n. Imagine drawing many samples of 117 TC scores each from a population of TC scores. Further assume that the mean of each sample is converted into a standardized (z) score by subtracting the mean of the sampling distribution and then dividing the difference by the *standard error (SE)* of the mean. Suppose we want a 95% confidence interval. If the scores are independently sampled from a normal population, Appendix Table C.2 tells us that .95 of the sampled z values will lie between -1.96 and 1.96. That is,

$$p\left(-1.96 \leq \frac{\bar{Y} - \mu}{\sigma_{\bar{Y}}} \leq 1.96\right) = .95 \qquad (5.10)$$

To obtain the bounds on μ, consider each inequality separately. First, consider

$$-1.96 \leq (\bar{Y} - \mu)/\sigma_{\bar{Y}}$$

Solving for μ, we have the upper bound:

$$\mu \leq \bar{Y} + 1.96\sigma_{\bar{Y}}$$

Similarly, we can solve for the lower bound. From the inequality

$$(\bar{Y} - \mu)/\sigma_{\bar{Y}} \leq 1.96$$

we arrive at

$$\bar{Y} - 1.96\sigma_{\bar{Y}} \leq \mu$$

Putting it all together, we have

$$p(\bar{Y} - 1.96\sigma_{\bar{Y}} \leq \mu \leq \bar{Y} + 1.96\sigma_{\bar{Y}}) = .95 \qquad (5.11)$$

Recall that $\bar{Y} = 224.684$ and $s = 31.302$. Dividing s by the square root of n, $\sqrt{117}$, we have 2.894, an estimate of $\sigma_{\bar{Y}}$. Because n is large and the statistic s is a consistent estimate of σ, we expect s to be very close in value to σ, and feel justified in using it in our calculations.[2] Substituting into Equation 5.11, we find that the lower and upper bounds of the 95% confidence interval (CI) for μ are

$$CI = \bar{Y} \pm 1.96\sigma_{\bar{Y}} = 224.684 \pm 5.672 = 219.012, 230.356$$

In words, we can be 95% confident that, for men over 50, the population mean TC falls somewhere between 219.01 and 230.36. Consistent with our earlier look at plots of the data, we see that the lower limit of the confidence interval, 219, is above the recommended maximum TC of 200, but we are reasonably confident that the population mean is not dangerously high for the population of over-50 men from which we have sampled.

What exactly do these numerical limits mean? In what sense do we have 95% confidence that the population mean is contained within them? We may not say that "the *probability* is .95 that μ lies between 219 and 230" because μ is either in this interval or it is not. Furthermore, if we were to draw another sample from the same population of TC scores, the mean would change, giving rise to

---

[2] As noted earlier, because n is large, the results based on the normal distribution are quite similar to those based on the t distribution; the confidence limits using the t distribution are 218.952 and 230.415. Generally, we base inferences about population means on the t distribution because we usually do not know the value of σ.

different limits. What 95% confidence means is that *if we draw many samples and find the 95% confidence interval for each sample, in the long run, .95 of these intervals will contain* μ. Therefore, our *confidence* is .95, or 95%, that the actual value of μ falls within the particular interval that we calculated.

The narrower the interval, the better our estimate of μ. Returning to Equation 5.11, we can see that the interval width depends on the *SE*; the smaller the variability of the sample mean, the smaller will be the distance between the two limits. Recalling that $\sigma_{\bar{y}} = \sigma/\sqrt{n}$, it follows that the interval decreases with increased sample size and with decreased variability. Therefore, we can increase the precision of our estimate by doing whatever we can to reduce error variance, and by collecting as many observations as is practical. A third factor, not immediately obvious in Equation 5.11, also affects the width of the confidence interval. Turning to Appendix Table C.2, note that if the level of confidence is set at .90, rather than .95, the critical z score is 1.645. Replacing 1.96 by 1.645, the new limits are 219.92 and 229.44; we have less confidence but a slightly narrower interval. There is a tradeoff between confidence and interval width.

5.5.3 A Test of the Null Hypothesis

We originally asked whether the mean of the sampled population of *TC* scores differed from a value of 200. The confidence interval limits we just calculated suggests that the answer is "yes." We reason as follows: First, we have 95% confidence that the computed interval, which has the limits 219 and 230, contains the population mean. Second, that interval does not contain 200. Thus, we conclude with 95% confidence that the population mean *TC* score differs from 200.

Most researchers tend not to calculate the confidence interval and, instead, directly test whether the population mean equals the theoretical value. We believe this is a mistake because it addresses the question, Is the mean 200?, rather than the question, What is the mean? Nevertheless, the practice of hypothesis testing is widespread. Furthermore, a presentation of the test permits us to again address related concepts such as Type 1 and Type 2 errors. For these reasons, we will use the standardized normal distribution to test whether μ differs from 200. In Section 5.7, we will present a more detailed discussion of the relation between the confidence interval and the significance test.

When we introduced the logic of hypothesis testing in Chapter 4, we emphasized that the logic of the procedure is the same for any situation (see Box 4.2). Thus, the first step is to establish a null and an alternative hypothesis; these are again designated H_0 and H_1 respectively. Of course, our hypotheses in Chapter 4 concerned the probability of an event, whereas we are now concerned with the value of a population mean. Letting μ_{TC} represent the mean of the population of *TC* scores, the null hypothesis is that μ = 200 and is stated as

$$H_0: \mu_{TC} = 200$$

and the alternative hypothesis is

$$H_1: \mu_{TC} \neq 200$$

Once these two hypotheses have been formulated, we need a test statistic whose value will enable us to decide between them. We will estimate the population mean with the mean *TC* from our sample, and then convert the sample mean to a z score. The z statistic will serve as our test statistic. Because the sample mean is normally distributed for a large sample, the sampling distribution for our test statistic, z, is also normally distributed.

Recall the general form of the z statistic (Equation 5.9): $z = [V - E(V)]/\sigma_V$. In order to test whether the mean TC score is significantly different from 200, we replace V by, $\overline{Y}_{TC}$, $E(V)$ by the population mean specified by H_0 (μ_{hyp}), and σ_V by the SE. Consequently, we have

$$z = \frac{\overline{Y}_{TC} - \mu_{hyp}}{\sigma/\sqrt{n}} \qquad (5.12)$$

Substituting the values presented earlier,

$$z = \frac{224.684 - 200}{2.894} = 8.53$$

This z score informs us that the observed mean is more than eight standard deviation units above the hypothesized mean of 200.

Now that we have a numerical value for our test statistic, we can use it to decide between H_0 and H_1. We do this by determining those values of z that would lead to rejection of H_0 in favor of H_1. Such values constitute the rejection region, the set of possible values of z that are consistent with H_1 and very improbable if H_0 is assumed to be true. Indeed, those values are so improbable if H_0 is assumed that their occurrence leads us to reject H_0. An arbitrarily chosen value, α (alpha), defines exactly how unlikely "so unlikely" is. Traditionally, researchers have set α at .05. We want very strong evidence against H_0 before we reject it.

Once we have decided on a value of α, we can establish a rejection region for our study. Because our alternative hypothesis is nondirectional, we will consider as evidence against the null hypothesis both sample means that are well below and sample means that are well above the hypothesized population mean of 200. Thus, we need to determine the values of z that cut off the lower 2.5% and the upper 2.5% of the normal distribution. Turning to Appendix Table C.2, we find that 1.96 is exceeded by .025 of the standardized normal curve; because the curve is symmetric, .025 of the area also lies below −1.96. Thus, if the null hypothesis is true, there is only a 5% probability of obtaining a value greater than 1.96 or less than −1.96. Equivalently, we reject H_0 if the absolute value of z, $|z|$, is greater than 1.96. Obviously, the z we calculated is much larger than 1.96 and therefore we reject H_0. The obtained value of the test statistic, 8.53, falls well into the rejection region, so we can reject the null hypothesis and conclude that the mean TC level of adult males over 50 is greater than the recommended maximum of 200.

Recall from Chapter 4 that there is an alternative approach that we may choose for testing hypotheses based on computing the p-value of the observed result (see Box 4.1). The p-value is the probability that the value of the test statistic would be at least as extreme as we actually obtained, if the null hypothesis was true. We reject the null hypothesis if $p \leq \alpha$. Here, the p is $p(z > 8.53) + p(z < -8.53)$; to three decimal places, $p = .000$.

5.5.4 One-Tailed vs Two-Tailed Tests

The two-tailed rejection region was selected for our hypothesis test because our alternative hypothesis was nondirectional; that is, we tested whether cholesterol scores were different from 200 in either direction (lower or higher than 200). However, because low cholesterol scores are good, our interest lies primarily in detecting high values. In that case the rejection region would be one-tailed, and the null and alternative hypotheses would be:

$$H_0: \mu_{TC} \leq 200 \quad \text{and} \quad H_1: \mu_{TC} > 200$$

In this situation, if the population of scores is normally and independently distributed, and we know the population variance, we again can use the z test. Accordingly, we turn to Appendix Table C.2. Again, the rejection region consists of those extreme values of z that are consistent with the alternative hypothesis. However, because our alternative hypothesis is directional, we concentrate our rejection region in just one tail of the sampling distribution; specifically, the region consists only of the largest 5% of the z distribution. Therefore, again assuming that $\alpha = .05$, we will reject H_0 if the z calculated from our data is greater than 1.645. In the one-tailed case, the p value is determined only by the part of the distribution beyond the value of the test statistic in the direction consistent with the alternative hypothesis.

The choice between one- and two-tailed tests should be made before the data are collected. To understand why, consider the following scenario. Suppose we originally hypothesized that the average TC score should be above 200; we have a one-tailed hypothesis. However, upon examining the data, we find that the sample mean is less than 200, and we now restate our hypotheses, testing at the .05 level for a significant difference in the direction opposite to that originally hypothesized. This procedure will result in rejecting the null hypothesis if the results fall in the upper .05 of the normal distribution ($z \geq 1.645$) *or* if the results fall in the lower .05 of the distribution ($z \leq -1.645$). Thus, if we operate in such a fashion, the actual probability of a Type 1 error is the probability of $z > 1.645$ or $z < -1.645$, or .10.

Why not always carry out the two-tailed test? Doing so would allow us to test for departures from the null hypothesis in both directions. The answer lies in a consideration of power. Note that the two-tailed test requires a cutoff of 1.96 in the right-hand tail of the normal distribution, whereas the one-tailed test requires a cutoff of 1.645. In other words, if the alternative hypothesis is that the population mean is greater than 200, the one-tailed test has a more lenient criterion for rejection. Therefore, as we illustrated with the binomial distribution of Chapter 4 (see Fig. 4.4), when the null hypothesis is true the one-tailed test has more power against that alternative.

5.5.5 Hypothesis Tests and Confidence Intervals

The relation between confidence intervals and hypothesis tests may be understood by considering the usual decision rule for a two-tailed test: Assuming $\alpha = .05$, reject H_0 if

$$\frac{\overline{Y} - \mu_{hyp}}{\sigma_{\overline{Y}}} > 1.96 \quad \text{or} \quad \frac{\overline{Y} - \mu_{hyp}}{\sigma_{\overline{Y}}} < -1.96$$

Some algebra will show that this is equivalent to the rule, reject if

$$\mu_{hyp} < \overline{Y} - 1.96\sigma_{\overline{Y}} \quad \text{or} \quad \mu_{hyp} > \overline{Y} + 1.96\sigma_{\overline{Y}}$$

However, $\overline{Y} \pm 1.96\sigma_{\overline{Y}}$ are the lower and upper limits of a 95% confidence interval on μ. Therefore, the null hypothesis will be rejected at the .05 level (two-tailed) whenever the hypothesized value of the population mean is less than the lower bound, or more than the upper bound, of a 95% confidence interval. In the example of the seasonal change in depression scores, the value zero was below the lower limit of the 95% confidence interval, allowing us to reject the hypothesis of no mean change in the sampled population at the .05 level of significance. Note that the confidence interval permits evaluation of any null hypothesis; any hypothesized parameter value that falls outside the limits will lead to rejection by a significance test (assuming α is set at 1 minus the confidence level), whereas null hypotheses that assert values of the parameter within the confidence interval will not be rejected.

A confidence interval provides several advantages over a hypothesis test:

1. *It provides a bounded estimate of the population parameter*, thus focusing attention on the parameter value rather than on whether that parameter has one specific value.

2. *The confidence interval permits tests of all possible null hypotheses simultaneously*, thus providing considerably more information than does the hypothesis test.
3. *The interval width provides information about the precision of the research.* A significant result, coupled with a very narrow interval, may suggest that power was so great as to enable us to reject even a trivial effect. On the other hand, a nonsignificant result, together with a wide interval, suggests that our experiment lacked precision, pointing to the need for either a less variable measure, more careful application of experimental procedures, or a larger sample.

If you recall the discussion from Chapter 4 of factors that influence power, you will note that the width of the interval is influenced by the same variables that influence power. The narrower the interval, the more powerful a test of any particular null hypothesis will be. As *n* increases and as *s* decreases, the confidence interval narrows, and power increases. Furthermore, increasing α and decreasing confidence have parallel effects. An increase in α increases power at the cost of increasing the Type 1 error rate. There is a similar tradeoff between confidence and the interval width; decreasing confidence yields a narrower interval, providing a more precise estimate but with less confidence in that estimate.

5.6 THE POWER OF THE *z* TEST

In planning an experiment, the researcher might wish to know what sample size would be needed to attain a certain degree of power in the null hypothesis test for a given effect size. Or another investigator might wish to know what the power would be if a different sample size was used in a replication of a previously published study. Or an investigator who has failed to reject the null hypothesis might wish to estimate how much power the experiment had in the first place. In the latter two cases, the researcher seeks to determine power for known values of *n*, σ (or an estimate), and a specific effect size (such as a difference between two means). Building on the developments in Chapter 4, we will provide an example of how power is calculated when *n*, σ, and a specific effect size are given. Further examples of the determination of power, and also of *n*, using available software, will be presented in Chapter 6.

5.6.1 Determining the Power of the Normal Probability (*z*) Test

A situation very similar to the example of the analysis of cholesterol scores is one in which we have two or more scores for each participant, each in different conditions. For example, in the *Seasons* study, the researchers were interested in seasonal change. Accordingly, we might obtain a single score for each subject by subtracting a score in one season from that in another season, thus obtaining a single change score. We did this for 215 female subjects, subtracting their spring Beck Depression scores from their winter depression scores; see the *D_Change Data* file; the link is on the *Seasons* page of the book's website (*sex* = 1 in the data file). The mean change score was .557 and the *SE* was .266. Using the methods of our analysis of total cholesterol scores, and assuming $H_0: \mu_{change} = 0$ and $H_1: \mu_{change} > 0$, the value of the *z* statistic, 2.094, is significant with a *p* of approximately .018. Therefore, we reject the null hypothesis.

Now suppose that a research group in another part of the country wants to know whether the effects of seasonal change on female depression scores can be replicated in their area, an area in which seasonal climates differ from those in Massachusetts. Further, suppose that their sample of female participants is limited to an n of 100. This is a smaller sample than the 215 tested by the University of Massachusetts researchers. Would this second group of researchers have reasonable power to reject the null hypothesis if it is false? To answer this question, we have to follow the steps outlined for the binomial test in Chapter 4.

The basic principles in computing power are the same that dictated the power calculations of Section 4.5.2 and Box 4.3. To carry out the calculations, we need the standard error of the mean. To find the numerical value of the SE, we assume that $\sigma_{change} = 3.897$, the value of s_{change} obtained in the *Seasons* study, so that $SE = 3.897/10$, or .390. We can now calculate power.

1. Assume that $\alpha = .05$ and that the null hypothesis is $H_0: \mu_{change} = 0$ and the alternative hypothesis is $H_1: \mu_{change} > 0$. Then the decision rule is: Reject H_0 if $z \geq 1.645$. This is depicted in the left-hand curve of Fig. 5.4 (derived from G*Power 3), which shows the distribution assumed under H_0 with mean 0 and a rejection region (labeled α) to the right of 1.645.

2. Establish H_A, the specific alternative hypothesis. A reasonable assumption is that the mean change in the population is the sample value that we observed in our Massachusetts study, .557. Because our rejection region under the null hypothesis was in terms of standard deviation units—z scores—we convert .557 to a z score:

$$z = (\mu_A - \mu_{hyp})/\sigma_{\bar{Y}}$$
$$= (.557 - 0)/.390$$
$$= 1.429$$

   Thus the mean of the distribution, assuming H_A, is 1.429. The right-hand curve of Fig. 5.4 depicts this alternative distribution, with the critical region being that part of the curve beyond the shaded area labeled β; that is, the region to the right of 1.645.

3. Calculate power by finding the area between $z = 1.645$ and $z = 1.429$. To do so, subtract 1.429 from these two numbers so that the right-hand distribution in Fig. 5.4 now has a mean of zero and a critical region to the right of $1.645 - 1.429$, or .216.

4. Because the alternative distribution has been converted to one with a mean of zero, we can find the shaded area in the right-hand panel from Appendix Table C.2. That area to the right of .216 is .41. This is the power of the test based on $n = 100$.

What this result means is that if the mean change score in the population is really .557, the planned experiment has only a .41 probability of resulting in a rejection of the null hypothesis that there is no change in depression over the two seasons. The rather low value of power for our example serves to remind us of the critical effect variability has on our inferences. Despite what many laboratory scientists would consider to be a large sample, power is low against what appears to be a reasonable alternative hypothesis (on the basis of an actual study) and, accordingly, the Type 2 error rate is very high. The situation is considerably better—though hardly great—if we used the actual n of 215; power against the specific alternative ($\mu = .557$) with an n of 215 instead of 100 is approximately .67. Clearly, the variability in Beck Depression scores makes it difficult to achieve high power to test hypotheses, even with relatively large samples.

The preceding developments detail the calculation of power using the z statistic and the normal distribution. However, it is important to understand those aspects of our procedure that are general to calculating the power of all statistical tests. The point is not that we need to know how to calculate power; computer software will usually do this for us. The point is that we should understand just what is meant by power, and the factors that affect it.

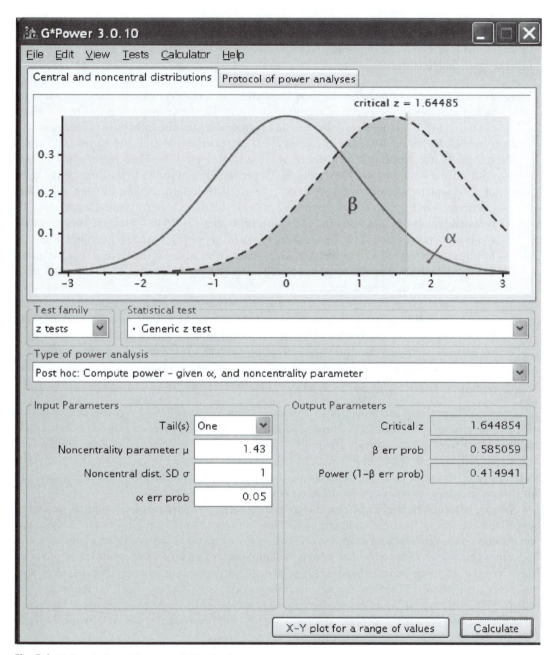

Fig. 5.4 Null and alternative normal distributions.

As we have just illustrated, although the relevant test statistic and sampling distribution vary across different situations, the steps involved in power calculations remain the same. Thus, the steps that we followed in computing power for a test based on the normal distribution were the same steps that we followed in computing power for a test based on the binomial distribution (see Box 4.3). Further, the factors affecting power are the same regardless of the test.

5.6.2 Factors Affecting Power

In general, the power of a test depends upon several factors, all of which have effects qualitatively similar to those noted in the discussion of power in Chapter 4.

1. *Power increases as α increases* because the increase in α requires an increase in the range of values included in the rejection region. If alpha is .10, the critical value in Fig. 5.4 shifts from 1.645 to 1.28, increasing the rejection region, and consequently the area above it.

2. *Power is affected by the nature of H_0 and H_1.* If the statement of H_1 is two-tailed, with alpha still at .05, the decision is to reject H_0 if $z < -1.96$ or $z > 1.96$. Then there would be two critical values in Fig. 5.4, -1.96 and 1.96. Power would correspond to the areas to the right of 1.96 and to the left of -1.96 under the H_A distribution. As we can see in the H_A distribution of Fig. 5.4, the probability of $z < -1.96$ if H_A is true is essentially zero, and the probability that $z > 1.96$ is less than the probability that $z > 1.645$. Therefore, the one-tailed test is more powerful against the specific alternative, $\mu_A = .557$. On the other hand, this one-tailed test has virtually no power against specific alternatives of the form $\mu < \mu_{hyp}$ whereas the two-tailed test has the same probability of rejecting H_0 against these alternatives as against those of the form $\mu > \mu_{hyp}$.

3. *Power is affected by the population variance and the sample size.* Decreased σ and increased n result in smaller standard errors. As the SE decreases, the sample mean is more likely to be close to the true parameter value. As we noted in considering confidence intervals, a smaller SE increases the probability of getting values of $\overline{Y}$ close to the true population mean. Accordingly, as σ decreases or n increases, we are more likely to reject the mean assumed under the null hypothesis, if that hypothesis is wrong.

Most null hypotheses are false at least to some extent. We should always consider whether we have had so large an n that an effect of little practical or theoretical importance was detected. This is one reason why confidence intervals are an important part of our analyses. Very large sample sizes may sometimes result in rejection of a null hypothesis even if the effect is trivial, but the confidence interval, by providing a bounded estimate of the effect, enables us to assess its importance. In subsequent chapters, we will consider other measures of the effect size.

We can influence variability by our choice of measures and experimental design, as well as by controlling extraneous factors that might contribute to chance variability. How large an n we need will depend on the other factors we noted and the power we want, as well as the smallest size effect we want to be able to reject with that power. A sample size of as little as 40 would have provided more than the .41 power we calculated if the variance of the depression scores had been less, or if μ_A had been larger than .557. Many sources, including books (e.g., Cohen, 1988; Kraemer & Thiemann, 1987), software, and websites, enable researchers to calculate the sample size needed to have a certain level of power against a specified alternative. We will illustrate the use of software available from the Internet for power analyses in the next chapter.

5.7 VALIDITY OF ASSUMPTIONS

The validity of the inferences that are based on the calculations of confidence intervals and hypothesis tests rests upon three assumptions. Scores are assumed to be independently and normally distributed, and have a known standard deviation, σ. Let us consider each of these assumptions in turn.

5.7.1 The Independence Assumption

Two scores, Y_i and Y_j, are independent of each other if the probability of any value of one is independent of the value of the other. In the notation of Chapter 3, we have two independent scores if $p(Y_j \mid Y_i) = p(Y_j)$. In other words, two scores are independent if knowing one score provides no information about the value of the other score. If scores are not independently distributed, the confidence interval for μ may be invalid and Type 1 error rates and power associated with tests of hypotheses about μ may be seriously affected. In the *Seasons* data, spring and winter scores are likely to be correlated, and therefore not independent; individuals who are more depressed than others in the winter will also tend to be so in the spring. For this reason we cannot treat the winter and spring samples as independent of each other.

Suppose that we had ignored the independence assumption for the spring and winter scores. For that data set, the confidence interval would have been overly wide and power would have been low relative to that in the correct analysis. The reason for this is that the standard error of the difference between two independent means is usually larger than that for two dependent means; Appendix 5.1 shows why this is so. By treating the means as independent when they are not, we use too large an estimate of the variability in this research design. In other research designs, the result of a failure to take nonindependence into account in the data analysis may result in an inflation of Type 1 error rate.

Of course, in our treatment of the depression scores, we did use the results for both seasons; however, we created a single change score for each participant. The mean and standard deviation we reported were based on these change scores. By computing the difference between the winter and spring scores for each subject, we incorporated information about the relation between the scores into the resulting change score. Further, because we have just one such score for each participant, we have satisfied the assumption of independence. Assuming that our subjects were randomly sampled, the change scores can be analyzed to provide inferences about μ_{change}, the mean of the population of change scores.

5.7.2 The Normality Assumption

Skewness and kurtosis statistics, together with various data plots from the Explore module, indicated that the distribution of depression change scores was symmetric, but not normal. However, the issue for any assumption is not whether it is correct but whether it is sufficiently close to being correct that our inferences are valid. In the example of the depression change scores, the departure from normality is not likely to be a problem. Our inferences are based on the assumption that the sampling distribution of the mean change score is normal. Even if the population of scores is not normal, the central limit theorem leads us to believe that the sampling distribution of the mean is approximately normal because we have a large number (215) of change scores.

5.7.3 The Assumption of a Known Value of the Standard Deviation

Although we can be certain that the value of s calculated from our data is not exactly the same as σ, s is an unbiased estimate of σ, and a consistent one. Consistency implies that as the sample grows larger, the probability increases that s lies close to σ. Because our sample size is large, using the sample value of the standard deviation in our calculations in place of the true (unknown) population value should not present a problem. Some evidence that violations of the normality and known-σ assumptions are not critical when n is large derives from a computer study we conducted.

We drew 2000 samples of 215 scores each from a population distribution with characteristics—mean, standard deviation, skewness, and kurtosis—similar to those of the sample of 215 scores. We then calculated a confidence interval for each sample. The proportion of samples yielding limits containing the mean of the simulated population was .945, quite close to the theoretical value of 95%. In terms of a two-tailed test of the null hypothesis, this implies a rejection rate of .055.

The close approximation of confidence and significance values to the theoretical values indicates that even if the population is not normally distributed, the normal probability function and an estimate of the population standard deviation can provide adequate inferences when the sample is large. This raises the question of how large is large. There is no simple answer to this. Using the population we simulated and drawing samples of size 30 instead of 215, .940 of the 2000 confidence intervals contained the true value of the population mean, a reasonable approximation to the theoretical value of 95%. However, the results may not be quite as satisfactory with small samples if the population distribution deviates more markedly from normality.

5.8 RELATIONSHIPS BETWEEN THE NORMAL AND OTHER DISTRIBUTIONS

5.8.1 The Normal As a Basis for Other Distributions

Three important distributions can be derived, starting with the assumption of a normally distributed standard deviate, or z score. These distributions are the chi-square (χ^2), the t, and the F. The χ^2 is most commonly applied in the analysis of frequency data. In such applications, it is used to determine how well a theoretical distribution fits an observed distribution, and in testing whether two or more categorical variables are independent. An example of the goodness-of-fit application would be in testing whether the distribution of letter grades in a class conformed to some theoretical distribution such as 15% As and Fs, 20% Bs and Ds, and 30% Cs. An example of the test of independence would be one in which we ask whether the distribution of letter grades is the same in the populations of male and female students. That is, is the distribution of grades independent of gender? An introduction to these applications of the χ^2 statistic may be found in almost every introductory statistics textbook, and entire textbooks have presented detailed treatments, particularly of tests of independence in multi-factor designs (e.g., Bishop, Fienberg, & Holland, 1975; Fienberg, 1977; Fliess, 1973).

The t distribution provides confidence intervals and hypothesis tests for single means, as in the total cholesterol example; for differences between means of correlated samples, as in the Beck Depression example; and for differences between means of two independent samples. As we stated previously in this chapter, the advantage of inferences based on the t distribution over those based on the normal distribution is that they do not rest on the assumption of a known population variance. When samples are small, the t provides more accurate confidence intervals and tests of hypotheses. In the next chapter, we will take a much closer look at the applications of the t distribution.

The most common application of the F distribution is in the analysis of variance (ANOVA). In ANOVA, the numerator of the F ratio is a variance of a set of sample means, and the denominator is a measure of chance, or error, variance. The F test in ANOVA allows us to simultaneously compare the means, correlated or independent, of any number of conditions. It addresses the question of whether the variance of these condition means is greater than what could reasonably be attributed to chance. If the F ratio is large enough, there is reason to believe that something more than chance variability is affecting the variance of the sample means; in that case, we have evidence that the experimental conditions are having an effect, and the null hypothesis that the population means are all equal can be rejected.

5.8.2 The Normal As an Approximation to Other Distributions

When we worked with the binomial distribution in Chapter 4, probabilities were obtained either by calculation, or by using tables of the binomial distribution. However, for large samples this is unnecessary, because we can estimate binomial probabilities from tables of the normal distribution. In Chapter 4, we showed that as the number of trials increased, the binomial distribution began to look more symmetric, and more like the normal distribution (see Fig. 4.2), particularly when the probability of a success on a trial, p, was .5. In fact, with n as small as 20, the normal distribution provides an excellent approximation to the tail probabilities of the binomial. The normal probability table in Appendix Table C.2 may be used to compute the probability of y or more successes when y is greater than pn. Simply calculate:

$$z = \frac{y - pn - .5}{\sqrt{p(1-p)n}} \tag{5.13}$$

where pn is the mean value of Y, $p(1-p)n$ is the variance of y, and the .5 is a *correction for continuity*. The correction reflects the fact that the binomial is a discrete distribution. Suppose we want the probability of 15 or more successes in 20 trials. Because 15 may be viewed as representing a point from 14.5 to 15.5 along a continuum, we "correct" 15 by subtracting .5; in other words, we find the area above 14.5 under the normal distribution. If $y < pn$, we add the .5 instead of subtracting it.

Table 5.2 presents tail probabilities $[p(Y \geq y)]$ when $n = 20$, $p = .5$ or .75, for values of y from 11 to 20. The normal approximation to the binomial is almost perfect when $p = .5$, and it is fair when $p = .75$. The approximation when $p = .75$ can be improved by increasing n. A rough rule of thumb is that in order to use the normal approximation to the binomial, the smaller of np and $n(1-p)$ should be greater than 5.

Table 5.2 Tail probabilities, $p(Y \geq y)$, for the binomial and normal distributions ($n = 20$)

	p = .5		p = .75	
y	Binomial	Normal	Binomial	Normal
11	.4119	.4115	.9861	.9899
12	.2517	.2512	.9591	.9646
13	.1316	.1318	.8982	.9016
14	.0577	.0588	.7858	.7807
15	.0207	.0221	.6172	.6019
16	.0059	.0070	.4148	.3981
17	.0013	.0018	.2252	.2193
18	.0002	.0004	.0913	.0984
19	.0000	.0001	.0243	.0354
20	.0000	.0000	.0032	.0101

5.9 SUMMARY

Chapter 5 has continued the development of inferential concepts and principles begun in Chapter 4. Central to both chapters has been the emphasis on the distributions of random variables, but in Chapter 5 we have used a continuous distribution to illustrate several important points concerning estimation and hypothesis testing:

- Every statistic that can be calculated has a sampling distribution whose properties are important in assessing criteria for estimators, and affecting the width of confidence intervals, and the power of hypothesis tests.
- The goodness of estimates of population parameters depends on several criteria. A good estimator is unbiased; the mean of its sampling distribution equals the parameter. A good estimator is consistent; as sample size increases, the estimator is more likely to be close to the estimated parameter value. And a good estimator is efficient relative to other estimators of the same parameter; its sampling distribution has a smaller variance about the parameter.
- The central limit theorem states that the sampling distribution of the mean will tend toward the normal for large samples even when the underlying population distribution is not normal. However, the speed with which the sampling distribution approaches normality as a function of sample size will depend on how closely the underlying distribution resembles the normal.
- Confidence intervals about population means will be narrower, and hypothesis tests involving means will be more powerful as the variability of the sampling distribution decreases; that is, as the standard error of the mean (the SE) decreases. The SE will decrease as sample size increases and as the sample variance decreases.

We illustrated the calculation of confidence intervals and hypothesis tests using probabilities obtained from the table of the normal distribution. Although in most instances, such calculations would be carried out with the t distribution, the concepts and principles are the same and extend to all the procedures in this book, and many others as well. The interpretation of p-values, confidence interval bounds, Type 1 errors, and power (or its complement, the probability of a Type 2 error) have been a focus of both Chapters 4 and 5. They are critical to interpreting the results of data analysis.

APPENDIX 5.1

The Variance of Linear Combinations

A *linear combination* of n observations, L, has the general form

$$L = w_1 Y_1 + w_2 Y_2 + \ldots + w_n Y_n$$

where the weights. the w_i, are any real numbers. A special case is one in which $n = 2$ and the weights are either both 1, in which case L is a sum, or 1 and -1, in which L is a difference. We consider this case first.

Variances of Sums and Differences.   The variance of a sum or difference of two variables depends both on the variances of the variables and on their covariance. The covariance is a function of the variances and the correlation coefficient; as we stated in Chapter 2, the sample correlation coefficient of two variables, X and Y, is defined as

$$r_{XY} = \frac{\Sigma(X - \bar{X})(Y - \bar{Y})/(n - 1)}{s_X s_Y} \tag{5.14}$$

and the covariance is defined as the numerator, $\Sigma(X - \bar{X})(Y - \bar{Y})/(n - 1)$. We will denote the covariance as s_{XY}. First consider the variance of $X + Y$; by definition of the sample variance,

$$s_{X+Y}^2 = \frac{1}{n - 1} \sum [(X + Y) - (\overline{X + Y})]^2$$

But

$$\overline{X + Y} = (1/n) \sum_i (X_i + Y_i) = \bar{X} + \bar{Y}$$

Therefore,

$$s_{X+Y}^2 = \frac{1}{n - 1} \sum [(X + Y) - (\bar{X} + \bar{Y})]^2$$

$$= \frac{1}{n - 1} \sum_i [(X_i - \bar{X}) + (Y_i - \bar{Y})]^2$$

$$= \frac{1}{n - 1} \sum_i [(X_i - \bar{X})^2 + (Y_i - \bar{Y})^2 + 2(X_i - \bar{X})(Y_i - \bar{Y})]$$

$$= s_X^2 + s_Y^2 + 2s_{XY}$$

where $s_{XY} = r_{XY} s_X s_Y$, the covariance of X and Y. Therefore,

$$s_{X+Y}^2 = s_X^2 + s_Y^2 + 2r_{XY} s_X s_Y \tag{5.15}$$

The variance of the difference scores has a similar form:

$$s_{X-Y}^2 = s_X^2 + s_Y^2 - 2r_{XY} s_X s_Y \tag{5.16}$$

The only difference in the two expressions is in the sign of the covariance term. Note that if the two variables are uncorrelated (i.e., $r = 0$), both the variance of $X + Y$ and $X - Y$ are $s_X^2 + s_Y^2$, the sum of the variances of X and Y.

Analogous expressions hold when we consider population parameters. The population variances for $X + Y$ and $X - Y$ are

$$\sigma_{X+Y}^2 = \sigma_X^2 + \sigma_Y^2 + 2\rho_{XY}\,\sigma_X \sigma_Y \tag{5.17}$$

and

$$\sigma_{X-Y}^2 = \sigma_X^2 + \sigma_Y^2 - 2\rho_{XY}\,\sigma_X \sigma_Y \tag{5.18}$$

where the Greek letter rho (ρ) is the population correlation coefficient. If X and Y are uncorrelated, the variances of both $X + Y$ and $X - Y$ are $\sigma_X^2 + \sigma_Y^2$.

The General Case.   We previously defined L as $L = w_1 Y_1 + w_2 Y_2 + \ldots + w_n Y_n$. The variance of L can be shown to be an extension of the formulas for two observations:

$$s_L^2 = \sum_j w_j^2 s_j^2 + \sum_{j \neq j'} \sum_{j'} w_j w_{j'} r_{jj'} s_j s_{j'} \tag{5.19}$$

For example, given two test scores, $T1$ and $T2$, and a final exam score, F, and supposing the grade is calculated by weighting the first two exams by 1/4 each and the final by 1/2, the variance of the grade is

$$s_{grade}^2 = (1/16)[s_{T1}^2 + s_{T2}^2] + (1/4)s_F^2 + (2)(1/4)(1/4)(s_{T1} s_{T2} r_{T1,T2}) + (2)(1/4)(1/2)(s_{T1} s_F r_{T1,F})$$
$$+ (2)(1/4)(1/2)(s_{T2} s_F r_{T2,F})$$

The Variance of the Mean.   An important consequence of these developments is that we can readily derive an expression for the variance of the mean of n independently distributed scores. The mean is $(1/n)(Y_1 + Y_2 + \ldots + Y_n)$. We view the variance of a score as the variance of scores in that position in the sample over many independent samples. Then $s_1^2 = s_2^2 = \ldots s_n^2 = s^2$ and each value of w is $1/n$. Because the scores are independently distributed, all covariances equal zero, and substituting into Equation 5.19,

$$\text{var}(\overline{Y}) = n \times s^2/n^2 = s^2/n$$

and the standard error of the mean is (as defined in Chapter 2)

$$SEM = \sqrt{s^2/n}$$

EXERCISES

The answers to several exercises involve calculating z scores and then using Appendix Table C.2. In some cases, it may be helpful to draw a normal curve, shading the area asked for. Also, in several exercises, we ask for the variance (or standard deviation) of means, or differences among means. We do this for cases in which the means are dependent and also for cases in which they are independent. A review of Appendix 5.1 will be helpful in finding the answers to those exercises.

5.1 A standard IQ test yields scores that are normally distributed with $\mu = 100$ and $\sigma = 15$. Y is a randomly selected score on the test.
   (a) What is the probability that a randomly selected student will score higher than 115?
   (b) (i) What is $p(Y > 130)$? (ii) $p(85 < Y < 145)$? (iii) $p(Y > 70)$? (iv) $p(70 < Y < 80)$?
   (c) What scores define the middle 80% of the distribution?
   (d) What is the 75th percentile (score such that it exceeds 75% of the scores)?
   (e) What is the probability that the mean IQ of a group of 10 randomly selected students will be greater than 105?
5.2 On a new test of logical reasoning, the mean and standard deviations for a population of males are $\mu = 170$ and $\sigma = 50$; for females, $\sigma = 200$ and $\sigma = 60$.
   (a) What is the probability that a randomly selected female will have a score greater than 170?
   (b) What is the probability that the mean of a group of nine randomly sampled females will be greater than 170?
   (c) Assume that many pairs of female (F) and male (M) scores are drawn from their respective

populations and a difference score, $d = F - M$, is calculated for each pair. What is the mean and standard deviation of the population of such difference scores (see Appendix 5.1)?

(d) What is the probability that a randomly selected female will have a higher score than a randomly selected male? [Note: $p(F > M) = p(F - M > 0)$.]

5.3 Assume that X and Y are independently and normally distributed variables. For X, $\mu = 30$ and $\sigma = 20$; for Y, $\mu = 20$ and $\sigma = 16$.

(a) What is the probability of sampling an X score (i) < 25? (ii) > 60? (iii) between 15 and 40?

(b) What is $p(X > \mu_Y)$?

(c) Let $W = X + Y$. (i) What is the mean of W? (ii) What is the variance of W? (iii) What is $p(W > 35)$?

(d) An individual's X score is at the 85th percentile (i.e., it exceeds .85 of the population of X scores); her Y score is at the 30th percentile of the Y distribution. What percent of the population of W scores does her W score exceed?

5.4 In this problem, we will use the normal probability distribution to test a hypothesis about a proportion.

A population of individuals has a disease, it is treated, and symptoms are no longer present. However, .4 of this population suffers a recurrence of the symptoms within 1 year. A new drug developed to prevent recurrence of the disease is tried on a sample of 48 patients. We wish to determine whether the probability of failure (i.e., recurrence of symptoms) is less than .4.

(a) Let π = the probability of failure in the population sampled. State H_0 and H_1.

(b) Let p = probability of failure in the sample. If the null hypothesis is true, the mean of the sampling distribution of p is π (.4) and its variance is $\pi(1 - \pi)/n$. In the study, only 12 of the 48 participants suffered a recurrence of symptoms after 1 year. Use the normal probability distribution to test the null hypothesis. State your conclusions.

(c) We might want a better sense of the true probability of recurrence of symptoms. Calculate a 95% confidence interval and interpret your result.

(d) In parts (b) and (c), we used the normal probability (z) table to draw inferences about a population probability. (i) What assumption about the sampling probability of p is implied by our methods? (ii) What justifies this assumption? (iii) Would the assumption be as justifiable if the sample had only 10 people in it? Explain.

5.5 A population of scores is uniformly distributed between 0 and 1. This means that all scores between 0 and 1 are equally likely and that $F(y)$ (the probability of sampling a score less than y) equals y. For example, $p(Y < .8) = .8$. The mean and standard deviation of this uniformly distributed population are .5 and $1/\sqrt{12}$.

(a) (i) What is $p(Y < .6)$? (ii) What is the probability that in a sample of two scores both are less than .6? Express your answer as a probability raised to a power. (iii) What is the probability that in a sample of 20 scores all are less than .6?

(b) Assume that we draw many samples of 20 scores and calculate the mean of each sample. Describe the shape of the sampling distribution. What are its mean and standard deviation?

(c) On the basis of your answer to part (b), what is the probability that the mean of a sample of 20 scores is less than .6?

(d) Briefly state your justification for your approach to part (c). Would the same approach be appropriate in answering part (a) (iii)? Explain.

5.6 We have a population in which $\pi = p(X = 1) = .2$ and $1 - \pi = p(X = 0) = .8$.

(a) (i) Calculate the population mean, μ_X, and variance, σ_X [$E(X)$ and $var(X)$]. Note that $E(X) = (\pi)(1) + (1 - \pi)(0)$ and $var(X) = E(X^2) - [E(X)]^2$. (ii) Assume that we draw samples of size 3 from this population. What would be the variance of the sampling distribution of the mean?

(b) Assume we draw samples of size 3. If we define the outcome of the experiment as a value of Y where $Y = \Sigma X$, there are four possible outcomes. Complete the following table (S^2 is the variance with n in the denominator whereas s^2 has $n - 1$ in the denominator):

Y	$p(Y)$		$\bar{X}$	S^2_X	$S^2_{\bar{X}}$	$s^2_{\bar{X}}$
0	$.8^3$	$= .512$				
1	$(3)(.8^2)(.2) = .384$					
2	$(3)(.8)(.2^2) = .096$					
3	$.2^3$	$.008$				

(c) Using the entries in the above table, find (i) $E(Y)$, (ii) $E(\bar{X})$, (iii) $E(S^2_{\bar{X}})$, and (iv) $E(s^2_{\bar{X}})$.

(d) How do $E(Y)$ and $E(\bar{X})$ compare with the value of $E(X)$ obtained in part (a)?

(e) How do $E(S^2_{\bar{X}})$ and $E(s^2_{\bar{X}})$ compare with the value of $\text{var}(\bar{X})$ obtained in part (a)?

(f) What do your answers to parts (d) and (e) say about which sample statistics are biased or unbiased estimators?

5.7 A national survey of a large number of college students in 1983 yielded a mean "authoritarianism" score of 52.8 and a standard deviation of 10.5. For all practical purposes, we may view these as population parameters.

(a) Suppose we wish to examine whether authoritarian attitudes have increased in the years since the survey by examining a random sample of 50 students. State H_0, H_1, and the rejection region assuming $\alpha = .05$.

(b) Assume that the mean of the sample of 50 scores is 56.0. Carry out the significance test and state your conclusion.

(c) Suppose the true population mean is now 57.00. What is the power of your significance test?

(d) Based on your sample (and assuming the population variance has stayed the same), what is the 95% confidence interval for the current population mean of authoritarianism scores?

(e) In part (d) you found the 95% confidence interval. What exactly *is* a 95% confidence interval? What exactly is supposed to happen 95% of the time?

5.8 Two random samples are available from a population with unknown mean. Sample 1 has n_1 scores and has a mean of $\bar{Y}_1$; sample 2 has n_2 scores and a mean of $\bar{Y}_2$. Consider two possible estimates of the population mean, μ_Y, that are based on both samples: One estimate is the unweighted mean of the sample means, UM, where

$$UM = \frac{\bar{Y}_1 + \bar{Y}_2}{2}$$

and the other is the weighted mean of the sample means, WM, where

$$WM = \frac{n_1 \bar{Y}_1 + n_2 \bar{Y}_2}{n_1 + n_2}$$

In answering the following questions, remember that $E(\bar{Y}_1) = E(\bar{Y}_2) = \mu_Y$.

(a) Is UM an unbiased estimator of the population mean? Show why or why not.

(b) Is WM an unbiased estimator of the population mean? Show why or why not.

(c) Assume that $n_1 = 20$ and $n_2 = 80$, and the population variance, σ^2, equals 4. Calculate the variance of UM.

(d) Calculate the variance of WM. Is UM or WM a better estimate of the population mean? Why?

(e) Is either UM or WM a better estimator of the population mean than $\bar{Y}_1$ or $\bar{Y}_2$? Why?

5.9 Assume that we have a treatment (T) and a control (C) population for which μ_T is larger than μ_C. Assume that both populations are normally distributed and have the same variance, σ^2.

(a) Let T and C be randomly sampled scores from their respective populations. Assume that μ_T is $.5\sigma$ larger than μ_C. Express the mean and variance of the sampling distribution of $T - C$ as a function of σ (see Appendix 5.1).

(b) What is the probability that a randomly chosen score from the treatment population will be higher than a randomly chosen score from the control population? [i.e., what is $p(T - C) > 0$?] It is not necessary to have numerical values for μ_T, μ_C, and σ.

(c) (i) what is the probability that the mean of nine randomly chosen scores from the treatment population will be larger than the mean of nine randomly chosen scores from the control population? (ii) What is the probability if μ_T is $.2\sigma$ larger than μ_C?

5.10 A population of voters consists of equal numbers of conservatives and liberals. Furthermore, .9 of the liberals prefer the Democratic candidate in the upcoming election, whereas only .3 of the conservatives prefer the Democratic candidate.

(a) What is P_D, the probability of sampling an individual from the entire population who prefers the Democratic candidate?

(b) The variance of a proportion p is $p(1 - p)/n$ (see Appendix B for the proof). With this in mind, what is the variance of the sampling distribution of p_D, the proportion of Democratic voters in a sample of 50 individuals who are randomly selected from the population of voters?

(c) Suppose you are a pollster who knows that the population is equally divided between liberals and conservatives, but you don't know what the proportion of Democratic voters is. You sample 50 individuals with the constraint that 25 are liberals and 25 are conservatives; this is referred to as stratified sampling.

  (i) From the information presented at the start of this problem, what is the variance of the sampling distribution of $p_{D|L}$, the proportion of Democratic voters in a sample of 25 liberals?

  (ii) What is the variance of the sampling distribution of $p_{D|C}$, the proportion of Democratic voters in a sample of 25 conservatives?

  (iii) The proportion of Democrats in the stratified sample is $p_D = (1/2)(p_{D|L} + p_{D|C})$. What is the variance of the sampling distribution of D when stratification is employed?

  (iv) In view of your answers to (b) and (c) (iii), discuss the effect of stratification.

5.11 Instruction in problem-solving methods raised the scores of a sample of 225 students by an average of 2 points. A difference between the *before* and *after* scores was calculated for each student and the standard deviation of the differences was 13.6.

(a) Find the standard error of the difference in the means.

(b) Using the result in part (a), find the .95 confidence interval for the difference in the means.

(c) Carry out the z test of the null hypothesis of no instructional effect; $\alpha = .05$.

5.12 Assume that we estimate the population variances from a previous study to be $s_1^2 = 160$ and $s_2^2 = 240$.

(a) Assume that there is a new experiment with n subjects in each of two groups, one from each population. Express the variance of the difference between the means as a function of the variance estimates and n. (Appendix 5.1 should be helpful here.)

(b) Using your results from part (a), calculate the n needed in each group in order to have a .95 confidence interval 5 points wide.

(c) Suppose that instead of two groups of subjects, we tested one group of n subjects under both of the conditions in part (a). Still assuming the same variances, and also assuming that the correlation of scores is .5, how many subjects should we run now to have a .95 confidence interval of 5 points? (Note: The variance of difference scores is $s_d^2 = s_1^2 + s_2^2 - 2s_1s_2r_{12}$.)

(d) Comparing your answers to (b) and (c), if you had a limited supply of subjects, which design would you choose? How does the size of the correlation affect the difference between the two designs?

5.13 Following are summary statistics for the total cholesterol scores for the winter ($TC1$) and spring ($TC2$) seasons for males; the data are at the website.

$$\overline{Y}_1 = 224.059 \qquad \overline{Y}_2 = 218.818$$
$$s_1 = 40.794 \qquad s_2 = 40.113$$
$$r = .855 \qquad n = 220$$

(a) Find the standard error of the difference in the means.

(b) Using the result in part (a), find the .95 confidence interval for the difference in the two seasonal means.

(c) Carry out the z test of the null hypothesis of no seasonal effect; $\alpha = .05$.

5.14 (a) Given the statistics in Exercise 5.13, how large should n be to have a .95 confidence interval of 4 points?

(b) Cohen (1988) has defined a standardized effect (d_z) as $\overline{d}/s_d$, where $\overline{d}$ is the difference between the means and s_d is the standard deviation of the difference scores. Calculate the standardized effect size for the data of Exercise 5.13.

(c) Assume that we wish to replicate our study of cholesterol differences in a new sample of males. If we have only 100 subjects available, what is the power to detect the standardized effect calculated in part (a)? Assume a one-tailed test with $\alpha = .05$.

5.15 In the *TC Data* file (see the *Seasons* page on the book's website), we created an educational level (EL) variable. If *Schoolyr* = 1, 2, or 3, $EL = 1$; if *Schoolyr* = 4, 5, or 6, $EL = 2$; and if Schoolyr = 7 or 8, $EL = 3$. $EL = 1$ corresponds to individuals with a high-school education or less, $EL = 2$ corresponds to those with education beyond high school but not including the bachelor's degree, and $EL = 3$ corresponds to those with a college or graduate school education.

(a) Calculate the standard error of the sampling distribution of the difference between the means of the $EL = 1$ and the $EL = 2$ groups.

(b) Calculate a 95% confidence interval for the difference in the TC population means between the $EL = 1$ and the $EL = 2$ groups. What can you conclude about this difference based on the confidence interval?

5.16 In this exercise, we use the *Mean_D* variable in the *Beck_D* file linked to the *Seasons* page on the book's website. This is an average of the four seasonal depression scores for those individuals who were tested in all four seasons. Note that there are missing values of the *Mean_D* measure because not all individuals were tested in all four seasons.

(a) Tabulate descriptive statistics separately for males and females, and compare these. Then graph the two data sets in any way you choose, relating characteristics of the plots to the statistics. Comment on location, spread, and shape.

(b) Using the statistics you obtained, construct a .95 confidence interval for $\mu_F - \mu_M$ (female – male *Beck_D* population means) and decide whether the male and female means differ significantly at the .05 level. Do you think the assumption of normality is valid?

(c) Outlying scores frequently influence our conclusions. Considering the male and female data separately, what values would be outliers?

(d) Redo parts (a) and (b) with the outliers excluded. How does this affect the results in parts (a) and (b)? (Note: If the file is sorted by sex and then by *Mean_D*, outliers can more easily be extracted.)

5.17 We plan a study of cholesterol levels in a population of patients. On the basis of the *TC* (total cholesterol) data in the present *Seasons* study, we assume that the population standard deviation is 30. We would like power = .80 to detect effects of small size (.2σ or 6 points) above a level of 200.

(a) What are the null and alternative hypotheses for the proposed study?

(b) What is the specific alternative hypothesis?

(c) How many subjects should we recruit for our study? Assume α = .05.

Chapter 6
The *t* Distribution and Its Applications

6.1 OVERVIEW

In Chapter 5, we constructed a confidence interval on the average total cholesterol (*TC*) for a population of older men, and also tested the hypothesis that the population mean was greater than 200. Having determined that the *TC* level was higher than recommended by most medical researchers, we might next design an experiment to test the effects of treatments intended to lower the *TC* level. In this chapter we will consider two possible ways to design the experiment. In the *independent-groups design*, there are two groups, one of which receives the treatment while a second group receives no treatment. Both groups are drawn from the same population. For example, we might request volunteers in a retirement community, and then randomly divide the volunteers into two groups, only one of which receives the treatment. The *correlated-scores design* involves testing the same subjects in two different conditions, or testing pairs of subjects with the members of each pair matched on relevant dimensions, such as initial level of *TC*. In the first approach, for example, a no-treatment baseline *TC* level is established and then subjects are retested, perhaps after 6 or 12 months' exposure to the treatment (for example, a prescribed diet).

In this chapter, we introduce the *t* distribution and present assumptions and calculations related to its application to data from the two designs just described. The major goals of the chapter are:

- *To compare the independent-groups and correlated-scores designs*, focusing on their relative merits in those instances in which both designs are applicable.
- *To provide a description of the t distribution*. This will involve the definition of the *t* statistic, a description of the distribution, both when the null hypothesis is true (the *central t distribution*) and when it is false (the *noncentral t distribution*).
- *To present confidence intervals, hypothesis tests, and power analyses based on the t distribution*, including the assumptions and calculations for the two designs under consideration.
- *To present a standardized effect size measure and its confidence interval*. The difference between means is the *unstandardized*, or *raw, effect*. It is a function of the variability in the

data, and therefore varies across experiments. Standardized effect sizes take that variability into account, providing a measure of effect size that is independent of the data scale.

The organization of this chapter is as follows. We first compare the independent-groups and correlated-scores designs. Following that, we define the t statistic and describe its distribution. We then present data sets and the related data analyses, including effect size estimation and power analyses, first for the independent-groups design, and then for the correlated-scores design.

6.2 DESIGN CONSIDERATIONS: INDEPENDENT GROUPS OR CORRELATED SCORES?

Consider a hypothetical experiment in which we wish to compare the effectiveness of a prescribed diet to reduce total cholesterol (TC) level with a control condition in which no diet has been prescribed. The first issue is how to design the experiment. As stated earlier, this study could be run in one of several ways. Before analyzing our hypothetical data set, we consider the relative merits of two approaches.

In the *independent-groups*, or *between-subjects, design*, $2n$ subjects are randomly divided into two groups with the restriction that there are the same number of subjects in each condition. In this case, all $2n$ scores are independent of each other. In the *correlated-scores*, or *paired samples, design*, each of n subjects is tested in each of two conditions, or two groups of n subjects each are selected so that one member of each group is matched on some relevant dimension (e.g., initial TC level) with one member of the other group. The design in which each subject is tested twice is often referred to as a *repeated-measures* or *within-subjects design*, and the design involving matching of subjects is often referred to as a *matched-pair design*. In these designs, a difference is calculated between the scores of each subject or between the scores of members of each matched pair, and the n difference scores are analyzed.

When both types of design are feasible, as they are in the study of effects of diet on TC level, the independent-groups design has two advantages. First, it involves more independent observations. Because each group provides an independent estimate of the population variance, each estimate is based on n independent scores, and altogether there are $2n$ independent scores. The correlated-scores design involves only n independent observations because only the n difference scores are independent. As we shall discuss in Section 6.3, the power of the t test increases and the confidence interval is narrower as the number of independent observations increases. Therefore—*if all other things are equal*—the independent-groups design has a power advantage. We will see shortly, however, that all other things usually are not equal in comparing the independent-groups and correlated-scores designs.

A second potential advantage of the independent-groups design is practical. Subjects are not required to return for a second session as is sometimes the case in the repeated-measures variation of the correlated-scores design, nor is there a need to obtain an additional measure to use to establish pairs, as in the matched-pairs variation.

Why, then, should we ever use a correlated-scores design? In the case of the repeated-measures design, a practical advantage is that the researcher requires half the number of subjects to make the same number of observations as the corresponding independent-groups design. However, the more important motivation for using a correlated-scores design lies in a comparison of the denominators of the t statistics for the two designs. As we shall see, in the independent-groups design, the standard error of the difference between the means (SE) is based on an average of the two group variances whereas in the correlated-scores design, the *SE* is based on the variance of the *n* difference scores. The latter *SE* will generally be smaller. To see why, consider a data set in which the experimental and control scores are perfectly correlated. For example, the scores for 10 subjects tested under both an experimental (E) and control (C) condition might be

					Subject					
Condition	1	2	3	4	5	6	7	8	9	10
E	5	10	3	7	12	13	9	4	8	15
C	7	12	5	9	14	15	11	6	10	17

Note that the difference between scores, $C - E$, is the same for all subjects in this example. In the correlated-scores design, the standard deviation of the difference, divided by the square root of *n*, is the denominator of the *t* statistic that is used in significance tests. In the preceding example, this standard deviation would be zero, and *any* difference between the *E* and *C* means would be significant. This would be true no matter how variable the scores within a condition were. Although we never have correlations this high, the correlations achieved by testing each subject under both conditions, or by matching subjects, will usually reduce the *SE* of the mean difference considerably compared to the variability of the individual scores. Therefore, the *t* statistic will usually be larger in the correlated-scores design. *TechNote 6_1* on the book's website (go to the *Technical Notes* page) more formally shows the effect of the correlation coefficient on the standard error of the difference between the means.

To sum up, both statistical and practical factors should influence the choice of design. With respect to statistical factors, although there are more independent observations in the independent groups design, the denominator of the *t* statistic (the *SE* of the mean difference) will be smaller in the correlated-scores design. Therefore, the *t* test usually will be more powerful and the confidence interval narrower when the two groups of scores are correlated than when they are independent. With respect to practical considerations, in some situations the correlated-scores design is difficult or impossible to implement. It would make no sense to use both methods of arithmetic instruction on the same subjects, although subjects could be matched on a pretest. Furthermore, some variables such as gender cannot be manipulated within subjects. The researcher also should be aware of the possibility of "contrast effects"; some experimental treatments (e.g., one amount of reward) have a very different effect when the same subject has been exposed to other treatments (e.g., other amounts of reward) than when the subject has experienced only that treatment.

In this chapter we will run a hypothetical experiment on the effects of diet on *TC* level both ways. We first consider the analysis of data when an independent-groups design is used. In this design, we ask whether total cholesterol (*TC*) level is lower for a group on a prescribed diet than for a control group. Following that, we present data for a similar experiment, but using a correlated-scores design in which the *TC* scores are obtained for the same individuals before and after the diet. However, before we can analyze the data for these two designs, we first need to know something more about the *t* statistic and its distribution.

6.3 THE *t* DISTRIBUTION

6.3.1 The *t* Statistic

In Chapter 5, we considered statistics that had the general form, $z = [(V - E(V)]/\sigma_v$ where V represents some statistic such as the sample mean, $\bar{X}$, or the difference between sample means, $\bar{X}_1 - \bar{X}_2$. $E(V)$ is the expected value of V, also referred to as the population parameter. For example, if $\bar{X}$ is the sample mean, $E(V)$ is the population mean, μ. The denominator of z is the standard error of the sampling distribution of V. In this chapter we consider a similar ratio, the t statistic; it has the general definition,

$$t = \frac{V - E(V)}{s_V} \tag{6.1}$$

where V and $E(V)$ are defined as before. The statistic s_V is the sample statistic that estimates σ_V, the *SE* of the sampling distribution of V. Note that the t statistic is identical to the z statistic except that the denominator of Equation 6.1 is an *estimate* of the standard error of V rather than its actual value. An implication of this difference is that the denominator of the z statistic is a constant over replications of the experiment whereas the denominator of the t statistic will vary over samples. As in the case of z, it is assumed that scores are independently and normally distributed.

The t distribution is tabled in Appendix C.3. When we turn to that table, we find that the entries in the first column correspond to something labeled *df*, which stands for *degrees of freedom*. The concept of degrees of freedom is closely related to sample size but is not quite the same thing. Because degrees of freedom are an important concept, not only for the t distribution but also for other distributions that play a role in data analysis, they deserve further discussion.

6.3.2 Degrees of Freedom (*df*)

The degrees of freedom associated with any quantity are the number of *independent* observations upon which that quantity is based. The meaning of "independent observations" is best illustrated by an example. Suppose that we had 10 markers of different colors to pass out to a group of children. The first nine children would have some choice in colors, but the last would not (i.e., no *df* remaining). Translating to a numerical example, suppose that we are asked to choose 10 numbers that sum to 50. We can freely choose any 9 values but the tenth must be 50 minus the sum of the first 9. In this case, there are 10 scores but because only 9 can be chosen independently, there are only 9 *df*. There is a restriction due to the fact that the numbers must sum to 50 and that costs us a "degree of freedom." The same situation occurs when we calculate a sample standard deviation. This requires us to subtract each score from the mean. However, as we stated in Chapter 2, the sum of deviations of all scores about their mean must be zero; that is, $\Sigma(Y - \bar{Y}) = 0$. Rewriting this last result, $\Sigma Y = n\bar{Y}$. If the sample mean is 5 and n is 10, we have the original example in which the sum of 10 scores must equal 50. Therefore, the sample standard deviation is based on $10 - 1$, or 9, *df*.

At this point, it looks as if the df are always just $n - 1$. That is true if the statistic of interest involves only one restriction. But suppose we draw two samples from some population; one sample is of size n_1 and the other of size n_2. We want to estimate the population variance but we have two estimates. As will be seen shortly, these can be averaged; however, the point now is that there are two restrictions if two sample variances are computed: the sum of the n_1 scores in the first sample must equal $n_1\bar{Y}_1$ and the sum of the n_2 scores in the second sample must equal $n_2\bar{Y}_2$. There are $n_1 - 1$ *df* associated with the variance for the first sample and $n_2 - 1$ *df* associated with that for the second sample. The *df* associated with a statistic involving some combination of these two variances will be $df = (n_1 - 1) + (n_2 - 1) = n_1 + n_2 - 2$. The message is that the *df* are not necessarily the number of scores minus 1. Rather,

df = *number of independent observations*

    = *total number of observations minus number of restrictions on those observations*

In the two-sample example, there are $n_1 + n_2$ observations and two restrictions caused by taking deviations about each of the sample means.

6.3.3 The Table of the *t* Distribution

Appendix Table C.3 contains critical values of the *t* statistic corresponding to various levels of significance and degrees of freedom. At the head of each column are two numbers corresponding to levels of significance for one- and two-tailed tests; each row of the table corresponds to a different number of *df*. As an example of the use of the table, find the column corresponding to a one-tailed proportion of .025 (and a two-tailed proportion of .05) and the row for *df* = 9. The critical value in the cell is 2.262. We interpret this to mean that when there are 9 *df*, a *t* of 2.262 is exceeded by .025 of the sampling distribution of *t*; .05 of the distribution is greater than 2.262 or less than −2.262. Now look down the same column to the row labeled infinity. The critical value in that cell is 1.96. This means that the probability is .025 of exceeding 1.96 and the probability of *t* > 1.96 or *t* < −1.96 is .05. This is exactly the critical value in Table C.2, the normal probability table. In general, the critical value of *t* decreases as *df* increases, rapidly approaching the critical value in Table C.2 for the normal distribution. Table C.3 usually provides more accurate inferences than Table C.2, although there is little difference when sample sizes are large. This is because s_V is a consistent estimator of σ_V; as sample size increases, the sample standard error more closely approximates the population standard error.

Assume that we want a .05 significance level for a test based on 35 *df* against a two-tailed alternative. We select the column labeled .05 for the two-tailed test and we want a row corresponding to 35 *df*. Table C.3 has values for 30 and 40 *df*, but not for 35, so we interpolate, taking a value halfway between 2.042 and 2.021, or 2.0315. The true value, 2.030, can be obtained from most statistical software packages; for example, it is available in SPSS using the IDF.T option found in the *Compute* menu listed among the *Transform* options. The approximation and the actual critical value yield very similar results.

With some knowledge of the *t* distribution, we are now ready to use it to draw inferences from data sets. We first consider the analysis of data from an independent-groups design.

6.4 DATA ANALYSES IN THE INDEPENDENT-GROUPS DESIGN

The data file, *Table 6_1 TC_IG* (found by a link from the *Tables* page on the website for this book) contains data for a design in which there are two independently sampled groups of 36 scores each. The first column in the file, labeled "Treatment," designates two types of treatment: control and diet. The second column, labeled *TC_level*, contains the total cholesterol scores for each of the two groups whose names appear in the first column. The group means and variances are presented in Table 6.1.

Ordinarily, we would begin our analyses by examining data plots and additional statistics but we will leave this data exploration stage as an exercise for the student. However, before proceeding

Table 6.1   Total cholesterol (TC) statistics from an independent-groups design

Group	Means	Variances
Control	224.50	2246.51
Diet	207.71	1581.75

to the inferential analysis of the TC data, we need to develop a formula for the standard error of the difference between the drug and control group means.

6.4.1 The Standard Error (SE) of $\bar{Y}_1 - \bar{Y}_2$

We earlier defined the t statistic as $t = [(V - E(V)]/s_V$. In the current example, the random variable, V, is the difference in TC level between the two group means: $\bar{Y}_C - \bar{Y}_D$ (control – diet means) or, in general, $\bar{Y}_1 - \bar{Y}_2$. S_V, the SE of the difference between the sample means, can be understood by considering a sampling experiment. Suppose we drew many independent pairs of random samples of sizes n_1 and n_2 from two independently and normally distributed populations of scores. If we carried out this sampling procedure, we could compute a difference between the means for each pair of samples drawn. The standard deviation of the sampling distribution of this difference, the SE, is the quantity to be estimated by the denominator of the t in the two-group study. The issue is how to calculate that estimate.

If the $n_1 + n_2$ scores are independently distributed, the variance of the sampling distribution of the difference between the two group means is the sum of the variances of the means (see Appendix B for proof of this). Then the SE of the difference is

$$\sigma_{\bar{Y}_1 - \bar{Y}_2} = \sqrt{\frac{\sigma_1^2}{n_1} + \frac{\sigma_2^2}{n_2}} \tag{6.2}$$

In addition to the assumption that the scores are drawn from independently normally distributed populations, using the t distributions of Appendix Table C.3 requires one additional assumption, that the two population variances are equal; that is, $\sigma_1^2 = \sigma_2^2 = \sigma^2$. This is usually referred to as the assumption of *homogeneity of variance*. Under this assumption, Equation 6.2 becomes

$$\sigma_{\bar{Y}_1 - \bar{Y}_2} = \sqrt{\frac{\sigma^2}{n_1} + \frac{\sigma^2}{n_2}} = \sigma \sqrt{\frac{1}{n_1} + \frac{1}{n_2}} \tag{6.3}$$

We have a single population variance (σ^2) and two possible estimates of it, the variances of the two groups of scores sampled in an experiment. To obtain the best single estimate of the σ, we need to average the two group variances, and take the square root of the result. Because variance estimates are consistent statistics, the estimate based on the larger group is more likely to be close to the true variance. Therefore, the best estimate of σ^2 is a weighted average of the two group variances. This is the *pooled variance estimate*, or, s_{pooled}^2, and is calculated as

$$s_{pooled}^2 = \left[\frac{n_1 - 1}{n_1 + n_2 - 2}\right] s_1^2 + \left[\frac{n_2 - 1}{n_1 + n_2 - 2}\right] s_2^2 \tag{6.4}$$

Note that the weight on each group variance in Equation 6.4 is obtained by dividing the df for that group by the sum of the *df* for the two groups, $[(n_1 - 1) + (n_2 - 1)]$. The *df* rather than the *n* are used in these weights because this yields an unbiased estimate of $\sigma^2_{\bar{Y}_1 - \bar{Y}_2}$. The pooled variance estimate can also be written as:

$$s^2_{pooled} = \frac{SS_1 + SS_2}{n_1 + n_2 - 2} \tag{6.5}$$

where the *SS* for a group is a sum of squared deviations of the scores about the mean of the group; that is,

$$SS_j = \sum_i (Y_{ij} - \bar{Y}_{.j})^2 \tag{6.6}$$

This quantity is usually referred to as the *sum of squares* and it will play an important role in the remaining chapters.

We can now state the expression for the estimate of the *SE* of the sampling distribution of the difference of two independent means:

$$s_{\bar{Y}_1 - \bar{Y}_2} = s_{pooled}\sqrt{\frac{1}{n_1} + \frac{1}{n_2}} \tag{6.7}$$

When $n_1 = n_2 = n$, as is frequently the case in experimental research, Equation 6.7 leads us to

$$s_{pooled} = \sqrt{(s_1^2 + s_2^2)/2} \tag{6.8}$$

and Equation 6.8 becomes

$$s_{\bar{Y}_1 - \bar{Y}_2} = s_{pooled}\sqrt{2/n} \tag{6.9}$$

For the *TC* data, from Equation 6.8,

$$s_{pooled} = \sqrt{(2246.51 + 1581.75)/2} = 43.75$$

and from Equation 6.9,

$$s_{\bar{Y}_1 - \bar{Y}_2} = 43.75\sqrt{2/36} = 10.31$$

With this estimate of the standard error, we can now proceed to draw inferences about the difference between the means of the control and diet populations.

6.4.2 Confidence Intervals for the Independent-Groups Design

The general form of the confidence interval, with confidence level $1 - \alpha$, is

$$p[V - (t_{df, \alpha/2} s_V) \le E(V) \le V + (t_{df, \alpha/2} s_V)] = 1 - \alpha \tag{6.10}$$

and the confidence limits are

$$CI = V \pm (t_{df, \alpha/2} s_V) \tag{6.11}$$

For our *TC* example, $df = (2)(36 - 1)$, or 70, and, assuming we want 95% confidence, $\alpha/2 = .025$. Then Equation 6.11 becomes

$$CI = (\bar{Y}_1 - \bar{Y}_2) \pm (t_{70, .025}s_{\bar{Y}_1 - \bar{Y}_2}) \tag{6.12}$$

The difference between the means is $224.50 - 207.71 = 16.79$ and its standard error (see Section

6.4.1) is 10.31. Turning to Appendix Table C.3, we find that the critical t value is 1.99. Putting our values together into Equation 6.12, we obtain the bounds for the 95% confidence interval:

$$CI = 16.79 \pm (1.99)(10.31) = -3.77, 37.35$$

Because these bounds encompass a value of zero we know that a two-tailed test at the .05 alpha level will not reject the null hypothesis of no difference between the diet and control means. Also, the fact that the confidence interval is quite wide suggests that our test of that hypothesis may be low in power, a point we will explore further in this chapter.

6.4.3 Interpreting Confidence Intervals

It is worth reviewing the interpretation of these bounds because they are often misinterpreted. In particular, note the following points:

1. Ninety-five percent confidence *does not mean* that there is a .95 probability that the computed bounds enclose the true value of $\mu_{control} - \mu_{diet}$. The bounds either enclose the population mean difference or they do not.
2. Ninety-five percent confidence *does not mean* that if the experiment were repeated many times, 95% of the observed differences between means would lie between −3.771 and 37.353, the bounds calculated from the TC data.
3. Ninety-five percent confidence *does mean* that if the experiment is repeated many times, and a new set of bounds is calculated each time, 95% of those bounds would contain the value of $\mu_{control} - \mu_{diet}$.

In summary, calculating a confidence interval accomplishes several things:

1. The CI bounds provide a range of plausible values for the parameter being estimated.
2. The CI width provides an index of precision of our estimate that is sensitive to the level of confidence, the variability, and the sample size.
3. The CI provides a test of an infinite set of null hypotheses. Those hypothesized values falling outside the interval can be rejected at $\alpha = 1 -$ confidence level, whereas those inside the interval cannot be rejected.

6.4.4 The t Test in the Independent-Groups Design

A direct test of $H_0: \mu_1 - \mu_2 = 0$ against the hypothesized alternative $H_1: \mu_1 - \mu_2 \neq 0$ follows from the preceding developments. The test statistic follows from Equation 6.1 and is

$$t = \frac{(\bar{Y}_1 - \bar{Y}_2) - (\mu_1 - \mu_2)_{hyp}}{s_{\bar{Y}_1 - \bar{Y}_2}} \tag{6.13}$$

Substituting numerical values, we obtain $t = 16.79/10.31 = 1.63$. This value of t is less than the critical value, 1.994, confirming that we cannot reject the null hypothesis. The exact p-value, obtained from SPSS, is .108. Note that this implies that a one-tailed test at the .05 level would also fail to reject H_0 because p would equal .054 for that test.

The validity of the confidence interval and the t statistic we calculated rest on certain assumptions. In the next few sections, we restate these assumptions and describe procedures to respond to their violations.

6.5 DATA ANALYSES IN THE CORRELATED-SCORES DESIGN

For reasons discussed earlier in this chapter, many comparisons of two conditions are made in a correlated-scores design in which each subject is tested in two conditions, or subjects are matched on some dimension related to the dependent variable. We illustrate the analyses of correlated-scores data with an artificial set of 36 pairs of total cholesterol (*TC*) scores.

The data file *Table 6_2 TC_CS* (from the *Tables* page on the book's website) has three columns. The first, labeled *Before*, contains the *TC* scores for the 36 subjects before receiving any treatment. The second column, labeled *After*, contains scores for the same individuals after one year on a diet prescribed by the researcher. The third column of scores, labeled *Change*, contains the difference in *TC* level, obtained by subtracting the *After* scores from the *Before* scores for each subject after some time period, perhaps 6 months. A positive score represents an improvement in *TC* level, and a negative score means that *TC* level was worse (higher) after being on the diet. In a real study, subjects might keep a diary describing the amounts and types of food eaten, and the researchers would probably test the subjects at regular intervals—perhaps once a week—during the study. However, we will focus on a single set of change scores.

In the correlated-scores experiment, our primary interest is in the change scores: What effect did the prescribed diet have on changes in *TC* level? Is there much variability in the effects among individuals? What can we conclude about the potential effects of the treatment for a population similar to the subjects in our study? A good place to begin is with the descriptive statistics and graphs provided by programs such as SPSS's Explore module. We leave this exploration of the data as an exercise but for convenience present means and standard deviations in Table 6.2.

Table 6.2 Descriptive statistics for data from a correlated-scores experiment

		Descriptive statistics		
	n	Mean	*SE* of the mean	Std. deviation
Before	36	224.50	7.90	47.40
After	36	208.17	10.69	64.12
Change	36	16.33	5.42	32.52

Following exploration of the data, we wish to use the sample of data to draw inferences about the population. First, what is the mean of the population of change scores, and what are reasonable bounds on the mean change? Second, is that change significantly greater than zero? That is, can we conclude that, on the average, a population represented by our sample would show a decrease in *TC* level as a result of the prescribed diet? We next turn to these questions.

6.5.1 Confidence Intervals in the Correlated-Scores Design

Our estimate of the mean of the population of change scores is $\overline{Y}_{change}$, the average of the 36 change scores. From Table 6.2, this is 16.333. In order to calculate confidence interval bounds on the mean of the population of change scores (μ_{change}), we need this value, but also the standard deviation of the 36 change scores (s_{change}), the number of change scores (n), and the critical value of t. Except that the critical value is obtained from the t rather than the normal probability distribution, confidence intervals and significance tests follow the procedures developed in Chapter 5. The general form of the confidence interval in the one-sample case is:

$$p\left[\bar{Y} - t_{n-1,\alpha/2} \frac{s}{\sqrt{n}} \leq \mu \leq \bar{Y} + t_{n-1,\alpha/2} \frac{s}{\sqrt{n}} \right] = 1 - \alpha \quad (6.14)$$

where $\bar{Y}$ is the sample mean, $s/\sqrt{n}$ is the SE of the mean, and $t_{n-1,\alpha/2}$ is the value of t such that $\alpha/2$ of the distribution on $n-1$ df lies to the right of it. In the example of the 36 TC change scores, $df = 35$, and therefore the critical t value for a 95% confidence interval is 2.03. From Table 6.2, we substitute the other necessary values into Equation 6.14 to obtain the lower (LB) and upper (UB) 95% bounds on μ_{change}:

$$LB = 16.333 - (2.03)(5.421) = 5.328 \quad \text{and} \quad UB = 16.333 + (2.03)(5.421) = 27.338$$

We have 95% confidence that the difference between the population means is between 5.33 and 27.34.

6.5.2 The *t* Test in the Correlated-Scores Design

The direct test of the null hypothesis parallels that developed in Chapter 5; the only difference is that we replace σ by an estimate, s, and use the t distribution as the basis for our test. We calculate

$$t_{n-1} = \frac{\bar{Y} - \mu_{hyp}}{s_Y/\sqrt{n}} \quad (6.15)$$

and, if the test is two-tailed, reject H_0 if $|t| > t_{n-1,\alpha/2}$. In the present example, $\mu_{hyp} = 0$, and the denominator is 5.421, the SE in Table 6.2. Therefore,

$$t = (16.333 - 0)/5.421 = 3.013$$

a much larger value than the critical value of 2.03. Accordingly, we reject the null hypothesis that the treatment had no effect, and conclude that the average change in the population is a reduction in total cholesterol level.

The population mean assumed by the null hypothesis is not necessarily zero. Suppose we knew that various treatments previously investigated in other laboratories had yielded an average TC reduction of 6. If we wished to ask whether the mean change was significantly different from 6, we would substitute 6 for μ_{hyp} in Equation 6.15, and solve for t. Alternatively, we note that 6 falls within the 95% confidence interval bounds previously computed. Accordingly, that null hypothesis cannot be rejected by a two-tailed test at the .05 level. Therefore, we cannot conclude that our diet differs in its average effect from previously investigated treatments.[1]

---

[1] Because an increase in TC level is of no interest, a one-tailed test might be more appropriate. With 35 df, the critical t value for the one-tailed test at the .05 level is 1.690. Because $t = [16.333 - 6]/5.421 = 1.906$, we may conclude that the mean reduction in the population of TC scores under our treatment was greater than that observed in previous experiments. However, it is important to understand that decisions about the directionality of the alternative hypothesis should be made before carrying out the test (see the discussion in Chapters 4 and 5).

6.6 ASSUMPTIONS UNDERLYING THE APPLICATION OF THE *t* DISTRIBUTION

Inferences based on data from the independent-groups design rest on the following assumptions:

1. The scores in each treatment population are independently distributed.
2. Both treatment populations have normal distributions of scores.
3. The variances of the two populations of scores are the same; this is the *homogeneity of variance* assumption.

The independence assumption is usually valid except in situations in which there is some interaction among subjects; this might happen when one subject responds in the presence of another. For example, suppose the scores were weights, rather than total cholesterol levels, and there were weekly weigh-ins observed by all subjects. The success or failure of some subjects might encourage or discourage others from adhering to a diet. In that case, the scores would not be independent.

As we noted in Chapter 5, even when the population is unlikely to be normally distributed, the sampling distribution of the mean tends to be normal when each mean is based on many scores. However, the sampling distribution of the mean is less well approximated by the normal distribution when the samples are small, particularly if there is extreme skew. We next consider the consequences of departures from normality. Following that, we consider the consequences of violations of the homogeneity of variance assumption. In both cases, we suggest some possible remedies for the consequences we discuss.

6.6.1 The Normality Assumption

The assumption that scores are normally distributed is often not met, so let us consider the possible consequences of violating the assumption and approaches to dealing with violations.

Consequences of Violating the Normality Assumption.   When data are not normally distributed, particularly if the distributions are skewed, the Type 1 error rate may be distorted. For example, when the nominal Type 1 error rate is .05, the true probability might be .08 or .02, depending on the direction of skew. Although our data are frequently skewed, as a result of the central limit theorem (see Chapter 5) the distortion of Type 1 error rates is usually slight with moderately large samples. "Moderately large" may be as small as 20 if $n_1 = n_2$ and if the two populations have symmetric distributions. More conservatively, except in cases of very extreme skew, *n* of 40 or more in both correlated-scores and independent-group designs will suffice to provide valid Type 1 error rates. Large data sets not only yield increased power and narrower confidence intervals, but also tend to provide more valid Type 1 error rates when the normality assumption is violated.

Although the Type 1 error rate may approximate its nominal value, another important consideration is that there may be a loss of power when populations are skewed or have outliers. In such cases, the sampling distribution of $\bar{Y}_1 - \bar{Y}_2$ will tend to be long-tailed (i.e., a greater proportion of extreme scores than would be found with the normal distribution); therefore, estimates of the difference between population means will be less precise, and variability may be greater than when the normality assumption holds. We next consider possible ways of addressing the potential loss of power due to departures from normality.

Dealing with Violations of the Normality Assumption. There are several possible modifications of, and alternatives to, the standard inference procedures based on the *t* distribution. These will result in more valid Type 1 error rates when samples are small and skewed and often will yield greater power when there are departures from normality even in large samples. Three possible approaches are:

1. *Transformations* of the data will often result in data distributions that more closely approximate the normal.
2. *Trimming outliers* will generally yield more powerful tests of the null hypothesis and narrower confidence intervals.
3. *Tests based on ranks* are available in most statistical packages and, by reducing the effect of extreme scores, often provide more powerful tests.

First, we consider why, when, and how to transform data. In transforming data, the same operation is applied to every score; for example, the square root of each score might be calculated and the analyses would then be based on the scores on this square-root scale. Transformations have been used to transform skewed distributions into more nearly normal distributions, to more nearly equate group variances, and to reduce the different effects treatments may have on different subjects' scores when data are obtained in several conditions from each subject. A transformation that achieves one purpose may not be best for other purposes; however, transformations that reduce heterogeneity of variance often also result in more normally distributed data.

Three very common transformations are (1) the *square-root* transformation; (2) the *logarithmic* transformation; and (3) the *reciprocal*—sometimes called the *inverse*—transformation. The square-root transformation is the weakest, causing the least change in the distribution, and the reciprocal is the most powerful of these transformations. In seeking to transform a skewed data distribution to normality, we first should view the results of the weakest possible transformation and, if that is not satisfactory, then investigate the effectiveness of more powerful transformations.

In Chapter 2, we viewed *Q–Q* plots (Fig. 2.5) of multiplication response times and multiplication speeds. As we noted then, the distribution of response speed, a reciprocal transformation of response time, more closely approximated the normal distribution. In general, we strongly recommend the approach taken in Chapter 2: before attempting transformations or other remedies, explore the statistics of the data, including indices of skew and kurtosis, as well as distributional plots. If the data appear skewed and a transformation is tried, again examine the results. Whether inferential methods are applied to transformed data, and if so, which transformation is used, should depend on looking at the data, not on the results of subsequent significance tests. A transformation should not be selected because it provides the largest value of the *t* statistic for testing the difference between means; rather, the criterion for choosing a transformation should be that it achieves a distribution that is more consistent with assumptions underlying the planned analyses.

Transformations are not always advisable. They work by changing relative distances among scores, compressing one tail of the distribution more than the other. The values on the new scale may not be as readily interpretable and the nature of relationships between the dependent and independent variables may be changed. For example, when there are more than two levels of the independent variable, a previously linear relationship between mean scores and the independent variable may now be curvilinear.

A further limitation is that confidence intervals on the transformed scale may be difficult to interpret. If a single sample of scores is transformed, the limits may be transformed back to the original scale. For example, if the *CI* is based on the square root of *Y*, the limits can be squared, thus returning to the original scale. However, if we obtain a *CI* on the difference between two means of data transformed by taking the square root of each score, retransforming those limits makes no sense. If the lower limit is negative, squaring the limits will yield two positive limits which will not contain zero, even though the difference being tested is not significant.

An alternative approach that can be useful in dealing with violations of the normality assumption is a *trimmed t test*. In Chapter 5, we saw that a trimmed mean can have a much smaller standard error than $\bar{Y}$ when the population distribution has a longer tail than the normal distribution (see Table 5.1). Arbitrarily trimming outliers and then calculating the conventional *t* statistic for the remaining scores is not appropriate because the test statistic will not necessarily be distributed as *t*. However, Tukey and McLaughlin (1963) proposed a statistic that has an approximate *t* distribution and takes advantage of the reduced standard error that results from trimming scores. Chapter 7 presents an example of this trimmed *t* test, and compares the results with that of the test performed on the untrimmed data. Details of the calculations are also presented there. In general, with either skewed or symmetric long-tailed distributions, the trimmed *t* test will have more power and the related confidence intervals will be narrower than when calculated in the usual way. Furthermore, when scores are normally distributed, Type 1 and 2 error rates are little affected by trimming.

Finally, a third approach to dealing with violations of the normality assumption is the use of *tests based on ranks*. This class of tests is usually referred to as *nonparametric* or *distribution-free*. When the data are obtained from two independent groups, the *Wilcoxon rank sum* or the equivalent *Mann–Whitney U* test can be applied. These essentially perform a *t* test on the mean ranks obtained by converting the data into ranks. The *U* test is available in many statistical packages; for example, SPSS's *Analyze* menu provides the test under Nonparametric Tests/Two Independent Samples. A detailed description of these and other nonparametric tests, including formulas, can be found in several sources (e.g., Gibbons, 1993; Hollander & Wolfe, 1999; Siegel & Castellan, 1988).

One caution is in order with respect to any nonparametric test for independent-groups data. These methods are applicable and provide a more powerful test of the hypothesis of identical distributions when the data distributions are not normal (Boneau, 1962; Zimmerman & Zumbo, 1993). However, contrary to some beliefs, there are important assumptions underlying these tests. In addition to the usual assumption of independence of scores, it is assumed that the population distributions have the same shape. If they do not, significant test results may reflect differences in variance, or in shape parameters, even though the averages are the same.

Which of the three approaches—transformations, trimming, tests of ranked data—will be appropriate in any situation depends on the data distribution as well as on the nature of the dependent variable. Transforming data makes sense if the data distribution is skewed and the original scale is arbitrary, as in some personality measures, or if the transformed scale makes as much sense as the original scale, as when response time is transformed into speed. The Mann–Whitney *U* test rests on the assumption that the two treatment distributions have the same shape, and has the added limitation that confidence intervals are difficult to construct. However, if the assumptions are met and all that is required is a significance test, this will provide a powerful alternative to the *t* test when data are not normally distributed and the population distributions are assumed to be the same shape. When the data distribution is symmetric but long-tailed, the trimmed-*t* test will often be most powerful and has the added advantage that confidence intervals can easily be constructed.

6.6.2 The Assumption of Homogeneity of Variance

It is common to encounter violations of the assumption that variances are the same in both experimental conditions. The consequences of such violations depend on a couple of considerations.

Consequences of Violating the Assumption of Homogeneity of Variance. The denominator of the equation for the two-sample *t* test is based on the pool of two variance estimates (see Equation 6.4); the underlying assumption is that the two group variances estimate the same population variance. If this is not true—if the population variances are heterogeneous—then the sampling distribution of the *t* statistic may not have a true *t* distribution. Table 6.3 gives a sense of what may happen in this case. We drew 2,000 pairs of samples of various sizes from two normal populations with identical means but different variances. Proportions of rejections for alphas equal to .01 and .05 are presented.

Two points about the results should be noted.

1. If the two sample sizes are equal, the difference between the empirical and theoretical Type 1 alpha rates tends to be at most 1%, except when *n* is very small (i.e., $n = 5$) and the variance ratio is very large (i.e., $\sigma_1^2/\sigma_2^2 = 100$).
2. If the *n*s are unequal, whether the Type 1 error rate is inflated or deflated depends upon the direction of the relation between sample size and population variance.

The relation between sample size and variance is that the denominator of the *t* is based on a weighted average of two variance estimates; the weights are proportions of degrees of freedom. Therefore, when the larger group is drawn from the population with the larger variance, the larger variance estimate receives more weight than the smaller estimate. The denominator of the *t* test tends to be large and the *t* small; the rejection rate is less than it should be. Conversely, when sample size and population variance are negatively related, the smaller variance estimate gets the larger

Table 6.3 Type 1 error rates for the *t* test as a function of population variances and sample sizes

n_1	n_2	σ_1^2/σ_2^2	$\alpha = .05$	$\alpha = .01$
5	5	4	.060	.014
5	5	16	.061	.019
5	5	100	.066	.024
15	15	4	.056	.010
15	15	16	.054	.015
15	15	100	.059	.017
5	10	4	.095	.031
5	10	.25	.021	.003
10	15	4	.073	.023
10	15	.25	.040	.006
10	20	4	.091	.031
10	20	.25	.021	.003
20	30	4	.067	.027
20	30	.25	.037	.004

weight; the denominator of the *t* statistic tends to be small and the *t* large; the rejection rate is inflated.

Unequal sample sizes should be avoided when possible. However, we recognize that there will be many cases in which sample sizes will differ, often markedly. For example, the response rate to questionnaires may be quite different for two populations such as men and women, or college- and non-college-educated. We do not advocate discarding data from the larger sample; this would increase sampling variability for statistics computed from that sample. Instead, we recommend an alternative to the standard *t* test.

Dealing with Unequal Variances: Welch's t Test.   One alternative to the standard *t* test is a *t* that does not use the pooled estimate of the population variance. The denominator of this statistic would be that of the *z* test for two independent groups with variance estimates instead of known population variances. We define

$$t' = \frac{(\bar{Y}_1 - \bar{Y}_2) - (\mu_1 - \mu_2)}{\sqrt{s_1^2/n_1 + s_2^2/n_2}} \tag{6.16}$$

This statistic is usually referred to as *Welch's t* (1938). If the scores have been drawn from normally distributed populations, *t'* is distributed approximately as *t* but not with the usual degrees of freedom. Instead, the degrees of freedom are

$$df' = \frac{(s_1^2/n_1 + s_2^2/n_2)^2}{\dfrac{s_1^4}{n_1^2(n_1 - 1)} + \dfrac{s_2^4}{n_2^2(n_2 - 1)}} \tag{6.17}$$

Many statistical packages compute values of both *t'* and *t* when an independent-groups *t* test is performed. Table 6.4 presents SPSS's output of the *t* statistics and confidence intervals (*CI*) for the

Table 6.4   SPSS output for the *t* test of the independent-groups *TC* means with unequal *n*

Group statistics treatment	n	Mean	Std. deviation	Std. error mean
Control	36	224.502	47.397	7.900
Diet	30	208.358	39.923	7.289

Independent samples test	Levene's test for equality of variances		*t* Test for equality of means							
	F	Sig.	t	df	Sig. (2-tailed)	Mean difference	Std. error difference	95% Confidence interval of the difference	
								Lower	Upper
Equal variances assumed	.470	.496	1.479	64	.144	16.144	10.919	− 5.668	37.957
Equal variances not assumed			1.502	63.988	.138	16.144	10.749	− 5.329	37.617

comparison of *TC* means in the control and diet groups after we created unequal group sizes by randomly dropping six scores from the diet group. The values of the *t* based on the pooled-variance estimate ("Equal variances assumed") and that of *t′* ("Equal variances not assumed") are almost identical. This is because the group sizes and standard deviations are not very different. Further evidence of homogeneity of variance is provided by Levene's (1960) test, which has a clearly nonsignificant result. In Levene's test, an average absolute deviation of scores about each group mean is calculated and the difference between these two averages is tested.

6.7 MEASURING THE STANDARDIZED EFFECT SIZE: COHEN'S *d*

In the experiment on the effects of diet on total cholesterol level, the difference between the two group means provides a measure of the size of the effect. However, that measure is on the original data scale. Although this has the advantage of being meaningful to the researcher, it has accompanying disadvantages: it is difficult to evaluate the importance of differences between means, or to compare such differences with effects of the same independent variable in other groups or laboratories, or to combine results of several experiments.

Another possible measure of the importance of an effect, the *p*-value associated with a hypothesis test, can be misleading. Very small effects, perhaps unimportant in any practical or theoretical sense, may be statistically significant because the sample sizes are large; conversely, important effects, even large differences, may not be statistically significant because the sample was too small, or variability too great, for the test to have much power.

In view of these concerns, several expressions for effect size have been proposed (e.g., Cohen, 1988; Kraemer, 2005; McGraw & Wong, 1992; Rosenthal & Rubin, 1994, 2003). In this section, we focus on *Cohen's d*, which evaluates the effect of a treatment relative to its standard deviation. Estimates of *d* have several uses:

1. They provide scale-free indices of the importance of the effect.
2. As we shall see in Section 6.8, they provide information required for power calculations.
3. They are used in meta-analyses, analyses which combine results from several studies.

There is increasing agreement that measures of effect size are important and should be reported along with the results of statistical tests. A growing number of journals now explicitly require that measures of effect size be reported, and the fifth edition of the *Publication Manual* of the American Psychological Association (2001) states, "For the reader to fully understand the importance of your findings, it is almost always necessary to include some index of effect size or strength of relationship in your Results section" (p. 25).

6.7.1 Estimating Cohen's *d*[2]

Cohen's *d* for the *independent-groups design* is defined as

$$d = [(\mu_1 - \mu_2) - \Delta]/\sigma \qquad (6.18)$$

---

[2] Our estimate of *d* for the independent-groups design is the statistic denoted by *g* by Hedges and Olkin (1985). Alternative estimates have been proposed (e.g., Glass, 1976). Also, Hedges and Olkin have noted that $\hat{d}$ is a biased estimate of *d*; the bias is small for large samples and can be corrected by $\hat{d}_{corrected} = \hat{d} \times [1 - 3/(4N - 9)]$.

where μ_1 and μ_2 are the actual population means, and Δ (Greek upper-case delta) is the population difference assuming H_0 is true; Δ is usually, but not always, 0. In the independent-groups design, assuming homogeneity of variance, the estimate of d is

$$\hat{d} = [(\overline{Y}_1 - \overline{Y}_2) - \Delta]/s_{pooled} \qquad (6.19)$$

where s_{pooled} was defined by Equation 6.4. In the TC example,

$$\hat{d} = (16.791 - 0)/43.751 = .384$$

In contrasting two independent means, Cohen (1988) suggests .2, .5, and .8 as guidelines for small, medium, and large standardized effect sizes. Following this recommendation, the standardized effect size of the experimental diet on TC level falls somewhere between small and medium.

Cohen has described two possible measures of effect size in the *correlated-scores design*. One, d_z, is the ratio of the difference between the means to the standard deviation of the difference scores. Using our TC change score data to illustrate (Table 6.2), our estimate is $\hat{d}_z = 16.333/33.524 = .502$. An important feature of d_z is that it is closely linked to statistical power; we will elaborate on this point in Section 6.8.2.

The second measure of effect size is $d = (\mu_1 - \mu_2)/\sigma$; this is estimated just as for the independent-groups design: The population means are estimated by the corresponding sample means and σ is estimated by averaging the two within-condition variances and taking the square root of the result. Again to use our TC change score data to illustrate, first converting the condition standard deviations to variances by squaring them, we compute our estimate of the pooled standard deviation by $\sqrt{(2,246.521 + 4,111.725)/2} = 56.384$.   Then, $\hat{d} = (224.5019 - 208.1694)/56.384 = .29$,   a relatively small effect.

Cohen preferred d to d_z because values of the former are comparable to those obtained from experiments involving the same conditions but in an independent-groups design. However, d_z is more directly linked to power calculations, as we shall discuss in Section 6.8.2. In any event, the two statistics are closely related; if s_{diff} is the standard deviation of the difference scores and s_{pool} is the square root of the average within-condition variance, then $\hat{d} = (s_{diff}/s_{pool})\hat{d}_z$.

6.7.2 Confidence Intervals on Cohen's *d*

In considering the difference between means, we saw that the confidence interval provided a sense of the plausible range within which the population parameter may fall. The interval bounds are an important adjunct to any parameter estimate; narrower intervals indicate a more restricted range of plausible values of the parameter being estimated. In constructing intervals for the raw difference between means, we had the formula provided by Equation 6.12. Unfortunately, no analytic solution exists for calculating confidence bounds on d; however, several programs exist for finding these bounds by computer-based search methods. Discussions of the rationale underlying the method may be found in several sources (e.g., Cumming & Finch, 2001; Hedges & Olkin, 1985; Steiger & Fouladi, 1997).

Cumming has a set of programs that can be purchased for a small fee at www.esci@latrobe.edu.au. These allow power calculations as well as confidence intervals, and provide graphics showing both the central and noncentral t distributions. The programs can be downloaded as Excel files. Alternatively, readers with access to SPSS may use freely downloaded syntax files developed by Wuensch.[3] They are available at the website http://core.ecu.edu/psyc/wuenschk/

---

[3] The website http://core.ecu.edu/psyc/wuenschk/SAS/SAS-Programs.htm provides similar programs for users of SAS.

SPSS/SPSS-Programs.htm.[4] *TechNote 6_2* (on our website) describes the input and output for the file to calculate confidence limits for Cohen's *d* for the independent-groups design (*TD-2-D sample.sps*). Running that syntax in SPSS verifies our calculation that $\hat{d} = .384$. It also provides the additional information that the 95% CI has bounds at $-.084$ and .849. In other words, the population value of *d* may be anywhere from virtually zero to a large positive treatment effect. The confidence interval limits not only set bounds on plausible values but remind us that the estimate by itself can be misleading. Wuensch's website also provides a file to calculate limits on d_z when the data are from a single sample (*TD-1-D sample.sps*). Using the differences between the *Before* and *After* scores from our hypothetical study of diet on cholesterol level, we estimated *d* to be .29 with 95% confidence interval bounds of .09 and .49. Wuensch's syntax file (and Cumming's program) estimates Cohen's d_z. As will usually be the case, the estimate of d_z is higher than that of *d*; it is .50. The bounds on that estimate are .15 and .85.

It should be noted that these estimates rest on the assumption of homogeneity of variance. In addition, because calculating the *CI* for *d* requires finding areas under the noncentral *t* distribution, it is also assumed that the population distribution is normal. In response to possible violations of these assumptions, Algina, Keselman, and Penfield (2005a, 2006) have proposed modifications of *d* that make use of the trimmed means and winsorized variances that are defined in Chapter 7.

6.7.3 *p*-Values, Effect Sizes, and Two Cautions

Researchers sometimes interpret the size of the *p*-value as an index of importance; the smaller the *p*-value, the more important the effect. However, it is not unusual to find that the effect associated with the smaller *p*-value actually has the smaller standardized effect size. Table 6.5 presents the results of two experiments that differed in the number of subjects. The larger *t* and smaller *p*-values in Experiment 2 might lead us to believe that the measure in Experiment 2 was more sensitive; the larger raw effect in Experiment 2 would seem to support that inference. However, the standardized effect size is almost twice as large in Experiment 1, indicating that Experiment 1 may have lacked power to reject the null hypothesis because of the relatively small sample. Although artificial, the

Table 6.5 A comparison of *p*-values (two-tailed) and effect sizes ($\hat{d}$) in two experiments

	Experiment	
	1	2
n	16	64
$\bar{Y}_1 - \bar{Y}_2$	15	40
s	33	152
t	1.818	2.105
p	.089	.039
$\hat{d}$	.455	.263

---

[4] Entering "Cohen d confidence interval" into a search engine such as Google brings up several websites featuring other freely downloadable calculators, including several that make use of the Microsoft Excel spreadsheet to calculate the limits. We have not investigated all of these; therefore, at a minimum, results should be compared with those in this chapter.

example shows that $\hat{d}$ can provide useful information, sometimes leading us to reconsider conclusions based on other statistics. It also illustrates the potential danger in using the size of the test statistic, or the *p*-value associated with it, or the raw effect size, as an index of importance.

Although effect size estimates provide important information to the researcher, we offer a couple of cautions concerning their use. First, estimates of Cohen's *d* are based on the assumption that group variances are homogeneous. When the variances for the two groups differ, $\hat{d}$ may be a poor estimate of *d*. This and other issues in using $\hat{d}$ as an index of effect size are discussed in several articles, together with possible solutions (Grissom & Kim, 2001; Kelley, 2005; Olejnik & Algina, 2000).

The second caution concerns Cohen's widely adopted benchmarks for effect sizes; namely, that *d* values of .2, .5, and .8 correspond to small, medium, and large effects, respectively. Although guidelines can be useful, it is important to emphasize that they are just that—guides, not mandates. Previous results, theoretical considerations, and practical goals are better bases for evaluating the importance of an effect size. We should ask: Is this effect large relative to those found in related studies in the research literature or in our laboratory? Smaller? About the same as in other studies of this type? Is our research goal—whether theoretical or applied—one for which even a small effect is important to recognize? In short, Cohen's *d* is just one perspective on the "importance" of an effect. By expressing the magnitude of an effect relative to variability, *d* provides useful information; however, it is entirely possible for an effect with a small value of *d* to have great practical or theoretical importance. There is a difference between statistical and practical significance.

6.8 DECIDING ON SAMPLE SIZE

Too many experiments waste time, effort, and resources because the researcher has failed to collect enough data to have sufficient power to detect differences that may be present in the population. Power should be taken into account in deciding on the sample size. Analyses that do this have been referred to as *a priori* or *prospective power analyses*.

6.8.1 *A Priori* Power Analyses in the Independent-Groups Design

How might we decide on the sample size of a planned experiment with two independent groups? We require an estimate of the smallest standardized population effect size we want to detect, and a minimum level of power to detect that effect. Understanding the role of these requirements in calculating power involves understanding how *t* is distributed when the null hypothesis is false. The relevant distribution is called the *noncentral t distribution* and we discuss it next. Following that discussion, we will consider a specific example of its application to the decision about sample size.

The Noncentral t Distribution.   As with the binomial (Chapter 4) and normal probability (Chapter 5) tests, we can conceive of two distributions, one when the null hypothesis is true and one when it is false by a specific amount. For example, in the *TC* experiment we might have one distribution corresponding to $H_0: \mu_{diet} - \mu_{control} = 0$ and an alternative distribution corresponding to $H_A: \mu_{diet} - \mu_{control} = 20$. The distribution of *t* assuming the null hypothesis is the *central t distribution*. As with other statistical tests, we first determine the rejection region in this distribution—the values of *t* that lead to rejection of the null hypothesis. That region can be obtained from Appendix Table C.3, or from most statistical software packages. Once we know the rejection region, we can calculate power by finding the probabilities of the *t* values in that region, assuming the alternative distribution; that is, assuming the *noncentral t distribution* under a specific alternative hypothesis.

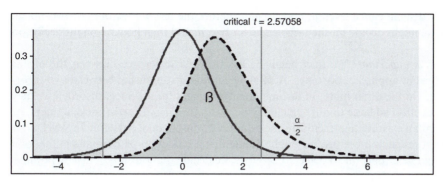

Fig. 6.1 Plot of the central and noncentral t distributions with $df = 5$.

Fig. 6.1 displays central (left) and noncentral (right) t distributions on 5 df. The figure was generated by G*Power, a versatile software package for calculating power.[5] In the example in the figure, $\alpha = .05$, the alternative hypothesis was two-tailed, and the actual (standardized) effect was .5 (arbitrarily chosen for the sake of illustration). Because the relation between $\hat{d}$ and t is simply $t = \hat{d}\sqrt{n}$, the distance between the means of the central and noncentral t distributions in Fig. 6.1 is $(.5)(\sqrt{6})$ or 1.22 units. The rejection region is the area to the left of the vertical line near -2.5 and to the right of the vertical line near 2.5. Power corresponds to the area under the right (noncentral t) distribution above the values required for rejection of H_0. Several points should be noted.

1. The noncentral t distribution has a different shape than the central t distribution; it is not just displaced. The location, variance, and shape of the noncentral t distribution are determined by the df and a *noncentrality parameter*, δ (the Greek letter delta). This is a measure of distance between the two distributions and incorporates information about variability (σ), sample size (n), and the raw effect size under the alternative hypothesis. In general, the noncentral t distribution tends to be skewed to the right, although both distributions will look more like the normal distribution as df increase.

2. Virtually none of the area under the noncentral distribution is to the left of the left critical value. If the alternative hypothesis is that the effect is positive, there is usually very little power to reject alternatives in the other direction.

3. If we hypothesize a larger alternative effect, the distance between the two distributions will increase; more of the area of the noncentral t distribution will lie to the right of the rejection region, displaying increased power.

Deciding on Sample Size: An Example. We found that the value of t for a comparison of diet and control group total cholesterol (TC) means was 1.63. Testing against the one-tailed alternative, $H_0 : \mu_{control} - \mu_{diet} > 0$, the corresponding p-value is slightly higher than .05. Suppose we decide to replicate the experiment. This requires us to state an effect size, a value of d under the specific alternative hypothesis. We also must state the power with which we wish to be able to reject H_0 given this effect, and the total sample size ($N = n_1 + n_2$) needed to achieve the desired power. Finally, we

---

[5] Help in using the program may be found at the G*Power 3 website, http://www.psycho.uni-duesseldorf.de/abteilungen/ aap/gpower3/. Users may freely download the program and also register in order to obtain updates. Additional help is provided by Faul, Erdfelder, Lang, and Buchner (2007), the developers of G*Power 3, who have written an excellent discussion of the program.

need to set the desired significance level, α, and decide whether the test will be one- or two-tailed. Let's consider how we might decide on the targeted effect size, d, and then how we might decide on the sample size.

What effect size is important? We may begin by asking what difference between the means would be of theoretical or applied importance. A small effect that distinguishes between two theories can be important. On the other hand, in testing a new treatment for a clinical disorder, we may wish to detect only an effect so large that it will clearly be worth the cost of further development, or will clearly be better than existing treatments. In the example of the effect of a diet on *TC* level, after reviewing the relevant research literature, we might decide that a reduction of 20 points in the total cholesterol level would be important to detect. Therefore, we decide that our alternative hypothesis should be $H_A: \mu_{control} - \mu_{diet} > 20$.

We now need an estimate of σ. In planning a replication of our *TC* experiment, we might base our estimate on our present data set; then $s_{pooled} = 43.751$. We could also examine estimates from related studies in the literature to see whether this is a reasonable estimate of the variance of change in total cholesterol level, and perhaps to improve our estimate. After some consideration, we decide that $s = 44$ is reasonable; dividing 20 by 44 yields $d = .47$.

Other options exist for setting the effect size. We might use the estimate from our pilot study of .38. However, we prefer to think first in terms of the raw effect size that is of interest, or is suggested by previous research. Another possibility in our example is based on noting that .47 is close to .5, Cohen's (1988) medium effect size. Therefore, for the purposes of easy communication to a future audience, we might set $d = .5$. Further discussion of the considerations involved in choosing an effect size in an *a priori* power analysis may be found in Lenth (2001).

What power do we want? Ideally, we want a sample size that will provide maximum power to detect the effect of interest. Unfortunately, there are practical considerations. The required sample size increases as either the target effect size decreases, or as the targeted power increases. The n needed, particularly for high power and small effect sizes, is much larger than most researchers realize. Suppose we decide on power = .8, a level of power that has been frequently suggested as reasonable. In that case, we would need $n = 57$. Increasing the desired power brings a cost; to have .90 power against the alternative, $d = .47$, we need 79 subjects in each group. Our sample size usually will be a compromise among considerations of the targeted effect, the power we would like to have to detect that effect, and the practical limitations of subject availability and the time required for data collection.

Calculating the Required Sample Size. We noted earlier that power calculations are based on the noncentral *t* distribution, whose location, variance, and shape are determined, in part, by a *noncentrality parameter,* δ. If our study involves two independent groups, δ is defined as:

$$\delta = \frac{\mu_1 - \mu_2}{\sigma\sqrt{(1/n_1) + (1/n_2)}} \tag{6.20}$$

From Equation 6.18, we can express δ as a function of d and the group sizes

$$\delta = d/\sqrt{(1/n_1) + (1/n_2)} \tag{6.21}$$

G*Power 3 takes values of d and the ratio of the *n*s as input and uses them to calculate δ in doing power computations. As an example, Fig. 6.2 presents our input (left-hand entries) to G*Power 3 and the resulting output (right-hand entries). We requested the *a priori* t test option for independent groups with power = .9, α = .05, the effect size = .47 (our specific alterative), and tested against

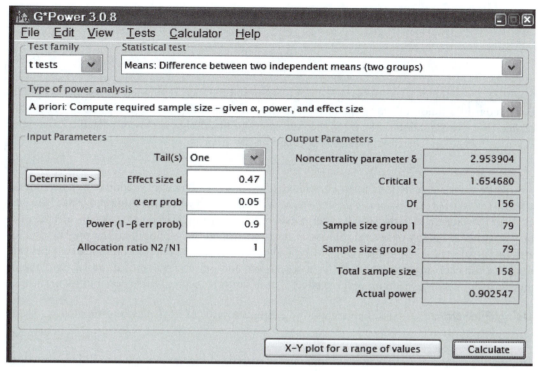

Fig. 6.2 Determining sample size with G*Power 3.

a one-tailed alternative. The total N of 158 is more than twice the N of 72 in our original experiment.

Suppose we had decided that a practical limit on the total sample size was 150 subjects. Generally, we will have to accept that power will suffer if there are constraints on the size of our sample. However, it is instructive to examine how changes in target effect size affect our calculation of sample size to achieve a given level of power. In our current example, a small increase in effect size from .47 to .5 enables us to achieve *a priori* power of .9 with 140 subjects. On the other hand, suppose that we were dealing with a much smaller presumed effect size. Even if we lowered our desired power to .8, if we set d to .25—small by Cohen's (1988) standards—we would require 398 subjects.

In summary, even moderate power to reject the null hypothesis when d is small requires quite large sample sizes. In many studies, both theoretically motivated and applied, power to detect an effect is too low because sample sizes are too small. Despite articles that have made this point (e.g., Cohen, 1962; Greenwald, 1993), researchers continue to underestimate the sample size needed for adequate power.

6.8.2 *A Priori* Power Analyses in the Correlated-Scores Design

In the case of the correlated-scores design, the definition of δ refers to a population of difference scores, rather than two independent populations of scores. Assuming a sample of n difference scores, as in the example of the TC change scores, δ is defined as

$$\delta = \frac{\mu_{difference}}{\sigma_{difference}/\sqrt{n}}$$

$$= \frac{\mu_{difference}\sqrt{n}}{\sigma_{difference}} \tag{6.22}$$

where $\mu_{difference}$ is the mean of the sampled population of difference, or change, scores and $\sigma_{difference}$ is the standard deviation of that population. Just as δ for the independent-groups design is closely related to d (see Equation 6.21), δ for the correlated-groups design is closely related to d_z, where, $d_z = \mu_{difference}/\sigma_{difference}$. Therefore, Equation 6.22 can be rewritten as

$$\delta = d_z\sqrt{n} \tag{6.23}$$

To do power calculations for a correlated-score design, G*Power 3 requires d_z as an input. Choose the *difference between two dependent means* option, and where the input requests *effect size* d_z, enter the value of d_z as the specific alternative to the null hypothesized value. Again, a value of d_z may originate from any of several sources. A researcher might have pilot data that may be used to estimate a value of d_z. Or a knowledge of typical effect sizes in the relevant literature may provide the basis for choosing a value of d_z. Or a researcher may select a value of d_z based on Cohen's guidelines for a small, medium, or large effect. Let us consider each of these possibilities in turn.

Using Pilot Data.   If pilot data are used to estimate a value of d_z, d_z may be estimated as:

$$\hat{d}_z = (\overline{Y}_1 - \overline{Y}_2)/s_{Y_1 - Y_2} \tag{6.24}$$

Or there is a simple relation between $\hat{d}_z$ and t in the correlated-scores case that is useful in estimating d_z:

$$\hat{d}_z = t/\sqrt{n} \tag{6.25}$$

Once an estimate is obtained, it may be inserted into G*Power 3 using the *t*-test/dependent means program. A more conservative approach would be to use a program such as Cumming's ESCI or Wuensch's syntax file (see Section 6.7.2) to obtain a confidence interval on d_z, and then insert into G*Power 3 a value of d_z from the lower range in the *CI*. This approach involves more steps, but it will produce a value of n that is more likely to guarantee the desired level of power because it recognizes that estimates of d_z are typically quite variable.

Using Knowledge of the Literature.   In many circumstances, a researcher plans to do an experiment that has an established context in a research literature. A review of related studies using the same paradigm will provide the researcher with the range of magnitudes of effects in the relevant literature. A prudent strategy would be to select a relatively small value of d_z from those observed, and use it as the basis for power calculations. If the true population standardized effect is larger than the selected estimate of d_z, the calculated value of n and the corresponding power will be greater than what is targeted, but that is better than having less power than desired.

Using Cohen's Guidelines.   In the event that there is no empirical basis for selecting a value of d_z on which to base power calculations, the researcher may rely on Cohen's guidelines for small, medium, and large effect sizes. Although Cohen's guidelines refer to d rather than d_z, there is a relation between d_z and d that can be exploited to obtain an estimate of d_z from d. Comparing Equations 6.20 and 6.22, we see that d and d_z differ only in their denominators. The relation between the standard deviation of the treatment populations, σ, and the standard deviation of the population of difference scores is:

$$\sigma_{Y_1 - Y_2} = \sqrt{\sigma_1^2 + \sigma_2^2 - 2\rho\sigma_1\sigma_2} \tag{6.26}$$

where ρ (rho) is the population correlation between scores in the two conditions. Assuming homogeneous variances, this can be rewritten as

$$\sigma_{Y_1 - Y_2} = \sigma\sqrt{2(1 - \rho)} \tag{6.27}$$

Substituting Equation 6.27 into Equation 6.22 and solving for d_z,

$$d_z = \frac{\mu_1 - \mu_2}{\sigma\sqrt{2(1 - \rho)}}$$
$$= d / \sqrt{2(1 - \rho)} \tag{6.28}$$

As an example of working from a value of d, suppose that we conducted an experiment with an independent-groups design. Despite a reasonable effect size of .5, the experiment failed to produce a significant effect. We decide to try again, but we choose a correlated-scores design for the follow-up. We wish to compute the n for .8 power assuming the same effect size found in the first experiment. In order to compute n for the correlated-scores design, we must translate our d-value of .5 to a value of d_z. We need to assume a value of ρ to do the conversion. In the absence of any information, we will assume a relatively low correlation of .3. Substituting in Equation 6.26, we compute $d_z = .42$. Using G*Power 3 for $d_z = .42$, $\alpha = .05$, power = .8, we calculate that n should be 37.

Cohen's guidelines for small, medium, and large values of d have been widely adopted, so it may be useful to translate those values into corresponding values of d_z. To do so, we will present values of d_z for values of ρ equal to .2, .5, and .8. Entries in Table 6.6 are values of d_z calculated using Equation 6.28 for the nine combinations of values of d and ρ. The values in the rows correspond to Cohen's (1988) guidelines for small, medium, and large effects.

6.9 POST HOC POWER

Having failed to reject the null hypothesis, researchers sometimes suggest that power was too low to detect a population effect. As support, they may calculate power based on the observed effect, perhaps using the *post hoc* option in G*Power, or SPSS's *Observed Power* option. For example, suppose we had two groups of 10 subjects each, and the observed $t = 1.9$, slightly short of the critical value of t of 2.1, required for a two-tailed test. Suppose that the researcher calculates $d = .85$. Noting that the effect is large by Cohen's guidelines, the researcher calculates post hoc power, which is only .44. With this information—a large effect and low power—the researcher claims that only the lack of power prevented a clear demonstration of statistical significance.

There are several problems with such post hoc (also called retrospective) power calculations.

Table 6.6 Values of d_z corresponding to nine combinations of d and ρ

Values of d	Values of ρ		
	.2	.5	.8
.2	.16	.20	.32
.5	.40	.50	.79
.8	.63	.80	1.26

Suppose that an investigator fails to reject the null hypothesis. A post hoc power calculation based on the observed effect size suggests low power, so the investigator concludes that the lack of significance was due to low power. However, this argument fails to recognize that sampling error makes it unlikely that the observed effect size is the same as the population effect size. Therefore, the estimate of power may be in error; it is possible that power was higher than indicated by the estimate and that there really is no effect to be detected. In short, null results are ambiguous.

There are other reasons to avoid post hoc power calculations. One is that post hoc power provides little, if any, more information than the *p*-value (Hoenig & Heisey, 2001; Lenth, 2001). Observed power and the *p*-value are inversely related because they are both functions of the observed effect size and the sample size. Stated differently, if the result of the *t* test was not significant, post hoc power was probably low.

Another problem is that post hoc power calculations often will be very unreliable estimates of the true power of the experiment. Calculating a confidence interval for *d* helps appreciate this point. Using Wuensch's syntax file, we find that the 95% *CI* for *d* in our current example has bounds of − .08 and 1.76; the standardized effect may be anywhere from a small negative effect to a very large positive effect. It may help us to understand the implication of these bounds if we put this result on a scale with which we are more familiar, that between zero and one. To do so, we inserted the .95 limits of *d* into G*Power, set alpha = .05 and *n* = 36, indicated a two-tailed test, and obtained a 95% *CI* on power. The resulting confidence limits on power were .053 and .961. That is, we estimate that the power of the experiment was anywhere between .053 (i.e., terrible) and .961 (i.e., excellent). Thus, we are left with almost as much uncertainty as if we had not calculated post hoc power.

In sum, we recommend against the practice of post hoc power computations. Instead, confidence intervals on both the raw and standardized effect sizes are much more useful. Confidence intervals on raw effect sizes are likely to be on a more meaningful scale; confidence intervals on standardized effect sizes provide comparability with other results. Post hoc power adds nothing to our understanding and the strategy of computing post hoc power misrepresents the essential ambiguity of a failure to reject the null hypothesis.

6.10 SUMMARY

This chapter focused on inferential statistics based on the *t* distribution, using two research designs to illustrate the use of those statistics. The following points are important to keep in mind:

- There are both practical and statistical considerations in selecting a research design. When several designs are practical, testing each subject under several conditions, or testing pairs of subjects matched on some relevant measure, will usually result in less error variance than the independent-groups design although there will be fewer degrees of freedom.
- Confidence intervals provide information that is not directly available from the *t* statistic alone. The interval provides a measure of the precision of our estimate of the treatment effect, and at the same time provides a test of the universe of possible null hypotheses. The width of the interval—and therefore the precision of the estimate of the treatment effect—was shown to decrease with (1) increases in sample size, (2) decreases in variance, and (3) increased alpha. Because it affects variability, the design of the experiment—for example, correlated scores or independent groups—is also a major factor.
- Effect size measures are an important addition to parameter estimates and significance tests: (1) they speak to the practical or theoretical significance of the effect, as distinct

from statistical significance; (2) they permit scale-free comparisons of effects from different conditions or experiments; (3) they are used in calculating the power of the statistical test; and (4) they provide a basis for meta-analyses in which results from several experiments are combined to provide a "big picture" of the effectiveness of an independent variable.

- We have emphasized statistical power, arguing that it should be a major consideration in the design of the experiment. Power is influenced by the same factors that affect the width of confidence intervals: sample size, variance, alpha level, and the experimental design. The use of freely available software, G*Power 3, was illustrated in decisions about sample size (*a priori*, or prospective, power).

- We presented arguments against calculating post hoc power based on the statistics of a completed experiment. The results of such analyses are misleading because they rest on the assumption that the sample statistics have the same value as the population parameters, and they are largely uninformative because post hoc power is an inverse monotonic function of the *p*-value associated with the observed *t* statistic.

- The validity of statistical methods rests on the validity of assumptions. We considered the assumptions underlying the methods presented, emphasizing the consequences of their violations as a function of such factors as sample size, shape of the population distribution, and the ratio of treatment population variances. We then suggested alternative analyses in response to these violations of assumptions.

Although later chapters will discuss analyses for designs that involve more than one factor, and more than two conditions, the material in the present chapter will be of central importance for two reasons. First, we have continued the development of inferential concepts that will be equally important in the subsequent chapters. Second, even when there are more conditions, the researcher's hypotheses and questions often translate into a comparison of two means, or a comparison of a single mean against some hypothesized value. Some of the comparisons will be superficially more complex than those of this chapter but they basically involve the same assumptions and calculations. Therefore, the material we have discussed here deserves close study.

EXERCISES

6.1 A sample of nine 30-day-old, protein-deficient infants are given a motor skills test. The mean for a normal population is 60. The data are

$$Y_1 = 40, 69, 75, 42, 38, 47, 37, 52, 31$$

(a) Find a 90% confidence interval for the mean of the protein-deficient population.

(b) Is the mean score of the protein-deficient children significantly below that of a normal population?

(c) After 3 months of a normal diet the scores of the nine children are

$$Y_2 = 48, 68, 77, 46, 47, 46, 41, 51, 34$$

Estimate the mean of the population after 3 months of a normal diet. Calculate the 90% confidence interval and test whether this sample mean is below the population value of 60. Assume $\alpha = .05$ for the significance test.

(d) Calculate difference scores and test whether there has been an improvement from the first test to the second. Assume $\alpha = .05$.

(e) Estimate Cohen's *d* for the comparison of the Y_1 and Y_2 means.

6.2 An investigator wants to determine whether the difficulty of material to be learned influences the anxiety of college students. A random sample of 10 students are given both hard and easy material to learn (order of presentation is counterbalanced). After completing part of each task, anxiety level is measured by a questionnaire. The anxiety scores are as follows:

Student	1	2	3	4	5	6	7	8	9	10	11	12
Hard task	48	71	65	47	53	55	68	71	59	31	80	77
Easy task	40	59	58	51	49	55	70	61	57	32	70	69

(a) Find the 95% confidence interval for the difference in the population means corresponding to the two conditions.

(b) Test whether anxiety is significantly different in the two difficulty conditions, using a matched-group *t* test. State H_0 and H_1 and indicate the rejection region for $\alpha = .05$.

(c) Redo parts (a) and (b), assuming that the experiment had been done with two independent groups of 12 subjects each. What are the strengths and weaknesses of each design? Note any differences in results of the analyses and the reasons for them in your answer, as well as any other considerations that you feel are important.

6.3 For a matched-group design, we wish to test $H_0: \mu_D = 0$ against $H_1: \mu_D > 0$ at $\alpha = .05$. Using a sample of 16 subjects, we find $\bar{D} = 2.0$ and $s_D = 5.6$.

(a) Carry out the *t* test.

(b) Calculate the standardized effect size, d_z.

(c) Using G*Power, what power did the *t* test have to reject the null hypothesis given the value of d_z calculated in part (b)? What would the power be if $n = 36$ instead of 16?

(d) What *n* would be required to have power equal to or greater than .80?

(e) In part (c), you should have found the power of the *t* test. Redo the power calculations in part (c), using the standardized normal distribution (see Chapter 5 for a review of the method, or use G*Power) for $n = 16$ and 36, and for the *n* in your answer to part (d). How good an approximation are these results to the results you obtained using the *t* distribution? Is the approximation better or worse as *n* increases? Why might this be?

6.3 In an independent-groups design, we have

Group 1	Group 2
$n_1 = 18$	$n_2 = 14$
$s_1^2 = 16$	$s_2^2 = 20$
$\bar{Y}_1 = 30.1$	$\bar{Y}_2 = 27.7$

(a) Find the 95% confidence interval for $\mu_1 - \mu_2$. Assuming we wish to test $H_0: \mu_1 = \mu_2$ against a two-tailed alternative, what can we conclude?

(b) Calculate the standardized effect size, *d*. Assuming this effect size, what power did the experiment have to reject the null hypothesis?

(c) Suppose we wished to redo the study with equal n and want .8 power to reject H_0, assuming the effect size calculated in part (b). What size n would we need?

(d) Using the n from part (c), and assuming the variances given in part (a), what would the width of the new confidence interval be?

6.5 In an independent-groups design we have

Group 1	Group 2
$n_1 = 21$	$n_2 = 11$
$s_1^2 = 8$	$s_2^2 = 30$
$\bar{Y}_1 = 30.2$	$\bar{Y}_2 = 27.0$

(a) Test the null hypothesis at $\alpha = .05$ against a two-tailed alternative using the pooled-variance t test.

(b) Test the null hypothesis at $\alpha = .05$ against a two-tailed alternative using the separate-variance (Welch) t test.

(c) Explain any differences in your conclusions in parts (a) and (b).

6.6 An arithmetic skills test is given to 8- and 10-year-old boys and girls. There are 10 children in each of the four cells of this research design. The means and standard deviations are given below:

		8 years	10 years
Boys	$\bar{Y} =$	58	72
	$s =$	2.7	2.1
Girls	$\bar{Y} =$	53	60
	$s =$	2.9	2.2

(a) (i) Calculate a 90% confidence interval for the difference in population means for 8- and 10-year-old girls ($\mu_{10,G} - \mu_{8,G}$). (ii) Assume you wish to test the null hypothesis against $H_1: \mu_{10,G} > \mu_{8,G}$. What can you conclude on the basis of the confidence interval?

(b) We wish to test whether the difference between boys and girls is significantly greater at age 10 than at age 8. (i) State H_0 and H_1 in terms of the four population means. (ii) Calculate the numerator of the t statistic that reflects whether the gender difference is greater at age 10 than at age 8. (iii) Calculate the standard error of the quantity calculated in part (ii); see Equation 5.19 in Appendix 5.1. (iv) Carry out a t test of your null hypothesis, briefly reporting the conclusion.

6.7 Several researchers have compared laboratory reading (subjects knew they would be tested for recall) with natural reading (subjects read material without knowing they would be tested). In one such study, two groups of eight subjects each (lab, natural groups) were tested twice on the same materials, once on each of two different days. Free-recall percentages (correct responses) were:

Lab	Day 1	45	60	42	57	63	38	36	51
	Day 2	43	38	28	40	47	23	16	32
Natural	Day 1	64	51	44	48	49	55	32	31
	Day 2	21	38	19	16	24	27	22	35

(a) For each group, find the 95% confidence interval for the population mean of the change in recall over the 2 days. For each group, is the change significant at the .05 (two-tailed) level?

(b) We wish to compare the two groups on day 2. Assuming a two-tailed test, can we reject H_0 at the .05 level?

(c) From part (a), we have a change score for each subject. We wish to test whether the amount of change is the same for the two populations of readers. State the null and alternative hypotheses. Do the test at the .05 level.

6.8 The data for this problem are in the *TC Data* file at the website.

(a) Calculate the standardized effect size (Cohen's *d*) for the winter–spring difference in *TC* scores (*TC*1 − *TC*2) for the *Sayhlth* = 2 (very good) and for the *Sayhlth* = 4 (fair) group. How would you characterize the effects in terms of Cohen's guidelines?

(b) Calculate the winter–spring confidence intervals for the two *Sayhlth* groups of part (a). In which is the confidence interval narrower? Also calculate the *t* statistic for each. Which has the larger *t*? The lower *p*-value?

(c) Considering the various statistics, discuss the effects of seasons (winter versus spring) on total cholesterol level.

6.9 In Exercise 6.8, we calculated an estimate of Cohen's *d*, a measure of the standardized effect size. When scores in two conditions (such as winter and spring) are correlated, an alternative measure is d_z, the ratio of the difference between the means to the standard deviation of the difference.

(a) Calculate d_z for each of the two *Sayhlth* groups we have been considering.

(b) Your result for d_z should differ from the result obtained when calculating *d*. In general, what will influence the size of the difference between these two measures of effect size?

(c) If we were to replicate the study for the two *Sayhlth* groups, assuming the effect sizes estimated from the present study, how many subjects would be needed in each condition to ensure power of at least .8 to reject the null hypothesis of no seasonal difference? Assume $\alpha = .05$ and a two-tailed test.

6.10 A group of 18 subjects, the experimental group (*E*), reads a passage designed to increase support for lowering the legal drinking age to 18 years. A second group of 18 subjects, the control group (*C*), reads a passage unrelated to this topic. Statistics for the two groups are as follows:

	E	*C*
Mean	4.0	3.2
Variance	2.25	1.44

(a) Calculate the 95% confidence interval. Based on the limits you calculated, is the difference between the means significant at the .05 level, two-tailed?

(b) Given the purpose of the experimental passage, reconsider whether the difference is significant.

6.11 (a) Estimate Cohen's d for the statistics given in Exercise 6.10.

(b) Assume your estimate of d is the actual population value. If we replicate the experiment, how large must each group be in order to have power = .8 against a one-tailed alternative?

(c) Suppose we assume the same value of d but decide to replicate the experiment using a design with a single group of subjects who are tested before and after reading the passage. A reasonable estimate of the correlation between *before* and *after* scores is .5. What should n be in this experiment to have power = .8?

6.12 In studies testing whether a single sample mean differs significantly from zero, we have the following t values and sample sizes (n):

t	2.0	4.5	2.0	4.5	2.0	4.5
n	16	81	36	36	4	225

(a) Calculate the value of Cohen's d statistic for each study.

(b) Is there a relationship between t and d? Explain your answer.

(c) Using software available from the Web (see Section 6.7.2), find the 95% confidence limits for each value of d.

(d) How does the sample size affect the interval width in part (c)?

6.13 Consider the following for four two-group experiments. In each experiment, the difference between the means is 3.3 for all four sets; and the variance is 22 for group 1 and 27 for group 2. The groups are of equal size within each experiment and the group sizes are:

Experiment =	1	2	3	4
$n =$	4	9	16	25

Calculate t, d, and find the p-value (two-tailed) and the post hoc power of the test. What are the relations among d, p, and post hoc power? Which is the best index of the importance of the effect? Why?

The next two problems are open-ended but represent the task faced by the investigator with a large data set.

6.14 The *Royer_acc* file at the website contains subtraction, addition, multiplication, and mean percent correct for male and female third- to eighth-graders who had accuracy scores for all three arithmetic operations. Considerable attention has been given to the relative quantitative skills of males and females. What differences, if any, are there between the sexes in performance? Support your conclusions with graphs, and any statistics—including significance test results, confidence intervals, and effect sizes—that you find relevant.

6.15 Using the *Royer_rt* file, discuss differences, if any, between the sexes, again supporting your answer with graphs and statistics.

Chapter 7
Integrated Analysis I

7.1 OVERVIEW

This is the first of several integrated analysis chapters designed with two purposes in mind.

- First, to help integrate concepts and procedures presented in the preceding chapters.
- Second, to help bridge the gap from theory to application.

Using new examples, these chapters review and extend the analyses presented in the previous chapters. The presentation of the material in these chapters follows the form of a research report, including the method used to collect the data, the results of both exploratory and inferential analyses, and a discussion of the results.

In this chapter, we consider a hypothetical independent-groups experiment on the effect of a drug on memory. We first consider the rationale for the experimental design, and then begin the data analysis by examining key descriptive statistics and data plots. We then estimate the raw and standardized differences between the means of the two treatment groups, construct confidence intervals, and test hypotheses; confidence intervals and hypothesis tests will be based on the t distribution. In response to evidence from the exploratory phase of possible violations of assumptions underlying these procedures, we calculate an alternative to the usual t test.

Following the analyses, we interpret the results, referring to the descriptive statistics and data plots obtained in the exploratory stage of the data analysis, as well as the results of hypothesis tests. In trying to understand our results, we not only have to account for causes of statistically significant effects but also consider whether nonsignificant trends represent chance variability or a lack of power due to factors such as small sample size, outliers, nonnormality of the distribution, or other violations of underlying assumptions.

7.2 INTRODUCTION TO THE RESEARCH

Assume that a pharmaceutical company has developed a new pill for retarding the memory decrement that accompanies aging even in normal individuals. Because the pill is expensive to develop, a small pilot study was designed to test its effects. If the results are promising, a larger, full-scale study will be conducted, using more subjects and more measures of memory. The researchers decided to test two groups, each having 25 subjects over 65. The experimental group took the memory pill once a day for 1 month prior to presentation of a list of 30 words and an immediate recall test. The control group was tested on the same list after taking a placebo for 1 month. The scores are in the Y column of the *IA1_memory* file on the book's website (go to *Data Files* and then *Tables* to find the link).

7.3 METHOD

7.3.1 Subjects

The pharmaceutical researcher posted a request for volunteers on the bulletin board of a local senior center. Volunteers were assessed in individual sessions to ensure that they were not suffering from any form of dementia. The assessment included a brief test of memory, an interview, and questions about facts that were judged to be common knowledge (e.g., the name of the vice-president of the United States). From the pool of potential volunteers, 50 were chosen, ranging in age from 65 to 75.

7.3.2 Experimental Design

As we discussed in Chapter 1, there are a number of options here. We could first test the subjects prior to their taking the memory pill and then again, sometime after taking the pill. The researcher decided against this, feeling that prior exposure to the testing situation might raise scores in the subsequent test, thus reducing the effect of the drug. Furthermore, a test–retest design would necessitate constructing a second memory test that was equated for difficulty with the first one. Still another possible problem was that age-related memory decline might accompany the period between test and retest, countering any possible benefit of the pill. Finally, just knowing they were given a pill designed to aid memory might have motivated subjects, producing an improvement unrelated to the pill itself. Modifications of the test–retest design can offset these potential problems; however, the researcher decided that the simplest procedure was to randomly assign the subjects to one of two conditions, experimental pill or control (placebo, a sugar pill). A single research assistant collected the data but did not know which subject was in which condition. As noted in Chapter 1, this is known as a double-blind procedure because neither the individual collecting the data, nor the subjects, knew who was in which condition.

Further modifications of this independent-groups design are possible. Restricting the assignment of subjects to ensure that the groups had equal numbers of men and women would facilitate investigating whether the effects of the pill were the same for both sexes, and equate any effects due to gender. A correlated-scores design in which subjects were assigned so that the groups were equated for age, or scores on the preliminary test given to all volunteers, would reduce error variance. However, these variables could be taken into account in regression analyses after the primary data were collected (e.g., analysis of covariance; see Chapter 25), or in a subsequent, larger experiment if this pilot study yielded promising results. Another possible design would involve a combination of the correlated-scores and independent-groups design; this would involve repeated testing of both experimental and control subjects, controlling for any changes due to prior exposure to the test, or age-related memory decline. Although several of these designs, as well as others, might result in less error variance or more control of nuisance variables that could bias the results, the experimenters opted for a relatively simple design in what was intended as a pilot study.

7.3.3 Procedure

Each subject was given a small bottle containing 28 pills. Half of the bottles contained the placebo and half the experimental pills. Each subject was assigned a different numbered bottle of pills and only the researcher knew the relationship between the numbers and the assigned experimental condition. Subjects were instructed to take one pill each day and to return to the laboratory on day 29. They were told that no side effects were expected but that, as a precaution, they should note any departures from their usual physical or emotional state.

On day 29, subjects were seated, and the research assistant slowly read a list of words aloud. These 30 test words were familiar English nouns of 5–7 letters in length. Immediately after they were read, the subjects wrote down in any order as many of the words as they could recall.

7.4 EXPLORING THE DATA

The score for each subject was the number of words recalled correctly. Spelling errors were ignored as long as the word clearly had been on the test list. For the present, we consider only the column of scores labeled Y in the *IA1_memory* file. We begin our analysis by obtaining the descriptive statistics and data plots that were illustrated in Chapter 2. Although we have used SPSS's Explore module for this purpose, most statistical software packages will provide similar output. Table 7.1 presents output from SPSS's Descriptive Statistics/Explore module, including measures of central tendency, variability, and shape. The medians and 5% trimmed means had similar values to those of the means, suggesting that the distributions are symmetric. We note that the drug did result in better average recall scores than the placebo taken by the control group. However, the mean difference of about 1.5 words recalled seems small and may not be of either practical or statistical significance. We will shortly calculate a standardized effect measure, Cohen's d, to obtain a better sense of the importance of the effect of the memory pill. Confidence intervals and significance tests will address the issue of statistical significance. First, however, we consider several of the other statistics in Table 7.1, and some data plots as well.

Before conducting any inferential tests, we should evaluate whether violations of test assumptions are a concern. A comparison of the variances (or standard deviations) indicates that the population variances are not dissimilar enough to affect the Type 1 error rate. The control-to-drug ratio of variances is less than 1.5, far less than any ratio of variances that would cause trouble when the ns are equal (see Table 6.3). SPSS and many other statistical software packages provide tests of homogeneity of variance. Panel a of Table 7.2, obtained from SPSS's Explore module, provides further evidence that the population variances do not differ significantly.[1] In these tests, each score is transformed into an absolute deviation from a measure of central tendency (the mean, median, or

---

[1] Table 7.2 was generated by selecting the "plots" option in the Explore module, then checking the "normal probability plots with tests," and then selecting any option except "none" under "Spread vs Level with Levene test."

Table 7.1   Statistics for the memory data (from SPSS's Explore module)

Method			Statistic	Std. error
Control	Mean		16.84	.750
	95% Confidence interval for mean	Lower bound	15.29	
		Upper bound	18.39	
	5% Trimmed mean		17.06	
	Median		17.00	
	Variance		14.057	
	Std. deviation		3.749	
	Minimum		5	
	Maximum		24	
	Range		19	
	Interquartile range		4	
	Skewness		− 1.071	.464
	Kurtosis		3.396	.902
Drug	Mean		18.36	.663
	95% Confidence interval for mean	Lower bound	16.99	
		Upper bound	19.73	
	5% Trimmed mean		18.43	
	Median		19.00	
	Variance		10.990	
	Std. deviation		3.315	
	Minimum		9	
	Maximum		27	
	Range		18	
	Interquartile range		3	
	Skewness		− .494	.464
	Kurtosis		3.311	.902

trimmed mean), and the group means of these absolute deviations are tested against each other. The result provides no evidence of a difference in the spread of scores of the two populations.

Whether the two populations are normally distributed is less certain. The ratio of the skew statistic to its standard error is 2.3, which is weak evidence of skewness in the control group's data. There is stronger evidence of kurtosis in the data of both groups; ratios of the statistics to their standard errors are greater than 3.5. This suggests that tails may be longer than in a normal distribution, a condition that might contribute to lowering the power of the test. Panel *b* of Table 7.2 also indicates that the populations may not be normally distributed; one test provides results with *p*-values less than .10 and the other more clearly indicates a significant departure from a normal distribution in both populations.

We can learn more about the distributions by examining plots of the data. The *Q–Q* plot in Fig. 7.1 was obtained from the Explore module by requesting "Normality plots with tests" under the "Plots" menu bar. The plot confirms that the data are not normally distributed but also indicates that this is largely attributable to several extreme scores. To determine which of these scores are outliers in the technical sense (see Chapter 2), we turn to the box plots in Fig. 7.2. These confirm that there are several outliers in the data set. They are the numbered circles; the numbers are the case numbers in the SPSS data file. The presence of outliers increases variability and they appear to be

Table 7.2 Tests of homogeneity of variance (panel *a*) and normality (panel *b*) for the memory data (from SPSS)

(*a*) Tests of homogeneity of variance

	Levene statistic	$df1$	$df2$	Sig.
Based on mean	.228	1	48	.635
Based on median	.190	1	48	.665
Based on median and with adjusted df	.190	1	47.700	.665
Based on trimmed mean	.174	1	48	.679

(*b*) Tests of normality

Method	Kolmogorov–Smirnov			Shapiro–Wilk		
	Statistic	df	Sig.	Statistic	df	Sig.
Control	.162	25	.088	.905	25	.023
Drug	.173	25	.052	.892	25	.012

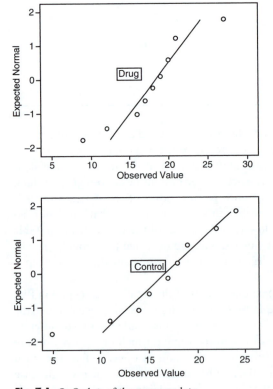

Fig. 7.1 *Q–Q* plots of the memory data.

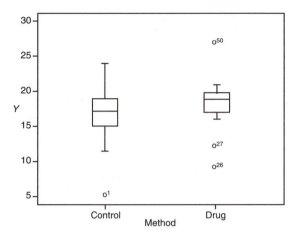

Fig. 7.2 Box plots of the memory data.

the source of departures from a normal distribution of scores. We should not just delete the outliers and then do the usual statistical tests because the variances based on trimmed data are biased estimates of the true population variances. However, after analyzing the entire data set, we will perform a trimmed-t test, using corrected variance estimates.

In sum, our exploration of the data has shown that the sample means are consistent with our hypothesis that the drug improves memory, has provided support for the assumption of the homogeneity of variance underlying subsequent analyses, and has shown that outliers are present that may reduce the power of the standard t test. With this information in hand, we proceed beyond the descriptive statistics to inferences about the population. We will first calculate confidence intervals for, and tests of, the difference between the group means and then, with the outliers in mind, recalculate employing the trimmed mean and winsorized variance.

7.5 CONFIDENCE INTERVALS AND HYPOTHESIS TESTS

Table 7.3 contains the results of an independent-groups t test on the means in Table 7.1. These analyses were generated using SPSS's Compare Means/Independent-Samples T-test module. Several points are apparent from the table:

1. Both Levene's test of homogeneity of variance and the similarity of results for the t ("Equal variances assumed") and t' ("Equal variances not assumed") tests support our earlier conclusion of the homogeneity of variance.
2. The confidence interval for the difference between the means is wide; we have 95% confidence that the memory pill (i.e., the drug) has anywhere from a .49 disadvantage to a 3.53 advantage.
3. Presumably, we are interested only if the drug has an advantage. Therefore, the alternative to the null hypothesis is one-tailed and the reported significance value of .135 ["sig. (2-tailed)"] should be halved; doing so, the one-tailed test yields $p = .068$. Thus, by conventional criteria, we cannot reject the null hypothesis of no difference between the two treatment population means.

Table 7.3   Output for the *t* test comparing the memory data group means (from SPSS)

	Levene's test for equality of variances		*t* Test for equality of means					95% Confidence interval of the difference	
	F	Sig.	*t*	df	Sig. (two-tailed)	Mean difference	Std. error of the difference	Lower	Upper
Equal variances assumed	.228	.635	1.519	48	.135	1.520	1.001	− .493	3.533
Equal variances not assumed			1.519	47.291	.136	1.520	1.001	− .493	3.533

7.6 THE STANDARDIZED EFFECT SIZE (COHEN'S *d*)

The differences between the group means is one measure of the effect of the drug. The standardized effect size provides an alternative measure that takes the variability into account. From Equation 6.19, $\hat{d} = (\overline{Y}_{Drug} - \overline{Y}_{Control})/s_{pooled}$. When the *n*s are equal, the pooled variance is just the average of the two variances. From the values in Table 17.1, $s^2_{pooled} = (1/2)(3.115^2 + 3.749^2)$, or 12.522. The square root of the pooled variance is 3.539; therefore, $\hat{d} = (18.36 - 16.84)/3.539 = .43$. By Cohen's (1988) guidelines, this is close to a medium-size effect for the comparison of two independent means. However, using Wuensch's syntax file (see Section 6.7.2), we found the 95% confidence interval bounds on the effect size to be − .13 and .99, indicating that the population effect was somewhere between a small advantage of the placebo and a very large advantage of the memory pill. Once again, we lack strong evidence that the pill aids memory.

7.7 REANALYSIS: THE TRIMMED *t* TEST

The results of analyses conducted to this point are ambiguous: on the one hand, they are suggestive of a positive effect of the new pill; on the other hand, the effect of the pill is not significant. We have found that the data are quite variable; in particular, there are several outliers in the data.

There are a couple of options for the researcher at this point. One is to conduct a Mann–Whitney *U* test on the data. This procedure copes better with outliers than the *t* test because it analyzes the rank-ordered observations. Further, the data meet the conditions under which the test is most appropriate; namely, the scores in the two conditions of the experiment are distributed similarly, with similar variances, kurtosis values, and skewness.

The other option for dealing with the outliers in the memory data set is the trimmed *t* test (Tukey & McLaughlin, 1963) cited in Chapter 6. When the tails of the distribution are longer than would be expected in a normal distribution, this test often will prove more powerful than the usual *t* test. Further, the trimmed *t* test has the advantages of permitting confidence interval calculations, effect size calculations, and power computations. For these reasons, we choose the trimmed *t* test as the better option for further analyses of the memory data set.

TechNote 7_1 on the book's website provides a detailed description of the test together with the necessary formulas. The numerator of the test statistic is the difference between the means of the two groups of scores after the k highest and lowest in each group have been removed; Wilcox (1997) has recommended that k be 20% of the scores.[2]

The trimmed scores are labeled T in the *IA1_memory* file. The denominator of t_{tk}, the standard error of the difference between the means, is based on the column labeled W; these *winsorized scores* are obtained by setting the k highest scores in each group to the value of the next highest, and the k lowest scores to the value of the next lowest. Because there are 25 scores in each condition, if we trim 20% from each tail, k is 5.

Upon carrying out the analysis, described in *TechNote 7_1*, we have

$$t_{tk} = (\bar{T}_1 - \bar{T}_2)/SE_{wk} = 1.60/.436 = 3.67$$

The statistic is distributed on $2(n - 1 - 2k)$, or 28 df, instead of the 48 associated with the usual t statistic. Nevertheless, the result is very significant. We can also recalculate the confidence interval; the critical value of t at the .05 (two-tailed) level is 2.048 and the 95% confidence limits are now

$$CI = 1.6 \pm (.436)(2.048) = .71 \text{ and } 2.49$$

This interval is much narrower than that found for the original data set, where the bounds were .49 to 3.53.[3]

Frequently, there will be reason to suspect that both the normality and homogeneity of variance assumptions are violated. Yuen (1974) proposed that the means in the numerator of Welch's t (described in Section 6.6.2), be replaced by trimmed means, and that the variances in that statistic, as well as in the formula for the degrees of freedom, be replaced by winsorized variances. This combination of Welch's t and the trimmed t guards against distortion of Type 1 error rates due to heterogeneity of variance and provides increased power when the distribution of data is long-tailed.

7.8 DISCUSSION OF THE RESULTS

After our original analysis of the data, we estimated that the memory drug has a medium size advantage over a placebo in the population of older adults. However, the difference was not significant, and confidence intervals on both the raw and standardized effects were wide. At that point, we could have decided (1) that further development and testing of our memory pill is not worthwhile or (2) that there is sufficient indication of an effect to merit further testing and development. The second choice rests on two assumptions: (1) that an effect of the size estimated is worth the cost involved in further testing and possible marketing; and (2) that the failure to reject the null hypothesis reflects a lack of statistical power.

Further support for the assumption that the pill does provide a memory advantage was found by reanalyzing the data, using the trimmed t test to reduce the variance caused by the long tails and,

---

[2] Rosenberger and Gasko (1983, p. 311) have provided a definition of the trimmed mean that is general enough to apply even when k is not an integer. However, we suggest the simpler approach of rounding k to the nearest integer when necessary.

[3] If you use a statistical package to analyze the W scores, it will report a different standard error than the one here. The reason is that it is dividing the sums of squared deviations by degrees of freedom based on the original data set, 48 in this example, rather than on the degrees of freedom adjusted for the fact that the data are winsorized.

particularly, the outlying scores. Although the reanalysis enabled us to reject the null hypothesis, we would feel more confident if we could replicate the result. We should design a large-scale study if we wish to further investigate the value of the pill. This would mean deciding on a larger sample size, and possibly additional measures of memory. Assuming that we believe that even a medium size effect warrants manufacture of the pill, we decide we want power $\geq .90$ to reject the null hypothesis of no advantage if Cohen's $d \geq .5$. Entering G*Power 3 with $\alpha = .05$, effect size $d = .5$, power = .9, and the *a priori* and *one-tail* options selected, we find that a total sample size of 140 (70 in each group) is required for further experimentation with these independent and dependent variables. Section 6.8 discussed the role of effect size and power in deciding on sample size, and Fig. 6.1 provided an example of the application of G*Power.

7.9 SUMMARY

All too often, researchers are concerned only with whether they have a significant effect. The current example illustrates the importance of considering both descriptive and inferential statistics. The exploratory stage of our analysis provided several pieces of important information:

- The memory pill had an advantage in the sample. Using the sample means and variances, we estimated that the population effect was medium in magnitude by Cohen's (1988) guidelines.
- Comparison of group variances, and significance tests comparing those variances, indicated that the assumption of homogeneity of variance underlying subsequent inferential analyses was not violated.
- A careful examination of the exploratory output indicated that the data departed significantly from the assumption of a normal distribution underlying the test and confidence interval based on the t distribution. Box plots of the data revealed the presence of outliers that could contribute to an increase in error variance and a resulting loss of power.

A t test on the full data set failed to reject the null hypothesis of no difference, and the confidence interval for the difference between the population means was wide. However, the results of the exploratory stage suggested that tests and confidence intervals based on trimmed data might provide stronger support for the memory pill. A reanalysis using the trimmed t statistic was performed; this resulted in a highly significant effect and a narrow confidence interval.

These are just some examples of the potential benefits of examining the data before carrying out statistical tests. We urge exploration of any data set, whether intended as a pilot study or as a more extensive study, and whether experimental or observational. As we stated both in Chapter 3 and in the overview to this chapter, such exploration may reveal patterns in the data that support our hypotheses, or suggest others we have not considered; they may also reveal departures from assumptions underlying our planned inferential analyses; and they may reveal outliers, scores that depart markedly from the distribution of our data. Although outliers should never be routinely discarded without examining their possible causes, their presence may suggest the need for other analyses.

Our analysis also went further in other respects than is often the case. We calculated confidence intervals on both the raw and standardized effect sizes. These emphasized how variable our data were and how wide the possible range of effects might be. The standardized effect size also helped us to decide on the effect size to input into an *a priori* power analysis to determine the sample size for a larger, more decisive, study of the effects of the drug we were studying.

In summary, after the data are collected, researchers should make use of one of several available statistical packages to explore the data, examining carefully both statistics and various data plots relevant to the assumptions of subsequent analyses. Confidence intervals and test statistics then should be calculated. Following careful exploratory and inferential analyses, the researcher is prepared to interpret the results and make decisions based upon them, including plans for replications or follow-up studies.

EXERCISES

7.1 **(a)** Scores of $-1, 0$, and 1 are assigned to underachievers, high achievers, and achievers, respectively, on the basis of a test of motivation. If the proportions of the population in each category are 1/4, 1/2, and 1/4, what are the population mean and variance?

(b) Assume that a sample of two students is drawn from the population. What are the possible values of the mean of the two scores? What is the probability of each value? Construct a table of the possible means and their probabilities. Note that this is the sampling distribution of the mean for samples of size 2.

(c) What are the mean and variance of the sampling distribution constructed in part (b)?

7.2 Assume that the selection criteria for personnel for a mission to Mars are based on tests of motivation (M), physical fitness (P), and intelligence (I). The following population parameters have been established:

	M	P	I
μ	62	66	60
σ^2	28	20	13

M, P, and I are independently and normally distributed. The selection criterion (C) is a weighted average of each individual's score: $C = .25M + .25P + .5I$.

(a) What are μ_C, the average criterion score in the population, and σ_C, the standard deviation of the population of criterion scores?

(b) Those selected for training for the mission must be in the top 5% of the population with respect to C. What criterion score will be our cutoff?

(c) The five-person crew of a previous mission had a mean criterion score of 64.5. Find the 90% confidence interval. Do the limits indicate that this crew's mean score was significantly below the current criterion score computed in part (b)?

7.3 In a study phase, each of 100 subjects is shown a series of six objects for five seconds each. In the following test phase, each subject is tested on six trials. On each trial, four objects are presented, one of which was present in the test phase. The subject's task is to choose the previously studied object on each test trial.

(a) If a subject is guessing, what is the probability of a correct response on a single test trial?

(b) Assuming guessing, state the probabilities of the possible outcomes (i.e., 0 correct, 1 correct, 6 correct) for a single subject.

(c) Assuming guessing, what is the number of subjects exhibiting each possible outcome?

(d) Assuming guessing, what is the expected mean number correct for each subject?

(e) What is the probability that by chance a subject will exceed the expected number correct?

7.4 In the experiment described in Exercise 7.3, the actual distribution of outcomes was

Number correct	0	1	2	3	4	5	6
Number of subjects	12	30	32	19	6	1	0

(a) Assign a plus to all subjects who had more than the expected value in your answer to Exercise 7.3 (d) and a minus to all others. Then, using Equation 5.13, test whether subjects have more correct responses than would be expected by chance.

   In part (a), we used the normal distribution to carry out a sign test of the null hypothesis of guessing. However, since we know the scores of the 100 subjects, we could calculate the observed mean and variance, and perform a t test of the null hypothesis.

(b) What is the observed mean of the 100 scores?

(c) What is the variance of the 100 scores?

(d) Calculate the t statistic and test the null hypothesis of chance performance.

7.5 Cobb and Hops (1973) compared reading scores for 12 experimental subjects who were trained by reinforcement and shaping techniques with those of 6 control subjects. Pretest and post-test scores are in the file, *EX7_5*. Group 1 is the experimental group.

(a) Calculate the 95% confidence intervals for the change scores for each group. State whether the change for each group is significant.

(b) Test the difference between groups in the average change score, assuming $\alpha = .05$ and the test is one-tailed.

7.6 The test in Exercise 7.5, part (b), is likely to have had low power because the group sizes were small. Suppose we replicate the study.

(a) Estimate Cohen's d for the difference between groups in mean change scores for the *EX7_5* data. Use this result to determine the group size needed to have power = .9, assuming $n_1 = n_2$ in a replication. Assume a one-tailed test.

(b) Assuming the group size you obtained in part (a), what power would you have for a one-tailed test that the control group improved from pre- to post-test? Estimate the effect size based on the data at the website.

7.7 In this chapter, we analyzed the memory data from an independent-groups design in which some subjects received a drug designed to improve memory and others received a placebo. We want to rerun the experiment, this time testing a group of subjects before and after taking the drug. We have estimated Cohen's d to be .43 for the data from the previous experiment and wish to use those data to decide on the sample size for the new experiment.

(a) Assuming the population variances are the same in both the experimental and control groups, we estimate that variance to be 12.5 from the data analyzed earlier. A reasonable estimate of the population correlation (ρ) is .6 for subjects tested in both conditions. Given that the population variance of difference scores is $\sigma_1^2 + \sigma_2^2 - 2\sigma_1\sigma_2\rho_{12}$, and assuming that $\sigma_1^2 = \sigma_2^2 = 125$, and $\sigma = .6$, estimate the standard deviation of the difference scores.

(b) From the independent-groups experiment, we estimate the difference between the two population means to be 1.52. Use this and your answer to part (a) to estimate Cohen's d_z.

(c) How many subjects should we run in this test–retest design in order to have .8 power to detect a memory improvement corresponding to the value of d_z calculated in part (b)?

7.8 A new drug was administered to several patients to reduce anxiety. One question is whether this drug has a different effect on cognitive processes than a previously prescribed drug. A clinical researcher compared response times (*RT*s) on a decision-making task for 30 subjects who had been taking the new drug (Group 1) with *RT*s for 20 subjects (Group 2) who had been taking a drug that had long been prescribed for anxiety. The data are in the *EX7_8* file at the website.

(a) Explore the data and describe any aspects that might affect the error rates of the *t* test comparing the group means.

(b) Select a transformation of the data and explore the transformed data. Did the transformation address your concerns?

(c) Test the hypothesis that the drug slows response times in cognitive tasks.

7.9 Another approach to the data of Exercise 7.8 is a trimmed *t* test.

(a) Perform this test using the *RT* data; see *TechNote 7_1* for a description and an example of the test.

(b) Compare the 95% confidence interval with that for the untrimmed data.

Part 2
Between-Subjects Designs

Chapter 8

Between-Subjects Designs: One Factor

8.1 OVERVIEW

In Chapter 8, we consider a basic research design in which there is a single independent variable with several levels that make up the conditions of the study, no subject is tested in more than one condition, and each subject contributes one score to the data set. Like any experimental design, the one-factor, between-subjects design has advantages and disadvantages.

The primary advantage of the design is that it is simple in several respects. First, data collection is simple. Only one observation is taken from each subject. No additional measures are required for the purpose of matching subjects in different conditions. Nor is there a need to be concerned about the order of presentation of treatments, or the interval between tests, as in designs in which subjects are tested in several conditions. Second, there are fewer assumptions underlying the data analysis than in most other research designs. More complex designs involve additional assumptions that, if violated, increase the likelihood of drawing incorrect conclusions from our data. Finally, there are fewer calculations than in other designs, and decisions about how to draw inferences based on those calculations are less complicated.

One disadvantage of the between-subjects design is that it requires more subjects than designs in which subjects are tested in several conditions. A second disadvantage is that there is less control of nuisance variables, and therefore the error variance is larger than in other designs. In particular, because subjects in different conditions differ in characteristics such as ability and motivation, it is more difficult to assess the effects of conditions than in designs in which such individual differences are better controlled.

In between-subjects designs, subjects may either be sampled from existing populations, or be assigned randomly to one of several experimental conditions, or treatment levels. An example of the former is the *Seasons* study[1] in which individuals were sampled from populations differing with respect to various factors, including gender, educational level, and occupation. Strictly speaking,

---

[1] See the *Seasons* data set on the website for this book.

that study would be classified as an observational study. True experiments involve random assignment of subjects to levels of an independent variable; the independent variable is said to be manipulated and the design is often referred to as *completely randomized*. Whether the levels of the independent variable are observed or manipulated, the data analysis has much the same form and the underlying assumptions are the same.

We view each group of scores as a random sample from a *treatment population*. The first question of interest is whether the means of these treatment populations vary. To address this question, we introduce the *analysis of variance*, or *ANOVA*, in which the total variability in the data set is partitioned into two components, one reflecting the variance of the treatment population means, and a second that reflects only the effects of nuisance variables.

In addition to testing whether the treatment population means are equal, we want some way of evaluating the practical or theoretical importance of the independent variable. Therefore, following the development of the ANOVA, we focus on several measures of importance. We also consider the role of statistical power in the research design and relate power to measures of importance.

Throughout this chapter, we will have made certain assumptions to justify the calculations presented. When those assumptions are violated, Type 1 and Type 2 error rates may increase. Therefore, the chapter also discusses such consequences, and alternative procedures that may improve the situation.

In summary, the main concerns of this chapter are:

- *Testing the null hypothesis that the treatment population means are equal.* This involves the ANOVA for the one-factor between-subjects design.
- *Measures of the importance of the independent variable.* These are derived from the ANOVA table.
- *The power of the test of the null hypothesis* and the relationship between power and the decision about sample size.
- *The assumptions underlying the ANOVA, measures of importance, and power of the significance test*, including the consequences of violations of assumptions and alternative methods that can be used in the face of violations.

8.2 AN EXAMPLE OF THE DESIGN

An example of an experiment, together with a data set, will make subsequent developments more concrete. Table 8.1 presents data from a hypothetical memory study in which 40 subjects were randomly divided into four groups of 10 each. Each subject studied a list of 20 words and was tested for recall a day later. Ten subjects were taught and instructed to use a memory strategy called the method of loci, in which each object on the list was associated with a location on campus; 10 subjects were told to form an image of each object on the list; 10 others were told to form a rhyme with each word; and 10 others—the control group—were just told to study the words.[2]

Fig. 8.1 presents the group means and 95% confidence intervals for those means. The three groups that were instructed to use a memory strategy had higher average recall scores than the control group, although the widths of the confidence intervals indicate that the data were quite variable. There is also some indication that the method of loci may be superior to the other two

---

[2] The data are also in a file labeled *Table 8_1 Memory Data*; a link is on the *Tables* page on the website for this book.

Table 8.1 Recall scores from a hypothetical memory study

	Control	Loci	Image	Rhyme	
	11	10	13	16	
	4	18	16	9	
	8	6	3	7	
	3	20	6	10	
	11	15	13	9	
	8	9	10	14	
	2	8	13	16	
	5	11	9	3	
	8	12	5	9	
	5	12	19	12	
$\overline{Y}_j =$	6.5	12.1	10.7	10.5	$\overline{Y}_j = 9.95$
$s_j^2 =$	10.056	19.433	25.567	16.722	

experimental methods. However, differences among the four means may just reflect differences in the effects of nuisance variables. By chance, the average ability or motivational level in one group of students may be higher than in the others; or other differences between individuals or between the conditions in which they were tested (e.g., the time of day, the temperature in the room) may account for the apparent differences among experimental conditions. A major goal of the data analysis is to separate out the effects of the instructional method from the effects of nuisance variables.

At this point, it would be wise to explore the data further, calculating additional statistics and plotting other graphs as described in Chapter 2. However, we will leave that as an exercise for the reader and proceed to address the question of whether the differences in Fig. 8.1 reflect true differences in the effects of the four study methods, or merely error variance. We begin by developing a framework for the analysis of variance.

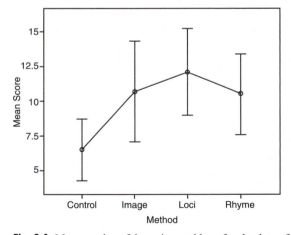

Fig. 8.1 Means and confidence interval bars for the data of Table 8.1.

8.3 THE STRUCTURAL MODEL

We view the various groups of scores in a study as random samples from populations selected for investigation. Then the question of whether the four study methods of Table 8.1 differ in their effectiveness can be rephrased as: Do the means of the four treatment populations differ? To answer this question, we need a way of linking the observed data to the hypothetical populations, of relating sample statistics to population parameters. We begin by constructing a *structural model*, a model that relates the scores to population parameters.

We start by assuming that the subjects in the experiment are identical in ability, motivation, and any other characteristics that would affect their scores. We further assume that they are identically treated—e.g., tested at the same moment in time, and under the exact same conditions. Under these very unrealistic assumptions, everyone in an instructional population, and therefore everyone in an instructional group, would have the same score; that score would be the treatment population mean. We can represent this state of affairs with the following notation:

$$Y_{11} = Y_{21} = Y_{31} = \ldots = Y_{i1} = \ldots = Y_{n1} = \mu_1$$
$$Y_{12} = Y_{22} = Y_{32} = \ldots = Y_{i2} = \ldots = Y_{n2} = \mu_2$$
$$Y_{13} = Y_{23} = Y_{33} = \ldots = Y_{i3} = \ldots = Y_{n3} = \mu_3$$

where there are n subjects in a group, Y_{ij} represents the ith score in the jth group, and μ_j is the mean of the *jth* population of scores. For example, Y_{52} would refer to the score of the fifth subject in the second group.

Of course, this is not realistic; the scores of individuals in an instructional group will vary, and therefore will differ from the instructional population mean, because of nuisance variables such as ability level, prior relevant experience, interest in the topic, or conditions at the time of testing. We can represent this complication by saying that the score of the ith subject in the jth group will differ from the treatment population mean, μ_j, by some amount—an *error component*, ε_{ij}. This means that an individual's score equals the mean of the treatment population plus an error component. That is,

$$Y_{ij} = \mu_j + (Y_{ij} - \mu_j)$$
$$= \mu_j + \varepsilon_{ij} \tag{8.1}$$

Note that ε_{ij} can be positive or negative; that is, nuisance variables can raise the score above the population mean, or lower it below that mean.

We can rewrite Equation 8.1 in a way that more directly expresses the relation between a score and the effect of the condition under which that score was obtained. First, we define one more population parameter, μ, the mean of all the treatment populations; i.e., $\mu = \Sigma\mu_j/a$, where a is the number of levels of the independent variable. Equation 8.1 is unchanged if we add and subtract μ from the right side:

$$Y_{ij} = \mu + (\mu_j - \mu) + \varepsilon_{ij} \tag{8.2}$$

Let $\alpha_j = (\mu_j - \mu)$; because α_j (Greek alpha) is the difference between the mean of the jth treatment population and the grand mean of all the populations, it represents the effect of the jth treatment on the scores in the jth population. Therefore, we can rewrite Equation 8.2:

$$Y_{ij} = \mu + \alpha_j + \varepsilon_{ij} \tag{8.3}$$

Equation 8.3 is a *structural equation*; it defines the structure of a score obtained in a one-factor between-subjects experiment. In words, the structure of a score is *score = grand mean + treatment effect + error component*

The parameters in Equation 8.3 are rather abstract and not very useful unless we tie them to statistics that we can calculate from our data. To do this, we need to estimate the population means, the treatment effects, and the errors. We have the following parameter estimates:[3]

Parameter	μ	μ_j	α_j	ε_{ij}
Estimate	$\overline{Y}_{..}$	$\overline{Y}_{.j}$	$\overline{Y}_{.j} - \overline{Y}_{..}$	$Y_{ij} - \overline{Y}_{.j}$

where Y_{ij} is the score of the ith person in the jth group, $\overline{Y}_{.j}$ is the mean of all the scores in the jth group, and $\overline{Y}_{..}$ is the mean of all the scores in the data set. For example, in Table 8.1, Y_{23} is 16, the score of the second person in the image condition; $\overline{Y}_{.4}$ is 10.5, the mean of the rhyme condition; and $\overline{Y}_{..}$ is 9.95, the grand mean.

With the structural equation as a basis, we now can begin to calculate the terms we need in order to draw inferences from our data.

8.4 THE ANALYSIS OF VARIANCE (ANOVA)

The ANOVA involves partitioning the variability of all the scores into two components, or *sums of squares*. These in turn are divided by their degrees of freedom to form *mean squares*, estimates of population variances. The ratio of mean squares, the *F ratio*, provides a test of the hypothesis that all the treatments have the same effect. In what follows, we consider each of these aspects of the ANOVA.

8.4.1 Sums of Squares

As Equation 8.3 implies, scores can vary because of the effects of the independent variable and because of the effects of uncontrolled nuisance variables. If we can separate those two sources of variance in our data, we will have the basis for deciding how much, if any, of the variance is due to the independent variable.

The structural equation suggests an approach to partitioning variability. If we rewrite Equation 8.3 by subtracting μ from both sides, we can express the deviation of a score from the grand mean of the population as consisting of a treatment effect and error; that is,

$$Y_{ij} - \mu = \alpha_j + \varepsilon_{ij}$$

Replacing the parameters in the preceding equation by the estimates we presented earlier, we have

$$Y_{ij} - \overline{Y}_{..} = (\overline{Y}_{.j} - \overline{Y}_{..}) + (Y_{ij} - \overline{Y}_{.j}) \qquad (8.4)$$

The next step in partitioning the total variability is to calculate the terms in Equation 8.4, and then square and sum them. The results are the sums of squares. For the data set of Table 8.1, the left side of Equation 8.4 leads to the *total sum of squares*:

$$SS_{total} = \sum_{j=1}^{4} \sum_{i=1}^{10} (Y_{ij} - \overline{Y}_{..})^2 = (11 - 9.95)^2 + \ldots + (12 - 9.95)^2 = 819.9$$

---

[3] These are *least-squares estimators*; that is, we can show that if these statistics are calculated for many samples, their variance about the parameter being estimated is less than that for any other estimator.

The first term to the right of the equal sign in Equation 8.4 is also squared and summed for each individual, yielding the *method sum of squares*:

$$SS_{method} = 10 \sum_{j=1}^{4} (\bar{Y}_{.j} - \bar{Y}_{..})^2 = 10[(6.5 - 9.995)^2 + \ldots + (10.5 - 9.95)^2] = 173.9$$

and finally we obtain the *residual sum of squares* which can be calculated either directly as

$$SS_{residual} = \sum_{j=1}^{4} \sum_{i=1}^{10} (Y_{ij} - \bar{Y}_{.j})^2 = (11 - 6.5)^2 + \ldots + (12 - 10.5)^2 = 646.0$$

or as the difference between the total and method sum of squares:

$$SS_{residual} = SS_{total} - SS_{method} = 819.9 - 173.9 = 646.0$$

The preceding results are based on the example of Table 8.1. In general, we designate the independent variable by the letter A, and we assume a levels of A with n scores at each level. Then,

$$\sum_{j=1}^{a} \sum_{i=1}^{n} (Y_{ij} - \bar{Y}_{..})^2 = n \sum_{j=1}^{a} (\bar{Y}_{.j} - \bar{Y}_{..})^2 + \sum_{j=1}^{a} \sum_{i=1}^{n} (Y_{ij} - \bar{Y}_{.j})^2 \qquad (8.5)$$

$$SS_{total} \qquad\qquad = SS_A \qquad\qquad\quad + SS_{S/A}$$

where S/A represents "subjects within levels of A" to remind us that the residual term reflects the variability of the scores within each level of A. A general proof that $SS_{total} = SS_A + SS_{S/A}$ is presented in Appendix 8.1.

8.4.2 Degrees of Freedom (*df*)

The three terms in Equation 8.5 are numerators of variances and, as such, must be divided by their corresponding degrees of freedom (*df*) in order to be converted into variances, or mean squares. The *df* associated with a particular *SS* term is the number of independent observations contributing to that estimate of variability. For our three *SS* terms, we have the following *df*:

1. *The total degrees of freedom, df_{total}.* The *total sum of squares*, SS_{total}, is the numerator of the variance of all an scores. Therefore, $df_{total} = an - 1$.
2. *The between-groups degrees of freedom, df_A,* scores. The *between-groups sum of squares*, SS_A, is n times the numerator of the variance of the a group means about the grand mean and is therefore distributed on $a - 1$ *df*.
3. *The within-groups degrees of freedom, $df_{S/A}$.* The *within-groups sum of squares*, $SS_{S/A}$, is the sum, or "pool" of the numerators of each of the group variances. Because each of the a group variances is distributed on $n - 1$ *df*, $SS_{S/A}$ is distributed on $a(n - 1)$ *df*. Note that

$$an - 1 = a(n - 1) + (a - 1)$$
$$df_{tot} = df_{S/A} + df_A \qquad (8.6)$$

Equation 8.6 demonstrates that the degrees of freedom are partitioned into two parts that correspond to the sums of squares. This partitioning of the degrees of freedom provides a partial check on the partitioning of the total variability. Although the partitioning in a one-factor design is simple, keeping track of the number of distinguishable sources of variance can be difficult in more complex designs. There are also designs in which it is a challenge to analyze the relations among the factors in the design. Therefore, when designs have many factors, it is wise to find the degrees of freedom associated with each source of variability and to check whether the *df* sum to the total number of scores minus one.

8.4.3 Mean Squares, Expected Mean Squares, and the *F* Ratio

The ratio of a sum of squares to degrees of freedom is called a *mean square*. In the one-factor design, the relevant mean squares are the *A* mean square, where

$$MS_A = SS_A/df_A$$

and the *S/A* mean square,

$$MS_{S/A} = SS_{S/A}/df_{S/A}$$

Under the assumptions summarized in Box 8.1, the ratio $MS_A/MS_{S/A}$ has a sampling distribution

---

Box 8.1 Parameter Definitions and Assumptions

1. *The parent population mean,* μ. This is the grand mean of the treatment populations selected for this study and is a constant component of all scores in the *a* populations. It is the average of the treatment population means:

$$\mu = \sum_{j=1}^{a} \mu_j/a$$

2. *The effect of treatment* A_j, α_j. This equals $\mu_j - \mu$ and is a constant component of all scores obtained under A_j but may vary over treatments (levels of *j*).
   2.1 Because the deviation of all scores about their mean is zero, $\Sigma_j\alpha_j = 0$.
   2.2 If the null hypothesis is true, all $\alpha_j = 0$.

   2.3 The population variance of the treatment effects is $\sigma_A^2 = \sum_{j=1}^{a} \alpha_j^2/a$.

3. *The error,* ε_{ij}. This is the deviation of the ith score in group *j* from μ_j and reflects uncontrolled, or chance, variability. It is the only source of variation within the jth group, and if the null hypothesis is true, the only source of variation within the data set. We assume that
   3.1 The ε_{ij} are independently distributed; i.e., the probability of sampling some value of ε_{ij} does not depend on other values of ε_{ij} in the sample.
   3.2 The ε_{ij} are normally distributed in each of the *a* treatment populations. Also, because $\varepsilon_{ij} = Y_{ij} - \mu_j$, the mean of each population of errors is zero; i.e., $E(\varepsilon_{ij}) = 0$.
   3.3 The distribution of the ε_{ij} has variance σ_e^2 (error variance) in each of the *a* treatment populations; i.e., $\sigma_1^2 = \ldots = \sigma_j^2 = \ldots = \sigma_a^2$. This is the assumption of *homogeneity of variance*. The error variance is the average squared error; $\sigma_e^2 = E(\varepsilon_{ij}^2)$.

---

called the *F* distribution *if the null hypothesis is true*. It provides a test of the null hypothesis that the treatment population means are all equal; that is, the *F* statistic tests the *null hypothesis*:

$$H_0: \mu_1 = \mu_2 = \ldots = \mu_j = \ldots = \mu_a = \mu$$

or, equivalently,

$$H_0: \alpha_1 = \alpha_2 = \ldots = \alpha_j = \ldots \alpha_a = 0$$

To understand the logic of the F test, we need to consider the relationship of the mean squares to the population variances. This requires us to determine the expected values of our two mean square calculations.

Suppose we draw a samples of n scores from their respective treatment populations, and calculate MS_A and $MS_{S/A}$. Now suppose that we draw another a samples of n scores, and again calculate MS_A and $MS_{S/A}$. We could repeat this sampling experiment many times and generate two sampling distributions, one for MS_A and another for $MS_{S/A}$. The means of these two sampling distributions are the expected values of the mean squares, or the *expected mean squares* (*EMS*). Given the structural model of Equation 8.3, and assuming that the ε_{ij} are independently distributed with variance, σ_e^2, the *EMS* of Table 8.2 can be derived (Kirk, 1995; Myers & Well, 1995). Consider each expected mean square in turn to understand the information provided by MS_A and $MS_{S/A}$.

Table 8.2   Sources of variance (*SV*) and expected mean squares (*EMS*) for the one-factor between-subjects design

SV	EMS
A	$\sigma_e^2 + n\theta_A^2$
S/A	σ_e^2

Note: $\theta_A^2 = \sum_j (\mu_j - \mu)^2/(a-1)$. We use the θ^2 (theta squared) notation rather than σ^2 to remind us that the treatment component of the *EMS* involves division by degrees of freedom; the variance of the treatment population means would be

$\sigma_A^2 = \sum_j (\mu_j - \mu)^2/a$.

$E(MS_A)$ states that the *between-groups mean square, MS_A,* estimates *error variance, σ_e^2,* plus n times the variance in the treatment population means, θ_A^2 (if there is any effect of the treatment). This result should make intuitive sense when you examine the formula for MS_A:

$$MS_A = \frac{n\sum_j^a (\bar{Y}_j - \bar{Y}_{..})^2}{a-1} \tag{8.7}$$

Equation 8.7 states that MS_A is the variance of the condition means times the sample size, n. Even if there were no differences among the treatment population means, the sample means would differ just by chance because there are different individuals with different characteristics in each group. The error variance, σ_e^2, reflects this. If there is also an effect of the treatment, the μ_j will differ and their variability will also be reflected in the value of MS_A.

$E(MS_{S/A})$ states that the *within-groups mean square, $MS_{S/A}$,* is an estimate of error variance. Again, this result may be understood intuitively by examining how $MS_{S/A}$ is calculated:

$$MS_{S/A} = \frac{SS_{S/A}}{a(n-1)}$$

$$= \frac{\sum_j \sum_i (Y_{ij} - \bar{Y}_j)^2}{a(n-1)} \tag{8.8}$$

Equation 8.8 may be rewritten as

$$MS_{S/A} = \left(\frac{1}{a}\right)\sum_j \left[\frac{\sum_i (Y_{ij} - \bar{Y}_j)^2}{n-1}\right]$$

The expression in the square brackets on the right side is the variance of the jth group of scores, and the entire right side is an average of the a group variances. Because subjects within a condition are treated identically, they should differ only due to error (see Eq. 8.1). If we assume that error variance is equal in each treatment population, $MS_{S/A}$ is an average of a estimates of the population variance, σ_e^2.

Given our understanding of what MS_A and $MS_{S/A}$ estimate, we are in a position to understand the logic of the F test, where $F = MS_A/MS_{S/A}$. First, *assume that the null hypothesis is true* and, also, that there is *homogeneity of variance*; that is

$$\mu_1 = \mu_2 = \ldots = \mu_j = \ldots = \mu_a \text{ and } \sigma_1 = \sigma_2 = \ldots = \sigma_j = \ldots = \sigma_a$$

Under these assumptions, MS_A is an estimate of the error variance common to the a treatment populations. In terms of $E(MS_A)$, $\theta_A^2 = 0$ so $E(MS_A)$ is an estimate of error variance, σ_e^2. Thus, if the null hypothesis is true, MS_A and $MS_{S/A}$ both estimate the same population error variance and their ratio should be about 1. Of course, it would be surprising if two independent estimates of the same population variance were identical; that is, the ratio of MS_A to $MS_{S/A}$ has a distribution of values. More precisely, *if H_0 is true*, the ratio, $MS_A/MS_{S/A}$, is distributed as F on $a - 1$ and $a(n-1)$ *df*. Critical values of F are tabled in Appendix Table C.5 and can also be obtained from various software packages and websites.

But what if the null hypothesis is, in fact, false? For example, suppose that the method of study does affect recall in the example of Table 8.1. Then the means of the groups of scores in Table 8.1 will differ not only because the scores in the different groups differ by chance, but also because the groups were studied by different methods. In other words, if H_0 is false, $\theta_A^2 > 0$ so $E(MS_A) = \sigma_e^2 + n\theta_A^2$. The situation with respect to the within-group variance does not change: $MS_{S/A}$ should not be affected by the independent variable because all subjects in a group receive the same treatment. Therefore, when H_0 is false, the ratio $MS_A/MS_{S/A}$ should be greater than 1.

In summary, under the assumptions of the null hypothesis, homogeneity of variance, and independently distributed scores, MS_A and $MS_{S/A}$ are two independent estimates of the population error variance, σ_e^2. If we also assume that the population of scores is normally distributed, the ratio of two independent estimates of the same population variance has an F distribution. Therefore, under the assumptions summarized in Box 8.1, the ratio $MS_A/MS_{S/A}$ is distributed as F. Because the numerator is based on an estimate of the variance of a population means, it has $a - 1$ *df*. The denominator has $a(n-1)$ *df* because the variance estimate for each group is based on $n - 1$ *df* and $MS_{S/A}$ is an average of a variance estimates.

Appendix Table C.5 presents critical values of the F distribution. As an example of its use, suppose we have three groups of 11 subjects each. Then the numerator $df = a - 1 = 2$, and the denominator $df = a(n-1) = 30$. Turning to the column headed by 2 and the block labeled 30, if $\alpha = .05$, we would reject the null hypothesis of no difference among the three treatments if the F we calculate is greater than 3.32. Interpolation may be needed for degrees of freedom not listed in the table. However, the critical F value is not necessary if the analysis is performed by any of several software packages. These packages usually calculate the F based on the data and provide the exact p-value for that F and the df for the design used.

8.4.4 The ANOVA Table

Panel a of Table 8.3 summarizes the developments so far, presenting the formulas for sums of squares, degrees of freedom, mean squares, and the F ratio for the one-factor between-subjects design. For any data set, most statistical software packages present this table with numerical results in some form. Panel b presents the output for the data of Table 8.1. The results are significant at the .05 level, indicating that there are differences among the means of the populations defined by the four different study methods. Fig. 8.1 suggests that this is due to the poorer performance of the control condition. However, there are a number of interesting questions that the omnibus F test leaves unanswered. Are all three experimental methods significantly superior to the control method? Do the means of the three experimental methods differ from each other? We will consider such comparisons of means within subsets of conditions in Chapter 10.

We might also ask whether the differences among the four population means are large enough to be of practical significance. As we noted when discussing effect size measures in Chapter 6, statistical significance is not the same as practical or theoretical significance.

Table 8.3   The analysis of variance for the one-factor between-subjects design

(a) General form of the ANOVA

Source	df	SS	MS	F
Total	$an-1$	$\sum_{j=1}^{a}\sum_{i=1}^{n}(Y_{ij}-\bar{Y}_{..})^2$		
A	$a-1$	$n\sum_{j=1}^{a}(\bar{Y}_{.j}-\bar{Y}_{..})^2$	SS_A/df_A	$MS_A/MS_{S/A}$
S/A	$a(n-1)$	$\sum_{j=1}^{a}\sum_{i=1}^{n}(Y_{ij}-\bar{Y}_{.j})^2$	$SS_{S/A}/df_{S/A}$	

(b) ANOVA of the data of Table 8.1

Source	Sum of squares	df	Mean square	F	p-value
Method	173.90	3	57.967	3.230	.034
Error	646.00	36	17.944		
Total	819.90	39			

8.5 MEASURES OF IMPORTANCE

The p-value in Table 8.3 informs us that the effects of the method of memorization are statistically significant, assuming that we had set alpha at .05. In addition, however, we need some indication of the practical or theoretical importance of our result. Generally, we seek a measure that assesses the magnitude of the effect of our treatment, A, relative to error variance. We will find that the EMS analyses that guided the logic of the F test will also be very useful in thinking about appropriate ways in which to assess the importance of an effect. We will consider several possible measures in this section. Several sources also present discussions of these and other measures (e.g., Kirk, 1996; Maxwell, Camp, & Arvey, 1981; Olejnik & Algina, 2000, 2003).

8.5.1 Measuring Strength of Association in the Sample: η^2 (Eta-Squared)

Greek-letter designations are usually reserved for population parameters, but η^2 is actually a sample statistic that is often used as a measure of association between the dependent and independent variables (Cohen, Cohen, West, & Aiken, 2003). It describes the proportion of variability in the sample as

$$\eta^2 = \frac{SS_A}{SS_{total}} \tag{8.9}$$

Referring to Table 8.3, we have

$$\eta^2_{method} = 173.9/819.9 = .212$$

Using SPSS, η^2 can be obtained by selecting *Analyze*, then *General Linear Model*, then *Univariate*. SPSS reports the R^2, which for the one-factor design is also the same as η^2. It also reports an *adjusted* R^2 as .146.[4]

Eta-squared has the advantage of being easily calculated and easily understood as a proportion of sample variability. However, the value of η^2 is influenced not only by the relative magnitudes of the treatment effect and error variance, but also by n, df_A, and $df_{S/A}$. In addition, σ_e^2 contributes to the numerator of η^2. For these reasons, other statistics that measure importance are often preferred. We turn to such estimates now, bearing in mind that our results rest on the assumptions underlying the derivation of the EMS; i.e., independence of the ε_{ij} and homogeneity of variance.

8.5.2 Estimating Strength of Association in the Population: ω^2 (Omega-Squared)

Whereas η^2 describes the strength of association between the dependent and independent variables by forming a ratio of sample sums of squares, ω^2 is a measure of the strength of association in the population; unlike η^2, it is a ratio of population variances:

$$\omega^2 = \frac{\sigma_A^2}{\sigma_e^2 + \sigma_A^2} \tag{8.10}$$

The numerator of the ratio is the variance of the treatment population means (the μ_j) or, equivalently, the variance of the treatment effects (the α_j):

---

[4] The adjusted $R^2 = [SS_A - (a-1)MS_{S/A}]/SS_{total}$

$$\sigma_A^2 = \frac{\sum_{j}^{a} (\mu_j - \mu)^2}{a} \tag{8.11}$$

$$= \frac{\sum_{j}^{a} \alpha_j^2}{a}$$

The denominator of ω^2 is the total population variance; that is, the treatment population error variance, σ_e^2, plus the variance of the treatment population means, σ_A^2. Thus, ω^2 assesses the magnitude of the treatment effect relative to the total variance in the design. We cannot know the ratio described by Equation 8.10 but we can derive estimates of σ_A^2 and σ_e^2 and therefore of ω^2. We begin with the *EMS* equations of Table 8.2:

$$E(MS_A) = \sigma_e^2 + n\theta_A^2 \tag{8.12}$$

and

$$E(MS_{S/A}) = \sigma_e^2 \tag{8.13}$$

To obtain an estimate of σ_A^2 we first subtract Equation 8.13 from Equation 8.12, and divide by n; then we have

$$\frac{MS_A - MS_{S/A}}{n} = \hat{\theta}_A^2$$

where the "hat" above θ_A^2 means "is an estimate of." Because the numerator of ω^2 as defined by Equation 8.10 involves σ_A^2, not θ_A^2, and noting that $\sigma_A^2 = [(a-1)/a] \times \theta_A^2$, our estimate of σ_A^2 is

$$\hat{\sigma}_A^2 = \left(\frac{a-1}{a}\right) \left(\frac{MS_A - MS_{S/A}}{n}\right) \tag{8.14}$$

We now have estimates of the numerator and denominator of ω^2, therefore, substituting into Equation 8.10, we have an estimate of ω^2 for the one-factor, between-subjects design:

$$\hat{\omega}^2 = \frac{[(a-1)/a](1/n)(MS_A - MS_{S/A})}{[(a-1)/a](1/n)(MS_A - MS_{S/A}) + MS_{S/A}} \tag{8.15}$$

We may write Equation 8.15 in a different form, one which allows us to calculate $\hat{\omega}^2$ from knowledge of the F ratio, a, and n. The advantages are that the expression is somewhat simpler and, perhaps more importantly, because most research reports contain this information, we can estimate the strength of association for data collected by other investigators. We begin by defining $F_A = MS_A/MS_{S/A}$. Then, multiplying the numerator and denominator of Equation 8.15 by an, and dividing by $MS_{S/A}$, we have

$$\hat{\omega}^2 = \frac{(a-1)(F_A - 1)}{(a-1)(F_A - 1) + na} \tag{8.16}$$

Let's review what Equations 8.15 and 8.16 represent. If we replicate the experiment many times, the average value of the right-hand term will approximately equal ω^2, the proportion of the total variance in the a treatment populations that is attributable to the variance of their means. We say "approximately equal" because the expected value of a ratio is not the same as the ratio of expected values. The approximation is reasonably accurate and the expression is much simpler than that for the exact expression.

One other aspect of Equation 8.16 should be noted. Because the numerator and denominator of the F reflect two independent estimates of the population error variance, when the null hypothesis is true or the effects of A are very small, the F may be less than 1. Then, $\hat{\omega}^2$ would be less than 0. Because a variance cannot be negative, we conclude that $\omega^2 = 0$; that is, none of the total population variance is attributable to the independent variable.

We can apply Equation 8.16 to the memory data in Table 8.1. In that experiment, $a = 4$, $n = 10$, and (from Table 8.3) $F = 3.230$. Then, inserting these values into Equation 8.16,

$$\hat{\omega}^2 = \frac{(3)(2.23)}{(3)(2.23) + 40} = .143$$

This is very close to the value of .146 noted earlier for adjusted R^2. That the values of R^2_{adj} and ω^2 are so close is not unusual; Maxwell, Camp, and Arvey (1981) reported that the two rarely differ by more than .02. With respect to assessing the importance of either measure, Cohen (1988) suggested that values of .01, .06, and .14 may be viewed as small, medium, and large, respectively. According to those guidelines, the proportion of variability accounted for by the study method may be judged to be large. Again, however, we caution that the importance attached to any value must be assessed in the context of the research problem and the investigator's knowledge of the research literature.

8.5.3 Cohen's f

In Chapter 6, we presented Cohen's d, a measure of the standardized effect for designs in which two means are compared. Cohen's f (1988) is a similar measure for situations in which the variance of more than two means is of interest. The parameter f is defined as

$$f = \sigma_A / \sigma_e \tag{8.17}$$

We can estimate f by substituting the estimate in Equation 8.14 in the numerator and $MS_{S/A}$ in the denominator. Then we have

$$\hat{f} = \sqrt{\frac{(a-1)(MS_A - MS_{S/A})}{anMS_{S/A}}} \tag{8.18}$$

which can also be written as

$$\hat{f} = \sqrt{(a-1)(F_A - 1)/an} \tag{8.19}$$

For the data of Table 8.1, substituting the F value from Table 8.3 into Equation 8.19, we have

$$\hat{f} = \sqrt{(3)(2.23)/40} = .409$$

Cohen has suggested that values of f of .1, .25, and .4 be viewed as small, medium, and large, respectively. Therefore, as with ω^2, the guidelines for f suggest that the standardized variance of the four reading method estimates is large. That ω^2 and f lead to the same conclusion about the size of the variance of effects follows from the relationship between them; given an estimate of f, we can also calculate an estimate of ω^2, and vice versa. The relations are

$$f^2 = \frac{\omega^2}{1 - \omega^2} \quad \text{and} \quad \omega^2 = \frac{f^2}{1 + f^2}$$

A useful property of f is that it is closely related to the noncentrality parameter of the F distribution; specifically,

$$\lambda = Nf^2 \tag{8.20}$$

The parameter, λ (lambda), determines areas under the noncentral F distribution, and therefore the power of the F test. Smithson (2001) provides an SPSS syntax file for obtaining a confidence interval on λ, and by making use of its relation to f and ω^2, confidence intervals on those measures can be obtained. The relation between f, λ, and power will be developed further in Section 8.8.

8.5.4 Measures of Importance: Limitations

In an introductory chapter to an edited collection aptly titled, "What if there were no significance tests?", Harlow (1997, pp. 5–6) reported that 11 of the book's other 13 chapters "were very much in favor" of reporting measures such as R^2, ω^2, and f, and the remaining two contributors "at least mildly endorsed such use." Similar support for measures such as these can be found in the American Psychological Association's guidelines for statistical usage (Wilkinson & Task Force, 1999), which urge researchers to report effect size statistics. Nevertheless, there are potential pitfalls. Values of these statistics may depend on the experimental design, the choice and number of levels of the independent variable, the dependent variable, and the population sampled. Estimates of ω^2 and f imply homogeneous variances and independence of observations (cf. Grissom & Kim, 2001, who discuss the variance assumption, and suggest alternative approaches for the two-group case). Another concern is that squared coefficients tend to be small and it is sometimes easy to dismiss an effect as trivial because of a small value of ω^2.

These arguments suggest that we must be careful when interpreting these measures, or when generalizing the results of any one study, or of making comparisons across studies that differ with respect to the factors just cited. In addition, we should treat guidelines such as those set forth by Cohen (1988) as suggestions, not as definitive boundaries between important and unimportant effects. Even a very small advantage of one therapy over another may be important. In theoretical work, a small effect predicted by a theory may be important support for that theory. In summary, if care is taken in interpreting measures of strength, statistics such as $\hat{f}$ and $\hat{\omega}^2$ are useful additions to the test statistics usually computed.

8.6 WHEN GROUP SIZES ARE NOT EQUAL

In the developments so far, our formulas have been based on the assumption that there are the same number of scores in each group. In this section, we present an example with unequal ns, and present formulas for sums of squares, expected mean squares, and measures of importance for this case.

The ns in conditions in a study may vary for one of several reasons. The populations may be equal in size but data may be lost from some conditions, perhaps because of a malfunction of equipment, or a subject's failure to complete the data-collection session. Usually, individuals can be replaced but sometimes this is impossible. In other instances, the treatments may affect the availability of scores; for example, animals in one drug condition may be less likely to survive the experiment than animals in another condition. In still other instances, usually when we collect data from existing populations, conditions may differ naturally in the availability of individuals for participation. For example, in clinical settings, there may be different numbers of individuals in different diagnostic categories.

Unequal n complicates calculations in the one-factor design, which might tempt some researchers to discard scores from some conditions to equate n. This is not a good idea for a couple of reasons. Discarding subjects to equalize the group ns will reduce error degrees of freedom and, consequently, power. Discarding subjects also may misrepresent the relative size of the populations sampled. If so, the effects of some conditions may be weighted too heavily or too lightly in the data analysis. Finally, computational ease should not be a consideration when software programs are available to handle the calculations.

8.6.1 The ANOVA with Unequal *n*

The ANOVA for unequal group sizes is a straightforward modification of the equal-n case, at least in the one-factor between-subjects design. (Complications arise when more than one factor is involved; these will be treated in Chapters 9 and 24.) Table 8.4 presents the ANOVA formulas and expected mean squares for the unequal-n case; the squared deviations in the SS_A formula and the n_j are weighted by the group size. Note that if the n_j are equal, these formulas reduce to the formulas in Table 8.3.

Table 8.4   The analysis of variance for the one-factor between-subjects design with unequal group sizes

Source	df	SS	MS	F	EMS
A	$a-1$	$\sum\limits_{j=1}^{a} n_j(\overline{Y}_{.j} - \overline{Y}_{..})^2$	SS_A/df_A	$MS_A/MS_{S/A}$	$\sigma_e^2 + \dfrac{1}{a-1}\sum\limits_j n_j\alpha_j$
S/A	$N-a$	$\sum\limits_{j=1}^{a}\sum\limits_{i=1}^{n_j} (Y_{ij} - \overline{Y}_{.j})^2$	$SS_{S/A}/df_{S/A}$		σ_e^2
Total	$N-1$	$\sum\limits_{j=1}^{a}\sum\limits_{i=1}^{n_j} (Y_{ij} - \overline{Y}_{..})^2$			

Note: n_j is the number of scores in the jth group and $N = \sum\limits_{j=1}^{a} n_j$.

Table 8.5 presents statistics based on Beck Depression scores for four groups of males who participated in the University of Massachusetts Medical School research on seasonal effects; the statistics are based on scores averaged over the four seasons. For the purposes of this example, we excluded some subjects (those having no or only some high-school education, and those with vocational training or an associate's degree). The remaining groups are HS (high-school diploma only), C (some college), B (bachelor's degree), and GS (graduate school).[5]

The statistics of Table 8.5 and the box plots of Fig. 8.2 indicate that the groups differ in their average depression score. Both means and medians are noticeably higher for those subjects who had only a high-school education; subjects with a graduate school education have lower scores but they

---

[5] The data may be found in the *Table 8_5 Male_educ* file; go to the *Tables* page of the book's website.

Table 8.5 Summary statistics for Beck Depression scores in four educational levels (the data are in the *Male-educ* file; go to the *Seasons* page on the book's website)

	Level of education			
	HS	C	B	GS
No. of cases	19	33	37	39
Median	6.272	2.875	2.265	3.031
Mean	6.903	3.674	3.331	4.847
Variance	34.541	5.970	9.861	26.218
Skewness ($g1$)	.824	.368	2.047	1.270
Kurtosis ($g2$)	.168	−.919	5.837	.745

Note: HS = high-school diploma only; C = some college; B = bachelor's degree; GS = graduate school.

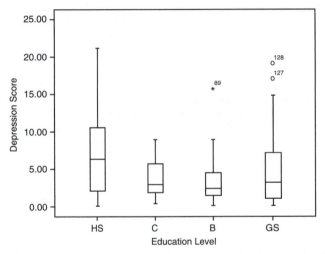

Fig. 8.2 Box plot of Beck Depression scores as a function of educational level.

are higher than those in the remaining two categories. Variances are also highest in the *HS* and *GS* groups; the differences among the variances as well as among the *H*-spreads in the figure warn us that heterogeneity of variance may be an issue. We also note that both the skew statistics and the long tails at the high end of depression scores in the figure indicate that the populations are unlikely to be normally distributed. A *Q–Q* plot (see Chapter 2) would confirm this.

Applying the formulas in Table 8.4, we obtain the ANOVA results in Table 8.6; these reveal that the means of the four groups differ significantly. However, the characteristics of the data revealed by

Table 8.6 ANOVA of the depression means in Table 8.5

Source	SS	df	MS	F	p
Education	186.501	3	62.167	3.562	.016
Error	2,164.061	124	17.452		
Total	2,350.562	127			

our preliminary exploration (Table 8.5, Fig. 8.2) indicate that the assumptions of the analysis of variance are violated. In Section 8.8, we discuss those assumptions, consider alternative analyses that respond to violations of the assumptions, and apply one such analysis to the depression scores.

8.6.2 Measures of Importance with Unequal *n*

As in the equal n design, $\eta^2 = SS_A/(SS_A + SS_{S/A})$. For the Beck Depression data, substituting values from Table 8.6, $\eta^2 = 186.501/2,350.562$, or .079. The formulas for ω^2 and Cohen's f undergo a very slight modification. We replace the n in Equation 8.14 by the average n, $\bar{n}$, where $\bar{n} = \sum_j n_j/a = N/a$.

We can simplify things further by replacing $a\bar{n}$ by N, the total sample size. Then the equations estimating, σ_A^2, ω^2, and Cohen's f apply with no further changes.

To estimate the population variance of the Beck Depression means as a function of educational level, substitute the mean squares from Table 8.6 into Equation 8.14, and with $\sum_j n_j = 128$,

$$\hat{\sigma}_A^2 = (3)(62.167 - 17.452)/128 = 1.048$$

We now can estimate ω^2 using Equation 8.16 with N replacing an. Then

$$\hat{\omega}^2 = \frac{(a-1)(F_A - 1)}{(a-1)(F_A - 1) + N}$$

$$= \frac{(3)(2.562)}{(3)(2.562) + 128} = .057$$

We use the same variance estimate to estimate Cohen's f:

$$\hat{f} = \hat{\sigma}_A/\hat{\sigma}_e$$

$$= \sqrt{1.048/17.245} = 0.245$$

Whether we view ω^2 or f, Cohen's guidelines suggest that the effect is of medium size.

In leaving the analysis of the effects of educational level on Beck Depression scores, we again caution that our exploration of the data suggested that both the normality and homogeneity of variance assumptions were violated, making suspect the results of significance tests and estimates of effect size. We will return to the general issue of violations of assumptions, and possible remedies, in Section 8.8.

8.7 DECIDING ON SAMPLE SIZE: POWER ANALYSIS IN THE BETWEEN-SUBJECTS DESIGN

Together with the practical constraints imposed by the available access to subjects and time, statistical power should be a primary consideration in deciding on sample size. In order to incorporate this into our decision about sample size, we need to decide on a value of power and we need a value of the minimum effect size we wish to detect. As we saw in our treatment of t tests in Chapter 6, there are several ways that we might proceed.

One possibility is that we use Cohen's guidelines to establish an effect size. For example, suppose that in designing the memory experiment described in Section 8.2, we had decided that we want power equal to at least .90 to reject an effect that was large by Cohen's guidelines; then $f = .4$.

How many subjects should we have included in the study? An easy way to answer this question is to use G*Power 3, available on the book's website. Fig. 8.3 shows the screen involved in the calculations. We selected *F tests* from the *Test Family* menu, the ANOVA for the one-way design from the *Statistical test* menu, and the *a priori* option from the *Type of power analysis* menu. We set the *Input*

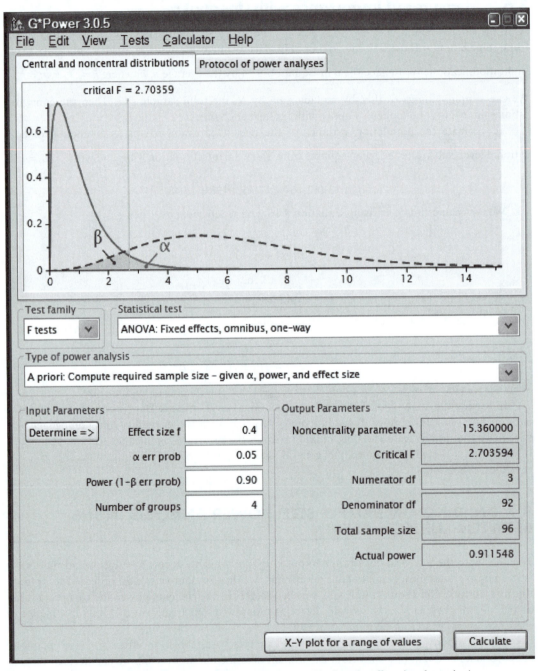

Fig. 8.3 G*Power 3 calculation of the *N* needed to have power = .90 when the effect size, *f*, equals .4.

Parameters as shown in the left-hand column. In the *Output Parameters* column, we find that the required total N is 96, or 24 in each group. The other output results should be self-explanatory except for the noncentrality parameter λ; $\lambda = N f^2$, or $96 \times .16$. This parameter is an index of the noncentral F distribution's distance from the central F distribution; when $\lambda = 0$, power equals the Type 1 error rate and as λ increases, so does the power of the test.

An alternative to using Cohen's guidelines is to base our assumed effect size on results from a pilot study. In this case, we would recommend using Equation 8.18 or 8.19 to obtain an estimate of f. We would then insert this into G*Power. For the data of Table 8.1, this estimate was .409. If we require power = .9, set $\alpha = .05$; then with four groups the required N is 92, slightly less than when we entered $f = .4$.

Finally, in some cases, we might have no single data set on which to base an estimate of f. However, practical or theoretical considerations, or a review of published results from several related studies, might suggest reasonable values of the treatment population means and of the population standard deviation. For example, in planning an experiment involving three groups, we might decide that the most likely values of the population means are 50, 60, and 70, and that the population standard deviation is about 20. Using G*Power 3, we enter $\alpha = .05$, power = .9, and the number of groups = 3, and then select the *determine* button. This brings up a panel in which we enter the hypothesized population means and the population standard deviation. Select "Calculate and transfer to main window." G*Power calculates

$$\sigma_A = \sqrt{[(50 - 60)^2 + (60 - 60)^2 + (70 - 60)^2] / 3} = 8.165$$

and divides by the standard deviation of 20 to yield $f = .408$. Transferring this value to the main window, the required total N is 81, or 27 in each of the three groups.

Post hoc, or retrospective power, is also available in G*Power, as well as in SPSS; in the latter, *Observed power* is an option in the univariate analysis program. However, as we discussed in Chapter 6, we have reservations about reporting power based on the observed set of statistics. Confidence intervals on the raw and standardized effects will prove more informative and be less misleading.

8.8 ASSUMPTIONS UNDERLYING THE *F* TEST

In Chapter 6, we discussed the consequences of violations of assumptions of independence, normality, and homogeneity of variance for the *t* test, and considered several possible remedies, including transformations, *t* tests that take heterogeneous variances into account, *t* tests based on trimming the data set, and tests based on ranks. The *F* test in the one-factor, between-subjects design rests on the same assumptions, and in addition the data should be consistent with the underlying structural model. The consequences of violations of assumptions, as well as the remedies proposed, parallel those discussed in Chapter 6. In the following sections, we consider each assumption in turn, describing both the consequences of violations and possible remedies.

8.8.1 The Structural Model

The analysis of variance for the one-factor design begins with the structural model of Equation 8.3. This equation implies that only one factor systematically influences the data, and the residual variability ($MS_{S/A}$) represents random error. However, researchers sometimes ignore factors that have been manipulated but are not of interest in themselves. If those factors contribute significant variability, the one-factor model is not valid for the research design. Common examples arise when half of the subjects are male and half are female, or when subject running is divided equally between two experimenters, or when the position of an object is counterbalanced in an experiment involving a choice. Although these variables may be irrelevant to the purpose of the research, they may affect the scores. If so, the $MS_{S/A}$ represents both error variance and variance due to gender, experimenter, or position. However, the variance due to these "irrelevant" variables will not contribute to MS_A. For example, if each method in our earlier example has an equal number of male and female subjects, sex of subject will not increase the *method* mean square. The analysis based on the one-factor model then violates the principle that the numerator and denominator of the F ratio should have the same expectation when H_0 is true. In such situations, the denominator has a larger expectation than the numerator because the irrelevant variable makes a contribution only to the denominator. The result is a loss of power, which can be considerable if the irrelevant variable has a large effect. We say that the F test is *negatively biased* in this case, meaning that the Type 1 error rate will be less than its nominal value if the null hypothesis is true. As a general rule, the researcher should formulate a complete structural model, one which incorporates all systematically varied factors, even those thought to be irrelevant or uninteresting. In the examples cited, this would mean viewing the study as involving two factors, the independent variable of interest and gender (or experimenter, or position), and carrying out the analysis described in Chapter 9.

8.8.2 The Independence Assumption

When only one observation is obtained from each subject, and subjects are randomly assigned to treatments or randomly sampled from distinct populations, the assumption that the scores are independently distributed is likely to be met. However, there are exceptions that sometimes are not recognized by researchers. For example, suppose we want to compare attitudes on some topic for males and females. Further suppose that before being tested, subjects participate in three-person discussions of the relevant topic. The scores of individuals who were part of the same discussion group will tend to be positively correlated. If this failure of the independence assumption is ignored (and it has been in some studies; see Anderson and Ager, 1978, for a review), there will be a *positive bias*—an inflation of Type 1 error rate—in an F test of the gender effect (Myers, DiCecco, & Lorch, 1981; Myers & Well, 1995). A class of analyses referred to as multilevel, or hierarchical (e.g., Raudenbush & Bryk, 2002), provides a general approach to this and other data analysis issues.

Another potential source of failure of the independence assumption is the "bottom-of-the-barrel" problem. Researchers at universities often feel that as the semester progresses, the performance of volunteer subjects in experiments tends to become poorer because less motivated subjects usually volunteer for research credit late in the semester. In this case, scores obtained close in time will tend to have higher correlations than those further apart in time.

8.8.3 The Normality Assumption

Violations of the normality assumption are relatively common and merit attention because they can reduce the power of the F test.

Consequences of Violating the Normality Assumption. As with the t test, the Type 1 error probability associated with the F test is little affected by sampling from non-normal populations unless the samples are quite small and the departure from normality extremely marked (e.g., Donaldson, 1968; Lindquist, 1953, pp. 78–90; Scheffé, 1959). This is true even when the independent variable is discretely distributed, as it is whenever rating data or response frequencies are analyzed. In all but the most skewed distributions, computer sampling studies indicate that Type 1 error rates are relatively unaffected when such measures are submitted to an analysis of variance (Bevan, Denton, & Myers, 1974; Hsu & Feldt, 1969; Lunney, 1970).

Although in most instances the Type 1 error rate is relatively unaffected by departures from normality, loss of power is a concern when distributions are long-tailed, skewed, or include outliers. In each of these situations, variability is high relative to the normal distribution. Thus, procedures that address the increased variability often have more power than the conventional *F* test. Several potential remedies are considered next.

Dealing with Violations of the Normality Assumption: Tests Based on Trimmed Data. As we explained in Chapter 6, merely deleting scores is not a valid procedure. However, a ratio of mean squares distributed approximately as *F* can be constructed by an approach similar to the trimmed *t* test illustrated in Chapter 7. An example should help us understand how this is done. Table 8.7 presents three groups of 11 scores each; the *Y* scores are the original values, sorted in ascending order within each group. Recognizing the presence of some outlying scores in each group's tail, we trimmed the lowest and highest two scores in each group, yielding the *T* data. We then replaced the deleted scores with the closest remaining scores to create the winsorized, *W*, set. We chose to delete two from each group's tail because this is roughly 20% of 11, the number of *Y* scores. Two ANOVAs, one on the *T* scores and one on the *W* scores, provide the values needed for the trimmed *F* test. The test is described and illustrated in Box 8.2.

Table 8.7   An example of original (*Y*), trimmed (*T*) and winsorized data (*W*)

	Y	5	6	8	8	10	10	10	10	10	11	14
Group 1	*T*			8	8	10	10	10	10	10		
	W	8	8	8	8	10	10	10	10	10	10	10
	Y	5	9	11	11	11	11	12	13	13	13	16
Group 2	*T*			11	11	11	11	12	13	13		
	W	11	11	11	11	11	11	12	13	13	13	13
	Y	9	10	10	10	10	11	11	11	12	12	15
Group 3	*T*			10	10	10	11	11	11	12		
	W	10	10	10	10	10	11	11	11	12	12	12

Box 8.2 The Trimmed *F* Test Applied to the Data of Table 8.7

After performing the ANOVAs on the *T* and *W* scores, do the following:

1. From the ANOVA of the *T* data, get the between-groups mean square, $MS_{BG,tk}$ (tk refers to trimming *k* scores from each tail); $MS_{BG,tk} = 9.19$.
2. From the ANOVA of the *W* data, get the within-groups sum of squares, $SS_{WG,wk}$; $SS_{WG,wk} = 27.455$. This is divided by the degrees of freedom for the trimmed data set, $a(n - 1 - 2k) = (3)(10 - 4) = 18$. Therefore, the winsorized error mean square, $MS_{WG,wk}$, is $27.455/18 = 1.523$.
3. The trimmed *F* statistic is $F = MS_{BG,tk}/MS_{WG,wk} = 27.455/1.523 = 18.269$, and is distributed on 2 and 18 *df*. Then $p = .000$.

For comparison purposes, the F statistic on 2 and 30 df for the Y data was 2.531; the corresponding p-value was .096. Clearly, in this example, the trimmed t test led to a considerably lower p-value. However, a word of caution is in order. In our example, the variances were roughly homogeneous and the distributions were roughly symmetric. Under other conditions, particularly if the group sizes vary, Type 1 errors may be inflated (Lix & Keselman, 1998). We will consider such cases in Section 8.8.4.

Dealing with Violations of the Normality Assumption: Tests Based on Ranked Data. In the _Kruskal–Wallis H Test_ (1952) and the _rank-transform F test_ (Conover & Iman, 1981), all scores are ordered with a rank of 1 assigned to the lowest score in the data set and a rank of N assigned to the largest, where N is the total number of scores. In case of ties, the median rank is assigned; for example, if the five lowest scores are 1, 4, 7, 9, and 9, they would receive ranks of 1, 2, 3, 4.5, and 4.5 respectively. The H test is available from the nonparametric menu of statistical packages such as SPSS, Systat, and SAS. In SPSS, select _Analyze_, then _Nonparametric_, and then k _independent groups_. Applying the Kruskal–Wallis H test to the data of Table 8.7, $p = .039$. As with the trimmed F test, the result is a lower value than that associated with the usual F test of the Y data.

In the rank-transform F test, the usual one-way ANOVA is performed on the ranks and the test statistic, F_R, is evaluated on $a - 1$ and $N - a$ df. H and F_R will generally result in similar p-values. This is not surprising given that they are related by the following equation:

$$F_R = \frac{(N - a)H}{(a - 1)(N - 1 - H)}$$

Both tests are more powerful alternatives than the usual F test when the populations are not normally distributed but have the same values of variance, skewness, and kurtosis; that is, when the populations have the same, non-normal distribution. Furthermore, they are only slightly less powerful than the F test when the distributions are normal. However, if the treatment populations do not have identical distributions, then H and F_R tests may reject the null hypothesis because of differences in the shapes or variances of the distributions. Therefore, the tests are not appropriate as tests of location when heterogeneity of variance is suspected (Oshima & Algina, 1992; Vargha & Delaney, 1998).

As we discussed in Chapter 6, when the data are skewed, transformations may provide a solution. Data transformations are also a possible response to heterogeneity of variance. We will discuss this option in the context of our treatment of the assumption of homogeneous variances.

8.8.4 The Homogeneity of Variance Assumption

Variances may differ across conditions for one of several reasons. One possible cause of heterogeneity of variance is an interaction of an experimental treatment with individual characteristics. For example, a drug tested for its effects on depression may result in a higher variance than, but the same mean score as, a placebo. This would suggest that some individuals had improved but others had been adversely affected by the drug. A second possible reason for unequal variances is that some populations are more variable than others on a particular task. For example, although boys may have higher average scores on some measure of mathematical ability, they may also have a higher variance. Still another factor in findings of heterogeneity of variance are floor, or ceiling, effects. Variability may be reduced in one condition relative to another because of a lower, or upper, limit on performance due to the measuring instrument. Finally, variances tend to be correlated with means, usually positively; the normal distribution is the sole exception in which the means and variances are independently distributed. For all of these reasons, variances are often unequal, or *heterogeneous*, in the populations sampled in our research. In what follows, we summarize some consequences of the failure of this assumption and we then consider alternatives to the standard *F* test.

Consequences of Heterogeneity of Variance.   When there are the same number of scores in all conditions, heterogeneous variances usually will cause Type 1 error rates to be slightly inflated. The inflation is usually less than .02 at the .05 level, and less than .005 at the .01 level, provided the ratio of the largest to smallest variance is no more than 4 to 1, and *n* is at least 5. Even larger ratios may not be a problem, but this will depend upon sample size, the number of groups, and the shape of the population distributions. The results of computer simulations employing these factors are discussed in articles by Clinch and Keselman (1982) and Tomarken and Serlin (1986).

When there are different numbers of scores in each condition, simulation studies clearly demonstrate that heterogeneous variances are a problem. Sampling from heavy-tailed and skewed distributions, and using variance ratios of largest to smallest as high as 16:1, Lix and Keselman (1998) found that error rates were as high as .50 in some conditions. Sampling from sets of either three or four normally distributed populations, Tomarken and Serlin found that at a nominal .05 level, the actual Type 1 error rate was as low as .022 when the group size was positively correlated with the variance (i.e., larger groups associated with greater variances) and as high as .167 when the correlation was negative. This is because the average within-group variance (i.e., the error term, $MS_{S/A}$) is increased when the largest groups have the largest variances and, conversely, is decreased when the largest groups have the smallest variances. Therefore, a positive relation between group size and variance will negatively bias the *F* test whereas a negative relation will positively bias the test.

There is evidence in the research literature that extreme variance ratios do occur (Wilcox, 1987), and simulation studies make clear that heterogeneity of variance can inflate Type 1 error rates or deflate power, depending upon various factors such as sample sizes and the type of distribution sampled. That leaves us with two questions. First, for a given data set, how do we decide whether to abandon the standard ANOVA for some remedial procedure? Second, If we do decide that unequal variances are a threat to the validity of the standard *F* test, what alternative should we use? We consider these questions next.

Detecting Heterogeneity of Variance.   As always, we urge that researchers begin the data analysis by examining summary statistics and plots of the data. Computer programs such as SPSS's Explore module are very helpful in this respect. Typically, they provide descriptive statistics, tests of homogeneity of variance, and box plots. The box plot for the Beck Depression data as a function of educational level was presented in Fig. 8.2 and, as we noted there, differences among the groups in shape and spread are quite evident. The range of variances in Table 8.5 suggest that the alpha level reported in Table 8.6 may not be the actual probability of a Type 1 error. For confirmation of this, we may wish to test whether the variances are homogeneous. Several tests of homogeneity of variance have been proposed. Some are overly sensitive to violations of the normality assumption (Bartlett, 1937; Cochran, 1941; Hartley, 1950; Levene, 1960) or lack power relative to other procedures (Box, 1953; Games, Keselman, & Clinch, 1979; Scheffé, 1959).

We recommend the Brown–Forsythe test (Brown & Forsythe, 1974*a*) based on deviations from the median. Sampling studies indicate it has only a slightly inflated Type 1 error rate and good power relative to various competitors even when *n*s are not equal and distributions depart markedly from the normal (Games, Keselman, & Clinch, 1979). In this test, the absolute residual of each score from its group median, $|Y_{ij} - \overline{Y}_{.j}|$, is computed, and these residuals are then submitted to the analysis of variance. Although these residuals do not directly represent the variance, their variance is an index of the spread of scores. For the depression scores summarized in Table 8.5, SPSS's Explore module reports the value of this statistic as 4.511 which, on 3 and 124 df, is very significant ($p = .005$). This indicates that the mean absolute residual varies significantly as a function of education level, confirming our sense that the spread of scores was indeed a function of the educational level.

Once we conclude that the population variances are not equal, the next question is: What shall we do about it? One possible response is to seek a transformation of the data that yields homogeneity of variance on the scale resulting from the transformation. A second possibility is to compute an alternative to the usual F test. We consider each of these approaches next.

Dealing with Heterogeneity of Variance: Transformations of the Data. Transformation of the data can sometimes result in variances that are more nearly similar on the new scale. Typical data transformations include raising scores to a power, or taking the natural logarithm of each score. These and other transformations have been used (1) to transform skewed distributions into more nearly normal distributions; (2) to reduce heterogeneity of variance; and (3) to remedy a condition known as "nonadditivity" in designs in which each subject is tested on several trials or under several treatment levels. A transformation which best achieves one purpose may not be equally suitable for other purposes, although it is true that transformations that equate variances do tend to yield more normally distributed scores. Our focus here will be on transformations designed to achieve homogeneous variances.

We begin by noting that transformations are not always a good option for a researcher. One potential problem is that values on the new scale may be less easily interpreted than on the original scale. For example, the percent correct on a test (y) is easily understood and communicated, but this is less true of the arc sine transformation ($\sin^{-1} \sqrt{y}$, the angle whose sine is the square root of y), often recommended to stabilize the variances of percentage scores. Another potential problem is that although variance-stabilizing transformations will usually maintain the ordering of the group means, the relative distances among means may change, creating problems when interpreting the effects of the factors manipulated. Suppose a researcher has predicted that response time will vary as a linear function of the levels of the independent variable. A test of linearity on a transformed scale will probably not support the prediction because the means on the new scale are likely to fall on a curve.

If the measurement scale is arbitrary, however, transfoming the data is one strategy for dealing with heterogeneous variances. In that case, how does the researcher identify a useful transformation for reducing the range of variances across experimental conditions? One possibility is to try several transformations. However, it is not appropriate to conduct a significance test after each transformation and choose the data scale that yields the largest F value. Such a procedure is bound to increase the probability of a Type 1 error if the population means do not differ. A more principled approach to identifying a variance-stabilizing transformation depends on observing a functional relation between the cell variances and cell means (Smith, 1976).

Emerson and Stoto (1983) described an approach that will frequently produce more nearly equal variances. The technique involves plotting the log of the H-spread (or interquartile range; see Chapter 2) as a function of the log of the median and then finding the slope of the best-fitting straight line. SPSS provides such a *spread versus level plot* in its Explore module if the "Plots" option is chosen and "Power Transformations" is checked. The output includes the value of the slope, which is used to transform the original score, Y, into the transformed score, Z, by the following *power transformation:*

$$Z = Y^{1 - slope} \qquad (8.24)$$

We obtained this plot for data from Royer's (1999) study of arithmetic skills in elementary schoolchildren.[6] Using SPSS's Explore module to analyze multiplication response times (RT), the slope of the spread-versus-level plot was 2.227 and the recommended power was therefore −1.227. We rounded this, letting $Z = Y^{-1} = 1/Y$, thus re-expressing response time as response speed, a measure that is easily understood. Table 8.8 presents the group means and variances on the original and new data scales. On the original RT scale, the ratio of largest to smallest variance is almost 15 to 1; on the speed scale, that ratio is only 1.4 to 1. We might also point out that the procedure illustrated here of rounding the recommended power to the nearest "meaningful" number makes sense from the perspective of communicating the transformation to an audience. For example, transforming by taking an inverse (power = −1) or square root (power = .5) or square (power = 2) will be more easily communicated and is unlikely to produce very different results than some "odd" number, such as −.742 or 1.88.

Often the researcher will not wish to transform the data because of the difficulty of interpreting effects (or lack of effects) on the new scale, or because a strong theory dictates the dependent variable. In other instances, it may be impossible to find a variance-stabilizing transformation.[7] Fortunately, there are other solutions that often can solve the heterogeneity problem. We turn now to consider modifications of the standard F test.

Dealing with Heterogeneity of Variance: Welch's F test.   Several alternatives to the standard F test of the equality of the a population means have been proposed (Alexander & Govern, 1994; Brown & Forsythe, 1974b; James, 1951, 1954; Welch, 1951), but no one test is best under all conditions. When the data are normally distributed and ns are equal, most of the procedures are reasonably robust with respect to Type 1 error rate; however, the standard F is slightly more powerful if the population variances are equal. When the variances are not equal, the choice of test depends upon the degree of skew and kurtosis, whether outliers are present, the degree of heterogeneity of variance, the relation between group sizes and group variances, and the total N (Clinch & Keselman, 1982; Coombs, Algina, & Oltman, 1996; Grissom, 2000; Lix, Keselman, & Keselman, 1996; Tomarken & Serlin, 1986).

Table 8.8 Means and variances of multiplication RT and speeds from the *Royer* data

	Grade			
	5	6	7	8
RT mean	3.837	1.998	1.857	1.935
RT variance	4.884	.612	.328	.519
Speed mean	.350	.560	.586	.583
Speed variance	.033	.028	.031	.038

---

[6] These data are in the file *Royer_RT*; go to the *Royer* data set on the book's website.

[7] Not all measures can be successfully transformed. For example, on the basis of the spread-vs-level plot, we found that the best transformation of the depression scores was to raise them to the −.106 power. However, following this transformation, and also after a log transform, variances still differed significantly by some tests, and the normality assumption was still violated.

Although there is rarely a clear-cut choice for any given data set, in a review of several simulation studies, Lix et al. (1996) concluded that the *Welch test, F_w,* provided the best alternative when both Type 1 error rates and power were considered. F_w performs well relative to various competitors except when the data are highly skewed (skew > 2.0) or group sizes are less than 10 (Lix et al., 1996; Tomarken & Serlin, 1986). Furthermore, the test is available in several statistical packages. In SPSS, both the standard test results and those for the Welch test are in the output of the *One-Way ANOVA* (*Compare Means*) option.

If you lack the appropriate software, Box 8.3 presents the necessary formulas. Substituting values from Table 8.5 in the equations in the box, we have:

	HS	C	B	GS
$w_j =$	.550	5.528	3.752	1.488
$\bar{Y}_{.j} =$	6.903	3.674	3.331	4.847

Then, $u = 11.318$, $\bar{Y}_{..} = 3.871$, $A = 2.594$, $B = 1.024$, $F = 2.533$, $df_1 = 3$, $df_2 = 1/.018 = 55$, and $p = .066$. The resulting p-value is considerably higher than the .016 we obtained using the standard F calculations. The discrepancy can be accounted for by noting that the correlation between n_j and s_j^2 is negative, $-.59$. There are only 19 subjects in the group having only a high-school education (HS) whereas the other groups all have at least 33 subjects. Because the larger groups have smaller variances, they have more weight in the denominator of the F test; that small denominator contributes to a larger F statistic with a resulting inflated probability of a Type 1 error. The Welch test has compensated for this by taking the inequalities in group sizes and variances into account.

Box 8.3 Formulas for the Welch (F_w) Test

$$F_W = \frac{A}{B}$$

where $A = \dfrac{1}{a-1} \sum w_j (\bar{Y}_{.j} - \bar{Y}_{..})^2$

$$B = 1 + \left[\frac{2(a-2)}{a^2-1} \right] \sum \frac{[1-(w_j/u)]^2}{n_j-1}$$

and $w_j = n_j / s_j^2;\ u = \sum w_j;\ \bar{Y}_{..} = \sum w_j \bar{Y}_{.j}/u$

$df_1 = a - 1$

$$\frac{1}{df_2} = \left[\frac{3}{a^2-1} \right] \sum \frac{[1-(w_j/u)]^2}{n_j-1}$$

A Robust F Test.   The normality and homogeneity of variance assumptions often are violated in the same data set. This is particularly a problem when *ns* are unequal, as in the Beck Depression data we analyzed. A promising approach is to apply the Welch *F* test to means based on data from which the highest and lowest 20% have been trimmed.(Keselman, Wilcox, Othman, & Fradette, 2002; Lix & Keselman, 1998). The test is described in Box 8.4. Because it uses trimmed means and winsorized variances, it may be helpful to refer to Chapter 7 where trimmed means and winsorized variances were defined and illustrated.

Box 8.4 Welch's (1951) _F_ Test with Trimmed Means and Winsorized Variances

1. Replace the n_j in Box 8.2 by $h_j = n_j - 2k_j$, where k_j is the number of scores trimmed from each tail of the jth group. For example, in the HS group of the depression analysis, $n_j = 19$. If we trim approximately 20% from each tail, $k = 4$ and $h = 19 - (2)(4) = 11$.
2. The $\overline{Y}_j$ are replaced by the trimmed means.
3. The s_j^2 are replaced by the winsorized group variances.
4. With these substitutions, the formulas for the Welch _F_ test in Box 8.3 apply directly.

8.9 SUMMARY

This chapter introduced the analysis of variance in the simplest possible context, the one-factor, between-subjects design. The developments in this chapter will be relevant in the analyses of data from other designs. These developments included:

- *The analysis of variance.* We illustrated the idea of a structural model that underlies the data and directs the partitioning of variability in the data. The structural model is the basis for determining what the variance calculations estimate in terms of population variance parameters. The *EMS*, in turn, justify the error terms for tests of the null hypothesis and are involved in estimating measures of the magnitude of effects.
- *Measures of importance.* We defined and applied to data several statistics that indicate the importance of the independent variable. Confidence intervals also were presented that provide a range of plausible values of the parameter being estimated.
- *A priori* power and sample size. We illustrated how sample size for a multi-group study can be determined, once the values of α, the desired power, and the effect size of interest are selected.
- *Assumptions underlying the significance test and the estimates of measures of importance.* We reviewed these assumptions, discussed the consequences of their violation, cited tests of the assumptions that are available in many software packages, and described procedures that respond to violations.

APPENDIX 8.1

Partitioning the Total Variability in the One-Factor Design

The following developments involve two indices of summation: i indexes a value from 1 to n within each group, where n is the number of individuals in a group; j indexes a value from 1 to a, where a is the number of groups. Appendix A provides an explanation of the use of this notation, using several examples.

Squaring both sides of Equation 8.1 yields

$$(Y_{ij} - \bar{Y}_{..})^2 = (Y_{ij} - \bar{Y}_{.j})^2 + (\bar{Y}_{.j} - \bar{Y}_{..})^2 + 2(Y_{ij} - \bar{Y}_{.j})(\bar{Y}_{.j} - \bar{Y}_{..})$$

Summing over i and j, and applying the rules of Appendix A, we have

$$\sum_j^a \sum_i^n (Y_{ij} - \bar{Y}_{..})^2 = \sum_j^a \sum_i^n (Y_{ij} - \bar{Y}_{.j})^2 + n\sum_j^a (\bar{Y}_{.j} - \bar{Y}_{..})^2 + 2\sum_j^a \sum_i^n (Y_{ij} - \bar{Y}_{.j})(\bar{Y}_{.j} - \bar{Y}_{..})$$

Rearranging terms, we can show that the rightmost (cross-product) term equals 0:

$$2\sum_j^a \sum_i^n (Y_{ij} - \bar{Y}_{.j})(\bar{Y}_{.j} - \bar{Y}_{..}) = 2\sum_j^a (\bar{Y}_{.j} - \bar{Y}_{..})\sum_i^n (Y_{ij} - \bar{Y}_{.j})$$

$$= 2\sum_j^a (\bar{Y}_{.j} - \bar{Y}_{..})(0) = 0$$

The last result follows because the sum of deviations of scores about their mean is zero.

EXERCISES

8.1 A data set has three groups of five scores each. Because the scores involve decimal values, each score is multiplied by 100.
  (a) How will the mean squares and F ratio be affected (relative to an analysis of the original data set)?
  (b) In general, what happens to a variance when every score is multiplied by a constant?
  (c) Suppose we just added a constant, say, 10, to all 15 scores. How would that affect the mean squares and F ratio?
  (d) Suppose we added 5 to all scores in the first group, 10 to all scores in group 2, and 15 to all scores in group 3? Should MS_A change? $MS_{S/A}$? Explain.

8.2 Following are summary statistics from a three-group experiment. Present the ANOVA table when (a) $n_1 = n_2 = n_3 = 10$ and (b) $n_1 = 6$, $n_2 = 8$, and $n_3 = 10$; the totals, or sums of scores, for the groups, the $T_{.j}$, and the variances are:

	A_1	A_2	A_3
Totals	30	48	70
Variances	3.2	4.1	5.7

8.3 The data are:

$$A_1: 27\ 18\ 16\ 33\ 24 \qquad A_2: 23\ 33\ 26\ 19\ 38$$

  (a) Perform the ANOVA.
  (b) Next, do a t test. How are the results of parts (a) and (b) related?

8.4 The F ratio is basically a test of the equality of the population variances estimated by its numerator and denominator. Therefore, it is applicable to the following problem. We have samples of reading scores from 5 boys and 11 girls. We form a ratio of the variances of the two samples, s_B^2/s_G^2.

(a) If many samples of sizes 5 and 11 are drawn, (i) what is the proportion of F values greater than 2.61 that we should expect? (ii) less than 4.47?

(b) What assumptions are implied in your approach to answering part (a)?

8.5 The file *EX8_5* at the website contains three groups of 15 scores.

(a) Explore the data; examine statistics and graphs relevant to assessing the normality and homogeneity of variance assumptions. What are the implications for a significance test?

(b) Calculate the F and Kruskal–Wallis H tests for these data and comment on the outcome, relating your discussion to your answer to part (a).

8.6 (a) A nonparametric test is only one way to reduce the effect of the straggling right tail of the data in Exercise 8.5. Explore the data after transformation by taking (1) the square root of each score and (2) the natural log of each score. Does either one better conform to the assumptions underlying the F test? Explain.

(b) Carry out the ANOVA with the transformation you selected in part (a). How do the results compare with those for the original F test in Exercise 8.5?

(c) Find the confidence intervals for the three means, using the Y data. Then do the same with the group means for the transformed scores. Transform the means of the transformed scores to the original scale. For example, if you had selected the square-root transformation, you would square the transformed means; if you had selected the log transformation, you would raise e to the power of the mean on the log scale (for example, if the mean on the log scale $= 3$, on the original scale we would have $e^3 = 20.09$). Do the same for the 95% confidence limits for each of the three means. Compare the results for the original and transformed data.

8.7 The following are the results of two experiments, each with three levels of the independent variable.

	Table 1			Table 2	
SV	df	MS	SV	df	MS
A	2	80	A	2	42.5
S/A	27	5	S/A	12	5

(a) For each of the two tables, calculate the Fs, and estimates of ω_A^2.

(b) What does a comparison of the two sets of results suggest about the effect of the change in n upon these two quantities?

(c) Calculate η_A^2 for each table. How does the change in n affect the value of η_A^2?

(d) Suppose $F = 1$. (i) What must the value of ω_A^2 be? (ii) What must the value of η_A^2 be (as a function of a and n)?

(e) Comment on the relative merits of the various statistics calculated as indices of the importance of A.

8.8 The result of an ANOVA of a data set based on three groups of 10 scores each is:

SV	df	SS	MS	F
A	2	192	96	3.2
S/A	27	810	30	

(a) Is there a significant A effect if $\alpha = .05$?

(b) Estimate Cohen's f for these results.

    (c) Assuming this is a good estimate of the true effect of A, what power did the experiment have?

    (d) How many subjects would be required to have power $= .8$ to detect a medium-sized effect? Use Cohen's guidelines.

8.9 According to a mathematical model for the experiment in Exercise 8.8, the predicted means are 10 in condition 1, 14 in condition 2, and 18 in condition 3. If the theory is correct, what sample size would be needed to achieve .8 power to reject the null hypothesis of no difference among the means? Assume that the error mean square is a good estimate of the population variance, and $\alpha = .05$.

8.10 In a study of the relative effectiveness of three methods of teaching elementary probability, students read one of three texts: the Standard (S), the Low Explanatory (LE), and the High Explanatory (HE). The data—scores on a test after a single reading—are in the file *EX8_10* on the website.

    (a) Explore the data. Are there any indications of departures from the underlying assumptions?

    (b) Test the null hypothesis that the texts do not differ in their effects.

    (c) Estimate ω^2 and Cohen's f. Verify that $\omega^2 = f^2/(1 + f^2)$ and $f^2 = \omega^2/(1 - \omega^2)$.

    (d) Based on these results, if you were to replicate the study, how many subjects would you run to have power $= .8$?

8.11 The *Sayhlth* file linked to the *Seasons* page on the website contains *Sayhlth* scores (self-ratings of health) of 1–4 (excellent to fair; three subjects with poor ratings in the *Seasons* file are not included). The four categories will be the independent variable in this exercise and the *Beck_D* score will be the dependent variable in the following analyses. The *Beck_D* score is an average of the four seasonal Beck Depression scores and is available only for those subjects whose scores were recorded in all four seasons. The distribution of *Beck_D* scores tends to be skewed and, as in most non-normal distributions, heterogeneity of variance is often a problem.

    (a) Explore the *Beck_D* (seasonal mean) data, using any statistics and plots you think are relevant, and comment on the relative locations, shapes, and variabilities of the scores in the four categories.

    (b) Using the four *Sayhlth* categories, plot the spread vs level; as stated in Chapter 8, this is the log of the H-spread plotted against the log of the median. Several statistical software packages make this plot available. Find the best-fit regression line for this plot and transform the *Beck_D* scores by raising them to the power, $1 - $ slope.

    (c) Explore the distribution of the transformed scores at each *Sayhlth* category. Has the transformation had any effect on the shape of the distributions or on their variances? Test for homogeneity of variance.

    (d) Next try a different transformation. Calculate $\log(Beck\_D + 1)$ and discuss the effects of this transformation.

    (e) What might be the advantages of transforming data to a scale on which they are normally distributed with homogeneous variances?

8.12 The *Sayhlth* file also categorizes individuals by employment category; 1 = employed full time; 2 = employed part-time; 3 = not employed.

    (a) Explore the *Beck_D* data in each *Employ* category, looking at relevant graphs and statistics. Comment on the validity of the ANOVA assumptions.

    (b) In Exercise 8.11, we considered transformations of the *Beck_D* data, one of which appeared to provide results more in accord with the ANOVA model. Use that transformation and again explore the data. Are the results more in accord with the ANOVA model?

(c) Do ANOVAs on the *Beck_D* scores and the transformed scores as a function of employment status. What do you conclude about the effects of employment?

(d) Does the Welch F test confirm or contradict your conclusion?

(e) Calculate Cohen's f for both the original and the transformed data. How would you characterize the effect sizes? In general, what can you say about the effect of employment status on depression scores?

8.13 Continuing with the *Sayhlth* file,

(a) Using the four *Sayhlth* categories as your independent variable, do separate *ANOVAs* of the *Beck_D* data for men and for women.

(b) Calculate Cohen's f for each sex and compare the effect sizes.

Chapter 9
Multi-Factor Between-Subjects Designs

9.1 OVERVIEW

In this chapter, we consider between-subjects designs that include two or more factors. In multi-factor designs, the experimental conditions are formed by creating every combination of levels of the independent variables. There are two advantages of such designs. (1) The obvious advantage is economy; the effects of each of several factors can be studied in the same experiment. (2) The second advantage is that the combined, or *interaction*, effects of several variables can be studied. A specific example may help illustrate these two points. Wiley and Voss (1999) had students read about the Irish potato famine of the first half of the nineteenth century. One factor was the format: whether the material was presented in a single, textbook-like chapter (text format) or divided among eight sources in a computer, web-like (web format) environment. The second factor was the instruction subjects received; they were told to write either a narrative (N), a summary (S), an explanation (E), or an argument (A) about what produced changes in Ireland's population between 1800 and 1850. Thus, there were eight conditions in the experiment corresponding to the two formats combined with the four types of instruction. Following reading, students were tested on the material.

Wiley and Voss had several hypotheses that could be tested in their design. One hypothesis was that the more difficult web format would lead to a deeper understanding by forcing readers to integrate material obtained from several sources. Therefore, one question was whether the formats differed in their average effects. A second hypothesis was that the argument instruction would promote "more conceptual understanding." Therefore, a second question was whether the instructions would differ in their average effect. Finally, a third question was whether the size of any difference in performance between the argument instruction and the other instructions would depend upon the format. This is a question of whether there is an *interaction* between format and instructions.

These questions point to the two main goals of this chapter:

- To extend the models, assumptions, and analyses of Chapter 8 to deal with multi-factor between-subjects designs.

- To introduce the concept of interaction, providing illustrations of its analysis and interpretation.

9.2 THE TWO-FACTOR DESIGN: THE STRUCTURAL MODEL

9.2.1 The Model Equation

In these designs, there are two independent variables, A and B, with a levels of A, b levels of B, and n scores in each of the ab cells. A score will be represented as Y_{ijk}, the ith score at the jth level of A and the kth level of B. We want to test hypotheses about population means and therefore need a model that relates the observed scores to the means of the populations formed by the combinations of the variables A and B, and to the error component of each score. These population parameters and the sample statistics that estimate them are presented in Table 9.1.

Consider a specific combination of levels of A and B, say, A_j and B_k. In terms of the *Wiley–Voss* experiment described in Section 9.1, this would be a cell formed by the combination of one of the two formats and one of the four instructions. Because the same combination of treatments is applied to everyone in that cell, the scores in the population corresponding to A_j and B_k should vary only because of error variance due to individual differences in factors such as ability, motivation, or physical state, or differences in other factors that can affect performance. Stating this more formally,

$$Y_{ijk} = \mu_{jk} + \varepsilon_{ijk} \tag{9.1}$$

where μ_{jk} is defined in Table 9.1 as the mean of the population formed by A_j and B_k, and ε_{ijk} is the error component of the ith score in the cell formed by A_j and B_k in the experiment.

Now consider the possibility that scores in different combinations of treatments may differ systematically. It is useful to express the deviation of a score from the grand mean of all the populations by subtracting μ from both sides of Equation 9.1:

$$Y_{ijk} - \mu = (\mu_{jk} - \mu) + \varepsilon_{ijk} \tag{9.2}$$

The μ_{jk} may vary for any of three reasons; namely, they correspond to different levels of A and B,

Table 9.1 Population parameters and estimates for a two-factor design

Population parameters	Estimates
μ_{jk} = mean of the population of scores at A_j and B_k	$\bar{Y}_{.jk} = \sum_i Y_{ijk}/n$
$\mu_{j.} = \sum_k \mu_{jk}/b$ = mean of the populations in condition A_j	$\bar{Y}_{.j.} = \sum_i \sum_k Y_{ijk}/nb$
$\mu_{.k} = \sum_j \mu_{jk}/a$ = mean of the populations in condition B_k	$\bar{Y}_{..k} = \sum_i \sum_j Y_{ijk}/na$
$\mu = \sum_j \sum_k \mu_{jk}/ab$ = mean of all ab populations	$\bar{Y}_{...} = \sum_i \sum_j \sum_k Y_{ijk}/nab$
$\varepsilon_{ijk} = Y_{ijk} - \mu_{jk}$ = error component of Y_{ijk}	$e_{ijk} = Y_{ijk} - \bar{Y}_{.jk}$

and to different combinations of those levels. We can represent this idea by the following identity:

$$(\mu_{jk} - \mu) = (\mu_j - \mu) + (\mu_k - \mu) + [(\mu_{jk} - \mu) - (\mu_j - \mu) - (\mu_k - \mu)] \tag{9.3}$$

A simpler notation is

$$\mu_{jk} - \mu = a_j + \beta_k + (\alpha\beta)_{jk} \tag{9.4}$$

Equation 9.4 states that $\mu_{jk} - \mu$ is a sum of three effects. The first of these, a_j, is the *main effect* of treatment A; its value represents the extent to which the average score in the population defined by the treatment A_j differs from the mean of all the scores in the ab populations. Similarly, β_k is the main effect of treatment B and reflects the extent to which the average score in population B differs from the average of all the scores in the ab populations. Finally, $(\alpha\beta)_{jk}$ is the *interaction effect* of A and B. The interaction is the difference between μ_{jk} and μ that remains after removal of the main effects of A and B; that is,

$$(\alpha\beta)_{jk} = (\mu_{jk} - \mu) - (\mu_j - \mu) - (\mu_k - \mu) \tag{9.5a}$$

This interaction effect is more often represented by simplifying the right-hand term in Equation 9.5a:

$$(\alpha\beta)_{jk} = \mu_{jk} - \mu_j - \mu_k + \mu \tag{9.5b}$$

From Equation 9.4, we can substitute for $\mu_{jk} - \mu$ in Equation 9.2. Recognizing that nuisance variables will also contribute to the observed data, we have the structural model underlying tests of hypotheses for the two-factor design:

$$Y_{ijk} - \mu = a_j + \beta_k + (\alpha\beta)_{jk} + \varepsilon_{ijk} \tag{9.6}$$

In words, the variability among scores in the populations has four possible sources: the effects of manipulating A; the effects of manipulating B; the joint, or interaction, effects of A and B; and the error component. A more detailed summary of the model components and related assumptions is presented in Box 9.1.

Box 9.1 Components of the Structural Model

1. *The error component,* $\varepsilon_{ijk} = Y_{ijk} - \mu_{jk}$. The errors are independently and normally distributed with mean zero and variance σ_e^2, within each treatment population defined by a combination of levels of A and B.

2. *The main effect of treatment A,* $a_j = \mu_j - \mu$. The factor A is assumed to have fixed effects; that is, the a levels have been arbitrarily selected and are viewed as representing the population of levels. Then $\sum_j a_j = 0$. The F test of the A main effect tests the null hypothesis that

    $$H_0: \mu_{1.} = \mu_{2.} = \ldots = \mu_{j.} = \ldots = \mu_{a.}$$

    or, equivalently,

    $$H_0: a_1 = a_2 = \ldots = a_j = \ldots = a_a = 0$$

3. *The main effect of treatment B,* $\beta_k = \mu_k - \mu$. This is also a fixed-effect variable and so $\sum_k \beta_k = 0$. The F test of the B main effect tests the null hypothesis that

    $$H_0: \mu_{.1} = \mu_{.2} = \ldots = \mu_{.k} = \ldots = \mu_{.b}$$

    or, equivalently,

    $$H_0: \beta_1 = \beta_2 = \ldots = \beta_k = \ldots = \beta_b = 0$$

4. The *interaction effect of A_j and B_k*, $(\alpha\beta)_{jk} = \mu_{jk} - \mu_j - \mu_k + \mu$. Because both A and B have fixed effects, $\Sigma_j(\alpha\beta)_{jk} = \Sigma_k(\alpha\beta)_{jk} = 0$. The relevant null hypothesis is

$$H_0: (\alpha\beta)_{11} = (\alpha\beta)_{12} = \ldots = (\alpha\beta)_{jk} = \ldots = (\alpha\beta)_{ab} = 0$$

Equation 9.6 provides the basis for the analysis of variance for the two-factor design. We will develop this relation between the analysis of variance and the structural model in Section 9.3. However, before doing so, we will try to provide a better understanding of what the main and interaction effects represent.

9.2.2 Understanding Main and Interaction Effects

Assume that we have a 2×4 design. Further assume that the population means are those in Panel *a* of Table 9.2. Note that the main effects (α_j and β_k) are calculated by subtracting the *grand mean* (obtained by averaging over all scores) from the *marginal means* (those obtained by averaging all the means in a row or column). For designs with equal n, the main effects are independent or

Table 9.2   Treatment population means and effects

(*a*) Original population means

	B_1	B_2	B_3	B_4	μ_j	$\alpha_j = \mu_j - \mu$
A_1	65	50	47	58	55	5
A_2	43	48	51	38	45	-5
μ_k	54	49	49	48	$\mu = 50$	
$\beta_k = \mu_k - \mu$	4	-1	-1	-2		

(*b*) Population means after removing the A (α_j) and B (β_k) main effects

	B_1	B_2	B_3	B_4	Mean
A_1	56	46	43	55	50
A_2	44	54	57	45	50
Mean	50	50	50	50	$\mu = 50$

(*c*) Interaction effects; $(\alpha\beta)_{jk} = (\mu_{jk} - \mu) - \alpha_j - \beta_k$

	B_1	B_2	B_3	B_4	Mean
A_1	6	-4	-7	5	0
A_2	-6	4	7	-5	0
Mean	0	0	0	0	

orthogonal. That is, knowing how the means of one factor vary across levels tells us nothing about how the means vary on the other factor.

In Panel *b*, we have the population means after the main effects have been subtracted. For example, in the A_1B_2 population, the cell mean after removal of the main effects that have contributed to it is $50 - 5 - (-1) = 46$. Note that although the marginal means are now identical, the adjusted cell means still vary. The reason for this variation is the presence of interaction effects. If we subtract the grand mean, μ, from each of the values in Panel *b*, we obtain the results in Panel *c* of Table 9.2; these are the interaction effects associated with each cell. In summary, one definition of interaction effects is that they are the difference between the cell mean and the grand mean, after removing the main effects of the independent variables.

It is useful to compare the pattern of means in Panel *a* of Table 9.2 with the pattern in Panel *a* of Table 9.3. The means in Table 9.3 show exactly the same main effects of *A* and *B* as the means in Table 9.2, as seen by comparing the corresponding values of α_j and β_k of the two tables. However, Table 9.3 does not present an interaction; in that case, we say that *A* and *B* have *additive effects* because the mean of each cell is determined by *adding* the main effect of *A* and the main effect of *B* to the grand mean. The absence of interaction effects is shown by subtracting the row and column effects from each mean. For example, in the A_1B_1 cell, $59 - 5 - 4 = 50$; doing the same for all cells, the values are all also 50, as shown in Panel *b*. An important point that is implicit in this comparison of Tables 9.2 and 9.3 is that the magnitudes of the main effects and interaction are unrelated, or *orthogonal* to one another, in a design where *n* is equal for all conditions. Thus, the presence of one or both main effects does not tell us anything about the magnitude of the interaction, and vice versa.

Another way of comparing the two tables is particularly useful for understanding the meaning of an interaction. In Panel *a* of Table 9.4, the effect of *A* is computed at each level of *B* for the data of Table 9.2; this is done by subtracting the A_2 mean from the A_1 mean. These *simple effects* of *A* are also computed in Panel *b* for the data of Table 9.3. The key observation is that the values of the simple effects of *A* differ over levels of *B* in Panel *a*, indicating that *A* and *B* interact. In contrast, the

Table 9.3 Treatment population means with no interaction effects

	B_1	B_2	B_3	B_4	μ_j	$\alpha_j = \mu_j - \mu$
A_1	59	54	54	53	55	5
A_2	49	44	44	43	45	-5
μ_k	54	49	49	48	$\mu = 50$	
$\beta_k = \mu_k - \mu$	4	-1	-1	-2		

(*b*) Population means after removing the *A* (α_j) and *B* (β_k) main effects

	B_1	B_2	B_3	B_4	Mean
A_1	50	50	50	50	50
A_2	50	50	50	50	50
Mean	50	50	50	50	$\mu = 50$

Table 9.4 Simple effects of A at each level of B $(\mu_{1k} - \mu_{2k})$ for the data of Tables 9.2 and 9.3

(*a*) Population means from Table 9.2 with interaction effects

	B_1	B_2	B_3	B_4	μ_i
A_1	65	50	47	58	55
A_2	43	48	51	38	45
$\mu_{1k} - \mu_{2k}$	22	2	−4	20	10

(*b*) Population means from Table 9.3 with no interaction effects

	B_1	B_2	B_3	B_4	μ_i
A_1	59	54	53	53	55
A_2	49	44	43	43	45
$\mu_{1k} - \mu_{2k}$	10	10	10	10	10

simple effects of A are constant over levels of B in Panel b, indicating no interaction. Thus, *an interaction means that the size of the effect of factor A differs over levels of factor B or*, equivalently, that the effect of factor B depends on the level of factor A. The same observation may be made graphically. The means for Panel a of Table 9.4 are graphed in Panel a of Fig. 9.1; the means for Panel b of Table 9.4 are graphed in Panel b of Fig. 9.1. The obvious difference in the two graphs is that the curves in Panel a are not parallel, whereas the curves in Panel b are. Thus, with respect to the population means, an *interaction is a departure from parallelism*. We say that the interaction is a significant source of variance when the size of the effects of one variable changes significantly across levels of the other variable.

9.3 TWO-FACTOR DESIGNS: THE ANALYSIS OF VARIANCE

The analysis of the variability in the data for the two-factor design follows the same logic developed for the one-factor design presented in Chapter 8. The structural model (Equation 9.6) suggests a way to partition the deviation of a score from the grand mean, $Y_{ijk} - \overline{Y}_{...}$, into several components. We derive these components in Section 9.3.1, and then develop formulas for the sums of squares based on them in Section 9.3.2. We then construct mean squares and, subsequently, F statistics to test null hypotheses about main and interaction effects.

9.3.1 Components of the Scores

In Section 9.2.1, we assumed the structural model

$$Y_{ijk} = \mu + \alpha_j + \beta_k + (\alpha\beta)_{jk} + \varepsilon_{ijk}$$

After subtracting μ from both sides and substituting treatment population means, we have

$$Y_{ijk} - \mu = (\mu_j - \mu) + (\mu_k - \mu) + (\mu_{jk} - \mu_j - \mu_k + \mu) + \varepsilon_{ijk} \qquad (9.7)$$

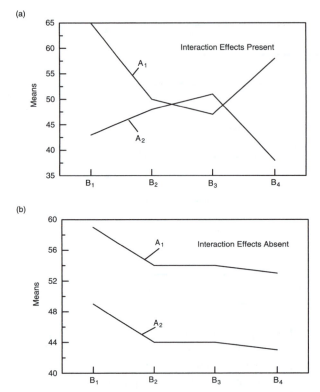

Fig. 9.1 Plots of the population means in Tables 9.2 and 9.3.

Substituting the estimates of these parameters from Table 9.1, we have the basis for the ANOVA:

$$(Y_{ijk} - \overline{Y}_{...}) = (\overline{Y}_{j.} - \overline{Y}_{...}) + (\overline{Y}_{.k} - \overline{Y}_{...}) + (\overline{Y}_{jk} - \overline{Y}_{j.} - \overline{Y}_{.k} + \overline{Y}_{...}) + (Y_{ijk} - \overline{Y}_{jk}) \qquad (9.8)$$

In words,

score − grand mean = main effect of A + main effect of B + interaction effect + residual error

9.3.2 Sums of Squares

Equation 9.8 forms the basis for the sums of squares; these are important components in tests of null hypotheses. Squaring both sides of Equation 9.8 and summing yields the sums of squares (*SS*) formulas in Panel *a* of Table 9.5. As a first step, we partitioned the total sum of squares into two components: a between-cells sum of squares and a within-cell (*S/AB*) sum of squares. The between-cell variability usually is not of interest in itself because it has several possible sources. For example, in the *Wiley–Voss* data set, the eight cell means may differ because they represent different formats, different instructions, or different combinations of formats and instructions. Although software packages do not include the between-subjects variability, SS_{cells}, we include it because it is involved in our conceptualization and calculation of the SS_{AB} and the $SS_{S/AB}$. The components of the between-cells sum of squares in Table 9.5 correspond to the main and interaction sources of variance that we wish to test.

The formulas presented in Table 9.5 define the sums of squares. Although statistical software

Table 9.5 The analysis of variance (ANOVA) table for the two-factor between-subjects design (*a*) and expected mean squares (*b*)

(*a*) ANOVA

Source	df	SS	MS	F
Total	$abn - 1$	$\sum\limits_{j}^{a}\sum\limits_{k}^{b}\sum\limits_{i}^{n}(Y_{ijk} - \overline{Y}_{...})^2$		
Between cells	$ab - 1$	$n\sum\limits_{j}^{a}\sum\limits_{k}^{b}(\overline{Y}_{jk} - \overline{Y}_{...})^2$		
A	$a - 1$	$nb\sum\limits_{j}^{a}(\overline{Y}_{j.} - \overline{Y}_{...})^2$	SS_A/df_A	$MS_A/MS_{S/AB}$
B	$b - 1$	$na\sum\limits_{k}^{b}(\overline{Y}_{.k.} - \overline{Y}_{...})^2$	SS_B/df_B	$MS_B/MS_{S/AB}$
AB	$(a-1)(b-1)$	$SS_{cells} - SS_A - SS_B$	SS_{AB}/df_{AB}	$MS_{AB}/MS_{S/AB}$
S/AB	$ab(n-1)$	$SS_{total} - SS_{cells}$	$SS_{S/AB}/df_{S/AB}$	

(*b*) Expected mean squares

SV	EMS
A	$\sigma_e^2 + nb\sum\limits_{j}\alpha_j^2/(a-1) = \sigma_e^2 + nb\theta_A^2$
B	$\sigma_e^2 + na\sum\limits_{k}\beta_k^2/(b-1) = \sigma_e^2 + na\theta_B^2$
AB	$\sigma_e^2 + n\sum\limits_{j}\sum\limits_{k}(\alpha\beta)_{jk}^2/(a-1)(b-1) = \sigma_e^2 + n\theta_{AB}^2$
S/AB	σ_e^2

Note: $\alpha_j = \mu_{j.} - \mu$, $\beta_k = \mu_{.k} - \mu$, and $(\alpha\beta)_{jk} = (\mu_{jk} - \mu) - \alpha_j - \beta_k = (\mu_{jk} - \mu_{j.} - \mu_{.k} + \mu)$. The θ^2 notation serves as a reminder that $\Sigma\alpha_j^2/(a-1)$ is not a variance; the variance of the treatment population means has a as the denominator.

usually will be available to perform the calculations, the formulas are presented to remind us that the sums of squares are indices of variability. For example, the SS_{total} is $abn - 1$ times the variance of all the scores, the SS_A is $bn(a-1)$ times the variance of the A marginal means, and the SS_{cells} is $n(ab-1)$ times the variance of the ab cell means. The tests of null hypotheses corresponding to the A, B, and AB sources of variance (SV) test whether those variances are greater than chance.

9.3.3 Degrees of Freedom

A formula for degrees of freedom is associated with each of the sources of variances. The df_{total} are $abn - 1$ because this SV represents the variability of all abn scores about the grand mean. The SS_{cells} is distributed on $ab - 1$ df because it involves the variability of the ab cell means about the grand mean. The df for the main effects have the same form as in Chapter 8; these SV reflect the variance of the a (or b) means about the grand mean and therefore one df is lost. The interaction degrees of freedom are

$$df_{AB} = (ab - 1) - (a - 1) - (b - 1) = (a - 1)(b - 1)$$

reflecting the adjustment of cell variability for the variability due to A and B. In practice, we can generate the degrees of freedom for an interaction just by multiplying the degrees of freedom for the interacting variables.

The $df_{S/AB}$ may be thought of as the difference between df_{total} and df_{cells};

$$df_{S/AB} = (abn - 1) - (ab - 1)$$

These degrees of freedom may also be viewed as the result of summing the degrees of freedom for variability within each cell; there are ab cells, each with $n - 1$ df, yielding $ab(n - 1)$ df. The two ways of thinking about degrees of freedom, as a difference between the total df and the cell df, or as a sum over cells, are equivalent: $(abn - 1) - (ab - 1) = ab(n - 1)$.

9.3.4 Mean Squares (*MS*), Expected Mean Squares (*EMS*), and *F* Ratios

As in the one-factor design, the MS of Table 9.5 are ratios of SS to df. Conceptually, however, the mean squares for the main effects are simple functions of variances. For example, MS_A is the variance of the a marginal means in the A conditions, multiplied by nb, the number of scores upon which each mean is based. Similarly, MS_B is the variance of the b marginal means in the B conditions, multiplied by na, the number of scores upon which each mean is based. The error mean square, $MS_{S/AB}$, is an average of the within-cell variances; it can be calculated as

$$MS_{S/AB} = (1/ab) \sum_j \sum_k s_{jk}^2$$

where s_{jk}^2 is the variance of the n scores in the cell defined by A_j and B_k.[1]

All three F ratios are formed by dividing by $MS_{S/AB}$. This is justified by the expected mean squares (*EMS*; see Panel b of Table 9.5). As we stated in Chapter 8, forming a ratio of two mean squares follows the rule that the numerator and denominator MS must have the same expectation when the null hypothesis corresponding to the numerator is true.

The *EMS* are derived by assuming the structural model of Equation 9.6, independence of the scores, and homogeneity of the population variances. In addition, if the treatment populations are normally distributed and the null hypothesis is true, the ratio of mean squares is distributed as F.[2]

We now have both a conceptual framework and formulas on which to base tests of hypotheses about main and interaction effects. We next apply this framework to the analysis of the inference verification test (*IVT*) data in Table 9.6. The complete data set, reported by Wiley and Voss (1999), includes a number of other measures and may be found in the *Wiley* file among the *Data Sets* pages on the website for this book.

---

[1]   Note that the mean square for the interaction is related to the variance of the cell means, but not as simply as is the case for the main effects. The variability associated with both main effects must be removed from the variability in the cell means; this happens at the level of the sums of squares calculations.

[2]   Strictly speaking, if the null hypothesis is true, we have the central F distribution whose cutoffs are presented in Appendix Table C.5. However, if the null hypothesis is not true, we have members of the noncentral F distribution family. The noncentral F distribution can be used to perform power calculations.

Table 9.6   Inference scores (percent correct) from Wiley and Voss (1999) with summary statistics

| Format | Instructions[a] | | | | |
	N	S	E	A	
	70	50	70	70	
	80	90	80	70	
	80	60	70	60	
Text	70	80	60	60	
	60	70	60	70	
	50	80	80	90	
	80	80	70	90	
	80	70	60	80	
$\bar{Y}_{Text,k} =$	71.25	72.5	68.75	73.75	$\bar{Y}_{Text} = 71.56$
$s^2_{Text,k} =$	126.79	164.29	69.64	141.07	
	100	70	60	100	
	80	70	60	90	
	60	80	80	100	
Web	60	50	80	80	
	60	90	80	90	
	70	60	60	100	
	90	100	80	70	
	90	70	80	90	
$\bar{Y}_{Web,k} =$	76.25	73.75	72.5	90	$\bar{Y}_{Web} = 78.1$
$s^2_{Web,k} =$	255.36	255.36	107.14	114.29	
$\bar{Y}_{j,Instruct} =$	73.75	73.13	70.63	81.88	$\bar{Y}_{..} = 74.84$

[a] N = Narrative, S = Summary, E = Explanation, and A = Argument.

9.3.5 The *Wiley–Voss* Example

Before considering the ANOVA, we should get some sense of the effects of our variables. Looking at the two marginal format means in the right-most column of Table 9.6, we find that performance for the web format ($\bar{Y}_{Web}$) was better than that for the text format ($\bar{Y}_{Text}$). This difference between the web and text formats is largely due to the argument (A) instructional condition; although the web format has a higher mean than the text format in all instructional conditions, the differences between web and text cell means are small except in the A column. Turning next to the marginal instructional means ($\bar{Y}_N$, $\bar{Y}_S$, $\bar{Y}_E$, and $\bar{Y}_A$), we find the IVT mean to be higher in the argument condition than in any of the others. Again, however, we must qualify this; the advantage of the argument condition is quite pronounced for the web format, but rather small in the text format. Whether we view the data as showing that the difference between format means depends on instructions, or as showing that the differences among instructional means depend on format, our focus should be on the interaction of format and instructions. This is clearer in the bar graph of Fig. 9.2. Although web learning has an advantage in all four instructional conditions, that advantage is clearly larger in the A condition than in any of the other three.

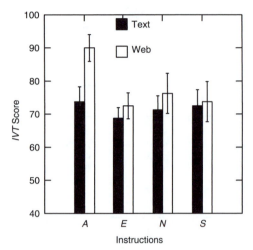

Fig. 9.2 Bar graph of the Wiley–Voss (1999) *IVT* data.

In addition to examining the means, we also checked for any departures from the assumptions underlying the hypothesis tests we wished to perform. Box plots and the Levene tests failed to reveal any violations of the assumption of homogeneity of variance severe enough to undermine conclusions based on the tests of main and interaction effects. Nor were any outliers present in the box plots. Finally, plots of residuals (deviations of scores from the cell means) and significance tests revealed no departure from normality. In summary, the ANOVA appears to provide appropriate tests for the *IVT* data.

The results of the analysis of variance for the data are presented in Table 9.7. As the experimenters hypothesized, a significantly higher proportion of inferences were correctly verified by subjects in the web than in the text format condition. This means that the average of the four populations of *IVT* scores obtained under the web format differs from the average of the four populations of *IVT* scores obtained under the text format. In terms of Table 9.6, it is the *marginal means*, $\overline{Y}_{Web}$ (78.13) and $\overline{Y}_{Text}$ (71.56), that differ significantly. We can conclude that, *averaging over levels of instruction*, the effects of the two formats differ significantly. However, this does not provide information about the effects of the formats at any particular level of instructions.

The experimenters also were interested in whether instructions would affect performance. They reported that the effect was "marginally significant" because the *p*-value was .07, short of the .05 level usually required for statistical significance. We will consider further the question of the effect

Table 9.7   The analysis of variance (ANOVA) table for the Wiley–Voss data

SV	df	SS	MS	F	p
Total	63	10,998.44			
Between cells	7	2,360.94			
Format (*F*)	1	689.06	689.06	4.47	.039
Instructions (*I*)	3	1,142.19	380.73	2.47	.071
FI	3	529.69	176.56	1.14	.337
S/FI	56	8,367.50	154.24		

of instructions later in this chapter when we calculate various measures of effect size for the *Wiley–Voss* data.

The *F* test of the *Format* × *Instructions* interaction tests the null hypothesis that the effects of one variable are the same under all levels of the other variable. One statement of the null hypothesis of no interaction is that the difference between the text and web population means is the same under all types of instructions. This may be represented as

$$H_0: (\mu_{Text, N} - \mu_{Web, N}) = (\mu_{Text, S} - \mu_{Web, S}) = (\mu_{Text, E} - \mu_{Web, E}) = (\mu_{Text, A} - \mu_{Web, A})$$

where, for example, $\mu_{Text, N}$ is the mean of the population of scores obtained under the text format and the narrative instructions.

An equivalent statement of the null hypothesis of no interaction is that the effects of instructions are the same at the two format levels. We could state this null hypothesis as

$$H_0: (\mu_{Text, N} - \mu_{Text, S}) = (\mu_{Web, N} - \mu_{Web, S})$$

and

$$(\mu_{Text, S} - \mu_{Text, E}) = (\mu_{Web, S} - \mu_{Web, E})$$

and

$$(\mu_{Text, E} - \mu_{Text, A}) = (\mu_{Web, E} - \mu_{Web, A})$$

Both forms of H_0 are ways of stating that the effect of one factor is the same at each level of the other factor (i.e., parallel functions).

The difference between the observed text and web means under argument (*A*) instructions appears considerably larger than the other differences, as evidenced in the means of Table 9.6 and the bar graph of Fig. 9.2. Nevertheless, the *F* test of the interaction fell well short of significance. This raises several questions. Given that the *Instructions* and the *Format* × *Instructions* sources of variance were not significant, is it proper to test more specific hypotheses related to those sources such as whether the narrative and argument means differ? If so, should we have different criteria for significance than for the usual *t* test? And what should our error term be? We will consider those questions, and attempt to further clarify the concept of interaction, in Chapter 10.

In sum, the analyses of the *Wiley–Voss* data are somewhat ambiguous. The effect of instructions is marginally significant. Graphically, there appears to be an interaction, but the *F* test does not confirm its reliability. The only significant result is the effect of format, showing better performance with the web presentation. However, there is some doubt about how to interpret this seemingly straightforward result because of the question about whether the effect of format is due to the results from the Argument condition.

At this point, we complete our presentation of the basic ANOVA by extending it to designs with more than two factors.

9.4 THREE-FACTOR BETWEEN-SUBJECTS DESIGNS

9.4.1 The General Case

Extending the two-factor design to the three-factor design is straightforward; the only new concept is the three-factor interaction. Therefore, we will present the general case of the three-factor design concisely so that we may reinforce the basic concepts already developed for the simpler one-factor and two-factor designs.

The general case of the three-factor between-subjects design involves a levels of A, b levels of B, c levels of C, and n scores in each of the abc cells. The relevant indices are

$$i = 1, 2, \ldots, n; j = 1, 2, \ldots, a; k = 1, 2, \ldots, b; \text{ and } m = 1, 2, \ldots, c$$

The structural model looks much like that for the two-factor experiment except that there are now three two-factor interactions and there is the added three-factor interaction:

$$Y_{ijkm} = \mu + \alpha_j + \beta_k + \gamma_m + (\alpha\beta)_{jk} + (\alpha\gamma)_{jm} + (\beta\gamma)_{km} + (\alpha\beta\gamma)_{jkm} + \varepsilon_{ijkm} \tag{9.9}$$

Definitions in terms of population means, together with estimates of those means, are presented in Table 9.8. The only new definition is that of the interaction effect for the cell $A_j B_k C_m$; this is the difference between the cell mean and the grand mean, adjusted for all main and first-order interaction effects that contribute to the cell.

The sums of squares follow directly from the parameter estimates by squaring each term in the Estimate column of Table 9.8, and summing over the indices. The results of this process are presented in Table 9.9 together with the degrees of freedom. The only new df term is $(a-1)(b-1)(c-1)$, the df_{ABC}. This follows by subtracting the main and two-factor df from $abc - 1$, the between-cells df.

The mean squares are obtained, as usual, by dividing sums of squares by degrees of freedom. $MS_{S/ABC}$, the average within-cell variance, is the error term against which all main and interaction terms are tested. As in other designs, expected mean squares, presented in Table 9.10, provide the rationale for this choice of error terms. These have been derived from the structural model (Equation 9.9) under the usual assumptions that the scores in the abc treatment populations are independently distributed and that the population variances all equal σ_e^2. In addition, all three factors are assumed to have *fixed effects*; that is, the levels have been arbitrarily selected and not randomly sampled from a universe of treatment levels.

9.4.2 Extending the *Wiley–Voss* Example

To illustrate the concepts and analyses, we add a hypothetical third factor to the design of the *Wiley–Voss* experiment. Assume that there are only two levels of instruction (I), Summary and Argument, and two formats (F), Text and Web. Further assume that subjects are divided with respect to experience (E)—either those who had prior experience searching the Internet (experts) or

Table 9.8 Parameters of the structural model for a three-factor design

Source	Population parameter	Estimate
A	$\alpha_j = \mu_{j..} - \mu_{...}$	$\overline{Y}_{.j..} - \overline{Y}_{....}$
B	$\beta_k = \mu_{.k.} - \mu_{...}$	$\overline{Y}_{..k.} - \overline{Y}_{....}$
C	$\gamma_m = \mu_{..m} - \mu_{...}$	$\overline{Y}_{...m} - \overline{Y}_{....}$
AB	$(\alpha\beta)_{jk} = (\mu_{jk.} - \mu_{...}) - \alpha_j - \beta_k$	$\overline{Y}_{.jk.} - \overline{Y}_{.j..} - \overline{Y}_{..k.} + \overline{Y}_{....}$
AC	$(\alpha\gamma)_{jm} = (\mu_{j.m} - \mu_{...}) - \alpha_j - \gamma_m$	$\overline{Y}_{.j.m} - \overline{Y}_{.j..} - \overline{Y}_{...m} + \overline{Y}_{....}$
BC	$(\beta\gamma)_{km} = (\mu_{.km} - \mu_{...}) - \beta_k - \gamma_m$	$\overline{Y}_{..km} - \overline{Y}_{..k.} - \overline{Y}_{...m} + \overline{Y}_{....}$
ABC	$(\alpha\beta\gamma)_{jkm} = (\mu_{jkm} - \mu_{...}) - \alpha_j - \beta_k$	$\overline{Y}_{.jkm} + \overline{Y}_{.j..} + \overline{Y}_{..k.} + \overline{Y}_{...m}$
	$\quad - \gamma_m - (\alpha\beta)_{jk} - (\alpha\gamma)_{jm} - (\beta\gamma)_{km}$	$\quad - \overline{Y}_{.jk.} - \overline{Y}_{.j.m} - \overline{Y}_{..km} - \overline{Y}_{....}$
Error	ε_{ijkm}	$Y_{ijkm} - \overline{Y}_{.jkm}$

Table 9.9 Degrees of freedom and sums of squares in a three-factor design

Source	df	SS
Total	$abcn - 1$	$\sum_i \sum_j \sum_k \sum_m (Y_{ijkm} - \bar{Y}_{....})^2$
Between cells	$abc - 1$	$n \sum_j \sum_k \sum_m (\bar{Y}_{.jkm} - \bar{Y}_{....})^2$
A	$a - 1$	$nbc \sum_j (\bar{Y}_{.j..} - \bar{Y}_{....})^2$
B	$b - 1$	$nac \sum_k (\bar{Y}_{..k.} - \bar{Y}_{....})^2$
C	$c - 1$	$nab \sum_m (\bar{Y}_{...m} - \bar{Y}_{....})^2$
AB	$(a-1)(b-1)$	$nc \sum_j \sum_k (\bar{Y}_{.jk.} - \bar{Y}_{.j..} - \bar{Y}_{..k.} + \bar{Y}_{....})^2$
AC	$(a-1)(c-1)$	$nb \sum_j \sum_m (\bar{Y}_{.j.m} - \bar{Y}_{.j..} - \bar{Y}_{...m} + \bar{Y}_{....})^2$
BC	$(b-1)(c-1)$	$na \sum_k \sum_m (\bar{Y}_{..km} - \bar{Y}_{..k.} - \bar{Y}_{...m} + \bar{Y}_{....})^2$
ABC	$(a-1)(b-1)(c-1)$	$n \sum_j \sum_k \sum_m (\bar{Y}_{.jkm} + \bar{Y}_{.j..} + \bar{Y}_{..k.} + \bar{Y}_{...m} - \bar{Y}_{.jk.} - \bar{Y}_{.j.m} - \bar{Y}_{..km} - \bar{Y}_{....})^2$
S/ABC (within cells)	$abc(n-1)$	$SS_{tot} - SS_{B.cells}$

those who were novices. Assume that there are 10 scores in each of the eight cells; i.e., $n = 10$ and $N = 80$. The means for this hypothetical experiment are presented in Table 9.11. The $MS_{S/cells}$ is presented as having a value of 154, but the relevant condition variances on which that value is based have been omitted. Note that we are dealing with the simplest case of a three-factor design, one in which there are only two levels of each of the three variables. The simplicity of the design enables us to concentrate on basic concepts. The design has the added advantage that it is a very common research design.

Main Effects. In the ANOVA, there will be three sources of main effects: instructions, format, and experience. We can view these main effects by calculating the marginal means separately for each factor. For example, the test of the format source of variance involves a comparison of the text and web marginal means. These means are obtained by averaging over the four combinations of instructions and experience. As can be seen in the right-hand column in the bottom panel of Table 9.11, the text and web means are 72.375 and 86.125. The significance test is a test of the null hypothesis that, *averaging over the four populations corresponding to the combinations of experience and instructions*, there is no difference between the population text and web means.

Table 9.10   Expected mean squares (*EMS*) for the three-factor design

SV	EMS
A	$\sigma_e^2 + nbc \sum_j \alpha_j^2/(a-1)$
B	$\sigma_e^2 + nac \sum_k \beta_k^2/(b-1)$
C	$\sigma_e^2 + nab \sum_m \gamma_m^2/(c-1)$
AB	$\sigma_e^2 + nc \sum_j \sum_k (\alpha\beta)_{jk}^2/(a-1)(b-1)$
AC	$\sigma_e^2 + nb \sum_j \sum_m (\alpha\gamma)_{jm}^2/(a-1)(c-1)$
BC	$\sigma_e^2 + na \sum_k \sum_m (\beta\gamma)_{km}^2/(b-1)(c-1)$
ABC	$\sigma_e^2 + n \sum_j \sum_k \sum_m (\alpha\beta\gamma)_{jkm}^2/(a-1)(b-1)(c-1)$
S/ABC	σ_e^2

Note: The parameters of the structural model are defined in Table 9.8.

Table 9.11   Means for a hypothetical extension of the Wiley–Voss experiment

		Summary	Argument	Mean
Novice	Text	71.25	73.75	72.50
	Web	76.50	90.00	83.25
	Mean	73.875	81.875	77.875
Expert	Text	70.50	74.00	72.25
	Web	88.25	89.75	89.00
	Mean	79.375	81.875	80.625
		Averaging over novices and experts		
	Text	70.875	73.875	72.375
	Web	82.375	89.875	86.125
	Mean	76.625	81.875	79.25

Note: Each cell contains 10 scores; i.e. $n = 10$, $N = 80$. The error mean square, $MS_{S/cells} = 154$.

To test this null hypothesis, we can calculate MS_F by computing the variance of the two marginal means, 94.53125, and then multiplying by the number of scores each mean is based on, 40, to obtain $MS_F = 3{,}781.25$. To construct the F test, divide MS_F by $MS_{S/cells} = 3{,}781.25/154 = 24.55$, which is significant on 1 and 72 degrees of freedom.

An astute reader might wonder whether the effect of format could be tested by a simple t test for independent means. In fact, we can calculate a t statistic:

$$t = \frac{\overline{Y}_{Web} - \overline{Y}_{Text}}{\sqrt{MS_{S/cells}\left(\frac{1}{n_{Web}} + \frac{1}{n_{Text}}\right)}}$$

$$= \frac{86.125 - 73.375}{\sqrt{154\left(\frac{1}{40} + \frac{1}{40}\right)}} = 4.59$$

Alternatively, noting that when the numerator has 1 degree of freedom, $F = t^2$; we could have calculated

$$F = \frac{(\overline{Y}_{Web} - \overline{Y}_{Text})^2 \Big/ \left(\frac{1}{n_{Web}} + \frac{1}{n_{Text}}\right)}{MS_{S/cells}} \tag{9.10}$$

The instruction and experience sources can be tested in a similar manner.[3] We encourage the reader to compute the mean squares for instruction and experience and confirm that they match the values in Table 9.12.

Table 9.12   The analysis of variance (ANOVA) table for the hypothetical data in Table 9.11

SV	df	SS	MS	F	p
Total	79				
Between cells	7	5,127.50	732.5		
Format (F)	1	3,781.25	3,781.25	24.55	.000
Instructions (I)	1	551.25	551.25	3.58	.05
Experience (E)	1	151.25	151.25	<1	
FI	1	101.25	101.25	<1	
FE	1	180.00	180.00	1.17	
IE	1	151.25	151.25	<1	
FIE	1	211.25	211.25	1.37	
S/FIE	72		154.00		

First-Order (Two-Factor) Interactions.   There are three possible two-factor interactions in a three-factor design. In the *Wiley–Voss* example, they are: *Format × Instructions (FI)*, *Format × Experience (FE)*, and *Instructions × Experience (IE)*. The *FE* interaction is of particular interest because computer experience should not have an effect in the text condition, but it well might in the

---

[3] Note that the t test computed in this example appropriately uses an error term based on the within-cell variances of the three-factor design. This is not the error term that would be calculated by a software program like SPSS if the user were to simply request a t test comparing the web and text formats. Rather, a simple t test that ignores the other two factors in the design would compute an error term that would be inflated by effects involving the two ignored factors.

web condition. The interpretation of this interaction is essentially the same as if F and E were the only factors in the experiment, except that in this case, the relevant means are obtained by averaging over the levels of the third variable, instructions. These means are in the right-most column in the upper two panels of Table 9.11. A better way to see the possible interaction is to redisplay the means:

		Experience	
		Expert	Novice
Format	Web	89.00	72.25
	Text	83.25	72.50

The pattern of means indicates that the advantage of the expert over the novice is, as hypothesized, greater when information is presented in the web format. The significance test of this interaction is a test of the null hypothesis that, *averaging over the two levels of instructions*, there is no difference between experts and novices in the magnitude of the effect of format.

Calculating the interaction sum of squares is generally too tedious to do by hand. However, in the case of interactions based on 1 df, we can represent the interaction as a difference between differences. This makes hand calculations more manageable; much more importantly, expressing a 2×2 interaction as a difference between simple effects is a better way to understand what is being tested. Let I indicate the interaction effect; then,

$$I_{FE} = (89.00 - 83.25) - (72.25 - 72.50) = 6.00$$

In words, the effect of format is 6 points greater for experts than for novices. Rearranging terms, this FE interaction can be rewritten as a difference between the sums of diagonal cell means:

$$I_{FE} = (89.00 + 72.50) - (83.25 + 72.25)$$

If we calculate the averages of the two diagonal sums, we have the basis for a test of the difference between two means; these are $(89.00 + 72.50)/2$, or 80.75, and $(83.25 + 72.25)/2$, or 77.75. As with our example in testing the main effect of format, we can test the FE interaction by comparing these two means via a t test:

$$t = \frac{80.75 - 77.75}{\sqrt{154\left(\frac{1}{40} + \frac{1}{40}\right)}} = 1.081$$

Alternatively, applying Equation 9.10, we can construct an F test:

$$F = \frac{(80.75 - 77.75)^2 \left/ \left(\frac{1}{40} + \frac{1}{40}\right)\right.}{154} = 1.169 = 1.081^2$$

The degrees of freedom for the error term are $abc(n - 1)$, or 72 in this design, assuming 10 subjects in each of the eight cells. The F of 1.17 is not significant on 1 and 72 df and therefore we lack sufficient evidence to reject the hypothesis of no interaction. In other words, we cannot conclude that the advantage of the web format over the text format is significantly greater for experts than for novices.

The tests of the *FI* and *IE* interactions follow from the example of the test of the *FE* interaction.

The Second-Order (Three-Factor) Interaction.   The eight cell means in Table 9.11 are plotted in Fig. 9.3. We assigned instructions to the x-axis, and had the experts' means in one panel and the novices in the other, with different lines for the two formats. However, this assignment of variables in the plot is arbitrary. We could have had the two formats, or the two types of instructions, in different panels. We will soon discuss some factors that may influence the decision when plotting means from a three-factor experiment. For now, let's focus on the interpretation of the second-order interaction.

In the left-hand panel of Fig. 9.3, we have plotted the interaction of format and instructions at the novice level of experience; we designate this interaction by *FI/N*. In the $2 \times 2 \times 2$ design, it is helpful to think of the three-factor interaction as a contrast of two-factor interactions. For example, in the novice panel on the left, the advantage of the web over the text format is larger in the argument than in the summary condition. However, the opposite is true in the expert panel on the right; there, the advantage of the web format over the text format is larger under summary than under argument instructions. Looking at the actual means, the *FI* interaction in the novice condition is

$$I_{FI/N} = (90.00 - 73.75) - (76.50 - 71.25)$$

The corresponding *FI* interaction in the expert condition is

$$I_{FI/E} = (89.75 - 74.00) - (88.25 - 70.50)$$

The *FIE* interaction is the difference between the two interactions; that is,

$$I_{FIE} = [(90.00 - 73.75) - (76.50 - 71.25)] - [(89.75 - 74.00) - (88.25 - 70.50)]$$

We can rewrite this as

$$I_{FIE} = (90.00 + 71.25 + 74.00 + 88.25) - (73.75 + 76.50 + 89.75 + 70.50)$$

The average of the four terms to the left of the minus sign is 80.875 and the average of the four

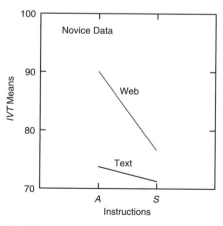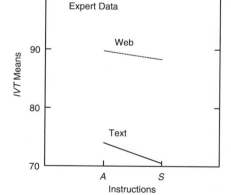

Fig. 9.3. A plot of the means in Table 9.8.

terms to the right of the minus sign is 77.625. We again have a basis for converting an interaction into a comparison of two means and therefore can test the three-way interaction with either a t test or an F test.

$$t = \frac{80.875 - 77.675}{\sqrt{154\left(\frac{1}{40} + \frac{1}{40}\right)}} = 1.171$$

or

$$F = \frac{(80.875 - 77.675)^2 \Big/ \left(\frac{1}{40} + \frac{1}{40}\right)}{154} = 1.372 = t^2$$

These significance tests are both relevant to the null hypothesis that the magnitude of the FE interaction does not differ for experts and novices. Based on 1 and 72 df, the F test does not approach significance. We conclude that the three-factor interaction is not significant. We cannot conclude that the FI population interaction differs as a function of the level of experience with computers. Nor does the FE interaction differ as a function of instructions, nor the IE as a function of the format. No matter which simple two-factor interactions are contrasted, the numerator of the F ratio always is equivalent to a contrast of the same two sets of four means.

9.4.4 More on 2^3 Interactions

A significant three-factor interaction means that the simple interaction effects of any two variables vary as a function of the level of the third variable. Researchers often understand this to mean that whenever the plot of the AB combinations looks different at different levels of C, the three-factor interaction is likely to be significant. However, plots like the one in Fig. 9.3 can be misleading with respect to the three-factor interaction. The following set of means should help us understand this point.

	C_1		C_2	
	B_1	B_2	B_1	B_2
A_1	22	11	34	23
A_2	20	14	23	17

Panel a of Fig. 9.4 presents a plot of the eight cell means under consideration. If these were population means, would you think that there is a second-order interaction? The pattern of means looks different at C_1 than at C_2; the lines cross in the C_1 panel, but not in the C_2 panel. As a result, students usually believe that an ABC interaction is present. In fact, if we calculate the interaction contrast, we find it is exactly zero, so there cannot be an ABC interaction. For example, calculating the AB interaction contrast at each level of C, and subtracting,

$$I_{ABC} = I_{AB/C_1} - I_{AB/C_2} = [(22 - 11) - (20 - 14)] - [(34 - 23) - (25 - 19)] = 0.$$

Sometimes plotting the data in different ways is helpful. In Panel b of Fig. 9.4, the data from Panel a have been replotted. Several points are now clearer than in Panel a. In particular, it should

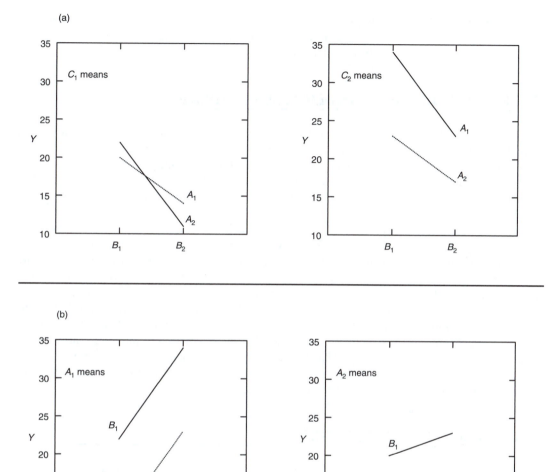

Fig. 9.4. Two ways of plotting a three-factor interaction.

be evident that there is no *BC* interaction, something that was not at all clear in Panel *a*. It also appears that there is an *AB* interaction because the difference between the B_1 and B_2 lines is greater in the A_1 panel than in the A_2 panel. Finally, it appears that there is no second-order interaction because the *BC* interaction contrast is zero in both panels. Of course, these are idealized data points, lacking the variability present in real data. However, the point still stands that it is often helpful to plot data in several ways. Different patterns may become evident, making clearer why certain effects in the ANOVA were significant whereas others were not.

The example of Panel *a* of Fig. 9.4 demonstrates that the pattern of means can be deceptive. However, some patterns will clearly signal the possibility of a three-factor interaction. If the lines in an *AB* plot are approximately parallel (i.e., there is no *AB* interaction) at one or more levels of *C*, but there is an interaction at least at one other level of *C*, an *ABC* interaction is indicated. Also, if the lines in one panel converge whereas those in other panels diverge, an *ABC* interaction is indicated. If the two *AB* plots are the same (or displaced by a constant amount), except for one point, there is reason to expect a three-factor interaction.

9.5 MORE THAN THREE INDEPENDENT VARIABLES

The analyses of data from between-subject designs involving more than three factors are in all respects straightforward generalizations of the material presented for two- and three-factor designs. However, designs with four or more factors become unwieldy in a couple of respects. Each variable and each possible combination of variables is a potential contributor to the total variability, and so is the variability among scores within each cell of the design. As the number of factors increases, the number of possible effects to be tested increase rapidly; with *f* factors there are $2^f - 1$ possible effects to test. For example, with five factors there are 31 possible effects: 5 main effects, 10 two-way interactions, 10 three-way interactions, 5 four-way interactions, and 1 five-way interaction.

The calculations of higher-order interactions follow directly from what we learned for two- and three-factor interactions. As might be guessed, the degrees of freedom for any higher-order interaction are a product of the degrees of freedom for the variables entering into the interaction. For example, an *ABCD* interaction would have $(a - 1)(b - 1)(c - 1)(d - 1)$ *df*. However, although the calculations are simple, the interpretation of such higher-order interactions is often difficult. We can say that a significant four-way interaction indicates that the interaction of any three variables is a function of the level of the fourth variable, but that is not very enlightening. Unless we have prior grounds for expecting such interactions to be significant, or can attribute the interaction to some subset of cell means, care should be taken before making too much of the result.

9.6 MEASURES OF EFFECT SIZE

In Chapter 8, we introduced η^2 and ω^2 as measures of effect size. Both measures assessed the magnitude of an effect against the total variability in the experiment. There are problems with this general approach to measuring effect size when we consider multi-factor designs. Namely, the introduction of more factors into a design will generally result in an increase in total variability. As a result, the assessment of the magnitude of the effect of some factor, *A*, will decrease as the number of factors in the design increases. In short, the use of η^2 or ω^2 as measures of importance does not allow comparisons across designs with different numbers of factors.

The solution that has been offered for this problem is to use either *partial* η^2 or *partial* ω^2 to assess effect size in a design. Partial η^2 is defined as $SS_{Effect}/(SS_{Effect} + SS_{S/cells})$. Partial ω^2 is defined similarly as $\sigma_{Effect}^2 / (\sigma_{Effect}^2 + \sigma_e^2)$. These measures do not depend on the number of factors in a design because they explicitly exclude other factors from consideration. However, partial η^2 and partial ω^2 do not solve the problem of comparability of measures across designs.

In order to create effect size measures that are comparable across designs, we must take into account the nature of the factors in the design. We will follow the lead of Olejnik and Algina (2003), who proposed a distinction between extrinsic and intrinsic factors in a design (also, see Cohen, 1973). An *extrinsic factor* is a variable that is manipulable and therefore independent of subject characteristics and other factors in a design. For example, the dosage level of a drug or the number of presentations of an item in a memory experiment are examples of extrinsic factors. An *intrinsic factor* is a variable that cannot be manipulated, although it might be controlled (e.g., by blocking on the factor) or measured. For example, in a learning experiment, intrinsic factors might include ability or prior experience with the task. The total variance in an experiment varies as a function of the number of extrinsic factors in the design. In contrast, total variance is not influenced by the number of intrinsic factors in a design because those factors contribute variability whether or not they are measured or controlled.

The distinction between extrinsic and intrinsic factors implies that the effect size statistic for a factor A should meet two criteria:

1. The statistic should not be affected by the contribution of extrinsic factors.
2. The baseline for assessing an effect size should include both random variance and variability associated with intrinsic factors.

Let us see how these criteria can be applied to the two measures of effect size we have been considering.

9.6.1 Eta-Squared (η^2) for the Multi-Factor Between-Subjects Design

The first criterion is readily met. For example, in a three-factor experiment in which all the factors have been manipulated, the statistic would be

$$\eta_p^2 \, (Effect) = \frac{SS_{Effect}}{SS_{Effect} + SS_{S/cells}} \tag{9.11}$$

As we have seen, this statistic is referred to as *partial* η^2. We use the subscript "p" in the notation to distinguish partial η^2 from the classical η^2 defined in Chapter 8. η_p^2 is an appropriate measure of effect size in a design that contains only extrinsic factors. It is not appropriate, however, if the design contains intrinsic factors, as in the next example.

Assume that one of the three factors in the experiment is the subject's experience with the task. Factors such as experience, or gender, or level of ability are intrinsic to the subject so they should be retained in the denominator of our calculation of η^2. Olejnik and Algina (2003) propose a statistic they call *general eta-squared*, which we will notate with a "g" in the subscript to distinguish it from classical and partial eta-squared. In a design with two extrinsic factors (A, B) and one intrinsic, C, η_g^2 for A now would be

$$\eta_g^2 \, (A) = \frac{SS_A}{SS_A + SS_C + SS_{AC} + SS_{BC} + SS_{ABC} + SS_{S/cells}} \tag{9.12a}$$

which is equivalent to

$$\eta_g^2 \, (A) = \frac{SS_A}{SS_{total} - SS_B - SS_{AB}} \tag{9.12b}$$

The reasoning behind this equation is that if we were comparing this statistic with one based on a one-factor design, the error variance in the one-factor design would include variability due to the intrinsic factor, C, and its interaction with other factors. Therefore, in order to have comparable values of η^2 for the two designs, we include the intrinsic sources of variability in the denominator of the statistic for the two-factor design.

Now suppose we wanted a measure of the effect size for the intrinsic factor, C, in a three-factor design. Then,

$$\eta_g^2(C) = \frac{SS_C}{SS_C + SS_{AC} + SS_{BC} + SS_{ABC} + SS_{S/cells}} \tag{9.13a}$$

which can be rewritten as

$$\eta_g^2(C) = \frac{SS_C}{SS_{total} - SS_A - SS_B - SS_{AB}} \tag{9.13b}$$

We may summarize developments as follows:

The denominator of η_g^2 includes the sums of squares for the effect of interest, for the within cell error term, and for all intrinsic effects and their interactions.

This rule holds whether the effect of interest is a main or interaction effect. As one further example, consider the design of Table 9.11 in which *Format* and *Instructions* are extrinsic factors and *Experience* is an intrinsic factor. If we wanted eta-squared for the *Format × Instruction* interaction,

$$\eta_g^2(FI) = \frac{SS_{FI}}{SS_{FI} + SS_E + SS_{FE} + SS_{IE} + SS_{FIE} + SS_{S/FEI}} = \frac{SS_{FI}}{SS_{total} - SS_I - SS_F}$$

Using the results in Table 9.12, $\eta_g^2(FI) = 101.25/(16,215.5 - 551.25 - 151.25) = .007$. Clearly, the interaction makes only a small contribution. Suppose that instead of experience, our third factor had been some manipulated variable—perhaps the time allowed for studying the material. In that case, the general eta-squared formula reduces to partial eta-squared:

$$\eta_g^2(FI) = SS_{FI} / (SS_{FI} + SS_{S/cells}) = \eta_p^2(FI)$$

and the proportion of variance when all factors are extrinsic is now $101.25/(101.25 + 11088)$, or .009, slightly larger than before, but still small.

We conclude our discussion of eta-squared with a caution. Statistical packages do not compute values of general η^2; for example, SPSS outputs values of partial eta-squared. As we have argued, partial eta-squared values generally are not comparable across different experimental designs, whereas general eta-squared values are comparable. Although it is tempting to report the partial η^2 values readily available in a computer output, investigators should calculate and report values of general eta-squared.

9.6.2 Omega-Squared (ω^2) for the Multi-Factor Between-Subjects Design

Although η_g^2 is easily calculated and interpreted, it is an overestimate of the population variance attributable to a factor. As we discussed in Chapter 8, $\hat{\omega}^2$ is more satisfactory in that respect. Most commonly, *partial* ω^2 has been reported. In a multi-factor design in which we wish to measure the effect of factor A, this parameter would be defined as

$$\omega_p^2(A) = \sigma_A^2 / (\sigma_A^2 + \sigma_e^2)$$

However, we prefer to again follow the approach suggested by Olejnik and Algina (2003). Therefore, we will focus our discussion on *general* ω^2. Because our estimate of ω_g^2 requires estimates of population variances., we first define a general formula for the estimate of the variance of any main or interaction effects, assuming that all levels of all variables have been arbitrarily selected; that is, that these are *fixed-effect variables*.[4] For such between-subjects design, the general formula is

$$\hat{\sigma}^2_{Effect} = df_{Effect} \times (MS_{Effect} - MS_{S/cells})/N \tag{9.14}$$

where N is the total number of scores. For example, for a three-factor between-subjects design, the estimate of the variance of the AB population interaction effects is

$$\hat{\sigma}^2_{AB} = (a-1)(b-1)(MS_{AB} - MS_{S/ABC})/abcn$$

Using the example of Table 9.11, the estimates of the population variances for the sources listed in Table 9.12 are

$\hat{\sigma}^2_F$	$\hat{\sigma}^2_I$	$\hat{\sigma}^2_E$	$\hat{\sigma}^2_{FI}$	$\hat{\sigma}^2_{FE}$	$\hat{\sigma}^2_{IE}$	$\hat{\sigma}^2_{FIE}$
45.341	4.966	0	0	.325	0	.716

Estimates have been set to zero when calculations based on Equation 9.14 had negative results, and σ^2_e is estimated by $MS_{S/cells}$.

Once the estimates of population variances have been calculated, we can calculate $\hat{\omega}^2$. We will follow the notational conventions introduced for η^2 to distinguish three variants of ω^2; namely, ω^2 without a subscript denotes the classical ω^2 introduced in Chapter 8, ω^2_p denotes partial ω^2, and ω^2_g denotes general ω^2. We need only a slight revision of the rule we formulated for calculating an estimate of general ω^2, $\hat{\omega}^2_g$:

The denominator of $\hat{\omega}^2_g$ includes the estimates of variances for the effect of interest, for the within cell error term, and for all intrinsic effects and their interactions.

Some examples should clarify this rule. Assume that we have three extrinsic factors; say, format, instructions, and time exposed to the material. Then, the estimate of *general* $\hat{\omega}^2$ for format is

$$\hat{\omega}^2_g(F) = \frac{\hat{\sigma}^2_F}{\hat{\sigma}^2_F + \hat{\sigma}^2_e} = \frac{(f-1)(MS_F - MS_{S/cells})/N}{(f-1)(MS_F - MS_{S/cells})/N + MS_{S/cells}}$$

Substituting either the previously calculated estimates of the variances or values of mean squares from Table 9.12, $\hat{\omega}^2_g(F) = .227$.

Now assume the design of Table 9.11 in which one factor, experience, is intrinsic. In that case,

$$\hat{\omega}^2_g(F) = \frac{\hat{\sigma}^2_F}{\hat{\sigma}^2_F + \hat{\sigma}^2_E + \hat{\sigma}^2_{FE} + \hat{\sigma}^2_{IE} + \hat{\sigma}^2_{FIE} + \hat{\sigma}^2_{error}}$$

Now the estimated variance due to experience and all its interactions contributes to the denominator. Substituting numerical estimates,

$$\hat{\omega}^2_g(F) = 45.341/(45.341 + 0 + .325 + 0 + .716 + 154) = .227$$

Because experience and its interactions contribute little variance in this experiment, the estimate is little changed from when we assumed that all factors were extrinsic. In either case, Cohen's suggested guidelines (see Chapter 8) indicate that format has a large effect.

To summarize developments thus far, we have presented an approach to computing measures of effect size that has as a goal comparability across designs. We endorse the approach advocated by

---

[4] This is independent of whether the factor is extrinsic or intrinsic.

Olejnik and Algina (2003) based on distinguishing extrinsic and intrinsic factors. We acknowledge that this approach is not yet widely adopted. However, general η^2 and general ω^2 do a better job of achieving the goal of comparability than do the more conventional statistics of partial η^2 and partial ω^2.

9.6.3 Cohen's *f* for the Multi-Factor Between-Subjects Design

As described in Chapter 8, Cohen (1988) defined *f* as

$$f = \sigma_{effect} / \sigma_{error} \tag{9.15}$$

For example, based on our previously calculated variance estimates,

$$\hat{f}_{Format} = \sqrt{45.341 / 154} = .54$$

As with $\hat{\omega}^2$, this is a large effect according to Cohen's guidelines. However, Equation 9.15 does not take into consideration whether the remaining factors are intrinsic or extrinsic. In order to increase compatibility across different designs, we might define *f* in a way consistent with the Olejnik and Algina (2003) approach to η^2 and ω^2. As with general ω^2, general *f* would involve a denominator that incorporates intrinsic effects, in addition to random error.[5] As with η_g^2 and ω_g^2, such a statistic would make sense in comparing effect sizes in two experiments, one of which involved a design in which intrinsic factors were controlled and one of which involved a design in which this was not the case.

Despite the advantage of f_g when comparing values of *f* based on data from different designs, we will limit our use to the classical formula for *f* in Equation 9.15. The reason for this is that *f* was viewed by Cohen as a parameter dictating the power of the *F* test, and is used in this way by the G*Power software cited earlier in this book. Because the denominator of *F* is based solely on the within-cell error variance, a value of *f* that includes intrinsic variation in its denominator would underestimate the power of the *F* test.

9.7 *A PRIORI* POWER CALCULATIONS

Assume that we wish to replicate the *Wiley–Voss* study. Further assume that our primary interest is whether the instructional effects vary. Cohen's $f = .262$ for instructions in Table 9.7. Suppose we want power $= .8$ to reject H_0 if the standardized effect is medium, as this value suggests. Fig. 9.5 shows the input to G*Power 3 and the resulting output. The total *N* of 179 translates to 22 subjects per condition, which is more than twice the number in the *Wiley–Voss* experiment.

9.8 UNEQUAL CELL FREQUENCIES

When cell frequencies are not equal, the ANOVA presented so far in this chapter has a problem. In this section, we describe the nature of the problem, and briefly introduce the different analyses that are available. Chapter 24 provides more detailed coverage within a regression framework.

---

[5] Let γ be the sum of all variance estimates involving an intrinsic factor; then, general *f* is $\hat{f}_g(Effect) = \sqrt{\hat{\sigma}_{Effect}^2 / (\hat{\sigma}_e^2 + \gamma)}$.

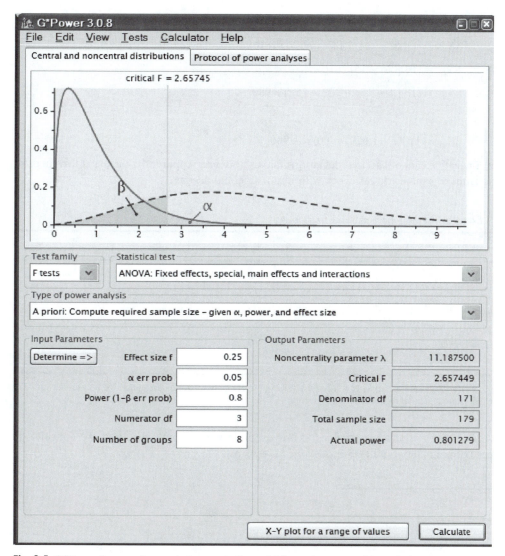

Fig. 9.5 G*Power 3 screen for *a priori* power in the multi-factor between-subjects design.

9.8.1 The Problem

In the developments thus far in this chapter, we considered only cases in which the number of scores is the same in each of the *ab* cells. As we stated in Chapter 6, when *n*s are not equal, heterogeneity of variance has a greater impact on Type 1 and 2 error rates. Furthermore, the sums of squares for main and interaction sources usually will not add to the SS_{cells} when each is calculated by ignoring the other effects. This is because when cell sizes are unequal and disproportional, the sums of squares are not independently distributed; the design is said to be *nonorthogonal*.

We can illustrate the problem by calculating sums of squares using the means in Table 9.13. Summing the squared deviations of the means about the grand mean and multiplying by the number of scores on which each mean is based, we have

$$SS_{cells} = (2)(20-15)^2 + (8)(25-15)^2 + (8)(5-15)^2 + (2)(10-15) = 1700$$

$$SS_A = (10)[(24-15)^2 + (6-15)^2] = 1,620$$

$$SS_B = (10)[(8-15)^2 + (22-15)^2] = 980$$

and

$$SS_{AB} = 1700 - (1,620 + 980) = -900$$

Of course, a negative sum of squared deviations makes no sense. Apparently, the usual formulas for calculating sums of squares do not work with nonorthogonal designs.

Table 9.13 Example with disproportionate cell frequencies

		B_1	B_2	$n_{j.}$	$\bar{Y}_{.j.}$
A_1	n_{1k}	2	8	10	
	$\bar{Y}_{.1k}$	20	25		24
A_2	n_{2k}	8	2	10	
	$\bar{Y}_{.2k}$	5	10		6
	$n_{.k}$	10	10	$n_{..} = 20$	
	$\bar{Y}_{..k}$	8	22		$\bar{Y}_{...} = 15$

Note: $\bar{Y}_{.j.} = \Sigma_k n_{jk} \bar{Y}_{.jk}/n_{j.}$; for example, $24 = [(2)(20) + (8)(25)]/10$. The column means are computed in a similar way. The grand mean (15) is the sum of all scores divided by the total N.

The reason for the strange results for our example will become clearer if we consider an extreme case of nonorthogonality. Suppose the ns were

	B_1	B_2
A_1	0	8
A_2	8	0

Now SS_A and SS_B are identical; both are based solely on the difference between the A_1B_2 and A_2B_1 cell means, and therefore the A and B main effects are perfectly correlated. In Table 9.13, the correlation is not perfect but it is still high. The magnitude of both SS_A and SS_B will still depend primarily (though not entirely) on the difference between the A_1B_2 and A_2B_1 means.

Fig. 9.6 contains a graphic representation of the situation when cell frequencies are unequal. The square represents the SS_{total}. The circles represent SS_A, SS_B, and SS_{AB}; overlap of circles represents the covariance of effects that results from nonorthogonality. Note that when cell frequencies are equal, the three circles do not overlap. Covariances can be positive or negative so that subtracting the covariance from a sum of squares might result in a smaller quantity (if the covariance is positive) or a larger one (if the covariance is negative). The presence of correlations among effects poses choices in data analysis and interpretation.

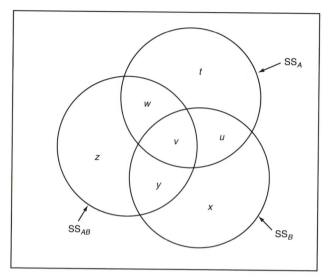

Fig. 9.6 The partitioning of variability in a two-factor design.

9.8.2 Three Types of Sums of Squares

There are three approaches available in many software packages for analyzing data when effects covary because cell frequencies are unequal. We will briefly describe each.

Type III sums of squares involve adjusting each main and interaction effect for the contributions of the others. For example, the adjusted SS_A would consist only of the area labeled t in Fig. 9.6. The Type III analysis is the default in most statistical software packages, including SPSS. It weights all the cell means equally and therefore is appropriate if it is assumed that the sampled populations are of equal size and the unequal ns reflect chance variation. Type III sums of squares should be calculated when the data come from true experiments in which the independent variables have been manipulated, and the loss of data is due to factors such as the random failure of subjects in various conditions to appear for the experiment.

Type II sums of squares involve adjusting an effect of interest for effects at the same or lower order, and for higher-order effects that do not include the effect of interest. In the two-factor design, this requires adjusting the sum of squares for each main effect for variability due to the other main effect, but not for the interaction. In Fig. 9.6, the Type II SS_A would be represented by the areas labeled t and w. This analysis implies that there are no interaction effects. Therefore, the interaction mean square can be averaged ("pooled"; see the next section) with the within-cell term, yielding more error degrees of freedom and potentially more power. However, such pooling runs the risk of failing to detect interaction effects that may exist, and of inflating the error term and thus increasing the rate of Type II errors when testing main effects. As a general rule, Type II sums of squares should not be calculated unless there is strong *a priori* reason to assume no interaction effects, and a clearly nonsignificant interaction sum of squares.

Type I sums of squares involve a hierarchical analysis. For example, suppose we are interested in the effects of educational level upon income. We might wish to control for other factors such as gender. In that case, we would first remove the sum of squares due to gender, and then calculate the sum of squares due to education. In terms of Fig. 9.6, if we represent education by A and gender by B, the sum of squares for gender would correspond to the full circle for SS_B and the education sum of squares, adjusted for gender, would correspond to the areas t and w. Type I sums of squares rest on the assumption that cell sizes represent population sizes, an assumption that is likely to be met when the independent variable is observed rather than manipulated (e.g., income level, occupation, or clinical diagnosis) or when some treatments are more aversive than others (e.g., subjects may find some diets more difficult to maintain in a study of weight loss).

Although the Type III sum of squares is usually the default, all three types of analyses are available in many software packages. We dropped scores randomly from the eight cells of the *Wiley–Voss* data set and used SPSS to analyze the data in order to note the similarities and differences among the three types of sums of squares.

9.8.3 A Numerical Example

The data set is linked to the *Wiley–Voss* page on the book's website and has the file name W*iley Unequal_N*. The means and cell frequencies are in Table 9.14. We analyzed the data using the univariate option in the *General Linear Model* menu of SPSS, but other statistical packages provide similar options. Table 9.15 presents the results of several analyses, each after choosing a different model.

The following points should be noted about the results in Table 9.15:

1. The within-cell error term is the same in all analyses in the table. It is obtained by calculating the sums of squared deviations of scores about their cell means, and then summing across cells; the degrees of freedom are $\Sigma_j(n_j - 1) = N - a$.

Table 9.14 Cell means (and frequencies) for an experiment with unequal n

	Instructions (A)			
Format	A_1 (Narrative)	A_2 (Summary)	A_3 (Explanation)	A_4 (Argument)
B_1 (text)	68.000 (5)	75.714 (7)	70.000 (4)	73.750 (8)
B_2 (web)	76.250 (8)	75.000 (2)	76.667 (8)	90.000 (8)

Table 9.15 Sums of squares (SS) for data with unequal cell frequencies

SV	df	Type III SS	Type II SS	Type Ia SS	Type Ib SS
Instructions (A)	3	801.57	854.97	683.77	854.97
		(t)	(t + w)	(t + w + v + u)	(t + w)
Format (B)	1	567.35	1004.54	1004.54	833.33
		(x)	(x + y)	(x + y)	(x + y + v + u)
AB	3	368.60	368.60	368.60	368.60
		(z)	(z)	(z)	(z)
Ss/AB	40	5409.76	5409.76	5409.76	5409.76

Note: The Type Ia *SS* is obtained when *A* is entered first in the *Univariate* dialog box; the Type Ib *SS* is the result of entering *B* first. The letters in parentheses refer to the corresponding areas in Fig. 9.6. See the text for further explanation.

2. The interaction term is also invariant across analyses. In all four cases, it is the sum of squares adjusted for the contributions of all other effects. This is $SS_{Between\ Groups}$ − $(SS_A + SS_B)$ where $SS_A + SS_B$ is obtained from either Type I analysis.

3. For the Type Ia SS, the A sum of squares was calculated while ignoring all other sources, and the B sum of squares was calculated after adjusting for (removing variability due to) A effects. For the Type Ib SS, the B sum of squares was calculated while ignoring all other sources, and the A sum of squares was calculated after adjusting for (removing variability due to) B effects.

4. The Type Ia sum of squares for B equals the Type II sum of squares for B. This is because both analyses adjust the B sum of squares for variability due to A. Similarly, the Type Ib sum of squares for A equals the Type II sum of squares for A because both adjust the A variability for the contribution of B.

The set of possible analyses was performed to illustrate the differences in results. However, in analyzing data from a study, only one of these analyses should be performed. Which one will depend upon whether variability in cell frequencies is assumed to be due to chance, in which case Type III is appropriate; whether there is strong reason to believe that the interaction effects are negligible, in which case Type II is appropriate; or whether it is assumed that there is a causal relationship among the factors in the study, in which case a Type I analysis is appropriate.

9.9 POOLING IN FACTORIAL DESIGNS

Pooling is the process by which two or more mean squares are averaged. This is often done when the investigator believes that some source of variance contributes only error variance and therefore pools that mean square with the error mean square. It is also done unintentionally when the investigator fails to consider some factor in the design. Because pooling affects tests of sources of interest, it merits a closer look.

9.9.1 What Is Pooling?

When two or more sources of variance are pooled, the sums of squares are added together and divided by the sum of the degrees of freedom. For example, in a two-factor design, the pool of the AB term and the S/AB term is

$$MS_{pool} = \frac{SS_{AB} + SS_{S/AB}}{df_{AB} + df_{S/AB}} \qquad (9.16)$$

Equation 9.16 can be rewritten as the weighted average of the two mean squares:

$$MS_{pool} = \left(\frac{df_{AB}}{df_{AB} + df_{S/AB}}\right) MS_{AB} + \left(\frac{df_{S/AB}}{df_{AB} + df_{S/AB}}\right) MS_{S/AB} \qquad (9.17)$$

This form of the equation raises the question: When is it proper to average two mean squares? The answer is that if the two mean squares estimate the same population variance, or variances, pooling is proper. In the example of Equation 9.17, the assumption is that both MS_{AB} and $MS_{S/AB}$ estimate σ_e^2 (i.e., $\sigma_{AB}^2 = 0$). The advantage of pooling two or more estimates of the population error variance is that MS_{pool} is distributed on more df than $MS_{S/AB}$; therefore, F tests based on the pooled error term may be more powerful than tests based on $MS_{S/AB}$. Of course, we never *know* that $\sigma_{AB}^2 = 0$. If it is not, we may lose power in using the pooled error term to test a false null hypothesis about a main effect. To see why, look again at Equation 9.17. If, contrary to the assumption upon which pooling is based, $E(MS_{AB}) = \sigma_e^2 + n\theta_{AB}^2$, then the weighted average of this expectation and of σ_e^2 will be larger than σ_e^2. As a result, the F test of a main effect will be *negatively biased*; the expectation of the error term involves more than just σ_e^2 and there will be too many Type 2 errors. Perhaps surprisingly, when the null hypothesis about the main effect is true, there may actually be an increase in Type 1 errors. The reason for this is that if MS_{AB} and $MS_{S/AB}$ do not both estimate σ_e^2, the ratio of MS_A (or MS_B) to MS_{pool} will not be distributed as F, and the tail area may be larger than the nominal α. In view of these considerations, it is not clear when, if ever, to pool. We consider this issue next.

9.9.2 When (If Ever) to Pool

One possible approach is to apply a sometimes-pool rule; interaction terms are tested against the within-cell error term, and the two mean squares are pooled if p is greater than some criterion value. With respect to the designs of the current chapter, a study by Mead, Bancroft, and Han (1975) is relevant. For a design with two fixed-effect factors and equal cell frequencies, even with the criterion α for the preliminary test of the AB source set at .50, the sometimes-pool rule often resulted in a loss of power when the null hypothesis about the main effect was false, and an increase in Type I error rate when it was true. Therefore, in designs in which all factors have fixed effects, we recommend never pooling. We will consider whether the sometimes-pool rule is advisable in other designs when we discuss those designs.

9.9.3 Unintended Pooling

Researchers often pool terms without realizing they have done so. Typically, in such cases there are one or more treatment variables and then one "nuisance" variable that the researcher regards as irrelevant. For example, the position of a reward may appear equally often in all experimental conditions of a discrimination study, or each of several experimenters may run an equal number of subjects in each condition. Ignoring such factors is essentially pooling them with the within-cell error term. As we noted in discussing Mead et al.'s (1975) results, such pooling runs the risk of a loss of power if the null hypothesis is false, or an increased Type I error rate if it is true. The message is simple: Include all factors in the analysis, whether they are of interest or not.

9.10 ADVANTAGES AND DISADVANTAGES OF BETWEEN-SUBJECTS DESIGNS

We will consider further tests of hypotheses in between-subjects designs in the next two chapters. However, this is a good point at which to review the major advantages and disadvantages of between-subjects factorial designs:

1. Assuming equal cell frequencies, the analysis of the data from the between-subjects design is much simpler than for most other designs.
2. For any given number of scores, the error degrees of freedom in the analysis of the between-subjects design will be larger than for any comparable design.
3. The requirements of the underlying model are more easily met by between-subjects designs

than by other designs, and violations of assumptions are less likely to affect the distribution of the F ratio.

4. However, there is one major disadvantage in using between-subjects designs. Because the error variance is largely due to individual differences, designs that permit the adjustment of the error variance for the differences among individuals often will enable more powerful tests and more precise estimates of population parameters, and often will do so with fewer data.

Because of the large error variance associated with between-subjects designs, these designs are most useful whenever subjects are relatively similar with respect to the dependent variable, or whenever a large N is available to compensate somewhat for the variability among individuals. Also, there are many experiments in which the nature of the independent variable (e.g., the method of instruction, or educational level of subjects) will constrain the design. However, there are many situations in which several different designs are feasible and desirable. In Chapter 13, we will introduce the idea of design efficiency, and consider the efficiency of alternative designs, and in Chapters 14–17, we will consider those designs and their analyses more closely.

9.11 SUMMARY

In this chapter, we considered experiments in which each subject contributed one score to a cell in a design in which all possible combinations of two or more factors were represented. Within this context, we covered the following topics:

- *The extension of the structural model to multi-factor designs.* Building on that model, we partitioned the total variability and degrees of freedom into components representing main, interaction, and error sources of variance.
- *The interpretation of interaction.* An interaction occurs when the magnitude of an effect varies over levels of another variable. One of the advantages of a multi-factor design is the ability to examine interactions among variables.
- *Measures of effect size.* We extended measures of importance to multi-factor designs, introducing modifications of the eta-squared and omega-squared measures presented in Chapter 8. In addition, we again considered Cohen's f.
- *Analyses when cell frequencies are unequal.* We explained why this may cause problems for the standard ANOVA, and briefly described alternative ways of calculating sums of squares, depending on what is assumed about population sizes and the presence of interaction, as well as the purpose of the study.

Thus far, we have focused on the omnibus F test. However, in most instances, other comparisons of means are of more interest. We turn next to that topic.

EXERCISES

9.1 **(a)** Perform an analysis of variance on the following data set (also available from the Exercises page on the book's website in the file *EX9_1*).

	B_1				B_2		
A_1	A_2	A_3	A_4	A_1	A_2	A_3	A_4
24	22	31	28	52	26	20	51
22	14	33	31	25	18	25	40
36	24	43	29	37	17	15	54

(b) Estimate the population main effects (the α_j and β_k) and the interaction effects [the $(\alpha\beta)_{jk}$] for the data in part (a).

(c) Using the estimated effects, calculate the main and interaction sums of squares. How do the results from parts (a) and (b) compare?

9.2 **(a)** State the *EMS* for the data in Exercise 9.1. Coefficients for variance components should be numbers, not letters.

(b) Based on the *EMS*, estimate Cohen's f for *B*.

(c) The number of observations in this study was quite small. Assuming the estimate in part (b), what total sample size (N) would be needed to have .8 power to test *B*?

9.3 A researcher publishes the following cell means and variances; $n = 10$. We wish to verify the results of the analysis and perform further tests.

	Means			Variances		
	B_1	B_2	B_3	B_1	B_2	B_3
A_1	2.6	4.3	6.5	2.75	5.00	5.50
A_2	4.3	3.6	3.4	1.75	2.25	3.75

(a) Carry out the ANOVA and present the tabled results.

(b) Test the simple effects of *A* at B_3.

(c) Test the simple effects of *B* at A_2.

(d) Briefly justify your choices of error terms for parts (b) and (c).

9.4 Suppose an article contains the following table of cell means from a between-subjects design with two factors and six scores in a cell:

	B_1	B_2	B_3
A_1	12	16	14
A_2	18	14	12

In addition, the article reports that only the *AB* interaction is significant, $F = 8.0, p = .002$.

(a) Reconstruct the entire ANOVA summary table.

(b) Test the simple effect of *B* at A_2. What assumption is needed to justify your test?

9.5 **(a)** Carry out the ANOVA for the data set in the file *EX9_5* on the book's website.

(b) Assuming *A* and *B* are both manipulated variables, calculate general η^2 for *B*.

(c) Repeat part (*b*), now assuming that *A* represents three different personality types.

9.6 **(a)** For the data set in the file *EX9_5*, calculate general ω^2 for *A, B,* and *AB*, assuming that *A* and *B* are both manipulated variables.

(b) Repeat part (a), now assuming that *A* represents three different personality types.

9.7 In the *Wiley–Voss* (1999) data set (in the *Wiley* file on the website), the variable *Causal* represents the number of causal connections subjects introduced into essays based on the information obtained. [Note: *Format* = 1 and 2 corresponds to *Text* and *Web*, respectively; *Instructions* 1 through 4 correspond to *Narrative* (*N*), *Summary* (*S*), *Explanation* (*E*), and *Argument* (*A*), respectively.]

(a) Are the assumptions underlying the analysis of variance met by the *Causal* scores? Justify your answer from any relevant statistics and plots.

(b) Carry out an ANOVA with *Format* and *Instructions* as the independent variables.

(c) Transform the data by *log*(*causal* + 1). How has this affected the results in parts (a) and (b)?

9.8 Consider each of the following sets of hypotheses. Which sources of variance should be significant? Plot means consistent with the theory.

(a) In a bar press experiment, we hypothesize that $Y = K \times D \times P$ where $Y =$ bar pressing rate (the dependent variable), *K* is a constant, $D =$ hours of deprivation, and $P =$ number of practice trials.

(b) In impression formation studies, we give subjects some information on the attractiveness (*A*) and intelligence (*I*) of an individual and then ask them to rate the individual. We believe that the rating, $R, = (A + I)/2$.

(c) Patients in a mental hospital are divided into experimental groups on the basis of their socioeconomic (*SE*) level (*SE*, three levels) and the kind of treatment they receive (*T*, two levels, psychotherapy and behavior therapy). The investigator predicts that (1) psychotherapy will be less effective than behavior therapy, and (2) psychotherapy will be more effective the higher the *SE* level of the patient, but that this will not be true for behavior therapy. In fact, no effect of *SE* level is predicted for the behavior therapy patients.

9.9 Assume that 40 subjects are divided into good and poor readers on the basis of a pretest. They then read either intact or scrambled text, and are tested for their recall. The means and variances (in parentheses) are:

Reading ability	Text	
	Scrambled	Intact
Good	63 (145)	67 (130)
Poor	37 (155)	54 (170)

(a) Construct the numerator of a *t* test of the *Ability* × *Text* interaction.

(b) What is the denominator of that *t* test?

(c) Calculate the *t* and report the level of significance. What is the value of the corresponding *F* statistic?

9.10 **(a)** Calculate general η^2 for the *Text* effects in Exercise 9.9.
(b) Estimate general ω^2 for the *Text* effects.

9.11 The file *EX9_11* at the website contains six groups of five scores in a two-factor experiment. There are three levels of A, amount of reward, and two experimenters each ran half of the subjects at each level of A.
(a) Present the ANOVA table, including the *EMS*.
(b) Estimate general ω^2 for A, treating A and E as extrinsic variables.
(c) Possible effects due to using more than one experimenter are often ignored. Write out the ANOVA table including *EMS*, assuming that E has no effect in the population.
(d) Estimate ω^2 for A for this analysis.
(e) Which is the more appropriate model? Why?

9.12 Assume that the following numbers represent population means in a three-factor design. Which sources contribute to the variance among the population of means? Explain your answer.

	C_1				C_2		
	A_1	A_2	A_3		A_1	A_2	A_3
B_1	21	27	30	B_1	9	5	10
B_2	17	23	26	B_2	23	19	24
B_3	14	20	23	B_3	22	18	23
B_4	16	22	25	B_4	22	18	23

9.13 Eighty subjects listened to a lecture (L) on either the general impact of global warming in Alaska or the impact on wildlife in Alaska. This was then followed by a movie (M) on either the impact of global warming in Alaska, or on wildlife in Alaska. They then rated their agreement on a series of questions about the environment and global warming. There were equal numbers of men and women. The results of the analysis of variance are:

Source	df	MS	F	p
Movie (M)	1	.445	7.18	.009
Lecture (L)	1	.273	4.40	.039
Sex (X)	1	.245	3.77	.056
ML	1	.341	5.50	.022
LX	1	.076	1.17	.283
MX	1	.089	1.37	.246
MLX	1	.142	2.29	.135
Ss/MLX	72	.065		

(a) Calculate general η^2 for the lecture and sex terms.
(b) Calculate general ω^2 for the movie term.

9.14 The *Wiley–Voss* file on the website contains several dependent variables. Here we analyze the *SVT* (sentence-verification task) measure.

(a) Plot the cell means, including standard error bars.

(b) Perform the ANOVA.

(c) Calculate the standardized effects (Cohen's f) for the main and interaction effects.

(d) Compare the relative sizes of the f values with the p-values for the ANOVA. If there is a difference in ordering, discuss why this has happened.

(e) What N would you need to have .8 power to reject H_0 if the *Format f* value was .25 (medium, by Cohen's guidelines)? What N would you need for the *Instruction* effect? Is there a difference? If so, why?

9.15 Assume that in a multi-factor experiment, $a = 4$, $b = 3$, and $c = 2$, and $N = 96$. Given that $MS_A = 56.8$ and the $F = 2.84$:

(a) What is n? $MS_{S/ABC}$?

(b) Estimate σ^2 and f^2 for the A effect.

(c) Assuming the effect size is medium (i.e., $f = .25$), what is the power to test the A effect (at $\alpha = .01$) if the study is redone with $n = 8$?

9.16 The file *EX9_16* on the website contains data modeled after that collected in a study by Bless, Bohner, Schwarz, and Strack (1990). These investigators manipulated the *mood* (1 = happy, 2 = sad) of their subjects, and presented them with a *message* (1 = strong, 2 = weak) designed to influence their attitude about student service fees. Subjects' *focus* (1 = content, 2 = language) was also varied. The dependent measure in our data set is the recommended fee (in dollars) after reading the message.

(a) Describe the pattern of the eight cell means. What main and interaction effects are suggested by these means?

(b) Perform an ANOVA on the data in the file. Discuss the results with reference to the plot of the means in part (a).

9.17 Following is a data set with unequal ns. The cell totals/ns (T_{jk}/n_{jk}) are

	B_1	B_2
A_1	20/2	40/4
A_2	16/8	4/2

(a) Calculate SS_{cells}. The equation is $SS_{cells} = \Sigma_j \Sigma_k n_{jk} (\overline{Y}_{\cdot jk} - \overline{Y} \ldots)^2$.

(b) In the same way you did part (a), calculate SS_A and SS_B. For example, $SS_A = \Sigma_j n_{j\cdot} (\overline{Y}_{\cdot j} - \overline{Y}_\cdot)^2$. Then subtract these from SS_{cells} to get SS_{AB}. Do you see any problem with this procedure? Explain.

(c) Calculate $\hat{\alpha}_1$ and $\hat{\alpha}_2$. This requires finding the marginal (row) means for A_1 and A_2 and subtracting the grand mean. If you have done this correctly, $\Sigma_j n_{j\cdot} \hat{\alpha}_j = 0$ (n_j is the total n for row j).

(d) Subtract $\hat{\alpha}_j$ from each cell mean in row j. Look at the table of means that results. Using these adjusted means, what are SS_B and SS_{AB}? How does this result compare with your answer in part (b)?

9.18 Consider the following table of cell means. We will adjust these means for the effects of A under different assumptions about cell frequencies and, by observing what happens to the column means, infer the consequences of equal, proportional, and disproportional cell frequencies for ANOVA. The cell means are:

	B_1	B_2	B_3
A_1	12	8	22
A_2	8	6	13
A_3	1	3	16

(a) Assume that the cell frequencies are all the same. (i) Calculate the row and column means. (ii) Calculate estimates of the row effects ($\hat{\alpha}_j$). (iii) Subtract each value of $\hat{\alpha}_j$ from the three cell means in the corresponding row. How do the column means of this adjusted (for A effects) matrix compare with those in part (i)?

(b) Assume the original cell means presented above. This time, however, assume the following cell frequencies (n_{jk}):

	B_1	B_2	B_3
A_1	4	8	12
A_2	3	6	9
A_3	1	2	3

Redo (i)–(iii) of part (a). Be careful in calculating the row, column, and grand means; the values being averaged must be weighted by their corresponding frequency. For example, the mean of the first row is $[(4)(12) + (8)(8) + (12)(22)]/24$. Similarly, the grand mean is the weighted average of the 12 cell means (or of the three row or column means).

(c) Again assume the original set of means. This time, the n_{jk} are

	B_1	B_2	B_3
A_1	5	10	4
A_2	5	5	10
A_3	10	3	5

Again do (i)–(iii).

(d) Review your answers to this problem and draw a conclusion about the effects of equal, proportional, and disproportional cell frequencies about the partitioning of variability in ANOVA.

9.19 Eighty students taking a class in statistics are divided into 20 study groups, each consisting of two women and two men. Ten of the study groups are instructed in class by one method, and the remaining 10 groups are taught by a different method. Much of the analysis is summarized next:

Source	df	MS	EMS
Method (M)	1	3627	$\sigma_e^2 + 4\sigma_{G/M}^2 + 400\theta_M^2$
Sex (X)	1	128	$\sigma_e^2 + 2\sigma_{GX/M}^2 + 400\theta_X^2$
MX	1	123	$\sigma_e^2 + 2\sigma_{GX/M}^2 + 200\theta_{MX}^2$
Groups/method (G/M)	18	420	$\sigma_e^2 + 4\sigma_{G/M}^2$
GX/M	18	32	$\sigma_e^2 + 2\sigma_{GX/M}^2$
Residual	40	30	σ_e^2

(a) Calculate the appropriate F statistics for M, X, and MX. Report whether each is significant. The investigator reanalyzes the data, pooling the GX/M with the residual error term. The resulting sources of variance are:

Source	df	MS	EMS
Method (M)	1	3,627	
Sex (X)	1	128	
MX	1	123	
G/M	18	32	
Pooled residual			

(b) What assumption would justify this reanalysis?

(c) In view of your answer to part (a), fill in the EMS column. Also provide the df and MS for the pooled residual.

(d) Recalculate the F ratios and report whether each is significant. What are the consequences of the reanalysis?

(e) What is the justification for the reanalysis?

Chapter 10
Contrasting Means in Between-Subjects Designs

10.1 OVERVIEW

In Chapter 8, we learned how to test the omnibus null hypothesis that the means of all populations sampled in an experiment are equal. Although a significant F indicates that not all of the population means are equal, it does not reveal the source of the differences among the means. For example, in the study of the effects of educational level on mean depression scores (see Table 8.5), we are left with questions such as: Does the mean for the population having only a high-school education differ from that for the population having some college education? Does the mean for the population with only a high-school education differ from the mean for a population with more than a high-school education; that is, from the mean of the other three populations? Within the context of a multi-factor designs we might ask these same questions, and also whether such differences depend on the sex of the subject.

Answering such questions requires calculating a test statistic and evaluating its significance. The calculations involve minor modifications of the t statistics presented in Chapter 6. Evaluating significance, however, is an issue when several tests are performed on a set of group means. Just as the probability of at least one head increases as the number of coin tosses increases, so does the probability of at least one Type 1 error increase as more significance tests are performed. The set of contrasts tested is referred to as a family, and the probability that the family contains at least one Type 1 error is referred to as the *familywise error rate*, or *FWE*. There are many factors that influence the *FWE* and many methods for controlling it.

The primary goals of this chapter are:

- To extend the t test for independent groups to testing contrasts of any form within a between-subjects design.
- To introduce a distinction between controlling the probability of a Type 1 error for an individual comparison, *EC* (for "error rate per comparison"), and controlling the probability of a Type 1 error within a family of comparisons, *FWE*.
- To distinguish among several different kinds of families of contrasts and present appropriate methods for controlling the *FWE* for each kind of family.

We first will develop these issues and applications in the context of a single-factor design. Once the procedures for testing contrasts are established, we will extend them to multi-factor designs, with emphasis on analyzing interactions.

10.2 DEFINITIONS AND EXAMPLES OF CONTRASTS

In Chapter 6, we reviewed procedures based on the *t* distribution for comparing a pair of means in the context of either testing hypotheses or constructing confidence intervals to estimate the difference between two means. In fact, the procedures introduced in Chapter 6 may be extended to more complex comparisons. In this chapter, we develop procedures for evaluating any type of contrast among means. We begin by defining a contrast.

A *contrast* of population means is denoted by the Greek letter *psi* (ψ) and is defined as a *linear combination* of the means; that is,

$$\psi = \sum_j w_j \mu_j \tag{10.1}$$

where μ_j denotes a population mean, w_j refers to a numerical weight, at least one w_j is not zero, and $\Sigma_j w_j = 0$.[1] To illustrate, consider the data set of Table 8.1. In this experiment, one group was taught to memorize words by the method of loci, a second group was told to form an image of each word, a third group was told to form a rhyme, and the fourth, a control group, was given no special instructions. We might wish to compare each of the strategies with the control condition. For example, the comparison of the control and image population means might be represented by

$$\psi_1 = \mu_{image} - \mu_{control} \tag{10.2a}$$

Rewriting Equation 10.2a to be explicit about the weights on the means and ordering the means according to their sequence in the data file gives

$$\psi_1 = (-1)\mu_{control} + (0)\mu_{loci} + (1)\mu_{image} + (0)\mu_{rhyme}$$

The control condition might be contrasted with the average of the three strategy conditions, in which case the contrast would be

$$\psi_2 = (1/3)(\mu_{loci} + \mu_{image} + \mu_{rhyme}) - \mu_{control} \tag{10.2b}$$

Again, being explicit about the weights on the means, Equation 10.2*b* may be written

$$\psi_2 = (-1)\mu_{control} + (1/3)\mu_{loci} + (1/3)\mu_{image} + (1/3)\mu_{rhyme}$$

Arguing that the image and loci strategies both involve imaging, the experimenter might ask whether their mean differs from the mean of the rhyme condition; then the contrast is

$$\psi_3 = (\frac{1}{2})(\mu_{loci} + \mu_{image}) - \mu_{rhyme} \tag{10.2c}$$

Again we may rewrite the contrast as

$$\psi_3 = (0)\mu_{control} + (\frac{1}{2})\mu_{loci} + (\frac{1}{2})\mu_{image} + (-1)\mu_{rhyme}$$

---

[1] The requirement that the weights sum to zero ensures that the contrasts deal with differences among means.

To construct a point estimate of a particular contrast on population means, $\hat{\psi}$, we simply substitute sample means for the corresponding population means:

$$\hat{\psi} = \sum_j w_j \overline{Y}_{.j} \tag{10.3}$$

For the contrasts in Equation 10.2, the point estimates are

$$\hat{\psi}_1 = (-1)(\overline{Y}_{control}) + (0)(\overline{Y}_{loci}) + (1)(\overline{Y}_{image}) + (0)(\overline{Y}_{rhyme}) \tag{10.4a}$$

$$\hat{\psi}_2 = (-1)(\overline{Y}_{control}) + (1/3)(\overline{Y}_{loci}) + (1/3)(\overline{Y}_{image}) + (1/3)(\overline{Y}_{rhyme}) \tag{10.4b}$$

$$\hat{\psi}_3 = (0)(\overline{Y}_{control}) + (1/2)(\overline{Y}_{loci}) + (1/2)(\overline{Y}_{image}) + (-1)(\overline{Y}_{rhyme}) \tag{10.4c}$$

Each of these equations estimates a different contrast of the four population means and therefore provides the basis for testing a different null hypothesis. Note that the zero weights in the first and third contrasts are not necessary for purposes of expressing the relevant contrast. However, it will be necessary to provide explicit weights for the means of all conditions when software is used to execute contrast computations, so it is good to get into the habit of providing weights for all conditions.

10.3 CALCULATIONS FOR HYPOTHESIS TESTS AND CONFIDENCE INTERVALS ON CONTRASTS

In Chapter 6, we presented calculations for the t statistic for two independent groups; that is, for *pairwise comparisons*. In this section we extend those calculations to contrasts involving more than two groups, such as those in Equations 10.4b and 10.4c. We also discuss the selection of weights when ns are unequal, and extend Welch's t' test of means when variances are heterogeneous to contrasts involving more than two groups.

10.3.1 Calculations When *ns* are Equal and Variances are Equal

A straightforward extension of the t test of Chapter 6 provides a test of contrasts in a one-factor design. We illustrate the test of contrasts using the data from the hypothetical memory experiment; those data were presented in Table 8.1 and are summarized in Table 10.1. The weights in the fourth row of the table are used for a test of the null hypothesis corresponding to Equation 10.2c:

$$H_0: (1/2)(\mu_{loci} + \mu_{image}) - (1)\mu_{rhyme} = 0$$

Table 10.1 Means and variances of the data in Table 8.1 with contrast weights

	Method			
	Control	Loci	Image	Rhyme
Mean	6.5	12.1	10.7	10.5
Variance	10.056	19.433	25.567	16.722
n	10	10	10	10
Weight	0	.5	.5	−1
Weight × 2	0	1	1	−2

Given the information in Table 10.1, we can now proceed to calculate the t statistic. The formula is

$$t = \hat{\psi} / s_{\hat{\psi}} = \frac{\sum_j w_j \bar{Y}_j}{\sqrt{MS_{S/A} \sum_j \frac{w_j^2}{n_j}}}$$

(10.5)

Note that the denominator involves $MS_{S/A}$, an average of all four within-group variances. Even though the control group mean is not included in the contrast, including the variance of the control group in the calculation of the error term is justified if we can assume homogeneous variances. The advantage of using $MS_{S/A}$ is that the estimate of error variance will be more accurate and our test will be more powerful because the error degrees of freedom are based on four groups rather than three.

We would not be justified in using $MS_{S/A}$ as the basis for computing our error term if the group variances differ, because doing so might bias the t test. In fact, the variances do not need to be very disparate before it makes sense to limit the error term to just the variances in the contrasted groups. For example, suppose $a = 3$, $n = 15$, and the group variances are 10, 12, and 29, respectively. Further, suppose the difference between the first two condition means is 2.5. If we test this difference using only the first two group variances, $F(1, 28) = 4.261$ and $p = .048$. However, if we assume homogeneous variances and use all three condition variances as the basis for our error term, the result is $F(1, 42) = 2.757$ and $p = 104$. Although this test is based on more df, the denominator of the F test is increased by the inclusion of the variance of the third group; consequently, the F ratio is smaller and nonsignificant. Even a nonsignificant result of a test of homogeneity of variance is not sufficient evidence to use $MS_{S/A}$ as our error term. In other words, we want to be quite confident of the assumption of homogeneity before we use $MS_{S/A}$ as the basis for our test. We will consider alternative analyses for the heterogeneous variance case in Section 10.3.4.

For the example of Table 10.1, we will assume homogeneity of variance. Therefore, given Equation 10.5 and the statistics in Table 10.1, we calculate

$$\hat{\psi} = (\tfrac{1}{2})(12.1 + 10.7) - (1)(10.5) = 0.9$$

$$MS_{S/A} = (10.056 + 19.433 + 25.567 + 16.722)/4 = 17.944$$

and

$$\sqrt{\Sigma \, w_j^2 / n_j} = \sqrt{1.5/10} = .3875 \quad \text{and} \quad \sqrt{MS_{S/A}} = \sqrt{17.944} = 4.236$$

Therefore,

$$t = \hat{\psi} / s_{\hat{\psi}}$$
$$= 0.9/[(4.236)(.3875)]$$
$$= .548$$

The df associated with the t test are the df on which the estimate of the error variance is based; these are the df associated with $MS_{S/A}$, or 36. The choice of an appropriate critical value of t will be deferred until we discuss the concept of familywise error rate. However, it is clear that the computed t value of .548 is not significant by any reasonable criterion.

The computations illustrated for the hypothesis test might have been used to compute a confidence interval to estimate the contrast, $(1/2)(\mu_{loci} + \mu_{image}) - (1)\mu_{rhyme}$. In Chapter 6, we learned how to construct an interval estimate on the difference between two population means. The generalization of that procedure to any contrast is

$$\hat{\psi} \pm (t_{critical})(s_{\hat{\psi}}) \tag{10.6}$$

Again, discussion of the selection of a critical value of t will be deferred for now. The contrast and standard error are computed the same way as for the hypothesis test, and the standard error is, again, based on 36 df in our example.

We have been considering a contrast where some of the weights on the means are fractions (i.e., ½ and ½). When using software to do such computations, it is necessary to express fractional weights as decimals (e.g., .5). In some cases, converting fractions to decimals results in a repeating decimal place (e.g., 1/3 converts to .33333. . . .). To avoid the imprecision caused by arbitrarily truncating a repeating decimal, it is useful to multiply the weights in a contrast by a constant to convert the weights to integers. For example, multiplying the weights in our example by 2 converts the weights to 1, 1, and −2 (see row 4 of Table 10.1). Multiplying the weights of a contrast by a constant has no effect on the value of a t test because both the numerator and denominator of the t ratio are multiplied by the same constant. However, a change in the weights of a contrast will affect a confidence interval: The point estimate and the width of the interval will be multiplied by the constant. Therefore, the upper and lower bounds of a confidence interval should be returned to its original scale by dividing the two boundary values by the constant. The reader should compute a t test and confidence interval for our example contrast, using the weights 1, 1, and −2 to verify that the value of the t ratio is unaffected by the changed weights, whereas the confidence interval boundaries are multiplied by 2.

Most statistical software packages will perform the calculations illustrated in this section, and will do so even if group sizes or variances are not equal. For example, SPSS's *One-Way ANOVA* module (in the *Analyze* menu) has a *Contrasts* option that enables the user to select group weights. To take advantage of available software, the researcher must become comfortable with specifying the weights on each condition mean, and with expressing the weights as integers. Finally, if the interest is in constructing confidence intervals, it is important to remember to convert the bounds on each interval back to the original scale.

10.3.2 Weighting Means When *ns* Are Unequal: Equal-Sized Populations Assumed

Suppose we wish to compare the speeds of solving arithmetic problems in four different grades (e.g., Royer et al., 1999; see the *Royer RT_speed* data file on the book's website). Table 10.2 presents mean variances and class sizes (*n*). Although there are different numbers of students in the different grades, this is likely to be due to chance; that is, there is no reason to view the four sampled populations as unequal in size. If the various populations are equal in size, then any means that are averaged should receive equal weight in a contrast. For example, when testing the average speed of fifth-graders against the combined average of the sixth-, seventh-, and eighth-graders, the weights would be −1, 1/3, 1/3, 1/3 or, equivalently, −3, 1, 1, and 1. Equal weighting of means that are averaged on one side of a contrast usually will also be appropriate in the analysis of data from any true experiment in which the independent variable is manipulated. Using the integer weights, we can use Equation 10.5 to calculate the statistic for the contrast of fifth-graders' mean speed against that of the combined mean of the sixth-, seventh-, and eighth-graders. You should verify that $t = \hat{\psi}/s_{\hat{\psi}} = .680/.130 = 5.233$. Because the estimate of variability in the calculation of the standard

Table 10.2 Summary information for the Royer response time data

	Grade				
	5	6	7	8	
Mean	0.350	0.560	0.586	0.583	
Variance	0.033	0.028	0.031	0.038	
n	23	26	21	20	$N = 90$

error is $MS_{S/A}$, the *df* associated with the test are $(90 - 4)$ or 86. Again, we defer selection of a critical value of t until our discussion of the *FWE*. Of course, we could also construct a confidence interval on the contrast. If we used the integer weights and resulting values of .680 for the contrast and .130 for the standard error, the upper and lower boundary values would be divided by 3 to return the interval to our original scale.

10.3.3 Weighting Means When *ns* Are Unequal: Unequal-Sized Populations Assumed

In many observational studies, differences in group sizes reflect differences in population sizes. A case in point is the *Seasons* study, which we cited previously. In Chapter 8, we tested the omnibus null hypothesis that mean depression scores were equal for four populations defined by their education level. The four groups were males with only a high-school education (*HS*), some college experience (*C*), a bachelor's degree (*B*), or graduate school experience (*GS*). Panel *a* of Table 10.3 presents group sizes, means, and variances.

Assume that one question of interest was whether the mean depression scores differed between males with a high-school education and all other males. Because the relative group sizes suggest that the *HS* population is considerably smaller than the others, we assume that the four populations vary in size. Then the mean of the last three populations, which we will denote as $\mu_{>HS}$ ("greater than high school"), would be a weighted average; that is,

$$\mu_{>HS} = \frac{w_C \mu_C + w_B \mu_B + w_{GS} \mu_{GS}}{w_C + w_B + w_{GS}}$$

and the null hypothesis of interest is

$$H_0: \mu_{HS} - \frac{w_C \mu_C + w_B \mu_B + w_{GS} \mu_{GS}}{w_C + w_B + w_{GS}} = 0$$

Because the t test of a contrast is not affected when all weights are multiplied by a constant, we can simplify things by multiplying the expression by $w_C + w_B + w_{GS}$, yielding the contrast

$$\psi = (w_C + w_B + w_{GS})\mu_{HS} - (w_C \mu_C + w_B \mu_B + w_{GS} \mu_{GS}) \tag{10.7}$$

and we can test the null hypothesis that this contrast equals zero.

Unless we know the actual sizes of the populations, we now need values of the *w*s. In many situations, the simplest and most reasonable will be the group sizes. Panel *c* of Table 10.3 presents output for Contrasts 1 and 2; the weights for the two contrasts are presented in Panel *b*. The weights

Table 10.3   Summary statistics (*a*), contrast coefficients (*b*), and test results (*c*) for depression scores as a function of educational level

(*a*) Statistics

Educational level	n	Mean	Variance
HS	19	6.903	34.541
C	33	3.674	5.97
B	37	3.331	9.861
GS	39	4.847	26.218

(*b*) Contrast coefficients

Contrast	Educational level			
	HS	*C*	*B*	*GS*
1	3	−1	−1	−1
2	109	−33	−37	−39

(*c*) Contrast test results (from SPSS)

	Contrast	Value of contrast	Std. error	t	df	Sig. (2-tailed)
Assumes equal variances	1	8.857	3.116	2.842	124	0.005
	2	318.922	113.204	2.817	124	0.006
Does not assume equal variances	1	8.857	4.181	2.118	20.527	0.047
	2	318.922	152.261	2.095	20.712	0.049

for Contrast 1 would be appropriate if we assumed that the populations are of equal size; that is not the case in this example, but Contrast 1 provides a comparison with Contrast 2, which uses weights based on the assumption that the group sizes reflect the population sizes. In Contrast 2, the weights on the means were calculated with Equation 10.7: the weight on the *HS* mean is the sum of the *n*s for the other three conditions; the weights on *C, B*, and *GS* are computed as −1 times the group size. Results are reported when equal variances are assumed and when they are not; we will discuss the calculations for the latter case in Section 10.3.4. For now, note that the assumption about variances can greatly influence the values of *t* and *p*.

Although the results for Contrasts 1 and 2 are very similar in this case, equal weighting and weighting by frequency can yield very different results; the distribution of group sizes is the critical factor. The reason results were similar in this example is that if we divide 109, −33, −37, and −39 by 36, we get 3.028, −.917, −1.028, and −1.083—not very different from 3, −1, −1, and −1.

We should point out that the issue of weights arises only with contrasts in which one or both subsets are based on at least two means. When testing pairwise comparisons (by far the most common situation), the weights will always be 1 and −1 for the two means involved in the comparison, and 0 for all other means.

10.3.4 Testing Contrasts When Variances Are Not Equal

In the situations we have considered to this point, $MS_{S/A}$ was used as our estimate of error variance in calculating the standard error for a contrast. However, there are two situations in which $MS_{S/A}$ is not an appropriate error term. In one case, the variances corresponding to the conditions involved in the contrast are very similar but different from the variances of those conditions not included in the contrast (that is, those having zero weight). The standard t is appropriate here, but the denominator should be based only on the variances corresponding to the included conditions. Degrees of freedom, due to the omitted group, are lost, but the standard error of the contrast is a valid denominator for the t test. For example, if there are three groups with variances 20, 21, and 5, and the means of the first two groups are to be compared, the variance of 5 should not be included in the denominator because the estimate of the standard error of the contrast will be too small, and the Type 1 error rate will be inflated.

The second situation is one in which there is heterogeneity of variance within the set of means that are to be contrasted. In this case, an extension of Welch's t test (t'; Welch, 1947; see Section 6.6.2) should be calculated. Recall that when variances are assumed to be homogeneous, the condition variances are pooled; however, when variances are assumed to be heterogeneous, the variances are not pooled and should be weighted differently according to the different weights on the corresponding means in the contrast. Also, the df are adjusted downward when unequal variances are assumed. The difference between the standard t results and those for t' are illustrated in panel c of Table 10.3 where two sets of results are presented for each of the two contrasts of the HS depression mean with the mean of the other three groups. One result is obtained assuming equal variances, and the t is calculated as in Equation 10.5. The second result is obtained when equal variances are not assumed.

To obtain the result when equal variances are not assumed, calculate

$$t' = \hat{\psi} / s_{\hat{\psi}} \tag{10.8}$$

where

$$s_{\hat{\psi}} = \sqrt{\sum_{j=1}^{a} \frac{w_j^2 s_j^2}{n_j}} \tag{10.9}$$

and the degrees of freedom are

$$df' = \frac{s_{\hat{\psi}}^4}{\sum_j \frac{w_j^4 s_j^4}{n_j^2(n_j - 1)}} \tag{10.10}$$

In summary, as can be seen in Table 10.3, the value of the test statistic depends both on whether the population variances are assumed to be equal and whether the populations are assumed to be equal in size.

10.4 EXTENDING COHEN'S *d* TO CONTRASTS

In Section 6.8, we introduced Cohen's *d*, a measure of the effect when there are two levels of the independent variable. This measure can be extended to contrasts in which several group means are involved. Assuming homogeneous variances, the general form of the standardized effect size for a contrast is

$$d = \hat{\psi}/\sqrt{MS_{S/A}} \qquad (10.11)$$

Using the memory data summarized in Table 10.1, and the contrast illustrated there,

$$d = 1.8/\sqrt{17.944} = .42$$

Thus, although the *t* calculated for the contrast was quite small (.548), the standardized contrast is of medium size according to Cohen's (1988) guidelines. Without consideration of confidence bounds, it is difficult to evaluate this statistic, but it does leave open the possibility that power may have been lacking in the original test.

10.5 THE PROPER UNIT FOR THE CONTROL OF TYPE 1 ERROR

10.5.1 Defining a Family of Tests

As we stated in the Introduction, the probability of a Type 1 error increases with the number of significance tests. Therefore, if the probability of each significance test is set without regard to how many tests might be conducted, the error rate for the entire collection of tests may rise to an unacceptable level. Statisticians and researchers generally are agreed that the proper unit for control of the Type 1 error rate is not the individual test but a set of contrasts called a *family*. Before we address the question of how to limit the Type 1 error rate for the family, we should clarify the idea of a family of contrasts.

It is useful to distinguish between the *error rate per contrast* (*EC*)—the probability that a single contrast results in a Type 1 error—and the *familywise error rate* (*FWE*)—the probability that a set, or family, of contrasts will contain at least one Type 1 error. For a family of *K* independent tests,

$$FWE = p(\text{at least one Type 1 error in the family})$$

$$= 1 - p(\text{no Type 1 errors in the family})$$

$$= 1 - p(\text{no Type 1 error on a single test})^K$$

The probability of a Type 1 error on a single test is the *EC*. Therefore,

$$FWE = 1 - (1 - EC)^K \qquad (10.12)$$

If a family consists of six independent tests each conducted at $EC = .05$, substitution in Equation 10.12 results in $FWE = 1 - (1 - .05)^6 = .265$; that is, even if the population means are all equal, the probability is .265 that one or more of the six tests will be significant. If the six tests are not independent, the exact value of *FWE* is difficult to calculate, but it is still greater than .05. In general, the larger the family, the more the *FWE* exceeds the *EC*. This suggests that in order to control *FWE*, we will need to adjust *EC* downward by an amount that will depend upon the size of the family of comparisons. This line of reasoning requires that we decide how to specify a family of contrasts. We will consider three alternatives.

An investigator working in a research area over a period of years might perform hundreds of experiments and test thousands of hypotheses. We might consider these thousands of tests to form a single family and set *FWE* equal to .05; however, this is not a reasonable specification of a family of tests, in part because it would result in an *EC* that would be infinitesimally small. Although this ultraconservative approach would result in a very low Type 1 error rate, the Type 2 error rate would soar to unacceptable levels. The experimenter could be confident that significant results revealed real effects but would miss finding many real effects. Because lowering the *EC* results in a reduction of power, the definition of family must be based on a compromise between concerns about Type 1 and Type 2 errors.

A more reasonable choice for a family of comparisons would be all of the tests conducted to analyze the results of an experiment. However, this approach to specifying families of comparisons is arbitrary because experiments may differ widely in the number of conditions they include, and thus the number of tests that might be performed. A researcher who performs simple experiments with few factors would perform fewer tests than a researcher who performs more complex, multifactor experiments with many conditions. This brings us to a third and more reasonable approach to specifying families of comparisons; namely, to identify families of tests with sources of variance in an experimental design. For example, in an experiment with three factors, a set of tests to understand the *AB* interaction would constitute one family of comparisons, and a set of tests to understand the main effect of *C* would constitute another. *FWE* would be controlled independently for the two families.

Identifying a family with the set of comparisons conducted to analyze a single source of variance seems a reasonable approach to defining families of contrasts in a few senses. First, it strikes a balance between control of Type 1 errors and power considerations by keeping the size of the family manageable. Related to this, compared to the two previously considered definitions of a family, this approach results in more consistency in the size of a family. Finally, there is a clear, substantive basis for the definition of a family when a family is identified with a source of variance.

Although the identification of a family of comparisons with a source of variance does a good job of addressing some important issues associated with controlling *FWE*, a researcher generally has many decisions to make regarding which contrasts to perform when analyzing a source of variance. For example, suppose we are comparing the effects of four different drugs on depression. There are six possible pairwise comparisons. In addition, we could compare each one of the drugs with the average of the other three, and with the average of two of the other three. That leads to a total of 22 possible significance tests. Many of the tests may be of interest, but we would suffer a substantial loss of power for each test if we conducted such a large set of tests while controlling *FWE* at a reasonable level. In short, the specification of a family of contrasts should involve a compromise between wanting to gain as much information as possible, and keeping the number of contrasts low enough to control *FWE* while still having reasonable power. In view of this, we should think hard about which hypotheses are of interest before we collect the data. We need to focus both the research design and the power of our significance tests on those questions that are of most interest to us.

10.5.2 Different Types of Families of Tests

In the sections that follow, we will describe several different methods for controlling *FWE*. The reason for the different methods has to do with the goals of procedures for controlling *FWE*. Any procedure for controlling familywise error rate attempts to (1) control *FWE* at a specified level (e.g., .05 or .10), while (2) maintaining good power to test individual contrasts. To meet these goals, a method must take into account both the size of the set of contrasts and the relations among those contrasts (e.g., independent or correlated). It is therefore useful to distinguish five categories of families of contrasts that differ in both these respects; these distinctions will help to organize the different procedures for controlling *FWE*.

1. *Planned contrasts.* A sensible research strategy is to include only those conditions in an experiment that are of interest, and to plan the contrasts to be tested before collecting the data. Focusing both the design and planned tests on only those contrasts that are important conserves time and effort in data collection and, by limiting the size of the family of contrasts, ensures more powerful tests of the contrasts when the familywise error rate is controlled.

2. *All pairwise comparisons.* Not all research can be planned to the point of specifying a set of contrasts *a priori*. A researcher must therefore be able to conduct tests based on an examination of the patterns of means that are actually observed. A simple, principled approach to analyzing a source of variance is to conduct the $(1/2)(a)(a-1)$ tests of differences between all pairs of group means to try to summarize patterns of effects.

3. *All comparisons with a control condition.* A relatively common experimental design includes a single control condition that serves as a baseline for evaluation of several experimental conditions. Assuming a conditions including the control, there will be $a-1$ significance tests of interest.

4. *Post hoc contrasts.* Despite thoughtful planning of contrasts, unanticipated differences may appear between means that may require more complex tests than simple pairwise comparisons. For example, it may appear that the mean across three experimental conditions is greater than the mean of a control condition. A researcher would, of course, want to explore those differences. However, the *FWE* is considerably larger in this situation than in the three preceding situations because the size of the family of tests is considerably larger, as we shall see.

5. *Contrasts when the independent variable is quantitative.* When the independent variable is defined by amount rather than type, the shape of the functional relation between the independent and dependent variable is usually of most interest. We will address the topic of trend analysis in Chapter 11.

To recap, the five categories of families differ in size and in the relations among the contrasts that comprise them. Thus, different methods for controlling *FWE* are appropriate for these different types of families. It will be useful to keep in mind that the same *t* test and confidence interval calculations may be applied in every case that we will consider. All that changes from one situation to another is the method of determining a critical value of *t*.

10.6 CONTROLLING THE *FWE* FOR FAMILIES OF *K* PLANNED CONTRASTS USING METHODS BASED ON THE BONFERRONI INEQUALITY

We begin with some very general methods that are applicable whenever several tests are planned. These methods apply not only to tests of differences among means, but also to tests of hypotheses about other parameters, such as proportions or correlations. *Note that it is not necessary that the omnibus F be significant prior to testing planned contrasts with the methods described in this section.*

In fact, power is lost by requiring a significant F before carrying out planned tests with these methods. What is critical is that the contrasts are decided on before the data are collected and a method for evaluating significance of the tests is used that maintains the familywise error rate at or below a reasonable level, presumably .05 or .10.

Equation 10.12 describes the relation between *FWE* and *EC* when the K tests are independent. Because this condition rarely holds, a more general statement of the relation is

$$FWE \le 1 - (1 - EC)^K \tag{10.13}$$

In other words, the *FWE* is equal to *or less than* the term on the right with the inequality holding when the tests are not independent. Furthermore, if K tests are conducted with error rates EC_1, $EC_2, \ldots, EC_K$,

$$FWE \le \sum_K EC_K \tag{10.14}$$

where EC_K is the probability of a Type 1 error for the Kth contrast. The relationship expressed in Equation 10.14 is known as the *Bonferroni inequality*, and it is the basis for several procedures for testing planned contrasts. From the inequality, it follows that if each of the K contrasts that make up the family is tested at $EC = FWE/K$, the probability of a Type 1 error for the family cannot exceed the *FWE*. If, for example, the family contains five planned contrasts, *FWE* will not be larger than .05 if each contrast in the family is tested at the .01 level.

In order to illustrate methods based on the Bonferroni inequality, we reconsider the memory experiment results summarized in Table 10.1. Table 10.4 contains an analysis of variance of those data, including results of tests of the three contrasts we considered earlier. The significance values for the three contrasts reported by SPSS are the *EC*s. According to this criterion, and assuming $\alpha = .05$, recall is significantly better in the image than in the control condition (Contrast 1), and the average of the three experimental methods yields significantly better recall than the control (Contrast 2). However, the reported *p*-values do not take into consideration the fact that three tests were performed on the means. Therefore, we will consider how each of two methods controls the *FWE* for this set of three tests.

10.6.1 The Dunn–Bonferroni Method (Dunn, 1961)

The Dunn–Bonferroni method for controlling *FWE* follows from Equation 10.14. If there are K contrasts, the *FWE* will not exceed a nominal value if the *EC* is set at that value divided by K. For example, assuming an *FWE* of .05, we test the three contrasts in Table 10.1 at the .0167 (.05/3) alpha level. The t statistics are those reported in Table 10.4; Equation 10.5 provides the formula for the t when variances are assumed equal, and Equations 10.8–10.10 provide the formulas for the t and df when variances are not assumed equal. If the exact *p*-value is available, we can control the *FWE* by comparing p with FWE/K and rejecting H_0 only for those contrasts where $p < FWE/K$. Looking at the SPSS output of Table 10.4 for our example, we would evaluate each of our three contrasts at the .0167 level. By this criterion, the contrast between the control and image conditions (i.e., Contrast 1) is no longer significant because the two-tailed *EC* is .033 (assuming homogeneity of variance).[2]

---

[2] Šidák (1967) proposed that, $H_{0k}: \psi_k = 0$ be rejected if $p_k \le 1 - (1 - FWE)^{1/K}$. Because $1 - (1 - FWE)^{1/K} > FWE/K$, this method has more power and a narrower confidence interval than the original Dunn–Bonferroni procedure. However, the difference is very small.

Table 10.4   Output for tests of three contrasts of means in a memory experiment (from SPSS)

(*a*) ANOVA

	Sum of squares	*df*	Mean square	*F*	Sig.
Between groups	173.900	3	57.967	3.230	.034
Within groups	646.000	36	17.944		
Total	819.900	39			

(*b*) Contrast coefficients

	Method			
Contrast	Control	Loci	Image	Rhyme
1	−1	0	1	0
2	−3	1	1	1
3	0	1	1	−2

(*c*) Contrast tests

	Contrast	Value of contrast	Std. error	*t*	*df*	Sig. (2-tailed)
Assumes equal variances	1	4.20	1.894	2.217	36	.033
	2	13.80	4.640	2.974	36	.005
	3	1.80	3.281	.549	36	.587
Does not assume equal variances	1	4.20	1.887	2.225	15.131	.042
	2	13.80	3.902	3.537	21.949	.002
	3	1.80	3.345	.538	20.466	.596

Confidence intervals based on the *FWE* have a form similar to those we encountered in Chapter 6; in general,

$$CI = \hat{\psi} \pm t_{FWE/K} s_{\hat{\psi}} \tag{10.15}$$

Consider Contrast 2 in Table 10.4. Inserting the means from Table 10.1, we have

$$\hat{\psi}_2 = (-3)(6.5) + (1)(12.1) + (1)(10.7) + (1)(10.5) = 13.80$$

Assuming equal variances, the standard error of this contrast is given in Table 10.4 as 4.640; it is calculated as in the denominator of Equation 10.5:

$$s_{\hat{\psi}} = \sqrt{MS_{S/A} \sum_j w_j^2 / n}$$

The critical value of t, t_{FWE}, can be obtained from statistical packages or by interpolation from Appendix Table C.7. For a two-tailed p equal to .0167, the critical $t = 2.51$ when $df = 36$.

Substituting values into Equation 10.14, the confidence bounds for ψ_2 are

$$CI = 13.80 \pm (2.51)(4.64) = 2.154, 25.446$$

We are not quite done. Recall that our original coefficients were 1, −1/3, −1/3, and −1/3; we multiplied by 3 to have integer entries in SPSS. We return to our original scale by dividing the interval bounds by 3. The final bounds are .718 and 8.482. We would follow the same procedure for constructing confidence intervals for the other two contrasts in our example.

When confidence intervals are based on the *FWE*, they are interpreted somewhat differently than when they are based on the *EC*. It may help to understand the distinction if we assume many random replications of the memory experiment. In each replication, a set of three confidence intervals, one for each of the planned contrasts in Table 10.1, is calculated. We expect that in 95% of the replications, all three intervals will contain the true (population) value of the contrast. Thus, we are 95% confident that all of the confidence intervals in the family are accurate statements; that is, we are 95% confident that all three intervals contain the value of the population parameter being estimated. These intervals based on the *FWE* are referred to as *simultaneous confidence intervals*.

10.6.2 Hochberg's Sequential Method (1988)

Sequential methods (also referred to as stepwise, or multistage) test contrasts in several stages. Some of these methods such as Duncan's (1955) and Newman–Keuls (Keuls, 1952; Newman, 1932) fail to adequately control the Type 1 error rate and therefore will not be considered. A limitation of all sequential methods is that confidence limits cannot be calculated. However, sequential methods confer a power advantage over the Dunn–Bonferroni procedure if the researcher is solely interested in a set of hypothesis tests.

There are several sequential methods for controlling *FWE* for a family of planned hypothesis tests. The simplest of these are Holm's sequentially rejective method (1979), and Hochberg's step-up method (1988). The Hochberg method is the more powerful of the two; it is described in Box 10.1. The power of this procedure can be increased, but at the cost of greater complexity (Hommel, 1988; Rom, 1990).

Box 10.1 Hochberg's (1988) Sequential Testing Method

1. Rank order the *K* contrasts according to their *p*-values with p_1 being the smallest and p_K being the largest. In the example of Table 10.4, the contrasts would be ordered: ψ_2, ψ_1, and ψ_3.
2. If $p_K \leq FWE$, all *K* null hypotheses are rejected. If not, consider the next largest *p*-value, p_{K-1}. If $p_{K-1} \leq FWE/2$, reject the null hypothesis corresponding to the *K* − 1 contrast and all remaining contrasts. If this test is not significant, test whether $p_{K-2} \leq FWE/3$, and so on.
3. Using the example of Table 10.4 and assuming *FWE* = .05, we first compare .587 with .05. This fails and we compare the next largest *p*-value, .033, against .05/2 or .025. This fails and we compare the last *p*-value, .005, against .05/3, or .0167. This is the only significant contrast, so we can reject only H_0: $\psi_2 = 0$.

To summarize, the choice between the Dunn–Bonferroni and the Hochberg procedures depends on whether the researcher wants confidence intervals. The Hochberg method is more powerful when conducting hypothesis tests, but does not yield confidence intervals.[3]

---

[3] Both the Šidák and Hochberg methods are available in several statistical packages, including SPSS and Systat, but the results are based on comparisons of members of all pairs of group means.

10.7 TESTING ALL PAIRWISE CONTRASTS

10.7.1 The Studentized Range Statistic

We present several methods for controlling *FWE* across a family of pairwise comparisons; all of the methods are based on q, *the Studentized range statistic*. This statistic is the range of a set of observations from a normally distributed population, divided by the estimated standard deviation of the population. If the observations are group means,

$$q = \frac{\overline{Y}_{max} - \overline{Y}_{min}}{s_{\overline{Y}}} \tag{10.16}$$

where $\overline{Y}_{max}$ and $\overline{Y}_{min}$ are the largest and smallest means in a set of a ordered means and $s_{\overline{Y}}$, the standard error of the mean, is

$$s_{\overline{Y}} = \sqrt{MS_e / n} \tag{10.17}$$

assuming homogeneity of variance and equal ns. Critical values of q can be found in Appendix Table C.9 as a function of the *FWE*, a (the number of means), and the df associated with the error mean square. Harter, Clemm, and Guthrie (1959) provide a more extensive table.[4]

The Studentized range statistic is closely related to t; the two statistics differ only in their denominators, so it is a simple matter to derive the relationship between t and q. If we were to carry out a t test of the difference between the largest and smallest means, assuming equal variances and group sizes in a one-factor design, the statistic would be

$$t = \frac{\overline{Y}_{max} - \overline{Y}_{min}}{\sqrt{MS_{S/A}\,(2/n)}} \tag{10.18}$$

$$= q/\sqrt{2}$$

Making explicit the relation between t and q makes it clear that the difference between the two classes of procedures is in the criterion for evaluating contrasts, rather than in the procedures for computing contrasts. Further, the relationship can be useful in comparing the results of procedures based on t (such as the Dunn–Bonferroni) with those based on q, and has also been the basis for dealing with unequal ns and unequal variances.

10.7.2 Tukey's (1953) *HSD* Test

Tukey's *HSD* (honestly significant difference) test controls the *FWE* for the set of all possible pairwise comparisons. It is a simultaneous method for testing hypotheses or constructing confidence intervals, meaning that a single critical value is used to evaluate all contrasts in a set. If the procedure is carried out without the help of software, it is helpful to compare differences against a critical difference. Specifically, a critical value of q is selected from Appendix Table C.9 and that value is multiplied by the standard error of the mean to find the critical difference between the two

---

[4] For significance levels other than those in Appendix Table C.9, users of SPSS can select the *Transform* option from the main menu, then *Compute Variable*; double-click on the *cdf.srange* option. Then, insert values for q (perhaps several trial values), a, and the error df. For example, in the left-hand panel, you may have a variable labeled p and in the right-hand panel, 2*(1 – CDF.SRANGE(5.05,4,19)). The p column of your data form should now show the value .02.

means that must be exceeded for significance. Once the critical difference is computed, it is a simple matter to evaluate any difference among group means. If the differences are ordered from largest to smallest, testing may stop once a nonsignificant difference is found because the remaining comparisons must also be nonsignificant.

A complete example of the procedure is presented in Box 10.2 using the summary statistics for the memory study that were presented in Table 10.1. Box 10.2 presents the necessary steps in testing all pairwise contrasts and for constructing simultaneous confidence intervals. The test is available in several statistical packages. For example, SPSS's *Post Hoc/Tukey* option reports the same bounds as in Box 10.2, and an exact *p*-value of .027 for the control versus loci difference.

Box 10.2 Applying Tukey's *HSD* Test to the Memory Data of Table 10.1

Hypothesis tests

1. Order the means in Table 10.1 from smallest to largest:

Method:	Control	Rhyme	Image	Loci
Mean:	6.5	10.5	10.7	12.1

2. From Appendix Table C.9, find the value of q required for significance when $FWE = .05$, $a = 4$, $n = 10$, and $df = a(n-1) = 36$. That value is approximately 3.81.

3. Calculate the standard error of the mean using the values of the variance in Table 10.1. Averaging the variance (assuming equal n), $MS_{S/A} = 17.944$, and

$$s_{\bar{Y}} = \sqrt{MS_{S/A}/n} = 1.340$$

4. We can now calculate a critical difference between means as $d_{crit} = SEM \times q_{crit} = 1.34 \times 3.81 = 5.1054$. All pairwise differences greater than this difference will be judged significant. For example, the largest difference (between the control and loci means) is 5.6 and is therefore significant. No other difference is larger than 5.1054, so this is the only significant difference when the *FWE* is controlled.

Confidence intervals

1. To construct confidence intervals, find the critical value of q and the standard error of the mean as above.

2. For any particular comparison of conditions, compute the difference between the means and compute an interval by: $\hat{\psi} \pm q_{(1 - confidence),a,df}\, s_{\bar{Y}}$. For example, the 95% confidence limits on the difference in mean recall of the control and loci populations are:

$$5.6 \pm (3.81)(1.34) = .495, 10.705$$

In many studies, only a few of the possible pairwise comparisons will be of interest. In such cases, is the Tukey test or the Dunn–Bonferroni procedure the better choice for controlling *FWE*? Dunn (1961) has demonstrated that when all possible pairwise comparisons are tested, the Tukey procedure has the narrower confidence interval and is the more powerful test. However, the advantage of the Tukey procedure declines as the *FWE* decreases, the *df* increases, or *K* decreases. Furthermore, if only a subset of all possible pairwise comparisons are planned and tested, a point is reached at which the Dunn–Bonferroni procedure is more powerful. For example, if there are four groups but only four or fewer of the possible six comparisons are tested, the Dunn–Bonferroni method requires a smaller value of t for significance than does Tukey's method.

If the researcher plans to test a subset of all possible pairwise comparisons, the relative power of the Dunn–Bonferroni and Tukey methods is easily assessed by comparing the critical values of the two procedures when both are expressed as t statistics: Calculate the ratio of critical values of the Dunn–Bonferroni to the Tukey method:

$$D\text{–}B \text{ to Tukey ratio} = \frac{t_{FWE,K}}{q_{FWE,K}/\sqrt{2}} \tag{10.19}$$

where K is the number of comparisons, and the t and q statistics are the values required for significance when K comparisons are made. When the ratio is less than 1, the Dunn–Bonferroni requires a smaller critical value, and will therefore be the preferred method.

In summary, if the researcher carefully plans only those pairwise comparisons that are truly of interest, power may be gained by using methods that focus only on the planned comparisons. Equation 10.19 provides a basis for deciding between the methods.

10.7.3 When *ns* are Unequal: The Tukey–Kramer Test

In the *Royer* study, the number of students in the fifth–eighth grades varied; see Table 10.2 for the group means, variances, and *ns*. A modification of Tukey's *HSD* test suggested by Kramer (1956) applies in such situations. The standard t statistic is calculated and compared with $q_{FWE,a,df_e}/\sqrt{2}$. Box 10.3 illustrates the test as applied to a comparison of the fifth- and sixth-grade mean speeds.

Box 10.3 An Example of the Tukey–Kramer Test When *ns* Are Not Equal

1. Find the critical value of q. In the example of the *Royer* speed data, $a = 4$ and the error df are 86. If $FWE = .05$, the critical q value is approximately 3.71.[a]
2. Obtain the critical value of t: $t = q_{FWE,a,df_e} / \sqrt{2} = 3.710/1.414 = 2.623$.
3. To test the difference between the fifth- and sixth-grade mean speeds, calculate the usual t statistic presented in Chapter 6 (with s_{pooled} replaced by $MS_{S/A}$). The Tukey–Kramer t equals the mean difference ($\hat{\psi}$) value divided by the std. error ($s_{\hat{\psi}}$);

$$t = \frac{\bar{Y}_{Grade6} - \bar{Y}_{Grade5}}{\sqrt{MS_{S/Grade}\left(\frac{1}{n_6} + \frac{1}{n_5}\right)}} = \frac{.560 - .350}{\sqrt{(.032)\left(\frac{1}{23} + \frac{1}{26}\right)}}$$

$$= .21/.051 = 4.101$$

which clearly exceeds 2.623.

[a] Harter, Clemm, and Guthrie (1959) provide a method of nonlinear interpolation when the exact *df* are not in the table. For example, when the $df = 86$, find $q_{.05,4,60} = 3.74$ and $q_{.05,4,120} = 3.69$ from the table, and the reciprocals of 86 (.0116), 60 (.0167), and 120 (.0083). The critical value for $df = 86$ is then given by

$$q_{.05,4,86} = 3.74 - \left(\frac{.0167 - .0116}{.0167 - .0083}\right)(3.74 - 3.69) = 3.710$$

10.7.4 When Variances Are Unequal

In Chapter 8, in our analysis of the effects of educational level upon mean depression scores of males in the *Seasons* study, we found that the variances were quite heterogeneous. Several methods have been proposed to deal with this problem. Most use Welch's t' and df' (see Section 10.3.4) but differ in the criterion against which t' is evaluated. In the Games–Howell test (1976), t' is compared with $q_{FWE,a,df'}/\sqrt{2}$. The procedure is illustrated in Box 10.4 using the *Seasons* depression data.

Box 10.4 The Games–Howell Procedure for Testing All Pairwise Comparisons When Variances Are Not Equal

1. Compute Welch's t' and df', using Equations 6.15 and 6.16. For the *HS* and *C* statistics of Table 10.3, panel *a*, we have:

$$t' = \frac{\bar{Y}_{HS} - \bar{Y}_C}{\sqrt{\dfrac{s_{HS}^2}{n_{HS}} + \dfrac{s_C^2}{n_C}}} = \frac{6.903 - 3.674}{\sqrt{\dfrac{34.541}{19} + \dfrac{5.970}{33}}} = 2.284$$

and

$$df' = \frac{\left(\dfrac{s_{HS}^2}{n_{HS}} + \dfrac{s_C^2}{n_C}\right)^2}{\dfrac{s_{HS}^4}{n_{HS}^2(n_{HS}-1)} + \dfrac{s_C^4}{n_c^2(n_C-1)}} = \frac{\left(\dfrac{34.541}{19} + \dfrac{5.970}{33}\right)^2}{\dfrac{34.541^2}{(19^2)(18)} + \dfrac{5.970^2}{(33^2)(32)}} \approx 22$$

2. Obtain the critical value of t from Appendix Table C.9. For our example with 22 *df*, interpolate in Appendix Table C.9 between $df = 20$ and $df = 24$, with $a = 4$, $FWE = .05$. The critical q value is approximately 3.93. Then

$$t_{.05,4,22} = 3.93 / \sqrt{2} = 2.779$$

3. Because $2.284 < 2.779$, we cannot reject H_0: $\mu_5 = \mu_6$. In similar fashion, values of t' and df' can be calculated for each of the remaining five pairwise comparisons. Note that the critical value of t must be recalculated for each test because the df' are likely to change for each comparison.

The Games–Howell method generally does a good job of controlling *FWE* with reasonable power. However, there are some circumstances under which *FWE* may be a bit inflated with Games–Howell. If the variances are fairly homogeneous and the group sizes are less than 50, the *FWE* for the Games–Howell method may sometimes be as high as .07 when the nominal probability is .05 (Dunnett, 1980; Games, Keselman, & Rogan, 1981). Even when the variances are not homogeneous, the *FWE* may be inflated with *n*s less than 6. However, the *FWE* is close to the nominal level under most other conditions. Furthermore, the test is more powerful than any of the several competitors that have been proposed and has narrower confidence intervals for each comparison. If the researcher is concerned about the possible inflation of the *FWE*, Dunnett's T3 test (Dunnett, 1980) appears to be the most powerful of several alternatives that maintain the *FWE* at less than or equal to the nominal value. The test requires tables of the Studentized maximum modulus distribution. Miller has described the procedure (1981, pp. 70–75) and has provided tables of the distribution. The test is also available in several statistical packages.

10.7.5 The Fisher–Hayter Test

The tests considered so far do not require a preliminary test of the omnibus null hypothesis; they control the *FWE* at or below its nominal level. In fact, requiring a significant omnibus *F* prior to these tests is likely to result in a loss of power. However, there are procedures for controlling the *FWE* that include an omnibus *F* test as a first stage; pairwise comparisons are conducted only if the initial *F* test is significant. In *Fisher's* (1935) *LSD* (least significant difference) procedure, the pairwise comparisons are tested by the usual *t* test at the .05 level in a second stage. However, because the *LSD* test has been shown to have an inflated *FWE* for $a > 3$, Hayter (1986) modified the test. The resulting Fisher–Hayter test maintains the *FWE* at or below its nominal level. In this test, a significant *F* test in the first stage is followed by tests of all pairwise comparisons using a standard *t* test, but each test is evaluated against the criterion $q_{FWE,\,a-1,\,df_e}/\sqrt{2}$. Note that in entering Appendix Table C.9, the column corresponding to $a - 1$ means provides the critical value.

Note that the Fisher–Hayter test is a sequential procedure involving two steps. As with other sequential testing methods, power is gained relative to simultaneous tests but at the loss of the ability to construct simultaneous confidence intervals. Therefore, the choice between the Fisher–Hayter test and the Tukey (or Tukey–Kramer) test depends on whether such confidence intervals are desired. Another consideration is whether variances are assumed to be homogeneous. The Fisher–Hayter test was derived under that assumption and therefore a test such as the Games–Howell or the Dunnett T3 should be used if homogeneity of variance is in doubt.

10.7.6 Pairwise Comparisons: Summing Up

The rather detailed set of recommendations for controlling *FWE* over families of pairwise comparisons results from an attempt to satisfy two criteria. The first is that we want a method that adequately controls the Type 1 error rate over the family. We have seen in previous chapters that two factors that often affect Type 1 error rates are heterogeneous variances and unequal *n* across conditions. We again find that the same two factors require adjustments of our procedures for controlling familywise error rates.

Given that we can identify alternative procedures that satisfactorily control Type 1 error rates, our second consideration is to choose the procedure that has the most power. Seaman et al. (1991) simulated tests of all pairwise comparisons under conditions of equal *n*s and equal variances. Over the conditions examined in their study, Seaman et al. found that the Fisher–Hayter method had a power advantage over the Tukey *HSD* method that varied between 2% and 9%; Tukey, in turn, had a power advantage of 2–3% over the Dunn–Bonferroni method. The other distinction among procedures that is relevant to power concerns is the distinction between simultaneous and sequential methods. Sequential tests have more power than simultaneous tests, although confidence intervals are not available when sequential methods are used.

Box 10.5 summarizes our recommendations with respect to the control of *FWE* over families of pairwise comparisons.

Box 10.5 Recommendations for Controlling *FWE* on Families of Pairwise Comparisons

1. If the researcher wants to construct confidence intervals to estimate the differences between group means:
   a. If the variances are homogeneous and *n*s are equal, use Tukey *HSD*.
   b. If the variances are unequal, use Games–Howell (or Dunnett T3 if the *n*s are fewer than 6).
   c. If the *n*s are unequal, use Tukey–Kramer.
   d. If only a subset of all pairwise comparisons are planned, use Equation 10.19 to determine whether Tukey HSD or Dunn–Bonferroni will have more power.
2. If the researcher only wants to conduct hypothesis tests:
   a. If the variances are homogeneous, use Fisher–Hayter.
   b. If the variances are unequal, use Games–Howell (or Dunnett T3 if the *n*s are fewer than 6).

We have excluded from our discussion of pairwise comparison procedures that are sometimes used; namely, Fisher's *LSD* test (1935), the Student–Newman–Keuls test (Keuls, 1952; Newman, 1939), and Duncan's multiple range test (1955). We advise against the use of these procedures because they yield *FWE*s that often are considerably in excess of the nominal value. We have also excluded several procedures that maintain the *FWE* at or below its nominal level and have slightly more power than the Fisher–Hayter method under some combinations of number of groups and group size (e.g., Peritz, 1970; Ramsey, 1978, 1981; Shaffer, 1979, 1986; Welsch, 1977). On the basis of various sampling studies, the very slight power advantage of these methods (usually 1% or 2%) does not warrant the added complexity they usually entail. Descriptions of these methods, together with results of sampling experiments, may be found in the article by Seaman et al. (1991); multiple comparison procedures are also reviewed by Zwick (1993), Shaffer (1995), and Toothaker (1993).

Finally, we note that some or all of the pairwise comparison procedures we have considered, as well as the Dunn–Bonferroni and Dunn–Šidák tests, are available in various statistical software packages. For example, SPSS can perform 12 different tests of pairwise comparisons (select the *Post hoc* option in the *Compare Means/One-Way ANOVA* or in the *General Linear Model/Univariate* menu). Although it is tempting to run several of these tests, we urge researchers to select one procedure in advance, and base conclusions on the results of that test.

10.8 COMPARING $a-1$ TREATMENT MEANS WITH A CONTROL: DUNNETT'S TEST

Dunnett (1955, 1964) proposed a test for studies in which the researcher plans to contrast each of several treatments with a control. If these are the only comparisons of interest, methods that control the *FWE* for a family consisting of *all* pairwise comparisons will be overly conservative; power will be lost and simultaneous confidence intervals will be wider than necessary. The Dunn–Bonferroni procedure with $K = a - 1$ will be an improvement but will still offer less power and wider intervals than the Dunnett test.

Assuming that the group sizes are equal and that variances are homogeneous, the test is quite simple. Box 10.6 illustrates the procedure using the data from the memory study. However, if

> **Box 10.6 Dunnett's Test Comparing the Experimental Means with the Control Mean in the Memory Study**
>
> 1. Compute the usual t statistic comparing the control with each experimental group; e.g., to compare the control and loci means
>
> $$t = \frac{\bar{Y}_{Loci} - \bar{Y}_C}{\sqrt{MS_{S/A}\left(\frac{2}{n}\right)}} = \frac{12.1 - 6.5}{\sqrt{17.944\left(\frac{2}{10}\right)}} = 2.96$$
>
> and for the comparison of the control group mean with the rhyme and image means, $t = 2.11$ and 2.22, respectively.
>
> 2. Evaluate the three t statistics against the critical value of $d_{FWE,a,df}$ in Appendix Table C.8, where a is the number of means including the control and df is the number of degrees of freedom associated with the ANOVA error term. In the present example, FWE (two-tailed) $= .05$, $a = 4$, and the error $df = 36$; the critical value is 2.48. Only the control and loci means differ significantly.
>
> 3. The confidence intervals have the same form as in the two-independent-group examples of Chapter 6; the bounds are
>
> $$(\bar{Y}_i - \bar{Y}_C) \pm s_{\hat{\psi}} d_{FWE,a,df}$$
>
> For example, for comparison of the loci mean with the control mean, the bounds are
>
> $$(12.1 - 6.5) \pm \sqrt{17.944\left(\frac{2}{10}\right)} \times 2.48 = .90, 10.30$$

the group sizes are not equal, replace $2/n$ in the equation for t by $1/n_j + 1/n_C$, and use the Dunn–Bonferroni procedure with $K = a - 1$. If any of the a group variances differ, use Welch's t' and again use the Dunn–Bonferroni procedure.

10.9 CONTROLLING THE FAMILYWISE ERROR RATE FOR POST HOC CONTRASTS

Sometimes observed patterns in the data suggest the presence of effects that had not been anticipated and that are not adequately captured by the set of all possible pairwise comparisons. When the corresponding null hypotheses are tested to determine whether these effects are significant, we should be quite conservative in evaluating the result. In testing contrasts "after the fact" we are, in effect, investigating the family of all possible outcomes. Therefore, the methods we present are quite conservative because they control for the probability of at least one Type 1 error in a very large set of possible contrasts.

10.9.1 Scheffé's Method

Assuming that the populations are normally distributed and have equal variances, Scheffé's (1959) method maintains the *FWE* at its nominal level when the family consists of all possible contrasts associated with a source of variance. Using the fifth–eighth-grade multiplication speeds in the study by Royer et al. (1999) as an example, assume that we had not anticipated the pattern of means in Table 10.2. After viewing the data, we observe that the sixth–eighth grades had very similar means, each higher than the fifth-grade mean. We might wish to test whether the mean of the fifth-grade response times differs significantly from that of the three combined sixth–eighth-grade times. Box 10.7 describes the Scheffé procedure, and illustrates its application to the contrast of the fifth-grade mean with the average of the other three means.

Box 10.7 Scheffé's Method to Test H_0: $(1/3)(\mu_6 + \mu_7 + \mu_8) - \mu_5 = 0$ (*Royer speed data*)

1. Calculate the t statistic to test the contrast of interest (see Equation 10.5).
2. Compare the computed value of t with $S = \pm \sqrt{df_1} \cdot F_{FWE, df_1, df_2}$ where df_1 and df_2 are the numerator and denominator degrees of freedom.
3. For the arithmetic experiment, $df_1 = 3$ and $df_2 = 36$; if $FWE = .05$, the critical F is approximately (from Appendix Table C.5) $F_{FWE, df_1, df_2} = 2.88$. Therefore,

$$S = \pm \sqrt{(3)(2.88)} = 2.94$$

4. Reject the null hypothesis if $t > S$ or $t < -S$. To test the null hypothesis, $t = 5.23$. Because $5.21 > 2.94$, we reject H_0.
5. The formula for the confidence interval bounds is

$$\hat{\psi} \pm s_{\hat{\psi}} \sqrt{df_1 \cdot F_{FWE, df_1, df_2}}$$

where $\hat{\psi} = .680$ and $s_{\hat{\psi}} = \sqrt{MS_{S/A} (\Sigma\, w_j^2 / n_j)} = .130$. Therefore, the bounds on $(\mu_6 + \mu_7 + \mu_8) - 3\,\mu_5$ are $.680 \pm (.130)(2.94) = .298, 1.062$.

6. To return to the original scale, these bounds must be divided by 3; the bounds on $(1/3)(\mu_6 + \mu_7 + \mu_8) - \mu_5$ are .099 and .354.

It is instructive to compare the confidence interval presented in Box 10.7 with the results we would have obtained if our contrast had been planned. Assume that the contrast was one of three planned for the experiment. In that case, we could have used the Dunn–Bonferroni method to compute the confidence interval. In contrast to the interval limits in Box 10.7, the Dunn–Bonferroni limits are

$$\hat{\psi} \pm t_{FWE/K} s_{\hat{\psi}}$$

The contrast and its standard error are .680 and .130 (see Box 10.7), and the t required for significance at the $.05/3 = .0167$ level (two-tailed) is 2.51. Substituting these values (and dividing the resulting limits by 3 to return to the original scale), we find the Dunn–Bonferroni limits to be .118 and .335. The Dunn–Bonferroni interval is narrower than the Scheffé interval in Box 10.7, revealing the price we pay in precision of estimation and power when contrasts are not planned. Whenever possible, it is a good strategy to plan all contrasts that might conceivably be of interest, and then use the Dunn–Bonferroni or Fisher–Hayter method. Although the power of these methods decreases as the number of planned contrasts increases, a rather large number of comparisons must be planned before the Scheffé criterion requires a smaller value of t for significance (see Perlmutter & Myers, 1973, for a more detailed comparison of the Dunn–Bonferroni and the Scheffé methods).

Experimenters who have used both the standard ANOVA tests and the Scheffé procedure have sometimes been surprised to find that the omnibus null hypothesis is rejected by the ANOVA test but that no contrasts are significant by the Scheffé criterion. The source of this apparent contradiction is that the overall F test has exactly the same power as the *maximum possible contrast* tested by the Scheffé procedure. That contrast may be of little interest, so it may not have been tested. It could be something like $(11/37)\mu_1 + (26/37)\mu_2 - (17/45)\mu_3 - (28/45)\mu_4$. In summary, although rejection of the omnibus null hypothesis indicates that at least one contrast is significant by the Scheffé criterion, there is no guarantee that any obvious or interesting contrast will be significant.

As with all the tests we have so far considered (except the Fisher–Hayter), there is no logical necessity that the Scheffé tests of contrasts be preceded by a significant omnibus F. On the other hand, if the omnibus F test is not significant, no contrast will be significant. Thus, there is little point in expending energy on a series of post hoc Scheffé tests unless first determining that the F test is significant.

10.9.2 The Brown–Forsythe Method When Variances Are Not Equal

Brown and Forsythe (1974b) proposed that Welch's t' and df' (Box 10.3) be used with a criterion similar to Scheffé's S when the test is post hoc and the assumption of homogeneity of variance is questionable. The only difference is that the critical value of S against which t' is evaluated is based on df' (see Equation 10.10).

10.10 CONTROLLING THE FAMILYWISE ERROR RATE IN MULTI-FACTOR DESIGNS

We have been considering the control of FWE in the context of examples taken from one-factor designs. Although the calculations and methods for control of error rates are the same in multi-factor designs, there are several additional issues. Consider a two-factor design with four levels of B (e.g., type of drug) and two levels of A (e.g., age). We may wish to compare the B marginal means to determine the relative efficacy of the different drugs. We might use the Tukey HSD procedure to control FWE. We may also wish to compare the means of the B conditions within each level of A (that is, the simple effects of drug at each age). Is each level of A a family with the FWE set at .05? Or should FWE be set at .025 at each level of A so that the FWE is .05 for the complete set of tests? And should the comparisons of marginal means and of simple effects be considered separate families, or one family? Suppose we are also concerned with testing interaction effects? Is this still another family of tests? Or should all the tests be considered a single family, thus controlling Type 1 error rates simultaneously for all hypotheses tested in the experiment, but sacrificing power? There are no generally agreed-upon answers to such questions. We will make some recommendations; however, depending on their designs and the questions they wish to address, investigators may decide on different approaches than the one we take in this section. Whatever the approach to controlling FWE, it is important that any report of research be clear about just how the FWE was controlled so that readers may perform their own evaluation of the significance of results.

In the remainder of this section, we illustrate some common tests of contrasts, and our recommendations for controlling the FWE, using a simple 2×4 set of means, each based on six scores. Table 10.5 contains the cell means and the A and B marginal means, together with the ANOVA summary.

Table 10.5   Cell means (a) and ANOVA (b)

(a) Cell means

	Drug type				
Age group	B_1	B_2	B_3	B_4	Mean
A_1	12	6	5	15	9.5
A_2	16	2	9	3	7.5
Mean	14	4	7	9	

(b) ANOVA (n = 6)

Source	df	SS	MS	F	p
Age group (A)	1	48	48	1.280	.265
Drug (B)	3	638	212.67	5.653	.003
AB	3	528	176	4.693	.007
S/AB	40	1,500	37.5		

10.10.1 Testing Hypotheses About Marginal Means

The results of the analysis of variance in Table 10.5 reveal that the drug type (B) has significant effects, and the significant interaction suggests that the sizes of these effects are different in the two age groups (A). Let us consider the effects of B first. Most likely, we would wish to compare pairs of the four drug means. Tukey's *HSD* method provides a way to control the familywise error rate for the six pairwise tests we will perform. Setting the *FWE* at .05 and turning to Appendix Table C.9, we find that the critical value of q, the Studentized range statistic, is 3.79 when $a = 4$ and the error $df = 40$. The standard error of the mean is $SEM = \sqrt{MS_{S/AB}/n} = 1.768$. Note that $n = 12$, which is the number of scores contributing to each mean at each level of B. As in Box 10.2, we multiply the critical value of q by the *SEM*, yielding a critical difference of 6.700. Only the difference between the marginal B_1 and B_2 means exceed this value; therefore, controlling the *FWE* at .05, the only significance pairwise difference is between these two drugs.

Sometimes the researcher may have an *a priori* hypothesis that specified that only certain comparisons, whether pairwise or more complex, would be significant. In that case, the Dunn–Bonferroni method should be followed. The per comparison error rate would be the desired familywise error rate divided by K, the number of tests; this would be the critical p-value for our significance tests.

Another possible scenario is that the researcher observes the means in Table 10.5 and decides at that point that the difference between the B_1 and B_2 means is large enough to warrant further investigation. Or, after viewing the means, the researcher decides that the B_1 mean is different enough from the other means that it should be tested against the average of the other three means. Such post hoc contrasts should be tested by the Scheffé procedure described in Box 10.7.

Two points should be noted about the developments so far. First, we have identified a family as a set of comparisons related to a single source of variance. If we had several levels of A, we also would have controlled the *FWE* at .05 for all comparisons of those marginal means. The second point is that we have assumed homogeneity of variance. As we discussed earlier in this chapter, modifications of the usual tests are indicated when this assumption is not met. In particular, the Tukey *HSD* method is not appropriate because the various means have different standard errors. In such a case, even if all pairwise comparisons are of interest, the Bonferroni procedure should be applied with the standard error of the difference between means based on the average within-cell variance of the cells involved in each comparison.

In sum, contrasts to analyze main effects within multi-factor designs follow the same recommendations and procedures presented earlier in the context of the one-factor design.

10.10.2 Testing Hypotheses About Simple Effects

Having found a significant difference between the marginal B_1 and B_2 means, we may ask whether this difference is significant in either or both age groups. Also, although no other differences among the marginal means were significant, it is possible that there are other significant differences in one of the two age groups. Therefore, a reasonable next step is to compare the drugs at each level of *A*. The issue is what familywise error rate will be acceptable. We view the set of all contrasts of simple effects as a single family and therefore recommend that the *FWE* at each level of *A* be .05 divided by the number of levels of *A*. In the example of Table 10.5, pairwise comparisons within each of the two age groups would be tested with the critical value of *q* at the .025 level. Although Appendix Table C.9 contains only .01, .05, and .10 values for the Studentized range, most software that performs the Tukey *HSD* test will allow entry of any criterion for significance; values are also available in the original Harter et al. (1959) technical report from which our table was adapted. The required value of *q* is 4.197 when $a = 4$ and the error $df = 40$.

It may seem that a first step would be to perform an omnibus *F* test at each level of *A*. However, the Studentized range statistic when applied to the largest difference between means is a test of the omnibus null hypothesis that all means are equal.[5] Therefore, we proceed directly to pairwise comparisons at each level of *A*. Assuming that the eight population variances are homogeneous, the critical difference is the standard error times the critical value of *q*; i.e., $d_{crit} = 2.5 \times 4.197$, or 10.493. At A_1, the difference between the B_4 and B_2 means, and that between the B_4 and B_3 means are the two largest, but neither exceeds the critical value. Accordingly, we cannot reject the hypothesis that the *B* population means at A_1 are equal. At A_2, however, there are significant differences; the B_1 mean differs significantly from the B_2 and the B_4 means. Our analysis of the simple effects of the drugs has provided important information. Although we cannot be sure that other differences among the drug effects do not exist (because we cannot accept the null hypothesis), we have found that in the second age group drug B_1 is clearly superior to drugs B_2 and B_4.

We have assumed that all pairwise comparisons within each level of a second factor are to be performed. There may be circumstances in which only some of the possible comparisons within each level are of interest. For example, assume that we have *a priori* hypotheses about three contrasts at A_1 and two more contrasts at A_2. In that case, the Dunn–Bonferroni procedure with $K = 5$ is appropriate; each test would be performed with $\alpha = .01$. On the other hand, assume that the same contrasts appear to be of interest only after viewing the cell means. In that case, the Scheffé procedure, described in Box 10.7, is appropriate with $df_1 = (a - 1)(b - 1)$.

---

[5] See Myers, 1979, for a discussion of the relative power of the *F* and Studentized range tests of the omnibus null hypothesis.

10.10.3 The Relation Between Tests of Interactions and Tests of Simple Effects

Contrasts of simple effects are of interest in their own right and, when the error rate is properly controlled, can be helpful in drawing more precise inferences about the effects of our variables. However, a common misconception is that such tests are performed only to help us understand the causes of a significant interaction. They may sometimes do so, particularly when differences among means are significant at one level of a factor but not at others, as in our analysis of the means in Table 10.5. In many cases, however, the pattern of results is inconsistent with what we would expect if our means were population means. We may have a significant interaction and fail to find any significant difference between means of one variable at any level of the second. Or the interaction may fail to be significant, but simple effects of one variable may differ significantly. The tests of interaction and of simple effects differ in power both because of differences in the criteria for significance and because of differences in the cell frequencies and variances involved.

A common result that sometimes puzzles researchers is illustrated by the following cell means:

	B_1	B_2
A_1	15	5
A_2	8	6

Assume nine scores in a cell and an average cell variance of 100. Then, the t test of interaction is

$$t_{interaction} = [(15 - 5) - (8 - 6)] / (10\sqrt{4/9}) = 1.20$$

The interaction is not significant. However, if we compare the simple effects of B at A_1 we have

$$t_{B/A_1} = (15 - 5) / (10\sqrt{2/9}) = 2.12$$

which is significant at the .021 level. The test at A_1 does not yield a significant result. Even controlling the FWE at .025 for each test comparing simple effects, we conclude that there is a difference between the B means at A_1. We now have an apparent contradiction: The test of the interaction does not provide evidence of an interaction in the population. However, the significant result of the test at A_1, coupled with a nonsignificant result of the test at A_2 (that t was .42), suggests that there is an interaction with B having effects at A_1 but not at A_2. The reason for this inequality is that the standard error of the interaction involves the variance of differences among four means, whereas the standard error for the simple effect involves the variance of only two means. Therefore, it is possible to have a pattern of test results for simple effects that is not consistent with the result of the test of interaction because the power of the test of the simple effects is greater than the power of the test of the interaction.

10.10.4 Testing Hypotheses About Interaction

Various proposals have been made about the proper follow-up analyses to perform to understand a significant interaction (Games, 1973; Marascuilo & Levin, 1972, 1973; Tukey, 1991). The most direct approach is to test embedded 2×2 interactions. For example, in Table 10.5, we might test the interaction involving the two age groups and the B_1 and B_4 drugs. This interaction effect size is

$(12 + 3) - (15 + 16) = -16$. Dividing this by its standard error, $\sqrt{MS_{S/AB}(4/n)}$, we have the t statistic or, squaring, we have the F. If this test had been planned, the alpha level would be set at .05. However, if such analyses are performed, they are typically post hoc. In that case, we have two options for controlling the familywise error rate. Assuming homogeneous variances, we can apply Scheffé's method; we calculate $S = \sqrt{(a-1)(b-1)F_{.05,\,(a-1)(b-1),\,ab(n-1)}}$. In our example, $(a-1)(b-1) = 3$ and $ab(n-1) = 40$. The F required for significance at the .05 level with 3 and 40 df is 2.84. Therefore, $S = 2.92$. An alternative is to view the set of six possible 2×2 interaction contrasts as a family and use the Bonferroni criterion. With the FWE set at .05, the alpha level for each t test is .05/6, or .0083. Assuming a two-tailed test, the critical value of $t = 2.78$, slightly smaller than the critical value of S. As in this example, the Bonferroni criterion will often be slightly more powerful though its advantage will be lost as the number of interaction contrasts increases. As in our example, when variances are homogeneous, the choice between methods rests on a comparison of the critical values (see Perlmutter & Myers, 1979). If variances are heterogeneous, the Bonferroni method should be used, with the error term and error df based on the contrast tested.

10.10.5 Using Software to Perform Further Analyses

In most software packages, simple effects can readily be tested by splitting the file. For example, using SPSS to test all pairwise comparisons among drugs for each age group, we would select the *Data* menu, and then indicate that the file is to be split by levels of A. A univariate analysis would then be performed on each of the a sets of means after selecting the Tukey *HSD* test from the available post hoc options. The *select cases* option available in most packages will enable selection of specified levels of factors, permitting tests of embedded 2×2 interactions. However, there are two caveats to keep in mind when splitting files or using *select cases* to conduct contrasts on subsets of observations in a data file. First, the error terms for the tests will be based just on the subset of observations selected for analysis. If variances are homogeneous in the experiment and the researcher wishes to take advantage of the increased number of df that result from pooling the variances across all conditions (i.e., using $MS_{S/AB}$ in the error term of each contrast), the researcher will need to recompute the denominator of the contrast. The second caveat is that the reported p-values are unlikely to reflect control of the familywise error rate. In general, the researcher must ensure that the appropriate criterion for significance has been applied, either through options in the software or, when these are lacking, by comparing the test statistic against the appropriate criterion.

10.11 SUMMARY

This chapter developed the following points:

- Contrasts are specific comparisons on a set of means that allow researchers to pose detailed questions of a data set.
- Procedures for conducting hypothesis tests and constructing confidence intervals on contrasts are straightforward extensions of the t test procedures covered in Chapter 6.
- In an experimental design of any complexity, there are many possible contrasts that might be of interest to a researcher. The probability that at least one Type 1 error will occur in a set, or family, of contrasts increases as a function of the size of the family. It is therefore important to control the probability of a Type 1 error across a family (i.e., FWE).

- There are many different kinds of families of contrasts of means. These include the family of comparisons planned prior to data collection; the family of all possible comparisons of members of pairs of group means; the family of all comparisons of experimental group means with a control mean; and the family of post hoc contrasts determined on the basis of viewing the data.
- Different methods have been developed for controlling the *FWE*, depending on the kind of family, and on whether confidence intervals are desired. Most of these methods involve the usual *t* statistic, or its close relative, the Studentized range statistic, or—when heterogeneity of variance is suspected, Welch's t'. The major difference among the methods is the criterion employed for judging a contrast of means to be significant.

Table 10.6 provides a summary of much of what has been presented in this chapter. This summary integrates several considerations affecting the choice of procedures for controlling Type 1 error. One reason for the many different procedures in Table 10.6 is that the control of Type 1 errors is influenced by considerations such as whether the assumption of homogeneity of variance has been met, and whether *n*s are equal across conditions. It is paramount that a given procedure controls Type 1 errors at close to the nominal level. Given that this criterion is met, power considerations are the second major reason for the many procedures presented in Table 10.6. Given two procedures that adequately control Type 1 error rates, we prefer the method that results in more powerful tests. Sequential methods provide more powerful tests, so they are preferred over simultaneous methods when hypothesis tests are conducted. However, sequential methods are not applicable to the construction of confidence intervals because there is no ordering within a set of confidence intervals. Finally, we emphasize again that contrasts should be planned whenever possible because a set of planned contrasts is almost always smaller than a set of unplanned contrasts. Thus, tests of planned contrasts generally have more power than tests conducted on other kinds of families. But perhaps the more important benefit of planning contrasts is that the careful thought that is required to specify the key research questions will probably lead to research designs that are more closely focused on those questions.

Table 10.6 Recommended procedures for controlling *FWE*

Family type	Simultaneous methods[a]		Sequential methods	
	Equal variances	Unequal variances	Equal variances	Unequal variances
Planned	Dunn–Bonferroni	Dunn–Bonferroni using Welch's t'	Hochberg	Hochberg using Welch's t'
All pairwise	Tukey *HSD* (equal *n*) or Tukey–Kramer (unequal *n*)[b]	Games–Howell or Dunnett T3	Fisher–Hayter	
Exptl vs control	Dunnett (equal *n*) or Dunn–Bonferroni (unequal *n*)	Dunn–Bonferroni using Welch's t'		
Post hoc	Scheffé	Scheffé using Welch's t'		

[a] Only the simultaneous methods allow the construction of simultaneous confidence intervals.
[b] Assuming *K* pairwise tests, the Bonferroni method will be more powerful than the Tukey under some conditions; Equation 10.19 provides the basis for the choice.

EXERCISES

10.1 There are five treatment conditions in a problem-solving study, each with $n = 20$. Two groups, $F1$ and $F2$, are given instructions designed to facilitate problem solving. The third group is a control group given neutral instructions. The fourth and fifth groups, $I1$ and $I2$, are given instructions designed to interfere with problem solving. The data are

	F1	F2	C	I1	I2
$\bar{Y}_j$	14.6	14.9	13.8	11.8	11.7
s_j^2	3	4	5	4	4

Test each of the following hypotheses with $\alpha = .05$. State H_0 and H_1.
(a) The average of the facilitation group population means is greater than the mean of the control population.
(b) The average of the interference population means is different from the mean of the control population.
(c) The average of the facilitation means is not the same as the average of the interference means.

10.2 (a) Assume that all three tests in Exercise 10.1 had been planned prior to data collection. Using the Dunn–Bonferroni method, construct 90% simultaneous confidence intervals for the three contrasts. Re-evaluate whether the null hypotheses in parts (b) and (c) should be rejected, using the Dunn–Bonferroni criterion with $FWE = .10$.
(b) Assume the contrasts were decided on after viewing the means. Use the Scheffé method to construct simultaneous confidence intervals. Re-evaluate whether the null hypotheses in parts (b) and (c) of Exercise 10.1 should be rejected with $FWE = .10$.

10.3 The following group means are each based on 10 scores:

A_1	A_2	A_3
24	16	14

(a) Calculate SS_A.
(b) Calculate the sum of squares for each of the following contrasts: (i) $\hat{\psi}_1 = \bar{Y}_{.1} - \bar{Y}_{.2}$; (ii) $\hat{\psi}_2 = (1/2)(\bar{Y}_{.1} + \bar{Y}_{.2}) - \bar{Y}_{.3}$; (iii) $\hat{\psi}_3 = \bar{Y}_{.1} - \bar{Y}_{.3}$. What should be true of the relation between SS_A and the sums of squares for $\hat{\psi}_1$ and $\hat{\psi}_2$? Why?
(c) We can remove the effect associated with $\hat{\psi}_1$ from the data by setting the means at A_1 and A_2 equal to their average. The adjusted means are

A_1	A_2	A_3
20	20	14

Redo part (b), (ii) and (iii). Are either of the sums of squares different from those calculated for the original (unadjusted) means? Explain, emphasizing the relation of the results to the concept of orthogonality.

10.4 **(a)** Suppose the group sizes in Exercise 10.3 were not equal; the n_j are 8, 10, and 12, respectively. Returning to the original means, calculate SS_A. Then calculate the sums of squares for $\hat{\psi}_1$ and $\hat{\psi}_2$. Now, what is the relation between the sums of squares for $\hat{\psi}_1$ and $\hat{\psi}_2$ and SS_A?

(b) Redefine the ψ_2 contrast so that it is orthogonal to that for ψ_1 for the samples sizes stated in this exercise. Calculate $SS_{\hat{\psi}_2}$. Does $SS_{\hat{\psi}_1} + SS_{\hat{\psi}_2} = SS_A$?

10.5 Consider the group means in Exercise 10.3. Assume that $MS_{S/A} = 900$.

(a) Assuming $n = 10$ in all three groups, calculate the standardized contrast, $\hat{\psi}_s$, for part (b, ii) of Exercise 10.3.

(b) Repeat part (a), but assume the unequal ns of Exercise 10.4 and define the contrast as in part (b). Assume that the error mean square still equals 900.

10.6 The following is suggested by a study conducted by Fenz and Epstein (1967). In a study of conflict in parachutists, GSR measures were obtained for five different groups of five subjects who differed with respect to when the measures were taken: 2 weeks before the jump (*BJ*-2), 1 week before (*BJ*-1), on the day of the jump prior to jumping (*DJ-P*), and on the day of the jump after jumping (*DJ-A*). There was also a control group who did not jump. The MS_{error} for the ANOVA = 4.0, and it is reasonable to assume homogeneity of variance. The means were

	BJ-2	*BJ*-1	*DJ-A*	*DJ-P*	*C*
Mean =	5	5	7	9	2

(a) Assume that the investigator had planned to compare each of the four experimental groups with the control (*C*). With $\alpha = .05$ (two-tailed), test the difference between the *DJ-P* and *C* means, using (i) the Dunn–Bonferroni procedure and (ii) the Dunnett procedure.

(b) Assume that the experimenter tested all possible pairwise comparisons. Redo the test in part (a), using the appropriate procedure for controlling the *FWE* at .05.

(c) Comment on the relative power of these three procedures, justifying your conclusion by citing relevant information in your preceding answers. Explain why these situations give rise to the differences in power that you indicate.

(d) Calculate the confidence intervals obtained with each of the three procedures and relate the results to your answer to part (c).

10.7 A sample of humanities majors is divided into three groups of 10 each in a study of statistics learning. One group receives training on relevant concepts *before* reading the text, a second receives the training *after* reading the text, and a third is a no-training *control*. Summary statistics on a test are:

	Before	After	Control
$\bar{Y}_{.j}$	20	14	13
s_j^2	72	62	76

(a) We want to test whether the mean of the *before* population is higher than the average of the other two populations combined. In answering the following parts, assume that $FWE = .05$. (i) State the null and alternative hypotheses. (ii) What is the estimate of the variance of the sampling distribution of $\hat{\psi}$ (assume homogeneity of variance)? (iii) Calculate the t statistic appropriate for testing H_0.

(b) Evaluate the test statistic you just calculated, assuming (i) the test was the sole contrast tested and had been planned before viewing the data; (ii) the test was a result of viewing the data.

10.8 We have five group means, each based on 10 scores, with $MS_{S/A} = 4.0$. The means are

A_1	A_2	A_3	A_4	A_3
8.6	9.5	9.2	8.0	10.4

(a) We plan five contrasts with $FWE = .05$. Test the contrast of A_5 against the average of the other four groups. State the criterion required for significance, and whether H_0 can be rejected.

(b) What is the result of the significance test if we decided on the contrast in part (a) after inspecting the data?

(c) Find the confidence intervals corresponding to the tests in parts (a) and (b). Explain the difference in widths.

(d) Suppose we did all possible pairwise tests. Actually calculate the test for A_1 against A_2. What is the criterion statistic? What conclusion do you reach about H_0?

(e) Suppose the only contrast we planned pitted the average of A_1 and A_2 against the average of the remaining three groups. Do the calculations and report the results, showing the criterion statistic.

10.9 In an attitude-change study, four groups of subjects are presented with persuasive messages about a topic. Two groups read the messages; a positive message for one group and a negative message for the other. Two other groups receive the messages by viewing a videotape. A fifth, control, group receives no message. Each group has its attitude assessed by a questionnaire in which larger scores mean a more positive attitude. There are seven subjects in each group and $MS_{S/A} = 20$. The group means are:

A_1 Video/positive	A_2 Video/negative	A_3 Read/positive	A_4 Read/negative	A_4 Read/negative
71	42	63	47	52

(a) Determine which experimental conditions differ significantly from the control, using the Dunnett test with $FWE = .05$.

(b) Test the hypothesis that the difference between the positive and negative messages is the same whether they are read, or are presented by videotape. Assume this is the only planned comparison.

(c) By how much would two groups have to differ before they would be considered significantly different by the Tukey test with $FWE = .05$?

10.10 The *Male_Educ* file on the *Seasons* page contains mean (over seasons) for four of the *Schoolyr* categories (3 = only high school, 5 = some post high school, 7 = bachelor's degree, 8 = graduate school). In what follows, assume that all pairwise differences are tested.

(a) Test the difference between the *Schoolyr* = 3 and *Schoolyr* = 5 *Beck_D* means, using (i) the Tukey–Kramer method, and (ii) the Dunn–Bonferroni method, assuming all pairwise comparisons and *FWE* = .05. Assume homogeneous variances. (iii) Compare the 95% confidence intervals.

(b) (i) Perform the Games–Howell test of the difference in part (a) and compare the results with those in part (a). In particular, which of these procedures should be used with these data? (ii) Calculate the Games–Howell confidence interval.

10.11 The *Sayhlth* file on the *Seasons* page of the website contains Beck Depression scores as a function of several factors.

(a) Test whether employment status significantly affects *Beck_D*, the mean (over seasons) of the Beck Depression scores.

(b) Calculate all simultaneous confidence intervals (*FWE* = .05) by the Tukey–Kramer method. Assume homogeneous variances.

(c) Redo part (b), using the Dunn–Bonferroni method. Assume homogeneous variances.

10.12 (a) Is the assumption of homogeneity of variance reasonable for the data in Exercise 10.11? Support your conclusion with statistical evidence.

(b) Assume that we wish to know whether the mean depression score for fully employed individuals (category 1) differs from that of those who are not fully employed (categories 2 and 3 in the *Sayhlth* file). Test whether the difference is significant, assuming this is the sole comparison tested and was planned prior to the collection of data.

10.13 Assume that 40 subjects are divided into good and poor readers on the basis of a pretest. They then read either intact or scrambled text, and are tested for their recall. The means are:

	Text	
Reading ability	Intact	Scrambled
Good	63	54
Poor	48	43

Assign weights to the cells and use them to calculate SS_ψ for reading ability, for text, and for their interaction.

10.14 Each cell in the following table contains a mean based on 10 scores:

	A_1	A_2	A_3
B_1	20	10	6
B_2	6	10	8

(a) Find the sums of squares accounted for by each of the following contrasts of the *A* marginal means: $\psi_1 = \mu_{1.} - (1/2)(\mu_{2.} + \mu_{3.})$; $\psi_2 = \mu_{2.} - \mu_{3.}$.

(b) Are the two contrasts orthogonal? Consider only the coefficients in your answer.

(c) Find SS_A and compare it with the sum of the two sums of squares found in part (a).

(d) Do either of the above contrasts vary as a function of B? Find the SS terms associated with each of the relevant significance tests. Add these terms and compare them with SS_{AB}.

10.15 Ninety children, varying in age ($A_1 = 5$, $A_2 = 7$, and $A_3 = 9$), are taught by one of three mnemonic methods (methods for memorizing; B_1, B_2, and B_3). All subjects are then shown a series of objects and their recall is scored. Thus we have nine groups of 10 subjects each. The cell means and variances are:

	Means			Variances		
	A_1	A_2	A_3	A_1	A_2	A_3
B_1	44	58	78	75	79	84
B_2	56	66	83	61	82	85
B_3	52	70	79	90	71	77

(a) Perform an ANOVA, using these statistics.

(b) B_2 and B_3 both involve the use of imagery whereas B_1 involves repeating the object names. Therefore, a contrast of the B_1 mean against the average of the B_2 and B_3 means is of interest. Calculate the 95% confidence interval for this contrast. Does the contrast differ significantly from zero?

(c) Test whether the contrast in part (b) is different at A_1 from at A_3.

10.16 (a) The file *EX10_16* on the *Exercises* page of the website contains a 3×3 data set. Table and plot the marginal and cell means. Describe the pattern of means.

(b) Carry out an ANOVA on the data and present the results in a table.

(c) With $FWE = .05$, calculate confidence intervals for pairwise comparisons of the A means; state which—if any—comparisons are significant.

10.17 Bless et al. (see *EX9_16*) also collected data from a control group ($n = 10$) that received no message but were asked to assess a fee. Assume that the mean for the control group is 48 and the standard deviation is 4.5. Test the difference between the control group and each of the eight experimental groups. Which of the experimental groups differed significantly ($\alpha = .10$) from the control group? Be explicit about the method for controlling the FWE and the selection of the error term(s).

Chapter 11
Trend Analysis in Between-Subjects Designs

11.1 OVERVIEW

In the preceding chapter, we presented calculations for comparing the mean scores of two groups, or of two subsets of groups. The independent variables in our examples were qualitative variables, variables whose "levels" differ in type such as type of therapy, method of instruction, and diagnostic category. In contrast, quantitative variables are variables whose levels differ in amount such as hours of therapy or instruction, drug dosage, and stimulus intensity. Even with variables such as these, contrasts of two means can be tested. However, when the independent variable is quantitative, it is often more informative to consider the overall relation between the treatment group means and the levels of the independent variable, rather than to make comparisons between two means. Such analyses of the function relating the dependent and independent variable are often referred to as *trend analyses*.

We may wish to test whether there is a trend for the population means to increase as the level of the independent variable increases. We may also want to test whether the function relating the means and the independent variable is significantly curved. In a design with multiple factors, we may want to compare functions for different populations of subjects. Beginning in Chapter 18, we present a more general regression framework within which to perform these tests. In this chapter, we present tests within the framework of ANOVA, with the caution that we assume a limited, although common, experimental context; namely, that there are equal number of scores at each level of the independent variable, and that those levels are equally spaced.

This chapter has two major goals:

- To provide a conceptual framework for trend analysis. That framework consists of (1) understanding how the between-groups sums of squares can be partitioned into $a - 1$ independent components, and (2) understanding how those components relate to the components of a curve.
- To present the computational formulas needed to calculate the sums of squares corresponding to the $a - 1$ components of a curve.

The $a - 1$ components of the between-groups sums of squares can each be viewed as a sum of squares for a contrast. We begin by developing that idea, and then show that by the proper choice of contrast weights, we can test contrasts that are independent of each other; the technical term is that they are *orthogonal*. We then discuss the selection of weights that enable us to test hypotheses about trends. These topics are first developed for a one-factor design, and then they are extended to a two-factor design.

11.2 SOME PRELIMINARY CONCEPTS

11.2.1 The Sum of Squares Associated with a Contrast

The t statistic presented in the previous chapter provides one approach to testing hypotheses about contrasts. An alternative, but equivalent, test is based on components of SS_A, the sums of squares for the between-groups source of variance. We develop this approach now in order to emphasize the continuity between the analysis of variance and test of contrasts, and to provide the base needed to develop the calculations used in trend analysis. A central idea is that any contrast of the group means corresponds to a component of the SS_A, the sum of squares for the variable, A. That component sum of squares, $SS_{\hat{\psi}}$, will be distributed on 1 df and the contrast can be tested by dividing it by $MS_{S/A}$.

Consider the square of the t statistic that was presented in Equation 10.5 for testing contrasts:

$$t^2 = \frac{\hat{\psi}^2}{s_{\hat{\psi}}^2} = \frac{(\Sigma\, w_j \overline{Y}_{.j})^2}{MS_{S/A}\, \Sigma\, w_j^2\, /\, n_j}$$

$$= \frac{(\Sigma\, w_j \overline{Y}_{.j})^2\, /\, (\Sigma\, w_j^2\, /\, n_j)}{MS_{S/A}}$$

The numerator, $(\Sigma w_j \overline{Y}_{.j})^2/(\Sigma w_j^2/n_j)$, is distributed as a sum of squares on one degree of freedom. We will denote this sum of squares by $SS_{\hat{\psi}}$; that is,

$$SS_{\hat{\psi}} = \frac{(\Sigma\, w_j \overline{Y}_{.j})^2}{\Sigma\, w_j^2\, /\, n_j} \tag{11.1}$$

Then

$$t^2 = \frac{SS_{\hat{\psi}}}{MS_{S/A}} \tag{11.2}$$

but a sum of squares on 1 df is a mean square, so that

$$t^2_{a(n-1)} = \frac{SS_{\hat{\psi}}}{MS_{S/A}} = F_{1,\,a(n-1)} \tag{11.3}$$

To illustrate the relation between contrasts and the ANOVA, we sampled 16 multiplication speed scores from each of four grades in the *Royer* (1999) study. Table 11.1 presents the mean speed for each grade, contrast weights for three contrasts, and the ANOVA table containing all relevant sums of squares, df, mean squares, and F tests. The contrasts represent (1) the difference between the mean for the eighth grade and the mean for the other three grades, (2) the difference between the seventh-grade mean and the mean of the combined fifth and sixth grades, and (3) the difference between the fifth- and sixth-grade means. Applying Equation 11.1, we obtain the sum of squares for each of these three contrasts. For example, for the first contrast,

$$SS_{\hat{\psi}} = \frac{[.350 + .560 + .586 + (-3)(.583)]^2}{[1^2 + 1^2 + 1^2 + (-3)^2]/16} = .085$$

If we assume equal condition variances, we may construct an F test, using Equation 11.3: $F(1, 60) = .085/.033 = 2.58$.

11.2.2 Orthogonal Contrasts

Note that the three contrast sums of squares in Table 11.1 add up to the between-groups sum of squares:

$$.085 + .183 + .353 = .621$$

$$SS_{\hat{\psi}_1} + SS_{\hat{\psi}_2} + SS_{\hat{\psi}_3} = SS_A$$

Think of the treatment sum of squares as a pie and each contrast as a piece of the pie. In the example of Table 11.1, the pieces do not overlap, and together they account for the whole pie. Here, the contrast of the fifth- and sixth-grade means (ψ_3) is the biggest piece, accounting for about 57% (.353/.621) of the variability among the treatment means.

Table 11.1 Contrasts of the means of arithmetic speeds

Group means and weights

Grade	$\bar{Y}_i$	w_1	w_2	w_3
5	.350	1	1	1
6	.560	1	1	−1
7	.586	1	−2	0
8	.583	−3	0	0

Contrasts

$\hat{\psi}_1 = (1)\bar{Y}_5 + (1)\bar{Y}_6 + (1)\bar{Y}_7 + (-3)\bar{Y}_8$
$\hat{\psi}_2 = (1)\bar{Y}_5 + (1)\bar{Y}_6 + (-2)\bar{Y}_7 + (0)\bar{Y}_8$
$\hat{\psi}_3 = (1)\bar{Y}_5 + (-1)\bar{Y}_6 + (0)\bar{Y}_7 + (0)\bar{Y}_8$

ANOVA (assuming $n = 16$ for all groups)

SV	df	SS	MS	F
A	3	.621	.207	6.27
ψ_1	1	.085	.085	2.58
ψ_2	1	.183	.183	5.55
ψ_3	1	.353	.353	10.70
S/A	60	1.95	.033	

As with any pie, the SS_A can be divided into pieces in many ways. For example, we might have a different set of contrasts:

$$\hat{\psi}_1 = (-3)\,\overline{Y}_5 + (-1)\,\overline{Y}_6 + (1)\,\overline{Y}_7 + (3)\,\overline{Y}_8$$

$$\hat{\psi}_2 = (-1)\,\overline{Y}_5 + (1)\,\overline{Y}_6 + (1)\,\overline{Y}_7 + (-1)\,\overline{Y}_8$$

$$\hat{\psi}_3 = (-1)\,\overline{Y}_5 + (3)\,\overline{Y}_6 + (-3)\,\overline{Y}_7 + (1)\,\overline{Y}_8$$

Again applying Equation 11.1, we find the corresponding sums of squares for these contrasts to be .421, .181, and .019; these values again sum to .621.

Will every set of contrasts result in sums of squares that add to SS_A? Not at all; in each of the preceding examples, the contrasts making up the set had a particular property that resulted in their accounting for different portions of the variability, for nonoverlapping pieces of the pie. When this is the case, the contrasts are said to be *orthogonal*. The maximum number of orthogonal contrasts in each set is equal to $a - 1$, the degrees of freedom of the treatment sum of squares. The sums of squares of $a - 1$ orthogonal contrasts will always add up to SS_A.

Before defining orthogonality more precisely, let us consider an example in which it does not occur. We will test

$$H_{01}: \mu_5 - \mu_6 = 0 \quad \text{and} \quad H_{02}: \mu_5 - (1/3)(\mu_6 + \mu_7 + \mu_8) = 0$$

If the mean of the fifth-grade population (μ_5) differs from that of the sixth-grade population (μ_6), there is a good chance that it will also differ from the combined mean of μ_6, μ_7, and μ_8, because that mean contains μ_6. In other words, there's a positive relation between the two contrasts. This lack of independence between the two contrasts is called *nonorthogonality*. It becomes evident in our example when we calculate the sums of squares corresponding to the two contrasts. The sums of squares for the tests of H_{01} and H_{02} are .353 and .615, respectively. The sum is clearly greater than SS_A, .621. The two pieces of the pie overlap.

We do not have to add the sums of squares to determine whether two contrasts are, or are not, orthogonal. Consider two contrasts, ψ_p and ψ_q, such that

$$\psi_p = \sum_j w_{jp}\mu_j \quad \text{and} \quad \psi_q = \sum_j w_{jq}\mu_j$$

If there are n scores at all levels of A, the criterion for orthogonality is

$$\sum_j w_{jp}w_{jq} = 0 \tag{11.4}$$

For example, we know that the first two contrasts in Table 11.1 are orthogonal because

$$(1)(1) + (1)(1) + (1)(-2) + (-3)(0) = 0$$

If the ns vary across treatment conditions, the criterion for orthogonality becomes

$$\sum_j \frac{w_{jp}w_{jq}}{n_j} = 0 \tag{11.5}$$

Several points about orthogonality deserve emphasis. First, a set of $a - 1$ orthogonal contrasts can be thought of as asking $a - 1$ logically independent questions that collectively "use up" all the degrees of freedom and variability associated with the independent variable. Note that the variability can be partitioned in different ways, so that it is possible to find different sets of orthogonal contrasts. Also, whether or not two contrasts are orthogonal depends on the contrast weights, not on the values of the means being contrasted. One way of thinking about this is that orthogonality depends on what questions are addressed by the contrasts, not on what the answers turn out to be. The second point is that we choose to test contrasts because they are of substantive interest, whether or not they are orthogonal to one another. For example, researchers commonly test sets of pairwise comparisons. These are often of interest and should be tested even though they are not orthogonal.

Summarizing, we have developed the idea that a sum of squares based on multiple degrees of freedom can be analyzed into components, each of which may be tested as a separate contrast. One way to conduct such analyses is to define $a - 1$ orthogonal contrasts that *partition* the SS for a source of variance; that is, the set of contrasts account for nonoverlapping components of the variance and together they account for all of the variance associated with the source. Trend analysis represents a special case in which the orthogonal contrasts represent independent components of a polynomial function.

11.3 TREND ANALYSIS IN A ONE-FACTOR DESIGN

11.3.1 Rationale

We can explore the nature of the functional relationship between the treatment means and the levels of the quantitative independent variable, X, by fitting the a data points ($\overline{Y}_j$, X_j) with a polynomial function. Suppose we estimate the linear function (i.e., polynomial of degree 1) that best describes the relation between the population means, μ_j, and our independent variable, X; that population function has the form

$$\hat{\mu}_j = \beta_0 + \beta_1 X_j \tag{11.6a}$$

Suppose that we find that the slope, β_1, is significantly different from zero. This tells us that there is a systematic tendency for the treatment means to increase (or decrease) as X increases.

We can expand our function to include a quadratic component (i.e., polynomial of degree 2); the resulting equation has the form

$$\hat{\mu}_j = \beta_0 + \beta_1 X_j + \beta_2 X_j^2 \tag{11.6b}$$

If the quadratic function fits the data significantly better than the linear function, this tells us that the best-fitting curve has a bend in it. This would be the case if, for example, Y first systematically increases with larger values of X, and then levels off or declines as X continues to increase.

We can expand our function further still by including a cubic component (i.e., polynomial of degree 3):

$$\hat{\mu}_j = \beta_0 + \beta_1 X_j + \beta_2 X_j^2 + \beta_3 X_j^3 \tag{11.6c}$$

If the additional component results in yet a significantly better fit, this allows us to say that the best-fitting curve has *two* bends in it. This would be the case if Y were to increase, then decrease, and then level off or increase again with larger values of X. Although theories in most research areas are rarely sophisticated enough to predict more than two or three bends, in principle we can explore whether there are more bends in the best-fitting function by considering polynomials of a higher order.

The goal of trend analysis is to test whether the various polynomial terms make significant contributions to the variance of the group means. However, the terms in, say, Equation 11.6c are not independent of each other. In trend analysis this function would be represented as a sum of *independent* (or *orthogonal*) linear, quadratic, and cubic components. We can associate a sum of squares with each of these components and test hypotheses about them. Calculations are a straightforward application of Equations 11.1 and 11.3. To illustrate these ideas, it may be useful to consider a concrete example.

In a study of stimulus generalization, a mild shock is paired with a rectangle of light 11 inches high and 1 inch wide. Subjects are then randomly divided into five groups of 10, each of which is tested on several trials in the presence of a rectangle of light, but with no shock. The independent variable is the height of the rectangle of light on these test trials. On each of several trials, the subjects are tested for generalization with a rectangle whose height is either 7, 9, 11, 13, or 15 inches. An average galvanic skin response (*GSR*) measure is obtained for each subject in each stimulus condition.[1]

The experimenters hypothesize that two processes are at work in this experiment. These are:

1. The magnitude of conditioned responses should vary directly with the magnitude of the test stimulus; this implies that *GSR* scores should increase as a function of the height of the rectangle of light.
2. There should be a generalization effect, a trend for *GSR* scores to be higher the closer the test stimulus is to the training stimulus. The result of this generalization process would be a symmetric, inverted, U-shaped curve with its peak at the 11-inch test stimulus.

According to the two hypotheses, the function relating population means to stimulus height should contain the sum of a straight line (Hypothesis 1) and an inverted U-shaped curve (Hypothesis 2). Panel *a* of Fig. 11.1 depicts what the components of the function relating *GSR* to stimulus height would look like according to the theory. The *Grand Mean* is the average of all 50 scores. The line labeled *Linear* is the straight line that best fits the observed group means after the grand mean has been subtracted from each. Similarly, the line labeled quadratic is the best-fitting, U-shaped curve after the group means have been adjusted for both the grand mean and the linear values. We will present computational formulas for the linear and quadratic curves in Sections 11.3.2 and 11.3.3.

The *Predicted* curve in Panel *b* is the sum of the three lines in Panel *a* and depicts the function that best fits the data if the two hypothesized processes are the only ones operating. The *Observed* function is the line connecting the group means obtained in the experiment. *Trend analysis* (sometimes referred to as *polynomial analysis*) permits us to test each component separately, and to test whether the deviation of the observed from the predicted function is significant. In this way, the researcher can address several questions about the function relating the population mean *GSR* and the stimulus height:

1. If we fit a straight line to the five means, will its slope be significantly different from zero? This addresses the hypothesis that there is an increase in the population means with increasing test stimulus height.
2. If we fit a symmetric, inverted, U-shaped curve to the five group means, will the points on this function vary significantly? This addresses the hypothesis that there is a generalization effect in the sampled population of *GSR* scores.

---

[1] The data for the five groups are on the book's website in the file *GSR Data*; follow links to *Data Files*, then *Tables*.

3. Are these two functions, together with the grand mean, sufficient to account for the relation between the treatment population means and X? A significant difference between the observed and predicted curves indicates that additional processes are needed to account for the data.

Given that we have identified our hypotheses with specific functional relations between the independent and dependent variables, how do we define appropriate contrasts to test the hypotheses? We begin by considering the linearity hypothesis: Is the slope of the straight line in Panel a of Fig. 11.1 significantly different from zero?

(a)

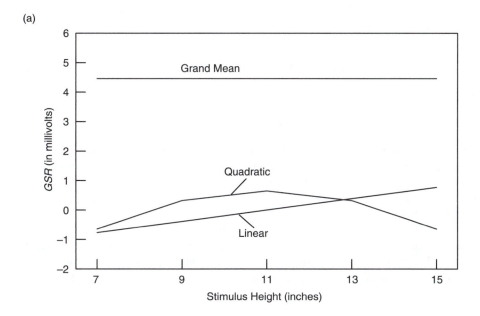

(b)

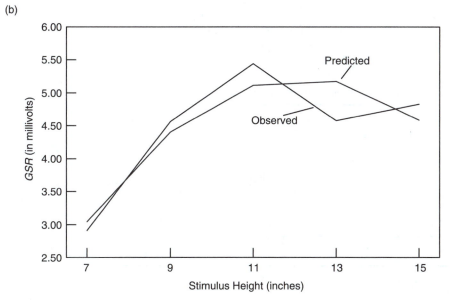

Fig. 11.1 Components of a predicted curve (a) and the predicted and observed curves (b).

11.3.2 Testing Linear Trends

In Equation 11.6a, the straight line that predicts the treatment population means from the levels of the independent variable has a slope (i.e., rate of change of predicted μ with X) of β_1 and a Y intercept (i.e., the value of the predicted value of μ when $X = 0$) of β_0. When we discuss regression starting with Chapter 18, we will present in detail how to estimate the βs that produce the best-fitting line, and how to test hypotheses about them. For the present purposes, however, we only provide formulas for the *least-squares estimates* of β_0 and β_1. These provide the best fit possible in the sense that they minimize the sum of squared differences between the observed and predicted means ($\overline{Y}_j$ and $\hat{\mu}_j$, respectively). Those formulas are

$$b_0 = \overline{Y}_{..} - b_1 \overline{X} \tag{11.7a}$$

and

$$b_1 = \Sigma_j (X_j - \overline{X}_.)(Y_{.j} - \overline{X}_.)/\Sigma_j(X_j - \overline{X}_.)^2 \tag{11.7b}$$

and the least-squares linear equation for predicting the jth group mean is

$$\overline{Y}_{pre,j} = b_0 + b_1 X_j \tag{11.8}$$

For the *GSR* and stimulus values presented in Table 11.2, using Equations 11.7a and 11.7b the least-squares estimates of the intercept and slope, b_0 and b_1, are .193 and 2.348. Substituting into Equation 11.8, we can obtain the predicted group *GSR* means on *GSR* from $\overline{Y}_{pre,j} = .193 + 2.348X$. If we then subtract the estimated grand mean of 4.46 from those predictions, we have the linear component displayed in Fig. 11.1.

Although we can—and, later, will—test for trend components by multiple regression, it is also possible to test trends by using contrasts with appropriately chosen weights. For example, in order to test whether there is a linear trend, we must determine whether the slope of the best-fitting linear equation is significantly different from 0. In Chapter 18, we show that the population slope is given by

$$\beta_1 = \frac{\displaystyle\sum_j [X_j - \overline{X}_.]\,[\mu_j - \mu_.]}{\displaystyle\sum_j [X_j - \overline{X}_.]^2}$$

Table 11.2   Group means, variances, and linear predictions for the *GSR* experiment

	Stimulus (X)	GSR ($\overline{Y}_j$)	S_Y^2	Linear prediction ($\overline{Y}_{linear,j}$)
	7	2.91	2.218	3.692
	9	4.56	2.563	4.078
	11	5.44	1.964	4.464
	13	4.58	2.881	4.850
	15	4.83	1.639	5.236
Means	11	4.464	2.253	4.464

Note: The predicted group means are $\overline{Y}_{linear,\,j} = .193 + 2.348X_j$.

The slope is equal to zero if its numerator is zero. The numerator is in the form $\psi_{linear} = \Sigma w_j(\mu_j - \mu)$ where $w_j = X_j - \bar{X}$. This can be rewritten as $\Sigma w_j\mu_j - \mu\Sigma w_j$. However, $\mu\Sigma w_j = 0$ because the sum of all deviations of a variable (X_j) about its mean $(\bar{X})$ must equal zero. Therefore, the null hypothesis of zero slope can be expressed as

$$H_0: \psi = \sum_j w_j \mu_j = 0 \quad \text{where } w_j = X_j - \bar{X} \tag{11.9}$$

We can test for linear trend with the contrast defined in Equation 11.9 by using the F statistic of Equation 11.3,

$$F = \frac{SS_{linear}}{MS_{S/A}} = \frac{(\Sigma w_j \bar{Y}_{.j})^2/(\Sigma w_j^2/n)}{MS_{S/A}} \tag{11.10}$$

The w_j for the GSR example of Section 11.3 are $X_j - \bar{X} = -4, -2, 0, 2,$ and 4, with $n = 10$ in all groups, and the error mean square, $MS_{S/A}$, equals 2.252 (see Table 11.2). Then,

$$SS_{linear} = [(-4)(2.91) + (-2)(4.57) + \ldots + (4)(4.83)]^2/[(16 + 4 + \ldots + 16)/10] = 14.822$$

Dividing by $MS_{S/A} = 2.252$, $F = 6.581$. The contrast sum of squares is distributed on 1 df and the error df are distributed on $a(n - 1)$, or 45, df. With $\alpha = .05$, we can reject the null hypothesis that the slope of the best-fitting straight line is zero.

Three points about this result should be understood:

1. The μ_j may vary even if the slope is zero; that is, they may vary even if there is no linear trend. To see this, suppose that the μ_j fall on a perfectly symmetric, inverted, U-shaped function. These means would exhibit no linear trend; a best-fitting straight line would have a slope (β_1) of zero. Nevertheless, there would be variability among the population means.
2. Evidence of a linear trend does not allow us to conclude that the population means are well fit by a straight line but only that the best-fitting straight line has a slope other than zero. Tests of curvature are required to decide whether a straight line fits the population function, or whether other, nonlinear, processes are involved.
3. Although it may not be immediately evident, the linear contrast sum of squares is essentially a measure of the variability of the predicted means; substituting the predicted means from Table 11.2, we could have calculated

$$SS_{linear} = 10 \times [(3.70 - 4.46)^2 + (4.08 - 4.46)^2 + \ldots + (5.24 - 4.46)^2] = 14.82$$

Computationally, the test statistic is identical to Equation 11.3, except for the way in which the weights have been selected. The advantage of recognizing that the numerator of that F test, SS_{linear}, can be written as a sum of squares for a single df contrast is that we do not have to calculate the slope and use it to calculate the predicted group means. Furthermore, we soon will show that tests of other trends, such as the quadratic curve in Panel a of Fig. 11.1, can also be viewed as tests of single df contrasts. The only difference is that when testing nonlinear trends, different sets of weights are required.

The linear weights for the generalization example were the deviations of the stimulus lengths about their average: $-4, -2, 0, 2,$ and 4. SS_{linear} is unchanged if we multiply or divide all the weights by a constant; this is because the squared constant appears in both numerator and denominator of the contrast sum of squares. Therefore, we can get the same value of SS_{linear} if we divide $X_j - \bar{X}$ by 2; the new weights are

$$w_{linear} = -2, -1, 0, 1, 2$$

These weights can be used in Equation 11.10 in place of $X_j - \bar{X}$ to test the linear trend whenever (1) the values of the independent variable are equally spaced, and (2) each mean is based on the same number of scores. If the X_j are equally spaced, $X_j - \bar{X}$ will differ from $w_{linear,j}$ by a constant multiplier and, as already noted, SS_{linear} will not be affected. For the general case in which spacing or ns are not equal, we need to use multiple regression (see Chapter 23).

Turn now to Appendix Table C.6, labeled "Coefficients of orthogonal polynomials." Find the block of coefficients for $a = 5$ (five levels of the independent variable) and look at the first row, the linear coefficients. These are the w_{linear} listed previously. The table also lists linear coefficients for other values of a; that is, for experiments in which there are more or fewer levels of the independent variable. For each row of linear coefficients: (1) $\Sigma w_{linear,j} = 0$; and (2) provided the values of X (the independent variable) are equally spaced, the linear coefficients are a straight line function of X. From now on, *if the values of X are equally spaced and the n_j are all equal*, Equation 11.1 can be used to calculate SS_{linear}, using the linear coefficients of Appendix Table C.6.

As you may have guessed, the coefficients in the rows labeled quadratic, cubic, etc., enable us to test other hypotheses about the shape of the function that best describes the treatment population means. We turn now to discuss these hypotheses and the related significance tests.

11.3.3 Testing Nonlinear Trends: A General Test

One question we might wish to ask is whether the group means in Table 11.2 depart significantly from the best-fitting straight line. The null hypothesis is that the population means fall on a straight line; there is no curvature. The experimenters expect generalization, implying that this null hypothesis should be false; the population means should deviate from a straight line. A general test of the null hypothesis of no curvature follows from recognizing that SS_A, the variability among the group means, can be partitioned into two components. The first of these is the SS_{linear} that we discussed in the preceding section. Recall that this reflects the difference between the best-fitting straight line and a line with slope of zero. The second component of SS_A is SS_{nonlin} ("sum of squares for nonlinearity"), which reflects the departure of the observed group means from the best-fitting straight line. This partitioning of SS_A follows from the identity,

$$(\bar{Y}_{.j} - \bar{Y}_{..}) = (\bar{Y}_{.j} - \bar{Y}_{linear,j}) + (\bar{Y}_{linear,j} - \bar{Y}_{..})$$

where $\bar{Y}_{linear,j}$ is the value of μ_j predicted by the best-fitting straight line. Squaring both sides of the preceding equation, and summing over subjects and groups, we have

$$n\Sigma(\bar{Y}_{.j} - \bar{Y}_{..})^2 = n\Sigma(\bar{Y}_{.j} - \bar{Y}_{linear,j})^2 + n\Sigma(\bar{Y}_{linear,j} - \bar{Y}_{..})^2 \qquad (11.11)$$

$$SS_A \quad = \quad SS_{nonlin} \quad + \quad SS_{linear}$$

To the extent that the observed group means differ from the means predicted by a straight line, the function has a nonlinear component (i.e., curvature). The sum of those squared differences (between the observed means and the means predicted by a straight line) is exactly what SS_{nonlin} reflects. Because SS_{linear} is distributed on 1 df, SS_{nonlin} must be distributed on $a - 2$ df. Another way of thinking about these df is that SS_{nonlin} represents the variability of a data points about a line; 2 df are lost because the line is determined by estimates of two parameters, β_0 and β_1, leaving $a - 2$ df.

It follows from Equation 11.11 that SS_{nonlin} is calculated as the difference between SS_A and SS_{linear}. Therefore, to test the hypothesis that the population means fall on a straight line, calculate

$$F_{a-2,a(n-1)} = \frac{(SS_A - SS_{lin})/(a-2)}{MS_{S/A}} \qquad (11.12)$$

Table 11.3 Tests of linearity and nonlinearity for the *GSR* data (from SPSS)

			Sum of squares	df	Mean square	F	Sig.
Between groups	(Combined)		35.261	4	8.815	3.914	.008
	Linear term	Contrast	14.822	1	14.822	6.581	.014
		Deviation	20.439	3	6.813	3.025	.039
	Quadratic term	Contrast	14.787	1	14.787	6.566	.014
		Deviation	5.651	2	2.826	1.255	.295
Within groups			101.351	45	2.252		
Total			136.612	49			

Table 11.3 presents the output from SPSS's tests of two orthogonal polynomial components, the linear and quadratic. Consider the row labeled "Linear term, Deviation"; the corresponding sum of squares, 20.439, represents $SS_{Between\ Groups} - SS_{linear}$. Accordingly, it is distributed on $df = (a - 1) - 1 = a - 2$, or 3 in this example. This linear deviation term provides a test of nonlinearity; because the F is significant ($F = 3.025$; $p = .039$), we can conclude that the group means depart significantly from a straight line.

In summary, the test of linearity reveals that there is a trend for the treatment population means to increase as X increases; the linear regression coefficient is significantly greater than zero. Furthermore, the test of deviations from the best-fitting straight line reveals that the straight line by itself is not sufficient to account for the variation in the population means. Consistent with the idea of stimulus generalization, the best-fitting function appears to be curved. We next consider the nature of that curve more closely.

11.3.4 Testing Nonlinear Trends: Orthogonal Polynomials

In the example of the generalization experiment (Table 11.2), we have so far established that there are both linear and nonlinear components of the population function. In many analyses, tests of these two components will be enough. However, more precise theories motivate more precise statistical tests. For example, in the generalization experiment the theory specifies two independent processes that combine to generate the treatment means. The absolute magnitude of the stimulus is thought to produce a linear effect; for each increment of one unit in X, the μ_j should increase by some constant amount. Distance of the test stimulus from the training stimulus results in a quadratic effect; if only this generalization effect were present, the μ_j would be a symmetric, inverted, U-shaped function of X. Note that this statement of the theory is more specific than just stating that there will be deviations from the best-fitting straight line. The theory says that the population means will be described significantly better by a *quadratic* or *second-order polynomial* function

$$\hat{\mu}_j = \beta_0 + \beta_1 X_j + \beta_2 X_j^2 \tag{11.13}$$

than by a linear function. In Equation 11.13, β_2 is often referred to as the *quadratic coefficient*.

Because there are five group means in the generalization example of Table 11.2, the data could conceivably be even better fit by a function having *cubic* (X^3) and *quartic* (X^4) terms.[2] Fig. 11.2

---

[2] We should note, however, that achieving better fits by adding polynomial components until we have almost as many components as levels of the independent variable is not useful. Just as any two data points must be perfectly fit by a straight line, any a data points must be perfectly fit by a polynomial equation of degree $a - 1$.

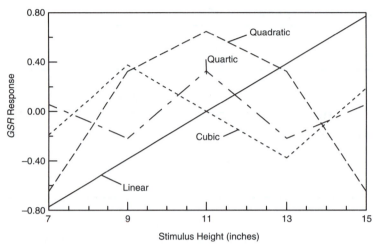

Fig. 11.2 Polynomial components of the *GSR* curve.

presents plots of all four orthogonal polynomial components of the function relating the group *GSR* means to the independent variable, stimulus height. We could test each of the four components to see whether each contributes significantly to the variability in the group means. Our theory, however, holds that only the linear and quadratic components are necessary to account for the variation among the treatment population means. Because the SS_{linear} was significant, we have already demonstrated the presence of a linear component. Now we would like to determine whether, in accord with the theory, the only significant nonlinear component is the quadratic.

In order to construct a test of the quadratic component of the function for our five group means, we make use of the orthogonal polynomial coefficients of Appendix Table C.6. Turning to the table, again focus on the block for which $a = 5$, but this time consider the row labeled *quadratic*. We wish to test H_0: $\beta'_{quadratic} = 0$ (where the prime on the β is to emphasize that we are using orthogonal contrast weights). To test the hypothesis, calculate

$$SS_{quad(A)} = \frac{\sum_j (w_{quad,j}\,\overline{Y}_{.j})^2}{\sum_j w^2_{quad,j} \Big/ n} \tag{11.14}$$

Substituting the coefficients from Appendix Table C.6 and the means from Table 11.2, we calculate

$$SS_{quad(A)} = \frac{[(2)(2.91) + (-1)(4.57) + \ldots + (2)(4.83)]^2}{[2^2 + (-1)^2 + \ldots + 2^2]/10} = 14.787$$

Dividing by $MS_{S/A}$, we have $F_{1,45} = 6.57$, which is significant with $p = .014$. That same result appears in the line labeled "Quadratic term, Contrast" in Table 11.3.

If this analysis is performed by SPSS, the results include a deviation following the quadratic term; the deviation is

$$SS_A - (SS_{linear} + SS_{quad})$$

which, as we can see in Table 11.3, is $35.261 - (14.822 + 14.787) = 5.651$. This residual combines the sums of squares for the cubic and quartic terms, and can be tested against the error mean square.

SPSS reports the result of the test of this deviation as $F = 1.255$, and $p = .295$. The numerator sum of squares for this test is on 2 df because it tests the sum of two single-df terms, the cubic and quartic. The test is performed as

$$F_{2, 45} = \frac{(SS_{deviation})/2}{MS_{S/A}} = \frac{2.826}{2.252} = 1.255$$

This result is not significant so we have no evidence that there are significant components other than the linear and quadratic.

We could also separately test the cubic and quartic terms by placing their coefficients in Equation 11.14, or by requesting such tests in the *Contrast* option in SPSS (or the equivalent in other programs). However, we did not perform such tests for several reasons. First, no other components were hypothesized; fishing for significant results that were not hypothesized may increase the Type 1 error rate. Second, components of higher than second order are difficult to interpret unless specified *a priori* by some theory. Finally, there is no evidence that other components were significant.

Although we caution against testing higher-order components that were not specified *a priori*, some properties of the full set of polynomial coefficients should be noted.

1. The plot of the coefficients in a given row of Appendix Table C.6 is closely related to the component we wish to test. In Fig. 11.2, we have plotted each row as a function of X. For example, the linear coefficients, the w_{lin}, lie on a straight line and the quadratic coefficients, the w_{quad}, lie on a symmetric, U-shaped function.
2. As with the linear coefficients, the coefficients in Appendix Table C.6 sum to zero. That is, $\Sigma_j w_{p,j} = 0$, where $w_{p,j}$ is the jth value in the pth row.
3. All pairs of rows are orthogonal by the definition provided by Equation 11.4 (Section 11.2). Recall that a necessary condition for two sets of weights, w_{jp} and w_{jq}, to be orthogonal is that $\Sigma_j w_{jp} w_{jq}$ must be zero. This requirement is met for the six pairs of rows here. For example,

$$\sum_j w_{lin, j} w_{quad, j} = (-2)(2) + (-1)(-1) + (0)(-2) + (1)(-1) + (2)(-2) = 0$$

Bear in mind that the values in Appendix Table C.6 are derived by assuming equal spacing of the levels of the independent variable, and equal numbers of scores at each level. If these conditions are met, the second and third points we have noted assure us that sums of squares based on these coefficients will be independently distributed, thus allowing tests of orthogonal components. As we noted earlier, such tests can also be carried out within a regression framework under more general conditions; Chapter 23 develops the appropriate method.

11.4 PLOTTING THE ESTIMATED POPULATION FUNCTION

In many studies, it is informative to plot the estimated population function. We did this in Panel *b* of Fig. 11.1 (the curve labeled *Predicted*). In order to understand how we arrived at that curve, we must understand its relation to the orthogonal polynomial coefficients in Appendix Table C.6. We can write the general polynomial function of order $a - 1$ as a sum of $a - 1$ orthogonal functions:

$$\mu_j = \beta_0' + \beta_1' w_{1,j} + \beta_3' w_{2,j} + \ldots + \beta_{a-1}' w_{a-1,j} \tag{11.15}$$

The b'_p, the estimates of the β'_p, are

$$b'_0 = \overline{Y}.. \tag{11.16}$$

and, for $p > 0$,

$$b'_p = \frac{\sum_j w_{p,j}\, \overline{Y}_{.j}}{\sum_j w^2_{p,j}} \tag{11.17}$$

For the example data set in Table 11.2, the intercept term is simply the grand mean of 4.64. The linear coefficient, b'_1, would be calculated as follows. First, we find the values of $w_{1,j}$ from Appendix Table C.6; when there are five groups, these are −2, −1, 0, 1, 2. Substituting these values and the group means into Equation 11.17,

$$b'_1 = \frac{(-2)(2.91) + (-1)(4.57) + \ldots + (2)(4.83)}{(-2)^2 + (-1)^2 + \ldots + 2^2}$$

$$= \frac{3.86}{10} = .386$$

The calculation of the quadratic coefficient, b'_2, would change only in the coefficients; from Appendix Table C.6, the coefficients are 2, −1, −2, −1, and 2, and the value of b'_2 is

$$b'_2 = \frac{(2)(2.91) + (-1)(4.57) + \ldots + (2)(4.83)}{(2)^2 + (-1)^2 + \ldots + 2^2}$$

$$= \frac{-4.55}{14} = -.325$$

Because our data provide evidence only for the contributions of linear and quadratic components, we calculated only, b'_0, b'_1, and b'_2. The resulting equation is

$$\hat{\mu}_j = 4.464 + .386w_{1j} - .325w_{2j}$$

Inserting the five linear and quadratic weights for w_{1j} and w_{2j}, respectively, gives the predicted values for *GSR* (3.04, 4.40, 5.11, 5.18, 4.59); these are the values plotted in Panel *b* of Fig. 11.1. If we had included the cubic and quartic components as well, the predicted curve would have fallen on the observed curve. However, our significance tests indicated that these two components do not reflect real trends in the population. Therefore, the deviations of the five group means about the function plotted in Panel *b* are attributed to chance variability, and the plotted function is our best estimate of the true population function.

11.5 TREND ANALYSIS IN MULTI-FACTOR DESIGNS

Consider an extension of the experiment on stimulus generalization in which 30 subjects are sampled from each of three populations: patients diagnosed as mildly schizophrenic (MS), patients diagnosed as severely schizophrenic (SS), and control patients (C). These 90 subjects are randomly assigned to each of the five stimuli used in our earlier example, so that we have 15 groups, each with

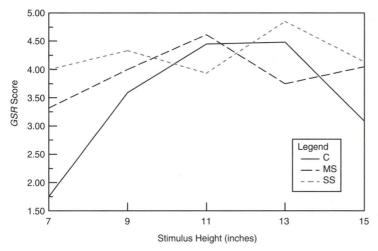

Fig. 11.3 Plot of the *GSR* means in Table 11.4.

Table 11.4 Group means for a two-factor experiment

| Category | Stimulus height (inches) | | | | | |
	7	9	11	13	15	Mean
C	1.750	3.950	4.450	4.483	3.083	3.543
MS	3.317	4.000	4.617	3.750	4.050	3.947
SS	4.000	4.333	3.933	4.850	4.133	4.230
Mean	3.022	4.094	4.300	4.361	3.756	3.907

six subjects. The mean *GSR* scores are plotted as a function of stimulus height for each clinical category in Fig. 11.3; the means also are contained in Table 11.4.[3]

Our hypothetical researcher is interested in answers to the following questions:

1. Averaging across the three populations of subjects, which orthogonal polynomial components of the function relating *GSR* to stimulus height in Fig. 11.3 are significant? For example, does the average function have a slope different from zero? Is there a significant departure from a straight line?
2. Of more interest, do these characteristics of the function differ among the three clinical categories? The researchers hypothesize that schizophrenic populations discriminate less well among stimuli, leading them to predict less of an increase in *GSR* scores with increasing stimulus length, as well as a flatter function.
3. Are the components (e.g., linear or quadratic) different for the control than for the average of the two schizophrenic populations?
4. Do the two schizophrenic populations differ with respect to any of the components?
   In order to answer these questions, we will need to carry out tests of several hypotheses. The next subsections present the necessary calculations; these are similar to those for the one-factor design.

---

[3] The complete data set is available on the website in the *GSR2 Data* file on the *Tables* page.

11.5.1 Analyzing the Components of the Average Function

The design in our example represents the general case in which there are a levels of A, b levels of B, and n subjects in each AB combination. In the example, A is clinical category, B is stimulus height, and $n = 6$. To calculate the sum of squares of the qth component of B, we use a formula very similar to Equation 11.14 for the one-factor design:

$$SS_{q(B)} = \frac{\sum_k (w_{q,k} \overline{Y}_{..k})^2}{\sum_k w_{q,k}^2 / an} \tag{11.18}$$

Here q refers to any polynomial component of B such as the linear, quadratic, or cubic; k indexes the levels of B; $w_{q,k}$ is the kth weight obtained from Appendix Table C.6 for the qth component; and an is the number of scores at each level of B. In our example, the linear component of stimulus height is

$$SS_{linear(B)} = \frac{[(-2)(3.022) + (-1)(4.094) + \ldots (2)(3.756)]}{10/18} = 5.408$$

We can calculate the quadratic sum of squares in a similar manner. Replacing the linear weights with the quadratic weights from Appendix Table C.6, and noting that the sum of squared weights is now 14 instead of 10, $SS_{quadratic(B)} = 15.750$.

The results of the complete ANOVA are contained in Table 11.5. There we see that both the linear and quadratic components of the stimulus source are significant. We conclude that the average of the C, MS, and SS population functions has a positive slope and a quadratic component. The deviation term is clearly quite small; the F is less than 1, indicating that the combined cubic and quartic components contribute little variability.

Table 11.5 ANOVA of the *GSR* data summarized in Table 11.4

Source	df	SS	MS	F	p
Category (A)	2	7.145	3.572	3.01	.059
Stimulus (B)	4	21.628	5.407	4.56	.002
Linear (B)	1	5.408	5.408	4.56	.036
Quadratic (B)	1	15.750	15.750	13.28	.000
Deviation (B)	2	.470	.235	0.20	.819
AB	8	19.240	2.405	2.03	.054
$A \times$ Linear (B)	2	1.992	.996	0.84	.436
$A \times$ Quadratic (B)	2	11.756	5.878	4.96	.009
$A \times$ Deviation (B)	4	5.492	1.373	1.16	.335
S/AB	75	88.943	1.186		

11.5.2 Analyzing the Components of Interaction: Comparing Curves

The second question we asked in the introduction to Section 11.5 was whether any polynomial component of the three curves in Fig. 11.3 varied as a function of clinical category. Looking at the figure, it appears that there is an interaction of category and stimulus height. We might wish to test whether this is attributable to differences in either slope or curvature, or both. The control (C) function in Fig. 11.3 clearly exhibits a generalization gradient with a positive slope. The mildly (MS) and severe (SS) schizophrenic functions are, as hypothesized, noticeably flatter with what appear to be lower slopes. To test whether these differences in slope and curvature are statistically significant, we broke the interaction sum of squares into components, much as we did with the stimulus sum of squares. Let's see how this was done.

Suppose we want to test the null hypothesis that the three slopes are the same. We calculate the linear sum of squares at each level of the category variable, and then subtract the linear sum of squares obtained in the analysis of the stimulus source. A difference among the slopes should be reflected in the variability of the three category slopes about their average; therefore, we calculate

$$SS_{linear(B) \times A} = SS_{linear(B)/A_1} + SS_{linear(B)/A_2} + SS_{linear(B)/A_3} - SS_{linear(B)} \tag{11.19}$$

where $SS_{linear(B) \times A}$ represents the variability in the slopes as a function of the level of A (clinical category in our example), and $SS_{linear(B)/A_j}$ is calculated as if only the data in the jth clinical category existed. The calculations in each category are the same as in a one-factor design. For example, to calculate the linear sum of squares for the clinical category, we weight the means in row C of Table 11.4 by the linear coefficients in Appendix Table C.6:

$$SS_{linear(B)/A_1} = \frac{[(-2)(1.75) + (-1)(3.95) + \ldots + (2)(3.083)]}{10/6}$$

Carrying this out for all three categories and substituting the results into Equation 11.19 together with the previously calculated $SS_{linear(B)}$, we have

$$SS_{linear(B) \times A} = 6.144 + .888 + .368 - 5.408 = 1.992$$

This is distributed on $a - 1$ degrees of freedom, or 2 in our example, because we are calculating the variability of a single degree of freedom components about their average. The error term against which the mean square is tested is the error mean square used in our previous F tests: $MS_{S/AB}$. The variation in the quadratic components as a function of clinical category, $SS_{quadratic(B \times A)}$, is calculated in the same way; the only change is the substitution of the quadratic sums of squares into Equation 11.19.

The results of the calculations of the sums of squares and F tests are reported in Table 11.5. We do not have sufficient evidence to conclude that the slopes differ, but there is a very significant difference among the three quadratic components; $p = .009$. The $A \times Deviation (B)$ term tests whether the combined cubic and quartic components vary significantly as a function of clinical category. Because they contribute little to the interaction variability ($p = .335$), we conclude that the clinical populations differ with respect to the curvature of the generalization functions, and that this is due to variation in the quadratic component of the function.

This approach also enables us to test each polynomial component in each category. For example, to test whether the slope for the control population is different from zero, and assuming that the variances are reasonably homogeneous across clinical populations, we divide 6.144 by $MS_{S/AB}$. If we have reason to suspect that the within-cell variances differ markedly across clinical categories, we would test 6.144 against the average within-cell variance based only on the cells in the control category. Similarly, we would test the slopes in the MS and SS conditions against the average within-cell variances for their respective clinical categories. The error degrees of freedom in that case would be $b(n - 1)$, or 25 in our example. We caution that a conservative approach should be taken in evaluating the results of the a tests; the Dunn–Bonferroni procedure seems best here.

11.5.3 Analyzing the Components of Interaction: Contrasting Polynomial Functions

It appears that the variation in the quadratic component as a function of clinical category is due to the difference between the control condition on the one hand and the two schizophrenic conditions on the other hand. Therefore, we might wish to test whether the quadratic component of the control curve differs from the average of the quadratic components of the two schizophrenic curves. We might also wish to test whether there is any difference between the quadratic components of the two schizophrenic curves in Fig. 11.3. Tests of such contrasts of polynomial components respond to the third and fourth questions raised in the introduction to Section 11.5.

Calculations of the sums of squares for these two contrasts of quadratic functions is aided by constructing tables such as those in Table 11.6. The uppermost row of weights in both panels (–2, 1, 2, 1, –2) are quadratic coefficients when there are five levels. The left column of weights are the weights for contrasting the control condition against the average of the other two (–2, 1, 1 in panel a) and for contrasting the two schizophrenic conditions (0, 1, –1 in panel b). The entries in the 15 cells are the products of these row and column weights; we will refer to them as the $w_{quadratic,jk}$. Given these 15 weights, the sums of squares are calculated as in the one-factor design. For the contrast of the control with the schizophrenic populations' quadratic components, we multiply each of the 15 cell means (in Table 11.4) by the corresponding product in Table 11.6, and continue as follows:

$$SS_{\psi_1} = \frac{n\left(\sum_j \sum_k w_j w_k \bar{Y}_{.jk}\right)^2}{\sum_j \sum_k (w_j w_k)^2}$$

$$\frac{6[(4)(1.75) + (-2)(3.95) + \ldots + (-2)(4.23)]^2}{4^2 + (-2) + \ldots + (-2)^2}$$

This is distributed on 1 df. Dividing by $MS_{S/AB}$, $F = 9.411$ and $p = .003$. We conclude that the quadratic curvature is different for the control population than for the schizophrenic populations. Carrying out a similar analysis for the contrast in Panel b of Table 11.6, $SS_{\psi_2} = .595$, and $F = .502$; there is no evidence that the quadratic components differ for the two schizophrenic populations.

The two sets of 15 coefficients in Table 11.6 are orthogonal to each other; that is, the sums of their cross-products are zero, as required by Equation 11.4. Because they are orthogonal and together exhaust the degrees of freedom for the $A \times quadratic$ (B) source, their sum yields that sum of squares; for the current example,

$$SS_{A \times quadratic(B)} = 11.161 + .595 = 11.756$$

the result in Table 11.5. Of course, it is not necessary that the contrasts tested be orthogonal but, as in the present example, they often address reasonable questions, and the results provide a computational check.

Contrasts of group trends, such as the comparisons of the *GSR* functions for the three clinical conditions, can be carried out by several software packages. Users of SPSS may find the syntax file *Partitioning Interaction.sps* useful. Using the *GSR2* data as an example, *Partitioning Interaction.sps* provides tests of, and confidence intervals for, contrasts between polynomial components. The file can be found on the *Syntax Files* page on the book's website. The *Syntax Readme* file has instructions for its use, as well as instructions for the use of other syntax files on the page.

Table 11.6 Weights for contrasts of the quadratic functions in Fig. 11.3

(*a*) Weights for contrasting the control quadratic component with the average of the two schizophrenic quadratic components

		7″ (B₁)	9″ (B₂)	11″ (B₃)	13″ (B₄)	15″ (B₅)
		-2	1	2	1	-2
C (A_1)	-2	4	-2	-4	-2	4
MS (A_2)	1	-2	1	2	1	-2
SS (A_3)	1	-2	1	2	1	-2

(*b*) Weights for contrasting the two schizophrenic quadratic components

		7″ (B₁)	9″ (B₂)	11″ (B₃)	13″ (B₄)	15″ (B₅)
		-2	1	2	1	-2
C (A_1)	0	0	0	0	0	0
MS (A_2)	1	-2	1	2	1	-2
SS (A_3)	-1	2	-1	-2	-1	2

11.6 SOME CAUTIONS IN APPLYING AND INTERPRETING TREND ANALYSIS

Trend analysis is a powerful tool for analyzing functional relations among variables. However, it is important to keep in mind that when variables have fixed effects, trend analysis provides statistical support only for conclusions about levels of the manipulated variable that were included in the experiment. For example, conclusions about the shape of the generalization function in our example have statistical support only for the values of stimulus height in the experiment. Would the function in Fig.11.1 decline further or level off if heights greater than 15 had been included? We might infer the answer to questions such as this, using our knowledge of the variables, theoretical considerations, and results of other studies. However, such extrapolation beyond the stimulus levels in the current experiment has a different status than the statistical inferences based on the stimulus levels in the study. The best advice is to include in the study the range of variables that are of possible interest, and to include a sufficient number of levels within that range to provide a good sense of the shape of the function.

Another concern is the routine application of trend analysis whenever one or more independent variables are quantitative. Any set of a data points can be fitted by a polynomial of order $a-1$, but if the population function is not a polynomial (a sine curve, or an exponential function, for example), the polynomial analysis can lead to an incorrect theory.

It is also dangerous to freely identify significant components with psychological processes. It is one thing to hypothesize a cubic component of a variable, then to test for its contribution, and to find it significant, thus substantiating the theory. It is another matter to assign psychological meaning to a significant component that has not been hypothesized prior to the collection of data. An unexpected significant component should be of interest and should alert the researcher to the possible need to re-examine the hypotheses that led to the study. However, such a result should be viewed with even more than the usual skepticism until validated by further research.

Finally, remember that when more polynomial components are tested, the probability of a Type 1 error increases unless a procedure such as the Dunn–Bonferroni (described in Chapter 10) is used to control the familywise error rate. However, when such methods are used, the more tests that are performed, the less power each has to detect true contributions to the population function. Think carefully about what may be contributing to the function of interest, and limit tests to the suspected components, going beyond those only when the data indicate that a component that is unanticipated may be contributing.

11.7 SUMMARY

This chapter presented a general description of the goals of trend analysis and a method of analysis specific to studies in which the levels of the independent variable are equally spaced and the group sizes are equal. We introduced several new topics:

- *The sum of squares for a contrast*. We noted that the F test based on the sum of squares for a contrast is the square of the t statistic previously described in the test of contrasts.
- *Orthogonal contrasts*. We stated criteria for determining when two sets of weights are orthogonal. When that condition is met, the sum of squares based on those weights is independently distributed.
- *Orthogonal polynomial coefficients and trend analysis*. Orthogonal polynomial coefficients are a special set of weights that enable calculation of sums of squares corresponding to independent components of a polynomial function. We illustrated their application to tests of trends and to the interpretation of test results with an example of a study of stimulus generalization.
- *Polynomial curve fitting*. We showed how the orthogonal polynomial coefficients could be used to fit a curve to data points, a curve that estimated the population function relating treatment population means to levels of the independent variable.
- *Multi-factor designs*. Finally, we extended the procedures for testing trends to multi-factor designs, showing how they could be used to test whether polynomial coefficients differ across two or more groups (i.e., testing interactions).

In future chapters, we will extend these developments to other designs, and to conditions in which levels of the independent variable are not necessarily equally spaced, and the numbers of observations at each level need not be the same. However, the present chapter provides the foundation for those developments.

EXERCISES

11.1 Four groups of eight subjects each are tested on a problem; time to solve is the dependent variable. The independent variable is the number of previous practice problems. The group means are

Practice	1	2	3	4
Time	6.49	4.82	4.25	3.80

The average within-group variance is 1.42.

(a) Calculate the values of b_0 and b_1, the least-squares linear regression coefficients defined by Equations 11.7a and 11.7b.

(b) Using the result in part (a), calculate the predicted mean for each of the four groups.

(c) (i) Based on these predicted means, calculate the SS_{linear}. (ii) Redo the calculations using the original means and the appropriate contrast weights (see Equation 11.10). Carry out the significance test. (iii) What would a significant F ratio tell us about the results of this experiment?

11.2 (a) Are the means in Exercise 11.1 adequately described by a straight line? Present evidence to justify your response.

(b) A different test of SS_{linear} is to test SS_{linear} against $MS_{residual}$; $SS_{residual} = SS_{total} - SS_{linear}$, $df_{residual} = (an - 1) - 1$, and $MS_{residual} = SS_{residual}/df_{residual}$. What is the underlying assumption of this test procedure? What are its potential advantages and disadvantages?

11.3 In a study of the effects of group problem solving, group size = 2, 3, 4, or 5. Professor Smith believes that "the more the merrier" and predicts that scores will increase as size increases. Professor Brown believes that "there can be too much of a good thing" and predicts that scores will improve and then drop as size increases. There are five groups in each size condition, and each group attempts 10 problems. The dependent variable is the number each group gets correct. The means and standard deviations for each size condition are

Size	2	3	4	5
Mean	2.8	4.6	7.6	6.0
Std. dev. (s)	1.643	2.074	2.302	2.550

Do a trend analysis. Which prediction do the results support?

11.4 (a) The F ratio for testing the pth polynomial component may be rewritten so that its square root is the t statistic of the form

$$t = \frac{b'_p}{\sqrt{MS_{S/A} \Big/ n \sum_j w_{j,p}^2}}$$

where b'_p is defined by Equation 11.17. Use this equation to test linear trend and confirm that the resulting t is the square root of the F ratio computed in Exercise 11.3.

(b) Find the 95% confidence interval for b'_1. Then convert this into a confidence interval for b_1, the slope of the line that best fits Y as a function of X.

11.5 A method used in some memory studies involves requiring subjects to respond yes or no within a predetermined interval to a probe of memory. One mathematical model predicts that response accuracy will be an S-shaped function of time. Assume that there are seven groups of six subjects, each of which is tested with a different response interval, ranging from 0.2 seconds to 1.4 in intervals of 0.2.

(a) Which trend component(s) should be significant?

(b) The file *EX11_5* contains the scores. The independent variable is *time* and the dependent variable is *d_prime (d′)*, a measure of accuracy. Test for the trend component(s) you listed in answer to part (a). Also test whether any other component(s) are significant.

11.6 For the data in the *Ex11_5* file, construct a plot based only on the significant components (see Equations 11.16 and 11.17). What does this plot represent?

11.7 The file *EX11_7* contains a data set from a hypothetical drug experiment. The four levels of the factor *A* represent drug dosages in mg. The dependent variable *Y* is a performance measure.

(a) Plot the means of the *Y* data against the levels of *A*; include standard error bars.

(b) Perform an ANOVA on the data, with tests of each of the three polynomial components of *A*.

(c) Discuss the results of part (b) with respect to the plot of the means.

11.8 The concept of orthogonal components may be clarified by further analysis of the data in the *Ex11_7* file.

(a) Using Equation 11.16, calculate b_3'. Then, calculate the cubic component for each group; $cubic = b_3' w_{cubic}$. The w_{cubic} values can be obtained from Appendix Table C.6.

(b) Subtract each cubic value calculated in part (a) from the *Y* scores in the corresponding group. Let $V = Y - cubic$. Find SS_A for the dependent variable, *V*. How is this quantity related to the linear and quadratic sums of squares in Exercise 11.7?

(c) Calculate the linear and quadratic sums of squares for the *V* variable. Compare the results with linear and quadratic sums of squares in Exercise 11.7.

11.9 In an experiment on memory, a passage was presented to subjects one word at a time at a rate of either 300, 450, or 600 words per minute. Either the texts were intact or the order of sentences was scrambled. The dependent variable was the percentage of idea units recalled. The summary statistics were:

	Means			Variances		
Rate =	300	450	600	300	450	600
Intact	66.250	59.875	43.375	68.492	79.549	81.415
Scrambled	54.375	49.750	45.875	33.977	54.214	55.267

There are eight subjects in each cell.

(a) There is some reason to believe that recall decreases as rate increases from 300 to 450 words per minute, but then levels off. What does the hypothesis predict about the polynomial components? Perform an analysis of trend to test the hypothesis.

(b) Test whether the contrasts indicated in part (a) are significantly different for the intact and the scrambled text conditions.

(c) Calculate the $SS_{Rate \times Text}$. How should the results in part (b) relate to this value?

(d) Discuss the results of these analyses.

11.10 Errors in a memory task are recorded for boys and girls of ages 5, 6, 7, and 8. There are five subjects in each of the eight cells, the average within-cell variance is 8.75, and the cell means are:

	\multicolumn{4}{c}{Age}			
	5	6	7	8
Boys	16.3	7.2	6.5	7.4
Girls	12.1	7.3	6.7	6.2

(a) Plot the means and carry out the ANOVA, including trend components of the age variable. Is the decrease in errors with age significant? Is the apparent curvature significant?

(b) There is some indication that the slope of the function relating errors and age is less negative for girls. Test whether this difference in slopes is significant.

11.11 The meaning of polynomial components of interaction such as the $Lin(Age) \times Sex$ term in Exercise 11.10 (part b) may be clearer if we redo part (b) in the following way. Calculate the equation (see Section 11.4) for the best-fitting straight line for the boys, and calculate the predicted mean errors at each of the four ages. Do the same for the girls. At this point you have a table of means much like the one in Exercise 11.10 except that those means were observed and these are predicted. Calculate the $Sex \times Age$ interaction sum of squares using the predicted means (remember that $n = 5$) and compare it to $SS_{lin(Age) \times Sex}$.

11.12 In an attempt to develop better approaches to postgraduate clinical training, a study compared three training methods (M). In order to determine whether there was some optimal point in time at which no further training was beneficial (within practical limits), a second variable, time (T; 3, 6, 9, or 12 months), was included. At the end of the training period, a committee of clinical faculty rated the individuals on a 10-point scale. There were five trainees in each cell and the error sum of squares was 87.84. The mean ratings are:

Method	\multicolumn{4}{c}{Time (in months)}			
	3	6	9	12
M_1	5.4	5.2	5.6	7.8
M_2	5.4	5.6	6.2	8.4
M_3	5.2	5.8	5.4	5.6

(a) Plot the means and describe any trends in the data. Then present the ANOVA table. Include tests of the polynomial components of T.

(b) We wish to know whether the linear trend for M_3 differs significantly from the average linear trend for M_1 and M_2. (i) State the null hypothesis in terms of the regression coefficients for the three training populations. Use the notation β_{11}, β_{12}, and β_{13} where the first subscript indicates linearity and the second subscript indicates the level of M. (ii) Carry out the significance test.

11.13 The file *EX11_13* contains an artificial data set modeled on results reported by Roediger, Meade, and Bergman (2001). They varied three factors in a study of social influence upon memory: (1) a confederate included false recalls in the presence of the subject [Context = Exptal (i.e., experimental)] or did not include such reports (Context = Control); (2) false items were highly related to items actually present in the to-be-remembered list or were low related (Related = high or low), and the time to view the items during the study period was either 15, 30, or 45 seconds. (In the actual study, the context and relatedness variables were within-subject factors, and there were only two viewing times.) The dependent variable in our file is the percent of false recognitions by the subjects.

(a) Plot the means and describe the trends in the data.

(b) Perform an analysis of variance, including trend tests you believe to be appropriate. Discuss the results.

11.14 In a study of visual processing, subjects are required to scan a row of d digits on a screen and report *yes* or *no*, depending on whether a target is among the digits in the row. One model of visual processing predicts that on negative trials the reaction time to respond *no* will be described by the equation $RT_{Neg} = k_1 + k_2 \times d$, and on positive trials by the equation $RT_{Pos} = k_1 + .5 \times k_2 \times d$, where k_1 and k_2 are numerical constants. Present sources of variance and degrees of freedom, including trend components of main and interaction effects, using asterisks to indicate which terms should be significant if the model is correct. Assume that there are $d = 2, 3, 4,$ or 5 digits on a trial.

11.15 Assume a theory predicts the following ANOVA results. Present a set of means consistent with the theory.

Source	df
A	1
B^*	3
$\text{lin}(B)^*$	1
$\text{quad}(B)$	1
$\text{cubic}(B)$	1
AB^*	3
$A \times \text{lin}(B)$	1
$A \times \text{quad}(B)^*$	1
$A \times \text{cubic}(B)$	1

Chapter 12
Integrated Analysis II

12.1 OVERVIEW

In this chapter, we review the material presented in the preceding chapters dealing with the analysis of data from between-subjects designs. We introduce a hypothetical two-factor experiment, and then analyze the data, including exploratory statistics, the ANOVA, and follow-up tests. Finally, we discuss the results.

12.2 INTRODUCTION TO THE EXPERIMENT

The effects of the organization of factual material upon memory for the material have been studied by several researchers. In one study (Myers, Pezdek, & Coulson, 1973), subjects read a series of 25 sentences, each of which related the name of one of five fictional countries with an attribute; there were five categories of attributes (e.g., climate, principal industry, language). The sentences were presented to subjects in five paragraphs, with each paragraph on a separate page. For the Name organization group, a paragraph consisted of five sentences describing five different attributes of a single country; each attribute was from a different category. For the Attribute organization group, each paragraph presented attributes for a single category for each country; for example, a page might state the different climates of the five countries, or the different languages. For the Random organization, the 25 facts were randomly placed, five to a paragraph. Subjects read each paragraph for 40 seconds and after reading all five paragraphs, wrote down as many of the 25 facts as they could recall. The Attribute organization resulted in significantly better recall than either of the other two types of organization; there was little difference between the Name and Random results.

In a hypothetical follow-up study, we imagine using the same materials but allowing subjects as much time as needed to produce perfect recall. Each of the three organizational groups is then divided into three delay groups to be retested after a delay of either 1, 2, or 3 days. With respect to the main effect of organization of the 25 facts, there are several possibilities: (1) the order of the Name, Attribute, and Random organization means may be the same as in the original study; (2)

when perfectly memorized, the differences among the three organizations may be eliminated in the delayed tests; (3) the groups that performed poorest in the original study (the name and random organizations) may do better than the attribute groups because subjects are likely to spend more time reaching the criterion of perfect recall and thus have the material better stored in memory. To examine these possibilities, we will conduct pairwise tests of the differences among the three organizations.

Although recall scores should be worse the longer the retest is delayed, the interaction of organization and delay will be of interest. Will the rate at which recall scores decrease as a function of delay be affected by the type of organization? This addresses the slopes of the three organizational curves, and requires a test of differences among their linear components. We might also ask whether the curves will differ in shape. This suggests a test of whether the quadratic components will differ. In the Results section, we will attempt to answer these questions.

12.3 METHOD

12.3.1 Subjects

The experimenters decided that the interaction of organization and delay of test was of primary interest, so they planned the experiment to have good power to detect an interaction effect of medium size (Cohen's $f = .25$). Using the *a priori* option in G*Power 3 (see Fig. 12.1), they specified 4 *df* for the numerator of the F test of the interaction and 9 for the number of conditions in the experiment. They found that 196 subjects would yield power of .8, which corresponds to approximately 22 subjects per condition. The 196 subjects were recruited from students in undergraduate psychology courses.

12.3.2 Experimental Design

The design was a 3 (organization of the texts) × 3 (delay of the test) with subjects randomly assigned to the nine cells of the design with the constraint that there were 22 in each cell.

12.3.3 Procedure

The experiment had three phases. In the first phase, subjects studied on their own time a 5-page booklet with five facts on each page, organized according to the organizational condition to which they had been assigned. They were told to study the materials until they had memorized all 25 facts and then return on an assigned day. In the second phase, subjects were tested in groups of nine; they had to remain until they could correctly reproduce all 25 facts they had previously studied. They were told that they could leave when they had produced a written sheet with all 25 facts correct, and that the purpose of the experiment was to see how much time was required to recall material they had previously studied. They were then assigned a day (1, 2, or 3 days later) on which they were to return to participate in "another experiment." In the third phase, subjects were tested for recall of the 25 facts. After completion of this phase, during debriefing they were asked whether they had studied the list between the second and third phase; none reported having done so.

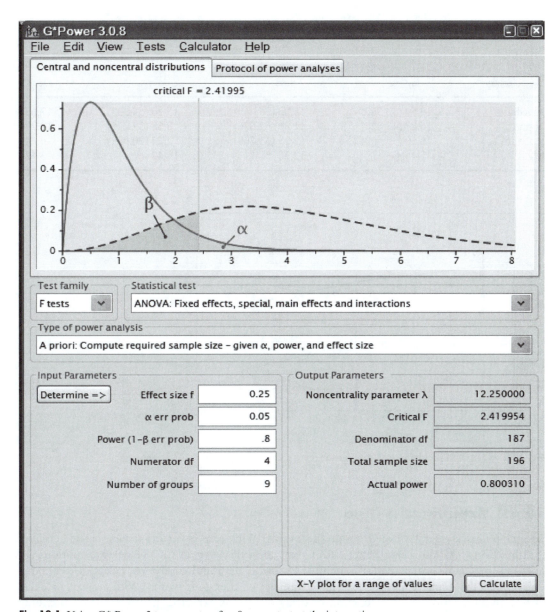

Fig. 12.1 Using G* Power 3 to compute *n* for .8 power to test the interaction.

12.4 RESULTS AND DISCUSSION

The score for each subject was the number of facts recalled correctly. Spelling errors were ignored as long as the category, attribute, and country name were correctly linked. The data are in a file on the *Tables* page of the website labeled *Table 12_1 IA2 Data*. The means and variances are presented in Table 12.1, and the means are plotted in Fig. 12.2.

Table 12.1 Means and variances (in parentheses) for a hypothetical text recall experiment

Organization	Delay			
	1 day	2 days	3 days	Mean
Attribute	19.59 (33.587)	18.05 (26.045)	15.36 (54.338)	17.67
Name	16.27 (43.827)	11.86 (67.076)	8.68 (37.275)	12.27
Random	16.50 (35.500)	7.23 (33.708)	7.23 (30.089)	10.32
Mean	17.45	12.38	10.42	13.42

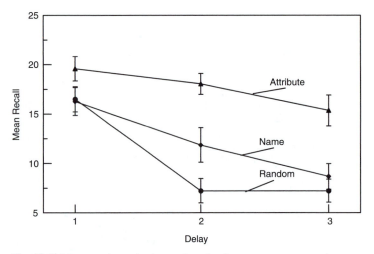

Fig. 12.2 Means and standard error bars for the text memory experiment.

12.4.1 Exploring the Data

Several points should be noted about the means. With respect to organizational effects, the Attribute organization yields better recall than the other two in all the delay conditions. In addition, the Name groups perform about the same as the Random groups, except after a 2-day delay when the Name condition has an advantage of over four words. With respect to delay effects, recall deteriorates as a function of delay of test, as expected; however, the drop is only about four items in the Attribute condition from days 1 to 3, whereas it is more than seven items in the Name and Random conditions for the same time period. These different rates of decay of memory suggest an interaction; specifically, they suggest that the linear component of the decay curves may differ among the organizational populations. The more pronounced curvature for the random groups indicates that there may also be a significant difference among the quadratic components.

We used the *Explore* option in SPSS's *Analyze* menu to examine possible violations of the normality and homogeneity of variance assumptions, (select *Normality plots with tests* under the *Plots* option). In almost all of the nine groups, the data departed significantly from normality according to results from both the Kolmogorov–Smirnov (Massey, 1951) and Shapiro–Wilk (1965) tests. However, the groups are large enough that we assume that the ratios of mean squares will be distributed approximately as F.[1]

To examine the possible violation of the homogeneity-of-variance assumption, we selected the *Plots* option in the *Explore* module of SPSS. We then selected *Power estimation* under *Spread vs Level with Levene Test*. This option uses the relation between the spread of scores and the group medians to estimate the power to which scores should be raised to reduce heterogeneity of variance. For these data the estimated exponent was 1.087; this is close to 1, indicating that a power transformation would be unlikely to reduce differences in group variances. With respect to tests of heterogeneity of variance based on absolute deviations about the group means, the p-value was .024; however, based on the deviations about the median, the p-value was .089. Considering that the ratio of the largest to the smallest of the nine group variances is only about 2 to 1 (see Table 12.1), and that with 8 and 189 df the tests are powerful enough to detect even trivial differences among the population variances, we conclude that variance heterogeneity was not a problem.

12.4.2 The ANOVA

Table 12.2 contains the results of the analysis of variance of the recall scores. The effects of organization and delay are both significant, whereas the interaction p-value falls short of the .05 level. The η^2 values are ratios of the effect sum of squares to the sum of the effect and error sums of squares and the f estimates were calculated, using the formulas in Table 9.13. These statistics reinforce the sense that the main effects contribute most of the variance among the nine cell means. By Cohen's guidelines, according to which $f = .4$ indicates a large effect, both organization and delay make large contributions to the population variance whereas their interaction contribution falls about halfway between small ($f = .1$) and medium ($f = .25$).

Let us analyze these effects further for a better understanding of the causes of the differences between organizations, and for a better sense of the shape of the function relating recall to delay.

Table 12.2 Analysis of variance of the recall scores summarized in Table 12.1

Source	Sum of squares	df	Mean square	F	p	Partial η^2	$\hat{f}$
Organization (O)	1,912.131	2	956.066	23.806	.000	.201	.480
Delay (D)	1,738.192	2	869.096	21.641	.000	.186	.457
OD	363.566	4	90.891	2.263	.064	.046	.160
Error	7,590.318	189	40.160				
Total	11,604.207	197					

R squared = .346 (adjusted R squared = .318).

12.4.3 Post Hoc Tests and Confidence Intervals

Turning to the effects of organization, the results of the Tukey *HSD* test in Table 12.3 reveal that the significant variance among the three organization means is largely due to the advantage of the

---

[1] In light of the violation of the normality assumption, we considered two alternatives to the usual ANOVA. One is the rank transform method described in Chapter 8. However, this test is valid only if there are no interaction effects (Akritas, 1990; Hora & Conover, 1984). We did perform an ANOVA based on trimmed means and winsorized variances (see Chapter 8) and arrived at the same conclusions as in the analysis of the original data, although the trimmed data distribution more closely approximated the normal.

Attribute condition over the Name and Random conditions; the difference between the latter two means is not significant.[2] The confidence intervals can be obtained as stated earlier in Box 10.2. The formula for the bounds and its application to the Attribute–Name contrast is

$$CI = \hat{\psi} \pm \left(q_{\alpha,a,ab(n-1)} / \sqrt{2} \right) \left(MS_{S/AB} \sqrt{2/ab} \right)$$

$$= 5.39 \pm \left(3.35 / \sqrt{2} \right) \left(1.103 \right)$$

Completing the calculation, the lower bound of the confidence interval is 2.79 and the upper bound is 8.00.

Because statistical significance does not always mean that an effect is of practical or theoretical importance (particularly when the large number of error degrees of freedom provide power to detect even very small—perhaps uninteresting—effects), we added a column containing estimates of Cohen's d to the SPSS output of Table 12.3. Each value is the mean difference divided by the square root of 40.16, the error mean square. The estimates of d are quite large for comparisons of the attribute mean with the other two organizational means, and relatively small for the comparison of the name and random means, providing further confirmation that the significant variance of the organizational means is largely due to the differences between the Attribute and the other two means.

Other contrasts are possible. Noting that the Name and Random organization means are similar to each other but markedly lower than the Attribute mean, we might wish to test the difference between their average and that for the Attribute subjects. Most statistical packages will enable such tests. For example, in SPSS the *Helmert* option calculates the confidence interval for that contrast and also for the contrast of the Name and Random means.[3]

Table 12.3 SPSS output of Tukey's *HSD* test of pairwise comparisons of the organizational (*O*) means and estimates of Cohen's *d*

O(*I*)	*O*(*J*)	Mean difference (*I* − *J*)	Std. error	Sig.	95% Confidence interval Upper bound	95% Confidence interval Lower bound	$\hat{d}$
Attribute	Name	5.39*	1.103	.000	2.79	8.00	.85
	Random	7.35*	1.103	.000	4.74	9.95	1.16
Name	Attribute	−5.39*	1.103	.000	−8.00	−2.79	.85
	Random	1.95	1.103	.182	−.65	4.56	.31
Random	Attribute	−7.35*	1.103	.000	−9.95	−4.74	1.16
	Name	−1.95	1.103	.182	−4.56	.65	.31

* The mean difference is significant at the .05 level.

Note: The standard error for these tests = $\sqrt{MS_{error}(2/66)}$; the use of the error mean square from the ANOVA rests on the assumption of homogeneity of variance, and 66 is the number of scores at each organizational level.

[2] As noted in Chapter 10, this and several alternative post hoc tests are available in many statistical packages. In SPSS, select *Analyze*, then *General Linear Model*, and then *Univariate*. Next select the independent (e.g., organization, attribute) and dependent variables (e.g., recall). To test pairwise differences among the organizational levels, select the *post hoc* option, and then select the test from the array presented. In this example, we chose *Tukey*.

[3] SPSS's *Help* file states: "*Difference* or reverse Helmert contrasts. Each level of the factor except the first is compared to the mean of the previous levels. In a balanced design, difference contrasts are orthogonal. *Helmert* contrasts. Each level of the factor except the last is compared to the mean of subsequent levels. In a balanced design, Helmert contrasts are orthogonal."

Table 12.4 Output from SPSS's univariate module

Contrast results (K matrix)

Organization Helmert contrast			Dependent variable recall
Level 1 vs. later	Contrast estimate		6.371
	Hypothesized value		0
	Difference (Estimate – Hypothesized)		6.371
	Std. error		.955
	Sig.		.000
	95% Confidence interval for difference	Lower bound	4.487
		Upper bound	8.256
Level 2 vs. level 3	Contrast estimate		1.955
	Hypothesized value		0
	Difference (Estimate – Hypothesized)		1.955
	Std. error		1.103
	Sig.		.078
	95% Confidence interval for difference	Lower bound	−.222
		Upper bound	4.131

The SPSS output is in Table 12.4.[4] The significance level reported there does not take into account that the test was post hoc. Therefore, to evaluate significance, use the Scheffé criterion:

1. From Table 12.4, calculate t either by dividing the contrast by the standard error (6.371/ .955) or by taking the square root of the value of F (44.473). In either case, $t = 6.67$.
2. Compare the computed value t of 6.67 with $S = \sqrt{df_1 \cdot F_{.05,df_1,df_2}} = \sqrt{2F_{.05,2,189}} = 2.47$. The result is significant.
3. The confidence interval bounds reported by SPSS also fail to take into consideration that the test is post hoc. From Chapter 10, the bounds are

$$
\begin{aligned}
CI\ bounds &= \hat{\psi} \pm s_{\hat{\psi}}S \\
&= 6.37 \pm (.955)(2.47) \\
&= 4.01, 8.73
\end{aligned}
$$

Because the contrast was selected after viewing the results, the bounds are based on the family of all possible contrasts and are therefore somewhat wider than those reported by SPSS in Table 12.4. We should also note that our syntax file used the weights 1, −.5, and −.5. Had we used other weights, the bounds would have required adjustment. For example, if we had used 2, −1, and −1, the values of the contrast and its standard error would have been twice those in Table 12.4. Accordingly, the bounds would have been divided by 2 to return to the original data scale.

12.4.4 Trend Tests

From the "Delay mean" column of Table 12.1 and from Fig. 12.1, it appears that the mean recall drops markedly from a delay of 1 day to a delay of 2 days, and then decreases less with a further

---

[4] We have also provided a more general approach in a file on the *Syntax* page of the book's website. The SPSS syntax file *Contrasts.sps* shows how many different contrasts can be evaluated.

delay to 3 days. This suggests that both linear and quadratic components are present in the average delay function. Most statistical packages will test this. In SPSS, the *Contrast* button in *GLM*'s *Univariate* menu allows access to various types of contrasts, including the polynomial. When the polynomial option is selected, the output includes the effect size, its standard error, the *p*-value, and confidence interval bounds for all polynomial components of the average curve.

Returning to Fig. 12.1, it also seems that the trends depend on the type of organization; the Attribute curve declines more slowly and is less curved than the curves for the Name and Random conditions. Although SPSS' *Univariate* option does not provide a test of the differences among the polynomial components of the three curves in Fig. 12.1, we can do so by using Equation 11.11 with the contrast weights replaced by polynomial coefficients from Appendix Table C.6. Box 12.1 presents the sums of squares formulas and shows how they apply to the recall data in our example.

Box 12.1 Calculating Polynomial Sums of Squares in a Two-Factor Design

1. Assume two factors, A and B; B is a quantitative variable. The sum of squares for the pth polynomial component of B is

$$SS_{p(B=)} = na\left(\sum_{k=1}^{b} \zeta_{p,k}\overline{Y}_{..k}\right)^2 \Bigg/ \sum_{k=1}^{b} \zeta_{p,k}^2$$

For the linear component of the average of the three delay curves,

$$SS_{linear(Delay)} = (66)[(1)(17.45) + (0)(12.38) + (-1)(10.42)]^2 /[1^2 + (-1)^2]$$

$$= 1630.89$$

2. The preceding calculation is for the average of the three organization curves in Fig. 12.1. We are also interested in whether the components vary as a function of organization. We first calculate $SS_{p(B)}$ at each level of A:

$$SS_{p(B)/A_i} = n\left(\sum_{k=1}^{b} \zeta_{p,k}\overline{Y}_{.jk}\right)^2 \Bigg/ \sum_{k=1}^{b} \zeta_{p,k}^2$$

For the linear component of the curve for Name organization,

$$SS_{linear(Delay)/Name} = (22)[(1)(16.27) + (0)(11.86) + (-1)(8.68)]^2 /[1^2 + (-1)^2] = 633.69$$

Similarly, the linear sums of squares for the Attribute and Random conditions are 196.82 and 945.26.

3. To obtain the sum of squares that represents the variation of the pth component of B over levels of A, calculate

$$SS_{A \times p(B)} = \sum_{j=1}^{a} SS_{p(B)/A_i} - SS_{p(B)}$$

In our example, the linear component of the organization $(O) \times delay$ sum of squares is $SS_{O \times linear(Delay)} = 196.82 + 633.69 + 945.26 - 1630.89 = 144.88$.

The calculations for the quadratic sum of squares in the preceding steps would be similar except that the weights (from Appendix Table C.6) are 1, -2, and 1.

Table 12.5 ANOVA of recall data with polynomial terms

Source	Sum of squares	df	Mean square	F	p
Organization (O)	1,912.13	2	956.07	23.81	.000
Delay (D)	1,738.19	2	869.10	21.64	.000
$\quad$linear(D)	1,631.03	1	1631.03	40.61	.000
$\quad$quad(D)	107.16	1	107.16	2.67	.104
OD	363.57	4	90.89	2.26	.064
$\quad O \times$ linear(D)	145.20	2	72.60	1.81	.203
$\quad O \times$ quad(D)	218.37	2	109.19	2.72	.068
S/OD	7,590.32	189	40.16		
Total	11,604.21	197			

Step 1 calculates the sum of squares for the pth polynomial component (linear or quadratic in our example) of the average curve. Step 2 does the same at each of the levels of organization. Step 3 can then be carried out on a calculator. The results of the complete analysis are presented in Table 12.5.

Several points should be noted about the relation of polynomial components to main, or interaction, terms. Because the linear and quadratic components of the delay source are orthogonal and exhaust the delay degrees of freedom, $SS_{linear(D)} + SS_{quad(D)} = SS_{delay}$. Also, MS_{delay} is the average of the mean squares of all its polynomial components. Similarly, the sum of all the orthogonal components of the interaction sum of squares will equal the interaction sum of squares, and the average of the component mean squares will equal the interaction mean square.

It is easy to lose sight of what the trend components represent. The F test of $linear(D)$ tests whether the straight line that best fits the average of the three curves in Fig. 12.1 has a slope significantly different from zero. That clearly is the case; we can conclude that the average recall score declines significantly as a function of delay of test.

The F test of $quad(D)$ tests whether the average of the three lines has a significant quadratic, or (inverted) U-shaped component. Because there are only three data points for this curve, the test of the quadratic component tests whether there is significant curvature. If there were more data points, ruling out a quadratic component would not rule out curvature because a cubic, or even higher order component might be contributing. In any event, despite the appearance of curvature in the data, the test of the quadratic component does not yield a significant result.

The F test of the $O \times linear(D)$ component tests whether the slopes of the Attribute, Name, and Random curves vary significantly; $MS_{O \times linear(D)}$ could be calculated as n times the variance of the three linear contrasts, divided by the sum of the squared weights (see Exercise 12.11). The $O \times quad(D)$ component can be interpreted in a similar way. Neither of these components were significant by the usual .05 criterion. We lack statistical evidence that organization affects either the rate of decline in recall with delay, or the curvature of the decay function.[5]

To sum up, the statistical analyses demonstrate that the type of organization influences recall; recall is better in the Attribute condition and in the Name or Random conditions, which do not differ. In addition, there is a linear decrease in recall over the delays included in the experiment.

---

[5] It might seem that this has to be the case because the OD source was not significant. However, suppose the OD sum of squares had been divided differently; e.g., $SS_{O \times lin(D)} = 63.57$ and $SS_{O \times quad(D)} = 300$. Now, for the quadratic component of the interaction, $F = 150/40.16 = 3.74$, which is quite significant with 2 and 189 df.

12.5 SUMMARY

In this chapter, we used data from a hypothetical two-factor experiment to review developments in Chapters 8–11.

- As always, we first explored the data, noting various trends in the means, and examining the spreads of scores and the shapes of distributions in the different conditions of the experiment.
- Following the ANOVA, we tested pairwise comparisons of the means for the qualitative variable, Organization, using Tukey's *HSD* method to control the familywise error (*FWE*) rate.
- Trend analyses were also performed to provide information about the shape of the average recall function of the quantitative variable, Delay, and to test differences among the delay curves as a function of organization.

EXERCISES

12.1–12.3   The website contains the files *EX12_1–EX12_3* on the *Exercises* page of the book's website. Each file contains a data set with three groups of scores. In each case, explore the data and on the basis of your exploration, decide on the appropriate test of the omnibus null hypothesis. The test might be the usual *F* test, an *F* test based on trimmed data, the Welch *F* test, a test based on a transformation, or a nonparametric test. Justify your choice and then carry out the test you have chosen.

12.4   An experiment on the effects of persuasion on attitude change yielded the following data:

	Movie	Lecture	Movie + lecture	Control	Neutral movie	Neutral lecture
Mean	5.4	3.0	6.4	−1.4	.8	−.6
Variance	13.1	11.8	11.1	15.1	16.3	16.6

There were five subjects in each cell. In what follows, *FWE* = .05, two-tailed.

(a) Test the mean of the left-most two conditions (movie, lecture) against the mean of the right-most two conditions (neutral movie, neutral lecture) assuming that it is one of four planned contrasts.

(b) Assume we wish to test each of the conditions against the control. Perform the test of the movie against the control mean.

12.5   Now assume the following means and variances for the experiment of Exercise 12.4:

	Movie	Lecture	Movie + lecture	Control	Neutral movie	Neutral lecture
Mean	5.4	3.0	6.4	−1.4	.8	−.6
Variance	7.2	8.0	8.8	24.1	15.3	20.6

(a) Redo part (a) of Exercise 12.4.

(b) Redo part (b) of Exercise 12.4.

12.6 The *Exercises* page on the website contains a data set, *EX12_6*. *Employment* = 1 (fully), 2 (part-time), and 3 (unemployed). The scores are subjects' ratings of their happiness.

(a) Explore the data. Is there any evidence that the assumptions underlying F and t tests are violated?

(b) Perform the usual ANOVA and also calculate Welch's F to test the null hypothesis that the population mean happiness scores do not differ.

(c) Assuming that all pairwise differences between the means are considered, calculate the confidence interval for the difference between the means of groups 1 and 2.

12.7 **(a)** The *Format* × *Experience* interaction in Table 9.12 may be viewed as a contrast; that is, as a sum of weights times means. State the weights and calculate the sum of squares for this contrast. The cell means are in Table 9.11.

(b) Do the same for the three-way interaction of *Format* × *Experience* × *Instructions*.

12.8 A researcher sampled the political attitudes of college students and older retirees. From each sample, subjects were chosen so that there were two age groups of 50, each further divided into five equal-size groups based on their political attitudes from very liberal (*LL*) to very conservative (*CC*). Each of the 100 subjects was then given a description of a hypothetical political candidate and asked to rate their support for such a candidate. The group means and variances (in parentheses) are

	Very liberal (LL)	Liberal (L)	Moderate (M)	Conservative (C)	Very conservative (CC)
Retirees	16.1 (107)	14.7 (99)	13.5 (124)	13.8 (113)	12.4 (118)
Students	18.5 (102)	16.9 (107)	8.5 (96)	3.2 (115)	1.4 (119)

Let A = political attitude and B = age group.

(a) Present the ANOVA table.

(b) Present the *EMS*.

(c) Calculate general ω^2 for A; i.e., the estimated proportion of variance due to political attitude.

12.9 **(a)** The researcher in Exercise 12.8 computes simultaneous confidence intervals for all pairwise differences. Assuming *FWE* = .05, what is the *CI* for the difference between the L and M marginal means? Is there a significant difference between the means?

(b) The researcher tests the difference between the mean of the two combined liberal groups and the mean of the combined two conservative groups. State the null hypothesis and calculate the test statistic.

(c) Consider each of the following situations for part (b). In each of the following cases, state the critical value for the test statistic and your conclusion (α = .05): (i) The test was decided on before the data were collected and it is the only follow-up test. (ii) The researcher also decides *a priori* to test two additional hypotheses. (iii) After viewing the means, the researcher decides on the contrast in part (b).

(d) Before collecting the data, the researcher wants to know whether the difference between moderates and the combined L and LL subjects is different for old and young subjects.

(i) State the null hypothesis. (ii) Calculate the confidence interval and state your conclusion about the null hypothesis.

12.10 Ninety-six subjects are asked to predict which of two lights will be lit on each of 100 trials. The more frequent light appears on 60% of the trials for 1/4 of the subjects, on 70% for another fourth, on 80% for another fourth, and on 90% for the remaining fourth. The subjects are further divided into three groups; one-third of the subjects are instructed to try to predict which light will appear on each trial (the predict group); one-third are instructed to maximize their total number of correct predictions over the 100 trials (the maximize group); and the remaining third are offered a reward of 5 cents for each correct prediction (the reward group). The cell means are

		Percent occurrence (P)				
		60	70	80	90	Mean
	Predict	61	69	82	91	75.750
Method (M)	Maximize	63	75	88	90	79.000
	Reward	75	88	94	93	87.500
	Mean	66.333	77.333	88.000	91.333	80.750

The error mean square $MS_{S/MP} = 50.600$ and $n = 8$. Calculate sums of squares, mean squares, and F ratios and present the ANOVA table, including the polynomial components of both P and MP. What do your results imply about the curves for the three groups?

12.11 Find the numerical value of the linear contrast at each of the three levels of M in Exercise 12.10. Then, calculate the variance of the three numbers, and divide by $(\Sigma_k w_k^2)/n$. The result should match your result in Exercise 12.10 for $MS_{M \times Linear(P)}$.

12.12 Calculate the bounds of the 95% confidence interval for the following planned comparisons of the slopes of the method functions in Exercise 12.10:

(a) Maximize vs Reward slope.

(b) Predict vs the average of the Maximize and Reward slopes.

Part 3: Repeated-Measures Designs

Chapter 13
Comparing Experimental Designs and Analyses

13.1 OVERVIEW

The preceding chapters were primarily concerned with analyses of data from a single experimental design, the completely randomized design. In a completely randomized design, each subject is randomly assigned to one of several experimental conditions. This is the simplest experimental design; as such, it provides a good foundation for developing the basic concepts of statistical inference and data analysis associated with ANOVA. However, random assignment of subjects to experimental conditions is only one of several approaches to designing experiments. Other experimental designs and statistical analyses offer important advantages compared to the completely randomized design; most notably, they often have a smaller error variance and, consequently, greater power. In the current chapter, we will introduce these alternatives and compare them to the completely randomized design and to one another. Our goal in this chapter is to consider general issues in choosing among alternative designs. Therefore, we will present only the simplest versions of the designs and we will assume simple, highly constrained, structural models. Development of the details of the new designs will be left to subsequent chapters.

The organization of the chapter is as follows:

- *Factors influencing the choice of a design* will be discussed first. The goal of this section is to identify the general considerations involved in selecting an approach to a research question.
- *Blocking designs* will be the first design considered because they are a straightforward extension of the completely randomized design. This approach can be used when a measure related to the dependent variable is available for each subject. Subjects are divided into blocks on the basis of this *concomitant variable*, resulting in smaller within-cell variance compared to the completely randomized design. In this context, we will also develop the concept of *relative efficiency* as a basis for comparing experimental designs.
- *Analysis of covariance* will follow blocking designs because ANCOVA also makes use of concomitant measures. The difference is that ANCOVA uses a concomitant measure as a *covariate* to provide a statistical adjustment to remove some of the error component of

each of the scores in the data set. To the degree that the covariate and the dependent variable are correlated, the error variance is reduced.

- The *repeated-measures design*, sometimes referred to as a *within-subjects design*, will be presented next. In the simplest version, each subject is tested in every condition or on every trial. Because the variability due to individual differences can be removed from the error variance, this design provides still another way of dealing with the effects of nuisance variables.

- *Latin squares.* In one variation of this design, subjects are tested in several conditions, but the order of presentations is counterbalanced so that an equal number of subjects receives each treatment in each position of the sequence of presentations. This allows removal not only of variability due to individual differences, but also of the variance due to the times at which treatments are administered. In another common variation, each subject is tested under several conditions, with each test on a different stimulus set. Then variability due to stimulus sets can be removed if assignment of treatments to sets is counterbalanced.

A central theme in comparing these alternative designs and statistical analyses is that they partition the same total variance in different ways, all with a shared goal of reducing error variance. A second, closely related theme of the chapter is that designs may be compared with respect to how effectively they reduce error variance. If design *A* results in less error variance than design *B*, we say that design *A* is *relatively efficient* compared to design *B*. Finally, a third theme of the chapter is that there are tradeoffs in choosing among designs. Generally, more efficient designs are more complex designs, and more complex designs have more things that can go wrong with them.

13.2 FACTORS INFLUENCING THE CHOICE AMONG DESIGNS

An important purpose of this chapter is to provide an understanding of the factors involved in deciding among experimental designs when a choice is available. One classification of such design factors has been proposed by Keren (1993; also see Chapter 1). He suggested three factors that should influence the choice of design; these are (1) theoretical, (2) methodological, and (3) statistical.

13.2.1 Theoretical Issues

Theoretical issues take precedence in determining design choices in the sense that the theoretical question motivating an experiment often places clear constraints on what types of designs are, and are not, appropriate. Theoretical considerations will typically dictate whether the researcher should take one observation per subject, or multiple observations. Keren (1993) provides an example. Suppose that a theory predicts the overall proportion of choices of one option versus another; in this instance, a between-subjects design is adequate. However, if the theory predicts sequences of choices—for example, the probability of option *A* being selected, given that on the preceding trial option *B* had been selected—the researcher clearly needs to test subjects in a series of trials in which both options are available. More generally, any study in which our theory predicts the effects of a series of responses upon subsequent responses requires a within-subjects design.

As Keren (1993) pointed out, theoretical issues often reduce to consideration of context effects. For example, experiments with rats (Crespi, 1944; Zeaman, 1949), monkeys (Schrier, 1958), and college students (Schnorr, Lipkin, & Myers, 1966) have shown that the effects of amount of incentive depend on whether each subject is tested at several different levels of incentive (i.e., a within-subjects design) or at only a single incentive level (i.e., a between-subjects design). In this example, the use of a within-subjects design is appropriate to test hypotheses about contrast effects, the effect of one incentive level as a function of whether the subject has previously been tested with a smaller or larger amount. The between-subjects design is appropriate if interest centers on the absolute, rather than the relative, effect of incentive.

13.2.2 Methodological Issues

The choice of a research design is often affected by practical concerns. For example, if a between-subjects design is considered, we must be able to recruit enough subjects to ensure sufficient statistical power. However, if the task is boring or unpleasant, it may be difficult to recruit subjects. As another example, if we wish to test the same subjects under several conditions, then completing the procedure may require either that subjects be available for long time periods or that they be willing to participate in multiple sessions.

Developmental studies provide one example of some of the practical concerns in choosing between designs. Suppose we want to study the development of math skills taught by an experimental method to children in all grades in an elementary school. Should we test children in different grades simultaneously (*cross-sectional design*) or repeatedly test the same children as they proceed through the grades (*longitudinal design*)? There are tradeoffs in making this choice. Cross-sectional studies avoid the possible loss of data as subjects move from the area or change schools. They also avoid the possibility that the study will be disrupted, or learning affected, by changes over time in factors other than the variable of interest (e.g., an event producing a marked social or economic change such as the Katrina hurricane of 2004). On the other hand, the longitudinal study eliminates variability due to differences among individuals in different age groups. For example, some children in the higher grades may have entered from another school and not been initially taught by the method of interest. At the least, this complicates the analysis of cross-sectional data because their data must be removed from analyses.

Even in laboratory studies in which multiple measures are obtained in a single session, there are potential issues. Possible practice or fatigue effects may be confounded with the effects of the independent variable when subjects are tested under several conditions, or if different subjects are tested at different times. In addition, repeated-measures designs may result in *carry-over effects* such that a subject's performance in a given condition may be affected by their experience in earlier conditions. As we noted in our discussion of theoretical issues, such context effects may be of interest; however, if they are not, the researcher must carefully weigh the possibility of carry-over effects.

13.2.3 Statistical Issues

Designs differ with respect to the degree to which they control nuisance variables; this translates into differences in error variance. Designs with less error variance translate into more powerful statistical tests and narrower confidence intervals given the same number of observations. Thus, an important basis for comparing designs is with respect to their error variances; the ratio of the error variances of two designs is a measure of their *relative efficiency*. In this chapter, we will consider the relative efficiency of various pairs of designs, and try to make clear why some designs are more efficient than others.

In sum, the choice of a research design must balance theoretical, methodological, and statistical considerations. Theoretical considerations and practical constraints sometimes dictate a single, appropriate design. However, the researcher often has choices, even after theoretical and methodological issues are taken into account. In that case, the relative efficiency of alternative designs should be a major consideration in selecting the research design.

In the remainder of this chapter, we will discuss the methodological and statistical pros and cons of the experimental designs cited earlier, as well as of the analysis of covariance. We will omit further consideration of theoretical issues in selecting a design because these are related to specific research questions. We will postpone discussion of variations and extensions of the basic designs and analyses, as well as many details of data analysis, assumptions underlying the analyses, and interpretations. A fuller treatment of the repeated-measures and Latin square designs will be presented in Chapters 14–17, and of analysis of covariance in Chapter 25.

13.3 THE TREATMENTS × BLOCKS DESIGN

13.3.1 The Design

Blocking usually refers to a design in which the subjects are matched with respect to a measure that is correlated with the dependent variable. For example, in an experiment comparing three methods of teaching fractions to elementary school students, we might take steps to match the distributions of arithmetic skills of the children assigned to the three methods. One way to do this would be to administer a pretest designed to measure basic arithmetic skills of 36 children, and then divide the children into four blocks based on their pretest scores. The nine children scoring highest would then be randomly assigned to one of the three instructional methods, so that within this block there would be three students in a cell. The same would be done with the next highest scoring nine students, and so on until we had four blocks based on pretest scores.

Although this is a common type of blocking design, blocking could be done on the basis of other variables that we assume will be related to performance on the dependent variable. If two experimenters are involved in testing subjects, and if there is reason to believe that responses may be influenced by the person administering the test, half of each experimental group could be tested by each experimenter. In this case, experimenter is the blocking variable. Similarly, if there is reason to believe that the time of day at which testing takes place can affect performance, we can either test all subjects at the same time of day or, if that is impractical, we can establish time of day as a blocking variable. In that case, if we had four testing times, 1/4 of each treatment group would be tested at each time.

Regardless of how it is accomplished, the primary purpose of blocking is to reduce error variance, thus increasing the power of the hypothesis test and decreasing the width of confidence intervals. We next consider how this occurs.

13.3.2 Blocking vs Completely Random Assignment

Suppose two investigators independently ran the experiment we described in which 36 students were divided into three treatment groups, each group taught by one of three instructional methods. Experimenter *CR* randomly assigns each of the 36 subjects to one of the three groups; the only restriction is that there are 12 students taught by each method. Experimenter *TB* follows the procedure described in the preceding section, using pretest scores to divide the students into four blocks, and then randomly assigning each of the nine students within a block to one of the three instructional methods, with the constraint that there are three students in a block taught by each method. The first design is a one-factor completely randomized design, with the data analyzed as described in Chapter 8. The data from the blocking design are analyzed as a two-factor design, as in Chapter 9.

The blocking design should result in a smaller error variance than the one-factor CR design based on the same total number of subjects. This is because the three subjects within each treatment × block ($A \times B$) cell will vary less in arithmetic knowledge than will the 12 subjects in a level of A in the CR design, so we can expect that their scores on the posttest will also be less variable. For example, consider the following set of 12 posttest scores, grouped into three levels of ability as measured on a pretest:

Low				Medium				High			
7	12	8	5	8	12	13	14	14	9	16	15

The variances of the posttest scores for low, medium, and high ability groups are 8.67, 6.92, and 9.67, respectively; the average within-group variance is 8.42 (i.e., $MS_{S/AB}$). However, if the 12 scores were not grouped by pretest level, their variance would be 12.63 (i.e., $MS_{S/A}$). Thus, the error variance will be smaller in a treatments × blocks design than in a completely randomized design, *provided that the pretest scores are correlated with the posttest scores.*

To further understand the effect of blocking, we consider the average result of many independent replications of two experiments differing in their design. Table 13.1 presents the average sums of squares and mean squares for 5,000 independent replications of the two experimental designs under consideration. The results in the table were obtained by using a computer program to draw 5,000 samples of 36 pretest and posttest scores from a population in which the correlation between the two measures was .4. In the CR design, the 36 posttest scores then were divided randomly among the three treatment levels; in the blocking design, the posttest scores were divided among four blocks in order of their pretest scores, and then randomly divided among the treatments within each block. A constant was added to all posttest scores at a given treatment level in both designs, with a different constant for each level, thus creating treatment effects. An ANOVA was then performed for the data in each design and the proportion of the 5,000 samples that resulted in a rejection at the .05 level was recorded as power. The numerical results presented in Table 13.1 are averages over the 5,000 replications of the simulated experiment. There are several points to note about the results:

1. The average SS_{total} is virtually identical for the two designs, the very small difference being due to chance variability involved in performing a finite number of replications.
2. The treatment variability, SS_A, is smaller in the blocking than in the CR design. To see why, consider the expected mean square for treatments, $E(MS_A)$. As we saw in Chapter 8, with 12 scores at each level $E(MS_A) = \sigma_e^2 + 12\theta_A^2$. But as the preceding numerical example demonstrated, we expect the error variance, σ_e^2, to be smaller in the $T \times B$ design than in the completely randomized design. Therefore, we expect the MS_A to be smaller in the blocking design.
3. The blocking design involves fewer error degrees of freedom than does the completely randomized design. The 33 df in the CR error term (S/A) are now divided among the B, AB, and S/AB terms in the $T \times B$ analysis.
4. Power, the proportion of significant results, is greater in the $T \times B$ ANOVA, despite the fact that the MS_A and the error df—factors that affect power—are smaller in that design.

Power is greater in the $T \times B$ design than in the CR design because $MS_{S/AB}$ is smaller than $MS_{S/A}$. To understand why the two error terms differ in magnitude, consider the sources of random variation in the two designs. The error term of the CR design is influenced by measurement error and individual differences, including differences in arithmetic skills. We can expect that differences in arithmetic skills will be responsible for much variation in performance in the experiment, so by measuring those differences and incorporating them into the experimental design via blocking, we remove that variability from the error term of the $T \times B$ design. This conceptual difference in the two designs is realized in differences in how they partition the same total variance: Whereas the CR design distinguishes just two sources of variability, the $T \times B$ design distinguishes four. The two additional terms of the $T \times B$ design—the block (B) source of variance and, to a lesser extent, the interaction (AB)—capture much of the variance contributing to $MS_{S/A}$ of the CR design. In short, by incorporating the pretest scores as a systematic source of variance in the design, we are left with a smaller residual error variance.

Table 13.1   Average results of analyses of variance for completely randomized and blocking designs, based on 5,000 replications

	Completely randomized design					Treatments (A) × blocks (B) design			
SV	df	SS	MS	Power	SV	df	SS	MS	Power
A	2	1,163.43	581.71	.550	A	2	1,123.40	561.70	.595
S/A	33	4,736.78	143.54		B	3	1,058.74	352.91	
Total	35	5,900.21			AB	6	746.19	124.37	
					S/AB	24	2,974.16	123.92	
					Total	35	5,902.49		

13.3.3 Relative Efficiency

We have presented an argument that the error term will be smaller and, consequently, power will be higher in the $T \times B$ design than in the CR design. However, the argument was based on a single example, so it is fair to question the generality of that conclusion. Will the $T \times B$ design always have more power than the corresponding CR design? If not, what factors determine the relative power of the two designs? When the $T \times B$ design does have a power advantage, is the added time, effort, and expense involved in executing the design worth the trouble? Key to answering these questions is the concept of *relative efficiency* (*RE*).

Two designs may be compared to determine their relative efficiency by computing the ratio of their MS_{error} terms. In our current example of the $T \times B$ and CR designs, the relative efficiency of the blocking design to the randomized design is

$$RE_{T \times B \, to \, CR} = \frac{MS_{S/A}}{MS_{S/AB}} \tag{13.1}$$

Treating the right-hand values in Table 13.1 as if they came from a single experiment, and substituting into Equation 13.1, we find the relative efficiency of our hypothetical experiment to be 1.159. A value greater than 1 indicates that the $T \times B$ design is more efficient than the CR design. Some algebra (see *TechNote 13_1* on the book's website) will show that *RE* is greater than 1 if the pooled mean square due to blocking (the *B* and *AB* sources) is greater than the error mean square; i.e., $RE > 1$ if $[(SS_B + SS_{AB})/a(b-1)] > MS_{S/AB}$. This condition will hold if there is a correlation between the blocking variable and the dependent variable. Typically, it is a simple matter for a researcher to identify a blocking variable that is related to the dependent variable, so the efficiency of the *T* × *B* design will generally be greater than that of the *CR* design.

A smaller error variance is not enough, however, to warrant using the blocking design because blocking results in a loss in error degrees of freedom relative to the completely randomized design. Recognizing this, Fisher (1935) proposed an adjustment to take into account the difference in error *df*:

$$Adjusted\ RE_{T \times B\ to\ CR} = \left(\frac{df_{S/AB} + 1}{df_{S/AB} + 3}\right)\left(\frac{df_{S/A} + 3}{df_{S/A} + 1}\right)\frac{MS_{S/A}}{MS_{S/AB}} \tag{13.2}$$

For our hypothetical experiment, the adjusted *RE* is $(25/27)(36/34)(1.159) = 1.136$. This value is still larger than 1, indicating that the decrease in error variance more than offsets the loss in degrees of freedom associated with blocking. Whether the adjusted *RE* is large enough to warrant the extra cost, effort, and time involved in collecting and using the pretest data for blocking in future studies is an issue our hypothetical researcher should consider.

One way to make the choice between the two designs more concrete is to translate the difference in design efficiency into its implications for power. We can estimate Cohen's effect size, *f*, from the right-hand side of Table 13.1. Recall from Chapter 8 that *f* is the ratio of $\hat{\sigma}_A$ to $\hat{\sigma}_e$. We can estimate $\hat{\sigma}_A$ from the results in the right-hand side of Table 13.1 as

$$\hat{\sigma}_A = \sqrt{\frac{(a-1)}{abn}(MS_A - MS_{S/AB})}$$

$$= \sqrt{\frac{2}{36}(561.70 - 123.92)} = 4.932$$

We can estimate $\hat{\sigma}_e$ by taking the square root of $MS_{S/AB} = \sqrt{123.92} = 11.132$. Our estimate of *f* is therefore

$$\hat{f} = \hat{\sigma}_A / \hat{\sigma}_e = 4.932/11.132 = .443$$

Using this estimate of effect size with G*Power, we can now estimate the *post hoc* power to be .601 for the *T* × *B* design. Note that this is quite close to the proportion of rejections reported in Table 13.1 for the 5,000 simulated replications of the blocking experiment. The same set of computations on the data for the *CR* design in Table 13.1 produces an estimated value for *f* of .412, and a corresponding value for power of .551. Comparing the power estimates for the two designs, we see that the power of the *CR* design is .05 less that than obtained for the blocking design.

The difference in power for the two designs seems small and, perhaps, does not merit the additional work of gathering the pretest data. A relevant question for the researcher considering which design to use in future related research is: How many additional subjects in the *CR* design would yield the same power as in the *T* × *B* design? Multiplying the total *N* of 36 by the adjusted relative efficiency of 1.136 yields approximately 41. Because we need a total *N* divisible by 3, the number of instructional conditions, we estimate power when $N = 42$ and $f = .412$. The estimated power is .628, slightly higher than we achieved with the blocking design. If it is practical to find six more subjects, it may be preferable in subsequent experiments just to randomly assign individuals to treatment conditions without collecting pretest data and blocking.

13.3.4 How Many Blocks?

If a blocking design is chosen, the researcher must decide how many blocks to use. As the number of blocks increases, the scores in the cells representing the combinations of treatments and blocks should be less variable, yielding a still smaller error term. However, the increase in blocks involves a loss of error degrees of freedom; if we had six instead of four blocks, n would equal 2, and the error $df = ab(n - 1) = 3 \times 2 \times (2 - 1) = 6$. There is a tradeoff; the reduction in error variance with more blocks leads to more power, but the loss of degrees of freedom with more blocks leads to less power. Feldt (1958) published a table of the optimal number of blocks; i.e., the number such that power is maximized. This optimal number of blocks depends on several factors:

1. *The correlation between X, the concomitant variable, and Y, the dependent variable.* If there is no correlation, blocking costs error degrees of freedom with no corresponding reduction in error variance because Y will not be affected by factors affecting X. As the population correlation coefficient increases, so does the optimal number of blocks.
2. *The total sample size, N.* Although increasing the number of blocks decreases the error degrees of freedom, this loss has less effect on power when the sample size is large; that is, when there are many error degrees of freedom to begin with.
3. *The number of levels of the independent variable, A.* As the number of levels of A decreases, the number of blocks that can be profitably used increases because the loss in error degrees of freedom is smaller when a is lower.

All of these factors—the likely correlation, the available sample size, and the number of treatment levels—should be considered before engaging in the added effort of collecting and using concomitant measures.

Before leaving this design, a few more words are in order. First, we have been considering estimates. We cannot *know* what will happen when we run experiments. Our estimates of error variance, effect size, and power will be useful to the extent that the estimates are accurate for the planned experiments. Second, the efficiency of the blocking design depends on N, a, and ρ, the correlation between concomitant variable and the dependent variable. This last factor is particularly important. Blocking requires more time, effort, and often expense than random assignment. That cost will result in more powerful tests and more precise estimates of effects only to the extent that the concomitant variable is a good predictor of performance.

Finally, we have spent considerable space on the blocking design to illustrate certain concepts in a layout that should be familiar from the preceding chapter. However, there are alternatives available to the researcher. One such alternative is the analysis of covariance; this analysis makes use of concomitant data in a different way from that of the blocking analysis. We introduce this approach to increased efficiency next.

13.4 THE ANALYSIS OF COVARIANCE

In both the blocking design and the analysis of covariance (ANCOVA), a concomitant variable is used to account for variance that would otherwise be treated as random (i.e., error). As we have seen, the blocking design reduces error by incorporating the concomitant variable, B, into the design and thus extracting variance associated with B from the error term. In ANCOVA, the concomitant variable, X, is not incorporated into the experimental design; rather, subjects are assigned randomly to conditions without regard to their scores on X. However, the correlation of X with the dependent variable, Y, is used to remove from SS_{total} the variance that is predictable from X. The resulting, *adjusted* SS_{total} is then partitioned into variability attributable to A and S/A. Thus, ANCOVA is similar to the blocking design in that it also uses the concomitant variable to reduce the error variance; however, it accomplishes the reduction statistically instead of incorporating X into the design of the experiment.

ANCOVA is best developed within a regression framework and therefore we postpone most details until Chapter 25. However, we will try to present a conceptual understanding, using a numerical example.

13.4.1 ANCOVA: A Numerical Example

Table 13.2 presents a data set. The independent variable, A, represents three instructional methods. As in the completely randomized design, 12 students were randomly assigned to each method. As in the blocking ($T \times B$) design, a pretest of basic arithmetic skills was administered because the pretest scores should be highly correlated with performance on the posttest. In Table 13.2, the X values are the pretest scores and the Y values are the posttest scores. Our interest is in the effects of the instructional methods on the posttest score.

Table 13.3 presents the results of two analyses: an analysis of variance in which the pretest scores are not relevant, and an analysis of covariance in which the pretest scores are used to account for some of the variance in the original data set. Note that the adjusted total sum of squares and error sum of squares in the ANCOVA are smaller than the unadjusted terms in the ANOVA. Those reductions can be explained by reference to correlations between the X and Y data. The adjusted total sum of squares is the proportion of the total sum of squares that *cannot* be predicted from X. Although we do not usually calculate the terms in Table 13.3 this way, we could obtain the adjusted sum of squares (3,613.905 in our example) by first calculating r, the correlation between all the X and Y scores. The square of r is the proportion of the variance of the Y scores that is predictable from our knowledge of X (see Chapter 25). Therefore, the proportion of the total sum of squares that is *not* predictable from X is $1 - r^2$, and the amount of the total variability not predicted is $SS_{total(adj)} = (1 - r^2)SS_{total(y)}$. In our example, $r^2 = .2411$ and $SS_{total(adj)} = (1 - .2411) \times 4764.75$, or

Table 13.2 Data to illustrate analysis of covariance

A_1	Y	53	59	69	57	55	63	54	81	59	63	59	71
	X	66	84	60	78	59	72	69	80	81	55	65	81
A_2	Y	79	74	80	69	66	65	72	71	62	73	69	79
	X	100	60	80	68	63	66	85	72	47	89	78	85
A_3	Y	60	70	80	57	50	83	97	91	86	78	52	81
	X	54	85	72	41	55	74	74	85	70	69	55	71

Note: Y is the dependent variable and X is the covariate.

Table 13.3 Analyses of the data of Table 13.2

Source	Sums of squares	df	Mean squares	F	p
		Analysis of variance			
A	953.667	2	476.333	4.123	.025
S/A	3,812.083	33	115.518		
Total	4,764.500	35			
		Analysis of covariance			
A	1,140.594	2	570.297	7.352	.002
S/A	2,482.210	32	77.569		
Total	3,622.804	34			

3615.969. Ignoring a small error due to rounding the value of the correlation coefficient, this is the adjusted total sum of squares in the ANCOVA results of Table 13.3. Similarly, the ANCOVA error variance is adjusted depending on the within-condition correlation of the covariate and dependent variable; as a result, the error term is reduced relative to the ANOVA.

Chapter 25 presents ANCOVA as a special case of multiple regression. For now, the important point to understand is that the increased efficiency of the covariance analysis is a function of the variability in Y predictable from X that would otherwise show up in the error term of an ANOVA. This reduction in error is achieved with the loss of only one error degree of freedom, but at the cost of more complexity and more assumptions.

13.4.2 Comparing ANCOVA to the *CR* and *T* × *B* Designs

We have indicated that when its assumptions are met, ANCOVA can provide more power than the *CR* analysis. But how does ANCOVA compare with analyses based on blocking? As stated earlier, Feldt (1958) derived the optimal number of blocks to be used in the blocking design. Using those numbers of blocks, he concluded that blocking followed by a two-factor ANOVA was more powerful than the one-way ANCOVA when the correlation was less than .4, but that ANCOVA was more powerful when the correlation was greater than .6; there was little difference when the population correlation was between .4 and .6. A simple rule for choosing between the two approaches might be to block if the expected correlation is less than .5, but randomly assign subjects and use ANCOVA if the expected correlation is greater than .5. However, Maxwell, Delaney, and Dill (1984) have offered two alternative design approaches that promise greater power than simply choosing between a blocking design and ANCOVA.

Maxwell et al. (1984) pointed out that the choices examined by Feldt were not the only possible ones. They found that the assignment of subjects to treatments on the basis of their concomitant scores *together with* an analysis of covariance on the dependent measure provided a power advantage over the two-way ANOVA that usually is performed on data obtained from the blocking design. This makes sense because treating the concomitant variable as discrete loses information. It does not take into consideration each observed value of X whereas ANCOVA, which treats X as continuous, does involve each value of X in the analysis.

Maxwell et al. also recommend a method proposed by Dalton and Overall (1977) for equating groups on the concomitant measure. The *alternate ranks method* requires ranking subjects on the basis of X. Then, assuming three treatment conditions—A, B, and C—the subject ranking highest on the pretest would be assigned to A, the next highest ranking to B, the next to C, and further assignments would be to C, then B, then A, and repeat for the remaining subjects. This ensures even closer matching on X than does the random assignment of subjects within blocks, and does not require the researcher to have an estimate of the correlation coefficient in order to decide on the number of blocks. When the dependent measure is analyzed by ANCOVA, the approach yields good power relative to other design and analysis combinations.

When used properly, ANCOVA and the variants just described can be an excellent tool for reducing error variance and thereby increasing power. In practice, ANCOVA is often used not only in designs involving random assignment of subjects, but also in designs that involve pre-established groups. In such circumstances, the covariate may differ across groups, leading to possible difficulties of interpretation. We will consider interpretative issues and provide further details on the analysis and its underlying assumptions in Chapter 25.

13.5 REPEATED-MEASURES (*RM*) DESIGNS

13.5.1 The Design

The designs discussed in the preceding sections are between-subjects designs in which N subjects are distributed among the a conditions, and each subject contributes exactly one score to the data set. In many studies, however, subjects contribute scores in several conditions. Such studies include experiments in which the conditions are levels of a manipulated independent variable, with the order of presentation randomized independently for each subject. These are often referred to as *subjects × treatments* designs. In still other repeated-measures studies, scores are recorded for the same individuals at several points in time; these are often referred to as *subjects × trials* designs. In these repeated-measures designs, instead of *an* subjects, there are *an* observations comprised of *n* subjects each tested in all *a* conditions.

Repeated-measures designs often are treated as a category of *randomized-blocks designs*. In the randomized-blocks design with *a* treatment levels, *a* subjects who are roughly matched on a concomitant measure are considered to form a block. Then, each of the members of the block is tested at a single level of A. Such blocks also may exist naturally; for example, as a litter of animals. Conceptually, the design is a treatments × blocks design with *b* blocks and $n = 1$. The ANOVAs for the randomized-block design and the repeated-measures design are the same. However, in the former, results generalize to a population of subjects each of whom has been exposed to only one treatment level whereas in the latter, results generalize to a population of subjects each of whom has been exposed to all *a* treatment levels.

13.5.2 The ANOVA

Suppose a researcher wishes to compare the tastes of four light beers. Having different subjects each rate only a single beer requires many subjects for only a few seconds each. A more efficient use of subjects is to have a smaller number each rate all four. The beers are presented for a single taste in a different random order to each of eight subjects with a short interval in between, during which subjects rinse their mouths. Table 13.4 presents ratings (Panel *a*) and ANOVA results (Panel *b*).

Table 13.4 Data and analysis for a repeated-measures design

(*a*) The data

Subject	Beer 1	Beer 2	Beer 3	Beer 4	Mean
1	2	5	3	3	3.25
2	4	6	5	4	4.75
3	5	7	4	5	5.25
4	3	4	3	4	3.50
5	6	7	6	5	6.00
6	2	5	4	3	3.50
7	4	5	6	4	4.75
8	3	6	4	6	4.75
Mean	3.63	5.63	4.38	4.25	4.47

(*b*) The ANOVA

SV	df	Sum of squares	Mean square	F
Subjects (*S*)	7	26.219	3.746	6.091
Beer (*A*)	3	16.844	5.615	9.136
Residual	21	12.906	.615	

In general, this subjects × treatments design involves *a* levels of the treatment variable and *n* subjects; here $a = 4$ and $n = 8$. Mean squares are calculated as in the two-way completely randomized or treatments × blocks designs. The term labeled "residual" in Table 13.4 is computed as an interaction of $S \times A$; the only unusual aspect of the calculations is that there is only one score per cell instead of a mean of several scores, as in a between-subjects design. The residual term serves as the error term to test the effect of *A*.

The design summarized in Table 13.4 is usually referred to as a one-way, repeated-measures design. In the case of the one-way, completely randomized design, recall that we were able to partition the total variance into just two sources of variance—the main effect of *A* and an S/A term that served as the error term. In the case of the repeated-measures design, however, the fact that each subject participates in all conditions of the experiment makes it possible to distinguish the main effect of subjects from the interaction of subjects with treatments (labeled "residual" in Table 13.4b). This finer partitioning of the variance in the repeated-measures design usually results in a substantial reduction of the error term (i.e., "residual") relative to the completely randomized design.

Earlier (see Section 13.3.2), we attributed the greater efficiency of the $T \times B$ design to the fact that blocking removed some individual difference variability from the error term, thus reducing the error term relative to the completely randomized design. The use of a concomitant variable in ANCOVA was similarly presented as statistically removing some individual difference variability from the error term, relative to the completely randomized design. In the case of the repeated-measures design, we are essentially blocking by subjects, with the result that differences in the performances of subjects are entirely removed from the error term of that design. Thus, the subjects × treatments design will typically result in a smaller error term than any of the designs we have considered to this point.

The *Subjects* source of variance (S) provides an indication of the potential increase in power if a *RM* design is used instead of a *CR* design. In many types of research, we would expect to find considerable individual differences in performance. This variability would be a component of the error term of the ANOVA for a *CR* design. Thus, the repeated-measures design will be more efficient than the completely randomized design (and other between-subjects designs) when there is substantial individual variability. However, if there is little variability among subjects' mean scores, it would suggest that we had not greatly reduced error variance relative to the *CR* design. In such a situation, the repeated-measures design could actually be less efficient than the completely randomized design because the *RM* design has fewer error degrees of freedom. In the example of Table 13.4, there are only 21 error degrees of freedom compared to 28 in a completely randomized design with the same number of scores. To better understand the issue of the efficiency of the *RM* design compared to the *CR* design, we next consider the expected mean squares.

13.5.3 Expected Mean Squares and Relative Efficiency

Panel *a* of Table 13.5 presents the results of 5,000 independent replications of a computer simulation of two experimental designs. In each replication of the completely randomized experiment, there were three groups of 10 scores; each of the 30 scores consisted of an error component and an individual difference component. The three groups of scores each had a different treatment effect added. For the replications of the repeated-measures experiment, the three scores for a simulated subject contained different errors of measurement, but all three scores had the same value of the individual difference error. The two types of errors were drawn from the same population as in the completely randomized simulations. Three treatment effects were added, as in the completely randomized experiment.

Table 13.5 Results of analyses of variance for completely randomized and repeated-measures designs, based on 5,000 replications (*a*) and expected mean squares (*b*)

(*a*) Simulation results

Completely randomized design					Repeated-measures design				
SV	df	SS	MS	Power	SV	df	SS	MS	Power
A	2	589.38	294.69	.235	A	2	391.53	195.77	.684
S/A	27	3,666.55	135.90		Subjects	9	3,024.17	336.02	
Total	29	4,255.93			Residual	18	650.68	36.15	
					Total	29	4,066.38		

(*b*) Expected mean squares

Completely randomized design			Repeated-measures design		
SV	df	EMS	SV	df	EMS
A	$a-1$	$\sigma_e^2 + \sigma_S^2 + n\theta_A^2$	A	$a-1$	$\sigma_e^2 + n\theta_A^2$
S/A	$a(n-1)$	$\sigma_e^2 + \sigma_S^2$	Subjects	$n-1$	$\sigma_e^2 + a\sigma_S^2$
			Residual	$(a-1)(n-1)$	σ_e^2

There are several points to note about the results in Panel *a* of Table 13.5.

1. Summing the average values of $SS_{Subjects}$ and $SS_{Residual}$, the result is 3674.85, within sampling error of the average $SS_{S/A}$ (3,666.55). This is because the average error sum of squares for the *CR* design contains variability due to measurement errors and individual differences. However, in the *RM* design, the variability due to differences in performance across subjects winds up in the subjects source of variance with the consequence that the $SS_{Residual}$ term in the *RM* analysis is usually much smaller than the $SS_{S/A}$ term of the *CR* analysis.

2. The SS_A is smaller in the *RM* design. This is because individual differences no longer contribute to the differences among the observed means in the *RM* design.

3. Despite having a smaller numerator mean square and fewer error degrees of freedom, the *RM* design resulted in considerably more power; i.e., the proportion of the 5,000 replications resulting in a rejection of the false null hypothesis was .684 as opposed to only .235 for the *CR* design. This power advantage reflects the fact that much of the error variance in the *CR* design was due to individual differences, and these did not contribute to the *RM* error term.

As we did in Section 13.3.3 with the blocking design, we can form an expression for the efficiency of the *RM* design relative to that of the *CR* design. We estimate the *CR* error term as $MS_{S/A} = (SS_S + SS_{Residual})/(df_S + df_{S/A})$. Incorporating Fisher's adjustment for the difference in degrees of freedom, and substituting our estimate of the *CR* error term, we have

$$AdjustedRE_{RM\ to\ CR} = \left(\frac{df_{Residual} + 1}{df_{Residual} + 3}\right)\left(\frac{df_{S/A} + 3}{df_{S/A} + 1}\right)\frac{MS_{S/A}}{MS_{Residual}} \tag{13.3}$$

$$= \left(\frac{(a-1)(n-1) + 1}{(a-1)(n-1) + 3}\right)\left(\frac{a(n-1) + 3}{a(n-1) + 1}\right)\frac{(SS_S + SS_{Residual}) / [a(n-1)]}{MS_{Residual}}$$

Using the data of Table 13.4 and the estimated $MS_{S/A}$, the relative efficiency in our example is $(22/24)(31/29)(1.397/.615) = 2.23$. It is clear that despite the loss of error degrees of freedom, the *RM* design is considerably more efficient than the completely randomized design. This translates into requiring many fewer subjects to achieve the same power as a completely randomized design.

In summary, when both designs are practical, the repeated-measures design will usually be more efficient, both in the use of subjects and with respect to error variance. The relative efficiency promises greater power and narrower confidence intervals. However, one caution is in order. We have assumed a very simple structural model in presenting our results. There are alternative, more complicated, and often more realistic models for data obtained with the repeated-measures design. We will consider this topic and other aspects of the design and analysis of related data in the next few chapters.

13.5.4 Advantages and Disadvantages of the *RM* Design

We have established that the repeated-measures design is usually a relatively efficient design compared to the between-subjects designs we considered earlier in the chapter. An advantage of this efficiency is that fewer subjects are required to achieve the same degree of statistical power in the *RM* design. This is important if the population is limited in size, as are many clinical populations; or when subjects are difficult to recruit, as when the task is very boring or dangerous; or when subjects are expensive animals such as monkeys. Even without these constraints on subject availability, the *RM* design may prove more practical than a between-subjects design. For example, if it takes very little time to obtain a score from a subject, it may be more efficient to run one subject in several conditions than to run several subjects each in a different condition.

Repeated-measures designs make efficient use of subjects, both in the sense of requiring fewer subjects than between-subjects designs, and in the sense of having less error variance. However, not all independent variables lend themselves to such designs. For example, subject variables such as gender, intelligence, and clinical category must be treated as between-subjects factors. Also, many experimental manipulations such as surgical procedures or instructional methods do not lend themselves to within-subject manipulation. For example, in an experiment designed to compare the effectiveness of different methods of teaching mathematics, knowledge achieved by being exposed to one of the methods cannot be miraculously expunged so that it can be relearned by a second method.

Although the between-subjects designs we considered in previous chapters may involve more error variance, they are relatively simple. Scores in different groups can be assumed to be independent and the within-cell variance can be used as the error term for testing any effect. We pay for the *RM* design's smaller error variance with some additional complexity:

- *Carry-over effects*: the influence of a treatment at one point in time upon a score in a later condition can complicate the interpretation of treatment effects.
- *Scores will be correlated* because each subject contributes several scores; as we will see in the next few chapters, this will have implications for the validity of the *F* test of treatments.

In short, like any other design, the *RM* design is not appropriate for all situations. However, when it is a suitable choice, its high efficiency makes it a very attractive option.

13.6 THE LATIN SQUARE DESIGN

13.6.1 An Example of the Design

Suppose we wish to measure accuracy on five tasks of varying structure. We intend to present each task for a block of trials, recording percent correct for each block. Because a trial block requires little time to complete, we decide to present the tasks in a series of five blocks such that there will be a score for each subject in each trial block. We have at least two options with respect to the design. If we have *n* subjects, we may construct *n* random sequences of the five trial blocks, assigning each subject to a sequence. For five subjects, the sequences in this repeated-measures design might look like the left side of Table 13.6. Note that some treatments appear more often than others in some sequential positions. For example, the fifth condition (A_5) is presented first to two subjects and second to another two. If there is an improvement with time in the situation, performance on this task would be at a disadvantage because its average position is early in the sequence of trial blocks. Although randomization ensures that the average sequential positions of the tasks will be equal over replications of the experiment, the practice effect does contribute to error variance, rendering the design less efficient than it would be if we could somehow remove these practice effects from the error variance.

The right side of Table 13.6 presents a counterbalanced design in which each treatment appears once in each row (subject) and column. Columns may represent blocks of trials, as in the preceding

Table 13.6 Design layouts for five subjects with random sequences and Latin squared sequences (A refers to a treatment condition, C to a trial block, and S to a subject)

	Random sequences						Latin squared sequences				
			Trial block						Trial block		
Subject	C_1	C_2	C_3	C_4	C_5	Subject	C_1	C_2	C_3	C_4	C_5
S_1	A_5	A_3	A_2	A_1	A_4	S_1	A_1	A_3	A_4	A_2	A_5
S_2	A_2	A_1	A_4	A_3	A_5	S_2	A_2	A_4	A_5	A_3	A_1
S_3	A_4	A_5	A_3	A_1	A_2	S_3	A_5	A_2	A_3	A_1	A_4
S_4	A_3	A_5	A_4	A_2	A_1	S_4	A_4	A_1	A_2	A_5	A_3
S_5	A_5	A_1	A_4	A_3	A_2	S_5	A_3	A_5	A_1	A_4	A_2

example, or sets of materials, as in many studies of language processing. The column variable is an independent variable in this *Latin square design* and we can now separate its effects from the error variance. Therefore, this design has the potential to be more efficient than the repeated-measures design in which treatments are randomly assigned to trial blocks, or material sets. Although the design on the right is potentially a very efficient one, therefore promising considerable power and precision of estimates, there are some potential drawbacks:

1. As we will see when we consider the ANOVA, the $df_{error} = (a-1)(a-2)$. If $a = 4$, the error $df = 6$, and power may be quite low. For this reason, it is often recommended that there be at least five levels of A. In most psychological research, there usually are several subjects in each row of the square, providing an additional source of variance, a potential error term with more degrees of freedom than in the design in which there is only one subject in each row.

2. As we will see when we consider the ANOVA, it is not possible to analyze interactions among the three factors. Furthermore, if such interactions are present in the population, they reduce the efficiency of the design and may bias the test.

3. There may be effects of one treatment level on a subsequent one. Such carry-over effects differ from trial block effects in that the latter involve a practice, acclimation, or fatigue effect associated with the position in time, whereas carry-over effects represent the effect of exposure to one treatment upon responses to a subsequent one. There are modifications of the basic Latin square design that are balanced so that the residual effect can be estimated (e.g., Williams, 1949) but the analysis becomes complicated.

Despite these limitations and potential drawbacks, the basic Latin square is a component of designs frequently used in research. Often, each row of the square represents a group of subjects, rather than a single individual. We will consider that variation of the design in Chapter 16; here we focus on the basic Latin square design.

13.6.2 Analyzing the Data

Suppose we are interested in studying the effects of the structure of a display upon the probability of detecting a target on a screen within some fixed interval of time. The display might be an open field (A_1), or be segmented into one to four vertical areas (A_2, A_3, A_4, and A_5). Subjects are tested in each of five counterbalanced blocks, and the proportion of correct detections is recorded. Panel a of Table 13.7 presents the design and the data. The five columns on the left represent the five trial blocks, with C_1 being the first and C_5 being the last. For example, the first subject (S_1) was first tested in a trial block with the A_1 (open field) display, then in a block with A_3 (two segments), and so on. On the right side of the panel, the scores have been rearranged so that all the scores from the same treatment level are in the same column.

There are three independent variables in this design: S, A, and C. These account for $3(a-1)$, or 12, degrees of freedom in this example. The total degrees of freedom are $a^2 - 1$, or 24. This leaves $(a^2 - 1) - 3(a - 1) = (a - 1)(a - 2)$ to be accounted for. This value, 12 in the example, is too small to permit calculation of any of the possible interaction terms, each of which requires 16 df (and 64 df for the three-way interaction). Therefore, the analysis rests on the assumption that the three variables do not interact, and the residual mean square corresponding to the $(a - 1)(a - 2)$ df is considered to represent only error variance.

The sums of squares for the three main effects can be calculated by the usual formulas. For example, the SS_A is a times the variance of the five treatment (A) means, and SS_C is a times the variance of the trial block (C) means. The *residual* sum of squares is obtained by subtraction of the

Table 13.7 Data and ANOVA for a Latin square design

(a) Data

	C_1	C_2	C_3	C_4	C_5		A_1	A_2	A_3	A_4	A_5
S_1	(A_1) 58	(A_3) 58	(A_4) 73	(A_2) 63	(A_5) 71		(C_1) 58	(C_4) 63	(C_2) 58	(C_3) 73	(C_5) 71
S_2	(A_2) 49	(A_4) 54	(A_5) 53	(A_3) 60	(A_1) 57		(C_5) 57	(C_1) 49	(C_4) 60	(C_2) 54	(C_3) 53
S_3	(A_5) 85	(A_2) 79	(A_3) 83	(A_1) 85	(A_4) 84		(C_4) 85	(C_2) 79	(C_3) 83	(C_5) 84	(C_1) 85
S_4	(A_4) 77	(A_1) 73	(A_2) 74	(A_5) 86	(A_3) 82		(C_2) 73	(C_3) 74	(C_5) 82	(C_1) 77	(C_4) 86
S_5	(A_3) 56	(A_5) 65	(A_1) 50	(A_4) 64	(A_2) 59		(C_3) 50	(C_5) 59	(C_1) 56	(C_4) 64	(C_2) 65
Mean	65	65.8	66.6	71.6	70.6		64.6	64.8	67.8	70.4	72.0

(b) ANOVA

SV	df	SS	MS	F
A	4	217.84	44.36	3.10
C	4	177.44	54.46	3.08
S	4	3,074.64	768.66	57.65
Residual	12	171.92	14.33	
Total	24	3,641.84		

three sums of squares for treatments, rows, and columns from the total sum of squares. We will have more to say about calculations in an extended discussion of this design and the related analysis in Chapter 16.

13.6.4 Efficiency of the Latin Square Relative to the Repeated-Measures Design

The error degrees of freedom for the repeated-measures design with a subjects and a treatment levels is $(a - 1)(a - 1)$, whereas that for the Latin square design is $(a - 1)(a - 2)$. However, despite fewer error degrees of freedom, the Latin square design will be more efficient than the repeated-measures design if the column variability makes a large contribution to the total variability. We can see this in the following estimate of the mean square error for the repeated-measures design (MSE_{RM}) derived from the Latin square ANOVA results (see *TechNote 13_2* on the website for the derivation):

$$est MSE_{RM} = \frac{(a - 1)MSE_{LS} + MS_C}{a} \tag{13.4}$$

where the terms on the right are the residual and column mean squares from the Latin square ANOVA. Applying Equation 13.4 to the data of Table 13.7, we have $est MSE_{RM} = (4 \times 14.33 + 54.46)/5 = 22.36$. The adjusted relative efficiency is

$$AdjustedRE_{LS\,to\,RM} = \left(\frac{df_{LS} + 1}{df_{LS} + 3}\right)\left(\frac{df_{RM} + 3}{df_{RM} + 1}\right)\frac{MSE_{RM}}{MSE_{LS}} \tag{13.5}$$

and substituting the estimate of MSE_{RM}, together with the other values from Table 13.7, $RE = (13/15)(19/17)(22.36/14.33) = 1.51$. Clearly, despite the loss of four error degrees of freedom, the Latin square design will provide greater power and more precise estimates of population parameters than will the repeated-measures design.

13.7 SUMMARY

Chapter 13 has introduced four new approaches to designing experiments and analyzing the data. Each approach seeks to reduce error variance with corresponding benefits for power and parameter estimates.

- The *treatments × blocks design* attempts to remove some sources of individual differences relevant to performance by establishing blocks of subjects using a concomitant variable.
- *ANCOVA* assigns subjects randomly to conditions, but uses a concomitant variable to statistically remove some sources of individual differences.
- The *repeated-measures design* involves testing subjects in all of the conditions of the experiment with the result that individual difference variance may be entirely removed from the error term of the design.
- The *Latin square design* is a variation of the subjects × treatments design in which the sequence of conditions is counterbalanced across subjects. This procedure permits removing not only the contribution of individual differences from the error mean square, but also the contribution of temporal effects due to fatigue or practice.

When executed successfully, both the $T \times B$ design and ANCOVA reduce error relative to the completely randomized design; the RM design reduces error further; and the Latin square design reduces error further still.

Although we have emphasized the increased efficiency of these four designs and analyses, relative efficiency is not the only consideration in selecting a research design. Thus, other advantages and some disadvantages of each design were noted:

- *The treatments × blocks design.* The assumptions underlying the analysis are the same as for any completely randomized design, and are the least restrictive of any of the procedures considered. However, the collection of an additional measure on which to base assignment of subjects to treatments may incur added time, effort, and cost.
- *The analysis of covariance.* The analysis is extremely versatile, capable of application to data from most research designs. However, there are some disadvantages associated with the use of ANCOVA. (1) Like the blocking design, analysis of covariance requires the collection of an additional measure. (2) The assumptions underlying the analysis are more stringent than those underlying the usual ANOVA. (3) As we will discuss in Chapter 25, when the scores on the covariate are influenced by the independent variable or when subjects at different levels of the independent variable are selected from different pre-existing groups, ANCOVA results are prone to misinterpretation.
- *The repeated-measures design.* The advantages of the RM design include: (1) fewer subjects are required than in completely randomized designs; and (2) it is a natural approach when interest resides in learning or forgetting curves, or in any other changes over time or trials. However, the advantages are accompanied by several potential disadvantages: (1) scores are correlated and as a result assumptions about the distribution of errors are more stringent than in completely randomized designs; and (2) a treatment may influence not only responses on the trial on which that treatment is applied but also responses to other treatments on subsequent trials. Such carry-over effects make it difficult to interpret comparisons among means.
- *The Latin square design.* Advantages include: (1) when used as a variant of the repeated-measures design, it has the advantages cited for that design; and (2) when subjects are tested under different conditions in a sequence of trials or trial blocks, both treatment and trial effects can be tested. Similarly, if each treatment is applied to a different set of stimulus materials, both the effects of treatments and of stimulus sets can be evaluated. However: (1) the design has the disadvantages cited for repeated-measures designs in general; (2) if only one square is used, the number of subjects must equal the number of conditions; and (3) that number should generally be at least five in order to have a large enough number of degrees of freedom to provide reasonable power.

In future chapters, we deal with these designs and the analysis of covariance in greater detail, considering assumptions and responses to their violations, as well as important extensions of the basic designs and analyses.

EXERCISES

13.1 A teacher compared three types of instructional methods (A) on mathematics final exam test scores (Y). In the research design, students were first divided into four blocks (B) of 15 each on the basis of a pretest score (X), then assigned to the three conditions. In summary, the design had three levels of A roughly matched for ability and four ability blocks, with five students in each $A \times B$ cell. The data are in the file *EX13_1* at the website.

(a) In analyzing the data, the teacher ignored the X data and also did not consider B as a factor in the design. Assuming that she had accomplished her purpose by equating the three instructional conditions, she analyzed the data as if from a one-factor, between-subjects design with 20 scores at each level. Do this analysis and explain the potential problem with it.

(b) Perform an analysis taking B into consideration and state your conclusions.

13.2 (a) The teacher in Exercise 13.1 could have randomly assigned 60 students to the three conditions without blocking. The last equation in *TechNote 13_1* (at the website) allows us to estimate the error variance for this design from the results for the blocking design. That equation is

$$est(MS_{S/A}) = \left[1 - \frac{a(b-1)}{abn - 1}\right] MS_{S/AB} + \frac{SS_B + SS_{AB}}{abn - 1}$$

Calculate the estimated error variance for a completely randomized design.

(b) Then calculate the estimated adjusted relative efficiency of the $T \times B$ to the CR design.

13.3 (a) From the ANOVA of the treatments $\times$ blocks design (Exercise 13.1, part (b)), estimate Cohen's f for the A source.

(b) Using the estimate of σ_A^2 from part (a) and the error variance estimated in Exercise 13.2, estimate Cohen's f for the A source for the CR design.

(c) Using the two estimates of f, compare the power of the two designs for this study.

(d) You should have found that the $T \times B$ design provides a more powerful test of A. How many students would be needed in the CR design to match the power obtained with the $T \times B$?

(e) Find the N needed to achieve .8 power for the $T \times B$ design. Then, using this value and the relative efficiency estimated in Exercise 13.2, find the N needed if you had used a completely randomized design.

13.4 Blocking is not always preferable to completely random assignment of subjects to treatments. What factors should influence the decision to divide subjects into blocks?

13.5 Analysis of covariance (ANCOVA) provides another approach to analyzing the data of Exercise 13.1. Consider the summary tables from the one-factor ANOVA and from the ANCOVA (ignoring B in both analyses).

ANOVA				ANCOVA		
Source	df	SS		Source	df	SS
A	2	861.233		A	2	1,006.147
S/A	57	10,096.700		S/A	56	9,873.610
Total	59	10,957.933		Total	58	10,879.757

(a) In this chapter, we stated that $SS_{total(adj)} = (1 - r^2)SS_{total(y)}$, or $r^2 = 1 - SS_{total(adj)}/SS_{total(y)}$. Calculate the correlation for the 60 XY scores and show that this relation holds for the two totals in the preceding tables.

(b) A similar relationship holds between the two error sums of squares: $SS_{S/A(adj)} = (1 - r_{S/A}^2)SS_{S/A(y)}$. The r in this case is an average of three correlations, one from each level of A. However, the best estimate is not obtained by adding the three correlation coefficients and dividing by three. Instead, $r_{S/A}^2 = (\Sigma_j SP_j)^2/[(SS_{S/A(X)})](SS_{Y(S/A)})]$ where SP_j is the sum of cross-products; $SP_j = \Sigma_i(X_{ij} - \bar{X}_{.j})(Y_{ij} - \bar{Y}_{.j})$, the numerator of the covariance of X and Y in group A_j. The sums of squares terms are as usually defined; they are the sums of squared deviations of scores about their group means, summed over groups. Although most software has an option for calculating these terms, for convenience, we provide them here. Calculate $r_{S/A}^2$ and use it to verify the relation between it and the two error sums of squares. Here are the necessary sums of cross-products and sum of squares.

	A_1	A_2	A_3
SS_X	1,736.000	3,591.750	1,874.200
SS_Y	2,624.550	2,418.950	5,053.200
SP_{XY}	−749.000	2,010.750	5.800

13.6 The following data set consists of three scores for each of four subjects:

	A_1	A_2	A_3
S_1	10	14	16
S_2	8	8	17
S_3	9	9	13
S_4	7	6	9

(a) Calculate the SS_{total}, SS_S, SS_A, and SS_{SA}; $SS_{SA} = SS_{total} - (SS_S + SS_A)$. Divide SS_S, SS_A, and SS_{SA} by their degrees of freedom to obtain the mean squares. Then, assuming the expected mean squares of Table 13.5, panel b, calculate the F test for A.

(b) Having used the repeated-measures design, we might wish to estimate for future experiments the error variance if we had used a completely randomized design with 12 subjects, four different subjects at each level of A. Using Equation 13.3 and the data of part (a), estimate what $MS_{S/A}$ would have been from the ANOVA in your answer to part (a). What is the adjusted relative efficiency?

13.7 (a) Cohen defined his effect size, f, for the repeated-measures design as σ_A/σ_W; σ_W^2 is the variance within treatment populations; $\sigma_W^2 = \sigma_S^2 + \sigma_e^2$. From the *EMS* of Table 13.5, estimate the variances based on the data in Exercise 13.6; then estimate f.

(b) In G*Power 3, select the following options: *F test, ANOVA: Repeated-measures, within factors*, and *Post hoc*. Then enter $\alpha = .05$, total sample size = 4 (the number of subjects), number of groups = 1, repetitions = 3 (number of within-subject conditions), correlation = .75, and epsilon = 1. Insert your estimate of f from part (a). Calculate post hoc power, assuming these values.

(c) Now use G*Power's option for *ANOVA Fixed effects Omnibus oneway*. Assuming the value of f calculated in part (a), estimate post hoc power for the completely randomized design.

(d) Assuming we wished to redo the experiment to detect a medium sized effect ($f = .25$) with power = .9 and $\alpha = .05$, how many observations would be required for each design?

(e) How does the relation between the required sample sizes change as r decreases?

13.8 Five experts taste each of six wines and rate each on a 100-point scale. The order of presentation is counterbalanced so that over the five subjects, each wine appears in each of the eight possible positions in the sequence of tastings. Let A be the wines and C be the position in time. The data, also present on the website in the file *EX13_8*, are organized by wines (A) and position in time (C):

A_1	A_2	A_3	A_4	A_5		C_1	C_2	C_3	C_4	C_5
82	83	80	84	81		82	83	80	84	81
89	84	91	84	79		84	79	89	84	91
88	86	87	88	84		86	87	88	84	88
88	86	89	95	77		77	88	86	89	95
86	86	78	78	79		78	78	79	86	86

(a) Often researchers ignore the blocking factor, C, and carry out the following ANOVA:

Source	df	SS	MS	F	p
Subjects (S)	4				
Wines (A)	4				
SA	16				

Complete the table.

(b) A similar analysis can be performed, ignoring A, and having subjects C, and SC as the sources. Do this analysis.

(c) Subtract SS_C from part (b) from SS_{SA} in part (a). Call the result $SS_{Residual}$. Also subtract SS_A from part (a) from SS_{SC} in part (b). How does this compare with the residual sum of squares?

(d) As we did for Table 13.7, we can carry out a complete Latin square ANOVA. The sources and *df*s are as follows:

Source	df	SS	MS	F	p
Subjects (S)	4				
Wines (A)	4				
Time (C)	4				
Residual					

Complete the table, testing A and C against the residual mean square. What are the differences between the results of this analysis and those in parts (a) and (c)?

13.9 **(a)** Applying Equation 13.4 to the data in Exercise 13.8, estimate the error term if each sequence of ratings had been randomized independently for each subject.

(b) Estimate the efficiency of the Latin square design relative to that of the repeated-measures design for this data set.

Chapter 14

One-Factor Repeated-Measures Designs

14.1 OVERVIEW

In Chapter 13, we introduced repeated-measures designs, distinguishing two types of experiments, subjects × trials and subjects × treatments. In subjects × trials experiments, the researcher is interested in changes in behavior as a function of time so the independent variable is trials or trial blocks. In subjects × treatments experiments, the order of presentation of the treatments is randomly permuted for each of the n subjects in order to guard against systematic effects related to time, such as practice or fatigue. In addition, the interval between treatment presentations should be long enough to minimize the risk that the effects of one treatment will influence responses to a subsequent treatment. Such carry-over effects may be due to fatigue, practice, or contrast with prior treatments.

Our introduction to the repeated-measures design in Chapter 13 emphasized its efficiency, both with respect to the need for fewer subjects and its smaller error variance relative to the completely randomized design. In developing our case for the small error variance of the repeated-measures design, we assumed that subjects and treatments (or trials) did not interact. The structural model corresponding to this assumption is called an *additive model*. It implies that if we exclude measurement error and plot the performance of the population of subjects as a function of treatment level (or trial), the curves will be parallel; in other words, the treatment effects will be the same for all subjects in the population.

The alternative to the additive model is a *nonadditive model* that includes a subjects × treatments interaction term. That is, it is assumed that treatment effects are different for different subjects. This is probably the more realistic model for most situations. However, because the additive model enables us to introduce certain ideas in a simpler context, we will begin developments with that model.

To summarize, the goals of this chapter are:

- To present two alternative models of the structure of the data: the additive model in which subjects × treatments ($S \times A$) interaction effects are not present in the population, and a nonadditive model in which they are assumed to be present. We consider possible problems arising from nonadditivity and possible solutions to those problems.

- To define several measures of the effect of the independent variable.
- To discuss the factors that influence decisions about sample size when planning experiments and the use of G*Power 3 to estimate the required sample size.
- To present tests of contrasts and trend for the repeated-measures design.
- To address the problem of missing observations in repeated-measures designs.
- To describe alternative test procedures based on ranks. These nonparametric procedures are designed to test hypotheses when the data do not conform to the assumptions underlying the analysis of variance.

14.2 THE ADDITIVE MODEL IN THE ONE-FACTOR REPEATED-MEASURES DESIGN

14.2.1 The Structural Model

We assume that the n subjects are a random sample from an infinitely large population of subjects. We view Y_{ij}, the score of the ith subject tested in the jth condition, or on the jth trial, as being composed of a *true score*, μ_{ij}, and measurement error, ε_{ij}; that is,

$$Y_{ij} = \mu_{ij} + \varepsilon_{ij} \tag{14.1}$$

If the different treatment levels all have the same effect on the scores and if all subjects in the population have the same scores, all the true scores will equal the grand mean of the population, μ. However, different treatments may have different effects and different subjects will score differently because of differences in ability, experience, or motivation. Therefore, the parameter μ_{ij} in Equation 14.1 can be viewed as being equal to the population mean plus the effects due to the jth treatment and the ith subject. Acknowledging this, Equation 14.1 is rewritten as

$$Y_{ij} = \mu + (\mu_i - \mu) + (\mu_j - \mu) + \varepsilon_{ij}$$

$$= \mu + \eta_i + \alpha_j + \varepsilon_{ij} \tag{14.2}$$

The parameters of this structural equation are defined in the upper panel of Box 14.1, and related assumptions are in the lower panel. The model of the data represented by Equation 14.2 is referred to as additive because scores are viewed as reflecting the sum of subject (η_i, eta-sub-i) and treatment (α_j) effects; no interaction is assumed to contribute to the data.

Box 14.1 Definitions and Assumptions for Parameters of the Additive Model

Parameter	Definition
$\mu_{i.}$	$\Sigma_j \mu_{ij}/a$
$\mu_{.j}$	$E(\mu_{ij})$
μ	$\Sigma_j \mu_{.j}/a$
η_i	$\mu_{i.} - \mu$
α_j	$\mu_{.j} - \mu$

The following conditions hold for α_j, η_i, and ε_{ij}:

1. The α_j, η_i, and ε_{ij} are distributed independently of each other.
2. If A is a fixed-effect variable,

    2.1 $\Sigma_j \alpha_j = \Sigma_j (\mu_{\cdot j} - \mu) = 0$.

    2.2 The variance of the treatment effects is $\sigma_A^2 = \sum_j \alpha_j^2 / a$.

    2.3 The null hypothesis about the effects of treatments is H_0: $\alpha_1 = \alpha_2 = \ldots = \alpha_j = \ldots = \alpha_a = 0$ or, equivalently, $\sigma_A^2 = 0$.
3. We assume that the subjects in the experiment are a random sample from an infinite population. We further assume that the population of η_i values is distributed independently and normally with mean zero and variance $\sigma_S^2 = E(\eta_i^2)$. Because the n subjects are viewed as a random sample from an infinite population,

    3.1 The sum of the n values of η_i sampled in the experiment is unlikely to sum to zero; that is, $\Sigma_i \eta_i \neq 0$.

    3.2 However, the average value of all such effects for the population of subjects will be zero; that is, $E(\eta_i) = 0$.
4. The error component, ε_{ij}, is assumed to be distributed independently and normally with mean $E(\varepsilon_{ij}) = 0$ and variance $\sigma_e^2 = E(\varepsilon^2)$.

14.2.2 Advantages of Additivity

Although we will consider both additive and nonadditive models and the analyses related to them, analyses based on data consistent with the additive model have these advantages:

1. *Simplicity of interpretation.* The interpretation of treatment effects is simple under the additive model because such effects are the same for all subjects. When effects of treatments vary over subjects, interpretation of the effects of the independent variable is unclear. It may be necessary to distinguish among subpopulations that differ in the effect of treatments.
2. *Design efficiency.* The presence of interactions increases variability and therefore reduces the power of statistical tests and the precision of estimates.
3. *Estimation of population variances.* Some measures of the importance of independent variables require estimates of components of variance; for example, σ_s^2, the variance of the population of subject means. As will be seen when expected mean squares are considered, unbiased estimates are available, assuming the additive model, but not when a nonadditive model is assumed.
4. *F tests.* Under the nonadditive model, only approximate F tests of some effects are possible.

In summary, tests of the effects of the independent variable and estimates of several measures of importance rest on the underlying structural model. Understanding the relation between the model, expected mean squares, and various statistics requires that we understand the distinction between two types of variables, fixed effects and random effects. We consider this distinction next.

14.3 FIXED AND RANDOM EFFECTS

Generally, the treatment levels in a study are based on theoretical considerations and the researcher's understanding of the domain. For example, in a study of the effects of dosage levels on treatment efficacy, a researcher might select four equally spaced dosages ranging across levels thought likely to differ in their effects. In a study of memory, a researcher might compare three strategies that are based on different theoretical principles. When the levels of an independent variable have been systematically chosen, as in these examples, we view the population of treatment levels as consisting of only those levels included in the study; we say that the independent variable has *fixed effects*. In contrast, the subjects in a study are not systematically selected; rather, they are usually viewed as having been randomly sampled from a wider population of potential subjects. For this reason, the subject variable is said to have *random effects*. Items in a study, such as pictures that are rated for some characteristic, or words whose recognition times are recorded, also are usually viewed as having random effects.

The distinction between fixed- and random-effects variables has implications for how we define the population parameters estimated by our data, and for the generality of conclusions based on the data analysis. With respect to parameter definitions, we see in Box 14.1 that the variance of the population treatment means, σ_A^2, is a variance for only those treatment levels included in the study, whereas the subject variance, σ_S^2, is defined for the population of subjects. With respect to the generality of conclusions, although we are always free to draw conclusions about a drug dosage or a strategy that was not in the study, such conclusions are extra-statistical generalizations. These may be based on extrapolation from the function relating depression scores to drug dosage, or the similarity we perceive between some strategy not included in the study and those that were. Conclusions about treatments that were not included in the study are not necessarily less correct than those about the included treatments, but they are less firmly grounded in the data analysis than conclusions about the treatments included in the study. In contrast, the variance of the mean scores of subjects in the experiment estimates the variance of the sampled population, and permits generalizations beyond the immediate sample.

The distinction between fixed- and random-effects variables has implications not only for the generality of conclusions but also for the expected mean squares. In turn, this influences our estimates of population parameters and the calculation of the F tests in the more complex designs of Chapters 15 and 16.

14.4 THE ANOVA AND EXPECTED MEAN SQUARES FOR THE ADDITIVE MODEL

An example of the use of a repeated-measures design is the *Seasons* study carried out by researchers at the University of Massachusetts medical school. Table 14.1 presents Beck Depression scores for each season for each of 14 men under the age of 35 who served in the *Seasons* study, and for whom scores were available in all four seasons.[1] Each row of the data set represents a different subject and each column represents a season. Fig. 14.1 plots the means together with the 95% confidence interval (*CI*) bounds obtained as

---

[1] The complete data set is on the *Seasons* page on the book's website; go to *Data Files*, then *Seasons*. The data in Table 14.1 are also in the file *Male_D under 35*.

$$CI = \overline{Y}_j \pm SEM \times t_{.025,39} \tag{14.3}$$

where SEM is the standard error of the mean and equals $\sqrt{MS_{error}/n}$, where n is the number of observations on which each condition mean, $\overline{Y}_{.j}$, is based. The t is the two-tailed critical value for $p = .05$, where the df are those on which the ANOVA error term is based. From Table 14.2, $SEM = \sqrt{5.307/14} = .616$; $t_{.025,39} = 2.023$, and $SEM \times t_{.025,39} = 1.246$. It is apparent from Fig. 14.1 that the mean depression scores are quite similar except for the mean in the summer season, which is noticeably lower. However, as the confidence intervals indicate, there is considerable variability within each condition.

Before proceeding to the ANOVA of the data, we used SPSS's Explore option. We will not take the space to reproduce the results, but we note that plots revealed that the data were extremely

Table 14.1 Seasonal depression scores for males under 35 years of age

Subject	Winter	Spring	Summer	Fall	Mean
1	7.500	11.554	1.000	1.208	5.316
2	7.000	9.000	5.000	15.000	9.000
3	1.000	1.000	0.000	0.000	0.500
4	0.000	0.000	0.000	0.000	0.000
5	1.059	0.000	1.097	4.000	1.539
6	1.000	2.500	0.000	2.000	1.375
7	2.500	0.000	0.000	2.000	1.125
8	4.500	1.060	2.000	2.000	2.390
9	5.000	2.000	3.000	5.000	3.750
10	2.000	3.000	4.208	3.000	3.052
11	7.000	7.354	5.877	9.000	7.308
12	2.500	2.000	0.009	2.000	1.627
13	11.000	16.000	13.000	13.000	13.250
14	8.000	10.500	1.000	11.000	7.625
Mean	4.290	4.712	2.585	4.943	4.133

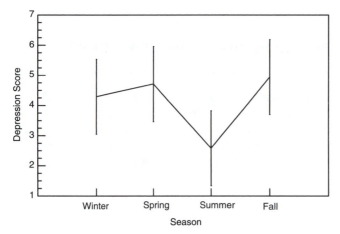

Fig. 14.1 Means of depression scores of Table 14.1 with confidence intervals.

skewed to the right, and statistical tests showed a very significant departure from normality. These results indicate that we may want to consider alternatives to the conventional ANOVA and we will do so later in the chapter. For now, we ignore this violation of assumptions and perform the tests of the *Seasons* effects.

Table 14.2 presents the results of an analysis of variance of the data, together with the expected mean squares (*EMS*). Equation 14.2 and the assumptions about its component parameters provide the basis for the *F* tests. Consistent with the three terms in the equation, we have three sources of variance representing subjects, treatment, and residual error variability. The mean squares for the subjects and treatment terms are calculated as in any two-factor design, and the residual sums of squares and *df* are obtained by subtraction from the totals. Assuming the additive model, the *F* tests are justified by the expected mean squares displayed in the table. The *EMS* indicate that, under the additive model, $MS_{residual}$ is the appropriate error term for testing null hypotheses about both S and A. In either test, if the null hypothesis is true, the numerator and denominator of the F ratio have the same expected value.

Table 14.2   ANOVA of the data in Table 14.1 and expected mean squares

SV	df	SS	MS	F	p	EMS
Subjects (S)	$n - 1 = 13$	$a\sum_i(\bar{Y}_{i.} - \bar{Y}_{..})^2$ $= 779.100$	SS_S/df_S $= 59.931$	MS_S/MS_{SA} $= 11.295$	0.000	$\sigma_e^2 + a\sigma_S^2$
Seasons (A)	$a - 1 = 3$	$n\sum_j(\bar{Y}_{.j} - \bar{Y}_{..})^2$ $= 47.778$	SS_A/df_A $= 15.926$	MS_A/MS_{SA} $= 3.001$	0.042	$\sigma_e^2 + n\theta_A^2$
Residual (SA)	$(n-1)(a-1)$ $= 39$	$SS_{total} - SS_S - SS_A$ $= 206.960$	SS_{SA}/df_{SA} $= 5.307$			σ_e^2
Total	$an - 1 = 55$	$\sum_i\sum_j(Y_{ij} - \bar{Y}_{..})^2$ $= 1033.838$				

Note: $\theta_A^2 = \sum_j(\mu_j - \mu)/(a-1)$.

14.5 THE NONADDITIVE MODEL FOR THE $S \times A$ DESIGN

In many studies, the effects of treatments may vary over subjects with the result that the additive model of Equation 14.2 fails to provide a valid description of the structure of the data. For example, the effects of rate of presentation of text material upon comprehension may depend upon such individual factors as reading ability, familiarity with the topic, current state of alertness, and motivation to perform well in the experiment. In such cases, although analyses can be carried out, F tests may be biased and estimates of population parameters may be lacking or imprecise. In what follows, we develop the nonadditive model and its consequences. Following that, we consider the possibility of transformations to a scale on which the effects of subjects and treatments are additive. Because that is often not possible, or not desirable, we then consider ways of correcting possible bias in the F tests of treatments.

14.5.1 The Structural Equation

For the nonadditive model, we add an interaction component to the additive model of Equation 14.2. Therefore, the equation for the nonadditive case is

$$Y_{ij} = \mu + \alpha_j + \eta_i + (\alpha\eta)_{ij} + \varepsilon_{ij} \tag{14.4}$$

Assumptions about the distribution of the terms that were in Equation 14.2 are unchanged. The interaction effect associated with the ij^{th} cell is defined as

$$(\eta\alpha)_{ij} = (\mu_{ij} - \mu) - \eta_i - \alpha_j$$

$$= (\mu_{ij} - \mu) - (\mu_{i.} - \mu) - (\mu_{.j} - \mu) \tag{14.5}$$

$$= \mu_{ij} - \mu_{i.} - \mu_{.j} + \mu$$

Because the independent variable, A, is a fixed-effect variable, the sum of the a interaction effects for any subject in an experiment equals 0; i.e. $\sum_{j=1}^{a}(\eta\alpha)_{ij} = 0$. However, because subjects are a random-effects variable, and therefore only n of the infinitely possible population effects at any level of A are sampled, $\sum_{i=1}^{n}(\eta\alpha)_{ij}$ rarely will equal zero, although the expectation of all population values is zero; i.e., $E(\eta\alpha)_{ij} = 0$. These properties of the $S \times A$ interaction effects have implications for the EMS, and therefore for the F tests. We consider this next.

14.5.2 Expected Mean Squares (EMS)

Table 14.3 presents the sources of variance (SV), degrees of freedom (df), and EMS under the additive and nonadditive models. The numerical values of the sums of squares and the mean squares are the same for the two models. Furthermore, in both cases, the A source of variance would be tested against MS_{SA}. However, there is a difference between the two cases: the interaction variance, σ_{SA}^2, contributes to the A and SA terms in the nonadditive case.

Why does the SA variance contribute to MS_A, the variance among the treatment means, but not to MS_S, the variance among the subject means? The answer lies in the distinction between fixed- and random-effects variables. Table 14.4 may help clarify this. The table presents the true scores and parameters for a population of four subjects with interaction effects calculated as in Equation 14.5. All ε_{ij} have been set equal to zero to simplify our discussion. Note that the treatment population (column) means are identical; therefore, the null hypothesis is true. Also note that the average interaction effect in each column and in each row is zero; this is an algebraic result of the definition of an interaction effect. Now assume an "experiment" in which S_1 and S_2 were selected by random sampling. Taking the "data" from the two subjects in the experiment, we find that the means at the

Table 14.3 Expected mean squares and F ratios for the $S \times A$ design

SV	df	Additive EMS	Additive F ratio	Nonadditive EMS	Nonadditive F ratio
S	$n-1$	$\sigma_e^2 + a\sigma_S^2$	MS_S/MS_{SA}	$\sigma_e^2 + a\sigma_S^2$	
A	$a-1$	$\sigma_e^2 + n\theta_A^2$	MS_A/MS_{SA}	$\sigma_e^2 + \sigma_{SA}^2 + n\theta_A^2$	MS_A/MS_{SA}
SA	$(n-1)(a-1)$	σ_e^2		$\sigma_e^2 + \sigma_{SA}^2$	

Table 14.4 Data for a population of four subjects with interaction effects present

	A_1		A_2		A_3			
	Y_{i1}	$(\eta\alpha)_{i1}$	Y_{i2}	$(\eta\alpha)_{i2}$	Y_{i3}	$(\eta\alpha)_{i3}$	μ_i	η_i
S_1	8	−1	10	1	9	0	9	−5
S_2	10	3	9	2	2	−5	7	2.5
S_3	11	−1	12	0	13	1	12	2.5
S_4	9	−1	7	−3	14	4	10	5
$\mu_j =$	9.5		9.5		9.5			

Note: S_1 and S_2 are samples from the population, and constitute the "experiment."

levels of A, the $\overline{Y}_j$, are 9, 9.5, and 5.5. Although the treatment population means, the $\mu_{.j}$, are identical, the sample means, the $\overline{Y}_j$, are not. This is not because of error of measurement because there is none in this artificial data set. It is entirely due to the fact that the *sampled* interaction effects are different at the three levels of A. This random sampling of only some of the population interaction effects at each treatment level is why σ_{SA}^2 contributes to the variability among the $\overline{Y}_j$, and therefore to MS_A. Which treatment means will be most raised or lowered relative to their population values will depend upon the pattern of interaction effects that have been sampled from each treatment population.

One other point follows from Table 14.4. Because A is a fixed-effects variable, each subject mean includes the average of all interaction components in the corresponding row. That average is zero and therefore the interaction variance does not contribute to differences among subject means and, accordingly, does not contribute to MS_S.

14.5.3 Consequences of Nonadditivity

To briefly summarize, there are several undesirable consequences of nonadditivity:

1. *No proper F test of subjects*. Given the *EMS* of Table 14.3, a test of the *Subjects* source of variance against the *SA* term would be negatively biased. However, subjects usually differ greatly in their average responses, and so this test is rarely performed.
2. *Unbiased estimates of some measures of effect size are not possible* under the nonadditive model. This is because it is not possible to obtain estimates of each of the variance components contributing to the effect size measures. Looking at the *EMS* in Table 14.2, it can be seen that it is not possible to algebraically isolate σ_e^2, σ_S^2, or σ_{SA}^2.
3. *The sphericity assumption may be violated*. This assumption, also called *circularity*, is an assumption about the variances and covariances of the data in the different conditions. We will define this and more fully discuss the consequences of violations in Section 14.6. For now, we merely note that biased *F* tests may result when variances differ among conditions, or when covariances differ among pairs of conditions.
4. *The efficiency of the design is reduced* because the interaction effects contribute added "noise" to the data set.

This last point can be seen by considering the ratio of *EMS* under the two models. If additivity holds, that ratio is

$$\frac{E(MS_A)}{E(MS_{SA})} = 1 + \frac{n\sum_j(\mu_j - \mu)^2/(a-1)}{\sigma_e^2} = 1 + \frac{n\theta_A^2}{\sigma_e^2}$$

However, if the nonadditive model is valid, the ratio is smaller:

$$\frac{E(MS_A)}{E(MS_{SA})} = 1 + \frac{n\sum_j(\mu_j - \mu)^2/(a-1)}{\sigma_e^2 + \sigma_{SA}^2} = 1 + \frac{n\theta_A^2}{\sigma_e^2 + \sigma_{SA}^2}$$

The SA interaction effects will reduce the precision of parameter estimates and the power of the significance test. However, such interaction variance will usually be less than the individual difference variance associated with completely randomized designs. Therefore, even when the data do not conform to the additive model, the repeated-measures design usually will yield more powerful tests of the null hypothesis than will the completely randomized design with the same number of observations.

As we discussed in Section 6.6.1, it is sometimes possible to find a transformation to a scale other than the original data scale, a scale on which the transformed data are additive. Even when this is possible, it may not be desirable. As we stated in Chapter 6, results on the new scale may not be as readily interpretable and the nature of relationships between the dependent and independent variables may be changed. Nevertheless, there are many cases in which the original scale was arbitrary and not intrinsically meaningful, or—as is often the case when response time is transformed to speed—the two scales provide equivalent information. In these cases, the transformation to additivity is desirable because, when the additivity assumption holds, it provides more precise estimates of population effects and a more powerful F test of those effects. With this in mind, we next consider how such transformations may be selected.

14.5.4 Tukey's Test of Nonadditivity and Transformations

Assuming that additivity of subject and treatment effects is desirable, we must decide whether the assumption is reasonable for a given data set and, if not, whether a transformation exists that will improve things. We might plot n curves, one for each subject, and attempt to decide whether they depart sufficiently from parallelism to justify concluding that subjects and treatments interact in the population. However, distinguishing between variability due to chance and variability due to inter-action effects is usually difficult, particularly if there are more than a very few subjects. Although it will not detect all forms of nonadditivity, Tukey's (1949) test is helpful, not just because it provides a significance test but also because a transformation to additivity can sometimes be found using some of the results of the calculations (Anscombe & Tukey, 1963). The test and related transform-ation are available in some statistical packages; for example, SPSS permits the calculation of Tukey's (1949) test of the null hypothesis of additivity, and includes with the test result the value of the exponent (the power to which each score should be raised) that best improves the fit of the transformed data to an additive model.[2]

Using SPSS, we applied the Tukey test to the *Seasons* data of Table 14.1. Although the F test of

---

[2] In SPSS, select the *Analyze* menu, then *Scale*, then *Reliability Analysis. Tukey's test of additivity* is then available from the *Statistics* option. Formulas and examples of the calculations also are available in Kirk (1995, pp. 412–413) and Myers (1979, p. 184).

nonadditivity was not significant at the .05 level, the p-value of .067 and the recommended transformation (i.e., that each score be raised to the power of .325) suggest that subjects and treatments may interact. After applying the recommended transformation to the scores, the F test of nonadditivity yields a p-value of .488, indicating that the transformation was successful in eliminating the subjects × treatments interaction. Furthermore, an ANOVA on the transformed data resulted in an F of 4.077, $p = .013$. That p-value is considerably smaller than the .042 on the original untransformed depression scores.

Because raising scores to a power of .325 seemed unnatural, we also tried a square root transformation of the scores in Table 14.1; that is, we raised each score to the .5 power, reasoning that this was not too far from the Anscombe–Tukey result. The outcome was similar to that obtained with the .325 transform. Now the test of nonadditivity resulted in a p-value of .891. The F test of the *Seasons* source of variance was again significant at the .013 level. The averages of the square roots of the scores in Table 13.1 were:

Winter	Spring	Summer	Fall
1.867	1.752	1.186	1.894

This pattern is similar to that for the original means; the mean depression score is different for summer than for the other three seasons. For these 14 men, both the original and the transformed data indicate that the men are more depressed in the summer than in the other seasons. However, the test on the square root scale provides stronger evidence of the effect of season on depression.

These results with a real data set show that data transformations may increase power and the precision of estimates of population parameters. However, it is important to realize that the tests of null hypotheses and parameter estimates are based on a different scale than the original. If the original scale is more meaningful, or the transformation badly distorts the pattern of means, the gain in efficiency may not be worthwhile. On the other hand, the original scale is often quite arbitrary; taking the square root, or log, or reciprocal of scores may be equally meaningful. Researchers may increase their comfort levels by transforming the means back to their original scale for purposes of presenting a summary of result (e.g., by squaring the means based on the transformed data).

14.6 THE SPHERICITY ASSUMPTION

In order for MS_A/MS_{SA} to have an F distribution, the data must meet an assumption that we did not encounter in the analysis of between-subjects designs. This is usually referred to as the *sphericity*, or *circularity*, assumption (Huynh & Feldt, 1976; Rouanet & Lepine, 1970). In the following pages, we define and provide examples of sphericity; in Section 14.10, we consider alternatives to the standard F test when the assumption is violated.

14.6.1 Sphericity Defined

Consider the typical subjects × treatments design with n subjects, each of whom is tested under a conditions. For each subject, we can calculate $(½)(a)(a - 1)$ differences, based on the number of pairs of treatments. For example, when there are three treatments, we can construct three pairings, and calculate the difference between the scores in each pair. We have done that in Table 14.5. The

Table 14.5 Data exhibiting sphericity

	A_1	A_2	A_3	$Y_{i3} - Y_{i2}$	$Y_{i2} - Y_{i1}$	$Y_{i3} - Y_{i1}$
S_1	21.050	7.214	26.812	19.598	−13.836	5.760
S_2	6.915	29.599	16.366	−13.233	22.684	9.451
S_3	3.890	21.000	41.053	20.053	17.110	37.163
S_4	11.975	12.401	18.896	6.495	.426	6.921
S_5	31.169	34.786	31.872	−2.914	3.617	.703
Mean	15.000	21.000	27.000	6.000	6.000	12.000
s^2	124.000	132.000	100.000	208.000	208.000	208.000

Note: In general, $MS_{SA} = (1/2)\Sigma s_d^2$.

left-most three columns of the table contain the scores for five subjects at three levels of A, and the right-most three columns contain all possible difference scores for each subject, with the value of the variances, s_d^2, at the bottom of the columns. These data fit the assumption of sphericity because the three values of the variance are the same; *sphericity exists when the population variances of all possible difference scores are equal.*[3] If this assumption is violated, Type 1 error rates will be higher than the nominal alpha level.

Nonsphericity, or heterogeneity of variance of difference scores, is similar in both form and consequences to heterogeneity of variance in the between-subjects designs of Chapters 8–12. In Chapter 8, the error term, $MS_{S/A}$, was the average of the group variances. If the null hypothesis is true and if there are n scores at each treatment level, then $E(MS_A) = E(MS_{S/A})$ even if the group variances are very different from each other. However, even though this heterogeneity of variance does not affect the ratio of expected mean squares, it does affect the sampling distribution of the ratio of mean squares. More precisely, when the null hypothesis is true and group sizes are equal, heterogeneity of variance inflates the probability of sampling large F values.

We have a similar situation in the repeated-measures design. The error term, MS_{SA}, is always one-half of the average of all values of s_d^2. This relation between the variances of the difference scores and MS_{SA} will hold for any number of levels of A, and will be true regardless of the values of the s_d^2. Therefore, MS_{SA}, and consequently the ratio of expected mean squares, will not be affected by differences among the variances of difference scores. However, the distribution of the F ratio will be affected and the Type 1 error rate will be inflated if the variances are very different, as is the case when group variances differ in the between-subjects design. A test of the sphericity assumption was derived by Mauchly (1940) and is available in some computer packages (for example, in SPSS's *GLM* module). However, if the population distributions are not normal, the Mauchly test tends to yield significant results even when the violation of the sphericity assumption is small (Keselman, Rogan, Mendoza, & Breen, 1980; Rogan, Keselman, & Mendoza, 1979). Therefore, care should be taken in interpreting the result of this test.

In Section 14.7, we will consider how to respond to violations of the sphericity assumption, but first we note a special case under which the sphericity assumption will hold.

---

[3] For the purposes of making the point clear, we have created data in which the sample variances of difference scores are identical. In a real data set, there would be some differences due to error variance; however, if the population variances were homogeneous, we would not expect marked differences among the sample variances.

14.6.2 Compound Symmetry

A stronger assumption than sphericity that is often discussed is *compound symmetry*. Compound symmetry exists if the population variances, σ_j^2, are the same for all treatments, and if the population covariances, $\rho_{jj'}\sigma_j\sigma_{j'}$, are the same for all pairs of treatments, where $\rho_{jj'}$ is the population correlation between the scores at A_j and $A_{j'}$, and $\rho_{jj'}\sigma_j\sigma_{j'}$ is the covariance. From developments in Appendix 5.1, the variance of the population of difference scores is

$$\sigma_d^2 = \sigma_j^2 + \sigma_{j'}^2 - 2\rho_{jj'}\sigma_j\sigma_{j'} \tag{14.6}$$

If compound symmetry holds in the population, all variances of difference scores will involve the same variances and covariances of scores and therefore they must be identical. However, although compound symmetry is sufficient, it is not necessary for sphericity. In Table 14.5, the variances of the individual scores are not the same; they are 124, 132, and 100. Nor are the covariances identical. They are 24 for conditions 1 and 2, 8 for conditions 1 and 3, and 12 for conditions 2 and 3. Nevertheless, the variances of the difference scores all equal 208.

14.7 DEALING WITH NONSPHERICITY

There are two data-analysis strategies that protect the researcher against inflation of Type 1 error rates due to nonsphericity. These are the *univariate F test with epsilon-adjusted degrees of freedom*, and the *multivariate analysis of variance*, or *MANOVA*. These methods involve calculating the covariances of scores. The reason for this lies in the relation, expressed in Equation 14.6, between the variances and covariances of scores and the variance of the difference scores.

14.7.1 The Epsilon-Adjusted F Test

When the assumption of sphericity is violated, the Type 1 error rate is inflated if the conventional F test is evaluated on the usual degrees of freedom. One approach to controlling the Type 1 error rate in this situation involves conducting an F test, but adjusting the degrees of freedom downward. When the sphericity assumption is violated, the ratio of mean squares is still distributed approximately as F, provided that the numerator and denominator degrees of freedom are multiplied by a factor, ε (epsilon); that is, $df_A = (a - 1)\varepsilon$ and $df_{SA} = (a - 1)(n - 1)\varepsilon$. The value of epsilon ranges between 1 when the sphericity assumption is met, and $1/(a - 1)$ when the assumption is severely violated. In general, as nonsphericity increases, the degrees of freedom decrease, with the result that a larger value of F is required for significance. In this way, the epsilon adjustment compensates for the inflation of Type 1 error rate caused by the failure of the sphericity assumption.

One estimator of ε, $\hat{\varepsilon}$ ("epsilon-hat"), was derived by Box (1954), and later extended to the mixed designs of Chapter 15 by Greenhouse and Geisser (1959). Subsequently, Huynh and Feldt (1976) developed a more liberal estimator, $\tilde{\varepsilon}$. Both estimators require calculations involving the elements of the variance–covariance matrix. Fortunately, common statistical programs do these calculations.

Panel *a* of Table 14.6 presents SPSS output for Mauchly's test of sphericity. The output includes not only the test results (W, chi-square, df, and the p-value), but also the two estimates of epsilon and the lower bound $[1/(a - 1)]$. Mauchly's test does not reject the null hypothesis of sphericity; $p = .408$. Turning next to the estimates of ε, the Greenhouse–Geisser (G–G, $\hat{\varepsilon}$) estimate of ε is less than 1. Contrary to results of the Mauchly test, $\hat{\varepsilon}$ indicates that the sphericity

Table 14.6   SPSS output for the data of Table 14.1: Mauchly's test of sphericity (*a*), ANOVA (*b*), and MANOVA (*c*)

(*a*) Mauchly's test of sphericity

Within-subjects effect	Mauchly's W	Approx. chi-square	df	Sig.	Epsilon[a]		
					Greenhouse–Geisser	Huynh–Feldt	Lower bound
Season	.648	15.078	5	.408	.832	1.000	.333

[a] May be used to adjust the degrees of freedom for the averaged tests of significance. Corrected tests are displayed in the tests of within-subjects effects table.

(*b*) Tests of within-subjects effects

Source		Type III sum of squares	df	Mean square	F	Sig.
Seasons	Sphericity assumed	47.778	3	15.926	3.001	.042
	Greenhouse–Geisser	47.778	2.495	19.151	3.001	.053
	Huynh–Feldt	47.778	3.000	15.926	3.001	.042
	Lower bound	47.778	1.000	47.778	3.001	.107
Error (seasons)	Sphericity assumed	206.960	39	5.307		
	Greenhouse–Geisser	206.960	32.433	6.381		
	Huynh–Feldt	206.960	39.000	5.307		
	Lower bound	206.960	13.000	15.920		

(*c*) Multivariate tests

Effect		Value	F	Hypothesis df	Error df	Sig.
Seasons	Pillai's trace	.392	2.365[a]	3.000	11.000	.127
	Wilks' lambda	.608	2.365[a]	3.000	11.000	.127
	Hotelling's trace	.645	2.365[a]	3.000	11.000	.127
	Roy's largest root	.645	2.365[a]	3.000	11.000	.127

[a] Exact statistic.

assumption is violated, and this causes a reduction in the degrees of freedom required to evaluate the *F* statistic in panel *b*. However, consistent with the results of the Mauchly test, the Huynh–Feldt (*H–F*, $\tilde{\varepsilon}$) estimate equals 1. These differences in the estimates lead to slightly different conclusions about the effects of seasons, as can be seen in panel *b* of Table 14.6. Using the *H–F* estimate of ε, the variation among the mean depression scores for the four seasons is significant at the .05 level; however, using the *G–G* estimate results in a failure to reject the null hypothesis.[4]

---

[4] Note that the *F* ratio is the same in all rows but the *p*-value ("Sig.") varies with variation in the *df*. The tabled mean squares in panel *b* are ratios of sums of squares to the degrees of freedom based on the corresponding degrees of freedom.

Both $\hat{\varepsilon}$ and $\tilde{\varepsilon}$ are biased estimates of ε, and there is debate as to which should be used. The H–F estimate, $\tilde{\varepsilon}$, is always at least as large as that of $\hat{\varepsilon}$ and therefore provides greater power. However, it also appears that $\tilde{\varepsilon}$ has a higher Type 1 error rate under many conditions (Gary, 1981). Thus, the conservative course is to rely on the G–G adjustment, $\hat{\varepsilon}$. In our example in Table 14.6, we fail to reject the null hypothesis of no effect of seasons upon Beck Depression scores.

The epsilon adjustment does not apply if A only has two levels. In that case, there is only one set of n difference scores and, therefore, only one variance of difference scores. Homogeneity of variance of difference scores becomes an issue only when A has more than two levels. In that case, the inflation in Type 1 error rate can be large if the df are not adjusted. Therefore, the univariate F should not be evaluated without an adjustment.

14.7.2 Multivariate Analysis of Variance (MANOVA)

If the data have a multivariate-normal distribution, the multivariate analysis of variance, or MANOVA, provides an alternative to the univariate test that does not require the assumption of sphericity. Although a detailed discussion of MANOVA is beyond the scope of this book, we will provide a brief introduction to the topic.

If there are a within-subject conditions, the null hypothesis of equality of population means is equivalent to assuming that a series of $a - 1$ pairwise differences are all equal to 0. One such null hypothesis would be

$$H_0: \mu_1 - \mu_2 = 0, \mu_2 - \mu_3 = 0, \ldots, \text{and } \mu_{a-1} - \mu_a = 0$$

This suggests transforming the a scores for each subject into a set of $a - 1$ difference scores. For example, the successive differences for the response times of subject 1 in Table 14.1 are $d_{12} = 7.5 - 11.554 = -4.054$, $d_{23} = 11.554 - 1 = 10.554$, and $d_{34} = 1 - 1.208 = -.208$. Similarly, difference scores can be obtained for all 14 subjects. The difference scores for each subject are then weighted and summed to create a single score; call this score U. For example, the U-score for subject 1 based on the successive differences is

$$U_1 = (w_1)(-4.054) + (w_2)(10.554) + (w_3)(-.208)$$

The derivation of the weights, the w_j, requires some knowledge of matrix algebra but the important point is that they have the property of maximizing a t ratio. That t looks very much like the standard one-sample t. It is the mean of the n values of U_i divided by the standard error of the mean:

$$t = \overline{U}/s_{\overline{U}} \tag{14.7}$$

The squared value of this t is ordinarily calculated with matrix algebra and is usually referred to as Hotelling's T^2 (Hotelling, 1931). The F ratio reported in panel c of Table 14.6 is T^2 multiplied by $(n - a + 1)/[(n - 1)(a - 1)]$. This statistic has the F distribution on $a - 1$ and $n - a + 1$ df. Because $n - a + 1$ must be greater than zero, the multivariate test, unlike the univariate, requires that n be greater than $a - 1$. Also, if $a = 2$, $(n - a + 1)/[(n - 1)(a - 1)] = 1$, and $F = t^2$. Stated differently, when there are only two conditions, the multivariate F reduces to the univariate because both are equivalent to calculating a squared t statistic for matched pairs.

In panel c of Table 14.6, we see four different multivariate statistics listed, all of which have the same value of F. When there is no between-subjects variable, these statistics will always result in the same F. In other instances, they will usually yield similar results. Several books discuss the various statistics and provide a far more detailed discussion of MANOVA as it applies to the designs of this and the next chapter. Harris (2001) and Morrison (2004) are two excellent sources.

The results of the univariate and multivariate F tests do not always agree. In the present example, the multivariate statistics have a p-value of .127, higher than any of the three ε-adjusted p-values. Other data sets will often yield the opposite result: significant multivariate results paired with nonsignificant univariate results. There is no simple answer to the question of which procedure to use, but there are some general principles that we next consider.

14.7.3 ANOVA or MANOVA?

One attraction of MANOVA is that it does not require the assumption of sphericity. For this reason, if other assumptions such as normality and independence of subjects are met, we can be sure of an honest Type 1 error. However, computer-sampling studies have shown that the Type 1 error rate for the epsilon-adjusted F test is quite close to the nominal alpha level. Therefore, the critical issue in deciding between procedures is their relative power. Unfortunately, the situation is complicated in this respect.

The relative powers of the two procedures depend on the value of ε, and on a and n, as well as on the pattern of correlations and means (Algina & Keselman, 1997; Davidson, 1972). When the population value of ε is 1, the univariate test will be more powerful because its denominator df, $(a-1)(n-1)$, will be greater than the multivariate df, $n-a+1$. As n increases, the error df will increase for both tests and the power advantage of the univariate test will decrease.

When sphericity does not hold, either approach may prove more powerful, depending upon a number of factors. Based on simulations, Algina and Keselman recommended the multivariate test if (1) $a \le 4$, $n \ge a + 15$, and $\tilde{\varepsilon} \le .90$, or (2) $5 \le a \le 8$, $n \ge a + 30$, and $\tilde{\varepsilon} \le .85$. These conditions are not met in the current example because the n is not large enough. This suggests basing conclusions on the univariate test of panel b. However, these rules will not apply in all situations. The simulations are not exhaustive; different results might be obtained with combinations of n, a, and ε other than those investigated. Furthermore, as Algina and Keselman state, even in their simulations "selection of the multivariate test according to these rules is not a guarantee of increased power; our results indicate that some percentage of the time this rule will result in choosing the wrong test" (1997, p. 215). Despite this caveat, it is apparent that MANOVA is more likely to have a power advantage as n increases relative to a, and as ε decreases. However, it helps to keep in mind that even if we choose the less powerful procedure, the consequences will not be severe provided the sample size is large enough to ensure high power against the effect size of interest, regardless of the test.

14.8 MEASURES OF EFFECT SIZE

Our analysis of the *Seasons* data in Table 14.2 informed us that differences among the seasonal depression means are statistically significant. However, there are additional questions to be asked of the data. For one, we would like some indication of the practical or theoretical importance of our result. There are several statistics that might be computed to answer this question. In this section, we will consider two measures of effect size based on the proportion of variability accounted for by our treatment, A. The measures, η^2 and ω^2, also were discussed in the context of between-subjects designs in Chapters 8 and 9, and developments here will be similar. We will also consider Cohen's f because of its relevance to power calculations.

14.8.1 η^2 (Eta-Squared), the Proportion of Sample Variability

In a one-factor between-subjects design, η^2 is calculated as

$$\eta^2(A) = \frac{SS_A}{SS_A + SS_{S/cells}} \tag{14.8}$$

In the one-factor, repeated-measures design, investigators often calculate *partial* η^2:

$$\eta_p^2(A) = \frac{SS_A}{SS_A + SS_{SA}} \tag{14.9}$$

From the sums of squares column of Table 14.2, $\eta_p^2(A) = 47.778/(47.778 + 206.96) = .188$. This is the computation performed in SPSS if an effect size measure is requested in the *General Linear Model/Repeated-Measures* module. However, a limitation of Equation 14.9 is that it is not comparable to Equation 14.8 because Equation 14.8 includes variability due to individual differences, whereas Equation 14.9 omits such variability. Therefore, following the recommendation of Olejnik and Algina (2003), we recommend calculating *general* η^2:

$$\eta_g^2(A) = \frac{SS_A}{SS_A + SS_{SA} + SS_S} \tag{14.10}$$

Again turning to the SS column in Table 14.2, $\eta_g^2(A) = 47.778/(47.778 + 779.1 + 206.96) = .046$. In the one-factor, repeated-measures design, the denominator of the general statistic is the total sum of squares, provided that the numerator represents a factor with fixed effects. Note that η^2 and *general* η^2 are identical in the one-factor, repeated-measures design; however, the denominator of the general statistic usually is not the total sum of squares for designs with multiple factors, so the two statistics are different in multi-factor designs. We will consider such designs in the next chapter.

As we stated in Chapter 8, η^2 has the advantage of being easily calculated and easily understood as a proportion of *sample* variance, but it tends to overestimate the proportion of *population* variance due to the independent variable. The next statistic to be considered provides a somewhat better estimate of the effect of the independent variable in the population.

14.8.2 ω_A^2 (Omega-Squared), the Proportion of Population Variance

Typically, researchers have reported estimates of *partial* ω_A^2, which is the variance among the population treatment means divided by the sum of that variance and the population error variance:

$$\omega_p^2(A) = \frac{\sigma_A^2}{\sigma_A^2 + \sigma_e^2} \tag{14.11}$$

As with η^2, we recommend calculating a statistic that takes individual differences into account so that values of ω^2 may be compared across designs. *General* ω^2 is defined as

$$\omega_g^2(A) = \frac{\sigma_A^2}{\sigma_A^2 + \sigma_e^2 + \sigma_S^2} \tag{14.12}$$

Assuming that the additive model applies to a data set, the expected mean squares in Table 14.2 suggest the following estimates of the variances:

$$\hat{\sigma}_A^2 = \left(\frac{MS_A - MS_{SA}}{n}\right)\left(\frac{a-1}{a}\right)$$

$$\hat{\sigma}_S^2 = \left(\frac{MS_S - MS_{SA}}{a}\right) \tag{14.13}$$

and

$$\hat{\sigma}_e^2 = MS_{SA}$$

Substituting these estimates into Equation 14.12 and multiplying the numerator and denominator by an, we have

$$\hat{\omega}_g^2(A) = \frac{(MS_A - MS_{SA})(a-1)}{(MS_A - MS_{SA})(a-1) + n(MS_S - MS_{SA}) + anMS_{SA}} \tag{14.14}$$

We can obtain this estimate from published research reports even when mean squares are not reported if we are provided the F ratios and degrees of freedom. Dividing the numerator and denominator of Equation 14.14 by MS_{SA}, and noting that $F_A = MS_A/MS_{SA}$ and $F_S = MS_S/MS_{SA}$, we have

$$\hat{\omega}_g^2(A) = \frac{(a-1)(F_A - 1)}{(a-1)F_A + nF_S + (a-1)(n-1)} \tag{14.15}$$

If F_A is less than 1, the estimate is assumed to be zero.

For the data set of Table 14.1, we substitute the F ratios and values of a and n into Equation 14.15, and find that

$$\hat{\omega}_g^2(A) = \frac{(4-1)(3.001-1)}{(4-1)(3.001) + (14)(11.295) + 39} = .030$$

We estimate that the variation in seasons accounts for about 3% of the total population variance.

In many circumstances, the nonadditive model will be a more accurate description of the data. In that case, the formula for general ω^2 must include σ_{SA}^2:

$$\omega_g^2(A) = \frac{\sigma_A^2}{\sigma_A^2 + \sigma_e^2 + \sigma_S^2 + \sigma_{SA}^2} \tag{14.16}$$

We still use Equation 14.14 or 14.15 to estimate the variance components, but the estimate is biased because it is not possible to obtain estimates of all four variance terms. Under the nonadditive model, Equation 14.14 estimates:

$$\omega_g^2(A) = \frac{\sigma_A^2}{\sigma_A^2 + \sigma_e^2 + \sigma_S^2 + [(a-1)/a]\sigma_{SA}^2} \tag{14.17}$$

Equation 14.14 underestimates the denominator of general ω^2 and consequently overestimates the proportion of variance due to A. However, the overestimate will be small except when the interaction variance is large and a is small.

In addition to the problem of obtaining an unbiased estimate, a possible criticism of general ω^2 is that the estimates are usually small, leading researchers to disregard effects that may in fact be of practical or theoretical import. However, values of any index of effect size should be judged within the context of the researcher's experience. Furthermore, although the same data set will provide larger values of η^2, that statistic is inflated by the presence of error variance. Even if the population treatment means are identical, the sample means almost surely will differ, yielding a value of the partial η^2 greater than zero.

14.8.3 Cohen's *f*

Cohen's f is defined as the ratio of the standard deviation of effects to the standard deviation of the populations of scores within each level of A:

$$f = \sigma_A/\sigma_W \tag{14.18}$$
$$= \sigma_A/\sqrt{\sigma_e^2 + \sigma_S^2 + \sigma_{SA}^2}$$

where σ_W is the standard deviation of the scores within any treatment population. Its square, the within-treatment variance, combines subject and error variance, making it comparable to the Cohen's f that we first introduced in Chapter 8 as a measure of effect size in a between-subjects design. For additive data (i.e., when $\sigma_{SA}^2 = 0$), an estimate of Cohen's f is

$$\hat{f}(A) = \sqrt{\frac{(MS_A - MS_{SA})(a-1)}{n(MS_S - MS_{SA}) + anMS_{SA}}} \tag{14.19}$$

Equation 14.19 may also be used when the data are nonadditive, but it will overestimate Cohen's f for the same reason that general ω^2 is overestimated by Equation 14.14 for nonadditive data.

Our interest in Cohen's f is that it has become a common measure of effect size. Also, it is the preferred measure of effect size in many programs for computing power, including G*Power 3.

14.9 DECIDING ON SAMPLE SIZE: POWER ANALYSIS IN THE REPEATED-MEASURES DESIGN

As with other designs, considerations of statistical power should be a major factor in deciding on sample size. We need several pieces of information to compute *a priori* power for the repeated-measures design. The steps for using G*Power 3 are presented in Box 14.2 and an output from the program is displayed in Fig. 14.2.

Box 14.2 Using G*Power 3 to Determine Sample Size in the Repeated-Measures Design

Fig. 14.2 contains the screen illustrating these selections and entries.

1. Select the *F* test family; the test option *ANOVA: Repeated-measures, Within subjects*; and the *a priori* option for the type of test.
2. Enter the Type 1 error rate (α) and the desired power. We will set these to .05 and .9, respectively.
3. Enter an epsilon value. We will assume sphericity; that is, we set $\varepsilon = 1.0$. A conservative approach would be to use the minimum value of $1/(a-1)$.
4. Enter the number of levels of the independent variable for *Repetitions*; there are four in the example of the *Seasons* study. *Number of groups* is the number of levels of between-subjects factors, and it is one in this case.
5. Enter an estimate of the correlation between conditions.
6. Select the *calculate* button.

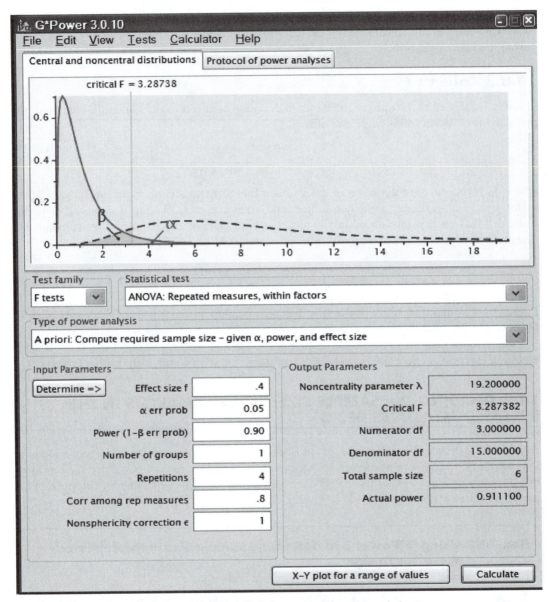

Fig. 14.2 G*Power's screen for *a priori* power analysis for a repeated-measures design.

To begin, we identify the test option as *ANOVA: Repeated-measures, within factors* and indicate that we want to do an *a priori* power calculation. We must decide what value of power we seek, the alpha-level we will use, and the design of the experiment we are planning. The power level and alpha-level are entered directly into the program; the design information requested is the number of between-subjects conditions (i.e., "number of groups") and the number of observations per subject (i.e., "repetitions"). For our example, assume that we have a single-factor, repeated-measures design with four levels of factor *A*. A repeated-measures design without any between-subjects factors has one group of subjects; thus, "1" is entered for the number of groups in our example, and "4" is entered for the number of repetitions.

Recall from our discussion in Chapter 8 that the power of the F test is determined, in part, by the magnitude of the effect of A, as well as the error variance associated with the test of A. Cohen's f is the input requested by G*Power 3 that provides information about the magnitude of the effect of A. With respect to error variance, Cohen's f also includes some information about the error variance; recall that the denominator of f is the within-condition variance. However, the error variance in a repeated-measures design is a function of both the variance within conditions and the correlation of scores between conditions. Thus, G*Power 3 requests a value for the correlation between the repeated-measures, ρ.

Finally, we also must provide enough information to calculate the degrees of freedom associated with the test of A. This information is needed because it establishes the critical value of F for our test of A. The values of the degrees of freedom are determined, in part, by the number of groups and the number of repetitions (scores per subject) in the design. Also, if the sphericity assumption is violated, the degrees of freedom must be adjusted downward by the correction factor, ε. Thus, G*Power 3 requests an input for ε. If it is assumed that the sphericity assumption will be met, the input should be 1; if the worst case violation of sphericity is assumed, the input should be $[1/(a-1)]$; an intermediate choice might be the average of these best- and worst-case scenarios. In the event that pilot data are available, the value of the Greenhouse–Geisser correction from an analysis of the data may be used.

How is a researcher to select values of Cohen's f and of ρ? One approach to providing values of f is to follow Cohen's guidelines and use .1, .25, and .4 for small, medium, and large effects, respectively. For repeated-measures designs, we suggest that a reasonable range of values of ρ is .2, .5, and .8 for small, medium, and large values, respectively. If a researcher wants .90 power to detect a large effect of A and assumes a strong correlation between conditions, the inputs to G*Power 3 will be $f = .4$ and $\rho = .8$. For the example we have been using, the total sample size required is only 6. The required sample size will be larger if we assume a smaller effect of A, or a weaker correlation among conditions, or that the sphericity assumption is not met. For example, if we assume $f = .1$, $\rho = .2$, and $\varepsilon = .33$ (worst case for a design with four levels of A), the required sample size is 633! As these examples make clear, researchers should do their best to make reasonable assumptions and, when in doubt, be conservative in their assumptions.

When a researcher has pilot data available, those data can be used to select values of f, ρ, and ε. Alternatively, a knowledge of the relevant literature and/or theoretical considerations may provide estimates of these parameters. G*Power 3 provides help with calculating f. Select the *determine* button (see Fig. 14.2) and, in the window that pops up, enter the estimates of the variance among the population means as the *Variance explained by special effect* and the within-population variance as *Variance within groups*. Then select the button labeled *Calculate and transfer to main window*. If the two variances were 4 and 25, a value of $f = .4$ (i.e., $\sqrt{4/25}$) would appear in the main window. Assuming that the other values—e.g., alpha, power, the correlation—have been inserted, selecting the *Calculate* button will yield the required sample size.

The output of G*Power 3 should be self-explanatory, with the possible exception of the noncentrality parameter, λ. Lambda characterizes the noncentral F distribution and is defined as

$$\lambda = \varepsilon naf^2 / (1 - \rho) \tag{14.20}$$

Inserting the output value of n, and the input values of ε, a, f, and the correlation (from the left column of Fig. 14.2), we have $(1)(6)(4)(.16)/.2 = 19.2$, the value of λ in Fig. 14.2. This value can be used in some programs (e.g., SPSS's *NCDF.F*) to calculate power.

14.10 TESTING SINGLE *df* CONTRASTS

14.10.1 Pairwise Comparisons

In many, perhaps most, studies, pairwise comparisons or more complex contrasts are of more interest than the omnibus *F* test. Contrasts are distributed on one degree of freedom, so sphericity is not an issue because there is only a single contrast score for each subject. In the example of seasonal effects upon depression, we might wish to test all pairwise comparisons. The calculations are straightforward and, in any event, paired *F* or *t* tests can be carried out by most statistical software. There are two issues, however:

1. *The error terms for the six possible pairwise comparisons.* Should each of the six comparisons in our example be tested against MS_{SA} or against the variance of the comparison under consideration?

2. *The control of familywise error (FWE) rate.* Should Tukey's *HSD* procedure, described in Chapter 9, be used or is an alternative to be preferred?

With respect to the error term issue, MS_{SA} is distributed on more error degrees of freedom, $(a-1)(n-1)$, and therefore the *F* test with this denominator is potentially more powerful. Nevertheless, the default error term in most statistical packages is the variance of the contrast being tested. For example, to test the difference between winter and summer mean depression scores, the mean ($\bar{d}$) and standard deviation (s_d) of the 14 differences are calculated. Then

$$t = \bar{d} / (s_d / \sqrt{n})$$

$$= 1.705 / (2.622 / \sqrt{14}) = 2.433$$

(Some software packages report the *F* statistic, which is just the square of the above *t*.) The reason for dividing by the standard error of the contrast instead of a denominator based on MS_{SA} is that if there is nonsphericity in the data set, the variances of difference scores may vary greatly across comparisons. Because MS_{SA} is a function of the average of these variances, it will be too small when testing some of the comparisons and too large when testing others. Boik (1981) showed that when the denominator of the *t* (or *F*) is based on MS_{SA} even small departures from sphericity can create serious distortions in Type 1 and 2 error rates and in the widths of confidence intervals.

With respect to the question of the method for controlling *FWE*, Tukey's *HSD* procedure would seem to be the natural approach. However, the test performs badly if there is nonsphericity. Maxwell (1980) compared the Type 1 error rates and powers of various methods of controlling the *FWE* and concluded that the Bonferroni approach, with the error term based on the contrast being tested, provided the best solution. In the *Seasons* example, we would calculate a different standard error of the mean difference for each of the six comparisons, compute the six *t* tests, and compare each *t* value against the critical value for *FWE* = .05, *df* = 13, and *K* = 6, which is 3.107. Alternatively, if computer software is used to compute each *t* test, the *p*-value in the output may be compared against .06/6, or .008.

14.10.2 A Contrast Involving More Than Two Means

More complex contrasts are sometimes of interest. For example, we might have hypothesized prior to data collection that summer depression scores would be lower than the average of the other three seasons because summer provides sunshine and vacations, both possibly enhancing moods. Then from Table 14.1,

$$\hat{\psi} = (1/3)(\bar{Y}_{winter} + \bar{Y}_{spring} + \bar{Y}_{fall}) - \bar{Y}_{summer}$$

$$= (1/3)(4.290 + 4.712 + 4.943) - 2.585 = 2.063$$

The test statistic is

$$t = \hat{\psi} / (s_{\hat{\psi}} / \sqrt{n}) \tag{14.21}$$

where $s_{\hat{\psi}}$ is calculated by first obtaining for each subject

$$\hat{\psi}_1 = (1/3)(Y_{i(winter)} + Y_{i(spring)} + Y_{i(fall)}) - Y_{i(summer)}$$

and $s_{\hat{\psi}}$ is the standard deviation of the contrast scores (the $\hat{\psi}_1$) of the n subjects. For example, the contrast score for the first subject is $\hat{\psi}_1 = (1/3)(7.5 + 11.554 + 10208) - 1 = 5.754$.

Given the individual contrast scores, a one-sample t test can be performed. The same result can also be obtained without first obtaining the contrast scores by using the contrast option available in many statistical packages. The result frequently will be a value of F, the square of the t, or 7.872 in our example. Whether t or F is reported, the p-value for our example will be .015, indicating that the average of summer depression scores is significantly lower than the average for the other three seasons. Note that because the test involves a single group of difference scores, sphericity is not an issue here.

There is the question of the control of FWE in this situation. Typically, multiple contrasts will be performed to understand the pattern of means associated with the effect of a source of variance. Again, the Bonferroni procedure should be used to control the FWE. This requires that the researcher plan the set of contrasts that will be conducted to analyze the effect of A. In the absence of such planning, the appropriate procedure for controlling FWE is the Roy–Bose method (1953), a multivariate extension of the Scheffé method.[5] Because use of this procedure will result in a substantial loss of power compared to the Bonferroni procedure, we strongly recommend that researchers make every effort to plan their comparisons.

14.10.3 Trend Analysis

In situations in which the independent variable is a set of points in time—e.g., trials, days, or even seasons—we may be interested in describing the trend, the slope, and shape of the function relating the means to the points in time. In the example of seasonal effects on depression scores, we might be interested in the function relating the Beck Depression scores to the four seasons, starting with winter. Most software packages provide the orthogonal polynomial analysis. For example, SPSS does so as part of its repeated-measures output (in the GLM module). In the absence of software, we can calculate contrast scores for each subject as described in the preceding section, and perform t tests. Again, we emphasize that unless there is clear evidence of sphericity, each polynomial component should be tested against its own standard error and the Bonferroni procedure should be used to control FWE.

14.11 THE PROBLEM OF MISSING DATA IN REPEATED-MEASURES DESIGNS

Missing data can be a problem in any kind of research. They are particularly troublesome in repeated-measures designs because when the general linear model (GLM) modules of the standard

---

[5] The Roy–Bose method is as follows. Assume a contrast—e.g., $C = \bar{Y}_1 - (1/2)(\bar{Y}_2 + \bar{Y}_3)$. C is considered to be significantly different from zero if $C > (n-1)(a-1)F_{FWE,(a-1),(n+a-1)}/(n+a-1)$.

statistical packages are used to conduct ANOVAs, all cases that have missing scores in any condition are completely dropped from the analysis.

There are many possible causes of missing data. There may be some equipment failure, or a subject may not show up for a session or may fail to respond to a questionnaire item or stimulus presentation. What are we to do? If we drop subjects who have scores in most but not in all conditions, or drop a condition because it contains too many missing data, a good deal of effort and a lot of information may be lost. More importantly, cases with complete data may differ systematically from those with missing data. If missing data occur nonrandomly, conducting analyses with only complete cases will provide biased estimates of population parameters and standard errors and thereby invalidate our inferences.

We can distinguish among three general types of missing data: data *missing not at random* (*MNAR*, or nonignorable missing data), data *missing at random* (*MAR*), and data *missing completely at random* (*MCAR*). To illustrate the distinction, consider a data set like the one presented in Table 14.1 in which depression scores are collected at different seasons of the year, except assume there are 28 subjects, 14 men and 14 women.

1. Missing data on Y are $MNAR$ if the probability of missing scores on Y is related to the value of Y. As examples, some subjects may have missing depression scores because they are too depressed to provide answers to some of the items on the depression questionnaire, or heavier subjects may be less willing to report their weight. In this sense, we can think of missing data as an extreme form of biased measurement error. In such situations, if we only use data from subjects without any missing scores, we are likely to underestimate depression and weight in the population. In general, if data are MNAR, complete case analysis will result in biased parameter estimates and invalid inferences.

2. Missing data on a variable Y are MAR if the probability of missing data is not associated with the value on Y *after controlling for the other variables in the data set*. For example, missing depression scores would be MAR if men are less likely to respond to items on the depression scale than women, but the tendency to have missing depression data is not associated with level of depression either for men or for women. If we use only complete cases in our analyses, MAR missing data can also result in biased results, though the problem is not as severe as for MNAR data. Here, for example, if men tend to have lower depression scores than women and more men are dropped from analyses because of missing data, their overall mean depression score will be higher because of the missing data.

3. Missing data on a variable Y are said to be $MCAR$ if the probability of missing data on Y is unrelated to the value of Y or to the values of any other variables in the data set. Perhaps data were not collected on a few trials because of an electrical power surge. Or a subject did not show up for a session because of bad weather. In our illustration, missing depression scores would not be more likely to occur for more depressed or less depressed individuals, nor for men or women. Subjects with complete data can be thought of as randomly selected from the original sample. If we analyze only complete cases, the presence of MCAR missing data results in less power, but no bias.

If the missing data are MAR or MNAR, the pattern of missing observations may provide useful information about our research question. We can code the missing data by 1s and the nonmissing data by 0s, and then look to see whether there are systematic tendencies for the missing data to be associated with particular values on the other variables. Better yet, we can use the built-in capabilities of our statistical packages to look for patterns of missing data. For example, SYSTAT contains a missing values analysis module that can be used to display patterns of missing data and to impute (i.e., provide estimates for) missing data in several different ways, using a variety of possible assumptions about the underlying model. It also offers Little's (1988) *MCAR* test. SPSS has a missing values analysis module (*MVA*—renamed *MV* starting with Version 17) with similar capabilities. It also is offered as an optional add-on in SPSS. These programs use sophisticated procedures that, in addition to displaying patterns of missing scores, are able to impute missing scores under a variety of assumptions. In addition, stand-alone, free software is also available for imputing missing data; for example, *NORM* (Schafer, 1999), which can be downloaded, along with some documentation, from http://www.stat.psu.edu/~jls/misoftwa.htlm. Of course, the best solution to the problem of missing data is to design the test materials and data collection procedures in ways that produce as few nonresponses as possible.

In addition to the availability of procedures to estimate missing scores, a set of statistical procedures have been developed during the last two decades to deal with designs that produce correlated scores. These procedures are called, depending on the context, mixed-effects, random coefficient, multilevel, or hierarchical linear models. Mixed models provide an approach to missing data, in addition to many other benefits. Good discussions may be found in several books and articles (e.g., Baayen et al., 2008; Brysbaert, 2007; Luke, 2004; Quené & van den Bergh, 2004; Raudenbush & Bryk, 2002).

Readers interested in pursuing the topic of missing scores can find several excellent references. Cohen et al. (2003) and the SYSTAT manual have readable chapters on the topic, and Allison (2002) offers an excellent, more comprehensive introduction. Two standard, more advanced texts on the problem of missing data are Little and Rubin (1987) and Schafer (1997). Also, a special section of the December 2001 issue of *Psychological Methods* was dedicated to new approaches to missing data in psychological research. The details of the estimation procedures are beyond the level of this book, but we will discuss the topic a bit more when we study correlation and regression.

14.12 NONPARAMETRIC PROCEDURES FOR REPEATED-MEASURES DESIGNS

In previous chapters, we have discussed the implications of violations of the assumptions of statistical tests. We have found that such violations may result in distortions of Type 1 error rates or in loss of power. In such situations, we have found that nonparametric procedures often have advantages over the conventional F and t tests. For example, in Chapter 8, two tests based on ranks were presented, the Kruskal–Wallis H test and the rank-transformation test (Iman & Conover, 1981). These tests are often more powerful than the F test when the treatment population distributions have heavy tails or are skewed. Similar analyses of ranked scores can be applied to data from repeated-measures designs. We will consider these as well as a test for situations in which all scores are either zeros or ones.

14.12.1 Friedman's χ^2 (Chi Square) Test

In the first procedure we consider, the scores for each subject are assigned ranks from 1 (for the lowest) to a (for the highest); tied scores are assigned the median, or midrank, of their ranks. The test statistic is approximately distributed as chi square under the null hypothesis that, for each subject, all possible sequences of ranks are equally likely. If this null hypothesis is true, differences between conditions in the mean ranks are due to chance rather than to the effects of the independent variable.

Several programs calculate Friedman's (1937) χ^2; for example, SPSS's *nonparametric* module (select *K Related Samples*) takes the original data as its input and yields a statistic distributed approximately as χ^2 when Friedman's χ^2 is selected from the available options. For the *Seasons* depression data of Table 14.1, the result is $\chi^2 = 6.738$, $p = .081$. In the absence of statistical software, formulas are available in several sources. Lehmann (1975, p. 265) provides details of the calculations and a numerical example.

14.12.2 The Rank-Transformation F Test (F_R)

An ANOVA based on ranks has been proposed by Iman, Hora, and Conover (1984; also see Hora & Iman, 1988). There are two steps:

1. Assign ranks to all *an* scores from smallest to largest, assigning midranks in case of ties. Note that, unlike Friedman's procedure, each subject's scores are not ranked separately.
2. Do the standard $S \times A$ ANOVA on the rank values. This means that once the Y_{ij} have been converted to R_{ij}, the transformed values can be submitted to any program that analyses data from a repeated-measures design.

When the R_{ij} transforms of the data of Table 14.1 are analyzed, $F = 3.44$ with $p = .026$ (see Exercise 14.11). The Greenhouse–Geisser and Huynh–Feldt epsilon estimates are .83 and 1, almost identical to those in the ANOVA of the original data, but the *p*-values are slightly lower, .035 and .026.

14.12.3 Which Test: F, Friedman's χ^2, or F_R?

When the distributions of scores in the treatment populations have the same shape and variance, the usual F test, χ_F^2, and F_R all test the null hypothesis of equal treatment population means. If those populations can also be assumed to be normal, or to have short tails (as when the data are ratings from a scale with only a few points), the F test will be most powerful. The relative power of the F and the rank-based tests changes when treatment populations are skewed or heavy tailed. In a study comparing F_R with F_F, an F test on data ranked by Friedman's method, Iman, Hora, and Conover (1984; also see Hora & Iman, 1988; Kepner & Robinson, 1988) found that with heavy-tailed or skewed distributions, both F_R and F_F usually have Type 1 error rates close to the nominal .05 level, and both are more powerful—often considerably so—than the F test on the original scores. As for the relative powers of F_R and χ_F^2 (or of F_R and F_F), this depends upon several factors including the number of conditions, the shape of the treatment population distribution, the within-subject correlation, and the variability of subject means. The power advantage moves to the Friedman tests as the correlation or subject effects increase. Because of the influence of so many factors, there is no simple rule-of-thumb, but we recommend F_R unless a is more than 5 and the data are very skewed. In both tests, the epsilon adjustment should be used to reduce degrees of freedom when nonsphericity is present.

14.12.4 Paired Scores: The Wilcoxon Signed-Rank (WSR) Test

Neither F_R nor χ_F^2 has good power when $a = 2$. When there are only two conditions, the Wilcoxon signed-rank, or *WSR*, test (1949) is an excellent alternative not only to these tests, but also to the standard t test. The *WSR* is only slightly less powerful than the correlated-scores t test when the data are normally distributed and can be considerably more powerful when the difference scores are symmetrically (but not necessarily normally) distributed with heavy tails (Blair & Higgins, 1985). However, two cautions are in order. First, if the distribution of difference scores is skewed, Type 1 error rates may be inflated for the *WSR* test. Second, power is lost for the *WSR* test when difference scores are zero because these scores are discarded in the *WSR* test. The *t* test will have a clear power advantage in this situation because difference scores of zero are retained in the *t* test.

The *WSR* test is available in several statistics packages. SPSS assumes large samples and uses a normal-distribution approximation which is quite good for samples as small as 20. Select *Analyze*, followed by *Nonparametric Tests*, and then *2 Related Samples*, and click on *Wilcoxon*. For smaller samples, formulas, examples, and tables of *p*-values are available in several books on nonparametric statistics; e.g., Bradley (1968) and Lehmann (1975).

14.12.5 Zero-One Data: Cochran's (1950) Q Test

A common research situation is one in which each subject responds on several trials or under several different conditions, and each response is classified in one of two ways. For example, suppose we record a success or failure for each subject on each of four mathematical problems which varied in their conceptual distance from a practice problem. The question is whether the probability of success depends upon the problem type. In general, $Y_{ij} = 1$ or 0, indicating a success or failure by subject i in condition j. If p_j is the probability of a success in the population of responses under A_j, the null hypothesis is

$$H_0: p_1 = p_2 = \ldots = p_j \ldots = p_a$$

The Q statistic is defined as

$$Q = SS_A / MS_{A/S} \tag{14.22}$$

$MS_{A/S}$ is the average of n variances where each variance is based on the a scores for a subject. Q is distributed as chi square when n is large and the population correlation for any pair of conditions is the same as for any other pair. Therefore, the null hypothesis is rejected when Q exceeds the critical value of χ^2 on $a - 1$ df.

The χ^2 distribution rests on the assumption that the variable of interest is normally distributed. Under the central limit theorem, this assumption is essentially true for proportions when n is large. For the Q test, the effective n does not include any subjects who have either all successes or all failures. Based on a review of several simulation studies, Myers, DiCecco, White, and Borden (1982) recommended that the effective number of subjects be at least 16. When n is small, empirical rejection rates of true null hypotheses are less than the nominal alpha, and power is quite low.

Again, many statistical packages include the Q test. For example, SPSS provides a Q test program; Select *Analyze*, *Nonparametrics*, *k related samples*, and *Cochran*. The 0/1 data can also be submitted to a repeated-measures ANOVA. In fact, Myers et al. (1982) report that the F and Q tests have very similar Type 1 error rates for $n \geq 16$; for smaller n, the F test's Type 1 error rate may be inflated.

14.12.6 Nonparametric Tests and Assumptions

Although it is often assumed that nonparametric tests are assumption-free, this is not the case. The Friedman and rank-transformation tests require the usual assumptions of ANOVA for repeated-measures, but with respect to the ranks rather than to the original scores. The *WSR* test is a test of the null hypothesis that the median is zero only if the population of difference scores is symmetric. Lastly, Cochran's Q test rests on the assumption that the correlations for pairs of treatments are the same in the population, and requires a sufficient sample size to warrant use of the chi-square tables to evaluate significance. Thus, deciding whether to analyze the data of a repeated-measures design with ANOVA versus one of the nonparametric tests requires that the researcher pay close attention to the characteristics of the data and their correspondence (or lack thereof) with the assumptions of the statistical procedures under consideration.

14.13 SUMMARY

In this chapter, we considered the analysis of data from a repeated-measures design in which subjects were tested on several trials, or at several randomly sequenced levels of an independent variable. Within that context, we addressed the following topics:

- *The distinction between additive and nonadditive structural models*, the problems that may be encountered when data include subject × treatment interactions, and possible solutions to these problems.
- *Measures of effect size*, including eta-squared, omega-squared, and Cohen's *f*.
- *The role of power considerations in deciding on sample size* in the repeated-measures design. We illustrated the use of G*Power for making those decisions.
- *Tests of contrasts and trend* in the one-factor, repeated-measures design.
- *Treatment of missing data*, including distinctions among bases for missing data, their implications for estimates of population parameters, and approaches to replacing missing observations.
- *Nonparametric tests* when the assumptions of the analysis of variance are violated. These include analyses of ranks when the original scores are not normally distributed, and Cochran's *Q* test when the scores are zeros and ones.

The design considered in this chapter involved only one factor other than subjects. In the next chapter, we build on this simple design, adding other factors either as between-subjects or within-subjects variables.

EXERCISES

14.1 The following data set consists of three scores for each of four subjects:

	A_1	A_2	A_3
S_1	12	14	15
S_2	9	8	10
S_3	10	9	12
S_4	8	6	7

(a) Carry out the ANOVA.
(b) Assuming additivity, present the *EMS*.

(c) Use your answer to part (b) to estimate general ω_A^2.

14.2 Consider the data set in the *EX14_2* file on the *Exercises* page of the book's website; follow the link from *Data Files*.

(a) For each subject, calculate the three difference scores d_{12}, d_{13}, and d_{23}, where d_{ij} represents the difference, $Y_{ij} - Y_{ik}$. Find the variances of each set of difference scores.

(b) Calculate the variance–covariance matrix for the original scores $(Cov(X, Y) = r_{xy}s_x s_y)$. Using those results, calculate the three variances of difference scores. The result should be the same as in part (a).

(c) Perform an ANOVA on the data and show that $MS_{SA} = (\frac{1}{2}) \times$ (average of the three variances calculated in the preceding two parts).

14.3 (a) Analyze the data set of *EX14_3* on the *Exercises* page of the website. Then use the error mean square (sphericity assumed) as the basis for a t test of the difference between the A_1 and A_2 means.

(b) Repeat the t test using the variance of d_{12}.

(c) Which analysis do you think should be preferred? Why?

14.4 Huynh and Feldt (1970) present the following variance–covariance matrix. Does it satisfy compound symmetry? Does it satisfy sphericity?

$$
\begin{array}{c} \\ A_1 \\ A_2 \\ A_3 \end{array}
\begin{array}{ccc} A_1 & A_2 & A_3 \\ \left[\begin{array}{ccc} 1.0 & .5 & 1.5 \\ & 3.0 & 2.5 \\ & & 5.0 \end{array}\right] \end{array}
$$

14.5 Consider the following data set:

	A_1	A_2	A_3	A_4
S_1	1.8	2.2	3.2	2.4
S_2	2.4	1.5	1.9	2.7
S_3	1.9	1.7	2.5	3.5
S_4	2.7	2.6	2.4	3.1
S_5	4.7	4.8	4.4	4.8
S_6	3.6	3.1	4.2	5.4
S_7	4.4	4.2	4.1	4.9
S_8	5.8	6.1	6.4	6.6

(a) Carry out the ANOVA on these data and find the lower and upper bounds on the p-value, assuming sphericity and nonsphericity, respectively. Assuming $\alpha = .05$, can you reach a conclusion with respect to the A source of variance?

(b) Assume that we planned all pairwise comparisons for the preceding data set. Find the 95% confidence interval for $\bar{Y}_4 - \bar{Y}_2$, controlling for the *FWE*.

14.6 Assume that the levels of A in Exercise 14.5 are equally spaced. Perform a trend analysis, testing each of the three polynomial components.

14.7 An educational psychologist wishes to develop a measure of articulation that can be used in examining the relation between reading comprehension and the ability to articulate words. She has 40 third-graders read aloud each of 20 words, and measures the time required for the response. A *subjects* $\times$ *words* ANOVA yields the following results:

SV	df	MS	F
Subjects (S)	39	208,305.017	244.158
Words (W)	19	739.141	.866
SW	741	853.157	

One measure of the reliability of a measuring instrument is r_{11}, the proportion of the total variance attributable to differences among the subjects.

(a) Because the variability due to words is clearly negligible, obtain an error mean square by pooling the W and SW mean squares.

(b) Estimate σ_S^2 and σ_e^2.

(c) Using the results from parts (a) and (b), calculate r_{11}.

14.8 Each of five subjects is tested at four equally spaced points in time on a visual detection task. The numbers of errors for each test are:

		Time		
Subject	1	2	3	4
1	9	6	7	5
2	11	8	6	6
3	6	8	7	5
4	13	10	10	9
5	12	8	9	6

(a) Time 1 provides a baseline. The experimenter plans to test whether the mean at Time 1 differs significantly from the combined mean for the other three times. State the null hypothesis and carry out the test with $\alpha = .05$.

(b) Calculate a confidence interval for the contrast in part (a).

(c) Test whether there is a significant linear trend.

(d) Test whether the means depart significantly from a straight line.

14.9 **(a)** Perform the ANOVA on the following data set, response times (in milliseconds) obtained under four different conditions for eight subjects:

Subject	A_1	A_2	A_3	A_4
1	2036	2220	2211	2316
2	2034	2042	2094	2077
3	2198	2612	2272	2348
4	2593	2629	2652	2647
5	2347	2408	2416	2479
6	2308	2352	2463	2358
7	2454	2501	2475	2461
8	2462	2394	2491	2659

(b) Assuming A is an extrinsic factor, estimate general ω_A^2 and general ω_S^2.

(c) Estimate Cohen's f, using Equation 14.19.

(d) Estimate Cohen's f, using the *Determine* option in G*Power 3. The *Variance explained by special effect* is the variance of the means, 2,459 (i.e., MS_A/n); the *Variance within groups* is the average within-condition variance, 36,993 [i.e., $(SS_S + SS_{SA})/(df_S + df_{SA})$]. Enter these values to calculate f. (Note: There should be one group and four repetitions; values of the correlation and epsilon are irrelevant when the *Determine* option is used.)

(e) Your two estimates should be different. Why is this?

14.10 We wish to rerun the experiment of Exercise 14.9 with power = .9 to detect a medium-sized effect: $f = .25$.

(a) Create a 3×3 table with cells containing the n needed for the following combinations of conditions: $\varepsilon = .6, .8$, or 1.0; correlation = .4, .6, .8.

(b) Briefly explain the effects of varying these factors on the required n and the reason for the effects.

14.11 (a) For the data of Exercise 14.9, test the effects of A, using Friedman's Chi square.

(b) Transform the data of Exercise 14.9 by $recip = (10^5)(1/Y)$ (in SPSS, $recip = (10**5)*(1/Y)$). Perform the ANOVA on the transformed data.

(c) On the basis of plots of the data, discuss any differences between the result of the ANOVA on the original data and those of parts (a) and (b).

14.12 Twenty people underwent a 1-week program aimed to help them quit cigarette smoking, The researchers running the program checked on the progress of the participants after 3, 6, and 9 months. The results follow with a 1 signifying that the individual has smoked at least once during the preceding 3-month period and a zero indicating that the individual has not smoked during that period.

	Subjects																			
Period	1	2	3	4	5	6	7	8	9	10	11	12	13	14	15	16	17	18	19	20
1	1	0	0	0	1	0	0	0	0	0	0	0	1	1	0	0	1	1	1	0
2	1	1	1	1	1	0	1	0	0	1	1	0	1	0	0	1	0	0	1	1
3	1	1	1	1	1	0	0	1	1	1	1	1	0	1	0	1	1	1	1	0

The investigators want to know whether there has been a significant change in the percentage of smokers over the three periods in the follow-up study. Perform an analysis to answer this question and state your conclusion.

14.13 The file *EX14_13* on the *Exercises* page of the book's website contains hours/weekday of exposure to daylight for the oldest group of subjects in the *Seasons* study. This was of interest to the researchers because it is believed that exposure to daylight affects mood.

(a) Perform an analysis of variance on the female (i.e., sex = 1) *DIRWDC* (direct exposure to daylight during weekdays) scores; 1 = winter, 2 = spring, 3 = summer, 4 = fall.

(b) Calculate general ω^2 for the effects of seasons.

(c) Perform a trend analysis and discuss the results.

14.14 (a) Transform the data in Exercise 14.13 by $Log(DIRWDC + 1)$ and redo parts (a)–(c). Comment on any differences in results.

(b) Using any graphs or descriptive statistics you find useful, comment on any changes in the distributions of scores due to the transformation.

Chapter 15
Multi-Factor Repeated-Measures and Mixed Designs

15.1 OVERVIEW

In this chapter, we extend our discussion of repeated-measures designs to designs involving two or more factors. These factors may all be within-subjects or a mix of within- and between-subjects factors. We refer to the latter as *mixed designs*; they also are called *split-plot designs* in reference to their early appearance in agricultural experiments. In both pure repeated-measures designs and mixed designs, it is important to distinguish between variables that have fixed effects and those that have random effects. As we shall see, this distinction has implications not only for the interpretation of results but also for expected mean squares and, consequently, for hypothesis tests and measures of effect size.

The chapter will be organized as follows: We first consider pure repeated-measures designs in which all independent variables except subjects have fixed effects. We then turn to mixed designs in which each subject is at only one level of *A* but is tested at all levels of *B*, and *A* and *B* are fixed-effect factors. We will extend each of these designs to designs with more than two factors. Following these developments, we introduce analyses involving a random-effects variable (in addition to subjects) and consider the implications for the expected mean squares and the *F* test. An approximate *F* test is presented for such situations. Finally, procedures for making specific comparisons within the designs are developed, and measures are presented for computing effect size and *a priori* power for both classes of design.

In summary, this chapter has these main goals:

- To extend the analyses of repeated-measures designs to within-subjects designs having more than one factor.
- To introduce mixed designs involving both between-subjects and within-subjects factors.
- To present designs with more than one random-effects factor and develop a general set of rules for generating expected mean squares for all of the designs we consider.
- To develop approximate *F* tests called *quasi-F* tests for analyses in which no single mean

square provides an appropriate error term against which to test some main and interaction effects.

- To present methods for doing contrasts and simple effects tests, for computing measures of effect size, and for doing *a priori* power computations involving repeated-measures and mixed designs.

15.2 THE $S \times A \times B$ DESIGN WITH A AND B FIXED

In a conventional, two-factor repeated-measures design, n randomly sampled subjects are each tested at every combination of levels of the other factors. Therefore, if there are two within-subjects factors, A and B, with a and b levels, respectively, each subject is tested ab times. For example, consider a hypothetical experiment modeled on a study of factors affecting facial recognition (Murray, Yong, & Rhodes, 2000). These investigators presented subjects with photos of several faces differing with respect to the type of *distortion* (three levels) and the *orientation* of the face (there are three levels in the example we will develop, instead of the seven in the actual experiment). Each of six subjects saw examples of each of the nine combinations of orientation and distortion, with the order of presentation of the nine combinations randomly determined for each subject. Subjects rated each face for bizarreness, with normal being 1 and very bizarre being 7.

15.2.1 The Structural Model and Expected Mean Squares (*EMS*)

We assume that Y_{ijk}, the score from subject i in the cell formed by A_j and B_k, is composed of a true score and error of measurement; i.e., $Y_{ijk} = \mu_{ijk} + \varepsilon_{ijk}$. We may rewrite this in terms of the grand mean and the deviation of the true score from that mean:

$$Y_{ijk} = \mu + (\mu_{ijk} - \mu) + \varepsilon_{ijk}$$

Under a general nonadditive model, we assume that individual differences (η_i), and the effects of A (α_j), and of B (β_k), and their interactions contribute to the difference between μ_{ijk} and μ. Substituting these effects for $\mu_{ijk} - \mu$, we have:

$$Y_{ijk} = \mu + \eta_i + \alpha_j + \beta_k + (\eta\alpha)_{ij} + (\eta\beta)_{ik} + (\alpha\beta)_{jk} + (\eta\alpha\beta)_{ijk} + \varepsilon_{ijk} \tag{15.1}$$

The parameters and their variances are defined in Table 15.1 and the sums-of-squares (SS) formulas and *EMS* are in Table 15.2. The *EMS* are similar to those for the $S \times A$ design of Chapter 14. As was the case there, A is tested against the SA mean square. Similarly, B and AB are tested against SB and SAB respectively.

15.2.2 An Example of the $S \times A \times B$ ANOVA

Table 15.3 (the data are also on the website in the file *Table 15_3 SAB Data* on the *Tables* page) presents the data for our hypothetical experiment on face perception. The scores in Table 15.3 are hypothetical averages of ratings of several photos in each condition, but the pattern of the means plotted in Fig. 15.1 is similar to the pattern in the Murray et al. (2000) article.

Table 15.4 presents the results of the ANOVA of the $S \times A \times B$ data in Table 15.3. The degrees of freedom and sums of squares can be verified using the formulas in Table 15.2. The F tests are based on the nonadditive model, assuming A and B both have fixed effects and subjects are a random sample from an infinitely large population of subjects. As the *EMS* in Table 15.2 dictate, A

Table 15.1   Components of the structural model for the $S \times A \times B$ design

Population parameter	Definition	Variance
η_i	$\mu_i - \mu$	$\sigma_S^2 = E(\eta_i^2)$
α_i	$\mu_j - \mu$	$\sigma_A^2 = \sum_{j=1}^{a} \alpha_j^2 \Big/ a$
β_k	$\mu_k - \mu$	$\sigma_B^2 = \sum_{k=1}^{b} \beta_k^2 \Big/ b$
$(\eta\alpha)_{ij}$	$(\mu_{ij} - \mu) - \eta_i - \alpha_j$	$\sigma_{SA}^2 = E\left[\sum_{j=1}^{a} (\eta\alpha)_{ij}^2 \Big/ a \right]$
$(\eta\beta)_{ik}$	$(\mu_{ik} - \mu) - \eta_i - \beta_k$	$\sigma_{SB}^2 = E\left[\sum_{k=1}^{b} (\eta\beta)_{ik}^2 \Big/ b \right]$
$(\alpha\beta)_{jk}$	$(\mu_{jk} - \mu) - \alpha_j - \beta_k$	$\sigma_{AB}^2 = \sum_{k=1}^{b} \sum_{j=1}^{a} (\alpha\beta)_{jk}^2 \Big/ ab$
$(\eta\alpha\beta)_{ijk}$	$(\mu_{ijk} - \mu) - \eta_i - \alpha_j - \beta_k - (\eta\alpha)_{ij} - (\eta\beta)_{ik} - (\alpha\beta)_{jk}$	$\sigma_{SAB}^2 = E\left[\sum_{k=1}^{b} \sum_{j=1}^{a} (\eta\alpha\beta)_{ijk}^2 \Big/ ab \right]$
ε_{ijk}	$Y_{ijk} - \mu_{ijk}$	$\sigma_e^2 = E(Y_{ijk} - \mu_{ijk})^2$

Note: $\mu_{ijk} = E(Y_{ijk})$, $\mu_{jk} = E(\mu_{ijk})$, $\mu_{ij} = \Sigma_k\mu_{ijk}/b$, $\mu_{ik} = \Sigma_j\mu_{ijk}/a$, $\mu_i = \Sigma_k\Sigma_j\mu_{ijk}/ab$, $\mu_j = E(\Sigma_k\mu_{ijk}/b)$, $\mu_k = E(\Sigma_j\mu_{ijk}/a)$, and $\mu = E(\mu_i) = \Sigma_j\Sigma_k\mu_{ijk}/ab$. The random effects—$\eta_i$, $(\eta\alpha)_{ij}$, $(\eta\alpha\beta)_{ijk}$, and ε_{ijk}—are assumed to be normally distributed with mean zero and variance, as noted in the table.

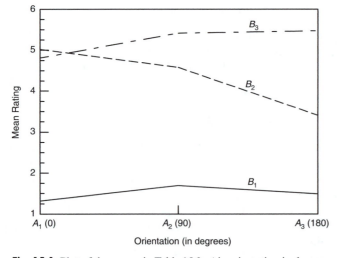

Fig. 15.1 Plot of the means in Table 15.3. *A* is orientation in degrees and *B* is the type of distortion

Table 15.2 ANOVA for an $S \times A \times B$ design; A and B have fixed effects

Source	df	SS	EMS	F
S	$n-1$	$ab\sum_{i=1}^{n}(\bar{Y}_{i..}-\bar{Y}_{...})^2$	$\sigma_e^2+ab\sigma_S^2$	
A	$a-1$	$nb\sum_{j=1}^{a}(\bar{Y}_{.j.}-\bar{Y}_{...})^2$	$\sigma_e^2+b\sigma_{SA}^2+nb\theta_A^2$	MS_A/MS_{SA}
SA	$(n-1)(a-1)$	$b\sum_{j=1}^{a}\sum_{i=1}^{n}(\bar{Y}_{ij.}-\bar{Y}_{...})^2$ $-SS_S-SS_A$	$\sigma_e^2+b\sigma_{SA}^2$	
B	$b-1$	$na\sum_{k=1}^{b}(\bar{Y}_{..k}-\bar{Y}_{...})^2$	$\sigma_e^2+a\sigma_{SB}^2+na\theta_B^2$	MS_B/MS_{SB}
SB	$(n-1)(b-1)$	$a\sum_{k=1}^{b}\sum_{i=1}^{n}(\bar{Y}_{i.k}-\bar{Y}_{...})^2$ $-SS_S-SS_B$	$\sigma_e^2+a\sigma_{SB}^2$	
AB	$(a-1)(b-1)$	$n\sum_{j=1}^{a}\sum_{k=1}^{b}(\bar{Y}_{.jk}-\bar{Y}_{...})^2$ $-SS_A-SS_B$	$\sigma_e^2+\sigma_{SAB}^2+n\theta_{AB}^2$	MS_{AB}/MS_{SAB}
SAB	$(n-1)(a-1)(b-1)$	$SS_{\text{total}}-SS_S-SS_A-SS_{SA}$ $-SS_B-SS_{SB}-SS_{AB}$	$\sigma_e^2+\sigma_{SAB}^2$	

Note: $\theta_A^2=\Sigma_j(\mu_j-\mu)^2/(a-1)$, $\theta_B^2=\Sigma_k(\mu_k-\mu)^2/(b-1)$, and $\theta_{AB}^2=\Sigma_j\Sigma_k[(\mu_{jk}-\mu)-\alpha_j-\beta_k]^2/(a-1)(b-1)$.

is tested against *SA*, *B* is tested against *SB*, and *AB* is tested against *SAB*. With respect to the results, *Orientation* (*A*), *Distortion* (*B*), and their interaction are all significant. The large *F* for *Distortion* is primarily due to the difference between the average bizarreness rating of the unaltered photo (*B₁*) and the means for the two altered photos. Adjusting the degrees of freedom by the Greenhouse–Geisser (*G–G*) or Huynh–Feldt (*H–F*) estimates of epsilon did not change the *p*-values markedly.

15.2.3 Repeated-Measures Designs with Three or More Factors

It is a straightforward matter to extend the $S \times A \times B$ design by including additional factors. For the current example, one possible extension might be to include a third within-subjects factor of the sex (*C*) of the faces in the photos. This added factor will double the number of conditions in the experiment: Photos will represent every combination of the two sexes with the three orientations and the three distortions. As before, every subject will see examples of all 18 conditions presented in random order.

Adding *C* increases the number of sources of variance from 7 to 15. There will be three main effects of interest (*A, B, C*), three interactions of interest (*AB, AC, BC*), and a three-way interaction (*ABC*); the *F* tests of these seven terms each involve a different error mean square (i.e., an interaction of subjects with the term being tested). Conceptually and computationally, there is nothing new here; we discussed the interpretation of three-factor interactions in Chapter 8. Furthermore,

Table 15.3   Data for a two-factor repeated-measures experiment (A is orientation, B is distortion)

Subjects	B_1			B_2			B_3		
	A_1	A_2	A_3	A_1	A_2	A_3	A_1	A_2	A_3
1	1.18	2.40	2.48	4.76	4.93	3.13	5.56	4.93	5.21
2	1.14	1.55	1.25	4.81	4.73	3.89	4.85	5.43	4.89
3	1.02	1.25	1.30	4.98	3.85	3.05	4.28	5.64	6.49
4	1.05	1.63	1.84	4.91	5.21	2.95	5.13	5.52	5.69
5	1.81	1.65	1.01	5.01	4.18	3.51	4.90	5.18	5.52
6	1.69	1.67	1.04	5.65	4.56	3.94	4.12	5.76	4.99

Cell and marginal means	A_1	A_2	A_3	$\bar{Y}_{..k}$
B_1	1.315	1.692	1.487	1.498
B_2	5.020	4.577	3.412	4.336
B_3	4.807	5.410	5.465	5.227
$\bar{Y}_{.j.}$	3.714	3.89	3.455	$\bar{Y} = 3.687$

Table 15.4   ANOVA of the data of Table 15.3

Source	df	SS	MS	F	Significance		
					p	G–G	H–F
S	5	.544	.109				
A (orientation)	2	1.749	.874	9.23	.005	.006	.005
SA	10	.947	.095				
B (distortion)	2	136.554	68.277	302.56	.000	.000	.000
SB	10	2.257	.226				
AB	4	8.560	2.140	7.75	.001	.011	.003
SAB	20	5.522	.276				
Total	53	156.133					

Note: G–G refers to the Greenhouse–Geiser correction for nonsphericity and H–F refers to the Huynh–Feldt correction.

the underlying assumptions of the analysis are the same as in the $S \times A$ and $S \times A \times B$ designs. Sphericity is still assumed and most software packages will adjust degrees of freedom for violations of this assumption. Also, as discussed in Chapter 14, MANOVA is an alternative approach available for dealing with violations of sphericity in the repeated-measures design.

15.3 MIXED DESIGNS WITH A AND B FIXED

Designs that incorporate a mixture of between- and within-subjects factors are called *mixed designs*. Our development relies on the univariate analysis of variance, although we note that there are other approaches to such designs.[1] Mixed designs involve at least one between-subjects variable and one within-subjects variable. They are a compromise between a desire to employ within-subjects factors to reduce error variance (and thus increase power and the precision of estimates) and the reality that certain variables simply cannot be treated as within-subjects factors. Examples of variables that are inherently between-subjects factors are those whose levels are observed rather than manipulated (e.g., individual differences variables such as gender, age, or clinical diagnostic category) and manipulated variables that entail carry-over effects (e.g., training method).

As an example of a mixed design, Table 15.5 (the data are also in the file *Table 15_5 Mixed Data* on the website; follow the link to the *Tables* page) presents a data set for a hypothetical

Table 15.5 Data for a design with one between-subjects (*A*) and one within-subjects (*B*) factor

Method of instruction		Time of test				$\bar{Y}_{ij.}$
		B_1	B_2	B_3	B_4	
A_1	S_{11}	82	48	41	53	56
	S_{21}	72	70	51	45	62
	S_{31}	43	35	30	12	30
	S_{41}	77	41	61	31	50
	S_{51}	43	43	21	29	34
	S_{61}	67	39	30	40	44
	$\bar{Y}_{.1k}$	64	46	39	35	$\bar{Y}_{.1.} = 46$
A_2	S_{12}	71	53	50	62	59
	S_{22}	89	67	76	68	75
	S_{32}	82	84	83	71	80
	S_{42}	56	56	55	45	53
	S_{52}	64	44	44	52	51
	S_{62}	76	74	64	74	72
	$\bar{Y}_{.2k}$	73	63	62	62	$\bar{Y}_{.2.} = 65$
A_3	S_{13}	84	80	75	77	79
	S_{23}	84	72	63	81	75
	S_{33}	76	54	57	61	62
	S_{43}	84	66	61	77	72
	S_{53}	67	69	55	69	65
	S_{63}	61	67	55	61	61
	$\bar{Y}_{.3k}$	76	68	61	71	$\bar{Y}_{.3.} = 69$
	$\bar{Y}_{..k}$	71	59	54	56	$\bar{Y}_{...} = 60$

[1] The alternatives include MANOVA and what are referred to as *mixed models* (also called mixed-effects models, hierarchical models, and multi-level models) that are implemented in statistical software packages (e.g., "mixed models" in SPSS and PROC MIXED in SAS). Although applicable to many designs including mixed-factors designs, a full treatment is beyond the scope of this book; however, a brief introduction is provided in Chapter 23.

experiment in which one group of students was taught algebra by a standard instructional method (A_1), a second group was given additional problems (A_2), and a third group received additional problems from a computer that provided immediate feedback (A_3). All three groups were tested at the end of the instructional period, and then were tested once every 2 weeks until four different tests had been given. Assume that the tests were equated for difficulty so that any differences could be attributed to the passage of time. This design permits us to compare the instructional methods (A), and also to see the time course (B) of performance following the end of instruction for each method. Notice that the design is a mixture of the between-subjects design of Chapter 8 and the within-subjects design of Chapter 14. If we average the four test scores for each subject, we have a between-subjects design and can conduct the ANOVA exactly as in Chapter 8. If, on the other hand, we retain the four test scores but ignore the instructional factor, we have an $S \times B$ design in which 18 subjects have scores at the four levels of B.

15.3.1 The Structural Model and *EMS* for the Mixed Design

In designs such as the one in Table 15.5, n subjects are tested at A_1, n other subjects are tested at A_2, and so on. All an subjects are tested at each of the b levels of the independent variable B. Therefore, $abn - 1$ df must be accounted for in the analysis of variance. With respect to notation, we refer to Y_{ijk} where i indexes the subject ($i = 1, 2, \ldots, n$), j indexes the level of the between-subjects variable ($j = 1, 2, \ldots, a$), and k indexes the level of the within-subjects variable ($k = 1, 2, \ldots b$). In Table 15.5, $n = 6$, $a = 3$, and $b = 4$.

As always, the structural model underlies the partitioning of the total variability in the ANOVA. The model equation for the data in Table 15.5 is

$$Y_{ijk} = \mu + \alpha_j + \eta_{i/j} + \beta_k + (\alpha\beta)_{jk} + (\eta\beta)_{ik/j} + \varepsilon_{ijk} \tag{15.2}$$

There are some important differences between this equation and Equation 15.1 for the $S \times A \times B$ design. These differences rest on the distinction between *nested variables* and *crossing variables*. Subjects are nested within levels of A because there are different subjects at each level of A; the same is true for SB interaction effects. We have indicated these nested relationships by inserting a slash before the j in the subscripts for subjects and SB effects within levels of A [$\eta_{i/j}$, $(\eta\beta)_{ik/j}$]. Because a subject is tested at only one level of A, there are no SA interaction effects. Also, because the SB effects are nested in levels of A, there are no SAB effects in the model. In contrast, there are SB interaction effects because subjects cross with B; that is, all subjects are tested at all levels of B. The parameters and their variances are defined in Table 15.6.

Table 15.7 contains the sources of variance, df and SS formulas, and the *EMS*. The sources of variance follow from Equation 15.2. In panel a, we have organized them into between- and within-subjects terms in order to emphasize the relationship to designs encountered previously. If we ignore the factor B, the design is a one-factor design with subjects nested within levels of A. As in the one-factor between-subjects design, $an - 1$ df are divided between the A and subjects-within-A sources. If we ignore A, we have the $S \times B$ design of Chapter 14; there is a subjects term (S), a B term, and an SB interaction. However, part of the SB variance is potentially due to the interaction of A and B, and so the SB variability is partitioned into an AB and a $B \times S/A$ term, as shown in Table 15.7.

From the *EMS* of panel b in Table 15.7, we see that the between-subjects factor, A, is tested against the S/A source. This is the same as in a one-factor between-subjects design. Differences among the a means reflect not only the effects of A and errors of measurement, but also individual differences because there are different subjects at each level of A. It is important to recognize that

Table 15.6 Components of the structural model for the mixed design

Population parameter	Definition	Variance
η_{ilj}	$\mu_{ij} - \mu_j$	$\sigma^2_{S/A} = E(\eta^2_{ilj})$
α_i	$\mu_j - \mu$	$\sigma^2_A = \sum_{j=1}^{a} \alpha^2_j \Big/ a$
β_k	$\mu_k - \mu$	$\sigma^2_B = \sum_{k=1}^{b} \beta^2_k \Big/ b$
$(\eta\beta)_{iklj}$	$(\mu_{ik} - \mu_j) - \eta_{ilj} - \beta_k$	$\sigma^2_{SB/A} = E\left[\sum_{k=1}^{b} (\eta\beta)^2_{iklj} \Big/ b \right]$
$(\alpha\beta)_{jk}$	$(\mu_{jk} - \mu) - \alpha_j - \beta_k$	$\sigma^2_{AB} = \sum_{k=1}^{b}\sum_{j=1}^{a} (\alpha\beta)^2_{jk} \Big/ ab$
ε_{ijk}	$Y_{ijk} - \mu_{ijk}$	$\sigma^2_e = E(Y_{ijk} - \mu_{ijk})^2$

Note: $\mu_{ijk} = E(Y_{ijk})$, $\mu_{jk} = E(\mu_{ijk})$, $\mu_{ij} = \Sigma_k \mu_{ijk}/b$, $\mu_{ik} = \Sigma_j \mu_{ijk}/a$, $\mu_i = \Sigma_k \Sigma_j \mu_{ijk}/ab$, $\mu_j = E(\Sigma_k \mu_{ijk}/b)$, $\mu_k = E(\Sigma_j \mu_{ijk}/a)$, and $\mu = E(\mu_i)$. The random effects—η_{ilj}, $(\eta\beta)_{iklj}$, and ε_{ijk}—are assumed to be normally distributed with mean zero and variance, as noted in the table.

Table 15.7 ANOVA formulas (*a*) and *EMS* (*b*) for the mixed design

(*a*) Partitioning degrees of freedom and sums of squares

Sources of variance	df	Sums of squares
Total	$abn - 1$	$\Sigma_k \Sigma_j \Sigma_i (Y_{ijk} - \overline{Y}_{...})^2$
Between-subjects (*S*)	$an - 1$	$b\Sigma_j \Sigma_i (\overline{Y}_{ij.} - \overline{Y}_{...})^2$
A (Instructions)	$a - 1$	$bn\Sigma_j (\overline{Y}_{.j.} - \overline{Y}_{...})^2$
S/A	$a(n - 1)$	$SS_S - SS_A$
Within-subjects (*W Ss*)	$an(b - 1)$	$SS_{\text{total}} - SS_S$
B (Time)	$b - 1$	$an\Sigma_k (\overline{Y}_{..k} - \overline{Y}_{...})^2$
AB	$(a - 1)(b - 1)$	$n\Sigma_j \Sigma_k (\overline{Y}_{.jk} - \overline{Y}_{...})^2 - SS_A - SS_B$
B × S/A	$a(n - 1)(b - 1)$	$SS_{W Ss} - SS_B - SS_{AB}$

(*b*) Expected mean squares (*EMS*)

Source	EMS
A	$\sigma^2_e + b\sigma^2_{S/A} + bn\theta^2_A$
S/A	$\sigma^2_e + b\sigma^2_{S/A}$
B	$\sigma^2_e + \sigma^2_{SB/A} + na\theta^2_B$
AB	$\sigma^2_e + \sigma^2_{SB/A} + n\theta^2_{AB}$
B × S/A	$\sigma^2_e + \sigma^2_{SB/A}$

the term σ_e^2 has a different meaning in the current design than it had in Chapter 8. In the one-factor design of Chapter 8, σ_e^2 encompassed both variability due to individual differences and measurement errors. However, in the current design, individual differences contribute only to between-subjects factors; therefore, σ_e^2 denotes only measurement errors and $\sigma_{S/A}^2$ denotes individual differences.

Continuing on to the within-subjects portion of the design, the B and AB terms are tested against the residual error, $MS_{B \times S/A}$. This is because the nested interaction effects of subjects and B contribute to both the B and AB variance. This is analogous to the way we tested effects in the repeated-measures designs in Chapter 14 and Section 15.2 of the current chapter.

15.3.2 Assumptions in the Mixed Design

As in any repeated-measures design, the univariate F test requires the assumption of sphericity; it is assumed that within each level of A, the population variances of difference scores for all pairs of B levels are the same. Violations of this assumption will result in inflation of Type 1 error rates. However, as in the pure within-subjects design, the epsilon-adjusted F test provides an approximately correct p-value. Whether testing B or AB, numerator and denominator df are multiplied by the Greenhouse–Geisser or Huynh–Feldt estimate of epsilon, reducing the df, and thus requiring a larger F value for significance than would be required without the adjustment.

Consider the b populations of scores at a level of A. Our second assumption is that the variances and covariances of these populations are the same at all levels of A. This assumption is made whether the univariate (ANOVA) or the multivariate (MANOVA) test is performed. However, the assumption is less critical than the sphericity assumption. Generally, if the group sizes are equal, the ratios of mean squares will be distributed as F, although the degrees of freedom for within-subjects terms may require correction if the sphericity assumption is violated.

15.3.3 ANOVA of Data from a Mixed Design

Fig. 15.2 displays a plot of the means from our hypothetical study of the effects of instructional method and time of test; curves are plotted for each instructional group (A) as a function of time (B). The average curve declines over time, although there is an increase for the A_3 method at the

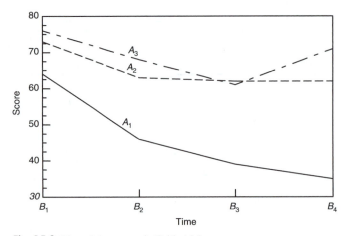

Fig. 15.2 Plot of the means in Table 15.5

Table 15.8   ANOVA of the data in Table 15.5

Source	df	Sum of squares	Mean square	F	p	G–G	H–F
A (Method)	2	7,248	3,624.00	7.76	0.005		
S/A	15	7,010	467.33				
B (Time)	3	3,132	1,044.00	18.72	0.000	0.000	0.000
AB	6	1,056	176.00	3.16	0.011	0.027	0.015
B × *S/A*	45	2,510	55.78				

fourth time. The decline seems most steep between the first and second test positions. There seems to be little difference in performance between groups A_2 and A_3, but both clearly have higher averages than the A_1 group.

Table 15.8 contains the results of an ANOVA of the data in Table 15.5. The denominators of the tests of the main and interaction effects follow the *EMS* of Table 15.7. Presumably because of the relatively poor performance of the A_1 group, the *A* main effect is significant. The significant *B* source of variance reflects the lowering of average scores over time. The *AB* interaction is also significant, reflecting the steeper decline in the A_1 curve and perhaps the upturn in the A_2 curve.

15.3.4 Mixed Designs with Additional Fixed Factors

Just as we were able to do with the $S \times A \times B$ design, we might also add factors to our mixed design. In our hypothetical experiment, we had three methods of instruction in math and we tested subjects at four different times; method was a between-subjects variable and time was a within-subjects variable. At each of the four tests, we might include two types of problems. For example, we might compare problems presented as stories with problems expressed directly in terms of variables such as *X* and *Y*. Now we again have subjects nested within levels of *A* (method), but subjects have scores for each of eight combinations of *B* (time of test) and *C* (type of problem).

Table 15.9 presents sources of variance (*SV*), *df*, and *EMS* for our expanded design. There

Table 15.9   Expected mean squares and error terms for a design with one between- and two within-subjects factors

SV	df	EMS	Error term
A	$a - 1$	$\sigma_e^2 + bc\sigma_{S/A}^2 + nbc\theta_A^2$	*S/A*
S/A	$a(n - 1)$	$\sigma_e^2 + bc\sigma_{S/A}^2$	
B	$b - 1$	$\sigma_e^2 + c\sigma_{SB/A}^2 + nac\theta_B^2$	*SB/A*
AB	$(a - 1)(b - 1)$	$\sigma_e^2 + c\sigma_{SB/A}^2 + nc\theta_{AB}^2$	*SB/A*
SB/A	$a(n - 1)(b - 1)$	$\sigma_e^2 + c\sigma_{SB/A}^2$	
C	$c - 1$	$\sigma_e^2 + b\sigma_{SC/A}^2 + nab\theta_C^2$	*SC/A*
AC	$(a - 1)(c - 1)$	$\sigma_e^2 + b\sigma_{SC/A}^2 + nb\theta_{AC}^2$	*SC/A*
SC/A	$a(n - 1)(c - 1)$	$\sigma_e^2 + b\sigma_{SC/A}^2$	
BC	$(b - 1)(c - 1)$	$\sigma_e^2 + \sigma_{SBC/A}^2 + na\theta_{BC}^2$	*SBC/A*
ABC	$(a - 1)(b - 1)(c - 1)$	$\sigma_e^2 + \sigma_{SBC/A}^2 + n\theta_{ABC}^2$	*SBC/A*
SBC/A	$a(n - 1)(b - 1)(c - 1)$	$\sigma_e^2 + \sigma_{SBC/A}^2$	

Note: *A*, *B*, and *C* are all assumed to have fixed effects.

are four groups of sources. The first includes A and S/A as in the mixed design with only one within-subjects factor. The only modification in the components of the *EMS* is in the multipliers of $\sigma_{S/A}^2$ and θ_A^2; the rule is that components of variance are multiplied by the number of scores on which each mean is based. There are bc scores for each subject and bcn scores at each level of A; therefore, these are the coefficients. The remaining groupings involve the within-subjects factors (B, C, and BC). A interacts with each of these, as does S/A. Note that the result of crossing S/A with each within-subjects factor is a nested interaction. Coefficients of the components of the *EMS* are determined as previously described. In short, the extension of the two-factor mixed design to a three-factor mixed design is straightforward.

15.3.5 Pretest–Posttest Designs

A common, special case of the mixed design is one in which there is a between-subjects treatment (A), and a pretest and a post-test score are obtained from each subject. Subjects are generally assigned randomly to the levels of A, and the pretest scores are obtained before the treatment is applied, so that there are no systematic differences in the pretest scores across levels of A. The post-test scores reflect the effects of the treatment, if there are any. Although this design is often analyzed as a mixed design, other analyses are preferable. Because the treatment is applied to the post-test scores but not the pretest scores, the two types of scores are described by different structural models. Several different analyses have been performed to test whether A affects posttest performance.

1. *Using the mixed design analysis.* It is natural to view the design as a mixed design and carry out the ANOVA of the preceding section. This has been frequently done with A as the between-subjects factor and *Trials* as the within-subjects factor (Huck & McLean, 1975; Jennings, 1988). With this analysis, the F test for the A main effect will be very conservative because the pretest scores cannot be affected by the treatment. The F for the $A \times Trials$ interaction is a more powerful test. It is equivalent to that obtained by performing a one-factor ANOVA on the gain (posttest–pretest) scores, which we consider next.

2. *Analysis of gain scores.* Gain scores are calculated by subtracting the pretest score from the post-test score for each subject; a one-factor ANOVA is then performed on these scores. This approach rests on the assumption that each treatment adds a constant to the pretest score. Because this model is less likely to be true than that assumed in the analysis of covariance, it will generally provide a less powerful test.

3. *Analysis of covariance.* When its assumptions are met, the most powerful analysis is provided by the analysis of covariance (see Chapters 13 and 25). Briefly, this analysis rests on the assumption that the posttest scores are linear functions of the pretest scores, and that the slopes of these functions are the same at each level of A. The analysis takes advantage of this relationship, reducing error variance in the post-test scores by removing variability accounted for by the pretest scores.

4. *Analysis of posttest scores only.* Because the treatment only affects the posttest scores, one could ignore the pretest scores and simply perform a one-factor ANOVA on the post-test scores. The resulting F would clearly test the effect of A upon posttest scores. However, although this approach does not violate any assumptions, it ignores data (the pretest scores) which could help reduce error variance, and therefore this approach will produce less powerful tests than those noted above.

We emphasize that the discussion in this section has presupposed random assignment of subjects to levels of A. Without random assignment, there may be systematic differences in the pretest scores across levels of A. If so, interpretation is more difficult, both for analysis of covariance and for analyses of gain scores (see, for example, Cronbach & Furby, 1970; Linn & Slinde, 1977). Further discussion of these issues is provided by Huck and McLean (1975), Jennings (1988), and Maxwell and Howard (1981).

15.4 DESIGNS WITH MORE THAN ONE RANDOM-EFFECTS FACTOR: THE FIXED- vs RANDOM-EFFECTS DISTINCTION AGAIN

Recall from Section 14.3 that the distinction between random- and fixed-effects refers to how levels of a factor are sampled. In the case of a fixed-effects factor, the levels of the factor are either chosen in such a way that they exhaust all possible levels or they are chosen selectively from among all possible levels. An example of the former is taking observations from all four seasons in the *Seasons* data set or observing both men and women in a study. Examples of the latter are common, such as our hypothetical experiment in which face orientation and face distortion are manipulated. For both of these factors, the experimenter intentionally chose the specific orientations and particular distortions to be included in the experiment. In both cases, the levels of the variables were presumably chosen to be a representative range of variation on each dimension.

In the case of a random-effects factor, the levels of the factor do not exhaust all possible levels of the variable nor are they selected in a systematic way. Instead, levels are a randomly chosen subset of a much larger potential set of observations. The sole example of a random-effects factor that we have encountered to this point is subjects. However, there are many types of experiments in which stimuli are a factor and should be treated as a random-effects variable. As one example, suppose a software company has designed a new font which they believe will make reading easier than more commonly used fonts. The human factors group in the company performs an experiment in which subjects are presented with the same set of words in each of the two fonts; the total number of presentations are randomly sequenced for each subject. The task is to say each word aloud as soon as it is presented; time to initiate pronunciation of each word is recorded to the nearest millisecond. The words are chosen from the population of words that are relatively low in English language frequency on the assumption that any differences in the time to recognize the words are more likely to show up when the task is relatively difficult. The software company is not interested in whether there is a difference in recognition time for only those words included in the experiment. Rather, the words used in the experiment are considered a random sample from a much larger population of low-frequency words. There is little point in marketing the new font unless the company is convinced that any observed advantage holds for the population of words sampled in the experiment.

Our example is not unusual. We often want to generalize our results to stimuli beyond those used in the study. Examples include sentences differing in syntactic construction in a psycholinguistic study, different concrete and abstract words in a memory experiment, pictures of faces illustrating different emotions in a personality experiment, and photographs of different species of insect in a discrimination-learning experiment for pigeons. In these examples, it is important to distinguish the stimuli (i.e., sentences, words, pictures, and photographs) from the categories from which they were sampled (i.e., different types of syntactic construction, concrete and abstract concepts, types of emotions, and species of insect). The researcher's substantive interest is in the categorical variables, which are fixed-effects factors; however, the stimuli are distinct sources of variability in the experiment and they are most appropriately considered random-effects factors.

Treating a factor as *random* instead of as *fixed* does not change the sources of variance, sums of squares, or degrees of freedom when an ANOVA is performed. However, it does change the expected mean squares, so that now different F tests may be required. To see how and why the expected mean squares are affected by the designation of factors as random or fixed effects, we must first look at the rules for generating expected mean squares.

15.5 RULES FOR GENERATING EXPECTED MEAN SQUARES

To illustrate the rules for generating expected mean squares, we will use the design summarized in Table 15.9. Recall that A is a between-subjects factor, whereas B and C are within-subjects factors; A, B, and C are all assumed to have fixed effects, whereas S is a random-effects factor.

There are six components of variance that might potentially contribute to any of the expected mean squares in Table 15.9. These are the variances due to subjects ($\sigma_{S/A}^2$), the interaction of subjects and B ($\sigma_{SB/A}^2$), and error variance (σ_e^2), as well as components corresponding to the fixed effects in the structural equation (θ_A^2, θ_B^2, and θ_{AB}^2). Referring to Table 15.9, only a few of these terms actually contribute to any given expectation, and therefore play a role in the selection of the error term, or in the estimation of effect sizes. Box 15.1 presents *"rules of thumb"* for generating EMS that apply to many common designs.

Box 15.1 Rules of Thumb for Obtaining Expected Mean Squares

1. Decide for each variable, including subjects, whether it has fixed or random effects. Assign a letter to represent the variable (e.g., *S, A, B, C*) and a letter to represent the number of levels (e.g., *n, a, b, c*).

2. Each EMS contains σ_e^2.

3. For each EMS, list for consideration all components whose subscripts include all the letters in the source under consideration. For example, for the EMS for AB in Table 15.10, we would list $nc\theta_{AB}^2$, $c\sigma_{SB/A}^2$, $n\theta_{ABC}^2$, and $\sigma_{SBC/A}^2$. Note that a component has three parts:
   (1) A coefficient such as *bc* or *nac* representing the number of scores at each level of the variable.
   (2) A σ^2 or θ^2 term depending on whether the subscripted variable is assumed to have random or fixed effects.
   (3) Subscripts designating the variable under consideration.

4. Define *essential* subscripts. If there is a slash as in *SB/A*, only those letters to the left of the slash are considered essential. For example, only *SB* is essential in the subscript *SB/A*. (In some designs, there can be several levels of nesting—e.g., students within classes within schools; only the letters to the left of the left-most slash are essential subscripts.)

5. Among the essential subscripts, if any letters that are not part of the source designation represent fixed effects, delete that component from the expected mean square. For example, under Rule 4 we would have listed $\sigma_{SBC/A}^2$ when considering the expectation for the AB source. Among the essential subscripts—*S, B,* and *C*—*C* is not part of the source designation (i.e., *AB*) and does have fixed effects. Therefore, $\sigma_{SBC/A}^2$ does not contribute to the EMS for AB.

The box illustrates the rules using the EMS for the AB source of variance in the design of Table 15.9. As a second example, consider how the rules of thumb might be used to find $E(MS_B)$. First, list σ_e^2 because it contributes to every EMS. Then add every additional component of variance that has subscripts containing B, multiplying each component by its appropriate coefficient. The result is

$$\sigma_e^2 + nac\theta_B^2 + nc\theta_{AB}^2 + c\sigma_{SB/A}^2 + na\theta_{BC}^2 + n\theta_{ABC}^2 + \sigma_{SBC/A}^2$$

Rules 4 and 5 dictate deletion of the $nc\theta_{AB}^2$, $na\theta_{BC}^2$, and $n\theta_{ABC}^2$ components because once B is deleted from the subscripts, we are left with A, C, or both; these subscripts denote fixed-effects variables. We also delete $\sigma_{SBC/A}^2$ because when we ignore B we still have C among the essential subscripts. However, $nc\sigma_{SB/A}^2$ is retained because when B is deleted from the essential subscripts of that component, we are left only with S, a subscript that denotes a random-effects variable. The final result is given in the B line of Table 15.9.

The design in Table 15.9 involves three fixed-effects factors and one random-effects factor. Readers should verify that the expected mean squares presented for all of the designs that we have considered to this point in the book are consistent with the rules of thumb. However, in all of the cases considered up until now, the only random-effects factor was subjects. The rules still apply when there is a second random-effects factor (e.g., stimuli); in fact, they are particularly important in such cases because without the rules to generate the *EMS*, the selection of error terms to test effects of interest is unclear. We provide two examples in the following subsections.

15.5.1 $S \times A \times B$ Design with Two Random-Effects Factors

In Section 15.4, we described a human factors experiment in which both subjects and words would be considered random-effects factors. Imagine that we conducted such an experiment involving n subjects, b words, and a fonts. A summary of the appropriate analysis of this design is presented in Table 15.10. The sources of variance and their df are what you would expect, but the expected mean squares for S, A, and SA are unexpected from the designs encountered to this point. We will work through the expected mean square for A to illustrate the application of the rules for this term.

There are eight distinct variance components in this design: measurement error, σ_e^2; variability due to subjects, σ_S^2; variability due to words, σ_B^2; variability due to the interactions of subjects with A, σ_{SA}^2, B, σ_{SB}^2, and SAB, σ_{SAB}^2; variability due to the interaction of words with A, σ_{AB}^2; and variability associated with the fixed-effects factor A, θ_A^2. The coefficients associated with each of these variance components is, as always, the product of the number of levels of all of the factors that are not represented in the subscript on the variance term (e.g., nb for A; a for SB). Consider how the rules apply to the generation of the expected mean square for the effect of interest, A.

First, list measurement error and every component that includes A in its subscript, along with the appropriate coefficients:

$$\sigma_e^2 + \sigma_{SAB}^2 + b\sigma_{SA}^2 + n\sigma_{AB}^2 + nb\theta_A^2 \tag{15.3}$$

Table 15.10 Expected mean squares for an $S \times A \times B$ design when B has random effects

Source	df	EMS[a]
S	$n-1$	$\sigma_e^2 + \underline{a\sigma_{SB}^2} + ab\sigma_S^2$
A	$a-1$	$\sigma_e^2 + \underline{\sigma_{SAB}^2} + b\sigma_{SA}^2 + \underline{n\sigma_{AB}^2} + nb\theta_A^2$
SA	$(n-1)(a-1)$	$\sigma_e^2 + \underline{\sigma_{SAB}^2} + b\sigma_{SA}^2$
B	$b-1$	$\sigma_e^2 + a\sigma_{SB}^2 + na\sigma_B^2$
SB	$(n-1)(b-1)$	$\sigma_e^2 + a\sigma_{SB}^2$
AB	$(a-1)(b-1)$	$\sigma_e^2 + \sigma_{SAB}^2 + n\sigma_{AB}^2$
SAB	$(n-1)(a-1)(b-1)$	$\sigma_e^2 + \sigma_{SAB}^2$

[a] Underlined components are absent if B is assumed to have fixed effects.

Next, apply Rules 4 and 5 in Box 15.1. Here these rules do not result in any deletions, so that Equation 15.3 is our final result for the expected mean squares for A. Compare this to what we found when B was a fixed-effects variable; in that case, the SAB and AB terms were dropped and the expected mean squares assumed its conventional form. In the current example, we find that the value of MS_A depends on not three, but five variance components; the sample means for the two font conditions may vary because of measurement error, because they are based on different combinations of subjects, words, and fonts (SAB), different combinations of subjects and fonts (SA), different combinations of fonts and words (AB), and different fonts (A). Looking at the EMS in Table 15.10, it will be seen that the expected mean squares for S and for SA are also affected by the inclusion of words as a random-effects factor in the design.

15.5.2 Mixed Design with Two Random-Effects Factors

The $S \times A \times B$ example can undergo further complications. We might have several groups of subjects, perhaps differing in reading ability or grade level. In general, we conceive of an experiment with a between-subjects variable, A, having fixed effects (e.g., grade level); a within-subjects variable, B, also having fixed effects (e.g., font); and a second within-subjects variable, C, having random effects (e.g., words). All combinations of the three factors appear in the design. To summarize the design under consideration: there are a groups of n subjects each and all subjects are tested on the same c items at each of b levels of a fixed-effects factor, B. We presented this design in Table 15.9 under the assumption that all three factors—A, B, and C—had fixed effects. Table 15.11 reproduces much of Table 15.9; the difference is that because C is now assumed to have random effects, the EMS now include additional terms. Those added terms are underlined in Table 15.11.

The underlined variance components are dictated by the rules of thumb introduced in Box 15.1. As an example of the application of the rules, consider the A source of variance. $\sigma^2_{C \times S/A}$ contributes to $E(MS_A)$ because A appears in the subscripts, and the essential subscripts, S and C, both represent variables having random effects. σ^2_{AC} also contributes to the expected mean square

Table 15.11 Expected mean squares for a mixed design in which C is assumed to have random effects

SV	df	EMS[a]
A	$a-1$	$\sigma^2_e + b\sigma^2_{C \times S/A} + bc\sigma^2_{S/A} + \underline{bn\sigma^2_{AC}} + nbc\theta^2_A$
S/A	$a(n-1)$	$\sigma^2_e + \underline{b\sigma^2_{C \times S/A}} + bc\sigma^2_{S/A}$
B	$b-1$	$\sigma^2_e + c\sigma^2_{B \times S/A} + \underline{na\sigma^2_{BC}} + \sigma^2_{BC \times S/A} + nac\sigma^2_B$
AB	$(a-1)(b-1)$	$\sigma^2_e + c\sigma^2_{B \times S/A} + \underline{n\sigma^2_{ABC}} + \sigma^2_{BC \times S/A} + nc\sigma^2_{AB}$
$B \times S/A$	$a(n-1)(b-1)$	$\sigma^2_e + \underline{\sigma^2_{BC \times S/A}} + c\sigma^2_{B \times S/A}$
C	$c-1$	$\sigma^2_e + b\sigma^2_{C \times S/A} + nab\sigma^2_C$
AC	$(a-1)(c-1)$	$\sigma^2_e + b\sigma^2_{C \times S/A} + nb\sigma^2_{AC}$
$C \times S/A$	$a(n-1)(c-1)$	$\sigma^2_e + b\sigma^2_{C \times S/A}$
BC	$(b-1)(c-1)$	$\sigma^2_e + \sigma^2_{BC \times S/A} + na\sigma^2_{BC}$
ABC	$(a-1)(b-1)(c-1)$	$\sigma^2_e + \sigma^2_{B \times C/A} + n\sigma^2_{ABC}$
$BC \times S/A$	$a(n-1)(b-1)(c-1)$	$\sigma^2_e + \sigma^2_{BC \times S/A}$

[a] Underlined terms are not present if C has fixed effects. If C has random effects, quasi-F statistics test A, B, and AB; those tests and the associated degrees of freedom follow from the developments in Section 15.4.2.

for A because, ignoring the A subscript, the remaining letter, C, represents a variable assumed to have random effects.

We have now seen two examples in which the designation of a factor as having random instead of fixed effects results in changes to the expected mean squares in the ANOVA, and therefore the appropriate F tests. *We emphasize that the identification of sources of variance, the computation of df, and the computations of SS and MS quantities are unaffected by the random- vs fixed-effects distinction. However, our conceptualization of what the MS calculations estimate in terms of population parameters is directly affected, as we have seen. These effects on the EMS, in turn, have direct implications for our F tests.*

15.6 CONSTRUCTING UNBIASED *F* TESTS IN DESIGNS WITH TWO RANDOM FACTORS

Consider the $S \times A \times B$ design whose analysis is summarized in Table 15.10. The question of interest in this design is whether there is an effect of type of font, A, on subjects' recognition of words, B. If we test MS_A against MS_{SA}, we cannot know whether a significant result is because $\theta_A^2 > 0$ (our null hypothesis is false) or because $\sigma_{AB}^2 > 0$. The error term should have an expectation of $\sigma_e^2 + b\sigma_{SA}^2 + n\sigma_{AB}^2 + \sigma_{SAB}^2$. As can be seen in Table 15.10, there is no single source of variance that has this expectation.

The same problem is encountered for the mixed design summarized in Table 15.11. The effects of interest in this example are the main effects of A and B, and the AB interaction. Examining the *EMS* terms for these three terms, it is apparent that no single MS in Table 15.11 provides an appropriate error term to test any of these effects. If we test MS_A against $MS_{S/A}$, for example, we again run the risk of inflating the Type 1 error rate.

We consider three possible responses to the problem of constructing an unbiased test of effects of interests in such designs. To anticipate, the approaches discussed in Sections 15.6.1 and 15.6.2 usually do not provide satisfactory solutions to the problem; however, we consider them because they help clarify the issue.

15.6.1 Preliminary Tests of Interaction

We may sometimes be fortunate to find that an effect of interest does not vary in magnitude across subjects (i.e., the additive model). For example, if the effect of type of font was the same for all of the subjects in our repeated-measures design, then the interaction, σ_{SA}^2, equals zero and may be dropped from all of the *EMS* terms in Table 15.10. In that event, the *EMS* for A simplifies to:

$$E(MS_A) = \sigma_e^2 + \sigma_{SAB}^2 + n\sigma_{AB}^2 + nb\theta_A^2$$

and MS_{AB} provides an appropriate error term to test A because

$$E(MS_{AB}) = \sigma_e^2 + \sigma_{SAB}^2 + n\sigma_{AB}^2$$

A similar situation results if the effect of A is constant over stimuli. In that case, σ_{AB}^2 equals zero and MS_{SA} then provides an appropriate error term for the test of A. This suggests a preliminary test of the SA and AB terms against MS_{SAB}. For example, if the test of MS_{SA} against MS_{SAB} does not yield a significant result, we might conclude that σ_{SA}^2 was zero and therefore MS_A could be tested against MS_{AB}.

We stated at the outset that this approach is not completely satisfactory. One limitation is that both the SA and AB interactions will often be significant; in those instances, the approach is not applicable. Less obviously, even when a nonsignificant interaction is observed, it is possible that the preliminary test will result in a Type 2 error; that is, we wrongly conclude that σ_{SA}^2 equals zero. In that case, the Type 1 error rate in testing A against AB will be increased beyond the nominal level. In studies related to this issue, Type 1 error rates have ranged from .07 to .11 with the nominal α level at .05 (Janky, 2000). Therefore, preliminary tests to justify F tests of A involve risks we ordinarily would prefer to avoid.

15.6.2 Separate Tests Against MS_{SA} (F_1) and MS_{AB} (F_2)

A frequent approach to the problem of lacking a single mean square to serve as an error term is to form two F ratios: MS_A is tested against both MS_{SA} and MS_{AB} with significance being required on both tests in order to conclude that A has an effect. The presumed logic of this approach is that the test against MS_{SA} allows generalizability to the subject population and the test against MS_{AB} allows generalizability to the item population. It is true that our goal is to generalize our results to both the population of subjects and the population of items from which we have sampled. However, even if both F tests are significant, we cannot claim that kind of generality. To see why, suppose our null hypothesis is true (i.e., $\theta_A^2 = 0$) but A interacts with S and B. Then the ratio of expected mean squares when we test A against SA is

$$\frac{\sigma_e^2 + \sigma_{SAB}^2 + b\sigma_{SA}^2 + \sigma_{AB}^2}{\sigma_e^2 + \sigma_{SAB}^2 + b\sigma_{SA}^2}$$

which is greater than 1. Similarly, if we test A against AB, the $S \times A$ variance will spuriously inflate the F ratio. In short, even if there is no effect of A in the population, the F_1 and F_2 tests could both be significant if A interacts with both subjects and items. This would lead to the erroneous conclusion that there were A main effects. A more defensible approach is to calculate an F statistic such that the ratio of mean squares is 1 when the null hypothesis is true. We next consider such a statistic.

15.6.3 Quasi-F (F') Tests

We have established that a test of A in the $S \times A \times B$ design summarized in Table 15.10 requires that we identify an error term whose expectation is $\sigma_e^2 + b\sigma_{SA}^2 + n\sigma_{SB}^2 + \sigma_{SAB}^2$. Given the expected mean squares of Table 15.10, no single mean square has the appropriate expected value, but we can form a combination of mean squares with the appropriate expectation. The combination ($MS_{AB} + MS_{SA} - MS_{SAB}$) meets that criterion; thus, we can create a *quasi-F ratio* whose numerator and denominator are equal if the null hypothesis is true. That ratio is:

$$F_1' = \frac{MS_A}{MS_{AB} + MS_{SA} - MS_{SAB}} \tag{15.4}$$

A second possible F test may be constructed, using the same four MS terms:

$$F_2' = \frac{MS_A + MS_{SAB}}{MS_{AB} + MS_{SA}} \tag{15.5}$$

The rationale, again, is that the expectations of numerator and denominator differ only with respect to the null hypothesis component. In Equation 15.5 the ratio of EMS is

$$\frac{(2)(\sigma_e^2 + \sigma_{SAB}^2) + b\sigma_{SA}^2 + n\sigma_{AB}^2 + bn\theta_A^2}{(2)(\sigma_e^2 + \sigma_{SAB}^2) + b\sigma_{SA}^2 + n\sigma_{AB}^2}$$

which equals 1 if the null hypothesis ($\theta_A^2 = 0$) is true. That the ratio of *EMS* terms equals 1 is a necessary but not a sufficient condition for the ratio of mean squares to be distributed as *F*. An important condition is that both the numerator and denominator must be distributed as chi-square variables divided by their degrees of freedom. Satterthwaite (1946) has shown that under the usual assumptions of analysis of variance, a linear combination of mean squares has approximately this sampling distribution.

The denominator of F_1' and the numerator and denominator of F_2' are special cases of *combinations of mean squares* (*CMS*) that have the general form

$$CMS = w_1 V_1 + w_2 V_2 + \ldots + w_k V_k + \ldots + w_K V_K \tag{15.6}$$

where w_k is any real number, and V_k is either a mean square or a variance. Such terms have degrees of freedom that are more complicated than the usual ones. The general form of the degrees of freedom for any combination of mean squares (*CMS*) is

$$df_{CMS} = (CMS)^2 \bigg/ \sum_k (w_k^2 V_k^2 / df_k) \tag{15.7}$$

where df_k are the degrees of freedom associated with the kth mean square. For F_1' in Equation 15.4, the numerator degrees of freedom are $a - 1$. The denominator of F_1' is

$$CMS = (1)(MS_{AB}) + (1)(MS_{SA}) + (-1)(MS_{SAB})$$

and inserting this and the degrees of freedom for each of the three mean squares into Equation 15.7, the denominator *df* for F_1' are

$$df_{denominator} = \frac{(MS_{SA} + MS_{AB} - MS_{SAB})^2}{MS_{SA}^2 / df_{SA} + MS_{AB}^2 / df_{AB} + MS_{SAB}^2 / df_{SAB}} \tag{15.8}$$

For F_2' the appropriate *df* for the numerator are

$$df_{num} = \frac{(MS_A + MS_{SAB})^2}{MS_A^2 / df_A + MS_{SAB}^2 / df_{SAB}} \tag{15.9}$$

and the denominator *df* are

$$df_{den} = \frac{(MS_{AB} + MS_{SA})^2}{MS_{AB}^2 / df_{AB} + MS_{SA}^2 / df_{SA}} \tag{15.10}$$

Simulation studies by Hudson and Krutchkoff (1968) and Davenport and Webster (1973) indicate that F_2' has a slight power advantage over F_1'. However, F_1' involves a simpler numerator and requires calculation of only denominator degrees of freedom. Software capable of calculating quasi-*F* statistics usually uses this form. *TechNote 15_1* on the website illustrates SPSS's approach to an $S \times A \times B$ design with *B* assumed to have random effects.

15.6.4 A Numerical Example

To illustrate the computations described in the preceding subsection, we use a hypothetical data set based on the previously described experiment for testing the effect of type of font on word recognition. Our hypothetical experiment involves eight subjects ($n = 8$), six words ($b = 6$), and two fonts ($a = 2$); time to report the word on a screen is measured in milliseconds. The data are in Table 15.12

Table 15.12 Response times (in msc) to items as a function of font

	Subject	I1	I2	I3	I4	I5	I6	$\overline{Y}_{i1.}$
	1	552	509	487	541	574	554	536
	2	628	735	816	842	614	652	715
	3	590	585	662	372	726	489	571
Font 1	4	496	594	549	547	587	590	561
	5	682	685	631	777	634	789	700
	9	746	775	774	693	817	777	764
	7	743	702	611	632	748	630	678
	8	569	581	588	514	595	623	578
$\overline{Y}_{.1k}$		626	646	640	615	662	638	$\overline{Y}_{.1.} = 638$
	1	713	588	335	624	513	767	590
	2	567	672	887	820	603	587	689
	3	734	598	774	217	1034	615	662
Font 2	4	508	672	644	521	593	598	589
	5	643	652	682	662	841	768	708
	9	890	900	871	717	888	844	852
	7	951	788	576	683	684	606	715
	8	406	672	579	551	775	623	593
$\overline{Y}_{.2k}$		677	693	669	599	741	676	$\overline{Y}_{.2.} = 676$

Note: Font and items are both within-subjects factors.

Table 15.13 ANOVA of the data in Table 15.12

SV	df	Sum of squares	Mean square	F	p
Subjects (S)	7	604,280	86,040		
Font (A)	1	34,846	34,846	11.451	.132
SA	7	32,356	4,622		
Items (B)	5	74,839	14,968	.721	.612
SB	35	726,103	20,746		
AB	5	19,601	3,920	.713	.618
SAB	35	192,451	5,499		

Note: To test A: $F'_1 = MS_A/(MS_{AB} + MS_{SA} - MS_{SAB}) = 34,846/3,043 = 11.451$. The error degrees of freedom are $(MS_{AB} + MS_{SA} - MS_{SAB})^2/[(MS_{AB}^2/df_{AB}) + (MS_{SA}^2/df_{SA}) + (MS_{SAB}^2/df_{SAB})] = 1.33$. B and AB are tested against SB and SAB, respectively.

and are also available on the website in the files labeled *Table 15_12 Font_S* (cases are subjects) and *Table 15_12 Font_I* (cases are items). The ANOVA results are presented in Table 15.13. Referring to the formulas for *EMS* for the case in which subjects and B are assumed to have random effects (Table 15.11), we find that the B and AB sources are tested against their respective interactions with subjects; only the A source requires a quasi-F test. The note at the bottom of Table 15.13 defines the appropriate error term and corresponding degrees of freedom for this test. Although the F-value for the test of font is 11.45, it is based on only 1 and 1.33 *df*, so the effect of font is not significant by this test.

The calculation of the *df* for a combination of mean squares is cumbersome. Fortunately, some software packages will calculate the quasi-*F* statistic and the degrees of freedom. In the case of repeated-measures designs, however, the data spreadsheet must be organized differently than for the more conventional design with all fixed-effects factors. The interested reader should consult *TechNote 15.1* at the website for a description of the input and analysis in SPSS.

15.6.5 Some Other Issues in Using Quasi-*F* Tests

The construction of quasi-*F* ratios provides a general solution to the problem of testing effects in designs with multiple random-effects factors. However, researchers often encounter an obstacle to this approach. In many studies, observations are missing and therefore not all $S \times A \times B$ combinations are available. If so, it will be impossible to calculate MS_{SAB} and, therefore, the quasi-*F* statistic cannot be calculated. A conservative remedy in this situation is to calculate a minimum quasi-*F* (*minF'*; Clark, 1973; Forster & Dickinson, 1976) :

$$minF' = MS_A/(MS_{AB} + MS_{SA}) \tag{15.11}$$

When observations are missing, *minF'* and the denominator *df* are calculated as a function of F_1 and F_2; the formulas are presented in Box 15.2 and a derivation is presented in *TechNote 15_2* at the book's website. The test based on *minF'* is somewhat conservative because it lacks an estimate of MS_{SAB}.

Box 15.2 Calculating the Minimum Quasi-*F* Statistic (*minF'*)

1. Find the average of the scores in each $S \times A$ combination; presumably there will be a few scores in each combination even if some values are missing. Compute

$$F_1 = MS_A/MS_{SA}$$

2. Find the average of the scores in each $A \times B$ combination. Compute

$$F_2 = MS_A/MS_{AB}.$$

3. Compute

$$minF' = \frac{F_1 F_2}{F_1 + F_2}$$

and

$$df_{error} = \frac{(F_1 + F_2)^2}{F_1^2/df_{AB} + F_2^2/df_{SA}}$$

The numerator *df* are just $a - 1$.

What about the effects of violations of the sphericity assumption upon the distribution of *F'*? Somewhat surprisingly, Maxwell and Bray (1986) have found evidence that nonsphericity does not inflate the Type 1 error rate for *F'*. Their article presents an interesting discussion of the reasons for this.

Finally, a comment on the power of quasi-*F* tests. We know that the number of subjects in an experiment is an important determinant of the power of statistical tests. This is because the more subjects, the less error there is in sample means as estimates of the corresponding population means.

When a researcher is planning an experiment that will necessitate quasi-F tests, the number of subjects remains an important design consideration. However, the number of items sampled in the experiment also becomes a consideration. Interactions of A with both subjects and items will contribute to the error variance against which treatment effects are evaluated. Therefore, there should be enough observations to have sufficient degrees of freedom associated with both subjects and items to ensure powerful tests of A. An added benefit of including a large number of subjects and items in a design is evidence that the distribution of F' more closely approximates to that of F as a, b, and n increase.

15.7 FIXED OR RANDOM EFFECTS?

It should be clear by now that designating effects as fixed or random has important implications for significance testing, as well as for the degree to which we can generalize our results. We will soon discover that the designation also has direct implications for parameter estimation (e.g., effect size). Therefore, we need to further consider the decision about classifying effects.

The decision to classify a variable as having fixed or random effects is not always a simple one. At one extreme, we have variables that clearly should be viewed as having fixed effects. The levels of the variable have been intentionally selected for inclusion in the experiment and, because of the way in which they have been selected, there is no basis for viewing them as a random sample of levels from a population of levels. This class includes most manipulated variables such as the type of distortion or the orientation of the photo in the Murray et al. (2000) experiment, or observed characteristics of individuals such as gender or clinical category. It also would include a variable such as seasons because the four seasons exhaust the population of possible seasons.

At the other extreme, we have random sampling from some well-defined population. This is rarely realized in practice and it is therefore difficult to determine the population to which our results can be generalized. Can we reasonably view our subjects as a random sample of adults, college students, college students interested in psychology, or college students who attend the particular university in which the study was run? The answer depends on the sampling process but also on the particular study. In studies of sensory processes like visual acuity, we might generalize to the population of adults having normal vision. In studies of human learning, we might define the population more narrowly, reserving judgment as to whether our conclusions will hold for populations having a markedly different average level of ability from that characterizing the institution in which our study was run. When in doubt, generalizations should be restricted to the more narrowly defined population.

Even though the population is rarely as well defined as we would like, it should be clear from the preceding comments that we do view subjects as a random-effects variable. Our justification is that other individuals are provided an equal opportunity to participate and might well serve if replications of the experiment were run.

Classifying stimuli such as words and pictures presents greater difficulty. For many experiments, we can argue on much the same grounds that we presented in discussing subjects that stimuli are a random sample from a (possibly ill-defined) population of potential items. That is, the specific stimuli selected were not chosen in such a way that they were the only items with an opportunity to be included in the experiment; rather, there were many other items that had an equal opportunity of being included under the sampling procedure used. In many other experiments, however, the choice of stimuli is so constrained that the items selected for the experiment virtually exhaust the stimuli that meet the sampling constraints. In studies involving responses to words, for example, restrictions are often placed on the grammatical class, length in both syllables and letters, familiarity, and number of associates of each word. The experimenter may find it difficult to meet those restrictions. Under such conditions, it is not clear that stimuli should be treated as having random effects. Two rough guidelines may be helpful. First, under the existing constraints, could independent investigators produce other samples of items? Assuming there is a reasonably large population of items, the second question is: Was there an equal likelihood that all members of the population could be included in the study? If the answer to this question is also positive, then it is reasonable to treat the stimuli as having random effects with all that this implies for our data analyses and the scope of our conclusions.

15.8 UNDERSTANDING THE PATTERN OF MEANS IN REPEATED-MEASURES DESIGNS

Table 15.4 reveals that the orientation of pictures of faces (A), the type of distortion (B), and the AB interaction all have very significant effects on bizarreness ratings. Ordinarily, to better understand the source of effects, we follow these overall F tests with tests and confidence intervals that more precisely target differences among the means. We might begin by testing comparisons among the marginal means. Comparisons of marginal means are of most interest when there clearly is no interaction, because then there is no evidence that the effects of one factor vary as a function of the level of the other factor. When an interaction is present, or even when there is some reason to anticipate an interaction prior to data collection, other tests should be of greater interest. Tests of simple effects, such as the difference between the B_2 and B_3 means at the A_2 orientation, might be helpful in understanding the pattern of means. Other possibilities include tests of interaction contrasts. For example, we may decide to test whether the difference between the B_2 and B_3 means is significantly greater at A_2 than at A_1.

In this section, we illustrate approaches to analyzing marginal means to understand main effects, and cell means to understand interactions. We first consider examples from repeated-measures designs, and then examples from mixed designs. We also discuss contrasts in designs with multiple random-effects factors. Finally, we consider the control of familywise error rate (FWE). Before dealing with the details of these analyses, we wish to emphasize that there are no definite answers to the questions of which analyses to carry out, and how to control the error rate. As we discussed in Chapter 10, we may have some reason before the data are collected to focus interest on differences among specific cell means, or to compare some subset of curves in a trend analysis. Perhaps more commonly, we want to analyze a pattern of means that was not anticipated. In these circumstances, we will suggest some systematic approaches that might be used to understand the pattern, or researchers may design specific contrasts to summarize the pattern. Such considerations will influence the choice of contrasts and the alpha-level set for each test.

15.8.1 Comparing Marginal Means

In a multi-factor design, the main effect of a factor may be of interest if its interpretation is not qualified by the presence of an interaction. In that event, the researcher will want to analyze the pattern of marginal means. Although complex contrasts can certainly be constructed if theoretical considerations or the observed pattern of means warrant, researchers most often compute pairwise comparisons among the marginal means. As we discussed in Section 14.10.1, the safest approach to testing any contrast in a repeated-measures design is to use an error term based only on the data involved in the contrast (cf. Boik, 1981). Therefore, if we decided to carry out paired comparisons on the marginal means of B for the data in Table 15.3, our error term would *not* be the SB term from the overall ANOVA presented in Table 15.4; rather, the error term would be the SB interaction based only on the two levels of B involved in the comparison. A simple way in which to conduct each comparison is to use the option available in most statistical software to select only the two levels of B you wish to include in the analysis, and then perform the usual ANOVA on that subset of data. The B source of variance in the resulting table will reflect the difference between the marginal means of the scores at the two levels of B selected for comparison, and the SB error term will be based on only those scores.

What should be our criterion for evaluating the contrasts we conduct? If k differences were selected *a priori* and were the only ones tested, we would set the *FWE* criterion at $.05/k$. If all pairwise comparisons are of interest, k would be the number of possible pairwise comparisons. In that case, the criterion *FWE* is $.05/3$ for our example.

One other question that arises is what our criterion should be if we test comparisons among both the B marginal means and among the A marginal means. As we discussed in Chapter 10, we consider comparisons among the levels of a variable to constitute a family; therefore, if we were to do the three pairwise comparisons of the A marginal means and also the three comparisons of the B marginal means, each test would be carried out at the $.05/3$ level.

15.8.2 Comparing Cell Means

We are often interested in the pattern of cell means, particularly if we have predicted an interaction or observed one after the initial ANOVA. One common approach to analyzing cell means is to conduct all pairwise comparisons of levels of A within each level of B, or vice versa. For the example of Table 15.4, we might compare the three levels of distortion within each level of orientation. There are nine possible such tests based on Table 15.3; i.e., at each level of A, we compare B_1 vs B_2, B_1 vs B_3, and B_2 vs B_3. If we wish to keep the *FWE* at or under $.05$ for the full set of tests, we would require an alpha level of $.05/9$, approximately $.005$, for significance of any one comparison (i.e., the Dunn–Bonferroni method). We selected *Compare Means*, then *Paired-Samples t Test* from SPSS's *Analyze* menu; then we selected the nine pairs we wanted to test. Only two of these comparisons were not significant at the $.005$ level: $A_1B_2 - A_1B_3$ ($p = .546$) and $A_2B_2 - A_2B_3$ ($p = .025$). Note that these are the two smallest differences in Fig. 15.1. This accounts for the interaction; it apparently is largely due to the lack of a difference in the distortion effects of B_2 and B_3 at A_1 and possibly at A_2. These results should focus the researcher on the question of why these effects are so different from the others that were tested.

Before turning to an alternative analysis of the cell means, it is useful to consider the nature of the t tests, and also provide an example of a confidence interval. Following are results for two of the nine contrasts in the SPSS output:

	Mean	Std. deviation	Std. error mean	95% Confidence interval of the difference		t	df	Sig. (2-tailed)
				Lower	Upper			
$A_2B_3 - A_2B_2$	0.833	0.642	0.262	0.159	1.508	3.177	5	.025
$A_3B_3 - A_3B_2$	2.053	0.950	0.388	1.056	3.050	5.294	5	.003

There are several points to note: First, the standard deviations of the differences are different for the two tests. This is because each difference is tested against a measure of the variability of that difference, not against an error term from the ANOVA (Table 15.4). Second, the test is conservative not only because of the criterion alpha (i.e., .05/9) but also because the degrees of freedom are $(n-1)$ or 5 in this example. Third, the confidence interval does not take into consideration the fact that we have nine tests. The appropriate CI should be based on the t required for significance at the .005 level, not the .05 level. From Appendix Table C.3, the critical t value at the .005 level (two-tailed) with 5 df is 4.773. Therefore, the CI bounds for the comparison between the A_2B_2 and A_2B_3 means ($\overline{Y}_{23} - \overline{Y}_{22}$) are $0.833 \pm (0.262)(4.773) = -0.418$ and 2.084.

15.8.3 Tests of Interaction Contrasts

A more direct way of understanding the reason for the significant AB interaction in Table 15.4 might be to test interaction contrasts. In Fig. 15.1, we note that $\overline{Y}_{13} - \overline{Y}_{12}$ is smaller than either $\overline{Y}_{23} - \overline{Y}_{22}$ or $\overline{Y}_{33} - \overline{Y}_{32}$. This suggests that we focus on these interaction contrasts: $\psi_1 = [(4.81 - 5.02) - (5.41 - 4.58)]$ and $\psi_2 = [(4.81 - 5.02) - (5.47 - 3.41)]$. One way to test these two interaction contrasts is to use the *Transform* option in SPSS to create two new "scores" for each subject: $(A_2B_3 - A_2B_2) - (A_1B_3 - A_1B_2)$ and $(A_3B_3 - A_3B_2) - (A_1B_3 - A_1B_2)$. We then select the *One-Sample t Test* option (under *Analyze/Compare Means*). For ψ_1, $t = 1.87$ and for ψ_2, $t = 4.917$.[2] If we had selected the two interaction contrasts before viewing the data, we would have used the Dunn–Bonferroni procedure to control the FWE at .05 by evaluating each contrast at alpha at $.05/2 = .025$. However, having determined that these were of interest after viewing Fig. 15.1 and noting that there are nine possible 2×2 contrasts, we set alpha at $.05/9 = .005$ (approximately). With 5 df, the critical value of t is 4.773 and therefore only the test of ψ_2 has a significant result. The AB interaction result in Table 15.4 seems to largely reflect this interaction embedded within the larger design.

15.8.4 Tests of Trends

In the current example, the factor of orientation (A) is a quantitative variable (i.e., three, evenly spaced degrees of rotation); thus, a particularly useful approach to understanding the face-rating data is to test a set of polynomial contrasts on orientation. These contrasts are easily obtained in SPSS in the *General Linear Model: Repeated-Measures* program by choosing the "contrasts" option, selecting the variable of orientation, and requesting "polynomial." The result is the trend analysis presented in Table 15.14, in which each source of variance is partitioned into a linear and quadratic component. The $lin(A)$ term provides a test of the null hypothesis that the average of the linear components (i.e., slopes) of the three curves in Fig. 15.1 does not differ from zero. The error term for $MS_{lin(A)}$ is the $S \times lin(A)$ term in Table 15.14. Because the test result is not significant at the .05 level, we cannot reject the null hypothesis. Note that the $quad(A)$ source of variance is significant, indicating that the average curvilinear component of the three curves in Fig. 15.1 does differ from zero. However, the important observation concerns the AB interaction. When the AB interaction variance is partitioned into its linear and quadratic components, we find that the $B \times lin(A)$ term is significant, but the $B \times quad(A)$ term is not. The significant $B \times lin(A)$ term indicates that

---

[2] The same results can be obtained by selecting only the cells involved in the 2×2 interaction contrast and performing an ANOVA. For example, the F test of the AB interaction for the ψ_1 contrast yields $F = 3.497$, the square of 1.870. However, using interaction contrast scores permitted us to test several interaction contrasts at once, and without the extraneous output that is part of the output of the repeated-measures ANOVA.

Table 15.14   ANOVA of the data of Table 15.3 with polynomial contrasts

Source	df	SS	MS	F	p	G–G	H–F
						\multicolumn{2}{Significance}	
S	5	.544	.109				
A (Orientation)	2	1.749	.874	9.23	.005	.006	.005
$lin(A)$	1	.606	.606	5.77	.061		
$quad(A)$	1	1.143	1.143	13.54	.014		
SA	10	.947	.095				
$S \times lin(A)$	5	.525	.105				
$S \times quad(A)$	5	.422	.084				
B (Distortion)	2	136.554	68.277	302.56	.000	.000	.000
SB	10	2.257	.226				
AB	4	8.560	2.140	7.75	.001	.011	.003
$B \times lin(A)$	2	8.543	4.272	12.514	.002	.003	.002
$B \times quad(A)$	2	.017	.086	.040	.961	.890	.915
SAB	20	5.522	.276				
$SB \times lin(A)$	10	3.413	.341				
$SB \times quad(A)$	10	2.109	.211				
Total	53	156.133					

Note: G–G refers to the Greenhouse–Geisser correction for nonsphericity and *H–F* refers to the Huynh–Feldt correction.

the best-fitting lines to the B_1, B_2, and B_3 functions in Fig. 15.1 have different slopes; the slopes for B_1 and B_3 are slightly positive whereas the slope for B_2 is decidedly negative. The non-significant $B \times quad(A)$ term suggests that the degrees of curvature of the three functions do not differ.

From the perspective of the trend analysis, the main contribution to the overall *AB* interaction seems to be a difference in the slopes of the three curves. This is consistent with our earlier conclusion that the difference between the B_2 and B_3 means is greater at A_3 than at A_1. We could pursue the comparison of trends further by performing three analyses, each of which includes only a pair of the levels of *B*. We would find, for example, that the difference between the slopes of the B_2 and B_3 curves [$B \times A(linear)$] is quite significant; $F_{1,5} = 24.181$.

15.8.5 Mixed Designs

Tests of contrasts in designs involving both between- and within-subjects factors follow the approaches previously established. When analyzing effects of between-subjects factors, the methods available are those described for completely randomized designs in Chapters 10 and 11. Software packages routinely offer procedures for conducting contrasts to understand main effects of between-subjects factors. For example, users of SPSS may request "options" in the *GLM/Repeated-Measures* module and have a choice of several multiple comparison procedures. The procedures each report all pairwise comparisons, but use different methods to control *FWE*. The researcher should be warned, however, that some of the options are not wise choices because they lack power as methods for controlling error rate across the set of all pairwise comparisons; e.g., Scheffé is not a good choice of procedures in this context.

If a researcher is interested in analyzing the main effects of a within-subjects factor or an interaction involving a within-subjects factor, the available options are the same as for any repeated-measures design. Most software packages will perform trend (polynomial) analyses on quantitative within-subjects factors, or pairwise comparisons of means at different levels of within-subjects factors. In addition, as described in the preceding subsections, interaction contrasts may be performed to analyze how a within-subjects comparison (e.g., polynomial or pairwise) varies over levels of a between-subjects factor. As we discussed in the context of repeated-measures designs, contrasts should be planned and the Dunn–Bonferroni procedure used to control *FWE*. If contrasts are unplanned, the control of the *FWE* with Dunn–Bonferroni is justified if the set of contrasts consists of all possible contrasts of the same form (i.e., all pairwise or all embedded 2×2 interactions).

15.8.6 Designs with Multiple Random-Effects Factors

In the examples of contrasts presented thus far, we have dealt only with designs in which all factors have fixed effects except subjects. When a second random-effects factor is included in a design, we found that tests of effects of interest often necessitated use of quasi-*F* ratios. This is because when both subjects and items are considered random effects, terms must be tested against both subject and item variability simultaneously. Similarly, when we conduct contrasts within designs in which both subjects and items have random effects, the error terms to test the contrasts must also take into account subject and item variability, so quasi-*F* tests are still in order.

Table 15.12 presented an example of a repeated-measures design with eight subjects, six words, and two fonts where the task was to recognize words as quickly as possible. Our interest in this experiment was whether the type of font influenced word recognition. The test of font required a quasi-*F* ratio where the denominator was based on a combination of three mean squares: ($MS_{S \times Font}$ $+ MS_{Words \times Font} - MS_{S \times Words \times Font}$). Imagine an extension of this simple design where four types of fonts are tested, instead of just two. Also, suppose that we included three levels of illumination of the computer screen to manipulate the visual conditions under which the words must be perceived. Thus, the extended design includes two factors that have random effects (i.e., subjects and the within-subjects factor of words) as well as two within-subjects factors that have fixed effects (i.e., font and illumination). Our substantive interest is in the effects of type of font and level of illumination on performance in the word-recognition task. Tests of effects of font, illumination, and their interaction would still require quasi-*F* ratios, as in the simpler design. If significant *F* tests resulted, we would surely want to make detailed comparisons between specific fonts, or levels of illumination, or combinations of fonts and illumination levels. How are we to carry out such comparisons?

As before, our general recommendation is that for any given comparison that a researcher wishes to make, only the data from the conditions to be compared should be included in the analysis. For example, if the researcher wished to compare the results for Gothic font with Times Roman font, data on those two fonts would be included, but the data for the other two fonts would be excluded from the analysis. An ANOVA would be conducted specifying two levels of font; all levels of the other variables (i.e., subjects, words, illumination) would be fully represented in the analysis. An *F* test of font would be conducted as in the overall ANOVA; the mean square for font would be tested against the combination ($MS_{S \times Font} + MS_{Words \times Font} - MS_{S \times Words \times Font}$). A significant result would allow the researcher to conclude that Gothic and Times Roman differed in their legibility.

It is important to understand that the combination of mean squares that is the error term is the same as in the ANOVA on the complete data set, but its value will differ because it is based on a subset of the data. If the sphericity assumption is met in the ANOVA on the complete data set, that would justify use of the error term from the overall analysis. In our experience, however, the sphericity assumption is frequently violated in the overall analysis.

15.8.7 Control of *FWE*

Control of *FWE* should always be a consideration when conducting multiple statistical tests. However, we saw in Chapter 14 that such control is complicated in repeated-measures designs by the likelihood that the sphericity assumption will be violated. We recommended that researchers generally plan not to use overall error terms from the ANOVA when conducting contrasts on subsets of conditions involving repeated-measures. Instead, tests of contrasts should be conducted with only the data from the conditions involved in the contrast. Such an approach eliminates from consideration many of the procedures used to control *FWE* when conducting contrasts involving between-subjects factors. Thus, our recommendation is that researchers plan contrasts or use a principled approach to define a set of contrasts (e.g., use a contrast option offered by the software program), and use the Bonferroni procedure to control *FWE*. In our example of analyzing performance changes over time in the experiment on algebra instruction, the use of polynomial contrasts to test the linear, quadratic, and cubic components of the performance functions, we would require significance of each test at the .05/3 = .0167 level under the Bonferroni procedure.

15.9 EFFECT SIZE

15.9.1 The *S* × *A* × *B* Design

Common measures of effect size include partial eta-squared and partial omega-squared. However, as was noted in Chapter 14, both measures suffer from the limitation that their denominators change across designs. Because it is desirable to have measures of effect size that are comparable across designs, we have argued for the use of general eta-squared and general omega-squared as measures of effect size (Olejnik & Algina, 2003).

The denominator of general eta-squared is the sum of several sums of squares terms; namely, SS_{Effect} plus the sum of every SS term that includes subject variability. For example, in the $S \times A \times B$ design, general eta-squared for A is computed as:

$$\eta_g^2 = \frac{SS_A}{SS_A + SS_S + SS_{SA} + SS_{SB} + SS_{SAB}} = \frac{SS_A}{SS_{Total} - SS_B - SS_{AB}} \tag{15.12}$$

However, as noted in Chapter 14, general eta-squared tends to overestimate the proportion of population variance due to a variable. For that reason, we prefer general omega-squared as a measure of effect size.

The definition of general omega-squared (ω_g^2) for the $S \times A \times B$ design is similar to that in Chapter 14 for the one-factor within-subjects ($S \times A$) design. For example, if A and B are extrinsic factors, we define ω_g^2 as

$$\omega_g^2(A) = \frac{\sigma_A^2}{\sigma_e^2 + \sigma_A^2 + \sigma_S^2 + \sigma_{SA}^2 + \sigma_{SB}^2 + \sigma_{SAB}^2} \tag{15.13}$$

Unfortunately, estimating $\omega_g^2(A)$ presents a problem because the interaction terms cannot be estimated from the expected mean squares in Table 15.2. An approximate solution is obtained if we assume that $\sigma_{SAB}^2 = 0$. With this modification, the *EMS* of Table 15.2 provide estimates of the

Table 15.15 Estimates of variance components based on the EMS of Table 15.2

Source	Estimator
A	$(a-1)(MS_A - MS_{SA})/abn$
S	$(MS_S - MS_{SAB})/ab$
SA	$(MS_{SA} - MS_{SAB})/b$
SB	$(MS_{SB} - MS_{SAB})/a$
SAB	MS_{SAB}

Note: Estimates rest on the assumption that $\sigma^2_{SAB} = 0$.

variances in Equation 15.13. Those estimates are presented in Table 15.15. Substituting into Equation 15.13, multiplying numerator and denominator by abn, and collecting all the MS_{SAB} terms, we have

$$\hat{\omega}^2_g(A) = \frac{(a-1)(MS_A - MS_{SA})}{(a-1)(MS_A - MS_{SA}) + n[(MS_S + aMS_{SA} + bMS_{SB}) + (ab - 1 - a - b)MS_{SAB}]} \quad (15.14)$$

To the extent that $\sigma^2_{SAB} > 0$, the expected value of the denominator of Equation 15.14 will underestimate the denominator of Equation 15.13, and therefore will overestimate $\omega^2_g(A)$; the denominator that is estimated is the same as in Equation 15.13 except that $(1 - 1/a - 1/b - 1/ab)\sigma^2_{SAB}$ replaces σ^2_{SAB}. Note that the error of estimation is smaller when a and b are larger.

What if B represents a random-effects factor? Such factors are usually extrinsic; for example, stimuli in a perception experiment or items in a psycholinguistic study. Therefore, Equation 15.13 still applies, but the estimates of population variances will differ from those on which Equation 15.14 is based. Still assuming that MS_{SAB} estimates only error variance (i.e., $\sigma^2_{SAB} = 0$), estimates of the components of Equation 15.13 can be derived from Table 15.10. We leave the formula as an exercise.

15.9.2 Omega-Squared in the Mixed Design

Estimation of ω^2_g in the mixed design follows the approach taken in the $S \times A \times B$ design. For convenient reference, Table 15.16 presents the formulas for A, B, and AB for a design in which subjects are nested within levels of A and are tested at all levels of B, where A and B are both assumed to have fixed effects.

Table 15.16 Estimates of general omega-squared (ω^2_g) for a design with one between-subjects (A) and one within-subjects factor (calculations are based on the data of Table 15.5)

Source	Formula for the estimate	Estimate
A	$\dfrac{(a-1)(MS_A - MS_{SA})}{(a-1)(MS_A - MS_{SA}) + an(MS_{S/A} - MS_{B \times S/A}) + abnMS_{B \times S/A}}$	.356
B	$\dfrac{(b-1)(MS_B - MS_{B \times S/A})}{(b-1)(MS_B - MS_{B \times S/A}) + an(MS_{S/A} - MS_{B \times S/A}) + abnMS_{B \times S/A}}$	.206
AB	$\dfrac{(a-1)(b-1)(MS_{AB} - MS_{B \times S/A})}{(a-1)(b-1)(MS_{AB} - MS_{B \times S/A}) + an(MS_{S/A} - MS_{B \times S/A}) + abnMS_{B \times S/A}}$	.059

Note: Estimates are based on the assumption that $\sigma^2_{BS/A} = 0$.

The right-most column of the table contains numerical estimates of ω_g^2 for the A, B, and AB sources. The definition of general omega-squared is exemplified by the formula for the A source:

$$\omega_g^2(A) = \frac{\sigma_A^2}{\sigma_A^2 + \sigma_{S/A}^2 + \sigma_e^2 + \sigma_{B \times S/A}^2} \tag{15.15}$$

We estimated σ_A^2 from the expected mean squares in Table 15.7. As can be seen in Table 15.16, our estimates of the remaining denominator components rest on the assumption that $\sigma_{B \times S/A}^2 = 0$. If $\sigma_{B \times S/A}^2 > 0$, the expectation of the denominator includes $[(b-1)/b]\sigma_{B \times S/A}^2$ instead of $\sigma_{B \times S/A}^2$. If B is a random-effects factor, Equation 15.15 still applies, but the expected mean squares are slightly different from those in Table 15.7 and the estimates of the population variances consequently differ from those in Table 15.16. Estimates of population variances were presented in Table 15.11 for a design in which there are two within-subjects factors, one of which is assumed to have random effects.

15.10 *A PRIORI* POWER CALCULATIONS

15.10.1 The $S \times A \times B$ Design

Suppose that we are planning a two-factor, repeated-measures design and we want to determine how many subjects to include in the procedure. The design will yield tests of the main effects of A and B, and of their interaction. If one of these tests is of particular interest, we might focus on it in calculating the number of subjects we need to achieve good power to test that effect. Or if one effect is expected to be smaller than the others, power computations based on that effect will ensure that the power of the other two tests will be at least as good.

Power calculations are readily performed with G*Power 3. If we wish to compute the required sample size to test the main effect of B, we select *ANOVA: Repeated-measures, within factors* and specify that we want to do an *a priori* power analysis. Several items of information must be provided. Suppose that we assume a small effect of .10, set alpha at .05, we want .90 power to detect an effect, and our design includes three levels of A and four levels of B. There is only one "group" of subjects because there are no between-subjects factors; there are four "repetitions" or levels of B. We will assume that the average correlation of scores between conditions is .5, and that the sphericity assumption is violated and $\varepsilon = .8$. For this combination of values, the required sample size is 210 subjects. This is quite large but if we are willing to sacrifice some power and allow for a larger effect, perhaps by setting power to .8 and the effect size to .25 (medium by Cohen's standards), the required N is only 27.

15.10.2 The Mixed Design

Power calculations can also be performed for mixed designs using G*Power 3. For example, suppose we are planning an experiment in which there will be three groups (A) of n subjects, each of whom will be tested in three different conditions (B). We decide that large effects of A are important to detect and therefore set $f = .4$. We want power = .8 to detect the effects of A if the null hypothesis is false. From previous research, we have estimated the within-subjects correlation coefficient to be .6. How many subjects will we need, assuming $\alpha = .05$? We select the *a priori* type of power analysis and *repeated-measures, between factors* option. After we enter the parameters, G*Power returns a value of 48 for the total sample size, or 16 subjects in each of the three groups. The actual power is .807.

We might ask how much power a sample size of 48 would give us to test the B factor, again assuming a large effect of .4. This time we select the *post hoc* power, select the *repeated-measures, within factors* option, and enter our parameters and 48 for the total sample size. Assuming sphericity (i.e., set $\varepsilon = 1$), power is 1. If we had selected the *a priori* option with the same parameters and asked what n was needed for power to equal .8, we would have needed only 12 subjects, 4 in each group.

The difference between the ns needed to achieve power in testing the between- and within-subjects factors reflects the fact that variability is greater between subjects than within subjects. Furthermore, this depends on the size of the correlation of scores across repeated-measures. As ρ increases, the n required to achieve a particular level of power to test the between-subjects factor, A, increases. In contrast, as ρ increases, the n required to achieve a particular level of power to test B decreases. This can be seen by substituting values of $\hat{\rho}$ into the G*Power screens for the between and within factors.

15.11 SUMMARY

Chapter 15 extended the repeated-measures designs of the previous chapter by inserting additional within-subjects factors. It also introduced mixed designs involving one or more between-subjects factors in addition to the within-subjects factors. Within this context, we covered the following topics.

- We first developed the structural model and ANOVA for multi-factor, repeated-measures designs assuming that all factors other than subjects had fixed effects.
- We then developed the structural model and ANOVA for mixed designs; i.e., designs with both within-subjects and between-subjects factors. We again assumed that all factors had fixed effects except subjects.
- We then modified the designs by assuming that one within-subjects factor, most commonly items, had random effects. Because this complicates the expected mean squares, we provided rules for generating the *EMS* that apply to many different designs.
- When within-subjects factors have random effects, consideration of the *EMS* reveals that tests of main and interaction effects against any single mean square will result in inflated Type 1 error rates. We considered several ways of addressing this problem, and concluded that a quasi-F ratio provided the most defensible solution. Because the decision as to whether a variable has fixed or random effects has important consequences for the data analysis, and for whether conclusions can be generalized beyond the subjects and items in the experiment, we discussed the considerations that should go into such decisions.
- Having established the relevant considerations for identifying multi-factor designs with repeated-measures and F tests of effects within such designs, we discussed contrasts within the designs and control of *FWE* when doing multiple contrasts.
- We extended measures of general omega-squared to multi-factor repeated-measures and mixed designs, noting that unbiased estimates of effect size are often not possible because not all variance components can be estimated.
- Finally, we discussed power computations in repeated-measures and mixed designs.

The designs considered so far in this book undergo further modifications in many experiments. In the next chapter, we will consider some frequently encountered variations of the designs we have so far discussed.

EXERCISES

15.1   Ten randomly sampled clerical workers (W) are observed on each of five randomly sampled occasions (O) with each of four word-processing programs (P). The programs have been selected for comparison purposes to decide which ones to buy for the entire work force. A score is obtained for each worker with each processor on each occasion. An analysis of variance is then carried out. The results are:

Source	df	MS
W	9	2580
P	3	2610
O	4	690
WP	27	330
WO	36	370
PO	12	640
WPO	108	320

   (a) Write out the *EMS* for the above table, first specifying which factors have random effects and which have fixed effects.
   (b) Calculate a quasi-*F* test of the P source. Let $\alpha = .05$.
   (c) Calculate an alternative to the quasi-*F* test of P. What is assumed in doing this test?

15.2   In research on personality, there has been much discussion of the relative importance of traits and situations. The basic research design involves n subjects and t tasks representing a random sample of situations. Measures are obtained for each subject (S_i) on each task (T_j) on each of b randomly sampled occasions (O_k).
   (a) Assuming the completely additive model, $Y_{ijk} = \mu + \eta_i + \alpha_j + \beta_k + \varepsilon_{ijk}$, present expressions for the *SV*, *df*, and *EMS*.
   (b) Present expressions for estimates of the variance components for subjects, tasks, and occasions.
   (c) Assume we have evidence from previous studies that subjects and tasks interact. State the revised model, the revised ANOVA table (*SV*, *df*, and *EMS*), and revised estimates of the variance components.
   (d) Assuming the model of part (c), state the formula for estimating $\omega_g^2 (S)$.

15.3   In the following data set, B represents statements which are rated before (A_1) and after (A_2) reading a persuasive communication.

	A_1			A_2		
	B_1	B_2	B_3	B_1	B_2	B_3
S_1	2	3	4	8	9	8
S_2	3	3	4	6	7	9
S_3	7	4	6	4	9	9
S_4	2	2	4	7	9	8
S_5	1	2	2	5	4	5

(a) Assume B is fixed and do an $S \times A \times B$ ANOVA.
(b) Find the mean at A_1 and at A_2 for each subject. Now do an ANOVA for this $S \times A$ design. How does this compare with the results in part (a)?
(c) Now assume B is a random-effects variable. Present the *EMS*.
(d) Test the A source of variance under the model of part (c).
(e) What is the problem with the ANOVA of part (b) when B has random effects?

15.4 The design is an $S \times A \times B$ with $n = 10$, $a = 3$, and $b = 5$. The following table summarizes part of the results.

Source	df	MS
S	9	250
A	2	64
B	4	71
SA	18	24
SB	36	32
AB	8	44
SAB	72	10

Find the values of the F ratios and p values for A, B, and AB in the following conditions:
(a) Both A and B have fixed effects.
(b) A has fixed effects but B represents randomly sampled items.

15.5 Find the values of general ω^2 for A in the following conditions (assume the table in Exercise 15.4 and that SAB estimates only error variance):
(a) Both A and B have fixed effects and are both extrinsic factors.
(b) Both A and B are extrinsic factors but now B represents randomly sampled items.
(c) A is an extrinsic factor, B is an intrinsic factor (e.g., personality type), and B has random effects.

15.6 In Section 15.8.3, we described two tests of interactions embedded within the design of Table 15.3.
(a) Are those two contrasts orthogonal to each other? Explain why or why not.
(b) The ψ_1 contrast may be represented by the following weights on the nine cell means:

A_1B_1	A_1B_2	A_1B_3	A_2B_1	A_2B_2	A_2B_3	A_3B_1	A_3B_2	A_3B_3
0	−1	1	0	1	−1	0	0	0

Ignore all cells having zero weights. Find the sum of squares on 3 *df* for the remaining four cells (A_1B_2, A_1B_3, A_2B_2, and A_2B_3). (Remember that $n = 6$.)
(c) Construct two contrasts that are orthogonal to ψ_1. From the means in Table 15.3, find the sum of squares associated with each, add the three terms, and compare your total with your answer in part (b).

15.7 Consider the following data set; A is a between-subjects factor, and B is a within-subjects factor.

		B_1	B_2	B_3
	S_{11}	23	16	12
A_1	S_{12}	27	17	14
	S_{13}	22	12	9
	S_{21}	32	27	22
A_2	S_{22}	33	25	18
	S_{23}	34	32	23

(a) Present the complete ANOVA table with all numerical results; assume that A and B both have fixed effects.

(b) Find the mean score for each subject. You now have a one-factor, completely randomized design. Perform an ANOVA using the mean scores as the data. (i) How does the F test of A compare with that calculated in part (a)? (ii) How does MS_A in this analysis compare with that obtained in part (a)? Explain the relation.

(c) $SS_{SB/A}$ is equivalent to the result of calculating the $S \times B$ sum of squares separately at each level of A and then summing the a terms. To demonstrate this, ignore the A_2 data and calculate the sum of squares for $S \times B$ at A_1 (SS_{SB/A_1}). Do the same thing at A_2 and check the sum of the two terms against $SS_{SB/A}$ calculated in part (a). Confirm that $MS_{SB/A}$ is the average of the two $S \times B$ mean squares.

15.8 A_1 and A_2 in Exercise 15.7 might have been two litters of three animals; in that case, we would assume that A has random effects. Assume that B represents trials and is a fixed-effect variable.

(a) State the expected mean squares for the various sources of variance.

(b) Recalculate any F ratios that are not the same as in Exercise 15.7.

15.9 Now assume that A_1 and A_2 in Exercise 15.7 have fixed effects and the levels of B correspond to three problems sampled randomly from some very large population of problems.

(a) Present the EMS under this model.

(b) Recalculate F tests where necessary.

15.10 An investigator interested in children's attention to violent acts on television runs an experiment with 120 subjects: half males and half females (sex, X) at each of three age levels (age, A). Each child views six scenes differing with respect to the level of violence (V, three levels) and the type of character; half the scenes involve animal cartoon characters and the other involve human characters (C, two levels). The dependent variable is a measure of attention during presentation of the scene.

(a) State the SV, df, and error terms for this design.

(b) In an alternative design, each of the 120 children might view only three scenes involving only one type of character; C would be a between-subjects variable. Present the SV, df, and EMS for this design. What tests will be affected by this change in design? In what way?

(c) Suppose the children are available for only short periods of time but the investigator has access to large numbers of subjects. What are the advantages and disadvantages of a design in which each subject is tested only once in some combination of V and C versus the original design [part (a)]?

15.11 In a study of the development of the concepts of conservation of quantity and weight, two standardized tasks (T, two levels) are presented to each of 72 children. Mastering the first task requires that a child grasp the notion of conservation of quantity whereas the second task depends on conservation of weight. The score is the number of trials required for the mastery of the task. Both age (A, three levels, 5, 7, and 9 years) and sex (X, two levels) are included as major variables in the design.

(a) Present the sources of variance associated with the design of this study as well as the df and EMS (using numbers where possible).

(b) State the error term and its df for tests of the following simple effects: (i) the effect of age for the conservation-of-quantity task (T_1); (ii) the effect of age for all male subjects on the T_1 task; (iii) the effects of task on the scores of all males.

15.12 Twenty-four participants were divided into two groups. A group heard a tape of music by either Mozart or Albinoni (group, $g = 2$). All subjects were tested on measures of spatial relations, arousal, mood, and enjoyment after listening to the music and also after a period of silence (condition, $c = 2$).

The means are (approximately)

Group	Condition	
	Music	Silence
Mozart	14.8	11.0
Albinoni	9.8	11.4

(a) Only F ratios were reported. We wish to be able to have some sense of the range of likely values of the effects reported. Find the 95% confidence interval on the difference between the group means if the reported F for *groups* is 6.20.

(b) The F for *groups* × *conditions* was 16.89. Find the 95% confidence interval for the interaction.

15.13 In a pilot study of the effects of diet upon the ability to withstand physical stress, 12 volunteers were divided into three groups of four subjects, with each group given a different diet. They then underwent a battery of physical tests on each of 4 successive days. A score was obtained on each day. The data are in the file *Ex15_13* at the book's website.

(a) Plot the performance curves for each group.

(b) Perform the ANOVA, including a complete trend analysis. Discuss the results in terms of the plot in part (a).

15.14 (a) For the *EX15_13* data set, calculate the 95% simultaneous confidence intervals on the pairwise differences among diet means (averaging over the 4 days), using Tukey's *HSD* (1953) procedure. Report any significant differences.

(b) After inspecting the data, the researcher notes that diet C yields better performance than A or B on day 4. Calculate a confidence interval for the difference between that mean and the average of the other two means, taking into consideration the fact that the test is post hoc ($FWE = .05$). Is the difference significant?

15.15 Two groups (A_1, A_2) of four subjects each are tested six times; there are two levels of B and three levels of C crossing to yield six scores for each subject. The data are in the *EX15_15* file on the *Exercises* page of the book's website.

(a) Report the results of tests of the *A* and *AB* terms, assuming all factors are fixed.

(b) Suppose *C* represents randomly chosen items. Again test the *A* and *AB* sources. How does this change the tests and the results?

15.16 We wish to test whether the differences between the *SVT* (sentence verification) and *IVT* (inference verification) from the Wiley–Voss study are affected by the *format* and *text* manipulations. The two measures can be found in the *EX15_16* file on the *Exercises* page of the website.

(a) Table the cell means and describe the resulting pattern. What effects are suggested?

(b) Perform an ANOVA with *format* and *text* as between-subjects variables and test (*SVT* vs *IVT*) as the within-subjects variable. Discuss the results, relating your discussion to the table of means.

15.17 In Exercise 15.16, there is a significant interaction between *format* and the type of test (*SVT* vs *IVT*). We may better understand this effect if we calculate some additional measures.

(a) Estimate Cohen's *f* for the effect of *format* on the difference between test scores.

(b) Calculate a 95% confidence interval for the interaction of *format* and *test*.

(c) We wish to have a measure of the effect of instructions on the difference between *SVT* and *IVT* scores. Estimate Cohen's *f* statistic for that difference (i) in the *text* and (ii) in the *web* condition.

Chapter 16
Nested and Counterbalanced Variables in Repeated-Measures Designs

16.1 OVERVIEW

Repeated-measures designs can be very efficient because they allow the removal of variability due to individual differences; however, they are not without their problems. As we have previously pointed out, because each subject contributes data in a number of different treatment conditions, we must be concerned with effects of the ordering of conditions and with repetition effects that may occur if the same items are repeatedly presented in different conditions. In the present chapter, we discuss two modifications of the standard repeated-measures design that address these issues.

An example will be useful for contrasting the standard repeated-measures designs of previous chapters with the hierarchical and Latin square designs discussed here. Suppose we want to investigate the effect of font type on the time taken to recognize words. In the most basic repeated-measures design, the levels of the font (A) and item (B) factors are *crossed*; that is, we record recognition times for the *same b* words presented in each of the a fonts. The ab trials would be sequenced randomly for each subject, perhaps with the restriction that the same word could not be presented on two successive trials. In the corresponding ANOVA, the $ab - 1$ df associated with the trials would be partitioned into components associated with the main effect of font ($a - 1$ df), the main effect of item ($b - 1$ df), and the font × item interaction ($(a - 1)(b - 1)$ df).

In contrast, in a hierarchical design, words would be *nested* within level of font. Each subject would be tested with a random sequence of ab different words, b *different* words for each font. The advantage of this hierarchical design is that it precludes the possibility that responding to a word in one font will influence responses to later presentations of the same word in other fonts. The disadvantage is that differences among the mean response times for the fonts will in part be due to differences among the sets of words presented in the different fonts. In other words, the hierarchical design eliminates effects due to stimulus repetition but at the cost of increased error variance. In the ANOVA for this hierarchical design, the $ab - 1$ df associated with trials are partitioned into components associated with the main effect of font ($a - 1$ df) and the effect of items nested within font ($a(b - 1)$ df). There can be no font × item interaction because different items are used in each font condition.

The Latin square designs can be used to address the variability inherent in presenting different lists of words at different levels of the independent variable. The assignment of lists to treatments can be counterbalanced so that some of the variability associated with lists can be removed if the proper analysis is performed. In our hypothetical experiment, four lists of words could be created. Each group of subjects would read each list of words in a different font with the assignment of lists to fonts counterbalanced over the groups such that each list appears equally often in each font across all subjects. The analysis of data from this Latin square design would allow removal of variance due to differences among the lists, increasing the efficiency of the design.

The Latin square design can also be used to counterbalance the order of treatment conditions, thereby allowing the removal of some of the variability associated with treatment order. In the example described above, if we had the same items in four different font conditions, responses to the four fonts might be collected in four trial blocks. Subjects would be divided into four groups and the assignment of fonts to trial blocks would be counterbalanced over groups so that each font would appear equally often in each block. The advantage of such counterbalancing is that this would equate the fonts with respect to practice or fatigue effects and enable the removal of variance due to such effects in the data analysis.

It is common to find that researchers have appropriately used counterbalancing and/or nesting in their designs, but then failed to perform statistical analyses that properly take these manipulations into account. When the analysis does not match the design, results may be severely biased (see, for example, Pollatsek & Well, 1995). Chapter 16 deals with the proper analysis of data from two repeated-measures designs:

- Designs in which stimuli are nested within treatment level; such designs are often referred to as *hierarchical* or *multi-level designs*.
- Designs in which factor levels are counterbalanced with respect to some potential source of error variance, such as position in time or sets of stimuli. These designs are referred to as *Latin square designs*.

16.2 NESTING STIMULI WITHIN FACTOR LEVELS

As discussed in Section 16.1, researchers often use different items in the different conditions. For example, if the effect of type of font on time to recognize words is being investigated, a different set of words may be presented in each font, probably with some attempt to match the sets of words for their average length and familiarity. As another example, if the dependent variable is a measure of the effect of the mood depicted in pictures of faces, there might be different faces in the various mood conditions, perhaps matched for age, race, and gender. In this hierarchical design, we say that words are nested within font conditions, or faces are nested within mood conditions.

In the font and mood examples, the independent variable was manipulated, and the use of a hierarchical design was the researcher's choice. In other experiments, the independent variable is observed. For example, the researcher may be interested in reading times for words that are or are not ambiguous, or words that are high or low in English-language frequency. In such cases, there is no choice; the items are naturally nested within levels of the independent variable.

In examples like those cited, the items are most often viewed as a random sample from a population of items. One approach frequently taken in the analysis is to reduce it to the subjects × treatments design of Chapter 13. This can be done by averaging over items so that each subject has a single mean score at each treatment level, and then using the means as the input to the ANOVA.

However, as we discussed in Chapter 15, this analysis is inappropriate because it ignores variability among items that potentially contributes to differences among the treatment means. Ignoring item variability inflates the probability of a Type 1 error because the error term does not include the variance of the scores on the items whereas the numerator of the F does. In what follows, a data set from a hypothetical experiment is used to illustrate the proper partitioning of the total sums of squares and degrees of freedom, and formulas for quasi-F tests are presented.

16.2.1 An Example of the Design

Table 16.1 presents means for a data set from a hypothetical experiment in which eight subjects were asked to categorize the mood depicted in each of 15 pictures. There were five pictures in each of three categories: sad, happy, and neutral; categories were validated in a pilot study. The time to push a button indicating a categorization response was recorded; the means of the eight response times for each of the 15 pictures are presented in Table 16.1 and the raw data are on the *Tables* page of the website in the file *Table 16_1 Nested Data*. In this example, items (B) are nested within moods (A) because the faces are different within each mood.

The study is a specific example of a general design in which there are n subjects, each of whom is tested with b different stimuli at each of a levels of A; in the above example, $n = 8$, $a = 3$ (moods), and $b = 5$ (faces within each mood). B is nested within levels of A (i.e., B/A) and is assumed to have random effects; A is assumed to have fixed effects. The distinction between fixed and random effects in this example stems from the fact that we have purposely chosen the three moods to be included in the experiment but have randomly sampled faces representing each mood. In what follows, we develop the analysis of data from this hierarchical design.

16.2.2 Partitioning the Sums of Squares and Degrees of Freedom

In the example represented by the data of Table 16.1, there are $a \times b$, or 3×5, pictures of faces so there are $ab - 1$, or 14, degrees of freedom for items. Part of the variability among the scores on the

Table 16.1 Mean response times (in ms) for items nested within moods

Response time (*RT*) means (averaged over subjects)								
Sad faces			Happy faces			Neutral faces		
Item		*RT*	Item		*RT*	Item		*RT*
1		1,419.25	6		1,286.75	11		1,588.13
2		1,698.75	7		1,643.25	12		1,894.63
3		1,359.88	8		1,478.88	13		1,701.88
4		1,503.00	9		1,472.63	14		1,807.00
5		1,047.25	10		1,336.88	15		1,541.00
Mean		1,405.63	Mean		1,443.68	Mean		1,706.53

The grand mean = 1,518.61

Note: Each mean is an average of the scores of the eight subjects. The complete data set is on the website in the file *Table 16_1 Nested Data*.

ab items is due to the *a* moods. This accounts for $a - 1$, or 2, of the 14 *df* for items. The remaining $a(b - 1)$, or 12, *df* account for the *B/A* term (faces within moods). In addition, each of *n*, or 8, subjects sees all of the pictures representing all three moods, so subjects cross with *A* and also with *B/A*. Therefore, our final set of sources of variance (*SV*) and *df* is:

SV	df
Subjects (*S*)	$n - 1$
Mood (*A*)	$a - 1$
SA	$(n - 1)(a - 1)$
Faces within mood (*B/A*)	$a(b - 1)$
SB/A	$a(n - 1)(b - 1)$

Several statistical packages provide analyses for data from designs in which one or more variables are nested within levels of other variables. Nesting of within-subjects factors can be handled within SPSS if the univariate module is used and an appropriate syntax file is written (see the file *Nested Designs* on the *Syntax* page on the book's website). However, there are alternatives if the available software does not handle nesting. One such alternative rests on the relationship between degrees of freedom for various terms. For example, the degrees of freedom for the *B/A* term are $a(b - 1)$, which equals $(b - 1) + (a - 1)(b - 1)$. This suggests that we can calculate the sums of squares for *B/A* by adding the sums of squares for *B* and *AB* from an ANOVA that treats *S, A,* and *B* as fully crossed variables. Similarly, *SB/A* can be calculated by adding the sums of squares for *SB* and *SBA*. In the example of Table 16.1, the analysis would proceed as if items 1, 6, and 11 were the same item; similarly for 2, 7, and 12, and so on. *S, A,* and *SA* are calculated as in the examples in Chapter 15. The resulting analysis is summarized in Table 16.2.

Table 16.2   ANOVA of the data of Table 16.1

SV	df	SS	MS	EMS
Subjects (*S*)	7	11,495,860	1,642,266	$\sigma_e^2 + 15\sigma_S^2$
Mood (*A*)	2	2,147,746	1,073,858	$\sigma_e^2 + 5\sigma_{SA}^2 + 8\sigma_{B/A}^2 + 400\theta_A^2$
SA	14	1,381,266	98,662	$\sigma_e^2 + 5\sigma_{SA}^2$
Items (*B/A*)	12	3,127,761	260,647	$\sigma_e^2 + 8\sigma_{B/A}^2$
SB/A	84	3,452,994	41,107	σ_e^2

16.2.3 Expected Mean Squares and Quasi-*F* Tests

The lack of a column of *F* values in Table 16.2 is not an oversight; the terms in the *EMS* column indicate the need for quasi-*F* ratios. The *EMS* follow the rules-of-thumb presented in Box 15.2. To illustrate, consider the expectation of the mean square for mood. As usual, error variance, σ_e^2, contributes to the expected mean square. In addition, because subjects are assumed to be a random sample from the population of potential subjects and no subscripts representing fixed effects other than *A* are present, σ_{SA}^2 also contributes. Similarly, the only essential subscript in the *B/A* term, *B*, represents items which we assume have been randomly sampled from their population. Therefore,

$\sigma^2_{B/A}$ is also present. Finally, the factor of interest, A, is represented by θ^2_A, with θ used instead of σ to remind us that we are dealing with a fixed effect.

Examining the *EMS* for A, it is clear that no single source of variance provides an appropriate error term to test A. Rather, we must form a combination of mean squares to create the error term, then compute a quasi-F' ratio. The relevant calculations are presented in Box 16.1.

Box 16.1 Quasi-*F* Test of *A* for the data of Table 16.1 (*B* Nested in Levels of *A*)

To test the effects of mood (A),

$$F' = MS_A/(MS_{SA} + MS_{B/A} - MS_{SB/A})$$

Substituting the *MS* values from Table 16.2 into this equation, we have

$$F' = 1{,}073{,}858/(98{,}662 + 260{,}647 - 41{,}107) = 3.375$$

The degrees of freedom for the numerator of this test are $a - 1 = 2$ and the denominator degrees of freedom are

$$df_{den} = \frac{(MS_{SA} + MS_{B/A} - MS_{S \times B/A})^2}{MS^2_{SA}/df_{SA} + MS^2_{B/A}/df_{B/A} + MS^2_{SAB}/df_{S \times B/A}}$$

$$= (98{,}662 + 260{,}647 - 41{,}107)^2/(98{,}662^2/14 + 260{,}647^2/12 + 41{,}107^2/84) = 15.88$$

Based on 3 and 16 *df*, the F' value of 3.375 is significant at $\alpha = .05$; therefore, we can conclude that the moods displayed in the pictures of faces affects the time required to categorize the faces.

16.2.4 Estimating Omega-Squared in the Hierarchical Design

As in previous chapters, we wish to estimate the proportion of variance due to the factor of interest that is relative to variances due to subjects and intrinsic factors, as well as error variance. Therefore, we define general omega-squared as

$$\omega^2_g(A) = \sigma^2_A/(\sigma^2_e + \sigma^2_A + \sigma^2_S + \sigma^2_{SA}) \tag{16.1}$$

Assuming n subjects, a levels of A, and b levels of B, our estimates of the parameters in Equation 16.1 are

$$\hat{\sigma}^2_A = \left(\frac{a-1}{a}\right)\left(\frac{MS_A - (MS_{SA} + MS_{B/A} - MS_{S \times B/A})}{bn}\right)$$

$$\hat{\sigma}^2_S = (MS_S - MS_{S \times B/A})/ab$$

$$\hat{\sigma}^2_{SA} = (MS_{SA} - MS_{S \times B/A})/b \tag{16.2}$$

$$\text{and}$$

$$\hat{\sigma}^2_e = MS_{S \times B/A}$$

Substituting values from Table 16.2 into Equation 16.2, the variance estimate for A is 12,594.3, the variance estimate for S is 106,743.9, the variance estimate for SA is 11,511, and the variance estimate for error is 41,107.[1] Putting these estimates together into Equation 16.1 gives an estimate for $\omega_g^2(A)$ of .073. This result indicates that the independent variable, mood, contributes moderate variance relative to the combined variance due to subject effects and error variance.

16.3 ADDING A BETWEEN-SUBJECTS VARIABLE TO THE WITHIN-SUBJECTS HIERARCHICAL DESIGN

16.3.1 An Example of the Design

The nesting design often involves a between-groups variable. For example, suppose that a researcher is interested in whether problem difficulty affects performance differently for experts and novices. Assume that there are five experts and five novices, and each subject is required to solve 12 problems, four of which are easy, four of intermediate difficulty, and four hard. In this example, problems are nested within difficulty levels and subjects are nested within levels of experience. The data are presented in Table 16.3. They are also in the website file *Table 16_3 nested mixed data*; follow links to the *Tables* page.

The means in panel *b* of the table indicate that solutions take longer for the hard problems, and longer for novices than experts. Furthermore, it appears that the advantage of the experts increases with increased problem difficulty. This is largely because problem difficulty has relatively little effect on expert performance. We next consider the ANOVA in Table 16.4 to see how to test these trends.

16.3.2 Partitioning Sums of Squares and Degrees of Freedom

As in our analysis of the data in Table 16.2, we have two within-subjects sources of variance: A (problem difficulty level) and B/A (problems nested within difficulty level). In the present design, we have the added between-subjects variable, C (experience), so subjects now are nested within levels of C. The SV column in the ANOVA of Table 16.4 includes these four sources of variance (C, S/C, A, B/A) as well as additional interaction terms. The AC term is the interaction of difficulty level with experience, and SS_{AC} is calculated as in all past designs. Because all problems are present at both levels of experience, C also crosses with the nested problems, giving rise to the CB/A term. If software that deals directly with nesting is unavailable, one way to calculate $SS_{C \times B/A}$ is to note that the degrees of freedom $a(b-1)(c-1) = (b-1)(c-1) + (a-1)(b-1)(c-1)$. This suggests treating the within-subjects factors as if they crossed, then adding together the sums of squares for the BC and ABC terms to obtain the nested BC interaction sum of squares.

16.3.3 Expected Mean Squares and Quasi-F (F') Ratios

Once again, the expected mean squares follow the rules of thumb. For example, consider $E(MS_C)$ in Table 16.4; S/C and CB/A both contribute to this expectation because we assume that both subjects (S) and problems (B) are randomly sampled from their respective populations, and they are the only essential (i.e., appearing to the left of the slash) subscripts other than C. The reader should

---

[1] If $F < 1$ for the test of S, σ_S^2 should be assumed to be 0, and S and SB/A should be pooled before estimating any of the other variance components. Similarly, if $F < 1$ for the test of SA, $\sigma_{S \times A}^2$ should be assumed to be 0, and SA should be pooled with SB/A before estimating other components. In both cases, the pooled term will be a more stable estimate of error variance than SB/A alone.

Table 16.3 Data from a design with problems (B) nested within levels of difficulty (A); experience (C) is the between-subjects factor

(*a*) Response times (each row contains the data for one subject)

C	A_1				A_2				A_3			
	B_{11}	B_{12}	B_{13}	B_{14}	B_{21}	B_{22}	B_{23}	B_{24}	B_{31}	B_{32}	B_{33}	B_{34}
1	4.4	5.2	5.8	4.5	5.5	5.7	4.2	4.8	5.4	4.2	5.6	5.6
1	4.4	6.0	6.1	4.3	5.7	5.3	4.0	6.4	5.5	3.7	5.2	6.7
1	5.0	5.9	6.3	4.8	5.3	6.8	4.6	6.2	6.3	5.1	4.9	5.3
1	4.4	5.0	5.5	3.4	5.2	5.2	3.5	4.9	5.8	4.6	5.4	4.5
1	4.8	5.5	5.3	5.4	4.9	5.1	4.0	5.2	5.1	4.5	5.2	5.1
C_1 Mean	4.60	5.525	5.80	4.48	5.32	5.62	4.06	5.50	5.62	4.42	5.26	5.44
2	5.0	7.8	9.8	6.0	8.4	8.7	5.9	8.4	8.9	5.1	7.9	9.5
2	3.9	6.6	8.6	5.2	6.1	8.3	4.9	6.1	7.6	3.9	7.7	9.0
2	3.9	5.6	6.5	3.6	6.5	7.2	4.1	6.2	7.6	2.8	5.6	7.1
2	6.1	7.1	8.3	5.7	6.9	9.1	5.2	6.5	9.5	6.4	7.5	8.9
2	6.0	7.8	9.1	6.6	7.9	9.9	5.9	8.0	8.8	5.4	7.0	9.2
C_2 Mean	4.98	6.98	8.46	5.42	7.16	8.64	5.20	7.04	8.48	4.72	7.14	8.74
Problem mean	4.79	6.25	7.13	4.95	6.24	7.13	4.63	6.27	7.05	4.57	6.20	7.09

(*b*) Condition means

	Easy (A_1)	Medium (A_2)	Hard (A_3)	Mean
Expert (C_1)	5.100	5.125	5.185	5.137
Novice (C_2)	6.460	7.010	7.270	6.913
Mean	5.780	6.068	6.228	6.025

Table 16.4 ANOVA of the data of Table 16.3

SV	df	SS	MS	EMS
Between-Subjects	$ac - 1 = 9$			
Experience (C)	$c - 1 = 1$	94.70	94.70	$\sigma_e^2 + ab\sigma_{S/C}^2 + n\sigma_{C \times B/A}^2 + nab\theta_C^2$
Subjects within C (S/C)	$c(n - 1) = 8$	41.76	5.22	$\sigma_e^2 + ba\sigma_{S/C}^2$
Within-Subjects	$ac(ab - 1) = 110$			
Problem difficulty (A)	$a - 1 = 2$	4.11	2.06	$\sigma_e^2 + nc\sigma_{B/A}^2 + b\sigma_{A \times S/C}^2 + nbc\theta_A^2$
AC	$(a - 1)(c - 1) = 2$	2.80	1.40	$\sigma_e^2 + n\sigma_{C \times B/A}^2 + b\sigma_{A \times S/C}^2 + nb\theta_{AC}^2$
AS/C	$c(n - 1)(a - 1) = 16$	5.00	.31	$\sigma_e^2 + b\sigma_{A \times S/C}^2$
Problems within A (B/A)	$a(b - 1) = 9$	111.47	12.39	$\sigma_e^2 + nc\sigma_{B/A}^2$
CB/A	$a(b - 1)(c - 1) = 9$	25.27	2.81	$\sigma_e^2 + n\sigma_{C \times B/A}^2$
SB/AC	$ac(n - 1)(b - 1) = 72$	18.70	.26	σ_e^2

apply the rules to verify the other expected mean squares in Table 16.4. Given the expected mean squares of Table 16.4, no single mean square provides an error term for C, A, or AC. Again, we are forced to construct quasi-F ratios. The F' test of the effect of experience (C) is illustrated in Box 16.2. We leave the remaining tests as an exercise.

Box 16.2 Quasi-*F* Test of *C* for the Data of Table 16.3 (*C* is Between Subjects, *B* is Nested in Levels of *A*)

To test the effects of experience (C),

$$F' = MS_C/(MS_{S/C} + MS_{C \times B/A} - MS_{Residual})$$

Substituting values of mean squares from Table 16.4 into the preceding equation, we have

$$F' = 94.70/(5.22 + 2.81 - .26) = 12.19$$

The numerator degrees of freedom $= c - 1$, or 1, and the denominator degrees of freedom are

$$\frac{(MS_{S/C} + MS_{C \times B/A} - MS_{Residual})^2}{MS_{S/C}^2/df_{S/C} + MS_{C \times B/A}^2/df_{C \times B/A} + MS_{Residual}^2/df_{Residual}}$$

$$= (5.22 + 2.81 - .26)^2/(5.22^2/8 + 12.81^2/9 + .26^2/72) = 14.09$$

$p = .004$; with $\alpha = .05$, we can conclude that more experienced problem solvers require significantly less time to solve.

16.4 THE REPLICATED LATIN SQUARE DESIGN

Although error variance is usually less when factors are varied within subjects rather than between subjects, it may be further reduced by using a Latin square design. Scores from an individual may vary because they are collected at different points in time, or in different locations, or because of variation among lists of items when items are nested within conditions. Using a Latin square to counterbalance the assignment of conditions with respect to such factors allows us to remove their effects from the error variance.

We introduced the Latin square in Section 13.5, using a single square to illustrate how the square is selected randomly from the population of possible squares. We discussed its advantages and disadvantages, with particular emphasis on its potential for reducing error variance relative to other designs. The reader will find it helpful to review that material before considering extensions of the design.

In the most common use of the Latin square design, there are n participants in each row of the square. We refer to this as a replicated square because we can view the design as involving n replications of a single square. Table 16.5 provides an illustration of this design. In the table, A is the treatment variable, B is the blocking variable, and G represents groups of n subjects; the groups correspond to the rows of the square and differ with respect to the assignment of treatments to blocks. The numbers in each cell are the cell means, each of which is based on five scores; that is, $n = 5$.[2] Blocks may be trial blocks, in which case the five subjects in Group 1 are tested first in condition

---

[2] The complete data set is on the website in the file *Table 16_5 LatinSqData*. The data appear twice in the file, once organized with the within-subjects variable as A and once with the within-subjects variable as B.

Table 16.5 An example of a Latin square with cell means (scores are number of errors in a detection experiment, A is number of noise elements, and levels of B are successive blocks of 25 trials)

Group	Blocks				
	B_1	B_2	B_3	B_4	Mean
G_1	7.6 (A_2)	10 (A_4)	8.2 (A_3)	6.4 (A_1)	8.05
G_2	9.6 (A_4)	11 (A_2)	7 (A_1)	8.6 (A_3)	9.05
G_3	8.6 (A_1)	10.4 (A_3)	7 (A_2)	10.2 (A_4)	9.05
G_4	9.6 (A_3)	7.8 (A_1)	9 (A_4)	3.8 (A_2)	7.55
Mean	8.85	9.8	7.8	7.25	8.425

The treatment means are:

A_1	A_2	A_3	A_4
7.45	7.35	9.2	9.7

Note: There are five subjects in each row (group) of the square. The complete data set is on the website in the file *Table 16_5 LatinSqData*.

A_2, next in condition A_4, and so on. Or the experiment might require detection of targets of four different sizes; size might be the treatment variable, A, and blocks might represent quadrants of the screen in which the target could appear. As still another example, A might represent study times for lists of words in a memory experiment and B would represent the lists. Many other examples of blocking variables are possible.

We will begin our analysis of the means in Table 16.5 by first discussing the partitioning of the sums of squares. Following that, we consider possible structural models, the expected mean squares based on these, and the hypothesis tests corresponding to each model.

16.4.1 Partitioning the Sums of Squares

To make the example in Table 16.5 less abstract, assume a hypothetical experiment in which 20 subjects must identify a target (e.g., a digit) in a noisy background within 1.5 seconds. The independent variable of interest is the number of noise elements (e.g., letters): $A = 6, 8, 10,$ or 12. A block contains the same number of noise elements for all 25 trials, although the target and the noise elements change from trial to trial. The numbers of errors (incorrect responses or failures to respond) in each block of 25 trials are the basis for the means in Table 16.5. The errors increase as the number of noise elements increases.

We may begin the process of partitioning the variance in the design by viewing it as a mixed design with one between-subjects factor of group and one within-subjects factor corresponding to the number of noise elements, A. That analysis is summarized in the left panel of Table 16.6. The reader may confirm these results by analyzing the individual scores in the website *Tables* file, *Table 16_5 LatinSqData*. However, our partitioning is incomplete in that it fails to recognize that the blocking variable, B, is a component of the experimental design. Because B was systematically incorporated in the design, we can measure the variance associated with B and remove it from the

Table 16.6   Three partitions of the sums of squares based on Table 16.5

SV	df	SS	SV	df	SS	SV	df	SS
Groups (G)	3	33.75	G	3	33.75	G	3	33.75
S/G	16	341.80	S/G	16	341.80	S/G	16	341.80
A	3	86.65	B	3	76.85	A	3	86.65
GA	9	129.55	GB	9	139.35	B	3	76.85
SA/G	48	533.80	SB/G	48	533.80	BCR^a	6	52.70
						WSR^b	48	533.80
Total	79	1,125.55	Total	79	1,125.55	Total	79	1,125.55

[a] BCR is the "between-cells residual"; $BCR = SS_{BCR} = SS_{GA} - SS_B = SS_{GB} - SS_A$.
[b] WSR is the "within-subjects residual"; $WSR = SS_{WSR} = SA/G = SB/G$.

Groups $\times$ *A* (*GA*) interaction. This is easily accomplished by conducting a second mixed-factors ANOVA in which B replaces A as the treatment variable, producing the output summarized in the middle panel of Table 16.6. The results of the two analyses are then used to obtain the partitioning summarized in the right panel of Table 16.6. In this analysis, we are able to distinguish not three, but four within-subjects sources of variability—the treatment variable, A; the blocking variable, B; a "between-cells residual" term computed as $(SS_{GA} - SS_B)$ or, equivalently $(SS_{GB} - SS_A)$; and a term that we will call "within-subjects residual," which corresponds to SA/G from our original analysis and SB/G from our second analysis. The df for the BCR term are computed as the difference between the df for the GA interaction and the df for the main effect of B; that is, $df_{BCR} = df_{G \times A} - df_B = (a-1)^2 - (a-1) = (a-1)(a-2)$. The df for the remaining terms are found in the usual fashion.

The right-most partitioning is the analysis we recommend for this experimental design. An astute reader may wonder why that partitioning does not explicitly contain a treatments $\times$ blocks (AB) interaction term. In fact, every possible combination of levels of A and B is represented in the design, so it is possible to recover information about the interaction. However, there is a confounding inherent in the design that prevents us from identifying a single term corresponding to the AB interaction. Groups may differ because each represents a different subset of assignments of treatments to blocks; i.e., a different subset of AB interaction effects (see Exercise 16.8). This accounts for $(a-1)$ of the $(a-1)(a-1)$ df associated with the interaction. The remaining AB interaction variability is embedded in the BCR source. A simple demonstration of this is to show that the sum of squares for AB is divided between the G and BCR sources; that is, $SS_{AB} = SS_G + SS_{BCR}$. From Table 16.5,

$$SS_{AB} = 5 \times [(7.6 - 8.425)^2 + (10 - 8.425)^2 + \ldots + (3.8 - 8.425)^2] - 86.65 - 76.85 = 86.45$$

But $SS_G + SS_{BCR} = 33.75 + 52.70$, which also equals 86.45. Therefore, we may view the *Groups* and *BCR* sources as each capturing some of the AB interaction variability. The AB interaction is confounded with the *Groups* and *BCR* sources.

With the partitioning of the variability established, we are now in a position to consider alternative models of the data, the corresponding expected mean squares, and the resulting F tests.

16.4.2 Expected Mean Squares and F Tests

We assume the following structural model for the replicated-square design:

$$Y_{ijkm} = \mu + \eta_{ilm} + \alpha_j + \beta_k + (\alpha\beta)_{jk} + \varepsilon_{ijkm} \tag{16.3}$$

where i indexes the subject within a row of the Latin square ($i = 1, 2, \ldots, n$), j indexes the level of A ($j = 1, 2, \ldots, a$), k indexes the level of B ($k = 1, 2, \ldots, a$), and m indexes the row within the square (the group; $m = 1, 2, \ldots, a$). The population of subject effects, the $\eta_{i|m}$, is assumed to be independently and normally distributed with mean zero and variance $\sigma_{S/G}^2$. The effects of A, the α_j, are assumed to be fixed. B may have fixed or random effects. If random, then the effects of B, the β_k, and the AB interaction effects, the $(\alpha\beta)_{jk}$, are distributed independently and normally with mean zero and respective variances σ_B^2 and σ_{AB}^2.

The expected mean squares for the replicated Latin square design are presented in Table 16.7. Note that there are two panels: one containing the *EMS* when B is assumed to have fixed effects and one when B is assumed to have random effects. In both panels, the AB interaction variance contributes to the *Group* and *BCR* expectations, as we showed in discussing the partitioning of sums of squares. For this reason, we use the label (AB') as a second designation of those sources; it is this designation that is operational when we apply the rules of thumb to determine *EMS*. Note that the AB interaction contributes to the A source of variance *when B has random effects*, as the rules of thumb dictate. This is the reason for the difference between the two panels in Table 16.7.

In the example of the detection experiment in which the number of noise elements was varied and counterbalanced over blocks of trials, it is reasonable to assume that trial blocks have fixed effects. In that case, the expected mean squares are those in the left panel of Table 16.7. and the error term for testing both A (number of noise elements) and B (trial blocks) is the same error term as in the mixed designs of Chapter 15 (remember that $SS_{WSR} = SS_{SA/G} = SS_{SB/G}$). This would be the case for any design in which the blocking variable is assumed to have fixed effects.

In other experiments, recall scores might be obtained for lists that have been studied for various amounts of time, or comprehensibility ratings might be obtained for lists of sentences varying in syntax, or brain activity might be recorded for sets of pictures varying in emotional content. In these examples, the blocks in Table 16.5 represent sets of stimuli. It is reasonable to assume that the stimuli have been randomly sampled from some large population of stimuli, and randomly divided into several sets. Suppose each group has a different pairing of set with study time or emotional content, with the pairings arranged so that the design forms a Latin square, as in Table 16.5. Then the appropriate error term for testing A (e.g., study time or emotional content) is the *BCR* source unless it can be assumed that $\sigma_{AB}^2 = 0$. In that case, A can be tested against the *WSR* mean square or—to achieve greater power—against the pool of the *WSR* and *BCR* mean squares.

Table 16.8 presents three sets of F tests and p-values based on the data of Table 16.5. The tests correspond to the assumption that B has fixed effects, or B has random effects, or the AB population variance is zero. As the *EMS* of Table 16.7 showed, when the effects of B are assumed to be

Table 16.7 Expected mean squares and error terms for the replicated-square design

	B has fixed effects			B has random effects	
SV	EMS	Error term	SV	EMS	Error term
Groups (AB')	$\sigma_e^2 + a\sigma_{S/G}^2 + na\theta_{AB}^2$	S/G	Groups (AB')	$\sigma_e^2 + a\sigma_{S/G}^2 + na\sigma_{AB}^2$	S/G
S/G	$\sigma_e^2 + a\sigma_{S/G}^2$		S/G	$\sigma_e^2 + a\sigma_{S/G}^2$	
A	$\sigma_e^2 + na\theta_A^2$	WSR	A	$\sigma_e^2 + n\sigma_{AB}^2 + na\theta_A^2$	BCR
B	$\sigma_e^2 + na\theta_B^2$	WSR	B	$\sigma_e^2 + na\sigma_B^2$	WSR
BCR (AB')	$\sigma_e^2 + n\theta_{AB}^2$	WSR	BCR (AB')	$\sigma_e^2 + n\sigma_{AB}^2$	WSR
WSR	σ_e^2		WSR	σ_e^2	

Table 16.8   Three analyses of the data of Table 16.5

SV	df	MS	B Fixed[a]		B Random[b]		$\sigma^2_{AB} = 0$[c]	
			F	p	F	p	F	p
$G(AB')$	3	1,125.00	0.53	0.67	0.53	0.67	0.53	0.67
S/G	16	21.36						
A	3	28.88	2.60	0.06	3.29	0.10	2.66	0.06
B	3	25.62	2.30	0.09	2.30	0.09	2.36	0.08
$BCR(AB')$	6	8.78	0.79	0.58				
WSR	48	11.12						
Pooled error	54	10.86						

[a] A and B are tested against WSR.
[b] A is tested against BCR.
[c] A and B are tested against the pool of BCR and WSR; $MS_{pooled\ error} = (6/54)(8.78) + (48/54)(11.12) = 10.86$; $df = 54$.

fixed the test of the treatment variable, A, is the same as in the mixed design of Chapter 15. The within-subjects error term is appropriate for testing both A and B main effects, as well as providing a test of the partial interaction (AB') of A and B.

When B is assumed to have random effects, following the rules stated in Chapter 15, σ^2_{AB} contributes to $E(MS_A)$ and the appropriate error term is MS_{BCR}. Unless there is a large effect of A, this F test will lack power because the df associated with BCR will typically be small except when the Latin square is large. Note that despite the big value of the F statistic in the random-effects case, the p-value is larger than in the fixed-effects test of A, reflecting the fewer degrees of freedom.

When B is assumed to have random effects, a more powerful test of A can be constructed if we have clear evidence that AB interaction effects (σ^2_{AB}) are negligible. In that case, the BCR and WSR mean squares can be pooled and used as an error term against which to test A. This has been done in the right-most two columns of Table 16.8, yielding increased error degrees of freedom and a slightly lower (though still not significant) p-value for the test of A. In fact, this analysis seems justified for the data set we are considering because a preliminary test of BCR against the WSR term produces a p-value considerably greater than .25 (Bozivich et al., 1956). But what if the preliminary test has a p-value less than .25? A transformation might be found that results in a scale on which there is no evidence of AB variance. Failing that, the investigator should consider redoing the experiment with an alternative design that does not involve the confounding associated with the Latin square.

One other issue deserves mention. Consider an experiment in which the blocking variable is sets of stimuli, perhaps sentences or pictures. Further suppose that a score, perhaps a rating or response time, is obtained for each item in each set. It may appear that—as we prescribed in Chapter 15—a quasi-F statistic should be calculated in order to take into account the variance due to items. However, the test against the BCR mean square (or, when appropriate, its pool with the WSR mean square) serves that function because variance due to the sets of items, and its interaction with treatments, is included in the expected mean squares (Raaijmakers, Schrijnemakers, & Gremmen, 1999).

16.4.3 Alternative Analyses of the Replicated Latin Square Design

It is not uncommon for researchers to conduct statistical analyses that are not entirely consistent with their experimental designs. The design currently under consideration is a good case in point.

One common but inappropriate approach to analyzing the replicated Latin square design is to ignore both the *Group* and blocking variables and treat it as a simple one-factor, repeated-measures design. The only sources of variance distinguished are subjects, *A*, and the *SA* interaction, with the effect of *A* being tested against *SA*. In terms of the recommended analysis summarized in the right panel of Table 16.6, the repeated-measures analysis corresponds to pooling the *Groups* sums of squares with the sums of squares for the *S/B* term, and—more importantly—pooling the sums of squares associated with *B* and *BCR* with the sums of squares for the *WSR* term. If *B* is assumed to have fixed effects, the pooling of the *B*, *BCR*, and *WSR* sums of squares has the unfortunate consequence of inflating the error term for the test of the treatment effect, *A*. As a result, the test of *A* will be negatively biased and Type 2 errors are likely to increase (Pollatsek & Well, 1995). Although the experiment was designed to reduce error variance through systematic manipulation of the blocking variable, the power of the statistical analysis is actually reduced because it is incompatible with the experimental design.

The other common statistical approach to the replicated Latin square design is to treat it as a mixed-factors design; that is, to conduct the ANOVA summarized in the left panel of Table 16.6. This analysis is an improvement over the simple repeated-measures analysis because it does distinguish the group variable. If *B* is assumed to have fixed effects, the resulting ANOVA produces an unbiased test of *A*. However, information about the effects of the blocking variable and its interaction with *A* are lost. Further, if *B* is assumed to have random effects and $\sigma^2_{AB} = 0$, the test of *A* against *SA/G* will be positively biased. Once again, the lesson is that the statistical analysis should be consistent with the experimental design.

16.4.4 Advantages and Disadvantages of the Latin Square Design

As we discussed in Chapter 13, the major advantage of the Latin square design is that it allows the researcher to remove error variance stemming from two sources, subjects and a blocking variable such as trials, or sets of stimuli. It also provides a test of the blocking variable. For example, if the assignment of treatments is counterbalanced over trials, we have the advantage over the subjects × treatments design of being able to estimate the function relating mean scores to trials, and of testing the slope and curvature of that function.

One potential disadvantage is that there are fewer degrees of freedom associated with the error term and therefore potentially lower power than in the subjects × treatments design. This is particularly true if the blocking variable, *B*, is best viewed as having random effects. In that case, the between-cell residual is the appropriate error term unless it can be assumed that there are no treatments × blocks interaction effects. The *BCR* error term will have few degrees of freedom unless the square is large; at least 5 × 5, or preferably larger.

The Latin square design shares with other repeated-measures designs one other potential problem: The responses to treatments may depend upon the treatments preceding it. For example, suppose *A* in Table 16.5 represents three drugs, and *B* represents successive days of testing. Further suppose that mean response times under drugs 3 and 1 differ. Is this because these drugs do differentially affect performance, or is it because drug 3 was preceded twice by drug 1 whereas drug 1 was preceded twice by drug 2? In other words, is the difference due to the drugs themselves or to different *carry-over effects* from the different drugs that preceded them? One response to this problem is to increase the period between treatments; for example, test every other day. A second response is a modified Latin square design, and this is to be considered in Section 16.6.

16.5 INCLUDING BETWEEN-SUBJECTS VARIABLES IN THE REPLICATED SQUARE DESIGN

Consider a hypothetical experiment in which time viewing an ambiguous word in a sentence is measured as a function of whether the preceding context in the sentence supported the less frequent sense of the word (A_1), was neutral with respect to the sense of the word (A_2), or supported the more frequent sense of the word (A_3). For example, a word such as *port* usually refers to a place where ships leave or enter, but it can refer to a type of wine; the preceding sentence can predict either of those meanings or be completely neutral. Assume that we create three lists of such words, approximately equated for length and total English-language frequency. These are the blocks in Table 16.9. Finally, assume that we wish to see whether context has different effects on the reading time for good (C_1) and poor (C_2) readers.

In general, we have an $a \times a$ Latin square, with n subjects in each row of the square at each level of C; therefore, there are acn subjects, each tested in a blocks. In the present example, $a = 3$, $c = 2$, $n = 4$, so that there are 24 subjects and a total of 72 scores. Table 16.9 presents the design and the means

Table 16.9 Cell means (of reading times in ms) for a replicated Latin square with a between-subjects factor

| Reader (C) | Row | Lists (B) | | | Row mean |
		B_1	B_2	B_3	
	1	338.00 (A_2)	346.00 (A_1)	341.50 (A_3)	341.83
Good (C_1)	2	344.75 (A_3)	345.50 (A_2)	355.25 (A_1)	348.50
	3	356.75 (A_1)	347.00 (A_3)	352.00 (A_2)	351.92
Mean		346.50	346.17	349.58	347.42
	1	359.75 (A_2)	367.25 (A_1)	360.75 (A_3)	362.58
Poor (C_2)	2	355.25 (A_3)	360.25 (A_1)	365.25 (A_2)	360.25
	3	353.25 (A_1)	351.50 (A_3)	353.25 (A_2)	352.67
Mean		355.08	359.67	359.75	358.50
Block mean		351.29	352.92	354.67	

| Reader | Context | | | Mean |
	A_1	A_2	A_3	
Good	352.67	345.17	344.42	347.42
Poor	361.92	357.75	355.83	358.50
Mean	357.29	351.46	350.13	

Note: A_1 = context supports subordinate meaning, A_2 = context is neutral, A_3 = context supports dominant meaning; B = lists of sentences; C = reader. Each of the six *Reader* $\times$ *Row* conditions represents a group of four subjects. The complete data set with columns organized both by A and by B is on the website in the file labeled *Table 16_9 LatinSqData_2 data*.

for the subjects in each cell of the design.[3] The means indicate that the context supporting the less frequent meaning (A_1) results in longer reading times. We also find that poor readers are slower than good readers, although the difference varies only slightly as a function of context. Finally, we note that reading times differ slightly over lists (the block means), but the differences seem small. Significance tests are in order but we must first consider the sources of variance and their expected mean squares.

The analysis is summarized in Table 16.10 for the case where B is assumed to have random effects. As indicated in the SV column and expected mean squares of Table 16.10, both the row and between-cells residual (BCR) terms reflect possible AB interaction effects. The $C \times Row$ and $C \times BCR$ terms reflect possible ABC interaction effects. This also is indicated in the SV and EMS columns of Table 16.10. These interaction effects are again a function of the confounding inherent in incomplete block designs; i.e., designs in which subjects are not tested in the complete set of combinations of A and B.

Main and interaction effects are calculated as in all preceding chapters. Recall that the term labeled "WSR" is simply $SA/C \times Rows$, using the notation familiar from repeated-measures designs. The only terms whose calculations might pose a problem are the BCR (between cells residual) and its interaction with C. These can be viewed as differences between terms derived from standard mixed-design ANOVAs. This observation again forms the basis for using computer packages to analyze the data. Any computer program capable of handling two between-subjects variables (C, Row) and one within-subjects variable (A or B) can then be used to do two analyses. In one analysis, specify A as the within-subjects variable and obtain SS_A; in the other analysis, specify B as the within-subjects variable and obtain $SS_{B \times Row}$. Then compute:

$$SS_{BCR} = (SS_{B \times Row} - SS_A) \quad \text{and} \quad SS_{C \times BCR} = (SS_{B \times C \times Row} - SS_{AC}).$$

Table 16.10 Analysis of the design of Table 16.9 (B is assumed to have random effects)

SV	df	EMS	Error term
C	$c - 1$	$\sigma_e^2 + a\sigma_{S/C \times Row}^2 + \underline{an\sigma_{BC}^2} + a^2n\theta_C^2$	quasi-F
Row (AB')	$a - 1$	$\sigma_e^2 + a\sigma_{S/C \times Row}^2 + acn\sigma_{AB}^2$	$S/C \times Row$
$C \times Row$ (ABC')	$(a-1)(c-1)$	$\sigma_e^2 + a\sigma_{S/C \times Row}^2 + an\sigma_{ABC}^2$	$S/C \times Row$
$S/C \times Row$	$ac(n-1)$	$\sigma_e^2 + a\sigma_{S/C \times Row}^2$	
A	$a - 1$	$\sigma_e^2 + nc\sigma_{AB}^2 + acn\theta_A^2$	BCR
B	$a - 1$	$\sigma_e^2 + \underline{acn\sigma_B^2}$	BCR
AC	$(a-1)(c-1)$	$\sigma_e^2 + \underline{n\sigma_{ABC}^2} + an\theta_{AC}^2$	$C \times BCR$
BC	$(a-1)(b-1)$	$\sigma_e^2 + an\sigma_{BC}^2$	BCR
BCR (AB')	$(a-1)(a-2)$	$\sigma_e^2 + nc\sigma_{AB}^2$	WSR
$C \times BCR$ (ABC')	$(a-1)(a-2)(c-1)$	$\sigma_e^2 + n\sigma_{ABC}^2$	WSR
WSR	$ac(a-1)(n-1)$	σ_e^2	

The EMS are based on the assumption that B has random effects. If B has fixed effects, the underlined components are deleted from the EMS, and the error terms change accordingly.

---

[3] The complete data set with columns organized both by A and by B is at the website in the file labeled *Table 16_9 LatinSqData_2 data*.

The results will be the same if SS_C is subtracted from $SS_{A \times Row}$ and SS_{BC} is subtracted from $SS_{A \times B \times Row}$. The entries in the *EMS* column in Table 16.10 were derived assuming that *B* has random effects, the most reasonable assumption when *B* represents sets of items. If *B* is a fixed-effects variable, as when *B* represents time periods, the expected mean squares and error terms are changed, as described in the note to Table 16.10.

Table 16.11 presents the numerical results for the analysis of the data set in Table 16.9. As noted below the table, extremely small between-cell variability led us to pool the *BCR*, $C \times BCR$, and *WSR* sources, yielding an error term on 40 degrees of freedom. The results are clear: good readers are faster than slow readers, context has an effect on reading times, and no interactions approach significance.

Table 16.11   ANOVA of the data in Table 16.9

SV	df	SS	MS	Error term	F	p
Reader (*C*)	1	2,211.13	2,211.13	$S/C \times Row$	8.33	0.01
Row	2	72.33	36.17	$S/C \times Row$	0.14	0.87
$C \times Row$	2	1,204.00	602.00	$S/C \times Row$	2.27	0.13
$S/C \times Row$	18	4,776.08	265.34	Pooled error[a]		
Context (*A*)	2	697.33	348.67	Pooled error	5.18	0.01
Blocks (*B*)	2	136.75	68.38	Pooled error	1.02	0.37
AC	2	34.33	17.17	Pooled error	0.25	0.78
BC	2	53.58	26.79	*WSR*	0.40	0.67
BCR	2	1.08	0.54	*WSR*	0.01	0.99
$C \times BCR$	2	11.08	5.54	*WSR*	0.08	0.92
WSR	36	1,341.17	74.51			

[a] Because the *F* test of *BC* yields a very small *F*, we assume that $\sigma^2_{BC} = 0$; therefore, *C* was tested against $S/C \times Row$. Similarly, the very small *F*s for *BCR* and $C \times BCR$ support pooling these terms with their error term, *WSR*. The pooled error term for testing all within-subjects terms is $MS_{pool} = (2/40)(0.54) + (2/40)(5.54) + (36/40)(74.51) = 67.36$.

16.6 BALANCING CARRY-OVER EFFECTS

When *B* represents time periods, there is a risk that the effects of treatments will be modified by preceding treatments. By the proper choice of squares, carry-over effects from the immediately preceding treatment can be balanced out. This can be done with a single square when there is an even number of treatments but requires two squares when *a* is an odd number. Assume that *a* is an even number, say, 4. Then the square is constructed in the following steps.

1. Number the treatments from 1 to *a*.
2. Enter numbers in order in every other cell of the first row:

B_1	B_2	B_3	B_4
1		2	

3. Fill the remaining cells with the remaining numbers in order, starting at the right of the row:

B_1	B_2	B_3	B_4
1	4	2	3

4. Fill each column in order from the first row:

B_1	B_2	B_3	B_4
1	4	2	3
2	1	3	4
3	2	4	1
4	3	1	2

Each number now precedes each other number exactly once. Treatment levels can now be assigned at random to the four numbers. Each row corresponds to a subject or to a group of subjects as in previous versions of the Latin square design.

When a is an odd number, say, 3, two squares are needed to balance carry-over effects from the immediately preceding treatment. To construct the squares, follow these steps.

1. Construct a row with $2a$ columns. Then write the numbers from 1 to a in order in every other cell:

B_1	B_2	B_3	B_1	B_2	B_3
1		2		3	

2. Write the same numbers in order, starting at the right of the row:

B_1	B_2	B_3	B_1	B_2	B_3
1	3	2	2	3	1

3. Fill in each column by proceeding sequentially from the number in the first row:

B_1	B_2	B_3	B_1	B_2	B_3
1	3	2	2	3	1
2	1	3	3	1	2
3	2	1	1	2	3

4. Split the columns midway and rearrange with the first a columns placed on top of the remaining a columns:

B_1	B_2	B_3
1	3	2
2	1	3
3	2	1
2	3	1
3	1	2
1	2	3

Each of the six rows corresponds to a subject or group of subjects. Each digit, representing a treatment level, precedes each other digit exactly twice.

The data from this *digram-balanced design* are analyzed as in the preceding sections. Because a treatment precedes all other treatments equally often, the carry-over contribution to treatment effects should be equated. However, the design equates only the effect of the immediately preceding treatment and does not deal with effects carried over several time periods. Cochran and Cox (1957, pp. 135–139) describe methods for calculating the sums of squares due to carry-over, and for removing that variability from the sums of squares for treatments. Namboodiri (1972) also describes other related designs.

16.7 GRECO-LATIN SQUARES

The designs presented in this chapter are a subset of the many possible variations of the Latin square design. They are an even smaller subset of incomplete block designs. We have limited our presentation to those designs we view as most useful and most often used by researchers. One possible extension occasionally referenced in the experimental literature is the Greco-Latin square. For example, suppose we vary the font in which words are presented for identification. If we have three types of fonts, we could create three lists, counterbalancing the assignment of words to lists. But what about the order in which the words are presented? We could randomly order the presentation of the words for each subject so that words from different lists randomly follow each other. However, we could also present each list in a block of trials. The Greco-Latin square permits us to do this. If the fonts are represented by the letters a, b, and c, lists by α, β, and γ, and the columns are successive trial blocks (hence "Greco-Latin"), the design might be represented by

$$\begin{bmatrix} b\beta & a\alpha & c\gamma \\ c\alpha & b\gamma & a\beta \\ a\gamma & c\beta & b\alpha \end{bmatrix}$$

where a subject or group is tested with the sequence of combinations of font and list indicated in a row of the square. Note that the layouts of the Latin letters and the Greek letters each meet the requirements for a Latin square. Furthermore, each combination of levels of A and B appears exactly once in each row and column.

The Greco-Latin design has the advantage of allowing us to control variance due to subjects, lists, and trial blocks. Or the Latin and Greek letters might both represent experimental factors, perhaps font and font size, thus enabling the researcher to efficiently investigate both factors. However, there are several potential problems. First, the introduction of another variable reduces the between-cell residual degrees of freedom; for a single square such as the one above, these degrees of freedom are $(a^2 - 1) - 4(a - 1) = (a - 1)(a - 3)$. This is zero when $a = 3$. To have any chance at rejecting a false null hypothesis, the Greco-Latin design should involve at least six rows and columns. The second problem is perhaps more serious. The introduction of another factor in this way sets up the possibility of still more interactions that may be confounded with main effects of interest. This may cost us a clean test of such main effects. The third problem is that if interactions between the Latin and Greek factors are present, we have no way of assessing them. It is rare that an investigator would want to forgo the opportunity to test for an interaction between two experimentally manipulated factors. In summary, when we wish to control for two nuisance variables, such as lists and trial blocks, the design is worth considering. However, if we wish to investigate two experimental factors, researchers usually will be better off with other designs.

16.8 SUMMARY

In this chapter, we described structural models and data analyses for two modifications of the repeated-measures designs of the preceding two chapters:

- *Hierarchical designs* involve the nesting of stimuli within levels of the independent variable. Nesting occurs when the nature of that variable necessitates nesting; for example, when the stimuli are pleasant, neutral, and unpleasant scenes. Nesting also occurs in some experiments to avoid repeating the same item in several conditions.
- *Latin square designs* involve assigning treatments to levels of a nuisance variable so that the assignment is counterbalanced over groups of subjects. The blocking variable can be trial blocks, locations of targets, lists of words, or any other potential source of within-subject error variance.

These designs have advantages and disadvantages relative to each other and to the repeated-measures and mixed designs of Chapter 15. Hierarchical designs, by nesting items within levels of the within-subjects factor, A, avoid effects of repeating stimuli. However, differences among sets of items contribute to the error variance against which the effects of A are tested. Latin squares reduce error variance due to blocking factors such as trial blocks of lists of items. However, they do so at a cost of error degrees of freedom, and therefore power of the hypothesis test. The choice of design will depend on factors specific to the research such as the nature of the independent variable, the response required of the subject, the number of available subjects, and the number of levels of the independent variable.

Before closing this chapter, we note that several books and articles have appeared recently, promoting multi-level, or hierarchical, models. These are very flexible in their application, and are particularly useful in dealing with designs such as those in this chapter. Many different assumptions about the effects of variables and the pattern of variances and covariances can readily be incorporated in this approach. Also, missing scores are not a problem. There is a price for these and other benefits in both the complexity of the approach and in the decisions imposed during the analysis of data. A discussion of the models and the analyses is beyond the scope of this book, but interested readers can consult several books and articles (e.g., Brysbaert, 2007; Luke, 2004; Quené & van den Bergh, 2004; Raudenbush & Bryk, 2002). Brysbaert's paper is particularly helpful for users of SPSS; it provides several examples of data and scripts containing commands to analyze the data using the SPSS *Mixed Model* option.

EXERCISES

16.1 To understand what the nested terms represent, it may help to note that sums of squares for nested terms such as items-within-moods (B/A in Table 16.2) represent a pooling of sums of squares across the levels of the higher-order factor (e.g., *Mood*). Furthermore, the mean square for a source such as B/A is an average of the mean squares at the levels of A. A possible use of this understanding is that it provides an approach to the ANOVA in the absence of software that calculates nested sums of squares. Do an ANOVA of the data within each mood of Table 16.1 (*Table 16_1 Nested Data* in the *Tables* page at the website), and then pool the sums of squares for B and SB and compare the result with $SS_{B/A}$ and $SS_{SB/A}$.

16.2 Assume that pairwise comparisons had been planned to test differences among the *Mood* means in Table 16.1. Perform the test comparing the sad and neutral moods (A_1 and A_3). What is the criterion p-value if the *FWE* rate is .05?

16.3 Fifty randomly sampled words are divided into five lists that differ with respect to meaningfulness (M). All 50 words are presented on a computer monitor to each of 20 subjects and the time to read each word aloud is recorded. Present all SV, df, and EMS, and the formula for the test of M, including the df.

16.4 A researcher wishes to study the effects of viewing televised violence upon the behavior of children. Fifteen cartoon episodes are drawn from a large random sample previously rated by adult viewers. Five of these are rated as low-violence episodes, five more are medium, and five more are high in violence. Thus there are three levels of violence (V) with five different episodes (E) at each level. There are 30 subjects, with equal numbers of 6-, 8-, and 10-year-olds. Viewing time is measured on each of 15 days with a different episode viewed on each day; the order of episodes is random. Present SV, df, and EMS, and the formula for the test of A and its degrees of freedom.

16.5 In a hypothetical experiment, on a given trial 10 subjects each read a sentence designed to prime a positive or negative attitude toward some personality trait. Following that, the subjects read a description of an individual which is ambiguous with respect to the trait and have to rate the individual on a 1 (very negative) to 7 (very positive) scale. The file *EX16_5* contains a data set with four conditions: A sentence primed either a positive (P) or negative (N) attitude, and was either relevant (R) or irrelevant (I) to the trait that was rated after reading the subsequent description. There are five different randomly sampled items (prime–description pairings) in each condition, so that there are 20 ratings for each of the 10 subjects. The variables are valence ($V = 1$ or 2, positive or negative), relevance ($R = 1$ or 2, relevant or irrelevant), and items (I, 5 different items within each of the four conditions). Perform the proper analysis and discuss the results.

16.6 Estimate general ω^2 for R, V, and RV for the design of Exercise 16.5.

16.7 Twenty subjects were tested in a visual detection experiment. Ten pictures of objects were presented three times, each time in a different context (C). A second factor was the English-language frequency (F) of the object's name; five objects were high frequent and five were low frequent.

(a) State the SV, df, and EMS. Assume a model in which the highest-order nested term estimates only σ_e^2.

(b) State the formula for the F ratios and error df for testing context (C) and frequency (F).

16.8 Assume the following 4×4 Latin square.

	B_1	B_2	B_3	B_4
G_1	A_1	A_4	A_2	A_3
G_2	A_3	A_2	A_4	A_1
G_3	A_4	A_1	A_3	A_2
G_4	A_2	A_3	A_1	A_4

A is a treatment variable and B is the position in the sequence of treatments. As is common in many experiments using the Latin square design, assume that each group (G) represents a different level of an independent variable; e.g., age or level of experience. Or a different treatment might be applied to each group in the design.

(a) Suppose the population effects of A are $\alpha_1 = -4$, $\alpha_2 = 0$, $\alpha_3 = 1$, and $\alpha_4 = 3$. Also, let the effects of B be $\beta_1 = -2$, $\beta_2 = 2$, $\beta_3 = 2$, and $\beta_4 = -2$. Assume $\mu = 10$ and there are five subjects in each group. Add the effects of A and B to μ to create the data set; for example, the score in the left-most cell for G_4 is $\mu + \alpha_2 + \beta_1 = 10 + 0 - 2 = 8$. No other effects are present in the data.

(b) Calculate the sums of squares for A, B, and G for these data.

(c) Now add in the following set of AB interaction effects. Let γ_{jk} represent the interaction effect of A_j and B_k.

	B_1	B_2	B_3	B_4
G_1	$\gamma_{11}=2$	$\gamma_{42}=1$	$\gamma_{23}=-2$	$\gamma_{34}=-2$
G_2	$\gamma_{31}=0$	$\gamma_{22}=-2$	$\gamma_{43}=0$	$\gamma_{14}=-3$
G_3	$\gamma_{41}=-3$	$\gamma_{12}=-3$	$\gamma_{33}=-2$	$\gamma_{24}=3$
G_4	$\gamma_{21}=1$	$\gamma_{32}=4$	$\gamma_{13}=4$	$\gamma_{44}=2$

Now what are the A, B, and G sums of squares for these data?

(d) What is the potential problem suggested by the preceding results?

16.9 Consider the following 4×4 Latin square:

$$
\begin{array}{c}
 & C_1 & C_2 & C_3 & C_4 \\
S_1 & 25(A_1) & 16(A_4) & 24(A_2) & 18(A_3) \\
S_2 & 19(A_2) & 19(A_1) & 13(A_3) & 12(A_4) \\
S_3 & 13(A_4) & 18(A_3) & 20(A_1) & 16(A_2) \\
S_4 & 17(A_3) & 19(A_2) & 18(A_4) & 17(A_1)
\end{array}
$$

(a) Calculate the SS_A, SS_C, SS_S, and $SS_{residual}$.

(b) Equation 13.4 estimates the MS_{SA}, assuming we had used a subjects × treatments design instead of the Latin square, and Equation 13.5 uses that estimate to obtain an estimate of the relative efficiency of the two designs. Estimate MS_{SA} from the data set above.

(c) What is your estimate of the relative efficiency of the two designs?

16.10 In a study of decision making, two factors were manipulated. The task either resembled one seen during a practice session or did not (experience, E), and the amount of information available was either high or low (information level, I). Each subject was tested under all four combinations of E and I with the assignment of EI combinations to four randomly sampled problems (P) counterbalanced through the use of a Latin square. Decision times were:

$$
\begin{array}{c}
 & P_1 & P_2 & P_3 & P_4 \\
S_1 & 1.4(E_1I_1) & 2.2(E_2I_2) & 1.5(E_1I_2) & 1.5(E_2I_1) \\
S_2 & 2.1(E_1I_2) & 1.5(E_1I_1) & 2.0(E_2I_1) & 2.4(E_2I_2) \\
S_3 & 2.8(E_2I_2) & 2.1(E_2I_1) & 1.4(E_1I_1) & 1.8(E_1I_2) \\
S_4 & 2.3(E_2I_1) & 2.1(E_1I_2) & 2.7(E_2I_2) & 1.6(E_1I_1)
\end{array}
$$

Perform the ANOVA.

16.11   A researcher wishes to investigate cognitive performance as a function of drug type (T) and dosage (D). Thirty-two subjects are randomly assigned to one of two drugs, and each subject is given a different one of four dosages of the same drug on four different occasions (O). A Latin square design is used with four sequences (R, row) of dosages and eight subjects in each sequence. Half of the subjects in each sequence receive D_1 and half receive D_2.

    (a) State the SV, df, and error terms.

    (b) Another way to run this study would be to create a single 8×8 Latin square with two subjects in each row (so there are still 128 total scores). The eight treatments would be all possible combinations of the drug (T) and dosage (D) levels. Write out the SV, df, and error terms for this case.

    (c) What are the advantages and disadvantages of the two designs?

16.12   A researcher is interested in gambling behavior under variations in initial stake (I), payoffs (P), and probability of winning (W). There are three levels of each of these variables. Eighty-one subjects are available for this experiment. Many possible experimental designs could be used. Suggest several alternative designs and discuss their relative merits.

16.13   When subjects are tested under different conditions at different points in time, carry-over (residual) effects are a potential problem. The digram-balanced design described in this chapter provides one possible solution.

    (a) Construct a digram-balanced design, assuming that there are six levels of the treatment variable.

    (b) Construct a digram-balanced design, assuming that there are five levels of the treatment variable.

16.14   The *Ex16_14* file in the *Exercises* page of the book's website contains a data set for a 4×4 Latin square design. There are 12 subjects with three in each row (R) of the square. A is the treatment factor and C is the column (or position in time) factor. Assume that C has fixed effects. Perform the ANOVA.

16.15   Presumably, you analyzed the *Ex16_14* data set correctly. However, some individuals might treat the data as if they were obtained from a subjects × treatments design. Pool terms from your answer to Exercise 16.14 to arrive at this incorrect ANOVA. How do the F and p-values relate to those previously obtained? Explain the reason for the difference in results.

16.16   The *Ex16_16* file contains data (very) loosely modeled after a study by Witvliet, Ludwig, and Vander Laan (2001). Subjects in that experiment were instructed to think of an individual who had mistreated or offended them. They imagined a response to this individual as they read four scripts representing hurting someone (S_1), bearing a grudge (S_2), empathizing (S_3), and forgiving (S_4). Various physiological measures were obtained in each of several segments of time in several counterbalanced blocks. The *Ex16_16* file contains heartbeat change scores similar to averages in the Witvliet article. There are 20 cases in the file, 5 in each of the four rows of a Latin square. The within-subject factors are S (the script) and C (the ordinal position in the sequence of presentation). Note that two scripts have negative valences (*SN1* and *SN2*) and two have positive valences (*SP1* and *SP2*); the effect of valence should be considered in the analysis. Perform the analysis and summarize your conclusions.

16.17   Assume that the experiment described in Exercise 16.16 was replicated with two groups of 20 subjects each; $H1$ and $H2$ represent high- and low-hostility groups as measured prior to the experiment. The data are in the *Ex16_17* file. Carry out the ANOVA and state your conclusions.

Chapter 17
Integrated Analysis III

17.1 OVERVIEW

In this chapter, we review and extend the developments in the preceding chapters on repeated-measures designs. To provide a context, we consider data from a hypothetical experiment. The design involves one between-subjects factor and two within-subjects factors; one of the within-subjects factors represents items nested within levels of the other within-subjects factor. This is another example of the hierarchical design of Chapter 16. We have the following goals in this chapter.

- To present an integrated analysis of the data in our example. This means exploring the data; carrying out the ANOVA, including quasi-F tests and contrasts where appropriate; and estimating measures of importance.
- To review the use of the Latin square design to investigate the factors in our example.
- To review the factors to consider in choosing between randomized assignment of items to levels of within-subjects variables and counterbalancing of the assignment.

17.2 INTRODUCTION TO THE EXPERIMENT

Fredrickson and Kahneman (1993) investigated the effects of duration of a film clip on the emotional response of individuals who witnessed the clip. Are pleasant clips deemed more pleasant when longer? Are unpleasant clips deemed more unpleasant when the unpleasant events take place for a longer time period? Our hypothetical experiment is a greatly simplified version of their study and the data are artificial, although designed to mimic the effect of duration of the film clip. We assume an experiment in which only unpleasant film clips are presented for varying time periods. Therefore, we varied duration with different clips nested within durations. We also varied the delay of the test; one group of subjects rated each clip immediately after viewing it whereas a second group rated each clip from memory after viewing all clips. In summary, we ask

1. What is the effect of duration of an unpleasant experience upon the viewer's perception of

the experience? A reasonable hypothesis is that continued exposure to an unpleasant stimulus will increase the viewer's discomfort.

2. Is the mean rating affected by the time gap between viewing and rating the clips? One possibility is that the negative effect of films viewed earlier will dissipate over time, resulting in a lower average rating of unpleasantness when ratings are made after all films have been viewed.

3. Does the effect of duration depend upon the time of testing? That is, do duration and time of test interact? The effect of duration may be more pronounced when each film clip is rated immediately after being viewed.

17.3 METHOD

17.3.1 Subjects

Assume that 24 college-age volunteers were randomly assigned to the two testing conditions, 12 to be tested in the immediate and 12 in the delayed condition.

17.3.2 Stimulus Materials

Thirty film clips were viewed and rated for unpleasantness by a group of 10 pilot subjects. From these, 15 with roughly equal distributions of unpleasantness ratings were included in the experiment. They were randomly divided into three groups of clips, and then edited so that five clips lasted approximately 30 s; five others had a 60-s duration, and the remaining five clips lasted 90 s. Each clip began with a title; e.g., "Aftermath of Hiroshima."

17.3.3 Design

There were two groups of 12 subjects each; they differed with respect to whether film clips were rated immediately after viewing or after all clips had been presented (variable C). The within-subjects factors were duration of the film clip (A) and clips (B/A); five clips were nested within each of the three durations.

17.3.4 Procedure

The order of viewing of the clips was randomized for each subject. The immediate-test group rated the film clip immediately after viewing. The delayed-test group viewed all 15 clips, and then was presented the titles as a reminder in the order of viewing and asked to rate each clip. Ratings were on a 100-point scale, with zero being "not at all unpleasant" and 100 being "very unpleasant."

17.4 RESULTS AND DISCUSSION

17.4.1 Exploratory Analyses

Table 17.1 presents the means for the delay × duration cells.[1] These means are also plotted, together with standard error bars, in Fig. 17.1. It appears that subjects find the clips more unpleasant the

---

[1] The complete data set is at the website in the file *Table 17_1 IA3 data*.

Table 17.1   Mean unpleasantness ratings of film clips

Delay of test	Duration (in seconds)			
	30 s	60 s	90 s	Mean
Immediate	47.867	54.383	57.933	53.394
Delayed	46.367	51.367	54.300	50.678
Mean	47.117	52.875	56.117	52.036

Note: Test delay is a between-subjects variable, and duration is a within-subjects variable. There are 12 subjects in each level of delay and each cell mean is based on ratings of five film clips.

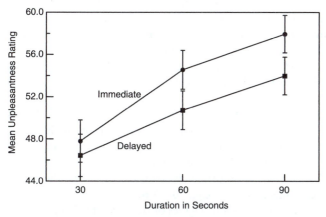

Fig. 17.1 Plot of ratings of film clips with standard error bars.

longer they are exposed to them, with a roughly linear increase with time. This is true of both delay-of-test conditions, although the rate of increase in ratings with duration of the clip is slightly greater when ratings occur immediately after each clip. The means are also higher in the immediate than in the delayed test condition. Finally, we note that the error bars are roughly similar in length across durations, indicating that the within-cell variances in the three durations do not differ greatly.

There are other considerations before we perform the analysis of variance. Is there evidence of any outliers that might distort the pattern of means? Are the data approximately normally distributed, as assumed by the ANOVA model? Are the variances homogeneous across items or across levels of the independent variables? To address these questions, we had SPSS save unstandardized residuals; similar options are available in other software packages. The complete set of residuals is also available in the *IA3 Residuals* file on the *Tables* page of the book's website. SPSS calculates each score's residual error as a sum of all between- and within-subjects error components associated with the score, thus removing the effects of the manipulated variables. We plotted box, stem-and-leaf, and Q–Q plots for each of the 15 film clips and obtained tests of normality for each set of residuals. There were no significant departures from normality, the variances were quite similar across factor levels, and only four outliers were detected among the 360 scores, fewer than we would expect by chance.

Another issue relevant to repeated-measures analyses is the assumption of sphericity. Maunchly's test revealed no significant violation and the Huynh–Feldt epsilon adjustment for degrees of freedom was 1.0 for both the duration and delay by duration sources. In summary, our exploration of the data suggested several trends for the effects of duration and test delay upon the mean ratings, and appeared consistent with assumptions underlying the analysis. We therefore proceed to the analysis of variance to test the trends noted.

17.4.2 Tests of Hypotheses

Users of SPSS may refer to the syntax file, *Nested Designs_2.sps*, that is on the website; its use is described in the *Syntax Readme* file. The syntax file provides quasi-F ratios as required to test various sources, and is also easily modified to deal with a design in which the within-subjects factors cross. In addition, any factor can be designated as fixed or random. Other statistical programs also can deal with nested variables. However, those users who have access to earlier or more limited versions of statistical software can use the analytical approach of Section 16.2. This involves first treating B (items) as if they crossed with A (duration). Table 17.2 presents the partitioning of sums of squares and degrees of freedom resulting from this approach. Combining the B and AB sums of squares and dividing by the sum of their associated degrees of freedom, we have the mean square for B/A in Table 17.3. Similarly, pooling the BC and ABC terms yields the BC/A nested interaction term in Table 17.3. Finally, we have pooled the SB/C and SAB/C to obtain the *Residual* (SB/AC) term in Table 17.3.

The error terms against which delay, duration, and their interaction are tested are derived from the expected mean squares in Table 17.4. Those *EMS* terms remind us that there is no single source of variance that provides an error term against which to test the duration, delay, and duration × delay effects. Instead, as described in Chapters 15 and 16, quasi-F statistics are calculated. These involve combinations of mean squares that have the appropriate expectations for testing the effects of interest. Formulas for F_1', the numerator mean square (e.g., MS_C) divided by its error mean square, are provided below Table 17.3; formulas for the error degrees of freedom are also presented there.

From Table 17.3, we see that duration has a significant effect. As film clips increased in length, so did viewers' feelings of discomfort as indicated by ratings of unpleasantness. The difference in

Table 17.2   Preliminary partitioning for the rating data summarized in Table 17.1[a]

Source	df	Sums of squares
Delay (C)	1	664.23
S/C	22	8,474.31
Duration (A)	2	4,986.87
AC	2	72.32
$A \times S/C$	44	1,176.21
Items (B)	4	45.02
BC	4	101.48
$B \times S/C$	88	3,168.17
AB	8	428.47
ABC	8	167.10
$AB \times S/C$	176	5,204.57

[a] For this preliminary partitioning, we treated items as though they crossed with duration. In Table 17.3, $SS_B + SS_{AB}$ yields the nested term $SS_{B/A}$. Similarly, $SS_{BC} + SS_{ABC} = SS_{CB/A}$, and $SS_{BS/C} + SS_{ABS/C} = SS_{Residual}$.

Table 17.3 ANOVA of the rating data summarized in Table 17.1

Source	df	Sums of squares	Mean square	F	p
Delay (C)	1	664.23	664.23	1.77	0.20
Error(C)[a]	20.81	7,820.31	375.86		
S/C	22	8,474.31	385.20		
Duration (A)	2	4,986.87	2493.34	72.33	0.00
Error(A)[b]	7.93	273.53	34.47		
AC	2	72.32	36.16	2.08	0.22
Error(AC)[c]	4.90	85.23	17.40		
$A \times S/C$	44	1,176.21	26.73		
Items/duration (B/A)	12	473.48	39.46		
$C \times B/A$	12	268.58	22.38		
Residual	264	8,372.73	31.72		

[a] $\text{Error}(C) = MS_{S/C} + MS_{C \times B/A} - MS_{Residual} = 375.863$;
$df_{error(C)} = MS^2_{error(C)}/[(MS^2_{S/C}/df_{S/C}) + (MS^2_{C \times B/A}/df_{C \times B/A}) + (MS^2_{Residual}/df_{Residual})] = 20.81$
[b] $\text{Error}(A) = MS_{B/A} + MS_{A \times S/C} - MS_{Residual} = 34.474$;
$df_{error(A)} = MS^2_{error(A)}/[(MS^2_{B/A}/df_{B/A}) + (MS^2_{A \times S/C}/df_{A \times S/C}) + (MS^2_{Residual}/df_{Residual})] = 7.93$
[c] $\text{Error}(AC) = MS_{A \times S/C} + MS_{C \times B/A} - MS_{Residual} = 17.399$;
$df_{error(AC)} = MS^2_{error(AC)}/[(MS^2_{C \times B/A}/df_{C \times B/A}) + (MS^2_{A \times S/C}/df_{A \times S/C}) + (MS^2_{Residual}/df_{Residual})] = 4.90$

Table 17.4 Expected mean squares for the design of Table 17.1

SV	df	EMS
Delay (C)	$c - 1 = 1$	$\sigma_e^2 + ab\sigma_{S/C}^2 + n\sigma_{C \times B/A}^2 + nab\theta_C^2$
Subjects within C (S/C)	$c(n - 1) = 22$	$\sigma_e^2 + ab\sigma_{S/C}^2$
Duration (A)	$a - 1 = 2$	$\sigma_e^2 + nc\sigma_{B/A}^2 + b\sigma_{A \times S/C}^2 + nbc\theta_A^2$
AC	$(a - 1)(c - 1) = 2$	$\sigma_e^2 + n\sigma_{C \times B/A}^2 + b\sigma_{A \times S/C}^2 + nb\theta_{AC}^2$
$A \times S/C$	$c(n - 1)(a - 1) = 44$	$\sigma_e^2 + b\sigma_{A \times S/C}^2$
Items within A (B/A)	$a(b - 1) = 12$	$\sigma_e^2 + nc\sigma_{B/A}^2$
$C \times B/A$	$a(b - 1)(c - 1) = 12$	$\sigma_e^2 + n\sigma_{C \times B/A}^2$
Residual	$ac(n - 1)(b - 1) = 264$	σ_e^2

mean unpleasantness ratings as a function of whether the test was immediate or delayed was not significant; therefore, we cannot conclude that increased delay lowers ratings of unpleasantness in the population sampled. Furthermore, the nonsignificant AC interaction means that we cannot conclude that the delay of test affects the rate of increase of unpleasantness ratings with increased duration, despite the somewhat steeper slope in the immediate condition in Fig. 17.1. It is possible that these effects are present in the sampled population, but, if so, we will require more subjects and items to have sufficient power to determine this.

We might wish to test other hypotheses about the means. We might ask whether the average of the two curves in Fig. 17.1 increases linearly with increased duration over the durations studied, or whether there is significant curvature. This implies tests of trend.

17.4.3 Testing Trend Components

Panel a of Table 17.5 presents the partitioning of the duration (A) sum of squares and its inter-actions into linear and quadratic components. This partitioning can be obtained from most recent

Table 17.5   Partitioning trend components for the rating data

(*a*) Partitioning the sum of squares

Source	df	Sums of squares
Duration (*A*)	2	4,986.672
linear(*A*)	1	4,860.000
quad(*A*)	1	126.672
Duration × test (*AC*)	2	72.317
linear(*AC*)	1	68.367
quad(*AC*)	1	4.050
Duration × subjects/test ($A \times S/C$)	44	1,176.211
linear($A \times S/C$)	22	739.733
quad($A \times S/C$)	22	436.478

(*b*) Results of the analysis

Source	df	Mean square	Error term[a]	Error df	F	p
linear(*A*)	1	4,860.000	41.366	9.25	117.49	.000
quad(*A*)	1	126.672	27.582	5.02	4.59	.085
linear(*AC*)	1	68.367	24.491	6.19	2.79	.144
quad(*AC*)	1	4.050	10.507	1.74	.39	.604
linear(*A*) × *S/C*	22	33.624				
quad(*A*) × *S/C*	22	19.840				

    [a] The error terms and their degrees of freedom are calculated by the formulas below Table 17.3 except that $MS_{A \times S/C}$ is replaced by $MS_{linear(A \times S/C)}$ or $MS_{quad(A \times S/C)}$, depending on whether a linear or quadratic component is being tested.

versions of statistical software packages.[2] If *B* is assumed to have fixed effects, the linear and quadratic components of *A* and *AC* are tested against the corresponding components of *AS/C*. However, in our example, *B* represents film clips, and, presumably, we would like to generalize our results to a population of similar items. As stated below panel *b*, the appropriate error terms are similar to those used in testing *A* and *AC*. For example, we tested *A* against

$$Error(A) = MS_{B/A} + MS_{A \times S/C} - MS_{Residual}$$

To test the linear component of *A*, the error term is

$$Error[linear(A)] = MS_{B/A} + MS_{linear(A) \times S/C} - MS_{Residual}$$

The results in panel *b* reveal that only the linear component of *A* is significant. Therefore, we conclude that over the range of film clip durations used in the experiment, averaging over both the immediate and delayed test conditions, mean ratings of discomfort increase linearly with duration. We cannot conclude that test delay affects the slope of this function, or that there is any departure from a straight line in the sampled population.

  [2] In the absence of such software, polynomial sums of squares can be calculated as described in Box 15.1.

17.4.4 Estimating General ω^2 (Omega-Squared)

A measure of the contributions of our variables to the variability in the data is desirable and is required by many journals. The expected mean squares in Table 17.4 lead directly to one such measure. Continuing with our example of the experiment in which film clips were rated for unpleasantness, we calculated estimates of general ω^2 for duration (A), delay (C), and their interaction. Although there are several different definitions of omega-squared in articles and books, we defined ω_g^2 as the ratio of the variance of the source of interest divided by that variance plus all variances involving subjects plus error variance. The variance and omega-squared estimates are contained in Table 17.6.

From the results in panel b of Table 17.6, it is clear that only the duration makes a more than negligible contribution to the variability in the data. The ratings were lower following a delayed test than an immediate test and this trend increased slightly with duration, but neither the F tests nor the ω^2 estimates indicated that these trends were true of the population means. In particular, the very small ω^2 estimates indicated that little variance is attributable to the delay or delay $\times$ duration factors. These estimates of variance ratios strongly support the conclusion that—for the durations and test delays of this study—only the duration of the film clips has an effect on the unpleasantness ratings.

17.5 AN ALTERNATIVE DESIGN: THE LATIN SQUARE

17.5.1 The Experimental Design

So far, we have assumed a design in which the order of presentation of the 15 film clips and their assignment to durations was randomized for each subject with the constraint that there are five

Table 17.6 Variance estimates and general ω^2 for a hierarchical design

(a) Variance estimates

Variance	Estimator	Estimate
Delay (C)	$[(c-1)/abcn](MS_C - MS_{error(C)})$	.80
Duration (A)	$[(a-1)/abcn](MS_A - MS_{error(A)})$	13.66
AC	$[(a-1)(c-1)/abcn](MS_{AC} - MS_{error(AC)})$	.10
S/C	$(MS_{S/C} - MS_{Residual})/ab$	23.57
B/A	$(MS_{B/A} - MS_{Residual})/nc$	0.32
$A \times S/C$	$(MS_{A \times S/C} - MS_{Residual})/b$	0
$C \times B/A$	$(MS_{C \times B/A} - MS_{Residual})/n$	0
Error	$MS_{Residual}$	31.72

Note: Because the variance estimates for $A \times S/C$ and $C \times B/A$ were negative, they were set to zero.

(b) Estimates of ω^2

Source	Estimator of ω_g^2	Estimate
Delay (C)	$\hat{\sigma}_C^2/(\hat{\sigma}_C^2 + \hat{\sigma}_e^2 + \hat{\sigma}_{S/C}^2 + \hat{\sigma}_{A \times S/C}^2)$	.014
Duration (A)	$\hat{\sigma}_A^2/(\hat{\sigma}_A^2 + \hat{\sigma}_e^2 + \hat{\sigma}_{S/C}^2 + \hat{\sigma}_{A \times S/C}^2)$	.198
AC	$\hat{\sigma}_{AC}^2/(\hat{\sigma}_{AC}^2 + \hat{\sigma}_e^2 + \hat{\sigma}_{S/C}^2 + \hat{\sigma}_{A \times S/C}^2)$	.002

Table 17.7   A Latin square design (a) and data (b)

(a) A Latin square design

Row	B_1	B_2	B_3
1	A_3	A_1	A_2
2	A_1	A_2	A_3
3	A_2	A_3	A_1

(b) A data set

Subject	Row	Delay = C_1 (immediate test)						Row mean

Subject	Row	A_1	A_2	A_3	B_1	B_2	B_3	Row mean
		Delay = C_1 (immediate test)						
1	1	51.0	61.8	63.4	63.4	51.0	61.8	
2	1	57.0	58.8	66.4	66.4	57.0	58.8	55.617
3	1	53.6	55.6	53.6	53.6	53.6	55.6	
4	1	41.6	48.6	56.0	56.0	41.6	48.6	
5	2	49.8	58.2	62.0	49.8	58.2	62.0	
6	2	36.6	44.8	49.6	36.6	44.8	49.6	51.450
7	2	46.4	56.4	60.6	46.4	56.4	60.6	
8	2	48.4	50.2	54.4	48.4	50.2	54.4	
9	3	54.8	62.2	63.2	62.2	63.2	54.8	
10	3	38.8	49.0	50.2	49.0	50.2	38.8	53.117
11	3	48.0	52.6	57.8	52.6	57.8	48.0	
12	3	48.4	54.4	58.0	54.4	58.0	48.4	
C_1 means		47.867	54.383	57.933	53.233	53.500	53.450	53.394
		Delay = C_2 (immediate test)						
13	1	57.8	62.8	61.4	61.4	57.8	62.8	
14	1	47.4	48.6	54.2	54.2	47.4	48.6	50.700
15	1	40.4	48.2	52.2	52.2	40.4	48.2	
16	1	42.2	48.0	45.2	45.2	42.2	48.0	
17	2	51.0	56.4	62.2	51.0	56.4	62.2	
18	2	37.8	43.8	47.8	37.8	43.8	47.8	50.200
19	2	46.6	53.8	56.0	46.6	53.8	56.0	
20	2	45.0	48.2	53.8	45.0	48.2	53.8	
21	3	47.0	50.8	55.6	50.8	55.6	47.0	
22	3	49.2	46.6	51.4	46.6	51.4	49.2	51.133
23	3	46.0	54.6	55.8	54.6	55.8	46.0	
24	3	46.0	54.6	56.0	54.6	56.0	46.0	
C_2 means		46.367	51.367	54.300	50.000	50.733	51.300	50.678
Overall means		47.117	52.875	56.117	51.617	52.117	52.375	52.036

Note: Scores are means of sets of five ratings for each subject, arranged by duration (A) and item set (B). C represents delay of test, and row refers to the assignment of durations to item sets.

stimuli shown at each duration. As discussed in Chapters 13 and 16, the Latin square design is potentially more efficient, capable of reducing error variance due to the order of testing or variability in the stimuli. With this in mind, we assume that the 15 film clips are divided into three sets of 5. These sets are assigned to durations in such a way that the assignment is counterbalanced over all subjects. Panel *a* of Table 17.7 illustrates the design in which each level of *B* represents a set of five film clips and the levels of *A* are the three durations of the study in which subjects rate how unpleasant each film clip was. As in the preceding sections, we assume that the ratings were made immediately after each clip or delayed until all clips were shown; this is represented by the letter *C*.

Panel *b* contains the means of the ratings of the film clips. These means are also in the file *Table 17_6 Lsq Data* on the *Tables* page of the book's website. They are presented twice, once organized by duration and once by item set. For example, 51 is the mean rating of five items seen by Subject 1 at the shortest duration, A_1; for Subject 1, these five items also make up the second set of film clips, B_2. The advantage of having two organizations of the cell means is that the same file can be analyzed with duration as the within-subjects factor, and a second time with the item set as the within-subjects factor. The complete Latin square analysis can be obtained from these two preliminary analyses.

17.5.2 The Data Analysis

Table 17.8 contains three possible partitionings of the sums of squares based on the data of Table 17.7. The left-most column presents a standard mixed-design analysis with rows (*R*) and test delay (*C*) as between-subjects factors and duration of the film clips (*A*) as a within-subjects factor. The middle partitioning replaces duration by set (*B*), referring to each set of five film clips, or items. Finally, the right-most partitioning drops the terms that reflect the interactions of the three Latin square factors (*A*, *B*, and *R*) because we lack sufficient degrees of freedom to include both the main effects and these interactions in this incomplete-block design.[3] The unanalyzed interaction effects

Table 17.8   Three partitions of the sums of squares based on Table 17.7

SV	df	SS	SV	df	SS	SV	df	SS
Delay (*C*)	1	132.85	Delay (*C*)	1	132.85	Delay (*C*)	1	132.85
Rows (*R*)	2	65.62	Rows (*R*)	2	65.62	Rows (*R*)	2	65.62
CR	2	45.17	*CR*	2	45.17	*CR*	2	45.17
S/CR	18	1,584.07	*S/CR*	18	1,584.07	*S/CR*	18	1,584.07
Duration (*A*)	2	997.33	Set (*B*)	2	7.13	Duration (*A*)	2	997.33
AC	2	14.46	*BC*	2	3.54	*AC*	2	14.46
AR	4	18.25	*BR*	4	1,008.45	Set (*B*)	2	7.13
ACR	4	4.71	*ABR*	4	15.63	*BC*	2	3.54
WSR	36	212.28	*WSR*	36	212.28	BCR^a	2	11.12
						$C \times BCR^b$	2	1.17
						WSR	36	212.28
Total	71	3,075.74	Total	71	3,075.74	Total	71	3,075.74

[a] $SS_{BCR} = SS_{AR} - SS_B = SS_{BR} - SS_A$
[b] $SS_{C \times BCR} = SS_{ACR} - SS_{BC} = SS_{BCR} - SS_{AC}$

[3] The Latin square is an incomplete-block design because each subject, or block, is tested only under some (actually $1/a$) of the possible combinations of factors *A* and *B*.

potentially contribute to the between-cell residual (BCR) variability and to the interaction with delay $(C \times BCR)$.

Before turning to the hypothesis tests based on the right-most partitioning in Table 17.8, compare the values of the sums of squares with similarly labeled terms in Table 17.3. Note that SS_C in Table 17.3 is exactly five times larger than the same term in Table 17.8. The same is true for SS_A and SS_{AC}. The reason for this is that in Table 17.8, the sums of squares are based on means of five items. As we said in Chapter 5, the variance of a mean is the variance of the scores divided by the number of scores. This also holds true for sums of squares.

Table 17.9 contains the tests of the Latin square data. The error terms are dictated by the expected mean squares presented earlier in Table 16.10. Those expectations indicate that the delay factor is tested by a quasi-F statistic. Alternatively, because the F test of BC yields a very small F, we could assume that $\sigma_{BC}^2 = 0$; in that case, C would be tested against $S/C \times Row$. This would not change the result, or even the p-value in this data set. Also, because the Fs for BCR and $C \times BCR$ when tested against WSR were less than 1, these terms might be pooled with their error term, WSR. If we did this, the pooled error term for testing all within-subjects terms would be $MS_{Residual} = (11.12 + 1.17 + 212.28)/40 = 5.61$. Again, using this error term to test A and AC would not substantially change the results. Of course, if the C, A, or AC results had been less clear-cut, the use of an error term on more degrees of freedom might have changed the result. Bear in mind, however, that we only even raise the possibility of pooling in this example, because preliminary tests of BC, BCR, and $C \times BCR$ yielded very small Fs.

Table 17.9 ANOVA of the data in Table 17.7

SV	df	SS	MS	Error term	F	p
Delay (C)	1	132.85	132.85	see *Note*	1.58	0.23
Row (R)	2	65.62	32.81	$S/C \times R$	0.37	0.70
$C \times R$	2	45.17	22.59	$S/C \times R$	0.26	0.77
$S/C \times R$	18	1,584.07	88.00			
Duration (A)	2	997.33	498.67	BCR	89.68	0.01
$A \times C$	2	14.46	7.23	$C \times BCR$	12.25	0.08
Set (B)	2	7.13	3.57	WSR	0.61	0.55
$B \times C$	2	3.54	1.77	WSR	0.32	0.73
BCR	2	11.12	5.56			
$C \times BCR$	2	1.17	0.59			
WSR	36	212.28	5.90			

Note: C is tested against $MS_{S/CR} + MS_{BC} - MS_{WSR} = 83.87$; the error df for testing C are 16.25; the formula is: $(MS_{S/CR} + MS_{BC} - MS_{WSR})^2 / [(MS_{S/CR}^2 / df_{S/CR}) + (MS_{BC}^2 / df_{BC}) + (MS_{WSR}^2 / df_{WSR})]$

17.5.3 Estimates of General Omega-Squared (ω_g^2)

The expected mean squares in Table 17.10 provide the basis for estimating ω^2 for the delay and duration terms, and their interaction. Because several of the variance estimates are negative, they were set to zero to simplify the calculations. As a result, the *Row*, C, CR, and S/CR terms all estimate the same population variances and were pooled. Similarly, all remaining terms with F ratios less than 1 were pooled with the WSR term to provide a single estimate of σ_e^2. Table 17.10

Table 17.10   Revised ANOVA table, variance estimates, and partial ω^2 for a Latin square design

(*a*) Revised ANOVA table with estimates of population variances

SV	df^a	EMS	$\hat{\sigma}^2$
Delay (*C*)	$c-1$	$\sigma_e^2 + a\sigma_{S/C}^2 + a^2 n\theta_C^2$	$[(c-1)/a^2 cn](MS_C - MS_{S/C}) = .775$
S/C^b	$c(an-1)$	$\sigma_e^2 + a\sigma_{S/C}^2$	$(MS_{S/C} - MS_{residual})/a = 23.898$
Duration (*A*)	$a-1$	$\sigma_e^2 + acn\theta_A^2$	$[(a-1)/a^2 cn](MS_A - MS_{residual}) = 13.703$
AC	$(a-1)(c-1)$	$\sigma_e^2 + an\theta_{AC}^2$	$[(a-1)(c-1)/a^2 cn](MS_A - MS_{residual}) = .052$
Residual^c	$c(an-1)(a-1)$	σ_e^2	$MS_{residual} = 5.346$

> ^{a} $a = 3$, $c = 2$, and $n = 4$.
> ^{b} $MS_{S/C} = (SS_{S/CR} + SS_R + SS_{CR})/c(an-1) = 77.039$.
> ^{c} $MS_{Residual} = (SS_B + SS_{BC} + SS_{BCR} + SS_{C \times BCR} + SS_{WSR})/c(an-1)(a-1) = 5.346$.

(*b*) Estimates of ω_g^2

SV	Estimator	Estimate
Delay (*C*)	$\hat{\sigma}_C^2/(\hat{\sigma}_e^2 + \hat{\sigma}_C^2 + \hat{\sigma}_{S/C}^2)$	.026
Duration (*A*)	$\hat{\sigma}_A^2/(\hat{\sigma}_e^2 + \hat{\sigma}_A^2 + \hat{\sigma}_{S/C}^2)$	.319
AC	$\hat{\sigma}_{AC}^2/(\hat{\sigma}_e^2 + \hat{\sigma}_{AC}^2 + \hat{\sigma}_{S/C}^2)$	.002

contains the revised ANOVA table, and formulas for the estimates of the population variances, and for the estimates of ω^2. As in our analysis of the hierarchical design, it is again clear that only the duration of the film clips has any effect on subjects' ratings of unpleasantness.

17.5.4 Which Design?

Whether we consider F tests or measures such as ω^2, the hierarchical and Latin square designs have yielded the same conclusions, although the ω^2 values are slightly larger in Table 17.10 than in Table 17.6. The similarity of results is not surprising because the analyses were based on the same data set. If we had actually run two experiments, using a different design in each, there would have been some differences in the two sets of rating data. This leaves the question of which design is preferable. Although there is no single answer, the following questions should be considered before choosing a design:

1. Is there reason to expect that items will contribute considerable variance? If so, counterbalancing the assignment of treatments to item sets will permit the removal of much of the item variability, increasing the efficiency of the Latin square design.
2. Is there reason to believe that treatments and items will interact? If so, the between-cell residual is likely to be inflated by that interaction variance, reducing the efficiency of the Latin square design.
3. How many factor levels will there be? Larger squares have more error degrees of freedom associated with both the *BCR* and *WSR* terms, thus increasing the effectiveness of the Latin square design. Although we used a small square for our example, generally it is wise to have squares with at least five levels of the Latin square factors.

If the Latin square is the design of choice, the data should be properly analyzed. We have found that in many, perhaps most, instances researchers have counterbalanced the assignment of factor levels and then analyzed the data as if the design were a standard repeated-measures (i.e., subjects × treatments) design, or a mixed design if there was a between-subjects factor. We did perform such an analysis in Table 17.10 but only after preliminary F tests (Table 17.9) of the terms we pooled indicated that the variances were negligible. We can justify this analysis only because we first performed the appropriate tests associated with the Latin square. If sources of variance are neglected that are substantial, ratios of mean squares may not be distributed as F and error rates may be increased. Furthermore, results of the row and BCR tests in the Latin square analysis provide indications of the presence of AB—treatment by item set—effects, If such effects are present, it should lead us to investigate whether our treatments are effective with some item sets and not with others and, if so, what distinguishes the "good" and "bad" item sets. Finally, in some instances the main effects of B are of interest; for example, if B represents successive trial blocks, we may wish to determine how performance changes over time.

17.6 SUMMARY

In this chapter, we reviewed and elaborated on the developments in Chapters 14–16, and extended the material in those chapters.

- We analyzed data from a standard mixed design and from a Latin square in which there was a between-subjects factor and items were nested within levels of a within-subjects factor.
- We reviewed the expected mean squares for these designs, using them to justify F tests and estimates of effect size in the form of partial ω^2.
- We reviewed the considerations involved in choosing between random assignment of items to levels and counterbalancing.

EXERCISES

17.1 **(a)** The *EX17_1* data set on the book's website contains percentages of target detections for 20 subjects for each of 3 days in a perception experiment. Explore the data and discuss the results of your exploration.

(b) Perform the ANOVA on the data including a trend analysis. What do you conclude?

(c) An arcsine transformation is sometimes performed on probabilities. Convert the percentages to probabilities, and then calculate the arcsine of the square root of the probabilities. Perform an ANOVA on the transformed data. Do the results change your conclusions?

17.2 A follow-up to the experiment in Exercise 17.1 is planned. Half of the targets (B) on each of the 3 days (A) will be digits and half letters. In addition, the background (C, noise elements) will be either digits or letters. Present the sources of variance, *df*, and *EMS*, and indicate the appropriate error terms to test the main and interaction effects of A, B, and C, and their interactions. Assume that $N = 44$ and use numerical values wherever possible (*df*s, *EMS* coefficients).

17.3 A different way of designing the experiment described in Exercise 17.2 is to have half of the targets on each day be letters and half digits, but maintain a constant background throughout the 3 days. However, context would be varied between groups with half of the subjects seeing a background of digits and half of the subjects seeing a background of letters. Present the sources of variance, *df*, and *EMS*, and indicate the appropriate error terms to test the main and interaction effects of *A*, *B*, and *C*, and their interactions. Assume $N = 44$ and use numerical values wherever possible (*df*s, *EMS* coefficients).

17.4 (a) Discuss the pros and cons of the designs in Exercises 17.2 and 17.3.

(b) What effects would changes in the correlation (ρ) and the degrees-of-freedom adjustment (ε) have on the power of the tests of targets and context in each design?

17.5 Because the tests of *CB/A* and *AS/C* in Table 17.3 yield *F*s less than 1, some components of variance in the expected mean squares of Table 17.4 may be assumed to be zero. Given this assumption, revise the *EMS*, and present a revised version of Table 17.3, including sources, *df*, mean squares, *F* ratios, and *p*-values. Does this revision change any conclusions based on Table 17.3?

17.6 Sixteen subjects read 15 short texts. Although all subjects were fluent in English, eight had learned it as a second language (*Group* = 1 or 2; native speaker or bilingual). Each text contained an ambiguous word whose meaning was made clear by a short region of text following the word. Time looking at the disambiguating region was measured. In five of the texts, the ambiguous word was preceded by a context supporting its meaning ($A = 1$); in five, the contexts were neutral ($A = 2$); and in the remaining five texts, the contexts implied the wrong interpretation, The data are at the book's website in the file *EX17_6*. Perform the ANOVA and discuss the results.

17.7 In studies such as that described in Exercise 17.6, scores are often missing and researchers calculate *minF'* to test hypotheses. The files *EX17_7S* and *EX17_7I* on the book's website were constructed by first randomly deleting a small number of scores from the *EX_17_6* files. The numbers in the *EX17_7S* file were calculated by averaging the remaining item scores in each level of *A* for each subject. The numbers in the *EX17_7I* file were calculated by averaging the scores in each level of *C* for each item. Calculate the *minF'* value and its degrees of freedom for the test of the *A* effect. Box 15.2 provides an example of the calculations.

17.8 Twenty air controllers were presented with a series of four simulated flight situations and their response times were recorded. The sequence of situations (*A*) was counterbalanced over four blocks of time (*B*). The data are on the website in the *EX17_8* file.

(a) Ignoring block and group variability, we can treat the design as a simple 20 subjects by four levels of *A* design. Present the sources of variance, *df*, sums of squares, mean squares, *F* ratios, and *p*-values, assuming this is the design.

(b) Reanalyze the data taking its Latin square properties into consideration. What is the relationship between the two sets of sums of squares in the analyses in parts (a) and (b)?

(c) What changes, if any, would there be in the analysis if *B* is assumed to have random effects?

17.9 The experiment described in Exercise 17.8 was replicated, but this time there were 24 subjects, 12 under 60 years old (*Age* = 1) and 12 more than 60 years old (*Age* = 2). The data are in the file *EX17_9; Group* refers to the order of the situations, *A* again refers to the situation, and *B* refers to the position in time. Perform the ANOVA and discuss the results.

17.10 We wish to further investigate the *Situation* $(A) \times Age$ interaction in Exercise 17.9.

(a) Create a new ANOVA table by combining terms from your answer to Exercise 17.8 so that you now have a mixed design with age as the sole between-subjects factor and A as the sole within-subjects factor. What justification might be given for this?

(b) Has the pooling affected your conclusion about the $A \times$ age interaction? Compare partial ω^2 for the two analyses (Exercises 17.9 and 17.10).

Part 4:
Correlation and Regression

Chapter 18
An Introduction to Correlation and Regression

18.1 INTRODUCTION TO THE CORRELATION AND REGRESSION CHAPTERS

Although the ANOVAs we have so far discussed are widely used to determine whether independent and dependent variables are related, they have some important limitations. Standard ANOVA treats factors as qualitative categorical variables even if they are inherently quantitative and continuous, thereby ignoring potentially useful information. In ANOVA, levels of a factor are merely considered to be *different* from one another. The *ordering* of levels or *how different* the levels are from one another is not considered, although supplementary procedures (e.g., trend analysis) that use ideas from regression can deal with quantitative factors. Also, the neat partitioning of variability into nonoverlapping components associated with main effects and interactions that is the hallmark of ANOVA only occurs when the factors are uncorrelated. Factors are uncorrelated in designed experiments with equal numbers of scores in each cell, but generally not otherwise.

We now begin a series of chapters that develop a general framework which incorporates both categorical and quantitative variables and can deal with correlated factors:

- Chapter 18 provides an introduction to the basic ideas of correlation and regression.
- Chapter 19 develops statistical inference and power analysis for correlation and considers some alternative measures.
- Chapter 20 extends the discussion of bivariate regression and considers inference and power analysis for regression.
- Chapters 21–23 develop regression procedures when there is more than one predictor variable. This use of regression is known as *multiple regression*.
- Chapter 24 introduces the idea of coding categorical variables so that they can be used along with quantitative variables in regression, thereby developing a very general framework for statistical analysis. We then show that ANOVA is a special case of regression.
- Chapter 25 deals with analysis of covariance (ANCOVA) within the regression framework.
- Chapter 26 presents several multiple regression analyses and focuses on interpretation.

- Certain extensions of the usual regression framework are also introduced in these chapters. We consider some "robust" regression procedures that are less sensitive to failures of assumptions than ordinary least-squares (OLS) procedures. We also briefly introduce logistic regression, as well as multilevel or hierarchical linear regression.

18.2 OVERVIEW OF CHAPTER 18

In Chapter 2 we considered how to graph and summarize distributions of single variables. We also briefly introduced scatterplots and the Pearson correlation coefficient as ways of exploring and summarizing bivariate data. Procedures for characterizing bivariate data are important because we rarely study individual variables in isolation; rather, we usually are interested in how variables are related to one another. For example, we may wish to know how cholesterol level varies with age or whether math skills are related to verbal skills in children. A major goal of this chapter is to discuss in more detail how to represent data in ways that allow us to see how, and how strongly, variables are related, and to present statistics that summarize important aspects of the relationship. A major focus will be to expand our understanding of the correlation coefficient as a measure of the degree to which two variables have a linear (i.e., straight-line) relationship. As we shall show, the value of the correlation coefficient depends on the similarity of the corresponding z scores of the variables being correlated, making it sensitive to the variances of these variables in the sample. This can lead to much confusion about how to interpret and how, or whether, to compare correlations.

Another major goal of the chapter is to develop the basics of linear regression. If two variables are systematically related, it should be possible to use information about one of the variables to predict the other. For example, knowing a father's height is useful in predicting the height of his son. Even though any single prediction may not be very accurate, if we consider many fathers and sons, on the average we can predict a son's height more accurately if we use information about the father's height than if we do not. As we would expect, the more closely the heights of fathers and sons are related, the better we can predict. We would like to develop procedures for making the best predictions possible with the information that we have available. Linear equations that use information about one variable to make optimal predictions about a second variable are referred to as *bivariate regression equations*.

In Chapter 18, we have the following goals:

- Provide examples of bivariate relationships and discuss how they may be represented with scatterplots.
- Discuss how to use "smoothers" or "fit lines" to extract systematic relationships between two variables in the face of random variability.
- Discuss the Pearson correlation coefficient as a measure of the strength of a linear relationship.
- Introduce least-squares linear regression, first with z scores and then with raw scores.
- Discuss major differences between regression and correlation.
- Introduce the concept of regression toward the mean and provide examples of how people misunderstand or fail to appreciate the consequences of this phenomenon.
- Consider measures of linear fit such as the coefficient of determination and the standard error of estimate.
- Discuss the interpretation of the correlation coefficient and factors that influence it.

18.3 SOME EXAMPLES OF BIVARIATE RELATIONSHIPS

Consider subtraction and multiplication accuracy scores (percent correct) for third-graders from the *Royer* data set on the arithmetic skills of grade-school children (included on the book's website). The basic statistics for the 28 third-grade students with values on both variables are given in Table 18.1. The multiplication accuracy scores tend to be lower than the subtraction scores, $t(27) = 3.09$, $p = .005$, and also exhibit greater variability,[1] $z = 2.78$, $p = .023$.

Table 18.1 Descriptive statistics for the 28 third-grade students who have both subtraction and multiplication accuracy scores (obtained using the SPSS Explore module)

Descriptives

			Statistic	Std. error
subacc	Mean		87.0240	2.30531
	95% confidence	Lower bound	82.2939	
	interval for mean	Upper bound	91.7541	
	5% Trimmed mean		88.1999	
	Median		89.1815	
	Variance		148.805	
	Std. deviation		12.19856	
	Minimum		46.67	
	Maximum		100.00	
	Range		53.33	
	Interquartile range		15.45	
	Skewness		−1.473	.441
	Kurtosis		3.129	.858
multacc	Mean		78.4690	3.42575
	95% confidence	Lower bound	71.4400	
	interval for mean	Upper bound	85.4981	
	5% Trimmed mean		79.8302	
	Median		79.4470	
	Variance		328.601	
	Std. deviation		18.12736	
	Minimum		29.41	
	Maximum		100.00	
	Range		70.59	
	Interquartile range		25.52	
	Skewness		−.835	.441
	Kurtosis		.813	.858

[1] Determined by using a test suggested by Sandik and Olsson (1982) for testing dependent variances. In this test, first the absolute deviations about the median are obtained for subtraction and for multiplication scores, and then the Wilcoxon signed-rank test is performed on these absolute deviations. For a more general discussion of tests for dependent variances, see Wilcox (1989).

18.3.1 Scatterplots

How can we best characterize the relationship between subtraction and multiplication accuracy in this sample of third-graders? We might expect that children with higher subtraction scores will also have higher multiplication scores, because we know that some children are better at arithmetic than others. Perhaps the best way of determining whether there is a relationship between two variables is to use a *scatterplot*, in which each data point has coordinates that represent the scores for one student. The scatterplot for the 28 third-graders for whom we have both multiplication accuracy and subtraction accuracy scores is presented in Fig. 18.1. Note that some statistical packages (in this case SYSTAT) allow us to present histograms or box plots along the borders of the scatterplot, so we can see information about both the univariate and joint distributions in the same display.

What we see in the scatterplot is a tendency for larger multiplication scores to go together with larger subtraction scores—we say there is a *positive* relationship between the two variables. If larger scores on one variable tend to go together with smaller scores on the other, we have a *negative* relationship. The scatterplot in Fig. 18.2 shows the mean time to answer multiplication problems plotted against multiplication accuracy. The graph shows a negative relationship, reflecting the tendency for children who are more accurate to take less time to answer.

We conclude this section with two additional examples of scatterplots that we will discuss later in the chapter. The first uses data obtained from an introductory college statistics class. Table 18.2 contains two scores for each of 18 students, the score on a math-skills pretest taken during the first week of class and the score on the final exam. The scatterplot for the 18 data points is presented in Fig. 18.3. Not surprisingly, the pretest and final scores co-vary; students who score higher on the pretest tend to do better on the final exam. If we could find the equation that did the best job in predicting the 18 final exam scores from the corresponding pretest scores, it would be useful both for describing the relationship between the two variables and for predicting final exam performance for students who take the pretest in future classes.

To obtain the second scatterplot, presented in Fig. 18.4, we first found the mean of the four seasonal total cholesterol scores (*TC*) for each of the 431 individuals who had scores in all four seasons in the *Seasons* study conducted by researchers at the University of Massachusetts Medical

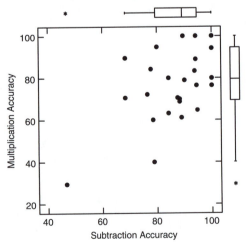

Fig. 18.1 Scatterplot for subtraction and multiplication accuracy for the 28 third-grade children having both subtraction and multiplication scores, with box plots for each variable on the borders.

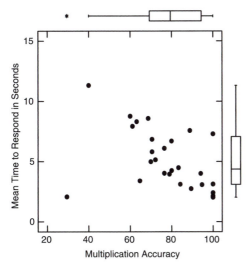

Fig. 18.2 Scatterplot for response time and multiplication accuracy for third grade.

School, and then plotted TC against age. Although there is a great deal of variability in the cholesterol scores, there seems to be a tendency for older people to have higher cholesterol scores. We used the SPSS chart editor to include a "fit line" (other statistical packages such as SAS and SYSTAT refer to such curves as "smoothers") to help us determine the nature of any systematic relationship between the two variables. We consider this procedure next.

Table 18.2 Statistics class example data

Pretest score	Final exam score
X	Y
29	47
34	93
27	49
34	98
33	83
31	59
32	70
33	93
32	79
35	79
36	93
34	90
35	77
29	81
32	79
34	85
36	90
25	66

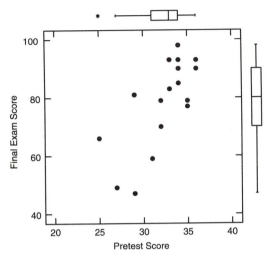

Fig. 18.3 Scatterplot for pretest and final exam scores in a statistics class.

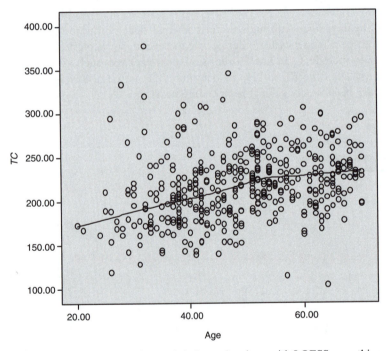

Fig. 18.4 SPSS scatterplot for total cholesterol and age with LOESS smoothing.

18.3.2 Extracting the Systematic Relationship Between Two Variables

Scatterplots can be very useful in helping us understand how, and to what extent, two variables are related. However, real data are often extremely messy. Any systematic relationship that exists between the variables may be obscured by variability due to factors such as individual differences and measurement error. In such cases we try to see through the "noise" in order to extract the "signal," that is, the underlying systematic relationship, if one exists. This can be difficult to do by eye, especially when there are many data points and a great deal of variability, as in the plot of cholesterol level against age in Fig. 18.4.

One way of trying to get at the underlying relationship is to use some type of averaging to reduce the complexity of the display. For example, we can find the average cholesterol score for each age and plot it against age, producing a plot of a "moving average" of cholesterol scores against age. Some statistical packages assist us in understanding the relationship by fitting curves called smoothers or fit lines to the data points in the scatterplot. There are many different types of smoothing functions available in SAS, SPSS, and SYSTAT, and a variety of options within each type.

An example of one kind of smoothing is provided by Fig. 18.4 which displays the scatterplot for cholesterol and age with LOESS smoothing, using SPSS. LOESS is a version of LOWESS (LOcal WEighted Scatterplot Smoothing; Cleveland, 1979; Cleveland, Devlin, & Grosse, 1988). For each value of X, LOWESS plots the Y score predicted by a procedure that gives more weight to data points near the value of X than data points that are further away (for details, see Cook & Weisberg, 1999). The resulting curve indicates a positive relationship between cholesterol and age that approximates a straight line.

In practice, we usually first look to see whether there is a systematic tendency for the variables to have a straight-line relationship because this is the simplest and most common way that two variables can be related. Then we look further to see whether there are systematic departures from linearity. The most common numerical measures that are used to summarize the relationship between two quantitative variables are those that (1) indicate how well a straight line "captures" the scatterplot, and (2) describe the straight line that gives the best fit.

18.4 LINEAR RELATIONSHIPS

A straight line can be represented by an equation of the form

$$Y = b_0 + b_1 X$$

where b_0 and b_1 are constants, because all points (X, Y) that satisfy this *linear equation* fall on a straight line. The constant b_1 is the *slope* of this line and indicates the rate of change of Y with X. We can see from the equation for a straight line that for every one-unit change in X, Y changes by b_1 units. The constant b_0 is the *Y-intercept*, the value of Y when X is equal to zero. This equation describes a perfect linear relationship between X and Y. In fact, perfect linear relationships do not occur in behavioral data, but there are many occasions when a line is a good approximate description of the relationship between two variables.

Each of the scatterplots in Fig. 18.5 contains a number of (X, Y) data points. If all of the data points fall exactly on a straight line, we say there is a perfect linear relationship between X and Y. This linear relationship is said to be positive if the slope of the line is positive; that is, if Y increases as X increases as in panel (a). The linear relationship is negative if Y decreases as X increases as in panel (b). In panel (c), there is a systematic increase in Y as X increases. However, not all the data points fall on the straight line that seems to best capture this systematic increase, although they cluster closely around it. In this case, we say that there is a strong positive linear relationship between X and Y, but not a perfect one. In panel (d), there is less clustering around the line,

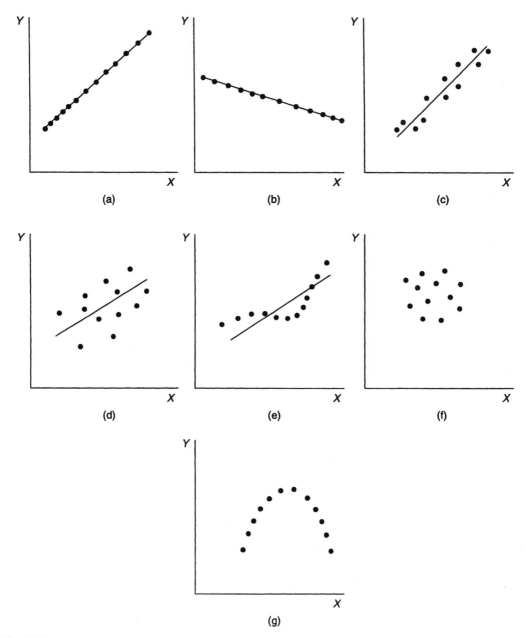

Fig. 18.5 Examples of scatterplots.

indicating a weaker linear relationship. In panel (e), there is a linear component to the relationship between X and Y; that is, the best-fitting straight line seems to capture part of how Y and X are related. However, not only do the points fail to cluster closely around the line, but there also seems to be a systematic nonlinear component to the relationship. In panels (f) and (g), there is no overall linear relationship between X and Y; no straight line passing through the center of either "cloud" of data points is better at characterizing the overall relationship between X and Y than a line parallel to the x-axis. In (g), however, X and Y are positively related for small values of X but negatively related for large values, whereas in (f) there does not seem to be any indication of a linear relationship for any part of the X distribution.

18.5 INTRODUCING CORRELATION AND REGRESSION USING z SCORES

18.5.1 Explaining the Pearson Correlation Coefficient

The Pearson correlation coefficient is a measure of the extent to which two quantitative variables are linearly related. We indicated in the previous section that the more tightly the data points are clustered around a straight line, the stronger the degree of linear relationship. However, if we plotted raw scores, the appearance of the scatterplot and the apparent degree of clustering around the best-fitting straight line would depend on the units in which X and Y are measured. This is not true for z scores, which have no units and are defined in terms of the relative standings of scores within their distributions. The correlation coefficient is a measure of similarity of the corresponding z scores of X and Y.

In Chapter 2, we indicated that each member of a set of scores X_1, X_2, X_3, ..., X_N can be converted to a z score using

$$z_{X_i} = \frac{X_i - \overline{X}}{s_X} \tag{18.1}$$

where $\overline{X}$ is the mean of the set of scores and s_X is the standard deviation. The z score that corresponds to X_i tells us the number of standard deviations that X_i is above or below the mean of the distribution. We also showed that the mean of a complete set of z scores is zero, and that the standard deviation and variance both have a value of 1.

The Pearson correlation coefficient for two variables, X and Y, is given by

$$r_{XY} = \frac{1}{N-1} \sum_{i=1}^{N} z_{X_i} z_{Y_i} \tag{18.2}$$

The symbol r is used to denote the Pearson correlation coefficient in a sample, and ρ (the Greek letter rho) denotes the correlation in a population. The correlation coefficient is basically the average of the products of corresponding z scores (it would be exactly the average if we divided by N instead of $N - 1$ when we obtained the standard deviations of X and Y). In Appendix 18.1, we show that if there is a perfect positive relationship between X and Y, then $z_Y = z_X$. In this case, the correlation is

$$r_{XY} = \frac{1}{N-1} \sum_{i=1}^{N} z_{X_i} z_{Y_i} = \frac{1}{N-1} \sum_{i=1}^{N} z_{X_i}^2 = 1$$

This result follows from the fact that the variance of a set of z scores is 1 and the expression for this variance is

$$\frac{1}{N-1} \sum_{i=1}^{N} (z_{X_i} - \bar{z}_X)^2 = \frac{1}{N-1} \sum_{i=1}^{N} z_{X_i}^2$$

because $\bar{z}_X$, the mean of a set of z scores, is equal to 0. If there is a perfect negative relationship, $z_Y = -z_X$, so that $r_{XY} = -1$. If there is no linear relationship between Y and X, there will be no systematic tendency for the products of the corresponding z scores, $z_{X_i} z_{Y_i}$, to be positive (when z_{X_i} and z_{Y_i} have the same sign) or negative (when they have opposite signs). Therefore, we would expect these products more or less to cancel out when averaged, so that r_{XY} is approximately equal to 0. In general, the value of r can range from -1 to $+1$; values of r close to the limits indicate strong linear relationships between X and Y, whereas values close to 0 indicate very weak linear relationships. Going back to the examples we introduced earlier in the chapter, for multiplication and subtraction accuracy for third-graders (Fig. 18.1), $r = .59$; for multiplication accuracy and the time taken to answer (Fig. 18.2), $r = -.49$; for final exam and pretest score (Fig. 18.3), $r = .73$; and for cholesterol level and age (Fig. 18.4), $r = .29$.

18.5.2 The Sample Covariance

The value of the Pearson correlation coefficient can always be obtained from Equation 18.2. However, other expressions for the Pearson correlation coefficient are often encountered. For example, if we substitute the expressions for z scores (Equation 18.1) into Equation 18.2, we get

$$r_{XY} = \frac{1}{N-1} \sum_{i=1}^{N} \left(\frac{X_i - \bar{X}}{s_X} \right) \left(\frac{Y_i - \bar{Y}}{s_Y} \right) \tag{18.3}$$

$$= \frac{s_{XY}}{s_X s_Y}$$

The symbol s_{XY} in Equation 18.3 denotes the sample *covariance* of X and Y, which we can write as

$$s_{XY} = \frac{1}{N-1} \sum_{i=1}^{N} (X_i - \bar{X})(Y_i - \bar{Y}) = r_{XY} s_X s_Y \tag{18.4}$$

The covariance is the *amount* of variance shared by X and Y.

The covariance provides information about the degree of linear relationship between X and Y. However, it is not usually employed as an index of strength of relationship because its value changes when we change the units of measurement of the variables. For example, if we measured the heights and weights of a number of people, and then found the covariance of height and weight, the numerical value of the covariance would be 12 times larger if we measured height in inches than if we measured it in feet. In contrast, the correlation coefficient would be the same in both cases. Correlation is the covariance of z scores.

18.5.3 Least-Squares Linear Regression Using z Scores

The correlation coefficient plays a major role in regression equations that predict one variable from another. Consider a set of N pairs of z scores (z_{X_i}, z_{Y_i}). Suppose we wish to predict z_Y from z_X by a linear equation; that is, an equation of the form $\hat{z}_{Y_i} = a + bz_{X_i}$, where we indicate the predicted value of z_{Y_i} by $\hat{z}_{Y_i}$, and a and b are the intercept and slope of the prediction line. How are we to determine the values of a and b that give the best predictions for the set of N paired z scores? We first have to specify what we mean by "best predictions." In one sense, this is easy—we will consider "best predictions" to be those that produce the least amount of error.

But we must also specify an appropriate measure of error to minimize. Suppose for the ith prediction, our predicted value is $\hat{z}_{Y_i}$ when the actual value is z_{Y_i}. Therefore, the ith prediction error is $z_{Y_i} - \hat{z}_{Y_i}$, and the mean error (ME) for the entire set of N predictions is given by

$$ME = \frac{1}{N}\sum_{i=1}^{N}(z_{Y_i} - \hat{z}_{Y_i}) = \frac{1}{N}\sum_{i=1}^{N}(z_{Y_i} - a - bz_{X_i}) \tag{18.5}$$

Although ME may seem like an intuitively appealing choice, it is not an appropriate measure of prediction error. For one thing, complete sets of z scores must sum to zero. Even if they did not sum to zero, positive and negative prediction errors would tend to cancel one another out, possibly producing small values of ME even when there are many large discrepancies between predicted and observed scores.

Other, more desirable candidates for a measure of error that does not allow for this cancelling out are the *mean absolute error* (MAE) and *mean squared error* (MSE), where

$$MAE = \frac{1}{N}\sum_{i=1}^{N}|z_{Y_i} - \hat{z}_{Y_i}| = \frac{1}{N}\sum_{i=1}^{N}|z_{Y_i} - a - bz_{X_i}| \tag{18.6}$$

and

$$MSE = \frac{1}{N}\sum_{i=1}^{N}(z_{Y_i} - \hat{z}_{Y_i})^2 = \frac{1}{N}\sum_{i=1}^{N}(z_{Y_i} - a - bz_{X_i})^2 \tag{18.7}$$

Both measures are useful. The MSE is mathematically easier to work with, and is the one used in introductions to regression. Regression equations obtained by minimizing the MSE are referred to as *ordinary least-squares* (OLS) regression equations. Because absolute deviations are less variable than squared deviations, the MAE is used in some developments of robust regression.

Using calculus, we can show that the MSE is minimized if $a = 0$ and $b = \frac{1}{N-1}\sum_{i=1}^{N}z_{X_i}z_{Y_i}$; that is, if the intercept is zero and the slope is the Pearson correlation coefficient, r. Therefore, the least-squares linear regression equation for predicting z_Y from z_X is given by

$$\hat{z}_{Y_i} = r_{XY}z_{X_i} \tag{18.8}$$

The slope of the regression line for predicting one z score from another is called the *standardized regression coefficient*[2] or the *beta weight*. When we predict z_Y from z_X the beta weight is the same as the correlation coefficient, r_{XY}.

If we stick with z scores and use the same set of data to find the least-squares linear equation that predicts z_X from z_Y, we obtain the same equation with X and Y interchanged.

$$\hat{z}_{X_i} = r_{XY}z_{Y_i} \tag{18.9}$$

One of the many important differences between correlation and regression is that the Pearson correlation coefficient is *symmetric* in X and Y. That is, if we interchange X and Y, the expression for r is unchanged and the interpretation remains exactly the same—the correlation between X and Y is exactly the same as the correlation between Y and X. There is no such symmetry when we

---

[2] Note that although z_Y and z_X are z scores, $\hat{z}_Y$ is not a z score, because, although the mean of the $\hat{z}_Y$s is zero, the variance is r^2, not 1. Note also that the correlation between z_Y and z_X is the same as the correlation of Y and X.

consider regression. Although the beta weight is r_{XY} in both Equations 18.8 and 18.9, these equations represent different regression lines.

Consider panel (a) of Fig. 18.6. Suppose that there is a moderate linear relationship between z_Y and z_X and that the elliptical envelope in the diagram contains a large number of standardized data points (i.e., paired values of z_X and z_Y). In the figure, the envelope is symmetrical about a straight line with a slope of 1 drawn through the origin; that is, the line with the equation $z_Y = z_X$. Now consider a series of vertical strips drawn through these data points; panel (a) shows two of these strips. Each strip can be thought of as containing data points that have roughly the same value of z_X but different values of z_Y. Now imagine finding the mean value of the z_Ys in each of these vertical strips—we would expect the mean to fall at about the middle of each strip. The least-squares regression line for predicting z_Y from z_X is approximately the line that connects these means. As we can see from the figure, the resulting regression line, $\hat{z}_{Y_i} = r_{XY}z_{X_i}$, has a slope less than 1 unless $z_Y = z_X$.

To consider what happens when we predict z_X from z_Y, look at panel (b) of Fig. 18.6, which has

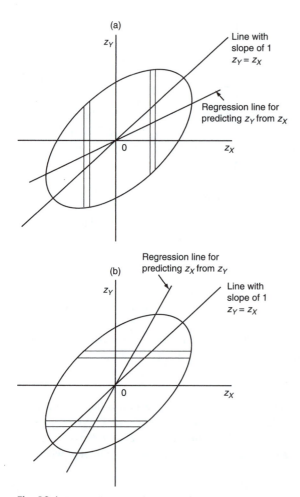

Fig. 18.6 Regression lines for predicting (a) z_Y from z_X and (b) z_X from z_Y when there is an imperfect relationship between X and Y.

the same data display as in panel (a). The regression line for predicting z_X from z_Y, $\hat{z}_{X_i} = r_{XY} z_{Y_i}$, is approximately the line that passes though the means of the *horizontal* strips that are drawn through the elliptical cloud of data points. As we can see by comparing panels (a) and (b), the two regression lines are different unless there is a perfect linear relationship. The reason for this has to do with the topic we consider next.

18.5.4 Regression Toward the Mean When Predicting z_Y from z_X

From Equation 18.8 and Fig. 18.7, we can see that unless there is a perfect linear relationship, the magnitude of $\hat{z}_{Y_i}$ will be smaller than that of z_{X_i}. If there is a perfect positive linear relationship, $\hat{z}_{Y_i} = z_{X_i}$; if there is no linear relationship, $\hat{z}_{Y_i} = 0$, the mean of the z_Y scores. This is because in the absence of any other information, it can be shown that the best least-squares predictor for a set of scores is their mean, and the mean z score is 0. Therefore, if there is a moderate positive linear relationship, $\hat{z}_{Y_i}$ should have a value somewhere between 0 and z_{X_i}. This tendency of predicted z scores to be less "extreme" than the z scores used to predict them is called *regression toward the mean* and is a characteristic of bivariate regression whenever two variables have equal variances and do not have a perfect linear relationship. The prediction equations we have been discussing are given the name "regression equations" in recognition of this characteristic. We will consider this issue in more detail when we discuss raw score regression in the next section.

18.6 LEAST-SQUARES LINEAR REGRESSION FOR RAW SCORES

18.6.1 Predicting Y from X

We have already discussed predicting z_Y from z_X using the regression equation $\hat{z}_{Y_i} = r_{XY} z_{X_i}$. However, we are often more concerned with finding the raw-score equation $\hat{Y}_i = b_0 + b_1 X_i$ that best predicts Y from X. We can do this by noting that

$$z_{X_i} = \frac{X_i - \bar{X}}{s_X} \quad \text{and} \quad \hat{z}_{Y_i} = \frac{\hat{Y}_i - \bar{Y}}{s_Y}$$

and then substituting into Equation 18.8 and solving for $\hat{Y}_i$. Alternatively, we can use calculus to derive formulas for the slope and intercept that minimize the measure of prediction error, $MSE = \frac{1}{N} \sum_i (Y_i - \hat{Y}_i)^2$ (see, for example, Myers & Well, 2003). Either way, we find

$$\hat{Y}_i = \bar{Y} + r \frac{s_Y}{s_X}(X_i - \bar{X}) \tag{18.10}$$

so that the slope and intercept for the regression of Y on X are given by

$$b_1 = r \frac{s_Y}{s_X} \tag{18.11}$$

$$\text{and} \quad b_0 = \bar{Y} - b_1 \bar{X} \tag{18.12}$$

Applying these equations to the statistics class data in Table 18.2 produces the linear regression equation that best predicts final exam performance (Y) from pretest score (X),

$$\hat{Y} = -36.08 + 3.55X$$

A difference of one point on the pretest translates into a predicted difference of about 3.55 points on the final exam. The prediction for the final exam score of a student who scored 30 on the pretest can be found by substituting 30 for X in the preceding equation. Our predicted score on the final is $-36.08 + (3.55)(30) = 70.42$, or 70, rounding to the nearest integer. Although this equation was developed in a data set in which we already knew both the pretest and final scores for each student, it serves as a useful way to represent how the two variables are related. Moreover, the equation can be useful in predicting the performance of students in future classes.

In contrast to what happens in correlation, X and Y play different roles in the regression of Y on X: X is the *predictor variable* and Y is the *criterion or dependent variable*, the variable that is predicted. In the general case where $s_X \neq s_Y$, the regression equation and the correlation coefficient tell us different things about the linear relationship. The regression equation describes the straight line that is best for predicting Y from X, whereas the correlation coefficient serves as a measure of how strongly Y and X are linearly related. If we solve for r in Equation 18.11, we get

$$r = b_1 \frac{s_X}{s_Y} \tag{18.13}$$

From this equation we can see that the same correlation may arise from different combinations of the slope and the standard deviations of X and Y. For example, both of the combinations $b_1 = 1$, $s_X = 3$, $s_Y = 5$ and $b_1 = .5$, $s_X = 6$, $s_Y = 5$ correspond to rs of .6. Because of this, we must be extremely cautious if we wish to compare the relationships between X and Y in different groups. Two groups that have the same regression slope may have different correlations, and two groups that have the same correlation may have different slopes. If we are primarily concerned with whether the rate of change of Y with X differs in two groups, we should compare the slopes, not the correlation coefficients.

18.6.2 Predicting X from Y

So far, we have discussed the regression equation for predicting Y from X that is optimal in the sense that it minimizes $\Sigma(Y - \hat{Y})^2/N$ (see panel (a) of Fig. 18.7). Exactly the same reasoning can be used to find the regression equation for predicting X from Y. In this case, the index of error that is minimized is $\Sigma(X_i - \hat{X}_i)^2/N$, the mean of the squared residuals when Y is used to predict X. These prediction errors are indicated in panel (b) of Fig. 18.7.

The expressions that have been developed for predicting Y from X can be transformed into expressions for predicting X from Y by simply interchanging X and Y in Equation 18.13. The regression equation becomes

$$\hat{X}_i = \bar{X} + r \frac{s_X}{s_Y}(Y_i - \bar{Y})$$

Of course, whether it makes any sense to predict X from Y depends on the situation. It is unlikely that we would want to predict pretest scores from final exam scores, because the pretest scores are available first.

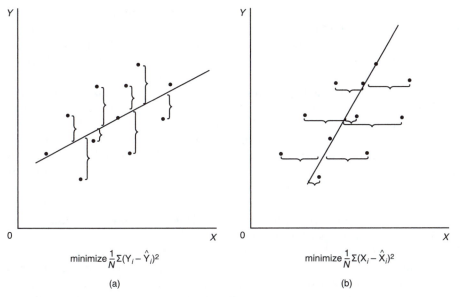

$$\text{minimize } \frac{1}{N}\Sigma(Y_i - \hat{Y}_i)^2$$

(a)

$$\text{minimize } \frac{1}{N}\Sigma(X_i - \hat{X}_i)^2$$

(b)

Fig. 18.7 Graphical representation of (a) the regression of Y on X and (b) the regression of X on Y.

18.6.3 Regression Toward the Mean in Predicting *Y* from *X*

We showed in Section 18.5.4 that whenever there is an imperfect linear relationship between X and Y, the values of z_Y associated with any given value of z_X will, on the average, be closer to zero than z_X is. We can extend this result to raw scores by rewriting Equation 18.10 as

$$\hat{Y}_i - \overline{Y} = r\frac{s_Y}{s_X}(X_i - \overline{X}) \tag{18.14}$$

Here we see that the best prediction for Y_i must be closer to $\overline{Y}$ than X_i is to $\overline{X}$ whenever $s_X = s_Y$ and r is less than 1.

Regression toward the mean must occur for predictions whenever two variables with equal variances are not perfectly linearly related. However, the finding that predicted scores are less extreme than those used to do the predicting often leads to faulty reasoning. Because people often ignore the fact that regression effects can be produced by random variability, measurement error, or any other factors that result in less-than-perfect correlation, they often feel compelled to provide more "interesting," elaborate, and often unwarranted, explanations.

We must keep the possibility of regression toward the mean in mind both when designing research and when considering many everyday life phenomena. Suppose we are interested in assessing the effects of some kind of instruction in children. Say, a group of children takes a multiple-choice achievement test, and then is given a period of instruction, followed by a second test. Usually, children who are near the top of the distribution on the first test will tend to show some decline in relative performance on a second test (just think what it takes to score at the top of the distribution), whereas children with extremely low scores on the first test will, on average, score relatively better on the second. This result seems to suggest that intervening instruction is more effective for the students who scored lower on the first test than for those who scored higher. However, even if instruction was equally effective for all children, we would expect regression toward the mean if the two tests did not measure exactly the same thing or if there were random fluctuations in children's alertness and success in guessing. Therefore, if we want to assess the effects of instruction, we must include an appropriate control group and conduct an experiment.

Another illustration is the so-called "sophomore slump." Individuals who perform particularly well in their first year of academics or athletics will, on average, perform relatively less well in their second. It is usually thought that this finding requires an explanation in terms of overconfidence and poor work habits that result from early success. However, such explanations may be unnecessary because even without any interventions or distractions, an individual's performance will generally fluctuate so that there are periods of better-than-usual performance and periods of worse-than-usual performance followed by performance that is more normal for the individual. This has far-reaching implications: Fluctuations in children's behavior may cause parents to overestimate the effectiveness of interventions such as punishment. Fluctuations in the intensity of symptoms in sufferers of many chronic diseases may cause patients to overestimate the effectiveness of alternative medicine and food supplements. Fluctuations in crime rates may cause observers to overestimate the effects of changes in social policy or gun laws.

Another important variation on this theme has to do with the misclassification of individuals on the basis of test results. People are classified as being gifted, learning disabled, depressed, or as having a high cholesterol level on the basis of tests that are not perfectly reliable. Because the test scores are subject to regression effects, we would predict that many of these classifications would change if a second test was given. Suppose being classified as "gifted" depends on scoring two or more standard deviations above the mean on a test. If we can assume normal distributions and that the results of a second test correlate .80 with those of the first, it can be shown that only about 43% of those individuals classified as gifted on the first test will be classified as gifted on the second (see Campbell & Kenny, 1999).

We conclude this section by noting that regression toward the mean is inevitable only if the variances of both variables are equal. As we can see in Equation 18.14, regression effects must occur for raw scores if

$$|r| \frac{s_Y}{s_X} < 1$$

However, if $s_Y > s_X$, regression toward the mean need not always occur for raw scores; in fact, if $|r| s_Y / s_X > 1$, we will have the opposite effect, which has been called egression from the mean (Ragosa, 1995). Although there are many situations in which regression effects occur for raw scores, there are others in which these effects occur for standardized, but not for raw, scores.

18.6.4 The Coefficient of Determination

The square of the correlation coefficient, r^2, is called the *coefficient of determination*, and is a commonly encountered measure of strength of linear relationship. The r^2 measure is usually described as *the proportion of the variance in Y accounted for or explained by X* (or, because the measure is symmetric in X and Y, as the proportion of the variance in X accounted for by Y). This language sounds impressive and vaguely causal, but all it actually means is that r^2 is the proportion by which squared prediction error is reduced if the regression equation is used to predict the Y scores instead of using $\overline{Y}$ to predict each of the Ys. The detailed interpretation is as follows:

1.   If we do not use any information about X in predicting the corresponding value of Y, the best least-squares prediction for each Y can be shown to be $\overline{Y}$, the mean of the Y scores. If

we use $\overline{Y}$ as the prediction for each of the Y scores, the sum of the squared prediction errors for the entire set of N predictions is the total variability in the Y scores, the sum of squares of Y, $SS_Y = \Sigma(Y_i - \overline{Y})^2$.

2. If we do use the information about X and predict using the regression equation, the sum of the squared errors for the set of predictions is $SS_{residual} = \Sigma(Y_i - \hat{Y}_i)^2$. Substituting the expression for $\hat{Y}_i$ from Equation 18.10 and simplifying, the sum of the squared residuals can be shown to be

$$SS_{residual} = (1 - r^2)SS_Y \tag{18.15}$$

3. The *amount* by which prediction error is reduced when the regression equation is used instead of the mean is, therefore,

$$SS_{regression} = SS_Y - SS_{residual} = SS_Y - (1 - r^2)SS_Y \tag{18.16}$$
$$= r^2 SS_Y$$

4. Therefore, the *proportion* by which prediction error is reduced (or the proportion of the variability in Y accounted for by the regression on X) is

$$\frac{SS_{regression}}{SS_Y} = \frac{r^2 SS_Y}{SS_Y} = r^2$$

The coefficient of determination, r^2, is therefore a measure of how well the linear regression equation fits the data. According to the Cohen (1977, 1988) guidelines, r^2 values of .01, .09, and .25 correspond to small, medium, and large linear relationships, respectively. For the statistics class data (Table 18.2), the correlation between the pretest and the final exam score is .725, so the coefficient of determination is $(.725)^2 = .53$. This tells us that the variability of the Y scores about the regression line is $(1 - .53) = .47$ of their variability about $\overline{Y}$. Therefore, if we use the regression equation to predict Y instead of using $\overline{Y}$, we will reduce the squared prediction error by about one half.

We should note that r^2 has frequently been misinterpreted, and that some of these misinterpretations have resulted in inappropriate claims being made in the literature. For example, the statement has been made in a number of psychology textbooks that children achieve about 50% of their adult intelligence by age 4. There is no valid basis for this statement; it is based on a misunderstanding of r^2. Specifically, it is based on the results of several longitudinal studies that found IQ scores at age 17 to have a correlation of about .7 with IQ scores at age 4 (see Bloom, 1964). The resulting r^2 of about .5 (or 50%) provides an indication of how predictable adult IQ is from IQ at age 4, using linear regression. However, this result says nothing about the relative *amounts* of intelligence at age 4 and age 17, and therefore provides no evidence for the statement.

18.6.5 Partitioning of Variability in Regression and the Standard Error of Estimate

Equation 18.17 indicates how the variability in the Y scores can be partitioned into two components—the variability of the predicted scores about the mean, and the variability of the actual Y scores about the regression line. Rewriting Equation 18.16, we have

$$SS_Y = SS_{regression} + SS_{residual}$$
$$= r^2 SS_Y + (1 - r^2)SS_Y \tag{18.17}$$
$$\Sigma(Y_i - \overline{Y})^2 = \Sigma(\hat{Y}_i - \overline{Y})^2 + \Sigma(Y_i - \hat{Y}_i)^2$$

Among other things, this helps us understand an important measure of error of prediction in regression called the *standard error of estimate*. Although r^2 is a commonly used measure of strength of relationship, measures such as the *variance of estimate* (basically, the mean of the squared raw-score prediction errors) or its square root, the *standard error of estimate*, provide more useful information than either r or r^2 about the accuracy of predictions based on the raw-score regression equation. The standard error of estimate is the most commonly used measure of variability of the data points around the regression line and is typically provided as part of the regression output by software packages. For the regression of Y on X, the standard error of estimate is defined as

$$s_{Y.X} = \sqrt{\frac{\Sigma(Y_i - \hat{Y}_i)^2}{N-2}} = \sqrt{\frac{SS_{residual}}{N-2}} = \sqrt{\frac{(1-r^2)SS_Y}{N-2}} \qquad (18.18)$$

In Equation 18.18, there are $N - 2$ *df* associated with $SS_{residual}$ because there are N data points and two restrictions; that is, two *df* are used up by estimating the intercept and slope of the regression equation. We will encounter the standard error of estimate again when we develop hypothesis testing and confidence interval estimates for regression statistics.

18.7 MORE ABOUT INTERPRETING THE PEARSON CORRELATION COEFFICIENT

Now that we have introduced linear regression and concepts such as the standard error of estimate, we are in a position to discuss the interpretation of the correlation coefficient in more detail. It is important to understand the characteristics of correlation coefficients and the factors that influence them because correlations seem to be the statistics of choice in some research areas. Moreover, they often serve as the raw material for more complex procedures such as factor analysis.

18.7.1 Ten Things to Remember About Correlation

1. *The Pearson correlation coefficient depends on the variabilities of X and Y.* Because the correlation coefficient is a measure of the similarity of the standardized values of X and Y, s_X and s_Y affect r because they influence the standardization of X and Y. From Equation 18.13, we have

$$r = b_1 \frac{s_X}{s_Y}$$

This means that for a given regression slope, different correlations will result from different standard deviations of X and Y. Even if the values for both the slope and standard error of estimate, $s_{Y.X}$, are held constant, Equations 18.13, 18.17, and 18.18 can be used to show that different values of r will result for different values of s_X and s_Y. For example,
   - For a given b_1 and $s_{Y.X}$, r increases with s_X.
   - For a given $s_{Y.X}$, r increases with b_1, s_X, and s_Y.
   - For a given s_X and $s_{Y.X}$, r increases with b_1 and s_Y.

   Therefore, if we are concerned with *how Y changes with X*, we should generally look at b_1, not r.
2. *Because the correlation coefficient depends on s_X and s_Y, it is a sample-specific measure.*

Given a population in which Y and X are linearly related with a population correlation of ρ, the value of r obtained in a sample will depend on how the sample is selected. If the sample is largely selected from only part of the distribution of X (say, any of the regions A, B, or C in Fig. 18.8), r will tend to be smaller than ρ because s_X will tend to be smaller than the value of σ_X in the population. Note that this dependence on the variability of X in the sample does not hold for the unstandardized estimate of slope, b_1.

This type of bias for correlations is frequently referred to as the *restriction of range* problem; all other things being equal, the sample correlation will be smaller if there is less variability in X. A frequently cited example of restriction of range is the low correlation between Graduate Record Examination (GRE) scores and success in graduate school as measured by grades or faculty ratings (e.g., Dawes, 1971), which has prompted calls for the abandonment of the GRE scores as predictive measures. However, even if GRE scores were an excellent measure of ability, the correlation with performance would be expected to be quite low because of the restricted range—only students with relatively high GRE scores get accepted into graduate programs.

Conversely, if we select a sample that overrepresents low and high values of X (i.e., is largely selected from regions A and C in Fig. 18.8), r will tend to be larger than ρ. Investigators interested in the relationship between two variables will sometimes drop the middle scores for one or both of them. Although this procedure may be acceptable for determining *whether* there is a linear component to the relationship, the correlation in this type of sample should definitely not be considered to be an estimate of the value of the correlation in the whole population.

This dependence on sample variability raises the question of what comparisons of correlations in different samples actually mean. Two correlations may be different not because the samples differ in the variability about the regression line or because the slopes are different, but merely because one of the samples has a broader range of X values. Because the correlation coefficient is sample specific and generally does not provide a description of the linear relationship between X and Y, some authors (e.g., Achen, 1982; Tukey, 1969) have recommended that the correlation coefficient not be used.

We agree with Achen and Tukey that characteristics of the regression equation such as

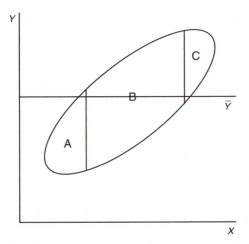

Fig. 18.8 Scatterplot with different regions marked to illustrate the effect of the variability of X and Y on the correlation coefficient.

the intercept, slope, and standard error of estimate describe a linear relationship more usefully than does r. Further, researchers should often be interested in the rate of change of Y with X (i.e., with b_1) even when they think they are interested in r. However, we do not believe that the correlation coefficient can or should be abandoned, although it should be used with an understanding of exactly what it does and does not measure.

3. *Size*. How large must a correlation coefficient be in order to indicate that there is a "meaningful" linear relationship? Cohen (1977, 1988) has discussed guidelines according to which rs of .10, .30, and .50 correspond to small, medium, and large effects. Cohen arrived at these values by noting the sizes of correlations encountered in the behavioral sciences, and by considering how strong a correlation would have to be before the relationship could be perceived by an observer. These values should be considered only as very rough guidelines and not as criteria for importance. In some contexts, even small correlations might be of great practical significance. We should also emphasize that unless the sample is large, the correlation may be quite different in the sample than in the population from which the sample was selected.

4. *Symmetry*. We have already noted that expressions for the correlation coefficient are *symmetric* in X and Y. The correlation between cholesterol level and age is the same as the correlation between age and cholesterol level. This is not the case for regression equations—the equation for predicting Y from X will be the same as that for predicting X from Y only if (a) there is a perfect linear relationship between X and Y and (b) X and Y both have the same mean and standard deviation—that is, if $Y = X$.

5. *Linearity*. The Pearson correlation coefficient is a measure of strength of the *linear* relationship between X and Y. It is not a measure of relationship in general because it provides no information about whether or not there is a systematic nonlinear relationship between the two variables. As can be seen in panels (e) and (g) of Fig. 18.5, two variables can have a systematic curvilinear component to their relationship in addition to, or instead of, a linear one. Therefore, finding a correlation coefficient of zero does not necessarily mean that the variables are independent. The data points in all four panels of Fig. 18.9 (see Table 18.3) have identical correlations and best-fitting straight lines. For each of the four panels, $r = .82$, and the slope of the least-squares regression line that predicts Y from X is 0.5. However, whereas panel (a) displays a moderate linear relationship with no curvilinear component, panel (b) displays a systematic curvilinear relationship that has a linear component. It cannot be emphasized strongly enough that if you want to understand how variables are related, you must plot them and not simply rely on statistics such as the correlation coefficient or the slope of the best-fitting regression line.

6. *What happens when units of measurement are changed?* The Pearson correlation coefficient, in contrast to other statistics such as the mean, standard deviation, covariance, and the unstandardized regression coefficient, is a *dimensionless* quantity. By this we mean that r is not expressed in terms of any units; it is simply a number between -1 and $+1$. Remember that r is the average product of pairs of z scores, and that a z score expresses in standard deviation units the location of a score in a distribution. The values of the z scores and thus of r do not change if we change the units in which we measure X and/or Y (i.e., if we multiply each score by a constant and/or add a constant to each score, as when we change units from ounces to kilograms, or from degrees Fahrenheit to degrees Centigrade). It follows that *just knowing the correlation between two variables tells us nothing about the mean or variance of either of the variables.* In contrast, changing units does affect b_1 and the raw-score variability about the best-fitting lines.

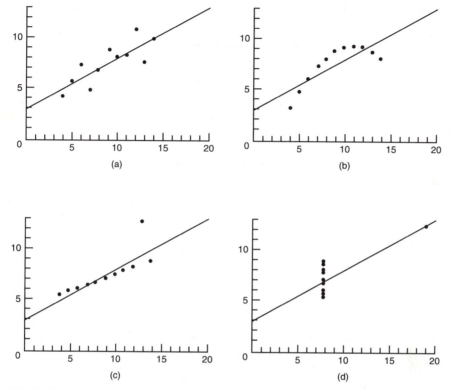

Fig. 18.9 Scatterplots for the Anscombe data sets in Table 18.3.

Unfortunately, the fact that the correlation coefficient has no units is one possible reason for its popularity. When we use r or r^2 or any other standardized measure of effect size, we do not think in terms of units and therefore may not pay close attention to our measures. What does a one-point difference on a seven-point anxiety scale really mean? And does the difference between 6 and 7 on the scale mean the same thing as the difference between 3 and 4? If we do not understand our measures, we will not recognize when they are not good measures of the underlying variables that are our real concern. As Tukey (1969, p. 89) puts it,

> Given two perfectly meaningless variables, one is reminded of their meaninglessness when a regression coefficient is given, since one wonders how to interpret its value. A correlation coefficient is less likely to bring up the unpleasant truth—we think we know what $r = -.7$ means.

7. *The correlation coefficient is not resistant.* The value of the correlation coefficient can be greatly influenced by the presence of extreme data points. Therefore, if there are extreme data points, it is important to identify them and, if possible, determine why they are extreme. In Fig. 18.10, we used SYSTAT to display the *influence plot* for multiplication and subtraction accuracy for the sample of third-graders. The influence plot is just a scatterplot in which each case is plotted as an open or filled circle that can vary in size. The size of the circle indicates how much the correlation would change if that point was omitted; whether the circle is filled or open indicates whether omitting the data point would make the correlation larger or smaller. The very large open circle in the left of the plot indicates that

Table 18.3   Four hypothetical data sets from Anscombe (1973). The left-most column of scores contains the X scores
used in all three data sets a, b, and c, and the next three columns are the three sets of Y scores used in these
data sets. The right-most two columns contain the X and Y scores for the fourth data set, d

	Data set					
	a–c	a	b	c	d	d
	Variable					
Case number	X	Y	Y	Y	X	Y
1	10.0	8.04	9.14	7.46	8.0	6.58
2	8.0	6.95	8.14	6.77	8.0	5.76
3	13.0	7.58	8.74	12.74	8.0	7.71
4	9.0	8.81	8.77	7.11	8.0	8.84
5	11.0	8.33	9.26	7.81	8.0	8.47
6	14.0	9.96	8.10	8.84	8.0	7.04
7	6.0	7.24	6.13	6.08	8.0	5.25
8	4.0	4.26	3.10	5.39	19.0	12.50
9	12.0	10.84	9.13	8.15	8.0	5.56
10	7.0	4.82	7.26	6.42	8.0	7.91
11	5.0	5.68	4.74	5.73	8.0	6.89

Note: From Anscombe, F. J. (1973). Graphs in statistical analysis. *The American Statistician, 27,* 17–21.

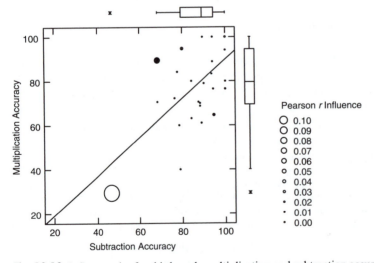

Fig. 18.10 Influence plot for third-grade multiplication and subtraction accuracy.

the corresponding data point has a large effect on the correlation. If we omit this one data
point, the correlation drops from .59 to .39. There are measures of correlation that are
more resistant than the Pearson coefficient because they diminish the importance of
extreme scores. An example is the *Spearman rho coefficient* for which the X and Y scores are
first ranked, and then the ranks are correlated. We will have more to say about such
measures in the next chapter.

8. *Correlation does not imply causation.* Because correlation is a measure of strength of relationship, it is tempting to consider the correlation coefficient as a measure of the extent to which changes in *X cause* changes in *Y*. However, *no statistic implies causation.* A correlation between two variables means that one is useful in predicting the other, but it does not necessarily mean that they are causally related. For example, the fact that in elementary school there is a positive correlation between shoe size and verbal ability does not mean that foot growth *causes* enhanced verbal ability, or vice versa. Rather, in this example the correlation follows from the fact that both physical and mental growth occur as children get older. It is very difficult, if not impossible, to determine causality without conducting a true experiment in which an independent variable is manipulated. However, despite repeated warnings, the tendency to lapse into causal thinking when dealing with correlation and regression is widespread. We will have much more to say about this when we get more deeply into regression.

9. *Measurement error.* If there is error in measuring *X* and/or *Y*, r_{XY} underestimates the "true" correlation coefficient that would be obtained if *X* and *Y* could be measured without error. This should not be surprising. If our data are contaminated by large amounts of measurement error, they can hardly be expected to reveal strong systematic relationships. To better understand the effect of measurement error on the correlation coefficient, assume that *X* and *Y* each consist of a true score and an error component; that is,

$$X = X_t + u \quad \text{and} \quad Y = Y_t + v$$

where X_t and Y_t are the true scores and *u* and *v* are error components. It can be shown that the equation that relates the observed correlation coefficient, r_{XY}, to the correlation coefficient for the true, errorless scores, $r_{X_tY_t}$, is

$$r_{XY} = r_{X_tY_t}\sqrt{r_{XX}}\sqrt{r_{YY}} \tag{18.19}$$

where the quantities r_{XX} and r_{YY} are the *reliability coefficients* for *X* and *Y*. A reliability coefficient estimates the proportion of the variance in the observed scores that is accounted for by the true scores; specifically

$$r_{XX} = \frac{\sigma_{X_t}^2}{\sigma_X^2}$$

From Equation 18.19, if the correlation between the true scores X_t and Y_t is .6 and the reliability coefficient for both *X* and *Y* is .7, then the observed correlation will be only .42. In fact, because the true correlation cannot be larger than +1 or less than −1, the observed correlation cannot be larger than $\sqrt{r_{XX}}\sqrt{r_{YY}}$ or more negative than $-\sqrt{r_{XX}}\sqrt{r_{YY}}$.

If we know the reliability coefficients for *X* and *Y*, we can use Equation 18.19 to estimate the correlation of the true scores; that is, we can estimate what the correlation would have been if both variables could be measured without error. Dividing both sides of Equation 18.19 by $\sqrt{r_{XX}}\sqrt{r_{YY}}$ results in an estimated correlation, r_C, that has been "corrected for attenuation,"

$$r_C = r_{XY}\left(\frac{1}{\sqrt{r_{XX}}\sqrt{r_{YY}}}\right) \tag{18.20}$$

If this is done, we should keep in mind that r_C is an *estimated* correlation, not a correlation directly obtained from observed scores. Correcting a correlation coefficient for attenuation does not change whether or not it is statistically significant; r_C has exactly the same level of significance as the uncorrected correlation coefficient, r (Hunter & Schmidt, 1990).

10. *The shapes of the X and Y distributions constrain the possible values of r.* The marginal distributions of X and Y place constraints on the possible values of the correlation between X and Y. If both X and Y have identical, symmetrical distributions, it is possible that any value of r from -1 to $+1$ might occur, depending on how the values of X and Y are paired. However, if X and Y have distributions that are different from one another, or if one or both of the distributions are asymmetric, the full range of correlations from -1 to $+1$ cannot occur, no matter how the values of X and Y are paired.

In Fig. 18.11, distribution (a) is positively skewed and distribution (b) is negatively skewed. If larger scores in (a) are paired with smaller scores in (b), and vice versa, it is possible to obtain a correlation of -1; however, it is not possible to obtain a correlation of $+1$. For one thing, there are no scores in (b) that have positive z scores as large as those in the upper tail of (b). For another, if we attempted to pair larger scores in (a) with those in (b), it would soon become apparent that there are not enough large scores in (a) to match up with those in (b). If we did the best we could (i.e., paired off scores that had the same rank order), the scatterplot would show that we had a curvilinear relation with a correlation less than $+1$. Similarly, if we had two variables whose marginal distributions were both positively skewed as in (a), or were both negatively skewed as in (b), it would be possible to have a correlation of $+1$, but not one of -1. Because of these constraints, we should plot the univariate distributions of X and Y as well as the scatterplot when we try to understand the relationship between X and Y.

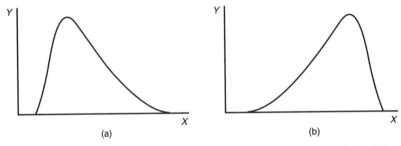

Fig. 18.11 Two skewed distributions to illustrate how the distributions of X and Y constrain the possible values of the correlation coefficient.

18.7.2 Concerns About Combining Data Across Groups

When data from different groups are combined, the correlation and regression statistics for the resultant data set may not characterize the relationship between X and Y in any of the groups. The problem occurs because the aggregate statistics reflect not only the relationship between X and Y within the different groups, but also the differences among the group means. Suppose, for example, that we were interested in finding the correlation between height and weight. Because men tend to be both taller and heavier than women, we would expect a situation like that depicted in panel (a) of Fig. 18.12, in which the correlation would be larger for the combined group than for either men or women. This expectation is confirmed if we consider the *Seasons* data set. Here, the correlation between height and weight is .29, both for men and for women considered separately. However, if we combine the data for men and women, the correlation is .53.

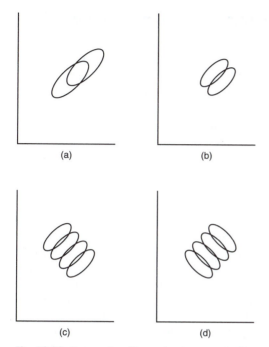

Fig. 18.12 Scatterplots illustrating how combining the data from different groups can affect the correlation coefficient.

As another example, if we correlated scores on verbal and math skills tests, we would expect positive correlations for both men and women. However, if the data conformed to the stereotypical view that women perform better than men on verbal tests but worse than men on math tests, we would have a situation like that depicted in panel (b) of Fig. 18.12, in which the correlation would now be lower in the combined group than for either men or women considered separately. In extreme cases, it is conceivable that X and Y could be positively correlated in each of a number of groups but negatively correlated when the groups were combined, as in panel (c), or negatively correlated in each group but positively correlated when combined, as in panel (d). The message is that we must be very cautious when combining data from meaningful subgroups.

The summary statistics for the combined data set may not only fail to describe each of the constituent groups appropriately, but they may also fail to describe *any* of the groups appropriately. This is important to keep in mind, not only when dealing with correlation, but also when considering more complicated analyses that may take correlations or covariances as inputs, such as factor analysis and structural equation modeling. If the correlations do not adequately characterize the subgroups making up a data set, neither will quantities based on these correlations, such as the factors obtained in a component or factor analysis. Of course, this caution does not apply only to correlation coefficients; it applies to any statistic. For example, the regression slope would be positive for each of the groups represented in panel (c) of Fig. 18.12, but would be negative for the combined data set.

18.7.3 Ecological Correlations: Correlations Based on Rates or Averages

Researchers sometimes compute the mean of X and Y scores for each of several groups, and then correlate the averages to assess the relationship between X and Y. For example, suppose that for the *Royer* data set we compute the average subtraction accuracy score and the average multiplication accuracy score for the third-, fourth-, fifth-, and sixth-graders. We then correlate the four pairs of means and find that $r = .82$. However, if we compute the correlation of the subtraction and multiplication scores within each grade, we get rs of .59, $-.18$, .23, and .43, for the third through sixth grades, respectively. The point illustrated here is that a correlation based on group *averages* may not tell us anything useful about the correlations based on the *individuals* within the groups.

There are two reasons for discrepancies between correlations based on group averages and correlations based on individuals within groups. For one thing, the group means do not convey information about the within-group variability. For another, factors that cause the variability across the groups may not be the same ones responsible for the within-group variability. For groups such as those represented in panel (c) of Fig. 18.12, we could have strong positive correlations in each of the groups, yet the correlation based on the group means could be strongly negative. In a classic study, Robinson (1950) illustrated the dangers of generalizing from correlations based on means to correlations based on individuals by showing that when measures such as race, national origin, and illiteracy were correlated, the results could differ dramatically depending on the unit of analysis. For measures of race and illiteracy, the correlation was .20 for individuals, .77 for the means of states, and .95 for the means of groupings of states (see Pedhazur, 1997, for a more complete discussion). Again, correlations between group averages do not communicate the relationship between X and Y between individuals within the groups.

18.8 WHAT ABOUT NONLINEAR RELATIONSHIPS?

So far, we have focused on describing the linear component of the relationship between two variables, and on measures of its strength. Indeed, correlation coefficients and regression slopes are by far the mostly commonly reported measures of relationship for quantitative variables. This is reasonable, given that an approximately linear relationship is the simplest and most common way that two variables can be related. However, there will certainly be situations when it is apparent from the scatterplot and the smoothers that the relationship has a nonlinear component. How are we to describe and measure the strength of this component or to describe the overall function that best seems to fit the data? We touched on this issue earlier when we discussed trend analysis, and will go into more detail when we discuss multiple regression.

18.9 CONCLUDING REMARKS

When we explore how two quantitative variables are related in a sample of data, the first step is to plot the data and look at both the scatterplot and the univariate distributions. Inspecting the scatterplot by eye and using smoothers or fit lines, we can try to extract, and describe, any underlying systematic relationship. We can use the Pearson correlation coefficient as a measure of the strength of linear relationship and the regression equation as a description of the straight line that allows the best prediction of one variable from the other. We can then try to determine whether there are any systematic departures from linearity, and if so, we can describe them. When we get to multiple regression, we will discuss how to fit various kinds of functions to the scatterplot.

We must also consider the possibility that the processes that determine how the variables are related may not be the same for all cases. Separate clusters of points may suggest the presence of subpopulations for which the variables are related differently or have different means. Outliers or "extreme" data should be examined closely because they may have a very large influence on statistics such as the correlation coefficient or regression slope. Extreme data points may come from subjects who perform in ways that are qualitatively different from the majority of subjects. Extreme data points may also arise because of errors in data collection or copying. If there are a few extreme outliers, we should examine our data records for errors, and we may wish to describe the data both when the extreme scores are included and when they are not. Statistical packages make it easy to identify outliers and to perform these analyses.

18.10 SUMMARY

Our goal in Chapter 18 has been to give some examples of bivariate relationships and to discuss how to extract and summarize them.

- When concerned with exploring the relationship between two variables, display the data in a scatterplot. Procedures such as using smoothers or fit lines are available to help extract systematic relationships from a background of noise.
- The Pearson correlation coefficient is a number between -1 and $+1$ that serves as a measure of the strength of the linear relationship between two variables.
- Least-squares bivariate linear regression produces the linear equation that best predicts one variable using information about the other. We developed linear regression, first for z scores, and then for raw scores.
- When two variables have an imperfect linear relationship and have the same variance, predictions of one variable from the other must regress toward the mean. Quite often there is confusion about this phenomenon, because people feel that an elaborate explanation is required.
- The coefficient of determination, r^2, is the proportion by which squared prediction error is reduced by using the regression equation, and the standard error of estimate, $s_{Y.X}$, is a measure of the amount of prediction error that remains.
- If we predict Y from X, the variability in the Y scores, SS_Y, can be partitioned into two components: $SS_{regression}$, the amount by which squared prediction error has been reduced by using the regression equation, and $SS_{residual}$, the amount of squared prediction error that remains.
- We have placed a great deal of emphasis on the interpretation of the Pearson correlation coefficient and on understanding the influences of different variables on the correlation.
- We must be careful about combining the data from different groups because the correlation and regression statistics for the combined group may not be appropriate for any of the constituent groups. Also, correlations based on the means of groups may be influenced by different variables than, and thus may be very different from, correlations based on individuals within the groups.

- A point that we have emphasized throughout is that if we want to understand how two variables are related, we should not just look at the correlations and regression slopes. *We must look at and plot the data.*

APPENDIX 18.1

Proof that $z_Y = \pm z_X$ when $Y = b_0 + b_1 X$

We want to show that if X and Y have a perfect linear relationship, $z_Y = z_X$ when the relationship is positive and $z_Y = -z_X$ when it is negative. For any data point (X, Y) that falls on a straight line, we have $Y = b_0 + b_1 X$. Substituting into the usual expressions for the mean and standard deviation and simplifying, we have $\bar{Y} = b_0 + b_1 \bar{X}$ and $s_Y = \pm b_1 s_X$, with $s_Y = + b_1 s_X$ when b_1 is positive and $s_Y = - b_1 s_X$ when b_1 is negative. Therefore, if there is a perfect linear relationship between X and Y,

$$z_Y = \frac{Y - \bar{Y}}{s_Y}$$

$$= \frac{b_0 + b_1 X - (b_0 + b_1 \bar{X})}{\pm b_1 s_X}$$

$$= \frac{X - \bar{X}}{\pm s_X}$$

$$= \pm z_X$$

EXERCISES

18.1   Given the following data,

X	Y
1	11
2	3
3	7
4	9
5	9
6	21

(a) Draw a scatterplot.
(b) What is the correlation between Y and X?
(c) What is the least-squares equation for the regression of Y on X?
(d) What is the proportion of variance in Y accounted for by X?
(e) Find the equation for the regression of X on Y.
(f) What is the proportion of the variance in X accounted for by Y?

18.2 Given the following data for three variables X, Y, and W:

W	X	Y
12	4	7
8	6	9
4	11	3
17	12	14
18	13	16

Using a statistical package, find the correlations among W, X, and Y. Standardize the variables and recompute the correlations. They should be identical. Why?

18.3 **(a)** A psychologist is interested in predicting Y from X in two distinct situations. She finds the following results:

Situation 1	Situation 2
$b_1 = 38.41$	$b_1 = .25$
$s_Y = 512.31$	$s_Y = 8.44$
$s_X = 2.00$	$s_X = 23.17$

In which situation is the correlation between X and Y higher?

(b) You are given a large number of data points (X, Y) and find that the correlation between X and Y is $r_{XY} = .70$. You now add 10 to each of the X scores. What happens to the correlation coefficient; i.e., what is the new correlation between Y and the transformed X?

(c) You have the same situation as in part (b)—except instead of adding 10 to each of the X scores, you multiply each of the Y scores by 3. Now what is the value of the correlation coefficient?

(d) Now perform both operations, multiply each Y score by 3, and add 10 to the product. What happens to the correlation coefficient?

18.4 **(a)** Using the *Royer* data set available on the book's website, find the correlation between multiplication accuracy (*multacc*) and the time taken to solve multiplication problems (*multrt*) for third-graders.

(b) Generate the scatterplot for these variables.

(c) The correlation coefficient is not very resistant to the influence of data points that deviate strongly from the best-fitting straight line. Here, case 64 can be shown to be the most influential data point; that is, its removal results in more change in r than the removal of any other data point. What is r if case 64 is removed?

18.5 For parts (a)–(c) indicate whether the use of the correlation coefficient is reasonable. If it is not, indicate why not.

(a) A social critic has long held the view that providing enriched programs for disadvantaged students is a waste of money. As evidence to support her position, she describes the following study:

Two thousand 8-year-old children were selected from economically deprived homes, given a battery of mental tests, and then randomly assigned to either Group 1 or Group 2. The 1,000 children in Group 1 entered special, enriched programs, while the 1,000 children in Group 2 continued in their regular classes. After 3 years, another battery of mental tests was given to all the children. It was found that the correlations between children's IQ scores at age 8 and their IQ scores at age 11 was just about the same in Group 1 as it was in Group 2. Our critic claims that finding very similar correlations in the enriched and regular groups strongly suggests that the enriched classes are ineffective in improving IQ.

(b) The research division of the Old Southern Casket and Tobacco Corporation has just released the results of a study that they argue is inconsistent with the negative health claims made against cigarette smoking. For a large sample of heavy smokers, a substantial positive correlation was found between the total number of cigarettes smoked during a lifetime and length of life, a result they claim leads to the conclusion that cigarette smoking is beneficial to health.

(c) It is found that for eighth-grade children there is a fairly strong negative correlation between the amount of television watched and school performance as measured by grades. It is claimed that this finding constitutes proof that watching television interferes with intellectual ability and has a negative effect on the ability to focus attention. Does this argument seem valid?

18.6 **(a)** A psychologist is interested in predicting Y from X in two distinct groups. She finds the following results:

Group 1	Group 2
$b_1 = 1$	$b_1 = 4$
$s_Y = 20$	$s_Y = 10$
$s_X = 10$	$s_X = 2$

In which situation is the correlation between X and Y higher?

(b) You are given a large number of data points (X, Y) and find that the correlation between X and Y is $r_{XY} = 0.70$. You now transform X by multiplying each of the X scores by 10 and adding 3 to the each of the products. You also transform Y by multiplying each of the Y scores by 2. What is the correlation coefficient between the transformed variables?

18.7 In a large study of income (Y) as a function of years on job (X), the data for 2,000 men and 2,000 women in a certain profession are

	Men		Women	
	Income (Y)	Years (X)	Income	Years
Mean	80	15	76	10
s^2	324	100	289	25
r_{XY}		.333		.235

Note: Income is recorded in thousands of dollars.

(a) Find b_{YX} (i.e., $b_{Income, Years}$, the regression coefficient for the regression of income on years of service) for men and for women. What is your best estimate of the amount by which salary increases per year for men and women? Is this result consistent with differences in the correlations? Explain.

(b) Using separate regression equations for men and women, what salary would you predict for men and for women with 10 years of experience? With 20 years of experience?

18.8 Using the *Seasons* data file available on the book's website, correlate height with weight, and then correlate height with weight separately for men and women. How might you account for the discrepancies among the three correlations.

18.9 For parts (a)–(c), indicate whether the use of the correlation coefficient and/or the conclusion drawn is reasonable. If it is not, indicate why not.

(a) A clinical psychologist reads a description of a study in which a correlation of −.80 was obtained between a measure of anxiety and a measure of emotional stability. Deciding to verify the result, he administers the same measures of anxiety and emotional stability to a random sample of patients in a Veterans Administration (VA) hospital. The observed correlation of −.20 between measures is not significant. He concludes that he has no evidence of any relationship (at least any linear relationship) between anxiety and emotional stability.

(b) Martians are tall and skinny and do not weigh very much. Jovians are shorter but weigh a lot more. Height and weight correlate pretty highly for each group, about $r = .60$. Would you expect the correlation between height and weight for a mixed group consisting of equal numbers of Martians and Jovians to be about the same, bigger, or smaller than .60? Why?

(c) It is reported in the press that getting a degree from a four-year college is highly correlated with lifetime earnings; i.e., it is worth several hundred thousand dollars a year in lifetime earnings.

18.10 Using the *Seasons* data set, verify that the correlation between cholesterol level (*TC*) and age is .506 for women but only .148 for women 50 years of age or over and .264 for women under 50 years of age. How do you explain the discrepancy? What are the corresponding results for men?

18.11 We are concerned with the correlation between two tests. The reliability of the first test is .64; that of the second test is .81.

(a) What is the largest correlation that we could possibly find?

(b) Suppose we actually find that the correlation is .40 in a sample of 40 subjects. What is our best estimate of what the correlation would be if we had perfectly reliable measures?

18.12 Using the data for men in the *Seasons* data set, if we consider individual men, the correlation between *TC* and age is .062. What is this correlation if we consider levels of the variable *agegrp*; that is, if we find the means value of *TC* and age at each level of *agegrp*, and use these as our data points?

18.13 (a) After each of two practice landings, pilot trainees discuss their performance with their instructors. The instructors find that trainees who make poor landings the first time tend to make better landings the second time, whereas trainees who make good landings the first time tend to do worse the second time. The instructors conclude that the criticism that follows poor performance tends to make pilots do better and that the praise that follows good performance tends to make them do worse. Therefore, the instructors decide to be critical of all landings, good or bad. Is this a reasonable strategy?

(b) After the first examination in a course, students who scored in the bottom 25% of the distribution are given special tutoring. On the next examination, all of these students score above the average for the whole class. Can we conclude that the tutoring was effective or could the results simply be due to regression toward the mean?

(c) An educational psychologist wants to see whether ability to spell has any effect on ability to read. To this end, he selects two groups of subjects, a group of poor spellers and a group of good spellers. However, he is worried that the poor spellers may not be as intelligent as the good spellers, so he creates a group of poor spellers and a group of good spellers that are equated on IQ. (To make this simple, let us assume that his procedure is to use only those subjects in both groups who scored 100 on an IQ test that he administered.) He now administers a reading test to both groups and finds that the good spellers do better on the average than the poor spellers. Does this mean that spelling ability affects reading ability?

(d) Keeping in mind what you know about regression toward the mean, explain how fluctuations in the intensity of pain and other symptoms may cause patients to overestimate the therapeutic effects of alternative medicine.

18.14 Assume that the correlation between the adult heights of fathers and sons is .5, and further, that the mean and standard deviations of the heights of adult males are 70.0 and 3.0 inches, respectively.

(a) Given the information that a father is 76 inches tall, what is the best linear prediction for the adult height of his son?

(b) Given that the adult height of a son is 73 inches, what is the best linear prediction for the height of his father?

(c) Given the phenomenon of regression toward the mean, why wouldn't we expect all men to have about the same height in a few more generations?

18.15 Students are classified as gifted and gain admittance to a special, enriched program of studies if they score more than two standard deviations above the mean on an entrance exam. George scores 2.1 standard deviations above the mean (at the 98th percentile) on form A of the test and is classified as gifted. Later, he is tested on form B, a parallel form of the entrance exam that has the same mean and standard deviation as form A, and correlates .90 with it.

(a) Would you expect George to be classified as gifted on the basis of his performance on this exam? Why or why not?

(b) What are the consequences of this finding?

(c) Mary takes form B of the test and scores 1.89 standard deviations above the mean. She then takes form A. What is the best prediction for Mary's score on form A?

18.16 Use a statistical package and the *Seasons* data set to calculate the correlations for women among the variables *beck_d1*, *beck_d2*, *beck_d3*, and *beck_d4* (scores on the Beck Depression Inventory obtained during winter, spring, summer, and fall, respectively).

(a) Do so, (1) choosing the listwise deletion option (i.e., exclude cases listwise in SPSS), in which data from a case are included only if there are no missing data on any of the four variables, and then (2) choosing the pairwise deletion option, in which the correlation between two variables is calculated without regard to whether there are missing data on the other variables.

(b) How would you characterize the differences between the two sets of correlations? Can you see any advantages of or problems with using either of these options?

Chapter 19
More About Correlation

19.1 OVERVIEW

In Chapter 18, we developed the Pearson correlation coefficient as a descriptive statistic. In Chapter 19, we extend our discussion of correlation by developing procedures for making inferences and by introducing other measures of correlation. The specific topics we consider are:

- *Statistical inference about correlation*. We consider confidence intervals and significance tests for population correlation coefficients (ρs) and the differences between them, and discuss how to calculate power. We also consider the assumptions that underlie the inference.
- *Partial* and *semipartial* (*or part*) *correlation*. In partial correlation, each of the variables being correlated, say, X and Y, is adjusted for the effects of other variables, so that these other variables can be "partialed out" of the correlation. In semipartial or part correlation, only X or Y is adjusted.
- *Special cases and alternative measures of correlation*. We discuss (1) the point-biserial and phi correlation coefficients, which are simply Pearson correlation coefficients in which one or both variables are dichotomous (i.e., can take on only two values); and (2) correlation coefficients such as the Spearman rho and the Kendall tau, in which the data consist of ranks.

19.2 INFERENCE ABOUT CORRELATION

So far, we have discussed the Pearson correlation coefficient as a descriptive statistic. We have not addressed the issue of what we can say about ρ_{XY}, the correlation between X and Y in a population, based on finding a correlation coefficient of r_{XY} in a sample selected from the population. Because we have focused on descriptive statistics to this point, we have not made any assumptions about the joint distribution of X and Y, although we have pointed out that certain characteristics of the distributions of X and Y can limit the range of possible values of r. However, we now turn to the topic of how to make inferences about correlation. This requires that we specify a model for the joint distribution of X and Y in the population.

19.2.1 A Model for Inference About Correlation

Many of the statistical tests for means discussed earlier in the book have assumed that the underlying populations of scores are normally distributed. When we discuss inference about the population correlation, we usually assume that X and Y are both random variables and that the population of (X, Y) pairs has a *bivariate normal distribution* (see Appendix 19.1 for the density function). Think of the bivariate normal distribution as the two-dimensional generalization of the univariate normal distribution.

We can graphically represent the bivariate normal distribution in several ways. In Fig. 19.1, the plane defined by the X and Y axes contains all possible pairings of X and Y. The bivariate normal density function can be represented by a bell-shaped surface that rises above the X–Y plane. The height of the surface above the X–Y plane represents the probability density. The intersections of the density surface with planes perpendicular to the X–Y plane and parallel to either the X or Y axis all define normal distributions. That is, for any value of either variable, the density function of the other variable is normally distributed.

The intersections of the bivariate normal surface with planes parallel to, but above, the X–Y plane define a family of ellipses, as shown in Fig. 19.2. Each point on one of these ellipses will have the same probability density, and therefore these ellipses are called isodensity contours. Because of the "peaked" shape of the surface, the smaller ellipses in Fig. 19.2 correspond to larger values of probability density. The more eccentric the ellipses (i.e., the less they look like circles), the larger the correlation between X and Y. A set of concentric circles corresponds to a correlation of zero.

Some characteristics of a bivariate normal distribution in X and Y are as follows:

- The marginal distributions (i.e., the distribution of one variable, collapsing over values of the other variable) of X and of Y are normal with variances σ_X^2 and σ_Y^2, respectively.

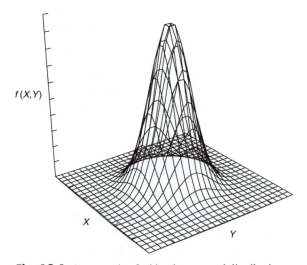

Fig. 19.1 An example of a bivariate normal distribution.

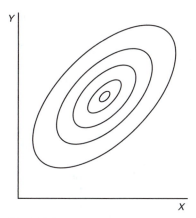

Fig. 19.2 Isodensity contours for a bivariate normal distribution.

- If X and Y have a correlation of zero, they are independent. That is, *given bivariate normality, the only possible systematic relationship between X and Y is a linear one*. The conditional means of Y (i.e., the means of the Y scores that correspond to particular values of X) fall on the straight line with the equation $\mu_{Y.X} = \mu_Y + \beta_{YX}(X - \mu_X)$ where $\beta_{YX} = \rho\sigma_Y/\sigma_X$ is the slope of the population regression equation that predicts Y from X. The conditional distributions of Y are normal with variance $\sigma_{Y.X}^2 = \sigma_Y^2(1 - \rho^2)$. The conditional means of X fall on the straight line with the equation $\mu_{X.Y} = \mu_X + \beta_{XY}(Y - \mu_Y)$ where $\beta_{XY} = \rho\sigma_X/\sigma_Y$ is the slope for the regression of X on Y, and the conditional distributions of X are normal with variance $\sigma_{X.Y}^2 = \sigma_X^2(1 - \rho^2)$.

The inferential procedures to which we now turn assume bivariate normal population distributions. If this assumption is violated, results may be biased.

19.2.2 Using the *t* Distribution to Test the Null Hypothesis H_0: $\rho = 0$

We can test whether there is a linear component to the relationship between X and Y in the population by considering the null hypothesis H_0: $\rho = 0$. When $\rho = 0$, the statistic

$$t = \frac{r}{\sqrt{\dfrac{1 - r^2}{N - 2}}} \tag{19.1}$$

has approximately a t distribution with $N - 2$ degrees of freedom. Therefore, we can use this expression as the test statistic with which to test the null hypothesis H_0: $\rho = 0$.[1] For example, the correlation between subtraction and multiplication accuracy for the 28 third-graders in the *Royer* data set is .594. The value of the t statistic with 26 *df* is $(.594)/\sqrt{(1 - .594)^2 / 26} = 3.77$, which yields, from Appendix Table C.3, $p < .001$. Therefore, we can reject the null hypothesis that H_0: $\rho = 0$.

---

[1] Note that there are other ways to test this hypothesis. We could use the Fisher Z transformation along with the normal distribution (see the next section), or we could work directly with the sampling distribution of r. SPSS uses the t test described in this section to test H_0: $\rho = 0$.

Power calculations for tests of the null hypothesis H_0: $\rho = 0$ are readily performed with available software. G*Power 3 can calculate the sample size necessary to obtain any desired level of power, given a specified effect size. Suppose we want the sample size necessary to have power = .80 for rejecting the null hypothesis H_0: $\rho = 0$, using a two-tailed t test with $\alpha = .05$. Further suppose that we expect the population correlation to be "medium sized," $\rho = .30$ according to Cohen's 1988 guidelines. To get G*Power 3 to calculate the desired sample size, select t *tests* as the *Test family*, and then select *Correlation* from the *Tests* menu and choose the *Point biserial model*.[2] For the type of power analysis, select *A priori*: Compute required sample size . . ., set $r = .30$, $\alpha = .05$, power = .80, and request a two-tailed test in the *Input Parameters* boxes. Now click on *Calculate*. G*Power 3 indicates that in order to have power equal to .80, it is necessary to have sample size of $N = 82$ (see Fig. 19.3).

It is important to estimate this required N so that we can decide whether it is worth using the resources necessary to achieve a reasonable level of power. If we simply went ahead with a study using, say, 30 subjects selected from a population in which ρ was .30, the estimated power for rejecting H_0: $\rho = 0$ against H_1: $\rho \neq 0$ at $\alpha = .05$ would only be about .38.

19.2.3 Using the Fisher Z Transformation

Although the t test for the null hypothesis $\rho = 0$ is quite robust with respect to the assumption of normality (see, for example, Edgell & Noon, 1984), it cannot be used to test null hypotheses about ρ other than $\rho = 0$, nor can it be used to develop confidence intervals for ρ. This is because the shape and the standard error of the sampling distribution of r depend on ρ. When ρ differs from 0, the sampling distribution of r is skewed, even for large sample sizes. The sampling distribution of r is negatively skewed if ρ is positive and positively skewed if ρ is negative. However, an appropriate transformation of ρ will allow us to test these other hypotheses and to find confidence intervals for ρ.

Fisher showed that if bivariate normality can be assumed, a logarithmic transformation

$$Z_r = \frac{1}{2} \log_e \left[\frac{1+r}{1-r} \right] \tag{19.2}$$

where $\log_e$ is the natural logarithm is approximately normally distributed with mean

$$Z_\rho = \frac{1}{2} \log_e \left[\frac{1+\rho}{1-\rho} \right]$$

and standard error

$$\sigma_r = \frac{1}{\sqrt{N-3}}$$

for sample sizes as small as $N = 10$. The effect of this *Fisher Z transformation*[3] is to stretch out the right tail of the sampling distribution for positive values of ρ and to stretch the left tail for negative values of ρ, in order to make the transformed distribution more symmetric. Thus, we can calculate confidence intervals for ρ by first using the normal distribution to find the confidence interval for

---

[2] G*Power 3 refers to the procedure that uses the t distribution to calculate power for this test as the "point-biserial model" because the procedure has a slight positive bias except for tests of the point-biserial correlation coefficient (see Section 19.4.1). For tests of the "usual" Pearson correlation coefficient for which X and Y are both quantitative continuous variables, this power calculation slightly overestimates power and underestimates the sample size required to achieve a desired level of power. This bias decreases with N and is negligible for $N > 30$.

[3] The Fisher Z transformation of r is the inverse of the hyperbolic tangent of r (i.e., $Z_r = \tanh^{-1} r$). This function is available on most scientific calculators.

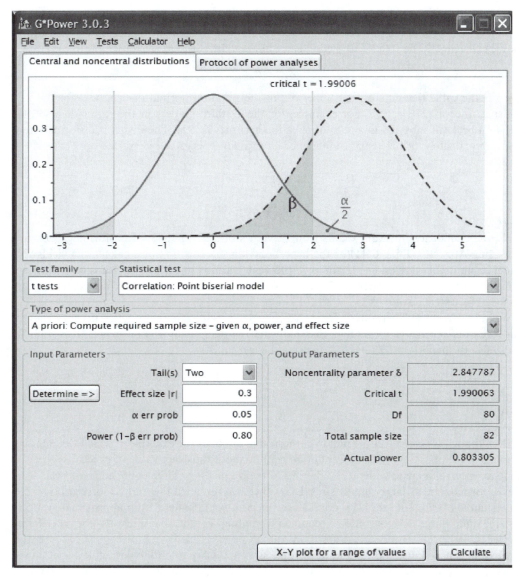

Fig. 19.3 G*Power 3 screen for calculating the sample size necessary to have power = .80 for a two-tailed t test of H_0: $\rho = 0$ at $\alpha = .05$ if ρ is really .30.

Z_ρ, and then transforming back to rs. The transformation also allows us to test null hypotheses of the form H_0: $\rho = \rho_{hyp}$, where ρ_{hyp} is not equal to 0.[4]

---

[4] Strictly speaking, the Z transformation is biased by an amount $r/2(N-1)$ (see Pearson & Hartley, 1954, p. 29). However, this bias will be negligible unless N is small and ρ is large, and we ignore it here. Note also that the sample correlation r is a biased estimator of ρ in normal populations, and the bias can be as much as perhaps .04 under realistic conditions (see Zimmerman, Zumbo, & Williams, 2003). An approximately unbiased estimator of ρ is

$$\hat{\rho} = r\left[1 + \frac{1 - r^2}{2N}\right]$$ but this estimator is rarely used.

Given an observed correlation r, we can find the value of the Fisher transformation, Z_r, using Appendix Table C.11, or the transformation menu found in most statistical packages, or using most scientific calculators. The $100(1 - \alpha)\%$ confidence interval for ρ is then given by

$$Z_r \pm z\, \sigma_r$$

where z is the value that cuts off the upper $\alpha/2$ of the standard normal distribution; for the 95% confidence interval, $z_{.025} = 1.96$. For example, for the 28 third-graders in the *Royer* data set, the correlation between subtraction and multiplication accuracy is .594. The Fisher transformation of .594 is approximately .684. The 95% confidence interval for Z_ρ is given by

$$.684 \pm (1.96)\,\frac{1}{\sqrt{25}}$$

$$= .684 \pm .392$$

That is, the confidence interval extends from Z values of .292 to 1.076. Transforming back to r scores using Appendix Table C.11 (or the hyperbolic tangent function of a calculator) yields 95% confidence limits of .284 and .792 for ρ. Note that because the Fisher Z transformation is a nonlinear function of r, the upper and lower limits of the confidence interval are not equally distant from the observed value of r.

We can reject the null hypothesis H_0: $\rho = \rho_{hyp}$ at $\alpha = .05$ for all values of ρ_{hyp} that do not fall in the confidence interval; that is, for all hypothesized values of ρ less than .284 or greater than .792. We can also test the hypothesis H_0: $\rho = \rho_{hyp}$ by using the test statistic

$$z = \frac{Z_r - Z_{\rho_{hyp}}}{\sqrt{\dfrac{1}{N-3}}} \tag{19.3}$$

Even though we can reject the null hypothesis that $\rho = 0$ for the example in which we found $r = .594$ in a sample of size $N = 28$, we cannot be certain about the exact value of ρ because the 95% confidence interval is quite wide. It is sobering to realize just how large confidence intervals for ρ are, even for moderately large sample sizes. Even if we had obtained the sample correlation of .594 from a sample of $N = 100$, the 95% confidence interval would extend from approximately .45 to .71—still quite large. We strongly recommend finding confidence intervals for correlation coefficients.

We can again calculate power and the sample sizes necessary to obtain desired levels of power. For example, suppose we want to test the hypothesis H_0: $\rho = .30$ against H_1: $\rho \neq .30$ at $\alpha = .05$, with power = .80, using Equation 19.3. If we assume that ρ is actually .50, we may use G*Power 3 to determine that the required sample size is $N = 140$.[5]

It is important to note that if *a priori* power calculations are based on a correlation estimate that comes from a small sample, the confidence interval for the required sample size may be so large that the power calculation will be of little use. For example, suppose we want to find the sample size necessary to have power = .90 to reject the hypothesis H_0: $\rho = .20$ against H_1: $\rho \neq .20$, at $\alpha = .05$, and

---

[5] To have the power calculation exactly match the test indicated by Equation 19.3, we must click on the *Options* button in the G*Power 3 screen and select *use large sample approximation (Fisher Z)*. Otherwise G*Power assumes that we are using the exact sampling distribution of r to conduct the test. However, because the Fisher Z transformation works well, we get almost the same value if we calculate power for the exact distribution test, $N = 139$.

that we base our calculations on the estimate $r = .594$, found in a sample of 28 third-graders. We can do so by specifying *Correlations: Difference from constant (one sample test)* in the *Statistical test* box of G*Power 3. Assuming $\rho = .594$, the sample size required to achieve power = .90 is 49. But the 95% *CI* for ρ extends from .284 to .792. If we use these two limits of the *CI* as our assumed values of ρ, we find that the required sample size is only 17 if $\rho = .792$, but it is 1,321 if $\rho = .284$!

19.2.4 What If the Assumption of Bivariate Normality Is Violated?

The model underlying statistical inference in this chapter assumes bivariate normality. However, we know that in real data sets, even univariate distributions rarely follow ideal normal distributions (e.g., see Micceri, 1989). Given the discussion in Section 19.2.1, we may alert researchers to a couple of conditions that indicate a violation of bivariate normality. Both conditions are easily detected. First, the bivariate normality assumption will be violated if the marginal distributions of X and/or Y are not normal. Second, even if the marginal distributions are normal, the assumption will be violated if there is any systematic relationship between X and Y other than a linear one. Recall that Q–Q plots are useful in detecting violations of the normality assumption (see Chapter 2). In addition, tests for violations of normality and linearity are discussed in Section 20.5.

As with any violations of the assumptions of a test, the concern is that either the Type 1 error rate will be inflated, or power will be adversely affected, or both. There have been a number of simulation studies to investigate the robustness of significance tests for correlation under violations of the normality assumption (e.g., Edgell & Noon, 1984; Havlicek & Peterson, 1977; Lee & Rodgers, 1998). The results show that tests of the hypothesis H_0: $\rho = 0$ are quite robust with respect to Type 1 error. Type 1 error rates are close to their nominal values, even for skewed distributions. The exception occurs when "composite" populations with large correlations are used (e.g., the population might be constructed by selecting half the data points from a population with $\rho = .7$ and the other half from a population with $\rho = -.7$). In this case, the actual Type 1 error rate may be two or three times as large as the stated value of α. Recall from Section 18.7.3 that combining data across distinct subgroups and computing a correlation on the resulting data set is generally not advisable for other reasons, as well. As we discussed, the aggregate statistic can seriously misrepresent the relationship between X and Y in any of the subgroups.

With respect to power considerations, other simulation studies have shown that severe violations of bivariate normality can result in substantial loss of power. For example, Lee and Rodgers (1998) calculated the power for the test of H_0: $\rho = 0$ when the true ρ was .4. They compared the power when samples were drawn from a normal population to the power when samples were drawn from a highly skewed population. For sample sizes of both 30 and 60, sampling from the skewed population resulted in less than half of the power of sampling from the normal population. This severe decline in power suggests that when the normality assumption is severely violated, we should consider alternatives to the usual tests.

An alternative procedure that may be useful when the normality assumption is not satisfied is *bootstrapping*. Bootstrapping is a general purpose, computationally intensive approach to inference (see, for example, Efron & Diaconis, 1983; Efron, 1988) in which the sampling distribution of a statistic can be obtained by repeatedly sampling, with replacement, from the observed sample. For example, a 95% confidence interval could be obtained for a correlation coefficient by selecting a large number of samples of size N from the observed sample, and then calculating the correlation coefficients for all of these samples and ordering them. If we selected 1,000 samples, the 95% confidence interval for ρ would be defined by the 25th and 976th largest correlations.

The bootstrapping option is available as part of some statistical packages. When we used bootstrapping in SYSTAT with 1,000 samples for the correlation between total cholesterol and age for women in the *Seasons* study, we found that the estimated 95% confidence interval extended from .386 to .605. This is sightly larger the interval from .397 to .599 that was found by the Fisher Z transformation approach discussed in the previous section.

19.2.5 Testing Whether Independent Correlations Are Significantly Different

Another natural question to ask about relationships between two variables is whether they differ in magnitude. For example, does the relationship between high-school GPA and college GPA differ for men and women? It is possible to test whether the correlation between X and Y is the same in two different populations. We can test H_0: $\rho_1 = \rho_2$ by using the test statistic

$$z = \frac{Z_{r_1} - Z_{r_2}}{\sqrt{\dfrac{1}{N_1 - 3} + \dfrac{1}{N_2 - 3}}} \tag{19.4}$$

As an example of using Equation 19.4 with real data, the correlation between subtraction and multiplication accuracy for the 28 third-graders in the *Royer* data set is .594; for the 25 fifth-graders, it is .225. To determine whether these correlations are significantly different at $\alpha = .05$, we can substitute in Equation 19.4. If we do so, we obtain

$$z = (.684 - .229)/.292 = 1.56$$

This is less than the upper critical value of $z_{crit} = 1.96$, so we do not have sufficient evidence to reject the null hypothesis that the correlations in the populations of third- and fifth-graders are equal.

Suppose that we wish to run the study again with a larger sample. We can readily do *a priori* power calculations for this test if we are willing to specify the size of the effect, $q = Z_{r_1} - Z_{r_2}$. For example, if we can assume that the two population correlations are .594 and .225, so that $q = .684 - .229 = .455$, we can use G*Power 3 to show that the sample size necessary to have power = .90 for a two-tailed test of H_0: $\rho_1 = \rho_2$ at $\alpha = .05$ is 105 in each group (see Fig. 19.4). However, we should be cautious about using these calculations when we design research using correlations from small samples. The 95% *CI* for the correlation between subtraction and multiplication accuracy for third-graders extends from .284 to .792, and the 95% *CI* for fifth-graders extends from −.206 to .583. In this situation, we should perform several different power calculations to assess the magnitude of the task before us. As above, we may estimate the required sample size based on the results of a previous study. Also, we can base our calculations on Cohen's guidelines that small, medium, and large values of q are given by .10, .30, and .50, respectively. Finally, we may base our calculations on the smallest values of q that are thought to be meaningful from either a theoretical or practical perspective, if such values are available.

It is important to note that equal differences in Zs are equally detectable and therefore can be said to represent equal changes in linear relationship at different points along the range of possible values (see Cohen, 1977, 1988). In contrast, *equal differences between the rs do not correspond to equal differences in relationship at different points along their range*. For example, the .3 difference between rs of .8 and .5 corresponds to a q of .45, whereas the .3 difference between rs of .4 and .1 corresponds to a q of only .32.

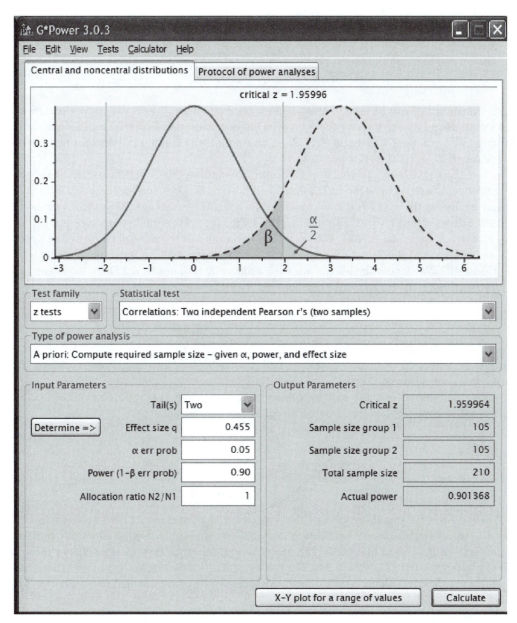

Fig. 19.4 G*Power 3 screen for calculating the sample size necessary to have power = .90 for a two-tailed *t* test of H_0: $\rho_1 = \rho_2$ at $\alpha = .05$ if ρ_1 is really .594 and ρ_2 is really .225.

As a second example of the application of Equation 19.4, in Section 18.7 we found that the correlations between total cholesterol level and age in the *Seasons* data set for women ($N = 211$) and men ($N = 220$) were .51 and .06, respectively. Substituting into Equation 19.4, we find $z = 5.15$, a value well beyond any entry in Appendix Table C.2. We conclude that the population correlations are different.

Equation 19.4 also provides a basis for obtaining confidence intervals for $Z_{\rho_1} - Z_{\rho_2}$. The 95% confidence interval is given by

$$Z_{r_1} - Z_{r_2} \pm 1.96 \sqrt{\frac{1}{N_1 - 3} + \frac{1}{N_2 - 3}} \tag{19.5}$$

Although Equation 19.5 can be used to find a confidence interval for $Z_{\rho_1} - Z_{\rho_2}$ we cannot transform back to obtain a confidence interval for $\rho_1 - \rho_2$. This is because the Fisher Z transformation is not linear, so $Z_{\rho_1 - \rho_2}$ is not the same as $Z_{\rho_1} - Z_{\rho_2}$. This nonlinearity is not a problem for hypothesis testing because if $Z_{\rho_1} \neq Z_{\rho_2}$, then $\rho_1 \neq \rho_2$.

However, Zou (2007) has provided a procedure for finding the confidence interval for the difference between two independent correlations. To find, say, the 95% confidence interval for $\rho_1 - \rho_2$, we start by finding the 95% CIs for each correlation, using the Fisher Z transform as we showed earlier. In the data for the previous example, the 95% CI for the correlation between age and TC for women, ρ_1, extends from .403 to .604. We denote the lower limit of the interval by l_1 and the upper limit by u_1. We then find the 95% CI for the corresponding correlation for men, ρ_2, as the interval from −.072 to .192. We denote the lower limit by l_2 and the upper limit by u_2. Then, the lower and upper limits of the 95% CI for the difference between the correlations, $\rho_1 - \rho_2$, are given by

$$L = r_1 - r_2 - \sqrt{(r_1 - l_1)^2 + (u_2 - r_2)^2}$$

and

$$U = r_1 - r_2 + \sqrt{(u_1 - r_1)^2 + (r_2 - l_2)^2}$$

Substituting the values for men and women, we find that the 95% CI for the difference between the two correlations extends from .28 to .61.

It is also possible to test the null hypothesis that more than two independent correlation coefficients are all equal. To test that J ρs are all equal, use the test statistic

$$\chi_{J-1}^2 = \sum_j (N_j - 3) Z_j^2 - \frac{\left[\sum_j (N_j - 3) Z_j \right]^2}{\sum_j (N_j - 3)} \tag{19.6}$$

where Z_j is the Fisher Z transformation of the jth correlation coefficient. For example, Table 19.1 presents the correlations between subtraction accuracy and multiplication accuracy for fourth-, fifth-, and sixth-graders; these are −.194, .225, and .431, respectively. The obtained value of the test statistic is $\chi^2 = 6.899 - (10.283)^2/68 = 5.344$. For $\alpha = .05$ and $(J - 1) = 2$ df, $\chi_{crit.05,2}^2 = 5.99$. Therefore, we do not have sufficient evidence to reject the hypothesis that the three population correlations are identical.

Table 19.1 Correlations between subtraction and multiplication accuracy for third-, fourth-, fifth-, and sixth-graders in the *Royer* data

Grade	Correlation	N	95% CI
Third	.594	28	.284 to .792
Fourth	−.194	28	−.528 to .194
Fifth	.225	23	−.206 to .583
Sixth	.431	26	.052 to .701

19.2.6 Testing Hypotheses About Dependent Correlations

In the preceding section, we focused on comparisons of correlations of the same two variables across different groups (e.g., the correlation between subtraction and multiplication scores for third- versus fifth-graders). In this section, our concern is with evaluating multiple correlations on the same set of subjects. Two questions are of interest: First, which variables are correlated? Second, which correlations differ in magnitude? We first consider the question of evaluating individual correlation coefficients.

When data on a number of variables have been collected from the same set of subjects, the correlations may be displayed as a *correlation matrix*. If the variables are X_1, X_2, X_3, and X_4, the correlation matrix is

$$
\begin{array}{c c c c c}
 & X_1 & X_2 & X_3 & X_4 \\
X_1 & \begin{bmatrix} 1 & r_{12} & r_{13} & r_{14} \\ X_2 & r_{21} & 1 & r_{23} & r_{24} \\ X_3 & r_{31} & r_{32} & 1 & r_{34} \\ X_4 & r_{41} & r_{42} & r_{43} & 1 \end{bmatrix}
\end{array}
$$

If there are k variables, the correlation matrix consists of k^2 elements. The k elements on the major diagonal (the one that goes from the upper left to the lower right) are each equal to 1 because any variable is perfectly correlated with itself. The $k^2 - k = k(k-1)$ off-diagonal elements can be divided into a set of $k(k-1)/2$ correlations above the diagonal and a set of equal size below it. The matrix is symmetric because elements on opposite sides of the diagonal are identical; $r_{12} = r_{21}$ and, in general, $r_{ij} = r_{ji}$ for all i and j.

When k is large, the number of correlations will be large. For example, if $k = 20$, $k(k-1)/2 = 190$. If we tested each correlation for significance at $\alpha = .05$, the Type 1 error rate for the entire family of correlations would be very high. Although most software packages will dutifully provide the significance level for each correlation coefficient as though it were the only one tested, it is as necessary to control Type 1 error here as when we perform multiple t tests on the differences between means. One way of controlling Type 1 error when we have numerous significance tests is to adjust the significance levels, using the Dunn–Bonferroni procedure described earlier. However, this adjustment will be conservative because the tests are not independent of one another.

In order to protect against excessive Type 1 error, Steiger (1980) has recommended the routine use of a simple test of the hypothesis that all off-diagonal elements of a correlation matrix are equal to zero. If this hypothesis cannot be rejected, tests on the individual correlations in the matrix are not likely to be meaningful unless motivated by *a priori* considerations. The hypothesis can be tested using the statistic

$$
\chi^2 = (N-3) \sum_{j > i} \sum Z_{ij}^2 \tag{19.7}
$$

with $k(k-1)/2$ *df*, where Z_{ij} is the Fisher Z-transformed value of r_{ij} and the summation is over the $k(k-1)/2$ squared Zs that correspond to the rs that are above (or below) the diagonal. For example, for the *Seasons* data set, if we correlate age, height, total cholesterol (*TC*), and body-mass index (*BMI*) for the 207 women having scores for all four variables, the correlation matrix is

	Age	Height	TC	BMI
Age	1	−.129	.513	.070
Height	−.129	1	−.198	−.093
TC	.513	−.198	1	.152
BMI	.070	−.093	.152	1

First, we find the Fisher Z transformations for each of the six correlations above the main diagonal. These are then squared and summed, yielding

$$\Sigma\Sigma Z_{ij}^2 = (-.130)^2 + (.567)^2 + (-.198)^2 + (.070)^2 + (-.093)^2 + (.153)^2 = .415$$

so, from Equation 19.7, $\chi^2 = (204)(.415) = 84.66$. Because the observed value of χ^2 is much larger than the critical value $\chi_{.05, 6}^2 = 12.59$, we can reject the hypothesis that all the off-diagonal correlations are zero. Had we failed to reject the overall null hypothesis, and if we had no *a priori* knowledge about the correlations, we would conduct no further tests on these correlations. However, given a significant result, we may then test individual correlations. Further, even if the null hypothesis is not rejected, we may test some of the individual correlations on *a priori* grounds. For example, the literature suggests that for women, there is a positive correlation between *age* and *TC*. Based on this sample, we find the 95% confidence interval for the correlation between *TC* and *age* extends from .41 to .61, and can therefore reject the null hypothesis that this correlation is zero in the population.

Let's now turn to the general question of whether a particular variable, X, has a different correlation with variable Y than with variable Z. For example, we may want to determine whether the correlation between *TC* and *age* is significantly different than the correlation between *TC* and *BMI*. Note that these are *dependent* rather than *independent* correlations because both are based on data from the same subjects. Although this is a reasonable question to ask, it is a difficult one to answer. Unfortunately, testing hypotheses about dependent correlations involves expressions that are complicated, not intuitive, and often very tedious to calculate, especially when the correlations to be tested do not have a variable in common. Because these tests have not been incorporated into the standard statistics packages, we must find macros for these packages, use specialized software, or find the values of the test statistics using a calculator. Tests of dependent correlations may also be performed by structural equation modeling programs (see Cheung & Chan, 2004, for a discussion of the problem and for the LISREL syntax necessary to perform the tests).

Some useful sources that discuss tests of dependent correlations are Meng et al. (1992), Olkin and Finn (1990, 1995), and Steiger (1980). Perhaps the simplest test for two dependent correlations that have a variable in common is given by Meng et al. (1992). Given the null hypothesis $H_0:\rho_{YX_1} = \rho_{YX_2}$, we can use the test statistic

$$z = (Z_{r_{YX_1}} - Z_{r_{YX_2}})\sqrt{\frac{N-3}{2(1 - r_{X_1 X_2})h}} \tag{19.8}$$

where
$$h = \frac{1 - f\bar{r}^2}{1 - \bar{r}^2}$$

and
$$f = \frac{1 - r_{X_1 X_2}}{2(1 - \bar{r}^2)} \quad \text{(where } f \text{ is not allowed to exceed 1)}$$

and $\bar{r}^2$ is the mean of $r_{YX_1}^2$ and $r_{YX_2}^2$. To test whether the correlation between *TC* and *age* (.513) is significantly different from the correlation between *TC* and *BMI* (.152), we may substitute into

Equation 19.8. We have $\overline{r^2} = .143$, $f = .543$, and $h = 1.076$, so that $z = 4.18$. Therefore, we may reject the null hypothesis at $p = .000$. Note that the test statistic given in Equation 19.8 is only appropriate if the two correlations have a common variable. If we wish to test the hypothesis H_0: $\rho_{XY} = \rho_{WQ}$, the test statistic is considerably more complicated (see Steiger, 1980).[6]

19.2.7 Some Cautions About Tests That Compare Correlations

In Sections 19.2.5 and 19.2.6, we discussed how to test whether two correlations differ in size. However, given that we have previously emphasized that correlations are dependent on sample characteristics such as the variance of X and Y, we should give serious thought to exactly what we are testing when we compare two correlations. Suppose, for example, we find that the correlations between income and number of years of education are significantly different for two ethnic groups. This means that there is a stronger linear relationship in one group than the other. However, the correlations may differ because the variances of income and/or years of education differ in the two groups, rather than because the rate of change of income with years of education is different. Also, a researcher who wishes to compare correlations should carefully evaluate whether constraints on the sampling of observations might have resulted in a biased estimate of ρ for either or both correlation coefficients.

Our second point is that we are often more interested in the slope of the regression line than the strength of the linear relationship. If our concern is about how much income changes with additional education and whether this differs across groups, we should compare regression slopes, not correlation coefficients. Just because the correlations are significantly different for the two groups does not necessarily mean that the regression slopes will be. Conversely, finding that the slopes are significantly different does not necessarily mean that the correlations are significantly different.

19.3 PARTIAL AND SEMIPARTIAL (OR PART) CORRELATIONS

In observational studies, many variables may be correlated with one another. In this section, we consider measures of the correlation between two variables that attempt to statistically control for the effects of other variables.

19.3.1 The Partial Correlation Coefficient

We noted in the last chapter that two variables may be correlated because they are both influenced directly or indirectly by other variables. For example, verbal ability is correlated with shoe size in young children because both verbal ability and shoe size increase with age. However, we may wish to

---

[6] We may test many different types of hypotheses about the elements of a correlation matrix by using Steiger's MULTICORR program (Steiger, 1979), which performs tests based on a statistical rationale developed by Dunn and Clark (1969). The program is free, and is available, along with documentation and source code, at Steiger's website, http://statpower.net. Although MULTICORR is a DOS (i.e., a pre-Windows operating system) program, it does run on Windows XP and is much easier to use than the corresponding computational formulas. If we use MULTICORR to test whether the correlation between TC and age is significantly different than the correlation between TC and BMI, we find that $\chi_1^2 = 17.819$. This corresponds to $z = 4.22$, a result very similar to the value of 4.18 provided by Equation 19.8.

ask whether there would still be a correlation even if the effects of age could somehow be *controlled* or *partialed out* of both variables. How can we find a measure of the relationship between size and verbal ability that is not contaminated by the effects of chronological age? By far the best way is to collect data from samples of children who are all approximately the same age. However, we can also attempt to control statistically for the effects of age in a sample of children of varying ages by finding a partial correlation.

If we use the notation r_{XY} = Corr (X, Y) to stand for the correlation between X and Y, then $r_{XY|W}$, the *partial correlation between X and Y with the effects of W partialed out*, is given by

$$r_{XY|W} = \text{Corr}\,(X\,|W,\,Y\,|W)$$

In this expression, $X\,|W = X - \hat{X}$, where $\hat{X}$ is the value of X predicted from the regression of X on W; therefore, $X\,|W$ is the part of X that is not predictable from W with linear regression. Similarly, $Y\,|W = Y - \hat{Y}$ is the residual that results when Y is regressed on W. It is possible to express $r_{XY|W}$ in terms of the simple correlations between X, Y, and W as follows:

$$r_{XY|W} = \frac{r_{XY} - r_{XW}\,r_{YW}}{\sqrt{(1 - r_{XW}^2)(1 - r_{YW}^2)}} \tag{19.9}$$

Suppose X represents shoe size, Y represents verbal ability, and W represents age. If the correlations of both size and verbal ability with age are .7 ($r_{XW} = r_{YW} = .7$), and the correlation between shoe size and verbal ability is .5 ($r_{XY} = .5$), then $r_{size,verbal|age}$ would have a value of $(.5 - .49)/(1 - .49) = .02$. In other words, if we take into account the relationship between shoe size and age, and between verbal skills and age, the correlation between size and verbal ability virtually disappears.

More than one variable may be partialed out of a correlation. Suppose that we wish to partial out the effects of variables W and Q from the correlation between X and Y. The partial correlation $r_{XY|WQ}$ is given by Corr$(X\,|\,WQ,\,Y\,|\,WQ)$ = Corr$(X - \hat{X},\,Y - \hat{Y})$, where $\hat{X}$ is the prediction of X based on a linear regression equation that contains both W and Q, and $\hat{Y}$ is the corresponding prediction of Y. The same logic holds no matter how many variables there are to be partialed out; the partial correlation can always be obtained by correlating the two sets of residuals that result when X and Y are regressed on these variables. Such partial correlations are readily obtained by using statistical packages that either produce the partial correlations directly, or provide the appropriate residuals that can then be correlated. If the raw data are not available but the first-order correlations are, Equation 19.10 indicates how to find the partial correlation between X and Y, partialing out W and Q. In effect, Equation 19.10 is first used to remove the effects of Q from r_{XY}, r_{XW}, and r_{YW}, and then is used again to remove the effects of W.

$$r_{XY|WQ} = \frac{r_{XY|Q} - r_{XW|Q}\,r_{YW|Q}}{\sqrt{(1 - r_{XW|Q}^2)(1 - r_{YW|Q}^2)}} \tag{19.10}$$

How are we to interpret the pattern of correlations that we observe when computing partial correlations? Often, the decision to calculate partial correlations is motivated by a desire to make causal statements. If $r_{XY|W}$ is about the same size as r_{XY}, it is said that W has no effect. If r_{XY} is significant but $r_{XY|W}$ is close to 0, it is said that either

1. r_{XY} is spurious, occurring because W influences both X and Y, not because X and Y influence one another; or
2. W is an intervening, or mediating, variable—perhaps W is influenced by X and in turn influences Y.

However, as we mentioned in the last chapter, the fact that two variables are correlated does not, by itself, mean that they are causally related.

How are we to interpret the results of an analysis based on partial correlations? When we compute $r_{XY|W}$, what is removed from X and Y are any components *predictable* from W. Consider an example in which X measures parents' education, Y measures their children's performance in elementary school, and W is the number of books in the home. If $r_{XY|W}$ is considerably smaller than r_{XY}—that is, if the correlation between school performance and parent's education is much smaller when the number of books in the home is partialed out—this does not necessarily mean that providing the family with lots of books will have any effect on the children's school performance, nor does it mean that providing the books will reduce the influence of parental education on the child's educational performance. Partialing number of books out of the correlation between parental education and school performance not only removes any *direct effect* of books on school performance, but it also removes any components of parental education and children's school performance *predictable* from number of books. We would expect the number of books to be correlated with parental education and intelligence, as well as with other potentially important variables such as socioeconomic level and parental encouragement of children's achievement. Therefore, when the number of books is partialed out of the correlation between X and Y, any effects of these other variables predictable from number of books are removed as well.

In sum, the pattern of correlations we observe does not tell us the source of the pattern. In particular, we must be very cautious about making causal inferences. If we have a well-developed causal theory, we can make decisions about which partial correlations make sense to compute and we can give them an interpretation within the context of the model. However, this does not work the other way around. We should not start with a bunch of partial correlations and use them to develop causal theories. The same pattern of results, say, a large r_{XY} but small $r_{XY|W}$, may be consistent with two or more very different causal models. These difficulties in interpretation also arise for other techniques in which there are a number of correlated variables and one or more of them are statistically "controlled" (e.g., analysis of covariance, multiple regression). We will be in a better position to discuss these issues further after we have considered multiple regression.

19.3.2 Confidence Intervals and Significance Tests for Partial Correlation Coefficients

Confidence intervals and significance tests for partial correlation coefficients are completely analogous to those calculated in Section 19.2. The null hypothesis H_0: $\rho_{XY|W} = 0$ can be tested by using

$$t = r_{XY|W} \sqrt{\frac{N-3}{1 - r_{XY|W}^2}} \text{ with } N - 3 \text{ } df$$

and the more general null hypothesis H_0: $\rho_{XY|W} = \rho_{hyp}$ can be tested by using

$$z = (Z_r - Z_{\rho_{hyp}})\sqrt{N-4}$$

where the Zs are Fisher transformations. The $100(1 - \alpha)\%$ confidence interval for ρ may be found by finding the limits for Z_ρ,

$$Z_r \pm z_{\alpha/2}\sqrt{\frac{1}{N-4}}$$

and then transforming back to the correlation scale.

In general, if r is the partial correlation with p variables partialed out, the expressions become

$$t = r\sqrt{\frac{N - 2 - p}{1 - r^2}} \text{ with } N - 2 - p \; df$$

and

$$z = (Z_r - Z_{\rho_{hyp}})\sqrt{N - 3 - p}$$

and the confidence limits on ρ can be obtained by transforming

$$Z_r \pm z_{\alpha/2}\sqrt{\frac{1}{N - 3 - p}}$$

19.3.3 The Semipartial (or Part) Correlation Coefficient

In addition to the partial correlation coefficient, it is possible to compute the semipartial correlation coefficient. This statistic has a useful interpretation in terms of multiple regression and will be discussed further in Chapter 21. For now, we simply indicate what it is and how to compute it.

The semipartial correlation coefficient $r_{Y(X|W)}$ is the correlation between Y and $X|W$, where $X|W = X - \hat{X}$, the residual when X is regressed on W. The coefficient may be obtained by regressing X on W, and then correlating the resulting residuals with Y, or by using Equation 19.11,

$$r_{Y(X|W)} = \frac{r_{XY} - r_{XW}r_{YW}}{\sqrt{1 - r_{XW}^2}} \tag{19.11}$$

Notice that the part of X that can be predicted by W has been removed, but no adjustment has been made to Y.

19.3.4 Constraints in Sets of Correlation Coefficients

Given three variables X, Y, and W, there are three correlation coefficients, r_{XY}, r_{XW}, and r_{YW}. The range of possible values that can be taken on by any one of these correlations is constrained by the values taken on by the other two. As the most extreme example, if W has a perfect linear relationship with both X and Y, then X and Y must have a perfect linear relationship. That is, if $|r_{XW}| = |r_{YW}| = 1$, then $|r_{XY}| = 1$. However, what can we say about the possible values of r_{XY} if r_{XW} and r_{YW} are both equal to some other value (e.g., .7)?

Because $r_{XY|W}$ is a correlation, it must take on a value between -1 and $+1$. If we solve equation 19.9 for r_{XY}, we have

$$r_{XY} = r_{XW}r_{YW} + r_{XY|W}\sqrt{(1 - r_{XW}^2)(1 - r_W^2)}$$

Therefore, the value of r_{XY} must lie between

$$r_{XW}r_{YW} - \sqrt{(1 - r_{XW}^2)(1 - r_{YW}^2)} \quad \text{and} \quad r_{XW}r_{YW} + \sqrt{(1 - r_{XW}^2)(1 - r_{YW}^2)}$$

Substituting into these expressions, we see that if $r_{XW} = r_{YW} = .7$, r_{XY} must have a value between $-.02$ and 1.00. A strong negative correlation between X and Y is not possible if X and Y both have large positive correlations with W. We view this finding as interesting on its own. However, another reason for mentioning these constraints is because correlation matrices that do not satisfy them—either because of missing data (see below) or because of adjustments to the correlations—may cause complications when they are used as inputs to multivariate procedures such as factor analysis or principal components analysis.

19.4 MISSING DATA IN CORRELATION

The constraint discussed in the previous section assumes that all correlations are calculated with data from the same cases. In other words, if a case is missing data on any of X, Y, or W, the case is dropped when any of the correlations are calculated (i.e., listwise deletion). If, instead, the correlation for any two variables is calculated without regard to whether there are missing data on other variables (i.e., pairwise deletion), then different correlations may depend on different subsets of the sample. This can result in inconsistent correlations (i.e., they violate the constraint discussed in the previous section), especially if the missing data are nonrandom. We should also note that if pairwise deletion is used and the missing data are MCAR (missing completely at random; see Chapter 14), pairwise deletion produces parameter estimates that are consistent and therefore approximately unbiased in large samples. In contrast, if the missing data are MAR (missing at random) or MNAR (missing not at random), pairwise deletion can lead to seriously biased parameter estimates. The practical implication of these observations is that listwise deletion should be used when observations are missing from datasets containing three or more variables.

19.5 OTHER MEASURES OF CORRELATION

In this section, we introduce several classes of correlation measures other than the usual Pearson product-moment correlation coefficient. We first discuss four measures used when one or both variables are dichotomous (i.e., they can take on only two possible values). The *point-biserial* and *phi* coefficients are simply the Pearson r with one and two dichotomous variables, respectively. The *biserial* and *tetrachoric* coefficients are different: They provide estimates of what the Pearson r would be if, instead of dichotomous variables, we actually had variables that were continuous and normally distributed. Finally, we discuss several measures of correlation used with ranked data. The first of these, the *Spearman rho coefficient*, is simply the usual Pearson r applied to data in the form of ranks. The *Kendall tau* and *Goodman–Kruskal gamma* coefficients employ a different measure of agreement based on the proportion of pairs of data points in which the rankings of X and of Y agree.

19.5.1 The Point-Biserial and the Phi Correlation Coefficients

We are frequently concerned with dichotomies such as male/female, pass/fail, correct/error, and experimental/control. Even though these are each categorical variables with two levels and there is nothing inherently quantitative about them, we can express each dichotomy as levels of a quantitative variable that may be correlated with other variables. For example, we can correlate a dichotomous variable with a continuous variable (e.g., passing or failing an individual test item with the overall test score), or correlate two dichotomous variables (e.g., male/female with pass/fail). We can find the correlation by assigning any two different numbers to the categories that make up the dichotomy. Usually the two numbers 0 and 1 are used, but the size of the correlation would be the same for any pair of numbers; e.g., if we used 31 and 57 to represent the two levels instead of 0 and 1, the correlation would be the same.

When the usual Pearson r formula is applied to a data set in which one variable is continuous and the other variable takes on the values 0 and 1, the result is called the *point-biserial correlation coefficient*. There are specialized formulas for the correlation that take advantage of the fact that one of the variables is dichotomous, but they will give the same numerical result as the Pearson r

applied to the same variables, and will not be presented here. The point-biserial correlation coefficient can be tested for significance by using the test statistic presented in Equation 19.1, and power for the test can be conveniently calculated by G*Power 3 by using the point-biserial model.

Given data from two independent groups, we could test the null hypothesis that the group population means are equal by a t test. If we do this, we get exactly the same observed t and test of H_0: $\rho = 0$ as if we

1. formed $N = n_1 + n_2$ data points (X, Y) in which each Y score was paired with either $X = 1$ if the score belonged to group 1, or $X = 0$ if the score belonged to group 2, and then
2. found r_{XY}, and tested H_0: $\rho = 0$ by using Equation 19.1.

Solving Equation 19.1 for r yields

$$r = \sqrt{\frac{t^2}{t^2 + N - 2}} = \sqrt{\frac{t^2}{t^2 + df_{error}}} \tag{19.12}$$

Because of this relationship, some authors recommend that r be used as a measure of effect size to accompany t tests and, because $F(1, df_{error}) = t^2(df_{error})$, that r be used as the measure of effect size for F tests in which $df_1 = 1$ (see, for example, Rosenthal, 1991).

As an illustration, if for the *Seasons* data set we correlate depression score (averaged over seasons) with sex (coded as 0 for men and 1 for women), we find $r = .134$. The positive correlation indicates that depression scores are higher for women. Using the t test statistic of Equation 19.1, we find that the correlation is significant, $t(328) = 2.455$, $p = .015$. If we perform a pooled-variance independent-groups t test on the same data with sex as the independent variable, we find that we can reject the hypothesis H_0: $\mu_{women} = \mu_{men}$, also with $t(328) = 2.455$ and $p = .015$. The point-biserial correlation coefficient may be used as a measure of effect size, although the standardized effect size measure $\hat{d} = (\bar{Y}_{women} - \bar{Y}_{men})/s_{pooled} = (6.217 - 4.720)/5.537 = .270$ seems to have a more direct interpretation.

When both X and Y are dichotomous variables and we apply the Pearson r formula, the result is called the *phi coefficient* (φ). As is the case for the point-biserial coefficient, specialized formulas for φ exist, but these always give the same result as applying the Pearson r to the dichotomous data. Table 19.2 contains the calculation of the correlation between survival (survive, die) and treatment (drug, no drug), using one of the expressions for φ. The example also demonstrates that, depending on the context, even a small correlation can correspond to an important effect. In the example, the value of the correlation between treatment and survival is .2; that is, only $.2^2 = .04$ of the variance in survival is accounted for by the treatment. Yet this small correlation corresponds to a 20% increase in survival rate when the drug is administered, a difference that is obviously important.

The φ coefficient is closely related to the χ^2 test for independence, and we can show that

$$\chi_1^2 = N \phi^2 \tag{19.13}$$

The χ^2 statistic with 1 df can be used to test the hypothesis that X and Y are independent in the population, whereas the φ coefficient (or φ^2, which can be interpreted as the proportion of variance accounted for) can be used as a measure of the strength of the relationship between X and Y.

Note that with large enough samples, even very small effects may be statistically significant. Using Equation 19.13 and Appendix Table C.4, we find that we can reject the null hypothesis that X and Y are independent at $\alpha = .05$, if $\chi^2 = N\varphi^2 > 3.84$ or $\varphi^2 > 3.84/N$. It follows that for $N = 1,000$, we would be able to reject the null hypothesis of independence even if φ^2 was only .00384, so that

Table 19.2 An example of the calculation of the phi coefficient

	X	
	1	0
Y 1	a	b
0	c	d

If there are a cases for which both X and Y are 1, b cases for which X is 0 and Y is 1, c cases for which X is 1 and Y is 0, and d cases for which X and Y are both 0, then the phi coefficient may be calculated as

$$\phi = \frac{ad - bc}{\sqrt{(a + b)(c + d)(a + c)(b + d)}}$$

Consider an example in which drug therapy and outcome are correlated. Assume the following contingency table:

	Outcome	
	Survive	Die
Drug	60	40
No drug	40	60

Treatment

the phi coefficient for treatment and outcome is

$$\phi = \frac{(60)(60) - (40)(40)}{\sqrt{(100)(100)(100)(100)}} = .20$$

$\phi = .062$. In this case the "significant" correlation would only account for about one-third of 1% of the variance.

The point-biserial correlation coefficient should not be confused with an estimate called the *biserial* coefficient. For both measures, one variable is dichotomous and the other is continuous. However, the biserial correlation coefficient is an estimate of what r would be if, instead of having a dichotomous variable, scores were available on an underlying normally distributed variable. The *tetrachoric correlation coefficient* is an analogous measure that may be used when there are two dichotomous variables that can be assumed to have underlying normal distributions. It estimates the r that would result if scores on these distributions were available. The biserial and tetrachoric coefficients are encountered in the testing literature and in structural equation modeling and should not be used unless the strong assumption of underlying normality is reasonable.

19.5.2 The Spearman Correlation Coefficient for Ranked Data

Sometimes we wish to obtain correlations for data that occur in the form of ranks. We may, for example, have two judges rank a set of stimuli according to some quality, and obtain the correlation between the two sets of rankings as a measure of reliability. Even if X and Y are continuous variables, we may wish to convert to ranks, either because we do not believe that equal differences in the X and/or Y scores necessarily correspond to equal differences in the underlying variable that is measured, or because we desire measures that are more resistant to the effects of outliers than the usual Pearson r.

The special case of the Pearson r for ranked data is referred to as the *Spearman correlation coefficient* (r_S) or sometimes as the *Spearman rho coefficient*. Although the value of the Spearman coefficient can always be obtained by applying any of the usual Pearson r formulas to the ranked data, one frequently encounters a fairly simple formula that takes advantage of the characteristics of ranks. If there are no ties, the ranks of N scores are the first N integers. Therefore, the mean of a set of N ranks is $(N + 1)/2$, and the variance of the ranks can be shown to be $N(N + 1)/12$. Substituting such expressions into the Pearson r formula and simplifying yields

$$r_S = 1 - \frac{6 \sum_i D_i^2}{N(N^2 - 1)} \tag{19.14}$$

where D_i is the difference between the X and Y ranks for the ith case. An example of a calculation using Equation 19.14 is given in Table 19.3.

Equation 19.14 should not be used if there are ties. Instead, when there are ties, all the scores in a group of ties are given the mean of the ranks they would have received had there been no ties. For

Table 19.3 Calculation of r_S and τ for a set of ranked data

X	Rank of X	Y	Rank of Y	D	D²
81	9	20	8	1	1
59	3	16	5	−2	4
37	1	12	2	−1	1
79	8	21	9	−1	1
63	5	19	7	−2	4
72	7	17	6	1	1
42	2	9	1	1	1
61	4	14	3	1	1
83	10	25	10	0	0
70	6	15	4	2	4

$$r_S = 1 - \frac{6 \, \Sigma_i D_i^2}{N(N^2 - 1)} = 1 - \frac{(6)(18)}{(10)(99)} = .89$$

To find τ, we need to find the number of inversions. For small data sets, this can readily be obtained by displaying the ordered ranks of X and the corresponding ranks of Y:

Ordered ranks of X	1	2	3	4	5	6	7	8	9	10
Corresponding ranks of Y	2	1	5	3	7	4	6	9	8	10

If we draw lines connecting the same ranks, the number of times pairs of lines cross one another is the number of inversions. For the current example, there are six inversions, so that

$$\tau = 1 - \frac{2(\textit{number of inversions})}{N(N - 1)/2} = 1 - \frac{(2)(6)}{(10)(9)/2} = .73$$

example, if after the nine largest scores have been ranked we find that four scores are tied for 10th place, each receives the rank of 11.5 (the mean of 10, 11, 12, and 13), and the next largest score receives a rank of 14. When this happens, the variances of ranks will not be the simple expressions assumed by Equation 19.14, so the Pearson r should be used on the ranks. Most statistical packages will perform both the ranking and the computation of the Pearson r.

For $N > 10$, we can test the null hypothesis that the ranks of X and Y have a correlation of zero in the population by using the test statistic given in Equation 19.1 with $N - 2$ df. Although this test is not appropriate for smaller samples, Zar (1972) has developed tables for the critical values of rho for small N; these have been reproduced in Siegel and Castellan (1988).

19.5.3 The Kendall Tau (τ) and Goodman–Kruskal Gamma (γ) Coefficients for Ranked Data

Kendall has developed a different approach to the problem of assessing agreement between two sets of ranks. Rather than using a measure of discrepancy that depends on the sum of the squared differences in the ranks of X and Y (i.e., the ΣD_i^2 quantity that appears in the formula for the Spearman coefficient), Kendall's approach depends on the number of agreements and disagreements in rank order when pairs of items are considered.

Suppose we have N objects $O_1, O_2, \ldots, O_N$ that receive two sets of rankings, X and Y. If the X and Y rankings are exactly the same, there will be no disagreement, and the Kendall τ will have a value of 1. We say that an *inversion* occurs if, for any two objects, say, O_i and O_j, O_i is ranked higher than O_j in one set of rankings, but lower than O_j in the other set. For N objects, there are $N(N - 1)/2$ possible pairings of objects. Therefore, if there are no ties, there are a maximum of $N(N - 1)/2$ possible inversions. The *Kendall τ coefficient* is defined as

$$\tau = 1 - \frac{(2)(\textit{number of inversions})}{\textit{maximum number of inversions}}$$

$$= \frac{\textit{number of agreements in order} - \textit{number of disagreements in order}}{\textit{total number of pairs}}$$

Various procedures exist for obtaining the number of rank inversions, but the simplest is the graphic method illustrated in Table 19.3. The graphic method is appropriate only if there are no tied ranks, and more general procedures when there are ties are outlined in Hays (1988) and Siegel and Castellan (1988). Packages such as SPSS, SYSTAT, and SAS all calculate *tau b*, which is a modification of τ that takes account of ties. However, the packages differ in whether or not they will perform significance tests; for example, SPSS will provide the results of significance tests for rho and tau, but SYSTAT will not.

For N greater than 10, the significance of τ can be tested by using the test statistic $z = \tau/\sigma_\tau$, where $\sigma_\tau = \sqrt{2(2N + 5)/9N(N - 1)}$ and z is approximately normally distributed under the null hypothesis. We can reject the null hypothesis that τ is equal to zero in the population at $\alpha = .05$ for the data in Table 19.3 because the obtained value of the test statistic, 2.94, is greater than the critical z of 1.96. Tables that can be used when $N \le 10$ can be found in Siegel and Castellan (1988).

The *Goodman–Kruskal gamma* (γ) is closely related to the Kendall τ and has essentially the same interpretation. The gamma is simply the ratio of the difference between the number of agreements and disagreements to their sum, after all ties have been thrown out; that is

$$\gamma = \frac{\textit{number of agreements in order} - \textit{number of disagreements in order}}{\textit{number of agreements in order} + \textit{number of disagreements in order}}$$

Both gamma and tau can be thought of as measures of *monotonicity*, the tendency for the underlying measures to increase or decrease together. The test for significance for gamma depends on an approximation that requires large samples (e.g., see Siegel & Castellan, 1988), and we shall not consider it here.

On what basis should we decide which measure to use? The Kendall τ is somewhat more appealing than Spearman rho because of its direct interpretation in terms of the proportion of agreements and disagreements in rankings. In contrast, rho is interpretable primarily by analogy to the usual Pearson coefficient. Concerns about power do not help much with the choice. Siegel and Castellan (1988) point out that although tau and rho will generally have different values when calculated for the same data set, when significance tests for tau and rho are based on their sampling distributions, they will yield the same p-values. However, if a normal approximation is used to perform the significance test, the tau is a better choice because its sampling distribution approaches normality more rapidly than that of the Spearman rho as sample size increases.

We found the correlation between cholesterol level and age for men, using the Pearson r, the tau, and the rho. As stated earlier, $r = .062$, and is not significant, $p = .363$. The Kendall tau b and Spearman rho values obtained from SPSS are slightly larger than r, .093 and .135; and they are both significant, $p = .044$ and .046, respectively. There are several reasons for this discrepancy. One reason is that monotonicity, the tendency for X and Y to increase (or decrease) together, is a weaker condition than linearity, and thus easier to satisfy. Another reason is that, because they are based on ranks, tau and rho are less influenced by outliers (i.e., more *resistant*) than the Pearson r. We conclude that there is a weak tendency for cholesterol level to increase with age for men.

19.6 SUMMARY

The first section of the chapter dealt with inference about correlation. Among the topics discussed were:

- The use of the t and normal distributions for testing hypotheses, and finding confidence intervals for ρ. We also discussed power, and the use of G*Power 3 to perform power calculations.
- The use of bootstrapping for finding confidence intervals for ρ when the assumption of bivariate normality was severely violated.
- Tests for whether the ρs in two independent populations were different, and the associated power calculations.
- Tests of hypotheses about dependent correlations; i.e., those obtained from the same subjects. We first discussed a test for the hypothesis that all the off-diagonal elements in a correlation matrix are equal to 0 in the population. We also discussed procedures for testing whether pairs of dependent correlations differed from one another. These tests are not generally offered by the standard software packages and we considered some specialized software for performing them.

The second part of the chapter dealt with partial and semipartial correlations. We showed how to calculate these correlations and that we could perform significance tests and form confidence intervals for them. However, we emphasized that the decision to find these correlations should be motivated by a well-developed causal model and that they should be interpreted within the context of the model. The final section of the chapter considered measures of correlation other than the Pearson correlation coefficient. The measures we discussed are summarized in Table 19.4.

Table 19.4 Summary of some of the types of correlations discussed in Section 19.4

Statistic	Equation or description
Point-biserial r	Pearson r where one variable is continuous and the other is dichotomous.
Phi coefficient, φ	Pearson r where both variables are dichotomous.
Biserial correlation	Given one continuous and one dichotomous variable, the biserial coefficient is an estimate of what the correlation would be if the dichotomous variable was continuous and normally distributed.
Tetrachoric correlation	Given two dichotomous variables, the tetrachoric coefficient is an estimate of what the correlation would be if both dichotomous variables were continuous and normally distributed.
Spearman rho, r_S	Pearson r for ranked data.
Kendall tau	$\dfrac{\text{number of agreements in order} - \text{number of disagreements in order}}{\text{total number of pairs of objects}}$
Tau b	This is a modification of the Kendall tau that takes account of ties.

APPENDIX 19.1

The Bivariate Normal Density Function

Both X and Y are assumed to be random variables and the density function that characterizes their joint distribution is

$$f(X, Y) = \frac{1}{2\pi\sigma_X\sigma_Y\sqrt{1 - \rho_{XY}^2}} \, e^{-B}$$

where

$$B = \frac{1}{2(1 - \rho_{XY}^2)}\left[\frac{(X - \mu_X)^2}{\sigma_X^2} + \frac{(Y - \mu_Y)^2}{\sigma_Y^2} - 2\rho_{XY}\frac{(X - \mu_X)(Y - \mu_Y)}{\sigma_X\sigma_Y}\right]$$

Although the equation for the density function may look formidable, we can think of it as a generalization of the one-dimensional normal distribution to two dimensions. In practice, we will not have to perform mathematical operations involving the density function, and will use tables and software that deal with it. However, we should be aware of the characteristics of the bivariate normal distribution and of its importance in making inferences about the population correlation. We can see that the equation represents a family of bivariate normal distributions, with each member of the family defined by a combination of the parameters μ_X, μ_Y, σ_X, σ_Y, and ρ_{XY}.

EXERCISES

19.1 It is found in an introductory statistics course with 19 students that scores on the final examination correlate $-.30$ with the number of hours studied.

  (a) Using the t distribution, test the null hypothesis H_0: $\rho = 0$, assuming a two-tailed test with $\alpha = .05$.

  (b) Test the same hypothesis, using the Fisher Z transform and the normal distribution.

  (c) Can we conclude that studying too much interferes with test taking?

  (d) Find the 95% confidence interval for the population correlation coefficient, ρ. Find the 50% confidence interval.

  (e) Assuming that the population correlation really is $-.30$, use GPower 3 to find the number of subjects necessary to have a power of .80 for rejecting H_0: $\rho = 0$, using a two-tailed test t test with $\alpha = .05$.

  (f) Using the normal distribution and the test in (b), find the number of subjects that would be necessary to have the power be .80 for the significance test.

19.2 Each year, a random sample of $N = 200$ freshmen admitted to the Elite Institute of Technology (EIT) must take a standardized skills test when they first enroll. Two years ago, the correlation between the test and first-year GPA was .22. Last year, after the test had been revised, the correlation rose to .35.

  (a) If the two entering classes can be considered random samples of EIT freshmen, test whether the two correlations are significantly different at $\alpha = .05$.

  (b) Assuming that the population correlations for the two versions of the test were actually .22 and .35, use G*Power 3 to determine how large N in each class would have to be in order to have a power of .80 to reject the null hypothesis that the population correlations were the same (assume two-tailed test with $\alpha = .05$).

  (c) According to Cohen's guidelines, qs of .10, .30, and .50 correspond to small, medium, and large effect sizes. How many subjects would be required to have a power of .90 for a two-tailed test of the medium-sized difference between the correlations of two groups? Use $\alpha = .05$.

  (d) Using Zou's procedure for finding the confidence interval for the difference between two correlations described in Section 19.2.5, find the 95% CI for the difference of the correlations obtained in part (a).

19.3 Using the information in Exercise 18.7, test whether the correlation between income and years on the job is significantly different for men and women. Use $\alpha = .05$, two-tailed.

19.4 For three independent groups, the data are as follows (use $\alpha = .05$ for any significance tests):

	G_1	G_2	G_3
n:	103	52	67
r:	.60	.45	.20

For the following, assume nondirectional alternative hypotheses with $\alpha = .05$:

  (a) Test H_0: $\rho_2 = 0$.

  (b) Test H_0: $\rho_1 = \rho_2$.

  (c) Test H_0: $\rho_2 = \rho_3$.

  (d) Find the 95% confidence interval for ρ_2.

19.5 A random sample of 39 students are given tests of abstract reasoning (A), quantitative reasoning (Q), and verbal skills (V). The resulting correlation matrix is

	A	Q	V
A	1.00		
Q	.30	1.00	
V	.50	.20	1.00

Note that these correlations are not independent because all the correlations are based on the same students.

(a) Test the hypothesis that all of the off-diagonal elements in the matrix (here the .30, .50, and .20 correlations) are equal to 0 in the population.

(b) Test the hypothesis that in the population, abstract reasoning correlates equally with verbal ability and with quantitative reasoning. That is, test H_0: $\rho_{AV} = \rho_{AQ}$ against the alternative hypothesis H_1: $\rho_{AV} \neq \rho_{AQ}$.

(c) Find $r_{AV|Q}$, the partial correlation between A and V with Q partialed out. Test whether it is significantly different from 0.

19.6 Steiger (1980) used as an example a longitudinal study of sex stereotypes and verbal achievement. Masculinity, femininity, and verbal achievement are measured at time 1 and time 2. A random sample of 103 observations are obtained. The resulting correlation matrix is

	M1	F1	V1	M2	F2	V2
M1	1.00					
F1	.10	1.00				
V1	.40	.50	1.00			
M2	.70	.05	.50	1.00		
F2	.05	.70	.50	.50	1.00	
V2	.45	.50	.80	.50	.60	1.00

Note that these correlations are *not independent* because all the correlations are based on the same students. If you can run Steiger's MULTICORR program on your computer,

(a) Test the hypothesis that in the population, the correlation between masculinity and femininity is the same at time 1 and time 2.

(b) Test the hypothesis that in the population, the correlation between V1 and M1 is the same as the correlation between V1 and F1.

19.7 If we have two binary variables X and Y, we can find the correlation between them (called the "phi coefficient", ϕ), using the expression in Table 19.2.

(a) What is the value of ϕ for the following 2×2 table?

		Item 2		
		Pass	Fail	
Item 1	Pass	20	20	40
	Fail	50	10	60
		70	30	100

(b) Given the marginal frequencies, what are the minimum and maximum values of ϕ that are possible?

(c) Given the marginal frequencies, for what cell values would ϕ be 0?

19.8 Sometimes we will find that a correlation has been computed between some variable X and another variable T which is the sum of a number of variables including X (e.g., $T = X + Y$). Under these circumstances, we can expect a positive correlation between X and T even if X is not related to Y because X is part of T. Show that in general

$$r_{X, T-X} = \frac{r_{XT} s_T - s_X}{\sqrt{s_X^2 + s_T^2 - 2 r_{XT} s_X s_T}}$$

where $r_{X, T-X}$ is the correlation between X and the part of T not containing X.

19.9 Note that the previous question has implications for the interpretation of correlations involving change or difference scores. Suppose that X refers to pretest scores and T to posttest scores. Therefore, $T - X$ refers to change scores. If we assume that $s_{pre} = s_{post}$, the equation in Exercise 19.8 reduces to

$$r_{X, T-X} = r_{pre, change} = \frac{r_{pre, post} - 1}{\sqrt{2(1 - r_{pre, post})}}$$

We would not expect a perfect correlation between pre- and posttest scores for a lot of reasons, including random error. Suppose $r_{pre, post} = .70$. What do we expect for $r_{pre, change}$? Remember, because of regression toward the mean, we would expect the correlation between pretest scores and change scores to be negative.

19.10 A researcher tries to develop a new questionnaire to measure some personality trait. The instrument is made up of a number of items, each of which is scored numerically. The total score, T, is supposed to represent the degree to which a person has the trait. The researcher likes the instrument, but thinks it will be too time-consuming to administer all of it, because it contains a large number of items—so she arbitrarily divides the instrument into two parts, each containing half the items. Let's refer to the score on one of the halves as X and the score on the other half as Y (so that $T = X + Y$). She finds that the correlation between X and T is high ($r_{XT} = .7$) and concludes that the correlation between the scores on the two halves of the instrument (r_{XY}) must also be pretty high, so that she can get by with using only one of the halves to measure the personality trait. If we can assume that the variances of X and Y are equal, what is r_{XY}?

Chapter 20

More About Bivariate Regression

20.1 OVERVIEW

In Chapter 20 we extend our coverage of bivariate linear regression in preparation for introducing multiple regression in Chapters 21–24. The primary goal of Chapter 20 is to discuss procedures for making inferences about bivariate regression. We also consider whether modifications of these procedures or their interpretation are required because of characteristics of the data set. The topics in Chapter 20 are:

- *Inference about bivariate regression.* We consider confidence intervals and significance tests for the population slope and intercept. We also consider a test for the equality of independent regression slopes, and discuss power calculations.
- *Inference about predictions.* We consider inferential procedures for the mean value of Y at a given value of X as well as for individual Y scores.
- *Regression in nonexperimental research.* The standard regression model assumes that the values of X are *selected* by the researcher as in an experiment. We therefore discuss regression in nonexperimental research in which X scores are generally *sampled* from a population.
- *The consequences of measurement error in Y and in X.* Increased measurement error in Y results in smaller values of R^2, wider confidence intervals, and less power for significance tests. Measurement error in the predictor variable, X, may cause more serious problems, especially if the errors are correlated with the values of the predictor.
- *Unstandardized vs standardized regression coefficients.* We will argue that in most contexts we should work with and interpret the unstandardized, rather than the standardized, regression coefficients.
- *Assumptions that underlie inference.* The confidence intervals, hypothesis tests, and power calculations depend on certain assumptions about the population. We discuss these assumptions and how to test them.

- *Identifying outliers and influential data points.* We consider how to identify outliers, as well as data points that strongly influence the regression.

We conclude the chapter by discussing several procedures for dealing with data sets that may cause difficulties for the usual, ordinary least-squares (OLS) regression:

- *Robust regression.* OLS estimation procedures are quite vulnerable to violations of assumptions and to the influence of outlying data points. Therefore, we consider several more resistant procedures, known collectively as *robust regression.*
- *Repeated-measures regression.* We briefly consider the situation in which groups of scores in the data set are related, especially when individual subjects contribute more than one data point to the regression.

20.2 INFERENCE IN LINEAR REGRESSION

20.2.1 The Standard Fixed Linear Regression Model

Our goal in this section is to develop a basis for making inferences in situations in which the systematic relationship between two variables, X and Y, is captured by a straight line. Making inferences requires that we make certain assumptions about the population of data points. We first consider the fixed regression model in which we select certain values of X, and for each of these selected values, we randomly sample values of Y. We assume that X and Y are related in the population according to the equation

$$Y_i = \beta_0 + \beta_1 X_i + \varepsilon_i \tag{20.1}$$

where Y_i is the value of the dependent variable for the ith case, β_0 and β_1 are the Y intercept and slope of the line, X_i is the value taken on by the predictor variable for the ith case, and ε_i is a random error component. We further assume that the error component, ε, is independently and normally distributed with mean 0 and variance σ_e^2; that is,

$$E(\varepsilon_i) = 0$$
$$\text{Var}(\varepsilon_i) = \sigma_e^2 \text{ for all } i \text{ (homogeneity of variance or homoscedasticity)}$$
$$\text{Cov}(\varepsilon_i, \varepsilon_{i'}) = 0 \text{ except when } i = i' \text{ (independence)}$$

Because we sample multiple values of Y at each value of X, there is a distribution of Y scores at each value of X. The *conditional distribution* of Y at a given value of X has a population mean, which we indicate by the symbol $\mu_{Y.X}$. Our assumptions about the population regression line imply that $\mu_{Y.X}$ lies on the straight line $\mu_{Y.X} = \beta_0 + \beta_1 X$, and that the deviation of Y from its conditional population mean is due solely to random error. If the systematic relationship between X and Y is not linear, our measure of error will include more than random variability, and the significance tests developed from this model may be biased. In this model, X is assumed to be a fixed-effect variable that is measured without error. In other words, we assume that the values of X have been selected by the researcher and that, if we replicated the study, exactly the same values of X would be used. If these conditions are satisfied, it can be shown that b_1 and b_0, the least-squares estimators of β_1 and β_0 that we developed in Chapter 18, are both unbiased (e.g., $E(b_1) = \beta_1$) and consistent (i.e., as the sample sizes are made larger, the estimates more closely approximate the parameter values). The estimators are

$$b_1 = r \frac{s_Y}{s_X} \tag{20.2}$$

and

$$b_0 = \bar{Y} - b_1 \bar{X} \tag{20.3}$$

As an example, consider the data presented in Table 20.1. In a hypothetical visual search experiment, 20 subjects each look at a screen and are presented with an array of letters. They are asked to indicate as quickly as they can whether a specified target letter is present in the array. Groups of five subjects are assigned to array sizes of two, four, six, and eight letters, and the times (in milliseconds) to respond correctly when the target letter is present are recorded. Each subject contributes one data point. Generally, when the letter arrays are larger, it takes longer to respond to the presence of a target letter, so the data are reasonably well fit by a linear equation. Here the assumption that X is a fixed-effect variable is satisfied because the array sizes are chosen by the researcher, and can be measured without error. Note that this is not the case for the statistics class example presented in Chapter 18, in which we select a sample of students and obtain values of X (pretest score) and Y (final exam score) from each student, so that both X and Y are random variables.

In the next few sections, we discuss how to make statistical inferences about the slope and intercept of the regression equation and about the predictions made by the equation. In every case, we can find confidence intervals for θ, the population parameter of interest, by finding

$$\hat{\theta} \pm t_{a/2} \, SE(\hat{\theta}) \tag{20.4}$$

and can test hypotheses about θ by using the test statistic

$$t = \frac{\hat{\theta} - \theta_{hyp}}{SE(\hat{\theta})} \tag{20.5}$$

Table 20.1   Data for the search experiment example

Size	Time
2	418
2	428
2	410
2	445
2	471
4	475
4	455
4	418
4	524
4	516
6	537
6	500
6	480
6	511
6	529
8	550
8	617
8	590
8	608
8	548

where $\hat{\theta}$ is the estimate of θ obtained from the sample and $SE(\hat{\theta})$ is the estimated standard error of $\hat{\theta}$. For example, the 95% confidence interval for β_1 is given by $b_1 \pm t_{.025}SE(b_1)$. We have already shown how to find b_1 in Chapter 18. To find the confidence interval, all we need in addition is $SE(b_1)$, the estimated standard error of b_1.

20.2.2 Inference about β_0 and β_1

Recall that the value of the intercept of the population regression line, β_0, is the conditional mean of Y when X has a value of zero. Estimates of β_0 are not always of interest, but there are circumstances in which they may be useful. For example, in the regression of cholesterol level (TC) on BMI, the intercept estimates the mean TC level for $BMI = 0$; this is not meaningful because there are no BMI scores of zero in the real world. On the other hand, if we regress TC on $BMIC$, where $BMIC$, the so-called *centered BMI score*, is given by $BMI - \overline{BMI}$, the intercept estimates the conditional mean of TC when BMI takes on its mean value. The slope of the population regression line, β_1, is almost always of interest. First, if it differs from zero, there is a linear relationship between X and Y. Second, the value of the slope tells us how much, on the average, Y increases (or decreases) with an increase of one unit in X.

The SPSS output for the regression of detection time on array size is given in Table 20.2. The output includes three tables. The B column in the coefficients table provides the unstandardized coefficients corresponding to the intercept (constant) and the slope (size). We see that the bivariate regression equation that best predicts reaction time (Y) from array size (X) is

$$\hat{Y}_i = 381.90 + 23.92X_i$$

The regression output also displays t tests for the significance of b_0 and b_1; in each case the t statistic is the ratio of the coefficient to its standard error. We see that both the slope and the intercept are significantly different from zero at $p = .000$. The standardized coefficients or beta column contains information about the regression of z_Y on z_X. Because the regression line must pass through the origin when the variables are standardized, the intercept must be 0. The standardized slope, or beta coefficient, has the same value as the correlation coefficient in bivariate regression.[1]

In the model summary table, R refers to the *multiple correlation coefficient*, $R_{Y.X} = \text{Corr}(Y, \hat{Y}) = .873$. This is the correlation between the actual value of Y and $\hat{Y}$, the value of Y predicted from the regression equation. For bivariate regression, the multiple correlation is the absolute value of r_{XY} because the magnitude of a correlation is unchanged by a linear transformation. Note that the multiple correlation coefficient can never be negative.

The model summary table also contains the *standard error of estimate* for the regression of Y on X,

$$s_{Y.X} = \sqrt{\frac{\Sigma(Y_i - \hat{Y}_i)^2}{N-2}} = \sqrt{\frac{SS_{residual}}{N-2}} = 31.452$$

a measure of the variability around the regression line that we discussed in Chapter 18. As we shall see, the standard error of estimate is a component of the standard errors of most of the parameter estimates we consider in this chapter.

---

[1] Unfortunately, both the standardized coefficients and the population parameters of the unstandardized coefficients are referred to as "betas." We will most often be concerned with unstandardized coefficients, and so will usually reserve the use of the β notation to refer to their population parameters. We will use b^* to refer to the sample standardized coefficient.

Table 20.2 SPSS regression output for the search experiment example

Model Summary

Model	R	R Square	Adjusted R Square	Std. Error of the Estimate
1	.873[a]	.763	.749	31.452

[a.] Predictors: (Constant), size

ANOVA[b]

Model		Sum of Squares	df	Mean Square	F	Sig.
1	Regression	57216.640	1	57216.640	57.839	.000[a]
	Residual	17806.360	18	989.242		
	Total	75023.000	19			

[a.] Predictors: (Constant), size
[b.] Dependent Variable: time

Coefficients[a]

Model		Unstandardized Coefficients		Standardized Coefficients	t	Sig.	95% Confidence Interval for B	
		B	Std. Error	Beta			Lower Bound	Upper Bound
1	(Constant)	381.900	17.227		22.169	.000	345.707	418.093
	Size	23.920	3.145	.873	7.605	.000	17.312	30.528

[a.] Dependent Variable: time

The ANOVA table output indicates the partitioning of variability. The total variability in the Y scores, $SS_Y = \Sigma(Y_i - \overline{Y})^2$, can be partitioned into two components, the variability accounted for by the bivariate regression equation,

$$SS_{regression} = \Sigma(\hat{Y} - \overline{Y})^2 = b_1^2 SS_X = r^2 SS_Y$$

and the variability not accounted for by the regression,

$$SS_{residual} = \Sigma(Y - \hat{Y})^2 = (1 - r^2)SS_Y$$

An ANOVA table containing these terms is given in Table 20.3. The F given in the right-most column of Table 20.3 is the ratio $MS_{regression}/MS_{residual}$. A significant F indicates that both r and b_1 are significantly different from zero; i.e., that the null hypotheses $H_0: \rho = 0$ and $H_0: \beta_1 = 0$ can both be rejected. The F can be used to test the significance of the correlation coefficient because it can be expressed as the square of the t that was presented in Chapter 19 as the test statistic for the null hypothesis $H_0: \rho = 0$. Also, the F can be written as the square of $t = b_1/SE(b_1)$, the test statistic for the null hypothesis $H_0: \beta_1 = 0$. Note that the square of the t for b_1, $(7.605)^2 = 57.836$, is, within rounding error, the same as the value of F in the ANOVA table.

Given the assumptions of the regression model, the least-squares estimates of the intercept and

Table 20.3 Explanation of the ANOVA table in the regression output for bivariate regression

SV	SS	df	MS	F
Regression	$\Sigma(\hat{Y}_i - \bar{Y})^2 = r^2 SS_Y = b_1^2 SS_X$	1	$\dfrac{SS_{regression}}{1}$	$\dfrac{MS_{regression}}{MS_{residual}}$
Residual	$\Sigma(Y_i - \hat{Y}_i)^2 = (1 - r^2)SS_Y$	$N - 2$	$\dfrac{SS_{residual}}{N - 2}$	
Total	$\Sigma(Y_i - \bar{Y})^2 = SS_Y$	$N - 1$		

slope, b_0 and b_1, can be shown to be unbiased estimators of the regression parameters β_0 and β_1 (see *TechNote 20_2* on the book's website). The estimated standard errors for b_0 and b_1 can be expressed as

$$SE(b_0) = s_{Y.X}\sqrt{\frac{1}{N} + \frac{\bar{X}^2}{SS_X}} \qquad (20.6)$$

and

$$SE(b_1) = \frac{s_{Y.X}}{\sqrt{SS_X}} \qquad (20.7)$$

where $s_{Y.X}$ is the standard error of estimate and $SS_X = \Sigma(X_i - \bar{X})^2$. These equations follow from the fact that, under the assumptions of the regression model, b_0 and b_1 can each be expressed as linear combinations of the Y scores. This discussion is elaborated and the expressions for the standard errors are derived in the Chapter 20 technical notes on the website.

Although the exact forms of the expressions for the standard errors are not entirely intuitive, they have characteristics that should seem reasonable. For example,

1. We would expect that the greater the variability of the data points around the regression line, the more uncertainty we should have about the location of the regression line. Therefore, the standard errors of b_0 and b_1 should increase as $s_{Y.X}$ increases.
2. We would expect to get more stable estimates of the regression parameters if the sample contains both large and small X values than if the sample contains only a narrow range of Xs. Therefore, the standard errors of both b_0 and b_1 should vary *inversely* with some measure of variability in the X scores such as s_X or SS_X.
3. Because the least-squares regression line must pass though the point $(\bar{X}, \bar{Y})$, variability in the slope will affect the Y intercept less if $\bar{X}$ is close to the y-axis (i.e., if $\bar{X}$ is close to $X = 0$). Therefore, the standard error of b_0 increases as $\bar{X}$ increases.

We can use the standard errors shown in Equations 20.6 and 20.7 to find confidence intervals and test hypotheses about the Y intercept and slope of the regression line. For the slope of the regression equation, the 95% confidence interval for β_1 is given by

$$b_1 \pm t_{.025,18}SE(b_1) = 23.92 \pm (2.101)(3.145) = 17.31, 30.53$$

We can test the null hypothesis H_0: $\beta_1 = \beta_{1_{hyp}}$ by using the test statistic

$$t = \frac{b_1 - \beta_{1_{hyp}}}{SE(b_1)} \text{ with } N - 2 \ df \qquad (20.8)$$

If we wished to test the null hypothesis $H_0: \beta_1 = 0$, a two-tailed t test for the slope is equivalent to the F test in the ANOVA table. This may be seen by squaring the expression for the t,

$$t^2 = \frac{b_1^2}{SE(b_1)^2} = \frac{b_1^2}{s_{Y.X}^2 / SS_X} = \frac{b_1^2 SS_X}{s_{Y.X}^2} = \frac{MS_{regression}}{MS_{residual}} = F$$

Suppose we wish to test the hypothesis $H_0: \beta_1 = 20$ against the alternative hypothesis $H_1: \beta_1 > 20$. The value of the test statistic is

$$t = \frac{23.92 - 20}{3.145} = 1.246$$

This result is, of course, consistent with the confidence interval limits previously calculated; those limits informed us that a two-tailed test cannot reject any hypothesized value of the slope between 17.31 and 30.53.

If we are concerned with the Y intercept, we can find confidence intervals and test hypotheses just as we did for the slope. For example, the 95% confidence interval for β_0 is

$$b_0 \pm t_{.025,18} SE(b_0) = 381.90 \pm (2.101)(17.227) = 345.71, 418.09$$

We know that the test of $H_0: \beta_0 = 350$ against $H_1: \beta_0 \neq 350$ at $\alpha = .05$ will not be significant because 350 lies within the 95% confidence interval for β_0.

20.2.3 Power Calculations

We can use G*Power 3 to perform *a priori* power tests for the hypothesis $H_0: \beta_1 = 0$ by entering information about α, the desired level of power, and the effect size,[2]

$$f^2 = \frac{R^2}{1 - R^2}$$

where R is the multiple correlation coefficient. According to the Cohen guidelines for regression, f^2 values of .02, .15, and .35 are considered "small," "medium," and "large." Given $f^2 = .15$, $\alpha = .05$, and desired power $= .80$, G*Power 3 indicates that a sample of size $N = 55$ is required for a "medium" effect size with one predictor variable (see Fig. 20.1 for the G*Power 3 dialog box). Similarly, sample sizes of 395 and 25 are required to obtain power $= .80$ for "small" and "large" effects in bivariate regression.

20.2.4 Testing Independent Slopes for Equality

In Chapter 18, we used the *Seasons* data set and regressed total cholesterol level (*TC*) on *age*, separately for the samples of 211 women and 220 men that had data on both variables. We found that the regression equations for women and men, respectively, were

predicted *TC* for women $= 131.70 + 1.71$ *age*   ($r = .51$)

and

predicted *TC* for men $= 211.91 + 0.20$ *age*   ($r = .06$)

In Chapter 19, we showed that the correlations between cholesterol level and age differed significantly, $z = 5.10$, $p = .000$. We can also test whether the regression slopes for men and women

---

[2] Under the assumptions described in Section 20.2.1, the noncentrality parameter is $\lambda = Nf^2$.

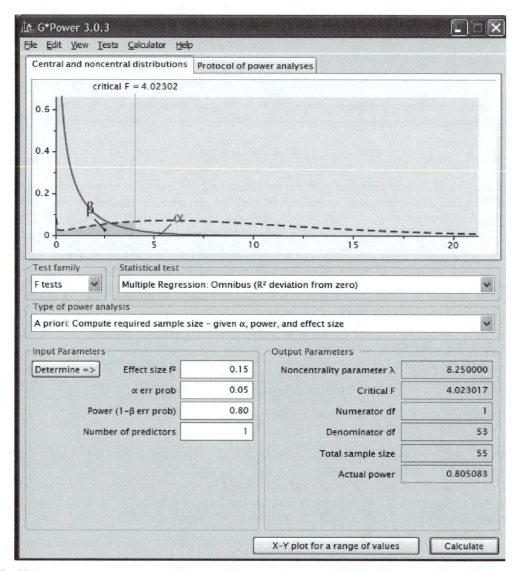

Fig. 20.1 G*Power 3 display for *a priori* power calculation for H_0: $\beta_1 = 0$, given medium-sized effect ($f^2 = .15$, according to Cohen's guidelines), $\alpha = .05$, and power = .80.

differ. As we discussed in Chapter 18, comparing slopes answers a different question than comparing correlation coefficients (see Exercise 20.5). The slope is a measure of the rate of change of Y with X. The correlation coefficient in an index of the strength of the linear relationship between Y and X, and can be thought of as a measure of the fit of the regression line. Correlation depends not only on the slope, but on the degree of scatter around the regression line as well as the variances of X and Y.

It is straightforward to compare two independent slopes in the context of multiple regression, as we will show in Chapter 23. However, even without using multiple regression, we can test the null hypothesis that two independent slopes are equal (H_0: $\beta_{11} - \beta_{12} = 0$), using the test statistic

$$t = \frac{b_{11} - b_{12}}{s_{Y.X} \sqrt{\dfrac{1}{SS_{X_1}} + \dfrac{1}{SS_{X_2}}}} \quad \text{with } N_1 + N_2 - 4 \text{ } df \tag{20.9}$$

where $s_{Y.X}$ is the best estimate of the standard error of estimate based on both groups (see Box 20.1). Substituting in the data for the regression of cholesterol and age for men and women, we have

$$t = \frac{1.712 - 0.198}{36.352 \sqrt{\dfrac{1}{28714.56} + \dfrac{1}{30944.92}}} = 5.08$$

so that the slopes are significantly different with $p = .000$.

Box 20.1 Testing for the Equality of Two Independent Regression Slopes

Suppose we wish to test whether the slopes are identical in populations 1 and 2; i.e., that H_0: $\beta_{11} - \beta_{12} = 0$. We can estimate the difference in the population slopes by $b_{11} - b_{12}$, and, because under the usual regression assumptions the bs can be expressed as linear combinations of the Ys, the ratio

$$\frac{(b_{11} - b_{12}) - (\beta_{11} - \beta_{12})}{SE(b_{11} - b_{12})}$$

is distributed as t with $df = N_1 + N_2 - 4$ if the null hypothesis is true. From Table 20.4 we know that $\text{Var}(b_1) = \sigma_e^2 / SS_X$. Further, because the groups are independent,

$$\text{Var}(b_{11} - b_{12}) = \text{Var}(b_{11}) + \text{Var}(b_{12})$$

$$= \sigma_e^2 \left(\frac{1}{SS_{X_1}} + \frac{1}{SS_{X_2}} \right)$$

where SS_{X_1} and SS_{X_2} are the sums of squares of X in groups 1 and 2. Therefore, we can estimate the standard error of $b_{11} - b_{12}$ by $SE(b_{11} - b_{12}) = s_{Y.X} \sqrt{\dfrac{1}{SS_{X_1}} + \dfrac{1}{SS_{X_2}}}$

where the best estimate of σ_e^2 is given by the weighted average of the estimates from group 1 and group 2:

$$s_{Y.X}^2 = \frac{df_1 s_{Y.X_1}^2 + df_2 s_{Y.X_2}^2}{df_1 + df_2} = \frac{SS_{residual_1} + SS_{residual_2}}{N_1 + N_2 - 4}$$

Combining this information, the test statistic

$$t = \frac{b_{11} - b_{12}}{s_{Y.X} \sqrt{\dfrac{1}{SS_{X_1}} + \dfrac{1}{SS_{X_2}}}} \quad \text{with } N_1 + N_2 - 4 \text{ } df$$

can be used to test the null hypothesis H_0: $\beta_{11} = \beta_{12}$.

Before leaving this topic, we note that the test of whether independent slopes differ depends on the assumption that the two within-group error variances are equal in the population. If this assumption is violated, the power of the test can be seriously affected, even when the sample sizes are equal. DeShon and Alexander (1996) and Overton (2001) discuss this problem and offer some possible remedies.

20.3 USING REGRESSION TO MAKE PREDICTIONS

In this section, we discuss inference about predictions of (1) the mean of the distribution of Y scores at a given value of X and (2) a single Y score in this distribution.

20.3.1 Obtaining a Confidence Interval for a Conditional Mean

There are occasions when it is useful to find the confidence interval for the predicted mean Y score for a given value of X. For example, a college admissions director might be interested in predicting the mean of the population of freshman grade point averages (GPA) for students with a high-school GPA of 3.0; this information might be relevant to selecting an admissions cutoff based on high-school GPA. According to the regression model, the expected value of Y at $X = X_j$ (i.e., the conditional mean) is $\mu_{Y.X_j} = \beta_0 + \beta_1 X_j$. We can show that

$$\hat{Y}_j = \hat{\mu}_{Y.X_j} = b_0 + b_1 X_j$$

is an unbiased estimator of $\mu_{Y.X_j}$, and that the estimated standard error is given by

$$SE(\hat{\mu}_{Y.X_j}) = s_{Y.X}\sqrt{h_{jj}} \tag{20.10}$$

where

$$h_{jj} = \frac{1}{N} + \frac{(X_j - \bar{X})^2}{SS_X} \tag{20.11}$$

is the so-called *leverage* of X_j. (See the Chapter 20 technical notes on the book's website for more detail.)

For the search experiment data, the best estimate for the conditional mean of Y at $X = 4$, $\mu_{Y.X=4}$, is given by $\hat{\mu}_{Y.X=4} = 381.90 + (23.92)(4) = 477.58$, and the estimated standard error is

$$SE(\hat{\mu}_{Y.X=4}) = (31.452)\sqrt{\frac{1}{20} + \frac{(4-5)^2}{100}} = 7.70$$

Therefore, the 95% confidence interval for $\mu_{Y.X=4}$ is

$$\hat{\mu}_{Y.X=4} \pm t_{.025,18}\, SE(\hat{\mu}_{Y.X=4})$$

$$477.58 \pm (2.101)(7.70) = 461.39, 493.77$$

As we can see from Equations 20.10 and 20.11, the standard error and therefore the confidence interval depend on the value of X_j. They are smallest when $X_j = \bar{X}$, and increase the more X_j deviates from $\bar{X}$. This can be seen in Fig. 20.2, which is the scatterplot for the search experiment data, with the regression line and the 95% confidence interval also displayed. Hypothesis tests may be conducted in the same way as in the previous section.

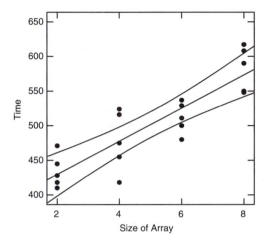

Fig. 20.2 Scatterplot for the search experiment data of Table 20.1 with the regression line and 95% confidence curves for the location of the line. Note that the width of the confidence interval increases with the distance of X from $\hat{X}$.

20.3.2 Obtaining a Confidence Interval for a New Value of Y at X_i

We just showed how to find a confidence interval for the conditional mean of the Y scores at $X = X_j$. Now, we show how to find a confidence interval for the Y score of a *new individual* who has $X = X_j$. That is, we wish to estimate *one of the scores* from the population of scores with mean $\mu_{Y.X_j}$, where $Y_{new\ j} = \mu_{Y.X_j} + \varepsilon$. In our college admissions example, this situation is relevant to a decision about the admission of a particular applicant to the college. The estimate of the conditional mean, $\hat{\mu}_{Y.X_j} = b_0 + b_1 X_j$, is an unbiased estimate of $Y_{new j}$. Therefore, if we wish to find the confidence interval for $Y_{new\ j}$, the variability associated with $\hat{\mu}_{Y.X_j}$ contributes to error in our estimate. However, we must also consider the variability of the individual Y scores around the conditional mean. The variance of estimate for $Y_{new\ j}$ is obtained by combining these two sources of variability, $s_{Y.X}^2 + s_{Y.X}^2 h_{jj} = s_{Y.X}^2(1 + h_{jj})$, so that the standard error of Y_{newj} is given by $s_{Y.X}\sqrt{1 + h_{jj}}$ where h_{jj}, the leverage, was defined by Equation 20.11.

For the search experiment data, the predicted reaction time for a new subject with an array size of 4 is $381.90 + (23.92)(4) = 477.58$, the same as the predicted conditional mean.

However, the estimated standard error is

$$31.452 \sqrt{1 + \frac{1}{20} + \frac{(4-5)^2}{100}} = 32.38$$

so that the 95% confidence interval for Y_{new} is $477.58 \pm (2.101)(32.38) = 477.58 \pm 68.03$. This interval is much wider than the 95% confidence interval for the conditional mean that we previously found to be 477.58 ± 16.19.

Note that finding this 95% confidence interval does not allow us to conclude that 95% of the population of Y scores corresponding to $X = 4$ lie within the interval 477.58 ± 68.03. As always, the correct interpretation of the confidence interval is based on what would be expected to happen during repeated sampling: Assume that:

1. We select many samples of size N, using the same values of X in each sample.

2. For each sample, we find the 95% confidence interval for the Y score of a new individual with $X = 4$.
3. For each sample we observe whether the Y score actually is contained within the confidence interval.

Then, if the assumptions of the model are valid, the 95% confidence intervals will contain the actual scores in 95% of the samples. Table 20.4 summarizes some of the population parameters that we might wish to estimate, the sample statistics that we use as estimators, and the standard errors that can be used to form confidence intervals.

Table 20.4 Summary of bivariate regression statistics

Statistic	Expression	Expected value	Estimated standard error for finding confidence interval
Slope	$b_1 = \dfrac{\Sigma(X_i - \bar{X})(Y_i - \bar{Y})}{SS_X}$		
	$= r\dfrac{s_Y}{s_X}$	β_1	$s_{Y.X}\dfrac{1}{\sqrt{SS_X}}$
			where $s_{Y.X} = \sqrt{\dfrac{SS_{residual}}{N-2}}$ is the standard error of estimate
Y intercept	$b_0 = \bar{Y} - b_1\bar{X}$	β_0	$s_{Y.X}\sqrt{\dfrac{1}{N} + \dfrac{\bar{X}^2}{SS_X}}$
Mean value of Y at X_j	$\hat{\mu}_{Y.X_j} = b_0 + b_1 X_j$	$\mu_{Y.X_j}$	$s_{Y.X}\sqrt{h_{jj}}$
			where $h_{jj} = \dfrac{1}{N} + \dfrac{(X_j - \bar{X})^2}{SS_X}$ is the leverage
New score at X_j	$\hat{Y}_{newj} = \hat{\mu}_{Y.X_j} = b_0 + b_1 X_j$	$\mu_{Y.X_j}$	$s_{Y.X}\sqrt{1 + h_{jj}}$
Residual of the jth case	$e_j = Y_j - \hat{Y}_j$	0	$s_{Y.X}\sqrt{1 - h_{jj}}$

20.4 REGRESSION ANALYSIS IN NONEXPERIMENTAL RESEARCH

In the regression model introduced in Section 20.2.1, X is assumed to be fixed and measured without error. In other words, the values of X scores are known constants. This condition will generally only be fully satisfied when X is an independent variable that is manipulated in an experiment. We can consider X to be a fixed-effect variable in the search experiment example because the researcher selects the array sizes to be used. When a statistical inference is made, conclusions are drawn about the populations of Y scores at these selected levels of X. However, regression is commonly used with data collected in nonexperimental research in which both X and Y take on values that can vary from sample to sample, and are therefore both random variables. For example, in the *Seasons* study that we have referred to throughout the book, a sample consisting of individuals between the ages of 20 and 70 was selected from the membership of a health maintenance organization and a number of variables were then measured. In the previous section we considered the regression of cholesterol level (Y) on age (X) from the *Seasons* data set. What should we do if both X and Y are random variables?

The usual strategy is to continue to treat X as though it was fixed; that is, to make our inferences conditional on the values of X that were obtained in the sample. In this case, we can use the same calculations for hypothesis tests and confidence intervals as for the fixed-X case that we discussed earlier. However, if we do so, we must remember that our inferences extend only to situations that have the same distribution of X scores as the current sample. Treating age as a fixed-effect X variable in the *Seasons* data set when interpreting the results of the test of equality of regression slopes for men and women in the previous section does not represent a great limitation on the inference. The age distributions for men and women are very similar and are fairly flat between the ages of 30 and 70. Moreover, age is one variable that we can usually expect to obtain without error.

But suppose we wish to treat X as a random variable that would be allowed to vary if we repeated the study. It can be shown that the least-squares estimates for the regression coefficients will be unbiased and consistent if we can assume that the values of Y are drawn from a normal population with mean $\mu_{Y.X} = \beta_0 + \beta_1 X + \varepsilon$ with constant variance σ_e^2, and that X and ε, the error component, are independent.[3] The estimated standard errors calculated assuming that X is fixed will now be somewhat too small because they do not take account of the random variability in X; however, for fairly large sample sizes (say, $N > 50$), this extra uncertainty does not usually have much practical importance (Berk, 2004).

The assumption that the error component is independent of X may be violated in nonexperimental research in which uncontrolled nuisance variables may vary systematically with the variables of interest. If we regress Y on X, using data from an observational study, there may be important variables left out of the equation that are correlated with X. If so, the effects of these variables will contribute to the error component, ε, which will then be correlated with X. In this case, b_1 will not be an unbiased or a consistent estimator of β_1. We discuss this issue in more detail in Chapter 23.

20.5 CONSEQUENCES OF MEASUREMENT ERROR IN BIVARIATE REGRESSION

Measurement error is always a bad thing, although a certain amount is unavoidable. However, the consequences of poor measurement can be worse in standard applications of regression than in ANOVA because error in measuring the predictor variable can cause a great deal of trouble, especially when the error is systematic.

First, consider measurement error in Y, the dependent variable. Increased measurement error in Y will contribute to the error term, causing s_Y and $SS_{residual}$ to be larger. Therefore, the standard error of estimate will be larger with the consequence that confidence intervals will be larger, significance tests will have less power, and R^2 will be smaller. Further, because the standardized regression coefficient is $b_1^* = r = b_1 s_X / s_Y$, increasing random error in Y systematically attenuates the sample standardized coefficient. However, if the increased error in Y is random, estimates of the unstandardized regression coefficient will be unbiased.

---

[3] Different authors make somewhat different assumptions when dealing with random-effects predictors. Useful discussions about what happens when both X and Y are random variables may be found in Fox, 1997, pp. 113–114; Hays, 1994, pp. 637–638; Mittelhammer et al., 2000, pp. 17–24 and 225–235; Neter et al., 1996, p. 85; and especially Berk, 2004, pp. 69–73.

The situation is worse when there is error in the predictor variable, X. We can see this by picturing a scatterplot for two variables that have a strong linear relationship—say, we regress height on weight. Now imagine that a random error component is added to each of the X (weight) scores. In the scatterplot, this will result in some of the X values being randomly moved to the left, and others to the right. This "smearing" of the X values will cause the slope of the regression of Y on X to become smaller. This consequence of error in the predictor variable is important, so let's consider it in more detail.

Although the usual regression model assumes that X is measured without error, the assumption is often not realistic. If we consider the situation where measurement error is present, we can express the observed value of X as consisting of two components: X_t, the "true" value (i.e., the value if there was no measurement error), and δ, an error component, so that

$$X = X_t + \delta$$

Therefore, the regression equation

$$Y = \beta_0 + \beta_1 X + \varepsilon$$

can be written as

$$Y = \beta_0 + \beta_1 X_t + (\varepsilon + \beta_1 \delta) \tag{20.12}$$

If we can assume that the measurement error in X is random and that the error component is uncorrelated with X_t, we have $E(\delta) = 0$ and $\sigma_X^2 = \sigma_{X_t}^2 + \sigma_\delta^2$. In the example of regressing height on weight, this situation might occur if the scale we used to measure weight was noisy but unbiased— say, on some trials it gives high readings and on others, low readings, but the tendency to read high or low is not related to any characteristic of the person being weighed.

If ε, δ, and X_t are all normally and independently distributed, the regression of Y on X will be linear with a slope of

$$\beta_1 = \beta_{1t} \left[\frac{\sigma_{X_t}^2}{\sigma_X^2} \right] = \beta_{1t} \, r_{XX} \tag{20.13}$$

where β_{1t} is the "true" slope (i.e., the slope of the equation that would be obtained by regressing Y on X_t) and $r_{XX} = \sigma_{X_t}^2 / \sigma_X^2$ is the *reliability* of X (i.e., the proportion of the variability in the actual X scores that is accounted for by the true scores). Even if X_t is not normally distributed, the result holds for large samples and approximately for small samples when the reliability is high. The implication of this result is that if there is error in measuring X, the obtained slope, b_1, underestimates the magnitude of the true slope and the amount of underestimation depends directly on the amount of measurement error. If there is a great deal of measurement error, the reliability will be low, and β_1 will be much closer to zero than the true slope.

The situation is worse if we cannot assume that X_t is independent of the error component. Suppose, for example, we do not use a scale to measure weight, but instead ask each subject to provide a self-report. Unfortunately, such estimates of weight will contain systematic as well as random error because the reported weights will tend to be less than the true weights, especially for subjects who are seriously overweight. Moreover, the degree of underreporting may be greater for some subgroups of subjects than others. The net result is a correlation between the predictor variable and the error component, violating the assumptions made in the last section for the case in which X is a random variable. *Given this type of violation, OLS regression provides neither unbiased nor consistent estimators.* Possible remedies for dealing with correlated predictors and error components exist, but they are beyond the scope of this text (see, for example, Berk, 2004).

Although discussion of measurement sometimes gets lost in treatments of regression, it is critically important. We should always try to use the most reliable measures we can, and should always be aware of the consequences of using poor measures. If we can get in trouble using measures of weight, think of what can happen if we use poorly constructed questionnaire scales to study emotionally charged predictors such as anxiety or hostility.

20.6 UNSTANDARDIZED vs STANDARDIZED REGRESSION COEFFICIENTS

When we regress Y on X, we get the regression equation

$$\hat{Y} = b_0 + b_1 X$$

We can also choose to look at the standardized regression equation; that is, the equation that would result if the regression was performed using z scores,

$$\hat{z}_Y = b_1^* z_X = r z_X$$

For example, in the statistics class example discussed in Chapter 18, the raw-score regression equation for predicting final exam score (Y) from the pretest score (X) is $\hat{Y} = -36.083 + 3.546X$ and the corresponding standardized regression equation is $\hat{z}_Y = .725 z_X$. The unstandardized coefficient b_1 is the change in $\hat{Y}$ (in units of Y) corresponding to a one-unit increase in X. For the statistics class example, each increase of one point on the pretest corresponds to a predicted increase of 3.546 points on the final exam. The standardized coefficient is the change in $\hat{z}_Y$ corresponding to an increase of one unit in z_X—or equivalently, b_1^* is the change in $\hat{Y}$ in s_Y units corresponding to an increase of one s_X unit in X. For the statistics class example, this means that an increase of one standard deviation in X corresponds to an increase of .725 in $\hat{z}_Y$ (or, equivalently, an increase of .725 s_Y in $\hat{Y}$).

For any given sample, the standardized and unstandardized coefficient will have the same sign, and their significance tests will yield identical results. But does one of these coefficients better characterize the nature of the relationship? Sources such as the publication manual of the American Psychological Association state that both the unstandardized and standardized coefficients should be reported in results sections. We have no problem with this; however, unless we are specifically interested in changes stated in terms of standard deviations or in terms of relative standing, we will usually be better off working with the unstandardized coefficients for the following reasons:

1. If the scales are meaningful, one-unit changes are more understandable than changes of one standard deviation.
2. If the scales are not meaningful or if there is a great deal of measurement error, the use of unit-free measures such as R^2 and standardized coefficients is more likely to obscure this fact. Standardizing poor measures will not help. As Achen (1977, p. 806) puts it, "To replace the unmeasureable by the unmeaningful is not progress."
3. The standard deviations of X and Y in two separate samples will be different, so that standardized regression coefficients are sample specific in the same way as correlation coefficients. In fact, for bivariate regression, the standardized regression coefficients *are* the correlation coefficients and therefore should usually not be used to make comparisons across groups.

4. The standardized regression coefficient is equal to the unstandardized coefficient multiplied by s_X/s_Y. Therefore, with two separate samples, A and B, we may find that the unstandardized coefficient is larger in A than in B but that the standardized coefficient is larger in B than in A because of differences in the standard deviations (see Exercise 20.5).

5. Finally, because the standardized coefficient depends on the variances of all the variables that contribute to the error term and therefore to s_Y, whether or not they are included in the model, it is less stable than the unstandardized coefficient when variances and covariances vary across samples.

20.7 CHECKING FOR VIOLATIONS OF ASSUMPTIONS

Because our conclusions can be seriously in error if there are severe violations of the assumptions, we next discuss how to check for violations. First, we emphasize that when we try to understand our data, we should not rely only on summary statistics such as the correlation coefficient or the slope of the regression line. It is also important to plot the data and to use the diagnostics that are usually provided by statistical packages. In Chapter 18, we presented data provided by Anscombe (1973). Fig. 18.9 presents scatterplots for four very different data sets that have identical values of N, $\bar{X}$, $\bar{Y}$, b_1, b_0, SS_X, $SS_{regression}$, $SS_{residual}$, $SE(b_1)$, and r. As we discussed in Chapter 18, although these summary statistics strongly suggest that the relationship between Y and X is the same for all four data sets, a comparison of the four scatterplots makes clear that this is not so. One plot (a) is well fit by a straight line whereas a second (b) is curved. A third plot (c) has just one point that departs from a straight line, and a fourth would have zero X variance if one point were deleted. To understand the relationship between Y and X, we must look at the scatterplot, determine whether there are systematic deviations from linearity, determine whether there are influential data points, and check the other assumptions that underlie inference.

20.7.1 Checking Regression Assumptions Using Residuals

Valuable information about whether the assumptions of the regression model are valid may be obtained by studying residuals; that is, differences between the observed and predicted values of Y. The residuals, $e_i = Y_i - \hat{Y} = Y_i - (b_0 + b_1 X_i)$, provide information about the population error components, $\varepsilon_i = Y_i - (\beta_0 - \beta_1 X_i)$. Statistical software packages generally provide residuals and standardized residuals and allow them to be plotted in a variety of ways. If the distribution of residuals differs strongly from that assumed for the error components, the assumptions of the model may not be satisfied. Moreover, the nature of the difference can tell us which assumptions have been violated and suggest appropriate remedial measures.

Residuals cannot provide us with information about the assumption $E(\varepsilon_i) = 0$ because when least-squares regression is used, the residuals are constrained to sum to zero. The residuals can, however, provide useful information about whether there are violations of the assumptions of linearity, homogeneity of variance, normality, and independence of error. If the assumptions of linearity and homoscedasticity (homogeneity of variance) are both valid, when residuals are plotted against either X or $\hat{Y}$, the data points should lie within a horizontal band, as indicated in panel (a) of Fig. 20.3. Any other pattern suggests that the assumptions are not valid or that some kind of error has been made. For example, plots such as that in panel (b) indicate that the relationship between Y and X is nonlinear and that the appropriate model should contain additional predictors such as X^2. Plots such as that in panel (c), in which the residuals are more spread out for some values

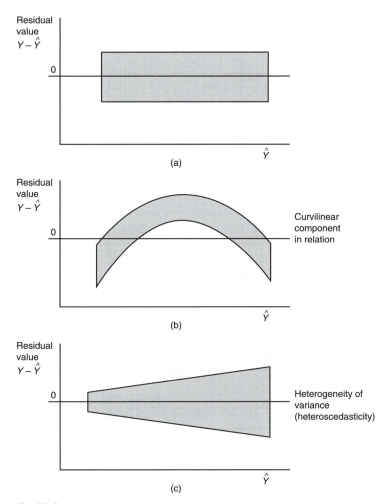

Fig. 20.3 Some possible patterns for plots of residuals vs predictions in regression.

of X or $\hat{Y}$ than others, indicate that the variance of estimate is not constant (the homoscedasticity assumption is violated). We plot residuals against predicted values of Y rather than against Y because it can be shown that e is not correlated with $\hat{Y}$ (or, therefore, with X) but has a correlation of $\sqrt{1 - r^2}$ with Y. We should also note that although plots of residuals against X and against $\hat{Y}$ provide equivalent information for bivariate regression (because Y is simply a linear function of X), this will not be the case when there is more than one predictor variable.

Another assumption of the regression model is that all relevant variables have been included in the model. If a relevant variable is omitted, the error component, ε, will consist of more than chance variability. We can determine whether an additional variable, W, belongs in the model by plotting the residuals against W. If the residual varies systematically with W, then W should be included in the model.

We used SPSS to regress total cholesterol level (TC) on age for women; the output for the regression is presented in Table 20.5. The coefficients table shows that the best-fitting regression line is predicted $TC = 131.87 + 1.712\ age$. The significant relationship between TC and age is

Table 20.5   SPSS output for the regression of *TC* on age for women

Model Summary[b]

Model	R	R Square	Adjusted R Square	Std. Error of the Estimate	Durbin-Watson
1	.506[a]	.256	.252	34.21896	2.084

[a.] Predictors: (Constant), age
[b.] Dependent Variable: *TC*

ANOVA[b]

Model	Sum of Squares	df	Mean Square	F	Sig.
1 Regression	84117.481	1	84117.481	71.838	.000[a]
Residual	244725.9	209	1170.937		
Total	328843.4	210			

[a.] Predictors: (Constant), age
[b.] Dependent Variable: *TC*

Coefficients[a]

Model	Unstandardized Coefficients		Standardized Coefficients	t	Sig.	95% Confidence Interval for B	
	B	Std. Error	Beta			Lower Bound	Upper Bound
1 (Constant)	131.870	10.053		13.117	.000	112.051	151.689
Age	1.712	.202	.506	8.476	.000	1.313	2.110

[a.] Dependent Variable: *TC*

Casewise Diagnostics[a]

Case Number	Std. Residual	tc	Predicted Value	Residual
251	−3.348	114.88	229.4288	−114.554
311	3.897	320.00	186.6398	133.36017
600	3.080	316.00	210.6017	105.39834
631	3.248	309.75	198.6207	111.12926

[a.] Dependent Variable: *TC*

demonstrated equivalently by the *t*-value of 8.476 for the test of the slope, and by the *F*-value of 71.838 (i.e., t^2) in the ANOVA table. We also used SPSS to plot the standardized residuals against the standardized predictions (see Fig. 20.4). In Fig. 20.4, the plot does not suggest any obvious curvilinearity or heteroscedasticity, although there are several outliers that we will examine more closely later.

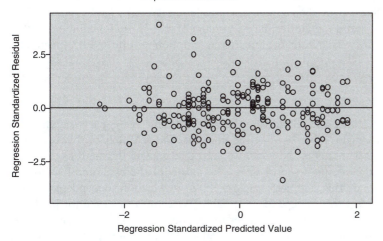

Fig. 20.4 Scatterplot of standardized residuals vs standardized predictions for the regression of *TC* on age for women (using SPSS).

20.7.2 An *F* Test for Departures from Linearity

The assumption that the conditional means of *Y* are a linear function of *X* in the population is basic to the inferential procedures that we have discussed in this chapter. Departures from linearity that are suggested by scatterplots or plots of residuals may be tested for significance by employing a procedure based on partitioning $SS_{residual}$ into two components, one based on systematic departures from linearity and the other based on *pure error*—that is, the variability around the conditional means of *Y* at the different values of *X*.

If the linear model is appropriate, the conditional *TC* means (i.e., the means of the *TC* values for different ages) all fall on a straight line. In this case, the variability about the straight line is the same as the variability about the means, so that $SS_{residual}$ consists only of pure error. If the linear model is not appropriate, $SS_{residual}$ consists of not only a pure error component that reflects variability about the conditional means, but also a "nonlinearity" component that reflects the extent to which the conditional means are not a perfect linear function of *X*. Assume that *X* takes on the values $X_1, X_2, \ldots, X_j, \ldots, X_a$, and that there are n_j values $Y_{1j}, Y_{2j}, \ldots, Y_{ij}, \ldots, Y_{n_j j}$ of *Y* at X_j. The predicted *Y* score at X_j is obtained from the linear equation $\hat{Y}_j = b_0 + b_1 X_j$. The identity

$$Y_{ij} - \hat{Y}_j = (Y_{ij} - \overline{Y}_{.j}) + (\overline{Y}_{.j} - \hat{Y}_j)$$

residual = pure error + nonlinearity

suggests the following partitioning of error variance:

$$\Sigma\Sigma\,(Y_{ij} - \hat{Y}_j)^2 = \Sigma\Sigma\,(Y_{ij} - \overline{Y}_{.j})^2 + \Sigma\Sigma\,(\overline{Y}_{.j} - \hat{Y})^2 \qquad (20.14)$$

$$SS_{residual} \quad = \quad SS_{pure\ error} \quad + \quad SS_{nonlinearity}$$

The pure error *SS* term is associated with $N - a$ *df*; there are $n_j - 1$ *df* at each of the *a* levels of *X*, and $N = \Sigma\, n_j$. The corresponding mean square, $\Sigma\Sigma(Y_{ij} - \overline{Y}_{.j})^2/(N - a)$, estimates the variance of the scores around the conditional means of *Y*. The nonlinearity *SS* term is obtained by subtracting

$SS_{pure\ error}$ from $SS_{residual}$. It has $a - 2$ *df* because there are a means and 2 *df* are used up in estimating the slope and intercept of the linear regression equation; equivalently, $(N - 2) - (N - a) = a - 2$. The corresponding mean square estimates a quantity that is the sum of $\sigma^2_{pure\ error}$ and a component that reflects the departure from linearity. Therefore, the linearity assumption may be tested by using

$$F = \frac{MS_{nonlinearity}}{MS_{pure\ error}} \tag{20.15}$$

with $a - 2$ and $N - a$ *df*.

Suppose we wish to test whether the relationship between *TC* and *age* departs significantly from linearity for women. Looking at Table 20.5, we see from the ANOVA table of the regression output that $SS_{residual} = 244{,}725.9$ with 209 *df*. Now, all we need to complete the analysis is to find $SS_{pure\ error}$, the variability of the cholesterol scores about the means of the cholesterol scores for different ages. The easiest way to do this is to perform an ANOVA in which the dependent variable is *TC* and *age* is treated as a categorical independent variable. We can do this even for predictor variables such as age that we would not usually consider to be categorical. The test only requires that some of the values of the predictor have more than one value of *Y* associated with them so that an estimate of $SS_{pure\ error}$ may be obtained. The results of the one-way ANOVA performed with SPSS are displayed in Table 20.6. We see that the sum of squares term for the "within groups" source of variance is 200,768.3 with 164 *df*; this is the $SS_{pure\ error}$ term in Equation 20.14. Subtracting this from $SS_{residual}$, we find $SS_{nonlinearity} = 43{,}957.6$ with 45 *df*. Substituting into the test statistic of Equation 20.15, we have $F = 976.84/1224.20 = 0.80$. This result does not provide evidence of a significant departure from linearity. We can summarize the steps to test for systematic departures from linearity as follows:

1. First find $SS_{residual}$: to do this, regress *Y* on *X*.
2. Then find $SS_{pure\ error}$: to do this, perform an ANOVA on *Y* with *X* as the factor; the within-groups *SS* in the ANOVA is $SS_{pure\ error}$.
3. Find $SS_{nonlinearity} = SS_{residual} - SS_{pure\ error}$ and $df_{nonlinearity} = df_{residual} - df_{pure\ error}$ and substitute into the test statistic given in Equation 20.15.

Table 20.6 Result of an ANOVA using data from women in which the dependent variable is total cholesterol level (*TC*) and the independent variable is age

ANOVA

TC

	Sum of Squares	df	Mean Square	F	Sig.
Between Groups	128075.1	46	2784.241	2.274	.000
Within Groups	200768.3	164	1224.197		
Total	328843.4	210			

20.7.3 Dealing with Heteroscedasticity

In the current example, when we regress *TC* on *age* for women, the assumption of homoscedasticity is reasonably well satisfied. But what should we do if there are severe violations of the assumption that can result in biased estimates and inflated standard errors? One possibility is to transform the *Y* variable; several possible transformations—and the potential pitfalls of using transformations—are discussed in Chapters 6 and 8. Another possibility, if the variability in the residuals varies systematically with X, is to use a procedure called *weighted least-squares (WLS) estimation* instead of the *ordinary least-squares (OLS) estimation* procedures that we have been using. WLS regression is identical to OLS regression except that residuals are not equally weighted. Instead, residuals based on values of the predictor variable for which there is less error variance are weighted more heavily than residuals based on predictor values that have more error variance. The rationale is that predictor values associated with less error are more useful for making predictions. In an appropriate WLS regression, the resulting values of b_1 and b_0 will have smaller standard errors and therefore narrower confidence intervals than they would have in the corresponding OLS regression. Some, but not all, of the standard statistical packages can conveniently handle weighted least-squares analyses. For example, SPSS offers a WLS option in the *Linear Regression* dialog box and a *Weight Estimation* option in the *Regression* menu to assist in determining which weights to use.

How do we decide which weights in a WLS regression? One approach is to set $w = (1/X)^{power}$. The *Weight Estimation* option in SPSS regression can help decide which power of $1/X$ to use as the weight. When regressing Y on X, we indicate that X is to be used as the basis of the weights. Then, SPSS tries out different powers of $1/X$, and indicates for which power the WLS model provides the best fit.

20.7.4 Normality

As indicated earlier, statistical packages are usually capable of constructing histograms and normal probability plots of the residuals. A virtue of the normal probability plot is that if the residuals are normally distributed, the points fall on a straight line and it is easier to detect departures from a straight line than from a normal histogram. Fig. 20.5 displays both a histogram with a normal smoother and a normal Q–Q plot for the standardized residuals of the regression of cholesterol on age for women. The distribution of residuals is slightly heavy-tailed and positively skewed. If there were large deviations from normality, we could consider transformations of the Y variable. Violations of the linearity and homogeneity of variance assumptions may cause the residuals to depart from normality, so that generally the linearity and homogeneity of variance assumptions should be checked and addressed before looking for violations of the normality assumption.

20.7.5 Independence

We assume that the error components, the ε_i, are independent of one another. If they are positively correlated, perhaps because of the omission of some important variables from the model, standard errors calculated by the usual ordinary least-squares procedures may underestimate the true standard errors of the regression coefficients and the confidence intervals, and hypothesis tests based on them will not be appropriate. The residuals cannot be strictly independent because they are all based on the same estimates of b_0 and b_1. Nonetheless, if N is reasonably large, this unavoidable dependency will be very small so that residuals can meaningfully be examined for evidence of lack of independence. This is typically done by examining the pattern of residuals as a function of time of observation. The rationale for doing this is that data are usually collected and recorded sequentially. If the error components are independent, the residuals should not vary systematically over time. Systematic variation may reflect changes in subjects, measuring devices, or surroundings. When the residuals are plotted against time or case number, the result should again look like panel (a) of Fig. 20.3.

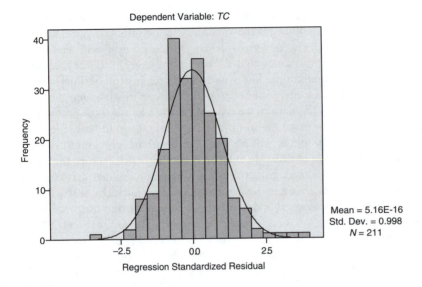

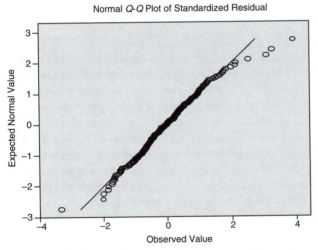

Fig. 20.5 A histogram with a superimposed normal distribution and a normal Q–Q plot of the standardized residuals for the regression of cholesterol level on age for women.

It is possible for error components to exhibit different kinds of serial correlations. For example, the residual corresponding to case i may tend to be similar (or dissimilar) in size to those corresponding to case $i-1$ or $i-2$. Several packages print values of the Durbin–Watson D statistic that forms the basis for a test of serial correlation in adjacent residuals. The D statistic

$$D = \frac{\sum_i (e_i - e_{i-1})^2}{\sum_i e_i^2} \tag{20.16}$$

will be small when sequentially adjacent residuals are positively correlated and large when they are negatively correlated. D is approximately equal to $2(1 - r_{i,i-1})$, where $r_{i,i-1}$ is the correlation between sequentially adjacent residuals. Therefore, D can range from 0 to 4, with larger deviations in either direction from a value of 2 providing stronger evidence of serial correlation. A more detailed discussion of the test, and appropriate tables for assessing significance, may be found in Draper and Smith (1998). Under some conditions, weighted least-squares can be used to perform the regression analysis when the data are serially correlated (e.g., see Draper & Smith, 1998). In the current example, as we can see from the model summary table in the regression output in Table 20.5, the Durbin–Watson statistic is close to 2, indicating that the serial correlation for adjacent residuals is close to zero.

20.8 LOCATING OUTLIERS AND INFLUENTIAL DATA POINTS

The results of an ordinary least-squares regression analysis can be markedly affected by a few extreme data points, so it is important to identify data points that are unusually influential. If these points can be located, checks can be made to determine whether they reflect different processes than the rest of the data, or occur because of recording or transcription errors. If so, they can be corrected or deleted from the data. If the influential points cannot be attributed to an error or failure of some sort, the appropriate way to deal with them depends on the specific research problem.

Given the presence of influential points, we can collect more data to lessen their effect. We can also make clear the impact of the influential points by reporting two sets of analyses, one including the influential cases and one deleting them. In situations in which predictions are important, the effects of influential points may be partially circumvented by isolating regions where the influence is relatively unimportant. It is also possible to use robust regression: procedures that are relatively resistant to the effects of outliers (see Huynh, 1982; Neter et al., 1996; Rousseeuw & Leroy, 1987).

It is frequently of interest to locate points that have outlying X and/or Y values, even though such points may not greatly influence the regression equation. These points can be examined for errors or to determine whether there is something special about them. Also, depending on the particular research problem, it may be reasonable to treat cases with extreme values of X differently, or to confine discussion to cases that do not have outlying values of X.

Table 20.7 contains output for the first 30 cases obtained from the SYSTAT statistics package when we regressed TC on *age* for women and requested that the residuals be saved. Six quantities are presented. The first two are the predicted value ($\hat{Y}$) and residual ($Y - \hat{Y}$) for each case. Note that estimates are provided for all of the women, including those who did not have complete cholesterol data. However, residuals and related variables can only be obtained for those with complete data. For the others, the missing data are indicated by dots. The quantity in the right-most column, SEPRED, is $SE(\hat{Y})$, which, as we have previously noted, takes on different values for different values of X. The remaining quantities are LEVERAGE (the h_{jj} that we have encountered on several occasions), COOK, and STUDENT. LEVERAGE measures the extent to which the case is an outlier with respect to the distribution of X values, COOK measures the influence exerted by the case on the regression equation, and STUDENT measures the extent to which the case has an outlying residual. In the remainder of this section, we provide an explanation of these and related measures, and indicate why they might be useful. Several packages allow us to save most of these measures (adding them to the original data set), along with a number of other diagnostic measures that we will describe below. In the subsections that follow, we will describe several measures of outliers and influential points.

Table 20.7 The first 30 cases of the SYSTAT residual output for the regression of cholesterol level on age for women[a]

Case	ESTIMATE	RESIDUAL	LEVERAGE	COOK	STUDENT	SEPRED
1	222.583	.	0.005	.	.	2.532
2	205.467	.	0.006	.	.	2.596
3	215.736	−63.486	0.005	0.008	−1.871	2.359
4	239.698	−9.198	0.012	0.000	−0.270	3.774
5	224.294	8.456	0.006	0.000	0.247	2.613
6	241.410	−59.535	0.013	0.021	−1.760	3.934
7	227.717	.	0.007	.	.	2.812
8	195.198	−15.823	0.009	0.001	−0.464	3.294
9	219.159	42.716	0.005	0.004	1.253	2.414
10	226.006	.	0.006	.	.	2.707
11	229.429	.	0.007	.	.	2.927
12	220.871	56.004	0.005	0.007	1.648	2.465
13	232.852	.	0.009	.	.	3.183
14	231.140	62.110	0.008	0.013	1.833	3.051
15	229.429	.	0.007	.	.	2.927
16	234.563	7.187	0.009	0.000	0.211	3.322
17	202.044	−58.669	0.007	0.010	−1.728	2.790
18	243.121	−13.246	0.014	0.001	−0.389	4.097
19	236.275	−14.025	0.010	0.001	−0.411	3.468
20	200.332	.	0.007	.	.	2.903
21	202.044	−24.419	0.007	0.002	−0.715	2.790
22	200.332	53.293	0.007	0.009	1.568	2.903
23	202.044	22.456	0.007	0.001	0.658	2.790
24	215.736	.	0.005	.	.	2.359
25	215.736	−41.361	0.005	0.004	−1.213	2.359
26	215.736	20.889	0.005	0.001	0.611	2.359
27	220.871	−34.871	0.005	0.003	−1.022	2.465
28	224.294	14.706	0.006	0.001	0.430	2.613
29	196.909	17.341	0.009	0.001	0.508	3.156
30	203.755	−27.005	0.006	0.002	−0.791	2.687

[a] The dots indicate missing data. These come from subjects who did not have cholesterol data recorded in each season.

20.8.1 Locating Outlying Residuals and Predictors

We first deal with detecting extreme residuals, and then with extreme values of the predictor. Measures for detecting these outliers are listed in Table 20.8.

Locating Outlying Residuals. Whether a given residual is an outlier depends not only on its absolute size but also on the distribution of the other residuals. Therefore, if one is interested in locating extreme outliers, it makes sense to use some sort of standardized measure in which the raw residual is divided by something like the standard deviation. Finding that a residual has a z score of 4.50 relative to the distribution of residuals informs us more directly that it is an outlier than finding that it has an absolute value of 34.58. Although there is nothing very complicated about this basic idea, the commonly used statistical packages provide a variety of measures termed *standardized* or

Studentized residuals. Unfortunately, different statistical packages use different names to refer to some of these measures.

We first note that the standard error for a given residual e_j is given by

$$SE(e_j) = s_{Y.X}\sqrt{1 - h_{jj}} \tag{20.17}$$

where h_{jj} is the leverage of X_j (see Equation 20.11). Dividing a raw residual by its standard error results in an *internally Studentized residual* (Velleman & Welsch, 1981),

$$t_j = \frac{e_j}{s_{Y.X}\sqrt{1 - h_{jj}}} \tag{20.18}$$

SPSS refers to this as the "Studentized residual." Although this measure seems a straightforward way to identify outlying data points, it has the important limitation that if a data point (X_j, Y_j) is far from the other data points, it may have a strong influence on the regression line (see the next section). An influential data point will pull the regression line towards itself, thereby reducing its residual, but in doing so, it will increase the residuals for many of the other data points. Because of this, a better way to obtain an index of the extent to which a data point is an outlier is to determine its distance from a regression line that does not depend on the data point under consideration, but rather is based on the other $N - 1$ data points.

The *deleted prediction* for the jth case is defined as

$$\hat{Y}_j^{(-j)} = b_0^{(-j)} + b_1^{(-j)}X_j \tag{20.19}$$

where $\hat{Y}_j^{(-j)}$ is the prediction of Y from X_j, using the regression equation in which the Y intercept and slope, $b_0^{(-j)}$ and $b_1^{(-j)}$, are obtained from the $N - 1$ cases that remain when the data point (X_j, Y_j) is not included.

The *deleted residual* for the jth case, $e_j^{(-j)}$, is defined as the difference between Y_j and its deleted prediction,

$$e_j^{(-j)} = Y_j - \hat{Y}_j^{(-j)} = \frac{e_j}{1 - h_{jj}} \tag{20.20}$$

The ratio of the deleted residual to its standard error is called the *externally Studentized residual*, and can be expressed as

$$t_j^{(-j)} = \frac{e_j^{(-j)}}{SE(e_j^{(-j)})} = \frac{e_j}{s_{Y.X}^{(-j)}\sqrt{1 - h_{jj}}} \tag{20.21}$$

where the deleted standard error of estimate

$$s_{Y.X}^{(-j)} = \sqrt{\frac{\sum_{i \neq j}(Y_i - \hat{Y}_i^{(-j)})^2}{N - 3}} \tag{20.22}$$

is based on the $N - 1$ data points that remain after case j has been deleted. The externally Studentized residual is what SYSTAT calls STUDENT in the saved residual output in Table 20.7, and what SPSS calls the *Studentized deleted residual*.

We recommend the use of externally Studentized residuals to identify outlying residuals because they can be tested by the t statistic defined in Equation 20.21. However, as usual, when a large number of significance tests are performed, Type 1 error rate should be controlled. This can be accomplished conveniently for the family of N residuals by using the Bonferroni inequality; that is,

Table 20.8   Measures for locating outliers

Measure	Equation	SPSS menu notation	Criterion
Measures for detecting extreme residuals			
Standardized residual	$r_j = \dfrac{e_j}{s_{Y.X}}$	*ZRESID	
Internally Studentized residual	$t_j = \dfrac{e_j}{s_{Y.X}\sqrt{1 - h_{jj}}}$	*SRESID	
Externally Studentized residual	$t_j^{(-j)} = \dfrac{e_j}{s_{Y.X}^{(-j)}\sqrt{1 - h_{jj}}}$	*SDRESID	$t_{.025/N}$
where	$s_{Y.X}^{(-j)} = \sqrt{\dfrac{\sum_{i \neq j}(Y_i - \hat{Y}_i^{(-j)})^2}{N - 3}}$		
Measures for detecting outlying values of predictors			
Mahalanobis distance	$D_j = \left[\dfrac{X_j - \bar{X}}{s_X}\right]^2 = \dfrac{(N-1)(X_j - \bar{X})^2}{SS_X}$		
Leverage	$h_{jj} = \dfrac{1}{N} + \dfrac{(X_j - \bar{X})^2}{SS_X}$		$2(p+1)/N$
Centered leverage (SPSS)	$c_{jj} = \dfrac{(X_j - \bar{X})^2}{SS_X} = h_{jj} - \dfrac{1}{N}$		$2p/N$

by conducting each test at the α / N level of significance. With $\alpha = .05$ and 211 cases, the critical t is approximately 3.73. Looking at saved Studentized deleted residuals in SPSS, we can see, for example, that case 311 is an outlier with an externally studentized residual of 4.068.

Locating Outlying Values of the Predictor.   The measures considered to this point are concerned with determining the extent to which Y_j differs from its predicted value. We might also be interested in the extent to which X_j differs from the mean of the X scores. Some statistical packages provide the *Mahalanobis distance*, which for bivariate regression is just a squared z score,

$$D_j = \left[\frac{X_j - \bar{X}}{s_X}\right]^2 = \frac{(N-1)(X_j - \bar{X})^2}{SS_X} \tag{20.23}$$

Another useful measure for identifying outliers in the X distribution that is commonly available in the regression output is the *leverage* that we discussed earlier.

$$h_{jj} = \frac{1}{N} + \frac{(X_j - \bar{X})^2}{SS_X}$$

The leverage is closely related to the Mahalanobis distance, and can be expressed in terms of it as

$$h_{jj} = \frac{1}{N} + \frac{D_j}{N-1}$$

It can be shown that the sum of the leverages for a data set is equal to $p + 1$, where p is the number of predictor variables; therefore, for bivariate regression, the h_{jj} must sum to 2 and have a mean value of $2/N$. Hoaglin and Welsch (1978) suggest that values of h_{jj} greater than $2(p + 1)/N$ should be considered large. Belsley, Kuh, and Welsch (1980) caution that this cutoff will identify too many points when there are only a few predictor variables, but recommend it because it is easy to remember and use. If we use SPSS, we should remember that when we ask for the leverages to be saved, what we get are *centered leverages*

$$c_{jj} = \frac{(X_j - \bar{X})^2}{SS_X} = h_{jj} - \frac{1}{N} = \frac{D_j}{N-1} \tag{20.24}$$

For centered leverages, Hoaglin and Welsch's suggested criterion is $2p/N$.

20.8.2 Influential Points

We should look at cases that have large residuals. However, we look even more closely at cases that have an unusually large influence on the regression equation, and thereby on the predictions made using it. Note that not all outliers will have large influences. As we shall see, cases that have large residuals and extreme values of X will have the greatest influence (see Equation 20.27). There are several measures that are commonly used to detect influential points. Each of the measures assesses the influence of a data point by comparing regression statistics when the data point is included, and when it is not included, in the regression. These measures are listed in Table 20.9.

One way of assessing the influence of the jth case on the regression equation is to compare the results of the analysis when the jth case is present with the results when it is deleted. Therefore, the difference in the fitted (i.e., predicted) value, $\hat{Y}_j$, when case j is included and when it is excluded from the regression equation, $DFFIT_j = \hat{Y}_j - \hat{Y}_j^{(-j)}$, can be considered an index of the effect of the jth case.

Table 20.9 Measures for detecting influential data points

Measure	Equation	Criterion
Measure of the influence of the jth data point on the fitted (predicted) value of Y_j		
DFFITS	$DFFITS_j = \dfrac{\hat{Y}_j - \hat{Y}_j^{(-j)}}{s_{Y.X}^{(-j)} \sqrt{h_{jj}}}$	$2\sqrt{(p + 1)/N}$
Measure of the influence of the jth data point on all fitted values		
Cook's distance	$CD_j = \dfrac{\sum_i (\hat{Y}_i - \hat{Y}_i^{(-j)})}{(p + 1)s_{Y.X}^2}$	$F_{.50, p+1, N-p-1}$
Measure of the influence of the jth data point on the kth regression coefficient		
DFBETAS	$DFBETAS_{jk} = \dfrac{b_k - b_k^{(-j)}}{SE^{(-j)}(b_k)}$	$2/\sqrt{N}$

Both $DFFIT_j$ and its standardized value,

$$DFFITS_j = \frac{\hat{Y}_j - \hat{Y}_j^{(-j)}}{s_{Y.X}^{(-j)} \sqrt{h_{jj}}} \tag{20.25}$$

where $s_{Y.X}^{(-j)}$ is as defined in Equation 20.22, can be requested for each data point in both SAS and SPSS. A number of criteria have been suggested for a case to be considered influential. SAS suggests a general cutoff of 2 and a size-adjusted cutoff of $2\sqrt{(p+1)/N}$ for $DFFITS$.

Cook (1977) proposed a measure that takes into consideration the effect of deleting case j on all N residuals. This measure, known as *Cook's distance*, can be expressed as

$$CD_j = \frac{\sum_i (\hat{Y}_i - \hat{Y}_i^{(-j)})^2}{(p+1)s_{Y.X}^2} \tag{20.26}$$

where $p = 1$ for bivariate regression and, in general, p is the number of predictor variables in the regression equation. Cook and Weisberg (1982) suggest that Cook's distance should be referred to an F distribution with $p + 1$ and $N - p - 1$ df. A value of Cook's distance is considered large if the F has a p-value greater than .5. For regressions with more than five or six predictor variables, this leads to a criterion Cook's distance value of about 1; however, for bivariate regression with a sample size of about 200, as in the current example, the criterion would be about 0.70.

Another useful expression for Cook's distance is

$$CD_j = \left(\frac{t_j^2}{p+1}\right)\left(\frac{h_{jj}}{1 - h_{jj}}\right) \tag{20.27}$$

where t_j is the internally Studentized residual of Equation 20.18. This expression makes it clearer that the influence of a data point depends on both its residual—captured by t_j^2—and the extent to which it is an outlier—captured by h_{jj}.

The final measures we consider here reflect differences in the regression coefficients b_0 and b_1 that result when case j is excluded from the analysis. The change in the value of the kth regression coefficient when the jth data point is not included in the regression is given by

$$DFBETA_{jk} = b_k - b_k^{(-j)} \tag{20.28}$$

where $k = 0$ for the Y intercept and $k = 1$ for the slope. The standardized change is given by

$$DFBETAS_{jk} = \frac{DFBETA_{jk}}{SE^{(-j)}(b_k)} \tag{20.29}$$

where the denominator is simply the usual standard error for b_k, except that $s_{Y.X}^{(-j)}$ replaces $s_{Y.X}$. The *DFBETAS* measure is available in both SAS and SPSS and has a suggested size-related cutoff of $2/\sqrt{N}$.

Cook's distance measure is extremely useful for identifying influential data points that influence the fit of the regression, and the *DFBETAS* measure is of particular interest if we are concerned with the stability of the regression coefficients. Given that packages such as SPSS readily provide these measures of influential data points, we can consider all of them. Looking back at our regression of *TC* on *age* for women in Table 20.5, case 311 seems to deserve special attention. It not only has an externally Studentized residual of 4.068, but also a *DFFITS* of .487, which is greater than the criterion of .195. It also has *DFBETAS* values of .452 and −.397 for b_0 and b_1, respectively, both of which exceed the criterion of .137. The Cook's distance for case 368 is .110. This does not exceed the criterion, but it is more than twice the size of the next largest value. When we examine case 311, we find that the data come from a woman who is relatively young (32 years old), but who has extreme *TC* (320) and *BMI* (41.1) values. There has not been any obvious error in recording the data. Although any one cholesterol reading can be in error, the cholesterol levels for case 311 are over 300 in each season. We cannot drop a data point from our analysis just because we do not like it, but we can assess whether and how much our conclusions would change if the data point was excluded. If we redo the regression analysis excluding case 311, the results are much the same: the slope changes from 1.71 to 1.79, the intercept from 131.87 to 127.49, and the correlation between the observed and predicted values from .51 to .54. In the present example, dropping an extreme outlier did not affect the overall regression greatly because we had a large number of data points. But what if it had? After checking to make sure that our extreme points did not result from some sort of equipment or clerical error, we could present the results both with the extreme points included and without them. If our basic conclusions were supported by both sets of analyses, we could feel more confident about them. We could also collect additional data. Or we could conduct analyses using some form of *robust regression*—the term refers to procedures that are less sensitive to extreme points and some violations of assumptions.

20.9 ROBUST REGRESSION

Because the mean of the squared residuals is minimized in standard OLS (ordinary least-squares) regression, data points with large residuals can have a great deal of influence. Robust regression procedures give less weight to cases with large residuals (see, for example, Huynh, 1982) by minimizing some quantity other than the mean of the squared residuals that is more resistant to the influence of extreme data points, such as the mean of the absolute residuals or the median of the squared residuals. We have already discussed a kind of robust analysis, weighted least-squares regression. Statistical packages offer many different robust regression procedures, either through separate menus or through nonlinear regression procedures that allow the user to specify the desired loss function (i.e., the quantity that is to be minimized by the regression).

The *least absolute deviations* (*LAD*) procedure, in which the sum of the absolute residuals is minimized, produces regression equations that are robust to outliers in the *Y* direction. When we used the nonlinear regression procedure in SPSS to perform a least absolute deviations regression of cholesterol level on age for women, we found an intercept of 133.21, a slope of 1.65, and a correlation between observed and predicted values of .51—values not very different from those obtained with the usual OLS regression using these data.

Another robust regression procedure, the *least median of squares* (*LMS*) procedure, in which the median of the squared deviations is minimized, produces regression equations that are robust to outliers in both the *X* and *Y* directions. When we used SYSTAT to perform a least median of squares regression, we found an intercept of 129.07 and a slope of 1.60, with a robust correlation between the actual and predicted *Y* scores of .67.

Robust regression procedures are particularly useful in situations in which there are groups of data points that collectively, but not individually, have a strong influence on the regression. In the current example, the results of the robust regression and the OLS regression are quite similar, reflecting the fact that the assumptions of OLS are reasonably well satisfied and that the regression is not severely distorted by outliers. In this case, we would report the results of the OLS regression because the method is well established and familiar to most researchers. The recommendations of Huynh (1982, pp. 511–512) are reasonable:

Perform the usual OLS regression along with a robust regression procedure. If the resulting estimates are in essential agreement, report the OLS estimates and relevant statistics. If substantial differences occur, however, take a careful look at the observations with large residuals and check to determine whether they contain errors of any type or if they represent significant situations under which the postulated regression model is not appropriate.

20.10 REPEATED-MEASURES DESIGNS AND HIERARCHICAL REGRESSION

We conclude the chapter by noting that the OLS regression procedures we have been considering will produce biased results when the data set consists of *groups of related scores* For example, we would normally run a search experiment of the type discussed in Section 20.2.1 as a repeated-measures design, collecting a number of detection times from each subject at each of the array sizes. If so, we would expect that scores collected from a given subject would tend to be more similar than scores collected from different subjects. If we ignored the fact that each subject provides a number of data points, and analyzed the data in the usual way, the test of the null hypothesis, H_0: $\beta_1 = 0$, would be biased because we would expect severe violations of the independence assumption (Lorch & Myers, 1990).

Suppose that we conduct a study in which 20 subjects search for target letters in arrays of letters and that we obtain 200 detection times from each subject, 50 at each of the four array sizes. The 20 subjects provide a total of 4,000 data points. Regression equations could be obtained by

1. Regressing detection time on array size using the combined data set (4,000 data points, 200 from each subject). Values of b_1 and b_0 could be obtained, as usual, by employing Equations 20.2 and 20.3; or
2. Regressing reaction time on array size separately for each of the 20 subjects, and then averaging the resulting 20 values of b_1 and b_0 to obtain values that best represent the entire group.

If each subject is tested at exactly the same levels of X and contributes the same number of data points at each level, both procedures will yield the same values for b_1 and b_0. However, if the first approach is used to test β_1 and β_0, the tests will be biased because the error term in this analysis pools between-subject and within-subject variability. The second procedure has the advantage that the values of b_1 and b_0 obtained for each subject can be treated as scores to be analyzed by conventional procedures for testing hypotheses about means (i.e., t-tests or F-tests). We can test the null hypothesis that β_1 is equal to some hypothesized value $\beta_{1\,hyp}$ by using a t-test with slope as the dependent variable. The test statistic is

$$t = \frac{\bar{b}_1 - \beta_{1\,hyp}}{s_{\bar{b}_1}} = \frac{\bar{b}_1 - \beta_{1\,hyp}}{s_{b_1}/\sqrt{N}} \quad \text{with } N-1 \; df$$

where $\bar{b}_1$ is the mean of the sample of N subject slopes and s_{b_1} is the estimated standard deviation of the N slopes; that is,

$$s_{b_1} = \sqrt{\frac{\sum_i (b_{1i} - \bar{b}_1)^2}{N-1}}$$

If, for example, the mean of the slopes for the 20 subjects is 22.75 and the estimated population standard deviation s_{b_1} is 5.45, so that $s_{\bar{b}_1} = s_{b_1}/\sqrt{20} = 1.22$, then the 95% confidence interval for β_1 is given by $22.75 \pm (2.093)(1.22) = 22.75 \pm 2.55$. The individual values of b_0 or b_1 could also be used in matched- and independent-groups t tests and in repeated-measures and between-subjects ANOVAs if we wished to test for equality of slopes or intercepts across conditions. We might, for example, want to test whether detection time vs array size slopes are equal for arrays consisting of letters and arrays consisting of digits.

Although the repeated-measures regression procedure just described is much superior to an analysis that ignores the hierarchical structure of the data, it is not ideal because it weights the regression coefficients for each subject equally, even though the standard errors of the individual regressions will be larger for some subjects than others. A number of multilevel modeling procedures, given names such as *hierarchical linear modeling* or *multilevel regression*, have been developed that address this issue (see, for example, Goldstein, 1995; Kreft & de Leeuw, 1998; Raudenbush & Bryk, 2002). We can think of these procedures as performing regressions for each subject and weighting the regression coefficients so that those coefficients based on more variable data are given less weight when used in higher-level analyses. Although we will briefly refer to these hierarchical regression analyses again when we deal with multiple regression, detailed coverage of the relevant estimation procedures is beyond the scope of this book.

20.11 SUMMARY

- Confidence intervals and significance tests for the population slope and intercept, as well as confidence intervals for predictions of Y scores for particular values of X, were discussed. We also considered how to test the equality of independent regression slopes.
- G*Power 3 was used to calculate power.
- In order to form confidence intervals, test hypotheses, or perform power calculations, we must make certain assumptions about the population. We first discussed the usual regression model which assumes that the predictor, X, is a fixed-effect variable that is measured without error. However, X is a fixed-effect variable only in studies in which the researcher selects the values of X and then observes values of Y at each of the selected values of X. Therefore, we considered the consequences for inference when both X and Y were random variables and X was measured with error, as is usually the case in nonexperimental research.
- We should be aware of the consequences of measurement error in both Y and X. Measurement error in X is particularly worrisome.
- In most contexts, we should be concerned with unstandardized, rather than standardized, regression coefficients.
- We can test for violations of linearity, homoscedasticity, normality, and independence.
- We can identify outliers and influential data points by using measures such as the leverage, Cook's distance, *DFFITS*, and *DFBETAS*.
- For certain violations of assumptions, or when there are outliers and influential data points, it may be useful to use more robust procedures such as weighted least-squares regression, least median of squares regression, and least absolute deviations regression.
- In some situations, subjects contribute data at several values of X. We briefly introduced procedures for dealing with these situations in which regression coefficients obtained for

each subject are used as the data in higher-level analyses, and indicated that these procedures can be extended to form the basis for hierarchical linear modeling.

EXERCISES

20.1 Use a statistical package to analyze the statistics class data (file *statistics class data* on the book's website).

(a) Regress final on pretest.

(b) Write out the regression equation. What are the values of the standard errors of estimate for b_0 and b_1, $SE(b_1)$, and $SE(b_0)$?

(c) Using the regression equation, estimate the mean of the population of final exam scores with a pretest score of (i) 24; (ii) 37. Find the 95% confidence interval for each of these population means.

(d) On the basis of your answers to (c), which estimate is more likely to be closer to the actual population value? Explain why, in terms of the leverages associated with the two pretest values.

(e) Find the 95% confidence interval for the final score of an individual student with a pretest score of 24.

20.2 The data set *EX20_2* contains response time (Y) to a target on a screen as a function of intensity level (X); the intensity levels have been coded from 1 to 5 for convenience. There are 10 subjects at each value of X.

(a) First, using a statistical package, plot the scatter diagram, including a smoother or fit line. Then, test whether there is a linear relationship between Y and X. Save the residuals for the regression.

   (i)   Write out the best-fitting linear equation, using the numbers from your regression analysis. Use this equation to predict Y for each of the five X values.

   (ii)   Is there a significant linear relationship? Report the appropriate test statistic and *df*.

(b) Now plot the residuals against the estimates. That is, produce a plot of residuals as a function of $\hat{Y}$. Include this graph with your answer. Does it suggest any problem with your analysis?

(c) Fill in the following table:

SV	df	SS	MS	F	p
Linearity					
Lack of fit (nonlinearity)					
Pure error					

Note that if you perform an ANOVA on Y with X, treating X as a categorical independent variable, the SS accounted for by X is the sum of the linear and nonlinear SS (i.e., accounts for all the variability in the group means). The error term of the ANOVA provides an estimate of the "pure error" variability (i.e., the residual variability when all the systematic effects are partitioned out).

(d) Now regress Y on both X and X^2. That is, Y should be the dependent variable and the predictor variables should be X and $XSQ = X*X$. Again, save the residuals. This estimates the parameters β_0, β_1, and β_2 for the population model

$$Y = \beta_0 + \beta_1 X + \beta_2 X^2 + \varepsilon$$

(i) Write out the equation for predicting Y with numbers taken from the output. Are β_1 and β_2 different from zero? Explain.

(ii) Does this model provide a better account of the data than the linear model? Explain.

(iii) Plot the residuals for this model against $\hat{Y}$. Do you see any problem now?

20.3 **(a)** Open the *Seasons* data set and select the data for women. Regress cholesterol level on age. Write out the regression equation and indicate the values of the standard error of estimate, $SE(b_1)$, and $SE(b_0)$.

(b) Using the regression equation, estimate the means of the populations of cholesterol scores for women of ages (i) 30 and (ii) 50. Find the 95% confidence interval for each of these population means.

(c) Which estimate is more likely to be closer to its actual population value, that for 30- or for 50-year-old women? Explain why.

(d) What is the 95% confidence interval for the cholesterol score of a randomly chosen 30-year-old woman?

20.4 Given the following data from a between-subjects experiment in which the dependent variable is a performance measure Y:

Drug dosage (D)			
10	20	30	40
27	38	69	60
17	32	64	57
14	10	59	55
20	26	57	30
15	29	35	50

(a) Regress Y on D. What is the best linear equation? Is the slope of the regression line significantly different from 0?

(b) Perform an ANOVA, using D as the independent variable. Is the D effect significant? How exactly does the null hypothesis in part (b) differ from that in part (a)?

20.5 We have previously considered data from a large study of income (Y) as a function of years on job (X); the data for 2,000 men and 2,000 women in a certain profession are

	Men			Women	
	Income (Y)	Years (X)		Income	Years
s^2:	324	100		289	25
r_{XY}:		.333			.235

Note: Income is recorded in thousands of dollars.

In Exercise 19.3 we found that the correlation between income and years of service was significantly larger for men than for women, $z = 3.38$, $p < .001$. Now, find b_{YX} (i.e., $b_{Income, Years}$), the regression coefficient for the regression of income on years of service for men and for women.

(a) What is your best estimate of the amounts by which salary increases per year for men and for women?

(b) Is the rate of increase significantly different for men and women?

(c) Is this result consistent with differences in the correlations? Explain.

20.6 In a search experiment, subjects are required to check for the presence of some target character in an array of characters. There are four different array sizes, $X = 2, 4, 6$, and 8. Ten subjects are assigned to each array size. The time to respond for each of the 40 subjects (Y) is recorded. The data for the four array sizes are

X_j:	2	4	6	8
$\bar{Y}_{\cdot j}$:	480	520	540	540
s_j^2:	360	315	324	333

Two reserachers, Anne and Reg, have different views about the analysis. Anne uses the ANOVA design model

$$Y_{ij} = \mu + \alpha_j + \varepsilon_{ij}$$

to test the hypothesis $H_0: \mu_1 = \mu_2 = \mu_3 = \mu_4$, and Reg assumes the linear regression model

$$Y_{ij} = \mu_Y + \beta_1(X_j - \bar{X}) + \varepsilon_{ij}$$

and tests the hypothesis $H_0: \beta_1 = 0$.

(a) Are Anne and Reg testing equivalent hypotheses? Briefly, justify your answer. If your answer is "no," are the two null hypotheses related? That is, if Anne's is false, should Reg's be true? Or if Reg's is false, should Anne's be true?

(b) Use ANOVA to test $H_0: \mu_1 = \mu_2 = \mu_3 = \mu_4$; and use regression to test $H_0: \beta_1 = 0$.

(c) Must SS_A always be larger than $SS_{regression}$?

(d) Determine whether there is a significant departure from linearity in the data, using $\alpha = .05$.

20.7 Groups of 40 men and 40 women each participate in the kind of search experiment described in the chapter. For each group, $SS_X = 200$. For men, we obtain $b_1 = 30.0$ and $s_e = 15.5$; for women, $b_1 = 20.0$ and $s_e = 12.2$. Test whether the slopes for men and women differ significantly at $\alpha = .05$.

20.8 (a) The search experiment described in Section 20.2 is rerun as a repeated-measures study. In one condition, letters are used as stimulus material. Each of the 10 men and 10 women in this condition is tested at all four array sizes, and slopes are obtained for each subject by performing separate regressions. The slopes are:

Men:	35	25	29	37	20	24	18	31	30	25
Women:	17	19	29	19	23	25	20	18	22	25

Find the 95% confidence interval for the difference in population slopes for men and women when letters are used.

(b) In a second condition using different subjects, digits (i.e., the numbers 0 through 9) are used as stimulus material. In this second condition, the slopes are

Men:	30	19	28	38	16	26	22	28	33	21
Women:	19	21	24	22	20	23	20	15	25	28

Test whether the slopes for men are significantly different from those for women in this condition. What exactly can you conclude from the significance test?

(c) From the results of both conditions, test the following, using slope as the dependent variable:

(i) The interaction between sex and type of stimulus material (letters vs digit).

(ii) The main effect of sex.

(iii) The main effect of type of stimulus material.

20.9 For a bivariate regression the multiple correlation coefficient R is .40. What does this tell you about the accuracy of predictions made with the regression equation?

20.10 Using the *Seasons* data set, we established in the chapter that the model assumptions were reasonably well satisfied for the regression of cholesterol level on age for women. We also established that the regression results were not strongly distorted by the presence of outliers and influential data points. Go through the same types of steps for the regression of cholesterol level on age for men and write a brief report about what you find.

Chapter 21

Introduction to Multiple Regression

21.1 OVERVIEW

In Chapters 18 and 20 we considered situations in which a dependent variable was regressed on a *single* predictor variable. Among the examples we discussed were the regressions of response time on stimulus array size, final exam score on pretest score, and cholesterol level on age. However, in most research situations, there are many relevant variables, and it is often useful to consider more than one predictor. If our goal is to generate accurate predictions, surely predictions should be better if we base them on more information. For example, in the statistics class example, we would expect to predict final exam performance better if we considered other measures of ability along with pretest score. If, on the other hand, our goal is to use regression for the much more difficult task of developing or testing an explanatory model, we may gain a better understanding of the situation if we study a number of variables simultaneously because dependent variables of interest are often influenced by many other variables.

In bivariate regression, our concern was estimating the parameters of the linear model

$$Y_i = \beta_0 + \beta_1 X_i + \varepsilon_i$$

Given our data sample, we found values of b_0 and b_1 that minimize the mean squared error obtained by using the prediction equation

$$\hat{Y}_i = b_0 + b_1 X_i$$

We can extend this discussion to multiple linear regression by considering models in which the dependent variable, Y, is expressed as a linear function of a number of predictor variables, X_1, X_2, X_3, . . ., X_p. Although the additional predictor variables result in more complexity and require the introduction of some new concepts, many of the basic ideas underlying bivariate and multiple regression are the same.

In multiple regression, if the population model is

$$Y_i = \beta_0 + \beta_1 X_{i1} + \beta_2 X_{i2} + \ldots + \beta_p X_{ip} + \varepsilon_i$$

we can estimate the βs by finding the values of b_0, b_1, b_2, . . ., b_p in the equation

$$\hat{Y}_i = b_0 + b_1 X_{i1} + b_2 X_{i2} + \ldots + b_p X_{ip}$$

that minimize $MSE = \dfrac{1}{N} \sum_i (Y_i - \hat{Y}_i)^2$ for the N data points in our sample.

In the next few chapters, we develop the basic ideas of multiple regression. Following the introduction in the current chapter, we go into more detail in Chapter 22 about inference, assumptions, and power calculations. In Chapter 23 we extend our discussion of some of the issues that complicate the use of multiple regression analysis to inform theory development and consider how to add and interpret curvilinear and interaction components. In Chapter 24, we show how to incorporate qualitative categorical variables into regression, thereby providing a powerful and flexible framework within which ANOVA and analysis of covariance (ANCOVA, Chapter 25) are special cases. In the current chapter, our goals are:

- *Introduce the basic terms and concepts of multiple regression.* We introduce some basic terms using an example with several predictor variables. We also illustrate the use of a statistical package (*SPSS*) to analyze the data and we explain the output.
- *Discuss the meaning of the regression coefficients and introduce some of their limitations in developing explanatory models.*
- *Discuss the partitioning of variance in multiple regression.*
- *Consider measures of fit.* Any regression equation developed from a sample will fit the sample better than it fits the population from which the sample was selected. Therefore, the multiple correlation coefficient, R, is positively biased. We discuss the use of cross-validation and adjustments to R in order to obtain more realistic measures of fit.
- *Introduce the concept of suppression.* Adding a predictor variable to a regression equation may improve prediction even if the added variable has little or no correlation with Y. This can occur if the added variable *suppresses* some of the extraneous variance in the predictors that are already in the equation.

21.2 AN EXAMPLE OF REGRESSION WITH SEVERAL PREDICTORS

In Chapter 20, we found that cholesterol level tends to increase with age in women. However, cholesterol level also changes systematically with other variables, such as weight. In the current section, we perform regressions involving total cholesterol level (*TC*), *age*, and body-mass index (*BMI*), which is defined as weight (in kilograms) divided by the square of height (in meters). In doing so, we use data from women in the *Seasons* study who were 20–65 years of age when they entered the study.

If we are interested in how *TC*, *BMI*, and *age* are related, the first step is, as always, to look at the data. Fig. 21.1 contains the scatterplot matrix for the three variables. The distribution of *BMI* scores is positively skewed and highly peaked, and from the descriptive statistics in panel (a) of Table 21.1, we find that both skewness and kurtosis are very large compared to their standard errors. The box plot for *BMI* scores in Fig. 21.1 indicates that there are outliers, and we can see these points clearly in the scatterplots. When we plot *TC* against *BMI* in Fig. 21.2 and apply a LOWESS smoother (see Chapter 18), it appears that the *BMI* outliers tend to have relatively low *TC* scores. Note from the box plot that *BMI* scores of 40 and above are outliers, and from the scatterplot we

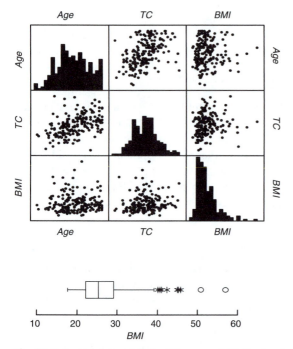

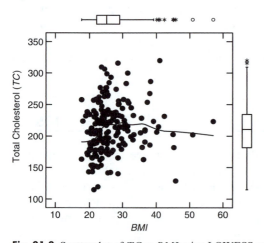

Fig. 21.1 Scatterplot matrix for *TC*, *age*, and *BMI* using data from all women 65 years of age or younger and box plot for *BMI*.

Fig. 21.2 Scatterplot of *TC* vs *BMI* using LOWESS smoothing for women 65 years of age or less.

see that these outliers introduce a strong curvilinear component to the relationship between *TC* and *BMI*. Because we are primarily concerned with describing the relationships among the variables for subjects who do not have extreme scores, we will exclude the data points of the nine subjects whose *BMI* scores were greater than 40. As can be seen in panel (b) of Table 21.1, when we exclude the outlying *BMI* scores, the ratios of the skewness and kurtosis measures to their standard errors are much smaller.

Table 21.1 Descriptive statistics for women aged 65 years or less

(a) For all cases with data on all three variables

Descriptive Statistics

	N	Minimum	Maximum	Mean	Std.	Skewness		Kurtosis	
	Statistic	Statistic	Statistic	Statistic	Statistic	Statistic	Std. Error	Statistic	Std. Error
Age	190	20.00	65.00	46.7421	10.59359	−.081	.176	−.735	.351
TC	190	114.88	320.00	211.6118	39.60712	.277	.176	−.010	.351
BMI	190	17.69	57.11	26.5991	6.30139	1.684	.176	3.906	.351
Valid N (listwise)	190								

(b) For cases with *BMI* of 40 or less

Descriptive Statistics

	N	Minimum	Maximum	Mean	Std.	Skewness		Kurtosis	
	Statistic	Statistic	Statistic	Statistic	Statistic	Statistic	Std. Error	Statistic	Std. Error
Age	181	20.00	65.00	46.9282	10.63016	−.116	.181	−.722	.359
TC	181	114.88	316.00	211.5801	39.17264	.239	.181	−.165	.359
BMI	181	17.69	39.12	25.6650	4.66999	.830	.181	.261	.359
Valid N (listwise)	181								

Information about the correlations among *TC*, *age*, and *BMI* is presented in Table 21.2, which contains SPSS output for the 181 women aged 20–65 years with *BMI*s of 40 or less who have scores on all three measures. The significant correlations of *TC* with both *age*, $r = .492$, $p = .000$, and with *BMI*, $r = .231$, $p = .002$, suggest that we might be able to predict *TC* better using information about both *age* and *BMI* than by using information about only one of these measures.

Tables 21.3, 21.4, and 21.5 contain the SPSS outputs for the regressions of *TC* (Y) on *age* (X_1), on *BMI* (X_2), and on both *age* and *BMI*, respectively. Let's consider the outputs for these three regressions.

Looking at the B columns of the coefficients panels in Tables 21.3 and 21.4, we can see that the regressions of *TC* on *age* and on *BMI* yield the equations

$$\hat{Y} = 126.531 + 1.812X_1 \tag{21.1}$$

and

$$\hat{Y} = 161.944 + 1.934X_2 \tag{21.2}$$

In Equation 21.1, the slope of 1.812 indicates that each 1-year increase in age is associated with an increase of 1.812 units in predicted *TC*. In Equation 21.2, we see that a one-unit increase in *BMI* is associated with an increase of 1.934 units in predicted *TC*.

Now consider the SPSS output for the regression of *TC* on both *age* and *BMI* in Table 21.5:

1. The B column in the coefficients panel provides the least-squares estimates of the *Y* intercept (b_0) and the *unstandardized regression coefficients* (or *unstandardized partial slope*

Table 21.2   Pearson correlation matrix for *TC*, *age*, and *BMI* for women aged 65 years or less with *BMI* less than or equal to 40

Correlations

		TC	Age	BMI
TC	**Pearson Correlation**	1	.492**	.231**
	Sig. (2-tailed)		.000	.002
	N	181	181	181
Age	**Pearson Correlation**	.492**	1	.116
	Sig. (2-tailed)	.000		.119
	N	181	181	181
BMI	**Pearson Correlation**	.231**	.116	1
	Sig. (2-tailed)	.002	.119	
	N	181	181	181

**. Correlation is significant at the .01 level (2-tailed).

coefficients) for X_1 and X_2, b_1 and b_2. These entries tell us that the best least-squares regression equation that includes both *age* and *BMI* as predictors is

$$\hat{Y} = 92.239 + 1.737X_1 + 1.474X_2 \tag{21.3}$$

The plot of Equation 21.3 is displayed in Fig. 21.3, along with the data points. Instead of the regression *line* that we obtained using bivariate regression, we now have a three-dimensional regression *plane*. If *BMI* is held constant, a one-unit (i.e., 1-year) change in *age* corresponds to an increase of 1.737 units in predicted *TC*. Similarly, if *age* is held constant, a one-unit change in *BMI* corresponds to an increase of 1.474 units in predicted *TC*.

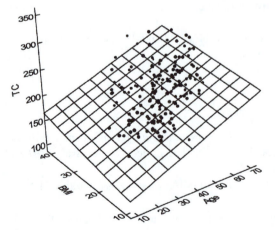

Fig. 21.3 Plane for the regression of total cholesterol level (*TC*) on *age* and *BMI*.

Table 21.3 SPSS output for regression of *TC* on *age* for women aged 65 years or less with *BMI* ≤ 40

Model Summary

Model	R	R Square	Adjusted R Square	Std. Error of the Estimate
1	.492[a]	.242	.238	34.20293

a. Predictors: (Constant), *age*

ANOVA[b]

Model		Sum of Squares	df	Mean Square	F	Sig.
1	Regression	66807.777	1	66807.777	57.108	.000[a]
	Residual	209401.4	179	1169.840		
	Total	276209.2	180			

a. Predictors: (Constant), *age*
b. Dependent Variable: *TC*

Coefficients[a]

Model		Unstandardized Coefficients		Standardized Coefficients	t	Sig.	95% Confidence Interval for B	
		B	Std. Error	Beta			Lower Bound	Upper Bound
1	(Constant)	126.531	11.538		10.967	.000	103.763	149.299
	Age	1.812	0.240	.492	7.557	.000	1.339	2.286

a. Dependent Variable: *TC*

2. The *Standardized Coefficient* (*Beta*) column of the coefficients panel contains the values of the regression coefficients that would result if the regression was performed with *z* scores.

3. In the model summary panel we see that the *multiple correlation coefficient*, *R*, is .522. This means that the *TC* values predicted by Equation 21.3 have a correlation of .522 with the actual *TC* values in the sample. The squared multiple correlation coefficient, *R square*, is sometimes called the *coefficient of multiple determination*. Here, its value is $.522^2 = .272$, so we may conclude that 27.2% of the variance in *TC* is "accounted for" by the regression on *age* and *BMI*. This means that by using the regression equation to predict the *Y* scores, the variability in the *Y* scores that is unaccounted for is reduced by the proportion .272. To be more specific, the residual variability that remains when the regression equation is used to predict the *Y* scores is $1 - .272 = .728$ of the residual variability that would result if $\bar{Y}$ was used to predict each of the *Y* scores. The *adjusted R square* is .264. The sample multiple correlation coefficient is a positively biased estimator of the population coefficient. The adjusted *R* results from one type of attempt to remove the positive bias (see Section 21.4).

4. Also, in the model summary panel, we see that the *standard error of estimate* is 33.603. As

Table 21.4   SPSS output for regression of *TC* on *BMI* for women aged 65 years or less with *BMI* ≤ 40

Model Summary

Model	R	R Square	Adjusted R Square	Std. Error of the Estimate
1	.231[a]	.053	.048	38.22356

a. Predictors: (Constant), *BMI*

ANOVA[b]

Model		Sum of Squares	df	Mean Square	F	Sig.
1	Regression	14682.972	1	14682.972	10.050	.002[a]
	Residual	261526.2	179	1461.040		
	Total	276209.2	180			

a. Predictors: (Constant), *BMI*
b. Dependent Variable: *TC*

Coefficients[a]

Model		Unstandardized Coefficients		Standardized Coefficients	t	Sig.	95% Confidence Interval for B	
		B	Std. Error	Beta			Lower Bound	Upper Bound
1	(Constant)	161.944	15.913		10.177	.000	130.543	193.346
	BMI	1.934	.610	.231	3.170	.002	.730	3.138

a. Dependent Variable: *TC*

with bivariate regression, the standard error provides a measure of how well the regression equation predicts cholesterol level. The equation provides a prediction, $\hat{Y}$, for each combination of X_1 and X_2. The standard error of estimate,[1] s_e, is the square root of the sum of the squared deviations of the actual cholesterol levels from the predicted levels, divided by the df, so that

$$s_e = \sqrt{\frac{\Sigma(Y_i - \hat{Y}_i)^2}{df}} = \sqrt{\frac{SS_{residual}}{df_{residual}}}$$

For the general case in which Y is regressed on p predictor variables, it can be expressed as

$$s_e = \sqrt{\frac{(1 - R^2_{Y.12\ldots p})SS_Y}{N - 1 - p}} \tag{21.4}$$

---

[1] A common notation is to use $s_{Y.12}$ to refer to the standard error of estimate when Y is regressed on X_1 and X_2, and $s_{Y.123}$ when Y is regressed on X_1, X_2, and X_3. We will use s_e when it is clear from the context what predictor variables are in the equation.

Table 21.5   SPSS output for regression of *TC* on *age* and *BMI* for women aged 65 years or less with *BMI* ≤ 40

Model Summary[b]

Model	R	R Square	Adjusted R Square	Std. Error of the Estimate	Durbin-Watson
1	.522[a]	.272	.264	33.60285	2.055

a. Predictors: (Constant), BMI, age
b. Dependent Variable: TC

ANOVA[b]

Model		Sum of Squares	df	Mean Square	F	Sig.
1	Regression	75220.300	2	37610.150	33.308	.000[a]
	Residual	200988.9	178	1129.151		
	Total	276209.2	180			

a. Predictors: (Constant), BMI, age
b. Dependent Variable: TC

Coefficients[a]

Model		Unstandardized Coefficients B	Std. Error	Standardized Coefficients Beta	t	Sig.	95% Confidence Interval for B Lower Bound	Upper Bound	Collinearity Statistics Tolerance	VIF
1	(Constant)	92.239	16.921		5.451	.000	58.846	125.631		
	Age	1.737	.237	.471	7.322	.000	1.269	2.205	.986	1.014
	BMI	1.474	.540	.176	2.730	.007	.408	2.540	.986	1.014

a. Dependent Variable: TC

Collinearity Diagnostics[a]

Model	Dimension	Eigenvalue	Condition Index	Variance Proportions (Constant)	Age	BMI
1	1	2.949	1.000	.00	.01	.00
	2	.037	8.954	.02	.79	.31
	3	.014	14.476	.98	.20	.69

a. Dependent Variable: TC

If the underlying model for the population is $Y_i = \beta_0 + \beta_1 X_1 + \beta_2 X_2 + \ldots + \beta_p X_p + \varepsilon_i$, the standard error of estimate provides an estimate of the standard deviation of ε.

5. The ANOVA table tells us that the total sum of squares associated with cholesterol scores is 276,209.2, and that it can be partitioned into two components: the sum of squares accounted for by the regression, $SS_{regression}$, and the sum of squares left unaccounted for, $SS_{residual}$, where

$$SS_{regression} = \Sigma(\hat{Y}_i - \overline{Y})^2 = R^2 SS_Y = 75,220.300$$

and

$$SS_{residual} = \Sigma(Y_i - \hat{Y}_i)^2 = (1 - R^2)SS_Y = 200,988.9$$

6. For each coefficient, a t statistic is formed by dividing b by its standard error. This tests the null hypothesis that the corresponding β is equal to 0. The t of 7.322 (with $p = .000$) for *age* indicates that when *BMI* is held constant, the rate of change of predicted *TC* with *age* is significantly different from zero. That is, there is a significant contribution of *age* to the predictability of *TC* over and above that provided by *BMI*. The t of 2.730 (with $p = .007$) for *BMI* indicates that there is a significant rate of change of predicted *TC* with *BMI* when *age* is held constant; that is, there is a significant contribution of *BMI* to the predictability of *TC* over and above that provided by *age*. The significant t for b_0, the constant (i.e., intercept) of the regression equation, indicates that we can reject the null hypothesis that $\beta_0 = 0$ in the population. We requested *confidence intervals*, so the coefficients panel contains the upper and lower bounds of the intervals for each coefficient. Even with a fairly large sample, the confidence intervals are quite wide. For example, the 95% confidence interval for the partial slope of predicted *TC* with *BMI* extends from 0.408 to 2.540.

7. We also requested *collinearity statistics*, measures that indicate the extent to which the predictor variables are correlated among themselves. As we shall see in Chapter 23, high correlations among the predictors, or *multicollinearity*, can present difficulties for multiple regression analysis and for the interpretation of the regression coefficients. Two useful measures are presented on the right side of the coefficients panel, the *tolerance* and the *variance inflation factor* (*VIF*). The tolerance is a measure of how *nonredundant* a predictor is with the other predictor variables. With only two predictor variables, the tolerance is 1 minus the square of the correlation between the two predictors. In general,

tolerance of the jth predictor variable $= 1 - R_{j.}^2$

where $R_{j.}^2$ is the square of the multiple correlation when X_j is regressed on all the other predictor variables in the equation. In other words, the tolerance is a measure of how well X_j can be predicted by the other predictor variable(s) in the equation.

The standard error of the coefficient of the jth predictor variable can be shown to be a function of its tolerance:

$$SE(b_j) = \frac{s_e}{\sqrt{SS_j}}\sqrt{\frac{1}{1 - R_{j.}^2}} = \frac{s_e}{\sqrt{SS_j}}\sqrt{\frac{1}{\textit{tolerance of } X_j}} \tag{21.5}$$

where s_e is the standard error of estimate defined earlier in this section, and

$$SS_j = \sum_i (X_{ij} - \overline{X}_j)^2$$

is the sum of squares of the jth predictor. The ratio under the right-most square root sign, 1 divided by the tolerance of X_j, is known as the *variance inflation factor* (*VIF*) for the predictor, which is also presented in the SPSS output. From Equation 21.5, we can see that as the tolerance of X_j decreases, the corresponding *VIF* increases, and consequently, so does the estimated *SE*. If the predictor X_j has a tolerance of 0 (i.e., if $R_{j.}^2 = 1$), this means that X_j can be perfectly predicted by a linear combination of the other predictors in the regression equation, and is therefore completely redundant. As a consequence, if any of the predictors has a tolerance of zero, we cannot obtain least-squares estimates of the regression coefficients because the set of equations that must be solved to find the b_js does not have a unique solution. In general, a t test of the regression coefficient b_j will have less power as the tolerance becomes smaller. This makes sense, because the more X_j is redundant with the other predictors, the less new information it provides, and the less we can expect it to increase the predictability of Y. Most statistical packages allow us to set a minimum tolerance below which a predictor will not be added to the regression equation. In the current analysis, the tolerance for both *age* and *BMI* is .986 and the *VIF* is 1.014, reflecting the fact that the correlation between *age* and *BMI* is small. The collinearity diagnostics panel contains additional measures that are useful for determining whether the degree of redundancy among the predictors is serious enough to present a problem for the regression. We discuss these measures further in Chapter 23.

21.3 THE MEANING OF THE REGRESSION COEFFICIENTS

In terms of the sample regression equation, the interpretation of the unstandardized regression coefficients is straightforward.[2] Consider the regression equation

$$\hat{Y} = b_0 + b_1 X_1 + b_2 X_2 \tag{21.6}$$

1. The intercept, b_0, is the value of $\hat{Y}$ when both X_1 and X_2 are equal to 0.
2. The regression coefficient b_1 is the rate of change of $\hat{Y}$ with X_1, *holding X_2 constant*. That is, if X_1 is increased by one unit and X_2 remains unchanged, the corresponding change in $\hat{Y}$ is b_1. The regression coefficient b_2 is the rate of change of $\hat{Y}$ with X_2, *holding X_1 constant*.

Unfortunately, what these coefficients say about the true model for the population is usually much less clear. When a regression equation does a good job predicting the dependent variable, it is tempting to use the equation not only to predict but also as an explanatory model—or at least to think of the regression coefficients in the equation as measures of the "importance" of the corresponding Xs in *influencing* (i.e., *causing* changes in) Y. However, unless the data come from a true experiment or we have a great deal of existing theory and detailed knowledge about how the data were generated, this temptation should be resisted. Although we consider the relationships between regression and explanatory models in more detail in Chapter 23, here we introduce some limitations that we must keep in mind when we are tempted to use regression equations as explanatory models and regression coefficients as measures of causal importance.

- *Regression deals with prediction, not causality*. We would expect that if changing X_1 causes important changes in Y, then X_1 should be a useful predictor of Y if we include it in a regression analysis. *However, the reverse is not necessarily true; a variable that is a very useful predictor may have no causal importance whatsoever*. The variable may be a good predictor and have a large regression coefficient because it happens to be correlated with other variables that are causally important but are not included in the equation. We should remember that X_1 may predict Y for a number of reasons, including the following:

  1. Some other variable (or variables) may influence both X_1 and Y. For example, shoe size

---

[2] Here, we focus on unstandardized regression coefficients. In Chapter 23 we consider in detail the reasons we generally prefer unstandardized to standardized regression coefficients.

is a good predictor of verbal ability in elementary school because both shoe size and verbal ability increase with age. As another example, the number of nonfiction books in a home is a good predictor of a child's success in elementary school even if the child never reads the books. The number of books is a good indicator of the family's affluence, intelligence, and level of education, and these variables do influence school performance.

2. Changes in Y may cause changes in X_1. An article in the journal *Circulation* reported that the use of diet soda drinks predicts the presence of metabolic syndrome (a constellation of metabolic risk factors likely due to insulin resistance). However, it is at least as plausible that individuals who develop symptoms of metabolic syndrome turn to diet foods as it is that the use of diet soda is one of the causes of metabolic syndrome.

3. Even if X_1 does have some causal influence on Y, the influence could be direct or indirect (or both). An indirect effect would occur if changes in X_1 caused changes in a third variable, X_2, and these changes in X_2 caused changes in Y. In this case we would call X_2 a *mediating variable*. A measure of the causal importance of a variable should consider both its direct and indirect effects. We discuss mediation in Chapter 23.

- *In observational studies, the true population model is almost certainly different from the regression equation we have developed.* Suppose the true model for the population is

$$Y = \beta_0 + \beta_1 X_1 + \beta_2 X_2 + \varepsilon \tag{21.7}$$

in which the error component, ε, refers to random error. If the usual regression assumptions are satisfied (see Chapter 22), the sample coefficients b_0, b_1, and b_2 in Equation 21.6 will be unbiased estimators of the corresponding population parameters in Equation 21.7. However, just because we perform a regression that predicts the Y scores in our sample fairly well does not necessarily mean that we have uncovered the correct population model.

One reason is that different data sets, possibly arising from different populations, can give rise to similar sample regression statistics. For example, we discussed the *Anscombe* data sets in Chapter 18 (see Fig. 18.9) in which identical bivariate regression statistics were obtained from four very different data sets. With more predictor variables, there is far more potential for different kinds of data structures to produce similar regression equations, as well as for different combinations of predictors to account for similar amounts of variance.

Also, as we discuss further in Chapter 23, we often work with relatively simple models that contain important variables as predictors. These models are often extremely useful for focusing our thinking and developing further research, but will rarely include all of the possible relevant predictor variables. As an example, consider the research question of how student performance is influenced by reductions in class size. This research is largely inconclusive because so many variables other than class size influence student performance—examples of relevant variables include characteristics of the student, family background, and school, as well as teaching style and course content (see Exercise 23.8).

These extraneous variables may not present a severe problem if we can conduct a true *experiment* in which variables of interest are manipulated and we use randomization and matching to control other variables. If so, a model such as that expressed in Equation 21.7 may be reasonable. The error component, ε, contains the effects of variables other than those that are manipulated, but these other variables are not systematically related to the manipulated variables.

However, suppose the data come from an *observational study* in which the variables of interest are systematically related to other important variables (for example, smaller classes are more likely to occur in more affluent school districts with better educated, more supportive parents and better-paid teachers). Unless these other variables are included in the model, ε is not really a random error component and may be correlated with the variables in the model. If important variables are omitted from the model, the b_js in Equation 21.6 will generally be biased estimators of the βs in Equation 21.7.

When important variables are left out of the regression equation, the regression coefficients of variables in the equation may, in part, reflect the effects of these omitted variables. We consider this point further in the next section.

- *Both the values and the interpretations of the regression coefficients may change when other predictor variables are added to or removed from the regression equation.* Consider the following regression equations in which Y is predicted by one, two, or three predictor variables:

$$\hat{Y} = b_{Y0.1} + b_{Y1}X_1 \tag{21.8}$$

$$\hat{Y} = b_{Y0.12} + b_{Y1.2}X_1 + b_{Y2.1}X_2 \tag{21.9}$$

and

$$\hat{Y} = b_{Y0.123} + b_{Y1.23}X_1 + b_{Y2.13}X_2 + b_{Y3.12}X_3 \tag{21.10}$$

Here, we use more elaborate subscripts on the regression coefficients to specify the predictor variables in the different regression equations. For example, $b_{Y0.12}$ is the intercept for the regression equation in which Y is regressed on both X_1 and X_2, and $b_{Y1.23}$ is the coefficient of X_1 in a regression equation in which Y is regressed on X_1, X_2, and X_3.

Unless the three predictor variables are uncorrelated, the coefficients of X_1 in the three equations, b_{Y1}, $b_{Y1.2}$, and $b_{Y1.23}$, will not have the same values. We have already seen this in our analyses of the cholesterol data summarized in Equations 21.1–21.3. The coefficient b_{Y1} represents the rate of change of $\hat{Y}$ with X_1; the coefficient $b_{Y1.2}$ represents the rate of change of $\hat{Y}$ with X_1 if X_2 is held constant; and the coefficient $b_{Y1.23}$ represents the rate of change of $\hat{Y}$ with X_1 if both X_2 and X_3 are held constant.

This "holding constant" of the other variables is represented explicitly in the expressions for the regression coefficients. For example, $b_{Y1} = r_{Y1}s_Y/s_1$ whereas

$$b_{Y1.2} = \left[\frac{r_{Y1} - r_{Y2}r_{12}}{1 - r_{12}^2} \right] \frac{s_Y}{s_1} = r_{Y1|2} \frac{s_{Y.2}}{s_{1.2}} \tag{21.11}$$

where $r_{Y1|2}$ is the partial correlation of Y and X_1 with the effects of X_2 partialed out, $s_{Y.2}$ is the standard error of estimate when Y is regressed on X_2, and $s_{1.2}$ is the standard error of estimate when X_1 is regressed on X_2. Although the expressions for b_{Y1} and $b_{Y1.2}$ are parallel in form, the terms in the equation for $b_{Y1.2}$ are all adjusted for X_2. Note that if $r_{12} = 0$, then $b_{Y1} = b_{Y1.2}$.

What the bs in Equations 21.8–21.10 have to say about the underlying model is complicated by the fact that we usually do not know the true model for the population. If X_1 and X_2 are correlated, the coefficient b_{Y1} will represent the rate of change of $\hat{Y}$ with X_1 in the sample, but it may not necessarily be a good estimator of how Y changes with X_1 in the population when X_2 is held constant. This is because if X_2 is left out of the regression equation, b_{Y1} will generally reflect the effects of *both* X_1 and X_2. If X_2 is now added to the equation, we obtain a coefficient of X_1 that represents the rate of change in $\hat{Y}$ with X_1 if X_2 is held constant.

To make this point more concrete, consider another example. Suppose we want to predict final exam performance in an introductory statistics course on the basis of two pretests: say that (1) pretest 1 measures algebra skills, (2) pretest 2 measures abstract mathematical reasoning skills, (3) people with better algebra skills also tend to have better abstract reasoning skills, and (4) performance on the final exam depends on both kinds of skills. If we regressed the final exam score only on algebra skills, we would be mistaken if we interpreted the regression coefficient as the measure of the importance of algebra skills in *influencing* the grade on the final.[3] The change in the predicted final exam score associated with a one-unit difference on pretest 1 reflects both the difference in algebra skills *and the associated difference in abstract reasoning skills*. However, if we regressed final exam score on both pretests, the coefficient of the pretest 1 variable would no longer reflect the predictive ability of abstract reasoning skills. In this case, the pretest 1 score coefficient would represent the rate of change of the predicted score on the final with algebra skills, *holding abstract mathematical reasoning skills constant*.

21.4 THE PARTITIONING OF VARIABILITY IN MULTIPLE REGRESSION

21.4.1 The Multiple Correlation Coefficient

In Chapter 18, we defined the correlation coefficient, r, as a measure of the degree of linear relationship between Y and X and introduced the coefficient of determination, r^2, as the proportion of the variability in one of the variables "accounted for" by the regression on the other. Both of these concepts have parallels when we investigate the relationship between a criterion variable, Y, and a collection of predictors, $X_1, X_2, X_3, \ldots, X_p$.

We define the multiple correlation coefficient, $R_{Y.123\ldots p}$, as the correlation between Y and $\hat{Y}$, where

$$\hat{Y}_i = b_0 + b_1 X_{i1} + b_2 X_{i2} + \ldots + b_p X_{ip}$$

is the prediction of Y obtained from the multiple regression equation that contains the p predictors. If Y is perfectly predicted by the multiple regression equation, then $R = 1$. If the multiple regression equation predicts no better than the equation $Y = \overline{Y}$, then $R = 0$. When there is a single predictor variable, X, the multiple correlation coefficient reduces to $R_{Y.X} = |r_{XY}|$, the absolute value of the bivariate correlation coefficient. Although the limits for r are ± 1, R can vary only between 0 and 1.

The proportion of the variability in Y accounted for by the regression on p predictor variables is $r^2_{Y\hat{Y}} = R^2_{Y.12\ldots p}$. Therefore, we can write

$$R^2_{Y.12\ldots p} = \frac{SS_{regression}}{SS_Y}$$

where $SS_{regression} = \sum_i (\hat{Y}_i - \overline{Y})^2$ is the amount of variability in Y accounted for by the regression.

---

[3] It would, however, be appropriate to interpret the regression coefficient as a measure of the importance of algebra skills as a *predictor* of final exam performance.

21.4.2 Partitioning SS_Y into $SS_{regression}$ and $SS_{residual}$

As was the case with bivariate regression, the variability of Y can be partitioned into a component accounted for by the regression, $SS_{regression}$, and a component not accounted for by the regression, $SS_{residual}$:

$$\Sigma(Y_i - \bar{Y})^2 = \Sigma(\hat{Y}_i - \bar{Y})^2 + \Sigma(Y_i - \hat{Y}_i)^2$$

$$SS_Y \quad = \quad SS_{regression} \quad + \quad SS_{residual}$$

where $SS_{regression} = R^2 SS_Y$ and $SS_{residual} = (1 - R^2)SS_Y$. It is convenient to express the partitioning of variability in an ANOVA table of the form of Table 21.6. SS_Y is associated with $N - 1$ df because one df is used to estimate the population mean. Of these $N - 1$ df, p are associated with the regression sum of squares because coefficients for each of the p predictors must be estimated. The remaining $N - 1 - p$ df are associated with the residual SS. Note that when there is only one predictor, $N - 1 - p = N - 2$, the result presented for bivariate regression.

Under standard assumptions that will be discussed in Chapter 22, if the p population regression coefficients $\beta_1, \beta_2, \ldots, \beta_p$ are all 0, the ratio

$$\frac{MS_{regression}}{MS_{residual}} = \frac{R^2 SS_Y/p}{(1 - R^2)SS_Y/(N - 1 - p)} = \frac{R^2/p}{(1 - R^2)/(N - 1 - p)} \tag{21.12}$$

will be distributed as F with p and $N - 1 - p$ df. Therefore, the ratio of mean squares tests the null hypothesis that $\beta_1 = \beta_2 = \ldots = \beta_p = 0$. In the current example, when we regressed TC on both *age* and *BMI* score (so that $p = 2$), we found $R = .522$. Substituting the square of this value into Equation 21.8, and replacing SS_Y by the total sum of squares in Table 21.6, we have

$$F = \frac{MS_{regression}}{MS_{residual}} = \frac{75,220/2}{200,989/(181 - 1 - 2)} = 33.308$$

Note that the numerator and denominator sums of squares are, within rounding error, the same as the values in the SPSS output of Table 21.5, and therefore the Fs are the same. The large F value provides the basis for rejecting the hypothesis that the population regression coefficients for both *age* and *BMI* are zero.

Table 21.6 ANOVA table for multiple regression

SV	df	SS	MS	F
Regression	p	$\Sigma(\hat{Y} - \bar{Y})^2$ or $R^2_{Y.1\ldots p}SS_Y$	$\dfrac{R^2_{Y.1\ldots p}SS_Y}{p}$	$\dfrac{MS_{reg}}{MS_{residual}}$
Residual	$N - 1 - p$	$\Sigma(Y_i - \hat{Y}_i)^2$ or $(1 - R^2_{Y.1\ldots p})SS_Y$	$\dfrac{(1 - R^2_{Y.1\ldots p})SS_Y}{N - 1 - p}$	
Total	$N - 1$	$SS_Y = \Sigma(Y_i - \bar{Y})^2$		

$MS_{residual}$ is the square of the standard error of estimate provided in the SPSS output. If all important systematic sources of variability are included in the regression equation so that the residual variability is due only to random error, $MS_{residual}$ estimates the random error variance, σ_e^2. If important sources of variability are omitted from the equation, $MS_{residual}$ will reflect these sources as well as random error, resulting in a biased F test.

21.4.3 Partitioning $SS_{regression}$

If the p predictor variables in a multiple regression are mutually uncorrelated, $SS_{regression}$ can be partitioned into nonoverlapping components associated with each of the predictors. Panel (a) of Fig. 21.4 represents this situation: X_1 and X_2 overlap with Y but not with each other, indicating that the variability in Y collectively accounted for by X_1 and X_2 is the sum of variabilities accounted for separately by X_1 and by X_2. In this situation,

$$SS_{regression} = SS_{Y.1} + SS_{Y.2}$$

where $SS_{Y.j} = r_{Yj}^2 SS_Y$ and r_{Yj} is the correlation between Y and X_j. Because for two predictors, $SS_{regression} = R_{Y.12}^2 SS_Y$, it follows that when the predictors are uncorrelated,

$$R_{Y.12}^2 = r_{Y1}^2 + r_{Y2}^2 = \sum_j r_{Yj}^2$$

More generally, if p predictors account for the nonerror variability in Y, and are mutually uncorrelated,

$$SS_{regression} = SS_{Y.1} + SS_{Y.2} + \ldots + SS_{Y.p}$$

and

$$R_{Y.12\ldots p}^2 = r_{Y1}^2 + r_{Y2}^2 + \ldots + r_{Yp}^2 = \sum_j r_{Yj}^2$$

In words, when the predictors are uncorrelated with one another, the proportion of the variability of Y they collectively account for is the sum of the proportions of variability accounted for by the individual predictors.

However, unless we have a true experiment, predictor variables are almost always correlated with one another. The predictors usually share variability, as in panel (b) of Fig. 21.4, where the correlation between X_1 and X_2 is indicated by the overlap of their circles. Note that if we add the overlap of Y with X_1 to the overlap of Y with X_2, the b area is added in twice. When any of p predictors are correlated, the proportion of variability in Y they account for is not the sum of the proportions associated with the individual predictors, but must be adjusted for overlapping variability.

An expression for R^2 that takes the correlations between predictors into account is

$$R_{Y.12\ldots p}^2 = \frac{\Sigma r_{Yj} b_j s_j}{s_Y} = \Sigma r_{Yj} b_j^* \tag{21.13}$$

where b_j is the unstandardized regression coefficient of X_j in the multiple regression equation; s_j and s_Y are the standard deviations of X_j and Y, respectively; and b_j^* is the standardized regression

(a)

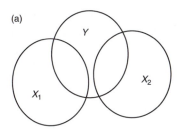

(b)

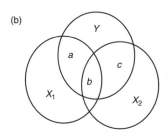

$R^2_{Y.1} = a + b$

$R^2_{Y.2} = b + c$ $\qquad\qquad$ $r^2_{Y(2|1)} = c$

$R^2_{Y.12} = a + b + c$ $\qquad$ $r^2_{Y(1|2)} = a$

Fig. 21.4 Representations of variability in the criterion variable, Y, accounted for by uncorrelated and correlated predictor variables. (a) Uncorrelated predictors: Variabilities accounted for by X_1 and X_2 do not overlap so that $R^2_{Y.12} = r^2_{Y1} + r^2_{Y2}$ (b) Correlated predictors: Variabilities accounted for by X_1 and X_2 overlap so that $R^2_{Y.12}$ is not the sum of the r^2_{Yj} s.

coefficient of X_j. For example, when TC (Y) was regressed on *age* (X_1) and *BMI* (X_2), we obtained the following results:

	TC	Age	BMI
b_j		1.737	1.474
r_{Y_j}		0.492	0.231
s_j	39.173	10.630	4.670

so that, substituting in Equation 21.12, we have

$$R^2 = [(0.492)(1.737)(10.630) + (0.231)(1.474)(4.670)]/39.173 = 0.272$$

the same value as that displayed in the SPSS output in Table 21.5. In the current example, the sum of the r^2 values for the correlations between TC and *age* and between TC and *BMI*, 0.295, is not very different from the value of 0.272 obtained above, because the correlation between *age* and *BMI* is small.

The increase in R^2 when X_2 is added to a regression equation that already contains X_1 is $r^2_{Y(2|1)}$, the square of the semipartial correlation coefficient introduced in Chapter 19. As we mentioned there, $r_{Y(2|1)}$ is the correlation of Y with the component of X_2 that is not predictable from X_1. In terms of panel (b) of Fig. 21.4, we may think of $r^2_{Y(2|1)}$ as the proportion of the Y circle that overlaps X_2 but not X_1. In general, the squared semipartial correlation coefficient $r^2_{Y(p+1|12...p)}$ is the increase in R^2 that follows from adding a $(p+1)^{st}$ predictor to a regression equation that already contains p predictors. That is,

$$r^2_{Y(p+1|12...p)} = R^2_{Y.12...p+1} - R^2_{Y.12...p} \tag{21.14}$$

In Equation 21.14, $r_{Y(p+1|12...p)}$ is the correlation between Y and $X_{p+1}|X_1, X_2, ..., X_p$, where the latter term represents the residuals of the regression of X_{p+1} on $X_1, X_2, ..., X_p$. Applying Equation 21.13 to the TC data, when age is added to a regression equation that already contains BMI as a predictor, the proportion of the variance of TC accounted for is increased by .219. If BMI is added to an equation when age is already included as a predictor, the increase is .030. Note that because age and BMI are somewhat correlated and therefore account for overlapping variability in TC, these increases are smaller than the proportions of variance accounted for by age and BMI when each is the only predictor in the equation. In Chapter 22, we discuss "partial F tests" that allow us to test whether the addition of one or more variables significantly increases the variability accounted for by a regression equation.

21.4.4 The Adjusted (or Shrunken) Multiple Correlation Coefficient and Cross-Validation

When a multiple regression equation is developed from a sample of data, the multiple correlation coefficient R and its square are commonly used indices of how well the equation fits the data in the sample. These measures are also often used as estimates of how the regression equation fits the population from which the sample was obtained. However, using R or R^2 as measures of fit can be misleading because R is a *positively biased* estimator of the population coefficient. Because of chance variability, a regression equation obtained from a sample always describes the sample better than the population from which the sample was drawn. Particularly if the sample is small and there are a large number of predictors, a regression equation that predicts well in the sample may predict poorly in the population.

With enough predictors, the regression equation *must* fit the sample well no matter how the predictors and the criterion are related in the population. Just as any two data points can be fit by a straight line, any $p + 1$ data points can be fit perfectly by a linear regression equation with p predictor variables—as long as none of the p predictors can be perfectly predicted by the remaining $p - 1$ predictors—and therefore, the resulting value of the sample R must be 1. With more than $p + 1$ data points, the R in the sample need not be 1, but will tend to be larger than R in the population as long as the N/p ratio (number of cases divided by the number of predictor variables) is small because of *capitalization on chance*; that is, because the regression equation takes advantage of chance fluctuations in scores that allow for increased predictability in the sample but not in the population. The bias in R can be reduced by working with larger samples. How large should samples be? Although the recommended sample size depends to some extent on the nature of the research problem and the purpose of the analysis, the N/p ratio should be large—perhaps 30 or more—if the size of R is to be taken very seriously.

A common adjustment for positive bias has been provided by Wherry (1931). The proportion of variance in the population that can be accounted for by the relationship between Y and a set of X_js is denoted by ρ^2_{XY}, which can be expressed as

$$\rho^2_{XY} = 1 - \frac{\sigma^2_e}{\sigma^2_Y}$$

If we replace the population variances by their unbiased estimates, we have

$$R^2_{adjusted} = 1 - \frac{SS_{residual} / (N - 1 - p)}{SS_Y / (N - 1)}$$

which can be rewritten as

$$R^2_{adjusted} = 1 - \left(\frac{SS_{residual}}{SS_Y}\right)\left(\frac{N - 1}{N - 1 - p}\right)$$

But $SS_{residual} / SS_Y = 1 - R^2$. Therefore, substituting into the last equation, we have Wherry's formula,

$$R^2_{adjusted} = 1 - (1 - R^2)\left[\frac{N - 1}{N - 1 - p}\right] \tag{21.15}$$

The adjusted (or "shrunken") squared multiple correlation coefficient is provided in the regression output of most statistical packages. For the regression of *TC* on *age* and *BMI*, Equation 21.15 yields an adjusted R^2 of $1 - (1 - .272)(180/178) = .264$, the same value, within rounding error, that is provided by the SPSS output in Table 21.5. Note that if we set the adjusted R^2 equal to zero and solve Equation 21.12 for R^2, we get

$$R^2 = \frac{p}{N - 1}$$

This gives the value of R^2 for which the adjusted R^2 will be 0. Using this equation, we can see that if we have 10 predictors and 50 cases, an R^2 value of .204 (or multiple R of .452) would correspond to an adjusted R of 0.

If our interest is prediction, the Wherry adjustment may not be ideal because we are less interested in how a regression equation fits the population than in how well the equation fits *another sample* drawn from the same population. Herzberg (1969; see the discussion in Stevens, 1986) gives two adjustment equations that attempt to estimate R^2 if we want to use the regression equation developed in sample 1 to make predictions for the data of sample 2. If the predictors are random variables, as is usual in non-experimental research, the adjustment equation is

$$R^2_{adj\ RP} = 1 - \left(\frac{N - 1}{N - p - 1}\right)\left(\frac{N - 2}{N - p - 2}\right)\left(\frac{N + 1}{N}\right)(1 - R^2) \tag{21.16}$$

If the predictors are fixed, the adjustment equation is

$$R^2_{adj\ FP} = 1 - \left(\frac{N - 1}{N}\right)\left(\frac{N + p + 1}{N - p - 1}\right)(1 - R^2) \tag{21.17}$$

The shrinkage is greater if we use the Herzberg equations instead of the Wherry equation. For example, given a sample of size 100 with 10 predictors and an R^2 of .50, $R^2_{adjusted} = .444$, whereas $R^2_{adj\ RP} = .374$ and $R^2_{adj\ FP} = .383$. In our current example, because of the high N/p ratio, there is not much shrinkage: $N = 181$, $p = 2$, and $R^2 = .272$, so that $R^2_{adjusted} = .264$ and $R^2_{adj\ FP} = .252$.

The best way of obtaining a more realistic estimate of the population R is to employ a procedure called *cross-validation* that avoids capitalizing on chance by developing the regression equation using one sample (called the screening sample) and testing it by a second sample (called the calibration sample). The cross-validated R is the correlation between (1) the predicted Y scores obtained when the regression equation developed in the screening sample is applied to the calibration sample and (2) the actual Y scores in the calibration sample. Because the regression coefficients are obtained from one sample and the value of R is obtained from a second sample, the cross-validated R cannot systematically capitalize on sampling variability.

The problem of capitalization on chance is most insidious when the variables used in the regression equation are chosen from a larger pool of possible predictors—a very common situation. Variables in the pool that are useful for predicting in the sample will be those chosen to be added to the regression equation and thus increase the multiple correlation. In this situation, chance variation in the sample may well be what determines the choice of variables for inclusion in the equation. If the N/p ratio is small and variables in the regression equation are chosen from a larger set of possible predictors, the shrinkage achieved by cross-validation can be dramatic.

We can illustrate this point by using the *Seasons* data set. We selected the data from the first 40 women aged 65 years or less with *BMI* scores of 40 or less. Then, we used *TC* as the dependent variable and arbitrarily chose *height*, *BMI*1, *host*1, *anger*1, *irrit*1, *anxiety*1, *dirwdc*1, *beck_d*1, *beck_d*2, *beck_d*3, and *beck_d*4 as 11 possible predictors. Using an automated procedure called stepwise regression (to be discussed later), we found that the regression equation containing five predictor variables that best predicts *TC* is

$$\hat{TC} = 78.143 + 2.706 \, BMI + 16.863 \, host1 - 1.605 \, anger1 + 16.461 \, dirwdc1 - 1.906 \, beck\_d1$$

Here, the regression equation is based on the 32 cases in the sample having data on the dependent variable and all five predictors, so the N/p ratio is 6.4 (the N/p ratio is only 2.9 if we count all 11 of the possible predictors we considered). The R obtained for the sample is .504, and the adjusted R is .333. We then cross-validated by (1) using the same equation to predict *TC* scores for the remaining 120 women with data on all the variables in the equation, and then (2) finding the correlation between the predicted and the actual *TC* scores for these 120 women. This correlation is very small, $r = .046$, so that the cross-validated R^2 is $.046^2 = .002$. The cross-validated R of .046 is a more realistic measure of how well the regression equation fits the population than the R of .506 obtained in the subsample that was used to generate the equation. In other words, because of the small sample and the large number of potential predictors, the regression equation predicts very poorly except in the sample that was used to generate it.

In summary, if the N/p ratio is small, the multiple correlation coefficient for a sample will overestimate the usefulness of the regression equation in the population and in other samples. This overestimation is larger when the predictors in the equation are chosen from larger pools of potential predictors. We strongly recommend the use of cross-validation to counter the effects of capitalization on chance.

21.5 SUPPRESSION EFFECTS IN MULTIPLE REGRESSION

If we compare the regression of Y on X_1 to the regression of Y on both X_1 and X_2 where the two predictors are correlated, $b_{Y1.2}$ is usually smaller than b_{Y1} because the effects of X_2 have been partialed out (see Equation 21.11). However, it is possible to have *suppression effects* in which the predictive effect of X_1 is greater when X_2 is also in the equation. Under certain conditions $X_1 | X_2$, that is, X_1 with the effects of X_2 partialed out, is a better predictor of $Y | X_2$ than X_1 is of Y, so that the coefficient of X_1 becomes larger when X_2 is added to the equation.

Suppose we add X_2 to a regression equation that already contains X_1. From Equation 21.14, the proportion of variance of Y accounted for by both predictors is given by

$$R^2_{Y.12} = r^2_{Y1} + r^2_{Y(2|1)} \tag{21.18}$$

where

$$r_{Y(2|1)} = \frac{r_{Y2} - r_{Y1}r_{12}}{\sqrt{1 - r^2_{12}}} \tag{21.19}$$

is the semipartial correlation between Y and the part of X_2 that is not predictable from X_1 (see Chapter 19).

In so-called *classical suppression*, $r_{Y1} > 0$, $r_{12} \neq 0$, and $r_{Y2} = 0$, so that X_2 overlaps variance with X_1 but not with Y. From Equation 21.19, the increased variability in Y accounted for by the addition of X_2 to a regression equation that contains X_1 reduces to

$$r^2_{Y(2|1)} = \frac{r^2_{Y1} r^2_{12}}{1 - r^2_{12}} \tag{21.20}$$

Also, the coefficient of X_1 when Y is regressed on both X_1 and X_2 is

$$b_{Y1.2} = \left[\frac{r_{Y1} - r_{Y2}r_{12}}{1 - r^2_{12}} \right] \frac{s_Y}{s_1} = \frac{b_{Y1}}{1 - r^2_{12}} \tag{21.21}$$

if $r_{Y2} = 0$. From Equations 21.18 and 21.20, we can see that given classical suppression, R^2 increases when X_2 is added to the regression equation even though it is uncorrelated with Y. From Equation 21.21 we see that $b_{Y1.2}$ is larger than b_{Y1} if $r_{12} \neq 0$, and increases in size as r_{12} increases. Also, given classical suppression, $b_{Y2.1} \neq 0$ even though $b_{Y2} = 0$. In what is called *net suppression*, r_{Y2} is not zero but is less than $r_{Y1}r_{12}$, so that even though X_2 now overlaps variance with both Y and X_1, $b_{Y1.2}$ is still larger than b_{Y1}.

Consider a hypothetical example in which suppression effects could occur: Suppose, for example, that

1. Y is a non-verbal performance measure of spatial judgment ability;
2. X_1 is the score on a paper-and-pencil test of spatial ability in which the subject follows a set of complex written instructions; and
3. X_2 is a test of reading ability.

Even if reading ability has little or no correlation with spatial ability, the scores on the reading test will be correlated with the results of the group test of spatial ability because of the need to follow the written instructions. In this case, $X_1 | X_2$, the score on the spatial ability test with reading ability partialed out, will be a better predictor of $Y | X_2$ than X_1 is of Y. This is because X_2 removes (or "suppresses") a source of variability in X_1 (i.e., reading ability), that is, error with respect to predicting Y.

21.6 SUMMARY

In Chapter 21, we have developed the basic ideas of multiple regression.

- We began by developing an example with several predictors. We used SPSS to analyze the data, and then explained the output.
- We discussed the meaning of the regression coefficients and introduced some of their limitations in developing explanatory models. We emphasized that the machinery of regression deals with prediction, not causality; that is, just because a regression equation *predicts* a dependent variable fairly well does not mean that it is the "correct" causal model of the research situation. Also, we pointed out that the coefficient of a predictor variable will generally take on different values when other predictors are added to, or removed from, the regression equation. This makes it very difficult to interpret the regression coefficients as measures of causal importance except within the context of a well-established model. We will continue this discussion in Chapter 23.
- We discussed the partitioning of variance in multiple regression and pointed out that just because adding a variable to a regression equations results in an increase in the variance that is accounted for, this does not mean that the variable has theoretical significance.
- We discussed cross-validation and adjusted measures of regression fit. Because any regression equation developed from a particular sample will always fit the sample better than it fits the population from which the sample was selected, the multiple correlation coefficient is positively biased. Adjustments to the multiple correlation coefficient and especially cross-validation provide more realistic measures of fit.
- We introduced the idea of suppression in regression, in which a variable with little or no correlation with the criterion variable can still improve predictability when added to a regression equation if it suppresses some of the variance of one or more of the other predictors.

EXERCISES

21.1 In a visual "search" experiment, subjects are presented with a display containing an array of letters and make a response when they detect the presence of a "target letter" that was specified beforehand. Arrays can differ in the number of letters they contain and (because of differences in brightness and contrast or the presence of visual "noise") how difficult it is to identify the letters. We simulated the results of such an experiment in which number of letters and identification difficulty were varied orthogonally, using the model

$$\text{Time} = 400 + 30 \times number + 2 \times diff + \varepsilon$$

where *number* stands for the number of letters in the array (2, 4, 6, or 8), *diff* stands for identification difficulty (10 or 20 units), and ε is a number selected randomly from a normal population with mean = 0 and standard deviation = 40 to generate the 24 cases. The data can be found in the file *EX21_1* on the book's website.

(a) Find the summary statistics and correlation matrix for these data.

(b) Regress time on number of letters and difficulty. Are the effects of *number* and *diff* significant at $\alpha = .05$? Are these significance tests equivalent to the tests of the number of letters and difficulty main effects in a standard ANOVA? Perform an ANOVA on time using the factors *number* and *diff* and compare the results with those that follow from the regression.

(c) What are the estimates of the parameters of the model that are obtained from the regression? How do these compare with the actual parameter values ($\beta_0 = 400$, $\beta_1 = 30$, and $\beta_2 = 2$) that were used to generate the data? What are the 95% confidence intervals for β_0, β_1, and β_2? We should emphasize that in the real world, we do not know what the parameters of the model are or even the form of the model. We use the sample data to infer something about the underlying model.

21.2 The file *EX21_2* contains values for three variables, Y, X_1, and X_2:

(a) Verify that X_1 and X_2 are uncorrelated.

(b) Verify that in this case (X_1 and X_2 uncorrelated), $R^2_{Y.12} = r^2_{Y1} + r^2_{Y2}$.

(c) For this data set, what is the relationship between (i) the regression coefficient for X_1 when Y is regressed on X_1 alone and (ii) the regression coefficient for X_1 when Y is regressed on both X_1 and X_2? Is this true in general? What is the relationship between the standard errors of b_1 in (i) and (ii)?

21.3 Values for Y, X_2, and X_3 are contained in the file *EX21_3*.

(a) Fit the model $Y = \beta_0 + \beta_1 X_1 + \beta_2 X_2 + \varepsilon$.

(b) From the data, does it seem that both X_1 and X_2 should be included in the regression model?

21.4 Calculate the adjusted R^2 given the following information:

(a) $R^2_{Y.1234} = .50$, $N = 10$.

(b) $R^2_{Y.1234} = .50$, $N = 40$.

(c) $R^2_{Y.1234} = .50$, $N = 200$.

(d) $R^2_{Y.12} = .30$, $N = 40$.

21.5 Given the 15 cases in *EX21_5*,

(a) Using only the first four cases, regress Y on X_1, X_2, and X_3. What is the value of $R_{Y.123}$? Comment on why $R_{Y.123}$ must take on the value that it does here.

(b) Use the regression equation obtained in part (a) to predict the values of Y for each of the 15 cases.

(c) Find the correlations between the scores predicted in part (b) and the actual Y values (i) for the first four cases and (ii) for the remaining 11 cases. Comment on the difference between these correlations.

21.6 Using pretty much the same procedure as in Exercise 21.5, find a value for the cross-validated R for the regression of TC on *age* and *BMI* for women aged 65 years or younger with *BMI*s less than or equal to 40. As we discuss in the chapter, the idea is to develop a regression equation on part of a sample, and then see how well that equation fits the remainder of the sample, in order to avoid the effects of capitalization on chance. Start by opening the *Seasons* file and selecting the data from women with *age* less than or equal to 65 and *BMI* less than or equal to 40. In SPSS, choose *Select Cases . . .* from the *Data* menu and in the *Select Cases* dialog box, select *If condition is satisfied*. In the *Select Condition: If* box, insert the conditions (*sex* = 1) and (*age* <= 65) and (*BMI* <= 40). To save the data set, in the *Select Cases* dialog box, choose (toward the bottom of the box) the option *Copy selected cases to a new dataset*. Insert a name for the data set, say, *tcforwomen*, and save it. There should be 187 cases in the data set, with 181 of them having data on all three of *TC*, *age*, and *BMI*. With about 180 cases and two predictors the N/p ratio is over 90:1; the cross-validated R should not be much less than the R obtained in the regression. There are several ways of proceeding. One way is to select, say, the first 94 cases, perform the regression of *TC* on *age* and *BMI*, and then see how well the regression equation obtained for the first 94 cases fits the remaining 93. To select the first 94 cases, in the *Select Cases* dialog box, choose the option *Based on time or case range* and insert 1 as the first case and 94 as the last case. Then perform the regression. You should find that the R is .544. Use the equation to predict *TC* for all cases. Now select cases 95–187 and correlate the predicted *TC* scores with the actual *TC* scores. Note that rather than using the first 94 cases and the last 93, SPSS allows the option of randomly selecting 50% (or any other percentage) of the sample.

21.7 Another way to find a value for the cross-validated *R* that lends itself to the capabilities of SPSS is to correlate the actual *TC* scores with the deleted predictions (what SPSS calls the adusted predicted value). We can get the adjusted predictions by clicking on the *Save* . . . button in the *Linear Regression* dialog box. In the *Linear Regression: Save* box, select *Adjusted* predicted scores. When the regression is performed, the adjusted predictions will appear in a column labeled *ADJ_1* that is added to the data set. The adjusted prediction for each case is based on the regression using the remaining $N - 1$ cases, thereby limiting the damage done by capitalization on chance. Find the correlation between the adjusted prediction of *TC* and actual *TC*.

21.8 You add three predictor variables to a regression that already contains two predictors.

(a) Is it possible for the *R* for the regression with seven predictors to be smaller than the *R* with only two predictors?

(b) Is it possible for the adjusted *R* to be smaller for the regression with seven predictors?

21.9 Starting with the *Seasons* file, select the data from men with ages less than or equal to 65 and *BMI* scores less than or equal to 40. Regress *TC* on *age* and *BMI*. What is R^2? Are the regression coefficients for *age* and *BMI* significantly different from 0?

21.10 Start with the analyses of Exercise 21.9. Now add height and weight as predictors. Comment on the differences in R^2 and the patterns of significant coefficients found in this analysis and the values found in Exercise 21.9. In particular, the coefficient of *BMI* in the previous exercise had the value 2.139 and was significant, $p = .004$. However, when weight and height are added as predictors the coefficient now has the value 0.221 with $p = .968$. How can these values be so different?

Chapter 22

Inference, Assumptions, and Power in Multiple Regression

22.1 OVERVIEW

Our goals in Chapter 22 are to consider the following topics:

- *Statistical inference in multiple regression.* We present statistical tests as well as confidence intervals for regression coefficients, predictions, and the multiple correlation coefficient. We also review the assumptions underlying these procedures and discuss the need to control overall Type 1 error.
- *Power calculations in multiple regression.* We show how power may be calculated for hypothesis tests of all the regression coefficients, a single regression coefficient, or a subset of the coefficients.
- *How to check for violations of the assumptions that underlie the inference model and how to detect outliers and influential points in multiple regression.*
- *Automated stepwise procedures.* Procedures that attempt to identify the "best" equation for making predictions include forward selection, backward elimination, and stepwise regression. Although the idea of letting a computer decide what is the most appropriate regression equation appeals to some researchers, these automated procedures have serious limitations and should never be used to develop explanatory models. We will discuss both the procedures and their limitations.

22.2 INFERENCE MODELS AND ASSUMPTIONS

As was the case for bivariate regression, the validity of our inferences rests upon a model and certain assumptions about the data. Also, we again distinguish between situations in which the predictors are fixed-effect variables and situations in which they are random variables. Fixed predictors generally occur in experimental studies in which the independent variables are manipulated; Y is a random variable but the values of the Xs are selected by the researcher and are therefore considered to be fixed over replications of the experiment. Predictors are considered to be random variables when they, as well as Y, are randomly sampled. Although somewhat different assumptions are made for fixed and random predictor variables, under certain conditions the procedures for testing hypotheses and forming confidence intervals are the same in both cases. However, we must remember that when the predictors are random variables but we treat them as fixed, our statistical inferences are limited to situations in which the distributions of predictor variables are the same as in the current sample.

Whether X is fixed or random, we assume that the model is

$$Y = \beta_0 + \beta_1 X_1 + \beta_2 X_2 + \ldots + \beta_p X_p + \varepsilon$$

$$= \mu_{Y \cdot X_1 X_2 \ldots X_p} + \varepsilon$$

where $\mu_{Y \cdot X_1 X_2 \ldots X_p}$ is the mean of the population of Y scores corresponding to a particular set of values for the p predictor variables. For the fixed-X situation, we assume that:

1. No predictor variable is completely redundant; i.e., no predictor variable, X_p, can be perfectly predicted from the other $p - 1$ predictors, using a linear equation. If this assumption is violated, the set of equations that must be solved in order to obtain the sample regression coefficients will not have a unique solution.
2. The error components associated with Y are normally and independently distributed with mean 0 and variance σ_e^2.
3. The values of the predictor variables are fixed and measured without error. This means that the values of the Xs will be exactly the same for each replication of the experiment.

If the Xs are random variables, we assume 1 and 2 and further assume that the distributions of the predictor variables are independent of ε.

22.3 TESTING DIFFERENT HYPOTHESES ABOUT COEFFICIENTS IN MULTIPLE REGRESSION

22.3.1 Testing the Hypothesis $\beta_1 = \beta_2 = \ldots = \beta_p = 0$

As we indicated earlier, if the p regression coefficients $\beta_1, \beta_2, \ldots \beta_p$ all have the value 0 in the population, the ratio

$$\frac{MS_{regression}}{MS_{residual}} = \frac{R^2 SS_Y / p}{(1 - R^2) \, SS_Y / (N - 1 - p)} = \frac{R^2 / p}{(1 - R^2) / (N - 1 - p)}$$

will be distributed as F with p and $N - 1 - p$ df under standard assumptions. Therefore, $MS_{regression} / MS_{residual}$ can serve as the statistic to test the null hypothesis that the p regression coefficients are all zero in the population. This test asks whether we have sufficient evidence to conclude that the model

$$Y = \beta_0 + \beta_1 X_1 + \beta_2 X_2 + \ldots + \beta_p X_p + \varepsilon$$

accounts for Y in the population better than the restricted model

$$Y = \beta_0 + \varepsilon$$

$$= \mu_Y + \varepsilon$$

If the restricted model is appropriate, then $\beta_1 = \beta_2 = \ldots = \beta_p = 0$, so that the best predictor for Y is $\hat{\beta}_0 = \hat{\mu}_Y = \overline{Y}$ and the multiple correlation coefficient in the population has the value 0.

In the current example, when we regress TC on age and BMI, we find

$$F = \frac{MS_{regression}}{MS_{residual}} = \frac{75,220.300 \, / \, 2}{200,988.913 \, / \, 178} = 33.308$$

and so we can reject the hypothesis that the population regression coefficients are zero for both *age* and *BMI*. The test assumes that $MS_{residual}$ is an estimate of the variance of the random error component. If important variables are left out of the regression equation, $MS_{residual}$ will reflect their effects as well as random error, and the test may be biased.

22.3.2 Testing the Hypothesis $\beta_j = \beta_{hyp}$ and Finding Confidence Intervals for β_j

A significant test of the overall regression equation logically implies that at least one of the predictors is linearly related to Y. Generally, we will want to examine how the individual X variables contribute to the prediction of Y. Under the usual assumptions, the ratio

$$\frac{b_j - \beta_j}{SE(b_j)}$$

will be distributed as t with $N - 1 - p$ df. Therefore, if we can estimate the standard error, we can test the hypothesis that the population intercept, β_0, or any of the population regression coefficients, β_j, are equal to any constant. In practice, the null hypothesis $\beta_j = 0$ is usually tested. Rejection of this hypothesis implies that X_j makes a significant contribution to the predictability of Y when it is added to the other variables in the equation.

Also, once we have obtained the appropriate SEs, we can obtain confidence intervals for each parameter using

$$b_j \pm t_{\alpha/2} SE(b_j)$$

In the current example, the value of $t_{.025}$ (178) is 1.973, and the relevant standard error values from Table 21.5 are 16.921 for the intercept, .237 for *age*, and .540 for *BMI*. Combining this information, the 95% confidence intervals for the intercept and the coefficients of *age* and *BMI* are 92.239 ± 33.392, 1.737 ± 0.468, and 1.474 ± 1.066, respectively.

22.3.3 Partial *F* Tests: Procedures for Testing a Subset of the β_js

We can use partial F tests to determine whether adding one or more predictors to a regression equation that already contains p predictors significantly increases the predictability of Y. If we consider just one additional predictor, X_{p+1}, a test of the model

$$Y = \beta_0 + \beta_1 X_1 + \beta_2 X_2 + \ldots + \beta_p X_p + \beta_{p+1} X_{p+1} + \varepsilon$$

against the restricted model

$$Y = \beta_0 + \beta_1 X_1 + \beta_2 X_2 + \ldots + \beta_p X_p + \varepsilon$$

is equivalent to testing the hypothesis H_0: $\beta_{p+1} = 0$. This approach provides a basis for comparing any two models where the restricted model includes a subset of the predictors in the full model.

We can represent the variability in Y accounted for by regression on the variables of the restricted model as

$$SS_{Y\cdot12\ldots p} = R^2_{Y\cdot12\ldots p} SS_Y$$

and the variability accounted for by the larger model when the predictor X_{p+1} is added as

$$SS_{Y\cdot12\ldots p+1} = R^2_{Y\cdot12\ldots p+1} SS_Y$$

Therefore the increment in variability associated with the predictor X_{p+1} is given by

$$SS_{increment} = SS_{Y\cdot p+1|12\ldots p} = (R^2_{Y\cdot12\ldots p+1} - R^2_{Y\cdot12\ldots p})SS_Y$$

This increment is associated with a single df because only one additional regression coefficient must be estimated in the larger model. Table 22.1 presents these results in the form of an ANOVA table. The hypothesis H_0: $\beta_{p+1} = 0$ can be tested using the ratio

$$F = \frac{MS_{increment}}{MS_{residual}}$$

where the denominator is the mean square associated with the variability not accounted for by the larger model; that is,

$$MS_{residual} = \frac{(1 - R^2_{Y\cdot12\ldots p+1})SS_Y}{N - p - 2}$$

The numerator of the F is associated with 1 df if a single predictor is added and the denominator with $N - p - 2$ df.

When a partial F test is used to test whether a *single* population regression coefficient is zero, the results produced are exactly equivalent to those of the t test discussed in the preceding section. If we use this procedure to test whether *BMI* adds significantly to the prediction of *TC* over and above *age*, $SS_{increment} = 8412.523$, $df_{increment} = 1$, and $MS_{residual} = 1129.151$, so that

$$F = \frac{MS_{increment}}{MS_{residual}} = \frac{8412.523}{1129.151} = 7.450$$

The F value obtained is the square of the t for the coefficient of *BMI* in the output for the regression of *TC* on *age* and *BMI* in Table 21.5.

Partial F tests can also be used to test hypotheses which state that some subset of the β_js is equal to zero. Suppose, for example, we start with a model containing p predictor variables

$$Y = \beta_0 + \beta_1 X_1 + \beta_2 X_2 + \ldots + \beta_p X_p + \varepsilon$$

and we add k more predictor variables so that the model is now

$$Y = \beta_0 + \beta_1 X_1 + \beta_2 X_2 + \ldots + \beta_p X_p + \beta_{p+1}X_{p+1} + \ldots + \beta_{p+k}X_{p+k} + \varepsilon$$

Again, the appropriate ANOVA table is given in Table 22.1. This general approach can be used to assess the effect of adding any set of predictors to the equation and tests the hypothesis that the regression coefficients for these added predictors are all equal to zero in the population.

Table 22.1 ANOVA table for testing the effect of adding k predictor variables to a model that already contains p predictors

SV	df	SS	MS
Larger model	$p + k$	$R^2_{Y.1\ldots p+k}SS_Y$	$\dfrac{R^2_{Y.1\ldots p+k}SS_Y}{p+k}$
Smaller model	p	$R^2_{Y.1\ldots p}SS_Y$	$\dfrac{R^2_{Y.1\ldots p}SS_Y}{p}$
Increment	k	$SS_{increment} =$ $(R^2_{Y.1\ldots p+k} - R^2_{Y.1\ldots p})SS_Y$	$SS_{increment}\,/\,k$
Residual	$(N - 1 - p - k)$	$(1 - R^2_{Y.1\ldots p+k})SS_Y$	$\dfrac{(1 - R^2_{Y.1\ldots p+k})SS_Y}{N-1-p-k}$

22.4 CONTROLLING TYPE 1 ERROR IN MULTIPLE REGRESSION

The need to control overall Type 1 error for each family of hypothesis tests is emphasized in most treatments of ANOVA. However, the issue is scarcely mentioned in many treatments of multiple regression, where inflation of Type 1 error can be a very serious problem (e.g., Dar et al., 1994). Given an interesting dependent variable and a collection of possibly useful predictors, we often see attempts to assemble combinations of predictors, often without regard to theory, that just happen to result in larger increases in R^2. Because this approach can capitalize on random error in the sample (see Chapter 21), it may not produce an equation with any explanatory value or even one that is effective for predicting in samples other than the one used to generate it. Trying out many different regression equations and looking at the tests for R^2, as well as the tests for all the individual regression coefficients, can result in highly inflated Type 1 error for the collection of tests. If we ignore this, we may add too many variables to the regression equation.

Looking at tests of individual regression coefficients is analogous to looking at tests of contrasts of means. If we have a large number of means but we have an *a priori* interest in comparing two specific means and test this comparison at $\alpha = .05$, we can say that the Type 1 error is .05. On the other hand, if we first find the two means that differ the most and test their difference at $\alpha = .05$, the effective Type 1 error is much larger because we had to consider all the pairwise differences in order to determine which one to test. Analogously, if we select a predictor variable from a large number of candidates solely because it results in a large increase in R^2, the effective Type 1 error is much larger than the nominal significance level used for the test. We can make several recommendations:

1. *Decisions about what sets of variables should be added to the regression equation should be driven by our knowledge and theories about our research question.* We should not just search through our potential predictors in a quest to find those that maximally increase R^2 because in some cases the most "effective" predictors will be those that have capitalized on chance variability in the sample. Also, some effective predictors may not be theoretically meaningful themselves, but rather gain their predictive power by being proxies for important variables that for some reason (e.g., measurement error) do not predict as well. The distinction we are trying to make here is analogous to that between dealing with planned contrasts and dealing with unexpected, but large differences among means in ANOVA.

2. *We should associate meaningful sets of predictors with families of tests.* For example, suppose we are interested in influences on classroom performance and have three sets of predictors. Say we are most interested in (1) student variables (measures of ability and motivation), then in (2) family variables (parental education, SES, support for education), and finally in (3) classroom variables (class size, teaching style). We could start by first including the set of student variables as predictors. If we determined that R^2 was significant for the set (say, at $\alpha = .05$), we could add the set of family variables and determine whether the increase in R^2 for the set was significant (again at $\alpha = .05$), and so on.

3. *We should also be mindful of the number of tests within each set.* Because the predictors in a meaningful set will almost always be correlated, we think that requiring adjustments such as the Bonferroni in which the k predictors within a set are each tested at the significance level α/k is too conservative a strategy. Nonetheless, we should be cautious and conservative when we interpret tests of the regression coefficients for the members of a set.

Cohen et al. (2003) have recommended extending the logic of Fisher's protected t test (Fisher, 1935) to multiple regression analyses. Fisher's protected t procedure as applied to ANOVA is as follows. First test for the significance of a categorical independent variable with a levels using α as the significance level. If the overall test is significant, then each of the $a(a - 1)/2$ pairwise comparisons between the levels of the variable may be tested at significance level α. Tests of the individual comparisons are said to be "protected" by the significant overall test. If the overall test is not significant, we are not allowed to perform significance tests on any of the pairwise comparisons in the set (unless, presumably, we have specified them *a priori*). As applied to multiple regression, a significant R^2 or increment in R^2 for a meaningful set of predictors would allow us to look at the significance tests for each of the regression coefficients in the set at the same level of significance. If the overall test for the set of predictors is not significant, we are not allowed to look at the tests for the individual predictors in the set.

Cohen et al. (2003) acknowledge some problems with this procedure, and it can be shown that the Fisher protected test does not completely control Type 1 error in ANOVA when the independent variable has more than three levels (Hayter, 1986). Nonetheless, the modified Fisher procedure at least acknowledges the issue of inflation of Type 1 error in multiple regression and offers an easily applied, if imperfect, control for it.

22.5 INFERENCES ABOUT THE PREDICTIONS OF Y

In bivariate regression, the expected value of Y corresponding to a value X_j of X is given by $\mu_{Y.X_j} = \beta_0 + \beta_1 X_j$, which can be estimated by $\hat{Y}_j = \hat{\mu}_{Y.X_j} = b_0 + b_1 X_j$. We showed in Chapter 20 that for bivariate regression, the estimated standard error associated with the prediction of Y at $X = X_j$ is given by

$$SE(\hat{\mu}_{Y.X}) = s_e \sqrt{h_{jj}} \tag{22.1}$$

and that the standard error associated with an individual score is

$$SE(\hat{Y}_j) = s_e \sqrt{1 + h_{jj}} \tag{22.2}$$

where s_e is the standard error of estimate and h_{jj}, the leverage of X_j, is

$$h_{jj} = \frac{1}{N} = \frac{(X_j - \bar{X})^2}{SS_X}$$

In multiple regression, we can find the estimated standard error for the prediction of Y associated with any combination of values of the p predictor variables in the regression equation. Because there is more than one predictor, the standard errors are most easily presented as matrix expressions. Although the expression for h_{jj} will now be more complicated because there is more than one predictor, it can be thought of and used in much the same way as in bivariate regression. If we want to find confidence intervals for the conditional means or individual scores corresponding to combinations of predictor values in our data set, we do not have to compute the leverage; we can simply ask that SPSS add the lower and upper confidence limits to our output, or ask that SYSTAT provide the leverage values that we can then use in Equations 22.1 and 22.2.

However, if we wish to find the standard error for the prediction of Y based on a combination of values for the p predictors, $X_{j1}, X_{j2}, \ldots, X_{jp}$, that did not occur in our sample, the estimated standard errors for $\hat{\mu}$ and $\hat{Y}$ are not directly made available in the computer output and must be calculated. We will not present the relevant matrix expressions or their derivation here. They are available, along with a worked-out example, in the brief development of multiple regression using matrix notation in the Supplementary Materials on the book's website (Chapter 21A).

22.6 CONFIDENCE INTERVALS FOR THE SQUARED MULTIPLE CORRELATION COEFFICIENT

A confidence interval for ρ^2, the squared population multiple correlation coefficient, is more informative than simply stating the sample R^2 along with the results of a significance test. Using an example given by Steiger and Fouladi (1997), suppose we obtain an R^2 of .40 in a regression using five predictor variables with $N = 45$. The shrunken estimator (i.e., the adjusted R^2) is .327 and if a significance test is performed, the p is .001. However, it is more useful to know that the 95% confidence interval for ρ^2 extends from .095 to .562. This interval tells us that the range of possible values is quite wide; converting from ρ^2 to ρ, the lower limit of the 95% CI is .31 and the upper limit is .75.

An expression for the variance of R^2 is given by

$$\text{Var}(R^2) = 4\rho^2(1 - \rho^2)^2 \left[\frac{(N - p - 1)^2}{(N^2 - 1)(N + 3)} \right] \tag{22.3}$$

where N is the total number of cases, p is the number of predictors, and ρ^2 is the square of the population multiple correlation coefficient (Olkin & Finn, 1995). For example, if we consider the regression of TC on age and BMI for women aged 20–65 years with BMI scores of 40 or less, and take the value of R^2 from Table 21.5 as our estimate of ρ^2, the variance of R^2 is estimated by

$$\frac{4(.272)(1 - .272)^2(181 - 2 - 1)^2}{(181^2 - 1)(181 + 3)} = .0030$$

Therefore, an estimate of the 95% CI for ρ^2 is given by

$$R^2 \pm z_{.025}SE(R^2) = .272 \pm 1.96\sqrt{.0030}$$

$$= .272 \pm .108$$

i.e., an interval that extends from approximately .164 to .380.

Steiger and Fouladi (1992) have developed a computer program, R2, that finds confidence intervals and performs significance tests and power calculations for R^2. The program is free and may be downloaded from Steiger's web page at http://statpower.net. Using R2 with the current example yields a 95% confidence that extends from .160 to .380, almost exactly the same values we calculated above.

We may also be interested in determining whether ρ^2 is equal in separate populations. Suppose we wish to test whether a battery of college-placement tests predicts college GPA equally well for city and suburban students, or whether a set of clinical variables predicts cholesterol levels equally well for men and women. When we regressed TC on age and BMI for the 183 men under the age of 65 with BMI of ≤40 who had data on all three variables in the $Seasons$ data set, we found $R^2 = .046$. This is less than the corresponding R^2 of .272 that we found for women. Do we have enough evidence to reject the hypothesis that ρ^2 is the same for women and men? If R_1^2 and R_2^2 are obtained from large independent samples with N_1 and N_2 observations, respectively, the distribution of their difference is approximately normal with a variance that can be estimated by

$$\mathrm{Var}(R_1^2 - R_2^2) = \frac{4}{N_1} R_1^2(1 - R_1^2)^2 + \frac{4}{N_2} R_2^2(1 - R_2^2)^2 \tag{22.4}$$

and the confidence interval may be approximated using

$$R_1^2 - R_2^2 \pm z_{\alpha/2}\, SE(R_1^2 - R_2^2) \tag{22.5}$$

For the regression of TC on age and BMI for women and men, the variance is

$$\mathrm{Var}(R_1^2 - R_2^2) = \frac{4}{181}(.272)(1 - .272)^2 + \frac{4}{183}(.046)(1 - .046)^2 = .0041$$

(where the subscripts 1 and 2 represent women and men), and the 95% confidence interval for the difference between the population squared multiple correlations for women and men is approximated by

$$R_1^2 - R_2^2 \pm 1.96\, SE(R_1^2 - R_2^2) = .272 - .046 \pm 1.96\sqrt{.0041}$$

$$= .226 \pm .126$$

This interval ranges from approximately .10 to .35. Because the interval does not contain 0, we can reject the null hypothesis that the ρ^2 values are equal for men and women. Furthermore, we are reasonably certain that the squared correlation is greater for women than for men, but probably not by more than .35.

How big must the samples be in order to provide a reasonable estimate of the confidence interval? There is no simple answer; several factors must be taken into account, including the assumed values of the population correlation coefficients, the number of predictors, and whether the sample sizes are equal. Based on their computer simulations, Algina and Keselman (1999) provide tables that indicate the sample sizes required for various combinations of factors.

It is also possible to use large-sample approximations to find confidence intervals for the difference between dependent R^2s (i.e., R^2s calculated on the same sample). As was the case with simple correlation coefficients, finding confidence intervals is more complicated when we use dependent measures because we must take account of their covariance. Alf and Graf (1999) and Zou (2007) discuss how to obtain these confidence intervals and present worked-out examples.

We should point out that the methods discussed in this section will not be accurate unless the assumption of multivariate normality is satisfied and the predictor variables have been specified in advance. As always, in situations in which the predictors have been selected from a larger pool of variables using some sort of stepwise procedure, it is important that cross-validation be used.

22.7 POWER CALCULATIONS IN MULTIPLE REGRESSION

There are many different kinds of power calculations that can be performed for multiple regression. Here, given the model

$$Y = \beta_0 + \beta_1 X_1 + \beta_2 X_2 + \ldots + \beta_j X_j + \ldots + \beta_p X_p + \varepsilon$$

we consider power for tests of the null hypotheses that

1. All p of the regression coefficients are equal to 0 in the population,
2. A particular coefficient is equal to 0, or
3. k of the p regression coefficients are equal to 0.

Most programs for calculating power require an estimate of the noncentrality parameter for the noncentral F distribution, defined as

$$\hat{\lambda} = N^* f^2 \tag{22.6}$$

where Cohen's effect size statistic for regression, f^2, is given by

$$f^2 = \frac{\Delta R^2}{1 - R^2} \tag{22.7}$$

Here, ΔR^2 is the increment in R^2 when k predictors are added to a set of $p - k$ predictors, and R^2 is the squared multiple correlation calculated for the full set of p predictors. When the predictors are fixed-effects variables, N^* is equal to the sample size, N; when the predictors are random variables, N^* is defined by Cohen (1988)[1] as

$$
\begin{aligned}
N^* &= df_{numerator} + df_{denominator} + 1 \\
&= k + (N - p - 1) + 1 \\
&= N - p + k
\end{aligned}
\tag{22.8}
$$

Maxwell (2000, p. 436) comments that Cohen's (1988) formulation appears to provide a small adjustment for the random nature of predictors that are usually encountered in psychological research. Therefore, a convenient way to perform *a priori* power calculations is to use G*Power 3 to determine the N^* required to achieve the desired level of power. If the predictors are fixed, then N, the required sample size, equals N^*; if the predictors are random,[2] then from Equation 22.8,

---

[1] Cohen's (1988) recommendation that $N^* = N - p + k$ represents a change from the 1977 edition of his power analysis book, in which he used $N^* = df_{residual} = N - p - 1$.

[2] Note that for cases 2 and 3 below, our recommended procedure for random-effects predictors may produce estimates of the required sample size that are slightly too large. This is because G*Power 3 bases the denominator df of the F statistic on N^* instead of N, and so the df will be too small by $p - k$. This can be ignored unless N is small and $p - k$ is large.

$N = N^* + p - k$. For fairly large values of N, the differences in estimated power obtained using N and $N - p + k$ will be small.

Gatsonis and Sampson (1989) have calculated exact power for random predictors assuming multivariate normality and pointed out that *a priori* power calculations based on Cohen's procedures are approximately accurate when the predictors are random but continuous. They suggest that a conservative course of action might be to increase the required sample size by 5, especially when the number of predictors is less than 10.

We now consider the three types of power calculations:

- *Case 1—power for tests that all of the regression coefficients are equal to zero in the population:* The test that all regression coefficients equal zero is equivalent to the test that the population squared multiple correlation, ρ^2, equals zero. For case 1, $p = k$, so that $N^* = N$, the required sample size, whether we have fixed- or random-effects predictors.

  As an example, suppose we want to estimate the sample size required to have power = .90 at $\alpha = .05$ for the test of the hypothesis that all population regression coefficients are zero. If we expect that $R^2 = .20$ when we regress the criterion variable on four predictors, the effect size is

$$f^2 = \frac{\Delta R^2}{1 - R^2} = \frac{R^2}{1 - R^2} = \frac{.20}{1 - .20} = .25$$

In G*Power 3, select

1. *F tests* as the *Test family*
2. *Multiple Regression: Omnibus (R^2 deviation from zero)* as the *Statistical test*, and
3. *A priori*: Compute required sample size given α, *power, and effect size* as the *Type of power analysis.*

Then insert the values $f^2 = .25$, *Power* = .90, $\alpha = .05$, and *Number of predictors* = 4 and click on *Calculate*. G*Power 3 indicates that the required sample size is 67.

- *Case 2—power calculations for the test that a particular coefficient is zero in the population.* Here $k = 1$, so that for random predictors $N^* = N - p + 1$, so that $N = N^* + p - 1$. As an example, suppose we plan to test whether adding a predictor to a regression equation that already contains three predictors will significantly improve the predictability of the dependent variable. This is the same as testing the significance of the coefficient of the predictor in a regression that contains all four predictors. Suppose that we want to find the N required to have power = .80 if R^2 with three predictors is .25 and we expect the fourth predictor to increase R^2 to .30, so that $f^2 = .05/(1 - .30) = .071$. In G*Power 3 (see Fig. 22.1), select

1. *F tests* as the *Test family*
2. *Multiple Regression: Special (R^2 increase)* as the *Statistical test*, and
3. *A priori: Compute required sample size given α, power, and effect size* as the *Type of power analysis.*

Then, insert $f^2 = .071$, $\alpha = .05$, *Power* = .80, *Numerator df* = 1, and *Number of predictors* = 4. If we click on *Calculate*, we find $N^* = 113$. If the predictors are fixed, $N = 113$. If they are random, $N = 113 + p - 1 = 116$.

As another example, we can find the number of cases required to yield power = .80 for

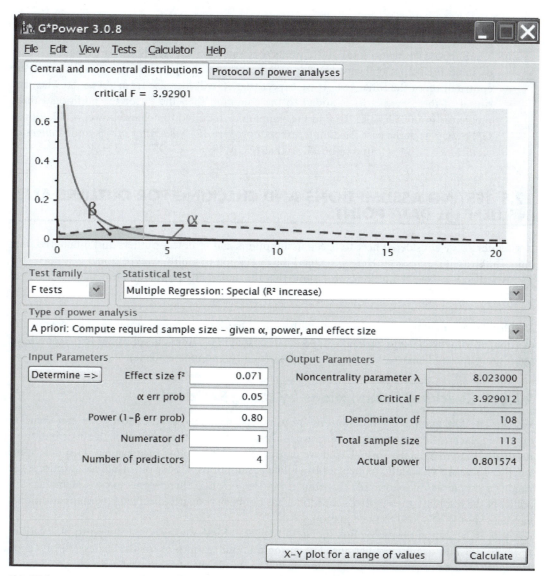

Fig. 22.1 G*Power 3 dialog box for finding N^* necessary to have power = .80 when one predictor variable is to be added to a regression equation containing three predictors, and is expected to increase R^2 from .25 to .30.

tests of small, medium, and large effects (according to the Cohen guidelines, f^2 = .02, .15, and .35, respectively) for one of four predictors in a regression. Note that this is the same as testing the effect of the predictor when it is added to a regression equation already containing the three other predictors. Using the procedure outlined above, for a medium effect size, G*Power 3 provides N^* = 55. If the predictors are random, the required number of cases is N = 55 + 4 − 1 = 58. The corresponding values for small and large effects are N = 398 and N = 28, respectively.

- *Case 3—power calculations for testing whether all members of a specified subset that contains k of the p coefficients are equal to zero.* Assuming that the predictors are random variables, we again use G*Power 3 to find N^*, and the required sample size is $N = N^* + p - k$ if the predictors are random-effects variables.

Suppose we have a total of five predictors and want to test whether a particular subset of three predictors collectively adds significantly to the prediction over and above the contribution of the other two. If we expect that R^2 will increase from .44 to .50 when the subset of three predictors is added to the equation, then the f^2 for the additional three predictors is .06/.50 = .12. To find the sample size required to achieve power = .80, we use G*Power 3 as in the case 2 example, except now $f^2 = .12$, *Numerator df* = 3, and *Number of predictors* = 5. N^* is found to be 95, so that $N = N^* + p - k = 95 + 5 - 3 = 97$.

22.8 TESTING ASSUMPTIONS AND CHECKING FOR OUTLIERS AND INFLUENTIAL DATA POINTS

In Chapter 20 we considered how to check assumptions and to detect outliers and influential data points in bivariate regression. Here we extend the discussion to multiple regression.

Whether X is fixed or random, we assume that the underlying population model is

$$Y = \beta_0 + \beta_1 X_1 + \beta_2 X_2 + \ldots + \beta_p X_p + \varepsilon$$

and that the error components associated with each of the Y scores are normally and independently distributed with mean 0 and variance σ_e^2. As we discussed in Chapter 20, we would like to check for the assumptions of linearity, homoscedasticity, normality, and independence.

22.8.1 Checking Assumptions by Using Residuals

We can check a number of assumptions by using the residuals, e—the closest we can come to observing the error components, ε. We can plot histograms of e to see whether the distribution of residuals is approximately normal, and we can generate scatterplots of e against $\hat{Y}$ to determine whether there are systematic tendencies to violate assumptions. Under our usual assumptions, the residuals should act like normally distributed random error. If there seems to be systematic variability in the residuals, then perhaps the model has not been properly specified—perhaps additional variables should be added to the equation.

As can be seen in the dialog box shown in Fig. 22.2, SPSS makes it convenient to plot various residual measures against predictions. The histogram and scatterplot for the regression of *TC* on *age* and *BMI* are presented in Figs 22.3 and 22.4. The standardized residuals have an approximately normal distribution. Also, although the scatterplot of e vs $\hat{Y}$ indicates that there are outliers that deserve to be looked at more closely, there are no strong suggestions of curvilinearity or heteroscedasticity.

We should also look at the *partial regression plots*. In bivariate regression, it really did not matter whether we plotted the residuals against the predicted scores or against the predictor variable, X. Because the predicted scores are just a linear transformation of the X scores, both plots provide the same information. This is not the case for multiple regression because there is more than one predictor variable. For multiple regression, in addition to the plot of residuals against predicted scores, we would like to see how the residuals vary as a function of each predictor, *taking the other predictors in the equation into consideration*. Note that SPSS will readily provide these partial regression plots for each predictor in the equation if we check *Produce all partial plots* in the *Linear Regression: Plots* dialog box shown in Fig. 22.2.

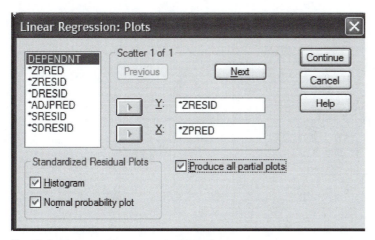

Fig. 22.2 SPSS dialog box used for obtaining residual and partial regression plots.

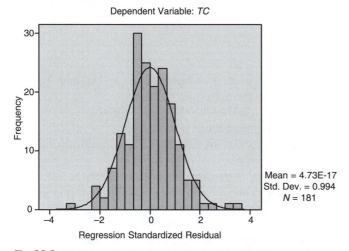

Fig. 22.3 Histogram for the standardized residuals with a superimposed normal curve for the regression of *TC* on *BMI* and *age* for women aged 20–65 with *BMI* scores no larger than 40.

Let's be more concrete in our description of partial regression plots. Suppose we have a criterion variable, Y, and three predictor variables, X_1, X_2, and X_3. We can obtain a partial regression plot for each of the predictor variables. The steps required to get the partial regression plot of Y against X_1 when X_2 and X_3 are also in the equation are the following:

1. Regress Y on X_2 and X_3, and obtain the residuals for this regression, $e_{Y.23}$.
2. Regress X_1 on X_2 and X_3, and obtain the residuals for this regression, $e_{1.23}$.
3. Now generate the scatterplot for $e_{Y.23}$ vs $e_{1.23}$.

These partial regression plots have the following useful properties:

- If we regress $e_{Y.23}$ on $e_{1.23}$, the slope is equal to $b_{Y1.23}$, the partial regression coefficient for X_1

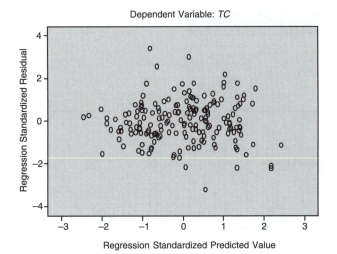

Fig. 22.4 Scatterplot of the standardized residuals vs the standardized predicted values of *TC* for women aged 20–65 with *BMI* scores no larger than 40.

in the regression equation that is obtained when Y is regressed on X_1, X_2, and X_3. The regression of Y on X_1 will not generally have the correct partial slope.

- The simple correlation between $e_{Y.23}$ and $e_{1.23}$ is equal to the partial correlation between Y and X_1 with the other predictor variables in the equation partialed out.
- The residuals from the regression line in this plot are exactly the same as those obtained when Y is regressed on all three predictors.
- If Y and X_1 are not linearly related, the partial regression plot will show both the linear and nonlinear components of the relation, *controlling for the other predictors*. This should help us decide whether we wish to add additional variables or other terms such as X_1^2 to the regression equation.
- We can also use these partial regression plots to determine whether the variability of the residuals varies as a function of X_j in the presence of the other predictors in the equation, thereby violating the assumption of homoscedasticity.

The partial regression plots for *TC* and *age* and for *TC* and *BMI* are displayed in Figs 22.5 and 22.6. There are some outliers and there also seems to be an increase in the variability of the *TC* residuals for larger values of the *age* residuals, suggesting a violation of the homoscedasticity assumption. We performed a weighted least-squares regression, using the SPSS weight estimation procedure for the *age* variable (see Chapter 20). When cases with greater ages were given less weight (the best estimated weight was $w_i = 1/age_i$) the partial regression coefficients were 1.750 and 1.753 for *age* and *BMI*, respectively, compared with the corresponding OLS regression estimates of 1.737 and 1.474. For both coefficients, the WLS estimates had slightly smaller *SE*s and *p*-values. The increase in the value of the coefficient for *BMI* when cases with greater age are given less weight suggests that the relationship between *TC* and *BMI* may differ for younger and older subjects, so that we may wish to consider whether there is an *age* × *BMI* interaction (we discuss how to do this in Chapter 23).

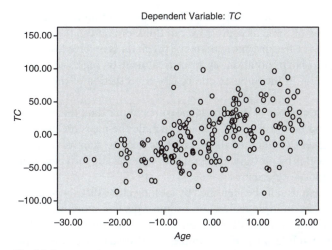

Fig. 22.5 Partial regression plot for *TC* vs *age* (i.e., the plot of the residuals for the regression of *TC* on *BMI* against the residuals for the regression of *age* on *BMI*).

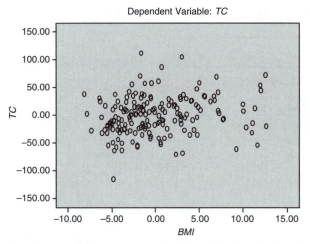

Fig. 22.6 Partial regression plot for *TC* vs *BMI* (i.e., the plot of the residuals for the regression of *TC* on *age* against the residuals for the regression of *BMI* on *age*).

22.8.2 Testing for Departures from Linearity

None of the residual plots show strong systematic departures from linearity. We can, however, test directly for curvilinearity in, and for interactions among, predictor variables. We take up these topics in Chapter 23.

22.8.3 Outliers and Influential Points in Multiple Regression

In discussing bivariate regression in Chapter 20, we introduced measures for identifying cases that had outlying residuals or outlying values of *X*, or had inordinate influence in determining the overall model fit or the value of the regression coefficient for X. The corresponding measures for multiple regression are just generalizations of these measures; we can think of and use them in the same way as in bivariate regression. However, because more than one predictor is involved, some of these measures are usually expressed in matrix notation. A brief treatment of regression using matrix notation is presented in Chapter 21A in the Supplementary Materials section of the book's website.

SPSS allows us to conveniently add a number of diagnostic measures to our data file when we conduct a regression (see the SPSS dialog box in Fig. 22.7). These include the measures listed in Table 22.2 that were all defined in Chapter 20. Each of these variables may be summarized and plotted. We can readily identify extreme cases by plotting histograms of the relevant variables. Here we briefly discuss several of the more important measures.

In bivariate regression, outliers in X can usually be identified by looking at the distribution of X or at the scatterplot of X vs Y. However, in multiple regression, we must depend more heavily on measures such as the leverage, h_{jj}, to identify outlying combinations of values on the predictors because multivariate outliers can occur in subtle ways. For example, the jth case may be an outlier because there are correlated deviations from the mean for several predictors; there need not be an extreme deviation for any single predictor.

Table 22.2 Variables that can be saved and added to the data set in multiple regression using SPSS

SPSS variable name	Referent
pre_1	unstandardized predicted value
zpr_1	standardized predicted value
adj_1	adjusted predicted value
sep_1	standard error of predicted value
res_1	unstandardized residual
zre_1	standardized residual
sre_1	Studentized residual
dre_1	deleted residual
sdr_1	Studentized deleted residual
mah_1	Mahalanobis distance
coo_1	Cook's distance
lev_1	centered leverage
sdb0_1	standardized DFBETA for the intercept
sdb1_1	standardized DFBETA for predictor 1
sdb2_1	standardized DFBETA for predictor 2
sdf_1	standardized DFFIT

Also, as we mentioned in Chapter 20, it can be shown that the sum of the leverages is $\Sigma h_{jj} = p + 1$ where p is the number of predictor variables; therefore, the mean value of h_{jj} is $(p + 1)/N$. Hoaglin and Welsch (1978) suggest that values of h_{jj} greater than $2(p + 1)/N$ should be considered large. Belsley, Kuh, and Welsch (1980) indicate that this cutoff will identify too many data points if p is small but recommend it because it is easy to remember and use. Other guidelines mentioned by Neter et al. (1996) are that h_{jj} values exceeding .5 indicate very high leverage whereas those between .2 and .5 indicate moderate leverage.

SPSS users should note that when leverages are requested, SPSS produces *centered leverages*,

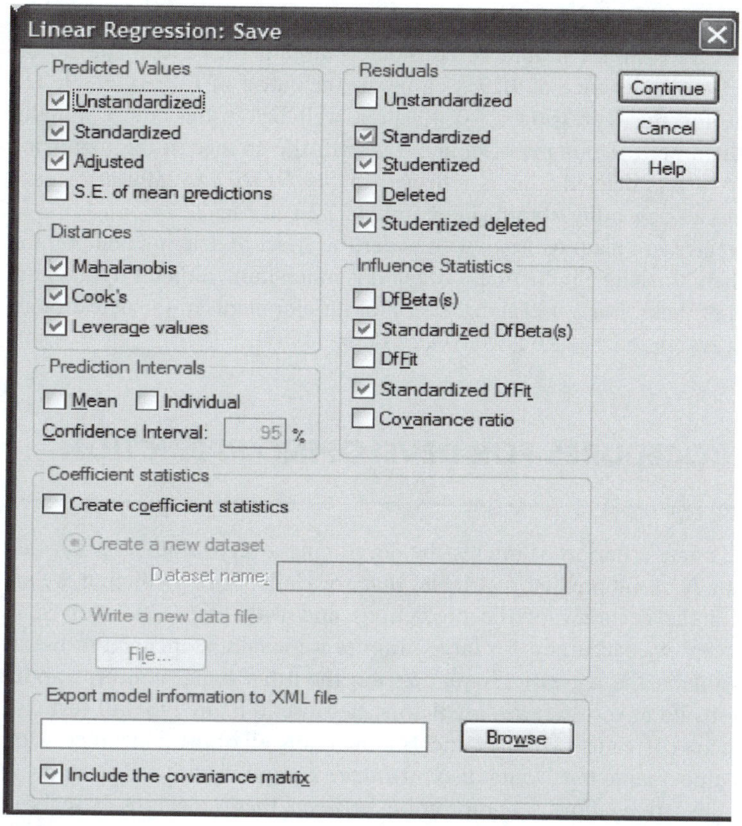

Fig. 22.7 SPSS dialog box used for saving measures of residuals as well as measures of influence into the data file.

$h_{jj} - 1/N$, for each case. To use the cutoff criteria, we can either modify the criteria so that they apply to centered leverages or simply transform the centered leverages to regular leverages by adding $1/N$ to each of them—here we do the latter. For the regression of *TC* on *age* and *BMI*, for women aged 20–65 years with *BMI*s of ≤40, the largest centered leverage is .055 so that the largest h_{jj} is .055 + 1/181 = .061, a low value according to the Neter et al. (1996) guidelines, although it is larger than the Hoaglin and Welsch criterion of .033. We can see from the data set that this leverage value comes from case 569 (ID = 1068), a woman with both predictor values (*age* = 64, *BMI* = 39) near their cutoffs.

As we pointed out earlier, cases with outlying residuals do not necessarily have the greatest influence on the regression equation or the fit. We introduced Cook's distance, CD_j, in Chapter 20 as a measure of the change that would result in the overall fit of the model if the jth case was omitted. CD_j can be written as

$$CD_j = \frac{\sum_i (\hat{Y}_i^{(-j)} - \hat{Y}_i)^2}{(p+1)s_e^2}$$

where $\hat{Y}_i^{(-j)}$ is the prediction of Y_i obtained from regression coefficients obtained with the jth case deleted. A simple guideline given by Cook and Weisberg (1982) is that a Cook's distance of 1 should be considered to be large. However, a guideline that takes sample size and number of predictors into account is that Cook's distance values should be considered large if they exceed the cutoff $F_{.50, p+1, N-p-1}$. Case 569 has a Cook's distance of .029, well below the cutoff of $F_{.50, 3, 178} = .79$. The largest Cook's distance value for the regression is .084, again well below the cutoff. Finally, although we do not discuss them here, if our major concern is with the change in the regression coefficients when a particular case is deleted, this is reflected in the *DFBETAS* values for each predictor variable; these values can be readily obtained (see Table 22.2 and Fig. 22.2).

Unfortunately, although regression diagnostics that consider the effect of deleting one point at a time work quite well when there is a single influential outlier, it is much more difficult to diagnose outliers when there are several of them. For a useful discussion of developments in the detection of multiple outliers and of robust regression, see Rousseeuw and Leroy (1987).

22.9 AUTOMATED PROCEDURES FOR DEVELOPING PREDICTION EQUATIONS

Sometimes we want to predict some criterion of interest by developing a regression equation that contains a subset of the potentially useful predictor variables that are available. In predicting, we are normally concerned both with the accuracy of the predictions and with the costs involved in making them. If our only concern was accuracy, for large samples we would be inclined to use as many valid predictors as possible in the regression equation; on the other hand, concerns about costs and simplicity would motivate us to use fewer predictors. Because in many types of research most of the predictor variables are correlated with one another, including all of them in a regression equation would not only be cumbersome but would also introduce a good deal of redundancy. A number of automated procedures that allow a compromise between these concerns have been developed to produce the best possible predictions with regression equations that contain relatively few predictors. These procedures include forward selection, backward elimination, and stepwise regression, and are available in many statistical packages. Using these procedures, it is often possible to select a subset of the potential predictors that account for nearly as large a proportion of the variability in Y as does the entire pool of predictors. Before describing them, we should emphasize that these automated procedures have been developed solely to produce the best prediction equations according to certain criteria. These equations need not be best nor even good in any explanatory or theoretical sense. Running an automated regression routine may be useful for predicting but is a poor way to develop theory.

22.9.1 Forward Selection

In the forward selection procedure, the regression equation is built up one variable at a time. On the first step, the predictor that has the highest correlation (positive or negative) is selected. If it fails to meet the criterion for inclusion, the procedure ends with no predictors in the equation, and the final equation is $\hat{Y}_i = \bar{Y}$. If the first predictor meets the criterion and is added to the equation, a second predictor is then selected and tested to determine whether it should be entered into the equation. The predictor selected is the one that would result in the greatest increment in R^2 if added to the equation. If the second predictor does not meet the criterion for inclusion, the procedure terminates with only a single predictor in the equation. If it does meet the criterion, on the third step, a third predictor is selected and tested, and so on. At each step, a partial F test is performed on the selected variable, and the criterion for inclusion is stated in terms of the critical value or the significance level of the F.

It should be noted that for procedures like forward selection, the usual significance levels obtained from the F distribution are not appropriate. This is because at each step a number of possible predictors are examined and only the one that produces the greatest increment in R^2 is tested. If only a single predictor is to be chosen from a pool of m possible predictors, the situation is analogous to choosing the largest member of a family of m contrasts and testing it for significance (see Section 22.4). As in the case of contrasts, if a single predictor is to be chosen, the Bonferroni procedure may be used to control Type 1 error; that is, to use $\alpha^* = \alpha/m$ as the criterion for significance, where α is the probability of at least one Type 1 error (see Chapter 10 for a discussion of the issue of familywise error rates and procedures for controlling them).

Wilkinson (1979) has discussed the case in which a subset of k predictors is to be chosen, where $1 < k < m$, and has provided tables of the upper 95th and 99th percentage points of the sample R^2 distribution in forward selection based on simulations (other tables and discussions of this problem can be found in Hocking, 1983; Rencher & Pun, 1980; and Wilkinson & Dallal, 1982). These tables are more conservative than the usual F tables. For example, with $N = 35$ and $\alpha = .05$, if all four members of a set of predictor variables are to be included in the regression equation, it is appropriate to use the standard F test to test R^2 for significance. When this is done, it is found that the sample R^2 has to exceed .26 in order to reject the hypothesis that the population multiple correlation coefficient is 0. However, if the four predictors are to be selected from a larger set of 20 predictors by a forward selection procedure, according to Wilkinson's tables, the sample R^2 must exceed .51 in order to reject the null hypothesis. Many researchers do not seem to be aware of this problem; for a sample of 66 published papers that reported significant forward selection analyses according to the usual F tests, Wilkinson found that 19 were not significant when his tables were used.

22.9.2 Backward Elimination

Whereas forward selection begins with no predictors in the equation and adds them to the equation one by one, backward elimination begins with all the predictors in the equation and removes them one by one until the final equation is obtained. At each step, the predictor in the equation that produces the smallest change in R^2 is tested to determine whether it should be removed from the equation. Again the criterion for removal is generally stated in terms of the significance level of a partial F test. If the selected variable is removed, another predictor is selected and tested on the next step. The procedure terminates when a predictor that has been selected for testing does not meet the criterion for elimination; the final equation includes that predictor and all the other predictors remaining in the equation at that point. In sum, the two automated procedures considered so far are flip sides of the same coin: whereas forward selection starts with no predictors and adds variables one-by-one to build an equation, backward elimination starts with all of the predictors and removes them one-by-one. However, despite the symmetry of this pair of procedures and their common goal, they can result in different final equations.

22.9.3 Stepwise Regression

Stepwise regression, the most popular of these procedures, is a combination of forward selection and backward elimination. The procedure is essentially the same as forward selection with the exception that after each new predictor has been added to the regression equation, all the predictors already in the equation are re-examined to determine whether they should be removed. A partial F

test is performed on the predictor already in the equation that produces the smallest increment in R^2. If the predictor no longer satisfies the criteria for inclusion, it is removed from the equation. Statistical packages allow the user to set the significance levels (or critical F values) for entering or removing a variable.

It is not difficult to see why it is sometimes desirable to remove a predictor that had been entered early in the analysis. For example, suppose that X_7 is highly predictable from X_4 and X_9 but is more highly correlated with Y than either of them. Even though X_7 may enter the equation early because of its high correlation with Y, it will become superfluous after X_4 and X_9 are entered. Even if X_7 contributes significantly to the predictability of Y by itself, it may not make a significant contribution over and above that provided by the other two variables.

It is important to emphasize that when predictor variables entered into the equation are selected from a larger pool, the significance levels printed out by stepwise programs are not "real" p-values. Because many researchers seem to be unaware of this fact, stepwise regression outputs are frequently misinterpreted. As Wilkinson has stated, stepwise regression programs are probably the most notorious source of "pseudo p-values" in the field of automated data analysis. As with forward selection, we recommend that Wilkinson's (1979) tables be used to test R^2 for significance.

We again emphasize that the sole motivation for the automated procedures described in this section is to develop useful prediction equations that include subsets of the available predictors. There is no reason to think that the equations they produce are reasonable explanatory models. Variables that are useful predictors need not be important components of a good theory or causal explanation of the situation. The automated procedures may include theoretically uninteresting variables in the regression equations they produce and they may not include the important variables. Consider, for example, a stepwise regression with several predictors that are highly correlated both with the criterion and with each other. The correlation between the criterion and the predictor included on the first step may be only marginally greater than the correlation between the criterion and the other predictors. Nonetheless, including the first predictor may prevent any of the others from being entered into the equation on subsequent steps. Even though the other predictors add significantly to the predictability of Y in the absence of the first variable, they may not do so when the first variable is in the equation. Forward regression procedures are more likely than backward elimination to exclude potentially useful predictors in situations that involve suppression (see Chapter 21). Even in situations in which both the suppressor variable and the variable whose variance is suppressed may be useful for predicting Y, it is possible that neither variable may make it into the equation unless the other variable is already there, if a forward selection procedure is used.

Because predictor variables are included in the regression equation if they are useful in the sample, stepwise procedures are extremely susceptible to capitalization on chance, especially when the sample is small. Recall that in the discussion of capitalization on chance in Chapter 21 we presented an example in which stepwise regression produced an equation that fit a sample fairly well ($R = .504$). Nonetheless, we demonstrated that the equation was of no use for predicting outside of that sample (cross-validated $R = .046$). If stepwise regression is ever to be used, it is important to use cross-validation in order to evaluate the usefulness of the resulting regression equation.

We conclude this section by restating that *using these automated stepwise procedures is a very poor way to develop theory*. Automated programs may be easy to use but are a poor substitute for thinking. Even minimal knowledge about the research situation along with careful exploration of the data should lead to better preliminary models than an automated procedure. We repeat this point because we keep encountering researchers who are ignorant of, or resistant to, this advice. As Wilkinson (1998) has stated in the SYSTAT manual:

Stepwise regression is probably the most abused computerized statistical technique ever devised. If you think you need automated stepwise regression to solve a particular problem, it is almost certain that you do not. Professional statisticians rarely use automated stepwise regression because it does not necessarily find the "best" fitting model, the "real" model, or alternative "plausible" models. Furthermore, the order in which variables enter or leave a stepwise program is usually of no theoretical significance. You are always better off thinking about why a model could generate your data and then testing that model. (p. 351)

22.10 SUMMARY

- In Chapter 22, we discussed statistical inference in multiple regression. We also considered the models underlying inference and introduced statistical tests and power as well as confidence intervals for the regression coefficients, the predictions, and the multiple correlation coefficient.
- We discussed how to check for violations of the assumptions that underlie the inference model and how to detect outliers and influential points in multiple regression.
- Finally, we considered some automated procedures available in statistical packages for finding the "best" prediction equations. Because many researchers seem to think that these automated procedures should be useful in developing theory, we tried to emphasize that they should not be used to develop explanatory models.

EXERCISES

22.1 In an experiment designed to determine the effects of drug dosage on performance, the following data (available as data set *EX22_1*) are obtained:

Dosage in milligrams			
10	20	30	40
6.8	10.4	10.7	8.9
2.8	6.4	14.4	12.5
5.2	13.1	15.9	12.7
4.8	8.7	10.6	7.4
	12.4		8.5
	7.2		

(a) Perform an ANOVA to test the effect of dosage on performance.
(b) Regress performance on dosage to determine whether there is a significant linear relationship between performance and dosage.
(c) Determine whether there is a significant nonlinear relationship between performance and dosage.
(d) Determine whether there is a significant quadratic component to the relationship by creating a new variable, *dosagesq*, formed by squaring dosage (in SPSS, use *Compute Variable . . .* on the *Transform* menu), and then regress performance on dosage and *dosagesq*. Find the best-fitting quadratic equation.

22.2   Data set *EX22_2* contains hypothetical data for verbal achievement of students in elementary school; potential predictor variables are *squality* and *tquality*, measures of school and teacher quality, and *sbackground* and *pbackground*, measures of student and parent background.

   (a) Do the school and teacher measures contribute to the predictability of verbal ability? Do the student and parent measures? Consider regression equations containing different combinations of predictors in arriving at your answer.

   (b) Perform a stepwise regression using one of the standard packages. Do you think that the regression equation identified by the stepwise regression is a reasonable explanatory model of the situation?

22.3   Using data from an observational study, we plan to perform a multiple regression analysis with six predictor variables. If we want to test the hypothesis that all population regression coefficients are equal to 0 at $\alpha = .05$, how many cases do we need to have a power of .80:

   (a) if we expect an R^2 of .30?

   (b) if $R^2 = .20$?

   (c) if $R^2 = .10$?

22.4   We perform a multiple regression with six predictors and find that $R^2 = .20$. Can we reject the null hypothesis that all the regression coefficients $= 0$ in the population if $N = 50$?

22.5   Suppose we wish to add a seventh predictor to a regression equation and expect it to increase R^2 from .30 to .35. How many cases are required to have power $= .90$?

22.6   Find the number of cases required to yield power $= .80$ for a test of a medium-sized effect ($f^2 = .15$) for a predictor to be added to a regression equation already containing five predictors.

22.7   Suppose we conduct a multiple regression analysis on data from an observational study with four predictor variables and $N = 40$. We find that adding variable X_4 to the other three predictors increases R^2 from .21 to .27. Can we reject the null hypothesis that the coefficient of variable X_4 has the value 0 in the population? Estimate how many cases we need to have a power of .80 to reject the null hypothesis if $\alpha = .05$.

22.8   Suppose we conduct a multiple regression analysis on data from an observational study with six predictor variables and $N = 80$. We find that adding both variables X_5 and X_6 to the first four predictors increases R^2 from .31 to .37.

   (a) Can we reject the null hypothesis that the coefficients of X_5 and X_6 equal zero in the population at $\alpha = .05$?

   (b) Estimate how many cases we need to have a power of .90 to reject the null hypothesis if we were to rerun the study.

22.9   Consider the data set *tcforwomen* on the book's website. If we regress *TC* on *schoolyr*, a crude measure of years of education, we find that *schoolyr* is a significant predictor of *TC*, $b = 1.42$, $t(178) = -3.02$, $p = .003$; more education is associated with lower cholesterol levels. This fits well with our stereotype that more educated people take better care of themselves and have better diets. However, there may be alternate explanations for this education effect. Try to think of one or more, and explore it by using the data set.

Chapter 23
Additional Topics in Multiple Regression

23.1 OVERVIEW

When we perform regressions, if our goal is to maximize prediction accuracy, we should look at measures of fit such as R or R^2. However, R is not a reasonable criterion for assessing the usefulness of explanatory models because it is not necessarily an index of causal effects, nor is it comparable across samples. Because predictions from an incorrect model can correlate more strongly with the dependent variable than predictions from the correct model, correlation has been referred to as "an instrument of the devil" when used to infer causation from confounded data (Birnbaum, 1973).

If our concern is with explanation or theory development, our goal is to understand the direct and indirect effects of the independent variables on the dependent variable of interest. Therefore, our focus should be on interpreting the regression coefficients. In Chapter 23, we discuss a number of issues that affect our ability to interpret regression coefficients. We introduced several of these issues in the three preceding chapters but expand upon them here:

- *What are the consequences of mis-specifying the regression model?* The omission of important predictor variables from the regression equation or the addition of extraneous variables may make it difficult to interpret the coefficients of predictors in the equation.
- *Measurement error and missing data*. To the extent that variables are not appropriately measured, subsequent statistical analyses are compromised. Having a poorly measured predictor results in the distortion of not only its own regression coefficient, but also the coefficients of other correlated predictors.
- *Multicollinearity*. When predictor variables are completely redundant, the regression cannot be performed. When they are highly redundant, the regression can be performed, but the regression coefficients are unstable and therefore difficult to interpret.
- *Unstandardized vs standardized regression coefficients*. One reason why it is difficult to interpret regression coefficients as measures of importance is that different regression coefficients generally have different units. One attempt to deal with this issue is to use standardized regression coefficients. We will argue that the kind of comparability achieved

by standardization is often not useful and that unstandardized coefficients are generally more interpretable and therefore more useful than standardized coefficients.

- *Direct vs indirect effects and mediating variables.* A predictor variable may indirectly affect the dependent variable by influencing *mediating* variables, which, in turn, influence the dependent variable. If we wish to construct an explanatory model or talk about the "importance" of a predictor, we must consider indirect effects as well as direct effects.

- *Testing for curvilinearity.* Because the relationship between the dependent variable and some predictors may not be purely linear, it is important to know how to detect and characterize curvilinearity.

- *Testing for interactions.* The nature of the relationship between the dependent variable and a predictor may depend on the values of other variables called *moderator variables*. We can test for these moderators by adding them, along with interaction terms, to the regression equations.

- *Distinguishing between curvilinearity and interactions.* Both the presence of curvilinear components and interactions represent deviations from pure linearity. Unfortunately, it can be difficult to distinguish between the presence of curvilinearity and interactions because the curvilinear and interaction terms will be correlated.

- *Logistic regression.* Important variables such as success/fail and live/die are categorical variables that have only two levels. In this chapter, we provide a very brief introduction to logistic regression, a kind of regression that can be used with dichotomous dependent variables, and we offer a more detailed introduction in the Supplementary Materials on the book's website.

- *Repeated-measures regression and multilevel or hierarchical regression.* Multilevel regression, or hierarchical linear regression (HLM), provides a very general framework for analyzing data when variables are nested within levels of other variables. For example, nesting occurs when students who are tested are part of an interactive group such as a class within a school, or when each subject is tested several times, so that measures are nested within subjects. Although a thorough treatment of HLM is beyond the scope of this book, we provide a brief introduction to some of the basic ideas.

23.2 SPECIFICATION ERRORS AND THEIR CONSEQUENCES

A regression equation is correctly specified if it contains the same variables as the true population model. If parameters of the population model

$$Y_i = \beta_0 + \beta_1 X_{i1} + \beta_2 X_{i2} + \ldots + \beta_p X_{ip} + \varepsilon_i$$

are estimated by the coefficients of the sample regression equation,

$$\hat{Y}_i = b_0 + b_1 X_{i1} + b_2 X_{i2} + \ldots + b_p X_{ip}$$

then, given the usual regression assumptions, the b_js can be shown to be unbiased estimators of the β_js. However, as we pointed out in Chapter 21, if the b_js are obtained from a regression equation that omits important predictors in the population model, or adds variables that are not in the model, they will generally be biased estimators of the β_js in the true population model.

Considering the consequences of mis-specification is important because in non-experimental research, we rarely work with "true" models. In developing explanations, we often start with crude, incomplete models, and then attempt to extend and refine them. As we conduct our analyses, questions may arise that lead us to collect more data and perform additional analyses, so that we modify our models in ways that help us better focus our thinking about the research question. Although we must be aware of their limitations, regression analyses can play a very useful role in advancing our understanding, even when the equations they produce cannot be thought of as representing complete, true models.

In many contexts, the most useful models are not "true" population models. Box (1979, p. 209; also see useful discussions in Berk, 2004, and King, 1991) has stated that "All models are wrong, but some are useful." Problems in the social sciences are often too complex to be represented completely by any specific theory or model, especially one that can be expressed as a single regression equation. Relatively simple models with few predictors that capture the essence of a research problem may contribute more usefully to scientific discourse and/or have more direct practical applications than more cumbersome complex models even if the larger models are more correct. However, when we work with models that do not match the true underlying population model, we must be aware of how regression coefficients may be affected when predictor variables are left out of, or added to, a regression equation.

Omitting Relevant Variables.   We pointed out in Chapter 21 that if an important variable in the true population model is omitted from a regression equation and if this omitted variable is correlated with one or more variables that are included in the equation, then the coefficients of the variables in the equation will reflect not only the effects of the corresponding predictors, but also the effects of the omitted variable.

Let's illustrate this point in more detail. Suppose that the true model in the population is

$$Y = \beta_{012} + \beta_{Y1 \cdot 2} X_1 + \beta_{Y2 \cdot 1} X_2 + \varepsilon$$

where we use the notation $\beta_{Y1 \cdot 2}$ to emphasize that the regression coefficient of X_1 comes from a model that includes both X_1 and X_2. If we regress Y only on X_1, thereby mis-specifying the model by omitting X_2 from the equation, we obtain the sample regression equation

$$\hat{Y} = b_{01} + b_{Y1} X_1$$

In Appendix 23.1, we show that the expected value of b_{Y1} is not $\beta_{Y1 \cdot 2}$, the coefficient of X_1 in the true model, but rather $\beta_{Y1 \cdot 2} + \beta_{Y2 \cdot 1} \beta_{21} = \beta_{Y1 \cdot 2} + \beta_{Y2 \cdot 1} \rho_{12} \sigma_2 / \sigma_1$. This expression contains $\beta_{Y1 \cdot 2}$ plus an additional term that depends on $\beta_{Y2 \cdot 1}$ as well as on the regression of X_2 on X_1, reflecting the fact that if X_2 is omitted from the regression, its effects on Y are partially expressed through X_1. Although things get more complicated when there are more predictors, the regression coefficients will generally be biased estimators of the population parameters if important variables are left out. The exception to this statement is when the omitted variables are *uncorrelated* with the variables that are included in the equation—we can see this above because the additional biasing term disappears when $\rho_{12} = 0$.

It is important to understand that it is the lack of correlation with other variables that allows us to make causal statements about independent variables on the basis of *experiments*. In well-designed experiments, the effects of nonmanipulated variables are controlled by procedures such as randomization and matching, so that variables in the model are not meaningfully correlated with those that are omitted. In contrast, in observational studies, nuisance variables may be hopelessly confounded (i.e., correlated) with the variables of interest in ways that make it impossible to sort out causality. In this case, the best we can do is to include the most important nuisance variables in our regressions and try to control for them statistically.

The message here is that although simple models may be very useful, if these models omit important variables that are correlated with variables in the model, we may arrive at faulty conclusions (see the example in Section 21.3).

Including Additional Variables. Because of the negative consequences of omitting important variables, researchers sometimes include additional variables in their regression equations in an attempt to make sure that nothing important has been left out. Adding variables that are not correlated with variables in the equation does not bias parameter estimates of the variables in the equation. However, including these additional variables will use up degrees of freedom. This will inflate the standard errors of the relevant variables, making parameter estimates less precise.

If, on the other hand, we add predictors that are correlated with variables in the equation, the coefficients will change. For example, suppose that we are interested in the effects of parental education on children's performance in elementary school and therefore regress some measure of children's school performance on the average number of years of parental schooling. If we now add other variables to the equation such as family income, class size, teacher pay, and number of books in the home—all measures correlated with parental education—the coefficient of years of parental schooling will change because it now reflects the effects of years of parental schooling *partialing out* the effects of these other variables.

23.3 MEASUREMENT ERROR IN MULTIPLE REGRESSION

As with other types of analyses, we need to have good measures of the variables when we use multiple regression. However, the consequences of measurement error differ depending on whether we are talking about the dependent variable or the predictor variables. Increased measurement error in the *dependent variable* increases the size of the error component, so that s_Y and s_e become larger and R^2 becomes smaller. This increases the size of confidence intervals and decreases the power of significance tests. However, if there are no major violations of assumptions, OLS estimates of the *unstandardized* regression coefficients remain unbiased. In contrast, because the *standardized* coefficient of X_j is the unstandardized coefficient multiplied by s_j/s_Y, standardized coefficients (the so-called beta weights) become smaller as measurement error in the dependent variable increases.

Now consider measurement error in the *predictor variables*. The usual regression inference model (see Chapters 20 and 22) assumes that predictor variables are fixed and measured without error. However, in many applications, values of the predictors are sampled and are measured with error. Measurement error in the predictors may result in serious problems, especially when some of the measurement error is systematic.

If the measurement error in the predictors is random, then at least the predictors may be independent of the error component for the model. The presence of random measurement error in any predictor will attenuate the estimate of the corresponding unstandardized regression coefficient. If the predictors are uncorrelated, the presence of random measurement error in one predictor will not systematically influence the estimated regression coefficient of any other predictor. If, on the other hand, the predictors in a multiple regression are correlated, as is usually the case, the result is more complicated. The coefficient of any predictor, X_j, is the rate of change of $\hat{Y}$ with X_j, partialing out the effects of the other predictor variables in the regression equation. When there is measurement error in predictors correlated with X_j, it is possible that too much or too little of the effects of the other variables may be partialed out. So, depending on the details, the unstandardized (b_j) and standardized (b_j^*) coefficients may be too large *or* too small.

The situation is at its worst when there is systematic error in the measurement of the predictors (e.g., when there are reporting biases; see Chapter 20), so that there are correlations between these predictors and the error component. If this happens, the OLS estimates of the coefficients will be neither unbiased nor consistent.

Some possible remedies are available. We can use instrumental variables; that is, we can try to use variables that are correlated with our predictors but not with the error component (see Berk, 2004). Or we can use structural equation modeling, a statistical technique for testing and estimating causal relationships that uses multiple indicators of underlying concepts, and explicitly models error. However, detailed discussion of both of these procedures is beyond the scope of the current discussion. At the level of coverage in this book, the best advice is to keep the issue of measurement in mind and to use the best possible measures available. It should go without saying that if we use poor and error-ridden measures, we can have little confidence in the results of our statistical analyses.

23.4 MISSING DATA IN MULTIPLE REGRESSION

In designing research, we should use measuring instruments and data collection procedures that minimize the occurrence of missing data, especially on the dependent variable. Depending on the details, the presence of missing data will result in our analyses having reduced power and may well result in biased parameter estimates and tests. The three options offered by SPSS to deal with missing data in the regression module are (a) exclude cases listwise (i.e., listwise deletion), (b) exclude data pairwise (i.e., pairwise deletion), and (c) replace with mean (i.e., mean substitution).

If we conduct multiple regressions using a set of variables and have some missing data, packages such as SPSS and SYSTAT allow us to use the *listwise deletion* option; that is, each regression is conducted by using only those cases with complete data on all the variables *used in the regression*. However, this approach may lead to different regressions being performed on somewhat different subsets of the data. For example, if we use the *Seasons* data set from the website and regress *TC* on *sex, age,* and *BMI*, the regression is performed by using the data from the 416 subjects with complete data on the four variables. If we add *Beck_d* (the mean score on the Beck Depression Scale over the four seasons) to the list of predictors, the regression is now based on the data from only the 313 cases with complete data on all five variables. If it is important to compare the results of the regressions, we may want to specify that only the data from the 313 subjects with complete data on all variables be used in both analyses.

If there are modest amounts of missing data, listwise deletion can have good properties. If the missing data are MCAR (that is, missing completely at random—see the discussion of missing data in Chapter 14), the data from complete cases can be thought of as randomly selected from the original sample. If so, estimates of the regression coefficients obtained by listwise deletion will be unbiased if all the usual regression assumptions are satisfied. The standard errors, of course, will be larger because they are based on fewer data.

It can be shown (e.g., see Allison, 2002) that if missing data on the dependent variable, Y, are *associated with* the values of Y and/or if missing data on the predictors are associated with the values of Y, then listwise regression will yield biased estimates (in this case, we can think of the missing data as an extreme case of systematic measurement error). However, as Allison points out, regression with listwise deletion is quite robust with respect to violations of the MAR assumption when the probability of missing data on Y and on the predictors does not depend on the values of Y.

Neither pairwise deletion nor mean substitution are recommended. The idea behind pairwise deletion is to use as much data as possible. Multiple regression can be performed, using the means, standard deviations, and correlations of all the variables in the regression equation. In pairwise deletion, these quantities are calculated by using whatever data are available. For example, if Y is the dependent variable and there are two predictors X_1 and X_2, we could obtain the correlation between Y and X_1 without regard to X_2, and the correlation between X_1 and X_2 without regard to Y. The problem is that if we use the pairwise deletion option in the standard statistical packages, the parameter estimates and test statistics may be biased unless the missing data are MCAR. In some cases, it may not be possible to perform certain higher-order analyses at all. Given pairwise deletion, the constraints normally expected in a correlation matrix (see Section 19.3.4) may not hold because different correlations may be obtained from substantially different subsets of cases and may be based on different numbers of observations.

Replacing missing scores on a variable by the variable mean (i.e., marginal mean imputation) is not recommended because it is well known that this procedure produces biased estimates of variances and correlations. As mentioned in Chapter 14, there are other, more sophisticated methods of imputing missing data that can produce unbiased estimates if the missing data are MCAR or MAR. Also, when there are repeated-measures, as, for example, in the case of depression scores measured at each season of the year, hierarchical regression modeling procedures that use all the available data can be used (see Section 23.11).

23.5 MULTICOLLINEARITY

Multicollinearity occurs when predictor variables included in a regression equation are correlated so that they can be predicted from the other predictors in the equation. If at least one predictor variable can be perfectly predicted from the others, there is perfect multicollinearity. Given perfect multicollinearity, an infinite number of regression equations will fit the data equally well, so the statistical packages cannot conduct a regression analysis. If we have only two predictors, one way of thinking about the problem is that if the predictors are perfectly correlated, so that X_1 and X_2 account for exactly the same variance in Y, there is no basis for attributing this variability to one or the other predictor.

A very useful way to think about the problem is to consider Figs 21.3 and 23.1. If Y is regressed on X_1 and X_2, the points ($\hat{Y}$, X_1, X_2) that satisfy the equation

$$\hat{Y} = b_0 + b_1 X_1 + b_2 X_2$$

will lie along the surface of a plane in the three-dimensional space defined by axes Y, X_1, and X_2. If X_1 and X_2 are not highly correlated, as in Fig. 21.3, the data points constrain the values of b_0, b_1, and b_2 that define the best-fitting regression plane. If the orientation of the plane was changed, b_0, b_1, and b_2 would take on different values, so that the predictions and therefore the fit of the regression equation would be different. However, if X_1 and X_2 are perfectly correlated, as in Fig. 23.1, the points ($\hat{Y}$, X_1, X_2) will lie along a straight line in the three-dimensional space, and any of the infinite number of planes that contain the line will fit the data equally well, making it impossible to specify unique values for b_0, b_1, and b_2. Fig. 23.1 shows two planes that fit equally well but which would have very different coefficient values.

It is rare to find perfect multicollinearity unless redundant variables such as subscale scores and total score, or age and year of birth, are included. However, it is not rare to find situations in which the predictors are highly collinear. In such cases, the software packages will perform the

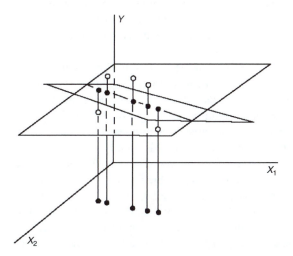

Fig. 23.1 Illustration of perfect multicollinearity: The open circles represent data points (X_1, X_2, Y). The lower group of filled circles represents the (X_1, X_2) coordinates of the data points. If X_1 and X_2 are perfectly correlated, these filled circles will fall on a straight line. The upper set of filled circles represents the points $(X_1, X_2, \hat{Y})$, where the $\hat{Y}$s are the best least-squares predictions of Y corresponding to (X_1, X_2). Note that these points fall on a straight line in the three-dimensional space, and that an infinite number of planes with different values of b_0, b_1, and b_2 will contain that straight line. Therefore, it is impossible to specify a unique regression plane.

regression,[1] but the values of the regression coefficients may be extremely unstable. The reason is that variability in Y that is shared by the predictors will be "split up" among them. The nature of this split will depend on the details of the data, and may vary widely from sample to sample, leading to dramatically increased standard errors for the regression coefficients.

The major software packages all provide diagnostic information that can be used to determine whether there is a potentially serious multicollinearity problem. In the SPSS output for the regression of *TC* on *age* and *BMI* in Table 21.5, the *Coefficients* panel displays information about the *Tolerance*, $(1 - R_j^2.)$, and *VIF* = 1/*Tolerance*, both measures that we discussed in Section 21.3. However, if we request collinearity diagnostics, we also get a table containing eigenvalues, condition indices, and variance proportions. Although a thorough explanation of these terms is beyond the scope of this discussion, a rough description is as follows: A principal components analysis (PCA) is first conducted to identify dependencies among the variables. Think of PCA as a data reduction technique in which we can determine whether most of the variability in the k predictor variables can be accounted for by fewer than k "components," where each component is a linear combination of the predictors. If so, this means there is redundancy in the predictors. The first principal component is obtained by finding the linear combination of predictor variables that accounts for the greatest amount of variability. The second principal component is the linear combination that is both

---

[1] When standard statistical packages such as SPSS, SAS, and SYSTAT are used, high correlations among predictors will not generally result in much difficulty if the only goal is prediction. However, multicollinearity can result in errors in the computational algorithms employed in spreadsheets such as Excel when one attempts to use them to perform multiple regression. Centering the variables (see the third remedy below and Section 23.9.4) can reduce the correlations among predictors, and can also reduce the sizes of the numbers used in calculations, thereby reducing rounding error. Nonetheless, spreadsheets and other nonstandard statistical software should not be used to perform serious statistical analyses, especially multiple regression.

uncorrelated with the first component and accounts for the greatest amount of the remaining variability, and so on. The eigenvalues are the amounts of variability accounted for by each of the principal components. If one or more of the eigenvalues are zero, this indicates that one or more of the variables are completely redundant, so there is perfect multicollinearity.

The *condition index* for each component is the square root of the ratio of the largest eigenvalue to the eigenvalue for that component. If the condition index for a component is large, this means that the component accounts for very little variability that has not already been accounted for by the other components, so that the set of predictors is redundant. According to Belsley, Kuh, and Welsch (1980), a condition index greater than 15 suggests a possible multicollinearity problem and a condition index greater than 30 suggests that there may be a serious multicollinarity problem.

The *variance proportions* are the proportions of variance of each regression coefficient estimate associated with each component. There is a serious multicollinearity problem when a component has a large condition index and high variance proportions (say, greater than .50) for two or more regression coefficients. We see in Table 21.5 that none of the condition indices exceed 15 for the regression of *TC* on *age* and *BMI*, so we do not have a serious multicollinearity problem for this analysis.

A number of possible remedies have been suggested if we find that there is a multicollinearity problem:

- *Deleting some of the predictors that are responsible for the problem*. If we have several measures of the same thing, this may be appropriate, although it is probably better to combine the measures—see below. However, if we have several different kinds of measures that are highly correlated, the cure may be worse than the disease. Deleting variables may result in specification errors and correlations between predictors and the error component that themselves can have very serious consequences, as we discussed earlier.
- *Combining clusters of highly related predictor variables into new variables that represent common underlying factors*. Deciding which variables to combine is best done on the basis of theoretical considerations. Procedures such as principal components analysis and factor analysis can also provide suggestions about possible underlying processes, thereby providing information about which variables might be combined.
- *Centering*. This involves replacing each score by the corresponding deviation score; that is, the score minus the mean of the variable. For example, when we regressed *TC* on *age* and *BMI* using data from women aged 20–65 with *BMI* scores not exceeding 40, the mean of the age scores was 46.928. We would center the age variable by replacing it with a new variable, *agec* = *age* − 46.928. Centering can be useful in providing more interpretable regression coefficients (e.g., see Sections 23.8 and 23.9) and will also often reduce multicollinearity.
- *Ridge regression* (e.g., Draper & Smith, 1998; Rozeboom, 1979). This procedure takes advantage of the fact that under certain conditions it may be more desirable to use biased estimates with small standard errors than unbiased estimates with larger standard errors.

23.6 UNSTANDARDIZED vs STANDARDIZED COEFFICIENTS IN MULTIPLE REGRESSION

As we mentioned earlier, standardized regression coefficients (sometimes called beta weights) are obtained if we perform the regression by using z scores. For any given predictor variable X_j, the standardized coefficient is given by

$$b_j^* = b_j s_j / s_Y$$

where b_j is the unstandardized coefficient and s_j and s_Y are the standard deviations of X_j and Y. The standardized coefficient b_j^* is the change in $\hat{Y}$ in s_Y units when X_j is increased by one s_j unit and the values of all other predictors in the equation are held constant.

Standardized coefficients can be useful if we are concerned with changes in relative standing within the Y and X_j distributions. Standardized coefficients are also related to the increases in the variance of Y accounted for (i.e., the increase in R^2) that occur when predictors are added to the regression equation. If the predictors are uncorrelated, $b_j^{*2} = r_{Yj}^2$, and it is the proportion of variance accounted for by X_j. If the predictors are correlated, the increment in R^2 achieved by adding X_j is $r_{Yj} b_j^*$. Many researchers consider the proportions of variance accounted for by predictors in a regression equation or their beta weights as measures of importance that can be used to develop theoretical models. However, we have argued that such measures are not a reasonable basis for determining the causal or theoretical importance of independent variables when we conduct observational studies and conduct regressions on correlated predictor variables. Pedhazur (1997) has provided a useful discussion of the *limitations* of using variance partitioning to assess the importance of correlated variables in multiple regression.

We discussed some of the problems with standardized coefficients in Section 20.6 when we considered bivariate regression. All five points mentioned there are also relevant for multiple regression. Briefly, they are: (1) if scales are meaningful, one-unit changes are more understandable than changes of one standard deviation; (2) standardizing may make us less aware of poor or unreliable scales of measurement; (3) standardized regression coefficients are sample specific; (4) differences in standard deviations may be the source of differences in the values of standardized coefficients across samples; and (5) standardized coefficients are less stable across samples than unstandardized coefficients. Here, we add the following:

- Scientific laws and policy recommendations are more naturally stated in terms of actual, raw scores rather than standardized scores. In many contexts, standardized coefficients are undesirable precisely because they confound the effects of variables with their standard deviations.
- Simple comparisons of unstandardized coefficients within a multiple regression equation are complicated by the fact that different predictors are expressed in different units. Researchers often argue that standardized regression coefficients have the advantage of being more "comparable" to one another than unstandardized coefficients because everything is in "comparable" standard deviation units. However, there is no reason to consider the standard deviations of two variables to be equivalent in any meaningful or useful sense, either in terms of practice or theory, unless we are interested in relative standing.[2] Comparisons of standardized coefficients within or across samples will depend on the variances of the samples which can change for any number of reasons. Moreover, it is harder to change some predictors by a standard deviation than it is to change others, especially if other correlated predictors are held constant.

---

[2] And then, really only if we are dealing with more or less normally distributed variables. Standard deviations are much less informative if we have highly skewed or lumpy distributions, or if we have important outliers.

23.7 REGRESSION WITH DIRECT AND MEDIATED EFFECTS

It is possible for an independent variable to influence the dependent variable directly, or it can influence the dependent variable indirectly, through its effect on a mediating variable. Fig. 23.2 provides an illustration of this distinction. In panel (a), we have a model in which X_1 exerts a direct effect on Y. This causal influence is indicated by the arrow, and the direction of the arrow indicates the direction of causality. In panel (b), we have a causal model that illustrates both direct and mediated effects. In this case, a change in X_1 directly affects Y but also affects Y indirectly through the mediator variable, X_2. There are many examples of the kinds of mediating influences illustrated in panel (b): changes in the workplace environment may influence job perception, which in turn influences productivity; or changes in parents' attitudes about education may change children's attitudes, which in turn influence academic performance. Theories specifying processes that intervene between independent and dependent variables are important in many fields of psychology. MacKinnon et al. (2002) have noted that a search of the *Social Science Citation Index* turned up more than 2,000 citations of the seminal Baron and Kenny (1986) paper that discussed ways of testing for a mediating effect.

We must consider the possibility of mediating effects if we try to determine the "importance" of a variable. Even if we include the correct variables in the regression equation and there is a causal relationship between X_j and the outcome, Y, the regression coefficient b_j does not estimate the total influence of X_j on Y. Rather, the regression coefficient reflects the *direct effect* of X_j on Y, that is, the rate of change of Y with X_j, *holding all of the other variables in the equation constant*. If changes in X_j cause changes in some of the other predictor variables, in turn causing changes in Y, we would have both direct and indirect effects. In assessing the importance of X_j, we must be concerned with both the direct and indirect effects. Given a valid causal model, structural equation modeling can be used to assess the total effect of changing a variable. However, as always, these estimates may be misleading if important variables are omitted from the model or if the model is otherwise invalid.

Again, consider the two causal models in Fig. 23.2. In panel (a), a change of one unit in X_1 causes a change of c units in Y. In panel (b), we have a causal model that illustrates both direct and mediated effects. For this model, changing X_1 by one unit directly causes a change in Y of c' units and a change in X_2 of a units. A change of one unit in X_2 causes a change of b units in Y. Therefore, the indirect effect of X_1 on Y though the mediator X_2 is ab, so that the total effect of X_1 on Y is $c' + ab$. Baron and Kenny (1986) have discussed four steps necessary to establish that a data set is consistent with the presence of mediation. These steps, translated into our terminology, are as follows:

Step 1.   Regress Y on X_1. If the regression coefficient b_{Y1} is nonzero, this is consistent with X_1 having a causal effect on Y.

Step 2.   Regress X_2 on X_1. If the regression coefficient b_{21} is nonzero, this is consistent with X_1 having a causal effect on the possible mediating variable X_2.

Steps 3, 4.   Regress Y on both X_1 and X_2. The coefficient of X_1, $b_{Y1 \cdot 2}$, is the rate of change of predicted Y with X_1 when X_2 is held constant, and so, *in terms of the model in panel (b)*, $b_{Y1 \cdot 2}$ is an estimate of c', the causal path from X_1 to Y. A finding that b_{Y1} is nonzero but $b_{Y1 \cdot 2}$ is zero is consistent with a model in which the entire effect of X_1 on Y is mediated by the intervening variable, X_2. A finding that $b_{Y1 \cdot 2}$ is nonzero, but smaller than b_{Y1} is consistent with partial mediation by X_2.

(a)

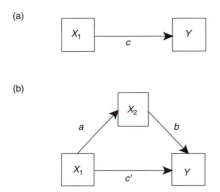

(b)

Fig. 23.2 Causal models illustrating direct and indirect (mediated) effects.

Some Cautions.   We emphasize that these interpretations are valid only in terms of the causal model given in panel (b) of Fig. 23.2. If our theory does not support this causal model, the best we can say is that our data are consistent with mediation, but are also consistent with other causal models as well, perhaps involving reverse causality and additional variables. Also, we would like to have a statistical test for any mediation effect. One that is widely used is the Sobel test, but a limitation of the test is that it is not very powerful. MacKinnon et al. (2002) offer a useful discussion of 14 methods for testing the statistical significance of a mediating effect. Finally, we should be aware that, as in any regression analysis, the results and interpretation may be distorted by measurement error. If, for example, the mediating variable X_2 is less reliable than X_1, the direct effect will appear larger, and the mediating effect will appear smaller than they should. If we want to pursue serious testing of a theory that involves mediation, we should use multiple indicators of the underlying latent variables and use structural equation modeling.

23.8 TESTING FOR CURVILINEARITY IN REGRESSION

23.8.1 Testing for Curvilinearity Using Continuous Predictor Variables

When we regressed *TC* on *age* and *BMI* (see Table 21.5), we found that there were significant effects of both predictor variables. However, it is possible that the relationship is not strictly linear and that the prediction of *TC* scores would be better if we included curvilinear components of the predictors as well. In general, given a dependent variable Y and a predictor X, we can test for a quadratic component by regressing Y on X^2 as well as X, so that the regression equation is

$$\hat{Y} = b_0 + b_1 X + b_2 X^2 \tag{23.1}$$

If the regression coefficient of the squared term is significant, we can then test for the presence of a cubic component by regressing Y on X^3, as well as X and X^2, yielding the equation

$$\hat{Y} = b_0 + b_1 X + b_2 X^2 + b_3 X^3 \tag{23.2}$$

and so on. *Note that we cannot test for the presence of a higher-level component without including the lower-level components as well.* For example, we cannot test for the presence of quadratic component by regressing only on X^2, because X^2 will usually be highly correlated with X. The regression of Y on X^2 alone would reflect both linear and quadratic effects, and we might get significance even if there was no quadratic component. If we wish to test for the presence of a quadratic component, we must partial out the linear component.

If we regress TC on BMI and BMI^2 for all women aged 65 or less in the *Seasons* data set, we find the regression equation

$$\hat{TC} = 79.561 + 8.118 \, BMI - 0.112 \, BMI^2 \tag{23.3}$$

Both the coefficients of BMI and BMI^2 are significant; $b_1 = 8.118$, $t\,(187) = 3.060$, $p = .003$ and $b_2 = -0.112$, $t\,(187) = -2.735$, $p = .001$, respectively.

There is one bend in a quadratic function. Because the partial regression coefficient of BMI^2 is negative, the rate of change of $\hat{TC}$ with BMI is negatively accelerated. That is, the amount by which $\hat{TC}$ increases as BMI increases becomes less as BMI gets larger, and for large enough values of BMI, $\hat{TC}$ starts decreasing as BMI increases. Had the coefficient of the quadratic component been positive, this would indicate that the rate of change of $\hat{TC}$ with BMI *increases* as BMI gets larger.

For Equation 23.1, we can show that the slope for any value of X is equal to $b_1 + 2b_2X$.[3] Therefore, the slope of the curve at $BMI = 25$ is $8.118 + (2)(-0.112)(25) = 2.518$, and the slope at $BMI = 35$ is $8.118 + (2)(-0.112)(35) = 0.218$. The maximum of the curve is found at $BMI = -b_1/2b_2 = -8.118/(2)(-0.112) = 36.241$. Substituting this value into the regression equation, we obtain $\hat{TC} \approx 227$.

23.8.2 Centering the Predictor

In order to make the regression coefficients more interpretable, we may also choose to subtract a constant, C, from each value of X. Ordinarily, C will be the mean of X; subtracting $\bar{X}$ from X is referred to as *centering*. If we subtract the mean from each value of X, Equation 23.1 becomes

$$\hat{Y} = b_0^c + b_1^c(X - \bar{X}) + b_2^c(X - \bar{X})^2 \tag{23.4}$$

where the superscript "c" on each regression coefficient indicates that the corresponding predictor has been centered about its mean.

If we expand this equation and compare it term-by-term with Equation 23.1, we find that $b_2^c = b_2$. That is, the regression coefficient of the squared term is the same whether or not the mean is subtracted from X before the regression is performed. This is a general finding. In any kind of polynomial regression, the regression coefficient of the highest-order term will be the same whether or not a constant is subtracted from X. We can also show that the slope of $\hat{Y}$ vs X is $b_1^c + 2b_2^c(X - \bar{X})$, so that we can interpret b_1^c as the slope at $X = \bar{X}$. Moreover, the significance test for b_1^c allows us to determine whether the slope differs significantly from zero at $X = \bar{X}$.

The mean BMI score for all women in the *Seasons* data set aged 65 years or less who have cholesterol data is 26.599. If we let $BMIC = BMI - 26.599$ and regress TC on $BMIC$ and $BMIC^2$, we find that

$$\hat{TC} = 216.047 + 2.144 \, BMIC - 0.112 \, BMIC^2 \tag{23.5}$$

Both the regression coefficients for $BMIC$ and $BMIC^2$ differ significantly from 0; $b_1^c = 2.144$, $t(187) = 3.459$, $p = .001$; $b_2^c = -0.112$, $t(187) = -2.735$, $p = .007$, respectively. Equations 23.3 and 23.5 are consistent with one another. However, in Equation 23.3, the constant in the equation and the coefficient of BMI represent the value of predicted TC and the slope of predicted TC vs BMI at

---

[3] If in Equation 23.1 we differentiate (i.e., use calculus) the expression for $\hat{Y}$ with respect to X, we obtain $b_1 + 2b_2X$. This tells us that slope at any value of X is given by $b_1 + 2b_2X$ so that b_1 is the slope of the curve at $X = 0$. If we set this expression equal to 0 and solve for X, we can see that $\hat{Y}$ has its maximum or minimum value at $X = -b_1/2b_2$.

$BMI = 0$—not very useful information, considering that no BMI in the data set was less than 15. In Equation 23.5, the BMI values have been centered, so the constant and coefficient of $BMIC$ represent the values of predicted TC and the slope at the mean value of BMI. Centering the predictor also results in lower correlations among the polynomial terms. For example, the correlations between BMI and BMI^2, BMI and BMI^3, and BMI^2 and BMI^3 are .986, .943, and .985, respectively. If the BMI variable is centered, the corresponding correlations are .696, .677, and .951. Note that although the constant usually subtracted from each value of X is the mean, any other constant, C, may be subtracted, so that the regression coefficient of $X - C$ is the slope at $X = C$.

We can now go on to test whether there is a cubic component (so that the curve has two bends), by adding X^3 to a regression equation that already contains X and X^2. We would get a cubic function if, for example, the value of the response variable rose, then fell, and then leveled off or rose again as the value of the predictor increased. In principle, we can test for higher-order components by adding larger powers of X to the regression. However, making predictions about curves with two bends in them largely exhausts the sophistication of existing theories in many research areas. If we are able to develop meaningful predictions about functions with three or more bends, we can test them by adding higher-order polynomial components to the regression.

23.8.3 Testing for Curvilinearity Using Quantitative Categorical Variables: Trend Analysis

Multiple regression can readily be used to perform the trend analyses that we discussed in Chapter 11 using contrasts with orthogonal polynomial weights. In fact, using multiple regression to perform trend analysis instead of using contrasts offers important advantages. The orthogonal polynomial contrast weights in Appendix Table C.6 assume equal numbers of subjects at each level of the independent variable and equal spacing between levels of the variable. If either of these equalities is violated, new orthogonal polynomial weights must be calculated. However, unequal n and unequal spacing present no difficulties if we perform trend analyses by using multiple regression. To do so, we regress Y first on X, then on X and X^2, then on X, X^2, and X^3, and so on, and we test the increments in variability accounted for when higher-order components are added to regressions that already contain the lower-order components.

For example, consider the addition accuracy scores for grades one to five in the *Royer* data set that are presented in Table 23.1 and plotted in Fig. 23.3. *Accuracy* first increases with *grade*, and then levels off. We would expect to find both a linear trend, because the best-fitting straight line has a positive slope, and a quadratic trend, because we have a negatively accelerated curve. The steps in the analysis are illustrated in Table 23.1. If we regress *accuracy* (Y) on *grade* (X), the variability accounted for by the regression is $R^2_{Y \cdot X} SS_Y = SS_{linear} = 4,690.170$. If we now regress Y on X and X^2, $SS_{quadratic}$ is the increment in $SS_{regression}$ that results when X^2 is added to a regression equation that already contains X. Similarly, if we regress Y on X, X^2, and X^3, SS_{cubic} is the increment in $SS_{regression}$ that results when X^3 is added to a regression equation that already contains X and X^2. All of these trend components have 1 df and can be tested against the within-groups error term, $MS_{error} = 219.318$. The ANOVA table in panel (b) of Table 23.1 presents the results of the tests. As expected, we find significant linear and quadratic trends, $F(1, 135) = 21.385$, $p = .000$, and $F(1,135)=8.495$, $p = .004$, respectively. We should note that because there are five levels of *grade*, and therefore 4 df if we treat grade as a categorical variable, the regression of Y on X, X^2, X^3, and X^4 must account for all of the variability in the group means; that is, $R^2_{Y \cdot X, X^2, X^3, X^4} SS_Y = 6,626.772 = SS_{Between}$. Just as any two points can be fit perfectly by a straight line, the points for the five group means can be fit perfectly by a fourth-degree polynomial.

Table 23.1 An example of trend analysis

(a) Percent addition accuracy as a function of grade for *Royer* data

	Grade (X)				
	1	2	3	4	5
n:	19	28	32	30	26
$\bar{Y}$:	71.82	84.66	91.97	92.34	91.98
s:	30.23	15.26	8.24	7.30	9.20

(b) Trend analysis for the data in panel (a)

$$SS_{linear} = R^2_{Y \cdot X} \, SS_Y = 4,690.170$$
$$SS_{quadratic} = (R^2_{Y \cdot X, X^2} - R^2_{Y \cdot X})SS_Y = 6,553.310 - 4,690.170 = 1,863.140$$
$$SS_{cubic} = (R^2_{Y \cdot X, X^2, X^3} - R^2_{Y \cdot X, X^2})SS_Y = 6,617.701 - 6,553.310 = 64.391$$
$$SS_{quartic} = (R^2_{Y \cdot X, X^2, X^3, X^4} - R^2_{Y \cdot X, X^2, X^3})SS_Y = 6,626.772 - 6,617.701 = 9.071$$

SV	df	SS	MS	F	p
Grade	4	6,626.772	1,656.693	7.554	.000
linear	1	4,690.170	4,690.170	21.385	.000
quadratic	1	1,863.140	1,863.140	8.495	.004
cubic	1	64.391	64.391	0.294	.589
quartic	1	9.071	9.071	0.041	.840
Error	130	28,511.337	219.318		

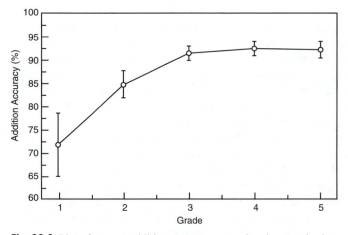

Fig. 23.3 Plot of percent addition accuracy vs grade using standard errors as error bars.

23.9 INCLUDING INTERACTION TERMS IN MULTIPLE REGRESSION

23.9.1 Introduction

The regression equation $\hat{Y} = b_0 + b_1 X_1 + b_2 X_2$ is *additive* because the effect on $\hat{Y}$ of changing the values of either of the predictors does not depend on the value of the other predictor. This kind of model will be unrealistic whenever the relationship between Y and a predictor, X_1, is moderated by (i.e., it depends on the value taken on by) another variable X_2. In this case we would say we have an interaction between X_1 and X_2.

We dealt with interactions in detail when we discussed ANOVA. In the context of ANOVA, we have an interaction when the effect of a factor is different for different levels of a second factor. We can translate this thinking directly to multiple regression analyses. However, we can extend the concept when we work with multiple regression because we can now deal not only with categorical factors, but with a mix of categorical and quantitative variables. Therefore, it is possible to construct models in which the effect of one factor is a specified function of the levels of a second factor.

23.9.2 Testing Interactions Between Quantitative and Dichotomous Predictors

Consider the regression of *TC* on *age* and *sex* for subjects in the *Seasons* study who are no older than 65 and have *BMI* scores no larger than 40. *Sex* is a dichotomous categorical variable and we can choose to code it by assigning men the value 0 and women the value 1. The regression output is provided in Table 23.2, which provides the coefficients for the regression equation

$$\hat{TC} = 178.009 + 0.900 \, age - 8.645 \, sex \tag{23.6}$$

Equation 23.6 is a misleading representation of the relationship of *TC* to *age* and *sex* because the relationship between *TC* and *age* differs for men and women. A better understanding of this relationship may be obtained by regressing *TC* on *age* separately for men and women, yielding

$$\hat{TC} = 221.143 - 0.0005 \, age \tag{23.7}$$

and

$$\hat{TC} = 126.531 + 1.812 \, age \tag{23.8}$$

These equations are plotted in Fig. 23.4. It is apparent that predicted *TC* changes little with *age* for men, but increases strongly with *age* for women. If we applied the test for equality of independent regression coefficients that we developed in Chapter 20, we would find that the regression slopes are significantly different.

We can easily test the interaction of age and sex by regressing *TC* on *age*, *sex*, and *Age × Sex*, a variable formed by multiplying *age* and *sex*. This regression equation is

$$\hat{TC} = 221.143 - 0.0005 \, age - 94.612 \, sex + 1.813 \, Age \times Sex \tag{23.9}$$

Note that Equations 23.7–23.9 are consistent: if we substitute *sex* = 0 and *sex* = 1 into Equation 23.9, we recover Equations 23.7 and 23.8. We can also readily interpret each of the coefficients in Equation 23.9. The coefficient of *age*, –0.0005, is the rate of change of predicted *TC* with *age* when *sex* = 0; that is, for men. The coefficient of *sex*, –94.612, is the rate of change of predicted *TC* with *sex* (i.e., the difference in predicted *TC* for men and women) for *age* = 0. We can better understand

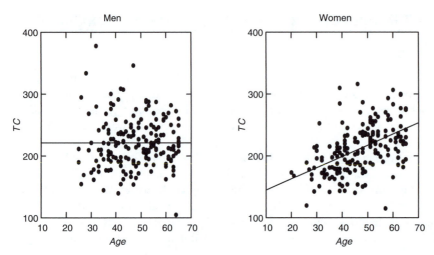

Fig. 23.4 Scatterplot of *TC* versus *age* for men and women with linear smoothers, using data from subjects aged 65 years or less with *BMI* ≤ 40.

Table 23.2   SPSS output for regression of *TC* on *age* and *sex* using data for subjects aged ≤ 65 years and *BMI* ≤ 40

Model Summary

Model	R	R Square	Adjusted R Square	Std. Error of the Estimate
1	.268[a]	.072	.067	38.54969

[a.] Predictors: (Constant), *sex*, *age*

ANOVA[b]

Model		Sum of Squares	df	Mean Square	F	Sig.
1	Regression	41436.19	2	20718.096	13.941	.000[a]
	Residual	536474.5	361	1486.079		
	Total	577910.7	363			

[a.] Predictors: (Constant), *sex*, *age*
[b.] Dependent Variable: *TC*

Coefficients[a]

Model		Unstandardized Coefficients		Standardized Coefficients		
		B	Std. Error	Beta	t	Sig.
1	(Constant)	178.009	9.562		18.616	.000
	Age	.900	.190	.240	4.723	.000
	Sex	−8.645	4.046	−.108	−2.137	.033

[a.] Dependent Variable: *TC*

the coefficient of the product term, 1.813, by regrouping the terms in Equation 23.9 and rewriting the equation as either

$$\hat{TC} = 221.143 - 94.612 \; sex + (-0.0005 + 1.813 \; sex) \; age \tag{23.10}$$

or as

$$\hat{TC} = 221.143 - 0.0005 \; age + (-94.612 + 1.813 \; age) \; sex \tag{23.11}$$

From these equations, we can see that the rate of change of predicted TC with age is a function of sex, namely, $-0.0005 + 1.813 \; sex$. Therefore, because the variable sex has only two levels, 1.813 can be interpreted as the difference between the slopes of predicted TC with age for women and men. Similarly, the change in predicted TC with sex, that is, the difference in predicted TC for men and women, is a linear function of age, $-94.612 + 1.813 \; age$. The coefficient of the interaction component, 1.813, can also be interpreted as the amount by which the predicted difference in TC levels for women and men becomes more positive (or less negative) for each additional year of age. For example, for $age = 60$, we would predict the difference to be $-94.612 + (1.813)(60) = 14.168$, whereas for $age = 30$, we would predict the difference to be $-94.612 + (1.813)(30) = -40.222$. That is, predicted TC for women is about 40 units lower than for men at age 30, but about 14 units higher at age 60.

As can be seen in the SPSS output in Table 23.3, the coefficient of the product term, 1.813, is significant, $t(363) = 4.909$, $p = .000$. Therefore, we can reject the null hypothesis that the rate of change of predicted TC with age is the same for men and women (or equivalently, the null hypothesis that the difference in predicted TC for men and women is the same at each value of age).

We should emphasize that when we test the interaction between two predictors, we must include both of the predictors in the regression equation along with the product of the two predictors, as we did in Equation 23.9. That is, to test the interaction, we evaluate the effect of the product term after the effects of the predictors that are the constituents of the product term have been partialed out by including them in the equation (see, for example, Cohen, 1978). It is *not* appropriate to test the interaction by including only the product term in the regression equation— although this is a common mistake. For one thing, the product term may be highly correlated with its constituents. In the current example, the product term has correlations of .168 and .953 with age and sex, respectively. It is also important to note that interactions with categorical moderator variables tend to have very small effect sizes (see Aguinis et al., 2005), so we must use large samples if it is important to investigate them.

23.9.3 Testing the Interaction Between Two Quantitative Predictors

In Chapter 21 we regressed TC on age and BMI for women aged 20–65 years and obtained the equation

$$\hat{TC} = 92.239 + 1.737 \; age + 1.474 \; BMI \tag{23.12}$$

This is the equation of a two-dimensional plane in the three-dimensional space that has as its axes predicted TC, age, and BMI (see Fig. 21.3). Because this equation is additive, if BMI is held constant, a 1-year increase in age corresponds to an increase of 1.737 units in predicted TC when BMI is held constant, *no matter at what value BMI is held constant*. Also, if age is held constant at any value, a one-unit increase in BMI corresponds to a 1.474-unit increase in predicted TC. However, it is possible that Equation 23.12 is unrealistic: the rate of change of predicted TC with age may differ for different values of BMI, or equivalently, the rate of change of predicted TC with

Table 23.3   SPSS output for regression of *TC* on *age*, *sex*, and *Age×Sex* using data for subjects aged ≤ 65 years with *BMI* ≤ 40

Model Summary

Model	R	R Square	Adjusted R Square	Std. Error of the Estimate
1	.360[a]	.130	.123	37.37274

[a] Predictors: (Constant), age×sex, age, sex

ANOVA[b]

Model		Sum of Squares	df	Mean Square	F	Sig.
1	Regression	75090.96	3	25030.320	17.921	.000[a]
	Residual	502819.7	360	1396.721		
	Total	577910.7	363			

[a] Predictors: (Constant), age×sex, age, sex
[b] Dependent Variable: *TC*

Coefficients[a]

Model		Unstandardized Coefficients		Standardized Coefficients			Collinearity Statistics	
		B	Std. Error	Beta	t	Sig.	Tolerance	VIF
1	(Constant)	221.143	12.773		17.313	.000		
	Age	.000	.260	.000	−.002	.999	.502	1.990
	Sex	−94.612	17.947	−1.187	−5.272	.000	.048	20.984
	Age×Sex	1.813	.369	1.120	4.909	.000	.046	21.554

[a] Dependent Variable: *TC*

BMI may differ for different values of *age*. We can investigate the possibility that *age* and *BMI* interact by creating a new variable *Age×BMI* that is the product of *age* and *BMI*, and regressing *TC* on *age*, *BMI*, and *Age×BMI*. As can be seen in the SPSS output in Table 23.4, the resulting regression equation is

$$\hat{TC} = -70.241 + 5.209 \, age + 7.844 \, BMI - 0.135 \, Age{\times}BMI \tag{23.13}$$

The coefficient of the product term is significant; $t \,(186) = -2.546$, $p = .012$. We can best understand the interpretation of this coefficient, −0.135, by grouping terms and rewriting Equation 23.13 as

$$\hat{TC} = -70.241 + 5.209 \, age + (7.844 - 0.135 \, age) \, BMI \tag{23.14}$$

and as

$$\hat{TC} = -70.241 + (5.209 - 0.135 \, BMI) \, age + 7.844 \, BMI \tag{23.15}$$

Now we can see that, according to Equations 23.14 and 23.15, the rate of change of predicted *TC* with *BMI* is a linear function of *age*, $7.844 - 0.135 \, age$, and the rate of change of predicted *TC* with

Table 23.4 Output for regression of *TC* on *age, BMI,* and *Age×BMI* using data for women aged ≤ 65 years and with *BMI* ≤ 40

Model Summary

Model	R	R Square	Adjusted R Square	Std. Error of the Estimate
1	.546[a]	.298	.286	33.09693

[a.] Predictors: (Constant), age×BMI, BMI, age

ANOVA[b]

Model	Sum of Squares	df	Mean Square	F	Sig.
1 Regression	82322.21	3	27440.736	25.051	.000[a]
Residual	193887.0	177	1095.407		
Total	276209.2	180			

[a.] Predictors: (Constant), age×BMI, BMI, age
[b.] Dependent Variable: *TC*

Coefficients[a]

Model	Unstandardized Coefficients		Standardized Coefficients	t	Sig.	Collinearity Statistics	
	B	Std. Error	Beta			Tolerance	VIF
1 (Constant)	−70.241	65.952		−1.065	.288		
Age	5.209	1.383	1.413	3.765	.000	.028	35.531
BMI	7.844	2.558	.935	3.067	.003	.043	23.441
Age×BMI	−.135	.053	−1.287	−2.546	.012	.016	64.420

[a.] Dependent Variable: *TC*

age is a linear function of *BMI*, $5.209 - 0.135\ BMI$. When we plot Equation 23.13 (see Fig. 23.5), we see that because we included the product term, we no longer have a plane, but rather a curved surface on which the slope for one predictor decreases as the value of the other predictor increases.[4] The slope of predicted *TC* with *age* decreases by 0.135 for each one-unit increase in *BMI*, and the slope of *TC* with *BMI* decreases by 0.135 for each one-unit increase in *age*. For example, according to Equation 23.15, the slope of predicted *TC* with *age* for $BMI = 20$ is $5.209 - (0.135)(20) \approx 2.51$ and for $BMI = 30$ it is approximately 1.16. The slope of predicted *TC* vs *BMI* at $age = 30$ is $7.844 - (.135)(30) \approx 3.79$, and for $age = 55$ it is approximately 0.42. *BMI* is a less useful predictor of *TC* for older subjects, and *age* is a less useful predictor of *TC* for subjects with large *BMI* values.

How do we interpret the other regression coefficients in Equation 23.13 and their tests of significance in Table 23.4? The coefficient of *age*, 5.209, is the slope of predicted *TC* with *age* for $BMI = 0$. The standard error, 1.383, and the corresponding *t* value of 3.765 are also conditional on

---

[4] If the coefficient of the product term was positive, the partial slope of predicted *Y* for one predictor would become larger as the value of the other predictor increased.

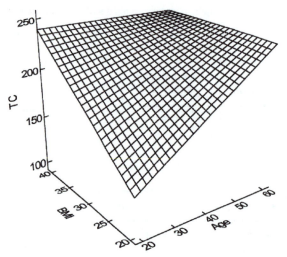

Fig. 23.5 Plot of the surface generated by the equation $\hat{TC} = -70.241 + 5.209\ Age + 7.844\ BMI - 0.135\ Age \times BMI$.

the value of $BMI = 0$. Similarly, the coefficient of BMI, 7.844, is the slope of predicted TC vs BMI for $age = 0$, and the standard error and t also hold only for $age = 0$.

We are not likely to be interested in what happens at $age = 0$ and $BMI = 0$, but we may well be interested in testing whether a coefficient is significant at a specified value of the other predictor. For example, we may wish to test whether the slope of predicted TC with BMI is significant at $age = 20$. There are several ways to conduct this test. We can find the value of the slope by substituting $age = 20$ into Equation 23.14. We can also develop expressions for the standard error of the slope at age = 20 and conduct the appropriate t test. However, the easiest way to perform this test of a simple effect is to transform the variable and redo the regression.

Suppose we create the variable $agem20 = age - 20$. Then we can regress TC on $agem20$, BMI, and $Agem20 \times BMI$, a variable obtained by multiplying $agem20$ and BMI. The resulting regression equation is

$$\hat{TC} = 33.931 + 5.209\ agem20 + 5.135\ BMI - 0.135\ Agem20 \times BMI$$

The interpretation of the coefficients is comparable to that of Equation 23.13. Here we are most interested in the coefficient of BMI, 5.135, which is the slope of predicted TC with BMI at $agem20 = 0$, that is, at $age = 20$. The coefficient is significantly different from 0, $t\ (177) = 3.765$, $p = .000$. So we can say that the slope for BMI is significant at $age = 20$. Note that the coefficient of the product term is not affected by transforming age to $age - 20$. The same approach can be used to test the coefficient at any other age. Similarly, we can test the coefficients of age at different levels of BMI by transforming BMI and redoing the regressions.

23.9.4 Using Centering to Reduce Multicollinearity

When we add a product term to a regression equation that already contains the terms making up the product, we are likely to have multicollinearity. This is because a product term will generally be highly correlated with its constituents. For example, in our continuing example using women aged 20–65 with BMI scores no greater than 40, age and BMI have correlations of .801 and .675 with the product term $Age \times BMI$. For the regression of TC on age, BMI, and $Age \times BMI$, the largest condition index (see Section 23.4) is 106, which is much greater than the value of 30 that suggests a possible serious problem with multicollinearity. Because of this, it is often suggested that regressions that include product terms should be conducted with centered variables (see, for example, Jaccard, Turrisi, & Wan, 1990).

Suppose we take the suggestion and center all the variables by replacing them by their deviation scores, resulting in the centered variables *agecent* (equal to *age minus the mean of the age scores*), *BMIcent, TCcent, and the product term Agecent* $\times$ *BMIcent* (note that we obtain the product term by multiplying the centered variables, not by multiplying the variables and then centering the product). The multicollinearity problem is no longer present. *agecent* and *BMIcent* have correlations of $-.007$ and $.009$ with the product term, the largest condition index for the regression of *TCcent* on *agecent*, *BMIcent*, and the product term is now 1.135, and all the tolerances are greater than .98.

Note that the algorithms built into the standard statistical packages were able to deal with the computational challenges presented by the regression with the uncentered variables, so that the coefficient of the product term is the same, -0.135, for both analyses. However, the coefficients of the lower-order terms are different and have more meaningful interpretations when the centered variables are used. Given centering, the coefficient of X_j represents the slope of predicted Y with X_j when the values of the other predictors equal their means.

23.9.5 Do We Have an Interaction or Curvilinearity or Both?

Because predictor variables are usually correlated, testing for an interaction or for curvilinearity is actually more complicated than we have so far discussed. Suppose the true model is

$$Y = \beta_0 + \beta_1 X_1 + \beta_2 X_2 + \beta_3 X_1^2 + \varepsilon$$

Because we never know what the true model is, we may not test for curvilinearity but instead decide to test for the presence of an interaction by regressing Y on X_1, X_2, and $X_1 \times X_2$. If we have enough power, we may find that the coefficient of $X_1 \times X_2$ is significant, not because the true model contains an interaction term, but because the product term in the regression is correlated with the squared term that is in the true model. Conversely, if the true model is

$$Y = \beta_0 + \beta_1 X_1 + \beta_2 X_2 + \beta_3 X_1 X_2 + \varepsilon$$

and we test for curvilinearity by regressing Y on X_1, X_2, X_1^2, and X_2^2, if we have sufficient power, we may find that the coefficients of one or both of the squared terms are significant, not because the squared terms are present in the model, but because of their correlations with the product term that is present in the model but left out of the regression equation.

Also, omitting terms from the regression can result in finding misleading interaction and curvilinear terms. We may find, for example, a positive interaction even when the true interaction is negative and we may find a negative quadratic component even when the coefficient of the squared term in the true model is positive. Suppose that the true model is

$$Y = \beta_0 + \beta_1 X_1 + \beta_2 X_2 + \beta_3 X_1^2 + \beta_4 X_1 X_2 + \varepsilon$$

where β_3 is positive and β_4 is negative. If we decide to test for the presence of the interaction by regressing Y on X_1, X_2, and $X_1 \times X_2$, but not on X_1^2, we may find that the coefficient of the product term is positive even though it is negative in the true model because of the correlation between the product term and the X_1^2 term that was not included in the model. Similarly, if we regress on X_1, X_2, and X_1^2, and omit $X_1 \times X_2$ from the equation, we may find that the coefficient of the squared term is negative, even though it is positive in the true model. Therefore, Ganzach (1997) recommends that we include both the interaction and the quadratic terms in the regression when either interaction or quadratic terms are evaluated. Not everyone agrees with Ganzach's recommendation because including the squared terms may lower the power for finding significant interactions. Aiken and West (1991) and Shepperd (1991) recommend against including squared terms when evaluating interactions unless there is theoretical justification for their inclusion. We recommend exploring the situation by trying it both ways.

If we regress *TC* on *age*, *BMI*, age^2, BMI^2, and *Age×BMI*, the interaction term is significant, $t(175) = -2.077$, $p = .039$, even though we include the squared terms in the regression, and the squared terms are not significant (this is the case whether or not we center the variables). Therefore, we conclude that there is a negative interaction between *age* and *BMI*.

There is yet another complication—the differential reliability of the terms in the regression. All other things being equal, predictors that are less reliable (i.e., have more measurement error) have smaller effect sizes and are tested with less power. Further, reliability will be lower for squared and product terms than for the first-order terms (see Busemeyer & Jones, 1983; MacCallum & Mar, 1995). For the typical situation in which the predictors are at least somewhat correlated, the attenuation will be worse for the quadratic terms than for the product terms. As a result of this differential reliability, when the predictors are measured with error, interaction effects will be under-estimated and quadratic terms will be underestimated even more. Therefore, if the true model contained interaction and quadratic effects of equal size, the power and observed effect size would tend to be larger for the interaction term. Because of these complications, we must be cautious about making strong conclusions from the data unless our measures are reliable.

23.10 LOGISTIC REGRESSION

In our coverage of regression to this point, we have considered only continuous dependent variables. However, we may encounter important dichotomous qualitative variables such as success/failure, live/die, pass/fail, etc. When such variables are used as predictors, we can assign any two different numbers, such as 0 and 1, to these levels and proceed as usual. However, when *dependent* variables are binary, we cannot apply the framework of least-squares regression that we have used to this point without severely violating major assumptions. Here, we have space only to make a few brief comments about logistic regression, a kind of regression that can be used with categorical dependent variables.

Logistic regression is different from the ordinary least-squares (OLS) linear regression in a number of ways. In OLS linear regression, the dependent variable *Y* is considered to be more or less continuous and is expressed as a linear function of the predictor variables. In binary logistic regression, the dependent variable can take on only two values, which we can consider to be 0 and 1, and the probability that $Y = 1$ is a nonlinear function of the predictor variable(s). For example, suppose X_i is the amount of exposure to some toxic substance, and let $Y = 1$ if this exposure results in death and $Y = 0$ if it does not, so that $p_i = p(Y | X = X_i)$ is the probability of dying, given the exposure level X_i. We would expect $E(Y_i) = p_i$ to be a nonlinear, "S-shaped" function of *X*; that is, it should be close to 0 for small values of *X*, and then increase with increasing levels of exposure until it approaches and stays close to 1. The logistic function has these characteristics. For one predictor variable, *p* expressed as a logistic function of *X* is

$$E(Y_i) = p_i = \frac{1}{1 + e^{-\beta_0 - \beta_1 X_i}} = \frac{e^{\beta_0 + \beta_1 X_i}}{1 + e^{\beta_0 + \beta_1 X_i}}$$

where $e = 2.718 \ldots$ is the base for natural logarithms. Note that no matter what the values are of the βs and the predictor variable, the value of the function cannot be smaller than 0 nor greater than 1. If we can assume that the logistic function is appropriate, a transformation of p_i can be expressed as a linear function of the predictor variables, and a regression can be performed.

The standard statistical packages can perform logistic regressions. However, because we assume that $E(Y)$ is a logistic function of the predictors, the procedures by which the regression coefficients are estimated are different from what we have used up to this point for linear functions. Estimates of the regression coefficients are obtained by using a procedure called *maximum likelihood estimation* instead of least-squares estimation. Because of this, the statistical package output for logistic regression looks quite different from that of OLS regression. Further, to complicate matters, notation and measures of fit vary widely across the statistical packages. Also, interpretation of the results of the analysis is, in part, based on nonlinear transformations of the regression coefficients. For example, e^{-b_1} can be shown to be the odds ratio for X_1—that is, the ratio of (the odds that $Y = 1$ when X_1 is increased by one unit) to (the odds that $Y = 1$ without the increase). Although logistic regression is not a difficult topic, there are new concepts that must be learned in order to conduct and interpret the analyses.

An introduction to logistic regression, including discussion of SPSS output, can be found in the supplementary materials on the book's website. More comprehensive introductions are available in Cohen et al. (2003), and Menard (2002). A standard reference is the book by Hosmer and Lemeshow (2001).

23.11 DEALING WITH HIERARCHICAL DATA STRUCTURES IN REGRESSION, INCLUDING REPEATED-MEASURES DESIGNS

23.11.1 Designs in Which Subjects Are Nested Within Groups

Suppose we wish to regress school performance on measures of parental education and income and collect data from, say, 400 students distributed across 20 different classrooms. We cannot simply ignore the fact that the students come from different classrooms and perform a single regression using the 400 data points. The significance tests for standard OLS regression assume that the data points are independent of one another; that is not likely to be the case here because even if the classroom means do not differ systematically from one another, we would expect that, on the average, measures from two students in the same classroom would be more similar than measures from two students selected from different classrooms. The result of this lack of independence is that we effectively have data from fewer subjects than we think we do, so that any significance tests that we perform will be positively biased.

Moreover, the mean levels of the dependent and predictor variables may differ systematically across classrooms; the classrooms may be sampled from different neighborhoods and different school systems. If so, combining data without regard to classroom may produce regression equations that do not characterize the relationships in any of the classrooms very well (see Chapter 18).

Nor can we avoid the problem by averaging the data for each variable within each classroom, and then performing a regression with one data point for each classroom. If we do this, we ignore all of the information about the variances of the variables and the relationships among them within the classrooms.

What we need is some sort of analysis that considers information about both individuals and classrooms, and allows us to consider variables that characterize both levels of this hierarchy. For example, class size, mean level of achievement, mean socioeconomic status (SES) level, and proportion of minority students characterize the class level, and minority status, parental education level, and SES might characterize the individual student.

In this example, we have a two-level hierarchy with students "nested" within classrooms. However, the hierarchy may have more than two levels: the different classrooms may come from different schools, and these schools may be selected from different school districts and geographical areas. Hierarchical structure is commonly encountered in many fields of research. Perhaps we wish to regress salary on educational level and years of experience, and select 50 workers from each of 10 different industries. Or perhaps we conduct family research, and consider individuals nested within families.

23.11.2 Designs in Which Measures are Nested Within Subjects: Repeated-Measures Designs

In the examples mentioned so far, individuals are at the lowest level of the hierarchy, but this need not be so. Repeated-measures designs have a hierarchical structure in which data on a number of different dependent variables are collected from each individual, so that scores on these variables are nested within individuals. For example, Table 23.5 contains the data for a hypothetical reading experiment described by Lorch and Myers (1990). Each of 10 subjects reads a paragraph consisting of seven sentences and reading times are recorded (in milliseconds) for each sentence. There are three predictor variables for each sentence: the serial position of the sentence in the text (SP), the number of words in the sentence ($WORDS$), and the number of new arguments in the sentence (NEW). We are interested in whether each of the predictors makes a significant contribution to the prediction of reading time over and above that provided by the other two predictors.

There are several ways of testing hypotheses and forming confidence intervals for the regression coefficients of the predictors. One of them is to regress reading time on the three predictors separately for each subject and then to perform subsequent analyses, using the regression coefficients as data. Table 23.6 contains the regression coefficients for each of the 10 subjects along with the mean, standard error, and t (i.e., the ratio of the mean to the standard error) for each coefficient. Because there are 10 subjects, there are 9 df associated with each t. Because $t_{CRIT.05,9} = \pm 2.262$, we can reject the hypotheses that $\beta_{SP} = 0$ and $\beta_{WORDS} = 0$ at $\alpha = .05$. We cannot reject the hypothesis that $\beta_{NEW} = 0$.

The strategy of using the "slopes as outcomes approach," that is, of performing regressions at the lowest level of the hierarchy and then using the resulting regression coefficients as data for analyses conducted at the next higher level, addresses some of the challenges presented by the

Table 23.5 Values of the predictor variables for the seven sentences and the reading times in milliseconds for each of the 10 subjects

Sentence	SP	WORDS	NEW	S1	S2	S3	S4	S5	S6	S7	S8	S9	S10
1	1	13	1	3429	2795	4161	3071	3625	3161	3232	7161	1536	4063
2	2	16	3	6482	5411	4491	5063	9295	5643	8357	4313	2946	6652
3	3	9	2	1714	2339	3018	2464	6045	2455	4920	3366	1375	2179
4	4	9	2	3679	3714	2866	2732	4205	6241	3723	6330	1152	3661
5	5	10	3	4000	2902	2991	2670	3884	3223	3143	6143	2759	3330
6	6	18	4	6973	8018	6625	7571	8795	13188	11170	6071	7964	7866
7	7	6	1	2634	1750	2268	2884	3491	3688	2054	1696	1455	3705

Table 23.6 Regression coefficients for the regression of reading time on *SP*, *WORDS*, and *NEW* for each of the 10 subjects

Subject	SP	WORDS	NEW
1	.23124	.39103	.22161
2	.30533	.43415	.34637
3	.20637	.40360	−.25294
4	.48300	.50203	−.27683
5	−.06210	.28778	.92680
6	1.10982	.80850	−.23336
7	.25448	.57498	.79643
8	−.33147	.11341	.33124
9	.66786	.50078	.16320
10	.46921	.56964	−.50621
Mean	.33337	.45859	.15163
SE	.12417	.05855	.14982
t	2.6849	7.8329	1.0121

hierarchical data structure. Also, note that this approach allows us to deal efficiently with missing data. If, for example, subject 2 is missing the data from sentence 4, and subject 5 is missing the data from sentences 2 and 7, we can simply obtain the regression coefficients for these subjects with the data that we do have.

However, there is a problem with this approach, especially when there are missing data or when the regression coefficients have larger standard errors for some subjects than for others. For the most appropriate analysis, the regression coefficients should be weighted less if they are based on poorer, or on less data, or if they have more extreme values. A collection of procedures that, in effect, perform these adjustments (i.e., think of weighting the coefficients by their reliability) and provide additional useful information is referred to as *multilevel modeling* or *hierarchical linear modeling* or *mixed-effects modeling*. These procedures are very useful for handling missing data, and use estimation algorithms that produce unbiased estimates of treatment effects if the missing data are missing at random (MAR). A proper discussion of this topic is beyond the scope of the present coverage. Introductions to hierarchical regression may be found in Cohen et al. (2003), Hox (2002), and Kreft and de Leeuw (1998), and an excellent, more comprehensive treatment is given by Raudenbush and Bryk (2002). SAS PROC MIXED is a comprehensive and flexible module that can perform these analyses. SPSS and SYSTAT have the capability to perform some multilevel analyses in their mixed-effects model modules. We have found the HLM (Raudenbush et al., 2000) software package to be well documented and reasonably user-friendly for dealing with hierarchical regression.

23.12 SUMMARY

In Chapter 23 we extended our coverage of multiple regression, largely dealing with issues related to interpreting the effects of predictor variables. We can briefly summarize much of the chapter by reviewing some cautions we must keep in mind if we seriously wish to consider the "importance" of a predictor variable. If we are concerned merely with prediction, or with describing the data, our task is relatively straightforward. However, if our goal is to associate the size of a regression coefficient with the causal importance of the corresponding predictor variable, using data that have not been collected in a true experiment, we must first understand that predictive usefulness is not the same as causal influence; that is, a variable that is a good predictor may have no causal importance whatsoever. Even if we have good reason to believe that the variable in question has a causal effect, the regression coefficient may not be a good index of its causal importance, for at least the following reasons:

- The units of the variable must be considered.
- The model may be mis-specified.
- There may be measurement error, either in the predictor variable we are concerned with, or in other variables in the model that are correlated with it.
- There may be nonrandomly missing data on the dependent variable or predictors.
- The predictor variables may be highly correlated.
- There may be mediating effects, so that part of the effect of the variable may be achieved by influencing other variables that, in turn, affect the dependent variable.
- There may be curvilinear effects or interactions with moderator variables that have not been considered.
- If the design has a hierarchical structure, this must be taken into account in the analysis or else any statistical tests may be positively biased.

These cautions suggest that it is difficult to make formal causal statements on the basis of regression analyses using data from an observational study, and even that we should view the results of our inferential tests with some skepticism because we are unlikely to have specified the "correct" model. However, despite its limitations, regression analysis can be an extremely useful component of a program for advancing knowledge about a research problem. Existing theory can suggest that certain regressions be performed. These regressions can provide useful descriptions of the data and can suggest modifications of the theory and speculations about causal effects that can often be pursued by conducting further research with a variety of techniques and tools, including controlled experiments where possible.

APPENDIX 23.1

To Show that b_{Y1} is Not an Unbiased Estimator of $\beta_{Y1 \cdot 2}$ if X_2 is Left Out of the Model

We begin by first expressing b_{Y1} as

$$b_{Y1} = \frac{\Sigma(X_1 - \bar{X}_1)(Y - \bar{Y})}{SS_1}$$

where $SS_1 = \Sigma(X_1 - \bar{X}_1)^2$ so that

$$E(b_{Y1}) = E\left(\frac{\Sigma(X_1 - \bar{X}_1)(Y - \bar{Y})}{SS_1}\right)$$

If we assume X is fixed, we can rewrite the preceding equation as

$$E(b_{Y1}) = \frac{\Sigma(X_1 - \bar{X}_1)E(Y - \bar{Y})}{SS_1}$$

Substituting the population model expressions for Y and $\bar{Y}$ and simplifying, we have

$$E(b_{Y1}) = \frac{\beta_{Y1 \cdot 2}\, \Sigma(X_1 - \bar{X}_1)^2 + E[\beta_{Y2 \cdot 1}\, \Sigma(X_1 - \bar{X}_1)(X_2 - \bar{X}_2)]}{SS_1}$$

$$= \beta_{Y1 \cdot 2} + \beta_{Y2 \cdot 1} E\left(r_{12}\sqrt{\frac{SS_2}{SS_1}}\right)$$

$$= \beta_{Y1 \cdot 2} + \beta_{Y2 \cdot 1} E(b_{21}) = \beta_{Y1 \cdot 2} + \beta_{Y2 \cdot 1}\beta_{21}$$

Note that because $\beta_{21} = \rho_{12}\, \sigma_2/\sigma_1$, if $\rho_{12} = 0$, then $E(b_{Y1}) = \beta_{Y1 \cdot 2}$.

EXERCISES

23.1 Hypothetical data from an experiment designed to determine the effects of drug dosage on performance may be found in the file *EX23_1*.

(a) Perform an ANOVA to test the effect of dosage on performance.

(b) Using multiple regression, perform a trend analysis on the same data.

23.2 Let's consider the distinction between standardized and unstandardized regression coefficients in a small data set. Use the file *statistics class data*. If we regress final exam score (Y) on pretest score (X), we find that the regression equation is $\hat{Y} = -36.083 + 3.546\,X$ and R is .725. The unstandardized coefficient is 3.546 and the standardized coefficient is 0.725.

(a) Now suppose we want to add two additional data points that are consistent with the regression equation but that change the variances of X and Y. Say we add pretest scores of 11 and 38, along with the final exam scores predicted with the regression equation, rounding off to the nearest whole number. What are the two predicted final exam scores?

(b) If we now regress final scores on pretest scores for this new data set (now with 20 cases), how should the new unstandardized regression coefficient differ from the previous one?

(c) How should the new standardized regression coefficient differ?

(d) How should the new value of R differ?

23.3 In the next few exercises, we use some data from the *Seasons* study to explore the relationships among the variables age, perceived health (*sayhlth*), level of education (*schoolyr*), body mass index (*BMI*), depression as measured by the Beck Depression Inventory (*beck_d*), and cholesterol level (*TC*). In doing so, we demonstrate the distinction between prediction and causality, and consider the limitations of our ability to answer questions with the available data.

Start by considering how level of education might be predicted by sex and age in the data set *Seasons exercises*. The amount of education that people receive has increased over recent generations, so we might expect age to be a (negative) predictor of level of education. Also, women have traditionally received less education than men, though in recent years such sex differences have been reduced. Perform some appropriate regressions to explore these issues.

23.4 Next, explore how perceived health (*sayhlth*—note that larger values on this measure correspond to poorer health) is predicted by sex and level of education. It is often stated that more educated people tend to be healthier and have longer life expectancies. Is this statement consistent with the information in the *Seasons exercises* data set? If so, why might this be the case? What kinds of additional information might be useful in investigating this issue further?

23.5 Now explore how sex, body-mass index (*BMI*), level of education (*schoolyr*), and level of depression (*beck_d*) relate to one another. Speculate about what kinds of mechanisms might be responsible for relationships among these variables. Is it possible to confirm these speculations? What can we say from these data about the causal influence of depression on *BMI* or of *BMI* on depression?

23.6 The purpose of this exercise is to explore the consequences of having additional measurement error.

(a) Start by using the *Seasons exercises* data file. To make the results comparable to those obtained in some previous analyses in the chapters, select subjects aged ≤ 65 years with *BMI*s of ≤ 40. Regress *TC* on age and *BMI* for both men and women. Interpret the output.

(b) Now, instead of using *BMI* as a predictor, simulate additional measurement error in *BMI* by creating a new variable *bmiplusnorm05*. This new variable is obtained by adding to each value of *BMI* a random number selected from a normal distribution with mean 0 and standard deviation 5. This new variable can readily be created in most statistical packages by using some sort of transform or compute statement, and we have included a variable created in this fashion in the data file. Note that because we are adding random components to the values of *BMI*, each time we generate the variable, the specific values will differ.

How should we expect the correlation between *TC* and *bmiplusnorm05* to differ from that between *TC* and *BMI*? How do we expect the regression of *TC* on age and *bmiplusnorm05* to differ from what was obtained in part (a)? Why?

(c) Repeat part (b) except replace *BMI* by *bmiplusnorm020*, obtained by adding to *BMI* a random number selected from a normal distribution with mean 0 and standard deviation 20.

(d) Now consider what should happen if we have more measurement error in the dependent variable *TC* (as opposed to the predictors). We have created a new variable *tcplusnorm040*, formed by adding to *TC* a random number selected from a normal distribution with mean 0 and standard deviation 40. How should we expect results to differ if we used this new variable as the dependent variable in the regression on *age* and *BMI* instead of using *TC*?

23.7 **(a)** A researcher is interested in relating measures of mother–child attachment to measures of externalization and criticism obtained from a series of interviews. A regression of the attachment measure on both externalization and criticism yields significant *t* tests for the coefficients of both predictor variables. What can be concluded?

(b) The researcher then decides to determine whether the joint effect of externalization and criticism is an important predictor of attachment. She creates a new variable by multiplying the externalization and criticism measures for each case. She then regresses attachment on the externalization and criticism measures as well as the new variable. The regression now shows that none of the *t* tests for the three predictors are significant. Is this an appropriate way to assess whether the joint effect of externalization and criticism is an important predictor of attachment? Why or why not? What is the most likely reason why the *t* tests for the coefficients of externalization and criticism are not significant in the second regression even though they were significant in the first regression described in part (a)? Considering the results of the two regressions together, what can be concluded?

23.8 Consider a timely research question: What is the effect of reducing class size on student performance in elementary school? If it can be established that reducing class size has a sufficiently large and enduring effect, then it may be worth investing the resources that would be required to achieve the reductions. Common sense suggests that children must learn more in smaller classes in which they can be given more individual attention. However, despite dozens of publications on the topic, there is still vigorous debate about whether the gain in learning is worth the extra resources required to achieve it, or even whether there is any meaningful gain at all. To get a flavor of this discussion, just enter "class size debate" in any Internet search engine. How can there possibly be so much disagreement about the results of class size research? Suppose we were to collect relevant data from observational studies, in which we sampled a large number of (naturally occurring) classes of different sizes, and compared the performance of students as a function of classroom size. How might the results of the study be questioned and what kinds of studies might be run that would be less subject to these criticisms?

23.9 Using the data file *Seasons exercises*, perform the analyses found in Section 23.9.2 to test the interaction of age and sex with the dependent variable *TC*. Compare with Table 23.3. Note: To make the results comparable, select subjects aged 65 years or less with *BMI* scores no larger than 40.

23.10 Perform the analyses found in Section 23.9.3 to test the interaction of age and *BMI*. Compare with Table 23.4.

Chapter 24
Regression with Qualitative and Quantitative Variables

24.1 OVERVIEW

We now consider how to include categorical variables with levels that differ *qualitatively* from one another within the regression framework. Examples of such variables are sex, with levels female and male; diagnosed mental illness, with levels schizophrenia, depression, and anxiety disorder; and treatment condition, with levels defined by different types of therapy. With the exception of the brief introduction to logistic regression in the last chapter and the occasional use of dichotomous predictor variables such as sex, our development of regression to this point has focused on variables that are quantitative and are treated as though they were continuous. However, qualitative categorical variables can also be incorporated into regression analyses, providing us with a general and powerful framework within which many of the analyses that we have discussed earlier can be considered as special cases, including ANOVA and ANCOVA. Viewing ANOVA and regression within the same framework can both increase our understanding of these analyses and how they are related, and allow us to deal with data from designs that cannot be handled easily by the standard ANOVA approach.

Our goals in Chapter 24 are the following:

- *Discuss how qualitative categorical variables can be coded so that they may be included within the multiple regression framework.*
- *Consider different kinds of ANOVA designs with between-subjects factors within the multiple regression framework. We will discuss single-factor designs and both orthogonal and nonorthogonal (i.e., unequal-n) factorial designs. We will defer the discussion of ANCOVA until the next chapter.*
- *Briefly consider how repeated-measures and mixed ANOVAs can be included within the multiple regression framework.*

24.2 ONE-FACTOR DESIGNS

24.2.1 Coding Qualitative Categorical Variables

It is important to distinguish between quantitative and qualitative categorical variables in regression. Suppose we have a factor with six levels that correspond to qualitatively different treatment conditions, and code this factor by using a single variable that assigns the numbers 1–6 to the treatments. *It is not correct to use this variable as a predictor in a regression analysis.* If we did, we would be treating the factor as though it was a *quantitative* variable—such coding implies that the treatment at level 3 is three times as large as the treatment at level 1, and that the treatment at level 4 is twice as large as the one at level 2. This makes no sense if we have a qualitative variable. Moreover, using a single coding variable only accounts for 1 *df*, whereas in ANOVA there are 5 *df* associated with a factor that has six levels.

If the treatments are *qualitatively* different from one another, we want a coding system which specifies that the treatments are different from one another without imposing any type of ordering. As we shall see, for a factor with *a* levels, $a - 1$ predictor variables are required to do the coding. In practice, we almost never have to generate these coding variables ourselves. Rather, the statistical software packages do it for us in their ANOVA or GLM (general linear model) modules. Here, we describe some ways of coding categorical variables because this allows greater insight into the analyses, and in some cases, allows us to better understand the options and output provided by the statistical packages.

Any qualitative categorical variable can be coded by defining one or more *dummy* (or *indicator*) *variables* that take on numerical values. These numerical values are not measures of the category levels; rather, they are best thought of as labels that together specify category membership. The coding is particularly simple when a categorical variable, A, has only two levels (e.g., sex). If factor A has only two levels, the dummy variable X could take on any value at one level and any different value at the other level. For the moment, assume these values are 1 and 2. The overall test of the regression of the dependent variable Y on X would then be exactly equivalent to the ANOVA F test for the categorical variable, A.

To be more specific, if we regress Y on X, the least-squares regression line must pass through the points $(1, \bar{Y}_{.1})$ and $(2, \bar{Y}_{.2})$, as can be seen in Fig. 24.1. This is because the regression line minimizes the mean squared deviations of the Ys, and the group means minimize the mean squared deviations in each of the groups. Because the regression line passes though the two group means, it accounts for all the variability in the group means, so $SS_{regression}$ must equal the between-group variability, SS_A. Also, $SS_{residual}$, the variability unaccounted for by the regression, must equal $SS_{S/A}$.

However, if the factor A has more than two levels, regression on a single dummy variable will not, in general, account for all of SS_A. Consider what happens with three levels: Panel (a) of Table 24.1 presents scores at levels A_1, A_2, and A_3 of the factor A. In panel (b) of the table, we code A with a single dummy variable, X_1, that takes on the values 1, 2, and 3. The points that represent the group means in the space defined by X_1 and Y will be $(1, \bar{Y}_{.1})$, $(2, \bar{Y}_{.2})$, and $(3, \bar{Y}_{.3})$, as shown in panel (a) of Fig. 24.2. In general, these three points will not be perfectly fit by a straight line. Therefore, if Y is regressed on X_1, the regression will usually not account for all the variability in the group means, and $SS_{regression}$ will be less than SS_A. However, we can account for all of SS_A if we define an additional dummy variable, X_2, that is not perfectly correlated with X_1—for example, the variable that takes on the values given in panel (b) of Table 24.1. Now if we represent the three group means in the three-dimensional space defined by Y, X_1, and X_2, as in panel (b) of Fig. 24.2, it is apparent that they can be perfectly fit by a two-dimensional regression *plane*. Therefore, when Y is regressed on

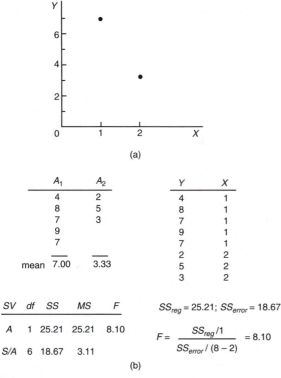

Fig. 24.1. (a) Plot of the means of A against X for the data in panel (b). Note that the two points representing group means can be fit perfectly by a straight line. (b) Data and results of ANOVA and multiple regression.

both dummy variables, all the between-group variability will be accounted for by the regression, so that $SS_{regression} = SS_A$, and the F test for the overall regression of Y on X_1 and X_2 is exactly equivalent to the ANOVA F test for the effect of the categorical factor, A.

This reasoning can be extended to factors with more levels by using additional dummy variables. In general, it will take as many dummy variables to code a factor as the number of degrees of freedom associated with it; for example, five dummy variables will be required to code a categorical variable with six levels. The only requirement on these dummy variables is that they be *linearly independent*; that is, none of them may be perfectly expressed as a linear combination of the others. If a variable can be expressed as a linear combination of the other dummy variables, it is redundant, and therefore cannot contribute anything to the specification of the categories.

24.2.2 Effect and Dummy[1] Coding

Although the variables X_1 and X_2 in our example appropriately partition the variability in Y into components associated with A and S/A, the coefficients associated with X_1 and X_2 are not particularly meaningful. Two more common approaches to coding categorical variables, *effect coding* and

---

[1] The term "dummy variables" is used to refer to the variables that code a categorical variable by using any of the coding procedures. The term "dummy coding" is used to refer to a specific kind of coding in which each dummy variable takes on the values 0 and 1 as described in the text.

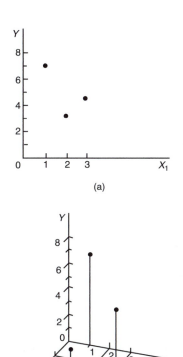

Fig. 24.2. (a) Plot of the means of A against X_1 for the data in Table 24.1. In general, the points representing the three means cannot be fit perfectly by a straight line. (b) Plot of the means of A against X_1 and X_2. The points representing the three means can always be fit by a plane if X_1 and X_2 are not perfectly correlated.

dummy coding, produce more interpretable regression coefficients. Both coding methods allow us to specify group membership so that a regression of the dependent variable on the dummy variables will produce an analysis identical to the ANOVA. The only difference between them is that the regression coefficients produced by the two coding systems have different interpretations.

Effect Coding. In discussing ANOVA as a special case of multiple regression, we may find it useful to consider the type of dummy variable coding called *effect coding* because, as we show below, it produces regression coefficients that estimate the ANOVA effects α_1, α_2, . . ., α_{a-1}, where $\alpha_j = \mu_j - \mu$. Effect coding represents group membership with dummy variables that contain 1s, 0s, and −1s, as illustrated by variables X_{E1} and X_{E2} in panel (b) of Table 24.1. Dummy variables for effect coding are defined as follows:

$$X_{Ej} = 1 \text{ for scores at level } A_j$$

$$= -1 \text{ for scores at some arbitrary level of } A, \text{ here } A_3$$

$$= 0 \text{ otherwise}$$

Because there are three levels of A in Table 24.1, we require two dummy variables to account

Table 24.1 Regression on dummy variables for a one-factor design

(a) Data and results of standard ANOVA for a one-factor design

A_1	A_2	A_3
4	2	4
8	5	5
7	3	3
9		6
7		

$\bar{Y}_{\cdot j} = 7.00 \qquad 3.33 \qquad 4.50$
$\bar{Y}_U = (7 + 3.33 + 4.50)/3 = 4.94$

SV	df	SS	MS	F
A	2	28.583	14.292	5.435
S/A	9	23.667	2.630	

(b) Dummy variable coding and some statistics obtained from the regressions of Y on X_1 and X_2 and on X_{E1} and X_{E2}

	Y	X_1	X_2	X_{E1}	X_{E2}	X_{D1}	X_{D2}
A_1	4	1	0	1	0	1	0
	8	1	0	1	0	1	0
	7	1	0	1	0	1	0
	9	1	0	1	0	1	0
	7	1	0	1	0	1	0
A_2	2	2	3	0	1	0	1
	5	2	3	0	1	0	1
	3	2	3	0	1	0	1
A_3	4	3	1	−1	−1	0	0
	5	3	1	−1	−1	0	0
	3	3	1	−1	−1	0	0
	6	3	1	−1	−1	0	0

The statistics for the regression of Y on X_1 and X_2, on X_{E1} and X_{E2}, or on X_{D1} and X_{D2} are $R = .740$; $SS_{regression} = 28.583$; $SS_{residual} = 23.667$; $F = MS_{regression}/MS_{residual} = 5.435$. The regression coefficients based on effect coding are:

$$b_{E0} = \bar{Y}_U = 4.94, \; b_{E1} = \bar{Y}_{\cdot 1} - \bar{Y}_U = 2.06, \text{ and } b_{E2} = \bar{Y}_{\cdot 2} - \bar{Y}_U = -1.61;$$

and the regression coefficients based on dummy coding are:

$$b_{D0} = \bar{Y}_{\cdot 3} = 4.50, \; b_{D1} = \bar{Y}_{\cdot 1} - \bar{Y}_{\cdot 3} = 2.50, \text{ and } b_{D2} = \bar{Y}_{\cdot 2} - \bar{Y}_{\cdot 3} = -1.17.$$

for all the between-group variability. The coding of X_{E1} and X_{E2} is presented in panel (b) of Table 24.1. As can also be seen there, the regression of Y on X_{E1} and X_{E2} produces a value of $SS_{regression}$ that is equal to the SS_A obtained from the standard ANOVA, and an overall F statistic for the regression that is equal to the ANOVA F.

We have stated that the regression coefficients resulting from effect coding correspond to the effects estimated in ANOVA. We can readily demonstrate this correspondence, first noting that the scores predicted by the regression equation for each of the groups must be the group means. For A_1, we have $\hat{Y} = \bar{Y}_{\cdot 1}$, $X_{E1} = 1$, and $X_{E2} = 0$. Substituting into the regression equation that predicts Y from X_{E1} and X_{E2}, we obtain

$$\bar{Y}_{\cdot 1} = b_{E0} + b_{E1}(1) + b_{E2}(0) = b_{E0} + b_{E1} \tag{24.1}$$

Similarly, for A_2 and A_3, respectively, we have

$$\bar{Y}_{\cdot 2} = b_{E0} + b_{E1}(0) + b_{E2}(1) = b_{E0} + b_{E2} \tag{24.2}$$

and

$$\bar{Y}_{\cdot 3} = b_{E0} + b_{E1}(-1) + b_{E2}(-1) = b_{E0} - b_{E1} - b_{E2} \tag{24.3}$$

Adding Equations 24.1–24.3, we obtain $3b_{E0} = \bar{Y}_{\cdot 1} + \bar{Y}_{\cdot 2} + \bar{Y}_{\cdot 3}$, so that

$$b_{E0} = \frac{\bar{Y}_{\cdot 1} + \bar{Y}_{\cdot 2} + \bar{Y}_{\cdot 3}}{3} = \bar{Y}_U$$

Here, $\bar{Y}_U$ is the unweighted average of the group means. If there are equal numbers of scores in each of the groups, $\bar{Y}_U$ will equal $\bar{Y}_{\cdot\cdot}$, the grand mean of all the scores.

We can now write the coefficients of the dummy variables as deviations from the unweighted mean of the group means. Substituting $b_{E0} = \bar{Y}_U$ into Equations 24.1 and 24.2, and solving, we obtain the formulas and numerical results for b_{E1} and b_{E2} that are presented in panel (b) of Table 24.1. For equal-n designs, the regression coefficients correspond exactly to the estimated main effect components of the ANOVA, the $\hat{\alpha}_j$s. That is, because $\bar{Y}_{\cdot j} = \hat{\mu}_j$ and $\bar{Y}_{\cdot\cdot} = \hat{\mu}$,

$$b_{E1} = \bar{Y}_{\cdot 1} - \bar{Y}_{\cdot\cdot} = \hat{\mu}_1 - \hat{\mu} = \hat{\alpha}_1$$

and

$$b_{E2} = \bar{Y}_{\cdot 2} - \bar{Y}_{\cdot\cdot} = \hat{\mu}_2 - \hat{\mu} = \hat{\alpha}_2$$

Furthermore, because of the requirement that $\Sigma \alpha_j = 0$, $\hat{\alpha}_3$ can be found as

$$\hat{\alpha}_3 = -\hat{\alpha}_1 - \hat{\alpha}_2 = -b_{E1} - b_{E2}$$

Dummy Coding. A second way to code categorical variables is to use *dummy coding*, for which the dummy variables only take on the values 0 and 1, as illustrated by X_{D1} and X_{D2} in panel (b) of Table 24.1. For dummy coding, the dummy variables are defined as

$$X_{Dj} = 1 \text{ for scores at level } A_j, \text{ and}$$

$$= 0 \text{ otherwise}$$

Note that because we only need $a - 1$ dummy variables to code a groups, one group, referred to as the *reference group*, will receive 0s on all the dummy variables.

Because there are three levels of A in the current example, we require two dummy variables to account for all the between-group variability. Scores at A_1 receive a 1 on X_{D1} and a 0 on X_{D2}; scores at A_2 receive a 0 on X_{D1} and a 1 on X_{D2}; and scores at A_3 receive values of 0 on both X_{D1} and X_{D2}. As we can see in panel (b) of Table 24.1, the regression of Y on X_{D1} and X_{D2} also produces a value of

$SS_{regression}$ equal to the SS_A obtained from the standard ANOVA. Although the variability accounted for by the regression is the same whether we use dummy or effect coding, the regression coefficients are different. If we use dummy coding, the intercept, b_{D0}, takes on the value of the mean of the *reference group* (the group that has 0s on all the indicator variables). For example, in Table 24.1, the value of the intercept is equal to the mean of condition A_3. The regression coefficients for each of the dummy variables, b_{D1} and b_{D2}, take on values equal to the differences between the group coded as 1 on the dummy variable and the mean of the reference group. We can see this by noting that because the regression accounts for all the between-group variability, the prediction for each score will be its group mean.

For the scores at A_3, each dummy variable has the value 0 so that

$$\bar{Y}_{.3} = b_{D0} + b_{D1}(0) + b_{D2}(0) = b_{D0}$$

Therefore, $b_{D0} = \bar{Y}_{.3}$. For scores at A_1, we have $\hat{Y} = \bar{Y}_{.1}$. Substituting $X_{D1} = 1$, and $X_{D2} = 0$ into the equation for the regression of Y on X_{D1} and X_{D2}, we obtain

$$\bar{Y}_{.1} = b_{D0} + b_{D1}(1) + b_{D2}(0) = b_{D0} + b_{D1}$$

Therefore, $b_{D1} = \bar{Y}_{.1} - b_{D0} = \bar{Y}_{.1} - \bar{Y}_{.3}$. Similarly, for scores at A_2, we have

$$\bar{Y}_{.2} = b_{D0} + b_{D1}(0) + b_{D2}(1) = b_{D0} + b_{D2}$$

so that $b_{D2} = \bar{Y}_{.2} - b_{D0} = \bar{Y}_{.2} - \bar{Y}_{.3}$.

Dummy coding might be particularly useful if the design contains a control group. If so, we could let the control group serve as the reference group, and the regression coefficients would then directly equal the differences between the treatment and control means. There are many other possible ways to code categorical variables. For example, categorical variables may be coded such that regression coefficients take on the values of contrasts of possible interest. Detailed discussions of these methods may be found in sources such as Cohen et al. (2003).

It is important to understand how categorical variables can be represented in regression because the choice of coding has direct implications for the interpretation of the intercept and the coefficients. Further, in some applications (e.g., use of the HLM software package), the value of each dummy variable must be coded in the data file. However, for the regression applications we are considering here, we rarely have to code the categorical variables ourselves. For example, once we have specified that we have a categorical factor, the general linear model module dialog box in SYSTAT allows us to choose whether to use effect or dummy coding. On the other hand, the corresponding module in SPSS does not provide a choice; it simply uses dummy coding. This does not present any particular problem, but we should be aware what the program is doing if we try to interpret the parameter estimates in the output.

No matter which coding procedure is used to code a factor A, when the dependent variable Y is regressed on the complete set of dummy variables,

$$SS_{between} = SS_A = R^2_{Y.A} SS_Y$$

where $R^2_{Y.A}$ is the square of the multiple correlation when Y is regressed on the $a-1$ dummy variables that code factor A, and

$$SS_{within} = SS_{S/A} = (1 - R^2_{Y.A})SS_Y$$

so that the test statistic for A is given by $F = \dfrac{MS_A}{MS_{S/A}} = \dfrac{R^2_{Y.A} SS_Y / (a-1)}{(1 - R^2_{Y.A})SS_Y / (N-a)}$.

24.3 REGRESSION ANALYSES AND FACTORIAL ANOVA DESIGNS

In Section 24.2, we saw how any categorical variable can be coded by a set of dummy variables and that a multiple regression analysis that uses these dummy variables as predictors provides all of the information, and more, that can be obtained from a one-factor ANOVA. In Section 24.3 we extend this discussion to multifactor ANOVA designs, first considering orthogonal designs and then the issues that arise in analyzing data from nonorthogonal or unbalanced (unequal-n) designs.

24.3.1 Orthogonal Designs

A regression analysis of a factorial design can be performed if both the factors and their inter-actions are coded by sets of dummy variables. Although it is generally more practical to analyze orthogonal designs with software designed to perform ANOVAs, it is useful to understand how such designs might be analyzed by regression. This will provide a deeper understanding of ANOVA as a special case of regression. In addition, greater facility with coding of categorical variables will provide the researcher with greater facility in the analysis of designs that consist of combinations of categorical and quantitative variables.

Panel (a) of Table 24.2 contains data from a 3×3 design with factors A and C (we use C rather than B to refer to the second factor because of the large number of bs already in the chapter). Panel (b) contains sets of effect dummy variables that code the design, where effect coding is used to code the categorical variables. Each set of dummy variables has as many members as the corresponding sources of variance have dfs. A and C are coded as though each were the only factor in the design, and the set of four dummy variables that code the AC interaction is obtained by multiplying each dummy variable in the A set by each one in the C set. Together, the eight dummy variables code membership in the nine cells of the design. Panel (c) contains the results of an ANOVA on the data.

With effect coding, the dummy variables *within* any one of the A, C, and AC sets are correlated. However, if the cell frequencies are all equal, the dummy variables in any set are uncorrelated with all the dummy variables in each of the other sets; therefore, the sums of squares associated with the different sets do not overlap. Let's use the notation $R_{Y.A}$, $R_{Y.AC}$, and $R_{Y.A,AC}$ to represent the multiple correlation coefficients that result when Y is regressed on the sets of dummy variables that code A, AC, and both A and AC, respectively. Then, because the sets of dummy variables corresponding to A, C, and AC are uncorrelated, we have

$$R_{Y.A,C,AC}^2 = R_{Y.A}^2 + R_{Y.C}^2 + R_{Y.AC}^2$$

Multiplying each of the squared correlations by SS_Y, we have

$$SS_{Between\ cell} = SS_A + SS_C + SS_{AC}$$

That is, the between-cells variability is partitioned into the main effects of A and C, and their interaction. Because we have enough coding variables to account for all the between-subjects vari-ability, $SS_{error} = SS_{residual} = (1 - R_{Y.A,C,AC}^2)SS_Y$, and tests of the A and C main effects and the AC interaction, respectively, are provided by

$$F = \frac{R_{Y.A}^2 / (a-1)}{(1 - R_{Y.A,C,AC}^2) / (N - ac)}$$

$$F = \frac{R_{Y.C}^2 / (c-1)}{(1 - R_{Y.A,C,AC}^2) / (N - ac)}$$

and

Table 24.2   Effect coding for an orthogonal 3×3 design

(a) Data

	C_1	C_2	C_3
A_1	53	88	56
	51	63	42
A_2	55	48	79
	78	42	50
A_3	79	80	69
	99	92	94

(b) Dummy variables formed by using effect coding

Effect:		A		C		AC			
	Y	X_1	X_2	X_3	X_4	X_5	X_6	X_7	X_8
A_1C_1	53	1	0	1	0	1	0	0	0
	51	1	0	1	0	1	0	0	0
A_1C_2	88	1	0	0	1	0	0	1	0
	63	1	0	0	1	0	0	1	0
A_1C_3	56	1	0	-1	-1	-1	0	-1	0
	42	1	0	-1	-1	-1	0	-1	0
A_2C_1	55	0	1	1	0	0	1	0	0
	78	0	1	1	0	0	1	0	0
A_2C_2	48	0	1	0	1	0	0	0	1
	42	0	1	0	1	0	0	0	1
A_2C_3	79	0	1	-1	-1	0	-1	0	-1
	50	0	1	-1	-1	0	-1	0	-1
A_3C_1	79	-1	-1	1	0	-1	-1	0	0
	99	-1	-1	1	0	-1	-1	0	0
A_3C_2	80	-1	-1	0	1	0	0	-1	-1
	92	-1	-1	0	1	0	0	-1	-1
A_3C_3	69	-1	-1	-1	-1	1	1	1	1
	94	-1	-1	-1	-1	1	1	1	1

SV	df	SS	MS	F
A	2	2,862.333	1,431.167	7.577
C	2	64.333	32.167	0.170
AC	4	1,399.333	349.833	1.852
Error	9	1,700.000	188.889	

$$F = \frac{R_{Y.AC}^2 / (a-1)(c-1)}{(1 - R_{Y.A,C,AC}^2) / (N - ac)}$$

These test statistics have exactly the same values as the ANOVA Fs for A, C, and AC that are presented in Table 24.2.

To carry out the ANOVA using a statistical package, we need only code each factor with a single variable that labels each level with a distinct symbol such as 1, 2, and 3, and then use the ANOVA or GLM module to analyze the data. If the variable is specified as a categorical variable or factor, the software creates the dummy variables and performs the analyses as described above. The programs differ somewhat in what must be specified in their GLM modules. For example, SPSS GLM assumes that each variable listed as a factor is categorical; continuous variables must be listed as covariates. On the other hand, in SYSTAT GLM, independent variables are assumed to be continuous unless specified as categorical.

24.3.2 Nonorthogonal Designs

In standard ANOVA, all factors are treated as though they are qualitative categorical variables that are independent of one another (i.e., the level at which a score is located on one factor provides no information about its location on other factors). It is this independence or *orthogonality* that makes it possible to partition the variability in factorial designs into distinct, nonoverlapping components associated with main effects and interactions in ANOVA. However, orthogonality requires that cell frequencies be equal, and this requirement is not realistic in many research contexts. Unequal cell frequencies introduce correlations among the factors, and these correlations cause the variance components associated with the different effects to overlap. Although we discussed unequal-n designs from an ANOVA perspective in Chapter 9 (Section 9.8), the complexities of unequal-n ANOVA are easier to understand within the multiple regression framework in which we expect variables to be correlated with one another.

Panel (a) of Table 24.3 contains data for a nonorthogonal design with factors A and C, panel (b) contains the effect coding for the design. Because of the unequal cell frequencies, the sets of dummy variables that code the A, C, and AC effects are no longer uncorrelated. Therefore, in general,

$$R_{Y.A,C,AC}^2 \neq R_{Y.A}^2 + R_{Y.C}^2 + R_{Y.AC}^2$$

because the variability associated with A, C, and AC overlaps, as represented by Fig. 24.3. This situation creates ambiguity in interpreting effects because it is unclear how to attribute variability that is shared by two or more sources. Multiple regression analyses allow a variety of possible adjustments for this overlap. Below we consider three types of adjustments and make recommendations about the conditions under which each seems most appropriate.

Method 1.   In considering the effect of A, we might decide to attribute to A only the variability *uniquely* associated with A. This is the variability in A that does not overlap with the other effects in the design and is represented by the area t in the upper circle of Fig. 24.3. It can be obtained from

$$SS_{A|C,AC} = (R_{Y.A,C,AC}^2 - R_{Y.C,AC}^2)SS_Y$$

where the subscript on the SS term on the left side of the equation is read "A adjusted for C and AC." When we adjust the sum of squares by removing the overlapping variability of all the other main or interaction effects, we obtain what are called *Type III sums of squares*. This is the default for most statistics packages.

Table 24.3 Effect coding for a nonorthogonal 3×3 design

(a) Data

	C_1	C_2	C_3
A_1	53	88	56
	51	63	42
		50	
		71	
A_2	55	48	79
	78	42	50
	39		62
A_3	79	80	69
	99	92	94
			80
			77

(b) Dummy variables formed by using effect coding

Effect:		A		C		AC			
	Y	X_1	X_2	X_3	X_4	X_5	X_6	X_7	X_8
A_1C_1	53	1	0	1	0	1	0	0	0
	51	1	0	1	0	1	0	0	0
A_1C_2	88	1	0	0	1	0	0	1	0
	63	1	0	0	1	0	0	1	0
	50	1	0	0	1	0	0	1	0
	71	1	0	0	1	0	0	1	0
A_1C_3	56	1	0	−1	−1	−1	0	−1	0
	42	1	0	−1	−1	−1	0	−1	0
A_2C_1	55	0	1	1	0	0	1	0	0
	78	0	1	1	0	0	1	0	0
	39	0	1	1	0	0	1	0	0
A_2C_2	48	0	1	0	1	0	0	0	1
	42	0	1	0	1	0	0	0	1
A_2C_3	79	0	1	−1	−1	0	−1	0	−1
	50	0	1	−1	−1	0	−1	0	−1
	62	0	1	−1	−1	0	−1	0	−1
A_3C_1	79	−1	−1	1	0	−1	−1	0	0
	99	−1	−1	1	0	−1	−1	0	0
A_3C_2	80	−1	−1	0	1	0	0	−1	−1
	92	−1	−1	0	1	0	0	−1	−1
A_3C_3	69	−1	−1	−1	−1	1	1	1	1
	94	−1	−1	−1	−1	1	1	1	1
	80	−1	−1	−1	−1	1	1	1	1
	77	−1	−1	−1	−1	1	1	1	1

Method 2. An alternative approach is to adjust the A effect only for the other main effect C, yielding the variability represented by areas t and w in the upper circle of Fig. 24.3,

$$SS_{A|C} = (R^2_{Y.A,C} - R^2_{Y.C})SS_Y$$

where the subscript on the SS term to the left is read "A adjusted for C." In general, Method 2 adjusts any effect for all effects of the same order or lower order (e.g., main effects are adjusted for other main effects, but not for interactions).

Method 3. Finally, we may decide not to adjust for the contributions of the other effects at all. This yields

$$SS_A = R^2_{Y.A}SS_Y$$

In terms of Fig. 24.3, the overlap of the circles is ignored; the effect of A is considered to be the sum of areas t, u, v, and w.

It should be clear that the three methods of analyzing effects in nonorthogonal designs will usually not produce equal estimates of effects of A. Because A will account for some variance in Y that is also accounted for by C and AC; SS_A, $SS_{A|C}$, and $SS_{A|C,AC}$ will generally not be equal. Depending on whether the covariations among the effects are positive or negative, the adjusted sum of squares may be smaller or larger than if there were no adjustment.[2] For the data in Table 24.3, $SS_{A|C,AC} = 4{,}139.42$, $SS_{A|C} = 3{,}609.95$, and $SS_A = 3{,}581.08$.

The three methods of adjusting the sums of squares result in different tests of the hypotheses of interest. Table 24.4 describes the three methods of analyzing nonorthogonal factorial designs and indicates the hypotheses tested by each of them. In all three methods, interactions are

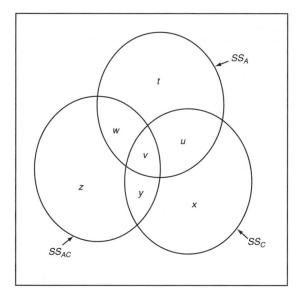

Fig. 24.3 Partitioning of variability in a nonorthogonal two-factor design.

---

[2] This example points out that the use of overlapping circles to represent overlapping variabilities, as in Fig. 24.3, is of limited utility. Here, the adjusted variabilities are larger than the unadjusted ones—something not obvious from the figure. This is because the representation does not distinguish between positive and negative covariation.

adjusted for all other effects in the design, resulting in tests of the usual interaction null hypothesis

$$H_0: \mu_{jk} - \mu_{j'k} - \mu_{jk'} + \mu_{j'k'} = 0 \quad \text{for all } j, j', k, \text{ and } k'$$

However, the three methods produce different tests of the main effects, as would be expected given their different ways of attributing variance to A. Given this, on what basis are we to decide which approach, if any, to use? Our view is that the proper analysis depends upon what the researcher assumes to be the basis of the confounding of sources of variance in the design.

If the variables in the study are manipulated, or if the data in the cells can be viewed as samples from naturally occurring, equal-sized treatment populations, then the unequal cell sizes in the sample reflect random sampling error. That is, we may plan to have equal cell frequencies, but fail to obtain them because of chance occurrences such as equipment failures or subjects failing to show up. In this event, it makes sense to give each cell in the design the same weight. The corresponding overall A null hypothesis that is of interest states that the unweighted averages of the c population means at each level of A are equal. That is,

$$\mu_1 = \mu_2 = \ldots = \mu_a.$$

where

$$\mu_{j.} = \frac{1}{c} \sum_k \mu_{jk}$$

is the unweighted mean of the cell means at the jth level of A. It can be shown (e.g., Myers & Well, 1995) that Method 1 tests this null hypotheses. Therefore, *Method 1 (which uses Type III sums of squares) is recommended when unequal cell frequencies occur by chance, as is usually the case in experimental designs*. This analysis is summarized in Table 24.4 and illustrated in Table 24.5.

Table 24.4 Three methods for analyzing nonorthogonal factorial designs

Method 1: Adjusting for all main and interaction effects

SV	df	SS
A	$a - 1$	$SS_{A|C,AC} = (R^2_{Y.A,C,AC} - R^2_{Y.C,AC})SS_Y$
C	$c - 1$	$SS_{C|A,AC} = (R^2_{Y.A,C,AC} - R^2_{Y.A,AC})SS_Y$
AC	$(a-1)(c-1)$	$SS_{AC|A,C} = (R^2_{Y.A,C,AC} - R^2_{Y.A,C})SS_Y$
Residual	$N - ac$	$SS_{residual} = (1 - R^2_{Y.A,C,AC})SS_Y$

Hypotheses tested:

A: $\mu_1 = \mu_2 = \ldots = \mu_a.$ where $\mu_{j.} = \dfrac{1}{c} \sum_k \mu_{jk}$ is the unweighted mean of the population means for the c cells in the jth row of A

C: $\mu_{.1} = \mu_{.2} = \ldots = \mu_{.c}$ where $\mu_{.k} = \dfrac{1}{a} \sum_j \mu_{jk}$ is the unweighted mean of the population means for the a cells in the kth row of C

AC: $\mu_{jk} - \mu_{j'k} - \mu_{jk'} + \mu_{j'k'} = 0$ for all j, k, j', k'

Usage: This method uses *Type III sums of squares* to test hypotheses about unweighted column and row means, and will usually be the method of choice when unequal cell frequencies occur by chance. This method is also known as Overall and Spiegel's (1969) method 1, Yates's (1934) weighted squares of means, and SPSS's classic regression approach.

Method 2: Adjusting for the effects of the same and lower order

SV	df	SS
A	$a - 1$	$SS_{A|C} = (R^2_{Y.A,C} - R^2_{Y.C})SS_Y$
C	$c - 1$	$SS_{C|A} = (R^2_{Y.A,C} - R^2_{Y.A})SS_Y$
AC	$(a - 1)(c - 1)$	$SS_{AC|A,C} = (R^2_{Y.A,C,AC} - R^2_{Y.A,C})SS_Y$
Residual	$N - ac$	$SS_{residual} = (1 - R^2_{Y.A,C,AC})\,SS_Y$

Hypotheses tested:

$$A: \sum_k \left[n_{jk} - \frac{n_{jk}^2}{n_{.k}} \right] \mu_{jk} - \sum_{j \neq j'} \sum_k \left[\frac{n_{jk} n_{j'k}}{n_{.k}} \right] \mu_{j'k} = 0 \quad \text{for } j = 1, 2, \ldots, a - 1$$

$$C: \sum_j \left[n_{jk} - \frac{n_{jk}^2}{n_{j.}} \right] \mu_{jk} - \sum_{k \neq k'} \sum_j \left[\frac{n_{jk} n_{jk'}}{n_{j.}} \right] \mu_{jk'} = 0 \quad \text{for } k = 1, 2, \ldots, c - 1$$

$AC: \mu_{jk} - \mu_{j'k} - \mu_{jk'} + \mu_{j'k'} = 0$ for all j, k, j', k'

Usage: Method 2 uses *Type II sums of squares*, which adjust an effect of interest for effects at the same or lower order, and for higher-order effects that do not include the effect of interest. If there is *no interaction*, Method 2 tests Method 1's hypotheses with somewhat more power than Method 1 itself. However, if there is the possibility of an interaction, Method 2 should be avoided because it tests data-dependent hypotheses that are not useful (see the hypotheses that are tested above). This method is also known as Overall and Speigel's method 2, Yates's fitting constants method, and SPSS's classic experimental design approach.

Method 3: Main effects not adjusted

SV	df	SS
A	$a - 1$	$SS_A = R^2_{Y.A}SS_Y$
C	$c - 1$	$SS_C = R^2_{Y.C}SS_Y$
AC	$(a - 1)(c - 1)$	$SS_{AC|A,C} = (R^2_{Y.A,C,AC} - R^2_{Y.A,C})SS_Y$
Residual	$N - ac$	$SS_{residual} = (1 - R^2_{Y.A,C,AC})\,SS_Y$

Hypotheses tested:

$A: \mu_{1*} = \mu_{2*} = \ldots = \mu_{a*}$ where $\mu_{j*} = \dfrac{1}{n_{j.}} \sum_k n_{jk}\mu_{jk}$ is the weighted mean of the population means for the c cells in the jth row of A

$C: \mu_{*1} = \mu_{*2} = \ldots = \mu_{*c}$ where $\mu_{*k} = \dfrac{1}{n_{.k}} \sum_k n_{jk}\mu_{jk}$ is the weighted mean of the population means for the a cells in the kth row of C

$AC: \mu_{jk} - \mu_{j'k} - \mu_{jk'} + \mu_{j'k'} = 0$ for all j, k, j', k'

Usage: This method tests main-effect hypotheses about the weighted row and column means. These tests may be desirable if the cell frequencies are proportional to the corresponding population sizes. This method is also known as Yates's method for proportional cell sizes.

Table 24.5   Results obtained by using the three methods with the data of Table 24.3

SV	df	SS	MS	F
		Method 1		
A	2	$SS_{A|C,AC} = 4{,}139.423$	2,069.712	11.639
C	2	$SS_{C|A,AC} = 21.074$	10.537	0.059
AC	4	$SS_{AC|A,C} = 1{,}103.074$	275.769	1.551
Residual	15	$(1 - R^2_{Y.A,C,AC})SS_Y = 2{,}667.833$	177.882	
		Method 2		
A	2	$SS_{A|C} = 3{,}609.950$	1,804.975	10.150
C	2	$SS_{C|A} = 60.468$	30.234	0.170
AC	4	$SS_{AC|A,C} = 1{,}103.074$	275.769	1.551
Residual	15	$(1 - R^2_{Y.A,C,AC})SS_Y = 2{,}667.833$	177.882	
		Method 3		
A	2	$SS_A = 3{,}581.083$	1,790.542	10.089
C	2	$SS_C = 31.601$	15.800	0.089
AC	4	$SS_{AC|A,C} = 1{,}103.074$	275.769	1.551
Residual	15	$(1 - R^2_{Y.A,C,AC})SS_Y = 2{,}667.833$	177.882	

An alternative scenario is that unequal cell sizes in a sample reflect systematic variation in the sizes of cell populations. This would often be the case in observational studies. If cell populations vary systematically in size, we may wish to test hypotheses in which the cell means are weighted according to population size. If we have reliable information about the relative sizes of the cell populations, we can use it to weight the cell means. If we do not have such information, we can use the cell frequencies as weights. In this case, the overall A null hypothesis of interest states that the weighted means of A are equal. That is,

$$\mu_{1*} = \mu_{2*} = \ldots = \mu_{a*}$$

where

$$\mu_{j*} = \frac{1}{n_{j.}} \sum_k n_{jk}\mu_{jk}$$

is the weighted mean of the cell means at the jth level of A. Method 3 provides tests of main effect hypotheses based on weighted row and column means. This analysis is summarized in Table 24.4 and illustrated in Table 24.5.

Finally, under what conditions might Method 2 be used? The Method 2 approach that has been favored by some statisticians (e.g., Cramer & Appelbaum, 1980) corresponds to a hierarchical series of model tests that starts with higher-order effects. On the rationale that main effects are not very meaningful in the presence of an interaction, this approach first tests the interaction by comparing the model

$$Y_{ijk} = \mu + \alpha_j + \gamma_k + (\alpha\gamma)_{jk} + \varepsilon_{ijk}$$

against

$$Y_{ijk} = \mu + \alpha_j + \gamma_k + \varepsilon_{ijk}$$

If there is no interaction, tests of the main effects are then conducted by comparing

$$Y_{ijk} = \mu + \alpha_j + \gamma_k + \varepsilon_{ijk}$$

against

$$Y_{ijk} = \mu + \gamma_k + \varepsilon_{ijk}$$

and

$$Y_{ijk} = \mu + \alpha_j + \gamma_k + \varepsilon_{ijk}$$

against

$$Y_{ijk} = \mu + \alpha_j + \varepsilon_{ijk}$$

The Method 2 tests correspond exactly to these model comparisons. The advantage of this approach is that if there is no interaction, tests of main effects are somewhat more powerful than if Method 1 is used.

Despite the potential power advantage that Method 2 may provide over Method 1, we do not recommend using Method 2. This is because if an interaction does exist, the hypotheses that it tests depend on the pattern of cell frequencies in ways that are of little, if any, interest. For example, the null hypothesis for the effect of A can be shown to be

$$\sum_k \left[n_{jk} - \frac{n_{jk}^2}{n_{.k}} \right] \mu_{jk} - \sum_{j \neq j'} \sum_k \left[\frac{n_{jk} n_{j'k}}{n_{.k}} \right] \mu_{j'k} = 0 \text{ for } j = 1, 2, \ldots, a - 1$$

(see Carlson & Timm, 1974). Another consideration is that Method 2 is likely to produce biased tests of the main effects. If a preliminary test of the interaction does not reject the null hypothesis, tests of the main effects are conducted and based on an assumption that the interaction is zero. But remember that failure to reject a null hypothesis runs the risk of a Type 2 error. Thus, even interactions that do not approach significance can result in biased tests of the main effects (see, for example, Overall, Lee, & Hornick, 1981). Therefore, we believe that Method 2 should not be used unless there is strong *a priori* reason to assume no interaction effects, and that a test for the interaction is not significant.

The three methods considered so far are not the only possible approaches to analyzing data from a nonorthogonal design. It is possible that a logical or theoretical analysis of the research problem might dictate the order in which the sets of dummy variables are entered into the regression equation and, therefore, the nature of the adjustments. Suppose, for example, that A and C indicate levels of child and parental educational achievement, respectively. It is reasonable to assume that parental education may influence a child's educational achievement but not the reverse. In this case, it may be desirable to consider the unadjusted effects of parental educational achievement but to adjust the effects of the child's education for that of the parents. Hierarchical designs produce what are called *Type I sums of squares*.

In summary, the ability to use categorical variables in multiple regression analyses enables us to adjust sums of squares in ways that result in tests of the hypotheses of factorial ANOVA in nonorthogonal designs. We can use the Method 1 approach to test hypotheses about unweighted cell means and the Method 3 approach to test hypotheses about weighted means. Also, if we have logically or theoretically determined orderings of factors, we can perform sequential adjustments.

Finally, we note that most statistical packages produce Type III sums of squares as their default, and therefore test hypotheses about unweighted means (i.e., they use Method 1). However, one should check the documentation or perform some test analyses to be sure. SPSS has caused some confusion in the past in its mainframe versions by defaulting to Method 2 for ANOVA commands and Method 1 for MANOVA.

24.4 TESTING HOMOGENEITY OF REGRESSION SLOPES USING MULTIPLE REGRESSION

In Chapters 20 and 23, we discussed tests for equality of slopes when one variable was regressed on another at different levels of a dichotomous (i.e., having only two levels) categorical variable. We selected subjects in the *Seasons* data set aged 65 years or less with *BMI* scores no larger than 40, and tested whether the rate of change of total cholesterol level (*TC*) with *age* was the same for men and women. Although we did not use the term there, the variable *sex* in the data set is a dummy variable that labels men by 0s and women by 1s. We showed that we could test the hypothesis that the rate of change was the same for men and women by regressing *TC* on *age, sex*, and an additional variable *Age×Sex* that was formed by multiplying *age* by *sex*. The resulting regression equation is

$$\hat{TC} = 221.143 - 0.0005 \, age - 94.612 \, sex + 1.813 \, Age \times Sex$$

Because the coefficient of the interaction term *Age×Sex* is significant, $t(363) = 4.909$, $p = .000$, we can reject the hypothesis that the slope of *TC* with *age* is equal for men and women.

What if the categorical variable has more than two levels? If so, we can still test the hypothesis of homogeneity of regression slopes by determining whether there is a significant interaction. That is, we can test whether the regression of *Y* on a continuous variable, *X*, depends on the level of *A* when *A* is a categorical variable with more than two levels. However, because now more than one dummy variable is needed to code the categorical variable, the interaction term will have more than 1 *df*, and we will need to use a partial *F* test to determine whether the interaction is significant.

Consider, for example, the categorical variable education level, *EL*. We might be interested not only in its main effect on *TC*, but also in its interaction with *age*. Let *EL* = 1 correspond to individuals with a high-school education or less (*schoolyr* = 1, 2, or 3), *EL* = 2 to education beyond high school but not including the bachelor's degree (*schoolyr* = 4, 5, or 6), and *EL* = 3 to at least a bachelor's degree (*schoolyr* = 7 or 8). For the moment, treat *EL* as a qualitative, categorical variable. *EL* seems to make a difference in *TC*. Using the same subjects as the previous analysis, mean *TC* is 227, 217, and 210 for *EL* = 1, 2, and 3, respectively, and an ANOVA with *EL* as the independent variable is significant, $F(2, 359) = 4.908$, $p = .008$.

Now let's consider whether the effects of *EL* on *TC* depend on the age of the subjects. Because *EL* has three levels, we can code it with two dummy variables—it does not matter whether we use effect, dummy, or any other kind of dummy variable coding. We can then code the interaction of *EL* with *age* by using two additional dummy variables, obtained by multiplying the two dummy variables used to code *EL* by *age*. If we have a continuous predictor variable *X* and a categorical variable *A* with *a* levels, the proportion of the variability in *Y* accounted for by a regression on *X* and the *a* − 1 dummy variables coding the categorical variable *A* is $R^2_{Y.X,A}$. If we now add the *a* − 1 dummy variables that account for the *AX* interaction to the regression, the proportion of variance accounted for is $R^2_{Y.X,A,AX}$. The *AX* interaction can be tested by the partial *F*

$$F = \frac{(R^2_{Y.X,A,AX} - R^2_{Y.X,A})SS_Y / (a-1)}{(1 - R^2_{Y.X,A,AX})SS_Y / (N - 2a)}$$

The numerator of the expression corresponds to the increment in the amount of variability accounted for by the interaction and has df equal to the number of dummy variables needed to code the interaction. The denominator is the amount of variability not accounted for by the regression equation that contains the interaction, divided by $df = N - 1 -$ (the number of predictors in the regression equation) $= N - 1 - [1 + 2(a - 1)] = N - 2a$. The bracketed quantity, $1 + 2(a - 1)$, represents the sum of the $a - 1$ df for the regression of Y on A, the $a - 1$ df for the AX interaction, and 1 df for the regression of Y on X.

Using the general linear model module of a standard statistics package to test the interaction, we would specify that EL is a categorical variable, age is a continuous variable (or is a covariate, if we use SPSS—see Appendix 24.1 for more detailed coverage about how to create EL and perform the test), and that we wanted to include the $EL \times age$ interaction in the model. The SPSS output for the analysis is provided in Table 24.6. The $EL \times age$ interaction is not significant; $F(2, 356) = 0.641$,

Table 24.6 SPSS GLM (general linear model) output for the test of (a) the EL factor, (b) the $EL \times age$ interaction for participants with $age \le 65$ years and $BMI \le 40$. Note that here EL is treated as a qualitative categorical variable with three levels

(a)

Tests of Between-Subjects Effects

Dependent Variable: TC

Source	Type III Sum of Squares	df	Mean Square	F	Sig.
Corrected Model	15270.392[a]	2	7635.196	4.908	.008
Intercept	16202490.4	1	16202490.38	10415.87	.000
EL	15270.392	2	7635.196	4.908	.008
Error	558445.173	359	1555.558		
Total	17519394.3	362			
Corrected Total	573715.565	361			

[a.] R Squared = .027 (Adjusted R Squared = .021)

(b)

Tests of Between-Subjects Effects

Dependent Variable: TC

Source	Type III Sum of Squares	df	Mean Square	F	Sig.
Corrected Model	44227.567[a]	5	8845.513	5.947	.000
Intercept	498491.490	1	498491.490	335.160	.000
EL	2149.938	2	1074.969	.723	.486
Age	25241.843	1	25241.843	16.971	.000
EL×Age	1905.416	2	952.708	.641	.528
Error	529487.998	356	1487.326		
Total	17519394.3	362			
Corrected Total	573715.565	361			

[a.] R Squared = .077 (Adjusted R Squared = .064)

$p = .528$. Therefore, we cannot reject the null hypothesis that the effects of EL do not vary with age (or, equivalently, that the rate of change of TC with age is the same at each level of EL).

The procedure can be readily extended to factorial designs. If we had Y and X scores for each cell of a 2×4 design with factors A and C, we could test the homogeneity of the regression slope in the eight cells of the design by performing analyses that produced partial F tests of the XA, XC, and XAC interactions.

Note that although we have been treating EL as a qualitative categorical variable, we could treat it as a crude quantitative variable. Although it has only three levels, they are ordered. If we regress TC on EL, treating it as a quantitative variable, we find that EL is significant, $b = -8.162$, $t(360) = -3.114$, $p = .002$; people with more education tend to have lower cholesterol levels. We can also test the interaction of EL with age by regressing TC on age, EL, and the product of age and EL. There is no evidence of an $age \times EL$ interaction, $b = -0.057$, $t(358) = -0.233$, $p = .816$.

24.5 CODING DESIGNS WITH WITHIN-SUBJECTS FACTORS

In a repeated-measures design, each subject is tested at every level of at least one independent variable, and subjects are considered to define levels of a factor, S, in the design. If there are n subjects, we can code S with $n - 1$ dummy variables in the same way as any other categorical variable.

Table 24.7 contains data for an $S \times A$ design with data from eight subjects at four levels of the repeated-measures factor, A. Using effect coding, we code the eight levels of S with the seven dummy variables labeled in Table 24.7 as S_1-S_7, the four levels of A with three dummy variables, and the SA interaction with 21 dummy variables ($SA11-SA73$) formed by multiplying every dummy variable in the S set by every dummy variable in the A set. The sums of squares can be found from

$$SS_S = R^2_{Y.S} SS_Y$$

$$SS_A = R^2_{Y.A} SS_Y$$

and

$$SS_{SA} = R^2_{Y.SA} SS_Y$$

From our earlier coverage of repeated-measures designs, we know that for an $S \times A$ design, the appropriate test for the A main effect is given by $F = MS_A / MS_{SA}$.

The coding procedure can be directly extended to designs in which there are several within-subjects variables, although the number of dummy variables required increases rather dramatically. If we had a $S \times A \times B$ design with eight subjects, four levels of A and two of B, coding all the main effects and interactions would require $abn - 1 = 63$ dummy variables, as many dummy variables as dfs for each source of variance. However, if a multiple regression program was used to analyze such a design, one would really only have to code the S, A, and B effects. Most software packages have some sort of compute or transform instruction that will create the variables needed to code the interaction effects.

Finally, the coding procedures can be extended to mixed designs that contain both within-subjects and between-subjects factors. Panel (a) of Table 24.8 contains a set of hypothetical data and the ANOVA table for a design that has one between-subjects variable, A, and one within-subjects variable, C, and panel (b) presents dummy variables that code the design. The A, C, and AC sources of variance can be coded as in a factorial between-subjects design, and S/A can be directly represented by coding subjects separately at each level of A, as indicated in Table 24.8. It is not

Table 24.7 Data and effect coding for an $S \times A$ design

Subject	A_1	A_2	A_3	A_4
1	1.4	3.2	3.2	3.0
2	2.0	2.5	3.1	5.8
3	1.4	4.2	4.1	5.6
4	2.3	4.6	4.0	5.9
5	4.7	4.8	4.4	5.9
6	3.2	5.0	6.2	5.9
7	4.0	6.8	4.5	6.5
8	5.0	6.1	6.4	6.6

		S							A			$S \times A$			
	Y	S_1	S_2	S_3	S_4	S_5	S_6	S_7	A_1	A_2	A_3	SA_{11}	SA_{21}	..	SA_{73}
A_1	1.4	1	0	0	0	0	0	0	1	0	0	1	0	...	0
	2.0	0	1	0	0	0	0	0	1	0	1	0	1	...	0
	1.4	0	0	1	0	0	0	0	1	0	0	0	0	...	0
	2.3	0	0	0	1	0	0	0	1	0	0	0	0	...	0
	4.7	0	0	0	0	1	0	0	1	0	0	0	0	...	0
	3.2	0	0	0	0	0	1	0	1	0	0	0	0	...	0
	4.0	0	0	0	0	0	0	1	1	0	0	0	0	...	0
	5.0	−1	−1	−1	−1	−1	−1	−1	1	0	0	−1	−1	...	0
A_2	3.2	1	0	0	0	0	0	0	0	1	0	0	0	...	0
	2.5	0	1	0	0	0	0	0	0	1	0	0	0	...	0
	4.2	0	0	1	0	0	0	0	0	1	0	0	0	...	0
	4.6	0	0	0	1	0	0	0	0	1	0	0	0	...	0
	4.8	0	0	0	0	1	0	0	0	1	0	0	0	...	0
	5.0	0	0	0	0	0	1	0	0	1	0	0	0	...	0
	6.8	0	0	0	0	0	0	1	0	1	0	0	0	...	0
	6.1	−1	−1	−1	−1	−1	−1	−1	0	1	0	0	0	...	0
A_3	3.2	1	0	0	0	0	0	0	0	0	1	0	0	...	0
	3.1	0	1	0	0	0	0	0	0	0	1	0	0	...	0
	4.1	0	0	1	0	0	0	0	0	0	1	0	0	...	0
	4.0	0	0	0	1	0	0	0	0	0	1	0	0	...	0
	4.4	0	0	0	0	1	0	0	0	0	1	0	0	...	0
	6.2	0	0	0	0	0	1	0	0	0	1	0	0	...	0
	4.5	0	0	0	0	0	0	1	0	0	1	0	0	...	1
	6.4	−1	−1	−1	−1	−1	−1	−1	0	0	1	0	0	...	−1
A_4	3.0	1	0	0	0	0	0	0	−1	−1	−1	−1	0	...	0
	5.8	0	1	0	0	0	0	0	−1	−1	−1	0	−1	...	0
	5.6	0	0	1	0	0	0	0	−1	−1	−1	0	0	...	0
	5.9	0	0	0	1	0	0	0	−1	−1	−1	0	0	...	0
	5.9	0	0	0	0	1	0	0	−1	−1	−1	0	0	...	0
	5.9	0	0	0	0	0	1	0	−1	−1	−1	0	0	...	0
	6.5	0	0	0	0	0	0	1	−1	−1	−1	0	0	...	−1
	6.6	−1	−1	−1	−1	−1	−1	−1	−1	−1	−1	1	1	...	1

Table 24.8 Dummy variable coding for a mixed design

(a) Data and ANOVA table

		C_1	C_2	C_3
	S_{11}	7	1	7
A_1	S_{21}	9	2	10
	S_{31}	7	3	8
	S_{12}	12	7	8
A_2	S_{22}	16	14	9
	S_{32}	19	11	12

SV	df	SS	MS	F
A	1	162.00	162.00	13.50
S/A	4	48.00	12.00	
C	2	85.33	42.67	17.66
AC	2	49.33	24.67	10.21
SC/A	8	19.33	2.42	

(b) Dummy variable coding for the design

	Y	A A_1	S/A S/A_{11}	S/A_{12}	S/A_{21}	S/A_{22}	C C_1	C_2	AC AC_{11}	AC_{12}
A_1S_1	7	1	1	0	0	0	1	0	1	0
	1	1	1	0	0	0	0	1	0	1
	7	1	1	0	0	0	−1	−1	−1	−1
A_1S_2	9	1	0	1	0	0	1	0	1	0
	2	1	0	1	0	0	0	1	0	1
	10	1	0	1	0	0	−1	−1	−1	−1
A_1S_3	7	1	−1	−1	0	0	1	0	1	0
	3	1	−1	−1	0	0	0	1	0	1
	8	1	−1	−1	0	0	−1	−1	−1	−1
A_2S_1	12	−1	0	0	1	0	1	0	−1	0
	7	−1	0	0	1	0	0	1	0	−1
	8	−1	0	0	1	0	−1	−1	1	1
A_2S_2	16	−1	0	0	0	1	1	0	−1	0
	14	−1	0	0	0	1	0	1	0	−1
	9	−1	0	0	0	1	−1	−1	1	1
A_2S_3	19	−1	0	0	−1	−1	1	0	−1	0
	11	−1	0	0	−1	−1	0	1	0	−1
	12	−1	0	0	−1	−1	−1	−1	1	1

really necessary to code SC/A because $SS_{SC/A}$ can be obtained as a residual

$$SS_{SC/A} = SS_Y(1 - R^2_{Y.A,S/A,C,AC})$$

However, SC/A could be coded by the eight dummy variables that would result from multiplying the values of variables in the C and S/A sets.

It should be noted that when there are different numbers of subjects at each level of A, the standard ANOVA and GLM modules will default to using Type III sums of squares. For example, SS_C will be obtained as $(R^2_{Y.A,C,AC} - R^2_{Y.C,AC})SS_Y$, not as $R^2_{Y.C} SS_Y$.

24.6 SUMMARY

The two goals we had in this chapter were to discuss how categorical variables can be coded so that they can be incorporated into the multiple regression framework and to reconsider, within this framework, several of the ANOVAs that we had discussed earlier. We did not include this second goal in order to encourage our readers to perform ANOVAs by coding categorical variables in terms of dummy variables and then using multiple regression—although they could do so if the standard ANOVA programs were not available. Rather, we believe that considering ANOVAs from the multiple regression perspective allows us to gain a deeper understanding of these analyses.

The generality and flexibility of the multiple regression framework offer some clear advantages. The standard ANOVA approach breaks down for disproportionate-n designs. Thinking in terms of multiple regression—a system in which nonorthogonality is the rule rather than the exception—facilitates consideration of the kinds of adjustments that might be made. In order to provide appropriate analyses of nonorthogonal designs, the standard "ANOVA" programs are really multiple regression programs. We hope that this chapter provides some understanding of how these programs might work and what options they allow. Finally, the ability to include categorical and continuous variables in the same analysis not only provides a framework for better understanding ANCOVA, but also makes it clear that it is not necessary—indeed, it is wrong—to transform inherently continuous variables into categorical ones (by, for example, using median splits) in order to analyze the data (see, for example, Fitzsimons, 2008).

APPENDIX 24.1

SPSS Notes

We have included on the book's website a file, *Age_BMI.sav*, that contains data from individuals in the *Seasons* study aged 65 years or less who had *BMI* scores no greater than 40. We use the file to illustrate the analysis of *TC* as a function of age and educational level (*EL*); however, there are many other variables in the file, enabling you to consider other possible regression analyses.

Our main purpose here is to show how we can analyze the interaction between a continuous variable (*age*) and a categorical variable (*EL*). On the book's website, we have included an SPSS syntax file (*EL_×_age.sps*) that does the analysis, and with revision can be used for other analyses. In general, the syntax file carries out the recoding and analyses that would require the following steps if we used the SPSS menus and dialog boxes:

1. *Recode the levels of schoolyr into the levels of the new variable EL*: Select the *Transform* menu, and then click on *Recode into Different Variables* ... In the *Recode into Different*

Variables . . . dialog box, select *schoolyr*, then, as the output variable, indicate *EL*, and then click on *Change*. Now click on *Old and New Values* . . . In the resulting dialog box, on the left side select *Range LOWEST through* and insert 3. Indicate on the right that the new value is 1. Then add to the *Old → New* box. Now specify that the old value 4 corresponds to the new value 2, and then do the same for the old values 5 and 6. Finally, specify that the old values 7 and 8 each correspond to the new value 3. Now click on *Continue*, and then on *OK*. This creates the appropriate new variable *EL*.

2. *Test for the EL effect, assuming EL to be a qualitative categorical variable*: On the *Analyze* menu, select *General Linear Model*, and then *Univariate* . . . In the *Univariate* dialog box, select *TC* as the *Dependent Variable* and *EL* as a *Fixed Factor*, and then click on OK.

3. *Test for the age × EL interaction*: On the *Analyze* menu, select *General Linear Model*, and then *Univariate* . . . In the *Univariate* dialog box, select *TC* as the *Dependent Variable*, *EL* as a *Fixed Factor*, and *age* as a *Covariate*. If we do not specify the appropriate model, SPSS will not include an interaction between a factor and a covariate. So click on *Model* . . . in the *Univariate: Model* dialog box, and select *Custom* to indicate that you want to specify the model. Insert *EL* and *age* in the model, and then, to include the *age × EL* interaction, highlight both *EL* and *age*, and then click on the insert arrow. Now click on *Continue*, and then on *OK* to perform the analysis.

4. *Treat EL as a quantitative variable*: We can also use *EL* as a crude quantitative variable with levels 1, 2, and 3. We can use *EL* as a predictor variable in regressions and test its interaction with age, as described in Chapter 23.

EXERCISES

24.1 Test scores are obtained from eight women and eight men. The data are as follows:

	Sex
Men	Women
27	35
18	33
16	26
27	21
24	38
30	28
32	38
26	32

(a) Find the correlation between sex and test score (i.e., the point-biserial correlation coefficient). Use a dummy variable for which men are given 1s and women are given 2s. Test the correlation for significance.

(b) Perform an independent-groups *t* test to determine whether there is a significant effect of sex.

(c) How many variables are needed to code for sex? Indicate how sex could be coded using (i) effect (1, −1) and (ii) dummy (1, 0) coding.

(d) Regress the dependent variable on the dummy (i.e., indicator) variables for (i) and (ii) above. Compare the significance levels with those found in (a) and (b). What are the interpretations of the regression coefficients for (i) and (ii)?

24.2 Create another dummy variable for sex, using 33 for men and -17 for women. Regress the dependent variable on this "nonsense" variable. What is the interpretation of this analysis?

24.3 Given the following data from a between-subjects design:

Condition

C_1	C_2	C_3
17	11	9
33	18	12
26	14	10
27	18	8
21		14

(a) How many linearly independent dummy (indicator) variables are needed to code the design?

(b) Code the design, using (i) dummy coding and (ii) effect coding.

(c) Regress the dependent variable on the indicator variables for (i) and (ii).

(d) What are the interpretations of the regression coefficients in each case?

24.4 Would the interpretations of the regression coefficients in Exercise 24.3 change if there were equal numbers of scores in each group? If so, how?

24.5 For the data set presented in Exercise 24.3, several coding schemes have been proposed. In each case, indicate whether regressing on the proposed set of dummy variables will result in $SS_{regression} = SS_{between}$. If a set of coding variables is not appropriate, indicate why it is not.

Condition	Set 1		Set 2		Set 3		Set 4		Set 5	Set 6		
	X_1	X_2	X_1	X_2	X_1	X_2	X_1	X_2	X_1	X_1	X_2	X_3
C_1	1	0	1	0	11	23	1	3	1	1	0	5
C_2	0	1	0	1	16	9	2	6	2	0	1	7
C_3	-1	-1	0	0	41	0	3	9	3	-1	-1	8

24.6 Given the following data from a 2×3 nonorthogonal (i.e., unbalanced or unequal-n) design:

	B_1	B_2	B_3
	72	49	40
	63	71	49
A_1	57	63	36
	52	48	50
	69		54
	75		

(Continued)

	B_1	B_2	B_3
	65	56	41
	45	55	42
A_2	53	49	57
	52	52	39
	57	45	
	57		

(a) Perform an ANOVA directly, using a statistical software package.

(b) Code the design, using effect coding (include variables for the main effects and the interaction).

(c) Are the dummy variables that correspond to the different effects correlated with one another?

(d) Assuming that the unequal ns have arisen by chance and we wish to test hypotheses about the unweighted means, perform the appropriate regression analyses and do what has to be done to test the A, B, and $A \times B$ effects. Exactly what hypotheses are tested? Compare your results with the ANOVA performed in (a).

(e) Suppose you regress on just the dummy variable corresponding to the A effect, omitting the dummy variables that code for B and the $A \times B$ interaction. What hypothesis is tested by using the SS_A obtained in this analysis?

24.7 The data file *EX24_7* contains information about a dependent variable, Y, a categorical factor, A, and a predictor variable, X. We have added two dummy variables X_1 and X_2 to code the factor X, and two additional dummy variables to code the interaction between A and X, $X_1 \times X$ and $X_2 \times X$.

(a) Use the GLM module of a statistical software package to test whether the slope of the regression of Y on X is homogeneous across the levels of the A factor.

(b) Perform the equivalent analysis, using the regression module and the dummy variables.

Chapter 25
ANCOVA as a Special Case of Multiple Regression

25.1 OVERVIEW

In Chapter 13, we briefly introduced analysis of covariance (ANCOVA) as one of several procedures that used information about a covariate (sometimes called a concomitant variable) to account for some of the error variance, thereby increasing the power of statistical tests on the factors of interest. Because ANCOVA is a procedure for analyzing data for a design that typically involves both categorical variables and quantitative variables, it is more naturally discussed as a type of regression rather than in terms of ANOVA. Therefore, we return to ANCOVA in this chapter to develop it more fully. Our goals in Chapter 25 are the following:

- *Discuss the rationale for ANCOVA.*
- *Introduce ANCOVA for a one-factor design as an example of multiple regression in which both quantitative and qualitative categorical variables are used as predictor variables.*
- *Present an example of the use of ANCOVA along with statistical package output.*
- *Discuss how group means can be adjusted for differences in the covariate.*
- *Consider the assumptions that underlie ANCOVA.*
- *Indicate how power calculations differ for ANOVA and ANCOVA.*
- *Consider ANCOVA for factorial designs.*
- *Briefly consider ANCOVA with more than one covariate and nonlinear ANCOVA.*

25.2 RATIONALE AND COMPUTATION

Treatments of ANCOVA from an analysis of variance perspective are notoriously opaque, given that at the heart of the technique, regression is used to remove variability in the dependent variable predictable from the covariate. We have already shown that we can use dummy variables to code a categorical variable (say, factor A), and then use regression to perform an ANOVA. The ANOVA can be thought of a comparison between two models, a full model that contains information about group membership

$$Y_{ij} = \mu + \alpha_j + \varepsilon_{ij(ANOVA)} \tag{25.1}$$

and a restricted model that does not,

$$Y_{ij} = \mu + \varepsilon_{ij} \tag{25.2}$$

We can obtain $SS_{between}$ as

$$SS_{between} = SS_A = R_{Y.A}^2 SS_Y$$

where $R_{Y.A}^2$ is the square of the multiple correlation coefficient that results when Y is regressed on a complete set of $a - 1$ dummy variables that code factor A, and the within-group variability can be obtained as

$$SS_{within} = SS_{S/A} = (1 - R_{Y.A}^2)SS_Y$$

so that the test statistic for A is given by

$$F = \frac{MS_A}{MS_{S/A}} = \frac{R_{Y.A}^2 SS_Y/(a-1)}{(1 - R_{Y.A}^2)SS_Y/(N-a)}$$

The null hypothesis tested is that the population means of Y are identical for each of the a levels of the factor A.

Performing a one-factor ANCOVA can be thought of as determining whether the categorical factor A has effects over and above those of a covariate, X, that is correlated with the dependent variable; or, equivalently, whether there are effects of A if we statistically adjust for differences in X. The hypothesis we wish to test is whether the Y population means would be identical for each of the a levels of the factor A *if each subject had the same value on X.* The ANCOVA can be thought of a comparison between two models in which Y is regressed on the covariate X:

1. A full ANCOVA model that also contains information about group membership

$$Y_{ij} = \mu + \alpha_j + \beta_{S/A}(X_{ij} - \bar{X}..) + \varepsilon_{ij(ANCOVA)} \tag{25.3}$$

where $\beta_{S/A}$ equals the weighted average of the slopes that would be obtained in separate regressions for each of the groups; i.e.,

$$b_{S/A} = \frac{\sum_j b_j SS_j}{\sum_j SS_j}$$

2. A restricted model that does not include information about group membership

$$Y_{ij} = \mu + \beta_{tot}(X_{ij} - \bar{X}..) + \varepsilon_{ij} \tag{25.4}$$

where β_{tot} is estimated by the slope of the regression of Y on X, ignoring group membership.

The test statistic for the ANCOVA does not contain SS_A and $SS_{S/A}$, but rather the corresponding sums of squares that have been adjusted for the covariate, called the *adjusted sums of squares*:

$$SS_{A(adj)} = (R_{Y.X,A}^2 - R_{Y.X}^2)SS_Y$$

and

$$SS_{S/A(adj)} = (1 - R^2_{Y.X,A})SS_Y$$

so that the ANCOVA test statistic is

$$F = \frac{MS_{A(adj)}}{MS_{S/A(adj)}} = \frac{(R^2_{Y.X,A} - R^2_{Y.X})SS_Y/(a-1)}{(1 - R^2_{Y.X,A})SS_Y/(N-a-1)}$$

where the F is distributed on $a-1$ and $a(n-1)-1$ df; note the loss of 1 degree of freedom because of the estimation of $b_{S/A}$.

Several points about Equations 25.3 and 25.4 should be noted. First, the slope parameters in the two models are not the same: β_{tot} is estimated by the slope of the overall regression of Y on X, ignoring group membership, whereas $\beta_{S/A}$, the *common slope* for the within-group regressions, can be shown to be estimated by the weighted average of the slopes that would be obtained in separate regressions for each of the groups; i.e.,

$$b_{S/A} = \frac{\sum_j b_j SS_j}{\sum_j SS_j}$$

Therefore, we cannot perform an ANCOVA by simply performing an ANOVA on the residuals of the first regression. The second point is a matter of notation. In ANCOVA, we use μ to refer to the mean of the Y scores and $\bar{X}$ to refer to the mean of the X scores because in the usual regression inference model, the standard assumption is that X is a fixed-effect variable and Y is random.

In practice, we conduct the ANCOVA by using any standard software package and specifying in the general linear model module that A is a categorical variable or factor and that X is a covariate. For a summary of the terms in the statistical outputs, see Table 25.1.

The reason to use ANCOVA is that using regression to remove the error variance predictable from a covariate may result in a smaller error term and also a reduction in bias of the group means due to the error variance. Comparing the ANOVA and ANCOVA models, we see that

$$\varepsilon_{ij(ANOVA)} = \beta(X_{ij} - \bar{X}..) + \varepsilon_{ij(ANCOVA)} = \varepsilon_{pred} + \varepsilon_{res}$$

That is, the error associated with the ith subject in the jth treatment condition can be considered to be made up of two components, a component predictable from the covariate (ε_{pred}) and a residual component (ε_{res}). In the ANOVA for a completely randomized design, both components contribute to the error variance, so that $\sigma^2_{ANOVA} = \sigma^2_{pred} + \sigma^2_{res}$, whereas in ANCOVA, only the residual component contributes.

To illustrate the advantage of ANCOVA compared to ANOVA, consider data from a study by Myers et al. (1983; see Table 25.2 and data set *pl with covariate*) in which subjects learned about probability. Subjects were each assigned to one of three instructional conditions based on reading different types of text: standard text (S), low-explanatory text (LE), or high-explanatory text (HE). The dependent variable was the proportion correct on a test administered after the instruction. When an ANOVA was performed, the null hypothesis that the population means for the three types of text were identical, i.e., $\mu_S = \mu_{LE} = \mu_{HE}$, could not be rejected, $F(2, 45) = 2.965$, $p = .062$. However, the main effect was significant, $F(2, 44) = 5.081$, $p = .010$, when a pretest measure of quantitative ability was used as a covariate in an ANCOVA. The data are presented in Table 25.2, and SPSS output for the ANOVA and ANCOVA is presented in panels (a) and (b) of Table 25.3.

Table 25.1 Explanation of the terms in one-factor ANOVA and ANCOVA outputs

SV	df	SS	Explanation
		ANOVA: Compare $Y_{ij} = \mu + \alpha_j + \varepsilon'_{ij}$ to $Y_{ij} = \mu + \varepsilon_{ij}$	
A	$a - 1$	$R^2_{Y.A}SS_Y$	"Between" variability in Y (i.e., variability accounted for by group membership)
S/A	$N - a$	$(1 - R^2_{Y.A})SS_Y$	"Within" variability in Y (i.e., the sum of the variabilities within each of the a groups)
Total	$N - 1$	SS_Y	Total variability in Y (i.e., variability about the mean)
		ANCOVA: Compare $Y_{ij} = \mu + \alpha_j + \beta_{S/A}(X_{ij} - \bar{X}..) + \varepsilon'_{ij}$ to $Y_{ij} = \mu + \beta_{tot}(X_{ij} - \bar{X}..) + \varepsilon_{ij}$	
A (adj)	$a - 1$	$(R^2_{Y.X,A} - R^2_{Y.X})SS_Y$	Variability accounted for by the full model over and above that accounted for by regression on X without regard for group membership
X	1	$(R^2_{Y.X,A} - R^2_{Y.A})SS_Y$ $= SS_{reg(within\ groups)}) =$ $SS_{reg(group\ 1)} + \ldots + SS_{reg(group\ a)}$ $= b^2_{S/A}\Sigma SS_{X_j}$	Variability accounted for by the full model over and above that accounted for by group membership alone; equivalently, the sum of the variabilities accounted for by separate regressions in each group but with a common slope
S/A (adj)	$N - a - 1$	$(1 - R^2_{Y.X,A})SS_Y$ $= SS_{error(group\ 1)} + \ldots + SS_{error(group\ a)}$ $= \Sigma(SS_{Y_j} - b^2_{S/A}SS_{X_j})$	Variability left unaccounted for by the full model; equivalently, the summed residual variability in the groups; i.e., the sum of the variabilities not accounted for by the a within-group regressions using the common slope, $b_{S/A}$
Total (adj)	$N - 2$	$(1 - R^2_{Y.X})SS_Y$ $= SS_Y - b^2_{tot}SS_X$	Variability left unaccounted for by regression of Y on X without regard for group membership

Note: If Y is regressed on X without regard to group membership, $SS_{reg} = r^2SS_Y = b^2_{tot}SS_X$ and $SS_{error} = SS_Y - b^2_{tot}SS_X$. Also, the common slope, $b_{S/A}$, is equal to the weighted average of the slopes, (b_js), that would be obtained in separate regressions, where the weights are the sums of squares of X for the groups.

Figs 25.1 and 25.2 may be useful in understanding the potential advantage in efficiency of ANCOVA over ANOVA. Fig. 25.1 schematically indicates how differences between two treatment groups may be easier to observe if the variability in Y that is predictable from X can be removed. The two ellipses in the central part of the figure represent clouds of data points for two treatment groups. As can be seen from the two marginal distributions plotted on the *right* vertical axis, the Y scores for the two groups overlap considerably. However, the distributions of the deviations of the data points from the regression lines that are plotted along the *left* vertical axis show greater separation. We should have more power if we were to test for the vertical separation of the population regression lines than if we test for differences among the marginal means.

In Fig. 25.2, the restricted model for two groups is illustrated in panel (a) and the full model is represented in panel (b). The test of the full against the restricted model asks whether we can account for more variability by including information about group membership; or, equivalently, whether we can account for more variability by performing separate within-group regressions with a single, common slope than by performing a single overall regression without regard to group

Table 25.2 Data for the one-factor ANCOVA example: Proportion correct in the Myers et al. (1983) study along with the quantitative aptitude score (X) for each subject

Standard		Low explanatory		High explanatory	
Y	X	Y	X	Y	X
.083	46	.083	64	.333	61
.167	41	.167	58	.333	61
.250	50	.250	51	.333	67
.250	60	.250	66	.417	52
.250	53	.250	52	.417	29
.333	74	.333	56	.500	38
.333	69	.333	68	.500	58
.333	51	.417	47	.500	60
.417	68	.417	72	.583	74
.500	49	.417	59	.583	59
.500	65	.417	61	.583	72
.500	42	.500	77	.583	48
.500	59	.583	51	.583	66
.583	69	.583	83	.667	75
.583	80	.667	93	.667	81
.750	71	.833	97	.917	90
Mean = .396	59.188	.406	65.938	.531	61.938
	$\overline{Y}.. = .444$		$\overline{X}.. = 62.355$		
$s^2 =$ .031	146.029	.038	225.929	.023	239.396

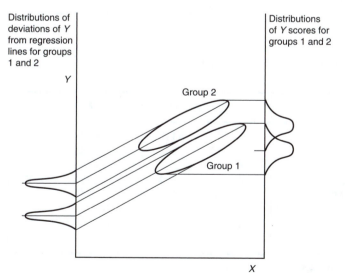

Distributions of deviations of Y from regression lines for groups 1 and 2

Distributions of Y scores for groups 1 and 2

Y

Group 2

Group 1

X

Fig. 25.1 Marginal distributions of Y scores (right side) and the distributions of the Y scores around the regression lines for two groups.

Table 25.3   SPSS GLM output for the test of (a) an ANOVA with text type as the factor, (b) an ANCOVA with text type as the factor and X (pretest score) as covariate, and (c) the test for the homogeneity of slope of Y vs X at the different levels of text

(a)

Tests of Between-Subjects Effects

Dependent Variable: Y

Source	Type III Sum of Squares	df	Mean Square	F	Sig.
Corrected Model	.182[a]	2	.091	2.965	.062
Intercept	9.479	1	9.479	309.389	.000
Text	.182	2	.091	2.965	.062
Error	1.379	45	.031		
Total	11.040	48			
Corrected Total	1.560	47			

[a] R Squared = .116 (Adjusted R Squared = .077)

(b)

Tests of Between-Subjects Effects

Dependent Variable: Y

Source	Type III Sum of Squares	df	Mean Square	F	Sig.
Corrected Model	.673[a]	3	.224	11.131	.000
Intercept	.000	1	.000	.016	.898
X	.492	1	.492	24.383	.000
Text	.205	2	.102	5.081	.010
Error	.887	44	.020		
Total	11.040	48			
Corrected Total	1.560	47			

[a] R Squared = .431 (Adjusted R Squared = .393)

(c)

Tests of Between-Subjects Effects

Dependent Variable: Y

Source	Type III Sum of Squares	df	Mean Square	F	Sig.
Corrected Model	.687[a]	5	.137	6.615	.000
Intercept	.001	1	.001	.038	.846
Text	.048	2	.024	1.146	.328
X	.480	1	.480	23.114	.000
Text * X	.014	2	.007	.341	.713
Error	.873	42	.021		
Total	11.040	48			
Corrected Total	1.560	47			

[a] R Squared = .441 (Adjusted R Squared = .374)

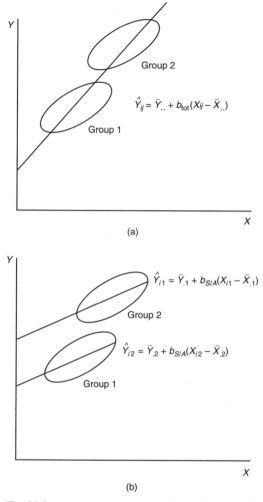

Fig. 25.2 (a) Schematic representation of the regression corresponding to the reduced model of Equation 25.7. All the data are used to obtain a single regression line without regard to group membership. (b) Schematic representation of the regressions corresponding to the full ANCOVA model of Equation 25.6. Note that because the model contains only a single slope parameter, the regression lines for the groups have a common slope, $b_{S/A}$.

membership. Rejection of the null hypothesis implies that the regression lines for the different populations do not all lie on top of one another.

25.3 ADJUSTING THE GROUP MEANS IN Y FOR DIFFERENCES IN X AND TESTING CONTRASTS

In the previous section, we showed how SS_A and $SS_{S/A}$ could be adjusted for differences in the covariate. Similarly, in certain situations, it is both possible and desirable to adjust the group means for covariate differences. To do the adjustment, we predict what the group means for Y would be if the value of the covariate was held constant. We define the *adjusted mean* of the scores for group j,

$\overline{Y}_{\cdot j(adj)}$, as the score predicted in group j, using the within-group regression equation with common slope $b_{S/A}$ *if the value of the covariate is equal to the grand mean of the covariate scores*; that is, if $X_{ij} = \overline{X}\ldots$.

Because for bivariate regression of Y on X,

$$\hat{Y} = \overline{Y} + b_1(X - \overline{X})$$

the regression equation for scores in group j is

$$\hat{Y}_{ij} = \overline{Y}_{\cdot j} + b_1(X_{ij} - \overline{X}_{\cdot j})$$

Substituting $b_{S/A}$ for b_1 and $\overline{X}..$ for X_{ij}, we have

$$\overline{Y}_{\cdot j(adj)} = \overline{Y}_{\cdot j} + b_{S/A}(\overline{X}.. - \overline{X}_{\cdot j})$$

or

$$\overline{Y}_{\cdot j(adj)} = \overline{Y}_{\cdot j} - b_{S/A}(\overline{X}_{\cdot j} - \overline{X}..)$$

The adjusted group means for the S, LE, and HE text conditions introduced in Section 25.2 are

$$\overline{Y}_{\cdot 1(adj)} = .369 - (.00732)(59.188 - 62.355) = .419$$

$$\overline{Y}_{\cdot 2(adj)} = .406 - (.00732)(65.938 - 62.355) = .380$$

and

$$\overline{Y}_{\cdot 3(adj)} = .531 - (.00732)(61.938 - 62.355) = .534$$

These three adjusted group means are the means predicted for each group for a covariate value equal to the grand mean on the covariate (i.e., 62.355 in the data set).

If the assumptions for ANCOVA are met, we can test contrasts based on the adjusted means that will generally be more powerful than those using unadjusted means. Suppose that working within the ANOVA framework, we wished to test the null hypothesis.

$$H_0: \psi = \mu_{HE} - \frac{\mu_S + \mu_{LE}}{2} = 0$$

Using the procedures described in Chapter 10, we would use the test statistic

$$t = \frac{\hat{\psi}}{s_{\hat{\psi}}} = \frac{\overline{Y}_{HE} - \dfrac{\overline{Y}_S + \overline{Y}_{LE}}{2}}{\sqrt{MS_{S/A} \Sigma \dfrac{w_j^2}{n_j}}} = \frac{.531 - \dfrac{.396 + .406}{2}}{\sqrt{(.031)(1.5/16)}} = .130/.054 = 2.411 \text{ with } 45 \text{ } df$$

and could reject the null hypothesis at $p = .019$.

An alternative approach to testing the contrast is to base it on the adjusted means (Huitema, 1980). The procedure is essentially the same as that for the unadjusted means, except that the comparison is among adjusted means and the error term contains corrections for the covariate. For a completely randomized design, the recommended test statistic is

$$t = \frac{\hat{\psi}_{(adj)}}{s_{\hat{\psi}(adj)}} = \frac{\overline{Y}_{HE(adj)} - \dfrac{\overline{Y}_{S(adj)} + \overline{Y}_{LE(adj)}}{2}}{\sqrt{MS_{S/A(adj)}\left(\Sigma \dfrac{w_j^2}{n_j}\right)\left(1 + \dfrac{MS_{A(X)}}{SS_{S/A(X)}}\right)}}$$

where $MS_{A(X)}$ and $SS_{S/A(X)}$ are the between mean square and the within sum of squares obtained when an ANOVA is performed on the covariate. Substituting into the equation, we have

$$t = \frac{\hat{\psi}_{(adj)}}{s_{\hat{\psi}(adj)}} = \frac{.534 - \dfrac{.419 + 380}{2}}{\sqrt{(.020)(1.5/16)\left(1 + \dfrac{184.333}{9170.312}\right)}} = .135/.044 = 3.089 \text{ with } 44 \ df$$

We can now reject the null hypothesis at $p = .003$. We obtained a larger value of the test statistic using the adjusted means, although we lost one error degree of freedom. In this example, the numerator of the t ratio is slightly larger for the adjusted means than for the unadjusted means. However, the main source of the difference in the two t-values is due to the fact that the error term is smaller after adjusting for the covariate (.044) than before the adjustment (.054).

The procedure we just illustrated for testing contrasts of adjusted means is appropriate when subjects are assigned at random to treatments. However, in observational studies where subjects are not randomly assigned to conditions, the recommended error term is different; specifically, it contains a correction that depends on the specific contrast that is tested,

$$s_{\hat{\psi}(adj)} = \sqrt{MS_{S/A(adj)}\left(\Sigma\frac{w_j^2}{n_j} + \frac{(\Sigma w_j \overline{X}_{\cdot j})^2}{SS_{S/A(X)}}\right)}$$

This equation follows from the expression we developed for the standard error of a predicted score when we considered bivariate regression. The implication for performing analyses is that researchers must select the error term that is appropriate to their research design. For a good discussion of these issues, see Huitema (1980).

As always, when several contrasts are tested, we should control Type 1 error across the set of comparisons. The procedures for controlling familywise error (FWE) rate were discussed in Chapter 10. If there are several planned contrasts, we can use the Dunn–Bonferroni method. For post hoc contrasts, if we wish to use the Scheffé test, the t statistics obtained above can be referred to the criterion $\sqrt{(a-1)F_{FWE,a-1,N-a-1}}$. For the Tukey post hoc test of pairwise differences, the same test statistics can be used with weights +1 and −1. If the covariate is a fixed-effect variable, the test statistic can be referred to $q_{FWE,a,df_{error}}/\sqrt{2}$, where q is a critical value of the Studentized range statistic that we used with the Tukey test in Chapter 10. There is one new consideration in the current context: If the covariate is a random variable, as is usually the case, Bryant and Paulson (1976) have shown that q should be replaced by $Q_{FWE,a,c,df_{error}}$, a value of the generalized Studentized range statistic in which c is the number of covariates. Tables of the generalized Studentized range statistic are available in Huitema (1980) and Kirk (1995).

25.4 ASSUMPTIONS AND INTERPRETATION IN ANCOVA

25.4.1 Introduction

When ANCOVA is used instead of ANOVA, increases in power may be achieved at the cost of greater complexity and more assumptions. The standard assumptions for ANCOVA break down into two groups. As in ordinary ANOVA, some assumptions are necessary for the ratio of adjusted mean squares to be distributed as F. However, unless certain additional assumptions are made, the ANCOVA F may test a different null hypothesis than ordinary ANOVA, and the adjusted means may be biased estimates of the population means. As with most other regression-related procedures, given that we have access to sophisticated statistical packages, the computations are the least of our worries. As always, the greatest challenges lie in interpretation. We now discuss the assumptions underlying ANCOVA and the consequences of violating them.

25.4.2 Normality and Homogeneity of Variance

In ANCOVA, it is assumed that the conditional distributions of Y at different values of X are normal and have equal variances. In general, the consequences of violating these assumptions are similar to those for ANOVA, with the exception that they depend to some extent on the distribution of the covariate (see Huitema, 1980, for a more detailed discussion of these assumptions). ANCOVA is unlikely to be severely biased by violations of these normality and homogeneity of variance assumptions provided there are equal numbers of subjects in each group and the covariate itself is approximately normally distributed.

25.4.3 Linearity

As we have so far discussed it, ANCOVA adjusts for differences in the covariate by removing the variability accounted for by a linear regression on X. If there is a systematic nonlinear component to the relationship between X and Y, the use of linear regression will not remove all the variability in Y potentially accounted for by X. The effect of moderate nonlinearity is a slight negative bias in the ANCOVA F test. However, strongly nonlinear relationships can result in severely biased F tests if linear ANCOVA is used (Atiqullah, 1964). Consider, for example, a situation in which there is a quadratic component to the relationship between Y and the covariate, X. If the curvilinearity is ignored and the X^2 that should be included in the model is omitted, it will contribute to the error component, thereby resulting in bias.

If the nature of the nonlinearities can be specified, transformations of Y or polynomial ANCOVA (see Section 25.7.3) may be used. It is recommended that the linearity assumption be checked as a preliminary step in using ANCOVA. Plotting the scatter diagrams for each group offers a quick check and a significance test for nonlinearity has previously been discussed.

25.4.4 Assumption of Homogeneity of Regression Slopes

In ANCOVA we adjust for differences in the covariate by using regression. In doing so, for each group we use a common slope, $b_{S/A}$, the pooled within-group regression coefficient, which is essentially an average of the slopes that would be obtained in separate within-groups regressions. This kind of adjustment makes the most sense if we can assume that the population slopes are the same in each of the groups. If the population group slopes differ, using any kind of "average" slope adjustment will not be appropriate for at least some of the groups. An analogy can be made between an adjusted A main effect in an ANCOVA in the presence of heterogeneous slopes and an A main effect in an ANOVA in the presence of an interaction between A and a second factor, B. If there is a large interaction, particularly if the curves cross, the F test of A may not adequately reflect the A effect at any level of B. Similarly, if the group regression coefficients vary, the effect of A is different for different values of X. Nonetheless, it is still useful to look at main effects even in the presence of interactions, and also to look at simple effects at different levels of the independent variables. Analogous procedures have been developed for ANCOVA.

It may help to describe the situation by using diagrams. When Y is adjusted for the effects of the covariate, X, treatment effects are interpreted in terms of vertical separation of the group regression lines instead of differences in the marginal group means. Suppose that the lines in each panel of Fig. 25.3 represent regression lines obtained separately for two treatment groups. Parallel lines, illustrated in panel (a), indicate that the treatment effects are the same for each value of the covariate. In this case, we can identify the treatment effects with the vertical distance between the lines. On the other hand, nonparallel lines, illustrated in panels (b) and (c), indicate that the treatment effects are not the same for each value of the covariate. In panel (b), the two lines intersect at $X = \bar{X}..$, but differ considerably for high and low values of X. In panel (c), there is a separation between the two lines at $X = \bar{X}..$, but the separation is larger for large X and smaller for small X. For panels (b) and (c), it does not make sense to consider the average separation of the two lines; rather, it is of more interest to determine for what values of X, if any, the separations are significant.

If the slopes of the population regression lines are reasonably homogeneous as evidenced by roughly parallel lines in the data set, we may proceed with the standard ANCOVA and be confident of conclusions regarding differences between adjusted group means. In practice, researchers usually first test the homogeneity of regression slope by testing the interaction of the group factor with the covariate (see Chapter 23). The interaction test can be accomplished with a statistical package such as SPSS, indicating in the general linear model module that *text* is the factor and X is the covariate, and requesting that the *text* $\times$ X interaction be included in the model (see Appendix 24.1 for an

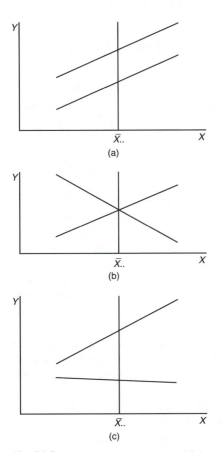

Fig. 25.3 Examples of regressions with homogeneous and heterogeneous slopes.

example of how to do this). If the interaction test is not significant, the ANCOVA is justified. Many textbooks recommend abandoning ANCOVA if the test is significant. However, the strict dichotomy between equal and unequal slopes is an oversimplification of the problem of comparing regression lines. Small differences in slope may not seriously affect the validity of the ANCOVA and, for large samples, homogeneity may be rejected even when the slope differences are small (and conversely, for small samples, the test for homogeneity may not have much power). Therefore, it may be worth proceeding cautiously with ANCOVA even in the presence of modest heterogeneity.

If the group slopes are sufficiently different to cause concern about interpreting an effect of groups in the ANCOVA, it is appropriate to analyze the interaction of the treatment with the covariate. Thus, in situations like those depicted in panels (b) and (c) of Fig. 25.3, we would be interested in determining how the groups differ at different values of X. Johnson and Neyman (1936) have developed a procedure for establishing regions of significance on the covariate. The Johnson–Neyman technique and related procedures are described in sources such as Huitema (1980), Hunka and Leighton (1997), and Ragosa (1980). Ragosa (1980) has also developed procedures for testing the average separation between regression lines and the separation at particular values of the covariate that are appropriate both when the lines have equal slopes and when they do not. Although these procedures are potentially useful, we do not describe them here because they have not, to the best of our knowledge, been implemented in any of the standard statistical packages. However, a good description is presented in Maxwell and Delaney (2004).

25.4.5 The Assumption That the Treatment and Covariate Are Independent

Many researchers use ANCOVA in observational studies "to adjust for initial group differences in the covariate" in the mistaken belief that the statistical procedure effectively eliminates any confounding of the covariate and the grouping variable. Thus, we emphasize that *ANCOVA should not be used to analyze designs in which the covariate varies systematically with the treatment*. If the treatment influences the covariate or is otherwise systematically related to it, performing an ANCOVA will not simply reduce error variance; rather, it may adjust between-group differences in ways that are difficult to understand and that may lead to biased tests.

It was appropriate to use ANCOVA to test the effect of text condition for the Myers et al. (1983) experiment because subjects were randomly assigned to the text conditions and there was no way that the treatment could influence the covariate. However, suppose everything else was kept the same except that subjects were given the quantitative reasoning test *after* the experiment instead of before they read the text material. In this case, we should not use the quantitative reasoning test as a covariate because material given in the text conditions might affect the subject's quantitative reasoning score. If so, and we went ahead and used it as a covariate, the regression adjustment built into the ANCOVA would not only remove some of the error variance in the dependent variable, but *it would also remove some of the effect of the treatment*.

To illustrate another kind of problem, suppose that rather than randomly assigning subjects to text conditions, the different text materials were presented to intact groups. For example, say the *LE* text was given to a class of psychology majors and the *S* and *HE* texts were given to classes of math and fine arts majors, thereby confounding text condition with major. We would say that we had a *nonequivalent-groups design*. As we noted at the start of this subsection, some researchers seem to believe that performing an ANCOVA can appropriately adjust the groups for their pre-existing differences. However, even though the groups may differ on the covariate, the confounding cannot be magically removed by performing an ANCOVA. The underlying groups may differ on many variables, and some of these differences are not likely to be fully predictable from a covariate. If treatments are applied to intact groups that differ from one another, ANCOVA presents the same kinds of difficulties that are always associated with interpreting the results of observational studies. Whenever the covariate varies systematically across conditions it becomes correlated with other variables that differ across groups, including the treatment itself. Performing an ANCOVA tends to adjust the effects of all of these variables, but to different degrees. In some cases, adjusting for some kinds of differences might exacerbate others.

Consider another example in which the independent variable and covariate might be correlated. Suppose an experiment is conducted to evaluate three different teaching programs. Students are given material to study on their own, and then are tested. Suppose the mean test score for subjects in Program 1 is higher than the means for Programs 2 and 3 and an ANOVA performed on the test scores is significant, suggesting that the three programs are not all equally effective. However, students assigned to Program 1 are observed to spend more time working with the material than students assigned to the other programs. If an ANCOVA using "study time" as the covariate reveals no significant differences, are we allowed to conclude that the three programs would be equally effective if study time was held constant? This interpretation is not necessarily correct. Statistically controlling for study time is not the same as experimentally controlling or manipulating it, so causal statements are not justified. We simply do not know from these data what would happen if study time was actually held constant. The materials used in Program 1 may be more understandable and interesting to work with than the materials used in the other programs. These qualities may be the cause of both the superior test performance and the greater study time. Using study time as a covariate will tend to remove the effects of any variables correlated with study time, including the characteristics of the program that are actually responsible for the superior performance. It is therefore entirely possible that Program 1 would produce superior performance even if study time was actually equated.

A related point addresses another approach that is sometimes used in the situation just described; namely, omitting observations in an attempt to equate groups. "Controlling" study time by throwing out data is not appropriate. Suppose that the mean daily study time is 40 minutes for the first group and 25 minutes for the other two groups. What if we analyze only the performance scores for students in the three groups who have comparable study times, say, 30–35 minutes? This is a poor strategy because in selecting students who have comparable study times, we may be selecting students who differ widely in other important characteristics. There is no reason to think that students in the first group whose study times are below that group's average are comparable in ability and motivation to students who have above-average study times in the other two groups. If we are interested in the effects of the program and of study time, there is no substitute for conducting a true experiment in which both variables are manipulated.

The assumption of independence of the treatment and covariate can be tested by performing an ANOVA on the covariate. In nonequivalent-group designs, a significant ANOVA result for a covariate measured before the treatments have been administered indicates that the ANCOVA Fs and adjusted means will almost certainly be biased. Unfortunately, a nonsignificant ANOVA cannot be taken as an indication that there will be no bias, although the bias is more likely to be small. In completely randomized designs, there will be no bias for covariates measured before treatments have been administered. However, ANOVAs should be performed on covariates measured during or following treatment.

25.4.6 Assumption That the Covariate Is Fixed and Measured Without Error

The standard model for making statistical inferences about regression assumes that the variable used to predict is a fixed-effect variable that is measured without error. In ANCOVA, this translates into the assumption that the covariate has these properties. However, the assumption that the covariate is a fixed-effect variable can generally be violated without serious consequences so long as we realize that if X is random, the statistical inference extends only to situations in which the distributions of X scores are comparable to those used in the current study.

If we randomly assign subjects to treatments or assign them to treatments entirely on the basis of their scores on the covariate, increased random error in both the dependent variable and covariate will result in reduced power but the results of the ANCOVA will not be biased. On the other hand, if we administer the different treatments to nonequivalent groups, measurement error in the covariate can result in increased bias and greater difficulties in interpretation. If the mean covariate value varies across groups and if the covariate is measured with error, the expected values of the adjusted Ys may differ even if the treatment has no effect. Fig. 25.4 illustrates the problem for two groups in which the true scores of X and Y are perfectly correlated and there are no treatment effects. In panel (a), X is measured without error and both group equations have the same slope and intercept. Therefore, the adjusted means for these groups must be the same and an ANCOVA would correctly reveal that there are no treatment effects. Panel (b) represents exactly the same situation, except that now X is measured with error. The effect of the measurement error will be to "spread out" the values of X and reduce the slopes for both groups. As can be seen in panel (b), the adjusted Y mean will now be larger for the group that has the larger values of X, even though there is no treatment effect. Because groups do not differ systematically from one another in randomized designs, measurement error in X will result in reduced power but will not cause the adjusted means to be biased. However, in nonequivalent-group designs, the measurement error in X may well introduce bias.

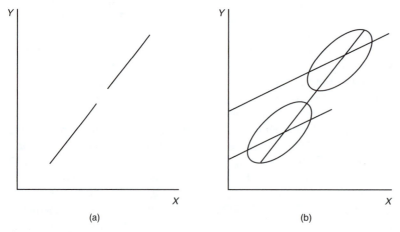

(a)   (b)

Fig. 25.4 Effect of measurement error on regression slopes. Both samples are from populations in which the true scores of Y and X are perfectly correlated and no treatment is applied. X is measured without error in panel (a) and with error in panel (b).

25.5 USING THE COVARIATE TO ASSIGN SUBJECTS TO GROUPS

If covariate values are available before an experiment is conducted, they can be used to assign subjects to conditions. For example, if the independent variable has a levels, the a subjects with the highest scores on the covariate can be randomly distributed across the treatment conditions, then the subjects with the next highest a scores, and so on. Compared to randomly assigning subjects to treatments without regard to the covariate values, this procedure will generally result in variances that are more similar across groups with respect to both Y and X. Maxwell, Delaney, and Dill (1984), using a simulation study, found that both ANCOVA and treatments × blocks ANOVAs were more powerful when assignment was made using the covariate than when it was not. Moreover, they found that the ANCOVA analysis was more powerful than the treatments × blocks ANOVA for several different values of ρ.

25.6 ESTIMATING POWER IN ANCOVA

When we discussed power for one-factor ANOVA, we considered the Cohen effect-size statistic

$$f_{ANOVA} = \sqrt{\frac{\sigma_A^2}{\sigma_e^2}}$$

According to Cohen's rough guidelines, large, medium, and small effect sizes in ANOVA correspond to f values of .40, .25, and .10, respectively. If we use these values in G*Power 3 for ANOVA and choose

1. *F tests* as the *Test family*;
2. *ANOVA, fixed effects, omnibus, one-way* as the *Statistical test*;
3. *A priori: Compute required sample size—given α, power and effect size* as the *Type of power analysis*;

then insert *Number of groups* = 3 (as in the current example), $\alpha = .05$, and desired power =.80, we find that the required numbers of subjects per group are 22, 52, and 323, respectively.

The major change when we perform power calculations for ANCOVA is that the error variance, σ^2, is adjusted for differences in the covariate and should therefore be smaller; that is, $\sigma_{ANCOVA}^2 = \sigma_{ANOVA}^2(1 - \rho^2)$, where ρ is the within-groups correlation between the dependent variable and covariate. Therefore, for ANCOVA, the quantity that should be used in place of f_{ANOVA} in G*Power 3 is the larger quantity

$$f_{ANCOVA} = f_{ANOVA} \sqrt{\frac{1}{1 - \rho^2}} \tag{25.5}$$

For large values of ρ, f_{ANCOVA} can be much larger than f_{ANOVA}; therefore, power may be considerably larger for an ANCOVA than for the corresponding ANOVA, and the required sample sizes will be smaller.

In the current example, the correlation between proportion correct on the test and pretest score is approximately .6 in each of the text groups. If we substitute $\rho = .6$ into Equation 25.5, we see that the ANOVA f values are each multiplied by $\sqrt{1/(1 - .6^2)} = 1.25$ when we perform ANCOVA power calculations. For large, medium, and small ANOVA effect sizes, the f values used in ANCOVA power calculations become .50, .3125, and .125. Using G*Power 3, we find that the required numbers of subjects in each group for $\alpha = .05$ and power $= .80$ are 14, 35, and 207 for large, medium, and small effect sizes, considerably smaller than the group sizes of 22, 52, and 323 found above for ANOVA. If the within-group correlations between the covariate and the dependent variable are smaller, say, $r = .3$, the power advantage for ANCOVA is reduced. The ANOVA f values are now multiplied by a smaller number, $\sqrt{1/(1 - .3^2)} = 1.048$, so that the ANCOVA sample sizes required to achieve power $= .80$ are 20, 48, and 291, respectively.

25.7 EXTENSIONS OF ANCOVA

25.7.1 Factorial ANCOVA

The multiple regression approach to ANCOVA can be readily extended to factorial designs. For example, if we consider a two-factor design described in the previous section, the ANCOVA tests for A, C, and AC are provided by

$$F_A = \frac{(R^2_{Y.X,A,C,AC} - R^2_{Y.X,C,AC})SS_Y / df_A}{(1 - R^2_{Y.X,A,C,AC})SS_Y / (N - 2 - df_A - df_C - df_{AC})}$$

$$F_C = \frac{(R^2_{Y.X,A,C,AC} - R^2_{Y.X,A,AC})SS_Y / df_C}{(1 - R^2_{Y.X,A,C,AC})SS_Y / (N - 2 - df_A - df_C - df_{AC})}$$

and

$$F_{AC} = \frac{(R^2_{Y.X,A,C,AC} - R^2_{Y.X,A,C})SS_Y / df_{AC}}{(1 - R^2_{Y.X,A,C,AC})SS_Y / (N - 2 - df_A - df_C - df_{AC})}$$

The statistical packages will perform the appropriate analyses if we specify A and C as factors, and X as the covariate.

25.7.2 Using More Than One Covariate

A researcher may wish to adjust for several sources of unwanted variability by using several covariates. For example, suppose we have a one-factor design and information about two covariates, X and W, that are each linearly related to Y. Performing an ANCOVA that uses both covariates tests whether A has significant effects over and above both X and W. The appropriate test statistic is the partial F:

$$F = \frac{(R^2_{Y.X,W,A} - R^2_{Y.X,W})SS_Y / df_A}{(1 - R^2_{Y.X,W,A})SS_Y / (N - 3 - df_A)}$$

Note that the denominator of this equation has one less df because of the additional covariate. The adjusted means are the scores predicted by the regression equation for each group if $X = \bar{X}..$ and $W = \bar{W}..$. Homogeneity of regression can be tested by using the partial F for the interactions between A and the covariates,

$$F = \frac{(R^2_{Y.X,W,A,AX,AW} - R^2_{Y.X,W,A})SS_Y / 2df_A}{(1 - R^2_{Y.X,W,A,AX,AW})SS_Y / (N - 3 - 3df_A)}$$

25.7.3 Nonlinear ANCOVA

The relationships between the dependent variable and potential covariates are not always linear. For example, according to the Yerkes–Dodson law, we would expect a curvilinear relationship between measures of motivation and performance. If we use standard ANCOVA procedures when there is substantial nonlinearity, the ANCOVA F tests may have little power and the adjusted means may be biased estimates of the treatment means. Therefore, it is a good idea to check for severe violations of nonlinearity by plotting scatter diagrams for each group. Also, significance tests for nonlinearity are available.

If the relationship between Y and X is nonlinear but monotonic (i.e., Y increases or decreases with X but not in a linear fashion), it may be worth checking to see whether there is a simple transformation of X such as log X or X raised to some power, for which the relationship between Y and the transformed X is approximately linear. If such a transformation can be found, the transformed value of X can be used as the covariate in a standard ANCOVA.

If the relationship between Y and X is not monotonic, a simple transformation will not achieve linearity. However, in this case it may be worthwhile to use polynomial ANCOVA, in which the ANCOVA model contains linear and higher-order polynomial components. For quadratic ANCOVA, it is assumed that the relationship between Y and X is of the form

$$Y = b_0 + b_1 X + b_2 X^2$$

For cubic ANCOVA, the polynomial function contains an X^3 term; and so forth. Quadratic ANCOVA is conducted by including both X and X^2 as covariates, so that for the one-factor design, the ANCOVA test for A becomes

$$F = \frac{(R^2_{Y.X,X^2,A} - R^2_{Y.X,X^2})SS_Y / df_A}{(1 - R^2_{Y.X,X^2,A})SS_Y / (N - 3 - df_A)}$$

Higher-order polynomial ANCOVA can be performed by adding X^3, X^4, and so on, as covariates. However, it is important to keep in mind that although more complex models will fit better, using more covariates results in fewer error dfs. Therefore, one should be careful not to use more complex models or more covariates than are necessary.

Finally, it should be noted that the powers of X (X, X^2, etc.) are highly correlated and using them in the same multiple regression will result in multicollinearity (see Chapter 23) that may cause computational difficulties for some software packages. These problems can generally be avoided by centering the covariates; that is, by using deviation scores. For example, $x = (X - \bar{X})$ and $x^2 = (X - \bar{X})^2$ may be used instead of X and X^2 in the regression.

25.8 SUMMARY

ANCOVA is a procedure in which a covariate can be used to account for some of the variability in the dependent variable, thereby achieving greater power for statistical tests at the cost of more assumptions and greater complexity. It is best understood as a special case of multiple regression. In Chapter 25, we:

- Developed the underlying logic of ANCOVA from a multiple regression perspective in which sources of variance are adjusted for differences on the covariate.
- Presented an example of ANCOVA and compared it with the corresponding ANOVA.

- Showed how group means could be adjusted for differences on the covariate and indicated how contrasts could be performed by using them.
- Discussed the major assumptions that underlie ANCOVA and considered some of the major issues involved in interpreting the results appropriately. In particular, we discussed the challenges posed by heterogeneity of regression slopes, by lack of independence between the covariate and the treatment, and by having measurement error in the covariate.
- Distinguished three designs in which ANCOVA is often used: (a) designs in which subjects are randomly assigned to treatments, (b) designs in which subjects are assigned on the basis of their score on the covariate, and (c) designs in which treatments are assigned to pre-existing non-equivalent groups. ANCOVA is an appropriate statistical procedure for analyzing designs (a) and (b), but its use with design (c) is problematic despite the fact that it is commonly used in that situation.
- Considered power calculations in ANCOVA.
- Briefly considered extensions to factorial designs, to the use of more than one covariate, and to nonlinear ANCOVA.

EXERCISES

25.1 Consider an experiment conducted to test the effectiveness of three software packages for teaching problem-solving skills to seventh-graders. Thirty-six seventh-graders are randomly selected and assigned to the software packages with the restriction that 12 children work with each of the packages. The levels of the independent variable (P) are the software packages the children worked with; the dependent variable (Y) is the score obtained on a problem-solving achievement test administered after the children have worked with a package for 6 months. There are also scores (X) obtained on a problem-solving pretest administered before the children were assigned to work with the software packages. The data are given in data set *EX25_1*.
  (a) Perform an ANOVA using P as the independent variable.
  (b) Perform an ANCOVA using P as the independent variable and X as the covariate.
  (c) Test whether the homogeneity of regression slope assumption is satisfied.
25.2 Eighteen subjects are assigned randomly to three treatment conditions A_1, A_2, and A_3. After the treatment is applied, values of Y, the dependent variable, are obtained. However, before the treatment is applied, values of X, a variable closely related to Y, are recorded. The data are in data set *EX25_2*.
  (a) Perform an ANOVA on Y.
  (b) Perform an ANOVA on X.
  (c) Test for homogeneity of regression in the three groups.
  (d) Perform an ANCOVA on Y, using X as the covariate.
  (e) How do the hypotheses tested by the ANOVA and the ANCOVA differ?
  (f) What are the adjusted means for the three treatment groups?
  (g) What is the interpretation of the adjusted means?
25.3 Discuss whether it is appropriate to perform ANCOVAs using X as the covariate in each of the following cases:
  (a) Measures of job satisfaction (Y) and performance evaluation by supervisors (X) are obtained for eight randomly sampled workers in each of the four departments of a company. The researchers desire to test whether job satisfaction is the same in each of the departments. The data are as follows:

D₁		D₂		D₃		D₄	
X	Y	X	Y	X	Y	X	Y
1.4	1.0	3.2	3.0	6.2	7.3	5.8	5.6
2.0	2.7	6.8	5.5	3.1	4.0	6.6	7.2
3.2	3.9	5.0	5.6	3.2	4.9	6.5	6.1
1.4	1.0	2.5	3.2	4.0	6.9	5.9	7.1
2.3	4.0	6.1	4.2	4.5	2.1	5.9	5.4
4.0	3.4	4.8	4.2	6.4	5.6	3.0	4.0
5.0	3.7	4.6	3.7	4.4	6.0	5.9	5.6
4.7	2.3	4.2	3.8	4.1	4.6	5.6	5.8

(b) Thirty children are each randomly assigned to one of three remedial math skills training programs. Before entering the programs, each child takes a standardized pretest (X). At the end of 6 months, a standardized achievement test (Y) is given to each of the children. The researchers wish to determine whether the training programs are all equally effective. The data are as follows:

A₁		A₂		A₃	
X	Y	X	Y	X	Y
29	61	39	79	41	78
37	73	34	66	36	66
26	54	35	76	29	56
32	63	39	84	33	61
31	62	35	73	42	70
37	76	27	75	35	65
33	72	35	66	32	59
39	80	29	85	42	80
33	73	34	62	39	65
36	72	26	79	36	64

25.4 If, for the data of problem 25.2, all the Y scores are regressed on all of the X scores, the regression equation obtained is

$$\hat{Y} = 9.974 + 1.816X$$

The residuals for this regression are as follows (and are given in data set *EX24_4*):

A₁	A₂	A₃
−5.771	2.045	2.128
−6.138	−0.771	1.412
−2.689	−0.872	6.780
−1.404	−1.670	3.780
−3.771	0.862	5.311
−3.955	1.045	3.678

Perform an ANOVA on these residuals. Is the ANOVA on the residuals equivalent to the ANCOVA of part (d) of Exercise 15.3? Why or why not?

25.5 With the data from Exercise 25.2, use some form of dummy coding to code A and then perform the ANCOVA using the regression module. (The data set with dummy coding can be found in *EX25_5*.)

25.6 Perform an ANCOVA for the following two-factor, between-subjects design:

	A_1		A_2	
	X	Y	X	Y
	24.4	15.9	22.5	24.2
	22.3	15.7	12.5	19.7
	23.3	19.2	14.2	19.2
B_1	15.8	13.4	18.6	17.9
	22.6	18.0	15.2	24.4
	24.9	22.5	23.2	28.0
	20.9	15.1	20.9	19.9
	19.6	13.7	18.1	28.2
	23.9	12.8	18.1	18.1
B_2	26.2	25.5	11.5	13.5
	18.8	17.0	22.4	19.3
	24.0	25.3	30.2	35.1

Chapter 26
Integrated Analysis IV

26.1 OVERVIEW

In the first part of this chapter, we discuss multiple regression analyses to explore the relationships between physical activity and depression, using real data collected as part of the *Seasons* study. We find that higher levels of leisure-time physical activity predict lower scores on the Beck Depression Inventory (*BDI*) for women, whereas higher levels of work- and household-related physical activity do not, when the three measures are included in a regression. However, there are a number of possible reasons for this pattern of results that cannot easily be sorted out without conducting an experiment in which physical activity is manipulated. Therefore, in the last part of the chapter, we discuss an experiment that might be designed to resolve the ambiguity, as well as the analysis of a hypothetical data set that might result.

26.2 INTRODUCTION TO THE STUDY

Lin et al. (2008) have reviewed some of the literature discussing the psychological benefits of physical activity. For example, the International Society of Sport Psychology (ISSP, 1992) has published a position statement in which it concludes that physical activity is related to decreases in mild to moderate depression, neuroticism, anxiety, and stress. Most studies that have examined the effect of physical activity on depression scores have considered leisure-time exercise such as walking, running, and cycling, and have found them to be associated with lower levels of depression.

For most people, leisure-related exercise comprises a relatively small part of their total physical activity. Friedenreich, Courneya, and Bryant (1998) found that a sample of 115 women were, on average, physically active approximately 55 hours per week. However, less than 10% of this time was spent on leisure-time exercise (about 4 hours); the rest was divided between occupational (22 hours) and household (28 hours) activity. Here, we use data collected as part of the *Seasons* study to assess the possible beneficial effects of leisure-time, occupational, and household physical activity. The relevant data are contained in the *Seasons physical activity* data set on the book's website.

26.3 METHOD

26.3.1 Subjects

The *Seasons* study[1] was a large project primarily directed at assessing seasonal variation in blood lipids. A detailed account of the methodology may be found in Merriam et al. (1999), and a statement of the lipid results is presented in Ockene et al. (2004). As a part of the study, data were collected on physical characteristics such as height and weight, diet, activity, psychological measures, education, marital and employment status, health, work environment, and exposure to sunlight, as well as blood lipid characteristics. There were two sets of eligibility criteria. The first required that subjects be between the ages of 20 and 70 years, have a telephone, be literate in English, and plan to remain in the area for a year. There was also a second set of criteria dealing with the subject's health record. Subjects could not be taking medication to lower lipids, be participating in a cholesterol- or weight-lowering diet, have a history of cancer within the past 5 years, or suffer from a psychiatric disease or other condition that would limit their participation in the study.

Subjects were recruited from the membership of the Fallon Healthcare System, a large health maintenance organization serving central Massachusetts. Of the 5,300 potential subjects contacted by telephone, 1,254 met the first set of requirements and made an appointment. Of these, 641 subjects (331 men and 310 women) kept their initial appointment, met all the eligibility requirements, and completed the baseline questionnaires. Of these, 285 men and 243 women were employed and able to provide data on occupational activity.

26.3.2 Measures Used in the Analyses

Several measures were taken on each subject.

Physical Activity.   In each of 15 telephone interviews spread through their five quarters of participation in the study, subjects were asked to recall the amount of time they spent in each of three categories of activity (leisure, occupational, and household) and at each of four intensities (light, moderate, vigorous, and very vigorous) during the previous 24-hour period. Estimates of physical activity energy expenditure were determined, using standard metabolic equivalent (MET) values. MET is a measure of the rate at which adults burn calories and is defined as the ratio of the activity metabolic rate to the resting metabolic rate: 1 MET is approximately 1 kcal per kilogram of body weight per hour and is roughly equivalent to the energy cost of sitting quietly. The weighted sums of different activity intensities were used: light activity = 1.5 METs; moderate = 4.0 METs; vigorous = 6.0 METs; and very vigorous = 8.0 METs. Activity scores in both hours of activity and the corresponding MET scores were averaged over the interview sessions yielding the variables *tot_hours_leisure* and *tot_MET_leisure*; *tot_hours_occup* and *tot_MET_occup*; and *tot_hours_house* and *tot_MET_house*.

Depression.   Depression was measured by the *BDI* (Beck & Steer, 1987), which has been found to be an effective screening instrument for detecting depression in community populations. This is a self-report questionnaire on which subjects rate symptoms and attitudes related to depression. Twenty-one items are each scored from 0 to 3 so that the *BDI* score can range from 0 to 63. Scores

[1] The *Seasons* study was funded by grant R01-HL52745 from the National Heart, Lung, and Blood Institute, Bethesda, MD, USA.

on items that received no response were imputed from the scores on the other items, yielding an overall *BDI* summary score.

Body Mass Index (BMI).   *BMI* scores were calculated for each subject from height and weight scores. *BMI* is defined as weight in kilograms divided by the square of height in meters. Current CDC guidelines for *BMI* are underweight = less than 18.5; normal weight = 18.5–24.9; overweight = 25.0–30.0; and obese = more than 30.0.

Education.   Subjects reported the highest level of education they had received on an 8-point scale: 1 = no high school; 2 = some high school, 3 = high-school diploma; 4 = vocational or trade school; 5 = some college; 6 = associates degree; 7 = bachelor's degree; and 8 = graduate degree.

Employment.   Subjects reported their employment status: 1 = full time; 2 = part time; and 3 = not employed.

Perceived Health.   Several measures of current health were collected. Here, we use a general self-report in which subjects reported their health as 1 = excellent; 2 = very good; 3 = good; 4 = fair; and 5 = poor. Therefore, larger scores on the health measure correspond to poorer self-perceived health.

26.4 PROCEDURE

Data collection took place between December 1994 and March 1998. Each subject was followed for a period of 15 months, a baseline quarter and four follow-up quarters. Demographic information was collected only at baseline. Depression scores and measures of physical activity were collected each quarter. Information on physical activity was obtained in three, 24-hour recall phone interviews during each of the quarters of data collection, a total of 15 interviews per subject. For the present purposes, depression and activity were each averaged across the five quarters to provide a single score on each measure for each subject.

26.5 RESULTS AND DISCUSSION

For the analyses in this chapter, we used data from subjects who were employed full-time (employed = 1; 252 men and 184 women) or part-time (employed = 2; 33 men and 59 women). The data are contained in the file *Seasons physical activity* that can be found on the book's website. The *BDI* score distribution is highly skewed for both men and women; skewness = 1.441 and 1.271, respectively. We therefore used a square root transformation of the $BDI = \sqrt{BDI + 1}$, reducing the skewness for the transformed variable to 0.668 for men and 0.512 for women. Although the patterns of significant results were very similar for the transformed and untransformed measure of depression, we usually present results for the transformed *BDI* scores.

It is well established that women score higher on the *BDI* than men (e.g., Piccinelli & Wilkinson, 2000). Some of this difference occurs because women are more willing to report symptoms of depression than men. However, even accounting for this response bias, women are considered to have higher levels of depression than men. We therefore performed regressions separately for men and women.

Table 26.1 Means and standard errors for age, education, *BMI*, perceived health, depression scores, and activity values (in MET units) for men and women who were employed. Independent-group t tests (Welch's t) were computed to test differences between men and women

Variable	Men $n = 285$	Women $n = 243$	t value	df	p
Age	45.649 (0.697)	45.181 (0.683)	0.480	524.155	.632
Education	5.782 (0.109)	5.370 (0.126)	2.465	500.677	.014
BMI	27.834 (0.263)	26.381 (0.378)	3.226	443.898	.002
Health	2.333 (0.050)	2.198 (0.052)	1.882	516.906	.060
BDI	5.492 (0.300)	6.793 (0.367)	−2.743	486.991	.006
Transformed BDI	2.376 (0.055)	2.615 (0.063)	−2.873	502.553	.004
Leisure activity	2.022 (0.121)	1.642 (0.114)	2.279	524.872	.023
Occupational activity	7.054 (0.431)	3.818 (0.256)	6.458	452.253	.000
Household activity	3.939 (0.188)	4.467 (0.179)	−2.034	524.471	.042

Table 26.1 displays the means and standard errors for age, education, *BMI*, self-perceived health, depression scores, and activity values (in MET units) for the 285 men and 243 women who were employed full- or part-time at the time of the study (i.e., employed = 1 or 2). Using Welch independent-groups *t* tests because of the unequal variances for men and women on some variables, we found significant sex differences for all these measures except for age and health. Men had significantly higher values for the education measures, for *BMI*, and for both leisure and occupational activity. Women had significantly higher values for both the raw and transformed depression measures and for household activity.

Following Lin et al. (2008), who also used data from the *Seasons* study, we regressed the transformed *BDI* score on the leisure-time, occupational, and household activity measures. The regression coefficients for the analysis with transformed *BDI* as the dependent variable are displayed in Table 26.2. The only significant coefficient was that of leisure activity for women, $t (239) = -2.281$, p = .023, suggesting that leisure-time physical activity is a predictor of lower depression scores for women, controlling for other kinds of physical activity, whereas household and occupational physical activity are not.

However, we must consider why it is that some individuals engage in more leisure-time physical activity than others. It is possible that healthier and fitter individuals tend to spend more energy in leisure-time physical activities. It also seems likely that these individuals will tend to have fewer symptoms of depression. In addition, individuals who expend more energy on occupational and household activities will have less energy left for leisure-time activities. These statements are

Table 26.2 Results of the regression of the transformed depression scores on leisure-time, occupational, and household physical activity

Predictor	Men			Women		
	B (SE)	β	p	B (SE)	β	p
Leisure physical activity (MET)	−.025 (.130)	−.056	.369	−.083 (.036)	−.150	.023
Occupational physical activity (MET)	.007 (.008)	.054	.385	.026 (.106)	.105	.111
Household physical activity (MET)	.006 (.018)	.021	.724	−.027 (.023)	−.077	.239

Table 26.3 Results of the regression of the leisure-time physical activity score on *BMI*, perceived health, and the occupational and household activity scores for men and women

Predictor	Men			Women		
	B (SE)	β	p	B (SE)	β	p
BMI	−.038 (.027)	−.083	.164	−.034 (.019)	−.113	.067
Health[1]	−.265 (.145)	−.109	.068	−.421 (.135)	−.191	.002
Occupational physical activity (MET)	−.073 (.016)	−.259	.000	−.094 (.027)	−.211	.001
Household physical activity (MET)	−.077 (.037)	−.119	.037	−.126 (.039)	−.196	.002

[1] Higher scores on the health variable correspond to worse perceived health.

supported by an exploration of the data that shows small but significant negative correlations between leisure-time physical activity and poorness of health ($r = -.217$, $p = .001$), *BMI* ($r = -.170$, $p = .008$), occupational activity ($r = -.187$, $p = .003$), and household activity ($r = -.168$, $p = .009$) for women, and much the same pattern for men.

To explore the relationships between leisure activity and the other two activities, *BMI* and health, we regressed the leisure-time activity score on the other four measures. The results are displayed in Table 26.3. For women, the regression coefficients were all negative and highly significant for the health and physical activity measures. In other words, poorness of health, occupational activity, and household physical activity were all negative predictors of leisure-time physical activity, controlling for the other predictors in the regression equation. A similar pattern was found for men, except that the regression coefficient for health was not significant.

Given the evidence of relationships among *BMI*, health, and the three types of activity, we reanalyzed the transformed *BDI* score on *BMI*, health, and the three activity measures. As can be seen in Table 26.4, rated poorness of health is a highly significant predictor of depression for both men and women, as is *BMI* for women. Controlling for *BMI* and self-perceived health, we now find that none of the physical activity measures were significant predictors of depression.

Another possible predictor of interest is completed education. Although we have only a crude measure of education (see the description in the Materials section), it is significantly positively correlated with leisure-time activity and significantly negatively correlated with *BMI*, poorness of health, depression, and occupational physical activity, for both men and women. If we add education to the list of predictors in Table 26.4, its regression coefficient is not significant and the pattern of significance for the other predictors is not changed for men or for women. However, if we

Table 26.4 Results of the regression of the transformed *BDI* score on *BMI*, perceived health, and the three types of physical activity scores for men and women

Predictor	Men			Women		
	B (SE)	β	p	B (SE)	β	p
BMI	.003 (.012)	.017	.777	.027 (.010)	.160	.010
Health	.408 (.065)	.369	.000	.315 (.076)	.259	.000
Leisure physical activity (MET)	−.001 (.027)	−.002	.979	−.035 (.036)	−.064	.322
Occupational physical activity (MET)	.008 (.007)	.064	.270	.027 (.015)	.110	.082
Household physical activity (MET)	.006 (.016)	.020	.725	−.027 (.022)	−.075	.230

Table 26.5   Results of the regression of the transformed *BDI* score on education level and the three types of physical activity scores for men and women

Predictor	Men			Women		
	B (SE)	β	p	B (SE)	β	p
Education	−.099 (.034)	−.197	.004	−.069 (.032)	−.138	.034
Leisure physical activity (MET)	−.015 (.028)	−.032	.601	−.070 (.036)	−.126	.058
Occupational physical activity (MET)	−.004 (.009)	−.034	.622	.021 (.016)	.087	.188
Household physical activity (MET)	.004 (.017)	.012	.839	−.027 (.023)	−.078	.232

regress transformed *BDI* on education and the three measures of physical activity, we see in Table 26.5 that education is a significant negative predictor of depression for both men and women, but that, controlling for education level, none of the regression coefficients for the activity measures are significant.

So what can we conclude about leisure-time activity and depression from this study? When considered along with the other activity measures, leisure-time physical activity is a significant predictor of lower *BDI* scores for women. However, our other analyses suggest that the predictive power of leisure-time exercise may come about because of its relationships with health, education, *BMI*, and the other measures of activity. Leisure-time physical activity may indeed have therapeutic effects with respect to depression, but it is extremely difficult to disentangle these from the effects of other variables we have considered in this observational study. If we want definitive answers to questions about the benefits of leisure exercise, we should design an experiment in which subjects are assigned to conditions that correspond to different amounts of leisure activity and the effects of variables such as education, *BMI*, and perceived health are controlled by randomization or by using blocking and including them as independent variables in a multifactor design.

26.6 A HYPOTHETICAL EXPERIMENTAL TEST OF THE EFFECTS OF LEISURE ACTIVITY ON DEPRESSION

To provide a test of the hypothesis that amount of leisure physical activity affects depression, consider a hypothetical experiment in which adult men and women perform different amounts of exercise each day. Thus, the experiment is a 2×2 (*Sex* $\times$ *Activity*) between-subjects design. Random assignment to activity condition is used to control for other factors evaluated in the preceding study (e.g., household activity, occupational activity, *BMI*). However, it is also decided to collect information on subjects' perceived health and education levels because both variables were found to correlate with depression scores in the *Seasons* study (see Tables 26.4 and 26.5). Scores on these two variables will be used as covariates to improve the power of the statistical test of the effect of leisure activity on depression scores.

To decide on the number of subjects to include in the study, *a priori* power analyses were conducted (see Section 25.7). Because we will again conduct separate analyses on the data for the men and women, the relevant design has one factor (activity, two levels) with two covariates (health and education). To convert Cohen's conventional *f* values for small, medium, and large effects of .1, .25, and .40 to the corresponding values for the ANCOVA, ρ^2 was estimated by regressing the transformed *BDI* scores on the health and education scores in the *Seasons* data set; R^2 was .156 for men and .120 for women. (The procedure of regressing the dependent variable on both covariates and using R^2 to estimate ρ^2 is an extension of the procedures presented in Section 25.7.) To be conservative in estimating the required number of subjects, the value of .120 was used. The resulting conversion of Cohen's values produced f values of .106, .2665, and .4264 for small, medium, and large effects, respectively. Using G*Power 3, the Ns required for power = .80 are 702, 114, and 46, respectively. Because the planned procedure is expensive in both time and resources, it was decided that 114 men and 114 women would be recruited for the experiment.

Subjects were solicited from the same lists of HMO clients used in the *Seasons* study. At the start of the experiment, all subjects completed a questionnaire in which they reported how much education they had completed and their perceived level of health, as in the *Seasons* study. They then received instructions about the nature of the activity condition to which they were assigned. One condition involved engagement in regular, vigorous exercise; the other, engagement in an alternative activity with minimal physical exercise. To ensure compliance with condition assignment, every subject agreed to report to the campus recreation center at a scheduled time every weekday to engage in the appropriate amount of exercise. Subjects in the exercise condition followed a regimen of a strenuous, 1-hour workout on each weekday (rate of energy expenditure estimated at 6 METs). Subjects assigned to the control condition participated in 1 hour of group discussion per day (estimated at 1 MET). All subjects participated in the experiment for 6 months. At the end of the 6-month period, all subjects took the *BDI*. Note that the difference in the energy demands of the two activities is relatively large compared to the observed variability in exercise found for the correlational study. This is an important advantage of the experiment; namely, it permits a more definitive comparison of exercise levels than occurs naturally. This, in turn, will mean a more powerful test of the effects of exercise than was possible in the observational study.

Hypothetical data from the experiment are contained in the *Activity experiment* data set on the book's website. The file includes the following variables: activity condition (0 = discussion; 1 = exercise); sex; education; health; and *BDI_transform*. The means for the education, health, and *BDI* variables are presented in Table 26.6, broken down by sex. Note that the number of observations is fewer than the 114 men and 114 women who started the study because some subjects failed to complete the procedure. However, there were very few dropouts and no clear evidence that the condition influenced the number of dropouts, so there were no concerns in proceeding with the analyses. Note that the values in Table 26.6 are similar to those found in the observational study (see Table 26.1).

Scatterplots were generated separately for the men and women relating the *BDI* scores to each of the covariates, health and education. There was no evidence of nonlinear relationships between *BDI* and either covariate. Preliminary regression analyses were conducted on the data for men and for women to test whether the group slopes were homogeneous. In these analyses, *BDI* was the criterion variable and sex, education, health, activity, and the interactions of activity with health

Table 26.6 Means and standard errors for education, health, and *BMI* (transformed) for men and women. Independent-group *t* tests (Welch's *t*) were computed to test differences between men and women.

Variable	Men $n = 110$	Women $n = 111$	t value	df	p
Education	5.35 (0.189)	4.98 (0.200)	1.357	218.437	.176
Health	2.509 (0.077)	2.270 (0.079)	2.164	218.942	.032
Transformed *BDI*	2.319 (0.082)	2.648 (0.104)	−2.492	207.770	.014

and with education were included. None of the interactions involving the covariates were significant, so the assumption of homogeneity of group slopes was considered to be satisfied.

Separate ANCOVAs were conducted on the data for the men and women, using the univariate ANOVA program in the GLM module of SPSS. In each analysis, the dependent variable was specified as *BDI_transform*, the factors were sex and activity, and the covariates were education and health. The results of the ANCOVAs are summarized in Table 26.7 (panels a and b), along with ANOVAs on the same data (panels c and d). The key result in both analyses is that depression scores were lower for subjects in the vigorous exercise condition than for subjects in the minimal exercise condition. For the men, the adjusted means in the exercise and control conditions were 2.077 and

Table 26.7 ANCOVA results for the Activity experiment for men (panel a) and women (panel b) and the ANOVA results for men (panel c) and women (panel d)

(a)

Source	Type III SS	df	Mean Square	F	p
Education	1.102	1	1.102	2.185	.142
Health	15.676	1	15.676	31.079	.000
Activity	6.588	1	6.588	13.062	.000
Error	53.465	106	0.504		
Total	80.009	109			

(b)

Source	Type III SS	df	Mean Square	F	p
Education	4.288	1	4.288	4.202	.043
Health	8.921	1	8.921	8.742	.004
Activity	4.897	1	4.897	4.799	.031
Error	109.195	107	1.021		
Total	132.107	110			

(c)

Source	Type III SS	df	Mean Square	F	p
Activity	8.541	1	8.541	12.908	.000
Error	71.467	108	0.662		
Total	80.009	109			

(d)

Source	Type III SS	df	Mean Square	F	p
Activity	7.203	1	7.203	6.286	.014
Error	124.903	109	1.146		
Total	132.107	110			

2.569, respectively; for the women, the adjusted means were 2.429 and 2.856, respectively. In fact, the effects of exercise were quite similar for men and women; an ANCOVA that included the data from both sexes showed main effects of both activity and sex (women's *BDI* scores were higher than men's), but no evidence of a significant interaction. Finally, we note that ANOVAs on the data showed exactly the same effects (see Table 26.7). Because the correlations of the covariates with the *BDI* scores were modest, the power advantage for the ANCOVAs was negligible.

In sum, because subjects were assigned at random to these two conditions and the activity variable was manipulated rather than observed, we can make a stronger case from our hypothetical experiment that leisure exercise decreases depression than we could from the observational study.

26.7 SUMMARY AND MORE DISCUSSION

In the first, observational study, we used several regression analyses to point out the difficulty of assessing the influence of different kinds of physical activity. The main question was whether leisure-time physical activity reduced symptoms of depression. We were unable to reach a definitive answer to this question because we could not separate the effects of leisure activity from the effects of other variables. Possible reasons why leisure-time physical activity may be a proxy for other measures include the following (as well as many more): people with higher *BMI* values tend to be more depressed and they also exercise less; people with less education tend to be more depressed and also tend to work in jobs which involve more physical activity, so they have less energy left to engage in leisure-related exercise; and so on.

The most direct way to assess the effect of leisure-time physical activity on depression is to conduct an experiment in which subjects are randomly assigned to different exercise conditions. That is what we did in the second, hypothetical study. In addition, we included health and education measures as covariates because both variables correlated significantly with depression in the observational study. Their inclusion in the design theoretically permitted a more powerful test of the relationship between leisure activity and depression. In fact, it turned out that the covariates were significantly, but not strongly, related to the dependent variable, so there was a negligible effect on power. A significant relationship between leisure activity and depression was found, suggesting that exercise tends to reduce depression. In the experiment, there is less ambiguity in interpreting the statistical relationship between the two measures because the random assignment of subjects to conditions eliminated serious confounding of leisure activity with other potential influences on depression.

Although a major goal of Section 26.6 was to consider how data from a follow-up experiment might be analyzed, it is useful to consider some design concerns that might limit the generality of the conclusions from such an experiment. We should be under no illusions that a single, simple experiment of the sort described above would settle the issue once and for all. Some issues that would impair our ability to arrive at definitive conclusions from our simple experiment include the following:

Issues Regarding the Selection of Subjects. The choice of subjects used in the experiment is critical. If subjects are selected from the HMO lists used in the *Seasons* study and are contacted by telephone and asked to participate in the experiment, on what basis will they decide whether or not to participate? If the study is described as being about depression, this may influence whether or not subjects with higher depression scores will decide to volunteer. Subjects will self-select, and this will be influenced by what they are told about the experiment.

Also, given the ranges of health and age of potential subjects, not all subjects may be capable of participating in a vigorous exercise condition. In any event, the effects of vigorous exercise might be different for different kinds of subjects. If we did not have access to the HMO patient pool and instead selected volunteers from university classes, subjects would be young adults with similar age, educational level, and health backgrounds. The results of the experiment would be useful, but would not readily generalize to the population at large.

Issues Regarding the Choice of Experimental and Control Conditions.   We must be careful about the control conditions that are used. In the experiment we described above, there were two conditions, a vigorous exercise condition and a minimal exercise condition in which subjects participated in a group discussion. It could be argued that the second condition is not an appropriate control. We might wish to have several exercise conditions, low, moderate, and vigorous. Part of the motivation is that although the effect of exercise on depression is not a completely closed question in the scientific literature, it is presented as a fact on the Internet—insert "exercise and depression" into a search engine and read what comes up. Because of this, we must assume that many subjects will have the expectation that an exercise program reduces depression. The consequence for us is that we must contend with placebo effects—the expectation would be that exercise should help and this expectation might have positive effects on depression. Therefore, we might be better off using a number of different activity conditions. Also, we might want to separate the "social" effects of getting out and going to the recreation center from the effects of the exercise per se. Therefore, we might want to add conditions in which subjects engaged in some exercise program at home. We might also want to look at the potentially different beneficial effects of leisure exercise for subjects who already engaged in different amounts of occupational or household activity. Given enough subjects, time, and resources, we could be successful in sorting this all out. But it would not be simple.

We should also note that it would have been possible to design a more powerful experiment than was presented above. In the *Seasons* study, the *BDI* was administered quarterly, and we can see that correlations for *BDI* scores obtained roughly 6 months apart are approximately .7 to .8 for both men and women. Therefore, we could have used a pretest–posttest design in which we administered the *BDI* both at the beginning and at the end of the experiment and used the pretest score as the covariate in the ANCOVA.

Finally, we should note that in many research contexts, it is not possible to conduct an experiment. We may be unable to manipulate the variables of interest or it may be unethical to do so. In this case, the best we can do is to conduct an observational study and try to control for possible moderator variables statistically. Although we do not go into details here, perhaps we can also use structural equation modeling to show that a plausible causal model is consistent with the data. The problem is that unless we are sufficiently constrained by our theories and knowledge of the research situation, we may be able to find several different causal models that are more-or-less consistent with the data.

EXERCISES

26.1   Using the data in the file *Seasons physical activity*, reproduce all the analyses reported in Tables 26.1–26.5. Remember that these analyses were based only on subjects who were employed either full- or part-time (employed = 1 or employed = 2).

26.2   Given the type of observational study described in Chapter 26, estimate the number of cases required to yield power = .80 for a test of a medium-sized effect ($f^2 = .15$) of leisure-time exercise on depression in a regression in which there are three additional predictors: age and measures of occupational and household exercise. This type of *a priori* power calculation is described in Chapter 22.

26.3 For the regression of depression on leisure-time, occupational, and household physical activity, the effect of leisure-time activity was significant for women, $b = -.083$, $p = .023$; see Table 26.2. Do what is necessary to determine whether this is a small, medium, or large effect according to the Cohen guidelines. Remember that for multiple regression, $f^2 = \dfrac{\Delta R^2}{1 - R^2}$. The guidelines, as well as how to obtain the f^2, were discussed when we considered power calculations in Chapter 22.

26.4 Let's explore some of the variables that are associated with depression, using the data set *phys_exercise_problems*.

   (a) Generate scatterplots of depression vs *BMI* for both men and women, and then use something like LOWESS smoothers or fit lines to explore the relationship between the two variables.

   (b) There seems to be a suggestion that, at least for men, there is a curvilinear relationship between depression and *BMI*. Test whether there is a significant curvilinear relationship and briefly discuss how it might be interpreted.

26.5 Considering only employed subjects, 252 men and 184 women were employed full-time and 33 men and 59 women were employed part-time. Can we reject the hypothesis that employment status and sex are independent?

26.6 Are the effects of leisure-time physical activity the same for women employed full- and part-time? Note that in SPSS, to select cases for women employed full-time, first click on the *Data* menu, and then on *Select Cases*. . . . Then, select *If condition is satisfied*, and insert the conditions (sex = 1) and (employed = 1), and then click on *OK*. To select cases for women employed part-time, insert the conditions (sex = 1) and (employed = 2). If there are differences, speculate about why they may be present.

26.7 Explore the relationship between scores on the depression measure and our crude measure of education.

26.8 Explore the relationship between our measure of perceived health and the measures of physical activity.

Part 5:
Epilogue

Chapter 27

Some Final Thoughts: Twenty Suggestions and Cautions

In this book, we have discussed how to describe and make inferences from data, with special emphasis on applications of ANOVA and the regression framework for statistical analysis. We use this final chapter to highlight 20 comments, cautions, and common errors that should be kept in mind when reading, conducting, and reporting research.

DESIGNING THE RESEARCH

1. *The generality of results depends on how the sample is selected.* The use of inferential statistics allows us to make statements about a population on the basis of a sample randomly selected from it. However, although there are formal procedures for selecting random samples from a population of interest, these are rarely used in most research contexts. There are several practical constraints that result in the use of nonrandom samples.

   One constraint is that matters of convenience often influence subject recruitment. In psychological research, many researchers take advantage of the availability of students enrolled in introductory psychology classes. Studies in cognitive, educational, social, and even clinical psychology heavily tap this source of subjects. This practice limits the generalizability of study findings, although the exact nature of the limits is often unclear and is likely to depend on the nature of the phenomena under investigation. Findings from a study of basic perceptual processes can probably be generalized to young adults regardless of educational level, ethnicity, socioeconomic status, and a host of other variables. On the other hand, findings from a study of reasoning are more likely to be restricted in generality, perhaps only applying to young adults with similar educational backgrounds.

   Also, subjects are usually self-selected. They choose whether to sign up for an experiment at a particular time during the semester, or whether to respond to a phone call requesting participation. In addition, many research studies have eligibility criteria that further constrain sampling. For example, the *Seasons* study was conducted through a medical school and had access to the members of a large HMO. Even so, of the 5,300 potential subjects initially contacted by telephone, only 641 agreed to participate, kept their initial appointments, met all the eligibility requirements (see Chapter 26), and completed the baseline questionnaires. These considerations mean that findings from a study may generalize only to those who reasonably match the characteristics of the subjects who self-select and meet eligibility criteria.

Related to issues of self-selection are attrition considerations. Subject attrition is common in some types of research. Animal research involving surgical procedures may result in deaths and longitudinal research with humans has to deal with dropouts, because either subjects lose motivation or researchers are unable to keep up-to-date contact information. In other types of research, the challenges of an experimental procedure may be daunting for some subjects, causing them to drop out, and this may occur more frequently in some experimental conditions than in others.

As an example of how attrition may bias results, consider that when we used the statistics class data set, the analyses that predicted final exam score from pretest score did not take account of the students who took the pretest, enrolled in the course, but dropped out before taking the final exam. It is unlikely that dropouts are a random sample of the students enrolled in a course, and we could look at their records to see whether we could have predicted that they would not complete the course. Quite likely, had the dropouts been required to stay in the course and take the final exam, they would have tended to do less well than non-dropouts.

We must keep in mind how the nature of the final sample limits the generality of our findings. When writing up results, we must describe our populations and samples as clearly as possible. If control or comparison groups are part of the design, we must specify exactly how they are defined. In short, we should always attend carefully to factors that may limit our ability to generalize our findings. We should also try to design our research materials and data collection procedures in ways that minimize the occurrence of missing data and subject attrition.

2. *Sophisticated statistical analyses may not mean much unless measures are valid and reliable.* Most statistics books say a great deal about statistical procedures but very little about measurement. We have commented throughout the book that researchers must try to make sure that their instruments are measuring the correct thing (i.e., they are valid) and do so with relatively little measurement error (i.e., they are reliable). Failure to do so may seriously compromise the results of any subsequent statistical analyses, no matter how sophisticated they may be. The consequences of poor reliability on a measure may be worse than just low power. For example, in multiple regression, poor reliability on a predictor may result in distorted regression coefficients for *other* predictors correlated with it. Also, measurement error may be systematic, as when subjects with high values on some emotionally charged measures tend to under-report them.

3. *The research design is important.* If our goal is to uncover the causal influence of some treatment, we should try, if possible, to design an appropriate experiment and use matching and randomization to control important nuisance variables. If we can perform an experiment, there are some designs that are more efficient than others, although often at the cost of more complexity and more assumptions (see Chapter 13). If the nature of the research problem precludes the manipulation of important independent variables and we are left with an observational study, then it will be difficult, if not impossible, to make valid causal statements—no matter how sophisticated our analyses may be. We can try to identify uncontrolled nuisance variables that may moderate the effects of possible causal variables,

and then measure them and try to adjust for their effects by modifying the design or the analyses. We can also generate a regression model or a more complicated "causal" structural equation model and determine whether the model is consistent with the obtained data. This may be a very useful step in the research process, but we must remember that testing such a model cannot, by itself, tell us whether the model is correct. We must keep in mind that there may be other plausible models that are also consistent with the data.

4. *Conduct a priori* power calculations. We have emphasized how statistical packages such as G*Power 3 can be used to determine the number of subjects necessary to achieve a specified level of power for finding significant results, given a specified effect size. If we fail to perform these calculations and perform a study with too few subjects, the result will be an expenditure of effort and resources without much chance of finding significant results. Also, if we base our calculations on a measure of effect size obtained from a small pilot study, we must remember that the confidence interval for this measure may be large, resulting in large confidence intervals on the estimated required number of subjects. We can estimate these limits by finding the required N at the upper and lower ends of the confidence interval for the effect size.

THE INITIAL ANALYSES

5. *Always explore the data.* Before conducting any statistical tests, always generate a thorough description of the data and consider it carefully. Almost all modern statistical packages provide graphical displays that allow us to summarize and display data. We should check for the presence of extreme outliers and data points that may have undue influence on the results. We must make sure that results do not occur because of anomalies that result from malfunctions in procedure or computer glitches during the data analysis. If we have outliers that cannot be explained by equipment failures or transcription errors, in many cases we can fall back on robust procedures, and/or we can determine the sensitivity of our findings to these questionable data points by determining whether we would come to the same conclusions whether or not these points are included. We should also check to see whether there are patterns of missing data that might bias our results.

6. *Correlations without scatterplots can be misleading.* The Pearson correlation coefficient is a very commonly used statistic that is a measure of the extent that two variables are linearly related. However, there may be a nonlinear component to the relationship between two variables in addition to, or instead of, a linear one. It is possible that there is an important systematic relationship between two variables even though their correlation is very small. Correlations are also very sensitive to the presence of outliers. If it is important to discuss correlations, we must look at the relevant scatterplots.

7. *Do not artificially categorize inherently continuous independent variables.* Because some researchers are more comfortable with t or χ^2 tests and ANOVA than with regression, we often see the use of median splits (i.e., placing all the values below the median into one category and all values above the median in another) in order to turn inherently continuous independent variables into dichotomous ones. This procedure throws away useful information and categorizes observations in an arbitrary way. For example, the smallest value and the value just below the median are placed in the same category even though they may be very different, but the value just below the median and the value just above it are placed in

different categories even though they may be very similar. Dichotomizing not only tends to reduce statistical power (cf. Irwin & McClelland, 2001) but can also create spurious significant effects if the independent variables are correlated (cf. Maxwell & Delaney, 1993). In the most egregious version of this kind of error, researchers start with data from an observational study, categorize several inherently continuous correlated variables, perform a multifactor ANOVA using these variables as factors, and then discuss the results as though they had conducted an experiment. This approach is unacceptable because it pretends that continuous variables are categorical and that correlated variables are not correlated. More detailed criticisms can be found in Fitzsimons (2008) and Pedhazur (1997).

8. *Be careful about combining data from different subgroups.* If we analyze the data from distinct subgroups without explicitly taking note of this in our model, then variability associated with differences among the groups will contribute to the error term and result in negatively biased tests. Moreover, the statistics for the combined data set may not match those for the data sets of any of the constituent groups. As an extreme example, we indicated in Chapter 18 that the correlation and regression coefficient could be positive for a combined data set, even though both of these statistics were negative in each of the constituent data sets. In ANOVA, a common error is to include factors in an experimental design (e.g., counterbalancing variables) but then to ignore them in the statistical analysis.

9. *Pay attention to assumptions.* The validity of many statistical test results depends on assumptions made about the population. If the assumptions are grossly violated, then the true p-values for these tests may differ greatly from their nominal values. We have presented procedures for checking major assumptions, and have discussed the consequences of violating them. We should use the capabilities of our statistical packages to examine residuals as well as to look at summary measures such as kurtosis and skewness. Even when Type 1 error rates are not badly distorted, power may be lost when the data do not conform to the assumptions underlying the method of analysis. In a number of chapters, we have discussed alternative procedures including data transformations, nonparametric tests, and tests that compensate for differences in variances, or that are resistant to the effects of outliers.

INTERPRETING THE RESULTS

10. *Interpret p-values and confidence levels correctly.* Remember that a p-value for a statistical test is the conditional probability $p(\text{data} | H_0 \text{ true})$. If $p = .01$, this means that if the null hypothesis is true, the probability of obtaining data at least as inconsistent with the null hypothesis as was obtained in the current sample is .01. This does *not* mean that the probability that the null hypothesis is true is .01. Neither the opposite conditional probability $p(H_0 \text{ true} | \text{data})$ nor $p(H_0 \text{ true})$ means the same thing as $p(\text{data} | H_0 \text{ true})$.

Also, if we were to take a large number of samples from the population and find the 95% confidence intervals for the population mean from each sample, we would expect 95% of these intervals to contain the population mean. However, because these intervals differ from one another, if we select the 95% confidence interval based on a single sample and note that it extends from, say, 5 to 10, this does *not* mean that 95% of the sample means lie between 5 and 10, nor does it mean that the population mean lies between 5 and 10 with probability .95.

11. *The finding of nonsignificant results does not necessarily mean that the null hypothesis is true.* Suppose we fail to reject the null hypothesis because the obtained *p*-value is not smaller than the specified significance level (i.e., *p* > .05). We cannot on this basis assume that the null hypothesis is true, but merely that we lack sufficient evidence to reject it. In some cases, the goal of a study is to argue that some null hypothesis is approximately true. We cannot make this case merely by finding nonsignificant results. This is because it is all too easy to find nonsignificant results by conducting a poor study with poor measures and little power that tells us almost nothing about the population. If we want to offer convincing evidence that the null hypothesis is approximately true, we must base our argument on confidence intervals for measures of effect size, or demonstrate that we had a very high level of power to find even a small effect, had one been present.

12. *Distinguish between statistical significance and effect size.* Researchers commonly look at the *p*-values provided by statistical tests to make comments about importance. However, the *p*-value depends not only on the size of the effect, but also on the size of the sample. Large sample sizes can result in highly significant results even when effect sizes are too small to be of any practical or theoretical importance. For example, Cohen (1990) discussed a *New York Times* article with the headline "Children's Height Linked to Test Scores" that reported a study involving nearly 14,000 children that showed a "definite" link between age- and sex-adjusted height with intelligence and achievement scores, even after controlling for a host of other factors such as birth order and physical maturity. Before ordering growth hormone, we should note that with a sample as large as 14,000, we would get *p* < .001 with a correlation as low as *r* = .0278. Using regression to predict IQ and height with a correlation of this size, we find that a predicted change in IQ from 100 to 130 would require about a 14-foot change in height, and a predicted four-inch change in height would require a change in IQ of about 230 points. We must consider not only significance levels, but also effect sizes.

13. *Remember that there are two kinds of significance test errors.* The probability of Type 1 error is $\alpha = p(\text{reject } H_0 | H_0 \text{ true})$; the probability of Type 2 error is $\beta = p(\text{fail to reject } H_0 | H_0$ false). The smaller we set α, the larger β will be. We must be aware of this tradeoff when we choose procedures to limit Type 1 error. The cost of guarding against false effects is that we may miss important effects that are present.

14. *Remember that measures of effect size are also statistics.* The APA task force recommends that measures of effect size always be presented for primary results, and more journals are now requiring that effect size measures be included in results sections. However, for any given study, the estimated effect size in a sample is just a statistic that has a sampling distribution of its own. Therefore, we should present confidence intervals when reporting effect size measures (e.g., see Chapter 6).

15. *Note that groups with significant differences and groups without significant differences are not necessarily significantly different from one another.* Suppose there is a significant main effect of condition (factor *C*) for group A_1, but the *C* effect is not significant for group A_2. We cannot on this basis say that the effects of *C* are different for groups A_1 and A_2. If we want to reject the null hypothesis that both groups have the same *C* effect, we must directly test that the *C* effect is significantly different for A_1 and A_2; that is, we must test the $A \times C$ interaction. Also, note that even if there is a significant *C* effect at A_1 but no *C* effect whatsoever at A_2, this interaction may not be significant. This is because interactions (i.e., differences of differences) have larger standard errors than differences. This issue is discussed in more detail in Chapter 10.

16. *Performing multiple statistical tests can increase the overall Type 1 error rate to unacceptable levels.* As we perform more statistical tests on the same data set, we are increasingly likely to commit Type 1 errors—that is, we are more likely to find spurious significant results. Procedures for controlling Type 1 error are well developed for certain kinds of tests, whereas they are virtually nonexistent for others. In Chapter 10 we discussed procedures for controlling Type 1 error for families of contrasts. We distinguished between planned (i.e., theory-driven) and unplanned contrasts, and discussed methods for controlling Type 1 error in both cases. However, there are other areas where such control is less commonly addressed. For multi-factor ANOVAs, common practice has been to test each main effect and interaction at the same significance level, usually .05, thereby resulting in a great potential inflation of Type 1 error in design with a large number of factors. Finally, we note that the control of Type 1 error is rarely explicitly addressed in multiple regression even though these procedures are extremely vulnerable to Type 1 error inflation, especially when predictors added to the equation have been selected from much larger pools of variables. In the regression chapters we distinguish between theory-driven analyses and what might be called ad hoc curve fitting (i.e., the assembling of collections of predictors that just happen to account for large values of R^2). We also discussed Steiger's (1980) recommendation to perform an omnibus test of all off-diagonal elements in a correlation matrix before looking at the individual correlations (Chapter 19). This is useful because with, say, 15 variables, there are $(15)(14)/2 = 105$ pairwise correlations. There is nothing wrong with looking at your data very carefully and in different ways—as the saying goes, if you torture your data long enough they will confess. The problem is that if you perform a very large number of tests without taking Type 1 error into account, they may confess to almost anything.

17. *Note that even a nonsignificant result can add to the cumulative evidence for an effect.* Suppose a researcher runs a study with 60 subjects and finds an unexpected effect that is fairly large and statistically significant. Further, suppose that the effect is of theoretical importance and was not predicted, so a second researcher decides to repeat the study with 40 subjects in an attempt to confirm its existence. If the effect is again significant, then there has been a successful replication and we have added confidence that the effect exists. But suppose the effect in the second study is not significant; say the estimated effect is in the same direction, but only about two-thirds the size of the effect found in the original study. How do we explain the "discrepancy" between the two studies? In fact, there is no discrepancy to explain. We would expect sampling variability in the estimate of the effect size and, in any event, would expect less significant results with the second study because it was run with fewer subjects. It is true that we now have two different estimates for the effect size, and that our best estimate of effect size is some average of the two. However, the fact that both studies found the effect to be in the same direction means that the case for the existence of the effect is stronger than if we did not have the findings for the second study, despite the fact that the results were not significant. It would take an effect size of zero or in the opposite direction in the second study to weaken the case for a significant effect. The field of meta-analysis (see, for example, Hunter & Schmidt, 1990; Rosenthal, 1991, 1995) has been developed to assess cumulative results across studies.

18. *Consider whether to compare correlations or unstandardized regression coefficients when looking at differences in bivariate relationships.* The unstandardized regression coefficient, b_1, is the slope of the linear equation that best predicts Y from X. The correlation

coefficient, r, is an index of the strength of the linear relationship between Y and X. These are related but different concepts, and we have argued that the slope is often the information that is most relevant to the researcher. Moreover, it is often difficult to interpret correlation coefficients. No matter how it is expressed, the Pearson correlation coefficient is a measure that depends on the similarity of corresponding z-scores. Because of this, the correlation coefficient and related measures such as the multiple correlation coefficient and standardized regression coefficients do not have units, and are sample specific; that is, the values of the correlations depend not only on the slope, but also on characteristics of the samples such as their variances in ways that unstandardized regression coefficients do not. As a consequence, correlations in two samples may differ because the variance of X differs, even if the rate of change of Y with X in the two samples is the same.

19. *Automated stepwise regression is not an appropriate basis for explanation.* Automated procedures that select variables to be included in a model such as stepwise regression should not be used to develop theory. Stepwise regression does not necessarily produce the best, good, or even plausible explanatory models. The p-values produced by stepwise regression programs are not "real" p-values because they do not take note of the fact that variables entered into the equation are selected from larger pools of possible predictor variables simply because they result in the largest increase in the multiple correlation coefficient. The order in which variables are added to a regression equation by an automated procedure is usually of no theoretical significance. Stepwise regression will capitalize on chance variation, especially in small samples. In Chapter 21 we considered an example of stepwise regression in which the multiple correlation coefficient was .504, but the cross-validated R was only .046. Even apart from the use of automated procedures, we have argued that attempts to maximize R^2 are not the best way to develop explanatory models.

20. *Regression equations generally are not explanatory causal models and regression coefficients are generally not measures of causal importance.* It is possible that a theory-driven causal model can be expressed as a set of regression equations, and we can perform these regressions to determine whether the model is consistent with the data. However, we cannot assemble a collection of predictors that just happen to account for a respectable proportion of the variability of an interesting outcome variable and thereby assume that we have a useful or plausible explanatory model. Among the points we mentioned in Chapters 21 and 23 were: (a) the machinery of regression deals with prediction, not causation, and a variable may be a good predictor without being causally important because the effects of variables that are not included in the equation are "absorbed" by predictors in the equation that are correlated with them; (b) because of this, both the values and interpretation of regression coefficients change when other correlated variables are entered into the equation; and (c) the regression coefficients do not take account of effects mediated by other variables in the equation because the interpretation of a regression coefficient is the rate of change of the outcome variable with the predictor, *holding all the other predictors constant.* It is also important to note that although changing one variable while holding constant a number of others is easy enough to understand in terms of the sample regression equation, it may not correspond to any plausible manipulation in the real world. Despite their limitations, regression analyses can be a very useful component of a program to advance knowledge and theory about a research problem by providing useful descriptions of the data and by suggesting questions and causal speculations that can be pursued by a variety of research techniques.

In earlier chapters, we have talked about data as our window on the world. Pursuing the metaphor, this window is almost always dirty, and if we are not careful, it may be distorted. In this book, we have discussed issues in research design, as well as how to describe and interpret data in ways that allow us best to cope with random noise and reduce bias. We have also tried to point out many of the pitfalls that should be avoided.

Appendix A
Notation and Summation Operations

We must have a common language to talk about the derivations and computational formulas that relate to psychological experimentation. Such a language exists in the notational system presented here. If you try to master it now, your efforts will be amply repaid. You will find first a few simple rules, which are then applied to some elementary statistical quantities.

A.1 A SINGLE GROUP OF SCORES

A.1.1 Some Basic Rules

In a group of scores like $Y_1, Y_2, Y_3, Y_4, \ldots, Y_n$, the subscript has no purpose except to distinguish among the individual scores. The quantity n is the total number of scores in the group. Suppose that $n = 5$ and we want to show that all five scores are to be added together. We could write

$$Y_1 + Y_2 + Y_3 + Y_4 + Y_5$$

or, more briefly,

$$Y_1 + Y_2 + \ldots + Y_5$$

Still more briefly, we write

$$\sum_{i=1}^{5} Y_i$$

This expression is read "sum the values of Y for all i from 1 to 5." In general, $i = 1, 2, \ldots, n$ (that is, i takes on the values of 1 to n), and the summation of a group of n scores is indicated by

$$\sum_{i=1}^{n} Y_i$$

The quantity i is the *index*, and 1 and n are the *limits* of summation.[1] When the context of the presentation permits no confusion, the index and limits are often dropped. Thus we may often indicate by ΣY that a group of scores are to be summed.

Three rules for summation follow.

■ RULE 1.   The sum of a constant times a variable equals the constant times the sum of the variable; or

$$\Sigma CY = C\Sigma Y$$

The term C is a constant in the sense that its value does not change as a function of i; the value of Y depends on i, and Y is therefore a variable relative to i. The rule is easily proved.

$$\Sigma CY = CY_1 + CY_2 + CY_3 + \ldots + CY_n$$
$$= C(Y_1 + Y_2 + Y_3 + \ldots + Y_n)$$
$$= C\Sigma Y$$

■ RULE 2.   The sum of a constant equals n times the constant, where n equals the number of quantities summed; or

$$\Sigma C = C + C + \ldots + C = nC$$

■ RULE 3.   The summation sign operates like a multiplier on quantities within parentheses.

■ EXAMPLE 1.

$$\sum_i^n (X_i - Y_i) = \sum_i^n X_i - \sum_i^n Y_i$$

Proof.

$$\Sigma(X - Y) = (X_1 - Y_1) + (X_2 - Y_2) + \ldots + (X_n - Y_n)$$
$$= (X_1 + X_2 + \ldots + X_n) - (Y_1 + Y_2 + \ldots + Y_n)$$
$$= \Sigma X - \Sigma Y$$

■ EXAMPLE 2.

$$\Sigma(X - Y)^2 = \Sigma X^2 + \Sigma Y^2 - 2\Sigma XY$$

Proof.

$$\Sigma(X - Y)^2 = (X_1 - Y_1)^2 + \ldots + (X_n - Y_n)^2$$
$$= (X_1^2 + Y_1^2 - 2X_1Y_1) + (X_2^2 + Y_2^2 - 2X_2Y_2) + \ldots + (X_n^2 + Y_n^2 - 2X_nY_n)$$
$$= (X_1^2 + X_2^2 + \ldots + X_n^2) + (Y_1^2 + Y_2^2 + \ldots + Y_n^2) - 2(X_1Y_1 + X_2Y_2 + \ldots + X_nY_n)$$
$$= \Sigma X^2 + \Sigma Y^2 - 2\Sigma XY$$

---

[1] To conserve space, when we wish to indicate an index of summation in a line of text or a fraction, we will often write it as a subscript. The expression $\Sigma_i Y_i$ should be considered equivalent to $\sum_i Y_i$.

A.1.2 Applying the Summation Rules

We can apply the rules of summation to prove the properties of means and variances stated in Chapter 2 (Table 2.1). Throughout this section it should be clear that we are summing over i from 1 to n even though the index and limits are not explicitly presented in each expression.

Properties of the Mean

1. $\Sigma(Y - \bar{Y}) = 0$; the sum of all deviations of scores about their mean is zero. Applying Rule 3, we get

    $$\Sigma(Y - \bar{Y}) = \Sigma Y - \Sigma \bar{Y}$$

    However, $\bar{Y}$ is a constant; its value is the same regardless of the value of the index of summation. Therefore, applying Rule 2, we rewrite the last equation as

    $$\Sigma(Y - \bar{Y}) = \Sigma Y - n\bar{Y}$$

    Because $\bar{Y} = \Sigma Y/n$, we can rewrite this as

    $$\Sigma(Y - \bar{Y}) = \Sigma Y - n\bar{Y} = \Sigma Y - n\left(\frac{\Sigma Y}{n}\right) = \Sigma Y - \Sigma Y = 0$$

2. $\Sigma(Y + k)/n = \bar{Y} + k$; if a constant is added to all scores, the mean is increased by that constant. Applying Rule 3 gives

    $$\frac{\Sigma(Y + k)}{n} = \frac{\Sigma Y + \Sigma k}{n} = \frac{\Sigma Y}{n} + \frac{\Sigma k}{n}$$

    Applying Rule 2 and noting that $\Sigma Y/n = \bar{Y}$, we have

    $$\frac{\Sigma(Y + k)}{n} = \bar{Y} + \frac{nk}{n} = \bar{Y} + k$$

3. $\Sigma k Y/n = k\bar{Y}$; if all scores are multiplied by a constant, the mean is multiplied by that constant. Applying Rule 1, we have

    $$\frac{\Sigma k Y}{n} = \frac{k\Sigma Y}{n} = k\bar{Y}$$

4. $\Sigma(Y - \bar{Y})^2$ is a minimum. Assume that there is some value $\bar{Y} + d$ such that the sum of squared deviations of all scores about it is smaller than the sum about any other value. This sum of squared distances is $\Sigma[Y - (\bar{Y} + d)]^2$. Expanding in accord with Rule 3, we have

    $$\Sigma[Y - (\bar{Y} + d)]^2 = \Sigma[(Y - \bar{Y}) - d]^2 = \Sigma(Y - \bar{Y})^2 + \Sigma d^2 - 2\Sigma d(Y - \bar{Y})$$

    Applying Rule 1, we rewrite the rightmost term as

    $$2\Sigma d(Y - \bar{Y}) = 2d\Sigma(Y - \bar{Y}) = (2d)(0)$$

    because $\Sigma(Y - \bar{Y}) = 0$. Applying Rule 2, we have

    $$\Sigma d^2 = nd^2$$

    Therefore,

$$\Sigma[Y - (\bar{Y} + d)]^2 = \Sigma(Y - \bar{Y})^2 + nd^2$$

which is as small as possible when $d = 0$; that is, when we sum the squared deviations of scores about their mean.

Properties of the Variance

1. Adding a constant to all scores leaves the variance unchanged. If a constant k is added to all scores the new variance is

$$\hat{\sigma}^2_{Y+k} = \frac{\Sigma[(Y + k) - (\overline{Y + k})]^2}{n - 1} = \frac{\Sigma(Y - \bar{Y})^2}{n - 1} = \hat{\sigma}^2_Y$$

2. Multiplying all scores by a constant k is equivalent to multiplying the variance by k^2 and the standard deviation by k. We have

$$\hat{\sigma}^2_{kY} = \frac{\Sigma(kY - \overline{kY})^2}{n - 1} = \frac{\Sigma k^2(Y - \bar{Y})^2}{n - 1}$$

By Rule 1 this becomes

$$\hat{\sigma}^2_{kY} = \frac{k^2\Sigma(Y - \bar{Y})^2}{n - 1} = k^2\hat{\sigma}^2_Y$$

z Scores

The properties proven allow us to show that the mean of a set of z scores is zero and its variance is 1. Recall that

$$z = \frac{Y - \bar{Y}}{\hat{\sigma}_Y}$$

To obtain the average of a set of n z scores, we sum them and divide by n, keeping in mind that $\Sigma(Y - \bar{Y}) = 0$. Then

$$\frac{\Sigma z}{n} = \frac{\Sigma(Y - \bar{Y})}{n\hat{\sigma}_Y} = \frac{(0)}{n\hat{\sigma}_Y} = 0$$

To prove that the variance (and therefore the standard deviation) of the z scores is 1, expand the formula for z as

$$z = \left(\frac{1}{\hat{\sigma}_Y}\right)Y - \left(\frac{1}{\hat{\sigma}_Y}\right)\bar{Y}$$

Note that $1/\hat{\sigma}_Y$ is a constant with respect to the index of summation i. Because adding (or subtracting) a constant from a variable does not change its variance (see the first property of the variance), the variance of z is the same as the variance of $(1/\hat{\sigma}_Y)Y$. But, from the second property of a variance, we know that the variance of a constant $(1/\hat{\sigma}_Y)$ times a variable (Y) is the squared constant times the variance of the variable. That is,

$$\hat{\sigma}^2_z = \left(\frac{1}{\hat{\sigma}_Y}\right)^2 \hat{\sigma}^2_Y = 1$$

A.1.3 Raw-Score Formulas

The summation rules can be applied to obtain raw-score formulas for quantities such as the variance and covariance. These raw-score or *computational* formulas contain sums of scores, squared scores, and cross-products rather than sums of squared differences and cross-products of difference scores. This allows them to minimize rounding error and makes them convenient to use with simple hand calculators that do not have variance and correlation keys.

The numerator of the expression for the variance of Y is $SS_Y = \Sigma(Y_i - \bar{Y})^2$. To get the raw-score formula for SS_Y, expand the quantity within the summation sign. Thus

$$\Sigma(Y - \bar{Y})^2 = \Sigma(Y^2 + \bar{Y}^2 - 2Y\bar{Y})$$

Applying Rule 3, we have

$$\Sigma(Y - \bar{Y})^2 = \Sigma Y^2 + \Sigma \bar{Y}^2 - \Sigma 2Y\bar{Y}$$

Noting that $\bar{Y}^2$ is a constant and applying Rule 2, we have

$$\Sigma(Y - \bar{Y})^2 = \Sigma Y^2 + n\bar{Y}^2 - \Sigma 2Y\bar{Y}$$

The quantity $2\bar{Y}$ is a constant and, by Rule 1, can be placed before the summation sign. Thus,

$$\Sigma(Y - \bar{Y})^2 = \Sigma Y^2 + n\bar{Y}^2 - 2\bar{Y}\Sigma Y$$

Now replace $\bar{Y}$ by $\Sigma Y/n$ to get

$$\Sigma(Y - \bar{Y})^2 = \Sigma Y^2 + \frac{n(\Sigma Y)^2}{n^2} - 2\left(\frac{\Sigma Y}{n}\right)\Sigma Y$$

Simplifying, we have

$$\Sigma(Y - \bar{Y})^2 = \Sigma Y^2 - \frac{(\Sigma Y)^2}{n} \tag{A.1}$$

Dividing the right-hand side of Equation A.1 by $n - 1$ gives the raw-score formula for $\hat{\sigma}_Y^2$.

We can find the raw-score formula for the covariance of X and Y,

$$\hat{\sigma}_{XY} = \frac{\Sigma(X - \bar{X})(Y - \bar{Y})}{n - 1}$$

by noting that Equation A.1 could be rewritten as

$$\Sigma(Y - \bar{Y})^2 = \Sigma(Y - \bar{Y})(Y - \bar{Y}) = \Sigma YY - \frac{(\Sigma Y)(\Sigma Y)}{n}$$

By analogy, the numerator of $\hat{\sigma}_{XY}$ has the raw-score formula

$$\Sigma(X - \bar{X})(Y - \bar{Y}) = \Sigma XY - \frac{(\Sigma X)(\Sigma Y)}{n}$$

Dividing by $n - 1$ yields the raw-score formula for $\hat{\sigma}_{XY}$.

A.2 SEVERAL GROUPS OF SCORES

The simplest possible experimental design involves several groups of scores. Thus one might have a groups of n subjects each, which differ in the amount of reward they receive for their performance on some learning task. In setting the data down on paper, there would be a column for each level of amount of reward—that is, for each experimental group. The scores for a group could be written in order within the appropriate column. In referring to a score, we should designate it by its position in the column (or experimental group) and by the position of the column. Table A.1 illustrates this procedure. Note that the first subscript refers to the position in the group (row), the second to the position of the group (column). Thus Y_{22} is the second score in group 2, and in general, Y_{ij} is the ith score in the jth group.

Table A.1   A two-dimensional matrix

			Groups		
	Y_{11}	Y_{12} ...	Y_{1j} ...	Y_{1a}
	Y_{21}	Y_{22} ...	Y_{2j} ...	Y_{2a}
	.	.	.	.
	.	.	.	.
Subjects	Y_{i1}	Y_{i2} ...	Y_{ij} ...	Y_{ia}
	.	.	.	.
	.	.	.	.
	Y_{n1}	Y_{n2} ...	Y_{nj} ...	Y_{na}

Suppose we want to refer to the mean of a single column. The term used previously, $\overline{Y}$, is obviously inadequate since it does not designate the row or column that we want. Even $\overline{Y}_1$ is not clear, since it might as easily refer to the mean of the first row as to the mean of the first column.[2] The appropriate designation is $\overline{Y}_{.1} = (1/n) \sum_i^n Y_{i1}$; the dot represents the summation over i, the index that ordinarily appears in that position. Similarly, the mean of row i would be designated by $\overline{Y}_{i.} = (1/a)\sum_j^a Y_{ij}$; summation is over the index j. The mean of all an scores would be designated by $\overline{Y}_{..} = (1/an)\sum\sum Y_{ij}$, or merely $\overline{Y}$.

Some examples using the double summation $(\Sigma_i \Sigma_j)$ may be helpful. Suppose we have

$$\sum_{j=1}^{a} \sum_{i=1}^{n} Y_{ij}^2$$

This is an instruction to set i and j initially at 1; the resulting score Y_{11} is then squared. Holding j at 1, we step i from 1 to n, squaring each score thus obtained and adding it to those previously squared. When n scores have been squared and summed, we reset the index i at 1 and step j to 2; the

---

[2] In the design we used for an example, the mean of the first row would not be a quantity of interest, since we stipulated that the order within each column was arbitrary. There are designs, however, giving rise to tables like Table A.1 for which it is as interesting to obtain row means as it is to obtain column means.

squaring and summing is then carried out for all Y_{i2}. The process continues until all *an* scores have been squared and summed. The process just described can be represented by

$$(Y_{11}^2 + Y_{21}^2 + \ldots + Y_{na}^2)$$

If we have

$$\sum_{j=1}^{a} \left(\sum_{i=1}^{n} Y_{ij} \right)^2$$

the notation indicates that a sum of *n* scores is to be squared. We again set *j* at 1, and after adding together all the Y_{i1}, square the total. The index *j* is then stepped to 2 and *i* is reset at 1; we get another sum of *n* scores, which is squared and added to the previous squared sum. We again continue until all *an* scores have been accounted for. The process can be represented by

$$(Y_{11} + Y_{21} + \ldots + Y_{n1})^2 + \ldots + (Y_{1a} + Y_{2a} + \ldots + Y_{na})^2$$

A third possibility is

$$\left(\sum_{j=1}^{a} \sum_{i=1}^{n} Y_{ij} \right)^2$$

which indicates that the squaring operation is carried out once on the total of *an* scores; we then have

$$[(Y_{11} + Y_{21} + \ldots + Y_{n1}) + \ldots + (Y_{1a} + Y_{2a} + \ldots + Y_{na})]^2$$

Note that the indices within the parentheses show how many scores are to be summed prior to squaring, and the indices outside the parentheses show how many squared totals are to be summed. When no parentheses appear, as in $\Sigma\Sigma Y^2$, we treat the notation as if it were $\Sigma\Sigma(Y^2)$. When no indices appear outside the parentheses, it is understood that we are dealing with a single squared term, as in $(\Sigma\Sigma Y)^2$. When several indices appear together, whether inside or outside the parentheses, the product of their upper limits tells us the number of terms involved. Thus, $(\Sigma_{j=1}^{a}\Sigma_{i=1}^{n} Y)^2$ indicates that *an* scores are summed before the squaring.

Our three illustrations of the double summation can be further clarified if we use some numbers. Let us use the three groups of four scores each shown in Table A.2.

Table A.2 Some sample data

	Group 1	Group 2	Group 3
	4	1	6
	1	7	4
	3	2	5
	2	4	4
$\Sigma_i Y_{ij} =$	10	14	19
$\Sigma_i Y_{ij}^2 =$	30	70	93

Now,

$$\sum_j \sum_i Y_{ij}^2 = 30 + 70 + 93 = 193$$

and

$$\sum_j \left(\sum_i Y_{ij} \right)^2 = (10)^2 + (14)^2 + (19)^2 = 657$$

and

$$\left(\sum_j \sum_i Y_{ij} \right)^2 = (10 + 14 + 19)^2 = 1849$$

As another example of how to use double summation, we might derive a raw score formula for the average group variance, often referred to as the *within-group mean square*. This is the sum of the group variances divided by a, the number of groups, or

$$\frac{1}{a} \left[\frac{\sum_{i=1}^n (Y_{i1} - \bar{Y}_{.1})^2}{n - 1} + \ldots + \frac{\sum_{i=1}^n (Y_{ia} - \bar{Y}_{.a})^2}{n - 1} \right]$$

More briefly, this average is indicated by

$$\frac{1}{a(n - 1)} \sum_j^a \sum_i^n (Y_{ij} - \bar{Y}_{.j})^2$$

Now, expanding the numerator (or "sums of squares") of this quantity, we get

$$\sum_{j=1}^a \sum_{i=1}^n (Y_{ij} - \bar{Y}_{.j})^2 = \sum_{j=1}^a \sum_{i=1}^n (Y_{ij}^2 + \bar{Y}_{.j}^2 - 2Y_{ij}\bar{Y}_{.j})$$

We "multiply through" by Σ_i, noting that $\bar{Y}_{.j}$ varies only with j; it is constant when i is the index of summation. Terms are also rearranged so that sums are premultiplied by constants:

$$\sum_j \sum_i (Y_{ij} - \bar{Y}_{.j})^2 = \sum_j \left(\sum_i Y_{ij}^2 + n\bar{Y}_{.j}^2 - 2\bar{Y}_{.j} \sum_i Y_{ij} \right)$$

Note that $\Sigma_i \bar{Y}_{.j} = n\bar{Y}_{.j}$. Although $\bar{Y}_{.j}$ is a variable relative to the index j, it is a constant relative to i, the index over which we are currently summing; therefore, Rule 2 applies.

Substituting raw-score formulas for the group means gives

$$\sum_j \sum_i (Y_{ij} - \bar{Y}_{.j})^2 = \sum_j \left[\sum_i Y_{ij}^2 + n\frac{(\Sigma_i Y_{ij})^2}{n^2} - 2 \left(\frac{\Sigma_i Y_{ij}}{n} \right) \sum_i Y_{ij} \right]$$

Simplifying gives

$$\sum_j \sum_i (Y_{ij} - \bar{Y}_{.j})^2 = \sum_j \left[\sum_i Y_{ij}^2 - \frac{(\Sigma_i Y_{ij})^2}{n} \right]$$

which can also be written

$$\sum_j \sum_i Y_{ij}^2 - \frac{\Sigma_j (\Sigma_i Y_{ij})^2}{n}$$

To simplify notation, we can use T (for "total") to replace ΣY. The sum of scores, for example, for group j is

$$T_j = \sum_i Y_{ij}$$

and the raw-score expression just derived can be rewritten as

$$\sum_j \sum_i Y_{ij}^2 - \frac{\Sigma_j T_j^2}{n}$$

Appendix B
Expected Values and Their Applications

The view of a population parameter as the expected value of a statistic is inherent in most inferential procedures. Furthermore, many important results are derived by taking expectations of statistics. The following discussion provides an introduction to these matters. We begin by defining an expected value, and we then present some rules for working with expectations. We then apply these rules to derive some results that were presented earlier in this book.

B.1 DEFINITIONS AND BASIC RULES

We repeat the earlier definitions of expected values (see Chapter 5) for convenience in dealing with the other material in this appendix. The expected value of a random variable, Y, may be viewed as a weighted average of all possible values Y can take. The weights are probabilities, $p(y)$, when Y is discretely distributed and densities, $f(y)$, when Y is continuously distributed. In the discrete case,

$$E(Y) = \sum_y yp(y)$$

and in the continuous case,

$$E(Y) = \int_y yf(y)\, dy$$

$E(Y)$ is read as "the expected value of Y" or "the expectation of Y." The y under the summation and integral signs is meant to remind us that the sum or integral is over all possible values of Y.

The symbol E is often referred to as an *expectation operator*, meaning that it is an instruction to sum or integrate the variable indicated. The expectation operator follows a set of rules similar to those presented in Appendix A for the summation operator. The most important of these rules are presented next.

■ **RULE 1.** *The expectation of a constant times a variable equals the constant times the sum of the variable:*

$$E(CY) = CE(Y)$$

This may be seen by writing

$$E(CY) = \Sigma(Cy)p(y) = C\Sigma yp(y) = CE(Y)$$

■ **RULE 2.** *The expectation of a constant is the constant:*

$$E(C) = C$$

If several events have the same numerical value C, the average value will equal C.

■ **RULE 3.** *E acts like a multiplier*. For example,

$$E(X + Y) = E(X) + E(Y)$$

To prove this, begin with the definition of $E(X + Y)$:

$$E(X + Y) = \sum_x \sum_y (x + y)p(x, y)$$

where the expression on the right indicates that each possible value of $X + Y$ is multiplied by its joint probability, and these products are then summed. Distributing this expression, we obtain

$$E(X + Y) = \sum_x \sum_y xp(x, y) + \sum_x \sum_y yp(x, y)$$

$$= \sum_x x\left[\sum_y p(x, y)\right] + \sum_y y\left[\sum_x p(x, y)\right]$$

$$= \sum_x xp(x) + \sum_y yp(y) = E(X) + E(Y)$$

A special case of this expression occurs when one variable is replaced by a constant; then

$$E(Y + C) = E(Y) + E(C) = E(Y) + C$$

This equation provides an immediate basis for asserting that

$$E(Y - \mu) = 0$$

because

$$E(Y - \mu) = E(Y) - \mu = \mu - \mu = 0$$

Another application of Rule 3 is

$$E(X + Y)^2 = E(X)^2 + E(Y)^2 + 2E(XY)$$

This leads to a proof of the statement in Chapter 2 that the variance of Y, $E(Y - \mu)^2$, equals $E(Y^2) - \mu^2$:

$$E(Y - \mu)^2 = E(Y^2) + E(\mu)^2 - 2E(Y\mu)$$

$$= E(Y^2) + \mu^2 - 2\mu E(Y), \quad \text{because } \mu \text{ is a constant}$$

$$= E(Y)^2 + \mu^2 - 2\mu^2, \quad \text{because } \mu \text{ and } E(Y) \text{ are the same entity}$$

$$= E(Y^2) - \mu^2$$

■ **RULE 4.** *IF X and Y are independently distributed, then* $E(XY) = E(X)E(Y)$. To prove this, we again begin with the definition of an expectation:

$$E(XY) = \sum_x \sum_y xy p(x, y)$$

$$= \sum_x \sum_y xy p(x) p(y)$$

because the joint probability $p(x, y) = p(x)p(y)$ if X and Y are independently distributed. Rearranging terms gives

$$E(XY) = [\Sigma x p(x)][\Sigma y p(y)] = E(X)E(Y)$$

A useful implication of this is that $E(X - \bar{X})(Y - \bar{Y}) = 0$ if X and Y are independent. This follows because $E(X - \bar{X})(Y - \bar{Y})$ then must equal $[E(X - \bar{X})][E(Y - \bar{Y})] = 0 \times 0$. Therefore, if X and Y are independent, their covariance (and consequently ρ) must equal zero.

B.2 APPLICATIONS TO ESTIMATION

We can now show that $\bar{Y}$ is an unbiased estimate of μ; that is, $E(\bar{Y}) = E(Y)$ or μ. We have

$$E(\bar{Y}) = E\left(\frac{\Sigma Y}{n}\right) = \frac{1}{n}E(\Sigma Y) \quad \text{by Rule 1}$$

$$= \frac{1}{n}\Sigma E(Y)$$

$$= \frac{1}{n}(n)E(Y) = E(Y)$$

We next show that $\hat{\sigma}^2$ is an unbiased estimator of σ^2; that is, $E(\hat{\sigma}^2) = \sigma^2$. Begin by considering the sum of squares, the numerator of $\hat{\sigma}^2$:

$$E[\Sigma(Y - \bar{Y})^2] = E\Sigma[(Y - \mu) - (\bar{Y} - \mu)]^2$$

$$= E[\Sigma(Y - \mu)^2 + \Sigma(\bar{Y} - \mu)^2 - 2(\bar{Y} - \mu)\Sigma(Y - \mu)]$$

$$= E[\Sigma(Y - \mu)^2 + n(\bar{Y} - \mu)^2 - 2n(\bar{Y} - \mu)^2]$$

$$= E[\Sigma(Y - \mu)^2 - n(\bar{Y} - \mu)^2]$$

$$= \Sigma E(Y - \mu)^2 - nE(\bar{Y} - \mu)^2 \quad \text{by Rule 3}$$

The average squared deviation of a quantity from its average is a variance; that is, $E(Y - \mu)^2 = \sigma^2$ and $E(\bar{Y} - \mu)^2 = \sigma^2/n$. Therefore,

$$E[\Sigma(Y - \bar{Y})^2] = n\sigma^2 - \frac{n\sigma^2}{n}$$

$$= (n - 1)\sigma^2$$

Therefore,

$$E\left(\frac{\Sigma(Y-\overline{Y})^2}{n-1}\right) = E[\hat{\sigma}^2] = \sigma^2$$

B.3 THE MEAN AND VARIANCE OF THE BINOMIAL DISTRIBUTION

Consider a series of n Bernoulli trials and let $X = 1$ or 0, depending upon whether the trial outcome was a success or failure; $p(X=1) = p$ and $p(X=0) = q$. The total number of successes in the n trials is $Y = \Sigma X$. We want to derive expressions for $E(Y)$ and $\text{Var}(Y)$, the mean and variance of the binomial distribution. We have

$$E(Y) = E(\Sigma X) = \Sigma E(X)$$

$$= \Sigma x p(x) \quad \text{by definition of an expected value}$$

$$= \Sigma[(1)(p) + (0)(q)] = \Sigma p = np$$

We derive the expression for the variance of the binomial distribution in a similar manner:

$$\text{Var}(Y) = \text{Var}(\Sigma X)$$

The variance of a sum of independent variables is the sum of their variances (see Section 2.5.2); therefore,

$$\text{Var}(Y) = \text{Var}(\Sigma X) = \Sigma \text{Var}(X)$$

The variance of X is $E[X - E(X)]^2 = E(X^2) - [E(X)]^2$; see the development under Rule 3, immediately preceding Rule 4. We showed above that $E(X) = p$, and

$$E(X^2) = (1^2)(p) + (0^2)(q) \quad \text{by definition of an expected value}$$

$$= p$$

Therefore, $\text{Var}(X) = E(X^2) - [E(X)]^2 = p - p^2 = p(1-p) = pq$. Finally, we have

$$\text{Var}(Y) = \Sigma \text{Var}(X) = \Sigma pq = npq$$

Appendix C
Statistical Tables

Table C.1 The binomial probability: $p(y, n, p)$

						p					
y	.05	.10	.15	.20	.25	.30	.35	.40	.45	.50
$n = 4$											
0	.8145	.6561	.5220	.4096	.3164	.2401	.1785	.1296	.0915	.0625
1	.1715	.2916	.3685	.4096	.4219	.4116	.3845	.3456	.2995	.2500
2	.0135	.0486	.0975	.1536	.2109	.2646	.3105	.3456	.3675	.3750
3	.0005	.0036	.0115	.0256	.0469	.0756	.1115	.1536	.2005	.2500
4	.0000	.0001	.0005	.0016	.0039	.0081	.0150	.0256	.0410	.0625
$n = 5$											
0	.7738	.5905	.4437	.3277	.2373	.1681	.1160	.0778	.0503	.0313
1	.2036	.3281	.3915	.4096	.3955	.3601	.3124	.2592	.2059	.1563
2	.0214	.0729	.1382	.2048	.2637	.3087	.3364	.3456	.3369	.3125
3	.0011	.0081	.0244	.0512	.0879	.1323	.1811	.2304	.2757	.3125
4	.0000	.0005	.0022	.0064	.0146	.0284	.0488	.0768	.1128	.1563
5	.0000	.0000	.0001	.0003	.0010	.0024	.0053	.0102	.0185	.0313
$n = 6$											
0	.7351	.5314	.3771	.2621	.1780	.1176	.0754	.0467	.0277	.0156
1	.2321	.3543	.3993	.3932	.3560	.3025	.2437	.1866	.1359	.0938
2	.0305	.0984	.1762	.2458	.2966	.3241	.3280	.3110	.2780	.2344
3	.0021	.0146	.0415	.0819	.1318	.1852	.2355	.2765	.3032	.3125
4	.0001	.0012	.0055	.0154	.0330	.0595	.0951	.1382	.1861	.2344
5	.0000	.0001	.0004	.0015	.0044	.0102	.0205	.0369	.0609	.0938
6	.0000	.0000	.0000	.0001	.0002	.0007	.0018	.0041	.0083	.0156
$n = 7$											
0	.6983	.4783	.3206	.2097	.1335	.0824	.0490	.0280	.0152	.0078
1	.2573	.3720	.3960	.3670	.3115	.2471	.1848	.1306	.0872	.0547
2	.0406	.1240	.2097	.2753	.3115	.3177	.2985	.2613	.2140	.1641
3	.0036	.0230	.0617	.1147	.1730	.2269	.2679	.2903	.2918	.2734
4	.0002	.0026	.0109	.0287	.0577	.0972	.1442	.1935	.2388	.2734
5	.0000	.0002	.0012	.0043	.0115	,0250	.0466	.0774	.1172	.1641
6	.0000	.0000	.0001	.0004	.0013	.0036	.0084	.0172	.0320	.0547
7	.0000	.0000	.0000	.0000	.0001	.0002	.0006	.0016	.0037	.0078
$n = 8$											
0	.6634	.4305	.2725	.1678	.1001	.0576	.0319	.0168	.0084	.0039
1	.2793	.3826	.3847	.3355	.2670	.1977	.1373	.0896	.0548	.0313
2	.0515	.1488	.2376	.2936	.3115	.2965	.2587	.2090	.1569	.1094
3	.0054	.0331	.0839	.1468	.2076	.2541	.2786	.2787	.2568	.2188
4	.0004	.0046	.0185	.0459	.0865	.1361	.1875	.2322	.2627	.2734
5	.0000	.0004	.0026	.0092	.0231	.0467	.0808	.1239	.1719	.2188
6	.0000	.0000	.0002	.0011	.0038	.0100	.0217	.0413	.0703	.1094
7	.0000	.0000	.0000	.0001	.0004	.0012	.0033	.0079	.0164	.0313
8	.0000	.0000	.0000	.0000	.0000	.0001	.0002	.0007	.0017	.0039
$n = 9$											
0	.6302	.3874	.2316	.1342	.0751	.0404	.0207	.0101	.0046	.0020
1	.2985	.3874	.3679	.3020	.2253	.1556	.1004	.0605	.0339	.0176
2	.0629	.1722	.2597	.3020	.3003	.2668	.2162	.1612	.1110	.0703
3	.0077	.0446	.1069	.1762	.2336	.2668	.2716	.2508	.2119	.1641
4	.0006	.0074	.0283	.0661	.1168	.1715	.2194	.2508	.2600	.2461

Table C.1 (continued)

						p					
y	.05	.10	.15	.20	.25	.30	.35	.40	.45	.50
5	.0000	.0008	.0050	.0165	.0389	.0735	.1181	.1672	.2128	.2461
6	.0000	.0001	.0006	.0028	.0087	.0210	.0424	.0743	.1160	.1641
7	.0000	.0000	.0000	.0003	.0012	.0039	.0098	.0212	.0407	.0703
8	.0000	.0000	.0000	.0000	.0001	.0004	.0013	.0035	.0083	.0176
9	.0000	.0000	.0000	.0000	.0000	.0000	.0001	.0003	.0008	.0020

$n = 10$

y	.05	.10	.15	.20	.25	.30	.35	.40	.45	.50
0	.5987	.3487	.1969	.1074	.0563	.0282	.0135	.0060	.0025	.0010
1	.3151	.3874	.3474	.2684	.1877	.1211	.0725	.0403	.0207	.0098
2	.0746	.1937	.2759	.3020	.2816	.2335	.1757	.1209	.0763	.0439
3	.0105	.0574	.1298	.2013	.2503	.2668	.2522	.2150	.1665	.1172
4	.0010	.0112	.0401	.0881	.1460	.2001	.2377	.2508	.2384	.2051
5	.0001	.0015	.0085	.0264	.0584	.1029	.1536	.2007	.2340	.2461
6	.0000	.0001	.0012	.0055	.0162	.0368	.0689	.1115	.1596	.2051
7	.0000	.0000	.0001	.0008	.0031	.0090	.0212	.0425	.0746	.1172
8	.0000	.0000	.0000	.0001	.0004	.0014	.0043	.0106	.0229	.0439
9	.0000	.0000	.0000	.0000	.0000	.0001	.0005	.0016	.0042	.0098
10	.0000	.0000	.0000	.0000	.0000	.0000	.0000	.0001	.0003	.0010

$n = 11$

y	.05	.10	.15	.20	.25	.30	.35	.40	.45	.50
0	.5688	.3138	.1673	.0859	.0422	.0198	.0088	.0036	.0014	.0005
1	.3293	.3835	.3248	.2362	.1549	.0932	.0518	.0266	.0125	.0054
2	.0867	.2131	.2866	.2953	.2581	.1998	.1395	.0887	.0513	.0269
3	.0137	.0710	.1517	.2215	.2581	.2568	.2254	.1774	.1259	.0806
4	.0014	.0158	.0536	.1107	.1721	.2201	.2428	.2365	.2060	.1611
5	.0001	.0025	.0132	.0388	.0803	.1321	.1830	.2207	.2360	.2256
6	.0000	.0003	.0023	.0097	.0268	.0566	.0985	.1471	.1931	.2256
7	.0000	.0000	.0003	.0017	.0064	.0173	.0379	.0701	.1128	.1611
8	.0000	.0000	.0000	.0002	.0011	.0037	.0102	.0234	.0462	.0806
9	.0000	.0000	.0000	.0000	.0001	.0005	.0018	.0052	.0126	.0269
10	.0000	.0000	.0000	.0000	.0000	.0000	.0002	.0007	.0021	.0054
11	.0000	.0000	.0000	.0000	.0000	.0000	.0000	.0000	.0002	.0005

$n = 12$

y	.05	.10	.15	.20	.25	.30	.35	.40	.45	.50
0	.5404	.2824	.1422	.0687	.0317	.0138	.0057	.0022	.0008	.0002
1	.3413	.3766	.3012	.2062	.1267	.0712	.0368	.0174	.0075	.0029
2	.0988	.2301	.2924	.2835	.2323	.1678	.1088	.0639	.0339	.0161
3	.0173	.0852	.1720	.2362	.2581	.2397	.1954	.1419	.0923	.0537
4	.0021	.0213	.0683	.1329	.1936	.2311	.2367	.2128	.1700	.1208
5	.0002	.0038	.0193	.0532	.1032	.1585	.2039	.2270	.2225	.1934
6	.0000	.0005	.0040	.0155	.0401	.0792	.1281	.1766	.2124	.2256
7	.0000	.0000	.0006	.0033	.0115	.0291	.0591	.1009	.1489	.1934
8	.0000	.0000	.0001	.0005	.0024	.0078	.0199	.0420	.0762	.1208
9	.0000	.0000	.0000	.0001	.0004	.0015	.0048	.0125	.0277	.0537
10	.0000	.0000	.0000	.0000	.0000	.0002	.0008	.0025	.0068	.0161
11	.0000	.0000	.0000	.0000	.0000	.0000	.0001	.0003	.0010	.0029
12	.0000	.0000	.0000	.0000	.0000	.0000	.0000	.0000	.0001	.0002

Table C.1 (continued)

						p					
y	.05	.10	.15	.20	.25	.30	.35	.40	.45	.50

$n = 13$

y	.05	.10	.15	.20	.25	.30	.35	.40	.45	.50
0	.5133	.2542	.1209	.0550	.0238	.0097	.0037	.0013	.0004	.0001
1	.3512	.3672	.2774	.1787	.1029	.0540	.0259	.0113	.0045	.0016
2	.1109	.2448	.2937	.2680	.2059	.1388	.0836	.0453	.0220	.0095
3	.0214	.0997	.1900	.2457	.2517	.2181	.1651	.1107	.0660	.0349
4	.0028	.0277	.0838	.1535	.2097	.2337	.2222	.1845	.1350	.0873
5	.0003	.0055	.0266	.0691	.1258	.1803	.2154	.2214	.1989	.1571
6	.0000	.0008	.0063	.0230	.0559	.1030	.1546	.1968	.2169	.2095
7	.0000	.0001	.0011	.0058	.0186	.0442	.0833	.1312	.1775	.2095
8	.0000	.0000	.0001	.0011	.0047	.0142	.0336	.0656	.1089	.1571
9	.0000	.0000	.0000	.0001	.0009	.0034	.0101	.0243	.0495	.0873
10	.0000	.0000	.0000	.0000	.0001	.0006	.0022	.0065	.0162	.0349
11	.0000	.0000	.0000	.0000	.0000	.0001	.0003	.0012	.0036	.0095
12	.0000	.0000	.0000	.0000	.0000	.0000	.0000	.0001	.0005	.0016
13	.0000	.0000	.0000	.0000	.0000	.0000	.0000	.0000	.0000	.0001

$n = 14$

y	.05	.10	.15	.20	.25	.30	.35	.40	.45	.50
0	.4877	.2288	.1028	.0440	.0178	.0068	.0024	.0008	.0002	.0001
1	.3593	.3559	.2539	.1539	.0832	.0407	.0181	.0073	.0027	.0009
2	.1229	.2570	.2912	.2501	.1802	.1134	.0634	.0317	.0141	.0056
3	.0259	.1142	.2056	.2501	.2402	.1943	.1366	.0845	.0462	.0222
4	.0037	.0349	.0998	.1720	.2202	.2290	.2022	.1549	.1040	.0611
5	.0004	.0078	.0352	.0860	.1468	.1963	.2178	.2066	.1701	.1222
6	.0000	.0013	.0093	.0322	.0734	.1262	.1759	.2066	.2088	.1833
7	.0000	.0002	.0019	.0092	.0280	.0618	.1082	.1574	.1952	.2095
8	.0000	.0000	.0003	.0020	.0082	.0232	.0510	.0918	.1398	.1833
9	.0000	.0000	.0000	.0003	.0018	.0066	.0183	.0408	.0762	.1222
10	.0000	.0000	.0000	.0000	.0003	.0014	.0049	.0136	.0312	.0611
11	.0000	.0000	.0000	.0000	.0000	.0002	.0010	.0033	.0093	.0222
12	.0000	.0000	.0000	.0000	.0000	.0000	.0001	.0005	.0019	.0056
13	.0000	.0000	.0000	.0000	.0000	.0000	.0000	.0001	.0002	.0009
14	.0000	.0000	.0000	.0000	.0000	.0000	.0000	.0000	.0000	.0001

$n = 15$

y	.05	.10	.15	.20	.25	.30	.35	.40	.45	.50
0	.4633	.2059	.0874	.0352	.0134	.0047	.0016	.0005	.0001	.0000
1	.3658	.3432	.2312	.1319	.0668	.0305	.0126	.0047	.0016	.0005
2	.1348	.2669	.2856	.2309	.1559	.0916	.0476	.0219	.0090	.0032
3	.0307	.1285	.2184	.2501	.2252	.1700	.1110	.0634	.0318	.0139
4	.0049	.0428	.1156	.1876	.2252	.2186	.1792	.1268	.0780	.0417
5	.0006	.0105	.0449	.1032	.1651	.2061	.2123	.1859	.1404	.0916
6	.0000	.0019	.0132	.0430	.0917	.1472	.1906	.2066	.1914	.1527
7	.0000	.0003	.0030	.0138	.0393	.0811	.1319	.1771	.2013	.1964
8	.0000	.0000	.0005	.0035	.0131	.0348	.0710	.1181	.1647	.1964
9	.0000	.0000	.0001	.0007	.0034	.0116	.0298	.0612	.1048	.1527
10	.0000	.0000	.0000	.0001	.0007	.0030	.0096	.0245	.0515	.0916
11	.0000	.0000	.0000	.0000	.0001	.0006	.0024	.0074	.0191	.0417
12	.0000	.0000	.0000	.0000	.0000	.0001	.0004	.0016	.0052	.0139

Table C.1 (continued)

						p					
y	.05	.10	.15	.20	.25	.30	.35	.40	.45	.50	
13	.0000	.0000	.0000	.0000	.0000	.0000	.0001	.0003	.0010	.0032	
14	.0000	.0000	.0000	.0000	.0000	.0000	.0000	.0000	.0001	.0005	
15	.0000	.0000	.0000	.0000	.0000	.0000	.0000	.0000	.0000	.0000	

$n = 16$

0	.4401	.1853	.0743	.0281	.0100	.0033	.0010	.0003	.0001	.0000	
1	.3706	.3294	.2097	.1126	.0535	.0228	.0087	.0030	.0009	.0002	
2	.1463	.2745	.2775	.2111	.1336	.0732	.0353	.0150	.0056	.0018	
3	.0359	.1423	.2285	.2463	.2079	.1465	.0888	.0468	.0215	.0085	
4	.0061	.0514	.1311	.2001	.2252	.2040	.1553	.1014	.0572	.0278	
5	.0008	.0137	.0555	.1201	.1802	.2099	.2008	.1623	.1123	.0667	
6	.0001	.0028	.0180	.0550	.1101	.1649	.1982	.1983	.1684	.1222	
7	.0000	.0004	.0045	.0197	.0524	.1010	.1524	.1889	.1969	.1746	
8	.0000	.0001	.0009	.0055	.0197	.0487	.0923	.1417	.1812	.1964	
9	.0000	.0000	.0001	.0012	.0058	.0185	.0442	.0840	.1318	.1746	
10	.0000	.0000	.0000	.0002	.0014	.0056	.0167	.0392	.0755	.1222	
11	.0000	.0000	.0000	.0000	.0002	.0013	.0049	.0142	.0337	.0667	
12	.0000	.0000	.0000	.0000	.0000	.0002	.0011	.0040	.0115	.0278	
13	.0000	.0000	.0000	.0000	.0000	.0000	.0002	.0008	.0029	.0085	
14	.0000	.0000	.0000	.0000	.0000	.0000	.0000	.0001	.0005	.0018	
15	.0000	.0000	.0000	.0000	.0000	.0000	.0000	.0000	.0001	.0002	
16	.0000	.0000	.0000	.0000	.0000	.0000	.0000	.0000	.0000	.0000	

$n = 17$

0	.4181	.1668	.0631	.0225	.0075	.0023	.0007	.0002	.0000	.0000	
1	.3741	.3150	.1893	.0957	.0426	.0169	.0060	.0019	.0005	.0001	
2	.1575	.2800	.2673	.1914	.1136	.0581	.0260	.0102	.0035	.0010	
3	.0415	.1556	.2359	.2393	.1893	.1245	.0701	.0341	.0144	.0052	
4	.0076	.0605	.1457	.2093	.2209	.1868	.1320	.0796	.0411	.0182	
5	.0010	.0175	.0668	.1361	.1914	.2081	.1849	.1379	.0875	.0472	
6	.0001	.0039	.0236	.0680	.1276	.1784	.1991	.1839	.1432	.0944	
7	.0000	.0007	.0065	.0267	.0668	.1201	.1685	.1927	.1841	.1484	
8	.0000	.0001	.0014	.0084	.0279	.0644	.1134	.1606	.1883	.1855	
9	.0000	.0000	.0003	.0021	.0093	.0276	.0611	.1070	.1540	.1855	
10	.0000	.0000	.0000	.0004	.0025	.0095	.0263	.0571	.1008	.1484	
11	.0000	.0000	.0000	.0001	.0005	.0026	.0090	.0242	.0525	.0944	
12	.0000	.0000	.0000	.0000	.0001	.0006	.0024	.0081	.0215	.0472	
13	.0000	.0000	.0000	.0000	.0000	.0001	.0005	.0021	.0068	.0182	
14	.0000	.0000	.0000	.0000	.0000	.0000	.0001	.0004	.0016	.0052	
15	.0000	.0000	.0000	.0000	.0000	.0000	.0000	.0001	.0003	.0010	
16	.0000	.0000	.0000	.0000	.0000	.0000	.0000	.0000	.0000	.0001	
17	.0000	.0000	.0000	.0000	.0000	.0000	.0000	.0000	.0000	.0000	

$n = 18$

0	.3972	.1501	.0536	.0180	.0056	.0016	.0004	.0001	.0000	.0000	
1	.3763	.3002	.1704	.0811	.0338	.0126	.0042	.0012	.0003	.0001	
2	.1683	.2835	.2556	.1723	.0958	.0458	.0190	.0069	.0022	.0006	
3	.0473	.1680	.2406	.2297	.1704	.1046	.0547	.0246	.0095	.0031	

Table C.1 (continued)

						p					
	y	.05	.10	.15	.20	.25	.30	.35	.40	.45	.50
	4	.0093	.0700	.1592	.2153	.2130	.1681	.1104	.0614	.0291	.0117
	5	.0014	.0218	.0787	.1507	.1988	.2017	.1664	.1146	.0666	.0327
	6	.0002	.0052	.0301	.0816	.1436	.1873	.1941	.1655	.1181	.0708
	7	.0000	.0010	.0091	.0350	.0820	.1376	.1792	.1892	.1657	.1214
	8	.0000	.0002	.0022	.0120	.0376	.0811	.1327	.1734	.1864	.1669
	9	.0000	.0000	.0004	.0033	.0139	.0386	.0794	.1284	.1694	.1855
	10	.0000	.0000	.0001	.0008	.0042	.0149	.0385	.0771	.1248	.1669
	11	.0000	.0000	.0000	.0001	.0010	.0046	.0151	.0374	.0742	.1214
	12	.0000	.0000	.0000	.0000	.0002	.0012	.0047	.0145	.0354	.0708
	13	.0000	.0000	.0000	.0000	.0000	.0002	.0012	.0045	.0134	.0327
	14	.0000	.0000	.0000	.0000	.0000	.0000	.0002	.0011	.0039	.0117
	15	.0000	.0000	.0000	.0000	.0000	.0000	.0000	.0002	.0009	.0031
	16	.0000	.0000	.0000	.0000	.0000	.0000	.0000	.0000	.0001	.0006
	17	.0000	.0000	.0000	.0000	.0000	.0000	.0000	.0000	.0000	.0001
	18	.0000	.0000	.0000	.0000	.0000	.0000	.0000	.0000	.0000	.0000
$n = 19$											
	0	.3774	.1351	.0456	.0144	.0042	.0011	.0003	.0001	.0000	.0000
	1	.3774	.2852	.1529	.0685	.0268	.0093	.0029	.0008	.0002	.0000
	2	.1787	.2852	.2428	.1540	.0803	.0358	.0138	.0046	.0013	.0003
	3	.0533	.1796	.2428	.2182	.1517	.0869	.0422	.0175	.0062	.0018
	4	.0112	.0798	.1714	.2182	.2023	.1491	.0909	.0467	.0203	.0074
	5	.0018	.0266	.0907	.1636	.2023	.1916	.1468	.0933	.0497	.0222
	6	.0002	.0069	.0374	.0955	.1574	.1916	.1844	.1451	.0949	.0518
	7	.0000	.0014	.0122	.0443	.0974	.1525	.1844	.1797	.1443	.0961
	8	.0000	.0002	.0032	.0166	.0487	.0981	.1489	.1797	.1771	.1442
	9	.0000	.0000	.0007	.0051	.0198	.0514	.0980	.1464	.1771	.1762
	10	.0000	.0000	.0001	.0013	.0066	.0220	.0528	.0976	.1449	.1762
	11	.0000	.0000	.0000	.0003	.0018	.0077	.0233	.0532	.0970	.1442
	12	.0000	.0000	.0000	.0000	.0004	.0022	.0083	.0237	.0529	.0961
	13	.0000	.0000	.0000	.0000	.0001	.0005	.0024	.0085	.0233	.0518
	14	.0000	.0000	.0000	.0000	.0000	.0001	.0006	.0024	.0082	.0222
	15	.0000	.0000	.0000	.0000	.0000	.0000	.0001	.0005	.0022	.0074
	16	.0000	.0000	.0000	.0000	.0000	.0000	.0000	.0001	.0005	.0018
	17	.0000	.0000	.0000	.0000	.0000	.0000	.0000	.0000	.0001	.0003
	18	.0000	.0000	.0000	.0000	.0000	.0000	.0000	.0000	.0000	.0000
	19	.0000	.0000	.0000	.0000	.0000	.0000	.0000	.0000	.0000	.0000
$n = 20$											
	0	.3585	.1216	.0388	.0115	.0032	.0008	.0002	.0000	.0000	.0000
	1	.3774	.2702	.1368	.0576	.0211	.0068	.0020	.0005	.0001	.0000
	2	.1887	.2852	.2293	.1369	.0669	.0278	.0100	.0031	.0008	.0002
	3	.0596	.1901	.2428	.2054	.1339	.0716	.0323	.0123	.0040	.0011
	4	.0133	.0898	.1821	.2182	.1897	.1304	.0738	.0350	.0139	.0046
	5	.0022	.0319	.1028	.1746	.2023	.1789	.1272	.0746	.0365	.0148
	6	.0003	.0089	.0454	.1091	.1686	.1916	.1712	.1244	.0746	.0370
	7	.0000	.0020	.0160	.0545	.1124	.1643	.1844	.1659	.1221	.0739

Table C.1 (continued)

					p					
y	.05	.10	.15	.20	.25	.30	.35	.40	.45	.50
8	.0000	.0004	.0046	.0222	.0609	.1144	.1614	.1797	.1623	.1201
9	.0000	.0001	.0011	.0074	.0271	.0654	.1158	.1597	.1771	.1602
10	.0000	.0000	.0002	.0020	.0099	.0308	.0686	.1171	.1593	.1762
11	.0000	.0000	.0000	.0005	.0030	.0120	.0336	.0710	.1185	.1602
12	.0000	.0000	.0000	.0001	.0008	.0039	.0136	.0355	.0727	.1201
13	.0000	.0000	.0000	.0000	.0002	.0010	.0045	.0146	.0366	.0739
14	.0000	.0000	.0000	.0000	.0000	.0002	.0012	.0049	.0150	.0370
15	.0000	.0000	.0000	.0000	.0000	.0000	.0003	.0013	.0049	.0148
16	.0000	.0000	.0000	.0000	.0000	.0000	.0000	.0003	.0013	.0046
17	.0000	.0000	.0000	.0000	.0000	.0000	.0000	.0000	.0002	.0011
18	.0000	.0000	.0000	.0000	.0000	.0000	.0000	.0000	.0000	.0002
19	.0000	.0000	.0000	.0000	.0000	.0000	.0000	.0000	.0000	.0000
20	.0000	.0000	.0000	.0000	.0000	.0000	.0000	.0000	.0000	.0000

Table C.2 The standardized normal distribution

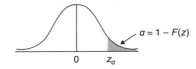

$$\alpha = 1 - F(z)$$

z	α	z	α	z	α	z	α	z	α
.00	.5000	.33	.3707	.66	.2546	.99	.1611	1.32	.0934
.01	.4960	.34	.3669	.67	.2514	1.00	.1587	1.33	.0918
.02	.4920	.35	.3632	.68	.2483	1.01	.1562	1.34	.0901
.03	.4880	.36	.3594	.69	.2451	1.02	.1539	1.35	.0885
.04	.4840	.37	.3557	.70	.2420	1.03	.1515	1.36	.0869
.05	.4801	.38	.3520	.71	.2389	1.04	.1492	1.37	.0853
.06	.4761	.39	.3483	.72	.2358	1.05	.1469	1.38	.0838
.07	.4721	.40	.3446	.73	.2327	1.06	.1446	1.39	.0823
.08	.4681	.41	.3409	.74	.2296	1.07	.1423	1.40	.0808
.09	.4641	.42	.3372	.75	.2266	1.08	.1401	1.41	.0793
.10	.4602	.43	.3336	.76	.2236	1.09	.1379	1.42	.0778
.11	.4562	.44	.3300	.77	.2206	1.10	.1357	1.43	.0764
.12	.4522	.45	.3264	.78	.2177	1.11	.1335	1.44	.0749
.13	.4483	.46	.3228	.79	.2148	1.12	.1314	1.45	.0735
.14	.4443	.47	.3192	.80	.2119	1.13	.1292	1.46	.0721
.15	.4404	.48	.3156	.81	.2090	1.14	.1271	1.47	.0708
.16	.4364	.49	.3121	.82	.2061	1.15	.1251	1.48	.0694
.17	.4325	.50	.3085	.83	.2033	1.16	.1230	1.49	.0681
.18	.4286	.51	.3050	.84	.2005	1.17	.1210	1.50	.0668
.19	.4247	.52	.3015	.85	.1977	1.18	.1190	1.51	.0655
.20	.4207	.53	.2981	.86	.1949	1.19	.1170	1.52	.0643
.21	.4168	.54	.2946	.87	.1922	1.20	.1151	1.53	.0630
.22	.4129	.55	.2912	.88	.1894	1.21	.1131	1.54	.0618
.23	.4090	.56	.2877	.89	.1867	1.22	.1112	1.55	.0606
.24	.4052	.57	.2843	.90	.1841	1.23	.1093	1.56	.0594
.25	.4013	.58	.2810	.91	.1814	1.24	.1075	1.57	.0582
.26	.3974	.59	.2776	.92	.1788	1.25	.1056	1.58	.0571
.27	.3936	.60	.2743	.93	.1762	1.26	.1038	1.59	.0559
.28	.3897	.61	.2709	.94	.1736	1.27	.1020	1.60	.0548
.29	.3859	.62	.2676	.95	.1711	1.28	.1003	1.61	.0537
.30	.3821	.63	.2643	.96	.1685	1.29	.0985	1.62	.0526
.31	.3783	.64	.2611	.97	.1660	1.30	.0968	1.63	.0516
.32	.3745	.65	.2578	.98	.1635	1.31	.0951	1.64	.0505
1.65	.0495	1.98	.0239	2.31	.0104	2.64	.0041	2.97	.0015
1.66	.0485	1.99	.0233	2.32	.0102	2.65	.0040	2.98	.0014
1.67	.0475	2.00	.0228	2.33	.0099	2.66	.0039	2.99	.0014
1.68	.0465	2.01	.0222	2.34	.0096	2.67	.0038	3.00	.0013
1.69	.0455	2.02	.0217	2.35	.0094	2.68	.0037	3.01	.0013
1.70	.0446	2.03	.0212	2.36	.0091	2.69	.0036	3.02	.0013

Table C.2 (continued)

z	α	z	α	z	α	z	α	z	α
1.71	.0436	2.04	.0207	2.37	.0089	2.70	.0035	3.03	.0012
1.72	.0427	2.05	.0202	2.38	.0087	2.71	.0034	3.04	.0012
1.73	.0418	2.06	.0197	2.39	.0084	2.72	.0033	3.05	.0011
1.74	.0409	2.07	.0192	2.40	.0082	2.73	.0032	3.06	.0011
1.75	.0401	2.08	.0188	2.41	.0080	2.74	.0031	3.07	.0011
1.76	.0392	2.09	.0183	2.42	.0078	2.75	.0030	3.08	.0010
1.77	.0384	2.10	.0179	2.43	.0075	2.76	.0029	3.09	.0010
1.78	.0375	2.11	.0174	2.44	.0073	2.77	.0028	3.10	.0010
1.79	.0367	2.12	.0170	2.45	.0071	2.78	.0027	3.11	.0009
1.80	.0359	2.13	.0166	2.46	.0069	2.79	.0026	3.12	.0009
1.81	.0351	2.14	.0162	2.47	.0068	2.80	.0026	3.13	.0009
1.82	.0344	2.15	.0158	2.48	.0066	2.81	.0025	3.14	.0008
1.83	.0336	2.16	.0154	2.49	.0064	2.82	.0024	3.15	.0008
1.84	.0329	2.17	.0150	2.50	.0062	2.83	.0023	3.16	.0008
1.85	.0322	2.18	.0146	2.51	.0060	2.84	.0023	3.17	.0008
1.86	.0314	2.19	.0143	2.52	.0059	2.85	.0022	3.18	.0007
1.87	.0307	2.20	.0139	2.53	.0057	2.86	.0021	3.19	.0007
1.88	.0301	2.21	.0136	2.54	.0055	2.87	.0021	3.20	.0007
1.89	.0294	2.22	.0132	2.55	.0054	2.88	.0020	3.21	.0007
1.90	.0287	2.23	.0129	2.56	.0052	2.89	.0019	3.22	.0006
1.91	.0281	2.24	.0125	2.57	.0051	2.90	.0019	3.23	.0006
1.92	.0274	2.25	.0122	2.58	.0049	2.91	.0018	3.24	.0006
1.93	.0268	2.26	.0119	2.59	.0048	2.92	.0018	3.25	.0006
1.94	.0262	2.27	.0116	2.60	.0047	2.93	.0017		
1.95	.0256	2.28	.0113	2.61	.0045	2.94	.0016		
1.96	.0250	2.29	.0110	2.62	.0044	2.95	.0016		
1.97	.0244	2.30	.0107	2.63	.0043	2.96	.0015		

Source: Adapted from Table 1 in Pearson, E. S. and Hartley, H. O. (1958). *Biometrika Tables for Statisticians*, Vol. 1, 2nd ed. Cambridge University Press: Cambridge, with the kind permission of the trustees of *Biometrika*.

Table C.3 Percentage points of the *t* distribution

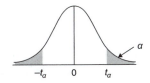

	Level of significance for a one-tailed test									
	0.4	0.25	0.1	0.05	0.025	0.01	0.005	0.0025	0.001	0.0005
	Level of significance for a two-tailed test									
df	0.8	0.5	0.2	0.1	0.05	0.02	0.01	0.005	0.002	0.001
1	0.325	1.000	3.078	6.314	12.706	31.821	63.657	127.32	318.31	636.62
2	.289	0.816	1.886	2.920	4.303	6.965	9.925	14.089	22.326	31.598
3	.277	.765	1.638	2.353	3.182	4.541	5.841	7.453	10.213	12.924
4	.271	.741	1.533	2.132	2.776	3.747	4.604	5.598	7.173	8.610
5	0.267	0.727	1.476	2.015	2.571	3.365	4.032	4.773	5.893	6.869
6	.265	.718	1.440	1.943	2.447	3.143	3.707	4.317	5.208	5.959
7	.263	.711	1.415	1.895	2.365	2.998	3.499	4.029	4.785	5.408
8	.262	.706	1.397	1.860	2.306	2.896	3.355	3.833	4.501	5.041
9	.261	.703	1.383	1.833	2.262	2.821	3.250	3.690	4.297	4.781
10	0.260	0.700	1.372	1.812	2.228	2.764	3.169	3.581	4.144	4.587
11	.260	.697	1.363	1.796	2.201	2.718	3.106	3.497	4.025	4.437
12	.259	.695	1.356	1.782	2.179	2.681	3.055	3.428	3.930	4.318
13	.259	.694	1.350	1.771	2.160	2.650	3.012	3.372	3.852	4.221
14	.258	.692	1.345	1.761	2.145	2.624	2.977	3.326	3.787	4.140
15	0.258	0.691	1.341	1.753	2.131	2.602	2.947	3.286	3.733	4.073
16	.258	.690	1.337	1.746	2.120	2.583	2.921	3.252	3.686	4.015
17	.257	.689	1.333	1.740	2.110	2.567	2.898	3.222	3.646	3.965
18	.257	.688	1.330	1.734	2.101	2.552	2.878	3.197	3.610	3.922
19	.257	.688	1.328	1.729	2.093	2.539	2.861	3.174	3.579	3.883
20	0.257	0.687	1.325	1.725	2.086	2.528	2.845	3.153	3.552	3.850
21	.257	.686	1.323	1.721	2.080	2.518	2.831	3.135	3.527	3.819
22	.256	.686	1.321	1.717	2.074	2.508	2.819	3.119	3.505	3.792
23	.256	.685	1.319	1.714	2.069	2.500	2.807	3.104	3.485	3.767
24	.256	.685	1.318	1.711	2.064	2.492	2.797	3.091	3.467	3.745
25	0.256	0.684	1.316	1.708	2.060	2.485	2.787	3.078	3.450	3.725
26	.256	.684	1.315	1.706	2.056	2.479	2.779	3.067	3.435	3.707
27	.256	.684	1.314	1.703	2.052	2.473	2.771	3.057	3.421	3.690
28	.256	.683	1.313	1.701	2.048	2.467	2.763	3.047	3.408	3.674
29	.256	.683	1.311	1.699	2.045	2.462	2.756	3.038	3.396	3.659
30	0.256	0.683	1.310	1.697	2.042	2.457	2.750	3.030	3.385	3.646
40	.255	.681	1.303	1.684	2.021	2.423	2.704	2.971	3.307	3.551
60	.254	.679	1.296	1.671	2.000	2.390	2.660	2.915	3.232	3.460
120	.254	.677	1.289	1.658	1.980	2.358	2.617	2.860	3.160	3.373
∞	.253	.674	1.282	1.645	1.960	2.326	2.576	2.807	3.090	3.291

Source: Adapted from Table 12 in Pearson, E. S. and Hartley. H. O. (1958). *Biometrika Tables for Statisticians*, Vol. 1, 2nd ed. Cambridge University Press: Cambridge, with the kind permission of the trustees of *Biometrika*.

Table C.4   Percentage points of the chi-square distribution

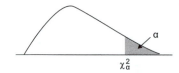

α \ df	0.995	0.990	0.975	0.950	0.900	0.750	0.500
1	$392704 \cdot 10^{-10}$	$157088 \cdot 10^{-9}$	$982069 \cdot 10^{-9}$	$393214 \cdot 10^{-8}$	0.0157908	0.1015308	0.454937
2	0.0100251	0.0201007	0.0506356	0.102587	0.210720	0.575364	1.38629
3	0.0717212	0.114832	0.215795	0.351846	0.584375	1.212534	2.36597
4	0.206990	0.297110	0.484419	0.710721	1.063623	1.92255	3.35670
5	0.411740	0.554300	0.831211	1.145476	1.61031	2.67460	4.35146
6	0.675727	0.872085	1.237347	1.63539	2.20413	3.45460	5.34812
7	0.989265	1.239043	1.68987	2.16735	2.83311	4.25485	6.34581
8	1.344419	1.646482	2.17973	2.73264	3.48954	5.07064	7.34412
9	1.734926	2.087912	2.70039	3.32511	4.16816	5.89883	8.34283
10	2.15585	2.55821	3.24697	3.94030	4.86518	6.73720	9.34182
11	2.60321	3.05347	3.81575	4.57481	5.57779	7.58412	10.3410
12	3.07382	3.57056	4.40379	5.22603	6.30380	8.43842	11.3403
13	3.56503	4.10691	5.00874	5.89186	7.04150	9.29906	12.3398
14	4.07468	4.66043	5.62872	6.57063	7.78953	10.1653	13.3393
15	4.60094	5.22935	6.26214	7.26094	8.54675	11.0365	14.3389
16	5.14224	5.81221	6.90766	7.96164	9.31223	11.9122	15.3385
17	5.69724	6.40776	7.56418	8.67176	10.0852	12.7919	16.3381
18	6.26481	7.01491	8.23075	9.39046	10.8649	13.6753	17.3379
19	6.84398	7.63273	8.90655	10.1170	11.6509	14.5620	18.3376
20	7.43386	8.26040	9.59083	10.8508	12.4426	15.4518	19.3374
21	8.03366	8.89720	10.28293	11.5913	13.2396	16.3444	20.3372
22	8.64272	9.54249	10.9823	12.3380	14.0415	17.2396	21.3370
23	9.26042	10.19567	11.6885	13.0905	14.8479	18.1373	22.3369
24	9.88623	10.8564	12.4011	13.8484	15.6587	19.0372	23.3367
25	10.5197	11.5240	13.1197	14.6114	16.4734	19.9393	24.3366
26	11.1603	12.1981	13.8439	15.3791	17.2919	20.8434	25.3364
27	11.8076	12.8786	14.5733	16.1513	18.1138	21.7494	26.3363
28	12.4613	13.5648	15.3079	16.9279	18.9392	22.6572	27.3363
29	13.1211	14.2565	16.0471	17.7083	19.7677	23.5666	28.3362
30	13.7867	14.9535	16.7908	18.4926	20.5992	24.4776	29.3360
40	20.7065	22.1643	24.4331	26.5093	29.0505	33.6603	39.3354
50	27.9907	29.7067	32.3574	34.7642	37.6886	42.9421	49.3349
60	35.5346	37.4848	40.4817	43.1879	46.4589	52.2938	59.3347
70	43.2752	45.4418	48.7576	51.7393	55.3290	61.6983	69.3344
80	51.1720	53.5400	57.1532	60.3915	64.2778	71.1445	79.3343
90	59.1963	61.7541	65.6466	69.1260	73.2912	80.6247	89.3342
100	67.3276	70.0648	74.2219	77.9295	82.3581	90.1332	99.3341
z	−2.5758	−2.3263	−1.9600	−1.6449	−1.2816	−0.6745	0.0000

Table C.4   (continued)

df \ α	0.250	0.100	0.050	0.025	0.010	0.005	0.001
1	1.32330	2.70554	3.84146	5.02389	6.63490	7.87944	10.828
2	2.77259	4.60517	5.99147	7.37776	9.21034	10.5966	13.816
3	4.10835	6.25139	7.81473	9.34840	11.3449	12.8381	16.266
4	5.38527	7.77944	9.48773	11.1433	13.2767	14.8602	18.467
5	6.62568	9.23635	11.0705	12.8325	15.0863	16.7496	20.515
6	7.84080	10.6446	12.5916	14.4494	16.8119	18.5476	22.458
7	9.03715	12.0170	14.0671	16.0128	18.4753	20.2777	24.322
8	10.2188	13.3616	15.5073	17.5346	20.0902	21.9550	26.125
9	11.3887	14.6837	16.9190	19.0228	21.6660	23.5893	27.877
10	12.5489	15.9871	18.3070	20.4831	23.2093	25.1882	29.588
11	13.7007	17.2750	19.6751	21.9200	24.7250	26.7569	31.264
12	14.8454	18.5494	21.0261	23.3367	26.2170	28.2995	32.909
13	15.9839	19.8119	22.3621	24.7356	27.6883	29.8194	34.528
14	17.1170	21.0642	23.6848	26.1190	29.1413	31.3193	36.123
15	18.2451	22.3072	24.9958	27.4884	30.5779	32.8013	37.697
16	19.3688	23.5418	26.2962	28.8454	31.9999	34.2672	39.252
17	20.4887	24.7690	27.5871	30.1910	33.4087	35.7185	40.790
18	21.6049	25.9894	28.8693	31.5264	34.8053	37.1564	42.312
19	22.7178	27.2036	30.1435	32.8523	36.1908	38.5822	43.820
20	23.8277	28.4120	31.4104	34.1696	37.5662	39.9968	45.315
21	24.9348	29.6151	32.6705	35.4789	38.9321	41.4010	46.797
22	26.0393	30.8133	33.9244	36.7807	40.2894	42.7956	48.268
23	27.1413	32.0069	35.1725	38.0757	41.6384	44.1813	49.728
24	28.2412	33.1963	36.4151	39.3641	42.9798	45.5585	51.179
25	29.3389	34.3816	37.6525	40.6465	44.3141	46.9278	52.620
26	30.4345	35.5631	38.8852	41.9232	45.6417	48.2899	54.052
27	31.5284	36.7412	40.1133	43.1944	46.9630	49.6449	55.476
28	32.6205	37.9159	41.3372	44.4607	48.2782	50.9933	56.892
29	33.7109	39.0875	42.5569	45.7222	49.5879	52.3356	58.302
30	34.7998	40.2560	43.7729	46.9792	50.8922	53.6720	59.703
40	45.6160	51.8050	55.7585	59.3417	63.6907	66.7659	73.402
50	56.3336	63.1671	67.5048	71.4202	76.1539	79.4900	86.661
60	66.9814	74.3970	79.0819	83.2976	88.3794	91.9517	99.607
70	77.5766	85.5271	90.5312	95.0231	100.425	104.215	112.317
80	88.1303	96.5782	101.879	106.629	112.329	116.321	124.839
90	98.6499	107.565	113.145	118.136	124.116	128.299	137.208
100	109.141	118.498	124.342	129.561	135.807	140.169	149.449
z	+0.6745	+1.2816	+1.6449	+1.9600	+2.3263	+2.5758	+3.0902

For $df > 100$ take

$$\chi^2 = df\left(1 - \frac{2}{9df} + z\sqrt{\frac{2}{9df}}\right)^3 \quad \text{or} \quad \chi^2 = \frac{1}{2}\left(z + \sqrt{2df - 1}\right)^2$$

according to the degree of accuracy required. z is the standardized normal deviate corresponding to α and is shown in the bottom line of the table.

Source: Adapted from Table 8 in Pearson, E. S. and Hartley, H. O. (1958). *Biometrika Tables for Statisticians*, Vol. 1, 2nd ed. Cambridge University Press: Cambridge, with the kind permission of the trustees of *Biometrika*.

Table C.5 Upper percentage points of the F distribution

df_2	α	1	2	3	4	5	6	8	12	24	∞
1	.001	405284	500000	540379	562500	576405	585937	598144	610667	623497	636619
	.005	16211	20000	21615	22500	23056	23437	23925	24426	24940	25465
	.01	4052	4999	5403	5625	5764	5859	5981	6106	6234	6366
	.025	647.79	799.50	864.16	899.58	921.85	937.11	956.66	976.71	997.25	1018.30
	.05	161.45	199.50	215.71	224.58	230.16	233.99	238.88	243.91	249.05	254.32
	.10	39.86	49.50	53.59	55.83	57.24	58.20	59.44	60.70	62.00	63.33
	.25	5.83	7.50	8.20	8.58	8.82	8.98	9.19	9.41	9.63	9.85
2	.001	998.5	999.0	999.2	999.2	999.3	999.3	999.4	999.4	999.5	999.5
	.005	198.50	199.00	199.17	199.25	199.30	199.33	199.37	199.42	199.46	199.51
	.01	98.49	99.00	99.17	99.25	99.30	99.33	99.36	99.42	99.46	99.50
	.025	38.51	39.00	39.17	39.25	39.30	39.33	39.37	39.42	39.46	39.50
	.05	18.51	19.00	19.16	19.25	19.30	19.33	19.37	19.41	19.45	19.50
	.10	8.53	9.00	9.16	9.24	9.29	9.33	9.37	9.41	9.45	9.49
	.25	2.56	3.00	3.15	3.23	3.28	3.31	3.35	3.39	3.44	3.48
3	.001	167.5	148.5	141.1	137.1	134.6	132.8	130.6	128.3	125.9	123.5
	.005	55.55	49.80	47.47	46.20	45.39	44.84	44.13	43.39	42.62	41.83
	.01	34.12	30.81	29.46	28.71	28.24	27.91	27.49	27.05	26.60	26.12
	.025	17.44	16.04	15.44	15.10	14.89	14.74	14.54	14.34	14.12	13.90
	.05	10.13	9.55	9.28	9.12	9.01	8.94	8.84	8.74	8.64	8.53
	.10	5.54	5.46	5.39	5.34	5.31	5.28	5.25	5.22	5.18	5.13
	.25	2.02	2.28	2.36	2.39	2.41	2.42	2.44	2.45	2.46	2.47
4	.001	74.14	61.25	56.18	53.44	51.71	50.53	49.00	47.41	45.77	44.05
	.005	31.33	26.28	24.26	23.16	22.46	21.98	21.35	20.71	20.03	19.33
	.01	21.20	18.00	16.69	15.98	15.52	15.21	14.80	14.37	13.93	13.46
	.025	12.22	10.65	9.98	9.60	9.36	9.20	8.98	8.75	8.51	8.26
	.05	7.71	6.94	6.59	6.39	6.26	6.16	6.04	5.91	5.77	5.63
	.10	4.54	4.32	4.19	4.11	4.05	4.01	3.95	3.90	3.83	3.76
	.25	1.81	2.00	2.05	2.06	2.07	2.08	2.08	2.08	2.08	2.08
5	.001	47.04	36.61	33.20	31.09	29.75	28.84	27.64	26.42	25.14	23.78
	.005	22.79	18.31	16.53	15.56	14.94	14.51	13.96	13.38	12.78	12.14
	.01	16.26	13.27	12.06	11.39	10.97	10.67	10.29	9.89	9.47	9.02
	.025	10.01	8.43	7.76	7.39	7.15	6.98	6.76	6.52	6.28	6.02

	α										
6	.05	4.36	4.53	4.68	4.82	4.95	5.05	5.19	5.41	5.79	6.61
	.10	3.10	3.19	3.27	3.34	3.40	3.45	3.52	3.62	3.78	4.06
	.25	1.87	1.88	1.89	1.89	1.89	1.89	1.89	1.89	1.85	1.70
	.001	15.75	16.89	17.99	19.03	20.03	20.81	21.90	23.70	27.00	35.51
	.005	8.88	9.47	10.03	10.57	11.07	11.46	12.03	12.92	14.54	18.64
	.01	6.88	7.31	7.72	8.10	8.47	8.75	9.15	9.78	10.92	13.74
	.025	4.85	5.12	5.37	5.60	5.82	5.99	6.23	6.60	7.26	8.81
	.05	3.67	3.84	4.00	4.15	4.28	4.39	4.53	4.76	5.14	5.99
	.10	2.72	2.82	2.90	2.98	3.05	3.11	3.18	3.29	3.46	3.78
	.25	1.74	1.75	1.77	1.78	1.78	1.79	1.79	1.78	1.76	1.62
7	.001	11.69	12.73	13.71	14.63	15.52	16.21	17.19	18.77	21.69	29.22
	.005	7.08	7.65	8.18	8.68	9.16	9.52	10.05	10.88	12.40	16.24
	.01	5.65	6.07	6.47	6.84	7.19	7.46	7.85	8.45	9.55	12.25
	.025	4.14	4.42	4.67	4.90	5.12	5.29	5.52	5.89	6.54	8.07
	.05	3.23	3.41	3.57	3.73	3.87	3.97	4.12	4.35	4.74	5.59
	.10	2.47	2.58	2.67	2.75	2.83	2.88	2.96	3.07	3.26	3.59
	.25	1.65	1.67	1.68	1.70	1.71	1.71	1.72	1.72	1.70	1.57
8	.001	9.34	10.30	11.19	12.04	12.86	13.49	14.39	15.83	18.49	25.42
	.005	5.95	6.50	7.01	7.50	7.95	8.30	8.81	9.60	11.04	14.69
	.01	4.86	5.28	5.67	6.03	6.37	6.63	7.01	7.59	8.65	11.26
	.025	3.67	3.95	4.20	4.43	4.65	4.82	5.05	5.42	6.06	7.57
	.05	2.93	3.12	3.28	3.44	3.58	3.69	3.84	4.07	4.46	5.32
	.10	2.29	2.40	2.50	2.59	2.67	2.73	2.81	2.92	3.11	3.46
	.25	1.58	1.60	1.62	1.64	1.65	1.66	1.66	1.67	1.66	1.54
9	.001	7.81	8.72	9.57	10.37	11.13	11.71	12.56	13.90	16.39	22.86
	.005	5.19	5.73	6.23	6.69	7.13	7.47	7.96	8.72	10.11	13.61
	.01	4.31	4.73	5.11	5.47	5.80	6.06	6.42	6.99	8.02	10.56
	.025	3.33	3.61	3.87	4.10	4.32	4.48	4.72	5.08	5.71	7.21
	.05	2.71	2.90	3.07	3.23	3.37	3.48	3.63	3.86	4.26	5.12
	.10	2.16	2.28	2.38	2.47	2.55	2.61	2.69	2.81	3.01	3.36
	.25	1.53	1.56	1.58	1.60	1.61	1.62	1.63	1.63	1.62	1.51
10	.001	6.76	7.64	8.45	9.20	9.92	10.48	11.28	12.55	14.91	21.04
	.005	4.64	5.17	5.66	6.12	6.54	6.87	7.34	8.08	9.43	12.83
	.01	3.91	4.33	4.71	5.06	5.39	5.64	5.99	6.55	7.56	10.04
	.025	3.08	3.37	3.62	3.85	4.07	4.24	4.47	4.83	5.46	6.94
	.05	2.54	2.74	2.91	3.07	3.22	3.33	3.48	3.71	4.10	4.96

Table C.5 (continued)

df_2	df_1 α	1	2	3	4	5	6	8	12	24	∞
	.10	3.28	2.92	2.73	2.61	2.52	2.46	2.38	2.28	2.18	2.06
	.25	1.49	1.60	1.60	1.60	1.59	1.58	1.56	1.54	1.52	1.48
11	.001	19.69	13.81	11.56	10.35	9.58	9.05	8.35	7.63	6.85	6.00
	.005	12.23	8.91	7.60	6.88	6.42	6.10	5.68	5.24	4.76	4.23
	.01	9.65	7.20	6.22	5.67	5.32	5.07	4.74	4.40	4.02	3.60
	.025	6.72	5.26	4.63	4.28	4.04	3.88	3.66	3.43	3.17	2.88
	.05	4.84	3.98	3.59	3.36	3.20	3.09	2.95	2.79	2.61	2.40
	.10	3.23	2.86	2.66	2.54	2.45	2.39	2.30	2.21	2.10	1.97
	.25	1.46	1.58	1.58	1.58	1.56	1.55	1.54	1.51	1.49	1.45
12	.001	18.64	12.97	10.80	9.63	8.89	8.38	7.71	7.00	6.25	5.42
	.005	11.75	8.51	7.23	6.52	6.07	5.76	5.35	4.91	4.43	3.90
	.01	9.33	6.93	5.95	5.41	5.06	4.82	4.50	4.16	3.78	3.36
	.025	6.55	5.10	4.47	4.12	3.89	3.73	3.51	3.28	3.02	2.72
	.05	4.75	3.88	3.49	3.26	3.11	3.00	2.85	2.69	2.50	2.30
	.10	3.18	2.81	2.61	2.48	2.39	2.33	2.24	2.15	2.04	1.90
	.25	1.46	1.56	1.56	1.55	1.54	1.53	1.51	1.49	1.46	1.42
13	.001	17.81	12.31	10.21	9.07	8.35	7.86	7.21	6.52	5.78	4.97
	.005	11.37	8.19	6.93	6.23	5.79	5.48	5.08	4.64	4.17	3.65
	.01	9.07	6.70	5.74	5.20	4.86	4.62	4.30	3.96	3.59	3.16
	.025	6.41	4.97	4.35	4.00	3.77	3.60	3.39	3.15	2.89	2.60
	.05	4.67	3.80	3.41	3.18	3.02	2.92	2.77	2.60	2.42	2.21
	.10	3.14	2.76	2.56	2.43	2.35	2.28	2.20	2.10	1.98	1.85
	.25	1.45	1.55	1.55	1.53	1.52	1.51	1.49	1.47	1.44	1.40
14	.001	17.14	11.78	9.73	8.62	7.92	7.43	6.80	6.13	5.41	4.60
	.005	11.06	7.92	6.68	6.00	5.56	5.26	4.86	4.43	3.96	3.44
	.01	8.86	6.51	5.56	5.03	4.69	4.46	4.14	3.80	3.43	3.00
	.025	6.30	4.86	4.24	3.89	3.66	3.50	3.29	3.05	2.79	2.49
	.05	4.60	3.74	3.34	3.11	2.96	2.85	2.70	2.53	2.35	2.13
	.10	3.10	2.73	2.52	2.39	2.31	2.24	2.15	2.05	1.94	1.80
	.25	1.44	1.53	1.53	1.52	1.51	1.50	1.48	1.45	1.42	1.38
15	.001	16.59	11.34	9.34	8.25	7.57	7.09	6.47	5.81	5.10	4.31
	.005	10.80	7.70	6.48	5.80	5.37	5.07	4.67	4.25	3.79	3.26

df	p										
16	.01	8.68	6.36	5.42	4.89	4.56	4.32	4.00	3.67	3.29	2.87
	.025	6.20	4.77	4.15	3.80	3.58	3.41	3.20	2.96	2.70	2.40
	.05	4.54	3.68	3.29	3.06	2.90	2.79	2.64	2.48	2.29	2.07
	.10	3.07	2.70	2.49	2.36	2.27	2.21	2.12	2.02	1.90	1.76
	.25	1.43	1.52	1.52	1.51	1.49	1.48	1.46	1.44	1.41	1.36
17	.001	16.12	10.97	9.00	7.94	7.27	6.81	6.19	5.55	4.85	4.06
	.005	10.58	7.51	6.30	5.64	5.21	4.91	4.52	4.10	3.64	3.11
	.01	8.53	6.23	5.29	4.77	4.44	4.20	3.89	3.55	3.18	2.75
	.025	6.12	4.69	4.08	3.73	3.50	3.34	3.12	2.89	2.63	2.32
	.05	4.49	3.63	3.24	3.01	2.85	2.74	2.59	2.42	2.24	2.01
	.10	3.05	2.67	2.46	2.33	2.24	2.18	2.09	1.99	1.87	1.72
	.25	1.42	1.51	1.51	1.50	1.48	1.47	1.45	1.43	1.39	1.34
18	.001	15.72	10.66	8.73	7.68	7.02	6.56	5.96	5.32	4.63	3.85
	.005	10.38	7.35	6.16	5.50	5.07	4.78	4.39	3.97	3.51	2.98
	.01	8.40	6.11	5.18	4.67	4.34	4.10	3.79	3.45	3.08	2.65
	.025	6.04	4.62	4.01	3.66	3.44	3.28	3.06	2.82	2.56	2.25
	.05	4.45	3.59	3.20	2.96	2.81	2.70	2.55	2.38	2.19	1.96
	.10	3.03	2.64	2.44	2.31	2.22	2.15	2.06	1.96	1.84	1.69
	.25	1.42	1.51	1.51	1.49	1.47	1.46	1.44	1.41	1.38	1.33
19	.001	15.38	10.39	8.49	7.46	6.81	6.35	5.76	5.13	4.45	3.67
	.005	10.22	7.21	6.03	5.37	4.96	4.66	4.28	3.86	3.40	2.87
	.01	8.28	6.01	5.09	4.58	4.25	4.01	3.71	3.37	3.00	2.57
	.025	5.98	4.56	3.95	3.61	3.38	3.22	3.01	2.77	2.50	2.19
	.05	4.41	3.55	3.16	2.93	2.77	2.66	2.51	2.34	2.15	1.92
	.10	3.01	2.62	2.42	2.29	2.20	2.13	2.04	1.93	1.81	1.66
	.25	1.41	1.50	1.49	1.48	1.46	1.45	1.43	1.40	1.37	1.32
20	.001	15.08	10.16	8.28	7.26	6.61	6.18	5.59	4.97	4.29	3.52
	.005	10.07	7.09	5.92	5.27	4.85	4.56	4.18	3.76	3.31	2.78
	.01	8.18	5.93	5.01	4.50	4.17	3.94	3.63	3.30	2.92	2.49
	.025	5.92	4.51	3.90	3.56	3.33	3.17	2.96	2.72	2.45	2.13
	.05	4.38	3.52	3.13	2.90	2.74	2.63	2.48	2.31	2.11	1.88
	.10	2.99	2.61	2.40	2.27	2.18	2.11	2.02	1.91	1.79	1.63
	.25	1.41	1.50	1.49	1.48	1.46	1.44	1.42	1.40	1.36	1.31
	.001	14.82	9.95	8.10	7.10	6.46	6.02	5.44	4.82	4.15	3.38
	.005	9.94	6.99	5.82	5.17	4.76	4.47	4.09	3.68	3.22	2.69
	.01	8.10	5.85	4.94	4.43	4.10	3.87	3.56	3.23	2.86	2.42

Table C.5 (continued)

df_2	α	df_1 1	2	3	4	5	6	8	12	24	∞
	.025	5.87	4.46	3.86	3.51	3.29	3.13	2.91	2.68	2.41	2.09
	.05	4.35	3.49	3.10	2.87	2.71	2.60	2.45	2.28	2.08	1.84
	.10	2.97	2.59	2.38	2.25	2.16	2.09	2.00	1.89	1.77	1.61
	.25	1.40	1.49	1.48	1.47	1.45	1.44	1.42	1.39	1.35	1.29
21	.001	14.59	9.77	7.94	6.95	6.32	5.88	5.31	4.70	4.03	3.26
	.005	9.83	6.89	5.73	5.09	4.68	4.39	4.01	3.60	3.15	2.61
	.01	8.02	5.78	4.87	4.37	4.04	3.81	3.51	3.17	2.80	2.36
	.025	5.83	4.42	3.82	3.48	3.25	3.09	2.87	2.64	2.37	2.04
	.05	4.32	3.47	3.07	2.84	2.68	2.57	2.42	2.25	2.05	1.81
	.10	2.96	2.57	2.36	2.23	2.14	2.08	1.98	1.88	1.75	1.59
	.25	1.40	1.49	1.48	1.46	1.44	1.43	1.41	1.37	1.34	1.29
22	.001	14.38	9.61	7.80	6.81	6.19	5.76	5.19	4.58	3.92	3.15
	.005	9.73	6.81	5.65	5.02	4.61	4.32	3.94	3.54	3.08	2.55
	.01	7.94	5.72	4.82	4.31	3.99	3.76	3.45	3.12	2.75	2.31
	.025	5.79	4.38	3.78	3.44	3.22	3.05	2.84	2.60	2.33	2.00
	.05	4.30	3.44	3.05	2.82	2.66	2.55	2.40	2.23	2.03	1.78
	.10	2.95	2.56	2.35	2.22	2.13	2.06	1.97	1.86	1.73	1.57
	.25	1.40	1.48	1.47	1.46	1.44	1.42	1.40	1.37	1.33	1.28
23	.001	14.19	9.47	7.67	6.69	6.08	5.65	5.09	4.48	3.82	3.05
	.005	9.63	6.73	5.58	4.95	4.54	4.26	3.88	3.47	3.02	2.48
	.01	7.88	5.66	4.76	4.26	3.94	3.71	3.41	3.07	2.70	2.26
	.025	5.75	4.35	3.75	3.41	3.18	3.02	2.81	2.57	2.30	1.97
	.05	4.28	3.42	3.03	2.80	2.64	2.53	2.38	2.20	2.00	1.76
	.10	2.94	2.55	2.34	2.21	2.11	2.05	1.95	1.84	1.72	1.55
	.25	1.39	1.47	1.47	1.45	1.43	1.41	1.40	1.37	1.33	1.27
24	.001	14.03	9.34	7.55	6.59	5.98	5.55	4.99	4.39	3.74	2.97
	.005	9.55	6.66	5.52	4.89	4.49	4.20	3.83	3.42	2.97	2.43
	.01	7.82	5.61	4.72	4.22	3.90	3.67	3.36	3.03	2.66	2.21
	.025	5.72	4.32	3.72	3.38	3.15	2.99	2.78	2.54	2.27	1.94
	.05	4.26	3.40	3.01	2.78	2.62	2.51	2.36	2.18	1.98	1.73
	.10	2.93	2.54	2.33	2.19	2.10	2.04	1.94	1.83	1.70	1.53
	.25	1.39	1.47	1.46	1.44	1.43	1.41	1.39	1.36	1.32	1.26

df	p										
25	.001	13.88	9.22	7.45	6.49	5.88	5.46	4.91	4.31	3.66	2.89
	.005	9.48	6.60	5.46	4.84	4.43	4.15	3.78	3.37	2.92	2.38
	.01	7.77	5.57	4.68	4.18	3.86	3.63	3.32	2.99	2.62	2.17
	.025	5.69	4.29	3.69	3.35	3.13	2.97	2.75	2.51	2.24	1.91
	.05	4.24	3.38	2.99	2.76	2.60	2.49	2.34	2.16	1.96	1.71
	.10	2.92	2.53	2.32	2.18	2.09	2.02	1.93	1.82	1.69	1.52
	.25	1.39	1.47	1.46	1.44	1.42	1.41	1.39	1.36	1.32	1.25
26	.001	13.74	9.12	7.36	6.41	5.80	5.38	4.83	4.24	3.59	2.82
	.005	9.41	6.54	5.41	4.79	4.38	4.10	3.73	3.33	2.87	2.33
	.01	7.72	5.53	4.64	4.14	3.82	3.59	3.29	2.96	2.58	2.13
	.025	5.66	4.27	3.67	3.33	3.10	2.94	2.73	2.49	2.22	1.88
	.05	4.22	3.37	2.98	2.74	2.59	2.47	2.32	2.15	1.95	1.69
	.10	2.91	2.52	2.31	2.17	2.08	2.01	1.92	1.81	1.68	1.50
	.25	1.38	1.46	1.45	1.44	1.42	1.41	1.38	1.35	1.31	1.25
27	.001	13.61	9.02	7.27	6.33	5.73	5.31	4.76	4.17	3.52	2.75
	.005	9.34	6.49	5.36	4.74	4.34	4.06	3.69	3.28	2.83	2.29
	.01	7.68	5.49	4.60	4.11	3.78	3.56	3.26	2.93	2.55	2.10
	.025	5.63	4.24	3.65	3.31	3.08	2.92	2.71	2.47	2.19	1.85
	.05	4.21	3.35	2.96	2.73	2.57	2.46	2.30	2.13	1.93	1.67
	.10	2.90	2.51	2.30	2.17	2.07	2.00	1.91	1.80	1.67	1.49
	.25	1.38	1.46	1.45	1.43	1.42	1.40	1.38	1.35	1.31	1.24
28	.001	13.50	8.93	7.19	6.25	5.66	5.24	4.69	4.11	3.46	2.70
	.005	9.28	6.44	5.32	4.70	4.30	4.02	3.65	3.25	2.79	2.25
	.01	7.64	5.45	4.57	4.07	3.75	3.53	3.23	2.90	2.52	2.06
	.025	5.61	4.22	3.63	3.29	3.06	2.90	2.69	2.45	2.17	1.83
	.05	4.20	3.34	2.95	2.71	2.56	2.44	2.29	2.12	1.91	1.65
	.10	2.89	2.50	2.30	2.16	2.06	2.00	1.90	1.79	1.66	1.48
	.25	1.38	1.46	1.45	1.43	1.41	1.40	1.38	1.34	1.30	1.24
29	.001	13.39	8.85	7.12	6.49	5.59	5.18	4.64	4.05	3.41	2.64
	.005	9.23	6.40	5.28	4.66	4.26	3.98	3.61	3.21	2.76	2.21
	.01	7.60	5.42	4.54	4.04	3.73	3.50	3.20	2.87	2.49	2.03
	.025	5.59	4.20	3.61	3.27	3.04	2.88	2.67	2.43	2.15	1.81
	.05	4.18	3.33	2.93	2.70	2.54	2.43	2.28	2.10	1.90	1.64
	.10	2.89	2.50	2.28	2.15	2.06	1.99	1.89	1.78	1.65	1.47
	.25	1.38	1.45	1.45	1.43	1.41	1.40	1.37	1.34	1.30	1.23

Table C.5 (continued)

df_2	α	1	2	3	4	5	6	8	12	24	∞
30	.005	9.18	6.35	5.24	4.62	4.23	3.95	3.58	3.18	2.73	2.18
	.001	13.29	8.77	7.05	6.12	5.53	5.12	4.58	4.00	3.36	2.59
	.01	7.56	5.39	4.51	4.02	3.70	3.47	3.17	2.84	2.47	2.01
	.025	5.57	4.18	3.59	3.25	3.03	2.87	2.65	2.41	2.14	1.79
	.05	4.17	3.32	2.92	2.69	2.53	2.42	2.27	2.09	1.89	1.62
	.10	2.88	2.49	2.28	2.14	2.05	1.98	1.88	1.77	1.64	1.46
	.25	1.38	1.45	1.44	1.42	1.41	1.39	1.37	1.34	1.29	1.23
40	.001	12.61	8.25	6.60	5.70	5.13	4.73	4.21	3.64	3.01	2.23
	.005	8.83	6.07	4.98	4.37	3.99	3.71	3.35	2.95	2.50	1.93
	.01	7.31	5.18	4.31	3.83	3.51	3.29	2.99	2.66	2.29	1.80
	.025	5.42	4.05	3.46	3.13	2.90	2.74	2.53	2.29	2.01	1.64
	.05	4.08	3.23	2.84	2.61	2.45	2.34	2.18	2.00	1.79	1.51
	.10	2.84	2.44	2.23	2.09	2.00	1.93	1.83	1.71	1.57	1.38
	.25	1.36	1.44	1.42	1.41	1.39	1.37	1.35	1.31	1.27	1.19
60	.001	11.97	7.76	6.17	5.31	4.76	4.37	3.87	3.31	2.69	1.90
	.005	8.49	5.80	4.73	4.14	3.76	3.49	3.13	2.74	2.29	1.69
	.01	7.08	4.98	4.13	3.65	3.34	3.12	2.82	2.50	2.12	1.60
	.025	5.29	3.93	3.34	3.01	2.79	2.63	2.41	2.17	1.88	1.48
	.05	4.00	3.15	2.76	2.52	2.37	2.25	2.10	1.92	1.70	1.39
	.10	2.79	2.39	2.18	2.04	1.95	1.87	1.77	1.66	1.51	1.29
	.25	1.35	1.42	1.41	1.39	1.37	1.35	1.32	1.29	1.24	1.15
120	.001	11.38	7.31	5.79	4.95	4.42	4.04	3.55	3.02	2.40	1.56
	.005	8.18	5.54	4.50	3.92	3.55	3.28	2.93	2.54	2.09	1.43
	.01	6.85	4.79	3.95	3.48	3.17	2.96	2.66	2.34	1.95	1.38
	.025	5.15	3.80	3.23	2.89	2.67	2.52	2.30	2.05	1.76	1.31
	.05	3.92	3.07	2.68	2.45	2.29	2.17	2.02	1.83	1.61	1.25
	.10	2.75	2.35	2.13	1.99	1.90	1.82	1.72	1.60	1.45	1.19
	.25	1.34	1.40	1.39	1.37	1.35	1.33	1.30	1.26	1.21	1.10
∞	.001	10.83	6.91	5.42	4.62	4.10	3.74	3.27	2.74	2.13	1.00
	.005	7.88	5.30	4.28	3.72	3.35	3.09	2.74	2.36	1.90	1.00
	.01	6.64	4.60	3.78	3.32	3.02	2.80	2.51	2.18	1.79	1.00

.025	5.02	3.69	3.12	2.79	2.57	2.41	2.19	1.94	1.64	1.00
.05	3.84	2.99	2.60	2.37	2.21	2.09	1.94	1.75	1.52	1.00
.10	2.71	2.30	2.08	1.94	1.85	1.77	1.67	1.55	1.38	1.00
.25	1.32	1.39	1.37	1.35	1.33	1.31	1.28	1.24	1.18	1.00

Source: Adapted from Table 18 in Pearson, E. S. and Hartley, H. O. (1958). *Biometrika Tables for Statisticians*, Vol. 1, 2nd ed. Cambridge University Press: Cambridge, with the kind permission of the trustees of *Biometrika*.

Table C.6 Coefficients of orthogonal polynomials

k	Polynomial	X=1	2	3	4	5	6	7	8	9	10	Σξ'²	λ
3	Linear	-1	0	1								2	1
	Quadratic	1	-2	1								6	3
4	Linear	-3	-1	1	3							20	2
	Quadratic	1	-1	-1	1							4	1
	Cubic	-1	3	-3	1							20	10/3
5	Linear	-2	-1	0	1	2						10	1
	Quadratic	2	-1	-2	-1	2						14	1
	Cubic	-1	2	0	-2	1						10	5/6
	Quartic	1	-4	6	-4	1						70	35/12
6	Linear	-5	-3	-1	1	3	5					70	2
	Quadratic	5	-1	-4	-4	-1	5					84	3/2
	Cubic	-5	7	4	-4	-7	5					180	5/3
	Quartic	1	-3	2	2	-3	1					28	7/12
7	Linear	-3	-2	-1	0	1	2	3				28	1
	Quadratic	5	0	-3	-4	-3	0	5				84	1
	Cubic	-1	1	1	0	-1	-1	1				6	1/6
	Quartic	3	-7	1	6	1	-7	3				154	7/12
8	Linear	-7	-5	-3	-1	1	3	5	7			168	2
	Quadratic	7	1	-3	-5	-5	-3	1	7			168	1
	Cubic	-7	5	7	3	-3	-7	-5	7			264	2/3
	Quartic	7	-13	-3	9	9	-3	-13	7			616	7/12
	Quintic	-7	23	-17	-15	15	17	-23	7			2184	7/10
9	Linear	-4	-3	-2	-1	0	1	2	3	4		60	1
	Quadratic	28	7	-8	-17	-20	-17	-8	7	28		2772	3
	Cubic	-14	7	13	9	0	-9	-13	-7	14		990	5/6
	Quartic	14	-21	-11	9	18	9	-11	-21	14		2002	7/12
	Quintic	-4	11	-4	-9	0	9	4	-11	4		468	3/20
10	Linear	-9	-7	-5	-3	-1	1	3	5	7	9	330	2
	Quadratic	6	2	-1	-3	-4	-4	-3	-1	2	6	132	1/2
	Cubic	-42	14	35	31	12	-12	-31	-35	-14	42	8580	5/3
	Quartic	18	-22	-17	3	18	18	3	-17	-22	18	2860	5/12
	Quintic	-6	14	-1	-11	-6	6	11	1	-14	18	780	1/10

Source: Adapted from Table 47 in Pearson, E. S. and Hartley. H. O. (1958). *Biometrika Tables for Statisticians*, Vol. 1, 2nd ed. Cambridge University Press: Cambridge, with the kind permission of the trustees of *Biometrika*.

Table C.7   Critical values of the Bonferroni *t* statistic (note that the tabled values are two-tailed)

df	FWE	Number of contrasts (K)									
		2	3	4	5	6	7	8	9	10	15
3	.01	7.453	8.575	9.465	10.215	10.869	11.453	11.984	12.471	12.924	14.819
	.05	4.177	4.857	5.392	5.841	6.232	6.580	6.895	7.185	7.453	8.575
	.10	3.182	3.740	4.177	4.541	4.857	5.138	5.392	5.625	5.841	6.741
4	.01	5.598	6.254	6.758	7.173	7.529	7.841	8.122	8.376	8.610	9.568
	.05	3.495	3.961	4.315	4.604	4.851	5.068	5.261	5.437	5.598	6.254
	.10	2.776	3.186	3.495	3.747	3.961	4.148	4.315	4.466	4.604	5.167
5	.01	4.773	5.247	5.604	5.893	6.138	6.352	6.541	6.713	6.869	7.499
	.05	3.163	3.534	3.810	4.032	4.219	4.382	4.526	4.655	4.773	5.247
	.10	2.571	2.912	3.163	3.365	3.534	3.681	3.810	3.926	4.032	4.456
6	.01	4.317	4.698	4.981	5.208	5.398	5.563	5.709	5.840	5.959	6.434
	.05	2.969	3.287	3.521	3.707	3.863	3.997	4.115	4.221	4.317	4.698
	.10	2.447	2.749	2.969	3.143	3.287	3.412	3.521	3.619	3.707	4.058
7	.01	4.029	4.355	4.595	4.785	4.944	5.082	5.202	5.310	5.408	5.795
	.05	2.841	3.128	3.335	3.499	3.636	3.753	3.855	3.947	4.029	4.355
	.10	2.365	2.642	2.841	2.998	3.128	3.238	3.335	3.422	3.499	3.806
8	.01	3.833	4.122	4.334	4.501	4.640	4.759	4.864	4.957	5.041	5.374
	.05	2.752	3.016	3.206	3.355	3.479	3.584	3.677	3.759	3.833	4.122
	.10	2.306	2.566	2.752	2.896	3.016	3.117	3.206	3.285	3.355	3.632
9	.01	3.690	3.954	4.146	4.297	4.422	4.529	4.622	4.706	4.781	5.076
	.05	2.685	2.933	3.111	3.250	3.364	3.462	3.547	3.622	3.690	3.954
	.10	2.262	2.510	2.685	2.821	2.933	3.028	3.111	3.184	3.250	3.505
10	.01	3.581	3.827	4.005	4.144	4.259	4.357	4.442	4.518	4.587	4.855
	.05	2.634	2.870	3.038	3.169	3.277	3.368	3.448	3.518	3.581	3.827
	.10	2.228	2.466	2.634	2.764	2.870	2.960	3.038	3.107	3.169	3.409
11	.01	3.497	3.728	3.895	4.025	4.132	4.223	4.303	4.373	4.437	4.685
	.05	2.593	2.820	2.981	3.106	3.208	3.295	3.370	3.437	3.497	3.728
	.10	2.201	2.431	2.593	2.718	2.820	2.906	2.981	3.047	3.106	3.334
12	.01	3.428	3.649	3.807	3.930	4.031	4.117	4.192	4.258	4.318	4.550
	.05	2.560	2.779	2.934	3.055	3.153	3.236	3.308	3.371	3.428	3.649
	.10	2.179	2.403	2.560	2.681	2.779	2.863	2.934	2.998	3.055	3.273
13	.01	3.372	3.584	3.735	3.852	3.948	4.030	4.101	4.164	4.221	4.440
	.05	2.533	2.746	2.896	3.012	3.107	3.187	3.256	3.318	3.372	3.584
	.10	2.160	2.380	2.533	2.650	2.746	2.827	2.896	2.957	3.012	3.223
14	.01	3.326	3.530	3.675	3.787	3.880	3.958	4.026	4.086	4.140	4.349
	.05	2.510	2.718	2.864	2.977	3.069	3.146	3.214	3.273	3.326	3.530
	.10	2.145	2.360	2.510	2.624	2.718	2.796	2.864	2.924	2.977	3.181
15	.01	3.286	3.484	3.624	3.733	3.822	3.897	3.963	4.021	4.073	4.273
	.05	2.490	2.694	2.837	2.947	3.036	3.112	3.177	3.235	3.286	3.484
	.10	2.131	2.343	2.490	2.602	2.694	2.770	2.837	2.895	2.947	3.146
16	.01	3.252	3.444	3.581	3.686	3.773	3.846	3.909	3.965	4.015	4.208
	.05	2.473	2.673	2.813	2.921	3.008	3.082	3.146	3.202	3.252	3.444
	.10	2.120	2.328	2.473	2.583	2.673	2.748	2.813	2.870	2.921	3.115
17	.01	3.222	3.410	3.543	3.646	3.730	3.801	3.862	3.917	3.965	4.152
	.05	2.458	2.655	2.793	2.898	2.984	3.056	3.119	3.173	3.222	3.410
	.10	2.110	2.316	2.458	2.567	2.655	2.729	2.793	2.848	2.898	3.089

Table C.7 (continued)

| df | FWE | \multicolumn{10}{c}{Number of contrasts (K)} |
		2	3	4	5	6	7	8	9	10	15
18	.01	3.197	3.380	3.510	3.610	3.692	3.762	3.822	3.874	3.922	4.104
	.05	2.445	2.639	2.775	2.878	2.963	3.034	3.095	3.149	3.197	3.380
	.10	2.101	2.304	2.445	2.552	2.639	2.712	2.775	2.829	2.878	3.065
19	.01	3.174	3.354	3.481	3.579	3.660	3.727	3.786	3.837	3.883	4.061
	.05	2.433	2.625	2.759	2.861	2.944	3.014	3.074	3.127	3.174	3.354
	.10	2.093	2.294	2.433	2.539	2.625	2.697	2.759	2.813	2.861	3.045
20	.01	3.153	3.331	3.455	3.552	3.630	3.697	3.754	3.804	3.850	4.023
	.05	2.423	2.613	2.744	2.845	2.927	2.996	3.055	3.107	3.153	3.331
	.10	2.086	2.285	2.423	2.528	2.613	2.683	2.744	2.798	2.845	3.026
25	.01	3.078	3.244	3.361	3.450	3.523	3.584	3.637	3.684	3.725	3.884
	.05	2.385	2.566	2.692	2.787	2.865	2.930	2.986	3.035	3.078	3.244
	.10	2.060	2.252	2.385	2.485	2.566	2.634	2.692	2.742	2.787	2.959
30	.01	3.030	3.189	3.300	3.385	3.454	3.513	3.563	3.607	3.646	3.796
	.05	2.360	2.536	2.657	2.750	2.825	2.887	2.941	2.988	3.030	3.189
	.10	2.042	2.231	2.360	2.457	2.536	2.601	2.657	2.706	2.750	2.915
35	.01	2.996	3.150	3.258	3.340	3.407	3.463	3.511	3.553	3.591	3.735
	.05	2.342	2.515	2.633	2.724	2.797	2.857	2.910	2.955	2.996	3.150
	.10	2.030	2.215	2.342	2.438	2.515	2.579	2.633	2.681	2.724	2.885
40	.01	2.971	3.122	3.227	3.307	3.372	3.426	3.473	3.514	3.551	3.691
	.05	2.329	2.499	2.616	2.704	2.776	2.836	2.887	2.931	2.971	3.122
	.10	2.021	2.204	2.329	2.423	2.499	2.562	2.616	2.663	2.704	2.862
60	.01	2.915	3.057	3.156	3.232	3.293	3.344	3.388	3.426	3.460	3.590
	.05	2.299	2.463	2.575	2.660	2.729	2.785	2.834	2.877	2.915	3.057
	.10	2.000	2.178	2.299	2.390	2.463	2.524	2.575	2.620	2.660	2.811
120	.01	2.860	2.995	3.088	3.160	3.217	3.265	3.306	3.342	3.373	3.494
	.05	2.270	2.428	2.536	2.617	2.683	2.737	2.783	2.824	2.860	2.995
	.10	1.980	2.153	2.270	2.358	2.428	2.486	2.536	2.579	2.617	2.761

TABLE C.8 Distribution of Dunnett's *d* statistic for comparing treatment means with a control (note that the tabled values are two-tailed)

df for MS$_{error}$	FWE	\multicolumn{9}{c}{Number of means (including control)}								
		2	3	4	5	6	7	8	9	10
	.10	1.94	2.34	2.56	2.71	2.83	2.92	3.00	3.07	3.12
	.05	2.45	2.86	3.18	3.41	3.60	3.75	3.88	4.00	4.11
6	.02	3.14	3.61	3.88	4.07	4.21	4.33	4.43	4.51	4.59
	.01	3.71	4.22	4.60	4.88	5.11	5.30	5.47	5.61	5.74
	.10	1.89	2.27	2.48	2.62	2.73	2.82	2.89	2.95	3.01
	.05	2.36	2.75	3.04	3.24	3.41	3.54	3.66	3.76	3.86
7	.02	3.00	3.42	3.66	3.83	3.96	4.07	4.15	4.23	4.30
	.01	3.50	3.95	4.28	4.52	4.17	4.87	5.01	5.13	5.24
	.10	1.86	2.22	2.42	2.55	2.66	2.74	2.81	2.87	2.92
	.05	2.31	2.67	2.94	3.13	3.28	3.40	3.51	3.60	3.68
8	.02	2.90	3.29	3.51	3.67	3.79	3.88	3.96	4.03	4.09
	.01	3.36	3.77	4.06	4.27	4.44	4.58	4.70	4.81	4.90
	.10	1.83	2.18	2.37	2.50	2.60	2.68	2.75	2.81	2.86
	.05	2.26	2.61	2.86	3.04	3.18	3.29	3.39	3.48	3.55
9	.02	2.82	3.19	3.40	3.55	3.66	3.75	3.82	3.89	3.94
	.01	3.25	3.63	3.90	4.09	4.24	4.37	4.48	4.57	4.65
	.10	1.81	2.15	2.34	2.47	2.56	2.64	2.70	2.76	2.81
	.05	2.23	2.57	2.81	2.97	3.11	3.21	3.31	3.39	3.46
10	.02	2.76	3.11	3.31	3.45	3.56	3.64	3.71	3.78	3.83
	.01	3.17	3.53	3.78	3.95	4.10	4.21	4.31	4.40	4.47
	.10	1.80	2.13	2.31	2.44	2.53	2.60	2.67	2.72	2.77
	.05	2.20	2.53	2.76	2.92	3.05	3.15	3.24	3.31	3.38
11	.02	2.72	3.06	3.25	3.38	3.48	3.56	3.63	3.69	3.74
	.01	3.11	3.45	3.68	3.85	3.98	4.09	4.18	4.26	4.33
	.10	1.78	2.11	2.29	2.41	2.50	2.58	2.64	2.69	2.74
	.05	2.18	2.50	2.72	2.88	3.00	3.10	3.18	3.25	3.32
12	.02	2.68	3.01	3.19	3.32	3.42	3.50	3.56	3.62	3.67
	.01	3.05	3.39	3.61	3.76	3.89	3.99	4.08	4.15	4.22
	.10	1.77	2.09	2.27	2.39	2.48	2.55	2.61	2.66	2.71
	.05	2.16	2.48	2.69	2.84	2.96	3.06	3.14	3.21	3.27
13	.02	2.65	2.97	3.15	3.27	3.37	3.44	3.51	3.56	3.61
	.01	3.01	3.33	3.54	3.69	3.81	3.91	3.99	4.06	4.13
	.10	1.76	2.08	2.25	2.37	2.46	2.53	2.59	2.64	2.69
	.05	2.14	2.46	2.67	2.81	2.93	3.02	3.10	3.17	3.23
14	.02	2.62	2.94	3.11	3.23	3.32	3.40	3.46	3.51	3.56
	.01	2.98	3.29	3.49	3.64	3.75	3.84	3.92	3.99	4.05
	.10	1.75	2.06	2.23	2.34	2.43	2.50	2.56	2.61	2.65
	.05	2.12	2.42	2.63	2.77	2.88	2.96	3.04	3.10	3.16
16	.02	2.58	2.88	3.05	3.17	3.26	3.33	3.39	3.44	3.48
	.01	2.92	3.22	3.41	3.55	3.65	3.74	3.82	3.88	3.93
	.10	1.73	2.04	2.21	2.32	2.41	2.48	2.53	2.58	2.62
	.05	2.10	2.40	2.59	2.73	2.84	2.92	2.99	3.05	3.11
18	.02	2.55	2.84	3.01	3.12	3.21	3.27	3.33	3.38	3.42
	.01	2.88	3.17	3.35	3.48	3.58	3.67	3.74	3.80	3.85
	.10	1.72	2.03	2.19	2.30	2.39	2.46	2.51	2.56	2.60

TABLE C.8 (continued)

df for MS$_{error}$	FWE	Number of means (including control)								
		2	3	4	5	6	7	8	9	10
20	.05	2.09	2.38	2.57	2.70	2.81	2.89	2.96	3.02	3.07
	.02	2.53	2.81	2.97	3.08	3.17	3.23	3.29	3.34	3.38
	.01	2.85	3.13	3.31	3.43	3.53	3.61	3.67	3.73	3.78
24	.10	1.71	2.01	2.17	2.28	2.36	2.43	2.48	2.53	2.57
	.05	2.06	2.35	2.53	2.66	2.76	2.84	2.91	2.96	3.01
	.02	2.49	2.77	2.92	3.03	3.11	3.17	3.22	3.27	3.31
	.01	2.80	3.07	3.24	3.36	3.45	3.52	3.58	3.64	3.69
30	.10	1.70	1.99	2.15	2.25	2.33	2.40	2.45	2.50	2.54
	.05	2.04	2.32	2.50	2.62	2.72	2.79	2.86	2.91	2.96
	.02	2.46	2.72	2.87	2.97	3.05	3.11	3.16	3.21	3.24
	.01	2.75	3.01	3.17	3.28	3.37	3.44	3.50	3.55	3.59
40	.10	1.68	1.97	2.13	2.23	2.31	2.37	2.42	2.47	2.51
	.05	2.02	2.29	2.47	2.58	2.67	2.75	2.81	2.86	2.90
	.02	2.42	2.68	2.82	2.92	2.99	3.05	3.10	3.14	3.18
	.01	2.70	2.95	3.10	3.21	3.29	3.36	3.41	3.46	3.50
60	.10	1.67	1.95	2.10	2.21	2.28	2.35	2.39	2.44	2.48
	.05	2.00	2.27	2.43	2.55	2.63	2.70	2.76	2.81	2.85
	.02	2.39	2.64	2.78	2.87	2.94	3.00	3.04	3.08	3.12
	.01	2.66	2.90	3.04	3.14	3.22	3.28	3.33	3.38	3.42
120	.10	1.66	1.93	2.08	2.18	2.26	2.32	2.37	2.41	2.45
	.05	1.98	2.24	2.40	2.51	2.59	2.66	2.71	2.76	2.80
	.02	2.36	2.60	2.73	2.82	2.89	2.94	2.99	3.03	3.06
	.01	2.62	2.84	2.98	3.08	3.15	3.21	3.25	3.30	3.33
∞	.10	1.64	1.92	2.06	2.16	2.23	2.29	2.34	2.38	2.42
	.05	1.96	2.21	2.37	2.47	2.55	2.62	2.67	2.71	2.75
	.02	2.33	2.56	2.68	2.77	2.84	2.89	2.93	2.97	3.00
	.01	2.58	2.79	2.92	3.01	3.08	3.14	3.18	3.22	3.25

Source: Adapted from tables in Dunnett, C. W. (1955). A multiple comparison procedure for comparing several treatments with a control. *Journal of the American Statistical Association, 50*, 1096–1121, and from Dunnett, C. W. (1964). New tables for multiple comparisons with a control. *Biometrics, 20*, 482–491, with permission of the author and the editors.

Table C.9 Critical values of the Studentized range distribution

Error df	FWE	\ Number of ordered means						
		2	3	4	5	6	7	8
2	.01	14.04	19.02	22.29	24.72	26.63	28.20	29.53
	.05	6.09	8.33	9.80	10.88	11.74	12.44	13.03
	.10	4.13	5.73	6.77	7.54	8.14	8.63	9.05
3	.01	8.26	10.62	12.17	13.33	14.24	15.00	15.64
	.05	4.50	5.91	6.83	7.50	8.04	8.48	8.85
	.10	3.33	4.47	5.20	5.74	6.16	6.51	6.81
4	.01	6.51	8.12	9.17	9.96	10.58	11.10	11.55
	.05	3.93	5.04	5.76	6.29	6.71	7.05	7.35
	.10	3.02	3.98	4.59	5.04	5.39	5.68	5.93
5	.01	5.70	6.98	7.80	8.42	8.91	9.32	9.67
	.05	3.64	4.60	5.22	5.67	6.03	6.33	6.58
	.10	2.85	3.72	4.26	4.66	4.98	5.24	5.46
6	.01	5.24	6.33	7.03	7.56	7.97	8.32	8.61
	.05	3.46	4.34	4.90	5.31	5.63	5.90	6.12
	.10	2.75	3.56	4.07	4.44	4.73	4.97	5.17
7	.01	4.95	5.92	6.54	7.01	7.37	7.68	7.94
	.05	3.34	4.17	4.68	5.06	5.36	5.61	5.82
	.10	2.68	3.45	3.93	4.28	4.56	4.78	4.97
8	.01	4.75	5.64	6.20	6.63	6.96	7.24	7.47
	.05	3.26	4.04	4.53	4.89	5.17	5.40	5.60
	.10	2.63	3.37	3.83	4.17	4.43	4.65	4.83
9	.01	4.60	5.43	5.96	6.35	6.66	6.92	7.13
	.05	3.20	3.95	4.42	4.76	5.02	5.24	5.43
	.10	2.59	3.32	3.76	4.08	4.34	4.55	4.72
10	.01	4.48	5.27	5.77	6.14	6.43	6.67	6.88
	.05	3.15	3.88	4.33	4.65	4.91	5.12	5.31
	.10	2.56	3.27	3.70	4.02	4.26	4.47	4.64
11	.01	4.39	5.15	5.62	5.97	6.25	6.48	6.67
	.05	3.11	3.82	4.26	4.57	4.82	5.03	5.20
	.10	2.54	3.23	3.66	3.97	4.21	4.40	4.57
12	.01	4.32	5.05	5.50	5.84	6.10	6.32	6.51
	.05	3.08	3.77	4.20	4.51	4.75	4.95	5.12
	.10	2.52	3.20	3.62	3.92	4.16	4.35	4.51
13	.01	4.26	4.96	5.40	5.73	5.98	6.19	6.37
	.05	3.06	3.74	4.15	4.45	4.69	4.89	5.05
	.10	2.51	3.18	3.59	3.89	4.12	4.31	4.46
14	.01	4.21	4.90	5.32	5.63	5.88	6.09	6.26
	.05	3.03	3.70	4.11	4.41	4.64	4.83	4.99
	.10	2.49	3.16	3.56	3.85	4.06	4.27	4.42
15	.01	4.17	4.84	5.25	5.56	5.80	5.99	6.16
	.05	3.01	3.67	4.08	4.37	4.60	4.78	4.94
	.10	2.48	3.14	3.54	3.83	4.05	4.24	4.39
16	.01	4.13	4.79	5.19	5.49	5.72	5.92	6.08
	.05	3.00	3.65	4.05	4.33	4.56	4.74	4.90
	.10	2.47	3.12	3.52	3.80	4.03	4.21	4.36

Table C.9 (continued)

Error *df*	*FWE*	Number of ordered means						
		2	3	4	5	6	7	8
17	.01	4.10	4.74	5.14	5.43	5.66	5.85	6.01
	.05	2.98	3.63	4.02	4.30	4.52	4.71	4.86
	.10	2.46	3.11	3.50	3.78	4.00	4.18	4.33
18	.01	4.07	4.70	5.09	5.38	5.60	5.79	5.94
	.05	2.97	3.61	4.00	4.28	4.50	4.67	4.82
	.10	2.45	3.10	3.49	3.77	3.98	4.16	4.31
19	.01	4.05	4.67	5.05	5.33	5.55	5.74	5.89
	.05	2.96	3.59	3.98	4.25	4.47	4.65	4.79
	.10	2.45	3.09	3.47	3.75	3.97	4.14	4.29
20	.01	4.02	4.64	5.02	5.29	5.51	5.69	5.84
	.05	2.95	3.58	3.96	4.23	4.45	4.62	4.77
	.10	2.44	3.08	3.46	3.74	3.95	4.12	4.27
24	.01	3.96	4.55	4.91	5.17	5.37	5.54	5.69
	.05	2.92	3.53	3.90	4.17	4.37	4.54	4.68
	.10	2.42	3.05	3.42	3.69	3.90	4.07	4.21
30	.01	3.89	4.46	4.80	5.05	5.24	5.40	5.54
	.05	2.89	3.49	3.85	4.10	4.30	4.46	4.60
	.10	2.40	3.02	3.39	3.65	3.85	4.02	4.16
40	.01	3.83	4.37	4.70	4.93	5.11	5.27	5.39
	.05	2.86	3.44	3.79	4.04	4.23	4.39	4.52
	.10	2.38	2.99	3.35	3.61	3.80	3.96	4.10
60	.01	3.76	4.28	4.60	4.82	4.99	5.13	5.25
	.05	2.83	3.40	3.74	3.98	4.16	4.31	4.44
	.10	2.36	2.96	3.31	3.56	3.76	3.91	4.04
120	.01	3.70	4.20	4.50	4.71	4.87	5.01	5.12
	.05	2.80	3.36	3.69	3.92	4.10	4.24	4.36
	.10	2.34	2.93	3.28	3.52	3.71	3.86	3.99
∞	.01	3.64	4.12	4.40	4.60	4.76	4.88	4.99
	.05	2.77	3.31	3.63	3.86	4.03	4.17	4.29
	.10	2.33	2.90	3.24	3.48	3.66	3.81	3.93

Error *df*	*FWE*	Number of ordered means						
		9	10	11	12	13	14	15
2	.01	30.68	31.69	32.59	33.40	34.13	34.81	35.43
	.05	13.54	13.99	14.39	14.75	15.08	15.38	15.65
	.10	9.41	9.73	10.01	10.26	10.49	10.70	10.89
3	.01	16.20	16.69	17.13	17.53	17.89	18.22	18.52
	.05	9.18	9.46	9.72	9.95	10.15	10.35	10.53
	.10	7.06	7.29	7.49	7.67	7.83	7.98	8.12
4	.01	11.93	12.27	12.57	12.84	13.09	13.32	13.53
	.05	7.60	7.83	8.03	8.21	8.37	8.53	8.66
	.10	6.14	6.33	6.50	6.65	6.78	6.91	7.03
5	.01	9.97	10.24	10.48	10.70	10.89	11.08	11.24

Table C.9 (continued)

Error df	FWE	Number of ordered means						
		9	10	11	12	13	14	15
	.05	6.80	7.00	7.17	7.32	7.47	7.60	7.72
	.10	5.65	5.82	5.97	6.10	6.22	6.34	6.44
6	.01	8.87	9.10	9.30	9.48	9.65	9.81	9.95
	.05	6.32	6.49	6.65	6.79	6.92	7.03	7.14
	.10	5.34	5.50	5.64	5.76	5.88	5.98	6.08
7	.01	8.17	8.37	8.55	8.71	8.86	9.00	9.12
	.05	6.00	6.16	6.30	6.43	6.55	6.66	6.76
	.10	5.14	5.28	5.41	5.53	5.64	5.74	5.83
8	.01	7.68	7.86	8.03	8.18	8.31	8.44	8.55
	.05	5.77	5.92	6.05	6.18	6.29	6.39	6.48
	.10	4.99	5.13	5.25	5.36	5.46	5.56	5.64
9	.01	7.33	7.50	7.65	7.78	7.91	8.03	8.13
	.05	5.60	5.74	5.87	5.98	6.09	6.19	6.28
	.10	4.87	5.01	5.13	5.23	5.33	5.42	5.51
10	.01	7.06	7.21	7.36	7.49	7.60	7.71	7.81
	.05	5.46	5.60	5.72	5.83	5.94	6.03	6.11
	.10	4.78	4.91	5.03	5.13	5.23	5.32	5.40
11	.01	6.84	6.99	7.13	7.25	7.36	7.47	7.56
	.05	5.35	5.49	5.61	5.71	5.81	5.90	5.98
	.10	4.71	4.84	4.95	5.05	5.15	5.23	5.31
12	.01	6.67	6.81	6.94	7.06	7.17	7.27	7.36
	.05	5.27	5.40	5.51	5.62	5.71	5.80	5.88
	.10	4.65	4.78	4.89	4.99	5.08	5.16	5.24
13	.01	6.53	6.67	6.79	6.90	7.01	7.10	7.19
	.05	5.19	5.32	5.43	5.53	5.63	5.71	5.79
	.10	4.60	4.72	4.83	4.93	5.02	5.10	5.18
14	.01	6.41	6.54	6.66	6.77	6.87	6.96	7.05
	.05	5.13	5.25	5.36	5.46	5.55	5.64	5.71
	.10	4.56	4.68	4.79	4.88	4.97	5.05	5.12
15	.01	6.31	6.44	6.56	6.66	6.76	6.85	6.93
	.05	5.08	5.20	5.31	5.40	5.49	5.57	5.65
	.10	4.52	4.64	4.75	4.84	4.93	5.01	5.08
16	.01	6.22	6.35	6.46	6.56	6.66	6.74	6.82
	.05	5.03	5.15	5.26	5.35	5.44	5.52	5.59
	.10	4.49	4.61	4.71	4.81	4.89	4.97	5.04
17	.01	6.15	6.27	6.38	6.48	6.57	6.66	6.73
	.05	4.99	5.11	5.21	5.31	5.39	5.47	5.54
	.10	4.46	4.58	4.68	4.77	4.86	4.94	5.01
18	.01	6.08	6.20	6.31	6.41	6.50	6.58	6.66
	.05	4.96	5.07	5.17	5.27	5.35	5.43	5.50
	.10	4.44	4.55	4.66	4.75	4.83	4.91	4.98
19	.01	6.02	6.14	6.25	6.34	6.43	6.51	6.59
	.05	4.92	5.04	5.14	5.23	5.32	5.39	5.46
	.10	4.42	4.53	4.63	4.72	4.80	4.88	4.95
20	.01	5.97	6.09	6.19	6.29	6.37	6.45	6.52

Table C.9 (continued)

Error df	FWE	\multicolumn{7}{c}{Number of ordered means}

Error df	FWE	9	10	11	12	13	14	15
	.05	4.90	5.01	5.11	5.20	5.28	5.36	5.43
	.10	4.40	4.51	4.61	4.70	4.78	4.86	4.92
24	.01	5.81	5.92	6.02	6.11	6.19	6.26	6.33
	.05	4.81	4.92	5.01	5.10	5.18	5.25	5.32
	.10	4.34	4.45	4.54	4.62	4.71	4.78	4.85
30	.01	5.65	5.76	5.85	5.93	6.01	6.08	6.14
	.05	4.72	4.82	4.92	5.00	5.08	5.15	5.21
	.10	4.28	4.38	4.47	4.56	4.64	4.71	4.77
40	.01	5.50	5.60	5.69	5.76	5.84	5.90	5.96
	.05	4.64	4.74	4.82	4.90	4.98	5.04	5.11
	.10	4.22	4.32	4.41	4.49	4.56	4.63	4.70
60	.01	5.36	5.45	5.53	5.60	5.67	5.73	5.79
	.05	4.55	4.65	4.73	4.81	4.88	4.94	5.00
	.10	4.16	4.25	4.34	4.42	4.49	4.56	4.62
120	.01	5.21	5.30	5.38	5.44	5.51	5.56	5.61
	.05	4.47	4.56	4.64	4.71	4.78	4.84	4.90
	.10	4.10	4.19	4.28	4.35	4.42	4.49	4.54
∞	.01	5.08	5.16	5.23	5.29	5.35	5.40	5.45
	.05	4.39	4.47	4.55	4.62	4.69	4.74	4.80
	.10	4.04	4.13	4.21	4.29	4.35	4.41	4.47

Error df	FWE	\multicolumn{7}{c}{Number of ordered means}

Error df	FWE	16	17	18	19	20	30	40
2	.01	36.00	36.53	37.03	37.50	37.95	41.32	43.61
	.05	15.91	16.14	16.37	16.57	16.77	18.27	19.28
	.10	11.07	11.24	11.39	11.54	11.68	12.73	13.44
3	.01	18.81	19.07	19.32	19.55	19.77	21.44	22.59
	.05	10.69	10.84	10.98	11.11	11.24	12.21	12.87
	.10	8.25	8.37	8.48	8.58	8.68	9.44	9.95
4	.01	13.73	13.91	14.08	14.24	14.40	15.57	16.37
	.05	8.79	8.91	9.03	9.13	9.23	10.00	10.53
	.10	7.13	7.23	7.33	7.41	7.50	8.14	8.57
5	.01	11.40	11.55	11.68	11.81	11.93	12.87	13.52
	.05	7.83	7.93	8.03	8.12	8.21	8.88	9.33
	.10	6.54	6.63	6.71	6.79	6.86	7.44	7.83
6	.01	10.08	10.21	10.32	10.43	10.54	11.34	11.90
	.05	7.24	7.34	7.43	7.51	7.59	8.19	8.60
	.10	6.16	6.25	6.33	6.40	6.47	7.00	7.36
7	.01	9.24	9.35	9.46	9.55	9.65	10.36	10.85
	.05	6.85	6.94	7.02	7.10	7.17	7.73	8.11
	.10	5.91	5.99	6.06	6.13	6.20	6.70	7.04
8	.01	8.66	8.76	8.85	8.94	9.03	9.68	10.13
	.05	6.57	6.65	6.73	6.80	6.87	7.40	7.76

Table C.9 (continued)

Error df	FWE	Number of ordered means						
		16	17	18	19	20	30	40
	.10	5.72	5.80	5.87	5.94	6.00	6.48	6.80
9	.01	8.23	8.33	8.41	8.49	8.57	9.18	9.59
	.05	6.36	6.44	6.51	6.58	6.64	7.15	7.49
	.10	5.58	5.66	5.72	5.79	5.85	6.31	6.62
10	.01	7.91	7.99	8.08	8.15	8.23	8.79	9.19
	.05	6.19	6.27	6.34	6.41	6.47	6.95	7.28
	.10	5.47	5.54	5.61	5.67	5.73	6.17	6.48
11	.01	7.65	7.73	7.81	7.88	7.95	8.49	8.86
	.05	6.06	6.13	6.20	6.27	6.33	6.79	7.11
	.10	5.38	5.45	5.51	5.57	5.63	6.07	6.36
12	.01	7.44	7.52	7.59	7.67	7.73	8.25	8.60
	.05	5.95	6.02	6.09	6.15	6.21	6.66	6.97
	.10	5.31	5.37	5.44	5.50	5.55	5.98	6.27
13	.01	7.27	7.35	7.42	7.49	7.55	8.04	8.39
	.05	5.86	5.93	6.00	6.06	6.11	6.55	6.85
	.10	5.25	5.31	5.37	5.43	5.48	5.90	6.19
14	.01	7.13	7.20	7.27	7.33	7.40	7.87	8.20
	.05	5.79	5.85	5.92	5.97	6.03	6.46	6.75
	.10	5.19	5.26	5.32	5.37	5.43	5.84	6.12
15	.01	7.00	7.07	7.14	7.20	7.26	7.73	8.05
	.05	5.72	5.79	5.85	5.90	5.96	6.38	6.67
	.10	5.15	5.21	5.27	5.32	5.38	5.78	6.06
16	.01	6.90	6.97	7.03	7.09	7.15	7.60	7.92
	.05	5.66	5.73	5.79	5.84	5.90	6.31	6.59
	.10	5.11	5.17	5.23	5.28	5.33	5.73	6.00
17	.01	6.81	6.87	6.94	7.00	7.05	7.49	7.80
	.05	5.61	5.68	5.73	5.79	5.84	6.25	6.53
	.10	5.07	5.13	5.19	5.24	5.30	5.69	5.96
18	.01	6.73	6.79	6.85	6.91	6.97	7.40	7.70
	.05	5.57	5.63	5.69	5.74	5.79	6.20	6.47
	.10	5.04	5.10	5.16	5.21	5.26	5.65	5.92
19	.01	6.65	6.72	6.78	6.84	6.89	7.31	7.61
	.05	5.53	5.59	5.65	5.70	5.75	6.15	6.42
	.10	5.01	5.07	5.13	5.18	5.23	5.62	5.88
20	.01	6.59	6.65	6.71	6.77	6.82	7.24	7.52
	.05	5.49	5.55	5.61	5.66	5.71	6.10	6.37
	.10	4.99	5.05	5.10	5.16	5.21	5.59	5.85
24	.01	6.39	6.45	6.51	6.56	6.61	7.00	7.27
	.05	5.38	5.44	5.49	5.55	5.59	5.97	6.23
	.10	4.91	4.97	5.02	5.07	5.12	5.49	5.74
30	.01	6.20	6.26	6.31	6.36	6.41	6.77	7.02
	.05	5.27	5.33	5.38	5.43	5.48	5.83	6.08
	.10	4.83	4.89	4.94	4.99	5.03	5.39	5.64
40	.01	6.02	6.07	6.12	6.17	6.21	6.55	6.78
	.05	5.16	5.22	5.27	5.31	5.36	5.70	5.93

Table C.9 (continued)

Error df	FWE	Number of ordered means						
		16	17	18	19	20	30	40
	.10	4.75	4.81	4.86	4.91	4.95	5.29	5.53
60	.01	5.84	5.89	5.93	5.97	6.02	6.33	6.55
	.05	5.06	5.11	5.15	5.20	5.24	5.57	5.79
	.10	4.68	4.73	4.78	4.82	4.86	5.20	5.42
120	.01	5.66	5.71	5.75	5.79	5.83	6.12	6.32
	.05	4.95	5.00	5.04	5.09	5.13	5.43	5.64
	.10	4.60	4.65	4.69	4.74	4.78	5.10	5.31
∞	.01	5.49	5.54	5.57	5.61	5.65	5.91	6.09
	.05	4.85	4.89	4.93	4.97	5.01	5.30	5.50
	.10	4.52	4.57	4.61	4.65	4.69	5.00	5.20

Source;: Adapted from Table II.2 in *The Probability Integrals of the Range and of the Studentized Range*. prepared by H. L. Harter. D. S. Clemm, and E. H. Guthrie. The original tables are published in WADC Tech. Rep. 58–484, Vol. 2, 1959, Wright Air Development Center, and are reproduced with the permission of the authors.

Table C.10 Critical values for the Wilcoxon Signed-Rank test

One-tailed	Two-tailed	5	6	7	8	9	10	11	12	13	14
						Number of pairs					
.05	.10	0	2	3	5	8	10	13	17	21	25
.025	.05		0	2	3	5	8	10	13	17	21
.01	.02			0	1	3	5	7	9	12	15
.005	.01				0	1	3	5	7	9	12
		15	16	17	18	19	20	21	22	23	24
.05	.10	30	35	41	47	53	60	67	75	83	91
.025	.05	25	29	34	40	46	52	58	65	73	81
.01	.02	19	23	27	32	37	43	49	55	62	69
.005	.01	15	19	23	27	32	37	42	48	54	61
		25	26	27	28	29	30	31	32	33	34
.05	.10	100	110	119	130	140	151	163	175	187	200
.025	.05	89	98	107	116	126	137	147	159	170	182
.01	.02	76	84	92	101	110	120	130	140	151	162
.005	.01	68	75	83	91	100	109	118	128	138	148
		35	36	37	38	39	40	41	42	43	44
.05	.10	213	227	241	256	271	286	302	319	336	353
.025	.05	195	208	221	235	249	264	279	294	310	327
.01	.02	173	185	198	211	224	238	252	266	281	296
.005	.01	159	171	182	194	207	220	233	247	261	276
		45	46	47	48	49	50				
.05	.10	371	389	407	426	446	466				
.025	.05	343	361	378	396	415	434				
.01	.02	312	328	345	362	379	397				
.005	.01	291	307	322	339	355	373				

Table C.11 Transformation of *r* to *Z*

r	Z	r	Z	r	Z	r	Z	r	Z
0.000	0.000	0.200	0.203	0.400	0.424	0.600	0.693	0.800	1.099
0.005	0.005	0.205	0.208	0.405	0.430	0.605	0.701	0.805	1.113
0.010	0.010	0.210	0.213	0.410	0.436	0.610	0.709	0.810	1.127
0.015	0.015	0.215	0.218	0.415	0.442	0.615	0.717	0.815	1.142
0.020	0.020	0.220	0.224	0.420	0.448	0.620	0.725	0.820	1.157
0.025	0.025	0.225	0.229	0.425	0.454	0.625	0.733	0.825	1.172
0.030	0.030	0.230	0.234	0.430	0.460	0.630	0.741	0.830	1.188
0.035	0.035	0.235	0.239	0.435	0.466	0.635	0.750	0.835	1.204
0.040	0.040	0.240	0.245	0.440	0.472	0.640	0.758	0.840	1.221
0.045	0.045	0.245	0.250	0.445	0.478	0.645	0.767	0.845	1.238
0.050	0.050	0.250	0.255	0.450	0.485	0.650	0.775	0.850	1.256
0.055	0.055	0.255	0.261	0.455	0.491	0.655	0.784	0.855	1.274
0.060	0.060	0.260	0.266	0.460	0.497	0.660	0.793	0.860	1.293
0.065	0.065	0.265	0.271	0.465	0.504	0.665	0.802	0.865	1.313
0.070	0.070	0.270	0.277	0.470	0.510	0.670	0.811	0.870	1.333
0.075	0.075	0.275	0.282	0.475	0.517	0.675	0.820	0.875	1.354
0.080	0.080	0.280	0.288	0.480	0.523	0.680	0.829	0.880	1.376
0.085	0.085	0.285	0.293	0.485	0.530	0.685	0.838	0.885	1.398
0.090	0.090	0.290	0.299	0.490	0.536	0.690	0.848	0.890	1.422
0.095	0.095	0.295	0.304	0.495	0.543	0.695	0.858	0.895	1.447
0.100	0.100	0.300	0.310	0.500	0.549	0.700	0.867	0.900	1.472
0.105	0.105	0.305	0.315	0.505	0.556	0.705	0.877	0.905	1.499
0.110	0.110	0.310	0.321	0.510	0.563	0.710	0.887	0.910	1.528
0.115	0.116	0.315	0.326	0.515	0.570	0.715	0.897	0.915	1.557
0.120	0.121	0.320	0.332	0.520	0.576	0.720	0.908	0.920	1.589
0.125	0.126	0.325	0.337	0.525	0.583	0.725	0.918	0.925	1.623
0.130	0.131	0.330	0.343	0.530	0.590	0.730	0.929	0.930	1.658
0.135	0.136	0.335	0.348	0.535	0.597	0.735	0.940	0.935	1.697
0.140	0.141	0.340	0.354	0.540	0.604	0.740	0.950	0.940	1.738
0.145	0.146	0.345	0.360	0.545	0.611	0.745	0.962	0.945	1.783
0.150	0.151	0.350	0.365	0.550	0.618	0.750	0.973	0.950	1.832
0.155	0.156	0.355	0.371	0.555	0.626	0.755	0.984	0.955	1.886
0.160	0.161	0.360	0.377	0.560	0.633	0.760	0.996	0.960	1.946
0.165	0.167	0.365	0.383	0.565	0.640	0.765	1.008	0.965	2.014
0.170	0.172	0.370	0.388	0.570	0.648	0.770	1.020	0.970	2.092
0.175	0.177	0.375	0.394	0.575	0.655	0.775	1.033	0.975	2.185
0.180	0.182	0.380	0.400	0.580	0.662	0.780	1.045	0.980	2.298
0.185	0.187	0.385	0.406	0.585	0.670	0.785	1.058	0.985	2.443
0.190	0.192	0.390	0.412	0.590	0.678	0.790	1.071	0.990	2.647
0.195	0.198	0.395	0.418	0.595	0.685	0.795	1.085	0.995	2.994

Answers to Selected Exercises

1.1 (a) The study is an experiment. Subjects were randomly assigned to each condition.

(b) The sample might best be characterized as a random sample of (presumably) overweight volunteers. The volunteer aspect is important because it is not clear that the effects of the diets would be the same if used by individuals less motivated to lose weight.

(c) One alternative approach is to observe individuals who have selected a particular diet. This might be done by advertising for individuals who are on the diets of interest, requesting that they volunteer as subjects in a study. This is not as attractive an option as the experiment for several reasons. For example, baseline information on weight and health prior to the start of the diet is likely to be lacking. One or more of the targeted diets may not be well represented in the volunteer sample. Individuals who chose different diets may differ systematically with respect to other factors that may influence weight loss.

1.3 (a) There are several factors other than long hours in day care that may increase aggressive behavior. Two possibilities are that (1) parents may be more likely to place more aggressive children in day care in order to reduce unpleasant interactions, or to provide a socializing experience; (2) parents who are more stressed may foster aggression in their children and may place those children in day care for longer hours in order to reduce their stress.

(b) Ideally, a measure of aggressive behavior prior to the first enrollment in day care should be obtained. If variation in aggressive behavior as a function of hours/day in day care manifests itself only after the first placement in day care, there is evidence that time in day care has an effect. (Of course this doesn't reveal whether the relation is due to the day-care environment, or absence from parents.) If children who were more aggressive after placement in day care were also more aggressive prior to first placement, there is an indication that factors such as those listed in part (a) are involved. Other measures such as measures of parental stress and rated quality of the home environment may also prove useful. Using the regression procedures referred to in this chapter, and developed in Chapters 20 and 21, we can investigate whether such measures predict variability in aggressive behavior beyond that predicted by hours in day care.

(c) An experiment could be performed by randomly assigning children to day care or to home care. To further reduce the influence of nuisance variables, care might be taken to equate the groups with respect to such factors as parents' working hours, parents' rating of their stress, and whether the child has one or two parents in the home. The advantage of the experimental approach is that random assignment ensures that there will be no systematic bias due to uncontrolled factors, and several factors may be controlled by equating the groups with respect to them. The disadvantage is that the approach is both unethical and impractical. It is unethical because if one treatment does cause problems, the researcher has subjected half of the children to an experience that may have a negative effect on their future. The experiment is impractical because it is doubtful that parents will allow a researcher to decide the preschool experience of their children.

1.5 Less education may cause lower income, less interesting jobs, and poorer health (because of lower income or because of less knowledge about practices that promote health). All of these consequences may, in turn, increase depression. Thus, there is some credibility to the idea that the difference in depression scores between high-school-educated and college-educated individuals is affected by education. However, further examination suggests other possibilities. For example, if the high-school-educated group came from families with less income, they may have been more likely to receive less education and also to be more depressed. It is also possible that other factors in the family environment mediated differences in both education and depression scores. Other factors may also be important. For example, from the data available on the website, we might try to determine whether there are systematic age differences between the two groups and, if so, whether depression is related to age within each educational level. If so, the difference in depression scores might be the result of differences in age.

CHAPTER 2

2.1 (a) $\bar{Y} = 30.563$; (b) $\tilde{Y}$ (median) $= 33.5$; (c) $(\Sigma Y)^2 = 239,121$; (d) $\Sigma Y^2 = 16,311$; (e) $s = 9.543$; (f) $H_L = 23.5$, $H_U = 37.5$.

2.3 (a) If the mean of six scores is 47, the sum must be 6×47, or 282. However, $\Sigma Y_i = 225$. Therefore, the sixth score must be $282 - 225$, or 57.

(b) The mean of the original five scores is 45. Adding a score equal to the mean will yield the smallest variance because the variance is the sum of squared deviations about the mean.

2.5 (a) $\displaystyle\sum_{i=1}^{5} (X_i + Y_i) = \sum_{i=1}^{5} X_i + \sum_{i=1}^{5} Y_i = 30 + 62 = 92$; (b) $\displaystyle\sum_{i=1}^{5} X_i^2 = 6^2 + 5^2 + \ldots + 11^2 = 232$;

(c) $\displaystyle\left(\sum_{i=1}^{5} X_i\right)^2 = 30^2 = 900$; (d) $\displaystyle\sum_{i=1}^{5} X_i Y_i = (6)(7) + (5)(11) + \ldots + (11)(9) = 315$;

(e) $\displaystyle\sum_{i=1}^{5} (X_i + 5Y_i^2 + 27) = \sum_{i=1}^{5} (X_i) + 5\sum_{i=1}^{5} (Y_i^2) + (5)(27) = 30 + (5)(888) + (5)(27) = 4,605$

2.7 (a) 286.533; (b) 245.840; (c) 2979.6.

2.9 Standardizing each of the three sets of scores equates their means (at 0) and standard deviations (at 1). The ranges, medians, and trimmed means are not necessarily ordered as they were for the original three distributions. However, each distribution of z scores has the same shape as before the transformation; the skewness and kurtosis values, and their standard errors, as well as the normal probability plot, are unchanged. The same cases are outliers as in the original data set. Standard scores are normally distributed only if the original scores are.

2.11 (a) Both mean and median depression scores (*Beck_D*) increase noticeably as *Sayhlth* scores increase from 1 to 4 (higher *Sayhlth* scores indicate poorer self-rating of health). Although we have not performed a significance test, the size of the differences and the large numbers of scores suggest that the effect will hold for other samples from the same population.

(b) Winter depression means and medians (*Beck_D1* scores) are highest in categories 1–3. However, individuals who rate themselves in fair health (*Sayhlth* = 4) have a somewhat higher average score in the fall season. This is particularly noticeable in the median scores.

2.13 (a) Relative to the class, the student's performance declined. The z score for Test 1 is $z_1 = (41 - 38.6)/4.616 = .520$ whereas $z_2 = (51 - 46.84)/9.496 = .438$.

(b) A score of 52 is the lowest integer value that transforms the Test 2 score into a z score exceeding .52. We arrive at this by solving $(X - 46.84)/9.496 > .52$. One point more on Test 2 would have yielded a z score of .543.

(c) The almost identical values of means and medians on each test suggest that the distributions are symmetric. This is confirmed by obtaining box plots. Finally, normal probability (*Q–Q*) plots indicate that the points lie fairly close to a straight line. A few of the upper and lower points depart slightly from a straight line, but this might occur by chance in any sample drawn from a normal population.

(d) The correlation between the two sets of test scores is .543. A scatterplot shows that Test 2 scores increase as Test 1 scores do, but there is considerable variability.

(e) Using Equations 2.10a and 2.10b, we have $b_1 = r \times s_y/s_x = 1.117$ and $b_0 = \overline{Y} - b_1\overline{X} = 3.737$. The regression equation is $\hat{Y} = b_0 + b_1X$; substituting for b_0 and b_1, and letting $X = 40$, the predicted value is 48.417.

2.15 (a) The correlation is .476. and it is significantly different from zero ($p < .001$). Of course, this moderately high correlation does not tell us the reason. It may reflect pitchers being more careful with players who hit more home runs, or such hitters having a better ability to distinguish between strikes and balls, or other factors.

(b) The correlation, .074, is very weak and, despite the large number of observations, is not significantly different from zero. There is no support for the existence of a relationship between offensive and defensive abilities.

(c) If you add the *BA*s and divide by the number of players, the Boston Red Sox mean is .268 and the New York Mets mean is .271. However, this method gives equal weight to all the individual averages even though there is a difference in the number of at-bats. We should add all the hits (*H*s) for the team and divide by the total of team at-bats (*AB*s). Then the Red Sox mean is .276 and the Mets mean is .274.

(d) The correlation is .682. Players with fewer at-bats tend to have lower averages. This is why the Red Sox mean team batting average was higher (.276) when the mean was correctly calculated, taking each player's *AB*s into consideration. When the averages are weighted by the number of at-bats, the low averages have less effect on the team mean average.

CHAPTER 3

3.1 (a) .2; (b) $.2^3 = .008$; (c) $(.8)(.2)(.8) = .128$; (d) $(3)(.128) = .384$; (e) $1 - p(\text{none correct}) = 1 - .8^3 = 1 - .512 = .488$; (f) $(3)(.2^2)(.8) = .096$; (g) $(.8^4)(.2) = .08192$.

3.3 (a) $p(A)\,p(B) = .42$; (b) $p(\tilde{A})\,p(\tilde{B}) = .12$; (c) $p(A)\,p(\tilde{B}) = .28$; (d) $p(\tilde{A})\,p(B) = .18$. (e) $1 - p(\tilde{A})\,p(\tilde{B}) = .88$; (f) $1 - p(\tilde{A}_1)p(\tilde{A}_2)p(\tilde{B}_1)p(\tilde{B}_2) = 1 - (.3)(.3)(.4)(.4) = .9586$; (g) $1 - p(A_1)p(A_2)p(B_1)p(B_2) = (.7)(.7)(.6)(.6) = .8236$.

3.5 (a) The completed table is as follows:

Test results	HIV	No HIV	Total
Positive	997	1,485	2,482
Negative	3	97,515	97,518
Total	1,000	99,000	100,000

(b) p(infected | positive test) = 997/2,482 = .402.

(c) p(not infected | negative test) = 97,515/97,518 = .99997

3.7 p(woman | schoolteacher) > p(schoolteacher | woman) > p(woman and schoolteacher).

3.9 (a) Given that there are 10 digits, the probability of matching any digit in the winning number by chance is 1/10. Because each digit is independent of the others, the probability of an exact match of all four digits is (1/10)(1/10)(1/10)(1/10) = 1/10000 = .0001.

(b) Because there are (4)(3)(2)(1) = 24 ways of ordering four digits, the probability of matching the four digits of the winning number in any order is 24/1000 = .0024.

3.11 The probability distribution is

Outcome	p(outcome)
2	1/36
3	2/36
4	3/36
5	4/36
6	5/36
7	6/36
8	5/36
9	4/36
10	3/36
11	2/36
12	1/36

From the distribution, we see that p(outcome $\geq$ 8) = 15/36.

CHAPTER 4

4.1 (a) p(reject | true) = α = .05

(b) p(don't reject | false) = β = 1 – power = .2

(c) One approach is to assume that 1,000 null hypotheses are tested. Then, from the information given, we have the entries without parentheses in the following table; the remaining entries (in parentheses) are obtained by addition and subtraction:

Hypothesis	Reject	Do not reject	Total
True	15	(285)	300
False	560	(140)	(700)
Total	(575)	(425)	1,000

From the table, p(true | nonreject) = 285/425 = .67.

(d) From the table, p(reject) = 575/1000 = .575.

4.3 Let C = the critical region. (a) $C > 10$; (b) $C = 5$; (c) $C < 3$; (d) $C < 5$ or $C > 16$.

4.5 (a) (i) H_0: π = .25, H_1: π > .25; (ii) $n = 5$; (iii) reject if y (number of matches) > 3.

(b) (i) H_0: π = .4, H_1: $\pi \neq$ .4; (ii) $n = 15$; (iii) reject if $y < 2$ or $y > 9$.

4.7 The output displayed below indicates that if $Y = 5$, we can reject null hypothesis H_0: $\pi = .5$ at $\alpha = .05$ whether we use a one- or two-tailed test.

Binomial Test

	Category	N	Observed prop.	Test prop.	Exact sig. (2-tailed)
Y1 Group 1	1	7	.35	.50	.263
Group 2	0	13	.65		
Total		20	1.00		
Y2 Group 1	1	5	.25	.50	.041
Group 2	0	15	.75		
Total		20	1.00		

4.9 (a) H_0: $\pi = .5$, H_1: $\pi \neq .5$; π is the probability that the imagery is better than the rote procedure. Let $n = 12$ and $\alpha = .05$. Then the decision rule is: reject if $y \geq 10$ or $y \leq 2$ where y is the number of subjects who performed better using the imagery method. Because $y = 9$, the null hypothesis cannot be rejected.

(b) Power $= p(y \leq 2$ or $\geq 10 \mid \pi = .9) = p(y \leq 2$ or $\geq 10 \mid \pi = .1) = .2824 + .3766 + .2301 + 0 = .89$. The same result is obtained when using G*Power 3.

CHAPTER 5

5.1 (a) $z = 1.00$; therefore, $p = .159$.

(b) (i) $z = (130 - 100)/15 = 2$, $p(z > 2) = .023$. (ii) $z_{upper} = (145 - 100)/15 = 3$, $p(z < 3) = 1 - .001 = .999$; $z_{lower} = (85 - 100)/15 = -1$, $p(z < -1) = .159$; $.999 - .159 = .840$. (iii) $z = (70 - 100)/15 = -2$, therefore, $p = 1 - .023 = .977$. (iv) $z_{70} = -2$, $z_{80} = -1.33$, $p = .092 - .023 = .069$.

(c) $z - 1.28$ and $z = 1.28$ contain the middle .80 of the area under the normal curve. Therefore, $1.28 = (Y_{upper} - 100)/15$. Solving algebraically, $Y_{upper} = 119.2$. Similarly, $Y_{lower} = 80.8$.

(d) $z_{.75} = .675 = (Y_{.75} - 100)/15$. Solving, $Y_{.75} = 110.125$.

(e) The appropriate denominator of the z is the standard error of the mean, therefore, $z = (115 - 105)/(15 / \sqrt{10}) = 2.108$. The area above this value is approximately .017.

5.3 (a) (i) $z = -.25$; therefore, $p = .401$. (ii) $z = 1.5$; therefore, $p = .067$. (iii) $z_{lower} = -.75$; the area above this is $1 - .227 = .773$. $z_{upper} = .5$; the area above this is .309. The area between the two z scores is $p = .773 - .309 = .464$.

(b) $p(X > \mu_Y) = p(X > 20)$; therefore, calculate $z = (20 - \mu_X)/\sigma_X = (20 - 30)/20 = -.5$. The proportion of the area in the X distribution above 20 (μ_Y) is $p = .69$.

(c) We require the population mean and variance of W. $\mu_W = \mu_X + \mu_Y = 50$. $\sigma_W = \sqrt{\sigma_X^2 + \sigma_Y^2} = 25.61$. Because X and Y are normally distributed, W is. Therefore, to get $p(W > 35)$, calculate $z = (35 - 50)/25.61 = -.59$. Then, $p = .72$.

(d) This requires finding the values of X and Y. From the information given $z_X = 1.035 = (X - 30)/20$. Solving, $X = 50.70$. Similarly, $z_Y = -.52 = (Y - 20)/16$ and $Y = 11.68$. Therefore, $W = 62.28$, $z_W = (62.28 - 50)/25.61 = .48$, which exceeds approximately .68 of the W population.

5.5 (a) (i) $p(Y < 6) = .6$. (ii) $p = .6^2$. (iii) $p = .6^{20}$.

(b) The sample will be symmetric and approximately normal. The mean will be the same as the mean of the original population, .5, and the standard deviation will be $\sigma/\sqrt{20} = .065$.

(c) $z = (.6 - .5)/.065 = 1.54$. The area below this z score is $1 - .06 = .94$.

(d) The central limit theorem states that as n increases, the sampling distribution of the mean approaches normality, justifying our approach to part (c). This approach is not correct for part (a) (iii) because there the distribution in question was the population distribution, which was not normal.

5.7 (a) H_0: $\mu = 52.8$; H_1: $\mu > 52.8$. Reject if $z > 1.645$.

(b) $\sigma_{\bar{x}} = 10.5/\sqrt{50} = 1.485$. Therefore, $z = (56 - 52.8)/1.485 = 2.15$. Reject H_0 and conclude that the population mean of authoritarianism scores has increased.

(c) The mean of 57 is 2.83 $\sigma_{\bar{x}}$ units above 52.8. Power is the area to the right of 1.645 under the distribution with mean at 2.83. Therefore, calculate $z = (1.645 - 2.83)/1.485 = -1.18$; power = the area above this z score, or $1 - .119 = .88$.

(d) $CI = 56 \pm (1.96)(1.485) = 53.09, 58.91$.

(e) Although the one interval calculated either contains μ or does not, we have .95 confidence in the following sense: If we were to draw many samples of size n from a normally distributed population with the assumed variance, .95 of the intervals calculated would contain the true mean.

5.9 (a) $E(T - C) = \mu_T - \mu_C = .5\sigma$; $\text{var}(T - C) = \sigma_T^2 + \sigma_C^2 = 2\sigma^2$.

(b) $p(T > C) = p(T - C > 0)$. Therefore, $z = [0 - E(T - C)]/\sqrt{\text{var}(T - C)} = (0 - .5\sigma)/\sigma\sqrt{2} = .5/\sqrt{2} - .35$; $p(z > -.35) = .64$.

(c) (i) $z = \dfrac{0 - .5\sigma}{(\sigma/3)\sqrt{2}} = -1.06$; $p = .86$. (ii) $z = \dfrac{0 - .2\sigma}{(\sigma/3)\sqrt{2}} = -.42$; $p = .66$.

This change in $p(T > C)$ with changing effect size corresponds to changes in power of a significance test of the difference. Similarly, if n were increased, p would increase because the denominator of the z (the standard error) would decrease. The power of a significance test would also increase.

5.11 (a) The standard error of the mean difference is $\sigma/\sqrt{n} = 13.6/15. = .907$.

(b) The bounds are $2 \pm (1.96)(.907) = .222, 3.778$.

(c) $z = 2/.907 = 2.205$. If $\alpha = .05$, any z greater than 1.96 or less than -1.96 allows us to reject the null hypothesis. Therefore, we conclude that the population mean score is higher following instruction. Note that this result is consistent with the fact that zero was not contained within the 95% CI calculated in part (b).

5.13 (a) Let $\bar{d} = \bar{Y}_1 - \bar{Y}_2$. Then $s_{\bar{d}} = \sqrt{(1/n)(s_1^2 + s_2^2 - 2rs_1s_2)} = 1.469$.

(b) $CI = \bar{d} \pm s_{\bar{d}}z_{.025} = 5.241 \pm (1.469)(1.96) = 2.36, 8.12$.

(c) $t = \bar{d} / s_{\bar{d}} = 5.241/1.469 = 3.57$. Total cholesterol levels are significantly higher in the winter than in the spring season. Note that this result is consistent with the fact that zero was not contained within the 95% CI calculated in part (b). The higher TC values in winter may reflect less exercise or diets that are more restricted to high cholesterol items (e.g., fewer vegetables in winter).

5.15 (a) The standard error of the sampling distribution of the difference between the means is

$$s_{\bar{d}} = \sqrt{(41.898)^2/112 + (33.896)^2/98} = 5.234.$$

(b) The 95% confidence interval is $CI = (228.931 - 215.455) \pm (5.234)(1.96) = 3.217, 23.735$. Because the interval does not contain zero, we conclude that the groups differ significantly in TC level by a two-tailed test with $\alpha = .05$.

5.17 (a) H_0: $\mu = 200$; H_1: $\mu > 200$.

(b) H_A: $\mu = 206$.

(c) The z corresponding to the targeted raw effect is $z = 6/(30/\sqrt{n}) = \sqrt{n}/5$. In order to have .8 power, this z must be .84 above the critical z of 1.645. Therefore,

$$z = \sqrt{n}/5 = 1.645 + .84; \quad n = [(5)(2.485)]^2 = 154.$$

CHAPTER 6

6.1 (a) $\bar{Y} = 47.889$, $s = 14.987$, and $SE = s/\sqrt{n} = 4.997$. The critical t value at the .10 (two-tailed) level on 8 df is 1.860. Therefore, $CI = 47.889 \pm (1.86)(4.997) = 38.60, 57.18$.

(b) Because the upper limit of the 90% CI is below the null hypothesis value of 60, it follows that the null hypothesis can be rejected at the .05 level in favor of the alternative that the mean motor skill score of the protein-deficient population is below 60. A t test yields $t = (47.889 - 60)/4.997 = -2.424$, $p = .021$.

(c) $\bar{Y}_2 = 50.889$, and $s = 13.365$, $SE = 4.455$. $t_{.05} = 1.86$. $CI = 50.889 \pm (1.86)(4.455) = 42.61, 59.17$. The mean is again significantly below 60; $t = -2.405$, $p = .038$.

(d) $\bar{Y}_1 - \bar{Y}_2 = 3$; the standard error of the mean difference is $SE = s_{diff}/\sqrt{n}$. Substituting numbers, $SE = 3.742/3 = 1.247$; $t = 3/1.247 = 2.405$ and for a one-tailed test with $df = 8$, $p = .021$.

(e) The variances of the Y_1 and Y_2 scores are 224.61 and 178.61. Therefore, our estimate of the population variance (assuming the population variances are the same both before and after the change in diet) is the square root of $(1/2)(224.61 + 178.61)$, or 14.20. Therefore, Cohen's $d = 3/14.20 = .21$, a small change according to Cohen's guidelines, although statistically significant.

6.3 (a) $t = 2/(5.6/4) = 1.43$. The null hypothesis can't be rejected.

(b) $d_z = 2/5.6 = .36$.

(c) Based on the noncentral t distribution (using G*Power 3 or any other software available to you), power $= .39$ when $n = 16$. When $n = 36$, power $= .68$.

(d) $n = 49$ yields the desired power of .80.

(e) The power values for various ns and the two distributions are:

	Distributions	
n	t	z
16	.39	.41
36	.68	.69
49	.80	.81

Two points should be noted: First, the z provides a reasonable approximation to the power of the t test, even when n is relatively small. Second, because the t distribution approaches the normal with increasing degrees of freedom, the approximation improves as n increases.

6.5 (a) $s_{pool}^2 = [(20)(8)+(10)(30)]/30 = 15.333$. The standard error of the difference of the means is $s_{\bar{d}} = \sqrt{s_{pool}^2\left(\frac{1}{21}+\frac{1}{11}\right)} = 1.457$. The $df = 30$; $t_{30,.025} = 2.042$. $t = 3.2/1.457 = 2.20$. Therefore, reject H_0.

(b) Applying Equation 6.16, we have $t' = 3.2/1.763 = 1.815$. From Equation 6.17, $df' = 13$. The null hypothesis cannot be rejected against a two-tailed alternative.

(c) The pooled-variance test gives heavy weight to the smaller variance, producing a positive bias (i.e., too many Type 1 errors) in the t test. The separate-variance test corrects this bias.

6.7 (a) With 7 df, $t_{7,.05} = 2.365$. For the *Lab* group, the standard error of the difference is $s_{\bar{d}} = s/\sqrt{n} = 6.116/2.828 = 2.163$; similarly, for the *Natural* group, the SE is 5.165. Therefore, the two confidence intervals are *Lab*: $CI = 15.625 \pm (2.365)(2.163) = 10.51, 20.74$; *Natural*: $CI = 21.5 + (2.365)(5.165) = 9.29, 33.71$. In both groups, performance deteriorated significantly from the first to the second test on the materials. However, the *Natural* group forgot more from the first to the second test; we will see in part (c) whether this difference between the groups is significant. Another difference between the groups is that the interval width is wider in the *Natural* group, indicating somewhat less precision in estimating the mean population change score.

(b) $s_{\bar{d}} = \sqrt{(111.979+59.352)/8} = 4.628$; therefore, $t = (33.375 - 25.250)/4.628 = 1.76$; $p = .10$. The difference is not significant.

(c) H_0: $\mu_{d\,Lab} = \mu_{d\,Natural}$; H_1: $\mu_{d\,Lab} \neq \mu_{d\,Natural}$; $s_{\bar{d}} = 5.599$; $t = 1.049$; $p = .31$. Again, there is no evidence to suggest that the groups differ. However, this may reflect a lack of power due to the small n.

6.9 (a) When *Sayhlth* = 2, $d_z = 4.560/20.318 = .224$. Note that this result can also be obtained by dividing the value of the t statistic by the square root of n. When *Sayhlth* = 4, $d_z = 11.087/19.375 = .572$.

(b) The denominator for d_z involves the same within-condition variances as that for d. However, there is an adjustment for the covariance, which depends on the magnitude of the correlation coefficient; $d_z = (\mu_1 - \mu_2)/\sqrt{\sigma_1^2 + \sigma_2^2 - 2\sigma_1\sigma_2\rho_{12}}$.

(c) We require a value of n large enough to have .8 power if the value of d_z is .22, the value for the *Sayhlth* = 2 condition. Turning to G*Power and indicating the t for dependent means, we need $n = 165$ for the *Sayhlth* = 2 condition. For the *Sayhlth* = 4 condition, d_z is .57. Here we require only 27 subjects.

6.11 (a) $\hat{d} = (4 - 3.2) / \sqrt{(1/2)(1.44 + 2.25)} = .59$. Or $\hat{d} = t \times \sqrt{2/n} = (1.77)(1 / 3)$. G*Power 3 will also do the calculation if you use the *determine* option in the post hoc t test menu (independent means t test).

(b) Using G*Power 3, the required total n is 74, or 37 subjects in a group.

(c) We need an estimate of d_z to calculate the required n. This is $\hat{d}_z = (4 - 3.2)/\sqrt{1.44 + 2.25 - (2)(1.2)(1.5)(.5)} = .58$. G*Power 3 will also calculate this value if the *determine* option is selected in the *a priori* t test menu (dependent means t test). Although this value is very slightly smaller than the d estimated in part (a), we need many fewer subjects; $n = 20$ to achieve .8 power.

6.13 Cohen's $d = 3.3/7 = .471$. The p and power values are:

	Experiments			
	1	2	3	4
$n =$	4	9	16	25
$p =$	.383	.176	.069	.023
power =	.143	.237	.351	.542

Although the standardized effect size, d, is constant, with increasing sample size p decreases and post hoc power increases. Both p and post hoc power are conditional probabilities; p is the probability of rejecting the null hypothesis if it is true and power is the probability of rejecting the null hypothesis if it is false, specifically, if the population effect size is the one estimated from our data, .471 in this example. Because both are dependent on n, neither is a good measure of the importance of the manipulation in our study. A second point to note is that despite having an effect that is estimated to be of roughly medium size, power is quite low even with a total of 50 scores.

6.15 Response time data are—like the accuracy data—quite similar for boys and girls. Again, effect sizes are very small, all less than .01, and all t statistics are less than 1. All distributions are skewed to the right, with the bulk of scores falling between 1 and 3 seconds. Perhaps the one notable difference between boys and girls is that the variances of the male scores are higher for all four measures.

CHAPTER 7

7.1 (a) $\mu = (1/4)(-1) + (1/2)(0) + (1/4)(1) = 0$. $\sigma^2 = (1/4)(-1)^2 + (1/2)(0)^2 + (1/4/)(1)^2 = .5$.

(b)

Samples	$\bar{X}$	$p(\bar{X})$
<−1, −1>	−1	1/16
<−1, 0>, <0, −1>	−.5	2/8
<−1, 1>, <1, −1>, <0, 0>	0	2/16 + 1/4 = 6/16
<1, 0>, <0, 1>	.5	2/8
<1, 1>	1	1/16

(c) The mean of the sampling distribution is $E(\bar{X}) = 0$. The variance is $\sigma_{\bar{X}}^2 = (1/16)(-1)^2 + (2/8)(-.5)^2 + (6/16)(0) + (1/16)(1)^2 + (2/8)(.5)^2 = .25$. Note that this is half of the variance of the population. In general, $\sigma_{\bar{X}}^2 = \sigma^2 / n$.

7.3 (a) $p(\text{correct}) = .25$.

(b) From Appendix Table C.1 with $n = 6$ and $p = .25$,

Number correct (x)	0	1	2	3	4	5	6
$p(x)$	.178	.356	.297	.132	.033	.004	0

(c) The number of subjects expected to have each outcome is $100 \times p(x)$.

(d) The expected number of successes in six trials is $(.25)(6) = 1.5$.

(e) $p(x > 1.5) = .297 + .132 + .033 + .004 = .466$.

7.5 (a) The relevant statistics are the following:

Group	Change	Critical t	Std. error
Experimental	10.67	2.201	1.906
Control	5.42	2.571	2.657

The form of the confidence interval is $CI = \bar{Y}_1 - \bar{Y}_2 \pm t_{.05,df} SE$. Substituting the preceding numbers, for the experimental group, we have $CI = 10.67 \pm (2.201)(1.906) = 6.47, 14.87$. Because the interval does not include zero, we can reject the hypothesis of no change in the population means at the .05 level. For the control group, the bounds are $5.42 \pm (2.571)(2.657) = -1.41, 12.25$. In this case, the null hypothesis cannot be rejected.

(b) The difference in the mean change scores is $10.67 - 5.42 = 5.25$. The standard error of this difference is 3.287. Therefore $t = 5.25/2.287 = 1.60$. With 16 df, the one-tailed critical $t = 1.746$. Therefore, we cannot reject the hypothesis that the population mean change scores differ.

7.7 (a) Assuming homogeneous variances, the standard deviation of difference scores is $\sigma_{diff} = \sqrt{2\sigma^2(1 - \rho)}$. Substituting 12.5 for σ^2 and .6 for ρ, we have $\sigma_{diff} = 3.16$.

(b) $d_z = 1.52/3.16 = .48$. An alternative approach is to note that $d_z = d/\sqrt{2(1 - \rho)}$; this is $.43/.89 = .48$.

(c) Using G*Power 3, selecting the t for dependent means and the *a priori* option, we need 29 subjects to have .80 power against $d_z = .48$.

7.9 After sorting the RT scores within each group, it is useful to get the descriptive statistics for each group: From SPSS, we have

Group = 1

	N statistic	Mean Statistic	Mean Std. error	Std. deviation statistic	Variance statistic
RT	30	857.13	75.040	411.009	168,928.671
T	18	771.61	42.922	182.102	33,161.193
W	30	787.17	41.875	229.357	52,604.695

Group = 2

	N statistic	Mean Statistic	Mean Std. error	Std. deviation statistic	Variance statistic
RT	20	667.30	75.827	339.110	114,995.589
T	12	610.58	40.902	141.689	20,075.902
W	20	630.95	41.273	184.580	34,069.945

(a) The difference between the trimmed means is $771.61 - 610.58 = 161.03$. The winsorized sum of squares (SS_W) for Group 1 is $(29)(52,604.625) = 1,525,536.155$; the SS_W for Group 2 is $(19)(34,009.945) = 646,188.385$. The pooled winsorized variance is the sum of these two values $(2,171,724.540)$ divided by the summed winsorized degrees of freedom. The winsorized df for each group are the number of scores that remain after trimming, minus one. Therefore, $df_W = 17 + 11 = 28$; the pooled variance is $s^3_{W,561.59} = 2,171,724,540/28 = 77,561.591$. Dividing the pooled variance by the total number of scores remaining after trimming ($18 + 12 = 30$), and taking the square root, we have the winsorized standard error of the difference between the means; this is $SE_W = \sqrt{77,561.59/30} = 50.847$ and $t = 3.17$, which is significant at the .001 level. Note that despite the loss of 20 degrees of freedom, the elimination of the straggling tail provides a much lower p value than previously obtained.

(b) The confidence interval is $CI = \bar{Y}_1 - \bar{Y}_2 \pm t_{.05,df}SE$. The required values are:

	$\bar{Y}_1 - \bar{Y}_2$	Critical t	Std. error
Untrimmed	189.83	2.000	110.90
Trimmed	161.03	2.048	50.85

Substituting into the equation for the confidence interval, the bounds for the untrimmed case are: $CI_{Untrimmed} = 189.83 \pm (2)(110.90) = -31.97, 411.63$; and the interval width $= 411.63 + 31.97 = 443.60$. The bounds for the trimmed case are: $CI_{Trimmed} = 161.03 \pm (2.048)(50.85) = 56.89, 265.17$. Because the trimmed bounds do not contain zero, we know that the difference is significant at the .05 level (two-tailed). Also, the trimmed CI interval width is 208.28, roughly half that for the untrimmed case, and therefore the estimate of the difference is considerably more precise.

CHAPTER 8

8.1 (a) The variances will be multiplied by 100^2. The F ratio will not change because both numerator and denominator increase by the same factor.

(b) The variance is increased by the square of the constant.

(c) Adding a constant to all scores will not change the mean squares or the F ratios.

(d) Because the spread of the group means changes, the MS_A changes. However, adding the same constant to all scores in a group will not change the within-group variance and therefore $MS_{S/A}$ is unaffected.

8.3 (a)

SV	SS	df	MS	F	p
A	44.1	1	44.1	.832	.39
S/A	424.0	8	53.0		

(b) $t = (27.8 - 23.6)/4.604 = .912$. Squaring t, $.912^2 = .832 = F$.

8.5 (a) The histograms, normality plots, and box plots indicate that the data are skewed with a long tail for the high scores. This is supported by the low p-value for the Shapiro–Wilk tests of normality for all three groups. However, the standard deviations are similar, as are the skew statistics. In summary, it is unlikely that Type 1 error rates are inflated, given the equal group sizes and roughly equal standard deviations. However, more powerful tests than the standard F may be found given the straggling right tail. A transformation to normality or a nonparametric test may provide added power.

(b) The ANOVA table is:

	Sum of squares	df	Mean square	F	Sig.
Between groups	3056.133	2	1,528.067	2.967	.062
Within groups	21,631.067	42	515.025		
Total	24,687.200	44			

The mean ranks for the three groups are 16.20, 22.87, and 29.93. SPSS's result for the Kruskal–Wallis (K–W) test is $p = .016$. The difference in results for the ANOVA and K–W tests probably reflects the fact that the transformation to ranks reduces the impact of the long tails on within-group variability, thus increasing power.

8.7 (a) Table 1: $F = 16$, $\hat{\theta}_A^2 = (MS_A - MS_{S/A})/n = (80-5)/10 = 7.5$;

$\hat{\sigma}_A^2 = [(a-1)/a]\hat{\theta}_A^2 = (2/3)(7.5) = 5$; $\hat{\omega}_A^2 = \hat{\sigma}_A^2/(\hat{\sigma}_e^2 + \hat{\sigma}_A^2) = 5/(5 + 5) = .5$.

Table 2: $F = 7.5$; all other values are unchanged.

(b) Increasing the sample size will not generally change the estimate of ω^2 unless the error mean square changes. As these results suggest, the major change will be in the F ratio, which will increase because the contribution of the treatments (θ^2) is multiplied by a larger n.

(c) $\eta^2 = SS_A / SS_{tot}$. Table 1: $\eta^2 = 160/(160 + 135) = .54$; Table 2: $\eta^2 = 85/(85 + 60) = .59$. With ω^2 fixed, increasing n results in a *decrease* in η^2.

(d) (i) If $F = 1$, $MS_{S/A} = MS_A$, and therefore $\hat{\omega}_A^2 = 0$. (ii) $\eta^2 = (a-1)MS_A / [(a-1)MS_A + a(n-1)MS_{S/A}]$. If $F = 1$, this becomes $(a-1)/(an-1)$.

(e) F reflects the sample size as well as treatment effects and error variance. As a result, reliance on F (or the associated p-value) may cause very small effects to appear important if n is very large. In Chapter 6 (Table 6.2), we saw a case in which the data set with the smaller standardized effect size resulted in the larger value of t, and in the present example we saw that ω^2 (or Cohen's f) might be invariant while F varied with n. As we also saw in the present example, η^2 is also affected by n. If we wish to compare effects across similar experiments differing in size, ω^2 is the better measure of effect size.

8.9 $\sigma_A^2 = \sum_j (\mu_{j.} - \mu_{..})^2/a$; $\mu_{j.} = 10, 14, 18$. Therefore, $\sigma = 10.667$ and $f = \sqrt{10.667/30} = 596$. We require $N = 33$, or $n = 11$.

8.11 (a) With respect to location, both means and medians increase from $Sayhlth = 1$ to $Sayhlth = 4$, with the most marked increase in depression scores occurring between the good (3) and fair (4) categories. Note that the lower bound of the 95% confidence interval for $Sayhlth = 4$ is higher than the higher bound for the $Sayhlth = 3$ category. A test of the means with $df = 3$ and 323 yields $F = 16.85$, a very significant result.

   The distributions are skewed, and tests of normality indicate the departure from normality for each group except the $Sayhlth = 4$ group. The lack of significance for that group most likely reflects the small sample of 15; the normal probability plot has a clear departure from a straight line.

   Standard deviations and H-spreads generally increase as ratings increase (i.e., as individuals rate their health as worse). All four tests of homogeneity provided by SPSS's Explore module yield $p < .01$.

(b) The best-fitting straight line for the spread vs level plot has a slope of .787. The usual strategy is to raise each score to a power equal to $1 -$ slope. This is .213. We rounded this and raised each score to .2.

(c) The test of the means still yields a very significant F, 14.102. The transformed scores still depart significantly from normality. However, the heterogeneity of variance has been greatly reduced; the Brown–Forsythe test has an associated p-value of .325, far from significant.

(d) This time, the test of the means yields $F = 16.219$. The distribution of the transformed scores no longer departs significantly from the normal as attested to by nonsignificant Kolmogorov–Smirnov tests for each $Sayhlth$ category. The variances are very similar; the Brown–Forsythe $p > .8$. With respect to meeting the assumptions underlying the ANOVA, $\log(Beck\_D + 1)$ does a good job.

(e) Since the transformations had little effect on the F test of means, why bother? Here are just a few reasons. First, confidence intervals and the proper interpretation of standardized effect size measures rest on the assumption of homogeneity of variance; confidence intervals are also affected by skew. Second, the $\log(Beck\_D + 1)$ transformation may reduce heterogeneity in comparisons for which the effects of variables are not as clear on the original scale. Third, if information is available about the parameters of the sampled population, an individual's z score can be calculated and inferences drawn about that person's score relative to the population on the transformed (presumably normally distributed) scale.

8.13 (a) The ANOVA for sex = 0 (men):

SV	SS	df	MS	F	p
Sayhlth	806.380	3	268.793	16.268	.000
S/Sayhlth	2,577.624	156	16.523		

The ANOVA for sex = 1 (women):

SV	SS	df	MS	F	p
Sayhlth	727.784	3	242.595	7.579	.000
S/Sayhlth	5,217.474	163	32.009		

(b) The estimate of the population variance for the men is $\hat{\sigma}_A^2 = [(a-1)/N](MS_A - MS_{S/A}) = (3/160)(268.793 - 16.523) = 4.730$. Therefore, $\hat{f} = \sqrt{\hat{\sigma}_A^2 / \hat{\sigma}_e^2} = \sqrt{4.730/16.523} = .54$. Similar calculations for the female data yield $\hat{f} = \sqrt{\hat{\sigma}_A^2 / \hat{\sigma}_e^2} = \sqrt{3.783/32.009} = .34$. The estimated effect of the *Sayhlth variable* for males is larger than that for females. However, according to the guidelines suggested by Cohen, the effect for males is large, and that for females nearly so.

CHAPTER 9

9.1 (a)

Source	SS	df	MS	F	Sig.
A	1,118.792	3	372.931	7.177	.003
B	77.042	1	77.042	1.483	.241
AB	1,003.458	3	334.486	6.438	.005
S/AB	831.333	16	51.958		

(b) The cell and marginal means, and main effects are:

	A_1	A_2	A_3	A_4	$\bar{Y}_{..k}$	β_k
B_1	27.333	20.000	35.667	29.333	28.083	−1.792
B_2	38.000	20.333	20.000	48.333	31.667	1.792
$\bar{Y}_{.j.}$	32.667	20.167	27.833	38.833	29.875	
α_j	2.792	−9.708	−2.042	8.958		

The main effects were estimated by subtracting marginal means from the grand mean. For example, $\hat{\alpha}_1 = \bar{Y}_{.1.} - \bar{Y}_{...} = 32.667 - 29.875$. The interaction effects are obtained as $(\bar{Y}_{.jk} - \bar{Y}_{...}) - \hat{\alpha}_j - \hat{\beta}_k$:

	A_1	A_2	A_3	A_4
B_1	−3.542	1.625	9.625	−7.708
B_2	3.542	−1.625	−9.625	7.708

Note that the sum of the main effects and the sums of the row and column interaction effects equal zero.

(c) $SS_A = (6)[2.792^2 + (-.9.708)^2 + (-2.042)^2 + 8.958^2] = 1,118.792$; $SS_B = (12)(2)(1.792^2) = 77.042$; $SS_{AB} = (3)[(-3.542)^2 + \ldots + 7.708^2] = 1,003.458$. The results are the same as in part (a).

9.3 (a) The analysis can be performed on a calculator with a mean and variance key. $MS_A = bn \times \text{var}(\overline{Y}_{j.}) = 7.350$ and, because there is one df, $SS_A = MS_A$. Similarly, $SS_B = (b-1) \times an \times \text{var}(\overline{Y}_{.k})$. $SS_{cells} = (ab - 1) \times n \times \text{var}(\overline{Y}_{jk})$. Finally, $SS_{AB} = SS_{cells} - SS_A - SS_B$. The error mean square ($MS_{S/AB}$) is the average cell variance. Therefore, the ANOVA table is:

SV	df	SS	MS	F	p
A	1	7.350	7.350	2.10	.153
B	2	23.333	11.667	3.33	.043
AB	2	57.600	28.800	8.23	.001
S/AB	54	189.000	3.500		

(b) $SS_{A/B_3} = (10)[(6.5 - 4.95)^2 + (3.4 - 4.95)^2] = 48.05$; $MS_{S/A/B_3} = (5.50 + 3.75)/2 = 3.625$. Therefore, $F = 48.05/3.625 = 13.255$. On 1 and 18 df, $p = .002$.

(c) $MS_{B/A_2} = 10 \times \text{var}(\overline{Y}_{.2k}) = 2.233$; $MS_{S/B/A_2} = (1.75 + 2.25 + 3.75)/3 = 2.583$. $F < 1$ and clearly not significant.

(d) The cell variances range from 1.75 to 5.50. Unless there is clear evidence of homogeneity of variance, the safest course is to base the error term for tests of simple effects on only those cells that are involved. The inclusion of variances that differ from those on which the targeted means are based can bias the F test.

9.5 (a)

Source	Sum of squares	df	Mean square	F	Sig.
A	972.028	2	486.014	3.097	.052
B	3,689.222	3	1,229.741	7.836	.000
AB	2,236.528	6	372.755	2.375	.040
S/AB	9,416.000	60	156.933		

(b) When both A and B are extrinsic factors, $\eta_g^2(A) = SS_A/(SS_A + SS_{S/AB}) = .094$. Similarly, $\eta_g^2(B) = SS_B/(SS_B + SS_{S/AB}) = .282$.

(c) When A is an intrinsic factor, variability due to AB contributes to *general* η^2. Therefore, $\eta_g^2(A) = SS_A/(SS_A + SS_{AB} + SS_{S/AB}) = .077$. $\eta_g^2(B) = SS_B/(SS_B + SS_{AB} + SS_{S/AB}) = .240$.

9.7 (a) Neither the homogeneity of the variance assumption nor the normality assumption seems to be met by these data. Variances appear to be correlated with the means, indicating heterogeneity of variance. Consistent with this, SPSS reports that Levene's F on 7 and 56 df equals 2.437, and is significant at the .03 level. Box plots and stem-and-leaf plots reveal a similar pattern for the H-spreads. With respect to the normality assumption, normal probability plots, the Kolmogorov–Smirnov test, and skewness and kurtosis statistics all indicate that the data are not normally distributed.

(b) The ANOVA table is

SV	df	SS	MS	F	p
Format (F)	1	26.266	26.266	4.705	.034
Instructions (I)	3	106.672	35.557	6.369	.001
FI	3	5.047	1.682	.301	.824
S/FI	56	312.625	5.583		

(c) The pattern of means is much the same as on the original scale although there is a more marked trend toward interaction; the effect of *format* decreases as we move from the narrative to the explanation condition. The most evident change is that the differences among the variances are much reduced; in fact, the Levene test of homogeneity, which previously yielded a p-value of .03, now yields $F_{7,56} = .384$, $p = .91$. In view of this, we redo the ANOVA, using the transformed scores:

SV	df	SS	MS	F	p
Format (F)	1	2.512	2.512	7.86	.007
Instructions (I)	3	8.059	2.686	8.41	.000
FI	3	1.387	.462	1.45	.239
S/FI	56	17.891	.319		

Although conclusions are essentially the same as on the original scale, p-values are lower.

9.9 (a) The numerator is $(63-67)-(37-54) = 13$.

(b) The variance of the linear combination (L) of four independently distributed means is $L = s_1^2/n + s_2^2/n + s_3^2/n + s_4^2/n$. Assuming homogeneity of variance, we replace the group variances by their average, $MS_{S/AB} = 150$, and n by 10, then, the denominator of the t statistic is $\sqrt{(4)(150/10)} = 7.746$.

(c) $t = 13/7.746 = 1.68$. F on one numerator df is $t^2 = 2.82$.

9.11 (a)

SV	df	SS	MS	F	p	EMS
A	2	194.867	97.433	3.903	.034	$\sigma_e^2 + 100\theta_A^2$
E	1	112.133	112.133	4.491	.045	$\sigma_e^2 + 150\theta_E^2$
AE	2	77.267	38.364	1.547	.233	$\sigma_e^2 + 50\theta_{AE}^2$
S/AE	24	599.200	24.967			σ_e^2

(b) $\hat{\omega}_g^2(A) = \hat{\sigma}_A^2/(\hat{\sigma}_A^2 + \hat{\sigma}_e^2)$; $\hat{\sigma}_A^2 = (MS_A - MS_{S/AE})(2/30) = 4.831$; $\hat{\sigma}_e^2 = 24.967$. Therefore, $\hat{\omega}_g^2(A) = .162$.

(c)

SV	df	SS	MS	F	p	EMS
A	2	194.867	97.433	3.336	.051	$\sigma_e^2 + 100\theta_A^2$
S/A	27	788.6	29.207			σ_e^2

(d) Our estimate of σ_A^2 is now 4.548, and $\hat{\omega}_v^2(A) = .135$.

(e) Neglecting a variable pools it and its interaction sums of squares with the error sum of squares. Because E contributed more than random error to $MS_{S/A}$, the p-value in the test of A was inflated, and we underestimated A's contribution to the population variance, as evidenced by the reduction in our estimate of $\omega_g^2(A)$. All factors should be included in the initial analysis and only neglected if there is strong evidence that they contribute nothing beyond error variance in the population.

9.13 (a) $\eta_g^2(L) = SS_L/(SS_L + SS_X + SS_{LX} + SS_{MX} + SS_{MLX} + SS_{S/MLX})$
$$= SS_{Total} - SS_M - SS_{ML}$$
Because they are distributed on 1 df, the sums of squares equal the mean squares except $SS_{S/MLX}$, which equals $72 \times .065 = 4.680$. Summing, $SS_{Total} = 6.291$; then $\eta_g^2(L) = .273/5.505 = .050$. Also, $\eta_g^2(X) = SS_X/(SS_{Total} - SS_M - SS_L - SS_{LM}) = .047$.

(b) $\hat{\omega}_g^2(M) = \hat{\sigma}_M^2/(\hat{\sigma}_M^2 + \hat{\sigma}_X^2 + \hat{\sigma}_{MX}^2 + \hat{\sigma}_{LX}^2 + \hat{\sigma}_{MLX}^2 + \hat{\sigma}_{S/MLX}^2)$. We need to estimate several population variances. Let MS stand for any of the mean squares, other than $MS_{S/MLX}$. Then the corresponding variance estimate is $(df_{MS}/N)(MS - MS_{S/MLX})$ where $df_{MS} = 1$, $N = 80$, and $MS_{S/MLX} = .065$. Multiplying by 100 (the ratio will not change), the variance estimates for the various sources in the preceding equation are

M	X	LX	MX	MLX	S/MLX
.475	.225	.014	.030	.096	6.500

and, after substitution and division, $\omega_g^3(M) = .065$.

9.15 (a) From the df for A, B, and C, we know there are 24 cells. Dividing N by 24, $n = 4$. Also, $MS_{S/ABC} = MS_A/F = 20$.

(b) $\hat{\sigma}_A^2 = \left(\dfrac{a-1}{a}\right)\left(\dfrac{MS_A - MS_{S/ABC}}{bnc}\right) = (3/96)(56.8 - 20) = 1.150$; $\hat{f}^2 = \hat{\sigma}_A^2/\hat{\sigma}_e^2 = 1.15/20 = .058$.

(c) From G*Power 3, we obtain power = .63.

9.17 (a) $SS_{cells} = \sum_j\sum_j n_{jk}(\bar{Y}_{.jk} - \bar{Y}...)^2 = (2)(10 - 5)^2 + (4)(10 - 5)^2 + (8)(2 - 5)^2 + (2)(2 - 5)^2 = 240$.

(b) $SS_A = \sum_j n_j.(\bar{Y}_{.j.} - \bar{Y}...)^2 = (6)(10 - 5)^2 + (10)(2 - 5)^2 = 240$; similarly, $SS_B = 52.267$. The combined variability due to A and B is greater than the variability among the four cell means, an impossible result. If we were to calculate SS_{AB} in the usual way (subtracting from SS_{cells}), we would have a negative sum of squares. The problem is that the A and B effects are correlated.

(c) $\hat{\alpha}_1 = 10 - 5 = 5$; $\hat{\alpha}_2 = 2 - 5 = -3$. Note that $\sum_j n_j.\hat{\alpha}_j = 0$.

(d) Adjusting for the effects of A, the cell means are now all 5. The SS_B and SS_{AB} are now both zero. This peculiar state of affairs exists because the A, B, and AB effects are perfectly correlated in this "data set." Although the correlation will not be zero with real disproportionate cell frequencies, calculations such as those in parts (a) and (b) will give misleading, and often absurd, results. Regression methods that provide more appropriate analyses are discussed in Chapter 24.

9.19 (a)

Source	df	MS	Error term	F	p
Method (M)	1	3,627	G/M	8.64	.009
Sex (X)	1	128	G/MX	4.00	.061
MX	1	123	G/MX	3.84	.066
Groups/Method (G/M)	18	420			
GX/M	18	32			
Residual	40	30			

(b) The reanalysis rests on the assumption that $\sigma_{GXIM} = 0$.

(c)

Source	df	MS	EMS
Method (M)	1	3,627	$\sigma_e^2 + 4\sigma_{G/M}^2 + 400\theta_M^2$
Sex (X)	1	128	$\sigma_e^2 + 400\theta_X^2$
MX	1	123	$\sigma_e^2 + 200\theta_{MX}^2$
Groups/Method (G/M)	18	420	$\sigma_e^2 + 4\sigma_{G/M}^2$
Pooled residual	58	30.62	σ_e^2

Note: The new residual mean square = $[(18)(32) + (40)(30)]/(18 + 40) = 30.621$.

(d) $F_X = 128/58 = 4.18$; with 1 and 58 df, $p = .045$. $F_{MX} = 123/58 = 4.02$; with 1 and 58 df, $p = .050$. Terms that previously were not significant now are.

(e) The F ratio for a test of $GXIM$ is less than 1, indicating that this term does not contribute to the variance in the population.

CHAPTER 10

10.1 (a) H_0: $(1/2)(\mu_{F1} + \mu_{F2}) - \mu_C \leq 0$; H_1: $(1/2)(\mu_{F1} + \mu_{F2}) - \mu_C > 0$. To test H_0, calculate

$$t = \frac{\hat{\psi}}{\sqrt{MS_{S/A}\sum_j w_j^2 / n}} = \frac{(1/2)(14.6 + 14.9) - 13.8}{\sqrt{(4)(.5^2 + .5^2 + 1^2)/20}} = 1.734$$

The error mean square is based on 5×20 scores, or 95 df; therefore, the p-value is .043. Reject H_0. Note that the group variances are quite similar; therefore, we averaged them to obtain the error mean square, $MS_{S/A}$. Also, note that doubling the weights to yield integers (1, 1, and −2) leaves t unchanged.

(b) H_0: $\mu_C - (1/2)(\mu_{I1} + \mu_{I2}) = 0$; H_1: $(1/2)(\mu_{I1} + \mu_{I2}) - \mu_C \neq 0$. Proceeding as in part (a), $t = 2.05/.548 = 3.743$, which is clearly significant.

(c) H_0: $(1/2)(\mu_{F1} + \mu_{F2}) - (1/2)(\mu_{I1} + \mu_{I2}) = 0$; H_1: $(1/2)(\mu_{F1} + \mu_{F2}) - (1/2)(\mu_{I1} + \mu_{I2}) \neq 0$. $t = 3/.447 = 6.708$. The null hypothesis can be rejected.

10.3 (a) $SS_A = (10)[(24 - 18)^2 + (16 - 18)^2 + (14 - 18)^2] = 560$.

(b) (i) $SS_{\hat{\psi}_1} = (24 - 16)^2 / (2/10) = 320$; (ii) $SS_{\hat{\psi}_2} = (20 - 14)^2 / (1.5/10) = 240$; (iii) $SS_{\hat{\psi}_3} = (24 - 14)^2 / (2/10) = 500$. Because the contrasts are orthogonal, $SS_{\hat{\psi}_1} + SS_{\hat{\psi}_2} = SS_A$.

(c) $SS_{\hat{\psi}_2}$ is unchanged because the contrast is orthogonal to the first contrast. However, $SS_{\hat{\psi}_3}$ is changed because it is not orthogonal to the first contrast. One way to think about this is in terms of a pie in which ψ_1 and ψ_2 represent nonoverlapping slices. Removing one does not change the size of the other. However, ψ_3 does overlap with the other two, so that removing either of the other two affects the size of ψ_3.

10.5 (a) $\hat{\psi}_s = \hat{\psi}/s_{pooled} = \sum_j w_j \overline{Y}_j/\sqrt{MS_{S/A}} = 6/30 = .2$.

(b) $\hat{\psi} = (8/18)(24) + (10/18)(16) - 14 = 5.556$. $\hat{\psi}_s = \hat{\psi} / 30 = .185$. Note that the effect size should be calculated on the original scale; i.e., do not multiply by 18 to create integer weights.

10.7 (a) (i) Let $\psi = \mu_B - (1/2)(\mu_A + \mu_C)$. Then H_0: $\psi = 0$; H_1: $\psi > 0$. (ii) $s_{\hat{\psi}}^2 = MS_{error}\sum_j w_j^2/n_j$. The error mean square is the average of the three variances, and all ns equal 10. Therefore, $s_{\hat{\psi}}^2 = (70)(1.5/10) = 10.5$. (iii) $t = \hat{\psi}/s_{\hat{\psi}} = 6.5/3.24 = 2.006$.

(b) (i) The standard t test, on 27 df, is appropriate if this test is the only one and has been planned. For α = .05 and a one-tailed alternative, reject H_0 if $t > 1.703$; therefore, reject H_0. (ii) The Scheffé method is appropriate here; t is compared with $S = \sqrt{df_1} \cdot F_{.05,df_1,df_2}$ where df_1 and df_2 refer to the numerator and denominator df (2 and 27). Substituting values, $S = \sqrt{(2)(3.35)} = 2.59$; $t = 2.01$, so we cannot reject H_0. Note that we treat this as a test against a two-tailed alternative. If we are "data-snooping," we are considering all possible differences in both directions that might be suggested by the data.

10.9 (a) $s_{\hat\psi} = \sqrt{(20)(2.7)} = 2.390$. The critical value of the Dunnett statistic is $d_{.05,30} = 2.62$. Reject H_0 if the absolute value of $t = (\bar{Y}_j - \bar{Y}_C)/\sqrt{MS_{error}\,(2/n)} > 2.62$, or $|\bar{Y}_j - \bar{Y}_C| > (2.62)(2.390)$. Therefore, the critical distance is 6.26, and all comparisons, except A_4 versus A_5, are significant.

(b) The null hypothesis is H_0: $(\mu_1 - \mu_2) - (\mu_3 - \mu_4) = 0$. Therefore, $\hat\psi = (29) - (16) = 13$, $s_{\hat\psi} = \sqrt{(20)(4/7)} = 3.381$, and $t = 13/3.381 = 3.85$, leading us to reject H_0.

(c) As in part (a), we calculate the critical distance by multiplying the critical value of t by $s_{\hat\psi}$. $q_{.05,5,30} = 4.10$; therefore, reject H_0 if $|t| > 4.10/\sqrt{2} = 2.90$, or if the absolute difference between two means is greater than $(2.90)\sqrt{MS_{error}(2/n)} = (2.90)(2.39) = 6.93$.

10.11 (a) $F = 86.679/28.895 = 3.00$; with 2 and 323 df, $p = .051$.

(b) For three groups, $q_{.05,323}$ is 3.325; therefore, the critical value of $t_{crit} = 3.31/\sqrt{2} = 2.351$. Let $\bar{D} = \bar{Y}_j - \bar{Y}_{j'}$ and $SE = s_{\bar{D}}$. The confidence limits are $\bar{D} \pm t_{crit} SE$ and $SE = \sqrt{MS_{error}(1/n_j + 1/n_{j'})}$. The numerical values are:

Employment categories	$\bar{D}$	SE	CI limits
1, 2	1.274	.872	−0.778, 3.326
1, 3	1.730	.783	−0.113, 3.573
2, 3	.456	1.053	−2.025, 2.936

(c) Because the number of comparisons, k, equals 3, $\alpha = .017$ (two-tailed), and with 323 df, $t_{crit} = 2.408$. The values of $\bar{D}$ and SE are the same as in part (b); the confidence intervals now are:

Employment categories	CI
1, 2	−.823, 3.372
1, 3	−.154, 3.514
2, 3	−2.080, 2.991

The D–B interval widths are about the same as the T–K. With both methods, all three intervals contain zero; therefore, none of the differences are significant when the FWE is controlled.

10.13 Ability: $SS_A = [(\bar{Y}_{.11} + \bar{Y}_{.12}) - (\bar{Y}_{.21} + \bar{Y}_{.22})]^2/(4/10) = 1690$;

Text: $SS_B = [(\bar{Y}_{.11} + \bar{Y}_{.21}) - (\bar{Y}_{.12} + \bar{Y}_{.22})]^2/(4/10) = 490$;

$SS_{AB} = [(\bar{Y}_{.11} + \bar{Y}_{.22}) - (\bar{Y}_{.12} + \bar{Y}_{.21})]^2/(4/10) = 40$.

10.15 (a)

SV	df	SS	MS	F	p
A	2	12,915.56	6,457.78	82.56	.000
B	2	1,202.22	601.11	7.68	.001
AB	4	431.11	107.78	1.38	.248
S/AB	81	6,336.00	78.22		

(b) $\hat{\psi} = (1/2)(68.333 + 67) - 60 = 7.667$. $S_{\hat{\psi}} = \sqrt{MS_{S/AB}\sum_k w_{\cdot k}^2/an} = \sqrt{(78.222)(1.5/30)} = 1.978$. The

confidence interval is $7.667 \pm (1.99)(1.978) = 3.73, 11.60$; the limits do not include zero. Therefore, the contrast differs significantly from zero.

(c) The contrast is $\hat{\psi} = [(1/2)(\bar{Y}_{\cdot 12} + \bar{Y}_{\cdot 13}) - \bar{Y}_{\cdot 11}] - [(1/2)(\bar{Y}_{\cdot 32} + \bar{Y}_{\cdot 33}) - \bar{Y}_{\cdot 31}] = [(1/2)(56 + 52) - 44] - [(1/2)(83 + 79) - 78] = 7$, and (assuming homogeneity of variance)

$$s_{\hat{\psi}} = \sqrt{MS_{S/AB}\sum_j\sum_k w_{jk}^2/n} = \sqrt{(78.222)(3/10)} = 4.844.\ t = 7/4.844 = 1.45;\ \text{on 81}\ df, \text{this is not}$$

significant. We cannot conclude that the contrast differs between the two age levels.

10.17 Dunnett's method is the appropriate method for comparing each of several groups with a control. The control group variance ($s^2 = 4.5^2$) is quite similar to the $MS_{S/AB}$ and therefore can be pooled with it. We can compare the t statistic with the critical value of Dunnett's d statistic (Appendix Table C.8), where $t = (\bar{Y}_E - \bar{Y}_C)/\sqrt{s_{pooled}^2(1/n_E + 1/n_C}$, and the E and C subscripts refer to experimental and control groups. In the present example, the pooled variance $= [(72)(21.432) + (9)(20.25)]/81 = 21.300$, $n_E = n_C = 10$, and the standard error is $s_{diff} = 2.064$. The critical value of d, with $\alpha = .10$ and 81 df, is approximately 2.43. We could calculate eight t statistics, comparing each with d, but a simpler approach is to note that if $t > d_{crit}$, then $|\bar{Y}_E - \bar{Y}_C| > s_{diff}d_{crit}$, or 5.02. The absolute differences between each mean and the control mean is:

Mood	Focus = content		Focus = language	
	Message		Message	
	Strong	Weak	Strong	Weak
Happy	4.70	1.10	3.30	8.70*
Sad	11.50*	1.10	3.20	2.10

The two differences marked by an asterisk are the only significant ones. In summary, means of experimental conditions differ significantly from the mean of a control only when subjects are sad and focused on the content of a strongly worded message, or when subjects are happy and focused on the language of a weakly worded message.

CHAPTER 11

11.1 (a) $\bar{X} = 2.5$, $\bar{Y} = 4.84$. Therefore,

$$X_j - \bar{X}. = \quad -1.5 \quad -.5 \quad .5 \quad 1.5$$
$$\bar{Y}_{\cdot j} - \bar{Y}.. = \quad 1.65 \quad -.02 \quad -.59 \quad -1.04$$

Let $SP = \sum_j(X_j - \bar{X})(\bar{Y}_{\cdot j} - \bar{Y}..) = -4.32$ and $\sum_j(X_j - \bar{X})^2 = 5.0$. Then $b_1 = SP/\sum_j(X_j - \bar{X})^2 = -.864$ and $b_0 = \bar{Y} - b_1\bar{X} = 4.84 - (-.864)(2.5) = 7.00$.

(b) $b_0 + b_1X = 6.136, 5.272, 4.408$, and 3.544.

(c) (i) $SS_{lin} = n\sum_j(\bar{Y}_{pre,j} - \bar{Y}..)^2 = 29.860$. (ii) Using integer weights $(-3, -1, 1, 3)$, $SS_{lin} = \dfrac{\hat{\psi}^2}{\Sigma w_j^2/n} = $

$\dfrac{(-8.64)^2}{(9 + 1 + 1 + 9)/8} = 29.860$. $F_{1,28} = 29.860/1.42 = 21.028$. (iii) The best-fitting straight line has a slope significantly different from zero.

11.3   The ANOVA table is:

SV	df	SS	MS	F	p
A	3	62.55	20.85	4.44	.019
Linear	1	39.69	39.69	8.45	.010
Quadratic	1	14.45	14.45	3.07	.099
Cubic	1	8.41	8.41	1.79	.200
S/A	16	75.20	4.70		

The results support Smith's hypothesis of an increasing trend with increased group size. However, n is small and a more powerful test might reveal the significant quadratic component that Brown predicted.

11.5   (a) According to the theoretical model, the function relating d' and time should increase with time and be S-shaped. This suggests linear and cubic polynomial components.

(b) The sums of squares for the polynomial components can be obtained as we did for the quadratic in Equation 11.14; only the weights change. Also, most statistical software will provide the trend analysis. In SPSS, select *Analyze*, then *Compare means*, and then *One-way ANOVA*. Before running the analysis, select the *contrast* option and indicate a polynomial contrast. The ANOVA results are:

SV	df	SS	MS	F	p
Time	6	8.700	1.450	20.47	.000
Linear	1	5.582	5.582	78.81	.000
Quadratic	1	.066	.066	.94	.339
Cubic	1	2.727	2.727	38.50	.000
Order 4	1	.000	.000	.00	.982
Order 5	1	.253	.253	3.57	.067
Order 6	1	.070	.070	.99	.326
S/Time	35	2.485	.071		

As the model predicts, only the linear and cubic components are significant.

11.7   (a) The following is a plot containing *SEM* bars.

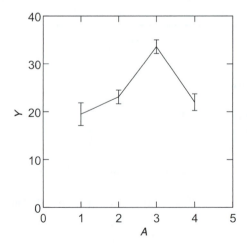

(b) The ANOVA table is:

SV	df	SS	MS	F	p
A	3	1160.1	386.7	13.651	.000
Linear	1	162.0	162.0	5.719	.022
Quadratic	1	577.6	577.6	20.390	.000
Cubic	1	420.5	420.5	14.844	.000
S/A	36	1019.8	28.328		

(c) The means at the A_1, A_2, and A_3 levels are increasing, contributing to the significant linear component. The downturn at A_4 is apparently responsible for the quadratic component. The inflection point at A_2 is the most likely reason for the cubic contribution.

11.9 (a) The hypothesis suggests that both the linear and quadratic components of the rate variable should be significant. $\hat{\psi}_1 = [(-1)(60.313) + 0 + (1)(44.625)] = -15.688$ and $SS_{Lin(Rate)} = 15.688^2/(1/16 + 1/16) = 1,968.781$. Similarly, $\hat{\psi}_2 = [(-1)(60.313) + (2)(54.813) + (-1)(44.625)] = 4.688$ and $SS_{Quad(Rate)} = 4.688^2/(1/16 + 4/16 + 1/16) = 58.594$. $MS_{error} = 62.152$. Therefore, the linear trend is significant ($F_{1,42} = 31.677$, $p = .000$) whereas the quadratic is not ($F < 1$).

(b) The $Lin(Rate) \times Text$ contrast is calculated as $[(-1)(66.250) + 0 + (1)(43.375)] - [(-1)(54.375) + 0 + (1)(45.875)] = -14.375$. Squaring this and dividing by $\sum_j \sum_k w_{jk}^2/n$, or 4/8, $SS_{Lin(Rate) \times Text} = 413.281$. Similarly, $SS_{Quad(Rate) \times Text} = 78.844$. The slopes of the functions differ significantly as a function of whether the text is intact or scrambled ($F_{1,42} = 6.65$, $p = .014$). The quadratic components do not differ significantly ($F_{1,42} = 1.27$, $p = .266$).

(c) $SS_{Rate \times Text} = 492.125 = 413.281 + 78.844$; the two sums of squares calculated in part (b) account for the variability due to interaction.

(d) Average scores deteriorate as rate increases, but the slope is significantly more negative in the intact condition, perhaps because in the scrambled condition, performance is poor even at the slow rate. There is no evidence for quadratic curvature, in either the quadratic component of rate or its interaction with the type of text.

11.11 For the boys ($j = 1$), the linear regression coefficient (the slope of the best-fitting straight line) is $b'_{1,boys} = \left(\sum_k w_{k1} \overline{Y}_{\cdot 1k} \right) \Big/ \left(\sum_k w_{k1}^2 \right) = [(-3)(16.3) + (-1)(7.2) + (1)(6.5) + (3)(7.4)]/20 = -1.37$. Similarly, the slope of the girls' means is $b'_{1,girls} = -.915$. The intercepts are $b'_{0,boys} = \overline{Y}_{\cdot 1} = 9.350$, and $b'_{0,girls} = \overline{Y}_{\cdot 2} = 8.075$. Then the predicted means are $\overline{Y}_{pre,1,k} = b'_{0,k} + b'_{1,k} w_{lin,k}$. Substituting, the predicted scores are 13.46, 10.72, 7.98, and 5.24 for boys, and 10.82, 8.99, 7.16, and 5.33 for girls. The sum of squares for the $Sex \times Age$ interaction based on these predicted means is 10.35, the value of $SS_{Lin(Age) \times Sex}$, in Exercise 11.10. In summary, the sum of squares for the linear component of interaction reflects departures from parallelism of the best-fitting straight lines.

11.13 (a) The means are

	Time =	15	30	45	Means
Exptal	High	.539	.201	.176	.305
	Low	.216	.041	.059	.105
Means		.378	.121	.118	.205
Control	High	.197	.166	.175	.179
	Low	.089	.112	.120	.107
Means		.143	.139	.148	.143

There are more false reports in the experimental condition than in the control condition; the experimental mean is .062 higher than the control. However, this seems entirely due to the 15-second viewing condition. Relatedness also appears to have an effect; there were more false recalls of items that were related to those actually studied. This is true even in the control groups although the effect is greater in the experimental groups.

(b) The ANOVA table, including trend components, is

SV	df	SS	MS	F	p
Context (C)	1	.092	.092	3.39	.069
Time (T)	2	.354	.177	6.51	.002
$Lin(T)$	1	.261	.261	9.59	.003
$Quad(T)$	1	.093	.093	3.43	.068
Related (R)	1	.445	.445	16.35	.000
$C \times T$	2	.357	.178	6.56	.002
$C \times Lin(T)$	1	.280	.280	10.37	.002
$C \times Quad(T)$	1	.077	.077	2.85	.095
$C \times R$	1	.098	.098	3.59	.061
$T \times R$	2	.077	.039	1.42	.247
$C \times T \times R$	2	.025	.012	.46	.634
Error	84	2.285	.027		

Objects highly related to those that actually were studied were more often falsely recalled; this effect was quite significant ($F_{1,84} = 16.35$, $p = .000$). Although false recalls occurred significantly more often in the experimental condition (in which the confederate gave false reports), this appears to be entirely due to the shortest viewing times. This is reflected in the significant context $\times$ time interaction, and particularly by its linear component.

11.15 An easy way to visualize what the data might look like is to build in the same linear effect at each level of A and then to add quadratic effects that cancel each other. For the linear component, we have

	B_1	B_2	B_3	B_4
A_1	−3	−1	1	3
A_2	−3	−1	1	3

For the quadratic component, we have

	B_1	B_2	B_3	B_4
A_1	−1	1	1	−1
A_2	1	−1	−1	1

Adding these. we arrive at a set of "means" that are entirely consistent with the starred sources corresponding to the theory:

	B_1	B_2	B_3	B_4	Mean
A_1	-4	0	2	2	0
A_2	-2	-2	0	4	0
Mean	-3	-1	1	3	

There are many other possible patterns that are consistent with the ANOVA table. Any linear transformation of the means (adding the same constant to them all, or multiplying all by the same constant) will result in sums of squares greater than zero only for the starred terms.

CHAPTER 12

12.1 Although we cannot reject the null hypotheses that the data are normally distributed, or that the population variances are homogeneous, the box plots indicate long tails and several outliers, a condition that indicates that the error variance may be inflated. This suggests that trimming the data might provide a more powerful test. Following the procedure in Box 8.2, we sorted the data in each group and trimmed 20% of the scores from each tail. The between-groups mean square based on the trimmed scores ($MS_{Groups,T}$) is 946.75. The winsorized within-groups sum of squares ($SS_{within,\,w}$) is 7,128.75, and the error degrees of freedom are $(3)(20 - 1 - 8) = 33$. Therefore, the F test of groups based on trimming $= 946.75/(7,128.75/33) = 4.383$; $p = .021$. The F test based on the untrimmed data yielded $p = .226$.

Two other alternatives might be considered; conversion to ranks would also reduce the effect of extreme scores. However, although the Kruskal–Wallis H test yields $p = .101$, it is not as effective in reducing the influence of outliers as the trimming procedure. Trimming also has the advantage of allowing us to use the winsorized standard error to obtain confidence intervals on the differences among group means. A second possibility is a transformation. SPSS's *spread-vs-level* plot reveals a monotonic relation between the log of the spread (the interquartile range) and the log of the median, and the note suggests raising each score to a power of 3.18. For simplicity, we cubed each score and performed an ANOVA, with no improvement over the standard F.

We emphasize that we have included these alternative procedures to illustrate the possibilities and for comparison purposes, but that, in practice, we would choose one method based on the exploration of the data. Trying a variety of tests and settling on the one that provides the lowest p-value greatly risks the possibility of a Type 1 error.

12.3 The test of the assumption of normality leads us to reject the assumption. Furthermore, although the tests of homogeneity of variance are not significant, there is a clear increase in spread as the medians increase (see the box plots and spread-vs-level plots). Histograms or stem-and-leaf plots show strongly skewed distributions. SPSS's *spread-vs-level* option reveals a monotonic increasing relationship between the log of the spread and the log of the median, and suggests raising scores to a power of .28. This is close enough to zero to encourage us to try a log transformation, which we consider somewhat more understandable and common in the literature. The results of the usual F test, the test on the log-transformed data, and the tests on scores raised to the .28 power are:

		Sum of squares	df	Mean square	F	Sig.
Y	Between groups	2,878.233	2	1,439.117	2.975	.059
	Within groups	27,571.500	57	483.711		
	Total	30,449.733	59			
Y_log	Between groups	5.844	2	2.922	3.508	.037
	Within groups	47.476	57	.833		
	Total	53.320	59			
Y_28	Between groups	2.202	2	1.101	3.528	.036
	Within groups	17.792	57	.312		
	Total	19.994	59			

The difference in results between the transformed and untransformed data seems largely a result of reducing the differences in the variances. Whichever transformation we consider, the group variances now are more homogeneous. The log transformation also appears to have resulted in data that more nearly conform to a normal distribution although this was not the case for the cubed data. Because the assumption of normality plays a role in other inferential procedures, we prefer the log transformation.

12.5 (a) For this problem, Welch's t' should be calculated because the variances differ markedly; refer to Equations 10.8–10.10. The test statistic is $t' = 8.2/\sqrt{(7.2 + 8 + 15.3 + 20.6)/5} = 8.2/3.197 = 2.57$. The degrees of freedom are $df' = 3.197^4/[(7.2^2 + 8^2 + 15.3^2 + 20.6^2)/(5^2 \times 4)] = 13.49$. Setting $\alpha = .05/4$, or .0125, and turning to Table C.3 with 13 df, the p-value is between .05 and .02 (two-tailed). Since .02 is greater than .0125, we cannot reject the null hypothesis. Note that even if $df = 14$, we reach the same conclusion.

(b) Again calculate the Welch t statistic: $t' = 6.8/\sqrt{(7.2 + 24.1)/5} = 6.8/2.502 = 2.72$. The degrees of freedom are $df' = 2.502^4/[(7.2^2 + 24.1^2)/(5^2 \times 4)] = 6.19$. Since five comparisons are tested, $\alpha = .01$. On so few degrees of freedom, we cannot reject H_0.

12.7 (a) Let N, E, W, and T represent Novice, Expert, Web, and Text, respectively. Then the null hypothesis is $(\mu_{N,T} - \mu_{N,W}) - (\mu_{E,T} - \mu_{E,W}) = 0$. Therefore, we have

	Novice		Expert	
	Text	Web	Text	Web
Mean	72.50	83.25	72.25	89.00
Weight	1	−1	−1	1

and with 20 scores in each cell, $SS_{F \times E} = [(72.50 - 83.25) - (72.25 - 89.00)]^2/(4/20) = 36/.2 = 180$, the result in Table 9.12.

(b) Similarly, with S and A representing Summary and Argument conditions, the null hypothesis is $[(\mu_{N,T,S} - \mu_{N,W,S}) - (\mu_{E,T,S} - \mu_{E,W,S})] - [(\mu_{N,T,A} - \mu_{N,W,A}) - (\mu_{E,T,A} - \mu_{E,W,A})] = 0$. Then, $SS_{F \times E \times I} = \{[(71.25 - 76.50) - (70.50 - 88.25)] - [(73.75 - 90) - (74 - 89.75)]\}^2/(8.10) = 211.25$.

12.9 (a) The L and M marginal means are 15.8 and 11.0, respectively. The cell variances are all quite similar; therefore, the Tukey HSD method will be applied. The formula for the confidence interval bounds is $CI = \bar{Y}_L - \bar{Y}_M \pm q_{.05,5,90}S_{\bar{Y}}$. The difference between the means is 4.8; the critical value of q at the .05 level, ranging over five means, with 90 df is approximately 3.75, and the standard error of the mean is $S_{\bar{Y}} = \sqrt{MS_{S/cells}/bn} = \sqrt{110/20} = 2.345$. Therefore, the bounds are $4.8 \pm (3.75)(2.345) = -3.99, 13.59$. Because the CI bounds enclose 0, we cannot reject the null hypothesis.

(b) The null hypothesis is $(1/2)(\mu_L + \mu_{LL}) - (1/2)(\mu_C + \mu_{CC}) = 0$. Multiplying by 2 to have integers, the test statistic is $t = [(17.3 + 15.8) - (8.5 + 6.9)]/\sqrt{MS_{S/cells} (4/20)} = 3.774$.

(c) (i) The criterion is $t_{.05, 90} = 1.99$; reject H_0 if $t > 1.99$ or $t < -1.99$. (ii) Because there are three planned tests, the criterion is $t_{.05/3, 90} = 2.46$; reject H_0 if $t > 2.46$ or $t < -2.46$. (iii) The Scheffé procedure should be used here. We need $S = \sqrt{4F_{.05, 4, 90}}$; the critical F is 2.48 and therefore the critical value $= 3.150$; reject H_0 if $t > 3.15$ or $t < -3.15$.

(d) (i) Let 1 refer to retirees and 2 to college students. Then H_0: $\psi = [(1/2)(\mu_{2,L} + \mu_{2,LL}) - \mu_{2,M})] - [(1/2)(\mu_{1,L} + \mu_{1,LL}) - \mu_{1,M})] = 0$. (ii) $\hat{\psi} = [(.5)(18.5 + 16.9) - 8.5] - [(.5)(16.1 + 14.7) - 13.5] = 7.3$. The

standard error is $s_{\hat{\psi}} = \sqrt{\left(\sum_j \sum_k w_{jk}^2/n\right)(MS_{S/cells})}$ or $s_{\hat{\psi}} = \sqrt{[(4)(.25/10) + (2)(1/10)](110)} = 5.745$. The

critical value of t is $t_{.05, 90} = 1.99$. Therefore, the CI limits are $7.3 \pm (1.99)(5.745) = -4.133, 18.733$. The null hypothesis cannot be rejected.

12.11 For the prediction method, $\Sigma_k w_k Y_{jk} = (-3)(61) + (-1)(69) + (1)(82) + (3)(91) = 103$. The linear contrasts for the other two methods equal 94 and 60. The variance of the three numbers is 514.333. Dividing by 20/8, the result is 205.733, the answer you should have obtained in Exercise 12.10.

CHAPTER 13

13.1 (a)

Source	SS	df	MS	F	Sig.
A	861.233	2	430.617	2.431	.097
S/A	10,096.700	57	177.135		
Total	10,957.933	59			

If the blocking factor contributes variance it will inflate the error term but will not affect the numerator because the levels of A are equated for the pretest score (blocks factor). In terms of expected mean squares, $E(MS_A) = \sigma_e^2 + bn\theta_A^2$. However, $E(MS_{S/A}) = \sigma_e^2 + [(b-1)an\theta_B^2 + (a-1)(b-1)n\theta_{AB}^2]/(abn-1)$; this is an average of the mean squares for S/AB, B, and AB. Therefore, if either B or AB contributes variability, the F test will be negatively biased.

(b) The correct ANOVA is:

Source	SS	df	MS	F	Sig.
A	861.233	2	430.617	3.411	.041
B	3,269.133	3	1,089.711	8.633	.000
AB	768.367	6	128.061	1.014	.427
S/AB	6,059.200	48	126.233		
Total	10,957.933	59			

The A effect is now significant; although the error df are reduced, the error mean square no longer reflects the rather large effects of blocks and thus the error term is much smaller than in part (a).

Note that $SS_{S/A}$ [from part (a)] equals $SS_{S/AB} + SS_B + SS_{AB}$. Equivalently, $MS_{S/A}$ is the average (weighted by degrees of freedom) of the three mean squares: $MS_A = [(48)(MS_{S/AB}) + (3)(MS_B) + (6)(MS_{AB})]/(48 + 3 + 6)$.

13.3 (a) $\hat{\sigma}_A^2 = (a - 1)(MS_A - MS_{S/AB})/abn = (2)(430.617 - 126.233)/60 = 10.146$. Then $\hat{f} = \sqrt{10.146/126.233} = .284$.

(b) Now $\hat{f} = \sqrt{10.146/175.409} = .241$.

(c) Using G*Power's post hoc ANOVA for main and interaction effects, power = .466 for the $T \times B$ design. Using the one-way option, power = .351 for the CR design.

(d) For the CR design, to achieve power = .466 with $f = .241$, $N = 84$, or 28 subjects at each level of A. The ratio of the estimated CR sample size to the size of the $T \times B$ experiment, 84/60, = 1.4, approximately the estimated relative efficiency of the two designs.

(e) From G*Power 3, for the $T \times B$ design with $f = .284$ and $\alpha = .05$, N must equal 123 to achieve power = .8. We estimate the N needed for the one-way design by multiplying 123 by the RE of 1.38 and get $N = 170$. To have a value divisible by 3, the number of groups, $N = 171$. As a check, select the *a priori* option for the one-way ANOVA F test, enter our estimated f of .241, $\alpha = .05$, power = .8, and three groups; the same result is obtained: $N = 171$. The relative efficiency of the two designs provides an estimate of the ratio of sample sizes needed to achieve a given level of power.

13.5 (a) For the 60 scores, $r = .084$. Therefore, $1 - r^2 = .993$, as does the ratio of the adjusted total SS (10,880) to the unadjusted total (10,958).

(b) $r_{S/A}^2 = (-749 + 2010.75 + 5.8)^2/[(1,736 + 3,591.75 + 1,874.2)(2,624.55 + 2,418.95 + 5,053.2)] = 1,267.55^2/(7,202.05 \times 10,096.7) = .022$. The adjusted error sum of squares from the ANCOVA (within rounding error) = $(1 - .022) \times SS_{S/A}$. Note that the reduction in the error variance due to taking X into consideration will increase as a function of the within-group correlation.

13.7 (a)

Variance	Variance estimate
A	$(32.25 - 3.917)(2/12) = 4.722$
S	$(18.333 - 3.917)/3 = 4.805$
Error	3.917
Within	$4.805 + 3.917 = 8.722$

$\hat{f} = \sqrt{4.722 / 8.722} = .736$.

(b) Power = .94.

(c) Power = .47. Despite the increased error degrees of freedom, because subject variability does not contribute to its error variance, the repeated-measures design provides a considerably more powerful test of the null hypothesis.

(d) The completely randomized design would require 207 subjects, each tested once. The repeated-measures design would require 19 subjects, each tested three times, for a total of 57 observations.

(e) As the correlation decreases, the repeated-measures design requires more subjects. If $r = 0$, the required $n = 69$; therefore, the total number of observations would be $3 \times 69 = 207$, the same number as with the completely randomized design.

13.9 (a) From Equation 13.4, $estMS_{RM} = [(a - 1)MSE_{LS} + MS_C]/a = [(4)(7.127) + 32.960]/5 = 12.294$.

(b) The adjusted relative efficiency is $AdjustedRE_{LS\,to\,RM} = \left(\dfrac{df_{LS} + 1}{df_{LSB} + 3}\right)\left(\dfrac{df_{RM} + 3}{df_{RM} + 1}\right)\dfrac{MSE_{RM}}{MSE_{LS}} =$

$(12/14)(19/17)(12.294/7.127) = 1.652$. The Latin square design is more efficient in this case; it will require fewer subjects to achieve the same power as the repeated-measures design.

CHAPTER 14

14.1 (a, b)

SV	df	MS	F	EMS
Subjects	3	23.556		$\sigma_e^2 + 3\sigma_S^2$
A	2	3.250	2.853	$\sigma_e^2 + 4\theta_A^2$
SA	6	1.139		σ_e^2

(c) $\hat{\sigma}_A^2 = [(a-1)/a]\hat{\theta}_A^2 = [(a-1)/a][(MS_A - MS_{S\times A})/n] = (2/3)(2.111/4) = .352$; $\hat{\sigma}_S^2 = (MS_S - MS_{SA})/a = 7.472$; $\hat{\sigma}_e^2 = 1.139$. Then $\hat{\omega}_g^2 (A) = \hat{\sigma}_A^2 / (\hat{\sigma}_A^2 + \hat{\sigma}_S^2 + \hat{\sigma}_e^2) = .352/(.352 + 7.472 + 1.139) = .039$.

14.3 (a) Using the ANOVA error term, $t_{10} = (5.200 - 3.867) / \sqrt{(4.938)(1/6 + 1/6)} = 1.333/1.283 = 1.039$; $p > .1$.

(b) Testing based on the standard error of the difference, $t_5 = (5.200 - 3.867)/\sqrt{1.048 / 6} = 1.333/.428 = 3.116$; $p < .05$.

(c) The variances in the three conditions are 2.943, 2.612, and 25.440. Therefore, the standard error based on the ANOVA error mean square is inflated by the variance due to the condition that was not included in the test of the difference between the A_1 and A_2 means. The test in part (b) is therefore preferred.

14.5 (a)

SV	SS	df	MS	F	p
A	3.763	3	1.254	6.350	0.003
SA	4.148	21	0.198		

If $\varepsilon = 1$, the df are unchanged, and $p = .003$. At its lower limit, $\varepsilon = 1/(a-1)$; then $df = 1$ and 7, and $p = .04$. Therefore, $.003 < p < .04$; in either case, assuming $\alpha = .05$, we conclude that the μ_j are not all equal.

(b) Using the Dunn–Bonferroni method (Tukey's *HSD* method assumes independently distributed means), if the $FWE = .05$, $\alpha = (.05/6) = .008$ (two-tailed). We want the value of t on 1 and 7 df that cuts off .004 in each tail. This is approximately 3.64. The means are 3.275 and 4.175 and the standard deviation of the difference is .804. Therefore, the 95% simultaneous confidence interval for this difference is $(4.175 - 3.275) \pm (3.64)(.804/\sqrt{8}) = -.135, 1.935$.

14.7 (a) $MS_e = (19/760)(739,141) + (741/760)(853.157) = 850.307$.

(b) $\hat{\sigma}_S^2 = (MS_S - MS_e) / a = (208,305.017 - 850.307)/20 = 10,372.736$.

(c) $r_{11} = \hat{\sigma}_S^2 / (\hat{\sigma}_S^2 + \hat{\sigma}_e^2) = 10,372.736/(10,372.736 + 850.357) = .92$.

14.9 (a) The means are

A_1	A_2	A_3	A_4
2,304.000	2,394.750	2,384.250	2,418.125

The ANOVA results are

SV	df	SS	MS	F	p	G–G	H–F
Subjects	7	890,801.72	127,257.39				
A	3	59,008.59	19,669.53	2.84	.062	.097	.076
Error	21	145,010.16	6,905.25				

G–G and H–F are the Greenhouse–Geisser and Huynh–Feldt corrections for nonsphericity; G–G Epsilon = .615; H–F Epsilon = .825. (Note: The mean square for subjects can be calculated by the usual formula, or, if using SPSS's *Repeated-measures* option, it is the error term in the output labeled "Tests of Between Subjects Effects.")

(b) $\hat{\omega}_g^2(A) = \dfrac{(a-1)(MS_A - MS_{SA})}{(a-1)(MS_A - MS_{SA}) + anMS_{SA} + n(MS_s - MS_{SA})}$

$= \dfrac{(3)(127,257.39 - 6,905.25)}{(3)(127,257.39 - 6,905.25) + (32)(6,905.25) + (8)(127,527.35 - 6,905.25)} = .031.$

(c) $\hat{f} = \sqrt{\hat{\sigma}_A^2 / (\hat{\sigma}_e^2 + \hat{\sigma}_S^2)} = \sqrt{\dfrac{(a-1)(MS_A - MS_{SA})/an}{MS_{SA} + (MS_S - MS_{SX})/a}} = .233.$

(d) In G*Power 3, first select the F test option, *ANOVA: Repeated-measures, within factors*, and then the *a priori* option. Select the *Determine* button and enter the values and select *Calculate*. The result is $f = .258$.

(e) G*Power calculates f as if the means and variances were the population values. Equation 14.19 *estimates* the population values and so takes error variance into account. The presence of error lowers the estimate relative to the value calculated by G*Power.

14.11 (a) Ranking the scores from 1 to 4 for each subject, the condition means are

A_1	A_2	A_3	A_4
1.250	2.500	2.125	3.250

The $SS_A = 22.750$ and $\chi_F^2 = SS_A/[a(a+1)/12] = 13.65$; $p = .003$. The nonparametric option in most statistical software packages will provide the same result.

(b)

Source		Type III sum of squares	df	Mean square	F	Sig.
A	Hypothesis	20.556	3	6.852	3.193	.045
	Error	45.067	21	2.146		
Subject	Hypothesis	309.430	7	44.204	20.598	.000
	Error	45.067	21	2.146		
$A \times Subject$	hypothesis	45.067	21	2.146		

(c) The box plots suggest that the tails of the distributions are long. Transformation to ranks or reciprocals reduces the effect of the more extreme scores on the error variance, resulting in a more powerful test.

Note: When analyzing real data, one test should be selected *a priori* on the basis of data exploration in order not to inflate the Type 1 error rate.

14.13 (a) The results of the ANOVA are

SV	SS	df	MS	F	p	G–G	H–F
Subjects	101.841	48	2.122				
Seasons	57.989	3	19.330	12.924	.000	.000	.000
Error	215.372	144	1.496				

G–G Epsilon = .658; *H–F Epsilon* = .687

(b) $\hat{\sigma}^2_{Seasons} = \left(\dfrac{a-1}{a}\right)\left(\dfrac{MS_{Seasons} - MS_{error}}{n}\right) = (.75)(17.834)/49 = .273$ and $\hat{\sigma}^3_{Subjects} = (MS_{Subjects} - MS_{error})/a$

$= (.626)/4 = .157$. Therefore, *General* $\hat{\omega}^2_g(Seasons) = \hat{\sigma}^2_{Seasons}/(\hat{\sigma}^2_{Seasons} + \hat{\sigma}^2_{error} + \hat{\sigma}^2_{Subjects}) = .273/(.273 + 1.496 + .157) = .142$.

(c) The results of the trend analysis are:

Source	Season	Type III sum of squares	df	Mean square	F	Sig.
Season	Linear	3.629	1	3.629	5.043	.029
	Quadratic	48.133	1	48.133	31.725	.000
	Cubic	6.227	1	6.227	2.767	.103
Error (season)	Linear	34.539	48	.720		
	Quadratic	72.824	48	1.517		
	Cubic	108.009	48	2.250		

The best-fitting straight line has a slope significantly zero. However, there is significant (quadratic) curvature in the population function.

CHAPTER 15

15.1 (a)

Source	EMS
W	$\sigma^2_e + 4\sigma^2_{WO} + 20\sigma^2_W$
P	$\sigma^2_e + 10\sigma^2_{PO} + 5\sigma^2_{WP} + \sigma^2_{WPO} + 500\theta^2_P$
O	$\sigma^2_e + 4\sigma^2_{WO} + 40\sigma^2_O$
WP	$\sigma^2_e + 5\sigma^2_{WP} + \sigma^2_{WPO}$
WO	$\sigma^2_e + 4\sigma^2_{WO}$
PO	$\sigma^2_e + 10\sigma^2_{PO} + \sigma^2_{WPO}$
WPO	$\sigma^2_e + \sigma^2_{WPO}$

(b) $F_1' = \dfrac{MS_P}{MS_{PO} + MS_{WP} - MS_{WPO}} = \dfrac{2610}{640 + 330 - 320} = 4.015$, The denominator df are

$$df'_{error} = \dfrac{(MS_{PO} + MS_{WP} - MS_{WPO})^2}{\dfrac{MS_{PO}^2}{(p-1)(o-1)} + \dfrac{MS_{WP}^2}{(w-1)(p-1)} + \dfrac{MS_{WPO}^2}{(w-1)(p-1)(o-1)}}$$

$$= \dfrac{650^2}{\dfrac{640^2}{12} + \dfrac{330^2}{27} + \dfrac{320^2}{108}} = 10.8$$

$p = .037$. We reject the null hypothesis that the programs have no effects.

(c) Testing WP against WPO, $F_{27,108} = MS_{WP}/MS_{WPO} = 1.03$, and $p = .44$. Assuming, therefore, that $\sigma_{WP}^2 = 0$, P can now be tested against MS_{PO}. The result is $F_{3,12} = 4.078$, $p < .05$.

15.3 (a)

Source	df	SS	MS	Error	F
S	4	36.467	9.117		
A	1	112.133	112.133	SA	30.170
B	2	9.800	4.900	SB	15.474
AB	2	4.067	2.034	SAB	.859
SA	4	14.867	3.717		
SB	8	2.533	.317		
SAB	8	18.933	2.367		

(b)

Source	df	SS	MS	F
S	4	12.156	3.039	
A	1	37.378	37.378	30.170
SA	4	4.956	1.239	

The mean squares in part (b) are 1/3 those in part (a) because each "score" is an average of three scores in the original data set.

(c) The *EMS* are in the following table. The terms in parentheses do not contribute to the expected mean square when *B* has fixed effects.

Source	EMS
S	$\sigma_e^2 + (a\sigma_{SB}^2) + ab\sigma_S^2$
A	$\sigma_e^2 + (\sigma_{SAB}^2) + b\sigma_{SA}^2 + (n\sigma_{AB}^2) + bn\theta_A^2$
B	$\sigma_e^2 + n\sigma_{SB}^2 + na\sigma_B^2$
SA	$\sigma_e^2 + (\sigma_{SAB}^2) + b\sigma_{SA}^2$
SB	$\sigma_e^2 + a\sigma_{SB}^2$
AB	$\sigma_e^2 + \sigma_{SAB}^2 + n\sigma_{AB}^2$
SAB	$\sigma_e^2 + \sigma_{SAB}^2$

(d) When the B effects are random, we require a quasi-F test of A. For example, $F_1' = MS_A/(MS_{SA} + MS_{AB} - MS_{SAB}) = 33.136$. From Equation 15.8, the error df is 1.84; then $p = .035$.

(e) Averaging over the levels of B and analyzing the data as if there were only a scores for each subject ignores the AB and SAB variability that contributes to the A mean square if B has random effects. Therefore, in such circumstances, that procedure will often lead to an inflated Type 1 error rate.

15.5 We first need to estimate the population variances. These are:

$\hat{\sigma}^2$	A and B fixed	B random
S	$(MS_S - MS_{SAB})/ab = 16.000$	$(MS_S - MS_{SB})/ab = 16.000$
A	$(a-1)(MS_A - MS_{SA})/abn = .533$	$(a-1)[MS_A - (MS_{SA} + MS_{AB} - MS_{SAB})]/abn = .080$
B	$(b-1)(MS_B - MS_{SB})/abn = 1.040$	$(MS_B - MS_{SB})/an = 5.200$
SA	$(MS_{SA} - MS_{SAB})/b = 2.800$	$(MS_{SA} - MS_{SAB})/b = 2.800$
SB	$(MS_{SB} - MS_{SAB})/a = 7.333$	$(MS_{SB} - MS_{SAB})/a = 7.333$
AB	$(a-1)(b-1)(MS_{AB} - MS_{SAB})/abn = 1.813$	$(MS_{AB} - MS_{SAB})/n = 27.200$
Error	$MS_{SAB} = 10.000$	$MS_{SAB} = 10.000$

(a) With A and B both extrinsic and having fixed effects, the results are

$$\hat{\omega}_G^2(A) = \hat{\sigma}_A^2 / (\hat{\sigma}_A^2 + \hat{\sigma}_S^2 + \hat{\sigma}_{SA}^2 + \hat{\sigma}_{SB}^2 + \hat{\sigma}_e^2) = .015$$

(b) If B is an extrinsic factor with random effects, the formulas for ω^2 remain the same, but the A, B, and AB variance estimates change. As a result, the value of general ω^2 for A is now .002.

(c) A still has fixed effects, and B is an intrinsic factor with random effects. Therefore, the B and AB variance estimates contribute to the denominator of the equation in part (b). Then the value of general ω^2 for A is .001.

15.7 (a) The results of the ANOVA are

Source	df	SS	MS	F	p
Between subjects	5	557.111			
A	1	490.889	490.889	29.65	.006
S/A	4	66.222	16.556		
Within subjects	12	478.666			
B	2	447.444	223.722	108.84	.000
AB	2	14.778	7.389	3.60	.077
SB/A	8	16.444	2.056		

(b) The results of the ANOVA based on the mean scores for the subjects is

Source	df	SS	MS	F	p
Total	5	185.704			
A	1	163.630	163.630	29.65	.006
S/A	4	22.074	5.519		

(i) The Fs in parts (a) and (b) are identical. (ii) The SS and MS in part (b) are 1/3 of their counterparts in part (a). The reason for this is that in part (a), $SS_A = bn \sum_j (\bar{Y}_{.j.} - \bar{Y}_{...})^2$, whereas in part (b), $SS_A = n \sum_j (\bar{Y}_{.j.} - \bar{Y}_{...})^2$.

(c) $SS_{SB/A_1} = 3.111$ and $SS_{SB/A_2} = 13.333$; the sum is 16.444, the result in part (a). Also, $MS_{SB/A_1} = .778$ and $MS_{SB/A_2} = 3.333$; the average is 2.056, the result in part (a).

15.9 (a)

Source	df	EMS
A	1	$\sigma_e^2 + \sigma_{SB/A}^2 + 3\sigma_{S/A}^2 + 3\sigma_{AB}^2 + 9\theta_A^2$
S/A	4	$\sigma_e^2 + \sigma_{SB/A}^2 + 3\sigma_{S/A}^2$
B	2	$\sigma_e^2 + \sigma_{SB/A}^2 + 6\theta_B^2$
AB	2	$\sigma_e^2 + \sigma_{SB/A}^2 + 3\sigma_{AB}^2$
SB/A	8	$\sigma_e^2 + \sigma_{SB/A}^2$

(b) To test the A effect, we form a quasi-F ratio. Then, $F' = MS_A / (MS_{S/A} + MS_{AB} - MS_{SB/A}) = 490.889/(16.556 + 7.389 - 2.056) = 22.426$. The error degrees of freedom are

$$df' = \frac{(MS_{S/A} + MS_{AB} - MS_{SB/A})^2}{MS_{S/A}^2 / df_{S/A} + MS_{AB}^2 / df_{AB} + MS_{SB/A}^2 / df_{SB/A}} = 4.97. \text{ With 1 and 5 } df, p = .005.$$

15.11 (a) The ANOVA table is

SV	df	EMS
Between subjects	71	
Sex (X)	1	$\sigma_e^2 + 2\sigma_{S/XA}^2 + 72\theta_X^2$
Age (A)	2	$\sigma_e^2 + 2\sigma_{S/XA}^2 + 48\theta_A^2$
XA	2	$\sigma_e^2 + 2\sigma_{S/XA}^2 + 24\theta_{XA}^2$
S/XA	66	$\sigma_e^2 + 2\sigma_{S/XA}^2$
Within subjects	72	
Task (T)	1	$\sigma_e^2 + \sigma_{ST/XA}^2 + 72\theta_T^2$
XT	1	$\sigma_e^2 + \sigma_{ST/XA}^2 + 36\theta_{XT}^2$
AT	2	$\sigma_e^2 + \sigma_{ST/XA}^2 + 24\theta_{AT}^2$
XAT	2	$\sigma_e^2 + \sigma_{ST/XA}^2 + 12\theta_{XAT}^2$
ST/XA	66	$\sigma_e^2 + \sigma_{ST/XA}^2$

S/XA is the error term for the between-subjects terms, and ST/XA is the error term for the within-subjects terms.

(b) The most conservative approach is to base the error term only on those scores involved in these tests of simple effects; this is the default in most statistical packages. For part (i), calculate the variances of T_1 scores within each age × sex combination, and average these. The $df = ax(n - 1) = (3)(2)(11) = 66$.

(ii) Average the T_j variances for each of the three male groups, $df = a(n - 1) = (3)(11) = 33$.

(iii) Calculate the ST mean square within each of the three male groups and average them. The $df = a(n - 1)(t - 1) = (3)(11)(1) = 33$.

15.13 (a)

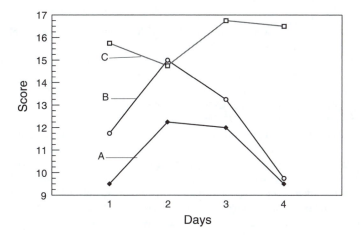

(b) The results of the ANOVA are

SV	df	SS	MS	F	p
Diet (D)	2	197.167	98.583	13.637	.002
S/D	9	65.063	7.229		
Days (d)	3	53.396	17.799	12.923	.000
$Lin(d)$	1	3.037	3.037	1.153	.311
$Quad(d)$	1	50.021	50.021	74.258	.000
$Cubic(d)$	1	.337	.337	.410	.538
$D \times d$	6	42.167	7.028	5.103	.001
$Lin(d) \times D$	2	9.300	4.650	1.765	.226
$Quad(d) \times D$	2	23.167	11.583	17.196	.001
$Cubic(d) \times D$	2	9.700	4.850	5.889	.023
$S \times d/D$	27	37.188	1.377		
$S \times Lin(d)/D$	9	23.713	2.635		
$S \times Quad(d)/D$	9	6.062	.674		
$S \times Cubic(d)/D$	9	7.413	.824		

The main effect of diet indicates that, averaging over days, the diet population means differ. The $Quad(d)$ term, together with the clear lack of significance for linear and cubic components of days, suggests that the average population function is adequately described by an inverted, U-shaped curve. The components of the interaction ($D \times d$) indicate that the main differences among the shapes of the three curves lies in their curvature. The best-fitting straight lines are nearly flat, accounting for the lack of a $Lin(d) \times D$ effect. The significant cubic and quadratic interaction components reflect the fact that the curve for C is essentially flat whereas the other two diets yield an initial improvement followed by a performance drop on the last day.

15.15 (a) $F_A = 80.083/8.750 = 9.152$; with 1 and 6 df, $p = .023$. $F_{AB} - 108/11.611 = 9.301$; with 1 and 6 df, $p = .023$.

(b) We now form quasi-F ratios to test A, and AB. To test the A source, $F' = MS_A/(MS_{S/A} + MS_{AC} -$

$MS_{SC/A}$) = 80.083/(8.750 + 21.271 − 2.271) = 2.885. The denominator df are $df_2 = \dfrac{(MS_{S/A} + MS_{AC} - MS_{SC/A})^2}{(MS^2_{S/A} / df_{S/A}) + (MS^2_{AC} / df_{AC}) + (MS^2_{SC/A} / df_{SC/A})} = 3.22$; $p = .18$. When we consider the variance due to the random factor C, the p-value is increased. If we wish to generalize to the sampled population of items, the result is no longer significant.

(c) For AB, $F' = MS_{AB}/(MS_{SB/A} + MS_{ABC} - MS_{SBC/A}) = 5.492$. The denominator df are 8.38 and $p = .05$.

15.17 (a) Viewing this as a two-factor design with a single measure (the difference score), we insert the value of the F test of *format* into the formula for $\hat{f}$ (see Equation 8.19). Then, $\hat{f} = \sqrt{(df_{Format} / N)(F - 1)} = \sqrt{(1/64)(10.747)} = .41$, a large effect under Cohen's guidelines.

(b) Subtracting the SVT mean from the IVT mean, we have −3.750 for the text format and 8.281 for the web format. Therefore, the interaction effect is 8.281 − (−3.750) = 12.031. To obtain a confidence interval, think of it as an interval containing the difference between the means of the text and web populations of difference scores. As usual, the general form of the confidence interval is $\bar{d} \pm ts_{\bar{d}}$, where $\bar{d}$ is the difference between the text and web mean differences, or 12.031, $s_{\bar{d}}$ is the standard error of this interaction effect, and t is the value that cuts off .025 in each tail of the t distribution. The standard error is $s_{\bar{d}} = \sqrt{(2 / 4n)MS_{error}}$. The "2" is because we are contrasting two means, and $4n$ is the number of scores on which each mean is based. The error mean square is obtained from the ANOVA of the $IVT - SVT$ difference scores. Therefore, $s_{\bar{d}} = \sqrt{(2 / 32)(197.154)} = 3.510$. The critical value of t is based on the error df; $t_{.05,56} \approx 2.00$. Therefore, $CI = 12.031 + (3.501)(2.00) = 5.03, 19.03$.

(c) Perform two ANOVAs on the difference scores calculated in part (a), one in each format condition. (i) In the text condition, $\hat{f} = \sqrt{(df_1 / N_{text})(F - 1)} = \sqrt{(3 / 32)(.110)} = .102$, a small effect. (ii) Because $F < 1$ in the web condition, our best estimate of f is zero. In either case, instructions have very little effect, relative to the error variance, on the difference between the two measures.

CHAPTER 16

16.1

Source	SS	df	MS
B/A_1	1,808,924.00	4	452,231.00
B/A_2	623,512.15	4	155,878.04
B/A_3	695,324.35	4	173,831.09

The sum of the three SS terms equals the sum of squares for B/A in Table 16.2. If the three SB mean squares are averaged, that average equals $MS_{SB/A}$.

16.3

SV	df	EMS
S	19	$\sigma_e^2 + 50\sigma_S^2$
M	4	$\sigma_e^2 + 20\sigma_{I/M}^2 + 10\sigma_{SM}^2 + 2000\theta_M^2$
I/M	45	$\sigma_e^2 + 20\sigma_{I/M}^2$
$S \times M$	76	$\sigma_e^2 + 10\sigma_{SM}^2$
$S \times I/M$	855	σ_e^2

To test M, a quasi-F is needed; $F' = MS_M/(MS_{IIM} + MS_{SM} - MS_{SIIM})$. The numerator $df = 4$ and the error $df = (MS_{IIM} + MS_{SM} - MS_{SIIM})/(MS_{IIM}^2/45 + MS_{SM}^2/76 + MS_{SIIM}^2/855)$.

16.5   The means for the four conditions are:

R_1V_1	R_2V_1	R_1V_2	R_2V_2
3.980	3.480	2.740	3.060

where $R = 1$ is relevant and $V = 1$ is positive. The output below is based on a modification of the SPSS syntax file, *Nested Designs.sps*, at the website.

Source	df	SS	MS	Error MS	Error df	F	p
R	1	.405	.405	2.541	12.482	.159	.696
V	1	34.445	34.445	2.692	13.086	12.794	.003
RV	1	8.405	8.405	2.763	13.301	3.042	.104
S	9	14.905	1.656	.997	144	1.661	.104
SR	9	9.345	1.038	.997	144	1.041	.411
SV	9	10.705	1.189	.997	144	1.193	.304
SRV	9	11.345	1.261	.997	144	1.265	.261
I/RV	16	40.000	2.500	.997	144	2.508	.002
SI/RV	144	143.600	.997				

Note: The error term for R is $MS_{RS} + MS_{IIRV} - MS_{SIIRV}$; for V it is $MS_{VS} + MS_{IIRV} - MS_{SIIRV}$; and for RV it is $MS_{RVS} + MS_{IIRV} - MS_{SIIRV}$. The error df for the quasi-F ratios follow the general form of Equation 15.7.

The main results are that mean ratings are significantly lower when negative attitudes are primed, and there is significant variability among item scores within each of the four conditions. The error terms follow from the expected mean squares. Note that those expected mean squares are not all the same as those produced by SPSS but follow our rules of thumb in Chapter 15.

   In the absence of software that directly handles nesting, we first proceed as if we have a pure mixed design in which the same items appear in all RV cells. Noting that $RV(I-1) = (R-1)(V-1)(I-1) + (R-1)(I-1) + (V-1)(I-1) + (I-1)$, SS_{IIRV} [the $I(RV)$ term in the SPSS output] is obtained as $SS_{IRV} + SS_{IR} + SS_{IV} + SS_I$.

16.7   (a)

Source	df	Expected mean squares
C	2	$\sigma_e^2 + 10\sigma_{SC}^2 + 20\sigma_{CIIF}^2 + 200\theta_C^2$
F	1	$\sigma_F^2 + 15\sigma_{SF}^2 + 60\sigma_{IIF}^2 + 3\sigma_{SIIF}^2 + 300\theta_F^2$
CF	2	$\sigma_e^2 + 5\sigma_{SCF}^2 + 20\sigma_{CIIF}^2 + 100\theta_{CF}^2$
S	19	$\sigma_e^2 + 3\sigma_{SIIF}^2 + 30\sigma_S^2$
SC	38	$\sigma_e^2 + 10\sigma_{SC}^2$
SF	19	$\sigma_e^2 + 3\sigma_{SIIF}^2 + 15\sigma_{SF}^2$
SCF	38	$\sigma_e^2 + 5\sigma_{SCF}^2$
I/F	8	$\sigma_e^2 + 3\sigma_{SIIF}^2 + 60\sigma_{IIF}^2$
$C \times I/F$	16	$\sigma_e^2 + 20\sigma_{CIIF}^2$
$S \times I/F$	152	$\sigma_e^2 + 3\sigma_{SIIF}^2$
$SC \times I/F$	304	σ_e^2

(b) To test C, the error term is $MS_{SC} + MS_{CIIF} - MS_{SCIIF}$. To test F, the error term is $MS_{SF} + MS_{IIF} - MS_{SIIF}$. The error df for the quasi-F ratios follow the general form of Equation 15.7.

16.9 (a) $SS_A = 79.5$, $SS_C = 166.5$, $SS_S = 56$, and $SS_{res} = 29$.

(b) The estimate of the repeated-measures error term, MS_{SA}, is $estMS_{SA} = [(a - 1)MS_{res} + MS_C]/a = [(3)(29/6) + (166.5/3)]/4 = 17.5$.

(c) From Equation 13.5, $RE_{LS\ to\ RM} = \left[\dfrac{df_{LS} + 1}{df_{LS} + 3}\right] \cdot \left[\dfrac{df_{RM} + 3}{df_{RM} + 1}\right] \cdot \left[\dfrac{MS_{SA}}{MS_{res}}\right] = \left[\dfrac{6 + 1}{6 + 3}\right] \cdot \left[\dfrac{9 + 3}{9 + 1}\right] \cdot \left[\dfrac{17.500}{4.833}\right] = 3.042$. The repeated-measures design is estimated to need about three times as many subjects as the Latin square to attain the same power.

16.11 (a)

Source	df
Drug type (T)	1
Row (R)	3
TR	1
Subjects/TR	24
Occasions (O)	3
Dosages (D)	3
TO	3
TD	3
Between-cells residual (BCR)	6
$T \times BCR$	6
Within-cells residual (WCR)	72

T, R, and TR are tested against Subjects/TR; all other terms are tested against WCR.

(b)

Source	df
Row (R)	7
Subjects/TR	8
O	7
T	1
D	3
TD	3
BCR	42
WSR	56

R is tested against Subjects/R; all other terms are tested against WSR.

(c) Design (b) involves fewer subjects and a simpler analysis. However, it requires more time to test each subject, and this may be a problem. With either design, there is the issue of whether dosage or drug type should be a within-subject factor. The answer depends on whether, and how quickly, the effects of a treatment, or treatment combination, wear off.

16.13 (a) One possible digram-balanced, 6×6 square is

$$
\begin{vmatrix}
1 & 6 & 2 & 5 & 3 & 4 \\
2 & 1 & 3 & 6 & 4 & 5 \\
3 & 2 & 4 & 1 & 5 & 6 \\
4 & 3 & 5 & 2 & 6 & 1 \\
5 & 4 & 6 & 3 & 1 & 2 \\
6 & 5 & 1 & 4 & 2 & 3
\end{vmatrix}
$$

(b) A digram-balanced, 5×5 square is

$$
\begin{vmatrix}
1 & 5 & 2 & 4 & 3 \\
2 & 1 & 3 & 5 & 4 \\
3 & 2 & 4 & 1 & 5 \\
4 & 3 & 5 & 2 & 1 \\
5 & 4 & 1 & 3 & 2 \\
3 & 4 & 2 & 5 & 1 \\
4 & 5 & 3 & 1 & 2 \\
5 & 1 & 4 & 2 & 3 \\
1 & 2 & 5 & 3 & 4 \\
2 & 3 & 1 & 4 & 5
\end{vmatrix}
$$

16.15 $SS_S = SS_R + SS_{S/R} = 1{,}300.417$. SS_A is unchanged. The remaining variability would be attributed to the SS_{SA}. Therefore, the new ANOVA table is

SV	df	SS	MS	F	p
Subjects	11	1,300.417			
A	3	384.250	128.083	3.95	.016
$S \times A$	33	1,071.250	32.462		

The F test of A is negatively biased because considerable variability due to C has been pooled with other terms to form a new error term. In this case, the result is still quite significant; however, if the original, correct, ANOVA had yielded a p-value of only slightly less than .05, we might have come to a different, nonsignificant, result for the analysis performed here.

16.17

SV	df	SS	MS	F	p
R	3	33.791	11.264	4.71	.008
H	1	.372	.372	.16	.696
RH	3	25.673	8.558	3.58	.025
Subjects/RH	32	76.599	2.394		
Script (S)	3	128.356	42.785	60.03	.000
V	1	118.922	118.922	166.79	.000
S/V	2	9.434	4.714	6.61	.002
HS	3	5.075	1.692	2.37	.075
HV	1	.098	.098	.14	.709
HS/V	2	4.977	2.489	3.49	.034
C	3	4.544	1.515	2.13	.102
BCR	6	2.195	.366	.51	.799
$H \times BCR$	6	1.009	.168	.24	.962
WSR	96	68.426	.713		

S/RH is the error term for the terms above it in the table and *WSR* is the error term against which the remaining terms are tested. After performing two ANOVAs, $SS_{H \times BCR} = SS_{Script \times R \times H} - SS_{CH}$.

CHAPTER 17

17.1 (a) The data are reasonably symmetric; skewness and kurtosis values are not large relative to their standard errors except for the kurtosis value for day 3, due to two outliers (cases 4 and 10) in the box plot for that day. There are no significant results of the tests of normality. We also used SPSS's *Reliability Analysis* option (in the *Analyze/Scale* menu) to perform Tukey's test of nonadditivity and found no evidence of nonadditivity; $p = .78$.
(b) The SPSS output:

Source		Type III sum of squares	df	Mean square	F	Sig.
Days	Sphericity Assumed	631.600	2	315.800	2.819	.072
	Greenhouse–Geisser	631.600	1.598	395.169	2.819	.086
	Huynh–Feldt	631.600	1.722	366.779	2.819	.081
	Lower bound	631.600	1.000	631.600	2.819	.110
Error (days)	Sphericity Assumed	4257.067	38	112.028		
	Greenhouse–Geisser	4257.067	30.368	140.184		
	Huynh–Feldt	4257.067	32.718	130.112		
	Lower bound	4257.067	19.000	224.056		

Tests of within-subjects contrasts

Source	Days	Type III sum of squares	df	Mean square	F	Sig.
Days	Linear	624.100	1	624.100	6.707	.018
	Quadratic	7.500	1	7.500	.057	.813
Error (days)	Linear	1,767.900	19	93.047		
	Quadratic	2,489.167	19	131.009		

The reduction in the *df* when adjusted indicates nonsphericity; the variance of the difference between scores on days 2 and 3 is more than twice that of the other two variances of difference scores. This suggests a departure from additivity not revealed by the Tukey test. That test is not sensitive to all departures from additivity (Myers, 1979, p. 185). The suggestion of nonsphericity accounts for why a multivariate analysis (MANOVA) indicates that mean performances do vary significantly ($p = .026$); that test does not involve the sphericity assumption.

The polynomial tests also indicate that the three means vary significantly. Even if we set $\alpha = .025$ to control the *FWE*, the slope of the best-fitting line clearly departs from zero. In summary, despite the nonsignificant result of the *F* test of *Days*, there is strong evidence that the means do vary.

(c) In SPSS, the transformation is—for example—ARC1 = ARSIN(SORT(.01*Day 1)). The results in this example are similar to those for the original data. Transformations are often helpful, but not always.

17.3

Source	df	EMS	Error term
Context (C)	1		S/C
Subjects within C (S/C)	44	$\sigma_e^2 + 6\sigma_{S/C}^2$	
Days (A)	2	$\sigma_e^2 + 2\sigma_{A \times S/C}^2 + 920\theta_A^2$	AS/C
AC	2	$\sigma_e^2 + 2\sigma_{A \times S/C}^2 + 460\theta_{AC}^2$	AS/C
AS/C	88	$\sigma_e^2 + 2\sigma_{A \times S/C}^2$	
Targets (B)	1	$\sigma_e^2 + 6\sigma_{SB/C}^2 + 1380\theta_B^2$	SB/C
BC	1	$\sigma_e^2 + 6\sigma_{SB/C}^2 + 690\theta_{Bc}^2$	SB/C
SB/C	44	$\sigma_e^2 + 6\sigma_{SB/C}^2$	
AB	2	$\sigma_e^2 + 46\theta_{AB}^2$	Residual
ABC	2	$\sigma_e^2 + 23\theta_{ABC}^2$	Residual
Residual (SAB/C)	88	σ_e^2	

17.5 Deleting $C \times B/A$ and $A \times S/C$ components of variance from the original EMS, we are able to pool $MS_{CB/A}$, $MS_{AS/C}$, and the original residual mean square to form a revised $MS_{Residual}$. Furthermore, there is no longer a need for quasi-F tests. Although F and p-values change slightly, and the analysis is much simpler, the basic conclusions are the same as those based on our original analysis. It may seem surprising that the p-value for the AC term is now higher than in the quasi-F test. The reason is that the large residual error mean square is now averaged with $MS_{A \times S/C}$ and $MS_{BC/A}$, rather than being subtracted from their sum as it was when forming the error term in the quasi-F test.

Source	df	MS	F	p	EMS
C	1	664.23	1.72	.20	$\sigma_e^2 + ab\sigma_{S/C}^2 + nab\theta_C^2$
S/C	22	385.20			$\sigma_e^2 + ab\sigma_{S/C}^2$
A	2	2,493.34	63.19	.00	$\sigma_e^2 + nc\sigma_{B/A}^2 + nbc\theta_A^2$
B/A	12	39.46			$\sigma_e^2 + nc\sigma_{B/A}^2$
AC	2	36.16	1.18	.31	$\sigma_e^2 + nb\theta_{AC}^2$
Residual	320	30.68			σ_e^2

17.7 From the *EX17_7S* file, $F_1 = MS_A/MS_{SA/C} = 30,283$, and from the *EX17_7I* file, $F_2 = 14.986$. Therefore, $minF' = F_1F_2/(F_1 + F_2) = 10.025$. In general, the denominator df are $(F_1 + F_2)^2/(F_1^2/df_2 + F_2^2/df_1)$ where df_1 and df_2 are the df for the F_1 and F_2 denominators, respectively. The F_1 error term is $MS_{AS/C}$ and the F_2 error term is $MS_{B/A}$ Therefore, the denominator df are $df' = (30.283 + 14.986)^2/(30.28^2/12 + 14.986^2/28) = 24.27$. The F of 10.025 distributed on 2 and 24 df is significant at the .001 level.

17.9

Source	df	SS	MS	F	p
Group (G)	3	159.916	53.306	0.989	0.423
Age	1	6,936.000	6,936.000	128.643	0.000
$G \times$ Age	3	45.250	15.083	0.280	0.839
$S/G \times$ Age	16	863.667	53.917		
Situation (A)	3	1,889.250	629.750	6.871	0.000
Blocks (B)	3	21.500	7.167	0.077	0.972
Age $\times A$	3	344.250	114.750	1.236	0.307
Age $\times B$	3	85.000	28.333	0.305	0.822
BCR (AB')	6	410.833	68.472	0.737	0.622
Age $\times$ BCR (Age $\times AB'$)	6	171.167	28.528	0.307	0.930
WSR	48	4458.000	92.875		

The younger age group ($Age = 1$) responds significantly more quickly. There is also significant variation among the mean response times to the four situations. Although the range of situation means is about half as large for the younger than for the older group, the $Age \times$ A interaction does not approach significance.

CHAPTER 18

18.1 (b) $r = .620$; (c) $\hat{Y} = 3 + 2X$; (d) $r^2 = .385$; (e) $\hat{X} = 1.577 + 0.192\,Y$; (f) $r^2 = .385$.

18.3 (a) Using $r = b_1 s_X / s_Y$, we find that the correlations are .15 and .69 for situations 1 and 2, respectively—even though the slope is much higher in situation 1.

(b), (c), and (d)These transformations all leave the z scores, and therefore the correlations, unchanged.

18.5 (a) The reasoning of the committee member is that because there is a high correlation between the pretest and posttest scores, no change in IQ has occurred. This reasoning is silly; the correlation is sensitive to the relative standing on the two tests but not the absolute scores. The correlation says nothing about the means. For example, if *all* the students in the enriched program had their IQ scores increase by 20 points between ages 8 and 11, the correlation would be the same as if their IQs changed by 0 points.

(b) Of course, the longer you live, the more time you have to smoke cigarettes. If we are concerned about the influence of smoking on longevity, we should look at the rate of cigarette smoking (cigarettes/day), not the total number.

(c) The data do not allow us to make a causal statement. It could be that less able or less motivated students spent less time on schoolwork and therefore had more time to watch TV. We cannot conclude that the TV watching *caused* the poor performance.

18.7 (a) Because $b_1 = rs_Y/s_X$, for men, $b_1 = (.333)\sqrt{324/100} = .599$ and for women, $b_1 = (.235)\sqrt{289/25} = .799$. The slope of the regression equation for predicting income from years of experience is greater for women even though the correlation is smaller. This is because the correlation reflects not only the slope, but also the variability in X and Y—and the variance of Y is much smaller for women than for men.

(b) To predict income from years of experience, we can use $\hat{Y} = \bar{Y} + b_1(X - \bar{X})$. For 10 years of experience, we predict for women, $\hat{Y} = 76 + .799(10 - 10) = 76.0$ and for men, $\hat{Y} = 80 + .599(10 - 15) = 77.0$. For 20 years of experience, the predictions are 84.0 for women and 83.0 for men.

18.9 (a) The patients in the VA hospital may constitute a restricted sample. For example, the anxiety scores may tend to be quite high. The sample should not be used to make inferences about the general population.

(b) The correlation between height and weight for the mixed group would be expected to be lower than .60. If the differences in mean height and weight for Martians and Jovians were great enough, the correlation might even be negative.

(c) This is a classic case of inferring causation from correlation. People who graduate from college may indeed make more money, but it is not obvious how much of their financial success can be attributed directly to graduating from college. Graduates may be smarter and more motivated and organized than nongraduates and therefore more successful. Graduates may also be more likely to come from wealthier and more stable families that are more willing to assist them.

18.11 (a) Because $r_{XY} = r_{X,Y,} \sqrt{r_{XX}} \sqrt{r_{YY}}$, the largest correlation that we could find would be $r_{XY} = \sqrt{r_{XX}} \sqrt{r_{YY}} = \sqrt{.64} \sqrt{.81} = .72$.

(b) The estimated correlation if we "correct for attenuation" due to low reliability is $.40/\sqrt{r_{XX}} \sqrt{r_{YY}} = .40/\sqrt{.64} \sqrt{.81} = .40/.72 = .56$.

18.13 (a) The strategy is not a good one. Given inconsistent behavior, very bad performance is likely to be followed by better performance, and exceptionally good performance may well be followed by performance that is not as good, whether or not feedback is given.

(b) The improvement cannot be explained as regression toward the mean. Regression toward the mean by itself would not account for above-average performance by the group that received tutoring.

(c) Not necessarily. Regression toward the mean complicates matching. Suppose that good spellers on the average have much higher IQs than poor spellers. If we were to form a mixed group of good and poor spellers matched for IQ on the basis of a single test, then the mixed group might largely consist of more intelligent good spellers who just happened to perform poorly on the IQ test and less intelligent poor spellers who performed well on the test. If they were to be given a second IQ test, the two groups might regress to different means.

(d) Many chronic diseases exhibit periods of exacerbation and remission. That is, there are periods of enhanced symptoms and periods of diminished symptoms. If we assume that patients are most likely to seek treatment when symptoms are at their worst, in many cases the symptoms can be expected to diminish, whether or not the treatment has any real effect. Nonetheless, the treatment may be given credit for the improvement. Critics (e.g., Singh & Ernst, 2008) have argued that when proper studies have been performed, virtually all of the supposed effects of alternative medical techniques such as homeopathy can be accounted for by some combination of placebo effects and regression to the mean.

18.15 (a) The best prediction for George on the second test is that he will score $\hat{z}_Y = rz_X = (.9)(2.1) = 1.89$ standard deviations above the mean. This second score does not classify him as gifted according to the two-standard-deviation criterion.

(b) This result should remind us that we should expect to see regression toward the mean when we retest children. If we give tests that have important consequences, we should make them as reliable as possible, and perhaps should administer several tests before making a decision.

(c) The best prediction for Mary's score on form A is $\hat{z}_Y = rz_X = (.9)(1.89) = 1.70$. It, too, shows regression to the mean. For more on this topic, see Campbell and Kenny (1999).

CHAPTER 19

19.1 (a) Using Equation 18.1, $t(17) = -1.30$, so we cannot reject H_0.

(b) $z = \dfrac{Z_r - Z_{hyp}}{\sqrt{\dfrac{1}{N-3}}} = \dfrac{-.310 - 0}{\sqrt{\dfrac{1}{16}}} = -1.24$, so again we cannot reject H_0.

(c) No, even if the correlation had been significant, we could not conclude that studying interferes with test performance. More likely, students having difficulty may study more, but still perform more poorly.

(d) The 95% CI for Z_ρ is given by $Z_r \pm z_{.025} \sqrt{\dfrac{1}{N-3}} = -.310 \pm (1.96)(1/4) = -.80, .18$. Translating back to correlations, the 95% CI for ρ extends from $-.66$ to $+.18$. The 50% CI for Z_ρ is $-.310 \pm (.675)(1/4) = -.48$ to $-.14$. Translating back to correlations, the interval extends from $-.44$ to $-.14$.

(e) To use G*Power 3 to calculate the number of subjects required to have power = .80 for the test in (a) if $\rho = -.30$, we select *t tests* as the *Test family; Correlation: Point biserial model* as the *Statistical test;* and *A priori . . .* as the *Type of power analysis.* The effect size is $|r| = .30$. G*Power indicates that we need $N = 82$ to get power of .80.

(f) If we intend to use the Fisher Z and perform the test in (b), to calculate the required sample size, we must select *Exact* as the *Test family, Correlations: Difference from constant (one sample case)* and *A priori . . .* as the *Type of power analysis.* Again, the effect size is .30. The population ρ (for the null hypothesis is 0. Now we must click on the *Options* tab and select *Use large sample approximation (Fisher Z).* The obtained result is $N = 85$.

19.3 For men $r = .333$, $Z_r = .346$, $N = 2000$. For women, $r = .235$, $Z_r = .239$, $N = 2000$.

$$z = \frac{Z_{r_1} - Z_{r_2}}{\sqrt{\dfrac{1}{N_1 - 3} + \dfrac{1}{N_2 - 3}}} = \frac{.346 - .239}{\sqrt{2/1997}} = 3.38.$$ So the difference is highly significant, $p < .001$.

19.5 (a) $\chi_3^2 = 36[.310^2 + .549^2 + .203^2] = 15.794$. The critical value of $\chi_{3,.05}^2$ is 7.815. So we can reject the hypothesis that the off-diagonal correlations are all 0 in the population.

(b) Using Steiger's MULTICORR program, we obtain $\chi_1^2 = 1.1791$, $p = .2270$. We can't reject the null hypothesis.

(c) The partial correlation is $r_{AV|Q} = \dfrac{.50 - (.30)(.20)}{\sqrt{(1 - .30^2)(1 - .20^2)}} = .47$.

The test statistic is $t = \dfrac{r}{\sqrt{\dfrac{1 - r^2}{N-3}}} = 3.20$ with 36 df. The partial correlation is significant.

19.7 (a) $\varphi = -.36$; (b) $\varphi_{max} = .56$, $\varphi_{min} = -.80$; (c) To obtain $\varphi = 0$, we need independence, so that, p(pass item 1 and pass item 2) $= p$(pass 1)p(pass 2) $= .4 \times .7 = .28$. The frequency of the pass–pass cell would then be $Np = 28$. The other frequencies may be filled in so as to preserve the marginals.

19.9 Substituting into the equation, we obtain $r_{pre,\ change} = -.39$.

CHAPTER 20

20.1 (a) Regressing final on pretest produces the following output:

Model Summary[b]

Model	R	R Square	Adjusted R Square	Std. Error of the Estimate	Change Statistics				
					R Square Change	F Change	df1	df2	Sig. F Change
1	.725[a]	.526	.496	10.638	.526	17.738	1	16	.001

a. Predictors: (Constant), pretest
b. Dependent Variable: final

ANOVA[b]

Model	Sum of Squares	df	Mean Square	F	Sig.
1 Regression	2007.497	1	2007.497	17.738	.001[a]
Residual	1810.780	16	113.174		
Total	3818.278	17			

a. Predictors: (Constant), pretest
b. Dependent Variable: final

Coefficients[a]

Model	Unstandardized Coefficients		Standardized Coefficients	t	Sig.	95% Confidence Interval	
	B	Std. Error	Beta			Lower Bound	Upper Bound
1 (Constant)	−36.083	27.295		−1.322	.205	−93.946	21.780
pretest	3.546	.842	.725	4.212	.001	1.761	5.332

a. Dependent Variable: final

(b) The regression equation is predicted final score = −36.08 + 3.55 pretest. The standard error of estimate is 10.64 and the standard errors of b_0 and b_1 are 27.295 and 0.842, respectively.

(c) Using the regression equation, estimates of the conditional means of the population of final scores for pretest = 24 and 37 are 49.02 and 95.12, respectively. To find the confidence intervals for the conditional means, we need the standard errors for the predicted final scores, $SE(\widehat{final}) = s_e\sqrt{h_{jj}} = $

$s_e\sqrt{\dfrac{1}{N} + \dfrac{(X - \bar{X})^2}{SS_X}}$. For pretest = 24, $N = 18$; $(X - \bar{X})^2 = (24 - 32.278)^2$; $SS_X = (N - 1)s_X^2 = 159.60$. So,

$SE(\widehat{final}) = (10.638)\sqrt{\dfrac{1}{18} = \dfrac{(24 - 32.278)^2}{159.60}} = 7.408$. Similarly, the SE for pretest = 37 is 4.708. The

95% CI for the conditional mean of final scores at pretest = 24 is given by $49.02 \pm t_{16,.025}\, SE = 49.02$ $\pm (2.12)(7.408) = 49.02 \pm 15.71$. Similarly, the 95% CI at pretest = 37 is given by 95.12 ± 9.98.

(d) The estimate at pretest = 37 is likely to be more accurate. Because it is closer to the mean of the pretest scores, it has a smaller leverage and therefore a smaller standard error.

(e) To find the 95% CI for the final score of a single student with pretest score = 24, we need the appropriate standard error given by

$s_e\sqrt{1 + \dfrac{1}{N} + \dfrac{(X - \bar{X})^2}{SS_X}} = (10.638)\sqrt{1 + \dfrac{1}{18} + \dfrac{(24 - 32.378)^2}{159.60}} = 12.96$, so the CI is 49.02 ± 27.48.

20.3 (a) For the 211 women having data on both cholesterol level and age, the regression of cholesterol level (Y) on age (X) yields $\hat{Y} = 131.870 + 1.712X$. The standard error of estimate is 34.219. $SE(b_0) = 10.053$ and $SE(b_1) = 0.202$.

(b) For 30-year-old women, $\hat{\mu}_{Y.X=30} = \hat{Y} = 131.870 + 1.712(30) = 183.23$. For 50-year-olds, $\hat{\mu}_{Y.X=50} = 217.47$. The 95% CIs for the conditional means may be found using $\hat{\mu}_{Y.X} \pm t_{.025,209}\, SE(\hat{\mu}_{Y.X})$, where

$SE(\hat{\mu}_{Y.X}) = s_e\sqrt{\dfrac{1}{N} + \dfrac{(X - \bar{X})^2}{SS_X}}$. We can find SS_X in several ways—one way is to note that $SE(b_1) = $

$s_e / \sqrt{SS_X} = 0.202$, so that $SS_X = (s_e/.202)^2 = (34.219/0.202)^2 = 28{,}696.70$. Now we need the mean X score for the 211 women having data on cholesterol and age; this is 48.398. Substituting, we find that $SE(\hat{\mu}_{Y.X})$ is 4.400 for 30-year-olds and 2.378 for 50-year-olds. Given that $t_{.025,209} = 1.971$, the 95% CI for 30-year-old women is 174.56, 191.90; for 50-year-olds, it is 212.78, 222.16.

(c) The interval is narrower (and hence the estimate is more likely to be closer to the population parameter) for 50-year-old women because 50 is closer to the mean age (43.898) than 30, and hence the standard error is smaller.

(d) Now the appropriate standard error is

$$s_e\sqrt{1 + \frac{1}{N} + \frac{(X - \bar{X})^2}{SS_X}} = (34.218)\sqrt{1 + \frac{1}{211} + \frac{(30 - 43.898)^2}{28{,}696.70}} = 34.415$$

and the 95% CI extends from 115.40 to 251.06.

20.5 (a) Using $b_1 = r s_Y / s_X$, we find there is a slope of .599 for men and .799 for women. Each additional year of service corresponds to about an additional \$600 ($.599 \times \$1{,}000$) for men and about \$800 for women.

(b) We can test whether the slope difference is significant by using the test statistic (see Box 20.1)

$$t = \frac{b_M - b_W}{SE(b_M - b_W)} = \frac{b_M - b_W}{s_e\sqrt{\dfrac{1}{SS_{X_M}} + \dfrac{1}{SS_{X_W}}}}$$

where $s_e^2 = \dfrac{SS_{residual}}{N_M + N_W - 4} = \dfrac{(1 - r_M^2)SS_{Y_M} + (1 - r_W^2)SS_{Y_W}}{3{,}996} = \dfrac{575{,}855.86 + 545{,}806.95}{3{,}996} = 280.70$, so that s_e = 16.75. Substituting, we find $t(3{,}996) = -2.38$, $p < .02$. The salary increment per year of experience for women is significantly *greater* than that for men.

(c) So here we have a situation in which the correlation is significantly larger for men than women even though the slope is significantly larger for women than for men. The reason for this apparent paradox is that the men have greater variability in their years of service. Here, the unstandardized regression coefficient tells one story and the standardized regression coefficient (here the correlation coefficient) tells another. It is important to understand the difference.

20.7 The null hypothesis that the population slopes are equal can be tested by using the test statistic $t = \dfrac{b_{1_M} - b_{1_W}}{SE(b_{1_M} - b_{1_W})}$ where $SE(b_{1_M} - b_{1_W})$ can be estimated by $s_e\sqrt{\dfrac{1}{SS_{X_M}} + \dfrac{1}{SS_{X_W}}}$ (see Box 20.1). In general, s_e^2 is the weighted average of $s_{e_M}^2$ and $s_{e_W}^2$, here 194.55, so $s_e = 13.95$. Therefore, we test the null hypothesis, using $t = \dfrac{30.0 - 20.0}{13.95\sqrt{\dfrac{1}{200} + \dfrac{1}{200}}} = 7.17$ with $N_M - 2 + N_W - 2 = 76$ df. We can reject the null hypothesis.

20.9 The R of .40 tells us that in the sample, the variability of the actual Y scores about the regression line is only 84% of their variability about the line $\hat{Y} = \bar{Y}$; i.e., the proportion of the variability accounted for by the regression is $.40^2 = .16$.

CHAPTER 21

21.1 (a)

Correlations[a]

		Time	No. of letters	Difficulty
Time	Pearson Correlation	1.000	.756**	.339
	Sig. (2-tailed)		.000	.105
No. of letters	Pearson Correlation	.756**	1.000	.000
	Sig. (2-tailed)	.000		1.000
Difficulty	Pearson Correlation	.339	.000	1.000
	Sig. (2-tailed)	.105	1.000	

** . Correlation is significant at the 0.01 level (2-tailed).
a. Listwise $N = 24$

Descriptive statistics								
No. of letters	2	2	4	4	6	6	8	8
Difficulty	10	20	10	20	10	20	10	20
Mean:	493.33	532.00	545.67	583.33	584.33	646.67	625.67	670.00
SD:	10.50	35.68	62.96	40.53	30.37	44.74	70.54	40.04

(b) The SPSS output for the regression of time on number of letters and difficulty is

Model Summary

Model	R	R Square	Adjusted R Square	Std. Error of the Estimate	Change Statistics				
					R Square Change	F Change	df1	df2	Sig. F Change
1	.829[a]	.687	.657	40.379	.687	23.022	2	21	.000

a. Predictors: (Constant), Difficulty, No. of letters

ANOVA[b]

Model	Sum of Squares	df	Mean Square	F	Sig.
1 Regression	75076.050	2	37538.025	23.022	.000[a]
Residual	34240.575	21	1630.504		
Total	109316.625	23			

a. Predictors: (Constant), Difficulty, No. of letters
b. Dependent Variable: Time

Coefficients[a]

Model	Unstandardized Coefficients		Standardized Coefficients	t	Sig.	95% Confidence Interval for B	
	B	Std. Error	Beta			Lower Bound	Upper Bound
1 (Constant)	402.375	31.923		12.605	.000	335.988	468.762
No. of letters	22.825	3.686	.756	6.192	.000	15.159	30.491
Difficulty	4.575	1.648	.339	2.775	.011	1.147	8.003

a. Dependent Variable: Time

In the regression, the effects of both number of letters and difficulty are significant, $t(21) = 6.192$, $p = .000$ and $t(21) = 2.775$, $p = .011$, respectively. If an ANOVA is conducted, we find significant main effects for both number of letters and difficulty, $F(3, 16) = 10.216$, $p = .001$ and $F(1, 16) = 6.091$, $p = .025$, respectively. The results of the regression are not equivalent to that of an ANOVA. The regression treats the predictors as quantitative variables and tests whether the rate of change of time with one of the variables is different from 0 in the population, holding the other variable constant. In the ANOVA, the test of the number main effect addresses the question of whether the population means for the different levels of number are all the same.

(c) The regression yields estimates of 402.375, 22.825, and 4.575 for β_0, β_1, and β_2. The 95% confidence intervals are 335.99–468.76, 15.16–30.49, and 1.157–8.00.

21.3 (a) Regressing Y on X_1 and X_2 yields the regression equation $\hat{Y} = -16.294 + 9.196X_1 + 9.941X_2$.

(b) In the initial regression, the coefficients of X_1 and X_2 both differ significantly from 0, $t(14) = 2.420$, $p = .030$ and $t(14) = 3.378$, $p = .005$, respectively. Therefore, both variables should be included.

21.5 (a) In SPSS, to choose the first four cases, (1) click on *Select Cases* . . . on the *Data* menu; (2) in the *Select Cases* dialog box, choose *Based on time or case range*, and then click on the *Range* button; (3) insert 1 as the *First Case* and 4 as the *Last Case*, then click on *Continue*. Now proceed with the regression. If we have three predictors and only four cases, unless one or more cases are completely redundant, the resulting regression equation must predict Y perfectly for the four cases, so that $R_{Y.123} = 1$. The regression equation is $\hat{Y} = 0.770 + 1.182X_1 + 1.627X_2 - 1.731X_3$.

(b) and (c)The predicted scores are obtained using the equation obtained in part (a). To find the prediction for each of the 15 cases, first we have to undo the selection of the first four cases. Choose *Select Cases* . . . from the *Data* menu, and then in the *Select Cases* dialog box, select *All cases*. Now, to generate the predictions of Y, choose *Compute Variable* . . . from the *Transform* menu. Insert prediction as the *Target Variable* and .770 + 1.182*X1 + 1.627*X2 − 1.731*X3 as the *Numeric Expression*.

　　To two decimal places, the predictions are identical to the first four Y scores, so the correlation must be 1. To find the correlation for the remaining 11 cases, select the cases between 5 and 15 and then find the correlation. The result is $r = .244$. A regression equation that fits a sample need not fit the population well if the N/p ratio is small.

21.7 The correlation between the adjusted predictions of TC and actual TC is .497.

21.9 Some of the output for the regression of TC on *age* and *BMI* for men is as follows:

Model Summary

Model	R	R Square	Adjusted R Square	Std. Error of the Estimate
1	.215[a]	.046	.035	39.43362

a. Predictors: (Constant), *BMI, age*

ANOVA[b]

Model	Sum of Squares	df	Mean Square	F	Sig.
1 Regression	13516.443	2	6758.221	4.346	.014[avg]
Residual	279901.835	180	1555.010		
Total	293418.278	182			

a. Predictors: (Constant), *BMI*, *age*
b. Dependent Variable: *TC*

Coefficients[a]

Model	Unstandardized Coefficients		Standardized Coefficients	t	Sig.
	B	Std. Error	Beta		
1 (Constant)	161.888	24.199		6.690	.000
Age	.010	.275	.003	.036	.971
BMI	2.139	.726	.215	2.948	.004

a. Dependent Variable: *TC*

As we can see, the coefficient of *BMI* is significant, $t(180) = 2.948$, $p = .004$. R^2 is .046 and the adjusted R^2 is .035.

CHAPTER 22

22.1 (a) For the data set, a standard ANOVA yields

SV	df	SS	MS	F	p
Dosage (*D*)	3	132.306	44.102	7.290	.003
Error (*S/D*)	15	90.740	6.049		

so there is a significant effect of dosage.
(b) The regression of performance and dosage has the output

ANOVA[b]

Model	Sum of Squares	df	Mean Square	F	Sig.
1 Regression	62.110	1	62.110	6.561	.020[a]
Residual	160.937	17	9.467		
Total	223.046	18			

a. Predictors: (Constant), dosage
b. Dependent Variable: performance

Coefficients^a

Model	Unstandardized Coefficients		Standardized Coefficients	t	Sig.
	B	Std. Error	Beta		
1 (Constant)	5.267	1.776		2.965	.009
Dosage	.165	.065	.528	2.561	.020

a. Dependent Variable: performance

There is a significant linear effect of dosage.

(c) To determine whether there is a significant nonlinear effect as well:

   (1) Find $SS_{pure\ error} = SS_{error}$ from the ANOVA = 90.740.

   (2) Find $SS_{nonlinearity} = SS_{residual} - SS_{pure\ error} = 160.937 - 90.740 = 70.197$.

   (3) $df_{nonlinearity} = df_{residual} - df_{pure\ error} = 17 - 15 = 2$.

   (4) Find $F(2,15) = \dfrac{MS_{nonlinearity}}{MS_{pure\ error}} = \dfrac{70.197/2}{90.740/15} = 5.802$. From Appendix Table C.4, $p < .025$.

There is a significant nonlinear component to the relationship between performance and dosage.

(d) If we regress performance on *dosage* and *dosagesq*, we get the output:

ANOVA^b

Model	Sum of Squares	df	Mean Square	F	Sig.
1 Regression	127.485	2	63.742	10.672	.001^a
Residual	95.561	16	5.973		
Total	223.046	18			

a. Predictors: (Constant), dosagesq, dosage
b. Dependent Variable: performance

Coefficients^a

Model	Unstandardized Coefficients		Standardized Coefficients	t	Sig.
	B	Std. Error	Beta		
1 (Constant)	−4.714	3.330		−1.416	.176
Dosage	1.122	.294	3.582	3.821	.002
Dosagesq	−.019	.006	−3.102	−3.308	.004

a. Dependent Variable: performance

There are significant linear and quadratic components. The best quadratic equation is $\hat{Y} = -4.714 + 1.122X - 0.019X^2$.

22.3 (a) $R^2 = .30$, so that $f^2 = .429$. Given six predictor variables, we can use G*Power 3 to determine the number of cases necessary to have power = .80 for the hypothesis test. We can insert values into the G*Power 3 dialog box as indicated below. We need $N = 39$.

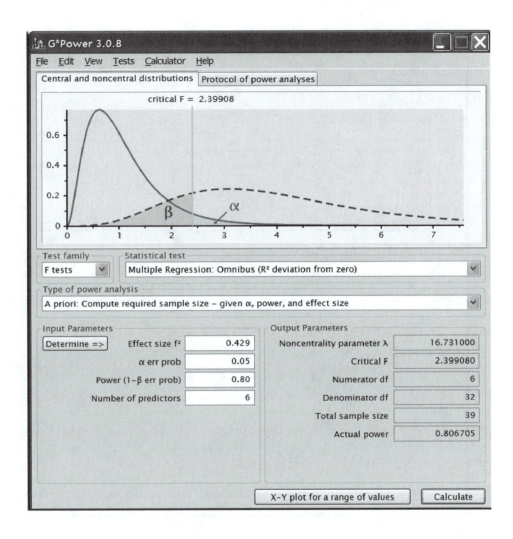

(b) If $R^2 = .20, f^2 = .25$, so that $N = 62$.

(c) If $R^2 = .10, f^2 = .111$, so that $N = 130$.

22.5 $f^2 = .077$, so that $N^* = 139$. $N = 139 + 7 - 1 = 145$.

22.7 If including X_4 in the regression equation results in R^2 increasing from .21 to .27, then $\Delta R^2 = .06$ and $f^2 = .06/(1 - .27) = .082$. To test whether the increment in predictability afforded by the addition of X_4 is significant, we form the partial-F ratio

$$F = \frac{(R^2_{Y.1234} - R^2_{Y.123})/1}{(1 - R^2_{Y.1234})/(N - p - 1)} = \frac{.06}{(1 - .27)/35} = 2.877$$

The obtained F is less than the critical $F_{.05, 1, 35}$ of 4.121 so the coefficient of X_4 is not significant. To determine the N necessary to have a power of .80 for the test of X_4, we find, using G*Power, that $N^* = 98$, so that $N = 98 + 4 - 1 = 101$.

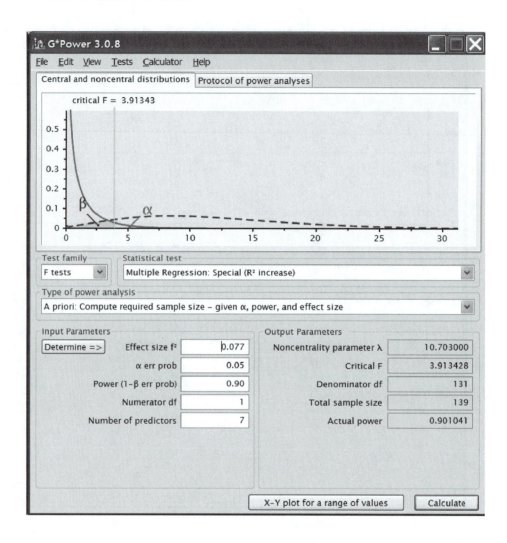

22.9 The coefficients table output for the regression of *TC* on *schoolyr* is as follows:

Coefficients[a]

| | Unstandardized Coefficients | | Standardized Coefficients | | |
Model	B	Std. Error	Beta	t	Sig.
1 (Constant)	233.887	8.004		29.222	.000
Schoolyr	−4.288	1.419	−.221	−3.022	.003

a. Dependent Variable: TC

However, we must also consider that older people have had less formal education (it used to be much less common to get a college degree), so that there is a negative correlation between *age* and *schoolyr*,

$r = -.22$, $p = .003$. This means that part of the "education" effect may really be due to age. If we regress TC on both *schoolyr* and *age*, we get the following:

Coefficients[a]

Model	Unstandardized Coefficients		Standardized Coefficients	t	Sig.
	B	Std. Error	Beta		
1 (Constant)	144.055	14.787		9.742	.000
Schoolyr	−2.338	1.293	−.120	−1.809	.072
Age	1.697	.245	.462	6.931	.000

a. Dependent Variable: TC

The coefficient of *schoolyr*, which in this regression represents the rate of change of TC with *schoolyr* holding age constant, is not significant. To pursue this issue further, we would want to determine whether there are effects of education in groups of people who are about the same age. One variable in the data set is *agegrp*, which has four levels: equal to or less than 40 years, 40–49, 50–59, and equal to or greater than 60. The regression of TC on *schoolyr* does not approach significance in any of the groups (though note that the samples are now much smaller). From these analyses it seems possible that much of the so-called education effect is due to age differences in education.

CHAPTER 23

23.1 (a) For the data set, a standard ANOVA yields

SV	df	SS	MS	F	p
Dosage (D)	3	132.306	44.102	7.290	.003
Error (S/D)	15	90.740	6.049		

(b) A trend analysis yields

SV	df	SS	MS	F	p
Dosage (D)	3	132.306	44.102	7.290	.003
linear	1	62.110	62.110	10.268	< .01
quadratic	1	65.375	65.375	10.808	< .01
cubic	1	4.821	4.821	0.797	ns
Error (S/D)	15	90.740	6.049		

So the linear and quadratic trends are significant, but the cubic trend is not.

(c) The best-fitting quadratic equation is $\hat{Y} = -4.714 + 1.122X - 0.019X^2$.

23.3 Education level tends to be significantly lower for older people, and is significantly lower for women than men—see Tables (a) and (b). When both *age* and *sex* are used as predictors in the same regression, each predictor contributes significantly, controlling for the effects of the other one—see Table (c). When *schoolyr* is regressed on *age* separately for men and women, the regression coefficient of *age* is significant for women (sex = 1), but not for men (sex = 0)—see Table (d). However, we lack sufficient evidence to claim that the coefficients for men and women are significantly different because the interaction between *age* and *sex* is not significant—see Table (e). Note that the interaction component is formed by multiplying *age* by *sex*.

(a)

Coefficients[a]

Model	Unstandardized Coefficients		Standardized Coefficients	t	Sig.
	B	Std. Error	Beta		
1 (Constant)	6.371	.303		21.025	.000
Age	−.020	.006	−.127	−3.228	.001

a. Dependent Variable: schoolyr

(b)

Coefficients[a]

Model	Unstandardized Coefficients		Standardized Coefficients	t	Sig.
	B	Std. Error	Beta		
1 (Constant)	5.688	.106		53.632	.000
Sex	−.545	.153	−.140	−3.571	.000

a. Dependent Variable: schoolyr

(c)

Coefficients[a]

Model	Unstandardized Coefficients		Standardized Coefficients	t	Sig.
	B	Std. Error	Beta		
1 (Constant)	6.680	.311		21.456	.000
Sex	−.563	.151	−.145	−3.716	.000
Age	−.021	.006	−.132	−3.387	.001

a. Dependent Variable: schoolyr

(d)

Coefficients[a]

Sex	Model		Unstandardized Coefficients		Standardized Coefficients	t	Sig.
			B	Std. Error	Beta		
0	1	(Constant)	6.327	.405		15.616	.000
		Age	−.013	.008	−.090	−1.630	.104
1	1	(Constant)	6.508	.445		14.623	.000
		Age	−.029	.009	−.178	−3.169	.002

a. Dependent Variable: schoolyr

(e)

Coefficients[a]

Model		Unstandardized Coefficients		Standardized Coefficients	t	Sig.
		B	Std. Error	Beta		
1	(Constant)	6.327	.416		15.201	.000
	Sex	.181	.601	.047	.302	.763
	Age	−.013	.008	−.085	−1.586	.113
	Age × Sex	−.016	.012	−.202	−1.280	.201

a. Dependent Variable: schoolyr

23.5 There are many regressions that can be performed with these four variables. Here we consider several that have either *BMI* or *depression* as the dependent variable. Noting the four output tables below, we can see that *depression* is a significant predictor of *BMI* and that, at least for women, *BMI* is a significant predictor of *depression*. It is possible to make a plausible case for causality in either direction and for reciprocal causality. However, it is very difficult to sort out the details. If we believe that people who are depressed are less active and have less healthy diets, we could collect data on diet and physical activity. It might be possible to get high-*BMI* people to change their diet and exercise habits and look to see whether there are changes in the depression scores. However, we are limited in our ability to change *BMI* by ethical considerations. For example, we would not ask normal subjects to increase their *BMI* scores.

Coefficients[a]

Model		Unstandardized Coefficients		Standardized Coefficients	t	Sig.
		B	Std. Error	Beta		
1	(Constant)	30.956	1.051		29.443	.000
	Schoolyr	−.704	.151	−.253	−4.649	.000
	Beck_D	.186	.053	.190	3.521	.000
	Sex	−2.018	.594	−.185	−3.395	.001

a. Dependent Variable: BMI

Coefficients[a]

Sex	Model		Unstandardized Coefficients		Standardized Coefficients	t	Sig.
			B	Std. Error	Beta		
0	1	(Constant)	30.967	1.251		24.745	.000
		Beck_D	.121	.070	.134	1.721	.087
		Schoolyr	−.655	.187	−.272	−3.507	.001
1	1	(Constant)	28.924	1.432		20.204	.000
		Beck_D	.221	.076	.217	2.887	.004
		Schoolyr	−.744	.231	−.242	−3.223	.002

a. Dependent Variable: BMI

Coefficients[a]

Model		Unstandardized Coefficients		Standardized Coefficients	t	Sig.
		B	Std. Error	Beta		
1	(Constant)	.268	2.154		.124	.901
	Schoolyr	−.209	.165	−.073	−1.268	.206
	Bmi	.206	.059	.201	3.521	.000
	Sex	1.727	.630	.154	2.740	.006

a. Dependent Variable: Beck_D

Coefficients[a]

Sex	Model		Unstandardized Coefficients		Standardized Coefficients	t	Sig.
			B	Std. Error	Beta		
0	1	(Constant)	2.020	3.199		.631	.529
		BMI	.158	.092	.143	1.721	.087
		Schoolyr	−.279	.221	−.105	−1.266	.207
1	1	(Constant)	1.213	2.747		.442	.659
		BMI	.227	.079	.231	2.887	.004
		Schoolyr	−.166	.241	−.055	−.686	.494

a. Dependent Variable: Beck_D

23.7 (a) Both externalization and criticism contribute significantly to attachment when the other predictor is held constant. Each contributes significantly to the prediction of attachment over and above the contribution of the other predictor variable.

(b) Adding the new variable to the regression equation is an appropriate way of determining whether the joint effect (i.e., the interaction) of externalization and criticism contributes to the predictability of attachment over and above the contributions made by the two measures by themselves.

Because of the correlation between the externalization and criticism measures and their product, it is important that the joint effect be evaluated in an equation that also contains the attachment and criticism measures. The interpretation of the coefficients of attachment and criticism is different in a regression equation that also contains the product term from an equation in which the product term is omitted. In the latter equation, the interpretation of the coefficient of externalization is the rate of change of attachment with externalization if criticism is held constant. In the former equation, the interpretation coefficient is the rate of change of attachment with externalization if the value of the criticism variable is zero.

CHAPTER 24

24.1 (a) We can create a sex variable with two levels, say, 1 for men and 2 for women. If we correlate sex with the dependent variable, we find $r(14) = -.509$, $p = .044$.

(b) We find that there is a significant effect of sex, $t(14) = 2.210$, $p = .044$. As we noted in Chapter 19, the test of the point-biserial correlation is equivalent to an independent-groups t test.

(c) Because it has only two levels, we only need a single dummy variable to code for sex. If men and women were assigned values of 1 and −1, we would have effect coding; if the values were 1 and 0, we would have dummy coding.

(d) For effect coding we have the output (here from SYSTAT):

Dep Var: Y   N: 16   Multiple R: 0.509   Squared multiple R: 0.259
Adjusted squared multiple R: 0.206   Standard error of estimate: 5.769

Effect	Coefficient	Std Error	Std Coef	Tolerance	t	P(2 Tail)
CONSTANT	28.187	1.442	0.000	.	19.545	0.000
EFFECT	−3.188	1.442	−0.509	1.000	−2.210	0.044

Analysis of Variance

Source	Sum-of-Squares	df	Mean-Square	F-ratio	P
Regression	162.563	1	162.563	4.885	0.044
Residual	465.875	14	33.277		

and for dummy coding, we obtain

Dep Var: Y   N: 16   Multiple R: 0.509   Squared multiple R: 0.259
Adjusted squared multiple R: 0.206   Standard error of estimate: 5.769

Effect	Coefficient	Std Error	Std Coef	Tolerance	t	P(2 Tail)
CONSTANT	31.375	2.040	0.000	.	15.384	0.000
DUMMY	−6.375	2.884	−0.509	1.000	−2.210	0.044

Analysis of Variance

Source	Sum-of-Squares	df	Mean-Square	F-ratio	P
Regression	162.563	1	162.563	4.885	0.044
Residual	465.875	14	33.277		

Note that the ANOVA tables are the same for both analyses; in both cases the sex variable accounts for all the variability in the means. However, the slope coefficients are not the same. The coefficient of EFFECT in the first analysis, −3.188, indicates that the mean for males is 3.188 units less than the average of the means for men and women, whereas the coefficient of DUMMY in the second analysis, −6.375, indicates that the mean of the scores for men is 6.375 units less than the mean of the scores for women.

24.3 (a) With three levels of the factor, we would need two dummy variables.

(b) The coding is as follows:

	Coding			
	Effect		Dummy	
Y	E1	E2	D1	D2
17	1	0	1	0
33	1	0	1	0
26	1	0	1	0
27	1	0	1	0
21	1	0	1	0
11	0	1	0	1
18	0	1	0	1
14	0	1	0	1
18	0	1	0	1
9	−1	−1	0	0
12	−1	−1	0	0
10	−1	−1	0	0
8	−1	−1	0	0
14	−1	−1	0	0

(c) (i) For effect coding the regression output is

Dep Var: Y N: 14 Multiple R: 0.846 Squared multiple R: 0.716
Adjusted squared multiple R: 0.664 Standard error of estimate: 4.335

Effect	Coefficient	Std Error	Std Coef	Tolerance	t	P(2 Tail)
CONSTANT	16.883	1.165	0.000	.	14.491	0.000
E1	7.917	1.616	0.928	0.720	4.900	0.000
E2	−1.633	1.710	−0.181	0.720	−0.955	0.360

Analysis of Variance

Source	Sum-of-Squares	df	Mean-Square	F-ratio	P
Regression	521.250	2	260.625	13.866	0.001
Residual	206.750	11	18.795		

(ii)

Dep Var: Y N: 14 Multiple R: 0.846 Squared multiple R: 0.716
Adjusted squared multiple R: 0.664 Standard error of estimate: 4.335

Effect	Coefficient	Std Error	Std Coef	Tolerance	t	P(2 Tail)
CONSTANT	10.600	1.939	0.000	.	5.467	0.000
D1	14.200	2.742	0.944	0.778	5.179	0.000
D2	4.650	2.908	0.291	0.778	1.599	0.138

Analysis of Variance

Source	Sum-of-Squares	df	Mean-Square	F-ratio	P
Regression	521.250	2	260.625	13.866	0.001
Residual	206.750	11	18.795		

Note that the ANOVA tables are exactly the same for the two regressions.

(d) The interpretations of the coefficients for the regression on the effect coding variables are $b_0 = \dfrac{\overline{Y}_{.1} + \overline{Y}_{.2} + \overline{Y}_{.3}}{3}$; $b_1 = \overline{Y}_{.1} - b_0$; and $b_2 = \overline{Y}_{.2} - b_0$. For the regression on the dummy coding variables, if the reference group, i.e., the group coded by 0s by both variables is group 3, the coefficients are $b_0 = \overline{Y}_{.3}$; $b_1 = \overline{Y}_{.1} - \overline{Y}_{.3}$; and $b_2 = \overline{Y}_{.2} - \overline{Y}_{.3}$.

24.5 Set 1 is appropriate—effect coding.

Set 2 is appropriate—dummy coding.

Set 3 is appropriate because using the proposed dummy variables will result in $SS_{regression} = SS_{between}$, although the coefficients will not be interpretable.

Set 4 is not appropriate—there are two coding variables, but values on X_2 are just the values on X_1 multiplied by the constant 3. X_1 and X_2 are perfectly correlated so we effectively only have one dummy variable.

Set 5 is not appropriate. There is only one dummy variable. $SS_{regression}$ will equal $SS_{between}$ only if the condition means are perfectly correlated with the values of X_1.

Set 6 is not appropriate because there are three dummy variables, but only two degrees of freedom for the effect of the condition variable. Regressing Y on any two of X_1, X_2, and X_3 will yield $SS_{regression} = SS_{between}$.

24.7 (a) As can be seen from the output, we cannot reject the null hypothesis that the slopes are the same at all three levels of A, $F(2, 42) = .341$, $p = .713$.

Tests of Between-Subjects Effects

Dependent Variable:Y

Source	Type III Sum of Squares	df	Mean Square	F	Sig.
Corrected Model	.687[a]	5	.137	6.615	.000
Intercept	.001	1	.001	.038	.846
X	.480	1	.480	23.114	.000
A	.048	2	.024	1.146	.328
A × X	.014	2	.007	.341	.713
Error	.873	42	.021		
Total	11.040	48			
Corrected Total	1.560	47			

a. R Squared = .441 (Adjusted R Squared = .374)

(b) To test for homogeneity of slope using the regression module and dummy coding, find

$$F = \frac{(R_{Y \cdot X, X_1, X_2, X_3, X_4}^2 - R_{Y \cdot X, X_1, X_2}^2)/2}{(1 - R_{Y \cdot X, X_1, X_2, X_3, X_4}^2)/42} = \frac{(.4406 - .4315)/2}{(1 - .4406)/42} = 0.345.$$

This is, within rounding error, the same as was found for the $A \times X$ interaction in part (a). We cannot reject the hypothesis that the population regression slopes are all the same.

CHAPTER 25

25.1 (a) The effect of P is not significant when an ANOVA is performed.

Tests of Between-Subjects Effects

Dependent Variable:Y

Source	Type III Sum of Squares	df	Mean Square	F	Sig.
Corrected Model	806.167[a]	2	403.083	2.221	.124
Intercept	133590.250	1	133590.250	736.147	.000
P	806.167	2	403.083	2.221	.124
Error	5988.583	33	181.472		
Total	140385.000	36			
Corrected Total	6794.750	35			

a. R Squared = .119 (Adjusted R Squared = .065)

(b) Using an ANCOVA, the effect of P is significant, $F(2, 32) = 4.074$, $p = .027$.

Tests of Between-Subjects Effects

Dependent Variable:Y

Source	Type III Sum of Squares	df	Mean Square	F	Sig.
Corrected Model	4675.907[a]	3	1558.636	23.539	.000
Intercept	3477.145	1	3477.145	52.514	.000
X	3869.741	1	3869.741	58.443	.000
P	539.495	2	269.748	4.074	.027
Error	2118.843	32	66.214		
Total	140385.000	36			
Corrected Total	6794.750	35			

a. R Squared = .688 (Adjusted R Squared = .659)

(c) We use the GLM module in one of the software packages to add a $P \times X$ term to the model. The interaction term is not significant, so we do not reject the hypothesis of homogeneity of slopes.

Tests of Between-Subjects Effects

Dependent Variable:Y

Source	Type III Sum of Squares	df	Mean Square	F	Sig.
Corrected Model	4838.365[a]	5	967.673	14.839	.000
Intercept	3540.735	1	3540.735	54.295	.000
P	75.463	2	37.731	.579	.567
X	3725.614	1	3725.614	57.130	.000
P × X	162.458	2	81.229	1.246	.302
Error	1956.385	30	65.213		
Total	140385.000	36			
Corrected Total	6794.750	35			

a. R Squared = .712 (Adjusted R Squared = .664)

25.3 (a) No, it is not appropriate to use ANCOVA here. We have a nonequivalent-groups design because the workers for whom we have satisfaction scores have not been randomly assigned to the four departments. Moreover, an ANOVA with X as the dependent variable yields a significant effect of department, $F(3, 28) = 5.602$, $p = .004$.

(b) No, it is not appropriate to use ANCOVA here. The data violate the assumption of homogeneity of slope. The test of heterogeneity of slope indicates that there is a significant interaction between the covariate X and the factor A, $F(2, 24) = 7.137$, $p = .004$.

25.5 The results are the same whether we use the GLM or code the factor and use regression. The results for the regression of (a) Y on X and (b) Y on X and the two dummy variables that code factor A are given in tables (a) and (b) below:

(a)

ANOVA[b]

Model	Sum of Squares	df	Mean Square	F	Sig.
1 Regression	610.230	1	610.230	42.689	.000[a]
Residual	228.714	16	14.295		
Total	838.944	17			

a. Predictors: (Constant), X
b. Dependent Variable: Y

(b)

ANOVA[b]

Model	Sum of Squares	df	Mean Square	F	Sig.
1 Regression	793.052	3	264.351	80.644	.000[a]
Residual	45.892	14	3.278		
Total	838.944	17			

a. Predictors: (Constant), X_2, X, X_1
b. Dependent Variable: Y

From table (a) we see that $R^2_{Y.X} SS_Y = 610.230$. From table (b) we have $R^2_{Y.X,A} SS_Y = 793.052$, so that

$$SS_{A(adj)} = (R^2_{Y.X,A} - R^2_{Y.X})SS_Y = 793.053 - 610.230 = 182.822$$

and $SS_{S/A(adj)} = (1 - R^2_{Y.X,A})SS_Y = 45.892$.
Therefore, the ANCOVA test statistic is

$$F = \frac{MS_{A(adj)}}{MS_{S/A(adj)}} = \frac{(R^2_{Y.X,A} - R^2_{Y.X})SS_Y / (a-1)}{(1 - R^2_{Y.X,A})SS_Y / (N-a-1)} = 27.886 \text{ with 2 and 14 } df.$$

This is the same as F given in the standard ANCOVA. Note that the SS for X obtained by regressing Y on X that is given in table (a) is not the same as the one given in the standard ANCOVA table; the SS in the ANCOVA table is given by $SS_X = (R^2_{Y.X,A} - R^2_{Y.A})SS_Y$.

CHAPTER 26

26.3 First, we must find $f^2 = \dfrac{\Delta R^2}{1 - R^2}$. When we regress depression on occupational and household physical activity for women, we find $R^2 = .024$. When we add leisure-time physical activity as a third predictor, R^2 increases to .044. Therefore, $\Delta R^2 = .020$, and $f^2 = .020/(1 - .044) = .021$. Recall that, according to the Cohen guidelines, f^2 values of .02, .15, and .35 correspond to small, medium, and large effect sizes, respectively.

26.5 Employment status and sex are not independent. There are several ways of showing this. We can find the value of the phi coefficient for the relationship between sex and employment (see Table 19.2) and test it for significance (see Equation 19.13). This yields $r = .167$, $p = .000$. We can also use a statistical package to perform the test. We first select cases in which subjects are employed either full- or part-time; i.e., if (employed = 1) or (employed = 2), then either perform a χ^2 test for independence or again find the correlation between the two dichotomous variables, sex and employment. The following output is from SPSS:

Correlations

		gender	presently employed
gender	Pearson Correlation	1.000	.167**
	Sig. (2-tailed)		.000
	N	528	528
presently employed	Pearson Correlation	.167**	1.000
	Sig. (2-tailed)	.000	
	N	528	528

**. Correlation is significant at the .01 level (2-tailed).

Testing the correlation does not usually test independence, but it does when both variables are dichotomous.

26.7 Our crude measure of education is a significant predictor of depression score for both men and women. As can be seen in Table 26.5, when education is included as a predictor along with the three measures of physical activity, education remains a significant predictor of depression score, but the activity measures do not (although leisure activity does not miss by much). Clearly, level of education is related to scores on the depression scale.

References

Achen, C. H. (1977). Measuring representation: Perils of the correlation coefficient. *American Journal of Political Science*, *41*, 805–815.

Achen, C. H. (1982). *Interpreting and using regression*. Beverly Hills, CA: Sage.

Aguinis, H., Beaty, J. C., Boik, R. J., & Pierce, C. A. (2005). Effect size and power in assessing the moderating effects of categorical variables using multiple regression: A 30-year review. *Journal of Applied Psychology*, *90*, 94–107.

Aiken, L. S., & West, S. G. (1991). *Multiple regression: Testing and interpreting interactions*. Newbury Park, CA: Sage.

Akritas, M. G. (1990). The rank transform method in some two-factor designs. *Journal of the American Statistical Association*, *85*, 73–78.

Alexander, R. A., & Govern, D. M. (1994). A new and simpler approach to ANOVA under variance heterogeneity. *Journal of Educational Statistics*, *19*, 91–101.

Alf, E. F., & Graf, R. G. (1999). Asymptotic confidence limits for the difference between two squared multiple correlations: A simplified approach. *Psychological Methods*, *4*, 70–75.

Algina, J., & Keselman, H. J. (1997). Detecting repeated-measures effects with univariate and multivariate statistics. *Psychological Methods*, *2*, 208–218.

Algina, J., & Keselman, H. J. (1999). Comparing squared multiple correlation coefficients: Examination of an interval and a test of significance. *Psychological Methods*, *4*, 76–83.

Algina, J., Keselman, H. J., & Penfield, R. D. (2005a). An alternative to Cohen's standardized mean difference effect size. *Psychological Methods*, *10*, 317–328.

Algina, J., Keselman, H. J., & Penfield, R. D. (2005b). Effect sizes and their intervals: The two-levels repeated-measures case. *Educational and Psychological Measurement*, *65*, 241–258.

Algina, J., Keselman, H. J., & Penfield, R. D. (2006). Confidence interval coverage for Cohen's effect size statistic. *Educational and Psychological Measurement*, *66*, 945–960.

Allison, P. D. (2002). *Missing data*. Newbury Park, CA: Sage.

American Psychological Association. (2001). *Publication manual of the American Psychological Association* (5th ed.). Washington, DC: Author.

Anderson, L. R., & Ager, J. W. (1978). Analysis of variance in small group research. *Personality and Social Psychology Bulletin*, *4*, 341–345.

Anscombe, F. J. (1973). Graphs in statistical analysis. *American Statistician*, *27*, 17–21.

Anscombe, F. J., & Tukey, J. W. (1963). The examination and analysis of residuals. *Technometrics*, *5*, 141–160.

Atiqullah, M. (1964). The robustness of the covariance analysis of a one-way classification. *Biometrika*, *51*, 365–373.

Baayen, R. H., Davidson, D. J., & Bates, D. M. (2008). Mixed-effects modeling with crossed random effects for subjects and items. *Journal of Memory and Language*, *59*, 390–412.

Balanda, K. P., & MacGillivray, H. L. (1988). Kurtosis: A critical review. *American Statistician*, *42*, 111–119.

Baron, R. M., & Kenny, D. A. (1986). The moderator–mediator variable distinction in social psychological research: Conceptual, strategic, and statistical considerations. *Journal of Personality and Social Psychology*, *51*, 1173–1182.

Bartlett, M. S. (1937). Properties of sufficiency and statistical tests. *Proceedings of the Royal Society*, *160*, 268–282.

Beck, A. T., & Steer, R. A. (1984). *Beck Depression Inventory: Manual*. San Antonio, TX: Psychological Corporation and Harcourt Brace Jovanovich.

Belsley, D. A., Kuh, E., & Welsch, R. E. (1980). *Regression diagnostics*. New York: Wiley.

Berk, R. A. (2004). *Regression analysis: A constructive critique*. Thousand Oaks, CA: Sage.

Bevan, M. F., Denton, J. Q., & Myers, J. L. (1974). The robustness of the *F* test to violations of continuity and form of treatment populations. *British Journal of Mathematical and Statistical Psychology*, *27*, 199–204.

Birnbaum, M. H. (1973). The devil rides again: Correlation as an index of fit. *Psychological Bulletin*, *79*, 239–242.

Bishop, Y. M. M., Fienberg, S. E., & Holland, P. W. (1975). *Discrete multivariate analysis: Theory and practice*. Cambridge, MA: MIT Press.

Blair, R. C., & Higgins, J. J. (1980). A comparison of the power of Wilcoxon's rank-sum statistic to that of Student's *t* statistic under various non-normal distributions. *Journal of Educational Statistics*, *5*, 309–335.

Blair, R. C., & Higgins, J. J. (1985). A comparison of the paired samples *t* test to that of Wilcoxon's signed-rank test under various population shapes. *Psychological Bulletin*, *97*, 119–128.

Bless, H., Bohner, G., Schwarz, N., & Strack, F. (1990). Mood and persuasion: A cognitive response analysis. *Personality and Social Psychology Bulletin*, *16*, 331–345.

Bloom, B. S. (1964). *Stability and change in human characteristics*. New York: Wiley.

Boik, R. J. (1981). *A priori* tests in repeated-measures designs: Effects of nonsphericity. *Psychometrika*, *46*, 241–255.

Boneau, C. A. (1962). A comparison of the power of the *U* and *t* tests. *Psychological Review*, *69*, 246–256.

Box, G. E. P. (1953). Nonnormality and tests on variances. *Biometrika*, *40*, 318–335.

Box, G. E. P. (1954). Some theorems on quadratic forms in the study of analysis of variance problems: Effect of inequality of variance in the one-way classification. *Annals of Mathematical Statistics*, *25*, 290–302.

Box, G. E. P. (1979). Robustness in the strategy of scientific model building. In R. L. Launer & G. N. Wilkinson (Eds.), *Robustness in statistics* (pp. 201–236). New York: Academic Press.

Bozivich, H., Bancroft, T. A., & Hartley, H. O. (1956). Power of analysis of variance test procedures for certain incompletely specified models. *Annals of Mathematical Statistics*, *27*, 1017–1043.

Bradley, J. V. (1968). *Distribution-free statistical tests*. Englewood Cliffs, NJ: Prentice-Hall.

Brown, M. B., & Forsythe, A. B. (1974a). Robust tests for the equality of variances. *Journal of the American Statistical Association*, *69*, 364–367.

Brown, M. B., & Forsythe, A. B. (1974b). The ANOVA and multiple comparisons for data with heterogeneous variances. *Biometrics, 30,* 719–724.

Bryant, J. L., & Paulson, A. S. (1976). An extension of Tukey's method of multiple comparisons to experimental designs with random concomitant variables. *Biometrika, 63,* 631–638.

Brysbaert, M. (2007). *The language-as-fixed-effect fallacy: Some simple SPSS solutions to a complex problem.* Paper presented at the Second Training Meeting of the EU Marie Curie Research Training Network: Language and Brain (Oviedo, Spain, April 2007).

Busemeyer, J. R., & Jones, L. E. (1983). Analysis of multiplicative combination rules when the causal variables are measured with error. *Psychological Bulletin, 93,* 549–562.

Campbell, D. T., & Kenny, D. A. (1999). *A primer on regression artifacts.* New York: Guilford.

Campbell, D. T., & Stanley, J. C. (1963). *Experimental and quasi-experimental designs for research.* Boston: Houghton-Mifflin.

Carlson, J. E., & Timm, N. H. (1974). Analysis of nonorthogonal fixed-effect designs. *Psychological Bulletin, 81,* 563–570.

Cheung, M. W.-L., & Chan, W. (2004). Testing dependent correlation coefficients via structural equation modeling. *Organizational Research Methods, 7,* 206–222.

Clark, H. H. (1973). The language-as-fixed-effect fallacy: A critique of language statistics in psychological research. *Journal of Verbal Learning and Verbal Behavior, 12,* 335–359.

Cleveland, W. S. (1979). Robust locally weighted regression and smoothing scatterplots. *Journal of the American Statistical Association, 78,* 158–161.

Cleveland, W. S., Devlin, S. J., & Grosse, E. H. (1988). Regression by local fitting: Methods, properties, and computational algorithms. *Journal of Econometrics, 37,* 87–114.

Clinch, J. J., & Keselman, H. J. (1982). Parametric alternatives to the analysis of variance. *Journal of Educational Statistics, 7,* 207–214.

Cobb, J. A., & Hops, H. (1973). Effects of academic survival skill training on low achieving first graders. *Journal of Educational Research, 67,* 108–113.

Cochran, W. G. (1941). The distribution of the largest of a set of estimated variances as a fraction of their total. *Eugenics, 11,* 47–52.

Cochran, W. G. (1950). The comparison of percentages in matched samples. *Biometrika, 37,* 256–266.

Cochran, W. G., & Cox, G. M. (1957). *Experimental designs* (2nd ed.). New York: Wiley.

Cohen, J. (1962). The statistical power of abnormal-social psychological research. *Journal of Abnormal and Social Psychology, 65,* 145–153.

Cohen, J. (1973). Eta-squared and partial eta-squared in fixed factor ANOVA designs. *Educational and Psychological Measurement, 33,* 107–112.

Cohen, J. (1977). *Statistical power analysis for the behavioral sciences* (rev. ed.). New York: Academic Press.

Cohen, J. (1978). Partialled products are interactions and partialled powers are curve components. *Psychological Bulletin, 85,* 858–866.

Cohen, J. (1988). *Statistical power analysis for the behavioral sciences* (3rd ed.). New York: Academic Press.

Cohen, J. (1990). Things I have learned (so far). *American Psychologist, 45,* 1304–1312.

Cohen, J., & Cohen, P. (1983). *Applied multiple regression/correlation analysis for the behavioral sciences* (2nd ed.). Hillsdale, NJ: Lawrence Erlbaum Associates, Inc.

Cohen, J., Cohen, P., West, S. G., & Aiken, L. S. (2003). *Applied multiple regression/ correlation analysis for the behavioral sciences* (3rd ed.). Mahwah, NJ: Lawrence Erlbaum Associates, Inc.

Conover, W. J., & Iman, R. L. (1981). Rank transformations as a bridge between parametric and nonparametric statistics. *American Statistician, 35,* 124–129.

Cook, R. D. (1977). Detection of influential observations in linear regression. *Technometrics, 19*, 15–18.

Cook, R. D., & Weisberg, S. (1982). *Residuals and influence in regression*. New York: Chapman & Hall.

Cook, R. D., & Weisberg, S. (1999). *Applied regression including computing and graphics*. New York: Wiley.

Coombs, W. T., Algina, J., & Oltman, D. O. (1996). Univariate and multivariate omnibus hypothesis tests selected to control Type I error rates when population variances are not necessarily equal. *Review of Educational Research, 66*, 137–179.

Cramer, E. M., & Appelbaum, M. I. (1980). Nonorthogonal analysis of variance—once again. *Psychological Bulletin, 87*, 51–57.

Crespi, L. P. (1944). Amount of reinforcement and level of performance. *Psychological Review, 51*, 341–357.

Cronbach, L. J., & Furby, L. (1970). How should we measure "change"—or should we? *Psychological Bulletin, 74*, 68–80.

Cumming, G., & Finch, S. (2001). A primer on the understanding, use, and calculation of confidence intervals that are based on central and noncentral distributions. *Educational and Psychological Measurement, 61*, 532–574.

Dalton, S., & Overall, J. E. (1977). Nonrandom assignment in ANCOVA: The alternative ranks design. *Journal of Experimental Education, 46*, 58–62.

Dar, R., Serlin, R. C., & Omer, H. (1994). Misuse of statistical tests in three decades of psychotherapy research. *Journal of Consulting and Clinical Psychology, 62*, 75–82.

Davenport, J. M., & Webster, J. T. (1973). A comparison of some approximate *F* tests. *Technometrics, 15*, 779–789.

Davidson, M. L. (1972). Univariate vs. multivariate tests in repeated-measures experiments. *Psychological Bulletin, 77*, 446–452.

Dawes, R. M. (1971). A case study of graduate admissions: Application of three principles of human decision making. *American Psychologist, 26*, 180–188.

DeCarlo, L. T. (1997). On the meaning and uses of kurtosis. *Psychological Methods, 2*, 292–307.

DeShon, R. P., & Alexander, R. A. (1996). Alternative procedures for testing regression slope homogeneity when group error variances are unequal. *Psychological Methods, 1*, 261–277.

Donaldson, T. S. (1968). Robustness of the *F* test to errors of both kinds and the correlation between the numerator and denominator of the *F* ratio. *Journal of the American Statistical Association, 63*, 660–676.

Downing, S. M., & Haladnya, T. M. (2006). *Handbook of test development*. Mahwah, NJ: Lawrence Erlbaum Associates, Inc.

Draper, N. R., & Smith, H. (1998). *Applied regression analysis* (3rd ed.). New York: Wiley.

Duncan, D. B. (1955). Multiple range and multiple *F* tests. *Biometrics, 11*, 1–42.

Dunn, O. J. (1961). Multiple comparisons among means. *Journal of the American Statistical Association, 56*, 52–64.

Dunn, O. J., & Clark, V. A. (1969). Correlation coefficients measured on the same individuals. *Journal of the American Statistical Association, 64*, 366–377.

Dunnett, C. W. (1955). A multiple comparison procedure for combining several treatments with a control. *Journal of the American Statistical Association, 50*, 1096–1121.

Dunnett, C. W. (1964). New tables for multiple comparisons with a control. *Biometrics, 20*, 482–491.

Dunnett, C. W. (1980). Pairwise multiple comparisons in the unequal variance case. *Journal of the American Statistical Association, 75*, 796–800.

Edgell, S. E., & Noon, S. N. (1984). Effect of the violation of normality on the *t* test of the correlation coefficient. *Psychological Bulletin, 95*, 576–583.

Efron, B. (1982). *The jackknife, the bootstrap, and other resampling plans*. Philadelphia: Society for Industrial and Applied Mathematics.

Efron, B. (1988). Bootstrap confidence intervals: Good or bad? *Psychological Bulletin, 104*, 293–296.

Efron, B., & Diaconis, B. (1983). Computer-intensive methods in statistics. *Scientific American, 248*, 115–130.

Emerson, J. D., & Stoto, M. A. (1983). Transforming data. In D. C. Hoaglin, F. Mosteller, & J. F. Tukey (Eds.), *Understanding robust and exploratory data analysis* (pp. 97–128). New York: Wiley.

Erdfelder, E., Franz, F., & Buchner, A. (1996). GPOWER: A general power analysis program. *Behavior Research Methods, Instrumentation, and Computers, 28*, 1–11.

Faul, F., Erdfelder, E., Lang, A. G., & Buchner, A. (2007). G*Power 3: A flexible statistical power analysis program for the social, behavioral, and biomedical sciences. *Behavior Research Methods, 39*, 175–191.

Feldt, L. S. (1958). A comparison of the precision of three experimental designs employing a concomitant variable. *Psychometrika, 23*, 335–353.

Fenz, W., & Epstein, S. (1967). Gradients of physiological arousal of experienced and novice parachutists as a function of an approaching jump. *Psychosomatic Medicine, 29*, 33–51.

Fienberg, S. E. (1977). *The analysis of cross-classified data*. Cambridge, MA: MIT Press.

Fisher, R. A. (1935). *The design of experiments*. Edinburgh, Scotland: Oliver & Boyd.

Fisher, R. A. (1952). *Statistical methods for research workers* (12th ed.). London: Oliver & Boyd.

Fitzsimons, G. J. (2008). Editorial: Death to dichotomizing. *Journal of Consumer Research, 35*, 5–8.

Fliess, J. L. (1973). *Statistical methods for rates and proportions*. New York: Wiley.

Forster, K. I., & Dickinson, R. G. (1976). More on the language-as-fixed-effect fallacy: Monte Carlo estimates of error rates for F_1, F_2, F', and min F'. *Journal of Verbal Learning and Verbal Behavior, 15*, 135–142.

Fox, J. (1997). *Applied regression analysis, linear models, and related methods*. Thousand Oaks, CA: Sage.

Fredrickson, B. L., & Kahneman, D. (1993). Duration neglect in retrospective evaluations of affective episodes. *Journal of Personality and Social Psychology, 65*, 45–55.

Friedenreich, C. M., Courneya, K. S., & Bryant, H. E. (1998). The lifetime total physical activity questionnaire: Development and reliability. *Medicine and Science in Sports and Exercise, 30*, 266–274.

Friedman, M. (1937). The use of ranks to avoid the assumption of normality implicit in the analysis of variance. *Journal of the American Statistical Association, 32*, 675–701.

Games, P. A. (1973). Type IV errors revisited. *Psychological Bulletin, 80*, 304–307.

Games, P. A., & Howell, J. F. (1976). Pairwise multiple comparison procedures with unequal *n*'s and/or variances: A Monte Carlo study. *Journal of Educational Statistics, 1*, 113–125.

Games, P. A., Keselman, H. J., & Clinch, J. J. (1979). Tests for homogeneity of variance in factorial designs. *Psychological Bulletin, 86*, 978–984.

Games, P. A., Keselman, H. J., & Rogan, J. C. (1981). Simultaneous pairwise multiple comparison procedures when sample sizes are unequal. *Psychological Bulletin, 90*, 594–598.

Ganzach, Y. (1997). Misleading interaction and curvilinear terms. *Psychological Methods, 2*, 235–247.

Gary, H. E., Jr. (1981). *The effects of departures from circularity on Type 1 error rates and power for randomized block factorial experimental designs*. Unpublished doctoral dissertation, Baylor University, Waco, TX.

Gatsonis, C., & Sampson, A. R. (1989). Multiple correlation: Exact power and sample size calculations. *Psychological Bulletin, 106*, 516–524.

Gibbons, J. D. (1993). *Nonparametric statistics: An introduction*. Newbury, CA: Sage.

Glass, G. V. (1976). Primary, secondary, and meta-analysis of research. *Educational Researcher, 5*, 3–8.

Goldstein, H. (1995). *Multilevel statistical models*. London: Edward Arnold.

Greenhouse, S. W., & Geisser, S. (1959). On methods in the analysis of profile data. *Psychometrika*, *55*, 431–433.

Greenwald, A. G. (1993). Consequences of prejudice against the null hypothesis. In G. Keren & C. Lewis (Eds.), *A handbook for data analysis in the behavioral sciences: Methodological issues* (pp. 419–448). Hillsdale, NJ: Lawrence Erlbaum Associates, Inc.

Grissom, R. J. (2000). Heterogeneity of variance in clinical data. *Journal of Consulting and Clinical Psychology*, *68*, 155–165.

Grissom, R. J., & Kim, J. J. (2001). Review of assumptions and problems in the appropriate conceptualization of effect size. *Psychological Methods*, *6*, 135–146.

Harlow, L. L. (1997). Significance testing introduction and overview. In L. L. Harlow, S. A. Mulaik, & J. H. Steiger (Eds.), *What if there were no significance tests?* (pp. 1–17). Mahwah, NJ: Lawrence Erlbaum Associates, Inc.

Harris, R. J. (1985). *A primer of multivariate statistics* (2nd ed.). New York: Academic Press.

Harris, R. J. (2001). *A primer of multivariate statistics* (3rd ed.). Mahwah, NJ: Lawrence Erlbaum Associates, Inc.

Harter, H. L., Clemm, D. S., & Guthrie, E. H. (1959). *The probability integrals of the range and of the Studentized range* (WADC Tech. Rep. 58–484). Wright-Patterson Air Force Base, Ohio: Wright Air Development Center.

Hartley, H. O. (1950). The maximum *F*-ratio as a short-cut test for heterogeneity of variance. *Biometrika*, *37*, 308–312.

Havlicek, L. L., & Peterson, N. L. (1977). Effect of the violations of assumptions upon significance levels for the Pearson *r*. *Psychological Bulletin*, *84*, 373–377.

Hays, W. L. (1981). *Statistics* (3rd ed.). New York: Holt, Rinehart & Winston.

Hays, W. L. (1988). *Statistics* (4th ed.). New York: Holt, Rinehart & Winston.

Hays, W. L. (1994). *Statistics* (5th ed.). New York: Holt, Rinehart & Winston.

Hayter, A. J. (1986). The maximum familywise error rate of Fisher's least significant difference test. *Journal of the American Statistical Association*, *81*, 1000–1004.

Hedges, L. V. (1981). Distributional theory for Glass's estimator of effect size and related estimators. *Journal of Educational Statistics*, *6*, 107–128.

Hedges, L. V., & Olkin, I. (1985). *Statistical methods for meta-analysis*. New York: Academic Press.

Herzberg, P. A. (1969). The parameters of cross validation. *Psychometrika* (Monograph supplement, No. 16).

Hill, M., & Dixon, W. J. (1982). Robustness in real life: A study of clinical laboratory data. *Biometrics*, *38*, 377–396.

Hillebrand, D. K. (1986). *Statistical thinking for behavioral scientists*. Boston: Duxbury.

Hoaglin, D. C., Mosteller, F., & Tukey, J. W. (1983). *Understanding robust and exploratory data analysis*. New York: Wiley.

Hoaglin, D. C., Mosteller, F., & Tukey, J. W. (1985). *Exploring data tables, trends and shapes*. New York: Wiley.

Hoaglin, D. C., Mosteller, F., & Tukey, J. W. (1991). *Fundamentals of exploratory analysis of variance*. New York: Wiley.

Hoaglin, D. C., & Welsch, R. (1978). The hat matrix in regression and ANOVA. *American Statistician*, *32*, 17–22.

Hochberg, Y. (1988). A sharper Bonferroni procedure for multiple tests of significance. *Biometrika*, *75*, 800–803.

Hocking, R. R. (1983). Developments in linear regression methodology: 1959–1982. *Technometrics*, *25*, 219–245.

Hoenig, J. M., & Heisey. D. M. (2001). The abuse of power: The pervasive fallacy of power calculations in data analysis. *American Statistician*, *55*, 19–24.

Hogg, R. V. (1974). Adaptive robust procedures: A partial review and some suggestions for future applications and theory. *Journal of the American Statistical Association*, *69*, 909–927.

Hogg, R. V. (1979). Statistical robustness: One view of its use in application today. *American Statistician*, *33*, 108–115.

Hogg, R. V., Fisher, D. M., & Randles, R. K. (1975). A two-sample adaptive distribution-free test. *Journal of the American Statistical Association*, *70*, 656–667.

Hollander, M., & Wolfe, D. A. (1999). *Nonparametric statistical methods* (2nd ed.). Hoboken, NJ: Wiley.

Holm, S. (1979). A simple sequentially rejective multiple test procedure. *Scandinavian Journal of Statistics*, *6*, 65–70.

Hommel, G. (1988). A stepwise rejective multiple test procedure based on a modified Bonferroni test. *Biometrika*, *75*, 383–386.

Hora, S. C., & Conover, W. J. (1984). The F statistic in the two-way layout with rank-score transformed data. *Journal of the American Statistical Association*, *79*, 668–673.

Hora, S. C., & Iman, R. L. (1988). Asymptotic relative efficiencies of the rank-transformation procedure in randomized complete-block designs. *Journal of the American Statistical Association*, *83*, 462–470.

Hosmer, D. W., & Lemeshow, S. (2001). *Applied logistic regression* (2nd ed.). New York: Wiley.

Hotelling, H. (1931). The generalization of Student's ratio. *Annals of Mathematical Statistics*, *2*, 360–378.

Hox, J. (2002). *Multilevel analysis: Techniques and applications*. Mahwah, NJ: Lawrence Erlbaum Associates, Inc.

Hsu, T. C., & Feldt, L. S. (1969). The effect of limitations on the number of criterion score values on the significance of the F test. *American Educational Research Journal*, *6*, 515–527.

Huck, S. W., & McLean, R. A. (1975). Using a repeated-measures ANOVA to analyze the data from a pretest–posttest design: A potentially confusing task. *Psychological Bulletin*, *82*, 511–518.

Hudson, J. D., & Krutchkoff, R. C. (1968). A Monte Carlo investigation of the size and power of tests employing Satterthwaite's synthetic mean squares. *Biometrika*, *55*, 431–433.

Huitema, B. E. (1980). *The analysis of covariance and alternatives*. New York: Wiley.

Hunka, S., & Leighton, J. (1997). Defining Johnson–Neyman regions of significance in the three-covariate ANCOVA using Mathematica. *Journal of Educational and Behavioral Statistics*, *22*, 361–387.

Hunter, J. E., & Schmidt, F. L. (1990). *Methods of meta-analysis: Correcting error and bias in research studies*. Newbury Park, CA: Sage.

Huynh, H. (1982). A comparison of four approaches to robust regression. *Psychological Bulletin*, *92*, 505–512.

Huynh, H., & Feldt, L. S. (1976). Estimation of the Box correction for degrees of freedom from sample data in randomized block and split-plot designs. *Journal of Educational Statistics*, *1*, 69–82.

Iman, R. L., & Conover, W. J. (1981). Rank transformations as a bridge between parametric and nonparametric statistics. *American Statistician*, *35*, 124–129.

Iman, R. L., Hora, S. C., & Conover, W. J. (1984). Comparison of asymptotically distribution-free procedures for the analysis of complete blocks. *Journal of the American Statistical Association*, *79*, 674–685.

Irwin, J. R., & McClelland, G. H. (2001). Misleading heuristics and moderated regression models. *Journal of Marketing Research*, *38*, 100–109.

ISSP (International Society of Sport Psychology). (1992). Physical activity and psychological benefits: A position statement. *The Sport Psychologist*, *6*, 199–203.

Jaccard, J., Turrisi, R., & Wan, C. K. 1990. *Interaction effects in multiple regression*. Newbury Park, CA: Sage.

James, G. S. (1951). The comparison of several groups of observations when the ratios of the population variances are unknown. *Biometrika, 38,* 324–329.

James, G. S. (1954). Tests of linear hypotheses in univariate and multivariate analysis when the ratios of the population variances are unknown. *Biometrika, 41,* 19–43.

Janky, D. G. (2000). Sometimes pooling for analysis of variance hypothesis tests: A review and study of a split-plot model. *American Statistician, 54,* 269–279.

Jennings, E. (1988). Models for pretest–posttest data: Repeated-measures ANOVA revisited. *Journal of Educational Statistics, 13,* 273–280.

Johnson, P. O., & Neyman, J. (1936). Tests of certain linear hypotheses and their application to some educational problems. *Statistical Research Memoirs, 1,* 57–93.

Kelley, K. (2005). The effects of nonnormal distributions on confidence intervals around the standardized mean difference: Bootstrap and parametric confidence intervals. *Educational and Psychological Measurement, 65,* 51–69.

Kepner, J. L., & Robinson, D. H. (1988). Nonparametric methods for detecting treatment effects in repeated-measures designs. *Journal of the American Statistical Association, 83,* 456–461.

Keren, G. (1993). Between-or within-subjects design: A methodological dilemma. In G. Keren & C. Lewis (Eds.), *A handbook for data analysis in the behavioral sciences: Methodological issues* (pp. 257–272). Hillsdale, NJ: Lawrence Erlbaum Associates, Inc.

Keselman, H. J., Rogan, J. C., Mendoza, J. L., & Breen, L. J. (1980). Testing the validity conditions of repeated-measures F tests. *Psychological Bulletin, 87,* 479–481.

Keselman, H. J., Wilcox, R. R., Othman, A. R., & Fradette, K. (2002). Trimming, transforming statistics, and bootstrapping: Circumventing the biasing effects of heteroscedasticity and nonnormality. *Journal of Modern Applied Statistical Methods, 1,* 288–309.

Keuls, M. (1952). The use of the Studentized range in connection with an analysis of variance. *Euphytica, 1,* 112–122.

King, G. (1991). Truth is stranger than prediction, more questionable than inference. *American Journal of Political Science, 35,* 1047–1053.

Kirk, R. E. (1995). *Experimental design: Procedures for the behavioral sciences* (3rd ed.). Belmont, CA: Brooks/Cole.

Kirk, R. E. (1996). Practical significance: A concept whose time has come. *Educational and Psychological Measurement, 56,* 746–759.

Koele, P. (1982). Calculating power in analysis of variance. *Psychological Bulletin, 92,* 513–516.

Kraemer, H. C. (2005). A simple effect size indicator for two-group comparisons? A comment on $r_{equivalent}$. *Psychological Methods, 10,* 413–419.

Kraemer, H. C., & Thiemann, S. (1987). *How many subjects? Statistical power analysis in research.* Beverly Hills, CA: Sage.

Kramer, C. Y. (1956). Extension of multiple range tests to group means with unequal numbers of replications. *Biometrics, 12,* 307–310.

Kreft, I., & de Leeuw, J. (1998). *Introducing multilevel modeling.* London: Sage.

Kruskal, W. H., & Wallis, W. A. (1952). Use of ranks in one-criterion variance analysis. *Journal of the American Statistical Association, 47,* 583–621.

Lee, W.-C., & Rodgers, J. L. (1998). Bootstrapping correlation coefficients using univariate and bivariate sampling. *Psychological Methods, 3,* 91–103.

Lee, Y. S. (1972). Tables of the upper percentage points of the multiple correlation coefficient. *Biometrika, 59,* 175–189.

Lehmann, E. L. (1975). *Nonparametrics*. San Francisco: Holden-Day.

Lenth, R. V. (2001). Some practical guidelines for effective sample-size determination. *American Statistician*, *55*, 187–193.

Levene, H. (1960). Robust tests for equality of variances. In I. Olkin (Ed.), *Contributions to probability and statistics: Essays in honor of Harold Hotelling* (pp. 278–292). Stanford, CA: Stanford University Press.

Levine, D. W., & Dunlap, W. P. (1982). Power of the *F* test with skewed data: Should one transform or not? *Psychological Bulletin*, *92*, 272–280.

Lin, L., Halgin, R. P., Well, A. D., & Ockene, I. (2008). The relationship between depression and occupational, household, and leisure-time physical activity. *Journal of Clinical and Sport Psychology*, *2*, 95–107.

Lindquist, E. F. (1953). *Design and analysis of experiments in education and psychology*. Boston: Houghton-Mifflin.

Linn, R. L., & Slinde, J. A. (1977). The determination of the significance of change between pre- and posttesting periods. *Review of Educational Research*, *47*, 121–150.

Little, R. J. A. (1988). Missing data in large surveys. *Journal of Business and Economic Statistics*, *6*, 287–301.

Little, R. J. A., & Rubin, D. B. (1987). *Statistical analysis with missing data*. New York: Wiley.

Lix, L. M., & Keselman, H. J. (1998). To trim or not to trim: Tests of location equality under heteroscedasticity and nonnormality. *Educational and Psychological Measurement*, *58*, 409–429.

Lix, L. M., Keselman, J. C., & Keselman, H. J. (1996). Consequences of assumption violations revisited: A quantitative review of alternatives to the one-way analysis of variance *F* test. *Review of Educational Research*, *66*, 579–620.

Lorch, R. F., & Myers, J. L. (1990). Regression analyses of repeated-measures data: A comparison of three different methods. *Journal of Experimental Psychology: Learning, Memory, and Cognition*, *16*, 149–157.

Luke, D. A. (2004). *Multilevel modeling*. Thousand Oaks, CA: Sage.

Lunney, G. H. (1970). Using analysis of variance with a dichotomous variable: An empirical study. *Journal of Educational Measurement*, *7*, 263–269.

Lutz, C., Well, A. D., & Novak, M. (2003). Stereotypic and self-injurious behavior in rhesus macaques: A survey and retrospective analysis of environment and early experience. *American Journal of Primatology*, *60*, 1–15.

MacCallum, R. C., & Mar, C. M. (1995). Distinguishing between moderator and quadratic effects in multiple regression. *Psychological Bulletin*, *118*, 405–421.

MacKinnon, D. P., Lockwood, C. M., Hoffman, J. M., West, S. G., & Sheets, V. (2002). A comparison of models to test mediation and other intervening variable effects. *Psychological Methods*, *7*, 83–104.

Marascuilo, L. A., & Levin, J. R. (1970). Appropriate post hoc comparisons for interaction and nested hypotheses in analysis of variance designs: The elimination of type IV errors. *American Educational Research Journal*, *7*, 397–421.

Marascuilo, L. A., & Levin, J. R. (1972). Type IV errors and interactions. *Psychological Bulletin*, *78*, 368–374.

Marascuilo, L. A., & Levin, J. R. (1973). Type IV errors and Games. *Psychological Bulletin*, *80*, 308–309.

Martin, P., & Bateson, P. (2007). *Measuring behaviour: An introductory guide*. Cambridge: Cambridge University Press.

Massey, F. J. (1951). The Kolmogorov–Smirnov test for goodness of fit. *Journal of the American Statistical Association*, *46*, 68–78.

Mauchly, J. W. (1940). Significance test for sphericity of a normal *n*-variate distribution. *Annals of Mathematical Statistics*, *11*, 204–209.

Maxwell, S. E. (1980). Pairwise multiple comparisons in repeated-measures designs. *Journal of Educational Statistics*, *5*, 269–287.

Maxwell, S. E. (2000). Sample size and multiple regression analysis. *Psychological Methods*, 5, 434–458.

Maxwell, S. E., & Bray, J. H. (1986). Robustness of the quasi *F* statistic to violations of sphericity. *Psychological Bulletin*, 99, 416–421.

Maxwell, S. E., Camp, C. J., & Arvey, R. D. (1981). Measures of strength of association. *Journal of Applied Psychology*, 66, 525–534.

Maxwell, S. E., & Delaney, H. D. (1993). Bivariate median splits and spurious statistical significance. *Psychological Bulletin*, 113, 181–190.

Maxwell, S. E., & Delaney, H. D. (2004). *Designing experiments and analyzing data: A model comparison perspective* (2nd ed.). Mahwah, NJ: Lawrence Erlbaum Associates, Inc.

Maxwell, S. E., Delaney, H. D., & Dill, C. A. (1984). Another look at ANCOVA versus blocking. *Psychological Bulletin*, 95, 136–147.

Maxwell, S. E., & Howard, G. S. (1981). Change scores—necessarily anathema? *Educational and Psychological Measurement*, 41, 747–756.

McGraw, L., & Wong, S. (1992). The common language effect size statistic. *Psychological Bulletin*, 111, 361–365.

Mead, R., Bancroft, T. A., & Han, C. (1975). Power of analysis of variance test procedures for incompletely specified fixed models. *Annals of Statistics*, 3, 797–808.

Menard, S. (2002). *Applied logistic regression* (2nd ed.). Thousand Oaks, CA: Sage.

Meng, X.-L., Rosenthal, R., & Rubin, D. B. (1992). Comparing correlated correlation coefficients. *Psychological Bulletin*, 111, 172–175.

Merriam, P. A., Ockene, I. S., Hebert, J. R., Rosal, M. C., & Matthews, C. E. (1999). Seasonal variation of blood cholesterol levels. *Journal of Biological Rhythms*, 14, 330–330.

Micceri, T. (1989). The unicorn, the normal curve, and other improbable creatures. *Psychological Bulletin*, 105, 156–166.

Miller, R. G. (1974). The jackknife—a review. *Biometrika*, 61, 1–17.

Miller, R. G., Jr. (1981). *Simultaneous statistical inference* (2nd ed.). New York: Springer-Verlag.

Mittlehammer, R. C., Judge, G. C., & Miller, D. J. (2000). *Econometric foundations*. Cambridge: Cambridge University Press.

Morrison, D. F. (1990). *Multivariate statistical methods* (3rd ed.). New York: McGraw-Hill.

Morrison, D. F. (2004). *Multivariate statistical methods*. Pacific Grove, CA: Duxbury Press.

Morrow, L. M., & Young, J. (1997). A family literacy program connecting school and home: Effects on attitude, motivation, and literacy achievement. *Journal of Educational Psychology*, 89, 736–742.

Murray, J. E., Yong, E., & Rhodes, G. (2000). Revisiting the perception of upside-down faces. *Psychological Science*, 11, 492–496.

Myers, J. L. (1959). On the interaction of two scaled variables. *Psychological Bulletin*, 56, 385–391.

Myers, J. L. (1979). *Fundamentals of experimental design* (3rd ed.). Boston: Allyn & Bacon.

Myers, J. L., DiCecco, J. V., & Lorch, R. F. (1981). Group dynamics and individual performances: Pseudogroup and quasi-*F* analyses. *Journal of Personality and Social Psychology*, 40, 86–98.

Myers, J. L., DiCecco, J. V., White, J. B., & Borden, V. M. (1982). Repeated measurements on dichotomous variables: *Q* and *F* tests. *Psychological Bulletin*, 92, 517–525.

Myers, J. L., Hansen, R. S., Robson, R. R., & McCann, J. (1983). The role of explanation in learning elementary probability. *Journal of Educational Psychology*, 75, 374–381.

Myers, J. L., Pezdek, K., & Coulson, D. (1973). Effects of prose organization on free recall. *Journal of Educational Psychology*, 65, 313–320.

Myers, J. L., & Well, A. D. (1995). *Research design and statistical analysis*. Hillsdale, NJ: Lawrence Erlbaum Associates, Inc.

Myers, J. L., & Well, A. D. (2003). *Research design and statistical analysis* (2nd ed.). Mahwah, NJ: Lawrence Erlbaum Associates, Inc.

Namboodiri, N. K. (1972). Experimental designs in which each subject is used repeatedly. *Psychological Bulletin*, *77*, 54–64.

Neter, J., Kutner, M. H., Nachtscheim, C. J., & Wasserman, W. (1996). *Applied linear statistical models* (4th ed.). Boston: WCB McGraw-Hill.

Newman, D. (1939). The distribution of range in samples from a normal population, expressed in terms of independent estimate of a standard deviation. *Biometrika*, *31*, 20–30.

Nunnally, J., & Berstein, I. (1994). *Psychometric theory* (3rd ed.). New York: McGraw-Hill.

Ockene, I. S., Chiriboga, D. E., Stanek, E. J., Harmatz, M. G., Nicolosi, R., Saperia, G., et al. (2004). Seasonal variation in serum cholesterol levels. *Archives of Internal Medicine*, *164*, 863–870.

Olejnik, S., & Algina, J. (2000). Measures of effect size for comparative studies: Applications, interpretations, and limitations. *Contemporary Educational Psychology*, *25*, 241–286.

Olejnik, S., & Algina, J. (2003). Generalized eta and omega squared statistics: Measures of effect size for some common research designs. *Psychological Methods*, *8*, 434–447.

Olkin, I., & Finn, J. (1990). Testing correlated correlations. *Psychological Bulletin*, *108*, 330–333.

Olkin, I., & Finn, J. (1995). Correlations redux. *Psychological Bulletin*, *118*, 155–164.

Oshima, T. C., & Algina, J. (1992). Type I error rates for James' second order test and Wilcox's H_m test under heteroscedasticity and non-normality. *British Journal of Mathematical and Statistical Psychology*, *45*, 225–263.

Overall, J. E., Lee, D. M., & Hornick, C. W. (1981). Comparison of two strategies for analysis of variance in nonorthogonal designs. *Psychological Bulletin*, *90*, 367–375.

Overall, J. E., & Spiegel, D. K. (1969). Concerning least squares analysis of experimental data. *Psychological Bulletin*, *72*, 311–322.

Overton, R. C. (2001). Moderated multiple regression for interactions involving categorical variables: A statistical control for heterogeneous variance across two groups. *Psychological Methods*, *6*, 218–233.

Pearson, E. S., & Hartley, H. (1954). *Biometrika tables for statisticians*. London: Cambridge University Press.

Pedhazur, E. J. (1997). *Multiple regression in behavioral research: Explanation and prediction*. Fort Worth, TX: Harcourt Brace.

Peritz, E. (1970). *A note on multiple comparisons*. Unpublished manuscript, Hebrew University, Jerusalem, Israel.

Perlmutter, J., & Myers, J. L. (1973). A comparison of two procedures for testing multiple contrasts. *Psychological Bulletin*, *79*, 181–184.

Piccinelli, M., & Wilkinson, G. (2000). Gender differences in depression: A critical review. *British Journal of Psychiatry*, *177*, 486–492.

Pollatsek, A., & Well, A. D. (1995). On the use of counterbalanced designs in cognitive research: A suggestion for a better and more powerful analysis. *Journal of Experimental Psychology: Learning, Memory, and Cognition*, *21*, 783–794.

Quené, H., & van den Bergh, H. (2007). On multi-level modeling of data from repeated-measures designs: A tutorial. *Speech Communication*, *43*, 103–121.

Raaijmakers, J. G. W., Schrijnemakers, J. M. C., & Gremmen, F. (1999). How to deal with "The language-as-fixed-effect fallacy": Common misconceptions and alternative solutions. *Journal of Memory and Language*, *41*, 416–426.

Ragosa, D. (1980). Comparing nonparallel regression lines. *Psychological Bulletin*, *88*, 307–321.

Ragosa, D. (1995). Myths and methods: "Myths about longitudinal research," plus supplemental questions. In M. Gottman (Ed.), *The analysis of change* (pp. 3–66). Mahwah NJ: Lawrence Erlbaum Associates, Inc.

Räkkönen, K., Matthews, K. A., Flory, J. D., Owens, J. F., & Gump, B. B. (1999). Effects of optimism, pessimism, and trait anxiety on ambulatory blood pressure and mood during everyday life. *Journal of Personality and Social Psychology*, *76*, 104–113.

Ramsey, P. H. (1978). Power differences between pairwise multiple comparisons. *Journal of the American Statistical Association*, *73*, 479–485.

Ramsey, P. H. (1981). Power of univariate pairwise multiple comparison procedures. *Psychological Bulletin*, *90*, 352–366.

Raudenbush, S. W., & Bryk, A. S. (2002). *Hierarchical linear models: Applications and data analysis methods.* Thousand Oaks, CA: Sage.

Raudenbush, S., Bryk, A., & Congdon, R. (2000). *Hierarchical linear and nonlinear modeling.* Chicago: Scientific Software International.

Rencher, A. C., & Pun, F. C. (1982). Inflation of *R*-squared in best subset regression. *Technometrics*, *22*, 49–54.

Robinson, W. S. (1950). Ecological correlations and the behavior of individuals. *American Sociological Review*, *15*, 351–357.

Rodgers, J. L., & Nicewander, W. A. (1988). Thirteen ways to look at the correlation coefficient. *American Statistician*, *42*, 59–66.

Roediger, H. L., III, Meade, M. L., & Bergman, E. T. (2001). Social contagion of memory. *Psychonomic Bulletin and Review*, *8*, 365–371.

Rogan, J. C., Keselman, H. J., & Mendoza, J. L. (1979). Analysis of repeated measurements. *British Journal of Mathematical and Statistical Psychology*, *32*, 269–286.

Rom, D. M. (1990). A sequentially rejective test procedure based on a modified Bonferroni inequality. *Biometrika*, *77*, 663–665.

Rosenberger, J. L., & Gasko, M. (1983). Comparing location estimators: Trimmed means, medians, and trimeans. In D. C. Hoaglin, F. Mosteller, & J. F. Tukey (Eds.), *Understanding robust and exploratory data analysis* (pp. 297–328). New York: Wiley.

Rosenthal, R. (1991). *Meta-analytic procedures for social research* (rev. ed.). Newbury Park, CA: Sage.

Rosenthal, R. (1995). Writing meta-analytic reviews. *Psychological Bulletin*, *118*, 183–192.

Rosenthal, R., & Rubin, D. B. (1983). Ensemble-adjusted *p* values. *Psychological Bulletin*, *94*, 540–541.

Rosenthal, R., & Rubin, D. B. (1994). The counternull value of an effect size: A new statistic. *Psychological Science*, *5*, 329–334.

Rosenthal, R., & Rubin, D. B. (2000). Contrasts and correlations in effect-size estimation. *Psychological Science*, *11*, 446–453.

Rosenthal, R., & Rubin, D. B. (2003). $r_{equivalent}$: A simple effect size indicator. *Psychological Methods*, *8*, 492–496.

Rouanet, H., & Lepine, D. (1970). Comparisons between treatments in a repeated-measurement design: ANOVA and multivariate methods. *British Journal of Mathematical and Statistical Psychology*, *23*, 147–163.

Rousseeuw, J. R., & Leroy, A. M. (1987). *Robust regression and outlier detection.* New York: Wiley.

Roy, S. N., & Bose, R. C. (1953). Simultaneous confidence interval estimation. *Annals of Mathematical Statistics*, *39*, 405–422.

Royer, J. M., Tronsky, L. M., & Chan, Y. (1999). Math-fact retrieval as the cognitive mechanism underlying gender differences in math test performance. *Contemporary Educational Psychology*, *24*, 181–266.

Rozeboom, W. W. (1979). Ridge regression: Bonanza or beguilement? *Psychological Bulletin*, *86*, 242–249.

Sandik, L., & Olsson, B. (1982). A nearly distribution-free test for comparing dispersion in paired samples. *Biometrika, 69*, 484–485.

Satterthwaite, F. E. (1946). An approximate distribution of variance components. *Biometrics Bulletin, 2*, 110–114.

Schafer, J. L. (1997). *Analysis of incomplete multivariate data.* London: Chapman & Hall.

Schafer, J. L. (1999). Multiple imputation: A primer. *Statistical Methods in Medical Research, 8*, 3–15.

Scheffé, H. (1959). *The analysis of variance.* New York: Wiley.

Schnorr, J. A., Lipkin, S. G., & Myers, J. L. (1966). Level of risk in probability learning: Within-and between-subjects designs. *Journal of Experimental Psychology, 72*, 497–500.

Schrier, A. M. (1958). Comparison of two methods of investigating the effect of amount of reward on performance. *Journal of Comparative and Physiological Psychology, 51*, 725–731.

Seaman, M. A., Levin, J. R., & Serlin, R. C. (1991). New developments in pairwise multiple comparisons: Some powerful and practicable procedures. *Psychological Bulletin, 110*, 577–586.

Shaffer, J. P. (1979). Comparison of means: An *F* test followed by a modified multiple range procedure. *Journal of Educational Statistics, 4*, 14–23.

Shaffer, J. P. (1986). Modified sequentially rejective multiple test procedures. *Journal of the American Statistical Association, 81*, 826–831.

Shaffer, J. P. (1995). Multiple hypothesis testing. *Annual Review of Psychology, 46*, 561–584.

Shapiro, S. S., & Wilk, M. B. (1965). An analysis of variance test for normality (complete samples). *Biometrika, 52*, 591–611.

Shepperd, J. A. (1991). Cautions in assessing spurious "moderator effects". *Psychological Bulletin, 110*, 315–317.

Šidák, Z. (1967). Rectangular confidence regions for the means of multivariate normal distributions. *Journal of the American Statistical Association, 62*, 626–633.

Siegel S., & Castellan, N. J. (1988). *Nonparametric statistics for the behavioral sciences* (2nd ed.). New York: McGraw-Hill.

Singh, S., & Ernst, E. (2008). *Trick or treatment: The undeniable facts about alternative medicine.* New York: Norton.

Smith, J. F. K. (1976). Data transformations in analysis of variance. *Journal of Verbal Learning and Verbal Behavior, 15*, 339–346.

Smithson, M. (2001). Correct confidence intervals for various regression effect sizes and parameters: The importance of noncentral distributions in computing intervals. *Educational and Psychological Measurement, 61*, 605–632.

Steiger, J. H. (1979). Multicorr: A computer program for fast, accurate, small-sample tests of correlational pattern hypotheses. *Educational and Psychological Measurement, 39*, 677–680.

Steiger, J. H. (1980). Tests for comparing elements of a correlation matrix. *Psychological Bulletin, 87*, 245–251.

Steiger, J. H., & Fouladi, R. T. (1992). R2: A computer program for interval estimation, power calculation, and hypothesis testing for the squared multiple correlation. *Behavior Research Methods, Instruments, and Computers, 4*, 581–582.

Steiger, J. H., & Fouladi, R. T. (1997). Noncentrality interval estimation and the evaluation of statistical models. In L. L. Harlow, L. L., Mulaik, & J. H. Steiger (Eds.), *What if there were no significance tests?* (pp. 221–257). Mahwah, NJ: Lawrence Erlbaum Associates, Inc.

Stevens, J. (1986). *Applied multivariate statistics for the social sciences.* Hillsdale, NJ: Lawrence Erlbaum Associates, Inc.

Stolberg, A. L. (2001). Understanding school- and community-based groups for children and adolescents. *PsycCRITIQUES, 46*, 55–56.

Thompson, W. F., Schellenberg, E. G., & Husain, G. (2001). Arousal, mood, and the Mozart effect. *Psychological Science, 12,* 248–251.

Tomarken, A. J., & Serlin, R. C. (1986). Comparison of ANOVA alternatives under variance heterogeneity and specific noncentrality structures. *Psychological Bulletin, 99,* 90–99.

Toothaker, L. E. (1993). *Multiple comparison procedures.* Newbury Park, CA: Sage.

Tukey, J. W. (1949). One degree of freedom for nonadditivity. *Biometrics, 5,* 232–242.

Tukey, J. W. (1952). A test for nonadditivity in the Latin square. *Biometrics, 11,* 111–113.

Tukey, J. W. (1953). *The problem of multiple comparisons.* Unpublished manuscript, Princeton University.

Tukey, J. W. (1969). Analyzing data: Sanctification or detective work? *American Psychologist, 24,* 83–91.

Tukey, J. W. (1977). *Exploratory data analysis.* Reading, MA: Addison-Wesley.

Tukey, J. W. (1991). The philosophy of multiple comparisons. *Statistical Science, 6,* 100–116.

Tukey, J. W., & McLaughlin, D. H. (1963). Less vulnerable confidence and significance procedures for location based on a single sample: Trimming/Winsorization. I. *Sankhyā: Indian Journal of Statistics, Series A, 25,* 331–352.

Vargha, A., & Delaney, H. D. (1998). The Kruskal–Wallis test and stochastic homogeneity. *Journal of Educational and Behavioral Statistics, 23,* 170–192.

Velleman, P., & Welsch, R. (1978). Efficient computing of regression diagnostics. *American Statistician, 35,* 234–242.

Welch, B. L. (1938). The significance of the difference between two means when the population variances are unequal. *Biometrika, 25,* 350–362.

Welch, B. L. (1947). The generalization of Student's problem when several different population variances are involved. *Biometrika, 34,* 28–35.

Welch, B. L. (1951). On the comparison of several mean values: An alternative approach. *Biometrika, 38,* 330–336.

Welsch, R. E. (1977). Stepwise multiple comparison procedures. *Journal of the American Statistical Association, 72,* 566–575.

Wherry, R. J. (1931). A new formula for predicting the shrinkage of the coefficient of multiple correlation. *Annals of Mathematical Statistics, 2,* 440–457.

Wilcox, R. R. (1987). New designs in analysis of variance. *Annual Review of Psychology, 38,* 29–60.

Wilcox, R. R. (1989). Comparing the variances of dependent groups. *Psychometrika, 54,* 305–315.

Wilcox, R. R. (1997). *Introduction to robust estimation and hypothesis testing.* San Diego, CA: Academic Press.

Wilcoxon, F. (1949). *Some rapid approximate statistical procedures.* New York: American Cyanimid Company.

Wiley, J., & Voss, J. F. (1999). Constructing arguments from multiple sources: Tasks that promote understanding and not just memory for texts. *Journal of Educational Psychology, 91,* 301–311.

Wilkinson, L. (1979). Tests of significance in stepwise regression. *Psychological Bulletin, 86,* 168–174.

Wilkinson, L. (1998). *SYSTAT 8 statistics manual.* Chicago, IL: SPSS, Inc.

Wilkinson, L., & Dallal, G. E. (1982). Tests of significance in forward selection regression with an *F*-to-enter stopping rule. *Technometrics, 24,* 25–28.

Wilkinson, L., & the Task Force on Statistical Inference (1999). Statistical methods in psychology journals: Guidelines and explanations, *American Psychologist, 54,* 594–604.

Williams, E. J. (1949). Experimental designs balanced for the estimation of residual effects of treatments. *Australian Journal of Scientific Research, Series A: Physical Sciences, 2,* 149–168.

Witvliet, C. V., Ludwig T. E., & Vander Laan, K. L. (2001). Granting forgiveness or harboring grudges: Implications for emotion, physiology, and health. *Psychological Science, 12,* 117–123.

Yates, F. (1934). The analysis of multiple classifications with unequal numbers in the different classes. *Journal of the American Statistical Association, 29*, 57–66.

Yuen, K. K. (1974). The two-sample trimmed *t* for unequal population variances. *Biometrika, 61*, 165–170.

Zar, J. H. (1972). Significance testing of the Spearman rank correlation coefficient. *Journal of the American Statistical Association, 67*, 578–580.

Zeaman, D. (1949). Response latency as a function of the amount of reinforcement. *Journal of Experimental Psychology, 9*, 466–483.

Zimmerman, D. W., & Zumbo, B. D. (1993). The relative power of parametric and nonparametric statistical methods. In G. Keren & C. Lewis (Eds.), *A handbook for data analysis in the behavioral sciences: Methodological issues* (pp. 481–517). Hillsdale, NJ: Lawrence Erlbaum Associates, Inc.

Zimmerman, D. W., Zumbo, B. D., & Williams, R. H. (2003). Bias in estimation and hypothesis testing of correlation. *Psicológica, 24*, 133–158.

Zou, G. Y. (2007). Toward using confidence intervals to compare correlations. *Psychological Methods, 12*, 399–413.

Zwick, R. (1993). Pairwise multiple comparison procedures for one-way analysis of variance designs. In G. Keren & C. Lewis (Eds.), *A handbook for data analysis in the behavioral sciences: Statistical issues* (pp. 43–71). Hillsdale, NJ: Lawrence Erlbaum Associates, Inc.

Author Index

Subject Index